C000121735

1 MONTH OF
FREE
READING

at

www.ForgottenBooks.com

By purchasing this book you are eligible for one month membership to ForgottenBooks.com, giving you unlimited access to our entire collection of over 1,000,000 titles via our web site and mobile apps.

To claim your free month visit:

www.forgottenbooks.com/free1008123

* Offer is valid for 45 days from date of purchase. Terms and conditions apply.

ISBN 978-0-332-23430-4
PIBN 11008123

This book is a reproduction of an important historical work. Forgotten Books uses state-of-the-art technology to digitally reconstruct the work, preserving the original format whilst repairing imperfections present in the aged copy. In rare cases, an imperfection in the original, such as a blemish or missing page, may be replicated in our edition. We do, however, repair the vast majority of imperfections successfully; any imperfections that remain are intentionally left to preserve the state of such historical works.

Forgotten Books is a registered trademark of FB &c Ltd.
Copyright © 2018 FB &c Ltd.
FB &c Ltd, Dalton House, 60 Windsor Avenue, London, SW19 2RR.
Company number 08720141. Registered in England and Wales.

For support please visit www.forgottenbooks.com

REPORTS

OF THE

COMMITTEE ON ACCOUNTS,

HOUSE OF REPRESENTATIVES,

FROM THE FOURTEENTH CONGRESS, 1815, TO THE FORTY-NINTH CONGRESS, 1887, INCLUSIVE.

IN ONE VOLUME.

COMPILED, UNDER THE DIRECTION OF THE JOINT COMMITTEE ON PRINTING

BY

T. H. McKEE,

CLERK, DOCUMENT ROOM, UNITED STATES SENATE.

STANFORD UNIVERSITY
GOV'T DOCUMENT DEPARTMENT

WASHINGTON:
GOVERNMENT PRINTING OFFICE.
1887.

9230

A11201

FORTY-NINTH CONGRESS, FIRST SESSION.

[PUBLIC RESOLUTION—No. 24.]

Joint resolution authorizing the preparation of a compilation of the reports of committees of the Senate and House of Representatives.

Resolved by the Senate and House of Representatives of the United States of America in Congress assembled, That there be prepared under the direction of the Joint Committee of Printing, a compilation of the reports of the Senate and House of Representatives from the Fourteenth to the Forty-eighth Congress, inclusive, classified by committees, arranged, indexed, and bound in suitable volumes for the use of the standing committees of the two Houses of Congress. And the sum of seven thousand seven hundred and fifty dollars, or so much thereof as may be found necessary, is hereby appropriated out of any money in the Treasury not otherwise appropriated, for the preparation of said work, which sum may be paid by the Secretary of the Treasury upon the order of the chairman of said Joint Committee, as additional pay or compensation to any officer or employee of the United States.

Resolved further, That the Clerk of the House and Secretary of the Senate be, and they are hereby directed, to procure and file, for the use of their respective Houses, copies of all reports made by each committee of all succeeding Congresses; and that the Clerk of the House and the Secretary of the Senate be, and they are hereby, authorized and directed at the close of each session of Congress, to cause said reports to be indexed and bound, one copy to be deposited in the library of each House and one copy in the room of the committee from which the reports emanated.

Approved, July 29, 1886.

2.

COMPILER'S NOTICE.

This compilation embraces all the printed reports made by both Houses of Congress from the commencement of the Fourteenth to the close of the Forty-ninth Congress. They are classified by committees and arranged in numerical order. The collection for each committee is divided into volumes of suitable size. Each committee has a separate index, a copy being bound in each volume.

The SPECIAL and SELECT reports are all compiled in one collection having one index, a copy of which is bound in each volume.

The plan throughout the compilation is to place each report to the committee from which it was reported, without reference to the subject-matter.

The House and Senate reports are compiled separately. Care will be required in noticing the chronological order, as in some instances an entire session or Congress may not appear in certain volumes from the fact that during this period no reports were made by this committee.

T. H. McKEE.

INDEX

TO

REPORTS OF COMMITTEE ON ACCOUNTS,

HOUSE OF REPRESENTATIVES.

FROM 1815, TO 1887, INCLUSIVE.

Subject.	Report.	Congress.	Session.	Volume.
ADAMSON, GEORGE, placing upon the roll of pages the name of	2041	47	2	1
BOYD, W. S., placing name of, on messenger roll	2039	47	2	1
CAPITOL POLICE, payment of one month's extra pay to certain	1732	48	2	1
CLAIMS, PRIVATE, indexing of, in House of Representatives	2135	48	1	1
Do	4064	49	2	1
CLERKS. (*See* COMMITTEE CLERKS; HOUSE OF REPRESENTATIVES.)				
COMMITTEE CLERKS,				
Assignment of	47	47	1	1
Payment of	383	47	1	1
COMMITTEES, clerks to, appointment of	5	49	1	1
COMPENSATION, employés of House of Representatives, reduction of	94	36	2	1
CONTINGENT EXPENDITURES. (*See* EXPENDITURES.)				
CONTINGENT FUND,				
Disbursement of, for 1867 and 1868	84	40	2	1
Do	36	40	3	1
Disbursement of, paying funeral expenses of deceased members	2035	47	2	1
COOK, L. B., relief of	1114	48	1	1
DECEASED MEMBERS OF CONGRESS, funeral expenses of	2035	47	2	1
DE KNIGHT, CLARENCE W., relief of	2040	47	2	1
DEMARS, CHARLES, relief of	1314	46	2	1
DEPRESSION OF LABOR. (*See* LABOR.)				
DIMOCK, Hon. DAVIS (deceased), salary for full term to widow of, as member from Pennsylvania	930	27	2	
DOORKEEPER OF HOUSE, payment of six months' salary to heirs of J. G Wintersmith, deceased	1829	49	1	1
ELECTIONS. (*See* ELECTION LAW.)				
EMPLOYÉS. (*See* HOUSE OF REPRESENTATIVES.)				
EXPENDITURES, reduction of	97	19	2	1
FUNERAL EXPENSES of deceased members, payment of	2035	47	2	1
GALT, FRANK, services as assistant journal clerk, compensation for	2014	48	1	1
HACKNEY, R. B., dismissal of, as Doorkeeper of the House	379	35	1	1
HALL OF REPRESENTATIVES, lighting by electricity, expediency and expense of	31	40	2	1
HOUSE OF REPRESENTATIVES,				
Clerks and other employés, reorganization of	94	36	2	1
Contingent fund, disbursement of, for years 1867 and 1868	84	40	2	1
Do	36	40	3	1
Contingent fund, regulating disbursements of	91	36	2	1
Contingent expenses of, reducing	97	19	2	1
Discharged employés of, granting additional pay to	29	49	1	1
Employés, one month's extra pay granted	982	48	1	1
Do	2178	48	2	1
Funeral expenses of deceased members of	2035	47	2	1
Officers of, defining duties of	750	25	2	1
Sergeant-at-arms, increasing force in office of	20	46	1	1
Additional pay of certain employés in investigation of	982	48	1	1
Do	2178	48	2	1
Appointment of stenographers by Speaker in	983	48	1	1
Telegraph operator of, increasing salary of	991	48	1	1
HOUSE POST-OFFICE. (*See* SESSION MESSENGERS.)				
HOWARD, WILLIE S., employment of, as page	310	49	1	1
KERR, R. W., payment for services rendered in indexing Journal and documents	2036	47	2	1

Subject.	Report.	Congress.	Session.	Volume.
LABOR, auditing the accounts of the chairman of the Select Committee on	1789	46	2	1
LEE, BUFORD, placing upon the laborers' roll the name of	2042	47	2	1
LORD, WILLIAM BLAIR, for relief	3052	49	1	1
LYLES, MINNIE, for relief	1754	47	1	1
McCRARY'S LAW OF ELECTIONS, purchase of 500 copies of	1731	46	2	1
MEMBERS OF CONGRESS. (*See* CONGRESS.)				
NEVENS, RICHARD, *et al.*, for relief	2186	48	2	1
NOYES, JOSEPH C., for relief	291	25	2	1
PAGE, GEORGE, payment for machine for cutting envelopes invented by	268	28	1	1
PETTIE, WINSHIP B., for relief	488	49	1	1
PRIVATE CLAIMS, indexing of, in House of Representatives	2135	48	1	1
Do	4004	49	2	1
PUBLIC DOCUMENTS, R. W. Kerr, for indexing, payment of	2036	47	2	1
PHILLIPS, EVERETT L., placing on the roll of pages the name of	2037	47	2	1
REPRESENTATIVES, clerks for	364	49	1	1
SERGEANT-AT-ARMS, additional force in the office of	20	46	1	1
SESSION MESSENGERS, House post-office, retention of, in the	3437	49	1	1
SOUTHERN CLAIMS. (*See* COMMISSIONER OF CLAIMS.)				
SPEAKER. (*See* HOUSE OF REPRESENTATIVES.)				
STATIONERY, expediency of allowing members a fixed sum for	764	25	2	1
STENOGRAPHERS. (*See* HOUSE OF REPRESENTATIVES.)				
TELEGRAPH OPERATOR. (*See* HOUSE OF REPRESENTATIVES.)				
WARDER, LUTHER F., for relief	489	49	1	1
WILLIAMS, ALFRED W., for relief	2038	47	2	1
WINTERSMITH, JAMES G., late Doorkeeper of the House, relief of estate of	1829	49	1	1
WIRT, JOHN L., for relief	29	34	3	1
WRIGHT, Hon. HENDRICK D., Select Committee on Depression of Labor, auditing accounts of, as chairman of	1789	46	2	1

O

REPORTS

OF THE

COMMITTEE ON AGRICULTURE,

HOUSE OF REPRESENTATIVES,

FROM THE ORGANIZATION OF THE COMMITTEE, MAY 3, 1820, TO THE CLOSE OF THE FORTY-NINTH CONGRESS, 1887, INCLUSIVE,

IN ONE VOLUME.

COMPILED, UNDER THE DIRECTION OF THE JOINT COMMITTEE ON PRINTING,

BY

T. H. McKEE,
CLERK, DOCUMENT ROOM, UNITED STATES SENATE.

WASHINGTON:
GOVERNMENT PRINTING OFFICE.
1887.

9214 AG H

FORTY-NINTH CONGRESS, FIRST SESSION.

[PUBLIC RESOLUTION—No. 24.]

Joint resolution authorizing the preparation of a compilation of the reports of committees of the Senate and House of Representatives.

Resolved by the Senate and House of Representatives of the United States of America in Congress assembled, That there be prepared under the direction of the Joint Committee of Printing, a compilation of the reports of the Senate and House of Representatives from the Fourteenth to the Forty-eighth Congress, inclusive, classified by committees, arranged, indexed, and bound in suitable volumes for the use of the standing committees of the two Houses of Congress. And the sum of seven thousand seven hundred and fifty dollars, or so much thereof as may be found necessary, is hereby appropriated out of any money in the Treasury not otherwise appropriated, for the preparation of said work, which sum may be paid by the Secretary of the Treasury upon the order of the chairman of said Joint Committee, as additional pay or compensation to any officer or employee of the United States.

Resolved further, That the Clerk of the House and Secretary of the Senate be, and they are hereby directed, to procure and file, for the use of their respective Houses, copies of all reports made by each committee of all succeeding Congresses; and that the Clerk of the House and the Secretary of the Senate be, and they are hereby, authorized and directed at the close of each session of Congress, to cause said reports to be indexed and bound, one copy to be deposited in the library of each House and one copy in the room of the committee from which the reports emanated.

Approved, July 29, 1886.

COMPILER'S NOTICE.

This compilation embraces all the printed reports made by both Houses of Congress from the commencement of the Fourteenth to the close of the Forty-ninth Congress. They are classified by committees and arranged in numerical order. The collection for each committee is divided into volumes of suitable size. Each committee has a separate index, a copy being bound in each volume.

The SPECIAL and SELECT reports are all compiled in one collection having one index, a copy of which is bound in each volume.

The plan throughout the compilation is to place each report to the committee from which it was reported, without reference to the subject-matter.

The House and Senate reports are compiled separately. Care will be required in noticing the chronological order, as in some instances an entire session or Congress may not appear in certain volumes from the fact that during this period no reports were made by this committee.

T. H. McKEE.

INDEX

TO

REPORTS OF THE COMMITTEE ON AGRICULTURE,

HOUSE OF REPRESENTATIVES.

FROM MAY 3, 1820, TO 1887.

Subject.	Report.	Congress.	Session.	Volume.
AGRICULTURAL COLLEGES, donating public land for college in Colorado	73	44	2	1
AGRICULTURAL COMMISSION, establishment of, to investigate and report upon the transportation of agricultural products	1889	47	2	1
AGRICULTURAL DEPARTMENT. (*See* DEPARTMENT OF AGRICULTURE.)				
AGRICULTURAL EXPEDITION to visit Eastern Asia for experimental purposes	27	38	2	1
AGRICULTURAL EXPERIMENTAL STATIONS, to establish	3909	49	2	1
AGRICULTURAL REPORT, printing of report for 1880	256	46	3	1
Do	2414	49	1	1
AGRICULTURAL SCHOOLS, establishment of	66	30	2	1
AGRICULTURAL SCRIP. (*See* LAND SCRIP.)				
AGRICULTURE, encouragement and promotion of	762	30	1	1
AGRICULTURE AND USEFUL ARTS, report of the Commissioner of Patents on	655	25	2	1
AMERICAN AGRICULTURAL SOCIETY, memorial to incorporate	57	46	3	1
AMERICAN FLAG, presented to the House by P. S. Du Ponceau, made from American silk	7	21	2	1
ANIMAL INDUSTRY. (*See* BUREAU OF ANIMAL INDUSTRY.)				
ANIMALS,				
Pleuro-pneumonia among	651	36	1	1
Do	344	46	3	1
Do	381	47	1	1
Do	119	48	1	1
Do	718	49	1	1
Do	1234	49	1	1
List of owners of, infected with pleuro-pneumonia (1886)	3418	49	1	1
Transportation and care in transit	105	43	2	1
Do	715	45	2	1
APPROPRIATIONS,				
Department of Agriculture	1461	46	2	1
Do	146	46	3	1
Do	469	47	1	1
Do	1819	47	2	1
Do	437	48	1	1
Do	2311	48	2	1
Do	1451	49	1	1
Do	3755	49	2	1
Increasing appropriation for Signal Service Bureau	1297	48	1	1
ARMY-WORM, appointment of commission to investigate origin and best means of destroying the cotton	250	45	2	1
ARTILLERY FIRING, production of rain by	786	43	1	1
ASIA, EASTERN, proposed expedition for agricultural and commercial purposes to	27	38	2	1
ATLANTA EXPOSITION, transportation of exhibit of Department of Agriculture to	10	47	1	1
BARTLETT, M. B., essay on agriculture	292	27	3	1
BUREAU OF AGRICULTURE,				
Annual appropriation bill for 1881	1461	46	2	1
Do	146	46	3	1
Do	469	47	1	1
Do	1819	47	2	1
Do	487	48	1	1
Do	2311	48	2	1
Do	1451	49	1	1
Do	3755	49	2	1

Subject.	Report.	Congress.	Session.	Volume.
BUREAU OF AGRICULTURE—Continued.				
Creating in Interior Department a	407	31	1	1
Exhibit at Atlanta Exposition	10	47	1	1
BUREAU OF ANIMAL INDUSTRY, establishment of	381	47	1	1
Do	119	48	1	1
Do	1234	49	1	1
BUREAU OF EMIGRATION, establishing in the Interior Department a	42	37	3	1
BUTTER AND CHEESE. (*See* OLEOMARGARINE.)				
CATTLE. (*See* ANIMALS.)				
CATTLE PLAGUE. (*See* ANIMALS.)				
CLARKE, JACOB B., grant of land to, at Greenbush, N. Y., for rearing of mulberry tree	49	20	2	1
COLMAN, NORMAN J., to adjudicate account as Commissioner of Agriculture	203	49	1	1
COLORADO, donating public land for agricultural college in	73	44	2	1
COMMISSIONER OF AGRICULTURE,				
Defining duties of	21	46	2	1
Directed to furnish detailed list of owners of cattle infected with pleuro-pneumonia (1886)	3413	49	1	1
Enlarging duties and powers of	380	47	1	1
Do	203	49	1	1
Furnishing seeds to destitute persons by	1075	47	1	1
Printing of annual reports of	135	43	2	1
CONTAGIOUS AND EPIDEMIC DISEASES, arresting ravages of pleuro-pneumonia among cattle	651	36	1	1
Do	344	46	3	1
Do	381	47	1	1
Do	119	48	1	1
Do	718	49	1	1
Do	1234	49	1	1
COTTON ARMY-WORM. (*See* ARMY-WORM.)				
COTTON SEED, exchange with Egypt of	195	43	1	1
COTTON WORM, continuance of commission to investigate ravages of	1318	46	2	1
DAIRY PRODUCTS. (*See* OLEOMARGARINE.)				
DEPARTMENT OF AGRICULTURE,				
Elevation of	100	48	1	1
Enlargement of duties and powers of	380	47	1	1
Do	203	49	1	1
Establishment of	595	27	2	1
Do	321	34	1	1
Do	21	37	2	1
Investigating system and workings of	385	46	3	1
Printing of annual reports of	135	43	2	1
To make an executive department of	428	46	2	1
DEPARTMENT OF INTERIOR, creating	66	30	2	1
Do	321	34	1	1
Do	21	37	2	1
DEY, ANTHONY, extension of time on patent for breaking and cleaning of hemp and flax	67	17	1	1
DU PONCEAU, P. S., donating silken flag, to House of Representatives, made of American silk by	7	21	2	1
EASTERN ASIA, expedition for agricultural and commercial purposes to	27	38	2	1
EGYPT, exchange of cotton seed with	195	43	1	1
ELVERS, PAUL HENREICH, prescription for cure of hog cholera	429	46	2	1
EMIGRANT BUREAU. (*See* BUREAU OF EMIGRATION.)				
ENTOMOLOGICAL COMMISSION, continuance of	1318	46	2	1
EPIDEMIC DISEASES. (*See* CONTAGIOUS AND EPIDEMIC DISEASES.)				
ESSAY, publication by M. R. Bartlett of	292	27	3	1
EXPEDITIONS, sending one to Eastern Asia for agricultural and commercial purposes	27	38	2	1
EXPERIMENTAL FARMS, creating	1004	47		1
Do	2034	48		1
Do	848	49		1
Do	871	49	1	1
EXPERIMENTAL STATIONS, agricultural	3000	49	2	1
FLAG, made from American silk, presentation of, to House of Representatives		21	2	1
FLEISCHMAN, CHARLES L., on restoring exhausted soil by means of a natural fertilizer	1133	46	2	1
FLORIDA,				
Encouragement of tropical plants in	451	22		1
Do	564	25	2	1
Establishment of a semi-tropical nursery by W. H. McKinney in	194	43		1
FREE TRADE, memorial of United Agricultural Societies of Virginia relative to	55	16	2	1
FRUIT PRODUCTS, cultivation and taxation of	1271	48		1
GERMANY, requesting co-operation of United States in exposition at Hamburg	1843	47	2	1
GREENBUSH, NEW YORK, granting Jacob B. Clarke public land in	49	20	2	1
HOG CHOLERA, adoption of Elvers's cure for	429	46		1
IMPORT DUTIES,				
Foreign-growth articles, increasing duties on	89	18	1	1
Modification of laws governing tax on imported articles	55	16	2	1
Do	763	30	1	1
Modification of laws governing tax on wool	574	28	1	1
INTERIOR DEPARTMENT. (*See also* DEPARTMENT OF INTERIOR.)				

Subject.	Report.	Congress.	Session.	Volume.
INTERIOR DEPARTMENT, creating a Bureau of Emigration in	42	27	3	1
INTERNAL REVENUE, articles manufactured from fruits, taxation of	1271	48	1	1
INTERNATIONAL EXPOSITION, exhibition of domestic animals at Hamburg	1848	47	2	1
INTERSTATE MIGRATION, on bill to encourage	21	48	2	1
IOWA TERRITORY,				
Granting Andrew Logan public land in	185	25	3	1
Promoting agriculture in	782	27	2	1
LAND SCRIP, agriculture college, disposition made by States of	88	42	2	1
LAW, J. H., and others, for a grant of public lands in United States for the purpose of promoting agriculture, memorial of	1069	27	2	1
LIVE STOCK (see ANIMALS), transportation of, to regulate	105	43	2	1
Do.	715	45	2	1
LOGAN, ANDREW, grant of land in Iowa Territory for the rearing of the silk-worm	185	25	3	1
MACDONALD, JAMES, extension of time on patent for breaking and cleaning of hemp and flax	87	17	1	1
M'KINNEY, W. H., petition praying Government aid in establishment of a semi-tropical nursery in Florida by	194	43	1	1
MADAGASCAR, proposed expedition for agricultural and commercial purposes to	27	28	2	1
MERRIAM, HORATIO C., *et al.*, petition modifying tax on wool	574	28	1	1
MIGRATION. (*See* INTERSTATE MIGRATION.)				
MULBERRY TREES, granting Government aid in rearing of	182	19	1	1
Do	49	20	2	1
Do.	289	21	1	1
Do	222	22	1	1
Do	815	25	2	1
OLEOMARGARINE, laws governing sale of	268	49	1	1
Do	2028	49	1	1
PATENT OFFICE, bureau in, for collecting and distributing seeds and plants, to establish	655	25	2	1
PERRINE, ANN F., relief of	78	26	2	1
PERRINE, HENRY, on memorial relative to tropical plants	454	22	1	1
Do	564	25	2	1
PLEURO-PNEUMONIA,				
Arresting ravages of	651	36	1	1
Do	844	46	3	1
Do	381	47	1	1
Do	119	48	1	1
Do	1234	49	1	1
Directing Commissioner of Agriculture to furnish a detailed list of the names of owners of cattle infected with (1886)	3413	49	1	1
PORK COMMISSION, compensation for	989	48	1	1
PRUSSIAN IMMIGRANTS, encouragement of	1069	27	2	1
PUBLIC DOCUMENTS, printing of agricultural report	135	43	2	1
Do	256	46	3	1
Do	3414	49	1	1
RAIN, production of, by artillery firing	786	13	1	1
SCHOOLS FOR AGRICULTURE. (*See* AGRICULTURAL SCHOOLS.)				
SEED, distribution of, in Texas	3704	49	2	1
SEEDS, distribution of, to destitute persons	1075	47	1	1
SEEDS AND PLANTS, establishing in the Patent Office a bureau of collection and distribution of	655	25	2	1
SIGNAL SERVICE BUREAU, increased appropriation for	1297	48	1	1
SILK FLAG, made from American silk, presentation of, to House of Representatives	7	21	2	1
SILK, promoting culture of	182	19	1	1
Do	289	21	1	1
Do	222	22	1	1
Do	82	22	2	1
SILK SPECIMENS, exhibition of	2480	40	1	1
SILK WORM, giving Government aid in the improvement of	182	19	1	1
Do	185	25	3	1
SMITH, JOSEPH L., *et al.*, establishment of department of agriculture and education	595	27	2	1
SUGAR BEET, promoting the culture of	815	25	2	1
SUGAR PALMS, making an appropriation for introduction of	668	46	2	1
SWINE PRODUCTS, appointment of commission to investigate traffic in	989	48	1	1
TARIFF, abolition and reduction of duties on imports	55	16	2	1
Do	763	30	1	1
TEXAS, distribution of seeds in	3704	49	2	1
TEXAS FEVER. (*See* ANIMALS.)				
TRANSPORTATION OF LIVE STOCK, care of, in railroad transit	105	43	2	1
Do	715	45	2	1
TROPICAL PLANTS, encouraging propagation of	454	22	1	1
Do	564	25	2	1
UTAH, asking Government aid in the improvement of lands in	424	45	2	1
VIRGINIA UNITED AGRICULTURAL SOCIETIES relative to free trade	55	16	2	1
WOOL, modification of tax on	574	28	1	1

REPORTS

OF THE

COMMITTEE ON ALCOHOLIC LIQUOR TRAFFIC,

HOUSE OF REPRESENTATIVES,

FROM THE ORGANIZATION OF THE COMMITTEE, MAY 16, 1879, TO THE CLOSE OF THE FORTY-NINTH CONGRESS, 1887, INCLUSIVE.

IN ONE VOLUME.

COMPILED, UNDER THE DIRECTION OF THE JOINT COMMITTEE ON PRINTING,

BY

T. H. McKEE,

CLERK, DOCUMENT ROOM, UNITED STATES SENATE.

WASHINGTON:
GOVERNMENT PRINTING OFFICE.
1887.

9252

FORTY-NINTH CONGRESS, FIRST SESSION.

[PUBLIC RESOLUTION—No. 24.]

Joint resolution authorizing the preparation of a compilation of the reports of committees of the Senate and House of Representatives.

Resolved by the Senate and House of Representatives of the United States of America in Congress assembled, That there be prepared under the direction of the Joint Committee of Printing, a compilation of the reports of the Senate and House of Representatives from the Fourteenth to the Forty-eighth Congress, inclusive, classified by committees, arranged, indexed, and bound in suitable volumes for the use of the standing committees of the two Houses of Congress. And the sum of seven thousand seven hundred and fifty dollars, or so much thereof as may be found necessary, is hereby appropriated out of any money in the Treasury not otherwise appropriated, for the preparation of said work, which sum may be paid by the Secretary of the Treasury upon the order of the chairman of said Joint Committee, as additional pay or compensation to any officer or employee of the United States.

Resolved further, That the Clerk of the House and Secretary of the Senate be, and they are hereby directed, to procure and file, for the use of their respective Houses, copies of all reports made by each committee of all succeeding Congresses; and that the Clerk of the House and the Secretary of the Senate be, and they are hereby, authorized and directed at the close of each session of Congress, to cause said reports to be indexed and bound, one copy to be deposited in the library of each House and one copy in the room of the committee from which the reports emanated.

Approved, July 29, 1886.

COMPILER'S NOTICE.

This compilation embraces all the printed reports made by both Houses of Congress from the commencement of the Fourteenth to the close of the Forty-ninth Congress. They are classified by committees and arranged in numerical order. The collection for each committee is divided into volumes of suitable size. Each committee has a separate index, a copy being bound in each volume.

The SPECIAL and SELECT reports are all compiled in one collection having one index, a copy of which is bound in each volume.

The plan throughout the compilation is to place each report to the committee from which it is reported, without reference to the subject-matter.

The House and Senate reports are compiled separately. Care will be required in noticing the chronological order, as in some instances an entire session or Congress may not appear in certain volumes from the fact that during this period no reports were made by this committee.

T. H. McKEE.

INDEX

TO

REPORTS OF COMMITTEE ON ALCOHOLIC LIQUOR TRAFFIC,

HOUSE OF REPRESENTATIVES.

FROM 1879 TO 1887, INCLUSIVE.

Subject.	Report.	Congress.	Session.	Volume.
ALCOHOLIC LIQUOR TRAFFIC, appointment of commission on subject of....	589	46	2	1
Do	132	47	1	1
Do	*1107	48	1	1
Do	2585	48	2	1
Do	*2281	49	1	1
COMMISSION ON LIQUOR TRAFFIC, appointment of	589	46	2	1
Do	132	47	1	1
Do	†1107	48	1	1
Do	2585	48	2	1
Do	†2281	49	1	1
CRIME, to lessen, by restriction of alcoholic liquor traffic	1293	48	1	1
DISTILLED SPIRITS,				
Restricting use of, to scientific, mechanical, and medicinal purposes	1293	48	1	1
Regulating sale of, in Territories	2586	48	1	1
DISTRICT OF COLUMBIA, limiting number of licensed liquor saloons in	1909	47	2	1
INTOXICATING LIQUORS, regulating sale of, in Territories	2586	48	2	1
LICENSE FEE, to increase retail, in District of Columbia	1909	47	2	1
LICENSED LIQUOR SALOONS, limiting number, in District of Columbia	1909	47	2	1
LIQUOR SALOONS, limiting number in District of Columbia of licensed	1909	47	2	1
MECHANICAL and MEDICINAL PURPOSES, restricting use of distilled spirits to uses of	1293	48	1	1
RETAIL LIQUOR TRAFFIC, legislation by General Government improper upon	2585	48	2	1
SCIENCE, restricting use of distilled spirits to uses of	1293	48	1	1
STATES, exclusive rights of, to legislate upon alcoholic liquor traffic	2585	48	2	1
TERRITORIES, regulating sale of intoxicating liquors in	2586	48	2	1

* And views of minority. † And views of minority, Part, 2.

REPORTS

OF THE

COMMITTEE ON AMERICAN SHIP-BUILDING,

HOUSE OF REPRESENTATIVES,

FROM THE FORTY-FIRST CONGRESS, 1870, TO THE FORTY-NINTH CONGRESS, 1887, INCLUSIVE.

IN ONE VOLUME.

COMPILED, UNDER THE DIRECTION OF THE JOINT COMMITTEE ON PRINTING,

BY

T. H. McKEE,

CLERK, DOCUMENT ROOM, UNITED STATES SENATE.

WASHINGTON:
GOVERNMENT PRINTING OFFICE.
1887.

9249

FORTY-NINTH CONGRESS, FIRST SESSION.

[PUBLIC RESOLUTION—No. 24.]

Joint resolution authorizing the preparation of a compilation of the reports of committees of the Senate and House of Representatives.

Resolved by the Senate and House of Representatives of the United States of America in Congress assembled, That there be prepared under the direction of the Joint Committee of Printing, a compilation of the reports of the Senate and House of Representatives from the Fourteenth to the Forty-eighth Congress, inclusive, classified by committees, arranged, indexed, and bound in suitable volumes for the use of the standing committees of the two Houses of Congress. And the sum of seven thousand seven hundred and fifty dollars, or so much thereof as may be found necessary, is hereby appropriated out of any money in the Treasury not otherwise appropriated, for the preparation of said work, which sum may be paid by the Secretary of the Treasury upon the order of the chairman of said Joint Committee, as additional pay or compensation to any officer or employee of the United States.

Resolved further, That the Clerk of the House and Secretary of the Senate be, and they are hereby directed, to procure and file, for the use of their respective Houses, copies of all reports made by each committee of all succeeding Congresses; and that the Clerk of the House and the Secretary of the Senate be, and they are hereby, authorized and directed at the close of each session of Congress, to cause said reports to be indexed and bound, one copy to be deposited in the library of each House and one copy in the room of the committee from which the reports emanated.

Approved, July 29, 1886.

COMPILER'S NOTICE.

This compilation embraces all the printed reports made by both Houses of Congress from the commencement of the Fourteenth to the close of the Forty-ninth Congress. They are classified by committees and arranged in numerical order. The collection for each committee is divided into volumes of suitable size. Each committee has a separate index, a copy being bound in each volume.

The SPECIAL and SELECT reports are all compiled in one collection having one index, a copy of which is bound in each volume.

The plan throughout the compilation is to place each report to the committee from which it was reported, without reference to the subject-matter.

The House and Senate reports are compiled separately. Care will be required in noticing the chronological order, as in some instances an entire session or Congress may not appear in certain volumes from the fact that during this period no reports were made by this committee.

T. H. McKEE.

INDEX

TO

REPORTS OF COMMITTEE ON AMERICAN SHIP-BUILDING,

HOUSE OF REPRESENTATIVES.

FROM 1870 TO 1887, INCLUSIVE.

Subject.	Report.	Congress.	Session.	Volume.
AMERICAN REGISTRY, amending law granting, to foreign-built ships	750	48	1	1
AMERICAN SHIPPING,				
Causes of decay and decline of	1827	47	2	1
Relative to construction and running of vessels	1827	47	2	1
AMERICAN TONNAGE, causes of reduction of	28	41	2	1
BUREAU OF NAVIGATION, providing for establishment of	281	48	1	1
CAROLINE MILLER (steamship), to grant American register to	311	49	1	1
Do	670	49	1	1
COMMERCE AND NAVIGATION,				
To establish Bureau of	1827	47	2	1
Removing burdens and encouraging American foreign carrying trade	5	48	1	1
Relative to appointment and compensation of shipping commissioners	362	48	1	1
To allow mail subsidies for encouragement of	363	48	1	1
Removing restrictions on purchase and registry of foreign vessels	493	48	1	1
To relieve vessels of compulsory pilot fees	791	48	1	1
To amend law relative to shipping commissioners	2494	48	2	1
To amend law relative to documenting vessels	2495	48	2	1
To abolish certain fees on vessels, and amend laws relative to shipping commissioners, seamen, and vessel owners	175	49	1	1
Do	4044	49	2	1
To remove restrictions on purchase of foreign vessels	1332	49	1	1
For relief of domestic vessels in foreign trade	3470	49	1	1
CONSULAR FEES exacted from American ships	1827	47	2	1
FEES (shipping commissioners'), repeal of law for	2494	48	2	1
Do	175	49	1	1
Do	4044	49	2	1
FOREIGN-BUILT SHIPS,				
Registration of	28	41	2	1
To allow purchase and registry of wrecked and repaired	493	48	1	1
Amending Revised Statutes authorizing purchase, by United States citizens of	750	48	1	1
To remove restrictions on purchase of	1332	49	1	1
GULF OF MEXICO, mail steamship service in	18	41	3	1
LUNDBORG, CHARLES G., making appropriation to build steamship according to design of	1849	48	1	1
MAIL STEAMSHIP SERVICE in Gulf of Mexico	18	41	3	1
MAIL, transportation of	1827	47	2	1
MERCHANT MARINE.				
To remove burdens on	5	48	1	1
Do	363	48	1	1
Do	2381	48	1	1
To encourage carrying trade of	750	48	1	1
Rise and fall of	28	41	2	1
NUEVO MOCTEZUMA (steamer), American register for	3540	49	2	1
OZAMA (steamship), to grant American register to	669	49	1	1
PILOTAGE,				
To repeal compulsory pilot fees	791	48	1	1
Granting right to masters and mates of vessels to pilot own vessels if competent	838	49	1	1
REVISED STATUTES, to amend and repeal,				
Section 4322, requiring copies of temporary documents of vessels to be filed at their home ports	4042	49	2	1
Sections 4153, 4177, 4371, documenting of vessels	2495	48	2	1
SAILORS, transportation of disabled	1827	47	2	1

Subject.	Report.	Congress.	Session.	Volume.
SEAMEN, fees for shipping, repeal law for	2494	48	2	1
Do	175	49	1	1
Do	4044	49	2	1
SHIP-BUILDERS, statements and views of	1827	47	2	1
SHIP-BUILDING (*see also* COMMERCE AND NAVIGATION),				
Tariff on	1827	47	2	1
SHIPPING COMMISSIONERS,				
To regulate appointment and compensation of	362	48	1	1
To amend law relative to	2494	48	2	1
Do	175	49	1	1
Do	4044	49	2	1
SHIP-OWNERS,				
Statements and views of	1827	47	2	1
Liability of	1827	47	2	1
SHIPPING, legislative obstructions to	1827	47	2	1
SHIPS,				
Registration of foreign-built	28	41	2	1
Restrictions on, in trade of	1827	47	2	1
STATISTICS OF FISHING VESSELS, to furnish	4043	49	2	1
STEAMBOAT INSPECTION SERVICE, to amend law relative to paying expenses of	3055	49	1	1
Do	3141	49	1	1
STEAMSHIP LINES OF THE WORLD	28	41	2	1
STEAMSHIP SERVICE in Gulf of Mexico	18	41	3	1
STEAM VESSELS, making appropriation to build steamship according to design of C. G. Lundborg	1849	48	1	1
STEAMSHIPS, subsidies to	28	41	2	1
SUBSIDIES, granting subsidies to steamships	28	41	2	1
TARIFF, on ship-building	1827	47	2	1
TONNAGE, AMERICAN,				
Causes of reduction of	28	41	2	1
Value of	28	41	2	1
TREASURY DEPARTMENT, to establish bureau of commerce and navigation in	281	48	1	1
VESSELS,				
Fishing, to furnish statistics of	4043	49	2	1
Liability of ship-owners	1827	47	2	1
Steamer Nuevo Moctezuma, American register to	3540	49	2	1
Taxation of, by State authority	1827	47	2	1
The running of American	1827	47	2	1
Amending Revised Statutes as regards documenting	2495	48	2	1
American, abolish certain fees for official services to	175	49	1	1
Do	4044	49	2	1
To relieve owners of vessels from paying pilot fees	838	49	1	1
For relief of domestic vessels in foreign trade	3470	49	1	1
YACHTS, to amend laws relative to	1637	49	1	1

○

REPORTS

OF THE

COMMITTEE ON APPROPRIATIONS,

HOUSE OF REPRESENTATIVES,

FROM THE ORGANIZATION OF THE COMMITTEE, MARCH 2, 1865, TO THE CLOSE OF THE FORTY-NINTH CONGRESS, 1887, INCLUSIVE.

IN FOUR VOLUMES.

COMPILED, UNDER THE DIRECTION OF THE JOINT COMMITTEE ON PRINTING,

BY

T. H. McKEE,

CLERK, DOCUMENT ROOM, UNITED STATES SENATE.

WASHINGTON:
GOVERNMENT PRINTING OFFICE.
1887.

9231

FORTY-NINTH CONGRESS, FIRST SESSION.

[PUBLIC RESOLUTION—No. 24.]

Joint resolution authorizing the preparation of a compilation of the reports of committees of the Senate and House of Representatives.

Resolved by the Senate and House of Representatives of the United States of America in Congress assembled, **That there be prepared under the direction of the Joint Committee of Printing, a compilation of the reports of the Senate and House of Representatives from the Fourteenth to the Forty-eighth Congress, inclusive, classified by committees, arranged, indexed, and bound in suitable volumes for the use of the standing committees of the two Houses of Congress. And the sum of seven thousand seven hundred and fifty dollars, or so much thereof as may be found necessary, is hereby appropriated out of any money in the Treasury not otherwise appropriated, for the preparation of said work, which sum may be paid by the Secretary of the Treasury upon the order of the chairman of said Joint Committee, as additional pay or compensation to any officer or employee of the United States.**

Resolved further, **That the Clerk of the House and Secretary of the Senate be, and they are hereby directed, to procure and file, for the use of their respective Houses, copies of all reports made by each committee of all succeeding Congresses; and that the Clerk of the House and the Secretary of the Senate be, and they are hereby, authorized and directed at the close of each session of Congress, to cause said reports to be indexed and bound, one copy to be deposited in the library of each House and one copy in the room of the committee from which the reports emanated.**

Approved, July 29, 1886.

COMPILER'S NOTICE.

This compilation embraces all the printed reports made by both Houses of Congress from the commencement of the Fourteenth to the close of the Forty-ninth Congress. They are classified by committees and arranged in numerical order. The collection for each committee is divided into volumes of suitable size. Each committee has a separate index, a copy being bound in each volume.

The SPECIAL and SELECT reports are all compiled in one collection having one index, a copy of which is bound in each volume.

The plan throughout the compilation is to place each report to the committee from which it was reported, without reference to the subject-matter.

The House and Senate reports are compiled separately. Care will be required in noticing the chronological order, as in some instances an entire session or Congress may not appear in certain volumes from the fact that during this period no reports were made by this committee.

T. H. McKEE.

INDEX

TO

REPORTS OF COMMITTEE ON APPROPRIATIONS,

HOUSE OF REPRESENTATIVES.

FROM 1865 TO 1887, INCLUSIVE.

Subject.	Report.	Congress.	Session.	Volume.
AGRICULTURAL DEPARTMENT. (*See* DEPARTMENT OF AGRICULTURE.)				
ALABAMA, sufferers from overflow of rivers in, appropriation for relief of	1506	49	1	4
ARMY,				
Appropriation for year ending,				
June 30, 1875	624	43	1	2
June 30, 1881	621	46	2	2
June 30, 1882	32	46	3	2
June 30, 1883	738	47	1	3
June 30, 1884	1832	47	2	3
June 30, 1885	1433	48	1	4
June 30, 1886	2366	48	2	4
AWARDS. (*See* TREATIES.)				
BALTIMORE, MARYLAND, erection of public buildings in	250	43	2	2
BLACKBURN, J. C. D., remuneration for supplies furnished to Kiowa, Comanche, and Apache Indians by	17	40	3	1
BOSTON, MASSACHUSETTS,				
Land for an extension of post-office in	1	43	1	2
Controversy concerning post-office in	1	43	1	2
BUREAU OF INDIAN AFFAIRS,				
Appropriation for current and continued expenses of	8	41	1	1
William Welsh, charges made by, relative to conduct of affairs in	39	41	3	1
CENSUS, completion of tenth, appropriation for	1	47	1	3
CHOCTAW INDIANS. (*See* INDIANS.)				
CLARA DOLSON (steamer), relief of owners of	80	42	3	1
Do	182	43	1	2
COLUMBIA INSTITUTION FOR DEAF AND DUMB, appropriation for	34	40	2	1
COMMISSIONER OF INDIAN AFFAIRS, William Welsh, charges made by, against	39	41	3	1
CONSULAR AND DIPLOMATIC EXPENSES, appropriation for year ending June 30, 1884	1814	47	2	3
Do	1430	48	1	4
Do	2190	48	2	4
COTTON CENTENNIAL EXPOSITION, appropriation to provide for celebration of	1432	48	1	4
CONSULAR AND DIPLOMATIC EXPENSES, appropriation for year ending,				
June 30, 1877	23	44	1	2
June 30, 1882	16	46	3	2
June 30, 1883	*115	47	1	3
June 30, 1884	1814	47	2	3
June 30, 1885	1430	48	1	4
June 30, 1886	2190	48	2	4
COURTS OF UNITED STATES, witness and juror fees, estimate of deficiency appropriations to pay	2484	49	1	4
DEFICIENCY APPROPRIATION for years ending,				
June 30, 1873 and 1874	476	43	1	2
Do	634	43	1	2
June 30, 1875	270	43	2	2
June 30, 1880	1577	46	2	2
June 30, 1881	381	46	3	2
June 30, 1882 (urgent deficiencies for)	378	47	1	3
June 30, 1882	1274	47	1	3

* Part 2.

Subject.	Report.	Congress.	Session.	Volume.
DEFICIENCY APPROPRIATION for years ending—				
June 30, 1883	1986	47	2	3
June 30, 1884 (rebate of tobacco tax to pay)	97	48	1	4
June 30, 1884	1791	48	1	4
June 30, 1885	2621	48	2	4
June 30, 1886 (for urgent)	733	49	1	4
June 30, 1886 (for printing, pensions, and pay of Army)	2436	49	1	4
June 30, 1886 (for general)	3109	49	1	4
June 30, 1886 (amendments of the Senate)	3447	49	1	4
June 30, 1887 (for printing and binding)	3485	49	2	4
June 30, 1887 (for general)	1463	49	2	4
DEMPSEY & O'TOOLE, claim for relief	91	42	2	1
DEPARTMENT OF AGRICULTURE, estimates for additional appropriation required for year ending June 30, 1868	9	40	2	1
DISTRICT OF COLUMBIA,				
Appropriation for the year ending,				
June 30, 1881	1125	46	2	2
June 30, 1882	138	46	3	2
June 30, 1883	930	47	1	3
June 30, 1884	1840	47	2	3
June 30, 1885	1299	48	1	4
June 30, 1886	2384	48	2	4
June 30, 1887	874	49	1	4
June 30, 1888	3744	49	2	4
Columbia Institute for Deaf and Dumb in the, appropriation for	34	40	2	1
FEES. (*See* COURTS OF UNITED STATES.)				
FORTIFICATIONS, appropriation for year ending,				
June 30, 1882	11	46	3	2
June 30, 1883	46	47	1	3
June 30, 1884	1841	47	2	3
June 30, 1885	2022	48	1	4
June 30, 1886	2638	48	2	4
June 30, 1887	3208	49	1	4
GREELY RELIEF EXPEDITION, appropriation for relieving and bringing home survivors of	51	48	1	4
HALL, G. A., claim for relief	353	45	2	2
HOUSE OF REPRESENTATIVES, revenue bills to originate in	14	40	2	1
INDIAN AFFAIRS. (*See* BUREAU OF INDIAN AFFAIRS.)				
INDIAN SERVICE IN NEW MEXICO. (*See* NEW MEXICO.)				
INDIANS,				
Appropriation to supply a deficiency for feeding Indians on the northern and southern reservations	29	40	3	1
Appropriations to carry out treaty stipulations with Choctaw Nation under treaty of 1855	35	40	2	1
Do	891	43	1	2
Annual appropriation for year ending,				
June 30, 1870	8	41	1	1
June 30, 1875	639	43	1	2
June 30, 1876	266	43	2	2
June 30, 1882	55	46	3	2
June 30, 1883	304	47	1	3
June 30, 1884	1812	47	2	3
June 30, 1885	953	48	1	4
June 30, 1886	2206	48	2	4
INTERNAL REVENUE, appropriation to supply deficiency for collecting tobacco tax	97	48	1	4
JURORS. (*See* COURTS OF UNITED STATES.)				
LEGISLATIVE, EXECUTIVE, AND JUDICIAL EXPENSES,				
Appropriation for year ending,				
June 30, 1875	139	43	1	2
June 30, 1875 (amendments of Senate)	608	43	1	2
June 30, 1876 (amendments of Senate)	107	43	2	2
June 30, 1877	221	44	1	2
June 30, 1881	1397	46	2	2
June 30, 1882	148	46	3	2
June 30, 1883	1276	47	1	3
June 30, 1884	1923	47	2	3
June 30, 1885	1557	48	1	4
June 30, 1886	2500	48	2	4
June 30, 1887	2495	49	1	4
June 30, 1888	*3916	49	2	4
Conferences, report on, for year ending,				
June 30, 1873	58	42	2	1
McCULLAH, JAMES A., claim for relief	594	43	1	2
MEXICAN PENSIONS, appropriation for	4110	49	2	4
MILITARY ACADEMY,				
Appropriation for support of, year ending,				
June 30, 1882	17	46	3	2
June 30, 1883	379	47	1	3

* Parts 1, 2, 3.

Subject.	Report.	Congress.	Session.	Volume.
MILITARY ACADEMY—Continued.				
Appropriation for support of, year ending,				
June 30, 1884	1818	47	2	3
June 30, 1885	322	48	1	4
June 30, 1886	2167	48	2	4
MISSISSIPPI VALLEY, appropriation for relief of sufferers from flood in	686	48	1	4
Do	1558	48	1	6
NAVAL SERVICE, appropriation for the support of, year ending,				
June 30, 1881	696	46	2	2
June 30, 1882	119	46	3	2
June 30, 1883	1433	47	1	3
June 30, 1884	1862	47	2	3
June 30, 1885	295	48	1	4
June 30, 1885 (for six months ending)	2166	48	2	4
June 30, 1885 (additional)	2191	48	2	4
June 30, 1886	2640	48	2	4
NEW MEXICO,				
Appropriation to supply deficiency in the appropriation for Indian service in	16	40	3	1
Appropriation to provide for the expenses of the meeting of the legislature of	97	48	1	4
NEW ORLEANS EXPOSITION. (*See* COTTON CENTENNIAL EXPOSITION.)				
PENSIONS,				
Appropriation for year ending,				
June 30, 1882	5	46	3	2
June 30, 1883	1412	47	1	3
June 30, 1884	1842	47	2	3
June 30, 1885	967	48	1	4
June 30, 1886	2168	48	2	4
June 30, 1886	2187	48	2	4
June 30, 1887	942	49	1	4
June 30, 1888	2560	49	2	4
Mexican, appropriation for	4110	49	2	6
POST-OFFICE DEPARTMENT, appropriation for year ending,				
June 30, 1876	119	43	2	2
June 30, 1877	441	44	1	2
June 30, 1879	473	45	2	2
June 30, 1881	1262	46	2	2
June 30, 1882	111	46	3	2
June 30, 1883	113	47	1	3
June 30, 1884	1817	47	2	3
June 30, 1885	591	48	1	4
June 30, 1886	2438	48	2	4
PUBLIC BUILDINGS IN BALTIMORE. (*See* BALTIMORE.)				
PUBLIC MONEYS, custody, expenditure, and transfer of	14	40	2	1
REVENUE, bills raising revenue to originate in House of Representatives	14	40	2	1
SIGNAL SERVICE AND TELEGRAPH COMPANIES. (*See* TELEGRAPHS.)				
SUNDRY CIVIL EXPENSES, appropriation for year ending,				
June 30, 1875	636	43	1	2
June 30, 1876	149	43	2	2
June 30, 1881	1566	46	2	2
June 30, 1882	262	46	3	2
June 30, 1883	1520	47	1	3
June 30, 1884	1960	47	2	3
June 30, 1885	1968	48	1	4
June 30, 1886	2627	48	2	4
June 30, 1887	2898	49	1	4
June 30, 1887 (amendments of Senate)	3431	49	1	4
June 30, 1888	3477	49	2	4
SUPPORT OF INDIANS. (*See* INDIANS.)				
TELEGRAPH,				
Connect the telegraph with the postal service, and to reduce rates of correspondence by	6	42	3	1
Priority of messages sent by Government over	69	42	2	1
Messages sent by Government, rates and compensation to companies for transmission of	69	42	2	1
TOBACCO, appropriation to supply deficiency for collecting tax on	97	48	1	4
TREATIES, appropriation to fulfill stipulation with Choctaw Indians, of 1855	35	40	2	1
Do	391	43	1	2
WELSH, WILLIAM, Commissioner of Indian Affairs, investigation of charges against, made by	39	41	3	1
WITNESSES. (*See* COURTS OF UNITED STATES.)				

O

REPORTS

OF THE

COMMITTEE ON BANKING AND CURRENCY,

HOUSE OF REPRESENTATIVES,

FROM THE ORGANIZATION OF THE COMMITTEE, MARCH 3, 1865, TO THE CLOSE OF THE FORTY-NINTH CONGRESS, 1887, INCLUSIVE.

IN THREE VOLUMES.

COMPILED, UNDER THE DIRECTION OF THE JOINT COMMITTEE ON PRINTING,

BY

T. H. McKEE,

CLERK, DOCUMENT ROOM, UNITED STATES SENATE.

WASHINGTON:
GOVERNMENT PRINTING OFFICE.
1887.

9247

FORTY-NINTH CONGRESS, FIRST SESSION.

[PUBLIC RESOLUTION—No. 24.]

Joint resolution authorizing the preparation of a compilation of the reports of committees of the Senate and House of Representatives.

Resolved by the Senate and House of Representatives of the United States of America in Congress assembled, That there be prepared under the direction of the Joint Committee of Printing, a compilation of the reports of the Senate and House of Representatives from the Fourteenth to the Forty-eighth Congress, inclusive, classified by committees, arranged, indexed, and bound in suitable volumes for the use of the standing committees of the two Houses of Congress. And the sum of seven thousand seven hundred and fifty dollars, or so much thereof as may be found necessary, is hereby appropriated out of any money in the Treasury not otherwise appropriated, for the preparation of said work, which sum may be paid by the Secretary of the Treasury upon the order of the chairman of said Joint Committee, as additional pay or compensation to any officer or employee of the United States.

Resolved further, That the Clerk of the House and Secretary of the Senate be, and they are hereby directed, to procure and file, for the use of their respective Houses, copies of all reports made by each committee of all succeeding Congresses; and that the Clerk of the House and the Secretary of the Senate be, and they are hereby, authorized and directed at the close of each session of Congress, to cause said reports to be indexed and bound, one copy to be deposited in the library of each House and one copy in the room of the committee from which the reports emanated.

Approved, July 29, 1886.

COMPILER'S NOTICE.

This compilation embraces all the printed reports made by both Houses of Congress from the commencement of the Fourteenth to the close of the Forty-ninth Congress. They are classified by committees and arranged in numerical order. The collection for each committee is divided into volumés of suitable size. Each committee has a separate index, a copy being bound in each volume.

The SPECIAL and SELECT reports are all compiled in one collection having one index, a copy of which is bound in each volume.

The plan throughout the compilation is to place each report to the committee from which it was reported, without reference to the subject-matter.

The House and Senate reports are compiled separately. Care will be required in noticing the chronological order, as in some instances an entire session or Congress may not appear in certain volumes from the fact that during this period no reports were made by this committee.

T. H. McKEE.

INDEX

TO

REPORTS OF COMMITTEE ON APPROPRIATIONS,

HOUSE OF REPRESENTATIVES.

FROM 1865 TO 1887, INCLUSIVE.

*Part 2.

Subject.	Report.	Congress.	Session.	Volume.
DEBT OF UNITED STATES, to pay interest upon, by substituting United States notes for national bank currency	328	43	2	3
DIVIDENDS, disposal of unclaimed, in hands of receivers of national banks	121	46	3	3
DORCHESTER, MASSACHUSETTS, Blue Hill National Bank in, to change location and name of	639	46	2	3
ENGRAVING AND PRINTING,				
Bureau of, to do only part of work on United States notes and other securities	150	43	2	2
To reorganize Bureau of Engraving and Printing	906	45	2	3
FALLS OF SAINT CROIX, WISCONSIN, relief of Benjamin W. Reynolds, depository of public moneys at	311	43	2	3
FINANCE, substitution of United States notes for the issues of national banks, testimony	328	43	2	3
FORT WORTH, TEXAS, First National Bank of, to increase capital stock of	6	48	1	3
FREEDMAN'S SAVINGS AND TRUST COMPANY,				
Petitions asking Government to adjudicate the claims of depositors in	58	43	2	3
To purchase real estate of, in Washington City	336	47	1	3
GOLD,				
Increasing relative value of	54	16	2	3
On expediency of increasing relative value of, to be coined at United States mint	54	16	2	3
For equalization of legal-tenders and bank-note currencies with	328	43	2	3
GOLD CERTIFICATES. (*See* CERTIFICATES.)				
GOLD EXCHANGE, investigation of	31	41	2	1
GOLD EXCHANGE BANK, investigation of	31	41	2	1
GOLD PANIC, 1869, investigation of	*31	41	2	1
GOVERNMENT ISSUES, providing for engraving and printing of	906	45	2	3
GREENBACKS. (*See* TREASURY NOTES.)				
GREENVILLE, PENNSYLVANIA, First National Bank at, change of name of	1968	47	2	3
HILLSBOROUGH, OHIO, to change name of National Bank of	2032	48	1	3
INTERNAL REVENUE STAMPS,				
To change present mode of engraving and printing of	906	45	2	3
To repeal law requiring use on bank checks of	1126	46	2	3
INVESTIGATION OF GOLD PANIC, September 21-27, 1869	31	41	2	1
INVESTIGATION, lock up of currency by national banks	5	42	3	3
JAMES SWEET NATIONAL BANK, to change name of	375	48	1	3
KITTANNING, PENNSYLVANIA, to establish national bank at	34	39	1	3
KUTZTOWN, PENNSYLVANIA, to change name of national bank at	1402	47	1	3
LANCASTER, MASSACHUSETTS, national bank at, to change name and location of	14	47	1	3
LARNED, KANSAS, First National Bank of, increase capital stock of	1035	48	1	3
LEGAL-TENDER NOTES,				
To prevent fraudulent withdrawal from circulation	5	42	3	3
Taxation of, by States	1002	47	1	3
LEGAL-TENDERS and BANK-NOTE CURRENCIES, for equalization of, with that of gold for all commercial purposes	328	43	2	3
LINCOLN, NEBRASKA, Marsh National Bank of, change name of	1300	48	1	3
LINCOLN, PENNSYLVANIA, National Bank of, change location and name of	40	49	1	3
LITTLE ROCK, ARKANSAS, Merchants' National Bank of, to change name of	2439	48	2	3
Do	36	49	1	3
LOANS, on real estate by national banks	180	46	2	3
Do	636	46	2	3
LOUISVILLE, KENTUCKY, Citizens' National Bank of, to increase capital stock of	716	49	1	3
MANCHESTER, NEW HAMPSHIRE, City National Bank of, to change name of	638	46	2	3
MARSHALLTOWN, IOWA, Commercial National Bank of, to change name and location of	3411	49	1	3
MEMPHIS, TENNESSEE, investigation of accounts of George N. Caelton, special agent, acting surveyor, and depository of public moneys in	108	39	1	3
MIDDLETOWN, PENNSYLVANIA, National Bank of, to change the location and name of	966	48	1	3
MILTON, MASSACHUSETTS, Dorchester Blue Hill National Bank of, to remove and change the name of	639	46	2	3
MINNEAPOLIS, MINNESOTA, First National Bank of, increase capital stock of	39	49	1	3
MINT OF UNITED STATES, on expediency of increasing relative value of gold to be coined at	54	16	2	3
MORTGAGES, to authorize national banks to make loans on real estate	180	46	2	3
Do	636	46	2	3
NATIONAL BANKS,				
Changing names of, providing regulations for	2377	49	1	3
Charters of, to extend	253	47	1	3
Conspiracy to lock up currency, investigation	542	42	3	3
First National Bank of Washington, D. C., examination and management of	300	43	1	3
German National Bank of Chicago, examination and management of	199	46	2	3
In Southern States, inquiry into operation of	82	39	1	3
Laws, to amend act of 1864	600	43	1	3
Loans on real estate, to authorize	180	46	2	3
Do	636	46	2	3

*And views of minority.

Subject.	Report.	Congress.	Session.	Volume.
NATIONAL BANKS—Continued.				
Location of, to allow Comptroller of Currency to change	1527	48	1	3
Do	104	49	1	3
Merchants' Bank of Poughkeepsie, N. Y., to issue duplicate bonds to, in lieu of lost	2555	49	2	3
National Bank of Barre, Vt., to replace unsigned stolen notes	1122	48	1	3
National bank at Kittanning, Pa., to establish	34	39	1	3
Notes of,				
To retire	328	43	2	3
Do	1169	48	1	3
Circulation of, to control	*595	48	1	3
Do	*201	49	1	3
Ocean National Bank of New York, examination and management of	1463	46	2	3
Osage National Bank, Iowa, to replace 1,800 unsigned $5 notes stolen from	1552	46	2	3
Receivers,				
Unclaimed dividends in hands of, disposal of	121	46	2	3
Appointment of, amend law providing for	118	47	1	3
Purchase of real estate by	871	49	1	3
Reports of, to the Comptroller of the Currency, providing for regulations for making oaths to	687	46	2	3
Reserve cities, providing additional	2616	49	1	3
Stockholders, liability of	202	49	1	3
Tax paid by, not to be refunded	113	46	3	3
Unclaimed dividends of, in hands of receivers, disposal of	121	46	2	3
To increase capital stock of the,				
Citizens' National Bank of Louisville, Ky	716	49	1	3
Commercial National Bank of Chicago, Ill	876	48	1	3
Do	2624	48	1	3
First National Bank of Fort Worth, Texas	6	48	1	3
First National Bank of Larned, Kans	1686	48	1	3
First National Bank of Minneapolis, Minn	39	49	1	3
First National Bank of Omaha, Nebr	2081	48	1	3
First National Bank of Shakopee, Minn	94	49	1	3
First National Bank of Wabash, Ind	322	48	1	3
National Bank of Bellaire, Ohio	190	49	1	3
To change name or location of, at:				
Bloomington, Ill	2182	48	2	3
Brooklyn, N. Y	2286	48	2	3
Cincinnati, Ohio	120	48	1	3
Dorchester, Mass	639	46	2	3
Hillsborough, Ohio	2032	48	1	3
Lancaster, Mass	14	47	1	3
Lincoln, Nebr	1300	48	1	3
Lincoln, Pa	40	49	1	3
Little Rock, Ark	2439	48	2	3
Do	36	49	1	3
Manchester, N. H	638	46	2	3
Marshalltown, Iowa	3411	49	1	3
Middletown, Pa	968	48	1	3
Nebraska City, Nebr	1402	47	1	3
New York City, N. Y	354	47	1	3
Do	354	47	1	3
West Greenville, Pa	1968	47	2	3
West Waterville, Me	377	48	1	3
Winona, Minn	37	49	1	3
Do	38	49	1	3
NATIONAL BANK NOTES (*see also* CURRENCY), percentage of circulation of notes to the deposit of Government bonds	1286	47	1	3
NATIONAL BANK STOCK, to prevent recovery of taxes levied on	118	46	3	3
NEBRASKA CITY, NEBRASKA, to change the name of James Sweet National Bank in, to Merchants' National Bank	375	48	1	3
NEW YORK CITY,				
National Mechanics' Banking Association to Wall Street National Bank, change name of	354	47	1	3
Ocean National Bank of, to investigate management of	1463	46	2	3
Investigation withdrawing United States legal-tender notes from circulation by	5	42	3	3
OMAHA, NEBRASKA, First National Bank of, increase capital stock of	2081	48	1	3
Do	491½	49	1	3
OSAGE, IOWA, to replace 1,800 unsigned $5 notes stolen from National Bank of.	1052	46	2	3
PANIC, investigation of national banks alleged to have locked up currency to produce a	5	42	3	3
PENNSYLVANIA, national bank at Kittanning in, establishment of another	34	39	1	3
POUGHKEEPSIE, NEW YORK, Merchants' National Bank of, relief of	2555	49	2	3
PRINTING UNITED STATES NOTES	150	43	2	2
READING, PENNSYLVANIA, Kutztown National Bank, change name and location to	1402	47	1	3
REAL ESTATE, loans on, by national banks, to authorize	180	46	2	3
Do	636	46	2	3
RECEIVERS OF NATIONAL BANKS (*see also* NATIONAL BANKS), to amend act appointing	118	47	1	3

* And views of minority.

Subject.	Report.	Congress.	Session.	Volume.
RESERVE CITIES, for national banks deposits, to increase number of	1037	47	1	3
Do	2616	49	1	3
REVISED STATUTES, to amend or repeal,				
Section 5137, permiting receivers of national banks to purchase real estate	871	49	1	3
Section 5151, relating to liability of stockholders of national banks	202	49	1	3
Sections 5171, 5176, relating to circulation of national bank notes	1037	47	1	3
Sections 5191, 5192, relating to reserve cities of national banks	2616	49	1	3
Section 5211, relating to verification of reports of national banks	637	46	2	2
REYNOLDS, BENJAMIN W., relief of	311	43	2	2
SHAKOPEE, MINNESOTA, First National Bank of	94	49	1	3
SIGNATURES on national bank notes to be written and not engraved	635	46	2	3
Do	252	47	1	3
SILVER CERTIFICATES. (*See* CERTIFICATES.)				
SIMPSON, THOMAS C., release of certain United States currency to	3654	49	2	[illegible]
SMALL BILLS (*see also* CURRENCY), issue of, circulation of	1455	49	1	[illegible]
SOUTHERN STATES, national banks in, inquiry into operations of	82	39	1	[illegible]
STAMPS (*see also* INTERNAL REVENUE STAMPS), to repeal law requiring stamps on bank checks	1126	46	2	[illegible]
STANDARD SILVER DOLLARS, limit coinage of	*1286	47	1	[illegible]
STOCKHOLDERS NATIONAL BANK, liabilities of	202	49	1	[illegible]
TRADE-DOLLAR, retirement of	550	47	1	[illegible]
TREASURY NOTES,				
Substitution of currency of national banks	328	43	2	3
To change present mode of engraving and printing	906	45	2	3
Taxation of by States	1002	47	1	3
To issue small bills for circulation	1455	49	1	3
UNITED STATES NOTES,				
Printing of	*150	43	2	2
Taxation of, by States	1002	47	1	2
WABASH, INDIANA, First National Bank at, increase capital stock of	323	48	1	3
WASHINGTON, DISTRICT OF COLUMBIA, First National Bank, examination of	300	43	1	3
WEST GREENVILLE, PENNSYLVANIA, First National Bank of, change of name of	1968	47	2	3
WEST WATERVILLE, MAINE, national bank in, to change name of, to the Messalonskee National Bank	377	48	1	3
WINONA, MINNESOTA, National Bank of Winona, change name of	37	49	1	3
Do	38	49	1	3

* And views of minority.

OF THE

COMPILED, UNDER THE DIRECTION OF THE JOINT COMMITTEE ON PRINTING,

BY

T. H. McKEE,

CLERK, DOCUMENT ROOM, UNITED STATES SENATE.

WASHINGTON:
GOVERNMENT PRINTING OFFICE.
1887.

9253

FORTY-NINTH CONGRESS, FIRST SESSION.

[PUBLIC RESOLUTION—No. 24.]

Joint resolution authorizing the preparation of a compilation of the reports of committees of the Senate and House of Representatives.

Resolved by the Senate and House of Representatives of the United States of America in Congress assembled, That there be prepared under the direction of the Joint Committee of Printing, a compilation of the reports of the Senate and House of Representatives from the Fourteenth to the Forty-eighth Congress, inclusive, classified by committees, arranged, indexed, and bound in suitable volumes for the use of the standing committees of the two Houses of Congress. And the sum of seven thousand seven hundred and fifty dollars, or so much thereof as may be found necessary, is hereby appropriated out of any money in the Treasury not otherwise appropriated, for the preparation of said work, which sum may be paid by the Secretary of the Treasury upon the order of the chairman of said Joint Committee, as additional pay or compensation to any officer or employee of the United States.

Resolved further, That the Clerk of the House and Secretary of the Senate be, and they are hereby directed, to procure and file, for the use of their respective Houses, copies of all reports made by each committee of all succeeding Congresses; and that the Clerk of the House and the Secretary of the Senate be, and they are hereby, authorized and directed at the close of each session of Congress, to cause said reports to be indexed and bound, one copy to be deposited in the library of each House and one copy in the room of the committee from which the reports emanated.

Approved, July 29, 1886.

COMPILER'S NOTICE.

This compilation embraces all the printed reports made by both Houses of Congress from the commencement of the Fourteenth to the close of the Forty-ninth Congress. They are classified by committees and arranged in numerical order. The collection for each committee is divided into volumes of suitable size. Each committee has a separate index, a copy being bound in each volume.

The SPECIAL and SELECT reports are all compiled in one collection having one index, a copy of which is bound in each volume.

The plan throughout the compilation is to place each report to the committee from which it was reported, without reference to the subject-matter.

The House and Senate reports are compiled separately. Care will be required in noticing the chronological order, as in some instances an entire session or Congress may not appear in certain volumes from the fact that during this period no reports were made by this committee.

T. H. McKEE.

INDEX

TO

REPORTS OF COMMITTEE ON CENSUS.

HOUSE OF REPRESENTATIVES.

FROM 1879 TO 1887, INCLUSIVE.

Subject.	Report.	Congress.	Session.	Volume.
ALASKA, to amend census act so as to include	588	46	2	1
AMERICAN CENSUS, historical view of	3	41	2	1
BIRTHS, prescribing form for entry of	3	41	2	1
CENSUS,				
Defects in present method of taking	3	41	2	1
History of taking	3	41	2	1
Supervisors of, additional compensation for	1204	47	1	1
To amend law relating to	588	46	2	1
COMPENSATION, additional pay for supervisors of elections	1204	47	1	1
CONGRESS, apportionment of Representatives in, among the several States under Tenth Census	120	46	3	1
Do	114	47	1	1
DEATHS, prescribing form for entry of	3	41	2	1
EUROPE, systems of public statistics in leading countries of	3	41	2	1
INDUSTRY, statistics of	3	41	2	1
INTERNAL COMMERCE, statistics on	3	14	2	1
MARRIAGES, prescribing form for entry of	3	41	2	1
MORTALITY, defects in schedules of	3	41	2	1
NINTH CENSUS, mode of taking	3	41	2	1
POPULATION, defects in schedules of	3	41	2	1
REPRESENTATIVES IN CONGRESS, apportionment among the several States under Tenth Census	120	46	3	1
Do	114	47	1	1
SOCIETY, statistics on	3	41	2	1
STATISTICAL SCIENCE, growth from beginning of nineteenth century to present day	3	41	2	1
STATISTICS, INTERNATIONAL, method of collecting	3	41	2	1
SUPERVISORS OF CENSUS, additional compensation for	1204	47	1	1
TENTH CENSUS, apportionment of Representatives in Congress among the several States under	120	46	3	1
Do	114	47	1	1
WRIGHT, CARROLL D., views of, on result of Tenth Census	2304	48	2	1
Do	2432	48	2	1

REPORTS

OF THE

COMMITTEE ON CLAIMS,

HOUSE OF REPRESENTATIVES,

FROM THE FOURTEENTH CONGRESS, 1815, TO THE FORTY-NINTH CONGRESS, 1887, INCLUSIVE,

IN THIRTY-TWO VOLUMES.

COMPILED, UNDER THE DIRECTION OF THE JOINT COMMITTEE ON PRINTING,

BY

T. H. McKEE,

CLERK DOCUMENT ROOM, UNITED STATES SENATE.

WASHINGTON:
GOVERNMENT PRINTING OFFICE.
1887.

9207 CL H

FORTY-NINTH CONGRESS, FIRST SESSION.

[PUBLIC RESOLUTION—No. 24.]

Joint resolution authorizing the preparation of a compilation of the reports of committees of the Senate and House of Representatives.

Resolved by the Senate and House of Representatives of the United States of America in Congress assembled, Tha there be prepared under the direction of the Joint Committee of Printing, a compilation of the reports of the Senate and House of Representatives from the Fourteenth to the Forty-ninth Congress, inclusive, classified by committees, arranged, indexed, and bound in suitable volumes for the use of the standing committees of the two Houses of Congress. And the sum of seven thousand seven hundred and fifty dollars, or so much thereof as may be found necessary, is hereby appropriated out of any money in the Treasury not otherwise appropriated, for the preparation of said work, which sum may be paid by the Secretary of the Treasury upon the order of the chairman of said Joint Committee, as additional pay or compensation to any officer or employee of the United States.

Resolved further, That the Clerk of the House and Secretary of the Senate be, and they are hereby directed, to procure and file, for the use of their respective Houses, copies of all reports made by each committee of all succeeding Congresses; and that the Clerk of the House and the Secretary of the Senate be, and they are hereby, authorized and directed at the close of each session of Congress, to cause said reports to be indexed and bound, one copy to be deposited in the library of each House and one copy in the room of the committee from which the reports emanated.

Approved, July 29, 1886.

COMPILER'S NOTICE.

This compilation embraces all the printed reports made by both Houses of Congress from the commencement of the Fourteenth to the close of the Forty-ninth Congress. They are classified by committees and arranged in numerical order. The collection for each committee is divided into volumes of suitable size. Each committee has a separate index, a copy being bound in each volume.

The SPECIAL and SELECT reports are all compiled in one collection having one index, a copy of which is bound in each volume.

The plan throughout the compilation is to place each report to the committee from which it was reported, without reference to the subject-matter.

The House and Senate reports are compiled separately. Care will be required in noticing the chronological order, as in some instances an entire session or Congress may not appear in certain volumes from the fact that during this period no reports were made by this committee.

T. H. McKEE.

INDEX

TO

REPORTS OF THE COMMITTEE ON CLAIMS,

HOUSE OF REPRESENTATIVES.

FROM 1815 TO 1887, INCLUSIVE.

Subject.	Report.	Congress.	Session.	Volume.
ABBOT, JAMES, claim for relief	55	21	1	5
ABBOTT, JOEL, Jr., claim for relief	25	18	2	2
ABBOTT, JOHN F., claim for relief	538	24	1	8
ABBOTT, SAMUEL W., claim for relief	705	44	1	27
Do	683	45	2	27
ABE (steamer), claim for relief of owners of	47	41	2	25
ABELL, JOSEPH, claim for relief	208	23	1	7
ACHEN, WILLIAM D., claim for relief	443	22	1	6
ACKLEY, EBY, claim for relief	53	30	1	15
ACRE, GEORGE, claim for relief	298	23	1	7
ACTON, H. C., claim for relief	826	47	1	29
ADA A. ANDREWS (schooner), claim for relief of owners	657	43	1	26
ADAMS, AARON, claim for relief	110	27	3	11
ADAMS, ALEXANDER H. (pension agent at Lexington, Ky.), for relief of sureties on official bond of	3789	49	2	32
ADAMS, GEORGE B., claim for relief	546	25	2	9
ADAMS, HENDERSON, claim for relief	27	39	1	25
ADAMS, HENRY and CATHARINE, claim for relief	336	29	1	13
ADAMS, J. H., claim for relief	602	47	1	29
Do	2160	48	2	30
Do	1882	49	1	31
ADAMS, JAMES, claim for relief	418	24	1	8
ADAMS, JOHN, claim for relief	55	19	1	3
Do	494	28	1	12
ADAMS, MARY A., claim for relief	13	42	2	26
ADAMS, RICHARD M., claim for relief	428	30	1	16
ADAMS, SAMUEL, claim for relief	512	44	1	27
ADAMS, THEODORE, claim for relief	49	36	2	22
ADAMS, WILLIAM L., claim for relief	16	45	3	27
ADDOMS, JOHN T. (executor), claim for relief	520	24	1	8
Do	24	25	2	9
Do	27	26	1	10
ADKINSON, D. O., claim for relief	1864	49	1	31
ADKINSON, W. G., claim for relief	1554	47	1	29
AFRICANS. (*See also* FREEDMEN.)				
AFRICAN SLAVES, rescued from slave ships, payment of bounty for	268	24	1	8
AGNEL, HYACINTHE ROBERT, claim for relief of heirs	428	47	1	29
AGNEW, NANCY, and others, claim for relief	49	22	2	6
AHERENFELDT, CHARLES, claim for relief	405	30	1	16
Do	3	31	1	18
ALABAMA,				
City of Mobile, moneys advanced during Creek war of 1836, to refund	304	24	2	8
Do	58	25	3	9
Claims of citizens for property impressed and losses by Indian depredations	301	24	2	8
Claims of the State for expenses incurred during the Creek war of 1836–'37	127	29	1	13
Creek Indian war, claim for losses sustained in suppressing	932	25	2	9
Physicians, claim for relief	1071	49	1	31
Do	2694	49	1	31
Volunteers,				
Captain Parks's company, 1837, service against Creek Indians	958	25	2	9
Compensation for services rendered by certain companies under command of Major Holt	258	24	2	8

Subject.	Report.	Congress.	Session.	Volume.
ALAMO CEMENT COMPANY, claim for relief	1290	49	1	31
ALBERT (brig), for relief of owners of	690	29	1	14
ALBERTSON, SARAH F., claim for relief	342	44	1	27
ALDEN, LUCIUS D., claim for relief	1718	46	2	28
ALEXANDER, H. H., claim for relief	4	44	2	27
ALEXANDER, JOHN E., claim for relief	624	25	2	9
Do	539	26	1	10
Do	48	27	2	11
ALEXANDER & CO., claim for relief	808	44	1	27
ALEXANDER SWIFT & CO., claim for relief	1999	47	2	29
ALLEGHENY COUNTY, PENNSYLVANIA, to reimburse certain citizens of, for damages in the construction of bridge across Ohio River	491	43	1	26
Do	596	47	1	29
ALLEN, ALBORNE, claim for relief	89	28	1	12
Do	105	29	1	13
Do	42	30	1	15
ALLEN, CHARLES N., claim for relief	410	30	1	16
ALLEN, CHARLES R., claim for relief	52	28	2	12
ALLEN, CLARK, claim for relief	65	24	1	8
Do	906	25	2	9
Do	168	27	3	11
ALLEN, D. B., & CO., claim for relief	303	43	1	26
ALLEN, E. G. (assignee), claim for relief	302	43	2	26
ALLEN, E. L., claim for relief of administrators of	1745	46	2	28
ALLEN, JOHN R., claim for relief	63	26	1	10
ALLEN, SPARTAN, claim for relief	680	26	1	10
ALLEN, STEPHEN, claim for relief	374	23	1	7
ALLEN, THOMAS, claim for relief	2	28	2	12
ALLIN, ERSKINE S., claim for relief	1814	49	1	31
ALLIS, RANDALL, claim for relief	241	22	1	6
ALLYN, FRANCIS, claim for relief	326	24	2	8
Do	17	29	1	13
Do	59	27	2	11
Do	74	28	1	12
Do	12	30	2	17
Do	35	33	1	19
ALVORD, STEPHEN W., claim for relief of sureties	725	47	1	29
AMADEN, THOMAS, claim for relief	458	36	1	22
AMAN, STEPHEN, claim for relief	44	26	1	10
Do	498	27	2	11
AMERICAN COLONIZATION SOCIETY, relief of certain Africans recaptured by the U. S. S. Yorktown	2	31	2	15
AMERICAN GROCER ASSOCIATION, claim for relief	1811	49	1	31
AMES, LEMUEL, claim for relief	50	18	1	2
AMES, RICHARD, claim for relief	656	30	1	17
ANDERSON, A. D., and others, claim for relief	24	46	1	29
ANDERSON, A. M., and others, claim for relief	3468	49	1	31
ANDERSON, ELBERT, claim for relief on Army contract, 1812	113	19	1	3
Do	57	21	2	5
Do	692	26	1	10
ANDERSON, GEORGE and JAMES, claim for relief	896	25	2	9
ANDERSON, HENRY JAMES (administrator), claim for relief	57	21	2	5
ANDERSON, JACOB, claim for relief	691	27	2	11
ANDERSON, JAMES W., claim for relief	428	26	1	10
ANDERSON, JOHN, claim for relief	24	15	1	1
Do	7	17	2	1
Do	493	22	1	6
Do	692	27	2	11
Do	27	29	1	13
Do	39	30	1	15
ANDERSON, JOHN, deceased, claim for relief of estate	167	27	2	11
Do	277	29	1	13
Do	396	33	1	19
ANDERSON, JOSEPH, claim for relief	1	41	1	25
ANDERSON, LEWIS, claim for relief	8	21	2	5
ANDERSON, SARAH, administratrix, claim for relief	57	51	2	5
ANDERSON, SAMUEL T. (purser U. S. Navy), settlement of accounts	47	18	2	1
Do	27	26	2	10
Do	142	27	2	11
ANDERSON, WILLIAM S., claim for relief	360	22	1	6
Do	7	23	1	7
ANDREWS, HENRY W., claim for relief	244	30	1	16
ANDREWS, J. H., claim for relief	332	27	2	11
ANGUS, SAMUEL, claim for relief of widow	183	35	1	21
APPEL, MORRIS, claim for relief	1596	46	2	28
ARBUTHNOT, WILLIAM, claim for relief	285	22	1	6
ARDREY, ROBERT G., claim for relief	427	47	1	29
ARFWERDSON, CHARLES D., claim for relief	174	36	1	22
ARIADNE (ship), settlement of prize case of	199	25	2	9
ARKANSAS, boundary between Missouri and	102	22	2	6
ARMES, JOSIAH C., claim for relief	6	38	1	25

Subject.	Report.	Congress.	Session.	Volume.
ARMISTEAD, WALKER K., claim for relief	190	19	1	3
ARMSTRONG, ANDREW, claim for relief	833	24	1	8
Do	603	27	2	11
ARMSTONG, EDWARD S., claim for relief	2649	48	2	30
ARMSTRONG, GEORGE, claim for relief	239	31	1	18
ARMSTRONG, JAMES B., claim for relief of heirs	659	43	1	26
Do	42	44	1	27
Do	97	47	1	29
ARMSTRONG, P. M., claim for relief of widow	7	44	2	27
ARMSTRONG, ROBERT and **WILLIAM**, claim for relief	742	25	2	9
ARMY.				
Band at Sackett's Harbor, N. Y., payment of	501	27	2	11
Children of deceased officers, special aid in education of	415	24	1	8
Compensation of officers of one grade performing duties of higher grade	77	23	2	7
Do	883	46	2	28
Compensation and allowances of the different corps of the Army on the same footing	415	34	1	8
Compensation of persons not mustered	108	37	2	25
Due-bills of quartermasters of, settlement of	115	22	2	6
Half-pay to widows and orphans of deceased soldiers	415	24	1	8
Sutlers' right of lien on soldiers' pay	89	22	1	6
Do	358	22	1	6
Do	9	24	1	7
ARNOW, JOSEPH and **PETER**, claim for relief	121	32	1	19
ARTHUR, CHESTER A., claim for relief	2711	49	1	31
ASH, GEORGE, claim for relief	62	25	3	9
ASHBURN, GEORGE W., claim for relief	19	39	2	25
ASHBURN, MARTHA A., claim for relief	302	43	1	26
Do	664	44	1	27
ASHLEY, GEORGE (administrator), claim for relief	175	36	1	22
ASHUELOT, (U. S. steamer), claim for relief of sufferers by wreck of	834	49	1	31
Do	3128	49	1	31
ASSASSINATION. (*See* CONSPIRATORS).				
ACHESSON, JOSEPH T., claim for relief	276	29	1	13
ATHERTON, CHARLES H., claim for relief	266	27	2	11
ATKINS, ALFRED, and others, claim for relief	190	34	3	20
Do	632	36	1	22
ATKINS, JAMES, claim for relief	422	43	1	26
Do	837	43	2	26
ATKINSON, ANDREW, claim for relief of administrator	216	35	2	21
ATKINSON, ROLLINS & CO., and others, claim for relief	190	34	3	20
Do	632	36	1	22
ATLANTA, GEORGIA, for relief of Masonic Hall Company of	29	45	3	27
ATLEE, JOHN S. (administrator), claim for relief	72	28	1	12
ATLEE, WILLIAM A., claim for relief of estate	72	28	1	12
ATWATER, CALEB, claim for relief	832	25	2	9
ATWELL & HAYDEN, claim for relief	296	24	1	8
ATWILL, EBENEZER, claim for relief	32	29	1	13
AUDITOR, FIFTH, OF UNITED STATES TREASURY, defining duties of	79	22	2	6
AUGUSTA, GEORGIA, corporation and citizens of, for relief	319	24	2	8
Do	1068	25	2	9
AUSMENT, WILLIAM D., claim for relief	116	29	1	13
AUSTIN, LORING, claim for damages growing out of military arrest in New York	60	15	1	1
AUSTIN & TAILER, claim for relief	694	24	1	8
Do	49	25	2	9
AVART, ROBERT, claim for relief of heirs of	339	22	1	6
Do	5	23	1	7
AVERILL, EBENEZER, claim for relief	8	18	2	2
AVERILL, JOSEPH K., claim for relief	981	25	2	9
AVERILL, WILLIAM, claim for relief	893	47	1	29
AVERY, HANNAH, claim for relief	39	31	2	18
AVERY, JOHN J., claim for relief	240	23	1	7
AXTON, JEREMIAH, claim for relief	212	23	1	7
AYERS, HENRY, claim for relief	2109	48	1	30
Do	2275	49	1	31
AYERS, JAMES H., claim for relief	70	48	1	30
Do	1009	49	1	31
AYMAR & CO. and others, claim for relief	190	34	3	20
Do	632	36	1	22
BABB, BENJAMIN, and others, claim for relief	1310	46	2	28
BABCOCK, FLOYD C., claim for relief	425	44	1	27
BACHE, SEMON & CO., claim for relief	3318	49	1	31
Do	3612	49	2	32
BACOT, ELIZABETH S. W., claim for relief	531	24	1	8
Do	25	25	2	9
Do	268	26	1	10
BAILEY, E. B., claim for relief	2712	49	1	31
BAILEY, MARTHA (administratrix), claim for relief	57	21	2	5
Do	91	21	2	5
Do	465	22	1	6
Do	27	23	1	7

Subject.	Report.	Congress.	Session.	Volume.
BAILEY, O. W., claim for relief	558	28	1	12
BAILEY, THEODORUS (administratrix), Army contract, settlement of	57	21	2	5
BAILEY, WILLIAM, claim for relief	359	24	1	8
Do	401	35	1	21
BAILEY & RINKER, claim for relief	171	19	1	3
BAILY & DELORD, claim for relief	192	24	2	8
Do	9	25	2	9
Do	24	26	1	10
Do	88	26	2	10
Do	401	35	1	21
BAIRD, ABSALOM, claim for relief of heirs	91	33	2	19
Do	680	36	1	22
BAKER, JAMES, claim for relief	414	24	1	8
Do	769	24	1	8
Do	16	25	2	9
BAKER, JOHN H., claim for relief	479	30	1	16
Do	401	31	1	18
BAKER, STEPHEN, claim for relief	69	15	1	1
BAKER, TIMOTHY, claim for relief	164	44	2	27
BAKER, WILLIAM, claim for care of wounded British prisoners left in Washington City at capture of, in 1814	480	22	1	6
Do	224	23	1	7
Do	424	23	1	7
Do	452	23	1	7
Do	12	24	1	7
Do	13	24	1	7
Do	4	24	2	8
BALCH, JOHN, JR., claim for relief	866	26	1	10
BALDWIN, ANNA MARIA, claim for relief	760	30	1	17
BALDWIN, IRA, claim for relief	348	27	2	11
BALDWIN, JOHN P., claim for relief	698	26	1	10
Do	695	27	2	11
BALL, EDWARD, claim for relief	142	38	1	25
Do	44	41	2	25
BALL, JOHN T., claim for relief	119	33	1	19
BALL & WASSON, claim for relief	423	30	1	16
BALLARD PAVEMENT COMPANY, claim for relief	1552	49	1	31
BALMER & WEBER, claim for relief	107	39	1	25
BALTIMORE, MARYLAND,				
Baltimore Bridge Company, claim for relief	419	44	1	27
Citizens of, for loss of vessels destroyed in war of 1812–'14, in defense of	11	16	2	1
Do	1	17	1	1
Do	6	18	2	2
Do	167	19	1	3
Do	221	20	1	4
Do	128	22	2	6
Common council of, for loans advanced to United States, claim for settlement	218	20	1	4
Night inspectors of port of, to compensate	2471	49	1	13
War of 1812, to pay expenditures in	519	49	1	31
BANK,				
Chillicothe, Ohio, loan to United States, settlement of, 1814	48	19	2	3
Do	45	21	1	5
First National, of Newton, Mass., for relief	3126	49	1	31
First National, of Portland, Oreg., claim for relief	3818	49	2	32
German National, of Louisville, Ky., relief	870	46	2	28
Do	324	47	1	29
Iron Mountain, of Saint Louis, Mo., for relief of	999	49	1	31
Phenix National, for relief	2504	49	1	31
State National, of Louisiana, relief of	1674	47	1	29
BANTA, ANDREW, claim for relief	568	24	1	8
BAPTIST AND UNITED BRETHREN CHURCH OF TYRONE, PENNSYLVANIA, claim for relief	81	39	1	25
BARBER, MERRITT, claim for relief	403	45	2	27
BARCLAY & LIVINGSTON, claim for relief	54	29	2	14
Do	65	30	1	15
BARGY, PETER, JR., claim for relief	809	25	2	9
Do	240	26	2	10
Do	486	27	2	11
BARGY, PETER, JR., *et al.*, removal of obstructions, mouth of Savannah River	248	21	1	5
Do	231	22	1	6
Do	248	26	2	10
BARKER, WILLIAM, *et al.*, claim for relief	2861	49	1	31
BARLOW, MARY, claim for relief	75	42	2	26
BARNES, FRANCIS, claim for relief	352	22	1	6
Do	475	22	1	6
Do	25	23	1	7
BARNES, JOHN, claim for relief of estate	301	26	1	10
Do	8	27	2	11
BARNES, JOSEPH, claim for relief	458	36	1	22
BARNES, S. & J., claim for relief	458	36	1	22
BARNES, WILLIAM, claim for relief	694	27	2	11

Subject.	Report.	Congress.	Session.	Volume.
BARNETT, EZRA B., claim for relief	17	44	1	27
BARNEY, JOSHUA, claim for relief	483	30	1	16
BARRETT, ANDREW J., claim for relief	668	43	1	26
Do	228	44	1	27
BARRON, JOHN V., claim for relief	164	27	2	11
BARRONTON, PERRY L., claim for relief	834	25	2	9
BARRY, ROBERT, claim for relief of administrator of	32	31	1	18
BARRY, WILLIAM B., claim for relief	92	35	1	21
BARTLE, ANDREW, claim for relief	370	26	1	10
BARTLETT, DAVID, claim for relief	362	23	1	7
Do	11	24	1	7
Do	48	25	3	9
Do	30	26	2	10
Do	35	27	2	11
BARTLETT, JOHN R., claim for relief	522	36	1	22
BARTLETT, RHOMAS T., claim for relief	630	44	1	27
BARTOL, GEORGE, Jr. (executor), claim for relief	176	24	1	8
BARTON, EDWARD, and others, for relief of	47	41	2	25
BASSETT, LESLIE, claim for relief	3895	49	2	32
BATES, DAVID G., claim for relief of estate	489	36	1	22
BATES, IRIS W., claim for relief	496	31	1	18
BATES, LINCOLN, claim for relief	287	33	1	19
BATTY, JOHN, claim for relief	126	28	2	12
BAUDOUIN, A., claim for relief	459	30	1	16
Do	76	31	1	18
Do	56	35	1	21
BAXTER, STEPHEN, claim for relief	61	16	1	1
BAYLESS, LOTT S., claim for relief	2426	49	1	31
BAYLIES, SAMUEL, claim for relief	9	18	2	2
BAYLOR, T. G., claim for relief	130	47	1	29
Do	355	48	1	30
BEACH, EDGAR A., claim for relief	3	44	2	27
Do	681	45	2	27
BEACHAM, THOMAS, claim for relief of heirs	108	23	2	7
Do	37	24	1	7
BEALE, ROBERT, claim for relief	436	23	1	7
BEALL, BENJAMIN, claim for relief	378	23	1	7
BEAMAN, JOHN W., claim for relief	2791	49	1	31
BEARD, B. H., claim for relief	165	25	3	9
BEARD, BETTY, claim for relief	306	26	1	10
BEARD, DAVID, claim for relief of heirs	41	26	1	10
Do	764	27	2	11
BEARD, HARRIET, claim for relief	367	26	1	10
BEARD, JAMES, claim for relief of widow	571	36	1	22
BEARD, PARTHENIA, claim for relief	713	24	1	8
Do	49	25	3	9
BEARD, STEPHEN, claim for relief	306	26	1	10
BEATTIE, WILLIAM and JOHN, claim for relief	976	47	1	29
BEATTY, JAMES, claim for relief of estate	167	34	3	20
Do	415	35	1	21
BEAUGRAND, JEAN BAP., claim for relief	35	21	2	5
BEAULEAN, THOMAS, claim for relief	458	36	1	22
BEAUMARCHAIS, CARON DE (heirs), claim for moneys advanced United States through French Government	111	15	1	1
Do	75	17	2	1
BEBEE, WASHINGTON S., claim for relief	41	30	2	17
BECK, JAMES PRESTON, claim for relief	74	39	1	25
BECK, JOHN J., claim for relief	361	24	1	8
Do	44	28	1	12
Do	136	28	1	12
BECK & WIRTH, claim for relief	198	43	1	26
BECKER, JOHN, claim for relief	3	39	1	25
BECKLEY, JOHN R., claim for relief	86	39	1	25
BECKLEY, R. D., claim for relief	598	49	1	31
BECKTILL, RIDDLE & HEADINGTON, claim for relief	173	20	1	4
BECKWITH, WEALTHY, claim for relief	766	24	1	8
BEDFORD, ROBERT, claim for relief	15	18	2	2
BEELER, LOUIS F., and others, claim for relief	482	30	1	16
BEENE, JONES C., claim for relief	1586	46	2	28
Do	325	47	1	29
BEGBIE, WISEMAN & CO., claim for relief	34	30	2	17
BELDEN, THOMAS, claim for relief	92	21	2	5
BELDING, H. K., claim for relief	676	45	2	27
Do	912	46	2	28
Do	463	47	1	29
Do	1679	48	1	30
Do	1551	49	1	31
Do	3102	49	1	31
BELL, CALEB, claim for relief	398	29	1	13
Do	486	30	1	16

Subject.	Report.	Congress.	Session.	Volume.
BELL, ELIJAH S., claim for relief	850	25	2	9
Do	403	22	1	6
Do	29	26	2	10
Do	697	27	2	11
Do	202	27	3	11
Do	502	28	1	12
BELL, FRANCIS M., claim for relief	828	49	1	31
BELL, ISAAC, claim for relief	491	25	2	9
Do	60	25	3	9
BELL, JOHN W., claim for relief	234	30	1	16
BELL, NICHOLAS H., claim for relief	548	25	2	9
BELL, PIROMIS H., claim for relief	3913	49	2	32
BELL, SAMUEL, claim for relief	491	25	2	9
Do	60	25	3	9
BELL, WILLIAM H., claim for relief	281	24	1	8
Do	11	25	2	9
BELLAMY, AARON, claim for relief	93	22	2	6
Do	38	22	1	7
BELLE, PEORIA (steamboat), for relief of owners of	72	42	3	26
BEDT, JOSEPH C., claim for relief	19	21	2	5
BENDER, GEORGE, claim for relief	475	23	1	7
Do	16	24	1	7
BENEDICT, JANE, claim for relief	371	23	1	7
BENJAMIN, CHARLES F., claim for relief	337	46	3	28
Do	86	47	1	29
BENNER, DANIEL J., claim for relief	903	46	2	28
Do	1477	47	1	29
BENNETT, JOSHUA, claim for relief	53	18	1	2
BENNETT, RANDOLPH, claim for relief	4	39	1	25
BENNS, CHARLES, claim for relief	27	22	2	6
Do	324	24	2	8
Do	76	25	2	9
Do	219	25	3	9
Do	2	29	1	13
Do	70	30	1	15
BENT, ST. VRAIN & CO., claim for relief	37	30	1	15
BENTLY, BENJAMIN, claim for relief	58	23	2	7
Do	291	27	3	11
BERAULT, MARY A. (administratrix), claim for relief	77	37	2	25
BERDAN, HIRAM (assignee of the Berdan Fire-Arms Manufacturing Company), settlement of claim	3791	49	2	32
BERRY, BENJAMIN, claim for relief	68	15	1	1
BERRY, JAMES R., claim for relief	2893	49	1	31
BESSELS, EMIL, service on board steamer Polaris, North Polar Expedition, claim for relief	306	46	3	28
BEYER, G. T., claim for relief	343	28	1	12
Do	225	29	1	13
BEZIOR, JULIA, claim for relief	437	23	1	7
BIBB, JOHN B., claim for relief	342	27	2	11
BIBB, JOHN G., claim for relief	679	26	1	10
BIDAMON, EMMA, claim for relief	66	34	1	20
BIDLE, RICHARD (administrator), claim for relief	3	20	2	4
Do	1	21	1	5
BIDOW & WILSON, claim for relief	55	45	2	27
BILLUPS, JOEL A., claim for relief	14	44	2	27
Do	696	45	2	27
BINGHAM, DANIEL H., claim for relief	29	37	3	25
Do	10	38	1	25
Do	28	39	1	25
BINGHAM, ELEAZER, claim for relief	184	27	2	11
BINGHAM, THOMAS, claim for relief	522	28	1	13
BINGHAM, W., & CO. (claim for relief)	367	35	1	21
BINNS, CHARLES, claim for relief of executor of	839	25	2	9
Do	38	25	3	9
BIRCKHEAD, JANE A., claim for relief	45	42	2	26
BIRD, DANIEL, claim for relief	837	25	2	9
BISCOE, GEORGE W. (owner of the schooner Speedwell), claim for relief	51	34	2	20
Do	146	34	2	20
Do	6	35	1	21
BISHOP, A. & F., claim for relief	458	36	1	22
BISHOP, A. J. & A. F., claim for relief	458	36	1	22
BISHOP, AMOS, claim for relief	458	36	1	22
BISHOP, W. & J., claim for relief	458	36	1	22
BISHOP, WILLIAM, claim for relief	11	20	1	4
BISHOP & COMPANY, claim for relief	299	43	2	26
BISSEL, LEWIS, claim for relief	263	24	2	8
Do	900	25	2	9
Do	50	26	1	10
BISSELL'S FERRY, CONNECTICUT, for relief of towns of Windsor and South Windsor, on account of damages done to	3958	49	2	32
BIXBY, FRANCIS M. & BUTLER H., claim for relief	78	39	1	25

Subject.	Report.	Congress.	Session.	Volume.
BOWHAY, WILLIAM P., claim for relief	465	36	1	22
Do	144	37	2	25
BOWIE, WASHINGTON, and others (executors), claim for relief	35	15	2	1
Do	20	16	2	1
BOWIE & KURTZ, owners of ship Allegany	35	14	2	1
Do	35	15	2	1
Do	20	16	2	1
BOWMAN ACT, settlement of private claims under	3497	49	2	32
BOYCE, PURNELL, claim for relief of heirs	330	22	1	6
BOYD, ROBERT, claim for relief of administrator	41	22	2	
BOYDEN, N., claim for relief	462	45	2	27
Do	342	46	2	28
BOYLE, ANDREW, claim for relief	280	22	1	6
BOYLE, CORNELIUS (administrator), claim for relief	426	45	1	21
BRADEN, EDWARD, & CO., claim for relief	1901	49	1	31
BRADFORD, A. C., claim for relief	3992	49	2	32
BRADFORD, THOMAS, claim for relief	90	19	1	3
BRADFORD, WILLIAM J. A., claim for relief	247	30	1	16
BRADY, FREEMAN, claim for relief	122	24	2	8
Do	63	25	2	9
BRADY, ROBERT, claim for relief	104	29	1	13
BRADLEY, GEORGE W., claim for relief	342	43	2	26
BRAGDON, ELIJAH, claim for relief of widow	414	30	1	16
BRAGG, HENRY, claim for relief	47	36	2	23
BRAINARD, DAVID L., *et al.*, claim for relief	1125	49	1	31
Do	3432	49	1	31
BRANCH PILOTS AT NEW ORLEANS, claim for relief	9	28		13
BRANNIN, RICHARD, and others, claim for relief	307	25	3	9
BRAXTON, JOHN S., claim for relief	401	45	2	27
Do	914	46	2	28
BRAYMAN, DANIEL, claim for relief	50	22	2	6
Do	337	27	2	11
Do	337	28	1	13
BRAZIL MAIL STEAMSHIP COMPANY, to refund to same certain port charges and custom-house dues wrongfully collected	84	41	2	25
BRENNAN, JOHN, claim for relief	152	43	1	26
BRERETON, AMELIA, claim for relief	379	29	1	13
Do	57	30	1	15
BREVARD, MARY K., claim for relief	1958	47	2	29
Do	740	48	1	30
Do	1233	48	1	30
BREVOORT, HENRY B., claim for relief	9	17	2	1
BREWER, AARON, claim for relief	698	27	2	11
BREWER, JAMES H., claim for relief	409	22	1	6
Do	9	23	1	7
BREWSTER, B. S., claim for relief	393	35	1	21
BRICE, JAMES, claim for relief	61	45	2	27
Do	2173	49	1	31
BRIDESBURG ARSENAL. (*See* FRANKFORD ARSENAL.)				
BRIDGES. (*See also* RIVERS AND HARBORS.)				
BRIDGE ACROSS THE POTOMAC, claim of O. H. Dibble for damage by annulment of contract for	142	23	2	7
BRIDGES, Ohio River, damages to transportation on, by	491	43	1	26
Do	596	47	1	29
BRIGGS, ALFRED M., claim for relief	49	41	2	25
BRINDLE, WILLIAM, claim for relief	242	45	2	27
BRINTON, WILLIAM T., claim for relief	63	42	3	26
BRISBOIS, MICHAEL, claim for relief	827	25	2	9
BRISTOL, CHARLES B., claim for relief	233	24	2	8
BRISTOW, JOHN T., claim for relief	98	44		27
BRODHEAD, JOHN M., claim for relief	655	26	1	10
BROADWELL, LEWIS H., claim for relief	393	35	1	21
BROCKENBOROUGH, AUSTIN, claim for relief	369	26	1	10
BRONSON, ALVIN, claim for schooner Penelope	84	16	1	1
Do	39	16	2	1
Do	40	17		1
Do	12	17	2	1
BRONSON, JOHN, claim for relief	147	23	1	7
BROOK, WILLIAM, and others, claim for relief	8	29	1	13
Do	13	30	1	15
BROOKE, ROBERT, claim for relief	81	19	1	3
BROOKS, O. A., & CO., claim for relief	387	35	1	21
BROOKS, THOMAS S., & CO., claim for relief	352	48	1	30
BROOME, JOHN, claim for relief	260	24	2	8
Do	1064	25	2	9
Do	115	25	3	9
BROPHEY, JOHN, claim for relief	75	23	2	7
BROSENNE, FREDERICK, claim for relief	7	41	2	25
BROUDT, ADAM, claim for relief	71	22	2	6
BROWN, AMOS W., claim for relief	467	24	1	8
BROWN, DANIEL, claim for relief	62	30	1	15
Do	96	30	1	15

Subject.	Report.	Congress.	Session.	Volume.
BROWN, ELIAS, claim for relief	456	36	1	22
BROWN, HARRIET, claim for relief	7	30	1	15
BROWN, HENRY B., claim for relief	5	44	2	27
Do	15	45	3	27
Do	1238	46	2	28
BROWN, JAMES, claim for relief of heirs	10	30	1	15
BROWN, JOHN, claim for relief	705	26	1	10
BROWN, JOHN J., claim for relief	2900½	49	2	33
BROWN, JOSEPH, claim for relief	729	25	2	9
Do	1286	46	2	28
Do	1312	46	3	28
Do	321	47	1	29
BROWN, JOSEPH C., claim for relief	102	22	2	6
Do	19	23	1	7
BROWN, JOSEPH R., claim for relief	317	30	1	16
BROWN, MORGAN, claim for relief	30	17	1	1
BROWN, MORGAR, claim for relief	5	17	2	1
BROWN, MORTIMER H., claim for relief	428	43	1	26
BROWN, RETURN B., claim for relief	186	27	2	11
BROWN, S. P., and others, claim for relief	45	41	2	25
BROWN, SAMUEL, claim for relief	140	24	2	8
BROWN, SOLOMON, claim for relief	458	36	1	22
BROWN, THOMAS, claim for relief	161	36	1	22
BROWN, WILLIAM, claim for relief	280	33	1	19
Do	215	35	2	21
Do	3	36	1	22
BROWNE, JONATHAN, Jr., and others, claim for relief	121	45	3	27
BROWNELL, EDWARD T., claim for relief	1504	46	2	28
BROWNING, MESHEEK, claim for relief	155	21	1	5
BROWNING, SAMUEL, claim for relief	2	38	2	25
BROWNLOW, WILLIAM G., claim for relief	1271	48	1	30
BROYLES, PERRY, claim for relief	325	43	1	26
BRUCE, JOHN, claim for relief	73	22	2	6
Do	193	23	1	7
BRUCE, WILLIAM, claim for relief of administrator	194	29	1	13
BRUNSON, JOHN, claim for relief	407	21	1	5
BRUSH, ADELAIDE, claim for relief	48	18	1	2
BRYAN, A. C., and others, claim for relief	469	30	1	16
BRYAN, JOHN A., claim for relief	302	33	1	19
BRYAN, RICHARD T., claim for relief	45	45	3	27
Do	104	45	2	27
Do	4160	49	2	32
BRYAN, THOMAS, claim for relief	235	30	1	16
BRYANT, WILLIAM, claim for relief of heirs	544	35	1	21
Do	15	36	1	22
BRYDEN, WILLIAM, claim for relief	373	23	1	7
Do	37	26	1	10
BUBER, JOHN, claim for relief	458	36	1	22
BUBER, WILLIAM, claim for relief	458	36	1	22
BUCK, CHARLES E., claim for relief	489	43	1	26
BUCKLAND, CYRUS, claim for relief	333	34	1	20
BUCKMINISTER, THOMAS, claim for relief of administrator	15	16	1	1
BUDLONG, HANNAH, claim for relief	679	24	1	8
Do	45	25	2	9
BUELL, DILLON, claim for relief	228	20	1	4
BUFORD, THOMAS, claim for relief	71	20	2	4
BUGGERT, HENRIETTA, claim for relief	1677	47	1	29
Do	1725	47	1	29
BULL, ARCHIBALD, claim for relief	583	29	1	14
Do	150	30	1	15
BULLARD, REUBEN N., claim for relief	24	22	2	6
Do	88	24	1	8
BULLOCH, ARCHIBALD S. (collector of port of Savannah), moiety of forfeiture (schooner Montevidiana)	63	17	1	1
Do	10	17	2	1
BULOW, JOHN J., Jr., claim for relief of heirs	176	27	3	11
Do	403	31	1	18
BURCHARD, JABEZ, claim for relief	655	48	1	30
Do	975	49	1	31
Do	2472	49	1	31
BURDSALL, REBECCA, claim for relief	1716	47	1	29
BURGESS, ANDREW, claim for relief	32	45	3	27
Do	426	48	1	30
BURGESS, EDWARD, claim for relief	*344	24	1	8
Do	6	25	2	9
BURGESS, WILLIAM S., claim for relief	390	45	2	27
Do	157	46	2	28
BURKE, JOHN, claim for relief	267	24	1	8
Do	203	27	3	11

* Parts 1, 2.

Subject.	Report.	Congress.	Session.	Report.
BURNETT, DAVID G., claim for relief	190	45	2	27
BURNHAM, GEORGE, and others, claim for relief	*420	43	1	26
BURNHAM, JOHN, claim for relief of heirs	305	33	1	19
BURNS, AMZI L., claim for relief	116	38	1	25
Do	80	39	1	25
BURNS, OTWAY, claim for relief	402	22	1	6
BURNS, W. W., claim for relief	245	46	2	28
Do	227	47	1	29
BURNSIDE, JAMES O. P., claim for relief	31	42	2	26
BURNSIDE, THOMAS, claim for relief	918	25	2	9
BURROUGH, ALBERT H. (administrator), claim for relief	324	31	1	18
BURROUGHS, FRANK J., claim for relief	3326	49	1	31
BURROWS, FRANK J., claims for relief	†2357	48	2	30
BURT, JOEL, claim for relief	255	24	1	8
BURWELL, W. P., claim for relief	611	44	1	27
Do	31	45	2	27
BUSH, JOHN P., claim for relief	2371	49	1	31
BUSTER, JOSHUA, claim for relief	999	25	2	9
BUTLER, EDWIN, claim for relief	73	42	3	26
BUTLER, JACOB, claim for relief	132	19	1	3
BUTLER, NATHANIEL, claim for relief	458	36	1	22
BUTLER, ROBERT, claim for relief	696	27	2	11
BUTLER, SAMUEL, claim for relief	220	23	1	7
BUTLER & PITKIN, claim for relief	1375	49	1	31
BUTTON, CHARLES W., claim for relief	628	44	1	27
Do	394	46	2	28
Do	161	47	1	29
BUTTON, ELISHA, claim for relief	66	28	1	10
Do	406	31	1	18
BUXTON, HANNAH, and others, claim for relief	24	38	1	25
BYERS, JAMES, and others, claim for relief	52	39	1	25
BYERS, JOHN and JAMES, army contract, 1818, settlement	11	17	1	1
BYINGTON, JOEL, claim for relief	224	20	1	4
Do	6	21	1	5
Do	497	22	1	6
Do	59	23	1	7
Do	47	26	1	10
Do	499	31	1	18
BYRNE, B. M., claim for relief	213	25	3	9
Do	422	35	1	21
BYRNES, JOHN, claim for relief of heirs	1239	48	1	30
CADDALL, JAMES S., claim for relief	179	44	1	27
CADWALLADER, JOHN F., claim for relief	1874	49	1	31
Do	2895	49	1	31
CAFFEY, MEDFORD, claim for relief	25	33	2	19
CALAHAN, ANDREW J., claim for relief	1389	47	1	29
CALDWELL, DAVID (clerk United States court, eastern district of Pennsylvania, 1826), settlement of accounts	390	24	1	8
Do	834	24	1	8
Do	12	25	2	9
CALDWELL, SAMUEL, claim for relief	114	21	2	5
CALER, JAMES, claim for relief	1097	47	1	29
CALHOUN, CHAUNCEY, claim for relief	151	25	3	9
Do	17	26	1	10
Do	8	26	2	10
Do	7	27	2	11
CALHOUND, JAMES S., claim for relief	1034	25	2	9
Do	654	26	1	10
CALIFORNIA, relative to payment of certain Indian war bonds issued by State of	669	43	1	26
CALL, ANSON, claim for relief	58	45	2	27
CALLAHAN, J. R., claim for relief	45	30	2	17
CALLAHAN, W. C., claim for relief	306	44	1	27
CALLAN, JAMES, claim for relief	195	24	1	8
Do	244	24	2	8
Do	65	25	2	9
CALVERT, GEORGE, claim for relief	128	37	2	25
Do	114	38	1	25
CALVERT, MADISON R., claim for relief	2009	48	1	30
CAMPBELL, ARCHIBALD, claim for relief of heirs	134	28	1	12
CAMPBELL, DAVID S., claim for relief	22	23	2	7
Do	30	24	1	7
CAMPBELL, HORACE S., claim for relief	129	35	1	21
CAMPBELL, JOHN, claim for relief	127	37	2	25
CAMPBELL, JOHN G., claim for relief	412	45	2	27
CAMPBELL, JOHN P., claim for relief	9	27	2	11
CAMPBELL, JOHN W., claim for relief	330	27	2	11
CAMPBELL, WILLIAM, claim for relief	464	23	1	7
CANAL COMPANY, Dismal Swamp, claim for relief	47	28	2	12
CANAL TRUST FUNDS, of the State of Wisconsin, relief of the State	20	39	2	25

* Parts 1, 2. † With views of the minority.

Subject.	Report.	Congress.	Session.	Volume.
CANARD, JAMES, relative to suits brought by certain insurance companies of New York against	757	30	1	17
CANDEE, G. W., claim for relief	627	49	1	31
CANFIELD, SAMUEL H., claim for relief	111	45	2	27
CANNON, DANIEL, claim for relief	618	36	1	22
CANNON, MARTHA, claim for relief	719	29	1	14
CANTWELL, L. C., claim for relief	898	46	2	28
CAPITOL BUILDING, for relief of stonecutters on extension of	306	33	1	19
CAPWELL, AMY C., claim for relief	1949	48	1	30
CARD, HENRY, claim for relief	18	24	2	8
CARLISLE, FREDERICK, claim for relief	1231	46	2	28
CARLTON, C. C., claim for relief	387	35	1	21
CARLTON, JAMES H., claim for relief of heirs	37	47	1	29
CARNES, PETER A., claim for relief	42	30	2	17
CARO, JOSEPH E., claim for relief	127	27	3	11
Do	128	28		12
CARPENTER, CEPHAS, and others, claim for relief	490	27	2	11
CARPENTER, DE FOREST W., claim for relief	2	44	2	27
Do	28	45	3	27
CARPENTER, GUY, claim for relief	206	27	3	11
Do	396	29	1	13
CARPENTER, IRA, claim for relief	392	25	2	9
Do	247	28	1	12
Do	171	29	1	13
Do	164	31	1	18
Do	47	35	2	21
CARPENTER, J. N., claim for relief	43	41	2	25
Do	368	43		26
CARPENTER, JEREMIAH, claim for relief	402	29		13
Do	758	30	1	17
Do	110	30	2	17
CARR, CHARLES F., claim for relief	86	42	2	26
CARR, JOHN, claim for relief	126	28	2	12
Do	434	29	1	13
CARROLL, DANIEL, claim for relief	11	14	2	1
CARROLL, LYSANDER H., claim for relief	652	48		30
Do	478	49	1	31
CARROLL, PATRICK, claim for relief	1842	46	2	28
Do	515	48	1	30
CARTER, CHAMPE, Jr., claim for relief	385	45	2	27
CARTER, CHARLES, claim for relief	2421	48	2	30
Do	2279	49	1	31
CARTER, JAMES R., claim for relief	1872	49	1	31
CARTER, SAMUEL, claim for relief	682	26	1	10
CARTY, MARY, claim for relief	238	30	1	16
CARVER (ship), for relief of owners of	94	42	3	26
CARVER, ELIAL, claim for relief	616	24	1	8
CARVER, NATHAN, claim for relief of administrator and executrix of	342	22	1	6
Do	39	30	2	17
Do	152	31	1	18
Do	301	33	1	19
Do	46	35	2	21
CARVER, WILLIAM K., claim for relief	603	47	1	29
CARY, EDWARD, claim for relief	153	20	1	4
Do	38	20	2	4
CASE, CALVIN, statement of, relating to loss of boats on Mississippi River	178	27	3	11
CASE, LEVI H., claim for relief	48	37	2	25
Do	4	38	1	25
CASEY, PATRICK, claim for relief	302	48	1	30
CASSEDY, CHARLES, claim for relief	394	21	1	5
CASSETY, JAMES M., claim for relief	673	47	1	29
CASSIDY, MARGARET, claim for relief	8	45	3	27
CATLETT, CHARLES J., claim for relief	413	22	1	6
CATLETT, HANSON, claim for relief of widow	47	21	2	5
CATON, JOSEPH M., and others, claim for relief	14	42	2	26
CATON, WILLIAM, claim for relief	322	23	1	7
CAYFORD, JOHN, claim for relief	176	24	2	8
CAZE, JAMES, and others, claim for relief	60	17	1	1
CAZE & RICHAUD, claim for property burned to prevent it falling into the hands of the enemy	60	17	1	1
Do	13	17	2	1
CENSUS, payment of enumerators of, 1860	52	43	1	26
CHAFFEE, JOHN, claim for relief	339	27	2	11
Do	201	27	3	11
Do	397	29	1	13
CHALMERS, JOHN, claim for relief	79	18	1	2
CHAMBERLAIN, CHARLES, claim for relief	3467	49	1	31
CHAMBERLAIN, E. M., claim for relief	83	31	2	18
CHAMBERLAIN, FRANK O., claim for relief	1561	46	2	28
CHAMBERS, THOMAS, claim for relief	305	48	1	30
Do	2014	49	1	31

Subject.	Report.	Congress.	Session.	Volume.
CHAMBERS & BROWN, claim for relief	2175	49	1	31
CHAMBLIN, TURNER, claim for relief	702	26	1	10
CHANCE (British bark), claim for relief of owners and crew	1481	49	1	31
Do	3025	49	1	31
CHANDLER, JOSEPH R., claim for relief	5	27	3	11
CHANDLER, THEOPHILUS P., claim for relief	570	46	2	28
Do	4	47	1	29
CHANEY, ELIZA JANE, claim for relief	79	39	1	25
CHANEY, THOMAS, claim for relief	602	30	1	17
CHAPIN, LUTHER, claim for relief, schooner Cuyahoga, captured	70	19	1	3
Do	73	19	2	3
Do	152	20	1	4
Do	14	20	2	4
Do	39	21	1	5
CHAPIN, VIRGINIUS P., claim for relief	212	35	2	21
Do	569	36	1	22
CHAPMAN, JOHN B., claim for relief	48	44	1	27
CHAPMAN, S. F., claim for relief	416	29	1	13
CHAPMAN, W. A	1667	47	1	29
CHAPPLE, JOHN, claim for relief	221	47	1	29
CHASE, JOSEPH, claim for relief	20	22	2	6
CHASE, THOMAS, claim for relief	167	19	1	3
CHANNCY, WOLCOTT, claim for relief	527	23	1	7
CHEATHAM, H., claim for relief	648	27	2	11
CHEATHAM, WILLIAM, and ADELICIA, to refund money illegally assessed and paid the Government under protest	116	46	2	28
Do	1016	48	1	30
Do	1009	49	1	31
CHECKS, DUPLICATE, regulating the issuing of	2156	48	1	30
CHEEARS, JAMES H., claim for relief of heirs of	928	25	2	9
CHEEK, JAMES, claim for relief	55	24	1	8
Do	385	27	2	11
CHEESEMAN, DAVID W., claim for relief	2	45	2	27
CHEEVER, WILLIAM D., claim for relief of executrix	85	26	2	10
Do	4	27	2	11
Do	232	30	1	16
CHEROKEE CLAIM, settlement of	3644	49	2	32
CHERRY, WILLIAM, claim for relief of heirs	408	29	1	13
CHESNUT, SAMUEL, claim for relief	195	19	1	3
Do	158	20	1	4
CHESTER, WILLIAM, claim for relief	151	43	1	26
CHEW, ANN MARIA B., claim for relief	640	27	2	11
CHEZUM, JAMES H., claim for relief	481	30	1	16
CHICAGO, employés in custom-house at	2268	49	1	31
Do	2271	49	1	31
CHILD, CHARLES W., claim for relief	843	25	2	9
CHILDERS, NATHANIEL, claim for service in taking fourth census	85	17	1	1
Do	47	18	1	2
Do	161	19	1	3
Do	121	21	1	5
Do	325	21	1	5
CHILDS, EVANDER, claim for relief	701	27	2	11
Do	639	29	1	14
CHILLICOTHE, OHIO, BANK OF, claim in settlement of loan to United States, 1814	45	21	1	5
Do	48	19	2	3
CHINN, GEORGE, claim for relief	306	22	1	6
Do	8	23	1	7
CHIPMAN, DE WITT C., claim for relief	496	43	1	26
CHISHAM, JOHN L., claim for relief	281	22	1	6
CHISHOLM, ROBERT, claim for relief	882	46	2	28
CHOCURA (gun-boat), prize-money to officers and crew of	12	42	2	26
CHOUTEAU, CHARLES P., claim for relief	1434	46	2	28
Do	79	47	1	29
CHRISMAN, JAMES S., claim for relief	180	44	1	27
CHRISTIAN, JEMIMA, claim for relief	8	36	1	22
CHRISTY, WILLIAM, claim for relief	271	24	1	8
CHURCH.				
Baptist, of Tyrone, Pa., claim for relief	81	39	1	25
Episcopal, Elizabeth City, Va., relief of wardens of	73	20	2	4
Presbyterian, Yorktown, N. Y., relief	492	31	1	18
United Brethren, of Tyrone, Pa., claim for relief	81	39	1	25
CHURCHILL, WARREN, claim for relief	877	46	2	28
CHURCHILL, SYLVESTER, claim for relief	23	26	2	10
CICOTT, FRANCIS, claim for relief	267	31	1	18
CLAGGETT, ELI, claim for relief	167	19	1	3
CLAIMS. (*See also* COURT OF CLAIMS; STATES.)				
Adjudicating, from citizens of disloyal States	10	39	1	25
Board of commissioners of, to refer all claims to	498	30	1	16
Captured or destroyed property, during war of 1812	11	14	2	1
Do	147½	15	1	1

Subject.	Report.	Congress.	Session.	Volume.
S. (See also COURT OF CLAIMS; STATES)—Continued.				
...ured or destroyed property, during war of 1812	177	15	1	1
Do	[illegible]	16	2	1
Do	8	17	1	1
Do	[illegible]	22	1	6
Do	[illegible]	22	1	7
Do	162	[illegible]	2	12
...t of Claims, jurisdiction of, in all claims against the United States (Bowman act)	[illegible]	47	1	[illegible]
Do	163	47	1	[illegible]
Do	[illegible]	49	1	31
Do	[illegible]	49	1	31
...rule, relative to private	[illegible]	27	2	11
...ce.				
...board of commissioners to settle	[illegible]	[illegible]	2	[illegible]
...before Congress, settlement of	[illegible]	[illegible]	2	[illegible]
...to correct error in schedule relative to claims under act of July 4, 1864	245	44	1	27
Do	121	[illegible]	2	[illegible]
..., for losses during war of 1812	[illegible]	15	1	1
..., A., claim for relief	[illegible]	[illegible]	1	[illegible]
..., DANIEL C., claim for relief of assignee	[illegible]	25	2	9
..., GEORGE W., and others, claim for relief	[illegible]	[illegible]	1	12
..., ISAAC, claim for relief	[illegible]	15	2	1
..., JACOB P., claim for relief	373	43	1	[illegible]
..., JOHN C., claim for relief of heirs	[illegible]	44	1	27
..., JONATHAN, claim for relief of estate and heirs	19	24	1	[illegible]
..., LORENZO N., claim for relief	[illegible]	[illegible]	1	[illegible]
..., M. F., claim for relief	[illegible]	45	2	[illegible]
..., REUBEN B., claim for relief	[illegible]	[illegible]	1	[illegible]
..., R. W., claim for relief	145	[illegible]	1	[illegible]
Do	[illegible]	[illegible]	1	[illegible]
Do	[illegible]	45	2	27
Do	[illegible]	47	1	[illegible]
Do	[illegible]	47	2	[illegible]
..., SATTERLEE, claim for relief	164	[illegible]	[illegible]	[illegible]
Do	727	[illegible]	1	17
..., THADDEUS, et al., claim for relief	[illegible]	17	[illegible]	1
..., WILLIAM J., claim for relief	[illegible]	41	2	25
...E, BENJAMIN, claim for relief of administrators	16	21	1	5
...E, CHRISTOPHER, claim for relief	172	24	1	8
Do	40	25	2	9
...E, LIZZIE D., claim for relief	1128	49	1	31
...E, R. L. B., claim for relief	125	37	2	25
Do	22	38	1	25
...E, ROBERT, & CO., claim for relief	1903	49	1	31
...CASSIUS M., claim for relief	365	30	1	16
Do	131	30	2	17
Do	150	33	2	19
Do	19	36	1	22
...HENRY (executor), claim for relief	505	23	1	8
...N, JOHN G., claim for relief	342	27	2	11
...TS, E. C., and others, claim for relief	342	46	2	28
...TS, R. H., claim for relief of estate	282	29	1	13
...TS, BRYAN & CO., claim for relief	137	26	2	10
...ONS, THOMAS, claim for relief	242	23	1	7
...NIN, J. C., claim for relief	709	44	1	27
...NING, WILLIAM, claim for relief	109	26	2	10
Do	149	27	3	11
...ittees, House of Representatives, employment of	53	39	1	25
...m-house at New York, claim for relief	722	29	1	14
...m-house at Philadelphia, claim for relief	544	35	1	21
Do	15	36	1	22
...ury Department, to give additional pay	598	30	1	17
...RALL, CAROLINE E., claim for relief	526	25	2	9
...AND, SAMUEL, Jr., claim for relief	104	18	1	2
...RD, EDWIN A., claim for relief	19	44	1	27
Do	59	45	2	27
...RD, JAMES, claim for relief	222	47	1	29
Do	1947	48	1	30
Do	472	49	1	31
..., ANDREW J., claim for relief	114	33	1	19
..., DUNCAN L., claim for relief	308	26	1	10
..., JAMES, claim for relief	31	31	1	18
...OHN L., claim for relief	36	26	2	10
Do	1	27	3	11
..., CHARLES, claim for relief	5	43	1	26
..., JOHN, claim for relief	224	43	1	26
Do	170	44	2	27
Do	48	45	2	27

Subject.	Report.	Congress.	Session.	Volume.
CLOYD, WILLIAM, claim for relief	13	19	2	3
Do	4	10	1	4
CLYMAN, JAMES, claim for relief	468	24	1	8
CLYMER, JOSEPH, claim for relief	425	45	2	27
Do	200	46	2	28
COALE & BARR, claim for relief	299	33	1	19
Do	110	35	1	21
Do	336	36	1	22
COAN, JOHN H., claim for relief	1771	47	1	29
COATS, JOHN, claim for relief		30	2	17
COATS, REYNELL, claim for relief	832	27	2	11
COATS, JAMES, claim for relief	153	43		26
COATS, MOSES H., claim for relief	261	31		18
COATS, NATHAN, claim for relief	575	26		10
COCHRON, GEORGE, claim for relief	162	30		15
COCHRAN, O. L., claim for relief	220	48		30
COCHRANE, R. E., claim for relief of widow	499	30	1	16
COCKE, JOHN, claim for relief	304	26		10
COFFINBERRY, JAMES M., claim for relief	8	44	1	27
COGSWELL, PEARSON, claim for relief	163	26	2	10
Do	132	30		17
COIT, THOMAS, claim for relief	55	26	1	10
COITE, WILLIAM J., claim for relief	642	43	1	26
COKER, THOMAS W., claim for relief	693	26	1	10
COLBURN, BENAIAH, and others, claim for relief	700	27	2	11
COLBY, HALL, claim for relief	310	43	2	26
COLDWELL, WILLIAM, claim for relief	714	24	1	8
COLEMAN, HENRY, claim for relief	388	25	2	9
COLGATE, CLINTON G., claim for relief	304	46	3	28
COLLEGE, NOTRE DAME, DU LAC, for relief of	966	45	2	27
Do	909	46	2	28
COLLIER, GEORGE, claim for relief	74	31		18
COLLIER, JAMES, claim for relief	127	24		8
Do	71	35	2	21
COLLIER & PETTIS, claim for relief	334	27	2	11
COLLINSWORTH, MARY B., claim for relief	10	30		15
COLLINS, A. G., claim for relief	400	43	1	26
COLLINS, BENJAMIN, claim for relief	110	22	2	6
COLLINS, CHARLES, claim for relief	1722	46	2	28
Do	461	47	1	29
COLLINS, DEMPSEY, claim for relief	987	25	2	9
COLLINS, JANE, claim for relief	41	34	3	20
COLLINS, TIPTON B., claim for relief	9	45	3	27
COLLINS, WILLIAM, claim for relief	2171	49		31
COLMAN, CHARLES, claim for relief	92	27	3	11
COLORED SOLDIERS AND SAILORS, pay and bounty to	1565	46	2	28
COLT, WILLIAM, claim for relief	528	25	2	9
COLUMBIA BANK OF PENNSYLVANIA, owners of bridge across Susquehanna River destroyed by United States forces, claim for relief	71	38		25
COMFORT, JOHN C., claim for relief	896	45	2	27
COMMITTEE CLERKS. (*See* CLERKS OF COMMITTEES.)				
COMMITTEE OF CLAIMS, HOUSE OF REPRESENTATIVES, authorized to employ clerk	789	27	2	11
COMPENSATION (*see also* SALARY; CONGRESS), preparation of manuscript matter without authority of Congress	17	35	2	21
CONANT, SHUBAEL, claim for relief as surety on paymaster's bond	246	23	1	7
Do	493	23		7
CONFISCATION OF MONEYS BY THE CONFEDERATE CONGRESS OF LOYAL CITIZENS OF UNITED STATES, liability of United States for	98	42	2	26
CONGRESS,				
Assignment of clerks to each committee in House of Representatives	53	39		25
Private claims pending before	3497	49	2	32
Salaries of members while absent, payment of	335	23		7
Do		24		7
CONKLING, A., claim for relief	97	30		15
CONLY, PATRICK, claim for relief	458	36		22
CONNECTICUT, claim for relief of	73	42	2	26
CONNER, BETSEY, claim for relief	609	27	2	11
CONSPIRATORS, distribution of the reward for the capture of those connected with the assassination of President Lincoln	99	39		25
Do	60	40	2	25
CONTESTED-ELECTION CASES, compensation and mileage of parties to, payment of	125	37	2	25
CONTINENTAL FIRE INSURANCE COMPANY, claim for relief	476	49	1	31
CONTRACTORS, constructing war vessels for United States Navy, relief	17	39	2	25
CONTRACTS WITH UNITED STATES, changing or abrogating	226	21	1	5
Do	518	23	1	7
Do	142	28	2	7
Do	190	29	1	13
Do	377	29	1	13

Subject.	Report.	Congress.	Session.	Volume.
TS WITH UNITED STATES, changing or abrogating	56	41	3	35
Do	463	42	1	39
, JOHN BAPTISTE, claim for relief of administrator	61	20	2	4
Do	38	21	1	5
R, JOHN P., claim for relief	246	24	2	8
Do	67	25	2	9
Do	47	27	2	11
Do	314	28	1	12
Do	84	28	2	12
Do	373	29	1	13
Do	160	30	1	15
Do	165	31	1	18
, FANNY S., claim for relief	280	40	2	31
SPER B., and others, claim for relief	501	27	3	11
Do	345	30	1	16
AAC, claim for relief	465	27	2	11
Do	738	29	1	14
Do	126	30	2	17
Do	237	31	1	18
MOTHY, claim for relief	165	27	2	11
Do	308	27	3	11
AVID, claim for relief	769	25	2	9
Do	473	30	1	16
LIZABETH, claim for relief	1007	25	2	9
AMES, claim for relief	42	18	2	2
Do	22	19	1	3
EMUEL, claim for relief	236	22	1	6
Do	385	23	1	7
THEOPHILUS, claim for relief	19	20	2	4
BENJAMIN, claim for relief	665	45	1	36
WILLIAM, claim for relief	695	26	1	10
Do	770	27	2	11
GRIFFITH, claim for relief	1	25	3	9
ALBERT G., claim for relief	420	36	1	18
D. H., claim for relief	7	44	1	27
JOHN B., claim for relief	109	30	2	17
JOSEPH, claim for relief	266	23	1	7
Do	3	24	1	7
WILLIAM, claim for relief	108	34	1	20
HUA M., claim for relief	1368	46	2	28
D, THOMAS, claim for relief	54	33	1	19
D, ZACHEUS, claim for relief	664	24	1	8
CHAEL, claim for relief	12	19	1	3
R. W., and others, claim for relief	342	46	2	28
IN, claim for relief	468	27	2	11
Do	2	27	3	11
J., claim for relief	458	36	1	22
, ISAAC, claim for relief	91	27	3	11
ISAAC, claim for relief	706	26	1	10
R, SYLVESTER, claim for relief	427	30	1	16
PETER, claim for relief	540	24	1	8
, TAUSSIG & CO., and others, claim for relief	379	46	3	28
Do	2473	49	1	31
AMOS B., claim for relief	162	34	1	20
EORGE B., claim for relief	3028	49	1	31
, THOMAS, claim for relief	900	46	2	28
CLAIMS (relative to those of North Carolina)	803	44	1	27
Do	7	45	3	27
L, RICHARD, claim for relief	696	24	1	8
, JOHN J., claim for relief	1816	49	1	31
SEWELL, claim for relief	1755	47	1	29
CLAIMS,				
commissioners of, to adjudicate all claims against the United States	730	25	2	9
Do	498	30	1	16
tion of, in investigating private claims	562	49	1	31
tion of, to extend to all claims referred by Congress or Executive epartments to	69	47	1	29
EVY, of Baltimore, Md., claim for relief	47	16	1	1
Do	36	17	1	1
Do	7	18	1	2
, JEAN B., claim for relief of administrator	26	17	2	1
, A. AUGUSTUS, claim for relief	637	29	1	14
OHN, claim for relief	126	15	1	1
Do	25	16	1	1
WILLIAM, claim for relief	397	36	1	22
C. J. (assayer), claim for salary	4153	49	2	32
JOHN, claim for relief	106	23	2	7
Do	151	24	1	8
AHAM, claim for relief	649	27	2	11
B., claim for relief	29	29	2	14
Do	66	30	1	15

Subject.	Report.	Congress.	Session.	Volume.
COX, EMILIE, claim for relief	52	20	1	4
COX, JAMES, claim for relief	16	26	1	10
Do	12	26	2	10
COX, JOHN (heirs of), claim for relief	586	29	1	13
Do	3	30	1	15
COX, JOHN P. (paymaster, United States Volunteers), claim for money stolen	80	18	1	2
Do	114	19	1	3
Do	52	20	1	4
Do	52	21	1	5
Do	467	22	1	6
COX, NATHANIEL, claim for relief of heirs	362	30	1	16
COX, WILLIAM, claim for relief	472	24	1	8
COXE, FERDINAND, claim for relief	182	35	1	21
COZAD, SAMUEL, captive by Indians, claim for ransom money and compensation for time	54	24	1	8
Do	213	24	2	8
COZZENS, WILLIAM B., claim for relief	56	33	1	19
Do	101	34	1	20
CRABB, HORATIO N., claim for relief	338	27	2	11
CRAIG, JOHN, claim for relief	167	19	1	3
CRANDALL, A. C., claim for relief	640	29	1	14
CRANE, J. W., claim for relief	200	27	3	11
Do	30	28	1	12
Do	514	29	1	13
CRANSTON, S. B., claim for relief	887	49	1	31
CRAWFORD, ANGUS M. A., claim for relief	336	27	2	11
CRAWFORD, JAMES S., claim for relief	3328	49	1	31
CRAWFORD, SAMUEL J., claim for relief	759	44	1	27
CREWS, H. B., claim for relief of assignee	25	24	1	87
CREWS, WILLIAM B., claim for relief	43	30	2	17
Do	2	31	1	18
CRITTENDEN, N. E., claim for relief	387	35	1	21
CRITTENDEN, ROBERT, claim for relief of assignee	339	21	1	5
CRITTENDEN, STEPHEN, claim for relief	44	23	2	7
Do	34	24	1	7
CRITTENDEN, THOMAS T., claim for relief	221	43	1	26
CROCKER, FRANKLIN, claim for relief	1722	47	1	29
CROOK, TIMOTHY D., claim for relief	493	43	1	26
CROOK, WILLIAM H., claim for relief	1179	47	1	29
Do	2112	48	1	30
Do	3697	49	2	32
Do	3699	49	2	32
CROOKS, JAMES, claim for relief	64	25	2	9
CROOKS, WILLIAM, claim for relief	129	23	1	7
Do	64	25	2	9
CROOKS, WILLIAM and JAMES, owners of the ship Lord Nelson, libel of	814	24	1	8
Do	243	24	2	8
Do	426	30	1	16
CROSBIE, H. R., claim for relief	60	37	3	25
Do	26	38	1	25
Do	1369	46	2	28
CROSKEY, JOSEPH, and others, claim for relief	957	25	2	9
Do	709	26	1	10
CROSS, ALEXANDER, claim for relief	604	36	1	22
CROSS, JAMES, claim for relief	471	23	1	7
CROSS, OSBORN, claim for relief	81	31	2	18
CROUCH, HAZEL W., claim for relief of administrator	849	25	2	9
CROW, ALBION T., claim for relief	491	24	1	8
Do	22	25	2	9
CROWN, THOMAS, claim for relief	54	26	1	10
Do	53	27	3	11
Do	557	28	1	12
Do	645	29	1	14
Do	306	30	1	16
Do	244	31	1	18
CRUMBO & MELCHER, claim for relief	3024	49	1	31
CRUMP, J. R., claim for relief	276	36	1	22
CRUSAT, MALVINA, claim for relief	328	31	1	18
CUBBAGE, GEORGE, claim for relief	569	24	1	8
CULLUMBER, JOSHUA, claim for schooner Two Brothers, impressed by United States	35	23	2	7
Do	38	24	1	7
CULVER, C. P., claim for relief	1876	47	2	29
Do	1419	48	1	30
Do	868	49	1	31
CULVER, WILLIAM, claim for relief	58	29	1	13
Do	4	29	2	14
Do	6	30	1	15
CUMBERLAND ROAD,				
Claim of contractors for work done on, west of Zanesville, Ohio	449	23	1	7
Do	455	23	1	7
Do	456	23	1	7

Subject.	Report.	Congress.	Session.	Volume.
CUMBERLAND ROAD—Continued.				
Forfeiting contract in Indiana	480	23	1	7
Right of way for, claims for individual damage	75	20	1	4
Do	245	20	1	4
Do	334	21	1	5
Do	251	22	1	6
Do	403	21	1	5
CUMBERLAND VALLEY RAILROAD COMPANY, to adjust and settle claims of	693	45	2	27
CUMMING, JOSEPH M., claim for relief	897	45	2	27
Do	1762	47	1	29
Do	2177	48	2	30
CUNNINGHAM, M., claim for relief	767	27	2	11
CUNNINGHAM, PATRICK, claim for relief	15	30	1	15
CURRIN, TIMOTHY, claim for relief of administrator	846	25	2	9
CUSTER, ELIZABETH B., claim for relief	191	45	2	27
CUSTER, JOHN W., claim for relief	245	28	1	12
CUTCHEON, JAMES, claim for relief	462	23	1	7
CUTTER, CHARLES W., claim for relief of sureties	163	36	1	22
CUTTING, HIRAM A., claim for relief	102	41	2	25
CUTTS, THOMAS, Jr., claim for relief	59	19	1	3
DABNEY, J. W., claim for relief	351	27	2	11
DADE, MAJOR, and others, to pension the widows and children of	415	34	1	8
DAHLER, CHARLES L., claim for relief	410	45	2	27
Do	1717	47	1	29
DAILEY, GEORGE H., claim for relief	179	47	1	29
DAILY, LAWRENCE, claim for relief	406	30	1	16
DAINGERFIELD, MARIA H., claim for relief	174	27	2	11
DAKEN, JONATHAN, claim for relief of heirs	707	27	2	11
DAKES, JOSEPH, claims for relief	246	22	1	6
DALE, SAMUEL, claim for relief	36	16	1	1
Do	75	18	2	2
Do	79	21	2	5
DALLAM & HAMBURGH, claim for relief	111	26	2	10
DALLAS, ALEXANDER J. (agent), claim of Pennsylvania for money passed to credit of	223	20	1	4
DAMAGES, recovery of, against officers of United States	159	19	1	3
Do	44	21	1	4
Do	244	20	1	4
Do	276	23	1	7
DANDON, DANIEL, claim for relief of heirs	69	32	1	19
DANIEL WEBSTER (ship), claim for relief	908	46	2	28
Do	200	47	1	29
DARDEN, SIMEON, claim for relief	508	30	1	17
D'AUTERIVE, MARIGNEY, claim for relief	58	19	1	3
Do	126	19	1	3
Do	27	20	1	4
Do	210	20	1	4
Do	26	21	1	5
DAUPHIN (ship), enslavement of crew of, by Algerines, and payment of ransom for	622	24	1	8
DAVENPORT, ARCHIBALD C., claim for relief	128	35	2	21
DAVENPORT, SAMUEL, claim for relief	458	36	1	22
DAVID, JOHN T. (paymaster, United States Volunteers), settlement of accounts	101	17	1	1
DAVIDGE, ROBERT A., claim for relief	402	35	1	21
DAVIESS, JAMES, claim for relief	249	21	1	5
DAVIS, C. R., and others, claim for relief	526	44	1	27
DAVIS, CHARLES B., claim for relief	314	23	1	7
DAVIS, DANIEL, claim for relief	413	24	1	8
Do	15	25	2	9
DAVIS, ELI, Jr., claim for relief	476	23	1	7
DAVIS, ELIZABETH, claim for relief	177	27	2	11
DAVIS, HANNAH, for relief	16	16	2	1
DAVIS, J. V., claim for relief	1549	47	1	29
Do	224	48	1	30
DAVIS, JAMES, claim for relief	56	27	3	11
DAVIS, JEFFERSON,				
Capture of, history of	60	40	2	25
Distribution of the reward offered for the capture of	90	39	1	25
Do	60	40	2	25
DAVIS, JEFFERSON, claim for relief	3196	49	1	31
DAVIS, JOHN B., claim for relief	224	47	1	29
Do	278	48	1	30
DAVIS, JONATHAN, claim for relief	482	24	1	8
Do	21	25	2	9
Do	44	25	3	9
DAVIS, JOSEPH, claim for relief	627	29	1	14
DAVIS, LEVI, claim for relief	710	25	2	9
DAVIS, ROBERT, claim for relief	10	20	1	4
Do	43	25	3	9
Do	467	27	2	11

Subject.	Report.	Congress.	Session.	Volume.
DAVIS, SOLOMON, claim for relief	2892	49	1	31
DAVIS, WILLARD, claim for relief	136	43	1	26
DAWSON, E. B., claim for relief	1326	49	1	31
DAWSON, GEORGE, claim for relief	734	24	1	8
DAWSON, JOHNSON A., claim for relief	110	39	1	25
DAY, L. MADISON, claim for property in New Orleans confiscated as belonging to Judah P. Benjamin	50	45	3	27
Do	9	46	2	28
Do	694	47	1	29
DAY, SYLVESTER, claim for relief of heirs	92	36	1	22
DAY, WILLIAM, claim for relief	458	36	1	22
DE AHNA, HENRY C., claim for relief	868	46	2	28
Do	1950	48	1	30
Do	1902	49	1	31
DEAN, DANIEL, claim for relief	705	27	2	11
Do	82	28	1	12
DEAN, GEORGE, claim for relief	458	36	1	22
DEAN, SAMUEL, claim for relief	458	36	1	22
DEARING, WILLIAM L. S., claim for relief	34	22	2	6
Do	128	23	1	7
Do	341	24	1	8
Do	842	29	1	14
DEBOIS, HANNAH, claim for relief	71	15	2	1
DECRITS, JOSEPH, claim for relief	33	18	2	2
DE ESCAUDON, FRANCISCA SANCHEZ, claim for relief	1552	47	1	29
DEGROAT, JOHN, claim for relief	377	30	1	16
DE GROOT, WILLIAM H., claim for relief	136	37	2	25
Do	26	37	3	25
Do	35	43	2	26
DEHON, THEODORE, claim for relief	601	47	1	29
DELANNEY, DAVID, claim for relief	50	22	2	6
DELANY, JOHN R., claim for relief	752	27	2	11
DE LA RONDE, PIERRE DENIS, for relief	25	16	2	1
DELASSIZE, JEAN VALLERY, claim for relief	156	19	1	3
DE LEON, EDWIN, claim for relief	692	45	2	27
Do	1693	46	2	28
DELAWARE, to pay State for interest on bonds for money advanced	249	20	1	4
DE LIRAC, G., claim for relief	156	30	1	15
Do	409	31	1	18
DELL, BENNETT M., claim for relief	410	28	1	12
Do	524	28	1	12
DE LOACH, CLAIBORNE, claim for relief of heirs	3027	49	1	31
DE LONG, FRANCIS, claim for relief	1417	48	1	30
DELORD, HENRY, claim for relief	359	24	1	8
Do	401	35	1	21
DELOSSUS, DON CARLOS DEHAULT, claim for relief	497	22	1	6
DELOZIER, TERRENCE, claim for relief	1235	48	1	30
Do	1295	49	1	31
DEMAREST, SAMUEL, claim for relief	50	16	1	1
Do	138	21	1	5
DEMISEN, JOHN F., claim for relief	2161	48	1	30
DENMON, MARTHA, claim for relief	134	28	1	12
DEMSTON, WILLIAM, claim for relief	48	30	1	15
DENHAM, DAVID R., and others, claim for relief	162	25	3	9
DENISON, CHARLES W., claim for relief	66	42	3	26
DENISON & ELY, claim for removal of armament and naval stores from Brooklyn to Sackett's Harbor	329	21	1	5
DENNIS, JAMES, claim for relief	299	23	1	7
Do	627	24	1	8
DENT, GEORGE W., claim for relief	704	27	2	11
Do	86	28	1	12
DENTON, CHARLES W., claim for relief	85	42	2	26
DENTON & SAGE, claim for relief	1681	48	1	30
Do	473	49	1	31
DEQUINDRE, ANTOINE, and others, militia claim during war of 1812	268	21	1	5
DERRICK, ANN P., claim for relief	1308	46	2	28
Do	518	47	1	29
DERRICK, W. S., claim for relief	298	34	1	20
DE RUSSEY, R. E., claim for relief	46	30	2	17
DESBROW, HENRY, claim for relief	224	27	3	11
DESERTERS, liability of persons arresting, when prosecuted for an assault	218	24	1	8
DESLONDE, ROSALIE P., for relief	12	16	2	1
DES MOINES RAPIDS, for relief of employés on work for improvement of	910	47	1	29
Do	225	48	1	30
DEVALL, CHARLES, claim for relief	151	28	2	12
DEVELIN, HENRY, and others, claim for relief	456	23	1	7
DEVINE, JAMES, claim for relief	1587	46	2	28
DEVINE, MILES, claim for relief	19	35	2	21
Do	337	36	1	22
DEVLIN, JOHN, claim for relief	312	33	1	19

Subject.	Report.	Congress.	Session.	Volume.
DEVLIN, JOHN S., claim for relief of administrators	155	28	2	12
Do	20	29	1	13
DEWEES, THOMAS B., claim for relief	68	48	1	30
DEWITT, EDWARD, respecting claim of	410	31	1	18
D'WOLF, JOHN, claim for relief	141	24	2	8
DIBBLE, O. H., claim for relief	142	23	2	7
Do	792	24	1	8
Do	50	25	1	10
Do	321	28	1	12
Do	725	29	1	14
Do	764	30	1	17
DICK, ELIAS D., claim for relief of administrator	30	20	2	4
Do	129	20	1	4
DICKERSON, MATILDA, claim for relief	246	27	2	11
DICKEY, JOHN O., claim for relief	44	30	1	15
DICKEY, MILUS W., claim for relief	274	25	3	9
DICKEY, THOMAS C., claim for relief	2224	49	1	31
DICKINS, ASBURY.				
Claim for relief	94	34	1	20
Do	224	35	1	21
Do	646	36	1	22
Claim for relief of heirs	30	43	1	26
Do	675	45	2	27
Do*	1727	46	2	28
DICKINSON, LEACH & CO., claim for relief	664	47	1	29
DICKSON, JOHN, claim for relief	25	31	1	18
Do	184	35	1	21
DICKSON, WILLIAM, claim for relief	869	25	2	9
DIEDRICK, ROBERT, claim for relief	245	27	3	11
DILLINGER, S., & SONS, claim for relief	876	49	1	31
DILLON, JOSIAH, claim for relief	445	28	1	12
DILLON, RICHARD, claim for relief	424	46	1	28
DIMICK, HORACE E., claim for relief	101	38	1	23
DIRECT TAX OF 1861,				
Amount apportioned among the several States and Territories and District of Columbia	*2486	48	2	30
To prohibit, being made set-off against claims of States	562	49	1	31
DISBROW, HENRY, claim for relief	796	27	2	11
Do	223	29	1	13
Do	18	31	1	18
DISBURSING OFFICERS OF UNITED STATES,				
Difference in exchange, claim for	596	24	1	8
Do	5	24	2	8
Liability of, for money lost or stolen from	157	21	1	5
Do	483	22	1	6
Do	525	23	1	7
Do	188	26	2	10
Do	20	40	2	25
Do	44	41	2	25
Liability of, for money lost by deposit in private banks	3	35	2	21
DISMAL SWAMP CANAL COMPANY, claim for relief	47	28	2	12
DISTILLING COMPANY, OF PEKIN, ILLINOIS, claim for relief	674	45	2	27
DISTRICT OF COLUMBIA,				
Additional compensation to metropolitan police	227	43	1	26
Do	30	45	3	27
Do	159	46	2	28
Bridge across Potomac in, purchase of, by	744	30	1	17
Direct tax, to provide for repayment of	*2486	48	2	30
Pennsylvania avenue in, claim for macadamizing	745	30	1	17
Refunding to city of Washington certain moneys, proceeds of lots donated to	65	39	1	25
DIXON, EPHRAIM D., claim for relief	667	27	2	11
Do	48	27	3	11
DIXON, JOSEPH, claim for relief	241	20	1	4
DOAK, THOMAS, claim for relief	884	46	2	28
Do	173	47	1	29
DODD, JOHN W., & CO., claim for relief	106	45	1	27
DODGE, ANDREW, claim for relief	470	23	1	7
Do	15	24	1	7
DODGE, WILLIAM C., claim for relief	1816	49	1	31
DOFT, GEORGE, claim for relief	168	27	2	11
DOFT, JAMES, claim for relief	89	27	3	11
DOLL, AARON T., claim for relief	30	38	1	25
DOLLY, PRESTON and MARIA, claim for relief	122	30	1	15
DOLTON, WILLIAM, claim for relief	1478	47	1	29
Do	597	49	1	31
DOMINGUES, MANUEL, claim for relief of heirs	499	27	2	11
DONALDSON, ALEXANDER, claim for relief	188	22	1	6
DONALDSON, WILLIAM, claim for relief	528	25	2	9
DONNELL, JOHN, claim for relief	167	19	1	3
Do	66	25	3	9

* Views of minority.

Subject.	Report.	Congress.	Session.	Volume.
DONNELLY, FRANK L., claim for relief	119	46	2	26
Do	522	47	1	29
DONOHUE, M. J., and others, claim for relief	342	46	2	26
DORSEY, JOHN M., claim for relief	665	45	2	27
Do	864	46	2	28
Do	865	46	2	28
Do	525	47	1	29
Do	219	48	1	30
DOUGHERTY, MARGARET, claim for relief	473	28	1	12
DOUGHTY & CARD, claim for relief	49	45	3	27
DOUGLAS, GEORGE L., claim for relief	308	48	1	30
DOUGLASS, DENISON, claim for relief	238	20	1	4
DOVE, RICHARD G., claim for relief	30	28	2	12
DOW, JESSE E., claim for prosecuting felonies against United States	343	24	1	8
Do	5	25	2	9
DOWNES, JOHN, claim for relief	46	23	2	7
Do	33	24	1	7
Do	728	24	1	8
Do	53	25	2	9
Do	98	25	3	9
Do	28	26	1	10
DOWNING, SAMUEL, claim for relief of surety	703	27	2	11
DOX, JACOB, claim for relief	18	15	2	1
DOXEY, JOSEPH C., claim for relief	350	27	2	11
Do	536	29	1	13
Do	40	30	1	16
Do	408	31	1	18
DOYLE, J. & E., claim for relief	458	36	1	22
DOYLE, MARGARET, claim for relief	456	36	1	22
DRAKEFORD, WILLIAM, claim for relief	16	17	2	1
DRANE, ANTHONY, claim for relief	121	24	1	8
DRAUGHN, MILES S., claim for relief	12	45	3	27
DREW, JAMES A., claim for relief	456	36	1	22
Do	395	43	1	25
Do	99	44	1	27
DRINKWATER, WEST, and others, claim for relief	10	34	1	20
DRUMMOND, RICHARD, owner of private armed schooner Roger, claim for prize money	176	20	1	3
DRURY, MATILDA, claim for relief	258	24	2	8
Do	84	28	1	12
Do	182	29	1	13
Do	257	30	1	16
DRURY, SAMUEL, claim for relief	755	24	1	8
DRYSDALE, JOHN, claim for relief	842	27	2	11
DUANE, JAMES C., claim for relief	2605	48	2	30
Do	3124	49	1	31
DUANE, WILLIAM, claim for relief	13	18	2	3
DUBOISE, SAMUEL, claim for relief of administrator	193	22	1	6
DUBOSE, SAMUEL, claim for relief of administrator	129	20	2	4
Do	80	20	2	4
Do	183	22	1	6
DUCKETT, JAMES M., claim for relief	57	33	1	19
DUDY, ELIZABETH, claim for relief	496	36	1	22
DUER, THOMAS, claim for relief	111	30	2	17
DUER, WILLIAM A., Army contract of 1791, additional compensation for	128	29	1	13
DUERSON, WILLIAM, claim for relief	155	31	1	18
DUFFIELD, MARGARETTA, claim for relief	71	15	2	1
DUFFIELD, MILTON B., claim for relief	459	45	2	27
Do	596	47	1	29
DUGAN, JOHN A., claim for relief	24	46	2	28
DUNCAN, JOHN, claim for relief of heirs	19	34	1	20
DUNCAN, KINGSBURY, and others, claim for relief	10	34	1	20
DUNCAN, MATTHEW, claim for relief	804	25	2	9
DUNCAN, SAMUEL, claim for relief of heirs	19	34	1	20
DUNCAN, SAMUEL C., claim for relief	480	23	1	7
DUNCAN & TAYLOR, claim for relief	217	24	2	8
DUNHAM, CYRUS L., claim for relief of heirs	899	48	1	30
DUNHAM, JACOB, claim for relief	702	27	2	11
DUNNINGTON, C. W. C., claim for relief	55	36	2	22
Do	149	43	1	25
DUPLICATE CHECKS, to issue in certain cases	74	47	1	29
Do	2156	48	1	30
DUPONT, ABRAHAM, claim for relief	828	25	2	9
DUPRE, WIDOW, for the relief of heirs of	73	21	1	5
DURKEE, HENRY, claim for relief	181	27	2	11
DUTTON, RICHARD H., claim for relief	44	43	1	25
DUVALL, EDWARD, claim for relief of administrator	688	24	1	8
Do	67	25	2	9
DUVALL, MERREN, claim for relief	46	18	1	2
DUVALL, P. S., & CO., claim for relief	430	35	1	21
DUVALL & CARNES, claim for relief	74	21	2	5

Subject.	Report.	Congress.	Session.	Volume.
..., RUFUS, claim for relief	307	35	1	21
FRANCES W., claim for relief	[illegible]	49	1	31
..., WILLIAM, claim for relief	[illegible]	22	2	6
Do	342	23	1	7
Do	573	24	1	8
Do	44	25	2	9
..., HENRY, claim for relief	[illegible]	[illegible]	1	19
..., WILLIAM,				
...m for relief	140	27	2	11
...m for relief of heirs of	174	34	2	20
...AM, J. N., claim for relief	90	35	1	21
..., RANSOM, claim for relief	184	25	2	9
...AN, ARTHUR W., claim for relief	76	47	1	29
..., ABIEL K., claim for relief	294	44	1	27
..., WILLIAM, claim for relief	471	24	1	8
Do	543	24	1	8
Do	542	24	1	6
WILLIAM, claim for relief of heirs	81	41	2	25
...F. GOUGH, claim for relief	2906	49	1	31
GEORGE W., AND OTHERS, claim for relief	94	46	2	28
...DSTON, SAMUEL A., claim for relief	152	23	1	7
...STON, WILLIAM C., claim for relief	458	45	2	27
..., JOSEPH, claim for relief	1064	25	2	9
...TSON, schedule of persons educated at expense of Government	415	24	1	8
...RDS, JAMES S., claim for relief of administrator	516	36	1	22
...Y, JACOB, claim for relief of administrator	98	24	1	7
...STON, BENJAMIN, claim for relief	709	27	2	11
..., NANCY, claim for relief	345	36	1	22
...HOUR LAW,				
...claims arising under	999	49	1	31
...arrearages of pay to certain employés of the Government	1367	45	2	28
Do	1922	46	2	28
...n of Government employés for extra compensation under the	11	44	2	27
..., JAMES, claim for relief	522	27	2	11
LAURENTIUS M., claim for correcting surveys of public lands, 1839	87	23	1	7
Do	16	23	2	7
Do	26	24	1	7
..., JAMES, claim for relief	441	23	1	7
...DGE, H. S., and others, claim for relief	534	36	1	22
..., JONATHAN, claim for relief	702	24	1	8
Do	51	25	2	9
...ETH CITY, VIRGINIA, claim for relief of Episcopal Church at	73	20	2	4
Do	14	21	1	5
...T, SAMUEL B., claim for relief	517	36	1	22
...T, W. W., claim for relief	220	43	1	26
ABNER Y., claim for relief	9	43	1	26
H. H., claim for relief	1010	49	1	31
Do	2553	49	1	31
JOHN, claim for relief	1761	47	1	29
Do	1653	48	1	30
Do	1654	48	1	30
Do	1098	49	1	31
JOHN H. (paymaster United States Volunteers), claim for relief	29	40	2	25
WILLIAM H. C., claim for relief	902	48	1	30
...K, GEORGE C., claim for relief	391	46	3	28
Do	555	47	1	29
Do	1217	49	1	31
...N, THOMAS C., claim for relief	1354	47	1	29
...ORTH, ISRAEL, claim for relief	267	23	1	7
...ORTH, TIMOTHY E., claim for relief	75	47	1	29
..., JOHN, claim for relief	292	28	1	12
..., ALBERT H., construction of machine for testing iron and steel	1584	46	2	28
Do	226	47	1	29
Do	484	48	1	30
Do	*2527	49	1	31
..., JAMES W., and others, claim for relief	163	36	1	22
..., JOSEPH, claim for relief	79	22	2	6
..., MATTHEW G., claim for relief	191	34	3	20
...ON, WILLIAM, claim for relief	596	24	1	8
...ERS,				
...ants of, under eight-hour law of all Government, to adjust	999	49	1	31
...go custom-house, for relief of	2358	49	1	31
Do	2371	49	1	31
...Moines Rapids, retained during suspension of work, payment of	919	47	1	29
...nal-revenue service, for relief of	2369	49	1	31
...H, JOHN, claim for relief	44	20	1	4
..., SAMUEL D., claim for relief	697	26	1	10
Do	118	27	3	11
Do	125	28	2	12
Do	161	29	1	13

* Views of minority.

Subject.	Report.	Congress.	Session.	Volume.
ENSEL, L. S., claim for relief	82	49	1	31
ENSIGN, ARIEL, claim for relief	386	21	1	5
EPLEY, ADAM L., claim for relief	4090	49	2	32
EPPES, RICHARD, claim for relief	187	20	1	4
Do	25	21	1	5
ERSKINE, ALLIN S. (heirs), claim of heirs for compensation for use of fire-arms invented by	3645	49	2	32
ERMATINGER, GEORGE, claim for relief	134	21	1	5
ERNI, HENRY, claim for relief	1366	46	2	28
ESKRIDGE, SAMUEL, claim for relief	100	23	2	7
ESLAVA, M. D., claim for relief of guardian of	287	23	1	7
Do	4	24	1	7
ESSEX (sloop), claim for relief of owners of	19	20	2	4
ESTE, EDWIN, claim for relief	836	47	1	29
ESTES, J. H., claim for relief	126	35	2	21
Do	459	36	1	22
ESTES, JAMES B., claim for relief	500	28	1	12
Do	185	33	1	19
ESTES, POLLY, claim for relief	944	25	2	9
ETHERIDGE, EMERSON, claim for relief	817	49	1	31
EUROPA (ship), claim for relief of owners of	908	46	2	28
Do	200	47	1	29
EVANS, BRITTON, claim for relief	430	26	1	10
Do	708	27	2	11
EVANS, HENRY F., claim for relief	789	24	1	8
EVANS, NICHOLS & CO., claim for relief	353	48	1	30
EVANS, ROBLEY D., claim for relief	3931	49	2	32
EVANS, ROXANA, claim for relief	298	28	1	12
Do	39	40	2	25
EVANS, SAMUEL P., claim for relief	3594	49	2	32
EVANS, SCIOTE, claim for relief	186	24	1	8
EVANS, THOMAS, claim for vessel impressed by the Government in 1812	538	23	1	7
EVELETH, EBEN, claim for relief	896	46	2	28
EVELETH, SARAH, claim for relief	51	27	3	11
EVERETT, JOB, claim for relief	456	36	1	22
EXTRA COMPENSATION to Govevnment clerks for extra work	378	23	1	7
EWING, B. N., claim for relief	183	47	1	29
EWING, REUBEN, and others, claim for relief	80	18	2	2
EWING, W. Y. C. & R. A., claim for relief	685	26	1	10
EXPRESS COMPANIES, relative to revenue laws governing the business of	1	44	2	27
Do	402	45	2	27
FAHNESTOCK, CHARLES E., claim for relief	16	44	2	27
Do	11	45	3	27
FAILEY, SAMUEL, claim for relief	458	36	1	22
FAIN, THOMAS, claim for relief	343	46	2	28
FAIRBANKS, E. & T., claim for relief	252	24	2	8
FAIRCHILDS, SAMUEL A., claim for relief	191	35	1	21
FARAN & McLEAN, claim for relief	705	49	1	31
FARDY, EMILY J., claim for relief	2176	49	1	31
FARMER, GEORGE W., claim for relief	9	30	2	17
FARMER, JOHN, claim for relief	289	27	3	11
FARNSWORTH, ADDISON, claim for relief	91	35	1	21
FARNSWORTH, NATHAN, claim for relief	268	31	1	18
FARRER, DEERIN, claim for relief	66	28	2	12
Do	99	29	1	13
FARROW, NIMROD. (*See* HARRIS & FARROW.)				
FAUCETT, ROBERT T., & CO., claim for relief	405	45	2	27
FAULKNER, C. R., claim for relief	31	46	1	28
FAULKNER, H. H., claim for relief	1420	48	1	30
Do	301	49	1	31
FAY, NAHUM, claim for relief	483	23	1	7
FEES, due from United States, collection of	17	23	2	7
Do	29	24	1	7
FELAND, JAMES, claim for relief	211	19	1	3
FELIX, FRANCES, claim for relief	93	20	1	4
FELL, JOSEPH G., and others, claim for relief	420	46	1	28
FELLOWS, HOMER, claim for relief	158	46	2	28
FELONIES, claims of persons for prosecuting, against United States	348	24	1	8
Do	5	25	2	9
FELT, JOHN, claim for relief	354	29	1	13
FELTON, C. N., claim for relief	421	43	1	26
Do	408	45	2	27
FELTON, SKELTON, claim for relief	559	28	1	12
FENLON, EDWARD, claim for relief	334	49	1	31
Do	2368	49	1	31
FENNER, JERAH, claim for relief	295	24	1	8
FENTON, ANDREW, claim for relief	521	30	1	17
FENWICK, MICHAEL, claim for relief of heirs	11	23	2	7
Do	106	24	1	8
Do	529	25	2	9

Subject.	Report.	Congress.	Session.	Volume.
FERGUSON, JOHN, claim for relief	170	36	1	22
Do	127	37	2	23
FERGUSON, SAMUEL, claim for relief	900	25	2	9
FERGUSON, WILLIAM R., claim for relief	868	25	2	9
FERRIS, ELIZA M., claim for relief of legal representatives	3083	49	1	31
FESSENDEN, ISAAC, claim for relief	54	27	2	11
Do	52	28	1	12
FIEDLER, ERNEST, claim for relief	168	34	3	20
FIELDING, DANIEL, claim for relief	98	19	1	5
FILLEBROWN, THOMAS, Jr., claim for relief	307	24	2	8
Do	90	25	2	9
Do	3	25	3	9
Do	36	26	1	10
FILLMORE, SEPTA,				
Claim for relief	19	17	2	3
Claim for relief of heirs	65	26	1	10
FINCH, LEMUEL S., claim for relief	568	29	1	14
Do	156	30	1	15
FINCH, WILLIAM H., claim for relief of heirs	2282	49	1	31
FINDLAY, WILLIAM (Representative from Pennsylvania, Fourteenth Congress), claim for salary while absent sick	335	22	1	7
Do	6	24	1	7
FINLAND, PATRICK, claim for relief	458	36	1	22
FIRST NATIONAL BANK OF NEWTON, MASSACHUSETTS, claim for relief	3126	49	1	31
FIRST NATIONAL BANK OF PORTLAND, OREGON, claim for relief	2818	49	2	32
FISHBACK, JAMES, claim for relief	107	45	2	27
FISHER, ANDREW, claim for relief	76	27	3	11
FISHER, GEORGE, claim for relief	102	26	2	10
Do	228	27	3	11
Do	346	30	1	16
FISHER, J. R., claim for relief	596	47	1	29
FISHER, JOSEPH, claim for relief	458	36	1	22
FISHING BOUNTIES UNDER ACT OF JUNE 19, 1813, payment of	335	35	1	21
Do	21	36	1	22
Do	173	36	1	22
FISK, HARRY, claim for relief	463	46	1	28
FISK, JAMES, collector of customs, district of Vermont, to reimburse for moneys stolen from	157	21	1	5
FITCH, JOHN B., inventor of steamboat, claim of heirs	124	29	1	13
FITCH, ROSWELL, claim for relief	43	30	1	15
FITCH, SOLOMON, and others, claim for relief	416	28	1	12
FITZGERALD, E. H., claim for relief	44	30	2	17
Do	241	31	1	18
Do	194	35	1	21
Do	520	36	1	22
FITZGERALD, EDWARD, claim for relief	682	29	1	14
FITZHUGH, L. H., claim for relief	26	46	1	28
FITZPATRICK, RICHARD, claim for relief	2176	48	2	30
Do	470	49	1	31
FITZPATRICK, WILLIAM, claim for relief	430	30	1	16
FLANIGAN, ANDREW, claim for construction of United States frigate Java	479	23	1	7
FLANNERY, JOHN, claim for relief	458	36	1	22
FLANNERY, PATRICK, claim for relief	458	36	1	22
FLANNERY, THOMAS, claim for relief	458	36	1	22
FLEANOR, NICHOLAS, claim for relief	135	28	1	12
FLEISHELL, JACOB J., claim for relief	691	45	2	27
FLEMING, ELIZABETH, claim for relief	1676	47	1	29
Do	2113	48	1	30
Do	2488	48	2	30
FLEMMING, SAMUEL H., claim for relief	1481	47	1	29
Do	1006	49	1	31
FLENING, WILLIAM, claim for relief	690	26	1	10
FLETCHER, A. BROOKS, claim for relief	3195	49	1	31
FLETCHER, ADDISON C., validity of certain letters-patent issued to, for self-canceling revenue stamp	*3766	49	2	32
FLETCHER, DAVID, claim for relief	26	22	2	6
FLETCHER, JOHN, claim for relief	306	43	2	26
Do	9	44	2	27
Do	87	47	1	29
FLETCHER, WILLIAM, claim for relief	25	22	2	6
FLINN, JAMES, claim for relief of widow	768	24	1	8
FLOOD, GEORGE W., claim for relief	4	35	2	21
Do	1508	46	2	28
FLOOD, MARY J., claim for relief	1669	47	1	29
FLORIDA,				
Claims arising under treaty of 1819, settlement of	*216	35	2	21
Claims of State of, settlement of	1230	46	2	28
Indian depredations claims, to settle	301	24	2	8
Indian war claims, to settle	308	49	1	31

* Views of minority.

Subject.	Report.	Congress.	Session.	Volume.
FLORIDA—Continued.				
Militia claim for relief of	209	25	2	9
Saint Augustine, for relief of citizens of	218	24	2	8
Do	724	25	2	9
Do	182	25	3	9
Union Bank, claim for money advanced Territory of	728	33	1	17
FLORIDA WAR. (*See* INDIAN WARS.)				
FLOYD, RACHEL J., claim for relief	2285	48	2	30
Do	596	49	1	31
FLYNN, WILLIAM, *et al.*, claim for relief	45	41	2	25
FOLGER, SAMUEL B., claim for relief	70	28	1	12
FONTANE, PHILIP J., claim for relief	526	28	1	12
FOOTE, GERVIS, claim for relief	88	28	1	12
FOOTE, WILLIAM S., claim for relief	132	32	1	18
FORBES, ABRAHAM, claim for relief	398	25	3	9
FORBES, WILLIAM, claim for relief	41	18	1	2
FORD, AUGUSTUS, claim for relief	669	33	1	17
FORD, CALVERT S., claim for relief	82	28	2	13
FORD, G. W., claim for relief	696	44	1	27
FORD, JOHN N., claim for relief	631	29	1	14
FORD, JONATHAN W., claim for relief	44	20	1	4
FORD, NATHAN, claim for relief	15	17	2	1
FORD, PETER, claim for relief	242	20	1	4
Do	5	21	1	5
FORD, ROBERT G., claim for relief	15	27	3	11
FORD, S. CALVERT, claim for relief	630	29	1	14
FORD, WILLIAM G., claim for relief	424	44	1	27
Do	667	45	2	27
Do	1370	46	2	28
FOREMAN, ANTHONY, claim for relief	367	21	1	5
FOREMAN, CHARLES, claim for relief	85	29	1	13
Do	54	30	1	15
FOREIGN STEAMSHIP COMPANIES, to adjust claims for tonnage duties paid by	661	49	1	31
FORMAN, F., claim for relief	710	25	2	9
FORSTER, ELISHA, claim for relief	473	24	1	8
FORSTER, THOMAS, claim for relief	25	37	2	25
FORSYTH, JOHN, claim for relief of heirs	269	28	1	12
Do	8	30	1	15
FORSYTHE, ROBERT A., claim for relief	286	21	1	5
FORSYTHE, WILLIAM, claim for relief	321	21	1	5
FOSTER, THOMAS, claim for relief	69	36	2	22
FOSTER, THOMAS, JR., claim for relief	419	24	1	8
FOULKE, CHARLES W., claim relief	1340	46	2	28
FOUNTAIN, GARRETT, claim for relief	12	18	1	2
Do	212	21	1	5
FOUQUET, NICHOLAS and MARC ANTOINE, claim for relief of heirs	519	47	1	29
FOURTH AUDITOR, rules of, in the settlement of claims to balances due deceased soldiers at the time of their death	167	27	3	11
FOWLER, BERNARD, claim for relief	477	23	1	7
Do	131	23	2	7
FOWLER, LAFAYETTE, claim for relief	2469	49	1	31
FOX, GEORGE WINTHROP, claim for relief	20	17	2	1
FOX, PETER C., claim for relief	275	35	1	19
FOX RIVER IMPROVEMENT, for the relief of certain laborers on	174	46	2	28
Do	521	47	1	29
FRAMPTON, H. R., claim for relief	594	44	1	27
FRANCIS, JOHN, claim for relief	159	28	2	13
FRANCISCO, JOHN, claim for relief	340	24	1	8
FRANKFORD, ARSENAL, for relief of sufferers by explosion at	521	47	1	29
FRANKLIN, SARAH B., claim for relief	96	44	2	27
Do	895	45	2	27
Do	866	46	2	28
FRANZ, E. D., claim for relief	182	44	1	27
FRANZONI VIRGINIA, claim for carving statuary for Capitol	296	23	1	7
Do	5	24	1	7
FRASER, ALEXANDER V., claim for relief	402	36	1	22
FRASER, JOHN, claim for relief	670	45	2	27
Do	1723	47	1	29
Do	300	49	1	31
FRASIER, CHARLES M., claim for relief	125	23	2	7
Do	45	24	1	8
FRAZEE, JOHN, claim for relief of widow	5	36	1	22
FRAZIER, JAMES, claim for relief	31	26	2	10
Do	167	27	2	11
FRAZIER, JOHN, & CO., claim for relief	290	28	1	13
FRAZIER, PRESTON, claim for relief	61	26	1	10
FREDERICK, CALVIN H., claim for relief	46	41	2	25
FREEDMEN, Africans captured by United States steamer Yorktown from the slaver pens	2	31	2	18
FREELAND, BENJAMIN, for relief	37	16	2	1
FREEMAN, RUTH, claim for relief	800	29	1	14

Subject.	Report.	Congress.	Session.	Volume.
GEDNEY, THOMAS, claim for relief of administrator	516	36	1	22
GEHON, FRANCIS, claim for relief	189	26	2	10
GELSTON, DAVID (collector of port of New York), settlement of accounts	276	23	1	7
Do	614	24	1	8
Do	38	25	2	9
GENTRY, ALLEN, claim for relief	1036	25	2	9
Do	276	26	1	10
GEORGIA,				
Augusta, claims of citizens of	319	24	2	8
Do	1068	25	2	9
Expenditures of State, in 1777 for common defense, to refund	370	45	2	27
Do	115	46	2	28
Do	38	47	1	29
Indian depredations claims, settlement of	301	24	2	8
Macon, to refund to, certain revenue taxes improperly collected from 1867 to 1837.	1432	46	2	28
Militia claims of, settlement of	549	28	1	12
Wilkes County, for relief of citizens of	322	24	2	8
GEORISH, WILLIAM, and others, claim for relief	253	35	2	21
GERARD, JOSEPH (Indian scout), murdered by the Indians in 1792, claim of heirs	174	28	2	12
Do	121	30	1	15
Do	82	33	1	19
GETMAN, CHARLES H., refund of duties on lumber imported	907	48	1	30
GIBBES & CO., claim for relief	25	44	2	27
GIBBONS, FRANCIS A., claim for relief	5	39	1	25
Do	86	39	1	25
GIBBONS, WILLIAM, claim for relief	111	3	1	18
GIBBS, WILLIAM, claim for relief	396	21	1	5
GIBERSON, A., claim for relief of heirs	458	36	1	22
GIBSON, CHARLES M., claim for relief	133	28	1	12
Do	28	29	1	13
GIBSON, DAVID, claim for relief of heirs	544	35		21
Do	15	36	1	22
GIBSON, WILLIAM D., claim for relief	431	30	1	16
GIBSON & CHASTAIN, claim for relief	141	38	1	25
GIDEON, JACOB, claim for relief	577	29	1	14
Do	86	30	1	15
Do	813	33	1	19
GIESEY, DRUSILLA, claim for relief	381	28	1	12
GIFFIN & HOAG, claim for relief	19	18	1	2
GILBERT, ABEL, and others, claim for relief	258	35	2	21
GILBERT, EPHRAIM F., claim for relief on stone contract	226	21	1	5
Do	715	26	1	10
Do	204	27	3	11
GILBERT, EUNICE, claim for relief	55	33	1	19
GILBERT, JACOB B., claim for relief	123	23	2	7
Do	35	24	1	7
GILBERT, JAMES H., claim for relief	3767	49	2	32
GILBERT, MAVINUS W., claim for sutler's stores furnished Army	88	17	1	1
Do	21	17	2	1
Do	88	19	1	3
Do	28	20	1	4
Do	339	23	1	7
Do	350	23		7
Do	7	24		7
Do	9	24	1	7
Do	81	24	2	8
GILBERT, W. J., claim for relief	108	37	2	25
GILBERT, WHITFORD, claim for relief	4	22	2	6
Do	14	23	1	7
GILBERT & GERRISH, claim for relief	258	35	2	21
Do	521	36	1	22
Do	77	38	1	25
Do	6	43	1	26
GILL, CHRISTOPHER, claim for relief	324	33		19
GILL, SAMUEL, claim for relief	128	24	1	8
GILL, WHITFORD, claim for relief	364	21	1	5
Do	4	22	2	6
GILMER, ELIZABETH H., claim for relief	225	47		29
Do	908	48		30
GILMORE, BESSIE S., claim for relief	3684	49	2	32
GILSON, THOMAS D., claim for relief	327	27	2	11
Do	4	27	3	11
GIVENEY, T., claim for relief	458	36	1	22
GLAEVECK, ADOLPHUS, claim for relief	332	36	1	22
GLASCOCK, THOMAS, claim for relief	58	17	2	1
GLASS, MOSES, claim for relief	458	36		22
GLEASON, O. E., claim for relief	597	47		29
GLEESON, ANDREW, claim for relief	1216	49		31
GLENN, JOHN (administrator), claim for relief	32	31	1	18

Subject.	Report.	Congress.	Session.	Volume.
GLOVER, CREAD, claim for relief	60	20	2	4
Do	23	21	1	5
GLOVER, HORACE, claim for relief	22	44	1	27
GLOVER, JAMES W., claim for relief	18	43	1	26
GODDARD, NATHANIEL,				
Owners of ship Ariadne	109	25	2	9
Do	30	26	1	10
Do	806	29	1	14
Claim for relief of executors of	417	35	1	21
GODFROY, GABRIEL, claim for relief	61	20	2	4
Do	35	21	1	5
Do	35	21	2	5
GODFROY & BEAUGRAND, claim for relief of	26	17	2	1
Do	128	22	1	6
GOETZ, FREDERICK, claim for relief of administrator	76	18	2	2
GOFF, ELI W., claim for relief	162	35	1	21
Do	468	36	1	22
GOIN, THOMAS, claim for relief	467	27	2	11
GOLRICK, J. R., claim for relief	2425	49	1	31
GOLDSMITH BROTHERS, claim for relief	114	39	1	25
GOLDSMITH & RODERICK, claim for capturing smugglers on coast of South Carolina	81	18	1	2
GOLLADAY & BOWLING, claim for relief	900	45	2	27
Do	1694	46	2	28
GOOCH, CORNELIUS D., claim for relief of heirs	712	27	2	11
GOOD, JOHN, claim for relief for right of way of Cumberland road	75	20	1	4
Do	345	20	1	4
Do	324	21	1	5
Do	261	22	1	6
GOODALE, AUGUSTUS B., claim for relief	27	45	3	27
GOODRICH, JAMES W., claim for relief	2273	49	1	31
GOODSELL, NATHAN, claim for relief	711	27	2	11
GOODSPEED, CHARLES, claim for relief	464	34	1	8
GOODWIN, LEWIS, claim for relief	304	43	2	26
Do	109	44	1	27
GORDAN, WILLIAM, claim for relief	116	15	1	1
Do	6	16	2	1
GORDON, DAVID, claim for relief	165	34	1	20
GORDON, VICTOR L., claim for relief	768	27	2	11
GORHAM, ALLEN, claim for relief	117	27	3	11
Do	644	27	2	11
Do	242	30	1	16
GORRISSEN, V. F., claim for relief	81	49	1	31
GOVERNMENT EMPLOYÉS. (*See* EMPLOYÉS.)				
GOVERNMENT OFFICERS, to reimburse for money lost or stolen	157	21	1	5
Do	483	22	1	6
Do	353	23	1	7
Do	188	26	2	10
GRADY, HENRY, claim for relief	141	25	3	9
GRAHAM, GEORGE D., claim for relief	1719	46	2	28
GRAHAM, HANNIBAL, claim for relief	96	36	1	22
Do	126	37	2	25
GRAHAM, JAMES, claim for relief	625	44	1	27
GRAHAM, JOHN, claim for relief	680	24	1	8
Do	46	25	2	9
GRAHAM, THOMAS B., claim for relief	341	30	1	16
GRAHAM, WILLIAM, claim for relief	83	24	2	8
GRAHAM, WILLIAM M., claim for relief	347	27	2	11
GRAND TRUNK RAILWAY, claim for relief	1549	49	1	31
GRANT, ALBERT, claim for relief	35	42	2	26
Do	415	44	1	27
Do	101	45	2	27
Do	897	46	2	28
Do	1668	47	1	29
GRANT, EDWAY A., claim for relief	1127	49	1	31
Do	2380	49	1	31
GRANT, JOHN M. (administrator), claim for relief	46	35	2	21
GRANT, ROBERT, claim for relief	539	24	1	8
GRATIOT, JOHN P. B., and others, claim for relief	591	30	1	17
GRATZ, BENJAMIN, claim for relief	45	38	1	25
GRAVES, GEORGE E., claim for relief	275	29	1	13
GRAY, GEORGE A., claim for relief	15	38	1	25
GRAY, HENRY C., claim for relief	307	48	1	30
GRAY, HENRY W., claim for relief	182	23	1	7
GRAY, JAMES, claim for relief	165	25	3	9
GRAY, JAMES W., claim for relief	306	26	1	10
GRAY, JOHN, claim for relief of heirs	306	26	1	10
Do	197	28	2	12
Do	131	29	1	13
GRAY, LUCY G., claim for relief	74	35	2	21
GRAY, WILLIAM, claim for relief	1350	49	1	31

Subject.	Report.	Congress.	Session.	Volume.
GRAY, WILLIAM H., claim for relief	24	44	1	27
Do	350	48	1	30
Do	2422	49	1	31
GRAY, McMURDO & CO., claim for relief	51	33	1	19
GREAT BRITAIN, compensation to owners of certain lands ceded by treaty of 1842 to	99	44	1	27
GREELY EXPEDITIONS IN 1881-'84, for relief of persons engaged in	3432	49	1	31
GREEN, ABBY, services rendered to prisoners confined in Libby Prison in 1863-'64, claim for relief	115	39	1	25
GREEN, JAMES, claim for relief	492	23	1	7
Do	131	23	2	7
GREEN, JANE A., claim for relief	94	41	2	25
GREEN, L. T., and others, claim for relief	342	46	2	28
GREEN, OCEOLA C., claim for relief	300	43	2	26
GREEN, PETER H., claim for relief	596	24	1	8
GREEN, RICHARD M., claim for relief	3931	49	2	32
GREEN, SIMON, claim for relief	39	26	1	10
GREEN, SOLOMON, claim for relief	490	27	2	11
GREEN, TIMOTHY, claim for relief	714	27	2	11
GREEN, WILLIAM, claim for relief	495	43	1	26
GREEN, WILSON A., claim for relief	1235	46	2	28
GREEN & TRAINOR, claim for relief	12	41	2	25
GREENE, JAMES H., claim for relief	928	47	1	29
GREENLEAF, ALBERT (navy agent), claim for relief	45	41	2	25
Do	3062	49	2	32
GREENSBURG LIMESTONE COMPANY, claim for relief	3325	49	1	31
GREER, WILLIAM, claim for relief	87	29	2	14
Do	55	30	1	15
Do	13	32	1	19
GREGG, BENJAMIN, claim for relief	4	36	1	22
GREGORY, LUCY, claim for relief of widow	46	35	2	21
GRESHAM, JOSEPH, claim for relief	52	24	1	8
GRICE, SAMUEL, claim for relief	6	22	1	6
GRIER, SAMUEL A., claim for relief	485	30	1	16
GRIESENBECK, JULIUS, claim for relief	147	43	1	26
GRIFFITH, SARAH, claim for relief	826	23	1	7
Do	5	28	2	12
GRIGSBY, JAMES M., claim for relief	1545	49	1	31
GRIGSBY, MARTIN, claim for relief	2371	49	1	31
GROEZINGER, GOTTLIEB, claim for relief	1611	49	1	31
GROOM, WRIGHT, claim for relief	237	24	2	8
GROUT, THEOPHILUS, claim for relief	489	23	1	7
GRUBB, CURTIS, claim for relief	630	24	1	8
Do	42	25	2	9
GRUBB, JACKSON, claim for relief	10	45	2	27
Do	28	46	2	27
GUEST, JOHN, claim for relief of administratrix	186	20	1	4
GUIGEY, ALEXANDER, claim for relief	458	36	1	22
GUIGEY, EDWARD, claim for relief	458	36	1	22
GUIGEY, JAMES, claim for relief	458	36	1	22
GUILBEAU, FRANCES, claim for relief	901	45	2	27
Do	2694	48	2	30
GUNN, CALVIN, claim for relief	998	49	1	31
GURLEY, E. J., claim for relief	804	44	1	27
Do	192	45	2	27
Do	201	46	2	28
Do	3	47	1	29
GUSTIN, SAMUEL L., claim for relief	172	46	2	28
GUTHRIE, A. J., claim for relief	697	47	1	29
Do	228	48	1	30
HABICHT, C. EDWARD (administrator), claim for relief	432	35	1	21
HADDOCK, JOHN A., claim for relief	19	38	2	25
HAGAN, MALICHI, claim for relief	160	30	1	15
HAGAR, JAMES M., claim for relief	1810	49	1	31
HAGERTY, WILLIAM, claim for relief	48	33	2	19
HAIGHT, JOHN, claim for relief	96	23	1	7
HAIL, WILLIAM P. A., claim for relief	498	31	1	18
HAILE, JOHN, claim for relief	115	15	1	1
HALE, DENNIS, claim for relief	458	36	1	22
HALE, ELISHA, claim for relief	458	36	1	22
HALE, JOSEPH, claim for relief	400	30	1	16
HALEY, D. W., claim for relief	210	24	2	8
Do	72	25	2	9
HALEY, WILLIAM, claim for relief	458	36	1	22
HALF PAY,				
Militia not mustered, widows and children of, who fell in active service	679	24	1	8
Widows and children of Army officers	415	24	1	8
Do	112	35	1	21
Do	*399	36	1	22

*Views of minority.

Subject.	Report.	Congress.	Session.	Volume.
HALFIN, HENRY, and others, claim for relief	13	45	3	27
HALIDAY, THOMAS,				
Claim for relief of administrator	242	27	2	11
Claim for relief of heirs of	74	24	1	8
HALL, ADAM, claim for relief	269	24	2	8
Do	704	26	1	10
HALL, CHAPIN, claim for relief	27	37	3	25
Do	3	38	1	25
HALL, CHARLES, claim for relief	564	28	1	12
HALL, ELIAS, claim for relief	197	35	1	21
HALL, HENRIETTA M., claim for relief	344	29	1	13
HALL, HIRAM, claim for relief	358	30	1	16
HALL, JAMES, claim for relief	117	24	2	8
Do	494	26	1	10
Do	240	31	1	18
Do	2421	48	2	30
Do	2279	49	1	31
HALL, JOHN, claim for relief	32	45	3	27
Do	426	48	1	30
HALL, JONATHAN, claim for relief	339	29	1	13
HALL, JOSEPH, claim for relief	460	24	1	8
Do	20	25	2	9
HALL, LARNETT, claim for relief	45	35	2	21
Do	168	36	1	22
HALL, LOT, claim for relief of heirs	16	36	1	22
HALL, NORMAN, claim for relief	118	39	1	25
HALL, P. P., claim for relief of heirs	94	36	1	22
HALL, RICHARD, claim for relief of heirs	717	27	2	11
HALL, WASHINGTON, claim for relief	32	31	1	18
HALL & COZZENS, claim for relief	396	36		22
HALL & STALKER, claim for relief	119	27		11
HALLOWES, MILLER, claim for relief	790	25	2	9
Do	762	27	2	11
HALSEY, FREDERICK, claim for relief	22	17	2	1
Do	584	23	1	7
HALSEY, LUTHER, claim for relief	788	27	2	11
HAMBAUGH, P. G., claim for relief of assignee of	278	29	1	13
HAMBLETON, SAMUEL, claim for relief	469	27	2	11
HAMBLEY, WILLIAM, claim for relief	7	18	2	2
HAMBLIN, J. & N., claim for relief	696	26		10
Do	766	27	2	11
HAMILTON, ARCHIBALD W. (captain), claim for imprisonment in British navy, 1812	124	15	1	1
Do	66	19	2	3
Do	190	20	1	4
HAMILTON, JOHN, claim for relief	376	30	1	16
Do	48	33	1	19
HAMILTON, JOHN R., claim for relief	503	43	1	26
HAMILTON, N. G., claim for relief	518	26	1	10
HAMILTON, ROBERT, JR., claim for relief	25	37	3	25
HAMILTON WOOLEN COMPANY, claim for relief	74	42	2	26
HAMILTON, J. & N., claim for relief	53	26	1	10
HAMMOND, CHARLES, claim for relief	458	36	1	22
HAMMOND, FRANCIS, claim for relief	2253	49	1	31
HAMMOND & DEXTER, claim for relief	983	27	2	11
Do	496	28	1	12
HAMPSON, JAMES, claim for relief	227	29	1	13
HAND, CHARLES J., claim for relief	502	23	1	7
HANKS, JACOB, claim for relief	1061	25	2	9
HANKS, JOHN F., claim for relief	39	42	3	26
HANNUM, J. C., claim for relief	519	43	1	26
HANSBOROUGH, JOHN, claim for relief of heirs	637	27	2	11
HANSELL, EMERICK W., claim for relief	426	44	1	27
HANSELL, GEORGE B., claim for relief	3105	49	1	31
HANSELL, WILLIAM Y., claim for relief	733	27	2	11
HANSON, THOMAS, claim for relief	89	24	1	8
HARBAUGH, DANIEL, claim for relief	70	35	2	21
HARBAUGH, YOST, claim for relief	222	48	1	30
HARBEN, WILEY, claim for relief	116	24	2	8
HARD, BENJAMIN F., claim for relief	153	27	2	11
HARDEMAN, SALLY, claim for relief	417	45	2	27
HARDESTY, RICHARD, claim for relief	403	21	1	5
Do	457	22	1	6
Do	357	23	1	7
Do	10	24	1	7
HARDIE, ALLEN W., claim for relief	86	23	1	7
HARDIN, claim for relief	1230	48	1	30
HARDING, JAMES, claim for relief	390	23	1	7
Do	155	43	1	26
HARDING, WINTHROP S., claim for relief	170	31	1	18
HARDWICKE, GEORGE W., claim for relief	1680	48	1	30

Subject.	Report.	Congress.	Session.	Volume.
HARDY, JOSEPH, claim for relief	297	34	1	20
HARDY & LONG, claim for relief	187	35	1	21
HARFORD, SARAH, claim for relief	207	23	1	7
HARKNESS, BYRON H., claim for relief	1744	46	2	28
Do	349	47	1	29
HARKNESS, THOMAS F., claim for relief	125	29	1	13
HARLEY, JOSEPH L., and others claim for relief	1433	46	2	28
HARMON, HANSON, claim for relief	367	45	2	27
HARMONY, MANUEL X., claim for relief	458	30	1	16
HARPER, JAMES H., claim for relief	178	20	1	4
HARPER, JOSEPH M., claim for relief	267	22	1	6
Do	26	23	1	7
HARRIS, B. W., claim for relief	492	43	1	26
HARRIS, JOHN, claim for relief	350	30	1	16
HARRIS, OLIVER, claim for relief	95	36	1	22
HARRIS, RICHARD. (*See* HARRIS & FARROW.)				
HARRIS, STEPHEN, claim for relief	107	23	2	7
HARRIS, WILLIAM, claim for relief	51	30	1	15
HARRIS, & FARROW, claim for construction of fortification on Dauphin Island, Mobile Bay	69	18	2	2
Do	181	20	1	4
Do	315	21	1	5
Do	245	24	2	8
Do	66	25	2	9
Do	39	25	3	9
Do	196	29	1	13
Do	167	30	1	15
Do	166	31	1	18
HARRISON, DAVID N., claim for relief	1981	47	2	29
Do	1421	48	1	30
HARRISON, GEORGE, claim for relief	148	27	3	11
HARRISON, JAMES, claim for relief	639	27	2	11
HARRISON, JAMES G., claim for relief	665	43	1	26
Do	416	44	1	27
Do	664	45	2	27
HARRISON, JAMES P., claim for relief	745	24	1	8
HARRISON, MARY W., claim for relief	5	29	1	13
HARRISON, PETER P., claim for relief	667	43	1	26
HARRISON, ROBERT, and others, claim for relief	216	35	2	21
HARRISON, THOMAS, claim for relief	1006	25	2	9
Do	68	26	1	10
HARRISON, PORTER & FISHBACK, claim for relief	1755	47	1	29
HARRISON & FISHBACK, claim for relief	1377	49	1	31
Do	2498	49	1	31
HART, ELI, claim for moneys advanced United States	23	16	1	1
Do	3	17	1	1
Do	19	17	1	1
De	37	17	1	1
Do	23	17	1	1
Do	24	17	2	1
Do	67	35	2	21
Do	68	35	2	21
HARTWICK, GEORGE, claim for relief	28	31	1	18
HARVEY, JAMES W., claim for relief	1721	47	1	29
Do	790	48	1	30
HARVEY, JOHN, claim for relief	517	25	2	9
HARVEY & LIVESEY, claim for relief	305	43	2	26
HASELTON, DANIEL, claim for relief	843	22	1	6
HASKELL, JOSIAH, claim for relief	254	29	1	13
HASKINS, WILLIAM, claim for relief	279	25	3	9
HASLET, WILLIAM, claim for the ship Liberty, captured by the French	18	14		1
HASSAM, THOMAS, claim for relief	393	35	1	21
HASELL, LOUISA H., claim for relief	1548	49		31
HATCH, ISAIAH claim for relief	80	36	2	22
HATHAWAY & HUBBELL, claim for relief	40	26		10
HAVENS, SYLVESTER, claim for relief	287	21		5
Do	452	22		6
HAWKINS, PHILEMON B., claim for relief	409	45	2	27
Do	886	46	2	28
HAWLEY, RICHARD & SONS, claim for relief	710	44	1	27
Do	112	45	2	27
Do	201	47		29
HAXTHAUSEN, JOSEPH, claim for relief	2174	49	1	31
HAY, EDWIN B., claim for relief	523	47	1	29
Do	1238	48	1	30
HAYDEN & ATWELL, claim for relief	296	24		8
HAYES, AHAZ, claim for relief	387	23		7
HAYNER, JOHN, claim for relief	135	21		5
HAYNIE, MARIAN F., claim for relief	2468	49		31
HAYS, H. H. B., claim for relief of sureties	632	25	2	9
Do	302	26		10

Subject.	Report.	Congress.	Session.	Volume.
HAYWARD, JOHN T. K., claim for relief	301	43	2	26
HAZLETON, DANIEL, claim for relief	74	22	2	6
Do	24	23	1	7
HAZZARD, EBENEZER, claim for relief	477	30	1	16
HEACOCK, REUBEN B., claim for relief	72	35	2	21
HEAD, E. B., claim for relief	162	44	2	27
Do	397	45	2	27
HEADY, WILLIAM J., claim for relief	351	30	1	16
HEARD, BENEDICT J., claim for relief	632	24	1	8
Do	325	24	2	8
Do	65	25	3	9
Do	753	30	1	17
HEARSEY, SOLOMON, claim for relief	831	25	2	9
HEARTT, WAITE & DODGE, claim for relief	161	44	1	27
HEATH, NATHANIEL H.,				
Claim for relief	41	14	2	1
Do	158	15	1	1
Claim for relief of heirs	11	34	1	20
HEATH, LABAN & CO., claim for relief	3125	49	1	31
HEBB, GEORGE V., claim for relief	25	46	1	28
Do	1013	46	2	28
HEBB, HOPEWELL, claim for relief	246	26	2	10
HEBBERT, EDWARD H., claim for relief	331	33	1	19
HEDGES, NICHOLAS, claim for relief	576	24	1	8
Do	33	25	2	9
Do	10	26	1	10
Do	11	26	2	10
HEDGPETH, WILLIAM, claim for relief	389	45	2	27
HEISKELL, HUGH L., claim for relief	746	24	1	8
HEMIUP, CHARLES S., claim for relief	1562	46	2	28
HENDERSON, JAMES, claim for relief	179	36	1	22
HENDERSON, JOHN, claim for relief	267	27	2	11
Do	672	43	1	26
HENDERSON, RAYMOND A., claim for relief	45	26	1	10
Do	66	26	2	10
HENDERSON, WILLIAM, claim for relief	139	15	1	1
Do	19	16	1	1
Do	5	17	1	1
HENLEY, ARTHUR H., claim for relief	34	18	1	2
HENRIE, DAN DRAKE, claim for relief	413	30	1	16
HENRY, A. G., claim for relief	253	30	1	16
HENRY, Mrs. A. L., claim for relief	649	36	1	22
HENRY, EULA E., claim for relief	3392	49	1	31
HENRY, GARDINER, claim for relief of widow	151	34	3	20
HENRY, GEORGE G. (administrator), claim for relief	482	25	2	9
HENRY, J. A., and others, claim for relief	342	46	2	28
HENRY, JACOB A., claim for relief	2552	49	1	31
HENRY, JOHN, claim for relief of administrator	167	27	2	11
HENRY, ROBERT, claim for relief	167	19	1	3
HENRY, WILLIAM, claim for relief of administrator	482	25	2	9
HENRY, WILLIAM M., claim for relief	11	41	3	25
HENRY, WILLIAM S., claim for relief of heirs	649	36	1	22
HERMAN, HENRY, claim for relief	1365	46	2	28
Do	3022	49	1	31
HERNANDEZ, JOSEPH M., claim for relief	1043	25	2	9
Do	104	27	3	11
Do	58	28	1	12
HERRON, JAMES, claim for relief	249	24	1	8
Do	60	25	2	9
HERTFORD, JOSEPH claim for relief	894	47	1	29
HERVEY, WILL R., claim for relief	656	43	1	26
Do	105	45	2	27
HEWETT, BENJAMIN, claim for relief	109	22	2	6
HICKEY, JOHN W., claim for relief	315	43	2	26
HICKEY, PHILIP, claim for relief	338	22	1	6
Do	21	23	1	7
HICKMAN, JOHN P., claim for relief of administrator	265	27	2	11
HICKMAN, NANCY B., claim for relief	84	21	2	5
HICKMAN, PASCHAL, claim for relief of administrator	434	23	1	7
HICKOK, SAMUEL, claim for relief	126	24	1	8
HICKS, A. W., claim for relief	118	46	2	28
HICKS, S. D., claim for relief	312	43	1	26
HICKS, WILLIAM, claim for relief	335	36		22
HIGGINS, JOHN L., claim for relief	458	36		22
HIGGINS, JOHN M., claim for relief	600	49	1	31
HIGHLYMAN, SAMUEL L., claim for relief	223	43	1	26
HIGHTOWER, RICHARD, claim for relief	72	18	2	2
HILL, HENRY, claims for relief	435	23		7
Do	292	24	1	8
Do	36	25	3	9
HILL, REES, claim for relief	715	24	1	

Subject.	Report.	Congress.	Session.	Volume.
HILLARY, RIGNALD (alias Nick), claim for relief of heirs of	63	30	1	15
HILLYARD, JOSHUA, claim for relief	28	26	2	10
Do	260	31	1	18
HILTON, LUKE, claim for relief	338	29	1	13
Do	165	36	1	22
HIME, DAVID, claim for relief	811	25	2	9
Do	42	25	3	9
HINE, JOHN, claim for relief	773	24	1	8
HINES, CHARLES W., claim for relief	715	27	2	11
HINKLEY, NATHANIEL, claim for relief	712	24	1	8
HITCHCOCK, HENRY, claim for relief	20	19	1	3
HIX, GEORGE, claim for relief	788	29	1	14
Do	46	30	1	15
HOAG, WILLIAM H., and others, claim for relief	131	28	1	13
HOBBS, J. M., claim for relief	2713	49	1	31
HOCKETT, JOHN W., claim for relief	101	28	2	12
Do	71	30	1	15
HODGES & LANSDALE and others, claim for relief	44	34	3	20
Do	64	36	2	22
HODGIN, JOHN, claim for relief	102	27	3	11
HODGKINS, WILLIAM, claim for relief	93	23	1	7
HODGSON, RICHARD M., claim for relief	93	41	2	25
HODSDON, ISAAC (captain, United States Army), claim for relief from civil proceedings of courts in New Hampshire	8	19	1	3
HODSON, WILLIAM, claim for relief of administrator	1046	25	2	9
Do	55	27	2	11
HOGAN, JAMES F., claim for relief	1969	49	1	31
HOGAN, JOHN, claim for relief of widow and heirs of	310	33	1	19
HOGAN, MICHAEL, claim for relief of administrator	89	29	2	4
Do	47	30	1	15
HOGAN, WILLIAM (administrator), claim for relief	89	29	2	14
Do	47	30	1	15
HOGG, CATHARINE, claim for relief	918	25	2	9
HOISINGTON, ABISHAI, claim for relief	754	24	1	8
HOIT, GATES, claim for services as United States spy in war of 1812	885	23	1	7
Do	771	24	1	8
Do	280	25	3	9
HOLBROOK, HENRY, claim for relief	26	26	2	10
Do	716	27	2	11
HOLDEN, FREDERICK A., claim for relief	9	37	3	25
Do	16	38	1	25
Do	24	38	1	25
HOLDEN, THOMAS, claim for relief	60	26	1	10
HOLGATE, HARVEY, claim for relief of heirs of	189	33	1	19
HOLGATE, HARVEY and MARGARET, claim for relief	419	29	1	13
HOLGATE, SAMUEL,				
Claim for relief	78	21	1	5
Do	398	23	1	7
Do	32	26	2	10
Claim for relief of administrators of	124	30	1	15
Do	173	36	1	22
HOLIDAY, ANN, claim for relief	411	23	1	7
HOLLADAY, BEN., claim for relief	1182	47	1	29
HOLLAND, WILLIAM T., claim for relief	212	30	1	15
HOLLENBOCK, GEORGE B., claim for relief	15	30	1	15
Do	53	30	1	15
HOLLIDAY, JOHN, claim for relief	62	18	1	2
HOLLINGSWORTH, LEVI, claim for relief	107	19	1	3
HOLLINGSWORTH, THOMAS and SAMUEL claim for relief	167	19	1	3
HOLLOWAY, J. B., claim for relief	894	46	2	28
HOLLOWAY, W. R., claim for relief	320	47	1	29
HOLMAN, JAMES D., claim for relief	197	45	2	27
HOLMES, A. F., claim for relief	387	35	1	21
HOLMES, PHILIP B., claim for relief	213	35	2	21
HOLMES AND PEDRICK, claim for relief	180	36	1	22
HOLROYD, SARAH E., claim for relief	2562	49	1	31
HOLT, SAMUEL D., claim for relief of Alabama troops under command of	258	24	2	28
HOLT COUNTY BANK, claim for relief	2420	48	2	30
HOMANS, BENJAMIN, claim for rleief	74	21	1	5
HOMANS, DANIEL, claim for marine hospital in Charleston, S. C., delay caused by change of site	518	23	1	7
Do	22	24	1	7
Do	58	27	2	11
Do	14	28	2	12
HOMER, W. B., claim for relief	881	46	2	28
HOOK, JOSIAH, JR. (collector of customs, Castine, Mass.), to indemnify, for property seized as	32	17	1	1
Do	46	18	1	2
HOOK, STEPHEN, claim for the arrest of persons charged with piracy, and compensation for time and expense as prosecuting witness	219	21	1	5

Subject.	Report.	Congress.	Session.	Volume.
HOOKER, H. C., claim for relief	1482	47	1	29
Do	806	48	1	30
HOOKER, SAMUEL F., claim for relief	161	15	1	1
Do	82	22	2	6
HOOPER, JAMES, claim for relief	4	39	2	25
HOOPER & WILLIAMS, claim for relief	521	36	1	22
Do	77	38	1	25
HOOPES, EDWARD, claim for relief	420	45	1	26
HOOVER, ANDREW, claim for relief	111	24	1	8
HOOVER, MANUEL, claim for relief	425	30	1	16
HOPKINS, BENJAMIN W., claim for relief of heirs	59	27	2	11
HOPKINS, Mrs. CARRIEE,				
Claim for relief	3651	49	2	32
Claim for relief of administrator	324	31	1	18
HOPPIN, FRANK M., claim for relief	518	44	1	27
HOPWOOD, JAMES, claim for relief	426	46	2	28
Do	322	47	1	29
HORNBROOK, P., claim for relief	193	45	1	26
HORNER, JOHN S., claim for relief	665	24	1	8
HORSES LOST IN MILITARY SERVICE OF UNITED STATES, settlement of claims for	12	17	1	1
Do	383	23	1	7
Do	843	24	1	8
Do	3	25	1	9
Do	921	25	2	9
Do	948	25	2	9
Do	1060	25	2	9
Do	929	27	2	11
HORTON, ELI, claim for relief	613	24	1	8
Do	37	25	2	9
HORTON, HIRAM, claim for relief	162	36	1	23
HORTON, IRA T., claim for relief	668	30	1	17
HORWITZ, ORVILLE (trustee), claim for relief	1007	49	1	31
Do	3395	49	1	31
HOULDER, THOMAS, claim for relief	463	23	1	7
HOUSE, CONRAD, claim for relief	844	25	2	9
Do	507	26	1	10
Do	12	27	2	11
Do	278	28	1	12
Do	320	29	1	13
HOUSE OF REPRESENTATIVES (*see also* CONGRESS), committee clerks, employment of	53	39	1	25
HOUSEMAN, JACOB,				
Claim for relief	215	24	2	8
Claim for relief of heirs	798	30	1	17
HOUSTON, S. D., claim for relief	67	48	1	30
HOW, JOHN (deceased), claim for relief of estate	1610	49	1	31
HOWARD, C. H., claim for relief	869	46	2	28
Do	321	47	1	29
HOWARD, JAMES B., claim for relief	1683	48	1	30
HOWARD, JAMES R., claim for relief	427	48	1	30
HOWARD, JOHN H., claim for relief	223	24	1	8
HOWARD, LEON, claim for relief	598	49	1	31
HOWARD, THOMAS M., claim for relief	805	44	1	27
HOWE, CHARLES, claim for relief	171	27	2	11
Do	638	27	2	11
HOWE, JOHN, claim for relief	188	25	3	9
Do	13	26	1	10
Do	14	26	2	10
Do	743	30	1	17
HOWELL, GILBERT, claim for relief	205	25	3	9
HOWELL, JOSEPH M., claim for relief	261	31	1	18
HOXIE, JOHN J. B., claim for relief	657	30	1	17
HUBBARD, ANN B. (administratrix), claim for relief	26	45	3	27
Do	402	47	1	29
Do	1312	49	1	31
HUBBARD, EBER, claim for relief	288	21	1	5
HUBBARD, EDWARD, claim for relief	1311	46	2	28
HUBBARD, HENRY, claim for relief	390	35	1	21
HUBBARD, HIRAM W., claim for relief	2274	49	1	31
HUBBELL, MARY (executrix), claim for relief	768	24	1	8
HUBBELL, W. W., claim for relief	23	46	1	28
HUDSON, WILLIAM, claim for relief of heirs	422	30	1	16
HUDSPETH, CHARLES M., claim for relief	563	29	1	13
HUGHES, A. K., claim for relief	113	30	1	15
HUGHES, DAVID M., claim for relief	267	27	2	11
HUGHES, HUGH, claim for relief of heirs of	222	29	1	13
HUGHES, SAMUEL, claim for gun foundry destroyed	75	15	1	1
Do	6	16	1	1
HUGO, SAMUEL B., claim for relief	427	35	1	21
HULE, C. H., claim for relief	1018	48	1	30

Subject.	Report.	Congress.	Session.	Volume.
HULL, DAVID, claim for relief	37	21	2	5
Do	770	24	1	8
HULL, ISAAC, claim for relief	52	27	2	11
HULL, GENERAL WILLIAM, claim for relief of widow and administrator of	63	19	2	3
Do	18	20	1	4
HULL & COZZENS, claim for relief	432	35	1	21
Do	7	37	3	25
Do	1	38	2	25
HULLFISH, GARRETT, claim for relief	33	38	1	25
HUMPHREY, ABEL, claim for relief	458	36	1	22
HUMPHREY, ALEXANDER,				
Claim for relief	94	23	1	7
Do	63	25	3	9
Claim for relief of heirs of	169	33	1	19
HUMPHREY, SYLVESTER, claim for relief	94	23	1	7
Do	169	33	1	19
HUMPHREYS, GAD, claim for relief	96	33	2	19
HUMPHREYS, HIRAM, claim for relief	45	25	3	9
Do	341	29	1	13
Do	269	36	1	22
HUMPHREYS, LETITIA (administratrix), claim for relief	216	35	2	21
HUNGERFORD, DEXTER, claim for relief	925	27	2	11
HUNGERFORD, E. V., claim for relief	70	29	1	13
HUNT, EPHRAIM, claim for relief	460	36	1	22
HUNT, JOHN E., and others, claim for relief	51	27	2	11
Do	12	27	3	11
HUNT, RUSSELL, and others, claim for relief	120	22	2	6
Do	20	23		7
HUNT, SAMUEL, claim for relief	62	42	3	62
HUNT, THOMAS, claim for relief	179	20	1	4
HUNT, THOMAS F., claim for relief	419	21	1	5
HUNTER, ARCHIBALD R. S., claim for relief	341	25	2	9
Do	569	28	1	12
Do	61	30	1	15
HUNTER, WILLIAM, claim for relief	62	26	1	10
HUNTINGTON, JEANETTE C., claim for relief	311	28	1	12
HUNTINGTON, WILLIAM, claim for relief	734	49	1	31
HUNTSMAN, GEORGE W., claim for relief of	55	40	3	25
HURD, Henry, claim for relief	458	36	1	22
HURTON, R. G., & CO., claim for relief	3394	49	1	31
HUSTON, ALMANZON, claim for relief	197	34	1	20
HUSTON, R. G., & CO., claim for relief	2008	48	1	30
Do	2840	49	1	31
HUSTON, ROBERT, claim for relief	46	19	2	3
Do	137	20	1	4
HYDE, WILLIAM H., claim for relief of heirs	1924	47	2	29
HYLAND, MARY, claim for relief	538	24	1	8
HYLIARD, CHARLES M., claim for relief	22	26	2	10
ILLINOIS,				
Black Hawk war, to compensate citizens for loss of property during	48	30	1	15
Citizens of, claim for property destroyed by Indians in 1832	579	24	1	8
Do	580	24	1	8
Indian depredations, for relief of sufferers from	351	25	2	9
IMPRESSMENT OF PROPERTY FOR PUBLIC USE, settlement of claims for	301	24	2	8
INCOME TAX, to refund to certain citizens of Tennessee	*102	47	1	25
INDIANA,				
Militia of, for services in 1836	197	24	2	8
Do	465	25	2	9
University of Notre Dame du Lac, to refund duties paid by	666	45	2	27
INDIAN DEPREDATIONS,				
Alabama, settlement of claims for	301	24	2	8
Florida, settlement of claims for	301	24	2	8
Do	162	25	3	9
Georgia, settlement of claims for	301	24	2	8
Settlement of claims for	1028	25	2	9
INDIAN HOSTILITIES, southern, claim of citizens of Wilkes County, Georgia, for advances made in suppressing	322	24	2	8
INDIAN LANDS, trespass upon, confiscation of property for	530	24	1	8
INDIAN OUTRAGES, compensation to heirs of those murdered during	121	30	1	15
INDIANS,				
Cherokees, claim of	2644	49	2	32
Choctaw tribe of, to grant bounty lands to	246	22	1	6
Horses stolen by, in Illinois and Michigan, payment to owners of	83	22	2	6
INDIAN WAR BONDS. (*See* BONDS.)				
INDIAN WARS,				
Alabama, claims for supplies and troops furnished in suppression of, 1836	127	29	1	13
Black Hawk war, to settle claims of Illinois citizens for losses incurred in	579	24	1	8
Do	580	24	1	8
Creek, Alabama militia in 1836, compensation	258	24	2	8
Do	382	25	3	9

* Parts 1, 2.

Subject.	Report.	Congress.	Session.	Volume.
INDIAN WARS—Continued.				
Creek, Alabama militia in 1836, compensation	958	25	2	9
Florida, claim of Augusta, Ga., for advances made during	819	24	2	8
Florida, to adjudicate claim of	303	49	1	31
Florida militia, to compensate, for services rendered in war of 1835–'36	209	25	3	9
Half pay, to widows and orphans of volunteers and regulars who fell in, claim for relief	415	24	1	8
Horses lost in, settlement of claims for	843	24	1	8
Property lost in, settlement of claims for	848	24	1	8
Seminole,				
To indemnify officers and volunteers for horses lost in	84	16	1	1
Do	26	16	2	1
Do	13	17	1	1
Volunteers in, payment of	84	16	1	1
INGALLS, J. E., claim for relief	494	43	1	26
INGERSOLL, CHARLES J., claim for relief	834	24	1	8
INGHAM, JOHN, claim for relief	297	23	1	7
INGLE, J. P., claim for relief	1	25	3	9
INGLE, JOSEPH, claim for relief	475	30	1	16
INSURANCE COMPANIES,				
Internal-revenue tax upon, bond of, to refund	476	49	1	31
Pacific, and others, claim for damages sustained in suits against United States marshal in eastern district of Pennsylvania	757	30	1	17
Banking houses in New York, taxes erroneously assessed on, to refer claim to Court of Claims	101	47	1	29
Bonds of insurance companies, to refund	476	49	1	31
INTERNAL REVENUE,				
Gaugers and other employés, relief of	2269	49	1	31
Macon, Ga., tax erroneously assessed upon, to refund	417	44	1	27
New York thirty-second district, relief of certain persons in	101	47	1	29
Vicksburg and Meridian Railroad Company, tax erroneously assessed upon, to refund	1292	49	1	31
IOWA,				
Des Moines Rapids Canal in, for relief of employés in	810	47	1	29
State penitentiary in, to donate land for	489	27	2	11
IRELAND, AMOS, claim for relief	690	45	2	27
IRELAND, C. H., claim for relief	1020	48	1	30
IRISH, F. M., claim for relief	152	28	2	12
IRON MOUNTAIN BANK, SAINT LOUIS, MISSOURI, claim for relief	999	49	1	31
IRVIN, ROBERT, claim for relief	144	20	1	4
IRVINE, ALEXANDER, owner of schooner Montevidiana confiscation of	63	17	1	1
Do	10	17	2	1
IRVINE, CALLENDER, claim for relief of administrator	187	27	2	11
IRVING, SARAH, claim for relief	45	33	2	19
IRWIN, JOSEPH C., claim for relief	1726	46	2	28
Do	1506	47	1	29
Do	660	49	1	31
ISABELITA (slave ship), capture and libel of	250	24	2	8
Do	629	25	1	8
IVES, ELISHA, claim for relief	142	21	1	5
IVINS, SAMUEL P., claim for relief	836	47	1	29
IVY, WILLIAM N., claim for relief	125	24	1	8
JACKSON, (steamer), for the relief of owners of	81	46	3	28
Do	78	47	1	29
JACKSON, CATHARINE, claim for relief	11	41	2	25
JACKSON, CHARLES, claim for relief	288	23	1	7
JACKSON, GEORGE W., claim for relief	736	29	1	14
JACKSON, JARVIS, claim for relief	379	30	1	16
JACKSON, JOHN, claim for relief	22	20	1	4
JACKSON, JOHN, claim for relief of administrator	749	27	2	11
JACKSON, JOSEPH, claim for relief	196	25	3	9
JACOBS, ENOCH, to compensate for services rendered Department of State	2470	49	1	31
JAMES, B. S., claim for relief	373	45	2	27
Do	2278	49	1	31
Do	3393	49	1	31
JAMES, HENRY L., claim for relief	163	44	2	27
Do	911	46	2	28
Do	174	47	1	29
JAMES, JOSEPH H., claim for relief	48	35	2	21
JAMES MITCHELL (ship), for relief of owners of	264	31	1	18
JAMISON, HORATIO G., claim for relief	490	23	1	7
JANE (brig), for relief of owners of	68	33	1	19
JANEY, JOSEPH, claim for relief	24	15	2	1
JANEY, JOSEPH,				
Claim for relief	45	16	1	1
Do	17	18	1	2
Claim for relief of heirs of	64	31	2	18
Do	48	34	3	20
JARDELLA, FRANCIS, claim for relief of heirs	5	24		7
JARDINE, JOHN, claim for relief	162	31		18
JARRETT, THOMAS, claim for relief	281	29		13
Do	29			18

Subject.	Report.	Congress.	Session.	Volume.
JARVIS, EDWARD, claim for relief	91	36	1	23
JEANNETTE EXPEDITION, claim for relief of survivors	662	49	1	31
Do	663	49	1	31
JEANS, JOSEPH, claim for relief of heirs of	109	19	1	3
Do	29	19	2	3
Do	208	20	1	4
Do	360	21	1	5
JEFFREY, SAMUEL, claim for relief	904	48	1	30
JENKINS, JAMES D., claim for relief	804	44	1	27
JENKINS, WILLIAM, claim for relief	415	29	1	13
JENKS, GEORGE C., claim for relief	95	44	2	27
Do	22	45	3	27
Do	1030	47	1	29
JENKS, SARAH K., claim for relief	68	33	1	19
JENKS, STEPHEN, & SON, claim for arms furnished United States	34	16	1	1
Do	168	20	1	4
JENNINGS, B., claim for relief	158	49	1	31
JENNINGS, GEORGE H., claim for relief	406	22	1	6
JENNINGS, ROBERT C., claim for relief	487	22	1	6
Do	10	22	2	6
Do	8	23	1	7
Do	206	23	1	7
JENNINGS, RODDY & CARTER, claim for relief	128	27	3	11
JEROME, JEAN B., claim for relief	33	16	2	1
Do	34	17	1	1
Do	26	17	2	1
Do	80	20	2	4
Do	34	21	1	5
JESSUP, WILLIAM, claim for relief	47	38	1	26
JETT, WILLIAM, claim for relief	406	23	1	7
JEWELL, ALBERT G., claim for relief	105	47	1	29
JEWELL, DORCAS, claim for relief	396	30	1	16
JOCKNICK, GUSTAVUS F., claim for relief	661	43	1	26
JOHNS, ELIAS, claim for relief	76	23	2	7
Do	535	24	1	8
Do	27	25	2	9
JOHNSON, ANN E., claim for relief of heirs	45	34	3	20
JOHNSON, DANIEL H., claim for relief	178	36	1	23
JOHNSON, DAVID H., claim for relief	76	35	2	21
JOHNSON, FRANCIS, claim for relief	561	28	1	12
JOHNSON, GEORGE, claim for relief as surety of Benjamin F. Bourne	356	21	1	5
Do	90	21	2	5
JOHNSON, GEORGE C., claim for relief	72	39	1	25
JOHNSON, GEORGE W., claim for relief	12	37	3	25
JOHNSON, HENRY D., claim for relief	94	31	1	18
JOHNSON, JAMES, claim for relief	519	36	1	23
Do	75	37	2	25
JOHNSON, JAMES L., claim for relief	75	39	1	25
JOHNSON, JOHN J., claim for relief	71	15	2	1
JOHNSON, JOSEPH P. and GEORGE W., claim for relief	481	26	1	10
JOHNSON, MARY E., claim for relief	1547	49	1	31
JOHNSON, MARY and MARGARET, claim for relief	1676	47	1	29
Do	2488	48	2	30
JOHNSON, MICHAEL,				
Claim for relief	341	27	2	11
Claim for relief of heirs of	111	35	1	21
JOHNSON, NANCY M. (administratrix), claim for relief	515	36	1	23
JOHNSON, ORLOFF, claim for relief	612	44	1	27
JOHNSON, RINALDO, claim for relief of heirs of	45	34	3	20
Do	64	36	2	23
JOHNSON, THOMAS S. J., claim for relief	85	33	1	19
JOHNSON, STERLING, claim for relief	81	21	2	5
JOHNSON, WALTER R.,				
Claim for relief	832	27	2	11
Claim for relief of administratrix of	575	36	1	23
JOHNSTON, ANN W., claim for relief	610	24	1	8
Do	73	25	2	9
JOHNSTON, GEORGE, and others, collector of customs, Boston, relief from action of courts of Massachusetts	159	19	1	3
Do	44	21	1	4
JOHNSTON, JOHN, claim for relief of administrator	677	30	1	16
JOHNSTON, STERLING, claim for relief	240	22	1	6
JOHNSTON, SUSAN (administratrix), claim for relief	515	24	1	8
JOHNSTON, WILLIAM, claim for relief	714	24	1	8
JONES, ANDREW A., claim for relief	192	29	1	13
Do	241	30	1	16
JONES, BENJAMIN F., claim for relief	576	48	1	30
Do	2674	49	1	31
JONES, DAVID W., claim for relief	906	48	1	30
Do	155	49	1	31
JONES, DE GAMEO, claim for relief	76	21	2	5

Subject.	Report.	Congress.	Session.	Volume.
S, **EMILIE** (executrix), claim for relief	515	36	1	22
S, **GEORGE M.**, claim for relief	73	28	1	12
S, **H. M.**, claim for relief	1048	48	1	30
S, **H. P., & CO.**, claim for relief	515	44	1	27
S, **J. H.**, claim for relief	67	44	1	27
S, **JAMES**, claim for relief	238	30	1	16
Do	333	31	1	18
S, **JOHN**, claim for relief	922	25	2	9
Do	747	27	2	11
Do	799	29	1	14
Do	110	45	2	27
S, **JOHN PAUL** (captain, United States Navy), settlement of accounts of	9	30	1	15
S, **M. P.**, claim for relief	548	47	1	29
S, **M. V.**, claim for relief	570	36	1	22
S, **NATHANIEL**, claim for relief	61	18	1	2
S, **PATRICK H.**, claim for relief	705	44	1	27
S, **PHILIP F.**, claim for relief	897	25	2	9
S, **RICHARD J.**, claim for relief	64	26	1	10
S, **THOMAS M.**, claim for relief	203	47	1	29
S, **THOMAS P.**, claim for relief of widow	515	36	1	22
S, **WILEY**, claim for relief of executor	731	27	2	11
S, **WILLIAM**, claim for relief	111	22	2	6
Do	270	24	2	8
Do	242	26	2	10
Do	99	34	1	20
S, **FOWLER, KIRTLAND & CO.**, claim for relief	40	40	3	25
Do	56	41	2	25
S & **SOUDER**, claim for relief	799	29	1	14
AN, **JOHN**, claim for relief	1228	48	1	30
AN, **RICHARD**, claim for relief	458	36	1	22
PH, **RICHARD**, claim for relief	396	45	2	27
N, **WILLIAM**, claim for relief	36	43	2	26
DAN, **B. & P.**, claim for relief	100	15	1	1
E, **HERBERT**, claim for relief	1600	46	2	28
E, **THOMAS L.**, claim for relief	726	30	1	17
MENT against a person upon a charge of assault while arresting a deserter, relief	128	24	1	8
CIAL PROCEEDINGS IN PENNSYLVANIA, to adjust account in certain	3321	49	1	31
ON, **MILES**, claim for relief of sureties	2	35	2	21
AN, **GEORGE W.**, claim for relief	1575	47	1	29
ER, **JOSEPH**, claim for relief	673	29	1	14
E, **ROBERT**, claim for relief	340	21	1	5
Do	195	22	1	6
Do	13	23	2	7
FLEISCH, **MARTIN**, claim for relief of heirs	48	43	1	26
AS,				
izens of, adjustment of claims of	789	48	1	30
ims of citizens for property destroyed during the troubles in, settlement of	104	36	2	23
Do	104	36	2	24
Do	77	41	2	25
blic lands, for relief of settlers and purchasers on	520	49	1	31
Do	3900	49	2	32
, **JOHN**, claim for relief	54	39	1	25
OR, **DANIEL**, claim for relief	205	47	1	29
NEY, **STEPHEN W.**, claim for relief	437	22	1	6
AN, **JAMES**, claim for relief	458	36	1	22
, **SAMUEL Y.**, and others, claim for additional pay as surgeon's mate	259	24	2	8
SAMUEL, claim for relief	365	21	1	5
TLEY, **E. T.**, claim for relief	24	46	1	28
, **MATTHEW IRWIN**, claim for relief	427	26	1	10
, **JAMES H.**, claim for relief	187	26	2	10
R, **C. M.**, claim for relief	883	25	2	9
R, **JONAS P.**, claim for relief	398	35	1	21
GG, **GILES**, and others, claim for relief	133	15	1	1
, **EDWARD F.**, claim for relief	130	28	1	12
, **IRAD** and **DATUS**, claim for relief	917	25	2	9
, **JOHN**, claim for relief	293	24	2	8
Do	48	26	1	10
, **L.**, claim for relief	458	36	1	22
, **PATRICK**, claim for relief	458	36	1	22
, **ROBERT N.**, claim for relief of heirs	49	27	3	11
, **THOMAS**, claim for relief	226	25	3	9
Do	458	36	1	22
LL, **JOSEPH**, claim for relief	11	28	1	12
Do	1	29	1	13
LL, **AMOS**, claim for relief	147	27	3	11
LL **WILLIAM**, claim for relief of representatives	2444	48	2	30
Do	3327	49	1	31
, **T. A.**, claim for relief	387	45	2	27

Subject.	Report.	Congress.	Session.	Volume.
KENDRICK, H. L., claim for relief	73	34	3	20
Do	93	35	1	21
KENNEDY, JOHN, claim for relief	788	24	1	8
KENNEDY, JOSEPH C. G., claim for relief	203	34	1	20
Do	185	35	1	21
Do	78	35	2	21
Do	265	36	1	22
Do	32	37	2	25
Do	28	38	1	25
KENNEDY, JOSEPH M., claim for relief	46	34	3	20
KENNEDY, JOSHUA,				
Claim for relief	357	22	1	6
Do	61	28	2	12
Claim for relief of heirs	689	29	1	14
Do	155	30	1	15
KENNEDY, MARTIN, claim for relief	507	23	1	7
KENNER, JAMES L., claim for relief	3	24	2	8
Do	59	25	2	9
KENTUCKY, to compensate the assistant United States marshals for services rendered in taking sixth census in State of	155	27	2	11
KER, MARY, claim for relief	96	28	2	12
KER, ROBERT B., claim for relief	342	27	2	11
KER, SAMUEL, claim for relief	343	27	2	11
KERCHNER, GALLUS, claim for relief	1743	46	2	28
KERLIN, JOHN, claim for relief of heirs	108	19	1	3
KERN, NICHOLAS, claim for reliefof sureties	137	23	2	7
Do	187	24	1	8
KERNAN, DANIEL, claim forrelief	114	46	2	28
KERR, SAMUEL, claim for relief	174	25	3	9
KERSHAW, MARIA, claim for relief	127	25	3	9
KETCHUM, ISRAEL, claim for relief	496	23	1	7
KETCHUM, W. SCOTT, claim for relief	723	25	2	9
Do	719	27	2	11
KETCHUM, ZEBULON, claim for relief	497	23	1	7
KEYES, GEORGE W., claim for relief	15	43	1	26
Do	1515	47	1	29
KEYWORTH, ROBERT, claim for relief	188	24	2	8
Do	74	25	2	9
KIDD, GEORGE W., claim for relief	134	30	2	17
KIERNAN, JOHN, claim for relief	516	44	1	27
KILBOURN, HENRY, claim for relief	331	21	1	5
KILGORE, JAMES, claim for relief	162	24	2	8
Do	190	25	3	9
KILGORE, WILLIAM, claim for relief	162	24	2	8
Do	190	25	3	9
KILGOUR, JAMES E. (executor), claim for relief	152	34	3	20
Do	64	36	2	22
Do	72	38	1	25
KILGOUR, WILLIAM, claim for relief	243	31	1	18
Do	836	47	1	29
KIMBRO, SAMUEL, claim for relief of widow	696	45	2	27
KINEO (gun-boat), prize money to officers and crew of	12	42	2	26
KING, AMANDA, claim for relief	478	29	1	13
KING, GIDEON, claim for relief of heirs	19	20	2	4
Do	15	21	1	5
KING, ISAAC, claim for relief	424	30	1	16
KING, JOHN, claim for relief	268	27	2	11
KING, JOHN A., claim for relief	718	27	2	11
KING, LYMAN, claim for relief	55	25	3	9
Do	43	26	1	10
Do	4	29	1	13
KING, PEYTON G., claim for relief	14	34	1	20
KING, W. R., claim for relief	180	47	1	29
KING, WILLIAM, claim for relief	157	19	1	3
KING, WILLIAM D., claim for relief	249	21	1	5
KING, ZENAS, claim for relief	559	29	1	13
Do	26	31	1	18
Do	176	36	1	22
KING & THURBER, owners of sloop Essex, claim for relief	34	19	1	3
KINGSBURY, JACOB, claim for relief of widow	847	25	2	9
KINKEAD, JOHN H., claim for relief	3080	49	1	31
KINGSLEY, ADAM, claim for arms furnished United States	171	15	1	1
KINSLEY & FRENCH, claim for relief	171	15	1	1
KINYON, WRIGHT & CO., refund of duties on lumber imported	997	48	1	30
KIRCHNER, GALLUS, claim for relief	100	47	1	29
KIRK, HYLAND C., et al., claim for relief	*1612	49	1	31
Do	*3766	49	2	32
KIRKHAM, ROBERT, claim for relief	891	35	1	21
KIRKPATRICK, JOHN (executor), claim for relief	187	24	2	8

* With views of minority.

Subject.	Report.	Congress.	Session.	Volume.
KLING, JAY, claim for relief	20	42	2	26
KLOPPER, HENRY A., claim for relief	429	35	1	21
KNIGHT, GEORGE J., claim for relief	1055	25	2	9
Do	226	29	1	13
Do	142	35	2	21
KNOWLES, HENRY, Sr., claim for relief	504	23	1	7
Do	20	24	1	7
KNOWLTON, SALLY, claim for relief	414	30	1	16
KNOWLTON, THOMAS, claim for relief of heirs	50	25	3	9
KNOX, HALDIMAN & CO., claim for relief	90	24	1	8
KNOXVILLE COMMERCIAL BANK, claim for relief	369	45	2	27
KOON, C. E., claim for relief	222	47	1	29
KORTZENBORN, CHARLES, claim for relief	1353	47	1	29
KOUNTZ, W. J., claim for relief	426	47	1	29
KRAMER, ELIZABETH, claim for relief	158	19	1	3
KREISMAN, HERMANN claim for relief	66	44	1	27
KREPPS, JOHN, claim for relief	184	24	2	8
Do	32	25	2	9
KUBISH, ERNEST, claim for relief	802	46	3	28
KURTZ, BOWIE, claim for relief	35	14	2	1
KURTZ, JOHN, claim for relief	85	15	2	1
Do	573	26	1	10
KUTTS, JOHN, claim for relief	405	23	1	7
KYLE, JOHN G., claim for relief	2474	49	1	31
LABATT, J. E., claim for relief	696	47	1	29
LABORERS EMPLOYED UPON GOVERNMENT WORKS BY CONTRACTORS, liability of United States for payment of	174	46	2	28
Do	521	47	1	29
LA CROIX, HURBERT, and others, claim for relief	46	20	2	4
Do	36	21	1	5
LADY FRANKLIN BAY EXPEDITION, for relief of enlisted men in	3432	49	1	31
LAGODA (bark), claim for relief	908	46	2	28
Do	200	47	1	29
LAKE, JOHN L., Jr., claim for relief	1226	48	1	30
LAKE, WILLIAM, claim for relief	150	47	1	29
LAMB, HENRY F., claim for relief	305	24	2	8
Do	632	24	1	8
LAMB, JOHN, claim for relief	845	27	2	11
LAMB, MARGARET M., claim for relief	520	44	1	27
LAMBERT, EDWARD A., claim for relief	568	28	1	12
LAMBERT, FRANCIS, claim for relief	623	25	2	9
LAND TITLES,				
Maine, to provide for quieting land titles in	254	34	3	20
Do	354	35	1	21
Do	458	36	1	22
Do	72	37	2	25
Missouri, to provide for quieting titles to lands in	36	40	2	25
LANDS, PUBLIC. (*See* PUBLIC LANDS.)				
LANE, GEORGE W., claim for relief	108	39	1	25
LANE, J. G., claim for relief	8	41	2	25
LANGDON, LOOMIS L., claim for relief	388	35	1	21
LANGDON, RICHARD C., claim for relief	325	23	1	7
Do	695	24	1	8
Do	67	26	2	10
LANGTRY & JENKINS, claim for relief	1	28	2	12
Do	190	29	1	13
LANGUILLE, FRANCIS B., claim for relief	80	16	1	1
Do	29	16	2	1
LANGWORTHY, GEORGE J., claim for relief	95	41	2	25
LANHAM, ROBERT, claim for relief	327	33	1	19
LANIN, J. F. D., claim for relief	786	27	2	11
LANMAN, CHARLES JAMES, claim for relief	546	35	1	21
Do	88	36	1	22
LANSING, ABRAHAM, claim for relief	573	24	1	8
Do	30	25	2	9
LAPETTER, REUBEN, claim for relief	491	27	2	11
LARCHE, FRANCIS, claim for relief	170	19	1	3
Do	236	20	1	4
Do	401	21	1	5
Do	40	21	2	5
LARENBURG, JACKSON, claim for relief	298	43	2	26
LARIMER, SARAH L., claim for relief	1546	49	1	31
Do	2700	49	1	31
LARMAN, JOHN Q., and others, claim for relief	1433	46	2	28
Do	202	47	1	29
LA SALLE COUNTY, ILLINOIS, citizens of, claim for property destroyed by Indians	579	24	1	8
LASSELLE, FRANCIS, and others, claim for relief	219	23	1	7
LATHAM, OBADIAH B. and OLIVER S., claim for relief	147	37	2	25
Do	69	38	1	25
Do	917	45	2	27
Do	889	46	2	28

Subject.	Report.	Congress.	Session.	Volume.
LATIMER, JOHN K., claim for relief	736	25	2	9
LATSHAW, WILLIAM D., claim for relief	631	36	1	22
LAUB, JOHN,				
Claim for relief	843	29	1	14
Claim for relief (administrator)	163	31	1	18
LAURENCE, HOEL, claim for relief	43	16	1	1
Do	28	17	2	1
LAWLER, THOMAS J., claim for relief	574	24	1	8
Do	31	25	2	9
LAWRENCE, ZACHARIAH, claim for relief	567	28	1	12
Do	319	29	1	13
Do	249	30	1	16
Do	404	31	1	18
LAWS,				
To provide laws for settlement of claims against the United States	498	30	1	16
LAWS, BOLITHA, claim for relief of administrator of	445	24	1	8
Do	724	24	1	8
	779	24	1	8
	19	25	2	9
	152	25	2	9
	688	27	2	11
	496	28	1	12
Do	147	28	2	12
Do	173	29	1	13
LAWSON, JOHN, claim for relief of heirs	757	29	1	14
LAY, JOHN O., claim for relief, army contract	278	21	1	5
LAYTON, CHARLES G., claim for relief	648	29	1	14
LAYTON, JOB M., claim for relief	20	33	1	19
LEAD MINES,				
Development of, claim of Lieut. Martin Thomas for	576	29	1	13
Do	60	30	1	15
On Indian lands, right of United States to collect rent upon	591	30	1	17
Do	297	34	1	20
Do	187	35	1	21
Do	89	36	1	22
Do	235	35	2	21
Sandy Mines in Missouri, right of United States to take possession of	39	30	1	15
LEAGUE, WILLIAM T., claim for relief	35	45	3	27
Do	876	46	2	28
Do	288	47	1	29
LEAKY, LEVI, claim for relief	402	30	1	16
LEATHERBERRY, PERRY A., claim for relief	368	47	1	29
Do	1422	48	1	30
Do	1815	49	1	31
LEATHERS, JOHN, claim for relief	2363	48	2	30
Do	479	49	1	31
LE BARON, JOHN K., claim for relief	975	48	1	30
Do	4079	49	2	32
LECKIE, ROBERT, claim for relief	86	22	2	6
LE COMPTE, PIERNES, claim for relief	8	20	1	4
LECROIX, HURBERT, claim for relief of widow	37	25	3	9
LEDDY, HUGH, claim for relief	46	38	1	25
LEDWITH, THOMAS, claim for relief	506	25	2	9
LEE, ASAHEL, and others, claim for relief	49	27	2	11
Do	1	27	3	11
LEE, BEAUFORT, claim for relief	2421	48	2	30
Do	2279	49	1	31
LEE, CHARLES H. and ELIZA, claim for relief	326	31	1	18
LEE, EDWARD, claim for relief	107	19	1	3
Do	217	21	1	5
LEE, EDWARD SUTHERLAND, claim for relief	655	30	1	17
LEE, FRANKLIN, claim for relief	668	45	2	27
Do	1590	46	2	28
LEE, HARVEY, claim for relief	1	27	3	11
LEE, HENRY, surety on bond of Paymaster J. Ricaud, release from liability	71	18	2	2
Do	123	19	1	3
Do	26	20	2	4
LEE, LEMUEL, claim for relief	1	27	3	11
LEE, OLIVER, claim for relief of heirs	478	30	1	16
Do	326	31	1	18
Do	86	33	1	19
LEE, R., claim for relief of widow	349	27	2	11
LEE, ROSWELL, claim for relief of heirs	426	24	1	8
Do	17	25	2	9
LEE, THOMAS B., claim for relief	648	27	2	11
LEE, WILLIAM G., claim for relief	64	39	1	25
LEECH, ANDREW, claim for relief	872	46	2	28
Do	176	47	1	29
LEEF, HENRY, claim for relief of heirs	104	31	1	18
Do	277	48	1	30
Do	1865	49	1	31

Subject.	Report.	Congress.	Session.	Volume.
EES, ISAAC W., claim for relief	1010	49	1	31
Do	2553	49	1	31
EGG, WILLIAM, claim for relief	211	19	1	3
Do	501	23	1	7
EITENSDORFER, EUGENE, claim for relief	189	45	2	27
ELAND, BALDWIN M., claim for relief	203	21	1	5
EMMON, JOHN C., claim for relief	38	43	2	26
ENFANT, BENJAMIN, claim for relief	266	23	1	7
ESTER, EBENEZER A., claim for relief	318	24	1	8
Do	8	25	2	9
Do	195	25	3	9
Do	9	26	1	10
Do	13	26	2	10
LESTER, W. W., claim for relief	1679	47	1	29
LEVY COURT OF MARYLAND. (*See* COURTS; MARYLAND.)				
LEVY, JONAS P., claim for relief	50	36	2	22
LEVY, MOSES E., claim for relief	236	25	3	9
LEWIS, ABEL M., claim for relief	16	43	1	26
Do	12	44	2	27
LEWIS, DAVID M., claim for relief	201	21	1	5
Do	346	24	1	8
LEWIS, HENRY, claim for relief	8	33	1	19
LEWIS, J. W. P., claim for relief (administrator)	432	35	1	21
LEWIS, JOSEPH N., claim for relief	301	46	3	28
LEWIS, MARY A., claim for relief	2012	48	1	30
LEWIS, MARY AURELIA, claim for relief	339	28	1	12
LEWIS, SAMUEL, claim for relief	790	29	1	14
LEWIS, WINSLOW, claim for relief	10	15	1	1
Do	378	25	2	9
LEWIS, WINSLOW and HENRY, claim for relief	10	15	1	1
LIABILITY OF UNITED STATES,				
Clerical work performed without authority of Congress	17	35	2	21
Do	5	47	1	29
Damage to real and personal property by forcible interference of U. S	323	24	2	8
Do	473	27	2	11
Do	38	31	2	18
Depreciation of Treasury notes, in payment of contracts	27	26	1	8
Funeral expenses of United States deputy marshal killed in discharge of official duties	489	23	1	7
Illegal acts of commercial agent at Apia, in the Navigators' Islands, against citizens of United States	212	35	2	21
Liens upon real property confiscated	50	45	3	27
Do	9	46	2	28
Do	694	47	1	29
Money lost on vessels at sea	84	39	1	25
Do	114	39	1	25
Moneys belonging to loyal citizens of United States confiscated by Confederate Congress	98	42	2	26
Moneys erroneously paid to United States marshal in sale of real estate, upon execution of United States	700	24	1	8
Money lost by deposit in private bank by disbursing officers	3	35	2	21
Payment of employés on Government works, where contractors fail	174	46	2	28
Do	521	47	1	29
Payment of reward for defaulting postmaster offered by private citizens	548	24	1	8
Ransom of crew of the ship Parago from Chinese pirates	401	31	1	18
Ransom of Indian captive, Samuel Cozad, and compensation for time	54	24	1	8
Do	213	24	2	8
River improvement performed without authority or contract	123	37	2	25
Slaves,				
Killed by United States soldiers, 1833	537	23	1	7
Captured by Creek Indians from the Seminoles, by military authority. Views of minority.	724	30	1	17
Do	102	31	1	18
Taken by British in Revolutionary war, claim for	471	36	1	22
Slave-ship Isabelita, prize case of	629	24	1	8
Toll over bridges on post-routes	373	29	1	13
Treasury notes destroyed by fire, to reimburse owner of	116	38	1	25
Vessel damaged by collision with United States war-ship	162	29	1	13
LIGHTFOOT, PHILIP, claim for relief	507	25	2	9
Do	342	27	2	11
LIGHTS. (This includes light-houses, beacons, beacon-lights, buoys, &c.; *see also under respective names of places.*)				
Poverty Island, for relief of workmen at	666	43	1	26
For relief of employés in twelfth United States district	471	49	1	31
LIGON, THOMAS, claim for relief	1000	25	2	9
LILLEY, ISAAC, claim for relief	947	25	2	9
Do	605	36	1	22
Do	28	37	3	25
LILLIE, JAMES, claim for relief	148	43	1	26
LILLY (light-house tender), claim for relief of officers and crew	724	49	1	31
LINCECUM, GENLAND, claim for relief	249	21	1	5

Subject.	Report.	Congress.	Session.	Volume.
LINCOLN, ABRAHAM, distribution of the reward offered for the arrest of Jefferson Davis and the conspirators in the assassination of	99	39	1	25
LINCOLN, JOTHAM (administrator), claim for relief on light-house contract on Florida Keys	1	21	2	5
Do	139	21	1	5
LINCOLN, SAMUEL BENE, claim for relief of administrator on light-house contract at Florida Keys	139	21	1	5
Do	29	22	2	6
Do	17	23	1	7
LINCOLN, SARAH F., claim for relief	17	43	1	26
LINGENFELTER, JOHN, claim for relief	720	27	2	11
LINN, H. C., claim for relief	1237	48	1	30
LINTON, THOMAS J., claim for relief	492	27	2	11
LINTS, J. J., claim for relief	574	36	1	22
Do	76	37	2	25
Do	5	38	2	25
Do	875	46	2	28
LIONBERGER, PETER, claim for relief	751	27	2	11
LITTLE, CHARLES L., claim for relief	577	28	1	10
LITTLE, DAVID, claim for relief	789	29	1	14
Do	593	30	1	17
LITTLE, JAMES, claim for relief	159	30	1	15
LITTLE, WILLIAM (administrator), claim for relief	49	18	2	3
LIVELY, E. H., claim for relief	898	45	2	27
LIVINGSTON, EDWARD, claim for relief	58	21	2	5
LIVINGSTON, KINCAID & CO., claim for relief	521	36	1	22
Do	77	38	1	25
LIVINGSTON, MADISON C., claim for relief	494	27	2	11
LOAN OFFICE CERTIFICATES OF OHIO LAND COMPANY, 1777, payment of	161	35	1	21
LOBBAN, J. M., claim for relief	179	49	1	31
LOBDELL, EBENEZER, claim for relief	324	25	2	9
Do	11	26	1	10
LOCKWOOD, ISAAC C., claim for relief	357	33	1	19
LOMBARD, GABRIEL, claim for relief	1002	25	2	9
LONG, ALTON, claim for relief	297	34	1	20
LONG, ELLEN CALL, claim for relief	1958	47	2	29
Do	740	48	1	30
Do	1233	48	1	30
LONG, JOHN, claim for relief	17	20	2	4
LONG, STEPHEN H., claim for relief	72	47	1	29
LOOMIS, DANIEL,				
Claim for relief	776	24	1	8
Claim for relief of heirs	337	33	1	19
LOOMIS, WALTER, claim for relief	28	21	2	5
Do	308	24	2	8
Do	190	26	2	10
LOOMIS & GAY, claim for relief	363	26	1	10
Do	796	29	1	14
LOOP, CHARLES B., claim for relief	323	47	1	29
LORD, JOHN, claim for relief of heirs	20	35	2	21
LORD NELSON (ship), libel and sale of, by United States	814	24	1	8
LORING, JOSEPH, claim for relief	621	24	1	8
LOUISIANA,				
Loyal creditors, whose moneys were confiscated by Confederate Congress in State of	98	42	2	26
State National Bank of, for relief of	1674	47	1	29
LOUISVILLE, KENTUKY,				
Baptist Orphans' Home, claim for relief	631	44	1	27
German National Bank, indemnity for coin coupons destroyed	870	46	2	28
Do	324	47	1	29
Savings Institution, claim for relief	466	25	2	9
Louisville and Bardstown Turnpike Company, claim for relief	30	42	2	26
LOVE, GEORGE, claim for relief	65	18	2	3
LOVE, JAMES W., claim for relief	521	44	1	27
LOVE, RUFUS KING, claim for relief	684	26	1	10
LOVELY, JOHN, claim for relief	458	36	1	22
LOW, DAVID W., claim for relief	2270	49	1	31
LOWE, SAMUEL A., claim for relief	34	45	3	27
Do	582	46	2	28
LOWERY, JACOB S., claim for relief	15	38	1	25
LOWRY, HEMAN, claim for relief	248	30	1	15
LOWREY, J. M., claim for relief	2693	48	2	30
Do	481	49	1	31
LOYAL CITIZENS, to ascertain the compensation justly due to loyal citizens of States not declared in insurrection	43	42	3	26
LUCAS, JACOB, claim for relief	1032	47	1	29
LUDLOW, CHARLES, claim for relief	301	22	1	6
LUDLOW, CORNELIUS V. C., claim for relief	244	28	1	12
LUKE, CHARLES H., claim for relief	80	47	1	29
LUNDY, WILLIAM, claim for relief	458	36	1	22

Subject.	Report.	Congress.	Session.	Volume.
R, SIDNEY P., claim for relief	688	45	2	27
Do	[illegible]	46	2	[illegible]
Do	6	47	1	[illegible]
, TIMOTHY, claim for relief	16[illegible]	[illegible]	1	[illegible]
, BERNARD, claim for relief	[illegible]	45	2	27
, THOMAS, claim for relief	[illegible]	43	1	[illegible]
, G., and others, claim for relief	[illegible]	26	2	[illegible]
WILLIAM, claim for relief	[illegible]	36	1	22
HOWARD, claim for relief	[illegible]	29	1	13
Do	16[illegible]	30	1	15
Do	[illegible]	33	1	19
HONORA V., claim for relief	2[illegible]	49	1	31
WILLIAM 2d, claim for relief	[illegible]	26	1	7
HUR, DUNCAN, claim for relief	[illegible]	27	2	11
R, BENJAMIN L., claim for relief	99	35	1	21
Y, JAMES, claim for relief	129	28	2	13
Do	[illegible]	30	1	15
Y, JOHN, claim for relief	316	33	1	19
DE, WILLIAM, claim for relief	470	24	1	8
NEY, JAMES C., claim for relief	1[illegible]	43	2	[illegible]
R, WILLIAM, claim for relief	[illegible]	28	1	13
BOY, JAMES, claim for relief	[illegible]	35	2	21
LESS, THOMAS F., for relief	427	24	1	8
Do	19	25	2	9
M, DWIGHT, claim for relief	5	41	2	[illegible]
Do	24	42	2	[illegible]
S, REBECCA, claim for relief	473	23	1	7
Do	64	27	3	11
TNEY, JOHN, claim for relief	14	16	2	1
Do	[illegible]	[illegible]	1	7
Do	[illegible]	24	1	8
Do	[illegible]	[illegible]	2	9
TY, E., claim for relief	4	48	1	[illegible]
TY, JAMES, claim for relief	1	20	2	4
Do	215	21	1	5
Do	100	23	1	7
TY, JOHN, claim for cattle found upon Indian lands in Alabama	[illegible]	24	1	8
Do	19	25	2	9
TY, JOHN L., claim for relief	1045	25	2	9
LY, THOMAS G., claim for relief	2	27	2	11
SLAND, JOHN, claim for militia fine	120	15	2	1
, THOMAS, claim for relief	209	27	3	11
TOCK, JOHN M., claim for relief	1553	49	1	31
Do	1870	49	1	31
RE, JOSEPH, claim for relief of administrator	389	35	1	21
RE, WILLIAM, claim for relief	94	20	1	4
OM, ANDREW, claim for relief	161	23	1	6
Do	623	24	1	8
AUGHEY, R. T., claim for relief	142	44	2	27
Do	370	47	1	29
ELL, JOHN C., claim for relief	76	38	1	25
, DAVID, claim for relief	686	24	1	8
ICK, PAUL, claim for relief	394	45	2	27
Do	901	48	1	30
ICK, TIMOTHY, claim for relief	1721	46	2	28
ICK, V. H., claim for relief	372	45	3	27
ICK, WILLIAM J., claim for relief of widow	166	36	1	22
, JOHN, claim for relief	368	25	2	9
LIS, MILO, claim for relief	1817	49	1	31
OCH, ADAM, claim for relief	129	19	1	13
Do	106	28	2	12
OM, ANDREW, claim for relief	161	23	1	7
UM, ARCHIBALD, claim for relief	52	26	1	10
Do	58	27	2	11
HEON, JAMES, claim for relief	67	26	1	10
Do	355	29	1	13
Do	740	29	1	14
ALD, HUGH, claim for relief	318	24	2	8
Do	71	25	2	9
ALD, JAMES, claim for relief of administrator	4	16	1	1
ALD, JOHN, claim for relief	458	36	1	22
ALD, WILLIAM (administrator), claim for relief	96	15	2	1
Do	4	16	1	1
ELL, JOHN, claim for relief	494	23	1	7
Do	19	24	1	7
AL, GEORGE, and others, claim for relief	34	17	1	1
Do	26	17	2	1
ERY, JOHN P., claim for relief	389	33	1	19
ATH, J. P., claim for relief	474	30	1	16
Y, T. F., claim for relief	1965	48	1	30
KE, THOMAS B., claim for relief	856	49	1	31

Subject.	Report.	Congress.	Session.	Volume.
McFERRAN, JOHN C., claim for relief	8	37	3	25
McGAHEN, GEORGE, claim for relief	748	29	1	14
McGAW, JAMES, claim for relief	89	33	2	19
McGINNIS, HUGH, claim for relief	354	23	1	7
McGLAUGHLIN, SARAH, claim for relief	458	36	1	22
McGRUDER, THOMAS C., claim for relief	117	39	1	25
McGUIRE, ROBERT, claim for relief	713	28	1	16
McHARG, JOHN, claim for relief	793	47	1	29
McINDOE, WILLIAM, claim for relief	696	44	1	27
Do	56	45	2	27
McINTIRE, JOHN, and others, claim for relief	59	26	1	10
McINTOSH, JOHN H., claim for relief	470	27	2	11
McINTOSH, RODERICK (master of schooner Bucephalus), claim for losses sustained in rescuing crew of schooner Astoria	4080	49	2	32
McIVER, JOHN, claim for relief	353	21	1	5
MACKALL, BENJAMIN, H., claim for relief	398	24	1	8
Do	13	25	2	9
MACKALL, JAMES, claim for relief	303	33	1	19
MACKALL, JOHN G., claim for relief	570	24	1	8
MACKALL, RICHARD, claim for relief	578	24	1	8
Do	601	25	2	9
Do	214	25	3	9
MACKAY, ELIZA, claim for relief	116	25	3	9
McKAY, NATHANIEL, claim for relief	36	42	3	26
MACKAY, SAMUEL, claim for relief	659	26	1	10
McKEE, JOHN, claim for relief	104	31	1	18
McKEE, J. H., claim for relief	412	30	1	16
Do	126	32	1	19
McKEE, MARTHA, claim for relief	320	24	2	8
MACKIE, THOMAS G., claim for relief	1924	47	2	29
McKINNEY, MICHAEL, claim for relief	456	36	1	22
McKINNIE, JOHN, claim for relief	129	25	3	9
McKNIGHT, BRENT & WOOD, claim for relief	243	30	1	16
McLAUGHLIN, HENRY, claim for relief	119	32	1	19
McLAUGHLIN, THOMAS A., claim for relief	47	45	3	27
Do	885	46	2	28
Do	695	47	1	29
Do	1782	48	1	30
Do	3700	49	2	32
McLEAN, JAMES, claim for relief	2381	49	1	31
Do	3341	49	1	31
McMAHON, JAMES, claim for relief in civil action for damages against, as prosecuting witness	548	24	1	8
Do	65	24	2	8
Do	28	25	2	9
McMANUS, THOMAS P., claim for relief	91	41	2	25
McMILLAN, ARTHUR, claim for relief	32	22	2	6
McMILLAN, ROBERT, claim for relief	2	43	1	26
McNAUGHT, WILLIAM, claim for relief	688	26	1	10
MACOMB, ALEXANDER, brigadier-general United States Army, claim for brevet pay	114	22	2	6
Do	265	24	1	8
Do	8	25	2	9
MACON, GEORGIA, to refund revenue taxes improperly collected from	417	44	1	27
Do	1	45	2	27
Do	1432	46	2	28
McPHERSON, EDWARD B., Jr., claim for relief	514	44	1	27
McPHERSON, JAMES, claim for relief	*194	24	2	8
Do	267	24	2	8
McPHERSON, NANCY, claim for relief	382	23	1	7
McQUISTON, JOHN C., claim for relief	9	41	3	25
McQUOWN, JOHN H., claim for relief	90	41	2	25
McKAVETT, HENRY, claim for relief	338	28	1	13
McROBERTS, ELLIE, claim for relief	3023	49	1	31
McROBERTS, WILLIAM, claim for relief	897	45	2	27
Do	1762	47	1	29
Do	2177	48	2	30
MADDING, LITTLE B., claim for relief	41	40	2	25
MADISON, CHANNING, claim for relief	698	24	1	8
MADRAZO, DON JUAN, owner of the slave-ship Isabelita, libel of	250	24	2	8
Do	629	25	1	8
MADRAZO, RAFAEL, claim for relief	369	43	1	26
MAGLENEN, JAMES, claim for relief of heirs of	172	25	3	9
Do	37	26	2	10
Do	46	27	2	11
MAGRUDER, GEORGE A., claim for relief	386	35	1	21
MAGUIRE, JAMES, claim for relief	135	24	1	8
Do	68	26	2	10
MAGUIRE, JOHN H., claim for relief	98	22	2	6
Do	18	23	1	7

* Parts 1, 2.

Subject.	Report.	Congress.	Session.	Volume.
ONEY, JAMES, claim for relief	238	30	1	16
S, to refund to the Brazilian Mail Steamship Company certain taxes illegally collected	84	41	2	25
E.				
oneys advanced for defense of frontier in war of 1812	76	41	2	25
tle to certain lands in State of, to quiet	254	34	3	20
Do	394	35	1	21
Do	458	36	1	22
EY, JAMES, claim for relief	700	24	1	8
ABY, FRANCIS, claim for relief	553	25	2	9
OY, LOUISA P., claim for relief	154	43	1	26
LEY, JESSE, claim for relief	402	23	1	7
N, WILLIAM, claim for relief	550	23	1	7
N, WILLIAM A., claim for relief	384	45	2	27
NEY, JAMES, claim for relief	402	22	1	6
SON, ROBERT P., and others, claim for relief	94	42	3	26
SCRIPT, preparation of, without authority of Congress, compensation for	17	35	2	21
Y, DANIEL, claim for relief	653	48	1	30
CHAL, JOSEPH, claim for relief	42	18	1	2
A (ship), enslavement of crew of by Algerians, and payment of ransom for	622	2	1	8
, DUNCAN, claim for relief	308	43	1	26
RS, JAMES R., claim for relief	3103	49	1	31
H, W. C., claim for relief	2356	48	2	30
HALL, JOHN, claim for relief of heirs	624	24	1	8
Do	41	25	2	9
HALL, PHILIP, claim for relief	41	25	2	9
HALL, S. T., claim for relief	1159	49	1	31
HALL, WILLIAM, claim for relief	400	29	1	13
TON, S. W., claim for relief	2647	48	2	30
Do	3897	49	2	32
TIN, ARMAND, claim for relief	747	29	1	14
TIN, CHARLES T., claim for relief	1330	46	2	28
TIN, J. R., claim for relief	854	49	1	14
TIN, JOEL, claim for relief	46	25	3	9
TIN, JOHN, claim for relief	159	28	2	12
Do	413	29	1	13
Do	203	30	1	15
TIN, RACHEL, claim for relief	879	46	2	28
TIN, WILLIAM F., claim for relief	369	47	1	29
LAND,				
ltimore,				
Claim of citizens of, for vessels lost in 1814	1	17	1	1
Do	6	18	2	2
Do	167	19	1	3
Do	221	20	1	4
Claim of, for balance due for advances made during war of 1812	218	20	1	4
lvert County,				
For destruction of jail and court-house occupied by Government forces	47	16	1	1
Do	36	17	1	1
Do	3	17	2	1
Do	7	18	1	2
Do	313	24	2	8
Reversing certain decisions made by levy court of	177	21	1	5
erest on advances made during the war of 1812 by State of, claim for	116	19	1	3
Do	189	20	1	4
Do	249	20	1	4
Do	303	48	1	30
Do	518	49	1	31
N, CHARLES, claim for relief	305	44	1	27
N, CHARLES H., claim for relief	195	45	2	27
N, EMANUEL, claim for relief	65	42	3	26
Do	31	45	3	27
Do	3957	49	2	32
N, JAMES M., claim for relief	1367	46	2	28
Do	1060	47	1	29
Do	2303	48	2	30
N, JOHN, claim for relief	628	29	1	14
N, JOSIAH, claim for relief	44	20	1	4
N, LUCRETIA, claim for relief	165	27	2	11
N, OLIVER P., claim for relief	146	43	1	26
NIC HALL COMPANY, ATLANTA, GEORGIA, claim for relief	29	45	3	27
Do	342	46	2	28
ACHUSETTS,				
ast defense, during war of rebellion, to reimburse State for moneys advanced for	103	41	2	25
Do	9	47	1	29
Do	39	47	1	29
ar of 1812, to refund to State moneys advanced for defense of frontier during	76	41	2	25
OLETTI, VINCENT, claim for relief	176	27	2	11
TERS, JOHN, claim for relief	835	25	2	9

Subject.	Report.	Congress.	Session.	Volume.
MATHER, THOMAS, commissioner to lay out road from Missouri to Mexico, compensation	416	21	1	5
MATHIS, MARSHALL H., claim for relief	636	99	1	14
MATHERS, ELIAS, and others, claim for relief	57	21	2	5
MATHEWS, FORMAN, claim for relief	18	44	2	27
MATHEWS, THOMAS, and others, claim for relief	1488	49	1	31
MATTHEWS, CHARLES S., claim for relief	117	24	2	8
Do	494	26	1	10
Do	240	31	1	18
MATTHEWS, WILLIAM B., claim for relief	69	21	2	5
MATTHEWS, WOOD and HALL, claim for relief	348	27	2	11
Do	414	28	1	12
Do	281	30	1	16
Do	44	32	1	19
MATTINGLY, EDWARD, claim for relief	150	34	3	20
MAURAW, J. R., and others, claim for relief	668	44	1	27
MAURICE, THEODORE W., claim for relief of heirs	532	24	1	8
MAURY, M. F., claim for relief	496	27	2	11
MAVER, WILLIAM N., claim for relief	256	28	1	12
MAXWELL, DAVID H., claim for relief	759	24	1	8
Do	55	25	2	9
MAY, JAMES, claim for relief	7	17	1	1
MAY, SAMUEL, claim for relief	501	22	1	6
Do	389	23	1	7
MAYER, HENRY F., claim for relief	25	39	1	25
MAYHEW, THADDEUS, claim for relief	154	15	1	1
Do	61	15	2	1
Do	54	16	1	1
MAYO, JOHN K., claim for relief	53	43	1	26
MEACHAM, A. B., claim for relief	51	45	3	27
Do	899	46	2	28
MEADE, HUGH K., claim for relief	780	29	1	14
MEADE, RICHARD W., claim against Government of Spain for private property taken for public use	95	38	2	22
Do	841	46	3	23
Do	837	47	1	29
MEADS, JAMES, claim for relief	401	29		13
MEARS, JOHN W., claim for relief	1885	49		31
MECHLIN, ALEXANDER H., claim for relief	592	30		17
MEEDS, ELEANOR M. T., claim for relief	141	44	2	27
MEEKER, MOSES, claim for relief	235	35		21
Do	89	36		22
MEEKER, SAMUEL, claim for relief, army contract	244	21		5
Do	364	22		6
MEGOWAN, JAMES F., claim for relief	237	30		16
MELDRUM, JOHN (administrator), for relief	85	16	2	1
MELLIFONT, JOHN, claim for relief	520	47		29
Do	2467	49		31
MELVILLE, DAVID, claim for relief	248	24	2	8
MENARD, PIERRE, claim for relief	843	30	1	16
MENARY, JOHN, claim for relief	88	21	2	5
MENDENHALL, CYRUS P., claim for relief	64	42	3	26
MENDENHALL, WILLIAM, claim for relief	99	19	1	3
MENNIE JAMES, claim for relief	30	22	2	6
MERCHANT, GEORGE, claim for relief	146	19	1	3
MERCHANT, L., & CO., claim for relief	69	40	2	25
MERLET, E., claim for relief of assignee	25	24	1	7
MERONEY, PHILIP D., claim for relief	547	25	2	9
MERRETT, WILLIAM H., claim for relief	392	45	2	27
MERRILL, J. H., claim for relief	1518	47	1	29
Do	903	48	1	30
MERRITT, EDWIN A., claim for relief	3317	49	1	31
MESLER, CHARLES V., claim for relief	1155	49	1	31
MESSENGER, HENRY A., claim for relief	8	41	3	25
METAL, ABRAHAM, claim for relief	721	27	2	11
METCALF, JOHN, claim for relief	41	25	3	9
Do	166	27	2	11
Do	109	27	3	11
METROPOLITAN POLICE, to grant additional compensation to police force in District of Columbia	227	43	1	26
Do	30	45	3	27
Do	159	46	2	28
METTEKIN, THOMAS (executor), claim for relief	187	24	2	8
MEYER, HENRY and FREDERICK W., claim for relief	170	34	3	20
MEYER, JAMES, claim for relief	43	35	2	21
MIAMI EXPORTING COMPANY, claim for relief	373	21	1	5
Do	310	24	2	8
MICHEL, JOHN, and others, claim for relief	190	34	3	20
Do	632	36	1	22
MICHIE, JOHN J., claim for relief	78	38	1	25

Subject.	Report.	Congress.	Session.	Volume.
MICHIGAN:				
Indiana, claim of citizens for services against	83	22	2	6
War of 1812, claim of citizens for losses incurred during	268	20	1	4
MICOU, J. M., and others, claim for relief	171	46	2	28
Do	542	46	2	28
MIDAS (bark), claim for relief	908	46	2	28
Do	200	47	1	29
MIDDLETON, ISAAC S., claim for relief	164	24	1	8
Do	689	26	1	10
Do	179	27	2	11
MILAM, ELIJAH, claim for relief	342	30	1	16
MILAN, GEORGE W., claim for relief	395	30	1	16
MILES, EVAN, claim for relief	1544	47	1	29
MILES, JOHN, claim for relief	169	20	1	4
MILES, SMITH M., claim for relief	674	24	1	8
Do	31	25	2	9
MILEY, AARON, claim for relief	678	45	2	27
MILITARY BAND, payment of, stationed at Sackett's Harbor	501	27	2	11
MILITARY ESTABLISHMENT OF 1811, compensation to enlisted men under	136	24	1	8
MILITARY SERVICE,				
Georgia State militia, to compensate	549	28	1	12
Property lost in, settlement of claims for	11	14	2	1
Do	84	16	1	1
Do	12	17	1	1
Do	842	24	1	8
Do	3	25	1	9
Do	948	25	2	9
Do	956	25	2	9
Do	1060	25	2	9
Do	929	27	2	11
MILITIA,				
Alabama,				
Three companies under Major Holt, service against Creek Indians, compensation of	258	24	2	8
Captain Parks's Company, 1837, service against Creek Indians	959	25	2	9
Indiana, service in protecting certain Indians in 1836	197	24	2	8
Do	465	25	2	9
Michigan volunteers, 1812, claims of	388	21	1	5
Do	219	22	1	7
Seminole Indian war, volunteers engaged in, payment of	84	16	1	1
MILLER, AMOS, claim for relief of heirs	5	18	2	2
MILLER, CHRISTOPHER, claim for relief of heirs	412	29	1	13
MILLER, FERDINAND O., claim for relief	245	35	1	21
MILLER, FREDERICK W., claim for relief	891	46	2	28
MILLER, E. P., claim for relief	374	26	1	10
MILLER, HAMILTON J., claim for relief	897	45	2	27
Do	1762	47	1	29
Do	2177	48	2	30
MILLER, HENRY, claim for relief	266	36	1	22
MILLER, HEZEKIAH, claim for relief	335	33	1	19
MILLER, JACOB, and others, claim for relief	401	22	1	6
MILLER, JOHN R., claim for relief	326	47	1	29
MILLER, SAMUEL, claim for relief	155	24	2	8
MILLER, THOMAS, claim for relief	69	15	1	1
MILLER, THOMAS C., claim for relief	629	29	1	14
MILLER, W. C., claim for relief	204	25	3	9
MILLER & BAKER, claim for relief	69	15	1	1
MILLIGAN, JOSEPH L., claim for relief	51	25	3	9
MILLIGAN, JOSEPH S., claim for relief	547	25	2	9
MILLIKEN, JOHN, claim for relief	1037	25	2	9
MILLS, CHARLES S., claim for relief	579	48	1	30
MILLS, PETER, claim for relief	42	26	1	10
MILONE, JOHN, claim for relief	101	41	2	25
MINER, REVES, claim for relief of administrator	49	18	2	2
MINIFIE, CHARLES, claim for relief	14	18	1	2
MINIS, DINAH, claim for relief	246	35	1	21
MINOR, SMITH, claim for relief	58	37	2	25
MINOR, WILTSHIRE, claim for relief	471	30	1	16
MINORS, enlistment of, in the Army, claim for time	21	15	1	1
MISSISSIPPI RIVER, loss of boats on, statement of	178	27	3	11
MISSOURI,				
Boundary between Arkansas and	102	22	2	6
Lands in State of, to quiet titles to	36	40	2	25
Volunteers, to indemnify, for loss of horses	948	25	2	9
MISSOURI RIVER, statement of boats lost on	178	27	3	11
MITCHELL, ALEXANDER, claim for relief of heirs	50	27	3	11
Do	566	28	1	12
MITCHELL, ANDREW, claim for relief of heirs	97	19	1	3
MITCHELL, JAMES, claim for relief	31	19	1	3
Do	10	20	2	4
Do	399	29	1	13

Subject.	Report.	Congress.	Session.	Volume.
MITCHELL, JAMES (British ship), salvage, claim for	267	31	1	18
MITCHELL, JOHN, claim for relief	112	18	1	2
MITCHELL, NATHANIEL, claim for relief	780	26	2	9
Do	156	27	2	11
MITCHELL, SAMUEL, claim for relief	400	21	1	5
Do	252	22	1	6
MITCHELL, WARREN, cotton claim, settlement of	424	46	2	28
Do	3	46	3	28
MITCHELL, WILLIAM, claim for relief	62	24	1	8
MITCHELL, WILLIAM S., claim for relief	627	44	1	27
MOBILE, ALABAMA, to reimburse city of, for expenses and moneys advanced during Creek war of 1836	304	24	2	8
Do	58	25	3	9
MOBILE AND OHIO RAILROAD COMPANY, to audit and settle the accounts of the	1735	47	1	29
MONEY, WILLIAM, claim for relief	7	35	2	21
Do	514	36	1	22
MONEY INCLOSED IN LETTERS, liability of United States for lost	30	20	1	3
Do	3788	49	2	32
MONROE, A. G., claim for relief	106	27	3	11
MONROE, JAMES, claim for relief	202	30	1	15
MONROE, JOHN, claim for relief	178	27	2	11
Do	88	27	3	11
Do	413	28	1	12
MONROE, U. P., claim for relief	56	39	1	25
MONTANARI, JOSEPH, claim for relief	192	43	1	26
MONTGOMERY, JOHN B., claim for relief	8	35	2	21
MOOERS, BENJAMIN, claim for relief	612	24	1	8
Do	36	25	2	9
MOORE, ALFRED L., claim for relief	347	24	1	8
MOORE, ALLEN R., claim for relief	31	17	2	1
Do	584	24	1	8
Do	26	25	2	9
MOORE, ELY, claim for relief of estate	2693	49	1	31
MOORE, EVA, and others, claim for relief	87	47	1	29
MOORE, FRANCES, claim for relief	746	29	1	14
MOORE, JACOB, claim for relief	109	30	2	17
MOORE, JENNIE K., claim for relief	695	45	2	27
Do	895	46	2	28
MOORE, JOSEPH E., claim for relief	1715	47	1	29
Do	1243	48	1	30
MOORE, JOSEPH P., claim for relief	51	36	2	22
MOOREHEAD, JAMES, claim for relief	670	30	1	17
MOORS, JEREMIAH, claim for relief	281	23	1	7
Do	722	27	2	11
Do	157	28	2	12
Do	126	29	1	13
Do	165	30	1	15
MORAN, WILLIAM P., claim for relief	855	49	1	31
MORELAND, CATHARINE E., claim for relief	750	29	1	14
MOREHEAD, ELIZA T., claim for relief	78	39	1	25
Do	301	43	1	26
MORGAN, ALEXANDER G., claim for relief	701	24	1	8
Do	50	25	2	9
MORGAN, JAMES M., claim for relief	841	27	3	11
MORGAN, JOHN, claim for relief	283	30	1	16
MORGAN, THOMAS P., claim for relief	2607	49	1	31
MORRILL, ABRAHAM, claim for relief	170	27	2	11
MORRIS, EDWARD, claim for relief	685	29	1	14
MORRIS, J. A., claim for relief	157	49	1	31
MORRIS, JOHN H., claim for relief	904	45	2	27
Do	1724	46	2	28
Do	71	47	1	29
MORRIS, JOSIAH, claim for relief	38	42	3	26
MORRIS, W. J., claim for relief	1	39	1	25
MORRIS, WILLIAM S., and others, claim for relief	1	44	1	27
MORRISON, ABRAHAM, claim for relief	57	25	3	9
Do	493	27	2	11
MORRISON, AMBROSE, claim for relief	79	38	1	25
MORRISSOM, JAMES, claim for relief of executors	133	21	1	5
Do	505	22	1	6
Do	11	23	1	7
MORRISSON, JESSE, claim for relief	787	24	1	8
MORRISON, SARAH B., claim for relief	655	43	1	26
Do	103	45	2	27
MORRISON, THOMAS D., claim for relief	1049	25	2	9
MORRISON, WILLIAM, claim for relief, Indian contract	64	19	2	2
Do	163	20	1	4
Do	63	21	1	5
MORRISON, WILLIAM M., claim for relief	3031	49	1	31
MORROW, JAMES, claim for relief	14	30	1	15

Subject.	Report.	Congress.	Session.	Volume.
E, ANDREW, claim for relief	189	22	1	6
E, COLLINS, claim for relief	307	48	1	30
E, SAMUEL A., claim for relief	97	28	2	12
S, OLIVER, and others, claim for relief	94	42	3	26
Do	29	45	3	27
Do	901	46	2	28
H. J. T., claim for relief	2184	48	1	30
Do	133	49	1	31
WILLIAM, claim for relief	1790	47	1	29
OW, JOHN, claim for relief of heirs	845	25	2	9
, CAROLINE, claim for relief	426	47	1	29
, DANFORD,				
im for relief	218	43	1	26
im for relief of administrator	494	47	1	29
WILLIAM B., claim for relief	416	29	1	12
RY, GEORGE, claim for relief	165	30	2	17
Do	74	38	1	25
, JANE, claim for relief	863	21	1	5
HEAD, WILLIAM, et al., reference of claims to Court of Claims	1621	48	1	30
ORD, L. E., claim for relief	826	47	1	29
EN, HENRY, claim for relief	344	46	2	28
Do	96	47	1	29
Do	974	49	1	31
ICAN, J. N., claim for relief of administrator	268	29	1	13
FORD, HANNAH R., claim for relief	820	25	2	9
Y, GEORGE W. (administrator), claim for relief	329	36	1	22
ERLYN, JOHN D., for relief	978	47	1	29
Do	2110	48	1	30
Do	3101	49	1	31
OE, GRAFTON, claim for relief	725	49	1	31
EY, G. B., claim for relief	227	36	1	22
HEY, JOHN, claim for relief	456	36	1	22
HY, BENJAMIN, claim for relief	394	26	1	10
Do	186	29	2	13
HY, CHARLES, claim for relief	433	46	1	28
Do	1342	48	1	30
Do	1323	49	1	31
Do	2743	49	1	31
HY, FRANK P., claim for relief	2629	49	1	31
HY, MARTIN and P. B., claim for relief	2451	49	1	31
HY, ROBERT C., claim for relief	411	45	2	27
Do	1595	46	2	28
Do	977	47	1	29
Do	425	48	1	30
HY, SARAH, claim for relief	572	24	1	8
Do	29	25	2	9
HY & GOOD, claim for relief	109	45	2	27
AY, ANTHONY, claim for relief	646	27	2	11
AY, J. A., claim for relief	20	44	2	27
AY, JOHN, claim for relief	757	24	1	8
AY, MARTIN, claim for relief	458	36	1	22
AY, THOMAS, claim for relief	371	24	1	8
AY, THOMAS, claim for relief of widow	344	27	2	11
LAWRENCE, claim for relief	116	15	1	1
Do	6	16	2	1
LE, DAVID, claim for relief	125	35	2	21
Do	93	36	1	22
S, LEONARD, claim for relief	1078	47	1	29
RS, REBECCA, claim for relief	873	46	2	28
ER, BENJAMIN, claim for relief	136	30	2	17
AMORE, ROBERT C., claim for relief	24	45	3	27
Do	892	46	2	28
Y, ABIGAIL, claim for relief of heirs	20	35	2	21
NAL BANKS,				
nix National Bank of New York, claim for relief	2504	49	1	31
te National Bank of Louisiana, claim for relief	1415	48	1	30
NAL ROAD. (See CUMBERLAND ROAD.)				
RRE, FRANCIS, claim for relief	7	14	2	1
RRE, ISIDORE, claim for relief	418	17	1	6
, UNITED STATES,				
ntracts, settlement of claims under	266	22	1	6
nsion fund, investment of	98	22	2	6
rgeon's mates, additional pay for	259	24	2	8
ar-vessels for the United States, relief of contractors	17	39	2	25
OR, JOHN, & CO., and others, claim for relief	433	35	1	21
OR, JOHN, & CO., claim for relief	7	37	3	25
, HENRY, claim for relief	2280	49	1	31
E, CHRISTOPHER (assignee), claim for relief	50	34	3	20
ASKA,				
aska, for money advanced in construction of capitol building in State of, to reimburse	77	39	1	25

Subject.	Report.	Congress.	Session.	Volume.
NEBRASKA—Continued.				
Public lands, for relief of settlers and purchasers on	520	49	1	31
Do	3900	49	2	32
NEELEY, JAMES C., claim for relief	238	30	1	16
NEILSON, WILLIAM, claim for relief	6	28	1	12
Do	193	35	1	21
Do	264	36	1	22
NELSON, ANDREW, claim for relief of heirs	830	22	1	6
NELSON, CHARLES L., claim for relief	129	37	2	25
NESSLE, WILLIAM H., claim for relief	43	44	1	27
NEWCOMB, JONATHAN, claim for relief	266	22	1	6
NEWELL, SAMUEL, claim for relief of administrator of	79	35	2	21
NEWELL, THOMAS M., claim for relief	80	34	3	20
NEW HAMPSHIRE, to reimburse the State for moneys advanced for bounties to soldiers during war of rebellion	23	41	3	25
NEWMAN, GEORGE T., claim for relief	1812	49	1	31
Do	3127	49	1	31
NEWTON, MASSACHUSETTS, FIRST NATIONAL BANK OF, for relief of	3126	49	1	31
NEWTON, THOMAS W. (assignee), claim for relief	389	21	1	5
NEW YORK CITY.				
Custom-house, clerks in, relief	722	29	1	14
Night inspectors in, additional compensation	2471	49	1	31
Sone and Fleming Manufacturing Company, claim for relief	1515	48	1	30
Thirty-second internal-revenue district, to settle claim of certain brokers in	101	47	1	29
NEW YORK STATE.				
Moneys advanced to United States, interest on, payment of	249	20	1	4
Do	143	37	2	25
Niagara County, citizens of, relief	31	16	2	1
NIAGARA COUNTY, NEW YORK, for relief of certain citizens	31	16	2	1
NIAGARA FRONTIER, property destroyed on, claim for, 1812	177	15		1
Do	31	16	2	1
Do	386	22	1	6
NICHOLAS, WILLIAM, claim for relief	36	26		10
NICHOLS, CALEB, claim for relief	61	14	2	1
NICHOLSON, THOMAS A., claim for relief	781	44	1	27
NICOLL, S. T., & CO., claim for relief	38	30	2	17
Do	31	31	1	18
NIGHTINGALE (sloop), for the relief of crew of	20	39	1	25
NILES, SAMUEL V., claim for relief	431	35	1	21
NILES WORKS, CINCINNATI, OHIO, claim for relief	1999	47	2	29
NIMMO, WILLIAM T., claim for relief of heirs	49	17	2	1
NOBLE, MOSES, claim for fishing bounties	385	35	1	21
Do	21	36	1	22
NOBLE, THOMAS H., claim for relief	742	30	1	17
NOCK, JOSEPH, claim for relief	290	27	3	11
Do	493	28	1	12
Do	377	29		13
Do	1307	43		20
NOKES, JAMES, claim for relief	62	38		25
NOTRE DAME DU LAC, UNIVERSITY OF, SAINT JOSEPH COUNTY, INDIANA, claim for relief	686	45	2	27
Do	909	46	2	28
NORRIS, JOHN, claim for relief of executors	195	29	1	13
NORRIS, WILLIAM B., claim for relief	101	30	1	15
NORTH CAROLINA, cotton claims of State of	808	44	1	27
Do	7	45	3	27
NORTH GERMAN LLOYD STEAMSHIP COMPANY, claim for relief	2563	49	1	31
NORTHUP, HENRY, claim for relief	95	23	1	7
NORTON, A. B., claim for relief	3021	49	1	31
NORTON, SILAS M., claim for relief	297	43	2	28
NORTON, STEPHEN, claim for relief	248	21	1	5
NORTON, THOMAS H., claim for relief	2381	49	1	31
NOURSE, JOHN, claim for relief	372	23	1	7
NOURSE, JOHN B., and others, claim for relief	483	36	1	22
NOURSE, JOSEPH, claim for extra compensation for disbursing certain funds in Treasury Department	844	24	1	8
Do	58	25	2	9
NOURSE, MICHAEL, claim for relief	95	34	1	20
Do	382	35		21
NULL, HENRY, claim for relief	283	24		8
NUTT, WILLIAM D., claim for relief	659	30		17
NYE, J. W., claim for relief	745	30		17
Do	161	31		18
Do	326	33		19
Do	6	41	2	25
OAKSMITH, APPLETON, claim for relief	420	44	1	27
O'BANNON, JENNINGS, claim for relief	28	16		1
O'BANNON, PRESLEY N., claim for relief	586	24		8
Do	34	25		9
OBER, HANSON & CO., claim for relief	84	39		25
O'BRIEN, GEORGE, claim for relief	396	35	1	21
O'CONNOR, MARY, claim for relief	1309	46	2	28

Subject.	Report.	Congress.	Session.	Volume.
OFFIELD, LEWIS D., claim for relief	419	30	1	16
OFFSET OF CLAIMS DUE UNITED STATES, by claims of private citizens	115	22	2	6
Do	202	23	1	7
Do	8	24	1	7
Do	123	30	1	17
OGDEN, DAVID B. (executor), claim for relief	170	29	1	13
OGDEN, ELIZA E., claim for relief	635	35	1	21
OGDEN, THOMAS L., claim for relief	86	18	1	3
OHIO,				
Bank of Chillicothe, in State of, for relief of	45	21	1	5
Miami Exporting Company, State of, for relief of	319	24	2	8
Volunteer militia, Second Regiment, for relief of	27	38	1	26
OHIO LAND COMPANY, 1777, loan office certificates, claim for settlement of	161	35	1	21
OHL, JOHN F., claim for relief	725	30	1	17
OKLAHOMA, protest against establishing the Territory of	89	43	2	26
O'LAUGHLIN, MARY, claim for relief	460	45	2	27
Do	96	45	3	27
OLIVE, FRANCIS (brig), claim for relief	1156	49	1	31
Do	21	45	3	27
Do	915	46	2	28
Do	1156	49	2	31
OLIVER, JOHN M., claim for relief	690	24	1	8
Do	39	25	2	9
OLMSTEAD, S. B., claim for relief	754	30	1	17
OMAHA, NEBRASKA, to reimburse city for money expended in erecting building for State capitol	77	39	1	25
O'NEILL, BERNARD, claim for relief	682	29	1	14
OPIE, LEROY, claim for relief of surety	703	27	2	11
ORANGE AND ALEXANDRIA RAILROAD COMPANY, claim for relief	494	31	1	18
Do	2	33	1	19
ORD, PACIFICUS, claim for relief	10	27	2	11
Do	369	28	1	12
Do	274	29	1	13
ORDNANCE PROJECTILES, improvements in, claim of Norman Wiard	43	41	3	25
Do	87	42	2	26
O'REILEY, ELIZABETH, claim for relief	697	24	1	8
ORMOND, JAMES, claim for relief	723	27	2	11
ORPHANS' HOME (Baptist) OF LOUISVILLE, KENTUCKY, claim for relief	631	44	1	27
OSBORN, SAMUEL, Jr., claim for relief	121	45	3	27
OSBORNE, ANNA W., claim for relief	658	43	1	26
Do	706	44	1	27
Do	1430	49	1	31
OSBORNE, THOMAS A., claim for relief	3104	49	1	31
Do	4091	49	2	32
OSBORNE, WILLIAM S., claim for relief	24	31	1	18
OSBURN, NEHEMIAH (contractor for erection of United States court-house in Baltimore, claim for relief	3930	49	2	32
OSWEGO DISTILLERY COMPANY, claim for relief	18	42	2	26
OTIS, JOHN, claim for relief	724	27	2	11
Do	149	29	1	13
Do	98	34	1	20
OTIS, WILLIAM, action against collector of customs, Barnstable, Mass., relief	244	20	1	4
OTTINGER, DOUGLASS, inventor of life-saving apparatus, claim for relief	196	35	2	21
OVERTON, SAMUEL, claim for relief	477	23	1	7
Do	131	23	2	7
OVIATT, SIDNEY F., claim for relief	17	44	2	27
Do	23	45	3	27
OWEN, AMASA, claim for relief	500	27	2	11
OWEN, CHARLES, and others, claim for relief	94	42	3	26
OWEN, JAMES (administrator), claim for relief	239	30	1	16
OWENS, ARTHUR R., claim for relief	703	26	1	10
OWENS, ELIZABETH, claim for relief	42	21	2	5
OWENS, JOSEPHINE C., claim for relief	193	45	2	27
OWENS, WILLIAM J., claim for relief	215	25	3	9
PACHECO, ANTONIO, claim for relief of administrator	472	27	2	11
Do	523	28	1	12
PACIFIC INSURANCE COMPANY OF NEW YORK, indemnity for losses sustained in suits against United States marshal of Pennsylvania	757	30	1	17
PADDOCK, JOSEPH, claim for relief	97	37	2	25
PAGE, FAIRCHILD, & CO., refund of duties on lumber imported	907	48	1	30
PAGE, DANIEL M., claim for relief	99	41	2	25
Do	19	42	2	26
PAIRO, HENRY T. (administrator), claim for relief	163	31	1	18
PALMER, AARON HAIGHT, claim for relief	17	35	2	21
Do	466	36	1	22
PALMER, BARNABAS, claim for relief	57	27	2	11
PALMER, JOHN A., index clerk, H. R., claim for relief	3967	49	2	32
PALMER, SALLE H., claim for relief	1720	46	2	28
PALMER, WILLIAM, claim for relief	343	22	1	6
Do	74	22	2	6
Do	24	23	1	7
Do	247	26	2	10

Subject.	Report.	Congress.	Session.	Volume.
PANKEY, J. E., claim for relief	517	44	1	27
PANLETT, WILLIAM W., claim for relief	841	25	2	9
PARISH, JASPER, claim for relief	163	21	1	5
PARISH, JOSEPH W., claim for relief	806	44	1	27
Do	1956	47	2	29
PARKE, HARVEY, claim for relief	156	28	2	12
Do	312	28	1	12
Do	801	29	1	24
PARKER, BENJAMIN, claim for relief	492	25	2	9
PARKER, DANIEL (Inspector-General United States Army), claim for compensation	77	23	2	7
Do	888	46	2	28
PARKER, DAVID S., claim for relief	13	44	2	27
Do	1550	47	1	29
PARKER, JANE, claim for relief	555	28	1	12
Do	31	28	2	12
PARKER, JOHN A., claim for relief	202	21		5
Do	188	24		8
Do	613	44		27
PARKER, PETER, claim for relief	181	35	1	21
PARKER, SOUTHEY, claim for relief of widow	838	27	2	11
Do	31	28	2	12
PARKINSON, JOHN S., claim for relief		27	3	11
PARKINSON, JOSEPH, claim for relief	790	48		30
PARKS, D. O., claim for relief	458	36		22
PARKS, ELIAS, claim for relief	43	15	2	1
PARKS, GEORGE F., claim for relief	458	36		22
PARKS, HANNAH, claim for relief	458	36	1	22
PARKS, JAMES, claim for relief	1563	46	2	28
PARSONS, GEORGE, claim for relief	337	29		13
Do	2	29	2	14
PARSONS, JOHN, claim for relief	35	47		29
PARTON, MADISON, claim for relief	4	33		19
PASCHALL, GEORGE W., claim for relief	448	26	1	10
PASKO, ABEL A., and others, claim for relief	544	25	2	9
PATCHEN, RALPH, claim for relief	71	15	2	1
PATRICK, WILLIAM, claim for relief	224	25	3	9
PATRIDGE, JESSE, claim for relief	458	36	1	22
PATTEE, WALLIS, claim for relief	85	41	2	25
PATTERSON, A. H., claim for relief	720	29	1	14
Do	749	30		17
Do	500	31		18
Do	300	33		19
PATTERSON, BERNARD M., claim for relief	248	22		6
PATTERSON, DANIEL T., claim for relief	87	24	2	8
Do	7	25		9
PATTERSON, MARTIN L., claim for relief	50	30		15
Do	11	33	1	19
PATTERSON, WILLIAM, claim for relief	167	19	1	3
PATTISON, JAMES J., claim for relief	406	24		8
Do	14	25	2	9
Do	199	27	3	11
PATTISON, JOHN I., claim for relief	14	15	1	1
PATTISON & CALDWELL, claim for relief	474	49	1	31
PATTON, MONTRAVILLE, claim for relief	660	43	1	26
PAXTON, JOSEPH, claim for relief	516	26	1	10
Do	100	28	2	12
PAY, to place the different corps of the Army on a footing of equality as regards their pay	415	34	1	20
PAYNE, D. L., claim for relief	29	46	2	28
PAYNE, JOHN A., claim for relief	577	48	1	30
PAYNE, JOHN H., respecting claim of	410	31	1	18
PAYSON, HENRY, & CO., claim for relief	167	19	1	3
PEALE, FRANKLIN, claim for relief	424	35	1	21
Do	464	36	1	22
Do	88	42	2	26
PEARCE, S. H., claim for relief	3319	49	1	31
PEASLEY & McCLARY, claim for relief	682	45	2	27
PECK, ADAM, claim for relief	32	21	2	5
PECK, MARY, claim for relief	282	25	3	9
PECK, PETER, claim for relief	408	21	1	5
PEDRICK, WILLIAM, claim for relief	213	35	2	21
PEEBLES, JAMES, claim for relief	188	27	2	11
PEEBLES, JOHN, claim for relief	64	25	3	9
PEEBLES, ROBERT, claim for relief	680	24	1	8
Do	46	25	2	9
PEGG, RANSDELL, claim for relief	104	34	1	20
PEIRCE, JOHN, claim for relief	277	23	1	7
PEIRCE, WILLIAM and JOHN, claim for relief	25	20	1	4
Do	2	24	1	8

Subject.	Report.	Congress.	Session.	Volume.
PEKIN, ILL., for the relief of City Distilling Company of	874	45	2	27
Do	1569	46	2	28
PELHAM, WILLIAM, claim for relief	371	42	1	22
PELLECIER, FRANCIS, claim for relief of administrator	57	28	1	15
Do	906	27	2	11
PELLETIER, ANTOINE, claim for relief	343	30	1	16
PEMBERTON, WILLIAM, claim for relief	16	18	2	2
PENNINGTON, JOHN, claim for relief	204	47	1	29
PENNOYER, JAMES, claim for relief	104	26	2	10
PENNSYLVANIA,				
Bank of Columbia, for relief of	71	38	1	25
Accounts in certain judicial proceeding in, to adjust	1066	49	1	31
Do	2331	49	1	31
Allegheny County, claim of citizens for damages sustained by construction of bridges across the Ohio River	491	48	1	30
Do	596	47	1	29
Interest due from United States on bonds issued for military purposes	349	20	1	4
Money passed to credit of Alexander J. Dallas for payment of militia, claim for	222	20	1	4
Volunteers, to reimburse certain officers of the Fiftieth Regiment of	15	44	2	27
PENRIFOY, T. D., claim for relief	263	25	3	9
PENROSE, CLEMENT T., claim for relief of widow	366	23	1	7
PENSIONS, to equalize the pensions to widows and children of persons serving in the different corps of the Army	415	24	1	8
PEPPER, CAREY B., claim for relief	160	47	1	29
PERCUSSION CAPS, machine for manufacture of, claim for invention of, by R. M. Boston	748	30	1	17
PERHAM, BENJAMIN, claim for relief	399	30	1	16
PERIAM, MARY and ELIZA, claim for relief	45	29	1	12
PERKINS, DANIEL W., claim for relief	79	46	2	28
Do	1696	47	2	29
PERKINS, JOHN B., claim for relief	665	24	1	8
Do	42	25	2	9
PERKINS, JOHN G., and others, claim for relief	25	28	2	15
PERKINS, JOSEPH and others, claim for relief	11	27	2	11
PERKINS, LAMEN A., claim for relief	86	47	1	29
PERKINS, MOSES, claim for relief of assignee	672	45	2	27
PERRIN, Mrs. F. A., claim for relief	407	45	2	27
PERRY, CHARLES A., & CO., claim for relief	690	49	1	31
PERRY, COLUMBUS F., claim for relief	671	45	2	27
Do	225	47	1	29
Do	908	48	1	30
PERRY, OLIVER H., claim for relief	212	24	2	8
PERRY, PAUL, claim for relief	35	22	2	6
PERRY, REUBEN, claim for relief	1000	25	2	9
PERRY, SAMUEL, claim for relief	173	28	2	12
Do	691	29	1	14
Do	11	30	2	17
Do	77	35	2	21
Do	461	36	1	22
PERRY & LIGON, claim for relief	119	30	1	15
PERSONAL INJURY, relief from judgment upon a charge of assault while arresting a deserter, relief	128	24	1	8
PESCUD, EDWARD, claim for relief	353	27	2	11
PETER, DAVID, claim for relief of executors	35	15	2	1
PETERS, LANDON C., claim for relief	34	26	2	10
PETERS & REED, claim for relief	305	43	1	26
PETERSON, JOHN P., claim for relief	2111	48	1	30
PETERY, MARY, claim for relief	421	35	1	21
PETIE, JOSEPH J., claim for relief	49	43	1	26
PETTIGREW, Z. M., claim for relief	909	48	1	30
PETTUS, WILLIAM G., claim for relief	74	31	1	18
PHELAN, JAMES, claim for relief	545	35	1	21
Do	90	36	1	22
PHELPS, GEORGE, claim for relief	16	35	2	21
PHELPS, HARLOW J., claim for relief	18	45	3	27
PHELPS, LIZZIE MANADIER, claim for relief	823	49	1	31
Do	2646	49	1	31
PHELPS, NOAH A., claim for relief	67	29	2	14
Do	214	30	1	15
PHELPS & LANDON, claim for relief	442	25	2	9
Do	26	26	1	10
Do	17	26	2	10
Do	18	27	2	11
PHENIX NATIONAL BANK, NEW YORK, claim for relief	2504	49	1	31
PHILADELPHIA, PENNSYLVANIA,				
Clerks in custom-house at, for relief of	544	35	1	21
Do	15	36	1	22
Express companies, claim of, for rebate on internal-revenue taxes	402	45	2	27
PHILIPS, ZACHARIAH, claim for relief	1027	25	2	9

Subject.	Report.	Congress.	Session.	Volume.
PHILLIPS, E. J., claim for relief	718	48	1	30
Do	475	49	1	31
PHILLIPS, GEORGE L., and others, claim for relief	220	24	2	8
PHILLIPS, SAMUEL G., claim for relief	597	25	2	9
PHILPOT, H. V., claim for relief	303	46	2	28
Do	5	47	1	29
PIATT, JOHN H., claim for relief of heirs	747	30	1	17
Do	325	31	1	18
Do	123	32	1	19
PICKARD, ISAIAH, claim for relief	689	45	2	27
PICKETT, A. J., claim for compensation	894	25	2	9
PICKETT, JOHN, and others, owners of brig Albert	690	29	1	14
PICKETT, J. T., claim for relief	580	48	1	30
PIERCE, AARON, claim for relief	756	24	1	8
PIERCE, GAD, claim for relief	32	17	2	1
PIERCE, JAMES, claim for relief	50	17	1	1
PIERIE, JOHN G., claim for relief	59	20	1	13
PIERNES, MADAM LE COMPTE, claim for relief	8	20	1	4
PIERSON, CHARLES E., claim for relief	194	45	2	27
PIERSON, HARVEY, claim for relief	786	24	1	8
Do	201	25	3	9
Do	560	28	1	12
PIERSON, MORRICE, claim for relief	786	24	1	8
PIGG, SAMUEL, claim for relief	238	30	1	16
PIGMAN, JOHN G., claim for relief	725	27	2	11
PILOTS, claim for relief of certain pilots at New Orleans	9	28	1	12
PILKINTON, EDWIN T., claim for relief of estate	1543	49	1	31
PILLSBURY, JOSIAH H., claim for relief	69	48	1	30
PIPER, WILLIAM J., claim for relief	685	45	2	27
PITTS, SAMUEL, claim for relief of administrator	543	35	1	21
PIX, CHRISTOPHER H., claim for relief	344	30	1	16
PLATT, NATHANIEL, claim for relief	514	23	1	7
Do	185	24	1	8
PLIASTON, STEPHEN, claim for relief	511	22	1	6
Do	79	22	2	6
PLOCHER, FERDINAND, claim for relief	1289	49	1	31
PLOWDEN, WALTER D., claim for relief	13	40	3	25
PLUMB, SAMUEL, claim for relief	71	15	2	1
PLUMMER, J. and G., claim for relief of assignee	50	34	3	20
PLUNKET, JOHN, claim for relief	75	31	1	18
POE, JOHN, claim for relief	5	30	2	17
Do	154	31	1	18
Do	97	34	1	20
POIDEOIN, MADAME, claim for money expended by United States consul on destitute seamen	99	15	1	1
POLLOCK, JOHN, claim for relief	505	23	1	7
Do	21	24	1	7
POLLOCK, WILLIAM J., claim for relief	246	44	1	27
POMAR, JOSEPH E., claim for relief	842	25	2	9
POMEROY, CHARLES, claim for relief	7		3	25
PONCE, JOHN, claim for relief	828	25	3	9
PONS (slaver), relative to the Africans recaptured by the U. S. S. Yorktown from the	2	31	2	18
POOL, ISAAC, claim for relief	2	18	2	3
POOL, RICHARD, claim for relief	517	23	1	7
POPE, BENJAMIN S., claim for relief	167	36	1	22
PORTER, ANDREW, claim for relief	869	25	2	9
PORTER, RICHARD H. and JAMES, claim for relief	1181	47	1	29
Do	2696	49	1	31
Do	2894	49	1	31
PORTLAND, OREGON, First National Bank of, claim for relief	3818	49	2	32
POSNER, J. G., claim for relief of heirs	37	19	1	3
POSNER, SYLVIA, claim for relief	489	22	1	6
POST & McCORD, claim for relief	3891	49	1	31
POSTMASTERS, claims for losses incurred by	1432	49	1	31
POST-OFFICE EMPLOYÉS, testimony of, in cases of plundered mail	30	20	1	3
POST-ROUTES, mail-carriers exempt from toll on all	378	29	1	1
POTTER, HEMAN B., claim for relief	23	17	1	
Do	4	17	2	1
POTTER, S. S., claim for relief	76	42	2	26
POTTER, WOODBURNE, claim for relief	1044	25	2	9
POUCHER, PETER, claim for relief	772	24	1	8
POUNDS, JOHN M., claim for relief	816	25	3	9
POVERTY ISLAND, for the relief of workmen at	666	43	1	26
Do	102	45	2	27
POVET, JOHN, claim for relief	85	23	1	7
POWELL, ALLEN H., claim for relief	683	26	1	10
POWELL, W. H., claim for relief	2370	49	1	31
POWERS, DAVID, claim for relief	107	25	3	9
POWERS, ELIZA HOWARD, claim for relief	303	43	2	26
Do	1945	48	1	30

1	29
2	1
1	1
1	1
2	1
1	1
1	6
1	7
2	11
3	11
1	12
1	12
2	12
2	12
3	20
3	8
1	80
1	5
2	25
1	6
2	82
1	7
2	8
1	1
1	2
1	81
3	11
2	7
1	7
1	12
1	14
2	8
2	26
2	25
2	8
2	9
1	29
1	18
1	80
1	29
2	82
1	15
1	7
1	14
1	16
1	80
1	81
2	27

Subject.	Report.	Congress.	Session.	Volume.
RANDALL, GEORGE, and others, claim for relief	652	26	1	10
Do	5	27	2	11
Do	14	27	3	11
RANDALL, WHEELER, claim for relief	51	26	1	10
RANDLE, WILLIAM H., claim for relief	2732	49	1	31
Do	2891	49	1	31
RATCLIFF, JOSEPH, claim for relief	521	23	1	7
RATHBONE, WILLIAM P., claim for relief	813	24	1	8
Do	30	25	3	9
Do	657	26	1	10
Do	9	26	2	10
RATHBUN, E. W., & CO., refund of duties on lumber imported	907	48	1	30
RAWLINS, JOHN O., for relief of sureties of	71	48	1	30
RAWLS, MORGAN, claim for relief	104	47	1	29
Do	2423	49	1	31
RAY, J. C., and others, claim for relief	622	29	1	14
RAY, JOSIAH, claim for relief	340	34	1	20
RAYNOLDS, JAMES, claim for relief	38	26	1	10
REA, JOHN A., claim for relief	45	47	1	29
READ, GEORGE B., claim for relief	781	29	1	14
Do	156	31	1	18
READ, JOHN B., claim for relief	2733	49	1	31
READ, JOSEPH S., claim for relief	304	43	1	26
RECEIVERS OF PUBLIC MONEYS, liability and settlement of accounts of	836	24	1	8
RECOGNIZANCE BOND, release from forfeiture of	188	21	1	5
REDDING, JOSEPH, claim for relief	599	25	2	9
REED, JOHN N., claim for relief	564	43	1	26
Do	63	44	2	27
Do	669	45	2	27
Do	24	46	1	28
Do	1232	46	2	28
REED, SAMUEL, claim for relief	49	30	1	15
REED, SILAS, claim for relief	318	43	2	26
REED, WALTER, claim for relief	1788	47	1	29
REEDER, GEORGE, claim for relief	45	30	1	15
REEDER, WILLIAM AND RICHARD H., claim for relief	732	27	2	11
REEDSIDE, JAMES, claim for relief of widow	334	34	1	20
REES, HENRY J., claim for relief	246	24	2	8
Do	67	25	2	9
REES, ORLANDO S., claim for relief	633	29	1	14
REEVES, B. H., commissioner to lay out a road from Missouri to Mexico, compensation	416	21	1	5
REEVES, MINOR, claim for relief	49	18	2	2
REID, JAMES W., claim for relief	141	38	1	25
REID, WILLIAM H. and others, claim for relief	72	42	3	26
Do	488	43	1	26
REILLY, BOYD, claim for relief	729	27	2	11
REILLY, JOHN, claim for relief	32	24	2	8
RELFE, JAMES H., claim for relief	191	27	2	11
REMBERT, ANDREW, claim for relief	966	25	2	9
REMINGTON, E., & SONS, claim for relief	3329	49	1	31
RENARD, ADOLPH, claim for relief	572	36	1	22
RENNER, DANIEL, and others, claim for relief	41	14	2	1
Do	11	34	1	20
RENNER, MARY B., claim for relief	804	29	1	14
Do	213	30	1	15
RENNER & HEATH, claim for relief	158	15	1	1
RESS, ROACH & RESS, claim for compensation	277	25	3	9
REW, JOHN A., & CO., claim for relief	416	45	2	27
REWARD,				
Distribution of, for capture of Wilkes Booth	99	39	1	25
Distribution of, for arrest of Jefferson Davis	99	39	1	26
REYNOLDS, ALEXANDER W., claim for relief	419	35	1	21
REYNOLDS, BENJAMIN, claims for relief	339	25	2	9
REYNOLDS, CHARLES C., claim for relief	522	44	1	27
Do	395	45	2	27
Do	904	46	2	28
REYNOLDS, JAMES, claim for relief of heirs	44	22	2	6
REYNOLDS, JOHN C., claim for relief	188	26	2	10
REYNOLDS, WILLIAM, claim for relief	654	30	1	17
RHETT, WILLIAM H., claim for relief	694	45	2	27
RHODES, G. T., claims for relief	84	24	2	8
RICE, JOSEPH (administrator), claim for relief	23	24	1	7
RICE, OWEN, *et al.* (assignees), claim for relief	532	23	1	7
RICE, WILLIAM, claim for relief	371	26	1	10
Do	765	27	2	11
Do	90	27	3	11
RICH, WILLIAM, claim for relief	15	28	2	13
RICHAUD, JOHN, claim for relief	60	17	1	1
RICHARDS, ELISHA F., claim for relief	560	29	1	14
Do	3	29	2	14
Do	104	30	1	15

Subject.	Report.	Congress.	Session.	Volume.
ROCKAWAY, W. R. (administrator), claim for relief	677	30	1	17
ROCKWELL, SAMUEL, claim for relief	733	27	2	11
ROCKWOOD, CEPHAS L., claim for relief	26	20	1	4
RODDY, JAMES, claim for relief	113	18	1	2
Do	487	22	1	6
Do	10	22	2	6
Do	187	24	2	8
RODDY, WILLIAM, claim for relief	74	37	2	25
RODGERS, JOHN B., claim for relief	120	32	1	19
RODRIGUEZ, JOHN, claim for relief	27	19	1	3
Do	19	20	1	4
Do	27	21	1	5
Do	526	29	1	[illegible]
ROGERS, ALLEN, claim for relief	589	27	2	11
ROGERS, ANN L., claim for relief	44	35	2	21
ROGERS, C. E., claim for relief	475	43	1	28
ROGERS, EDWIN, claim for relief	17	45	3	27
ROGERS, GEORGE, claim for relief	456	36	1	22
ROGERS, GEORGE T., and others, claim for relief	24	46	1	28
ROGERS, ISAIAH, claim for relief	278	25	3	9
ROGERS, JOHN B., claim for relief	254	30	1	16
ROGERS, THOMAS (executor), claim for relief	839	25	2	9
Do	38	25	3	9
ROGERS & BOND, claim for relief	182	27	2	11
ROLFE, HENRY P., claim for relief	418	45	2	27
Do	177	47	1	29
ROLLINS, PINKNEY, claim for relief	1484	47	1	29
ROOTS, LOGAN H., claim for relief	44	41	3	26
ROSE, ELIJAH, claim for relief	620	29	1	14
ROSE, MALITTY, claim for relief	1818	49	1	31
ROSE, JOHN, claim for relief of heirs	454	23	1	7
ROSE, ROBERT H., claim for relief	859	25	2	9
ROSECRANTZ, PETER, claim for relief	69	40	2	26
ROSENBAUM, LOUIS, claim for relief	181	44	1	27
ROSS, JAMES, claim for relief	187	19	1	3
ROSS, JOHN G., claim for relief	367	21	1	5
ROTHCHILD, JOSEPH B., claim for relief	150	43	1	26
ROUFF, E., and others, claim for relief	342	46	2	28
ROUNDTREE, WILLIAM T., claim for relief	82	45	3	27
Do	426	48	1	30
ROUSE, JAMES, or JACQUES, claim for relief of heirs	598	25	2	9
ROUSE, LEWIS, claim for relief, army contract	76	19	1	3
Do	98	19	2	3
Do	45	20	1	4
Do	110	21	1	5
Do	104	22	2	6
ROWLAND, E. S., claim for relief	3034	49	1	31
ROWLETT, WILLIAM M., claim for relief	172	27	2	11
RUDD, HENRY, claim for relief	112	39	1	26
RUDOLPH, JOHN, claim for relief	623	29	1	14
RUFFEE, CHARLES A., claim for relief	3899	49	2	32
RUGGLES, FREDERICK W., claim for relief	1718	47	1	29
RULAND, ISAAC, claim for relief	556	25	2	9
Do	58	26	1	10
RULE, WILLIAM, claim for relief	341	44	1	27
RUMPH, JAMES, claim for relief	243	35	1	21
RUMSEY, JAMES, inventor of the steamboat, claim of heirs (*see also* SELECT REPORTS OF THE HOUSE)	403	29	1	13
RUNDLETT, JAMES, claim for relief	5	24	2	8
RUNYON, GEORGE W., claim for relief	236	30	1	16
RUSCO, ALBERT P., claim for relief	519	23	1	7
RUSH, R., claim for relief	839	27	2	11
RUSHTON, JEREMIAH, claim for relief	380	30	1	16
RUSS, JOSEPH, and others (assignees), claim for relief	529	23	1	7
Do	25	24	1	7
RUSS, JOHN P. (executor), claim for relief	731	27	2	11
RUSSELL, GILBERT C., claim for erection of fortifications in Mobile Bay	62	18	2	2
Do	149	19		3
Do	69	33		19
RUSSEL, H. W., claim for relief	87	24	2	8
Do	61	25	2	9
RUSSELL, JOHN, claim for relief	458	36		22
RUSSELL, THOMAS, claim for relief	458	36	1	22
RUSSELL, THOMAS A., claim for relief	31	27	2	11
RUSSELL, WILLIAM, claim for relief	794	24	1	8
RUSSELL, WILLIAM H., claim for relief	678	30		17
Do	416	35		21
RUSSELL, MOSES R., claim for relief	81	47	1	29
RUSSELL, SAMUEL, claim for relief	331	27	2	11
Do	55	27	3	11
RUTHERFORD, WILLIAM, claim for relief	67	42	3	26

Subject.	Report.	Congress.	Session.	Volume.
RUTTER, JOSEPH H. J., claim for relief	18	38	2	25
RYAN, DAVID, claim for relief	2881	49	1	31
RYAN, NORMAN H., claim for relief	670	43	1	26
RYAN, WILLIAM, claim for relief	520	23	1	7
SACKETT'S HARBOR, NEW YORK, for relief of band stationed in 1814 at	501	27	2	11
SAINT, DANIEL, claim for relief	97	36	1	25
Do	103	36	1	25
SAINT AUGUSTINE, FLORIDA, claim of citizens for property destroyed	218	24	2	8
Do	724	25	2	9
Do	216	25	2	9
ST. CLAIR, F. O., claim for relief	1950	49	1	31
ST. JOHN, A. F. and N. C., claim for relief	1298	49	1	31
ST. JOHN, HENRY, claim for relief	615	24	1	8
SAINT LOUIS, MISSOURI, Iron Mountain Bank of, for relief	989	49	1	31
ST. VRAIN, FELIX, claim for relief of sureties	296	29	1	13
SALARY, Relative to compensation to members when absent from Congress	6	24	1	7
SALT, use of, in reducing silver from its solution in nitric acid, claim of Franklin Peale for discovery of	424	35	1	21
Do	464	36	1	22
SALT WORKS, AT MANCHESTER, KENTUCKY, destroyed by United States forces, payment of claim of owners	141	38	1	25
SALTMARSH AND FULLER, claim for relief	201	38	1	3
SAN ANTONIO, TEXAS, for relief of Alamo Cement Company of	1290	49	1	31
SANDERS, CAROLINE R., claim for relief	840	29	1	14
SANDERS, WILLIAM, claim for relief	309	43	1	26
SANDERS, WILLIAM G., claim for relief	216	24	2	8
Do	677	26	1	10
Do	580	27	2	11
SANDERSON, SAMUEL, claim for relief	365	24	1	8
Do	4	25	2	9
SANDS, CHARLES J., claim for relief	425	43	1	26
SANDS, JOHN, claim for relief	458	36	1	22
SANDS, SAMUEL, claim for relief	459	36	1	22
SANDS & WALTON, claim for relief	456	36	1	22
SANGER, HENRY K. claim for relief	311	43	1	26
Do	461	45	2	27
Do	694	47	1	29
SANGER, HENRY P. and HENRY K., claim for relief	68	43	2	26
SAN ROMAN, JOSEPH, claim for relief	662	43	1	26
SANTERMAN, WILLIAM G., claim for relief	110	45	2	27
SAPP, JOHN, claim for relief	192	21	1	5
SARTAIN, JOEL, claim for relief	34	23	2	7
Do	36	24	1	7
SASSER, ISAAC, claim for relief	578	26	1	10
SAUNDERS, ALEXANDER H., claim for relief	716	26	1	10
Do	647	27	2	11
SAUNDERS, JOHN, claim for relief	29	23	2	7
Do	31	24	1	7
SAVAGE, TEAKLE (administrator), claim for relief	445	24	1	8
Do	724	24	1	8
Do	779	24	1	8
Do	19	25	2	9
Do	152	25	3	9
Do	688	27	2	11
Do	495	28	1	12
Do	147	28	2	12
Do	173	29	1	13
SAWYER, JAMES LUCIUS, claim for relief	16	21	2	5
SAWYER, JOSEPH, claim for relief	279	29	1	13
SAWYER, SUSANNAH A., claim for relief	330	36	1	22
SAWYER, WILLIAM and others, claim for relief	124	37	2	25
SAXON, WILLIAM, claim for relief	714	24	1	8
SAYLER, W. A., claim for relief	220	43	1	26
SAYLES, SAMUEL L., claim for relief	576	26	1	10
SAYLOR, AUGUSTUS D., claim for relief	1157	49	1	31
SAYRE, BENJAMIN, claim for relief	206	25	3	9
Do	280	29	1	13
Do	361	30	1	16
Do	358	33	1	19
Do	43	34	3	20
Do	122	35	1	21
Do	401	36	1	22
SCAIFE, CHARNER T. (administrator), claim for relief	423	35	1	21
Do	20	36	1	22
SCARBOROUGH, S. E., claim for relief	2475	49	1	31
SCHAUMBURG, JAMES W., claim for relief	1376	49	1	31
SCHENK, ALEXANDER D., claim for relief	221	48	1	30
Do	309	48	1	30
SCHIEFFELIN, JACOB and HENRY H., Great Britain prize claim	42	16	2	1
SCHIEFFELIN, R. L., claim for relief	473	30	1	16
SCHLEY, WILLIAM (executor), claim for relief	87	19	1	3

Subject.	Report.	Congress.	Session.	Volume.
SCHOLEFIELD, HELEN M. claim for relief	327	47	1	29
SCHOONMAKER, ZACHARIAH (paymaster United States Volunteers), to reimburse for, moneys stolen	34	17	2	1
SCHORR, BARBARA, claim for relief	92	41	2	25
SCHRACK, LEWIS, claim for relief	231	20	1	4
Do	4	21	1	5
SCHUCHARDT, WILLIAM, claim for relief	3320	49	1	31
SCHWATKA, F. G., claim for relief	585	47	1	29
Do	428	48	1	30
SCHWARTZTRAWBER, PHILIP, claim for relief	408	28	1	12
Do	13	28	2	12
SCOPY, MATTHEW, claim for relief of heir	394	29	1	13
SCOTT, ALMEDUS, claim for relief	411	30	1	16
SCOTT, CYRUS C., claim for relief	439	25	2	9
Do	372	26	1	10
Do	341	28	1	12
SCOTT, JOHN L., claim for relief	658	26	1	10
SCOTT, JONATHAN, claim for relief	340	29	1	13
SCOTT, PRESLEY, claim for relief	653	26	1	10
SCOTT, SAMUEL P., claim for relief	128	24	1	8
SCOTT, THOMAS, claim for relief	59	30	1	15
SCOTT, WILLIAM W., claim for relief	126	25	2	9
SCREWS, WALLACE W., claim for relief	581	46	2	28
Do	77	47	1	29
SCRIBNER, B. F., claim for relief	2701	49	1	31
SCRIVENER, JOHN, claim for relief	795	24	1	8
Do	1046	25	2	9
Do	55	27	2	11
Do	631	29	1	14
SCROGGS, GUSTAVUS A., claim for relief	214	43	2	26
SCUDDER, CHARLES L., claim for relief	2841	49	1	31
SEARS, MARY,				
For relief	18	16	2	1
Claim for relief of executor	176	24	1	8
SEAT, SAMUEL B., claim for relief	1883	49	1	31
Do	2032	49	1	31
SEAWELL, WASHINGTON, claim for relief	525	23	1	7
Do	24	24	1	7
SECOND AUDITOR, relative to additional clerks in office of	598	30	1	17
SEELEY, JULIA E., claim for relief	704	44	1	27
Do	707	44	1	27
Do	910	46	2	28
Do	330	47	1	29
SELDEN, WILLIAM, claim for relief	87	41	2	25
SELMA AND MERIDIAN RAILROAD COMPANY, claim for relief	788	48	1	30
Do	2432	49	1	31
SEMINOLE WAR. (*See* INDIAN WARS.)				
SENER, JACOB and ELIZABETH, claim for relief	371	45	2	27
Do	1675	47	1	29
Do	1844	47	2	29
SENGSTACK, C. P., claim for relief	315	28	1	12
SENGTELLER, LOUIS A., claim for relief	1553	47	1	29
SENTER, DEWITT C., claim for relief	21	44	1	27
SENTER, GEORGE W., claim for relief	726	27	2	11
SETHERS, JESSE, claim for relief	714	24	1	8
SETTLERS ON PUBLIC LANDS IN STATES OF NEBRASKA AND KANSAS, claim for relief of	3900	49	2	32
SEVERANCE, JOHN F., claim for relief	913	46	2	28
Do	156	47	1	29
Do	227	48	1	30
SEWALL, HENRY, claim for relief	146	23	1	7
SEWALL, ROBERT, claim for relief	148	23	1	7
Do	254	28	1	12
Do	98	29	1	13
SEWELL, COULSON & PORTER, claim for relief	1877	49	1	31
Do	2498	49	1	31
SHACKLEY, EPHRAIM, claim for relief	94	35	1	21
SHAFER, JACOB, claim for relief	2	18	1	2
SHAFFER, PETER	128	28	2	12
Do	97	29	1	13
Do	215	30	1	15
SHANNON, S., claim for relief of heirs	199	28	1	12
SHANNON, WILLIAM and HUGH, claim for relief	59	20	1	4
SHAPLEY, WILLIAM, claim for relief	670	29	1	14
SHARP, ABBIE, claim for relief	310	48	1	30
Do	858	49	1	31
SHARP, JAMES, claim for relief	247	23	1	7
SHARRETTS, G. E. W., claim for relief	40	45	2	27
Do	3324	49	1	31
SHATTUCK, JAMES F., claim for relief	9	41	2	25
SHAUMBURGH, BARTHOLOMEW, claim for relief	431	22	1	6

Subject.	Report.	Congress.	Session.	Volume.
, C. C., claim for relief of widow	1502	46	2	28
, JOHN, claim for relief of executor	170	29	1	13
, JOSEPH, claim for relief	531	23	1	7
, JOSHUA, claim for relief	53	28	2	12
Do	418	35	1	21
, WILLIAM, claim for relief	282	24	2	8
, WILLIAM D., claim for relief	30	31	1	18
JAMES, claim for relief	458	36	1	22
RER, JOSEPH, claim for relief	264	24	1	8
BY, SUSAN A., claim for relief	38	40	3	25
ARD, ALEXANDER K., claim for relief	177	48	1	30
Do	654	48	1	30
ARD, DAVID, claim for relief	408	30	1	16
ARD, HORACE B., claim for relief	32	42	2	26
ARD, ISAAC, claim for relief	407	30	1	16
ARD, PELATIAH, claim for relief	107	27	3	11
Do	136	30	2	17
ARD, WILLIAM, claim for relief	665	45	2	27
Do	864	46	2	28
Do	865	46	2	28
Do	525	47	1	29
Do	219	48	1	30
IARD, JOSEPH, claim for relief	701	26	1	10
IERD, MOSES, Government contract, Cumberland road, claim for extra work	258	20	1	4
BURNE, JONATHAN W., claim for relief of administrator	633	24	1	8
Do	638	29	1	14
EY, BENJAMIN, claim for relief	333	22	1	6
Do	4	23	1	7
DAN, FREDERICK, claim for relief	4	38	2	25
IAN, ABNER, claim for relief	899	25	2	9
IER, JOSEPH (guardian), claim for relief	68	33	1	19
WOOD, DANIEL, claim for relief	469	24	1	8
D, EDWARD M., claim for relief of heirs	1240	48	1	30
ITO, SARAH, claim for relief	26	18	2	2
ULT, DIXON, and others, claim for relief	304	43	2	26
EY, ETHER (administrator), claim for relief	15	16	1	1
EY, E. R., claim for relief	899	49	1	31
IAN, CHARLES, claim for relief	267	27	2	11
IAN, STEPHEN, claim for relief	727	27	2	11
EY, JAMES Q., claim for relief	1417	48	1	30
IAKER, GEORGE R., claim for relief of heirs	106	31	1	18
IAKER, INDIANA, claim for relief	157	30	1	15
), JOSEPH, claim for relief	5	19	1	3
T, CELIA C., claim for relief	423	44	1	27
T, O. F., Mrs., claim for relief	421	44	1	27
Do	422	44	1	27
Do	404	45	2	27
VE, HENRY M., claim for relief of heirs	88	33	2	19
Do	577	46	2	28
PHIRE & ROSS, claim for relief	711	26	1	10
REN, R., claim for relief	458	36	1	22
L, J. B., claim for relief of heirs	544	35	1	21
Do	15	36	1	22
T, FRANK, claim for relief	2428	49	1	31
LD, CHARLES F., land grant, claim for damages against	323	24	2	8
Do	473	27	2	11
Do	38	31	2	18
Y, G. O., commissioner to lay out a road from Missouri to Mexico, compensation	416	21	1	5
Y, HENRY H., claim for relief	*1722	49	1	31
Do	*3772	49	2	32
Y, SOLOMON, claim for relief	87	18	1	2
, JOSEPH, claim for relief	38	17	2	1
ER, reducing, from its solution in nitric acid by use of common salt, claim of Franklin Peale for discovery of	424	35	1	21
Do	464	36	1	22
S, CHARLES, claim for relief of heirs	12	34	1	20
NDS, PRISCILLA C., claim for relief	118	33	1	19
NTON, ISAAC P., claim for relief of heirs of	3	33	1	19
SON, MORGAN, claim for relief	657	25	2	9
Do	769	27	2	11
SON, STEPHEN and others, claim for relief	747	24	1	8
SON, THOMAS, claim for relief	49	26	1	10
TON, GEORGE, claim for relief	402	31	1	18
Do	9	33	1	19
LAIR, ARTHUR, claim for relief	599	25	2	9
ARD, THOMAS, claim for relief	340	25	2	9
E, ALBERT O., claim for relief	239	47	1	29

* Views of minority.

Subject.	Report.	Congress.	Session.	Volume.
SIZER, SAMUEL D., claim for relief	417	29	1	13
SKINNER, FLORA, claim for relief	3026	49	1	31
SLAVES, claim for, taken by British in Revolutionary war	471	36	1	22
SLOAN, JAMES, claim for relief	782	29	1	14
Do	659	30	1	17
SLUDER, Mrs. JULIA A. (executrix), claim for relief	3771	49	2	32
SMALLEY, HENRY, claim for relief	123	37	2	25
SMART, ROBERT, claim for relief	366	21	1	5
SMILEY, ALEXANDER, claim for relief	296	49	1	31
SMITH, AARON, claim for relief	248	22	1	7
SMITH, ADAM, claim for relief	467	25	2	9
SMITH, AMBROSE D. (*see also* SMITH, JAMES P.), claim for relief	35	17	2	1
SMITH, ANTON, claim for relief	113	41	2	25
SMITH, CATHARINE M., claim for relief	775	24	1	8
SMITH, CHARLES, claim for relief	838	25	2	9
SMITH, CHAUNCEY, claim for relief	6	36	1	22
SMITH, ELLIOT, claim for relief	268	31	1	18
SMITH, FREDERICK, claim for relief	82	41	2	25
SMITH, FREDERICK W., claim for relief	562	28	1	12
SMITH, GAMALIEL E., claim for relief	567	24	1	8
Do	1065	25	2	9
Do	18	26	1	10
Do	78	27	3	10
SMITH, GUY W., claim for relief	483	22	1	6
SMITH, HENRY C., claim for relief	204	43	1	26
SMITH, HENRY H., claim for relief	337	46	2	28
SMITH, ISAAC, claim for relief	458	36	1	22
SMITH, JABEZ, claim for relief	395	29	1	13
SMITH, JACOB, claim for relief	557	23	1	7
SMITH, JAMES, claim for relief	64	21	1	5
SMITH, JAMES C., claim for relief	1691	46	2	28
SMITH, JAMES P., claim for relief	35	17	2	1
SMITH, JAMES Y., claim for relief	666	30	1	17
SMITH, JANE, claim for relief	112	35	1	21
Do	399	36	1	22
SMITH, JEREMIAH, JR., claim for relief	148	28	2	12
SMITH, JESSE, *et al.*, claim for offset in United States courts against the United States, in suit of	115	22		6
Do	202	23		7
Do	8	24		7
SMITH, JOEL M., claim for relief	214	35		21
Do	160	36		22
SMITH, JOHN B., claim for relief	38	18		2
Do	508	30		17
SMITH, JOHN L., claim for relief	89	33	2	19
SMITH, JOSEPH, claim for relief	12	18	2	2
SMITH, LUCY A., claim for relief	97	41	2	25
SMITH, NATHAN and CHARLES H., claim for relief	128	20	1	13
SMITH, NATHANIEL G., claim for relief	519	44	1	27
Do	309	45	2	27
SMITH, PATRICK, claim for relief	643	27	2	11
Do	72	29	1	13
SMITH, PETER, claim for relief	1005	25		9
SMITH, RICHARD, and others, claim for relief	268	21		5
SMITH, RUFUS C., claim for relief	425	47		29
SMITH, SAMUEL, and others, claim for relief	455	23		7
SMITH, THOMAS, claim for relief	2429	49	1	31
Do	4002	49	2	32
SMITH, THOMAS A., claim for relief	471	25	2	9
SMITH, THURGAR & CO., claim for relief	57	29	1	13
Do	54	29	2	14
Do	65	30		15
SMITH, WILLIAM, claim for relief	456	22	1	6
SMITH, WILLIAM G., claim for relief	322	33	1	19
SMITH, WILLIAM J., claim for relief	1843	48	1	30
Do	2273	49	1	31
Do	2490	49	1	31
SMITH, WILLIAM T., and others, claim for relief	121	45	2	27
Do	908	46	2	28
Do	200	47	1	29
SMOOT, BENJAMIN S., claim for relief	61	21	2	5
Do	89	22	2	6
SMYTH, BERNARD, claim for relief	354	48	1	30
SNAVELY, WILLIAM, claim for relief	647	30		17
SNIDER, DANIEL, claim for relief	788	25	2	9
SNIDER, JACOB, claim for relief	100	18	1	2
SNOW, ISAAC, claim for relief of heirs	565	28	1	12
SNYDER, ALONZO, claim for relief	137	43	1	26
Do	1834	46	2	28
Do	1059	47	1	29
SNYDER, JOHN, claim for relief of heirs	58	30	1	15

Subject.	Report.	Congress.	Session.	Volume.
SNYDER, WILLIAM C., claim for relief	10	44	2	27
SOMERS, PATRICK, claim for relief	458	36	1	22
SONE AND FLEMING MANUFACTURING COMPANY, NEW YORK CITY, claim for relief	1515	48	1	30
Do	3330	49	1	31
SOPER, ENOS, claim for relief	574	26	1	10
SOPER, ROBERT, and others, claim for relief	16	42	2	26
SORRELLS, JACKSON T., claim for relief	322	43	2	26
Do	418	44	1	27
SOUDER, CHARLES, claim for relief	922	25	2	9
SOULE, FRANK, claim for relief	178	49	1	31
SOULE, GEORGE W., claim for relief	1019	48	1	30
SOUTH CAROLINA,				
Arms furnished to militia in 1812, claim for	141	23	1	6
Field officers of fourth brigade State troops of	3122	49	1	31
Interest on bonds issued for military purposes, payment of	249	20	1	4
War of 1812, claim for advances made during	246	20	1	4
Do	141	22	1	6
SOUTH WINDSOR, CONNECTICUT, for relief of town of, on account of damages done to Bissell's Ferry	3958	49	2	32
SPAIN, claim of citizens for loss of slaves under treaty of February 19, 1819, with	723	27	2	11
Do	908	27	2	11
SPARKS, ORSON, claim for relief	33	20	1	4
Do	27	20	2	4
Do	3	21	1	5
SPARKS, THOMAS P., and others, claim for relief	1433	46	2	28
SPEAKMAN, JOHN, claim for relief of heirs	537	29	1	13
SPENCE, ROBERT T., claim for relief of administrator	750	27	2	11
SPENCER, DANIEL, claim for relief	763	27	2	11
Do	362	29	1	13
SPENCER, GEORGE D., claim for relief	728	27	2	11
Do	127	28	2	12
Do	18	29	1	13
SPENCER, JOHN, claim for relief	183	23	1	7
SPENCER, NANNIE, claim for relief	15	45	2	27
SPENCER, PELEG, claim for relief	169	23	1	7
SPENCER, SAMUEL B., claim for relief	133	30	2	17
SPICER, THOMAS, claim for relief	829	25	2	9
SPILLERS, WILLIAM H., claim for relief	544	24	1	8
Do	317	25	3	9
SPITZER, SOLOMON, claim for relief	1569	47	1	29
Do	2698	48		30
Do	1294	49	1	31
SPOTSWOOD, NORBORNE B., claim for relief	159	24	1	8
SPRAGUE, EPHRAIM, claim for relief	642	27	2	11
SPRAGUE, THOMAS S., claim for relief	395	35	1	21
SPRINGFIELD MANUFACTURING COMPANY, claim for arms furnished	535	23	1	7
Do	21	23	2	7
Do	40	24	1	7
Do	372	25	2	9
Do	305	26	1	11
Do	6	27	2	11
SQUIRRELL, JACOB, claim for relief of administrator	39	21	2	5
STAFFORD, SPENCER, claim for relief on postmaster's bond (Albany, N. Y.)	524	23	1	7
STALKER, GILBERT,				
Claim for relief	1	28	1	12
Do	498	31	1	18
Claim for relief of administrator of	20	36	1	22
STALKER & HILL, claim for relief	755	29	1	14
Do	118	30	1	15
STALL, MARIA B., claim for relief	564	29	1	13
STANDISH, JOHN H., claim for relief	1237	46	2	28
STANDLEY, ANDREW W., *et al.*, owners of brig Albert, claim for relief	690	29	1	14
STANIFORD, DANIEL, claim for relief	523	23	1	7
STANSBURY, CHARLES F., claim for relief	2	37	3	25
STANSBURY, TOBIAS E., claim for relief	125	15	1	1
Do	45	19	2	3
Do	9	22	2	6
STANSBURY, WILLIAM, claim for relief	45	19	2	3
Do	9	22	2	6
STANWOOD & REID, and others, claim for relief	190	34	3	20
Do	632	36	1	22
STATE NATIONAL BANK OF LOUISIANA, claim for relief	1674	47	1	29
Do	1415	48	1	30
STATES,				
Disloyal, claims of citizens of	10	39	1	25
War of 1812, adjudicating losses of, during	147½	15	1	1
Do	249	20	1	4
War tax of 1861, to prohibit, being made set-off against claims of	562	49	1	31
STAUBER, SAMUEL B., and others, claim for relief	576	44	1	27

Subject.	Report.	Congress.	Session.	Volume.
STEAMBOAT,				
Invention of, claim of Robert Fulton	300	24	2	8
Do	551	24	1	8
Do	744	24	1	8
Do	588	27	2	11
Do	127	28	1	12
Do	3	28	2	12
Do	256	30	1	16
Claim of John Fitch	124	29	1	13
Claim of James Rumsey	403	29	1	13
STEARNS, CATHARINE, claim for relief	2	20	1	4
STEBBINS, JOHN C., and others, claim for relief	250	24	2	20
STEEDMAN, CHARLES, claim for relief	88	41	2	25
STEELE, AUGUSTUS, claim for relief	761	27	2	11
Do	80	31	2	19
STEELE, GEORGE, claim for relief	497	28	1	12
STEELE, HIRAM, claim for relief	57	22	2	6
STEELE, RICHARD W., claim for relief	142	19	1	3
Do	67	19	2	3
STEENROD, DANIEL, contract on Cumberland road, claim for relief	835	24	1	8
Do	588	25	2	9
Do	298	25	3	9
Do	87	28	1	12
Do	255	29	1	13
Do	251	30	1	16
Do	78	31	1	18
Do	49	33	1	19
STEIN, JOHN, claim for relief	90	28	2	12
STEINMAN, JOHN, and others, claim for relief	61	19	1	3
STELSON, ABNER, claim for relief	120	22	2	7
Do	39	24	1	7
STEPHENS, FREDERICK, claim for relief	178	34	1	20
STERLING, JOHN, claim for relief	458	36	1	22
STERRELT, SAMUEL, claim for relief	167	19	1	3
STETSON, AMASA, claim for difference between specie and Treasury notes, 1812	95	17	2	1
STEUART, JOHN C., and others, claim for relief	756	29	1	14
STEVENS, EDWIN, claim for relief	1949	49	1	31
STEVENS, JOHN A., claim for relief of heirs	7	38	2	25
STEVENS, JOSEPH L., claim for relief	83	45	2	27
Do	874	46	2	28
Do	73	47	1	28
STEVENSON, JOHN, claim for relief	840	24	1	8
STEVENSON, ROBERT, and others, claim for relief	842	46	2	28
STEVENSON, SAMUEL, claim for relief	126	28	2	12
STEWART, CHARLES, claim for relief	106	30	2	17
Do	103	31	1	18
STEWART, CHARLES B., claim for relief of widow	792	47	1	29
STEWART, FRANCIS B., claim for relief	671	48	1	26
STEWART, JAMES, claim for relief of heirs	302	49	1	31
STEWART, MATTHEW, claim for relief of heirs	794	29	1	14
Do	69	30	1	15
STICKNEY, BENJAMIN FRANKLIN, claim for relief	487	23	1	7
Do	18	24	1	7
STIENROD, DANIEL, claim for relief	835	24	1	8
STILES, GEORGE P., claim for relief	197	35	2	21
STILES, JOHN S., and others, naval supplies, contract for, relief	128	22	2	6
Do	530	23	1	7
Do	625	24	1	8
STOCKS, WILLIAM, claim for relief	201	30	1	15
STOCKTON, GEORGE, claim for relief	19	21	2	5
Do	401	23	1	7
STOKER, HENRY, claim for slave killed by United States soldiers	1008	25	2	9
Do	836	28	1	12
STOKES, WILLIAM B., claim for relief	317	49	1	31
STONE, DAVID, claim for relief	541	25	2	9
STONE, F. A., claim for relief	372	43	1	26
STONE, H., claim for relief	883	25	2	9
STONE, MARY S., claim for relief	1787	47	1	29
STONE, THOMAS J., claim for relief	681	26	1	10
Do	342	27	2	11
STONESIFERT, JACOB, claim for relief	634	29	1	14
STOTESBURY, CHARLES, claim for relief	2172	49	1	31
STOUT, WILLIAM, claim for relief	128	25	3	9
STOWE, WILLIAM P., claim for relief	184	44	1	27
STRACHAN, ROBERT, claim for relief	826	49	1	31
Do	[illegible]	49	1	31
STRATTON, THOMAS T., claim for relief	1918	47	2	29
Do	2010	48	1	30
STREET, J. M., claim for relief	437	22	1	6

Subject.	Report.	Congress.	Session.	Volume.
, WILLIAM W., claim for relief	77	27	3	11
Do	[illegible]	46	2	28
ER, G. W., claim for relief	1884	46	1	30
LAND, VINCENT J., claim for relief	401	36	1	16
Do	941	27	2	11
R, THOMAS, claim for relief	[illegible]	45	3	27
R, WILLIAM, claim for relief	810	25	2	9
, MOSES M., claim for relief	748	27	3	11
ER, GEORGE F., receiver of public moneys at Saint Louis, Mo	396	24	1	8
, ADAM D., claim for relief	817	26	1	10
, D. McV., claim for relief	102	33	1	25
, BENNET & CO., claim for relief	169	34	3	20
RICHARD, claim for relief	1345	46	2	28
ON, CHARLES, claim for relief	251	25	3	9
Do	372	26	1	10
Do	346	28	1	12
N'S MATES, claim for additional pay	289	24	2	8
N, SAMUEL, claim for relief	3035	48	1	31
, lien on soldiers' pay for goods sold	30	22	1	6
Do	258	22	1	6
Do	97	22	2	6
Do	6	23	1	7
Do	250	23	1	7
Do	9	24	1	7
, MILO, claim for relief	48	37	3	25
Do	4	38	1	25
& CASE, claim for relief	23	36	2	22
, JOHN A., claim for relief	297	46	3	29
, EPHRAIM, claim for relief	169	19	1	3
, MOSES, claim for relief	956	24	1	8
, FRANCAISE, claim for relief	145	23	1	7
FRANCES, claim for relief	135	28	2	12
AMOS, and others, claim for relief	109	20	1	4
RICHARD H., claim for relief	45	42	1	25
RD, A. P. (Governor of Alaska), claim for salary	2668	49	2	32
, JAMES V., claim for relief	1944	48	1	30
K, ANDREW, claim for relief	589	25	2	9
T, ARTHUR, claim for relief	566	24	1	8
T, JOHN, claim for relief	1418	48	1	30
Do	604	49	1	31
T, WILLIAM, claim for relief	664	49	1	31
T, ENOCH B., claim for relief	189	35	1	21
OOSA (United States Steamer), claim for relief of sufferers by wreck of	825	49	1	31
Do	3402	49	1	31
AUGUSTINE, claim for relief	490	22	1	6
HILL, WILKINS, claims for relief	63	19	1	3
Do	107	21	1	5
RONA, PETER, claim for relief	866	45	2	27
Do	1692	46	2	28
Do	1786	47	1	29
ATHANIEL, claim for relief	48	41	2	25
O, LOUIS FITZGERALD, claim for relief	547	35	1	21
NATHANIEL P., claim for relief	482	23	1	7
Do	17	24	1	7
THOMAS, claim for relief	580	26	1	10
Do	344	28	1	12
, ISAAC D., claim for relief of heirs	161	30	1	15
e, to refund in certain cases	102	47	1	25
al-revenue, on bonds of banking and insurance companies	476	49	1	31
al-revenue, imposed in thirty-second collection district of New York, claim to refund, referred to Court of Claims	101	47	1	25
al-revenue, to refund, to Vicksburg and Meridian Railroad Company	1292	49	1	31
DIRECT, apportioned among the several States and Territories and District of Columbia	*2486	48	2	30
, B. O., claim for relief	795	29	1	14
Do	151	30	1	15
, DAVID, claim for relief	41	17	2	1
GEORGE W., claim for relief	1233	46	2	28
JAMES, claim for relief	94	22	2	6
Do	552	23	1	7
Do	422	26	1	10
, JANE, claim for relief	582	23	1	7
, JONATHAN, claim for relief	133	21	1	5
Do	23	25	2	9
SAMUEL H., claim for relief	5	35	2	21
Do	334	36	1	22
, THOMAS W., claim for relief	275	25	3	9
Do	15	26	1	10

* Views of minority.

Subject.	Report.	Congress.	Session.	Volume.
TAYLOR, VINCENT, claim for relief	386	22	1	7
TAYLOR, WILLIAM RUFUS (administrator), claim for relief	517	24	1	8
Do	23	25	2	9
TEALL, HIRAM & CO., claim for relief	841	29	1	14
TEAL, NATHANIEL, claim for relief	786	24	1	8
TEDROW, J. L., claim for relief	306	43	1	26
TEED, THEODORE, claim for relief	2153	48	1	30
Do	1837	49	1	31
TENNESSEE,				
Citizens of Bedford and other counties, to refund income tax collected from	102	47	1	29
Do	(*)	47	1	29
Seminole war claims, payment to citizens of	84	16	1	1
Do	26	16	2	1
Do	13	17	1	1
Volunteers in war with Mexico, muster and pay of	196	24	2	8
Do	597	30	1	17
TENNESSEE RIVER IMPROVEMENT, to audit unadjusted contracts of	2	36	1	22
TERRITORY OF KANSAS (*see also* KANSAS), claims of citizens for relief	104	36	2	23
TERRY, ENOS, claim for relief	40	17	2	1
Do	74	18	1	2
TESTING IRON, STEEL, and OTHER BUILDING MATERIAL, claim of A. H. Emery for constructing machine for, at Watertown Arsenal, New York	1584	46	2	28
Do	226	47	1	29
Do	484	48	1	30
Do	2527	49	1	31
THACHER, NORMAN, claim for relief	3896	49	2	32
THACHER, THOMAS, claim for relief	1975	47	2	29
Do	1506	48	1	30
THARP, WILLIAM, claim for relief	374	21	1	5
Do	97	22	2	6
Do	230	24	2	8
Do	63	25	2	9
THAYER, ELI, and others, claim for relief	24	33	1	25
THOMAS, A. A., claim for relief	2114	48	1	30
Do	1156	49	1	31
THOMAS, ALEXANDER, claim for relief	2421	48	2	30
Do	2279	49	1	31
THOMAS, DAVID, claim for relief	578	29	1	14
Do	28	29	2	14
Do	95	30	1	15
THOMAS, GREGORY, and others, claim for relief	162	29	1	13
THOMAS, ISRAEL, claim for relief	129	28	1	12
THOMAS, JOHN (major-general), settlement of accounts	33	16	2	1
THOMAS, JOHN L., claim for relief	697	44	1	27
Do	188	45	2	27
THOMAS, JOHN & CO., claim for relief	41	17	1	1
Do	39	17	2	1
THOMAS, JOSEPH S., claim for relief	41	23	1	7
Do	233	24	1	8
Do	33	26	2	10
THOMAS, LOUIS G. and E. K., claim for relief	68	33	1	19
THOMAS, MARTIN (lieutenant U. S. Army), ordnance officer, claim for developing the lead mines of United States	76	18	2	2
Do	576	29	1	13
Do	60	30	1	15
THOMAS, WILLIAM, claim for relief	315	25	3	9
THOMAS, WILLIAM W., claim for relief	228	48	1	30
THOMPSON, A. H., claim for relief	1682	48	1	30
THOMPSON, E. A., claim for relief	115	33	1	25
THOMPSON, E. P., claim for relief	1671	47	1	29
Do	2011	48	1	30
Do	1828	49	1	31
THOMPSON, ELIZABETH, claim for relief	5	28	2	12
THOMPSON, FRANCIS B., claim for relief	661	24	1	8
THOMPSON, JOHN,				
Claim for relief	2	22	2	6
Do	12	23	1	7
Claim for relief of widow	69	22	2	6
Do	181	23	1	7
THOMPSON, JOHN A., claim for relief	3898	49	2	32
THOMPSON, JOHN C., claim for relief	1232	48		30
Do	2859	49		31
THOMPSON, JOSIAS, claim for relief	556	23	1	7
Do	63	24	1	8
Do	663	25	2	9
Do	23	26	1	11
Do	471	27	2	11
THOMPSON, S. A., claim for relief	307	33	1	19

* Part 2.

Subject.	Report.	Congress.	Session.	Volume.
ON, SAMUEL, claim for relief	805	22	1	6
Do	2	23	1	7
Do	735	27	2	11
ON, THOMAS, claim for relief	563	28	1	12
Do	98	28	2	12
ON, WILLIAM, claim for relief	35	19	1	3
Do	6	20	1	4
Do	85	28	1	12
ON, WILLIAM H., claim for relief	14	45	3	27
JAMES, and others, claim for relief	57	21	2	5
URGH, GEORGE, claim for relief	790	24	1	8
, WILLIAM P., claim for relief	2276	49	1	31
THOMAS E., claim for relief	233	30	1	16
N, Dr., and others, claim for relief	167	19	1	3
KER, L. A., claim for relief	422	44	1	27
MORTON, J., claim for relief	595	27	2	11
Do	782	29	1	14
Do	28	30	1	15
JR, EZRA, claim for relief	19	20	2	6
Do	15	21	1	5
Do	73	35	2	21
AAC P., claim for relief estate	2491	49	1	31
Do	3020	49	1	31
ORNELIUS, claim for relief	690	24	1	8
Do	508	25	2	9
Do	21	26	1	10
Y, THOMAS J., claim for relief	895	47	1	29
HORATIO, claim for relief	258	23	1	7
D, JAMES, claim for relief	308	22	1	6
Do	125	23	1	7
Do	1	24	1	8
D, WILLIAM S., claim for relief of heirs	158	27	3	11
SAMUEL, claim for relief	362	24	1	8
Do	558	25	2	9
N, LACON R., claim for relief	719	43	1	20
Do	1278	49	1	31
DEPREDATIONS UPON UNITED STATES LANDS, claims for sstalement	388	29	1	13
Do	384	29	1	13
, WILLIAM, claim for relief of estate	2024	47	2	29
Do	2492	49	1	31
Do	3390	49	1	31
RTH, M. D., claim for relief	682	45	2	27
Do	1841	46	2	28
O DESTROYED IN WAR OF 1812, claim for	44	34	3	20
Do	45	34	3	20
Do	48	34	3	20
Do	49	34	3	20
Do	50	34	3	20
Do	51	34	3	20
ERNARD, claim for relief of heirs	639	29	1	14
Do	255	30	1	16
Do	157	31	1	18
Do	122	32	1	19
ARRY I., claim for relief	1123	49	1	31
Do	1124	49	1	31
AMUEL P., claim for relief	47	45	2	27
Do	49	45	2	27
HOMAS W., claim for relief	29	18	1	1
& EATON, claim for relief	880	46	2	28
NS, DANIEL, respecting claim of	410	31	1	18
, JAMES, claim for relief	321	24	2	8
Do	1046	25	2	9
, JOHN, claim for relief	55	27	3	11
E DUES, foreign steamship companies, illegal exaction of	661	49	1	31
E TAXES, to refund to the Brazil Mail Steamship Company, illegally collected	84	41	2	25
, JOHN A., claim for relief	809	47	1	29
, WILLIAM H., claim for relief	372	29	1	13
Do	92	33	1	19
, JOSEPH G., claim for relief	52	36	2	22
Do	24	37	2	25
ALBERT, claim for relief	894	45	2	27
IRAM S., claim for relief	1921	47	2	29
HOMAS B., claim for relief	846	25	2	9
ND, CHARLES, claim for relief	42	17	2	1
Do	64	28	2	12
ND, L. B., and others, to release as surety on bond of John C. Dexter	3736	49	2	32
ND, JACOB, claim for relief	130	23	1	7
ND, WILLIAM, claim for relief	76	39	1	25

Subject.	Report.	Congress.	Session.	Volume.
TOWNSLEY, THOMAS F., claim for relief	267	23	1	7
Do	4	24	1	7
TRACY, ELISHA, claim for relief	354	21	1	5
TRAFTON, JOHN, claim for relief	32	27	2	11
TRAINER, JOHN B., claim for relief	392	46	3	28
Do	70	47	1	29
TRAMEL, GEORGE S., claim for relief	1590	46	2	28
TRASK, J. NELSON, claim for relief	1227	48	1	30
TRAVERSE, WILLIAM, claim for relief	965	25	2	9
TRAVILLA, ROBERT, claim for relief	1672	47	1	29
TREASURY DEPARTMENT,				
Clerical force in office of Second Auditor, to increase	598	30	1	17
Drawback of duties on goods re-exported	458	30	1	16
First Comptroller, relating to duties of	645	27	2	11
TREASURY NOTES, loss of, by fire, to reimburse owners of	116	38	1	25
TREATIES, compensation to owners of certain lands ceded by United States to Great Britain in 1842	99	44	1	27
TRECHEL, G. C., claim for relief of heirs of	544	35	1	21
Do	15	36	1	22
TREDEGAR IRON COMPANY OF RICHMOND, VIRGINIA, claim for relief	621	29	1	14
TREFETHEN, WILLIAM, claim for relief	2002	49	1	31
TREUTLEN, JOHN R., claim for relief	2424	49	1	31
TRIMBLE, ISAAC R., claim for relief of trustees	1886	49	1	31
TRIMBLE, MARY J., claim for relief	1678	47	1	29
TRIPLETT, T. H., claim for relief	480	49	1	31
TROW, BARTHOLOMEW, claim for relief of heirs	334	25	2	9
TROWBRIDGE, SABIN, claim for relief	677	45	2	27
Do	902	46	2	28
Do	95	47	1	29
TRUFTON, JOHN, claim for relief	24	26	2	10
TRUST FUND, to reimburse the State of Wisconsin for advances made from canal trust fund	20	39	2	26
TRYON, WILLIAM, claim for relief	106	25	3	9
Do	26	27	2	11
TSCHIFFELY, FREDERICK D., claim for relief	11	19	2	3
TUCK, SAMUEL B., claim for relief	105	26	2	10
Do	734	27	2	11
Do	3	27	3	11
Do	71	28	1	12
TULLER & FISHER, claim for relief	87	39	1	26
TUPPER, SAMUEL, claim for relief of widow	322	21	1	5
TURK, HIRAM K., claim for relief	555	25	2	9
TURMAN, BENJAMIN, claim for relief of heirs	501	28	1	12
TURNBULL, GEORGE, claim for relief	247	22	1	6
TURNER, ALEXANDER, claim for relief	188	35	1	21
TURNER, DANIEL, claim for relief	458	36	1	22
TURNER, J. D., claim for relief	80	38	1	25
TURNER, WILLIAM J., claim for relief	599	30	1	17
TURNIPSEED, DANIEL, claim for relief	672	29	1	14
TURNPIKE COMPANY, WASHINGTON AND ALEXANDRIA, claim for relief	54	41	2	26
TURVIN, WILLIAM, claim for relief of heirs	244	35	1	21
TUTT, ANN MASON, claim for relief	241	26	2	10
TUTT, JOHN A. S., claim for relief of heirs	1296	49	1	31
TWEEDY, JOHN, claim for relief	388	45	2	27
Do	133	47	1	29
TWELFTH UNITED STATES LIGHT-HOUSE DISTRICT, for relief of employés at	471	49	1	31
TWIGGS, DAVID E. (colonel United States Army), claim for relief	487	22	1	6
Do	485	22	1	6
TWIST, MARTHA, claim for relief	29	28	2	12
TWITCHELL, TIMOTHY, claim for relief	241	22	1	6
TYNER, THOMAS, claim for relief	786	24	1	8
Do	56	25	2	9
TYRONE, PENNSYLVANIA,				
Baptist church at, relief	81	39	1	26
United Brethren church at, relief	81	39	1	26
TYSON, BRYANT, claim for relief	1327	49	1	31
TYSON, JOHN S., claim for relief	633	24	1	8
Do	638	29	1	14
UNCAPHER, ISAAC, claim for relief of assignee	302	43	2	26
UNDERWOOD, JOHN, claim for relief	22	26	1	10
Do	60	27	2	11
UNDERWOOD, WILLIAM, claim for relief	733	27	2	11
UNION BANK OF FLORIDA, claim for relief	726	30	1	17
UNITED STATES,				
Board of commissioners, to refer all claims to	496	30	1	16
Legislation relative to claims against the	496	30	1	16
Claims against	154	48	1	30
Liability of the United States for private property destroyed in time of war by forces hostile to	386	22	1	6

Subject.	Report.	Congress.	Session.	Volume.
UNITED STATES—Continued.				
Liability of the United States for private property destroyed in time of war by forces hostile to	413	22	1	6
Do	414	22	1	6
Do	490	22	1	6
Do	492	22	1	6
Do	501	22	1	6
UNITED STATES COURTS. (*See* COURTS OF THE UNITED STATES.)				
UNIVERSITY OF NOTRE DAME DU LAC, to refund custom duties paid by	666	45	2	27
Do	909	46	2	28
UNKART & DREYER, claim for relief	802	29	1	14
UNLAND, ERNEST F., claim for relief	1098	47	1	29
UPHAM, SAMUEL O., claim for relief	906	46	2	28
Do	103	47	1	29
UPTON, JAMES, claim for relief	458	36	1	22
UPTON, WILLIAM, claim for relief	458	36	1	22
UTAH EXPEDITION, to adjudicate claims of	2650	48	2	30
UTICA STEAM WOOLEN COMPANY, claim for relief	50	33	1	19
VAIL, WILLIAM, claim for relief	84	42	2	26
VALETTE, ELI, claim for relief of heirs of	544	35	1	21
Do	15	36	1	22
VALLEJO, MARIANO G., claim for relief	7	36	1	22
VAN BIBBER, ANDREW A., claim for relief	662	24	1	8
VAN BRUNT, RULIF, claim for relief	334	33	1	19
VAN CAMP, AARON, claim for relief	212	35	2	21
Do	569	36	1	22
VANCE, JACOB, claim for relief	342	27	2	11
VANCE, JACOB L., claim for relief	51	28	2	12
Do	193	29	1	13
Do	314	29	1	13
VANCE, JAMES and WILLIAM, claim for relief	1591	46	2	28
Do	1234	48	1	30
VAN COTT, JOHN, claim for relief	391	45	2	27
VANDERBILT, CORNELIUS, claim for payment of bills accepted by Post-Office Department	722	25	2	9
VAN DUYN, ABRAM, claim for relief of heirs	1564	46	2	28
VAN HORN, JAMES, claim for relief	328	33	1	19
VAN KLEECK, LAWRENCE L., claim for relief	67	21	2	5
VAN NESS, EDWARD, claim for relief	67	34	1	20
VANNETHEN, JOHN, & CO., claim for relief	254	24	2	8
VANNETHEN, JOHN, claim for relief	582	25	2	9
VAN VOORHIS, DANIEL, claim for relief	277	23	1	7
VARIAN, LEMUEL W., claim for relief	687	26	1	10
VAUGHAN, JAMES B., claim for relief	3	22	2	6
Do	13	23	1	7
VAUGHN, WILLIAM, claim for relief	25	27	2	11
VEAZIE, JAMES H., claim for relief	708	44	1	27
VEITCH, JOHN, claim for relief	63	36	2	22
VENABLE, CHARLES H., claim for relief	400	35	1	21
VESSELS.				
Brig Albert, for relief of owners of	690	29	1	14
Brig Cadmus, violation of maritime laws, relief of owners of	224	29	1	13
Collisions of private, with United States war-ships, liability of United States for	162	29	1	13
Schooner Walter B. Chester, relief of owners	1033	47	1	29
Ship Ariadne, American, settlement of prize case of	199	25	2	9
Do	20	26	1	10
Do	808	29	1	14
Ship Experiment, capture of, claim of owner for relief	2	30	1	15
Do	805	29	1	14
Ship James Mitchell (British), salvage, claim for	264	31	1	18
Steamship companies (foreign) tonnage dues, illegal exaction of	661	49	1	31
Sunk in harbor of Baltimore for defense of city	11	16	2	1
Do	1	17		1
Do	6	18		2
Do	167	19		3
Do	221	20		4
Do	128	22		6
United States steamer Ashuelot, for relief of crew of	824	49		31
Do	3128	49		31
United States war-ship Hornet, settlement of accounts of purser of	78	22		6
Do	781	24		8
Do	1027	27		11
Do	313	28		12
Do	4	28		12
Do	435	29		13
Do	250	30		16
United States steamer Tallapoosa, for relief of sufferers by wreck of	825	49		31
Do	3402	49		31
Whaling, Midas, Progress, and others, claim of owner for conveying ship-wrecked seamen to Honolulu	121	45		27

Subject.	Report.	Congress.	Session.	Volume.
VESSELS,				
Whaling, Midas, Progress, and others, claim of owner for conveying shipwrecked seamen to Honolulu	908	46	2	26
Do	200	47	1	28
VICKSBURG AND MERIDIAN RAILROAD COMPANY, claim for relief	1729	47	1	28
Do	1282	49	1	31
VIGO, FRANCIS, claim for moneys advanced United States, 1778	216	30	1	15
Do	117	33	1	19
VILLARD, ANDREW J., claim for relief	26	15	1	1
VIRGINIA, interest on bonds issued by, for military purposes	11	18	2	2
Do	189	20	1	4
Do	249	20	1	4
Do	203	46	1	25
Do	*518	49	1	31
VLEIT, GARRET, claim for relief	848	25	3	9
Do	19	26	1	10
Do	10	26	2	10
Do	843	27	2	11
VOGHT, JOHN F. H., claim for relief	405	30	1	15
Do	3	31	1	16
VOLIN, LOUIS, claim for relief	905	46	2	26
VOLLUM, EDWARD P., claim for relief	1723	46	2	26
Do	181	47	1	28
VOLUNTEERS, MISSOURI, to indemnify for loss of horses	948	25	2	9
VON SCHMIDT, ALLEXEY W., claim for relief	976	48	1	30
VON SCHMIDT, PETER, claim for relief	797	29	1	14
VROMAN, GILBERT, claim for relief	901	25	2	9
WADDILL, ABEL, claim for relief	10	30	1	15
WAGGAMAN, J. H., claim for relief	69	35	2	21
WAGGONER, ANDREW, claim for relief	65	28	2	12
WAGNER, WILLIAM F., claim for relief	74	34	3	20
Do	186	35	1	21
WAGSTAFF, SAMUEL, claim for relief	392	21	1	5
WAKEFIELD, HARVEY, claim for relief	368	25	2	9
WALDO, MOLLIE B., claim for relief	1583	46	2	26
Do	1922	47	2	28
WALDRAN, W. B., claim for relief	1918	47	2	28
WALDRON, CHARLES, claim for relief	214	24	2	8
Do	20	27	3	11
Do	158	30	1	15
WALES, GEORGE W., and others, claim for relief	190	34	3	20
Do	632	36	1	22
WALES, T. B., & CO., claim for relief	190	34	3	20
Do	632	36	1	22
WALKER, C. H., claim for relief	698	44	1	27
Do	57	45	2	27
WALKER, DABNEY, claim for relief	390	43	1	26
WALKER, EBENEZER, claim for relief	690	45	2	27
WALKER, GIDEON, claim for relief	81	28	1	12
Do	477	29	1	13
Do	647	29	1	14
Do	252	30	1	16
Do	12	31	1	18
WALKER, JOHN, claim for relief	786	24	1	8
Do	308	30	1	16
WALKER, MARY E., claim for relief	696	45	2	27
WALKER, T. A., claim for relief	673	45	2	27
WALKER, WILLIAM C., and others, claim for relief	5	38	1	25
WALKER, ZACHARIAH, claim for relief	725	29	1	14
WALLACE, ROBERT, claim for relief	1035	25	2	9
Do	823	29	1	14
Do	166	30	1	15
WALLEN, ELIAS, claim for relief	234	24	1	8
Do	214	24	2	8
Do	228	25	3	9
WALLER, HENRY, claim for relief	553	23	1	7
WALLER, JOHN, claim for relief	1677	48	1	30
WALLIS, JOSEPH, claim for relief	36	22	2	6
WALN, S. MORRIS, claim for relief	41	30	1	15
WALNUT GROVE MINING COMPANY, claim for relief of trustees of	420	43	1	26
WALTER, JACOB F., claim for relief	84	24	1	8
WALTER B. CHESTER (schooner), for relief of owners of	1083	47	1	28
WALTON, GEORGE W., claim for relief	108	26	2	10
Do	772	27	2	11
WALTON, JAMES, claim for relief	456	36	1	22
WALTON, JOSEPH, & CO., claim for relief	1391	49	1	31
WALTON, THOMAS, claim for relief	458	36	1	22
WAMACK, SUSAN A., claim for relief	857	49	1	31
WANNALL, CHARLES P., claim for relief	1081	47	1	28

* Views of minority.

Subject.	Report.	Congress.	Session.	Volume.
WARD, DAVID, claim for relief	893	46	2	28
Do	1946	48	1	30
Do	1126	49	1	31
WARD, JOSEPH D., claim for relief	107	30	2	17
Do	184	33	1	19
WARD, LAFAYETTE, claim for relief	222	43	1	26
WARD, NAHUM, claim for settlement of loan office certificates of Ohio Land Company of 1777	161	35	1	21
Do	172	36	1	22
WARD, WILLIAM., claim for relief	458	36	1	22
Do	1008	49	1	31
Do	3321	49	1	31
WARD, ZEB, claim for relief	2504	49	1	31
WARE, FRANCIS, claim for relief of heirs	1483	47	1	29
WARING, JOSEPH H., claim for relief	23	27	3	11
WARMAN, JAMES, claim for relief	778	29	1	14
WARNER, RICHARD, and others, claim for compensation	196	24	2	8
WARNER, ROBERT, claim for relief	388	45	2	27
WARREN, JOHN, & SON, claim for relief	98	38	1	25
WARREN, STEPHEN, claim for relief	187	33	1	19
WAR OF REBELLION,				
Citizens of disloyal States, claims of, payment	10	39	1	25
Massachusetts, to reimburse, for moneys expended for coast defense during	103	41	2	25
Do	9	47	1	29
Do	39	47	1	29
New Hampshire, claims of, for bounty moneys advanced to soldiers during	23	41	3	25
WAR VESSELS, contractors for, relief	17	39	2	25
WAR WITH GREAT BRITAIN, 1812,				
Half pay to widows and orphans of volunteers who fell in, for relief	415	24	1	8
Maryland, claim for interest on advances made during	116	19	1	3
Do	189	20	1	4
Do	219	20	1	4
Massachusetts, to refund moneys advanced for defense of frontier in	76	41	2	25
Michigan, for relief of sufferers in, arising from	268	20	1	4
New York, to reimburse, for moneys advanced during	143	37	2	25
Niagara, for relief of sufferers at, during	31	16	2	1
Property destroyed during, settlement of claims for	11	14	2	1
Do	177	15	1	1
Do	886	22	1	6
River Raisin claim for property destroyed at	33	16	2	1
States,				
To adjudicate losses of, during	147½	15	1	1
To adjudicate claims of, for moneys advanced during	519	49	1	31
Vessels sunk at Baltimore during, for relief of owners of	11	16	2	1
Virginia, claim of, for interest on bonds issued to assist in carrying on	11	18	2	2
Do	189	20	1	4
Do	249	20	1	4
WAR WITH MEXICO,				
Commerce and exporters, effect upon, caused by the	458	30	1	16
Tennessee volunteers, muster and pay	196	24	2	8
Do	597	30	1	17
WASHBURN, DANIEL B., claim for relief	3593	49	2	32
WASHBURN, HENRY and THOMAS, claim for relief	156	49	1	31
WASHINGTON, DISTRICT COLUMBIA, to refund to city of, the sum expended in improving streets, &c., adjacent to the property of the United States	85	39	1	25
WASHINGTON, LUND, claim for relief	241	27	2	11
Do	143	27	3	11
Do	382	28	1	12
WASHINGTON TREATY OF 1842. (*See* TREATIES.)				
WASHINGTON AND ALEXANDRIA TURNPIKE COMPANY, claim for relief	54	41	2	25
WATERMAN, BENJAMIN, claim for relief	324	23	1	7
WATKINS, ELEANOR B., claim for relief	646	29	1	14
Do	484	30	1	16
WATKINS, JAMES H., claim for relief	106	47	1	29
WATKINS, RICHARD, claim for relief	363	24	1	8
WATSON, ALEXANDER, claim for relief	1001	25	2	9
Do	694	26	1	10
Do	135	30	2	18
WATSON, CHABOT & CO., claim for relief	153	31	1	12
WATSON, E., claim for relief	458	36	1	23
WATSON, JAMES B., claim for relief	278	29	1	12
WATSON, JAMES C., claim for relief	132	28	1	13
Do	535	29	1	17
Do	724	30	1	17
Do	102	31	1	18
WATSON, JOHN, construction of vessel for United States without contract, destroyed by enemy, relief	33	20	1	4
Do	27	20	2	4
Do	3	21	1	5
Do	631	24	1	8

Subject.	Report.	Congress.	Session.	Volume.
WATSON, JOHN W., and others, claim for relief	304	43	2	26
WATTS, ELLEN, claim for relief	1585	46	2	28
WATTS, HENRY H., claim for relief	398	46	3	28
WAY, FRANCES M., claim for relief	425	46	2	28
Do	220	47	1	29
WAY, SAMUEL A., and others, claim for relief	190	34	3	20
Do	632	36	1	22
WEAD, D. D., claim for relief	6	44	2	27
Do	679	45	2	27
WEAD, JACOB, claim for relief	42	36	2	23
WEBB, ELI, claim for relief	339	24	1	8
WEBB, JOSEPH, claim for relief of heirs	205	27	3	11
Do	243	28	1	12
WEBBER, JOHN, claim for relief	485	22	1	6
Do	10	23	1	7
WEBBER, MARY C., claim for relief	113	45	3	27
WEBER, JACOB, claim for relief	18	38	1	25
WEBSTER, DAVID, claim for relief	1730	47	1	29
Do	787	48	1	30
Do	154	49	1	31
WEBSTER, J. McA., claim for relief	3123	49	1	31
WEBSTER, JOHN A., claim for relief	188	19	1	3
WEED, E. J., claim for relief of administrator	155	28	2	12
Do	29	29	1	13
Do	56	30	1	15
WEED, JACOB, claim for relief of administrators	162	36	1	22
WEEDMAN, MARY, claim for relief	771	27	2	11
WEEDON, W. W. (mail contractor), for relief of administrator and sureties of	3790	49	2	32
WEEKS, GEORGE, claim for relief	516	25	2	9
WEEKS, JAMES, Jr., claim for relief	96	41	5	2
WEER, WILLIAM, claim for relief	420	35	1	21
WELLER, SAMUEL, claim for relief	130	27	3	11
WELLS, GEORGE M., claim for relief	697	45	2	27
WELLS, JAMES H., claim for relief of widow	196	45	2	27
WELLS, JOHN, claim for relief	30	21	1	5
WELLS, RIMVAH, Jr., claim for relief	48	30	1	15
WELLS, THOMAS, claim for relief	26	39	1	25
WELSH, W. W., claim for relief	1017	48	1	30
WENDELL, JOSEPH H., claim for relief	33	22	2	6
WERNER, CHRISTOPHER, claim for relief	758	24	1	8
Do	54	25	2	9
WERTHEIMER, MORRIS J., claim for relief	2	38	2	25
WESCOTT, JOSEPH, & SON, claim for relief	907	46	2	28
Do	175	47	1	29
WEST, B. F., & CO., claim for relief	54	43	1	26
Do	247	44	1	27
WEST, SARAH JANE, claim for relief	105	31	1	16
WEST, WILLIAM W., claim for relief	836	25	2	9
WESTERN YEARLY MEETING OF FRIENDS, claim for relief	2839	49	1	31
WESTFALL, ALFRED, claim for relief	1062	25	2	9
WESTMORELAND, THOMAS P., claim for relief	2646	48	2	30
Do	978	49	1	31
WESTON, GEORGE M., claim for relief	394	35	1	21
WESTWOOD, JOHN S., claim for relief of estate	429	26	1	10
WETMORE, ALPHONZO (paymaster, U. S. Army), settlement of accounts of	228	23	1	7
WHARTON, JAMES E., claim for relief	40	40	3	25
WHARTON, SAMUEL, claim for relief	54	17	2	1
WHARTON, THOMAS J., claim for relief	341	46	2	28
Do	329	47	1	29
WHEATLEY, THOMAS, claim for relief	15	20	2	4
WHEATON, JOSEPH (Deputy Quartermaster-General),				
Settlement of accounts as	15	16	2	1
Do	43	17	2	1
Claim for relief of estate	77	37	2	25
WHEATON, WILLIAM R., claim for relief	3467	49	1	31
WHEEDON, F., claim for relief	106	26	2	10
WHEELER, F. L., claim for relief	2013	48	1	30
WHEELER, WILLIAM P., claim for relief	382	45	3	27
WHISTLER, JOHN, claim for relief	77	15	1	1
WHITAKER, J. L., claim for relief	1416	48	1	30
WHITALL, JOHN A., claim for relief	1343	46	2	28
WHITCOMB, RASSELAS, *et al.*, claim for relief	960	25	2	9
WHITE, FREDERICK,				
Claim for relief	28	17	2	1
Claim for relief of heirs	689	24	1	8
WHITE, GEORGE, claim for relief	458	36	1	22
WHITE, J. & D. *et al.*, claim for relief	141	38	1	25
WHITE, JAMES B., claim for relief	37	43	2	26
Do	600	47		29
Do	1226	47	1	29
Do	651	48	1	30

Subject.	Report.	Congress.	Session.	Volume.
WHITE, JOHN, claim for relief	161	24	1	8
Do	224	29	1	12
WHITE, JOHN C., claim for relief	1542	47	1	29
WHITE, JONATHAN, claim for relief	518	44	1	27
WHITE, JOSEPH F., claim for relief	28	17	1	1
WHITE, JUDITH (collector of customs), claim for money stolen in transit	322	22	1	7
WHITE, ROBERT D., claim for relief	1869	46	2	28
WHITE, VIRGINIA B., claim for relief	763	44	1	27
WHITE, WILLIAM, claim for relief	458	36	1	22
WHITE, WILLIAM L., claim for relief	1509	47	1	29
Do	429	25	1	[illegible]
WHITE, HORTON & GARRARD, AND OTHERS, claim for relief	141	38	1	25
WHITEHEAD, WILLIAM A., claim for relief	169	25	3	9
Do	28	27	2	1
WHITEHEAD, WILLIAM H., claim for relief	168	26	2	10
WHITEKNOCT, JONAH, claim for relief	456	36	1	22
WHITFIELD, JOHN W., et al., claim for relief of estates	2628	49	1	31
WITHERS, THOMAS C., claim for relief	45	19	1	3
WHITLOCK, AMBROSE W. (paymaster United States troops), to reimburse for money stolen from	39	16	1	1
WHITMAN, A. F., claim for relief	696	45	2	27
WHITNEY, DANIEL, claim for relief	469	23	1	7
Do	14	24	1	7
WHITNEY, B. P., claim for relief	429	30	1	16
WHITSON, HARRISON, claim for relief	43	28	2	12
Do	787	29	1	14
WHITTELSEY, A. T., claim for relief	1236	46	2	28
WIARD, NORMAN, ordnance projectiles, improvements in, claim for relief	43	41	3	25
Do	87	42	2	26
WICKHAM, WILLIAM, claim for relief	28	24	2	8
WECKIZER, JOHN H., claim for relief	171	36	1	22
WIGG, WILLIAM HAZZARD, claim for relief	6	35	2	21
Do	471	36	1	22
WIGHTMAN, JOHN, claim for relief of estate	2605	49	1	31
Do	3092	49	1	31
WILBUR, JAMES M., claim for relief	678	46	2	28
Do	3814	49	2	32
WILCOX, EBENEZER, claim for relief	451	24	1	8
WILDER, CHARLES S., claim for relief	19	45	2	27
WILDERMAN, JACOB, claim for relief	41	20	2	4
Do	41	21	1	4
WILKES COUNTY, GEORGIA, claim for relief	322	24	2	8
WILKEY, H. C., claim for relief	2430	49	1	31
WILKINS, CHARLES				
Claim for relief	96	18	1	2
Claim for relief of executors of	133	21	1	5
Do	53	23	2	7
Do	32	24	1	7
WILKINS, JOHN, claim for relief of administrator of	3	20	2	4
Do	1	21	1	5
WILKINSON, ASEL, claim for relief	65	23	1	7
WILKINSON, D. AND J., claim for relief	14	26	1	10
Do	3	27	2	11
Do	75	27	3	11
Do	821	29	1	13
WILKINSON, JOHN, claim for relief of heirs	40	25	3	9
Do	14	26	1	10
Do	15	26	2	10
WILLARD, JOHN, claim for relief as surety on paymaster's bond	3	20	1	4
Do	95	20	1	4
WILLETT, EDWARD, claim for relief	19	22	2	6
Do	16	23	1	7
WILLETT, ELIZABETH C., claim for relief	57	39	1	25
WILLIAMS, C. A., and others, owners of schooner Eva, claim for relief	4159	49	2	32
WILLIAMS, CHARLES N., claim for relief	1516	47	1	29
WILLIAMS, E. H., claim for relief	849	25	2	9
WILLIAMS, ELIZABETH, claim for relief	188	21	1	5
WILLIAMS, HENRY, claim for relief	63	15	1	1
Do	108	21	1	5
WILLIAMS, HENRY CLAY, claim for relief	10	41	3	25
WILLIAMS, J. D. and M., and others, claim for relief	190	34	3	20
Do	682	36	1	22
WILLIAMS, JAMES, claim for relief	33	27	2	11
WILLIAMS, JOHN LEE, claim for relief	241	22	1	6
WILLIAMS, J. P., claim for relief of widow	2419	48	2	30
Do	2696	48	2	30
WILLIAMS, JOHN R., claim for relief	219	24	2	8
Do	102	28	2	12
Do	191	29	1	13
Do	5	30	1	13
WILLIAMS, THOMAS, claim for relief	23	22	2	6

Subject.	Report.	Congress.	Session.	Volume.
WILLIAMS, WILLIAM G., claim for relief	315	33	1	19
WILLIAMS, WILLIAM H., claim for relief	56	25	3	9
WILLIAMS & GRAHAM, claim for relief	168	30	1	15
WILLIAMSON, A. J., claim for relief	338	33	1	19
WILLIAMSON, MILISANT and JOHN, claim for relief	538	24	1	8
WILLIS, LEWIS B., claim for relief	9	20	1	4
Do	2	28	1	13
WILLIS, STEPHEN F., claim for relief	116	39	1	25
WILLS, JAMES B., claim for relief	840	25	2	9
Do	163	25	3	9
WILLSON, JOSEPH, claim for relief	20	24	2	8
WILMOT, AMOS, claim for relief	75	35	2	21
WILSON, GEORGE, claim for relief	61	19	2	3
WILSON, H. B., claim for relief	2024	47	2	29
Do	3390	49	1	31
WILSON, JOHN, claim for relief	708	24	1	8
Do	52	25	2	9
Do	686	26	1	10
Do	183	33	1	19
Do	87	36	2	22
Do	38	37	2	25
Do	89	41	3	25
WILSON, J. A., claim for relief	3788	49	2	32
WILSON, PERRY P., claim for relief	336	46	3	28
Do	752	47	1	29
WILSON, WILLIAM, claim for relief	221	29	1	13
WILSON, WILLIAM B., claim for relief	60	42	3	26
WIND RIVER VALLEY, WYOMING TERRITORY, for relief of settlers in	1884	49	1	31
WINGERD, JANE J., claim for relief	18	35	2	21
WINGERD, JOHN B., claim for relief	731	29	1	14
WINDSOR, CONNECTICUT, relief on account of damages done to Bissell's Ferry.	3958	49	2	32
WINSLOW, DANIEL, claim for relief of sureties	314	33	1	19
Do	202	34	1	20
WINSLOW, GEORGE A., claim for relief	678	26	1	10
Do	42	27	3	11
WINTER, CHARLES, and others, claim for relief	311	33	1	19
WINTERINGER, NATHAN, claim for relief	417	24	1	8
Do	497	31	1	18
WIRT, SARAH A., claim for relief	418	30	1	16
WISCONSIN,				
Canal trust fund of the State of, relief of State	20	39	2	25
Lower Fox River in, for relief of laborers on improvement of	174	46	2	28
Do	521	47	1	29
WISDOM, JOHN H., claim for relief	159	44	2	27
WISE, ENOCH G., claim for relief	793	24	1	8
WISLIZEMES, ADOLPHUS, claim for relief	404	30	1	16
WITHERS, THOMAS C., claim for relief	55	19	2	3
WITHERSPOON & SUFFELL, claim for relief	32	45	2	27
WITNESSES IN UNITED STATES COURTS, claim for loss in attendance in certain cases	219	21	1	5
Do	408	22	1	6
Do	8	23	1	7
WOLCOTT, BENAJAH, claim for relief	202	20	1	4
WOLFE, UDOLPHO, and others, claim for relief	190	34		20
Do	632	36		22
WOLFE & CO., and others, claim for relief	190	34		20
Do	632	36		22
WOLVERTON, HIRAM, claim for relief	248	21	1	5
WOOD, CHARLES, claim for relief	117	24	2	8
Do	494	28	1	10
Do	240	31	1	18
WOOD, CHARLES O., claim for relief	3030	49	1	31
WOOD, DAVID, and others, claim for relief	190	34	3	20
Do	632	36	1	22
WOOD, GEORGE, claim for relief	247	24	2	8
WOOD, JAMES, claim for relief	353	29	1	13
WOOD, JAMES B., claim for relief	173	36	1	22
WOOD, NATHANIEL B., claim for relief	7	20	2	4
Do	2	21		5
WOOD, OLIVER, claim for relief	1291	48		30
WOOD, PALMER G (first lieutenant), claim for relief	3991	49		32
WOODBRIDGE, JOHN E., claim for relief	592	24		8
WOODBURY, ELLIOTT, claim for relief	168	33		19
WOODBURY, JACOB T., and others, owners of brig Albert, claim for relief	690	29		14
WOODLEE, MARY, claim for relief	1420	48	1	30
Do	301	49	1	31
WOODRUFF, A. B., claim for relief	18	44	2	27
WOODWARD, ISAIAH, claim for relief	399	35	1	21
WOODWARD, ROBERT, claim for relief	768	27	2	11
WOODWARD, WILLIAM, claim for relief	62	24	1	8
Do	755	30	1	17

Subject.	Report.	Congress.	Session.	Volume.
WOODWORTH, BENJAMIN, claim for relief	165	19	1	3
WOOL, JOHN E., claim for relief	116	33	1	19
WOOLSEY, MELANCTHON T., claim for relief	791	24	1	8
Do	57	25	2	9
WORDEN, L. J., claim for relief	2427	49	1	31
WORK, G. P., claim for relief	887	46	2	28
WORK, SAMUEL, claim for relief	458	36	1	22
WORSELEY, PARDON, claim for relief	490	43	1	26
Do	1241	48	1	30
WORSTER, ALEXANDER, enlistment of a minor in the Army, claim for time	21	15	1	1
Do	20	16	1	1
WORTHINGTON, SAMUEL, claim for relief	779	20	1	14
WRIGHT, HENRY (administrator), claim for relief	194	29	1	13
WRIGHT, J. P., claim for relief	1728	46	2	28
Do	599	47	1	29
WRIGHT, JOHN T., claim for relief of administrator	86	41	2	25
Do	51	43	1	26
WRIGHT, THOMAS T., claim for relief	149	28	2	12
WYOMING TERRITORY, for relief of settlers in Wind River Valley	1884	49	1	31
YARNELL, PETER, claim for relief	400	21	1	5
Do	253	22	1	6
YATES, FRANK D., and others, claim for relief	99	47	1	29
YATES, JOHN VAN NESS, claim for relief on postmaster's bond, Albany, N. Y.	524	23	1	7
YEARTY, JACOB, claim for relief	397	30	1	16
YEOMANS, STEPHEN P., claim for relief	872	46	2	28
Do	176	47	1	29
YONGE, WILLIAM, claim for relief	600	30	1	17
YORK, LAVINA, claim for relief	107	26	2	10
YORKTOWN, NEW YORK, Presbyterian church at, relief	492	31	1	18
YORKTOWN (United States steamer), relative to the care and support of the negroes recaptured from the slave ship Pons by the	2	31	2	18
YOUNG, JAMES, claim for relief	297	25	3	9
Do	119	34	3	20
Do	160	35	1	21
YOUNG, JAMES R., claim for relief	83	41	2	25
Do	415	43	1	26
YOUNG, ROBERT, claim for relief of heirs	49	34	3	20
YOUNG, WILLIAM, claim for relief	709	25	2	9
YOUNG, WILLIAM P., claim for relief	195	35	1	21
ZANE, H. H., claim for relief	241	47	1	29
ZANTZINGER, WILLIAM P. (purser United States war ship Hornet), claim for relief	78	22	2	6
Do	781	24	1	8
Do	1027	27	2	11
Do	313	28	1	12
Do	4	28	2	12
Do	435	29	1	13
Do	250	30	1	16
ZARRACHA FREDERICK, claim for relief	428	35	1	21
Do	240	47	1	29
ZINK, S. H., claim for relief	352	30	1	16
ZOCK, FRANCIS, claim for relief	103	18	1	2
Do	336	29	1	13

C

REPORTS

OF THE

COMMITTEE ON COINAGE, WEIGHTS, AND MEASURES,

HOUSE OF REPRESENTATIVES,

FROM THE ORGANIZATION OF COMMITTEE, JANUARY 21, 1864, TO THE CLOSE OF THE FORTY-NINTH CONGRESS, 1887, INCLUSIVE.

IN ONE VOLUME.

COMPILED, UNDER THE DIRECTION OF THE JOINT COMMITTEE ON PRINTING,

BY

T. H. McKEE,

CLERK, DOCUMENT ROOM, UNITED STATES SENATE.

WASHINGTON:
GOVERNMENT PRINTING OFFICE.
1887.

9244

FORTY-NINTH CONGRESS, FIRST SESSION.

[PUBLIC RESOLUTION—No. 24.]

Joint resolution authorizing the preparation of a compilation of the reports of committees of the Senate and House of Representatives.

Resolved by the Senate and House of Representatives of the United States of America in Congress assembled, That there be prepared under the direction of the Joint Committee of Printing, a compilation of the reports of the Senate and House of Representatives from the Fourteenth to the Forty-eighth Congress, inclusive, classified by committees, arranged, indexed, and bound in suitable volumes for the use of the standing committees of the two Houses of Congress. And the sum of seven thousand seven hundred and fifty dollars, or so much thereof as may be found necessary, is hereby appropriated out of any money in the Treasury not otherwise appropriated, for the preparation of said work, which sum may be paid by the Secretary of the Treasury upon the order of the chairman of said Joint Committee, as additional pay or compensation to any officer or employee of the United States.

Resolved further, That the Clerk of the House and Secretary of the Senate be, and they are hereby directed, to procure and file, for the use of their respective Houses, copies of all reports made by each committee of all succeeding Congresses; and that the Clerk of the House and the Secretary of the Senate be, and they are hereby, authorized and directed at the close of each session of Congress, to cause said reports to be indexed and bound, one copy to be deposited in the library of each House and one copy in the room of the committee from which the reports emanated.

Approved, July 29, 1886.

COMPILER'S NOTICE.

This compilation embraces all the printed reports made by both Houses of Congress from the commencement of the Fourteenth to the close of the Forty-ninth Congress. They are classified by committees and arranged in numerical order. The collection for each committee is divided into volumes of suitable size. Each committee has a separate index, a copy being bound in each volume.

The SPECIAL and SELECT reports are all compiled in one collection, having one index, a copy of which is bound in each volume.

The plan throughout the compilation is to place each report to the committee from which it was reported, without reference to the subject-matter.

The House and Senate reports are compiled separately. Care will be required in noticing the chronological order, as in some instances an entire session or Congress may not appear in certain volumes from the fact that during this period no reports were made by this committee.

T. H. McKEE.

INDEX

TO

REPORTS OF COMMITTEE ON COINAGE, WEIGHTS, AND MEASURES,

HOUSE OF REPRESENTATIVES.

FROM 1864 TO 1887, INCLUSIVE.

Subject.	Report.	Congress.	Session.	Volume.
ARIZONA, to establish assay office in	33	46	3	1
ASSAY OFFICE,				
To establish, in Arizona	323	46	2	1
To establish, at Deadwood, Dak	524	46	2	1
Do	744	47	1	1
Do	969	48	1	1
To establish, at Saint Louis, Mo	1462	46	2	1
To establish, at Socorro, N. Mex	2126	48	1	1
BULLION,				
To exchange silver bullion for silver dollars	535	46	2	1
Charges for melting	33	46	3	1
To exchange gold coin for gold bars	862	47	1	1
BULLION CLUB OF NEW YORK, to replace smaller national bank notes with gold and silver coin, petition of	264	46	2	1
CALENDAR (Gregorian), to change	290	45	3	1
COINS AND COINAGE,				
To change laws governing	569	47	1	1
Coin,				
Minor, redemption of	3968	49	2	1
Subsidiary silver, to supply	3969	49	2	1
To punish for defacing	143	45	3	1
To punish for counterfeiting United States coins	533	46	2	1
To establish uniform system of coinage	62	39	1	1
Punishment for counterfeiting United States coins	533	46	2	1
Defacing coin, punishment for	533	46	2	1
Double eagles, limiting coinage of	952	48	1	1
Gold coin,				
To discontinue coinage of one and three dollar pieces	509	47	1	1
To exchange, for gold bars	862	47	1	1
Goloid coin,				
Process of coining	918	45	2	1
Do	64	45	3	1
Creation of an international	136	45	3	1
Half-dollar, recoinage of	640	46	2	1
Metric coinage, to establish	203	46	2	1
Do	24	47	1	1
Do	542	47	1	1
Metric system, adoption of	14	46	1	1
Silver coinage, providing for	*524	49	1	1
Stella coin, creation of an international	136	45	3	1
COUNTERFEITING UNITED STATES COIN, punishment for	533	46	2	1
CURRENCY,				
Circulating small notes	264	46	2	1
Retiring of notes less than five dollars	1730	48	1	1
DEADWOOD, DAKOTA, to establish assay office at	524	46	2	1
Do	744	47	1	1
Do	969	48	1	1
DECIMAL SYSTEM OF WEIGHTS AND MEASURES, new plan for a	137	45	3	1
DEFACING COIN. (*See* COIN AND COINAGE.)				
DOUBLE EAGLES, limiting coinage of	952	48	1	1
FIVE-DOLLAR TREASURY NOTES, to retire	1730	48	1	1
FREE COINAGE OF SILVER (*see also* COINS AND COINAGE), to provide for	*524	49	1	1

* Views of minority.

Subject.	Report.	Congress.	Session.	Volume.
GOLD COIN.				
To exchange, for gold bars	862	47	1	...
GOLD AND SILVER COIN, to replace smaller notes with	264	46	2	...
GOLOID COIN.				
Creation of an international	136	45	3	1
Process of coining	918	45	2	1
Do	64	45	3	1
GREGORIAN CALENDAR, to change	290	45	3	1
HALF-DOLLAR (*see also* COIN AND COINAGE), providing for recoinage of	640	46	2	1
IMPORTERS, requiring them to use metric system of weights and measures	649	47	1	1
INTERNATIONAL COIN, to establish an	136	45	3	1
LOUISVILLE, KENTUCKY, subtreasury at, to establish	1643	49	1	1
MAILS (United States), transmitting of silver coin through	1260	46	2	1
METRIC COINAGE.				
Adoption of	14	46	1	1
To establish	918	45	2	1
Do	64	45	3	1
Do	136	45	3	1
Do	203	46	2	1
Do	24	47	1	1
Do	542	47	1	1
METRIC SYSTEM (*see also* COIN AND COINAGE),				
Adoption in weights and measures of	53	45	3	1
Do	14	46	1	1
Use in coinage of	64	45	3	1
To be used by importers	649	47	1	1
MINOR COIN, issue and redemption of	3968	49	2	1
MINT, Philadelphia, Pa., extension of	1625	46	2	1
Do	740	47	1	1
Saint Louis, Mo., to establish	267	46	2	1
Do	741	47	1	1
Do	1549	48	1	1
NOTES LESS THAN FIVE DOLLARS, to retire	1730	48	1	1
PAPER MONEY, circulation of small notes	264	46	2	1
PHILADELPHIA, PENNSYLVANIA, to extend mint building at	1625	46	2	1
Do	740	47	1	1
Do	1107	47	1	1
RECOINAGE.				
Trade dollars, providing for	3616	49	2	...
Half-dollar, providing for	640	46	2	...
REVISED STATUTES, to amend or repeal,				
Sections 3511, 3513, change name of gold and silver coin	569	47	1	
Sections 3569, 3570, to use metric system of weights and measures	649	47	1	
SAINT LOUIS, MISSOURI,				
To establish mint at	267	46	2	
Do	741	47	1	
Do	1549	48	1	
To establish assay office at	1462	46	2	
SILVER, providing for coinage of, free	*524	49	1	
SILVER BULLION, to exchange, for silver dollars	535	46	2	
SILVER COIN.				
Subsidiary, to supply	3969	49	2	
Transmitting of, through mails	1260	46	2	
SILVER COINAGE, metric system, providing for	542	47	1	
SILVER HALF-DOLLAR (*see also* COIN AND COINAGE), recoinage of, providing for	640	46	2	
SMALLER NOTES, to replace, with small gold and silver coin	264	46	2	
SOCORRO, NEW MEXICO, to establish assay office at	2126	48	1	
STELLA COIN, creation of an international	136	45	3	
TIME, to establish a uniform measure of	290	45	3	
TRADE DOLLAR.				
Exchanging the	566	47	1	
Recoinage of	567	47	1	
Do	†324	48	1	
Do	2037	49	1	
Do	3616	49	2	
Redemption of	2037	49	1	
Retirement of	534	46	2	
Do	568	47	1	
Do	324	48	1	
Do	2037	49	1	
Do	3616	49	2	
WEIGHTS AND MEASURES.				
Providing a uniform system of	62	39	1	
Adoption of metric system of	‡53	45	3	
Do	14	46	1	
Providing a new decimal system of	137	45	3	
Metric system to be used by importers	649	47	1	

*Views of minority. †Parts 1, 2. ‡Part 1.

REPORTS

OF THE

OMMITTEE ON COMMERCE,

HOUSE OF REPRESENTATIVES,

FROM THE FOURTEENTH CONGRESS, 1815, TO THE FORTY-NINTH CONGRESS, 1887, INCLUSIVE.

IN ELEVEN VOLUMES.

COMPILED, UNDER THE DIRECTION OF THE JOINT COMMITTEE ON PRINTING,

BY

T. H. McKEE,

CLERK, DOCUMENT ROOM, UNITED STATES SENATE.

WASHINGTON:
GOVERNMENT PRINTING OFFICE.
1887.

9221 COM H

FORTY-NINTH CONGRESS, FIRST SESSION.

[PUBLIC RESOLUTION—No. 24.]

Joint resolution authorizing the preparation of a compilation of the reports of committees of the Senate and House of Representatives.

Resolved by the Senate and House of Representatives of the United States of America in Congress assembled, That there be prepared under the direction of the Joint Committee of Printing, a compilation of the reports of the Senate and House of Representatives from the Fourteenth to the Forty-eighth Congress, inclusive, classified by committees, arranged, indexed, and bound in suitable volumes for the use of the standing committees of the two Houses of Congress. And the sum of seven thousand seven hundred and fifty dollars, or so much thereof as may be found necessary, is hereby appropriated out of any money in the Treasury not otherwise appropriated, for the preparation of said work, which sum may be paid by the Secretary of the Treasury upon the order of the chairman of said Joint Committee, as additional pay or compensation to any officer or employee of the United States.

Resolved further, That the Clerk of the House and Secretary of the Senate be, and they are hereby directed, to procure and file, for the use of their respective Houses, copies of all reports made by each committee of all succeeding Congresses; and that the Clerk of the House and the Secretary of the Senate be, and they are hereby, authorized and directed at the close of each session of Congress, to cause said reports to be indexed and bound, one copy to be deposited in the library of each House and one copy in the room of the committee from which the reports emanated.

Approved, July 29, 1886.

COMPILER'S NOTICE.

This compilation embraces all the printed reports made by both Houses of Congress from the commencement of the Fourteenth to the close of the Forty-ninth Congress. They are classified by committees and arranged in numerical order. The collection for each committee is divided into volumes of suitable size. Each committee has a separate index, a copy being bound in each volume.

The SPECIAL and SELECT reports are all compiled in one collection having one index, a copy of which is bound in each volume.

The plan throughout the compilation is to place each report to the committee from which it was reported, without reference to the subject-matter.

The House and Senate reports are compiled separately. Care will be required in noticing the chronological order, as in some instances an entire session or Congress may not appear in certain volumes from the fact that during this period no reports were made by this committee.

T. H. McKEE.

INDEX

TO

REPORTS OF COMMITTEE ON COMMERCE,

HOUSE OF REPRESENTATIVES.

FROM 1815 TO 1887, INCLUSIVE.

Subject.	Report.	Congress.	Session.	Volume.
ABRAHAMS, A. H. & CO., for relief	892	27	2	4
ADMIRAL (schooner), for relief of owners and crew	404	22	1	1
Do	107	23	1	1
ADULTERATION, food and drugs, to prevent	634	47	1	10
Do	3777	49	2	11
AFRICA, western coast of, commercial relations with	283	27	3	5
ALABAMA RIVER, to bridge, at Selma, Ala	650	46	2	9
ALASKA, to construct revenue cutter for service in	802	48	1	11
ALBANY, NEW YORK, marine hospital at, to erect	255	35	1	8
ALBEMARLE SOUND, to construct canal to connect waters of Atlantic Ocean with	891	27	2	4
Do	251	29	1	6
ALIENS, relative to employment as engineers and pilots on vessels	801	48	1	11
Do	106	49	1	11
ALLENDER, JAMES, for relief	307	44	1	9
Do	1507	47	1	10
AMERICA (sloop), to change name of	1453	46	2	9
Do	1627	46	2	9
AMERICAN CHAMBER OF COMMERCE, to incorporate	8	46	1	9
AMERICAN COLONIZATION SOCIETY. (*See* COLONIZATION SOCIETY; LIBERIA.)				
AMERICAN EXPOSITIONS, to authorize Executive Departments to loan certain articles to	374	49	1	11
AMERICAN PACKET COMPANY, discharge of passengers at docks of	220	46	3	9
AMERICAN REGISTRY. (*See* VESSELS; REGISTERS.)				
AMERICAN SHIP BUILDING. (*See* SHIP-BUILDING.)				
AMERICUS, PRESTON AND LUMPKIN RAILROAD, bridge Flint River	3107	49	1	11
AMSTERDAM, NETHERLANDS, to provide for representation of United States in international exhibition at	1692	47	1	10
ANCLOTE, FLORIDA, port of entry	77	45	3	9
ANDREW HARDER (propeller), to change name of	326	46	3	9
ANIMALS, inspection of, for exportation	1036	48	1	11
Do	2368	48	2	11
ANN (boat), for relief of owner and crew of	275	27	3	4
ANNAPOLIS, MARYLAND, transfer of naval hospital at, to be used as marine hospital	1451	46	2	9
ANNE (schooner), for relief of owners	47	17	1	1
ANNIE JOHNSON (bark), authorizing issue of American register to	665	46	2	9
ANOKA, MINNESOTA, bridge across Mississippi River at	1332	48	1	11
APALACHICOLA, FLORIDA,				
Custom-house, post-office, and court-house at, to erect	61	36	1	8
Debenture, to extend right of, to port of	279	27	3	4
Marine hospital at, to erect	258	35	1	8
Do	60	36	1	8
APPRENTICES. (*See* SEAMEN.)				
APPROPRIATIONS,				
Public works, providing for	*46	40	2	8
Rivers and harbors, improvement of, for,				
1858	251	35	1	8
1877	154	44	2	9
1881	151	46	3	9
1882	1263	47	1	10
1883	1977	47	2	10
ARKANSAS, to establish ports of entry in	540	26	1	8

* Views of minority.

Subject.	Report.	Congress.	Session.	Volume.
ARKANSAS RIVER,				
Bridge across,				
By Texas and Saint Louis Railroad	1154	47	1	10
At Van Buren, Ark	1155	47	1	10
ARMINGTON, ASA, and others, for relief	60	29	1	6
ARNOLD, REMINGTON, Jr., for relief	404	22	1	1
ARROW ROCK, MISSOURI, bridge across Missouri River near	340	46	3	9
ARTHUR KILL. (*See* STATEN ISLAND SOUND.)				
ARCTIC (bark), to grant American register to	44	44	1	9
ARTIST (sloop), authorizing change of name of	490	36	1	8
ASIATIC COMMERCIAL COMPANY, to incorporate	268	43	1	9
ASSAY OFFICE, to establish coinage department in United States, in New York City	106	37	2	8
ATCHAFALAYA RIVER, Light-House Board over, to extend operations of	1068	47	1	10
ATCHISON, KANSAS, port of entry	637	36	1	8
ATCHISON BRIDGE COMPANY, to bridge Missouri River	1457	49	1	11
ATLANTIC COAST (*see also* LIGHTS), of light-houses on, condition of	282	27	3	5
ATLANTIC MUTUAL INSURANCE COMPANY, for relief	36	33	1	7
ATLANTIC OCEAN, construction of direct communication between the waters of Albemarle Sound and	801	27	2	4
Do	251	29	1	6
ATLANTIC AND GREAT WESTERN CANAL, granting aid to	76	42	3	9
ATWATER & DAGGETT, for relief	102	23	1	1
ATWOOD, JOSHUA, for relief	68	27	2	4
BAKER, BARNABAS, Jr., for relief	411	28	1	6
Do	59	28	2	6
Do	265	29	1	6
BAKER, JOSEPH, for relief	259	30	1	6
BALTIMORE, MARYLAND,				
Defense of, to indemnify owners of vessels that were sunk in 1812 for	70	20	2	1
Do	144	21	1	1
Marine hospital at, to erect	124	28	2	6
Do	1451	46	2	9
Tonnage duty on coasting vessels, to repeal act authorizing city council to impose	445	22	1	1
BANGOR, MAINE,				
Custom-house, to enlarge and repair	65	39	1	8
Do	1700	46	2	9
Port of entry at, to make	123	28	1	6
BARCLAY & LIVINGSTON, for relief	65	30	1	6
Do	10	35	1	8
BARGES. (*See* VESSELS.)				
BARRONDALE (British vessel), to grant American register to	1694	47	1	10
BASCOM, OLIVER (assignee), for relief	626	36	1	8
BATES & LACON, for relief	163	29	1	6
Do	729	30	1	6
BAYLEY, CHRISTOPHER T., for relief	342	22	1	1
Do	101	22	2	1
BAYOU BARNARD, MISSISSIPPI, bridge over, to erect	1079	49	1	11
BAYOU BARTHOLOMEW, bridge over, to erect	2452	48	2	11
BAYOU BLEU, survey and improvement of	837	29	1	6
BAYOU LA FOURCHE, survey and improvement of	837	29	1	6
BEACONS. (*See* LIGHTS.)				
BEAMISH, HENRY, for relief	643	24	1	3
Do	78	25	2	3
BEDLOE'S ISLAND, NEW YORK, to transfer, for marine hospital purposes	666	46	2	9
Do	399	47	1	10
BEHRING STRAIT, survey of coast and islands of	82	36	2	8
BELL'S ROCK, VIRGINIA, light-house on	162	46	2	9
BENJAMIN D. JACKSON (schooner), for relief of owners and crew of	35	26	1	3
BENJAMIN, MEIGS & CO., for relief	31	26	1	3
BENTON BRIDGE COMPANY, bridge Missouri River	1551	48	1	11
Do	2911	49	1	11
BERRI & KEESE, for relief	319	30	1	6
BIG KANAWHA RIVER, to improve navigation on	806	47	1	10
BILLINGS, SAMUEL, for relief	875	27	2	4
Do	582	29	1	6
BILLS OF LADING,				
Forms of, to regulate	1665	48	1	[illegible]
Negotiation of, to facilitate	80	45	3	[illegible]
BINGLEY, CHARLES W., for relief	179	29	1	[illegible]
BLACK RIVER, LOUISIANA, bridge across, to erect	1644	47	1	[illegible]
BLAKE, ANDREW, for relief	384	28	1	
Do	60	28	2	
Do	266	29	1	
BLOOMING YOUTH (schooner), for relief of owners and crew of	172	27	3	
BŒUF RIVER, LOUISIANA, bridge across, to erect	2453	48	2	[illegible]
BOGGS & THOMPSON, for relief	30	36	1	
BOILERS (*see also* STEAM VESSELS),				
Inspection of, on steamboats	9	35	1	
Do	141	35	2	
Do	9	36	1	

Subject.	Report.	Congress.	Session.	Volume.
)LLERMAN, ANTHONY, for relief	350	22	1	1
)OKS, remission of duties on, imported for church purposes	740	24	1	2
Do	79	25	2	2
)STON, MASSACHUSETTS,				
Custom-house at, to erect new	448	24	1	2
Marine hospital near, to erect	649	30	1	6
)STON HARBOR, MASSACHUSETTS, light-house on Deer Island	1461	49	1	11
)WES, JOHN R., for relief	57	33	2	7
)WLEY, OLIVER, for relief	183	36	1	8
)WLING GREEN, KENTUCKY, port of delivery	238	34	3	
)WMAN, JOHN, and others, for relief	74	26	1	3
RAINERD, MINNESOTA, dam across Mississippi River at	1336	48	1	11
Do	105	49	1	11
RANDYWINE SHOAL, DELAWARE BAY, light-house on	740	27	2	4
RAYDON & CHASE, for relief	185	23	1	1
REAKWATERS (*see also* RIVERS AND HARBORS),				
Crow Shoal, at Cape May, in Delaware Bay	1050	25	2	2
Do	322	34	1	7
Do	358	34	1	7
Do	180	35	1	8
REED, EBENEZER, for relief	398	22	1	1
REWSTER, CHARLES, for relief	185	36	1	8
RIDGEPORT, CONNECTICUT,				
Collector of the district of Fairfield, Conn., giving permission to reside in	687	27	2	4
Immediate transportation of dutiable goods, to extend privilege of to	3483	49	2	11
RIDGES (*see also* under titles of respective rivers over which proposed to be built, and under titles of respective railroads asking authority to build),				
To construct, over navigable rivers	1892	47	2	10
Do	1041	48	1	11
Do	1308	49	1	11
To remove, over navigable rivers	1456	47	1	10
Do	1640	47	1	10
To make, post-roads	1892	47	2	10
Across,				
Arkansas River,				
Texas and Saint Louis Railroad	1154	47	1	10
At Van Buren, Ark	1155	47	1	10
Black River, in Louisiana	1644	47	1	10
Chattahoochee River, Savannah Pacific Short-Line Railroad	1642	47	1	10
Coosa River, East and West Railroad	1829	47	2	10
Cumberland River, at Nashville	993	47	1	10
Cumberland River, Tennessee, near Nashville	3828	49	2	11
Detroit River, at Detroit	1574	46	2	9
East River, New York, between New York and Long Island	3801	49	2	11
Flint River, Savannah Pacific Short-Line Railroad	1642	47	1	10
Illinois River, near Columbiana	1970	47	2	10
Lake Pontchartrain, New Orleans and Northeastern Railroad	1289	47	1	10
Lewis and Clarke River, in Oregon	2023	47	2	10
Little River, Louisiana	1644	47	1	10
Mississippi River,				
At Dubuque, Iowa	3800	49	2	11
At Fort Madison or Keokuk	3799	49	2	11
At Grand Tower, Ill	4154	49	2	11
Near Keithsburg, Ill	443	47	1	10
At Memphis, Tenn	3831	49	2	11
At New Boston, Ill	992	47	1	10
At Red Wing, Minn	1740	46	2	9
At Rock Island, Ill	250	35		8
At Saint Louis, Mo	1047	47	1	10
Between Wabasha and Reed's Landing, Minn	397	47	1	10
At Winona, Minn	3829	49	2	11
Missouri River,				
Near Arrow Rock, Mo	340	46	3	9
Do	231	47		10
Chillicothe and Kansas City Railroad	1971	47	1	10
Duluth, Pierre and Black Hills Railroad Company	3802	49	2	11
At Hamburg, Mo	230	47	1	10
Hannibal and Southwestern Railroad Company	231	47	1	10
In Winona County, Iowa	990	47		10
Between Kansas City and Sibley, Mo	3830	49	2	11
Between Omaha and Council Bluffs	3502	49	2	11
Do	3972	49	2	11
At Pierre, Dak	3802	49	2	11
Sioux City and Pacific Railroad Company	232	47	1	10
At Sioux City, Iowa	4033	49	2	11
Near Yankton, Dak	3803	49	2	11
Ocmulgee River, Savannah Pacific Short-Line Railroad	1642	47	1	10
Oconee River, Savannah Pacific Short-Line Railroad	1642	47	1	10
Ogeechee River, Savannah Pacific Short-Line Railroad	1642	47	1	10
Ohio River,				
Amend act of December 17, 1872, authorizing	814	47	1	10

Subject.	Report.	Congress.	Session.	Volume.
BRIDGES—Continued.				
Across				
Ohio River,				
To remove certain	622	44	1	9
Do	78	45	2	9
Osage River, in Missouri	339	46	2	9
Ouachita River, Texas and Saint Louis Railroad	1154	47	1	10
Pearl River, New Orleans and Northeastern Railroad Company	1269	47	1	10
Red River,				
In Cook County, Texas	1080	49	1	11
Do	1081	49	1	11
In Louisiana	1644	47	1	10
Do	3618	49	2	11
Do	3904	49	2	11
Texas and Saint Louis Railroad	1154	47	1	10
Rio Grande River, at El Paso, Texas	1288	47	1	10
Sabine River, in Louisiana	1644	47	1	10
Saint John's River, Fla., Sandford and Indian River Railroad	1643	47	1	10
Saint Lawrence River, at Montreal, Canada	1645	47	1	10
Saint Louis River, between Minnesota and Wisconsin	3971	49	2	11
Sainte Marie River, between Michigan and Canada	1455	47	1	10
Sunflower River, Georgia Pacific Railroad Company	3627	49	2	11
Tennessee River, near Mussel Shoals Canal	4128	49	2	11
Thames River, near New London, Conn	1969	47	2	10
Tombigbee River,				
Georgia Pacific Railroad	3627	49	2	11
Tombigbee Railroad Company	4129	49	2	11
West Pascagoula River, Mississippi, New Orleans, Mobile and Texas Railroad Company to maintain draw in	3614	49	2	11
White River, Texas and Saint Louis Railroad	1154	47	1	10
Willamette River, Oregon Pacific Railroad	1641	47	1	10
Do	1869	47	2	10
Yazoo River, Georgia Pacific Railroad Company	3627	49	2	11
Young's River, above Naluski Creek, Oregon	2022	47	2	10
BRIGGS, NATHANIEL, for relief	96	20	1	1
BRISTOL, RHODE ISLAND, removal of collector's office to Warren from	651	29	1	6
BRITISH AMERICA. (*See* CANADA.)				
BRODIE, ALEXANDER O., for relief	160	21	1	1
Do	80	22	1	1
BROUGHTON, GLOVER, for relief	94	29	1	6
BROWN, SAMUEL W., for relief	198	24	1	2
BROWN'S FERRY, TEXAS, bridge across Red River at	1080	49	1	11
Do	1081	49	1	11
BROWNSVILLE, TEXAS, custom-house from Point Isabel to	237	34	3	7
BUCK, ANTHONY, for relief	61	14	2	1
BUCKSVILLE, SOUTH CAROLINA, port of entry at	859	27	2	4
BUFFALO, NEW YORK,				
Custom-house at, to enlarge	236	34	3	7
Marine hospital at, to construct	256	35	1	8
BUFFALO (schooner), for relief of owners and crew	55	23	2	1
Do	43	24	1	2
Do	69	26	1	2
Do	738	27	2	4
BUOYS. (*See* LIGHTS.)				
BUREAU OF INTERSTATE COMMERCE. (*See* INTERSTATE COMMERCE.)				
BUREAU OF INTERNATIONAL COMMERCE, to establish	1037	48	1	11
BUREAU OF NAVIGATION, extension of the hydrographic duties pertaining to	6	38	2	8
BUREAU OF PUBLIC HEALTH, to establish	1230	49	1	11
BURLINGTON, IOWA, to erect public buildings at	258	35	1	8
BUSCARIO & PUIG, for relief	571	29	1	6
Do	123	30	1	6
BUTTER AND CHEESE. (*See* OLEOMARGARINE.)				
CABLE COMPANY, CENTRAL AND SOUTH AMERICAN, construction of	1454	46	2	9
CAIRO, ILLINOIS,				
Bridge, Ohio River, at	3111	49	1	11
Custom-house, post-office, and court-house at, to construct	38	39	1	8
CATER, JAMES, for relief	8	44	2	9
Do	61	45	3	9
CALIFORNIA, additional customs districts in	645	36	1	8
Do	70	46	2	9
Do	394	47	1	10
Do	760	47	1	10
CALLOWAY, SHADE, for relief	3	34	3	7
Do	190	35	1	8
Do	16	36	1	8
CALUMET RIVER, to improve harbor at mouth of	78	34	1	7
CAMDEN, NEW JERSEY, surveyor of customs at, to reduce salary of	159	27	3	4
CANADA,				
Drawback of duties on trade with, to extend privilege of	328	27	2	4
Do	335	27	2	4

Subject.	Report.	Congress.	Session.	Volume.
[A]—Continued.				
[recip]rocal trade with	4	32	2	7
[recip]rocity treaty with, appointment of commission to arrange	9	44	1	9
Do	*389	44	1	9
[...]DRY DOCK MANUFACTURING COMPANY, to construct dry docks in connection with Des Moines Rapids Canal	72	45	3	9
(*see also* under titles of respective corporations),				
[Atlan]tic and Great Western, to grant aid to construct	76	42	3	9
[Atlan]tic Ocean and Albemarle Sound, to connect waters of	801	27	2	4
[...]nd Oswego, to enlarge	76	42	3	9
[...]of Niagara on the American side, to construct ship-canal around	76	42	3	9
[...] River to Ohio River, to complete a water highway from	76	42	3	9
[...]ville and Portland Canal, to enlarge	327	34	1	7
[...]ville and Portland Canal Company, to pay bonds of	218	42	1	8
[...] FORK RIVER, bridge across, in Tennessee	2629	48	2	11
Do	3220	49	1	11
[...]D HARBOR, MASSACHUSETTS, improvement of	79	34	1	7
[...]AR RIVER, lights on	1263	48	1	11
[H]ATTERAS, NORTH CAROLINA, light-ship at	1387	49	1	11
[...]AY, NEW JERSEY, breakwater at, to construct	180	35	1	8
[...]RFORD, OREGON, to purchase right of way to light-house at	847	49	1	11
[SA]N BLAS, FLORIDA, light-house at	1973	47	2	10
[...]ED AND ABANDONED PROPERTY, to repeal eighth section of act of July 2, 1864, relative to, taken in States declared in insurrection	24	38	2	8
[...]S. (*See* VESSELS.)				
[...]N ISLAND, NEW YORK, light-house on	198	49	1	11
[...]N, NORWOOD & CO., for relief	82	37	2	8
[...]L, WILLIAM, for relief	27	40	2	8
[...], MAINE, custom-house at	438	29	1	6
Do	18	34	1	7
[...] HILL, RHODE ISLAND, light-house at	828	49	1	11
[...]KEYS, FLORIDA,				
[collec]tion district at, to establish	578	29	1	6
[marin]e hospital at, to erect	648	46	2	9
[port o]f entry at, to establish	833	27	2	4
Do	61	28	1	6
[...]L AND SOUTH AMERICAN CABLE COMPANY, contract for dispatch of Government messages with	1454	46	2	9
[...]RLAIN, DAKOTA, bridge across Missouri River at	1617	49	1	11
[...] AND ANCHORS, testing of	1978	48	1	11
Do	2845	49	1	11
[...]IN, ISAAC, and others, for relief	55	23	2	1
Do	43	24	1	2
Do	69	26	1	3
Do	738	27		4
[...]ER PRICE (ship), for relief of owners and crew of	751	30		6
Do	177	31	1	7
[CHARLE]STON, SOUTH CAROLINA,				
[churc]h of Saint Philip in, to remit duty on organ for	307	26	1	3
Do	471	27	2	4
[custo]m-house at, to repair	196	28	1	6
[marin]e hospital at, to erect	83	20	1	1
Do	150	21	1	1
[...]TTE AND ISABELLA (steam tug), to change name of	660	46	2	9
[...]graphic office, distribution of	325	48	1	11
[...]and current, to test Lieutenant Maury's	112	30	2	6
[...]LAIN & PONVERT, for relief	134	22	1	1
[CHATTA]NOOGA, TENNESSEE,				
[...] over Tennessee River at	2724	49	1	11
[...]f delivery at, to establish	133	46	3	9
[...]M, MASSACHUSETTS, Stage Harbor, light-house at	698	45	2	9
[CHATTA]HOOCHEE RIVER, GEORGIA, bridge across	1642	47	1	10
[...] COUNTY, OREGON, to bridge Young's Bay in	1466	49	1	11
Do	2555	49	1	11
(*See* OLEOMARGARINE.)				
[...]A, MASSACHUSETTS, to discontinue marine hospital at, and dispose of land connected therewith	649	30	1	6
[...]Y, RICHARD, for relief	404	36	1	8
[CHESAP]EAKE BAY, light-ship at, entrance to	1464	49	1	11
[CHICAG]O, ILLINOIS,				
[collect]ion district at, to establish	203	28	1	6
[harbo]r at, to complete	70	34	1	7
[...]in harbor of, to erect on tower of water-works crib	991	47	1	10
[marin]e hospital at, to erect	124	28	2	6
[...]ARR & CO., for relief	329	31	1	7
[...]AIL SERVICE. (*See* POSTAL SERVICE.)				
[CHINCOT]EAGUE BAY, VIRGINIA, to locate day-beacon on Killick Shoals, in	817	45	2	9
[...] COOLY TRADE. (*See* COOLY TRADE.)				
[...]'A RIVER, bridge across, in Wisconsin	1270	48	1	11
Do	766	49	1	11

*Views of minority.

Subject.	Report.	Congress.	Session.	Volume.
CHURCH OF SAINT PHILIP, CHARLESTON, SOUTH CAROLINA, for remission of duties on organ	307	26	1	3
Do.	471	27	2	4
CINCINNATI, OHIO, to make port of entry	81	14	2	1
Do.	642	36	1	8
CITIZENSHIP, to secure to free colored seamen the privileges of full	*80	27	3	4
CITY POINT, VIRGINIA, marine hospital at	110	28	2	3
CIVIL LIST, establishment of retired	187	36	1	8
CIVIL RIGHTS, colored seamen, proceedings respecting laws of Southern States affecting	80	27	3	4
CLARK, FERDINAND, for relief	64	24	2	2
Do	88	25	2	2
Do	12	33	1	7
CLARKSVILLE, TENNESSEE, port of delivery	639	35	1	8
CLEMENTS, JACOB, for relief of assignees	41	20	1	1
Do	290	23	1	1
Do	1047	25	2	2
CLEMENTS, SAMUEL (assignee), for relief	41	20	1	1
Do.	290	23	1	1
Do.	1047	25	2	2
CLERKS, New Orleans custom-house, claim for arrears of pay	114	28	2	6
CLEVELAND, OHIO,				
Marine hospital at,				
To erect	124	28	2	6
Authorizing lease of, to city for hospital purposes	197	43	1	9
CLUSKY, CHARLES B., for relief	752	30	1	6
COAL, drawbacks of duties upon foreign	245	26	2	3
COAST DEFENSE ASSOCIATION, to incorporate	1332	46	2	9
COAST SURVEY,				
Charts of, distribution of	6	35	2	3
Revenue steamer to, transfer of	187	30	2	6
COASTING TRADER (schooner), for relief of owners and crew of	35	26	1	3
Do.	474	27	2	4
Do.	195	28	1	6
COASTWISE,				
Merchandise transported, drawback on	72	20	1	1
Requiring statistical returns of	66	20	2	1
COB POINT BAR, WICOMICO RIVER, MARYLAND, to establish light-house at	3493	49	2	11
COD HOOK (schooner), for relief of owners and crew of	270	27	2	4
CODE OF SIGNALS. (*See* MARINE SIGNALS.)				
COFFEE (*see also* IMPORT DUTIES), remission of duties when imported in Dutch vessels	188	28	2	6
COINAGE, department of, in New York City assay office	106	37	2	3
COLBY, A. and E. G., for relief	253	35	1	3
COLLECTION DISTRICTS. (*See* CUSTOMS DISTRICTS.)				
COLLECTION LAWS, to amend and consolidate	145	33	2	7
COLLECTOR OF CUSTOMS. (*See* CUSTOMS OFFICERS.)				
COLLISIONS AT SEA. (*See* VESSELS.)				
COLONIZATION SOCIETY, affairs of the	283	27	3	5
COLORED SEAMEN. (*See* SEAMEN.)				
COLUMBIA RIVER, Light-House Board to extend operations of	1036	47	1	10
COMMERCE AND NAVIGATION (*see also* FOREIGN VESSELS; IMPORTS AND EXPORTS; LAKE AND MARINE SHIPPING; MARINE SIGNALS; SEAMEN; SHIP-BUILDING; STEAM VESSELS; VESSELS),				
Act of July, 1832, to explain and amend Section 18, relating to	12	22	2	1
Africa, commerce with western coast of	283	27	3	5
American merchant marine, to enlarge	835	27	2	4
Appointment of joint select committee on, in House of Representatives	1805	47	1	10
Apprenticeship in the merchant marine, providing a system of	97	33	2	7
Do	177	34	1	7
Burdens on American shipping, to remove	1831	47	2	10
Condition of	165	21	1	1
Do.	835	27	2	4
Encouragement of, providing for	165	21	1	1
Foreign regulations for, requiring Secretary of State to lay annually before Congress the history of	9	34	1	7
Measures to increase	6	38	2	8
Obstructing, by bridges of navigable waters	1456	47	1	10
Do.	1640	47	1	10
Reciprocal relations with foreign countries, to establish	835	27	2	4
Steam vessels, to establish laws and regulations for construction and equipment of	125	18	1	1
Steam vessels, security and safety of passengers on	9	35	1	8
Do	141	35	2	8
Do.	9	36	1	8
Steam vessels, to amend titles 48 and 52 of Revised Statutes, relating to	97	44	1	9
Do.	292	44	1	9
Do.	387	44	1	9
Do.	388	44	1	9
Do.	82	45	2	9
Subsidies, for supporting	109	35	1	6

* Views of minority.

* Parts 1, 2.

*Parts 1, 2.

Subject.	Report.	Congress.	Session.	Volume.
hooner), for relief of owner and crew of	173	27	2	4
Do	386	28	1	6
Do	259	28	1	6
and F. & CO., for relief	309	26	1	3
ACKS (*see also* IMPORT DUTIES),				
f March 1, 1823, to repeal, on merchandise transported from port to port.	72	20	1	1
lachicola, Fla., to extend right of debenture to port of	279	27	3	4
ntered for exportation, to allow, on foreign	245	26	2	3
ge made from foreign materials, to allow on	165	21	1	1
rtations with benefit of, extending time for	39	20	1	1
from foreign wheat, to allow, on	835	27	2	4
Do	258	36	1	8
gn goods conveyed overland to Mexico, to allow, on	540	28	1	6
when manufactured into cordage and exported, to allow, on	229	24	2	2
age of, to extend	590	24	1	2
Do	304	25	2	2
a, additional allowance on refined	51	20	1	1
and Mexico, to allow, on inland trade with	328	27	2	4
Do	885	27	3	4
Do	399	28	1	6
JOSHUA, for relief	888	27	2	4
(*see also* ADULTERATION), importation of impure, regulating	633	36	1	8
CKS, to authorise construction, in connection with Des Moines Rapids Canal	72	45	2	9
JE, IOWA, bridge across Mississippi River at	327	48	1	11
Do	2485	49	1	11
ITZ, GEORGE F., for relief	688	25	2	2
. (*See* IMPORT DUTIES.)				
TKINS, for relief	378	30	1	6
Do	58	33	2	7
GEORGE, Jr., for relief	136	24	2	2
Do	84	25	2	2
Do	73	26	1	3
ANT (steam-yacht), to change name of	1331	46	2	9
PASS, TEXAS, bridge across Rio Grande River at	800	48	1	11
RIVER, MICHIGAN, light-house at	656	46	2	9
VER, NEW YORK, bridge across, between New York and Long Island.	3801	49	2	11
HOMASTON, MAINE, to establish collection district at	113	30	2	6
RT, MAINE, custom-house at	581	29	1	6
I., for relief	54	36	2	8
GE, LEVI, for relief	38	26	1	3
Do	476	27	2	4
Do	139	28	1	6
Do	264	29	1	6
GE, T., for relief	97	26	2	3
ICITY, lighting navigable rivers by	2250½	48	2	11
TH MARY (schooner), for relief of owners	523	36	1	8
, WILLIAM, for relief	62	28	1	6
Do	56	28	2	6
Do	541	29	1	6
ILLIAM H., for relief	35	20	1	1
), TEXAS, bridge across Rio Grande at	1288	47	1	10
IN C., for relief	690	25	2	2
K, JOSEPH, for relief	246	30	1	6
TION (*see also* IMMIGRATION), collection of statistics of	3607	49	2	11
ERS. (*See* STEAM VESSELS.)				
NNSYLVANIA,				
or of, improvement of	135	37	2	8
-house at, to erect	857	47	1	10
NAL, enlargement of	76	42	3	9
A, CALIFORNIA, port of entry	760	47	1	10
BENJAMIN, for relief	883	27	2	4
Do	387	28	1	6
ILLE, INDIANA, local board of steamboat inspectors at	182	36	1	8
ATIONS, expedition to explore Pacific Ocean and South Seas	94	23	2	1
ATION OF MEATS, inspection of	3777	49	2	11
S (*see also* IMPORTS AND EXPORTS), collection of statistics of	3607	49	2	11
MASSEY, for relief	62	27	2	4
Do	128	32	1	7
, WILLIAM, for relief	514	29	1	6
Do	259	30	1	6
VEN, MASSACHUSETTS, light on bridge at	1229	49	1	11
(schooner), for relief of owners	198	24	1	2
Do	238	25	3	2
Do	72	26	1	3
IVER, MASSACHUSETTS, to erect custom-house and post-office at	570	28	1	6
(schooner), for relief of owners and crew	248	24	1	2
VOTH, NATHAN, for relief	35	26	1	3
Do	474	27	2	4
Do	195	28	1	6
Do	811	30	1	6

Subject.	Report.	Congress.	Session.	Volume.
FARRINGTON, WILLIAM, to recompense for relief rendered crew of United States schooner George Douglas	903	25	2	2
FAYETTEVILLE, NORTH CAROLINA, port of entry	647	46	2	9
FEES. (*See* CONSULAR AND DIPLOMATIC SERVICE.)				
FELCH, JACOB, for relief	648	30	1	6
Do	98	33	2	7
FELT, JONATHAN, Jr., for relief of administrator of	71	26	2	3
FERGUSON & MILHADO, for relief	36	31	1	7
Do	28	32	1	7
FERGUSON & REID, for relief	273	27	3	4
Do	253	28	1	6
FISH AND FISHERIES,				
Oysters, to investigate destruction of	3965	49	2	11
Propagation of, to protect, in certain parts of Atlantic Ocean	7	46	1	9
Do	85	46	2	9
Statistics of	2042	49	1	11
FLINT RIVER, GEORGIA, bridges across	1642	47	1	10
Do	3107	49	1	11
FLORES (schooner), for relief of crew and owners of	185	36	1	8
FLORIDA,				
Customs district in, to establish, at Cedar Keys	573	29	1	6
Rivers and harbors in, improvement of	886	27	3	4
Spanish vessels, extending privileges to all ports of entry in, to	22	30	2	1
FLORILLA (schooner), for relief of owner and crew	174	27	3	4
Do	80	34	1	7
FLOUR, drawback of duties on flour manufactured from foreign wheat and exported	885	27	3	4
Do	258	30	1	6
FLYNN'S KNOLL, NEW YORK, for light-house on	740	27	2	4
FOG SIGNALS. (*See* LIGHTS)				
FONTANE, PHILIP J., for relief	601	30	1	6
FOOD, adulteration of	634	47	1	10
Do	3777	49	2	11
FORBES, J. G. and R. B., for relief	30	26	1	3
FOREIGN COMMERCE. (*See* COMMERCE AND NAVIGATION.)				
FOREIGN COMMERCIAL COMPANY, to incorporate	34	46	3	9
FOREIGN INTERCOURSE, relative to	70	17	1	1
FOREIGN PORTS (*see also* WAREHOUSING), landing and storing of cargoes from	367	30	1	6
Do	141	30	2	6
FOREIGN REGULATIONS OF COMMERCE, to be reported to Congress	9	24	1	7
FOREIGN VESSELS,				
Annie Johnson, to issue American register to bark	665	46	2	9
Arctic, (Hawaiian bark), American register to	44	44	1	9
Gulnare (steamship), to issue American register to	221	46	3	9
Spanish vessels, law concerning tonnage duty on	64	24	2	2
Do	88	25	2	2
Unloading of, to amend section 2771 Revised Statutes in relation to	4	46	2	9
Do	662	46	2	9
FORT HOWARD, WISCONSIN, to establish marine hospital at	235	34	3	7
FOSTER, EZEKIEL, for relief	302	22	1	1
Do	12	22	2	1
FOSTER, JAMES, for relief	266	30	1	6
FOULWEATHER BLUFF, WASHINGTON TERRITORY, fog bell and steam whistle, on	69	45	3	9
FOWLE, GEORGE M., for relief	64	29	1	6
FRANCIS, JOSEPH, resolution for thanks of Congress and medal to	529	49	1	11
FRAUDS,				
Bills of lading, to punish	80	46	3	9
States declared in insurrection, to prevent in	24	38	2	8
FRAZIER, JAMES, for relief	513	29	1	6
FREE BLACKS (*see also* COLONIZATION SOCIETY), to form on west coast of Africa a colony of	283	27	3	5
FREE COLORED SEAMEN. (*See* SEAMEN.)				
FREIGHT. (*See* INTERSTATE COMMERCE.)				
FREY, FREDERICK, & CO., for relief	157	24	2	2
FRIENDSHIP (schooner), for relief of owners and crew	254	22	1	1
FULLERTON, WILLIAM, and others, for relief	477	27	2	3
FULSOM & GARDINER, for relief	181	36	1	8
FURGUSON, JAMES, for relief	28	32	1	7
GAFFNEY, DANIEL, for relief	96	29	1	6
GAINESVILLE AND CHICKASAW BRIDGE COMPANY, bridge Red River	1080	49	1	11
Do	1081	49	1	11
GALVESTON, TEXAS, marine hospital at	49	47	1	10
GALAXY (schooner), for relief of owners and crew	376	23	1	1
GALENCIA, JACOB, for relief	1048	25	2	2
GALLIPOLIS, OHIO, creating steamboat inspection district at	120	47	3	10
GALLISON, JAMES, for relief	189	25	1	2
GARRIGA, FRANCIS, to recompense for relief rendered crew of United States ship Philadelphia	903	25	2	2
GAS, light-houses for illuminating	1748	46	2	9

Subject.	Report.	Congress.	Session.	Volume.
RKS OF PHILADELPHIA, memorial on importation of machinery	127	32	1	7
STH, for relief	348	24	1	2
L JACKSON (schooner), for relief of owners	134	22	1	1
, JOHN D., for relief	257	24	2	2
Do	292	25	2	2
TOWN, D. C., to extend privileges of immediate transportation without appraisement of imported goods to port of	76	45	2	9
TOWN, SOUTH CAROLINA, light-house at mouth of Sampit River, harbor of	641	46	2	9
A PACIFIC RAILROAD COMPANY, bridges across the Sunflower, Yazoo, and Tombigbee Rivers, in Mississippi	3827	49	2	11
A RAILROAD COMPANY, for relief	368	33	1	7
D, NATHANIEL, and others, for relief	172	33	1	7
XCHANGE (schooner), for relief of crew and owners of	13	34	1	7
OGE, ISRAEL, and others, for relief	172	27	3	4
Do	545	29	1	6
, CHARLES, for relief	186	23	1	1
Do	736	27	2	4
I, WILLIAM, for relief	305	25	2	2
EORGE, for relief	47	23	2	1
Do	51	24	1	2
I SHOALS, MICHIGAN, fog-bell buoy on	223	46	3	9
MARAIS, MINNESOTA, light-house on Lake Superior at	699	45	2	9
Do	2385	48	2	11
RIVER, MICHIGAN, for improvement of	415	28	1	6
DANIEL, and others, for relief	188	28	1	6
Do	58	28	2	6
Do	260	29	1	6
HARBOR, WASHINGTON TERRITORY,				
house at, to erect at entrance	1567	47	1	10
f entry, to establish	260	35	1	8
y, to improve and	260	35	1	8
BEDS, NEW JERSEY, light-house in Raritan Bay, on shoals known as	786	45	2	9
BRITAIN,				
ercial intercourse between the United States and, to regulate	50	19	2	1
Do	835	27	2	4
imposed by, upon American tonnage	126	18	1	1
Do	835	27	2	4
rocity treaty with, to appoint commissioners to negotiate a new	22	37	2	8
Do	39	38	1	8
Do	9	44	1	9
Do	*389	44	1	9
y of 1815, relative to existence of any law in contravention of	126	18	1	1
with, giving notice for abrogating treaty made in behalf of British provinces in North America by	39	38	1	8
SHOALS, MARYLAND, light-house on	1213	47	1	10
WICOMICO RIVER, light-house at mouth of	856	47	1	10
Do	3452	49	1	11
, PHILIP and ELIPHALET, for relief	421	29	1	6
D. R., and others, for relief	41	36	2	8
JOSEPH W., for relief	461	23	1	1
Do	50	24		2
Y, DAVID, for relief	202	25		2
, WILLIAM, for relief	817	25		2
REBECCA, for relief	164	26		3
RE (steamship), granting American register to	221	46		9
OCKS, RHODE ISLAND, light-house on	1389	49		11
ON, NATHANIEL, for relief	248	24		2
N (schooner), for relief of owners and crew	185	23		1
AY ROCK, MASSACHUSETTS, light-house on	822			9
HARLES B., for relief	245	27		4
WAY, WILLIAM, for relief	54	19	2	1
ND, PARDON T., for relief	186	36	1	8
K, MAINE, port of entry at	2542	48	2	11
Do	1085	49	1	11
Do	1984	49	1	11
H (brigantine), for relief of owners	102	23	1	1
GER (schooner), to grant register to	144	32	1	7
S OF REFUGE,				
ukee, to reimburse city for expenditures incurred in construction of one at	1500	46	2	9
Beach, Lake Huron, control of	655	46	2	9
Do	233	47		10
G, WILLIAM, for relief	266	30		6
RP, JOHN, for relief	524	30		6
T (schooner), for relief of owners and crew of	476	27	2	4
Do	139	29	1	6
Do	264	29		6
, HERMAN, for relief	783	25		2
RD, CONNECTICUT, port of entry at	3221	49		11

* Views of minority.

Subject.	Report.	Congress.	Session.	Volume.
HARVEY & STAGG, for relief	310	26	1	3
Do	506	28	1	6
HASKELL, WILLIAM, and others, for relief	254	23	1	1
HASSLER, F. R., for relief of administrator	14	36	2	8
HAVRE DE GRACE, MARYLAND, surveyor at port of, to increase salary	212	27	2	4
HAZARD, FLORIDA, port of entry	887	27	2	4
HEDGE, JAMES, for relief	82	19	1	1
HELENA, ARKANSAS, port of delivery	853	47	1	10
HELL GATE, NEW YORK, lights at	1153	47	1	10
Do	1231	48	1	11
HEMP, allowing drawback of duties on imported hemp, when manufactured into cordage and exported	229	24	2	3
HENRIETTA (schooner), for relief of owners and crew of	96	29	1	6
HERALD (ship), for relief of owners of	94	29	2	6
Do	572	29	1	6
HICKMAN, KENTUCKY, marine hospital at	643	36	1	8
HIDDEN, JOSEPH, for relief	224	28	1	6
HIGGINS, A. G., for relief	259	30	1	6
HIGHWAY FOR LIVE STOCK, to establish	1328	49	1	11
HODGES, JOHN H., for relief	290	27	2	4
Do	572	29	1	6
Do	575	29	1	6
HOFFMANN, SAMUEL, for relief	210	25	2	2
Do	79	27	3	4
HOG ISLAND SHOAL, RHODE ISLAND, light-ship at	[illegible]	49	1	11
HOLMES, JOSEPH, for relief	316	26	1	3
Do	729	27	2	4
Do	261	29	1	6
Do	259	30	1	6
HOLMES, JOSIAH, for relief	313	26	1	3
Do	67	27	2	4
HOMER, JAMES, for relief	17	17	1	1
HOPKINS, SOLOMON, for relief	206	34	1	7
HOPS, to fix standard weight of bales and tare on	1974	48	1	11
HORTEN, IRA T., for relief	332	31	1	7
HORTEN, JOHN, and others, for relief	270	27	2	4
HOSPITAL FUND. (*See* MARINE HOSPITAL FUND.)				
HOSPITALS. (*See* MARINE HOSPITAL.)				
HOWARD, CALEB, for relief of executor	440	22	1	1
HUDSON RIVER, NEW YORK,				
Bridge across, between Stormking and Breakneck Mountains, to allow	806	48		11
Light-house at Danskammer Point on, to erect	1229	47		10
Navigation of, to improve	150	22		1
Piers of Poughkeepsie Bridge Company in, to remove	1454	47		10
HUMPHREY, ALEXANDER and SYLVESTER, for relief	81	17		1
HUMPHREYS, WILLIAM, Jr., for relief	548	29		6
Do	13	34		7
HUNT, STEPHEN W., for relief	1020	25		2
Do	169	25	3	3
HURTER & PATTENS, port charges, to purchase copies of	1040	48	1	11
HUTCHINSON, ROBERT and THOMAS, for relief	30	26		3
HYANNIS, MASSACHUSETTS, marine hospital at	16	34	1	7
HYDE, WILLIAM A., for relief	347	45	2	9
HYDROPHOBIA, to investigate	3463	49	1	11
HYDROGRAPHIC OFFICE, for distribution of charts of	325	48	1	11
ILLINOIS, custom districts of Chicago, to establish	203	28	1	6
ILLINOIS CENTRAL RAILROAD, bridge Ohio River	3111	49	1	11
ILLINOIS RIVER,				
Beacons and buoys for, to provide	1008	47	1	10
Bridges across,				
To authorize construction of	863	49		11
To construct near Columbiana	1970	47		10
Lights for, to provide	1003	47		10
IMMIGRATION,				
Act of July 4, 1864, to amend relative to encouragement of	48	39		8
Commission on, to appoint	1948	47	2	10
IMMIGRANTS,				
Arrival of, tabular statement of number entered at New York City from 1871 to 1882	650	47		10
Landing of, to provide for care on	121	47		10
Number entered at New York City from 1871 to 1882, tabular statement of	650	47		10
Protection of, on the high seas, to amend statutes for	1567	46		9
Do	1699	47		10
Statistics of, to collect more accurate	3607	49	2	11
Vessels carrying, regulating	121	47	1	10
IMPORT DUTIES,				
Amending section 18 of act of July 14, 1832	12	22	2	1
Investigations of system	165	21	1	1
Do	21	30	2	6

Subject.	Report.	Congress.	Session.	Volume.
ORT DUTIES—Continued.				
Collection of,				
To repeal thirty-seventh section of act of March 1, 1823	72	20	1	1
Rules and methods in the Treasury Department	740	24	1	2
Do.	81	25	2	2
Suits arising under	107	37	2	8
Discriminating,				
American cargoes in Cuba	115	21	2	1
Do.	468	23	1	1
Swedish and Norwegian cargoes	36	19	2	1
Drawbacks,				
Cordage made from foreign materials	165	21	1	1
Extend privilege of	590	24	1	2
Do.	304	25	2	2
Flour made from foreign wheat	835	27	2	4
Do	258	30	1	6
Foreign coal entered for exportation	245	26	2	3
Foreign goods conveyed overland to Mexico	540	26	1	3
Hemp imported, when manufactured in cordage and exported	229	24	2	2
With Texas, Mexico, and British American provinces	328	27	2	4
Do.	835	27	2	4
Do.	399	28	1	6
Iron, manufactured by rolling, and on hammered	126	18	1	1
Refunding, on goods destroyed by fire	321	30	1	6
Do.	34	31	1	7
Do.	202	33	1	7
Do.	86	34	1	7
Do.	10	35	1	8
Remission of,				
Bibles and religious works	740	24	1	2
Do.	79	25	2	2
Coffee in Dutch vessels	188	28	2	6
State of Michigan, certain duties on railroad iron	478	28	1	6
Rates of duty on,				
Cotton and woolen goods	49	14	1	1
Do.	61	14	2	1
Coffee	282	21	1	1
Do.	283	21	1	1
Drugs	633	36	1	8
Tea	282	21	1	1
Do.	283	21	1	1
Umbrellas	697	25	2	2
Wire	111	20	1	1
Warehousing laws for, establishing	93	20	2	1
Do.	65	21	1	1
Do.	367	30	1	6
MPORTATIONS, to encourage commerce and internal trade by facilitating direct	21	39	2	8
NDIANAPOLIS, INDIANA, port of entry	667	46	2	9
Do.	854	47	1	10
NDUSTRY (schooner), for relief of owners and crew of	316	26	1	3
Do	739	27	2	4
Do	201	29	1	6
NES, GEORGE, for relief	200	21	1	1
Do.	11	22	1	1
Do.	27	23	1	1
Do.	80	24	1	2
Do.	485	24	1	2
Do.	261	24	2	2
Do	307	25	2	2
NSPECTION LAWS OF THE STATES, to regulate disposal of surplus duties collected under	650	47	1	10
NSPECTORS (*see also* CUSTOMS OFFICERS; STEAM VESSELS),				
Steamboat,				
To establish at Albany, Ind., local board of	247	35	1	8
To establish at Evansville, Ind., local board of	182	36	1	8
To establish at Napoleon, Ark., local board of	248	35	1	8
Inspection of vessels propelled by steam, required	9	35	1	8
Do.	141	35	2	8
Do.	9	36	1	8
NSURRECTION, to repeal section 8, act of July 2, 1864, relative to States declared in	24	38	2	8
NTERIOR DEPARTMENT. (*See* DEPARTMENT OF THE INTERIOR.)				
NTERNAL TRADE, to encourage, by facilitating direct importations and commerce	21	39	2	8
NTERNATIONAL COMMERCE, to establish a bureau of	1037	48	1	11
NTERNATIONAL ELECTRICAL EXHIBITION, to appoint scientific commission for	1444	48	1	11
NTERSTATE COMMERCE (*see also* COMMERCE),				
Bureau in Interior Department on, to establish	1399	47	1	10
Commission to investigate questions relative to, to create	*1399	47	1	10

* Parts 1, 2.

Subject.	Report.	Congress.	Session.	Volume.
INTERSTATE COMMERCE—Continued.				
Commission to investigate questions relative to, to create	596	48	1	11
Do	902	49	1	11
Common carriers, to prohibit unjust discrimination by	245	45	2	9
Discriminations, to prohibit unjust, by common carriers	245	45	2	9
Interior Department, to establish bureau in, on	*1399	47	1	10
Regulations for, to provide	76	42	3	9
Do	245	45	2	9
Do	1399	47	1	10
Do	2554	49	1	11
INTERSTATE RAPID TRANSIT RAILWAY, bridge Kansas River	1393	49	1	11
INVESTIGATION, conduct of N. P. Trist, United States consul at Havana	707	26	1	3
IRON and STEEL, discriminating duties between rolled iron and hammered iron imported from Great Britain	126	18	1	1
IRONDEQUOIT BAY, LAKE ONTARIO, to improve channel of	1274	46		9
IRWIN, JAMES, for relief	74	33		7
ISLE OF PINES (schooner), to change name of	10	46		9
J. H. DUSENBERRY (schooner), to change name of	661	46		9
JACKSON, GEORGE R., & CO., for relief	14	36		8
JACKSONVILLE, FLORIDA, port of entry, to discontinue	887	27		4
JACOCKS, JOHN H., for relief	755	25		2
JACQUELINE, JOHN M., for relief	33	26		3
JANES, JOSEPH, for relief	384	20		3
JAMES RIVER AND KANAWHA CANAL, to complete a water highway from the James River to the Ohio River	76	42	3	9
JELLISON, ZACHARIAH, for relief	635	36	1	8
JERSEY CITY, NEW JERSEY, to construct custom-house and warehouse at	38	39	1	8
JOHN GEORGE (schooner), for relief of owner and crew of	466	27	2	4
JOHNSON, JAMES D., and others, for relief	144	38	1	8
JOSEPH OF WAREHAM (schooner), for relief of owners	99	26	2	3
Do	135	27	3	3
JUNIOR (ship), for relief of owner	41	36	2	8
KALAMAZOO RIVER, MICHIGAN, for improvement of	415	28	1	6
KANSAS CITY, MISSOURI,				
Bridge, to construct, across Missouri River between Sibley and	3830	49	2	11
Port of delivery	872	47	1	10
KANSAS CITY AND MEMPHIS RAILROAD BRIDGE COMPANY, bridge Mississippi River	2225	49	1	11
KANSAS RIVER, bridge across	1393	49	1	11
KATE BROWN (brig), for relief of owners	141	33	1	7
KATE SUTTON (yacht), to change name of	1329	46	2	9
KEITHSBURG, ILLINOIS, bridge Mississippi River at	763	49	1	11
KELLETT, CHARLES A., for relief	416	30	1	6
KENT (steamship), authorizing inspection of boiler	1038	48	1	11
KENT ISLAND, MARYLAND, light-house and fog-bell at Bloody Point Bar on	643	46	2	9
KEOKUK, IOWA, marine hospital at	241	34	3	7
Do	95	35	1	8
KERN, JOHN, for relief	257	24	2	2
Do	292	25	2	2
KETCHAM, THOMAS, for relief	349	24	1	2
KEWAUNEE, WISCONSIN, life-saving station at	4034	49	2	11
KEY WEST, FLORIDA, marine hospital at	396	28	1	6
KIFF, DANIEL, for relief	268	22	1	1
Do	367	23	1	1
KILL VON KULL. (*See* STATEN ISLAND SOUND.)				
KILLICK SHOALS, VIRGINIA,				
Day beacon in Chincoteague Bay on	817	45	2	9
Light-house on, to erect	1068	48	1	11
KIMBERLY, ELI, for relief	838	25	2	2
KINGSTON, STEPHEN, for relief	195	23	1	1
KNIGHT, J. B., for relief	269	27	2	4
KNOWLES, JOSEPH, Jr., for relief	225	28	1	6
Do	262	29	1	6
Do	81	34	1	7
KNOWLES, Z., for relief	174	27	3	4
Do	226	28	1	6
Do	62	28	2	6
Do	95	29	1	6
Do	80	34	1	7
L. BOARDMAN (steamer), to change name of	1626	46	2	9
LABELS OR TRADE MARKS, to prevent use of false	527	36		8
LABOR, AMERICAN, to protect	835	27		4
LA CROSSE, WISCONSIN, immediate transportation of goods in bond from	390	44		9
LADIES' SEAMAN'S FRIEND SOCIETY, to donate old marine hospital and grounds in San Francisco, Cal., to	248	44		9
LA FAYETTE, LOUISIANA, port of delivery at	278	27	[illegible]	4
Do	126	28	1	6
LA FAYETTE CREEK, GEORGIA, bridge across	2439	49	1	11
LAFEVER & GALLIER, for relief	848	24	1	2
LAKE CHAMPLAIN, light-house at Whitehall Narrows, on	946	49	1	11
Do	2441	49	1	11

* Parts 1, 2.

Subject.	Report.	Congress.	Session.	Volume.
LAKE CHARLES, LOUISIANA, deputy collector of customs at	10	46	1	9
LAKE COAST LIGHTS. (*See* LIGHTS.)				
LAKE HURON, light-house at Port Sanilac, on	1043	48	1	11
LAKE PONTCHARTRAIN, LOUISIANA,				
Light-house at Mandeville on, to erect	199	48	1	11
Bridge across	1289	47	1	10
Right of way for water-works, granting	1639	47	1	10
LAKE SUPERIOR,				
Light-house at Grand Marais, Minn., on	699	45	2	9
Improvement of	316	34	1	7
LAMBERTON, NEW JERSEY, port of, to change name	1396	49	1	11
LAMPHEERS, NEW YORK, light-house at	863	47	1	10
LA PLATA RIVER, SOUTH AMERICA, survey and navigation of	252	35	1	8
LAPWING (schooner), for relief of owners and crew of	15	34	1	7
LAREDO, TEXAS, bridge across Rio Grande River, at	798	48	1	11
LAVAL, JOHN, for relief	80	26	1	3
LAWSON & BRICE, for relief	172	22	1	1
LEAVENWORTH, KANSAS, bridge across Missouri River at	804	48	1	11
LEE, HENRY, for relief	71	14	2	1
LEEF, HENRY, for relief	47	30	2	6
Do	254	34	1	7
Do	12	35	1	8
LEEF, JULIA, for relief	705	45	2	9
LEEF, JULIET, for relief	15	46	1	9
LEGGETT, THOMAS H., & CO., for relief	150	29	1	6
Do	500	30	1	6
LEON (Spanish brig), to compensate owners for rescuing crew of United States ship Minerva	34	22	1	1
LEVI ELDRIDGE (schooner), for relief of officers and crew of	235	25	3	2
LEVY, NATHAN, for relief	705	24	1	2
Do	238	25	3	2
Do	72	26	1	3
LEWES, DELAWARE, port of delivery at	2366	48	2	11
Do	2765	49	1	11
LEWIS AND CLARKE'S RIVER, OREGON, bridge over	2028	47	2	10
LEXINGTON (schooner), for relief	61	27	2	4
LEXINGTON (ship), for relief of owners	98	26	2	3
LIBERIA, establishment of colony of free blacks in	283	27	3	5
LIFE-CARS, Douglas Ottinger's patent for, to purchase	403	35	1	8
LIFE-SAVING SERVICE,				
Efficiency of, to promote	470	47	1	10
Organization of, to provide for	426	45	2	9
Stations, to establish additional	1083	49	1	11
LIFE-SAVING STATIONS,				
Kewaunee, Wis., to establish station at	4034	49	2	11
Louisville, Ky., to establish at	645	46	2	9
LIGHT-HOUSE BOARD (*see also* LIGHTS),				
Atchafalaya River, to extend its operations to	1068	47	1	10
Columbia and Willamette Rivers, to extend operations over	1036	47	1	10
Illinois River, to extend operations over	1003	47	1	10
Inspections by, cost of	986	49	1	11
Jurisdiction of, to amend act of June 23, 1874, extending	1272	46	2	9
Sacramento and San Joaquin Rivers, California, to extend over	3608	49	2	11
Saint John's River, to extend operations over	1272	46	2	9
LIGHT-HOUSE DISTRICTS, to increase number of	1147	49	1	11
LIGHT-HOUSE ESTABLISHMENT, expenditures from 1816 to 1842, statement showing	811	27	2	4
Inspectors in, appointment of additional	811	27	2	4
Regulations for, to provide better	811	27	2	4
Reorganization of	811	27	2	4
LIGHTS (this title includes light-houses, light-ships, beacons, fog-signals, buoys, and all things under control of Light-House Board),				
Atlantic and Pacific Oceans and great lakes, to establish, along coast of	3619	49	2	11
Appropriation for surveys and erection of light-houses, &c	752	25	2	2
Do	837	27	2	4
Bell's Rock, Virginia, light-house in York River on	162	46	2	9
Booth Bay, Me., light-house	739	47	1	10
Borden Flats, Mount Hope Bay, Massachusetts, light-house on	1269	46	2	9
Brandywine Shoal, Delaware, light-house on	740	27	2	4
Cape Hatteras, North Carolina, light-ship at	1387	49	1	11
Cape San Blas, Florida, light-house at	1973	47	2	10
Carlton Island, New York, light on	198	48	1	11
Castle Hill, Rhode Island, light-house at	528	49	1	11
Chatham, Mass., light-house at Stage Harbor	698	45	2	6
Chesapeake Bay, light-ship at entrance to	1464	49	1	11
Chicago, Ill., light in harbor of	991	97	1	10
Chincoteague Bay, Virginia, day beacon on Killick Shoals in	817	45	2	9
Cob Point Bar, Maryland, light-house on	3493	49	2	11
Crab-tree Ledge, Maine, light-house at	1460	49	1	11
Croatan, N. C., light-house at	1385	49	1	11
Danger signals, to amend laws relating to	682	47	1	10

Subject.	Report.	Congress.	Session.	Volume.
LIGHTS—Continued.				
Deer Island, Boston, Mass., light-house at	1461	49	1	11
Destruction Island, Washington Territory, light-house and fog-signal on	1558	47	1	10
Detroit River, light-house	1153	47	1	10
Dog Island, Florida, light-house at	1973	47	2	10
Do	1362	48	1	11
Eagle River, Mich., light-house at	656	46	2	9
Eastern coast of the United States, condition of	282	27	3	5
Electricity, to authorize experiments for lighting rivers	2250½	48	2	11
Erie, Pa., light-house at	857	47	1	10
Flynn's Knoll, New York, light-house at	740	27	2	4
Foulweather Bluff, Washington Territory, to erect fog-bell on	69	45	3	9
Georgetown Harbor, South Carolina, light-house at mouth of Sampit River	641	46	2	9
Graham Shoals, Michigan, fog-bell buoy on	223	46	3	9
Grand Marais, Minn., light-house	699	45	2	9
Do	2385	48	2	11
Gray's Harbor, Washington Territory, light-house	1557	47	1	10
Great Shoals, Maryland, light-house on	1218	47	1	10
Great Wicomico River, light-house at mouth of	856	47	1	10
Do	3452	49	1	11
Gull Rocks, Newport, R. I., light-house on	1889	49	1	11
Half-Way Rock, Massachusetts, light-house at	822	46	2	9
Hell Gate, New York,				
Electric lights at	1133	47	1	10
Site for light at	1231	49	1	11
Hog Island Shoal, Rhode Island, light-ship at	1888	49	1	11
Hudson River, light-house at Danskammer Point	1229	47	1	10
Illuminating gas in light-houses, beacons, and other aids to navigation	1748	46	2	9
Kent Island, Maryland, light-house and fog-bell at Bloody Point Bar on	643	46	2	9
Killick Shoal, Virginia, light-house on	1668	48	1	11
Lake Michigan, light-house at Little Traverse Bay	116	45	2	9
Do	70	45	3	9
Lake Pontchartrain, light-house at Mandeville, La	855	47	1	10
Lake Superior,				
Fog-signal on Stannard's Rock in	114	45	2	9
Light-house at grand Marais, Minn. on	699	45	2	9
Lampheers, New York, light-house at	863	47	1	10
Light-house districts, to increase number of	1147	49	1	11
Light-houses,				
Authorizing surveys and examinations of proposed sites for	838	27	2	4
To establish additional buoys and	5	32	2	7
Little Traverse Bay, Lake Michigan, light-house at	116	45	2	9
Do	70	45	3	9
Do	570	47	1	10
Livingston's Creek, New York, light-house at	863	47	1	10
Louisiana Point, New York, light-house at	392	47	1	10
Lower Cape Fear River, North Carolina, lights on	1263	48	1	11
Lubec Narrows, Maine, light-house at	1462	49	1	11
Mackinac, Mich., light-house on Round Island at	419	45	2	9
Mandeville, Pontchartrain, light-house at	199	48	1	11
Manistique, Mich., light-house at	658	46	2	9
Do	398	47	1	10
Marine signals, to create an international commission upon	682	47	1	10
Maumee Bay, Ohio, light-house and range beacons	753	47	1	10
Menomonee Harbor, Wisconsin, light-house at entrance to	823	45	2	9
Milwaukee, Wis., light-house	327	36	1	8
Minot's Rock, Boston Harbor, light-house on	437	28	1	6
Mississippi River, light-ship and lights at mouth	1465	49	1	11
Moosehead Lake, Maine, beacon lights in	635	49	1	11
Mosquito Inlet, Florida, light-house at	391	47	1	10
Mount Hope Bay, Massachusetts, light-house	1269	46	2	9
New Bedford and Fair Haven, Mass., for light on bridge at	1229	49	1	11
Patuxent River, Maryland, lights at	1212	47	1	10
Pensacola, Fla., light-house at	1384	49	1	11
Point Robinson, Washington Territory, fog-signal at	1074	47	1	10
Point Saint George, California, light-house and fog-bell at	267	46	3	9
Do	890	47	1	10
Point Sur, California, light-house at	526	49	1	11
Point Wilson, Washington Territory, fog-signal	386	44	1	9
Port Sanilac, Mich., light-house at	1043	48	1	11
Private, to prohibit establishment of	3966	49	2	11
Puget Sound, Washington Territory, fog-signal on Sandy Point in	71	45	3	9
Racine, Wis., fog-signal and lake-coast light	423	45	2	9
Raritan Bay, New Jersey, light-house on shoals known as Great Beds in	786	45	2	9
Red River, Louisiana, extending operations of Light-House Board over	865	47	1	10
Richmond's Island, Maine, light-house	858	47	1	10
Saint Croix and Chippewa Rivers, extending operations of Light-House Board over	864	47	1	10
Saint John's River, Florida,				
Buoys at mouth of	890	27	2	4
Lights on	1152	47	1	10

Subject.	Report.	Congress.	Session.	Volume.
LIGHTS—Continued.				
Saint John's River, Florida—Continued.				
Lights on	197	48	1	11
Sakonnet Point, Rhode Island, light-house at	1944	47	2	10
Sandy Point, Maryland, changing light at	870	47	1	10
San Francisco, Cal., fog-signal at Lewis Point	1230	47	1	10
San Luis Obispo, Cal.,				
Light-house at	824	45	2	9
Do	525	49	1	11
Fog-signal at	868	47	1	10
Saybrook, Conn., beacon light at	867	47	1	10
Seul Choix Point, Michigan, light-house at	1568	49	1	11
South Farallon Island, California, fog-bell on	788	45	2	9
South Pass, Mississippi River, light-ship at	859	47	1	10
Southwest Pass, Vermillin Bay, Louisiana, light-house at	1556	47	1	10
Squaw Island, Lake Michigan, light-house on	654	46	2	9
Supply steamer for light-house districts, to construct	1459	49	1	11
Do	1463	49	1	11
Tarrytown, N. Y., light-house at	863	47	1	10
Thunder Bay, Michigan, light-house at	821	45	2	9
Two Bush Island, Maine, light-house on	1271	46	2	9
Whale's Back, New Hampshire, light-house on	437	28	1	6
Whitehall Narrows, New York, light-house at	946	49	1	11
Widows' Island, Maine, light-house on	1270	46	2	9
LILLY (schooner), for relief of owner	87	23	2	1
Do	75	26	1	3
Do	787	27	3	4
LITTLE, HENRY, for relief	648	30	1	6
Do	98	33	2	7
LITTLE FALLS WATER-POWER COMPANY, to allow them to dam Mississippi River	1675	48	1	11
Do	846	49	1	11
LITTLEFIELD, CARROLLTON AND WESTERN RAILROAD COMPANY, bridge across Illinois River	1970	47	2	10
LITTLE RIVER, LOUISIANA, bridge across	1644	47	1	10
LITTLE TRAVERSE, MICHIGAN, light-house at	116	45	2	9
Do	70	45	3	9
Do	570	47	1	10
LIVE STOCK, (*see also* ANIMALS),				
Importation of, to provide for	1644	49	1	11
Transportation of, investigation	2638	49	1	11
LIVE-STOCK HIGHWAY, to establish	1228	49	1	11
LIVINGSTON'S CREEK, NEW YORK, light-house at	863	47	1	10
LIZZIE (schooner), to change name of	132	46	3	9
LORD, SAMUEL, for relief	834	27	3	4
LORD, SAMUEL S., for relief	211	23	1	1
LOUISIANA, New Orleans customs district, to extend limits of	638	36	1	8
LOUISIANA NORTH AND SOUTH RAILROAD, bridge across Red River	3218	49	1	11
LOUISIANA POINT, NEW YORK, light-house at	392	47	1	10
LOUISVILLE, KENTUCKY,				
Life-saving station at, to establish	645	46	2	9
Marine hospital at, to erect	745	27	2	4
Do	124	28	2	6
LOUISVILLE AND PORTLAND CANAL,				
Bonds of, providing for payment of	218	43	1	9
Enlarging the	327	34	1	7
Purchase by United States of the individual stock of the	6	20	1	6
LOUISVILLE EXPOSITION, to remit duties on exhibits	3412	49	1	11
LOW, JAMES W., and others, for relief	330	31	1	7
LUBEC NARROWS, MAINE, light-house at	1462	49	1	11
LUCE, ELISHA, for relief	173	27	3	4
Do	57	28	2	6
Do	386	28	1	6
Do	259	29	1	6
LUCY ANN (schooner), for relief of officers and crew of	233	25	3	2
Do	385	26	1	3
Do	385	28	1	6
Do	263	29	1	6
Do	17	34	1	7
LUCY BLAKE (schooner), for relief of owners of	524	36	1	8
LURAND (schooner), for relief of owner and crew of	875	27	2	4
LUSHER, EDWARD, for relief of assignee	626	36	1	8
LYNCHBURG, VIRGINIA, port of entry	242	34	3	7
M. S. PERRY (steamer), to change name of	131	37	2	8
McCOLGAN, JOHN, for relief	153	25	2	2
Do	312	26	1	3
Do	456	27	2	4
McCULLOCH, ADAM, for relief	145	27	3	4
MACHIAS, MAINE, custom-house at	18	34	1	7
McINTYRE, JAMES, for relief	444	28	1	6
McKEE, JOHN, for relief	47	30	2	6

Subject.	Report.	Congress.	Session.	Volume.
McKEE, JOHN, for relief	206	34	1	7
Do	12	35	1	8
Do	705	45	2	9
MACKIE, THOMAS G., for relief	347	45	2	9
MACKINAC, MICHIGAN, light-house and fog-signal on Round Island at	419	45	2	9
McLANE, E. J., for relief	9	33	2	7
McLELLAN, JACOB, for relief	171	33	1	7
McLELLAN, JAMES H., & CO., for relief	347	28	1	6
MAIL CONTRACTS. (*See* POSTAL SERVICE.)				
MAINE,				
Customs districts, Bangor, to change	1700	46	2	9
Customs districts, in East Thomaston, to establish	113	30	2	6
Port of entry, to establish, on Penobscot River in	78	19	2	1
MANDEVILLE, LOUISIANA, light-house at	855	47	1	10
Do	199	48	1	11
MANISTIQUE, MICHIGAN, light-house at	658	46	2	9
Do	306	47	1	10
MANN'S MARINE DANGER SIGNAL. (*See* SIGNALS.)				
MANUFACTURES,				
Domestic, on subject of	105	15	1	1
Home fabrics from cotton and wool, to encourage	49	14	1	1
Do	61	14	2	1
MAP OF TRANSPORTATION ROUTES, to authorize preparation of	99	48	1	11
MARIAH (yacht), to change name of	1830	46	2	9
MARINE CANAL COMPANY OF NANTUCKET, relative to aiding the	213	27	3	4
MARINE DANGER SIGNALS. (*See* SIGNALS.)				
MARINE HOSPITAL,				
To erect, establish, and locate,				
Albany, N. Y	255	35	1	8
Bedloe's Island, New York	666	46	2	9
Do	399	47	1	10
Baltimore, Md	124	28	2	6
Do	1451	46	2	9
Boston, Mass	649	30	1	6
Buffalo, N. Y	256	35	1	8
Cedar Keys, Fla	648	46	2	9
Charleston, S. C	83	20	1	1
Do	150	21	1	1
Chelsea, Mass	649	30	1	6
Chicago, Ill	124	28	2	6
City Point, Va	110	28	2	6
Cleveland, Ohio	124	28	2	6
Do	197	43	1	9
Fort Howard, Wis	235	34	3	7
Galveston, Tex	49	47	1	10
Hickman, Ky	643	36	1	8
Hyannis, Mass	16	34	1	7
Keokuk, Iowa	241	34	3	7
Do	95	35	1	8
Key West, Fla	396	28	1	6
Louisville, Ky	745	27	2	4
Do	124	28	2	6
Memphis, Tenn	254	35	1	8
Milwaukee, Wis	239	34	3	7
Morgan City, La	843	46	3	9
Napoleon, Ark	745	27	2	4
Natchez, Miss	745	27	2	4
New Bedford, Mass	569	29	1	6
Do	120	30	1	6
New Berne, N. C	400	47	1	10
New London, Conn	569	29	1	6
Do	120	30	1	6
New Orleans, La	1450	46	2	9
Do	48	47	1	10
Do	1304	48	1	11
Newport, R. I	81	36	2	8
Ocracoke, N. C	889	27	2	4
Paducah, Ky	745	27	2	4
Do	124	28	2	6
Do	232	34	3	7
Pittsburgh, Pa	745	27	2	4
Do	124	28	2	6
Plattsburg, N. Y	258	35	1	8
Portland, Me	468	22	1	1
Do	151	23	1	1
Do	85	24	1	2
Do	82	25	2	2
Port Townsend, Wash	1211	47	1	10
Saint Joseph, Fla	237	25	3	2
Saint Joseph, Mo	258	35	1	8
Saint Louis, Mo	745	27	2	4

Subject.	Report.	Congress.	Session.	Volume.
E HOSPITAL—Continued.				
ent, establish, and locate—Continued.				
Saint Louis, Mo	457	[illegible]	1	6
Saint Paul, Minn	[illegible]	[illegible]	[illegible]	[illegible]
Staten Island, New York, property for hospital on	[illegible]	[illegible]	1	[illegible]
E HOSPITAL FUND, liability of seamen to contribute to	[illegible]	[illegible]	[illegible]	[illegible]
E HOSPITAL SERVICE,				
ciency of, to increase	[illegible]	[illegible]	[illegible]	[illegible]
Do	[illegible]	[illegible]	1	[illegible]
Do	[illegible]	[illegible]	1	[illegible]
Do	[illegible]	[illegible]	1	[illegible]
tern waters, extending system over	[illegible]	[illegible]	[illegible]	[illegible]
le fisheries, for seamen disabled in	275	31	1	7
E SIGNALS (see also SIGNALS; VESSELS),				
of, to introduce a uniform	21	[illegible]	1	[illegible]
and vessels, amending system of	[illegible]	[illegible]	1	[illegible]
LEWIS, for relief	[illegible]	[illegible]	1	1
Do	[illegible]	[illegible]	1	1
JAMES, for relief	[illegible]	[illegible]	2	1
LA (schooner), for relief of owners and crew of	211	[illegible]	1	[illegible]
(schooner), for relief of owners	[illegible]	[illegible]	1	1
Do	[illegible]	[illegible]	1	[illegible]
E. CANWELL (schooner), to change name of	[illegible]	[illegible]	2	[illegible]
FRANCIS (schooner), for relief of owners and crew of	[illegible]	[illegible]	1	[illegible]
APONY RIVER, VIRGINIA, bridge across	[illegible]	[illegible]	2	9
Y, MERINO D., for relief	[illegible]	[illegible]	2	[illegible]
E BAY, OHIO, light-house and range-beacons in	[illegible]	47	1	10
Lieut. M. F., to test wind and current charts of	[illegible]	[illegible]	2	6
OWER (schooner), for relief of owners	47	[illegible]	2	1
Do	[illegible]	24	1	2
EMENT. (See VESSELS.)				
inspection of exported	[illegible]	[illegible]	2	11
R, HIRAM L., for relief	[illegible]	[illegible]	2	[illegible]
LIS, DAVID, for relief	[illegible]	[illegible]	2	2
HIS, TENNESSEE,				
ge across Mississippi River at	[illegible]	[illegible]	1	11
Do	[illegible]	[illegible]	1	11
Do	[illegible]	[illegible]	2	11
ine hospital at, to construct	[illegible]	35	1	8
Do	60	36	1	8
lic buildings at, to construct	641	36	1	8
IINEE RIVER,				
ge across	2440	49	1	11
it-house, to erect, at mouth of	823	45	2	9
ANT MARINE (see also COMMERCE AND NAVIGATION),				
renticeship in, system of	97	33	2	7
Do	177	34	1	7
es of decline in	342	46	3	9
ANT VESSELS. (See VESSELS.)				
IAN. (See LONGITUDE.)				
IAN TIME, to telegraph daily to ports of entry	681	47	1	10
LL, EDWARD, for relief	355	38	1	7
LL, MOSES, for relief	704	24	1	2
IORA (schooner), for relief of owners and crew of	186	36	1	8
SYSTEM. (See COINS AND COINAGE; WEIGHTS AND MEASURES.)				
).				
id trade with,				
Ports of entry on Arkansas and Red Rivers, establishment of	540	26	1	3
To extend privilege of drawback of duties on	328	27	2	4
Do	835	27	2	4
Do	390	27	1	6
AN,				
rt duties on railroad iron, to remit to State	478	28	1	6
nboat inspectors in, to regulate compensation of	1646	47	1	10
AN (barge), to allow American register to	1138	49	1	11
ES, LOVEL G., patent, for protection of lives in case of collision of vessels	281	28	1	6
DOLPHUS, & CO., for relief	159	31	1	7
CITY BRIDGE COMPANY, bridge across Yellowstone River	1397	49	1	11
D, WILLIAM, for relief	730	30	1	6
D, A. A., for relief	159	35	1	8
, JAMES, for relief	85	20	1	1
, NOAH, for relief	977	25	2	2
Do	130	33	1	7
, ROBERT, for relief	751	25	2	2
Do	211	25	3	2
Do	70	26	1	3
Do	71	26	1	3
chooner), for relief of owners and crew	187	23	1	1
UKEE, WIS.,				
or at, improvement of, to reimburse city for	120	41	2	8

Subject.	Report.	Congress.	Session.	Volume.
MILWAUKEE, WIS.—Continued.				
Harbor at, improvement of, to reimburse city for	1500	46	2	9
Light-house at, to establish	327	36	1	8
Marine hospital at, to establish	239	34	3	7
MINERVA (ship), compensate owners of Spanish brig Leon for rescue of crew of.	84	22	1	1
MINNEAPOLIS INDUSTRIAL EXPOSITION, authorizing loan of certain articles to	3223	49	1	11
MINNESOTA RIVER, navigation of, to fix head of	119	47	1	10
MINNIE R. CHILD (steamboat), to change name of	658	46	2	9
MINOT'S ROCK, BOSTON HARBOR, light-house on	437	28	1	6
MINTS, UNITED STATES, to establish a branch in New York City	490	31	1	7
MISSISSIPPI RIVER,				
Bridges across, at,				
Anoka	1332	48	1	11
Dubuque, Iowa	327	48	1	11
Do	3800	49	2	11
Fort Madison or Keokuk	3799	49	2	11
Grand Tower, Ill	4154	49	2	11
Keithsburg, Ill	443	47	1	10
Memphis, Tenn	1567	48	1	11
Do	3831	49	2	11
Rock Island, Ill	250	35	1	8
Saint Louis, Mo	1647	47	1	10
Do	2341	49	1	11
Saint Paul, Minn	1267	48	1	11
Wabasha and Read's Landing, Minnesota	397	47	1	10
Winona, Minn	3829	49	2	11
Bridges across, by corporations,				
Central Missouri Railroad	2667	48	2	11
Do	522	49	1	11
Do	1307	49	1	11
Chicago, Burlington and Northern Railroad	2485	49	1	11
Chicago, Saint Paul and Saint Louis	1268	48	1	11
Davenport and Rock Island Bridge Company	1331	48	1	11
Kansas City and Memphis Railroad Bridge Company	3225	49	1	11
New York and Council Bluffs Railroad	763	49	1	11
Red Wing (Minn.) Ponton Bridge Company	1396	49	1	11
Red Wing (Minn.) Transit Company	1740	46	2	9
Rock Island and Southwestern Railroad Company	992	47	1	10
Saint Paul, Minneapolis and Minnetonka	1337	48	1	11
Winona Ponton Bridge Company	1309	49	1	11
Dams at,				
Brainerd, Minn	1336	48	1	11
Do	105	49	1	11
Little Falls, Minn	1675	48	1	11
Do	846	49	1	11
Saint Cloud, Minn	1303	48	1	11
Improvement at,				
Des Moines and Rock Island Rapids	69	34	1	7
Do	349	35	1	8
Falls of Saint Anthony and Sauk Rapids	72	34	1	7
Falls of Saint Anthony and mouth of Minnesota River	72	34	1	7
Light-ship and lights at mouth, to construct	1465	49	1	11
Do	3620	49	2	11
Pilotage on, to enact laws regulating	178	27	2	4
Reservoirs, to construct, for improvement of navigation of the	1701	46	2	9
MISSISSIPPI RIVER LOGGING COMPANY, sheer booms in the Mississippi River by, to construct	664	46	2	9
MISSISSIPPI WATER-POWER AND BOOM COMPANY, to allow to construct dam at Brainerd, Minn	1336	48	1	11
Do	105	49	1	11
MISSOURI, ports of entry in	540	26	1	3
MISSOURI RIVER,				
Bridges across at,				
Arrow Rock, Mo	340	46	2	9
Do	231	47	1	10
Hamburg, Mo	230	47	1	10
Harrison County, Iowa	990	47	1	10
Kansas City, Mo.	1456	49	1	11
Kansas City and Sibley, Mo	3830	49	2	11
Leavenworth, Kans	804	48	1	11
Nebraska City	3403	49	1	11
Sibley, Mo	803	48	1	11
Sioux City, Iowa	232	47	1	10
Do	4038	49	2	11
Yankton, Dak	3803	49	2	11
Bridges across, by corporations,				
Atchison (Kans.) Bridge Company	1457	49	1	11
Atchison and Nebraska Railroad	1042	48	1	11
Benton Bridge Company	1551	48	1	11
Do	2911	49	1	11

Subject.	Report.	Congress.	Session.	Volume.
MISSOURI RIVER—Continued.				
Bridges across, by corporations—Continued.				
Chillicothe and Kansas City Railroad	1971	47	1	10
Chicago, Milwaukee and Saint Paul Railroad	1394	49	1	11
Do	1617	49	1	11
Chicago and Central Kansas	1265	48	1	11
Dakota Central Railroad	1567	49	1	11
Duluth, Pierre and Black Hills Railroad Company	3802	49	2	11
Hannibal and Southwestern Railroad Company to	231	47	1	10
Nebraska City, Beatrice and Salina Railroad	1334	48	1	11
Do	1044	48	1	11
New York and Council Bluffs Railroad	1354	49	1	11
Saint Joseph and Rio Grande Railroad	1353	49	1	11
Saint Louis and Kansas City Short-Line Railroad	1392	49	1	11
Do	1395	49	1	11
Salina, Lincoln and Decatur Railroad	1566	48	1	11
Improvement of, to appoint commission on	1528	48	1	11
MOBILE, ALABAMA, harbor at, to improve	539	29	1	6
Do	86	34	1	7
MONTGOMERY, ALABAMA, port of delivery	640	36	1	8
MOODY, GEORGE, for relief	211	23	1	1
MOOSEHEAD LAKE, MAINE, beacon lights in	635	49	1	11
MORDECAI, M. C., for relief	892	27	2	4
MORGAN, CHARLES, for relief	355	33	1	7
MORGAN, CHARLES W., and others, for relief	495	31	1	7
MORGAN CITY, LOUISIANA, marine hospital at	343	46	3	9
MORSE, JONAH, for relief	275	27	3	4
MORSE, Prof. S. F. B. (*See* TELEGRAPH.)				
MOSQUITO INLET, FLORIDA, light-house at	391	47	1	10
MOUNT DESERT FERRY, MAINE, port of entry at	2542	48	2	11
Do	1085	49	1	11
Do	1984	49	1	11
MOUNT HOPE BAY, MASSACHUSETTS, light-house on Berden Flats in	1269	46	2	9
MUNN, JOHN G., and others, for increase of salary	388	26	1	3
MUSCATINE, IOWA, public buildings at	258	35	1	8
NAGG'S HEAD, connecting waters of Albemarle Sound with Atlantic Ocean at	251	29	1	6
NANTUCKET, MASSACHUSETTS, custom-house and post-office at	68	29	2	6
NANTUCKET ISLAND, signal station on	1301	48	1	11
NAPOLEON, ARKANSAS,				
Marine hospital at, to erect	445	27	2	4
Steamboat inspectors at, to establish local board of	247	35		8
NASH, JOHN, for relief	106	34		7
NASHVILLE, TENNESSEE, custom-house and post-office building at	19	34		7
NASHVILLE, JACKSON AND MEMPHIS RAILROAD, bridge across Tennessee River	634	49	1	11
NATCHEZ, MISSISSIPPI, marine hospital at	745	27	2	4
NATCHEZ, RED RIVER AND TEXAS RAILROAD COMPANY, bridges across Black River, Little River, Red River, and Sabine River	1644	47	1	10
NATIONAL INDUSTRIAL EXPOSITION of colored people of United States, at Birmingham, Ala., appropriation for	4047	49	2	11
NAVAL HOSPITALS, Annapolis, Md., to transfer to Secretary of Treasury to be used as a marine hospital	1451	46	2	9
NAVIGATION. (*See* COMMERCE AND NAVIGATION.)				
NAVIGATION LAWS, to consolidate	145	33	2	7
NAVY-YARD, Philadelphia, Pa., to build dry dock at	253	29	1	6
NEBRASKA CITY, NEBRASKA, bridge Missouri River at	1044	48	1	11
Do	1334	48	1	11
Do	3403	49	1	11
NETHERLANDS,				
Amsterdam Industrial Exhibition, providing for United States participating in	1692	47	1	10
Coffee from, to exempt from duties when imported in Dutch vessels	188	28	2	6
NEW ALBANY, INDIANA, steamboat inspectors, board of, to establish	247	35	1	8
NEW BEDFORD, MASSACHUSETTS,				
Light on bridge at	1229	49	1	11
Marine hospital at, to erect	569	29	1	6
Do	120	30	1	6
NEW BERNE, NORTH CAROLINA, marine hospital at	400	47	1	10
NEWBURG, NEW YORK, port of entry	200	48	1	11
NEWBURYPORT, MASSACHUSETTS, custom-house at	67	22	2	1
NEW LONDON, CONNECTICUT,				
Public wharf for custom-house at, to construct	214	27	3	4
Marine hospital at, to erect	569	29	1	6
Do	120	30	1	6
NEW ORLEANS, LOUISIANA,				
Custom-house at,				
To erect	55	28	2	6
For relief of clerks in	114	28	2	6
Customs district of, to extend	638	36	1	8
Harbor of, to improve	254	47	1	10

Subject.	Report.	Congress.	Session.	Volume.
POINT SAINT GEORGE, CALIFORNIA, light-house and fog-bell on	267	46	2	9
Do	390	47	1	10
POINT SUR, CALIFORNIA, light-house at	536	49	1	11
POINT WILSON, WASHINGTON TERRITORY, fog-signal on	386	44	1	9
POLLARD, CALVIN, for relief	348	24	1	2
POLLEN & COLGATE, for relief	900	27	2	4
POND, SABINE, for relief	179	19	1	1
PORT ANGELES, WASHINGTON TERRITORY, port of entry	119	37	2	8
PORT CHARGES OF THE WORLD, to purchase copies of	1040	48	1	11
PORTLAND, MAINE, marine hospital at	468	22	1	2
Do	151	23	1	1
Do	85	24	1	2
Do	82	25	2	2
PORTLAND, OREGON,				
Port of entry	2367	48	2	11
Port, to extend limits of	2764	49	1	11
PORT SANILAC, MICHIGAN, light-house at	1043	48	1	11
PORT TOWNSEND, WASHINGTON TERRITORY,				
Marine hospital at	1311	47	1	10
Port of entry at	119	37	2	8
Immediate transportation of goods in bond to	2369	48	2	11
PORTS OF DELIVERY,				
To establish at,				
Lewes, Del	2366	48	2	11
Do	2765	49	1	11
Rockport, Mass	250	48	1	11
Salamanca, N. Y	1671	48	1	11
Seattle, Wash	1335	48	1	11
Springfield, Mass	903	49	1	11
Do	1963	49	1	11
Tacoma, Wash	1335	48	1	11
PORTS OF ENTRY (*see also* under titles of respective localities),				
Abolishing distinctions in	590	24	1	2
Do	304	25	2	2
Arkansas, to establish, in	540	26	1	3
Florida, to extend privileges to Spanish vessels to all in	23	20	2	1
Missouri, to establish, in	540	26	1	3
To establish at,				
Anclote, Fla	77	45		9
Atchison, Kans	637	36		8
Bangor, Me	123	28		6
Bowling Green, Ky	238	34		7
Bucksville, S. C	859	27		4
Cedar Keys, Fla	833	27		4
Do	61	28		6
Chattanooga, Tenn	133	46		9
Cincinnati, Ohio	81	14		1
Do	642	36		8
Clarksville, Tenn	639	36		8
Crescent City, Cal	760	47		10
Denver, Colo	171	44		9
Do	395	47		10
Eureka, Cal	760	47		10
Fayetteville, N. C	647	46		9
Gray's Harbor, Wash	260	35	1	8
Hazard, Fla	887	27	2	4
Helena, Ark	858	47	1	10
Indianapolis, Ind	667	46	2	9
Kansas City	872	47	1	10
La Fayette, La	278	27	3	4
Do	126	28	1	6
Lynchburg, Va	242	34	3	7
Maine (on the Penobscot River)	78	19	2	1
Montgomery, Ala	640	36		8
Newburg, N. Y	200	49		11
Port Angeles, Wash	119	37		8
Portsmouth, Ohio	659	46		9
Oakland, Cal	79	45		9
Oconto, Wis	644	36	1	8
Sabine Pass, Texas	636	36	1	8
Saint Joseph, Mo	872	47	1	10
Saint Vincent, Minn	657	46	2	9
Do	17	47	1	10
San Luis Obispo, Cal	70	46	3	9
Do	394	47	1	10
Stonington, Conn	681	27	2	
Tampa, Fla	65	28	1	
Do	682	46	2	
Do	4101	49	2	1
West Point, Va	185	44	1	
Do	173	46	2	

Subject.	Report.	Congress.	Session.	Volume.
[illegible]TS OF ENTRY—Continued.				
To establish at,				
Wilmington, Cal	70	48	3	9
Do	294	47	1	10
[illegible]SMOUTH, OHIO, port of entry	690	49	2	9
[illegible]TUGAL, High duty levied on rice imported from United States to	115	21	2	1
[illegible]T & McCORD, for relief	285	46	3	9
[illegible]-OFFICE BUILDINGS. (See PUBLIC BUILDINGS; also names of respective localities.)				
[illegible]TAL SERVICE,				
China mail,				
Contracts for carrying	732	43	1	9
Subsidizing line between China and the United States	762	43	1	9
[illegible]TER, CHARLES, for relief	186	27	2	4
[illegible]TS, NATHAN (assignee), for relief	41	20	1	1
[illegible]TS & CLEMMENTS, for relief	290	22	1	1
Do	1067	20	2	2
[illegible]UGHKEEPSIE BRIDGE COMPANY, to remove piers in Hudson River belonging to	1496	47	1	10
[illegible]NTICE, JOSHUA, for relief	25	20	1	1
[illegible]NTISS, ORRIN, and others, for relief	707	27	2	4
[illegible]SIDENT OF THE UNITED STATES, veto of river and harbor bill by	741	29	1	6
[illegible]OCTOR, AMOS, for relief	474	28	1	6
Do	171	32	1	7
[illegible]TECTION PAPERS, issued to American seamen, to repeal all laws authorizing	189	24	2	2
[illegible]OVIDENCE, RHODE ISLAND, custom-house at, to repair	66	27	2	4
[illegible]OVINCETOWN, MASSACHUSETTS, harbor of, protection of	13	28	1	5
[illegible]BLIC BUILDINGS,				
Custom-house, removal of, from Jacksonville to Hazard, Fla	287	27	2	4
To erect, at,				
Albany, N. Y., marine hospital at	255	36	1	8
Apalachicola, Fla.,				
Custom-house, post-office, and court-house	61	36	1	8
Marine hospital	252	35	1	8
Do	60	36	1	8
Baltimore, Md., marine hospital	134	28	2	6
Do	1451	46	2	9
Boston, Mass.,				
Custom-house	448	24	1	2
Marine hospital near	649	30	1	6
Buffalo, N. Y., custom house at	236	34	3	7
Marine hospital at	256	35	1	8
Burlington, Iowa, certain public buildings	258	35	1	8
Cairo, Ill., custom-house and court-house	38	39	1	8
Castine, Me., custom-house	438	29	1	6
Do	18	34	1	7
Cedar Keys, Fla., marine hospital	648	46	2	9
Charleston, S. C., marine hospital	83	20	1	1
Do	150	21	1	1
Chicago, Ill., marine hospital	124	28	2	6
City Point, Va., marine hospital	110	26	2	3
Cleveland, Ohio, marine hospital	124	28	2	6
Eastport, Me., custom-house	581	29	1	6
Fall River, Mass., custom-house and post-office	570	28	1	6
Fort Howard, Wis., marine hospital	235	34	3	7
Galveston, Tex., marine hospital	49	47	1	10
Hyannis, Mass., marine hospital	16	34	1	7
Jersey City, N. J., custom-house and warehouse	38	39	1	8
Keokuk, Iowa,				
Marine hospital	241	34	1	8
Do	95	35	1	8
Custom-house	96	35	1	8
Key West, Fla., marine hospital	296	28	1	6
Louisville, Ky., marine hospital	745	27	2	4
Do	124	28	2	6
Machias, Me., custom-house	18	34	1	7
Memphis, Tenn.,				
Marine hospital	254	35	1	8
Do	60	36	1	8
Custom-house and post-office	641	36	1	8
Milwaukee, Wis., marine hospital	239	34	3	7
Morgan City, La., marine hospital	343	46	3	9
Muscatine, Iowa, public buildings	258	35	1	8
Nantucket, Mass., custom-house and post-office	68	29	2	6
Napoleon, Ark., marine hospital	745	27	2	4
Nashville, Tenn., custom-house	19	34	1	7
Natchez, Miss., marine hospital	745	27	2	4
New Bedford, Mass., marine hospital	569	29	1	6
Do	120	30	1	6
New Berne, N. C., marine hospital	400	47	1	10

Subject.	Report.	Congress.	Session.	Volume.
PUBLIC BUILDINGS—Continued.				
To erect, at,				
Newburyport, Mass., custom-house	67	22	2	1
New London, Conn., marine hospital	869	29	1	6
Do	120	30	1	6
New Orleans, La.,				
Custom-house	55	28	2	6
Marine hospital	1450	46	2	9
Do	48	47	1	10
Newport, R. I., marine hospital	81	36	2	8
Ocracoke, N. C., marine hospital	880	27	2	4
Paducah, Ky.,				
Marine hospital	745	27	2	4
Do	124	28	2	6
Marine hospital repairs	283	34	3	7
Peoria, Ill., certain ones at	258	35	1	8
Perth Amboy, N. J., custom-house	75	34	1	7
Petersburg, Va., custom-house	233	34	3	7
Pittsburgh, Pa., marine hospital	745	27	2	4
Do	124	28	2	6
Plattsburg, N. Y., marine hospital	258	35	1	8
Plymouth, Mass., custom-house	74	34	1	7
Point Isabel, Tex., custom-house	258	35	1	8
Portland, Me., marine hospital	408	22	1	1
Do	151	23	1	1
Do	85	24	2	2
Do	82	25	2	2
Port Townsend, Wash., to purchase buildings for marine hospital at	1211	47	1	10
Rochester, N. Y., custom-house	257	35	1	8
Saint Joseph, Fla., marine hospital	237	25	3	2
Do	258	35	1	8
Saint Louis, Mo., marine hospital	745	27	2	4
Do	437	29	1	6
Saint Paul, Minn.,				
Custom house	115	34	3	7
Marine hospital	950	45	2	9
Savannah, Ga., custom-house	682	24	1	2
Do	103	28	2	6
Toledo, Ohio, enlarge custom-house	76	34	1	7
Trenton, N. J., custom-house	259	35	1	8
Vicksburg, Miss., custom-house	240	34	3	7
PUBLIC DOCUMENTS, Hydrographic Office, distribution of charts of	325	48	1	11
PUGET SOUND, WASHINGTON TERRITORY,				
Fog-signal on Sandy Point in, to erect	71	45	2	9
Vessels in, to regulate clearing of	1287	47	1	10
PUIG, MIR & CO., for relief	76	34	3	7
QUARANTINE SYSTEM, to establish a national	392	43	1	9
QUARANTINE STATIONS,				
Ship Island, Mississippi, to remove	3998	49	2	11
Coast of Texas, to establish station on	50	47	1	10
QUINCY, MARIUS, for relief	305	25	2	2
RACINE, WISCONSIN, fog-signal and lake coast light at	423	45	2	9
RAFT. (*See* RED RIVER; RIVERS AND HARBORS.)				
RAILROADS,				
Arkansas Midland, bridge across White River, Ark	1302	48	1	11
Astoria and Winnemucca, bridges across,				
Young's and Lewis and Clarke's Rivers	2023	47	2	10
Certain rivers	2025	49	1	11
Do	2453	49	1	11
Atlantic and Pacific Ship, to incorporate	*717	49	1	11
Bellingham Bay, to build bridges	2442	49	1	11
Central Missouri, to bridge Mississippi River	2067	48	2	11
Do	522	49	1	11
Do	1307	49	1	11
Chicago, Burlington and Northern, to bridge Mississippi River	2185	49	1	11
Chicago, Freeport and Saint Paul, to bridge Saint Croix River	1232	49	1	11
Chicago, Milwaukee and Saint Paul, to bridge Missouri River	1394	49	1	11
Do	1617	49	1	11
Chicago, Saint Louis and New Orleans, to bridge Ohio River	3111	49	1	11
Chicago, Saint Paul and Saint Louis, to bridge Mississippi River	1268	48	1	11
Chillicothe and Kansas City, to bridge Missouri River	1971	47	1	10
Chippewa Falls and Western, to bridge Saint Croix River	1269	48	1	11
Cincinnati, Green River and Nashville, to bridge Cumberland River	2083	48	1	11
Covington and Cincinnati, to bridge Ohio River	1578	49	1	11
Dakota Central, to bridge Missouri River	1567	49	1	11
Duluth, Pierre and Black Hills, construction of bridge across Missouri River at Pierre Dak., by	3802	49	2	11
East and Middle Tennessee, to bridge Cumberland and Canary Fork Rivers	2639	48	2	11
Do	3220	49	1	11
East and West, to bridge the Coosa River	1829	47	2	10

*Parts 1, 2.

Subject.	Report.	Congress.	Session.	Volume.
RAILROADS—Continued.				
East and West, to bridge the Coosa River	2289	48	2	11
Do	372	49	1	11
Georgia, for relief	368	33	1	7
Gulf and Chicago Air Line Railway Co., to build bridges	1458	49	1	11
Hannibal and Southwestern, to bridge Missouri River	231	47	1	10
Minneapolis, Sault Sainte Marie and Atlantic, bridge across Saint Croix River	1266	48	1	11
Do	3110	49	1	11
New Orleans and Carrollton, for relief	90	28	1	6
New Orleans and Northeastern, to bridge Lake Pontchartrain and Pearl River	1289	47	1	10
New York and Council Bluffs,				
To bridge Mississippi River at Keithsburg, Ill	763	49	1	11
To bridge Missouri River	1354	49	1	11
North Louisiana,				
Ouachita River, to erect bridge at or near Monroe, La	209	45	2	9
Red River, near Shreveport, La., to erect bridge across	200	45	2	9
Ohio Central, to grant right of way at Great Kanawha locks	765	49	1	11
Oregon Pacific, to bridge Willamette River	1641	47	1	10
Do	326	48	1	11
Red River, cancellation of certain bonds given on iron imported	436	20	1	6
Richmond and Southwestern, construction of bridge over Pamunkey and Mattapony Rivers by	1273	46	2	9
Saint Joseph and Rio Grande, to bridge Missouri River	1353	49	1	11
Saint Louis and Kansas City Short Line, to bridge Missouri River	1392	49	1	11
Do	1396	49	1	11
Saint Louis and San Francisco, to bridge Arkansas River at Van Buren, Ark	1155	47	1	10
Saint Paul and Duluth, to bridge Saint Louis River	2469	49	1	11
Saint Paul, Minneapolis, and Minnetonka, to bridge Mississippi River	1837	48	1	11
Salina, Lincoln, and Decatur, to bridge Missouri River	1566	48	1	11
Sanford and Indian River, to bridge Saint John's River, Florida	1648	47	1	10
Savannah Pacific Short Line, to bridge the Ogeechee, Oconee, Ocmulgee, Flint, and Chattahoochee Rivers in State of Georgia	1642	47	1	10
Staten Island Rapid Transit, to bridge Staten Island Sound	*1667	48	1	11
Talladega and Coosa Valley, to bridge Coosa River	1082	49	1	11
Texas and Saint Louis, to build bridges across the Red, Ouachita, Arkansas, and White Rivers	1154	47	1	10
Tombigbee, bridge across Tombigbee River	4129	49	2	11
West Feliciana, for relief	368	33	1	7
Winona, Alma and Northern, to bridge certain rivers	1270	48	1	11
Do	766	49	1	11
RALLI, JOHN, for relief	101	36	2	8
RAM ISLAND, MAINE, light-house on	739	47	1	10
RARITAN BAY, NEW JERSEY, light-house at Great Beds in	786	45	2	9
REBECCA D. (schooner), to change name of	1328	46	2	9
RECIPROCITY TREATY (*see also* COMMERCE AND NAVIGATION),				
British North American colonies, reciprocal trade with	4	32	2	7
Great Britain and United States	22	37	2	8
Do	39	38	1	8
RED RIVER, LOUISIANA,				
Bridges across	200	45	2	9
Do	1150	47	1	10
Do	1644	47	1	10
Do	1080	49	1	11
Do	1081	49	1	11
Do	3218	49	1	11
Improvements in raft region of, to complete	85	34	1	7
Light-House Board, to extend operations over	865	47	1	10
RED RIVER OF THE NORTH, bridge across	3618	49	2	11
Do	3804	49	2	11
RED WING PONTON BRIDGE COMPANY, bridge across Mississippi River	1398	49	1	11
RED WING AND TRENTON TRANSIT COMPANY, bridge across Mississippi River	1740	46	2	9
REEDY ISLAND, harbor at, to improve	352	34	1	7
REGISTRY OF VESSELS (*see also* VESSELS),				
Foreign-built vessels, laws relative to registry of	14	17	17	1
Granting,				
Annie Johnson (bark)	665	46	2	9
Arctic (bark)	44	44	1	9
Barrondale (British vessel)	1694	47	1	10
Diana (ship)	14	17	1	1
Gulnare (steamship)	221	46	3	9
Harbinger (schooner)	144	32	1	7
RESERVOIRS, improvement of Upper Mississippi River	1701	46	2	9
RESTAURADER (brig), for relief	574	29	1	6
Do	123	30	1	6
RETIRED CIVIL LIST. (*See* CIVIL LIST.)				
REVENUE CUTTERS. (*See* REVENUE MARINE SERVICE.)				
REVENUE LAWS,				
Amending laws regulating collection of import duties	93	20	2	1
Effect of, on American commerce	165	21	1	1

* Parts 1, 2.

Subject.	Report.	Congress.	Session.	Volume.
REVENUE LAWS—Continued.				
Effect of, on foreign commerce	835	27	2	4
Revision of, to provide for	740	24	1	2
Do	81	25	2	2
Do	145	33	2	7
REVENUE MARINE SERVICE				
Vessel for service in Alaska	802	48	1	11
Efficiency of, to increase	415	30	1	6
Do	926	47	1	10
Do	1264	48	1	11
Do	2896	48	1	11
Expenses of transportation of shipwrecked seamen, to reimburse service for	3224	49	1	11
Officers of, to retire	2897	49	1	11
Steam revenue cutter				
For service in Delaware Bay	80	35	2	5
For service in New York Harbor	38	34	1	7
To substitute, for sailing vessels	634	36	1	6
REVENUE STEAMERS (*see also* STEAM VESSELS), respecting transfer to Coast Survey Service of certain	137	36	2	6
REVISED STATUTES, to amend,				
Act of April 18, 1874, which relates to vessels not propelled by steam or sail	115	45	2	9
Sections 2517, 2518, Bangor customs district, Maine	1700	46	2	9
Section 2552, collection districts in Virginia	652	47	1	10
Sections 2582, 2583, 2607, 2684, customs districts in California	394	47	1	10
Do	760	47	1	10
Sections 2586, 2587, customs districts	393	47	1	10
Section 2771, unloading of foreign vessels	4	46	2	9
Do	663	46	2	9
Sections 2990, 2997, bonded goods in transit	76	45	3	9
Section 2996, unloading cargoes of sailing vessels	869	47	1	10
Section 4214, yachts	652	46	2	9
Section 4233, danger signals	651	47	1	10
Do	682	47	1	10
Section 4414, steamboat inspectors	1646	47	1	10
Section 4417, inspection of hulls	388	44	1	9
Section 4458, steam-vessel inspection fees	51	47	1	10
Do	52	47	1	10
Section 4472, steamboat regulations	1756	47	1	10
Section 4482, life-preservers for river steamboats	388	44	1	9
Section 4488, life-boats for ocean and river steamers	388	44	1	9
Section 4489, penalty for violating laws regulating steam vessels	388	44	1	9
Section 4567, right of seamen to lay complaints before consular officer	3615	49	2	11
Section 5254, piers and cribs in rivers	16	47	1	10
Titles 48 and 52 relating to commerce and navigation and laws regulating steam vessels	97	44	1	9
Do	292	44	1	9
Do	387	44	1	9
Do	388	44	1	9
Do	62	45	2	9
Title 53, relating to merchant seamen	438	44	1	9
REZE, FREDERICK, for relief	735	24	1	2
Do	79	25	2	2
RHODE ISLAND, customs districts, removal of collector's office from Bristol to Warren	651	29	1	6
RICE IMPORTED FROM PORTUGAL, high duty levied upon	115	21	2	1
RICHMOND ISLAND, MAINE, light-house on	858	47	1	10
RICHMOND, LEMUEL C., for relief	264	25	3	2
RIGHT OF WAY to Crescent City Aqueduct Company to lay conduits under Lake Pontchartrain	1689	47	1	10
RIGHTS. (*See* CIVIL RIGHTS.)				
RINGGOLD, BENJAMIN, for relief	943	25	2	2
RIO GRANDE RIVER.				
Bridges across,				
At Eagle Pass, Tex.	800	48	1	11
At El Paso	1288	47	1	10
At Laredo	798	48	1	11
RITTER, JACOB, for relief	30	26	1	3
RIVERS AND HARBORS,				
Improvement and survey of,				
Act of July 11, 1870, supplemental to	623	44	1	9
Do	78	45	3	9
Appropriations for				
Annual for 1858	251	35	1	5
Annual for 1881	151	46	3	9
Annual for 1882	1283	47	1	10
Annual for 1883	1977	47	2	10
Expenditures, tabular statement of works provided for in bill of 1877	154	44	2	9
Bayou Bleu, Louisiana	837	29	1	6
Bayou La Fourche, Louisiana	837	29	1	6
Calumet River, Illinois	78	34	1	7
Cape Cod Harbor, Massachusetts	79	34	1	7

Subject.	Report.	Congress.	Session.	Volume.
...ND HARBORS—Continued.				
..., Ill., harbor at	78	34	1	7
...hoal at Cape May	[illegible]	35	2	2
...re Bay	118	20	1	1
...re Breakwater	322	34	1	7
Do	239	34	1	7
Do	652	45	3	9
...nee Rapids, to continue improvement of	69	34	1	7
Do	342	35	1	8
...nn., harbor at	196	27	3	8
... rivers and bays	390	27	2	4
...River, Michigan	425	22	1	6
...Harbor, Washington Territory	393	35	1	8
...River, New York	189	33	1	1
...uoit Bay Channel, Lake Ontario	1574	45	3	9
...on, Mich	425	29	1	6
...western, to improve	167	33	1	6
Do	318	34	1	7
...ippi River,				
...contract	66	34	1	7
...r Lake Concordia, Louisiana	9	46	1	9
...ween Sauk Rapids and Saint Anthony's Falls, and from the mouth of ... Minnesota River to Falls of Saint Anthony	72	34	1	7
...er-booms in	664	46	2	9
...Bay	698	29	1	6
Do	36	34	1	7
...rleans Harbor	264	47	1	10
...rk Harbor, to prevent deposit of rubbish in	742	47	1	10
...ctions of navigable waters by bridges, removal of	1636	47	1	10
Do	1049	47	1	10
...ver, to improve	294	34	3	7
...ntown Harbor, Massachusetts	12	35	1	8
...ver, completion of improvements in the raft region of	62	34	1	7
...Island in Delaware River	262	34	1	7
... Inlet, North Carolina	317	21	1	1
...ver, Minnesota	72	34	1	7
...harles Harbor, Missouri	649	46	2	9
...ohn's River, Florida	590	27	2	4
...a River, to make public highway of	365	29	1	6
...rd Harbor, Connecticut	662	46	2	9
... River, Massachusetts	77	34	1	7
...o improvement of	741	30	1	6
...gan Harbor, Illinois	71	34	1	7
...River	87	34	1	7
...BIEL, for relief	495	23	1	1
Do	48	24	1	2
... INLET, to improve the navigation of	317	21	1	1
...ON, JAMES, for relief	35	20	1	1
..., DAVID and EBENEZER, for relief	108	25	3	2
...ER, NEW YORK, custom-house and post-office building at	257	35	1	8
...AND, ILLINOIS, bridge across Mississippi River at	250	35	1	8
...AND RAPIDS, continuing improvement of	69	34	1	1
...AND AND SOUTHWESTERN RAILROAD COMPANY, bridge ...ross Mississippi River	993	47	1	10
...T, MASSACHUSETTS, port of delivery	250	48	1	11
... WILLIAM R., for relief	355	23	1	7
...OSIAH, for relief	348	24	1	2
...S & SON, for relief	97	36	1	8
...ER, MINNESOTA, to improve navigation of	72	34	1	7
... ARGENTINE CONFEDERATION, to establish consulate at	252	35	1	8
...LAND, MICHIGAN, light-house and fog-signal at Mackinac on	419	45	2	9
...BRASKA, bridge across Missouri River at	1042	48	1	11
... CHARLES H., & CO., for relief	196	27	3	4
... JOHN H., for relief	385	26	1	2
Do	385	28	1	6
Do	263	29	1	6
Do	17	34	1	7
...ASS, TEXAS,				
...m district at, to establish	636	36	1	
...ntry	636	36	1	8
...IVER, bridge across	1644	47	1	10
...NTO RIVER, CALIFORNIA, to extend jurisdiction of Light-House ...ard to	3606	49	2	11
...THAN, for relief of executors	374	26	2	2
...ELS. (*See* VESSELS; MARINE SIGNALS; COMMERCE AND NAVIGATION.)				
...GUSTINE CREEK, GEORGIA, bridge across	2439	49	1	11
...ARLES, MISSOURI, harbor of, to improve	649	46	2	9
...OUD WATER-POWER COMPANY, dam across Mississippi River	1303	48	1	11
...OIX, relating to commerce of United States with island of	117	21	2	1
...OIX RIVER, WISCONSIN,				
...ver	1232	49	1	11

Subject.	Report.	Congress.	Session.	Volume.
SAINT CROIX RIVER, WISCONSIN—Continued.				
Bridge over	1269	48	1	11
Do	1266	48	1	11
Do	1270	48	1	11
Do	766	49	1	11
Light-House Board over, extending operations of	864	47	1	10
Piers and cribs, to be constructed in	16	47	1	10
SAINT JOHN'S RIVER, FLORIDA,				
Buoys additional, on bar at mouth of	890	27	2	4
Bridge across	1643	47	1	10
Light-House Board over, extending jurisdiction	1272	46	2	9
Do	1152	47	1	10
Do	197	48	1	11
SAINT JOSEPH, FLORIDA, marine hospital at	237	25	3	2
SAINT JOSEPH, MISSOURI,				
Marine hospital at, to erect	258	35	1	8
Port of delivery at, to establish	872	47	1	10
SAINT LAWRENCE RIVER, bridge across	1645	47	1	10
SAINT LOUIS, MISSOURI,				
Bridge across Mississippi River at	*2341	49	1	11
Marine hospital at, to erect	745	27	2	4
Do	437	29	1	6
SAINT LOUIS RIVER, bridge across	2469	49	1	11
Do	3971	49	2	11
SAINT PAUL, MINNESOTA,				
Bridge across Mississippi River at	1267	48	1	11
Custom-house and post-office at, to erect building for	115	34	3	1
Marine hospital at, to erect	950	45	2	9
SAINT PHILIP CHURCH, CHARLESTON, SOUTH CAROLINA, for relief	307	26	1	3
Do	475	27	2	4
SAINT VINCENT, MINNESOTA, port of entry	657	46	2	9
Do	17	47	1	10
SAINTE MARIE RIVER, MICHIGAN, bridge across	1455	47	1	10
Do	3110	49	1	11
SAKONNET POINT, RHODE ISLAND, light-house at	1944	47	2	10
SALAMANCA, NEW YORK, port of delivery at	1671	48	1	11
SALARIES,				
Customs officers, to regulate and fix salaries of	480	24	1	2
Do	472	25	2	2
Inspectors of steamboats in Michigan and district of Superior, to regulate	1646	47	1	10
Inspectors of steam vessels, to increase compensation of	571	47	1	10
Inspectors of customs, to increase	354	34	1	7
Seamen, to change system of advance wages to	1757	47	1	10
Surveyor at Camden, N. J., to reduce salary of	159	27	3	4
Surveyor at Havre de Grace, to increase	212	27	3	4
SALEM, OREGON, bridge across Willamette River	3062	49	1	11
Do	3159	49	1	11
SALT-WATER FISH. (*See* FISH AND FISHERIES.)				
SAMPLES. (*See* COMMERCIAL TRAVELERS.)				
SAMPSON, THOMAS, authorizing award of life-saving medal to	642	46	2	9
Do	355	47	1	10
Do	873	49	1	11
SAN FRANCISCO, CALIFORNIA,				
Duties collected, to refund, on goods destroyed by fire in	202	33	1	7
Do	86	34	1	7
Fog-signal, to establish, on Lime Point, in harbor of	1290	47	1	10
Property in, to relinquish certain, of the United States, to	248	44	1	9
SAN FRANCISCO (steamship), to reward the officers and crew of	97	39	1	8
SAN JUAN ISLAND, WASHINGTON TERRITORY, to extend and enlarge the duties and jurisdiction of the deputy collector of customs at	1741	46	2	9
SAN JOAQUIN, CALIFORNIA, Light-House Board to, to extend jurisdiction	3608	49	2	11
SAN LUIS OBISPO, CALIFORNIA,				
Fog-signal at, to build	868	47	1	10
Light-house at, to construct	824	45	2	9
Do	525	49	1	11
Port of entry, to make	70	46	3	9
Do	394	47	1	10
SAND BEACH, MICHIGAN, government and control of harbor of refuge at	655	46	2	9
Do	233	47	1	10
SANDS, JOHN, for relief	144	27	3	4
Do	446	28	1	6
SANDUSKY, OHIO, Solicitor of Treasury authorized to execute quit-claim deed of land in	518	28	1	6
SANDY POINT, CHESAPEAKE BAY, light at, to change	870	47	1	10
SANDY POINT, WASHINGTON TERRITORY, fog-signal in Puget Sound, to erect	71	45	3	9
SANFORD, THOMAS, for relief	515	29	1	6
SAVANNAH, GEORGIA, custom-house at	682	24	1	2
Do	108	28	2	6
SAYBROOK BAR, CONNECTICUT, beacon light at	867	47	1	10

*Parts 1, 2.

Subject.	Report.	Congress.	Session.	Volume.
SEAMEN,				
Apprentices, requiring all vessels to employ	349	22	1	3
Do	97	32	2	7
Do	177	34	1	7
Complaints before consular officer, to amend Revised Statutes relating to right to lay	3615	49	2	11
Deserting, wages to accrue to United States, forfeiture of	490	28	1	6
Desertion in foreign countries of American, causes of increase of	490	28	1	6
Disabled, care and relief of	360	25	2	2
Do	178	31	1	7
Free colored, to render effectual the privileges of citizenship to	*80	27	2	4
Marine hospitals for seamen engaged in whale-fishery, to erect	569	29	1	6
Do	139	30	1	5
Do	178	31	1	7
Merchant, to amend title 53 Revised Statutes, relating to	628	46	1	9
Passports to American, to abolish protections and provide	182	24	2	3
Shipment and discharge of, to modify acts regulating, in foreign ports	490	28	1	6
Do	84	47	1	10
Do	85	47	1	10
Sick and disabled, care and relief of	360	25	3	2
Do	178	31	1	7
Wages, to change system of advance	1787	47	1	10
SHIP ISLAND, MISSISSIPPI, quarantine station, to remove	2096	49	2	11
SEARS, WINTHROP, and others, for relief	501	24	1	3
Do	77	25	2	2
SEATTLE, WASHINGTON TERRITORY, port of delivery	1295	48	1	11
SECRETARY OF STATE, to amend act of August 16, 1842, requiring foreign regulations of commerce to be laid before Congress by the	9	34	1	7
SEELEY, JAMES, for relief	602	25	2	2
SELMA, ALABAMA, bridge across Alabama River at	650	46	2	9
SEUL CHOIX POINT, MICHIGAN, light-house at	1596	49	1	11
SHEER-BOOMS, construction of, in Mississippi River	604	46	2	9
SHEFFIELD, AMOS, and others, for relief	438	23	1	1
SHEFFIELD LAND, IRON, AND COAL COMPANY, bridge across Tennessee River	2912	49	1	11
SHEKAGUA RIVER, to make public highway of	565	29	1	6
SHIP-BUILDING,				
American ships, to be built by American mechanics and out of American materials	782	46	1	9
Do	1831	47	2	10
Condition of, appointing joint committee to investigate	1805	47	1	10
SHIP-CANALS. (*See* CANALS.)				
SHIP-OWNERS, limiting and defining the liability of	33	31	1	7
Do	1665	48	1	11
SHIVERICK, THOMAS, for relief	53	20	2	1
SHOEMAKER, JACOB, for relief of widow and children of	219	24	1	2
SIBLEY, MISSOURI, bridge of Missouri River at	803	48	1	11
SIGNAL SERVICE, to establish signal stations on Nantucket Island	1301	48	1	11
SIGNALS (*see also* MARINE SIGNALS),				
International commission upon marine, to create	682	47	1	10
Marine danger, to establish system of	907	45	2	9
Do	11	46	1	9
SIMMONS, JOSEPH, for relief	30	26	1	3
SIOUX CITY, IOWA, bridge across Missouri River at	4033	49	2	11
SIOUX CITY AND PACIFIC RAILROAD COMPANY, to bridge across Missouri River	232	47	1	10
SLAVE TRADE (*see also* AFRICA), suppression of	283	27	3	5
SMALLY, HENRY, for relief	85	33	2	7
Do	434	35	1	8
SMILAX (schooner), for relief of owners and crew of	183	36	1	8
SMITH, ELLIOTT, for relief	35	26	1	3
Do	474	27	2	4
Do	193	28	1	6
Do	811	30	1	6
SMITH, GILBERT A., for relief	87	23	2	1
Do	64	24	1	2
Do	234	25	2	2
Do	75	26	1	3
SMITH, ISAAC, for relief	48	33	2	7
Do	75	34	3	7
Do	108	35	1	8
SMITH, NATHAN, and others, for relief	502	24	1	2
Do	83	25	2	2
Do	238	25	3	2
Do	314	26	1	3
Do	66	27	2	4
SMITH, STEVENS, for relief	235	23	1	1
SMITH, THURGAR & CO., for relief	407	29	1	6
SMITH, THURBAR & CO., for relief	65	30	1	6
SMITH & HERSEY, for relief	80	31	1	7

* Majority and minority.

Subject.	Report.	Congress.	Session.	Volume.
TIME BALLS, to place on custom-houses	681	47	1	10
TIPPETT, EDWARD D., for relief	8	35	1	8
TITUS, WALTER, & CO., for relief	150	29	1	6
TOBACCO, removal of restrictions of foreign nations upon introduction of	835	27	2	4
TOLEDO, OHIO, custom-house at, to enlarge	76	34	1	7
TONAWANDA, NEW YORK, bridge at	1333	48	1	11
TONNAGE (*see also* STATISTICS), to regulate measurement of vessels for	1228	47	1	10
TONNAGE DUTIES,				
Coasting vessels, to repeal act authorizing city council of Baltimore, Md., to impose, on	445	22	1	1
Congress, assent of, to any acts passed by States laying duties on vessels entering their ports	741	30	1	6
Cuba, imposed on United States vessels in the island of	115	21	2	1
Do	468	23	1	1
Law, to repeal	165	21	1	1
Spanish vessels, tonnage duty on	64	24	2	2
Do	88	25	2	2
Swedish and Norwegian vessels, to exempt, from payment of discriminating	36	19	2	1
TOPOGRAPHICAL BUREAU, relative to placing the Light-House Establishment under charge of the	811	27	2	4
TRADE MARKS, to prevent use of false	527	36	1	8
TRANSPORTATION IN BOND, to make Portland, Oreg., and Port Townsend, Wash., ports of entry for	2367	48	2	11
TRANSPORTATION OF LIVE STOCK. (*See* LIVE STOCK.)				
TRAVERS, SAMUEL H., for relief	182	44	2	9
TREADWELL, MOSES, for relief	514	24	1	2
TREASURY DEPARTMENT. (*See* DEPARTMENT OF TREASURY.)				
TREATIES,				
Commercial, termination of certain	835	27	2	4
Commissions to investigate and ascertain on what basis a treaty of reciprocal trade can be negotiated for the benefit of the United States and Canada, to appoint	9	44	1	9
Do	*389	44	1	9
Florida treaty, to extend article 15 of, to all ports of entry in Florida	23	20	2	1
Great Britain, new reciprocity treaty with	22	37	2	8
Do	39	38	1	8
TRENTON, NEW JERSEY, land for site for public buildings at	259	35	1	8
TRIST, N. P., investigation of conduct of, United States consul at Havana	707	26	1	3
TRYON (schooner), for relief of owners of	115	23	2	1
TURPENTINE, transportation of, in vessels	43	33	2	7
TWO BROTHERS (schooner), for relief of owners	50	24	1	2
Do	384	28	1	8
Do	60	28	2	6
Do	266	29	1	6
TWO BUSH ISLAND, MAINE, light-house on	1271	46	2	9
TWO SONS (schooner), for relief of owner and crew of	786	27	2	4
UMBRELLAS, defining law relative to import duties on	697	25	2	2
UNCLE AMASA (schooner), for relief of owners	24	34	3	7
UNITED STATES, authority over open sea and its fisheries, possessed by the Government of the	7	46	1	9
Do	85	46	2	9
URANUS (schooner), for relief of owners and crew of	181	36	1	8
UTICA, NEW YORK, abolishing office of inspector of customs at	574	29	1	6
VAIL, AARON, relief of representatives of	869	36	1	8
VAN BUREN (schooner), for relief of owners	49	24	1	2
VERMILLION BAY, LOUISIANA, light-house at Southwest Pass	1556	47	1	10
VESSEL FISHERIES OF UNITED STATES. (*See* FISH AND FISHERIES.)				
VESSELS. (*See also* FOREIGN VESSELS; SHIP-BUILDING; SEAMEN; STEAM-VESSELS, and under respective names of vessels),				
Act of April 18, 1874, relating to vessels not propelled by steam or sail, to amend	115	45	2	9
Aliens as engineers and pilots on, employment of	801	48	1	11
Apprentices on all, requiring the employment of	97	33	2	7
Cargoes from sailing vessels, unloading of	869	47	1	10
Coasting vessels, to reduce	1443	48	1	11
Collisions of, to adopt revised international regulations for preventing	731	48	1	11
Immigrants in sail or steam, to regulate carrying of	121	47	1	10
Do	1699	47	1	10
Landing of goods and personal effects, to amend law relative to	2451	48	2	11
Liability of owners, to amend law relative to	2639	48	2	11
Do	1145	49		11
Measurement of vessels for tonnage, to regulate	1228	47		10
Passengers, to regulate carriage of, in merchant	25	32		7
Pilot fees, to relieve certain ships from compulsory	392	44		9
Registers, to schooner Harbinger	144	32	1	7
Registration of	380	25	2	2
Revenue steamers to the Coast Survey service, transfer of	137	30	2	6
Signal lights for sail, system of	249	35	1	8
Tonnage of, altering mode of admeasuring vessels employed in United States merchant service	835	27	2	4

*Views of minority.

Subject.	Report.	Congress.	Session.	Volume.
SELS—Continued.				
Towing vessels, to license, to carry passengers	1146	49	1	11
Do	2653	48	2	11
Turpentine, transportation of	44	33	2	7
Ventilation of passenger, to provide for the	25	32	1	7
Yachts, to amend laws relative to licensing	15	47	1	10
To change name of,				
America (sloop)	1453	46	2	9
Do	1627	46	2	9
Arctic (sloop)	490	36	1	8
Charlotte and Isabel (tug)	660	46	2	9
E. B. Bryant (yacht)	1331	46	2	9
Isle of Pines (schooner)	10	46	3	9
J. H. Dusenberry (schooner)	661	46	2	9
Kate Sutton (yacht)	1329	46	2	9
L. Boardman (steamer)	1626	46	2	9
Lizzie (schooner)	132	46	3	9
M. S. Perry (steamer)	131	37	2	8
Mariah (yacht)	1330	46	2	9
Mary E. Caswell (schooner)	1501	46	2	9
Michigan (barge)	1138	49	1	11
Minnie R. Child (steamer)	653	46	2	9
Rebecca D. (schooner)	1328	46	2	9
J. W. Bradbury (propeller)	1327	46	2	9
Smilax (schooner)	183	36	1	8
Solferino (brig)	182	44	2	9
Susan Jane (schooner)	132	37	2	8
W. P. Cox (schooner)	646	46	2	9
TO, respecting veto by President of river and harbor bill of March 3, 1847	741	30	1	6
KSBURG, MISSISSIPPI, custom-house at	240	34	3	7
TOR, THEODORE, for relief	688	25	2	2
GINIA, to change boundaries of fourth customs district in	652	47	1	10
Do	3908	49	2	11
Do	4181	49	2	11
WEL, JOHN C. and THOMAS, for relief	14	17	1	1
P. COX (schooner), to change name of	646	46	2	9
J. GORDON (steam yacht), to change name of	673	46	2	9
GES (see also SEAMEN; SALARIES), forfeiture of deserting seamen's	490	28	1	6
LN, S. MORRIS, for relief	331	31	1	7
R OF 1812, to indemnify certain owners of vessels sunk in Baltimore Harbor during	70	20	2	1
Do	144	21	1	1
AREHOUSES, relative to erection of additional public	165	21	1	1
AREHOUSING, to amend laws relative to	93	20	2	1
Do	103	27	3	4
Do	437	28	1	6
Do	438	28	2	6
Do	411	29	1	6
Do	367	30	1	6
Do	141	30	2	1
ARREN, RHODE ISLAND, removal of collector's office from Bristol to	651	29	1	6
ASHINGTON TERRITORY, Port Townsend to Port Angeles, to change location of port of entry from	119	37	2	8
ATLINGTON, FRANCIS, for relief	167	25	3	2
ATSON, WESTGATE, for relief	54	19	2	1
AUKEGAN, ILLINOIS, harbor at, to improve	71	34	1	7
EIGHTS AND MEASURES,				
Metric system, adoption of	285	27	3	5
Directing complete set of standard, to be furnished each State by	259	24	1	2
Do	449	24	1	2
ELLES, HENRY S., for relief	64	43	1	9
EST PASCAGOULA RIVER, New Orleans, Mobile and Texas Railroad, to maintain draw in bridge across	2913	49	1	11
EST POINT, VIRGINIA, port of entry and delivery	185	44	1	9
Do	173	46	2	9
ESTERN WATERS,				
Marine hospital on	380	25	2	2
Improving rivers and harbors in	137	28	1	6
HALE FISHERIES (see also SEAMEN), erection of marine hospitals for disabled seamen engaged in	569	29	1	6
Do	120	30	1	6
HALE'S BACK, NEW HAMPSHIRE, light-house on	437	28	1	6
HARVES, to construct, at New London, Conn	214	27	3	4
HEELWRIGHT, EBENEZER, for relief	315	26	1	3
Do	63	28	1	6
Do	92	29	1	6
HITE CLOUD, KANSAS, bridge across Missouri River at	1265	48	1	11
HITE, STEPHEN, for relief	263	25	3	2
HITE RIVER,				
Bridges over,				
Arkansas Midland Railroad, to bridge	1302	48	1	11

Subject.	Report.	Congress.	Session.	Volume.
WHITE RIVER—Continued.				
Bridges over—Continued.				
Texas and Saint Louis Railroad, to bridge	1154	47	1	10
Improvement of, navigation	87	34	1	7
WHITEHALL NARROWS, NEW YORK, light at	946	49	1	11
WHITMARSH, CHARLES, for relief	189	25	3	2
WICKHAM, WILLIAM, for relief	308	25	2	2
Do	32	26	1	3
WIDOW'S ISLAND, MAINE, light-house on	1270	46	2	9
WILDMAN, ZALMON, for relief of heirs	512	28	1	6
WILLAMETTE RIVER.				
Bridges over,				
City of Salem to build	3062	49	1	11
Do	3159	49	1	11
Oregon Pacific Railroad, to build	1641	47	1	10
Do	1869	47	2	10
Do	326	48	1	11
Light-House Board, to extend operations of, to	1636	47	1	10
WILLIAM (brig), granting register to	51	18	1	1
WILLIAMS, CALEB, for relief	1020	25	2	2
Do	169	25	2	2
WILLIAMS, LEMUEL, for relief	172	29	1	6
WILLIAMS, STEPLES & WILLIAMS, for relief	79	31	1	7
Do	27	32	1	7
WILLIS, GEORGE, for relief	240	25	3	2
Do	34	26	1	3
WILLIS, LEWIS B., for relief	433	24	1	2
Do	201	25	2	2
WILLIS, STEPHEN F., for relief	403	36	1	8
WILMINGTON, CALIFORNIA, port of entry	70	46	2	9
Do	394	47	1	10
WIND AND CURRENT CHARTS, to test Lieutenant Maury's	112	30	2	6
WINES, to revise duties on	111	20	1	1
WINONA, MINNESOTA, bridge across Mississippi River at	3829	49	2	11
WINONA PONTON BRIDGE COMPANY, bridge across Mississippi River	1309	49	1	11
WINONA AND SAINT PETER'S RAILROAD COMPANY, for relief	28	40	2	8
WINSLOW, ISAAC and T. S., for relief	308	26	1	3
Do	901	27	2	3
WISCONSIN RIVER, bridge across	768	49	1	11
WOODBURY, JOHN, Jr., for relief	198	24	1	2
WOODS, HENRY, for relief	396	36	1	8
WORMSTEAD, JOSEPH W., for relief	47	24	1	2
WRIGHT & BROTHER, and others, for relief	687	25	2	2
YACHTS,				
E. B. Bryant, to change name of steam yacht	1331	46	2	9
Kate Sutton, to change name of	1329	46	2	9
Licensing, to amend law relative to	15	47	1	10
Mariah, to change name of yacht	1330	46	2	9
Revised Statutes, to amend section 4214 relating to	652	46	2	9
W. J. Gordon, to change name of steam yacht	673	46	2	9
YAQUINA, OREGON, to establish collection district at	398	47	1	10
YELLOW FEVER, to appoint commission to examine	*375	49	1	11
Do	375	49	1	11
Do	2914	49	1	11
YELLOWSTONE RIVER, Miles City Bridge Company to bridge	1397	49	1	11
YOUNG, THOMAS and GEORGE, for relief	523	36	1	8
YOUNG'S BAY, OREGON, Clatsop County to bridge	1466	49	1	11
Do	2555	49	1	11
YOUNG'S RIVER, OREGON, bridge across	2023	47	2	10

* Views of minority.

o

REPORTS

OF THE

MITTEE ON THE DISTRICT OF COLUMBIA,

HOUSE OF REPRESENTATIVES,

FROM THE FOURTEENTH CONGRESS, 1815, TO THE FORTY-NINTH CONGRESS, 1887, INCLUSIVE,

IN FIVE VOLUMES.

COMPILED, UNDER THE DIRECTION OF THE JOINT COMMITTEE ON PRINTING,

BY

T. H. McKEE,

Clerk, Document Room, United States Senate.

WASHINGTON:
GOVERNMENT PRINTING OFFICE.
1887.

9208 D.C

FORTY-NINTH CONGRESS, FIRST SESSION.

[PUBLIC RESOLUTION—No. 24.]

Joint resolution authorizing the preparation of a compilation of the reports of committees of the Senate and House of Representatives.

Resolved by the Senate and House of Representatives of the United States of America in Congress assembled, That there be prepared under the direction of the Joint Committee of Printing, a compilation of the reports of the Senate and House of Representatives from the Fourteenth to the Forty-eighth Congress, inclusive, classified by committees, arranged, indexed, and bound in suitable volumes for the use of the standing committees of the two Houses of Congress. And the sum of seven thousand seven hundred and fifty dollars, or so much thereof as may be found necessary, is hereby appropriated out of any money in the Treasury not otherwise appropriated, for the preparation of said work, which sum may be paid by the Secretary of the Treasury upon the order of the chairman of said Joint Committee, as additional pay or compensation to any officer or employee of the United States.

Resolved further, That the Clerk of the House and Secretary of the Senate be, and they are hereby directed, to procure and file, for the use of their respective Houses, copies of all reports made by each committee of all succeeding Congresses; and that the Clerk of the House and the Secretary of the Senate be, and they are hereby, authorized and directed at the close of each session of Congress, to cause said reports to be indexed and bound, one copy to be deposited in the library of each House and one copy in the room of the committee from which the reports emanated.

Approved, July 29, 1886.

COMPILER'S NOTICE.

This compilation embraces all the printed reports made by both Iouses of Congress from the commencement of the Fourteenth to the lose of the Forty-ninth Congress. They are classified by committees nd arranged in numerical order. The collection for each committee divided into volumes of suitable size. Each committee has a separate ndex, a copy being bound in each volume.

The SPECIAL and SELECT reports are all compiled in one collection aving one index, a copy of which is bound in each volume.

The plan throughout the compilation is to place each report to the ommittee from which it was reported, without reference to the subject-atter.

The House and Senate reports are compiled separately. Care will be required in noticing the chronological order, as in some instances an entire session or Congress may not appear in certain volumes from the fact that during this period no reports were made by this committee.

T. H. McKEE.

INDEX

TO

;TS OF COMMITTEE ON THE DISTRICT OF COLUMBIA,

HOUSE OF REPRESENTATIVES.

FROM 1815 TO 1887, INCLUSIVE.

Subject.	Report.	Congress.	Session.	Volume.
H., for relief	319	34	1	1
EL HEBREW CONGREGATION, Washington, D. C., for relief	1723	49	1	5
ING in D. C., tax sales in Georgetown	187	21	1	1
eal estate, in D. C., license tax law, to amend	3461	49	1	5
RIA, D. C.,				
ourt in, providing for residence of one of judges of, in	591	27	2	1
ion, for relief	255	24	2	1
Do	269	24	1	1
use at,				
ect	773	25	2	1
pair roof of	458	28	1	1
Asylum and Female Free School at, granting public land in aid of	35	28	1	1
Do	312	29	1	1
e, retrocession of, to Virginia	325	29	1	1
RIA CANAL COMPANY, D. C., memorial of president and direct- of	498	23	1	1
COLLEGE FOR THE BLIND, D. C., to incorporate	872	49	1	5
TRUST COMPANY, D. C., to incorporate	4003	49	2	5
A, D. C., to change name of Uniontown to	171	49	1	5
A BRIDGE, D. C.,				
William Benning to improve and control	106	19	1	1
ige, to make	137	29	1	1
Do	643	30	1	1
ige on present site, to erect	257	43	1	4
Do	596	43	1	4
AL SUBJECTS, D. C., delivery of dead bodies of criminals and pau- s to colleges for	2257	48	2	5
Do	873	49	1	5
T BRIDGE, D. C., to purchase	1958	48	1	5
Do	2300	49	1	5
stment of colored criminals of the District of Columbia in	23	38	2	2
NT CERTIFICATES, D. C., redemption of outstanding	1105	47	1	4
Do	1776	47	1	4
NT LAW, 1820, D. C., complaint against	83	19	1	1
NTS, D. C., made by M. G. Emory (mayor), refunding	1201	47	1	4
Do	1314	48	1	5
TEAM COAL GAS COMPANY, D. C., incorporation of	1108	46	2	4
D, HENRY, for relief	417	23	1	1
E AND OHIO RAILROAD, settlement of taxes made by D. C. Com- ssioners, to ratify	1109	46	2	4
RES in D. C., to tax	1523	48	1	5
). C.,				
to,				
ting additional	76	14	1	1
Do	332	28	1	1
wal of	56	16	1	1
Do	56	18	2	1
Do	332	28	1	1
ive to	4	27	1	1
TER, Jr., for relief	100	35	1	2

Subject.	Report.	Congress.	Session.	Volume.
BARGY & VAN ALSTINE, for relief of assignee	106	29	1	1
Do	594	30	1	1
Do	216	34	1	1
Do	217	34	1	1
BENNETT, H. M., for relief	82	47	1	4
BENNING, WILLIAM, for relief	106	19	1	1
BILLS OF SALE. (*See* MORTGAGES.)				
BOARD OF FOREIGN MISSIONS, property in District, to hold	2697	49	1	5
BOARD OF PUBLIC WORKS, D. C., workmen under, payment of	1200	47	1	4
BOILERS. (*See* STEAM BOILERS.)				
BONDS, D. C.,				
Executors, amending law regulating	318	48	1	5
Do	1629	49	1	5
Do	2645	49	1	5
Interest on, payment of	774	43	1	4
BOTTLERS in D. C., to protect	987	49	1	5
BOWEN, WILLIAM, for relief	1199	47	1	4
Do	1954	48	1	5
BOYLE, CORNELIUS, for relief of heirs	1112	46	2	4
BRIDGES in D. C.,				
Across Eastern Branch,				
To make free	137	29	1	1
Do	643	30	1	1
To construct a new	106	19	1	1
Do	137	29	1	1
Do	643	30	1	1
Do	257	43	1	4
Do	596	43	1	4
Do	2703	49	1	5
Across Potomac River,				
Aqueduct, to purchase	1956	48	1	5
Do	2200	49	1	5
Long Bridge, purchase of	484	22	1	1
At Three Sisters, to construct	470	48	1	5
Do	1958	48	1	5
Do	2300	49	1	5
BROWN, B. PEYTON, *et al.*, petition against taxing church property in District	1573	46	2	4
BURGLARY. (*See* SAFE BURGLARY.)				
BURROWS, JOSEPH, *et al.*, memorial for straightening F and G streets in Washington	318	22	1	1
CANALS in D. C., Tiber Creek, to provide for filling	690	47	1	4
CAPITOL, NORTH O STREET AND SOUTH WASHINGTON RAILROAD,				
To incorporate	129	46	3	4
To provide for extension of	1102	47	1	4
CARROLL, ANN C., for relief	1370	47	1	4
CARROLL, DANIEL, for relief of devisees	176	48	1	5
CASEY, STEPHEN, for relief	2007	47	2	4
CERTIFICATES, IMPROVEMENT, D. C., providing for funding of	207	46	3	4
CHESAPEAKE AND OHIO CANAL COMPANY, D. C., to amend act of incorporation	48	29	2	1
Do	126	30	1	1
CHILDREN in D. C., providing for protection of	1444	46	2	4
Do	1957	48	1	5
CHITTENDEN BROTHERS, contractors for building dam across Potomac River at Great Falls, claim for relief	3686	49	2	5
CHURCH OF THE ASCENSION in D. C., for relief	2580	48	2	5
CHURCHES in D. C., exempting from taxation	1573	46	2	4
Do	980	48	1	5
CLARK, E. B., for relief of heirs	1115	46	2	4
CLARKE, BAILEY L. and MASON E., for relief	515	23	1	1
CODE OF LAWS, D. C., providing for	269	21	1	1
Do	96	22	2	1
Do	683	46	2	4
Do	8	47	1	4
COGSWELL FOUNTAIN, acceptance of, by District	1372	47	1	4
COLLATERAL TRUST AND INDEMNITY COMPANY, D. C., to incorporate	492	48	1	5
COLORED CRIMINALS. (*See* CRIMINALS IN D. C.)				
COLUMBIA TURNPIKE COMPANY, D. C., to forfeit charter of	36	41	3	2
COLUMBIA COLLEGE, D. C., memorial of president of board of trustees	290	21	1	1
Do	334	22	1	1
COLUMBIAN INSTITUTION FOR DEAF, DUMB, AND BLIND, D. C., for relief	60	35	1	2
CONNOLLY, JOHN, for relief	128	46	3	4
Do	1998	47	2	4
Do	928	48	1	5
CONTAGIOUS DISEASES in D. C., to prevent spread of	215	20	1	1
CONTRACTS in D. C., made by board of public works, defining liabilities under	2181	48	1	5
CONVEYANCES in D. C., acknowledgments of	491	48	1	5
COOK, MATTHEW, for relief	1260	47	1	4
COOK, PATRICK, for relief	1992	47	2	4
Do	247	48	1	5

Subject.	Report.	Congress.	Session.	Volume.
CORCORAN ART GALLERY, to exempt from taxation	3049	49	1	5
CRIMINALS AND PAUPERS. (*See also* ANATOMICAL SUBJECTS.)				
CRIMINALS in D. C., enlistment of colored criminals in Army and Navy of United States	23	38	2	2
DEATH DAMAGES in D. C., recovery of	2379	48	2	5
DEBT of D. C.,				
Eight per cent. improvement certificates	207	46	3	4
Funding of, to provide for	774	43	1	4
Moneys to credit certain, on	3429	49	1	5
Settlement of	302	47	1	4
DE GROOT, WILLIAM H., for relief	182	35	2	2
Do	103	36	1	2
DE KRAFFT, FREDERICK C., for relief	351	24	1	1
DENMEAD, FRANCIS, for relief	2646	49	1	5
Do	3459	49	1	5
DENTISTRY in D. C., to regulate practise of	2258	48	2	5
DETECTIVES' BONDS in D. C., to compel compliance with the law	2043	47	2	4
DISTILLED SPIRITS in D. C., to regulate manufacture and sale of	2581	48	2	5
DISTRICT ATTORNEY of D. C., safe **burglary in office of**	785	43	1	4
DISTRICT OF COLUMBIA,				
Affairs in, investigation of	72	42	2	3
Do	7	42	3	3
Do	647	43	1	4
Do	702	44	1	4
Do	64	44	2	4
Alleys in,				
To change	1373	47	1	4
O street, to close	430	47	1	4
Title to, in square 635	729	49	1	5
Do	1012	49	1	5
To vacate	1106	48	1	5
American Trust Company to incorporate	4003	49	2	5
Anatomical subjects in, to authorize delivery of dead bodies of criminals and paupers to colleges for	2257	48	2	5
Do	873	49	1	5
Assessment certificates, providing for redemption of outstanding	1105	47	1	4
Do	1371	47	1	4
Do	1776	47	1	4
Assessments in, to refund to certain citizens	1314	48	1	5
Banks in, recharter of	76	14	1	1
Do	56	16	1	1
Do	56	18	1	1
Do	4	27	1	1
Do	332	28	1	1
Bills of sale in, to amend law on personal property in	1907	47	2	4
Bonds, interest on	774	43	1	4
Bottlers in, to protect	987	49	1	5
Bridges.				
Aqueduct, to purchase	470	48	1	5
Do	1958	48	1	5
Do	2300	49	1	5
Eastern Branch, to construct new	257	43	1	4
Do	596	43	1	4
Do	2703	49	1	5
Eastern Branch, to make free	137	29	1	1
Do	643	30	1	1
Long Bridge, to purchase	484	22	1	1
Twin Sisters, to construct	470	48	1	5
Do	1958	48	1	5
Do	2300	49	1	5
Three Sisters, to build	470	48	1	5
Do	1958	48	1	5
Do	2300	49	1	5
Canals in, for filling Tiber Creek	699	47	1	4
Charter of,				
Collateral, Trust, and Indemnity Company in, to grant	492	48	1	5
Mutual Fire Insurance Company, to amend	361	48	1	5
National Safe Deposit Company of, to amend	1775	48	1	5
Do	2705	49	1	5
Sixth Street and Bladensburg Railroad, to grant	959	48	1	5
Southern Maryland Railroad, to change	1712	48	1	5
United States Gas, Electric Light and Fuel Company in, to grant	1116	48	1	5
Washington Traction Railway, to grant	2299	49	1	5
Children in, for protection of	1444	46	2	4
Do	1957	48	1	5
Churches in, relative to taxation of	1573	46	2	4
Do	980	48	1	5
Civil and criminal code, provide for	269	21	1	1
Do	96	22	2	1
Contagious diseases in, prevent spread of	215	20	1	1
Contracts of board of public works, to define	2131	48	1	

Subject.	Report.	Congress.	Session.	Volume.
DISTRICT OF COLUMBIA—Continued.				
Conveyances in, acknowledgments of	481	48	1	5
Court, levy, reorganization of, in	721	29	1	1
Criminal code, to provide	2120	48	1	5
Criminals in, enlistment of colored, in Army and Navy of United States	23	38	2	3
Death damages, to provide for recovering	2870	48	2	5
Debt of, to fund bonded	774	43	1	4
Do	287	46	3	4
Do	362	47	1	4
Do	3428	49	1	5
Dentistry in, to regulate practice of	2256	48	2	5
Detectives in, to compel compliance with law	2048	47	2	4
District attorney, safe burglary in office of	765	43	1	4
Elevators in, authority to supervise and control construction and operation of	3798	49	2	5
Engineering, to regulate steam engineering in	2874	48	1	5
Executors in,				
To amend law relative to bonds of	818	48	1	5
Do	1629	49	1	5
Do	2645	49	1	5
Foreign, to allow suits by	2373	49	1	5
Financial affairs in, investigation of	1424	48	1	5
Firemen's Insurance Company of Washington and Georgetown, extending charter of	4088	49	2	5
Fire companies in, to organize and encourage	207	21	1	1
Fire escapes in, to require in hotels and boarding houses	1812	48	1	5
Firemen, to provide relief for those disabled in service in District	979	48	1	5
Fires in, protection against	3051	49	1	5
Fishing season in, to define	1975	47	1	4
Gaming in, to more effectually suppress	1272	47	1	4
Government of	337	22	1	1
Do	35	41	3	3
Highways in, to forfeit charters of	86	41	3	3
Imprisonment in, for debt, to abolish	732	24	1	1
Inspection of wood in, to repeal laws for	1576	47	1	4
Insurance in, to regulate	3426	49	1	5
Jail in, for the erection of	211	35	2	3
Do	41	36	1	3
Justices of peace, to extend jurisdiction of	342	47	1	4
Land records in, to improve system of indexing	1777	47	1	4
Land titles in,				
To certain United States property	1012	46	2	4
To quiet certain	1271	47	1	4
Do	1775	47	1	4
Do	4016	49	2	5
Quieting	1734	47	1	4
To amend law relative to	1953	48	1	5
Lands in,				
Retrocede to Virginia land allotted to	325	29	1	1
Subdivisions to be made by Commissioners of	4019	49	2	5
Laws, appointment of commission to provide code of	269	21	1	1
Do	96	22	2	1
Do	663	46	2	4
Do	8	47	1	4
Licenses tax in, assessment and collection of	813	47	1	4
Liquor in, to regulate manufacture and sale of	2561	48	2	5
Do	4014	49	2	5
Lottery tickets in, prohibiting sale of	174	20	1	1
Do	1631	49	1	5
Mechanics' liens in, to amend law relative to	1686	48	1	5
Minors in, protection of	4017	49	2	5
Mortgages in, to amend law relative to, on personal property	1967	47	2	4
National Guard in, to maintain order during competitive drill and parade of	3702	49	2	5
Negroes in, sale of, for court charges	43	19	2	1
Do	60	20	2	1
Physicians to the poor in, compensation of	4039	49	2	5
Police, metropolitan, in,				
Organization of	836	27	2	1
Increase of	4015	49	2	5
Payment of	59	41	2	3
Regulation of	1427	48	1	5
Relief for those disabled in service	979	48	1	5
Police court in,				
Lease of Unitarian church for	*418	45	2	4
To regulate service of process in	2301	49	1	5
Pool-selling in, to prohibit	1630	49	1	5
Poultry, undrawn, in, to prevent sale of	1853	49	1	5
Prisoners in, commitment of	815	45	2	4
Public buildings,				
Furnishing illuminating gas for	6	27	1	1
To repair roof of court-house in Alexandria, D. C	456	28	1	1

* And views of minority.

Subject.	Report.	Congress.	Session.	Volume.
DISTRICT OF COLUMBIA—Continued.				
Railroads in,				
Capitol, North O Street and South Washington, to incorporate	129	46	3	4
Fifteenth Street, to incorporate	352	47	1	4
M Street Cross-Town, to incorporate	350	47	1	4
Metropolitan, extending line of	127	46	3	4
Southern Maryland, amend act incorporating	1103	47	1	4
Southern Maryland, to extend	1712	48	1	5
Thirteenth Street, to incorporate	351	47	1	4
Washington and Atlantic, extension of	1512	47	1	4
Washington and Chesapeake, to extend their limits	197	46	3	4
Washington and Point Lookout, extension	1513	47	1	4
Real estate in, to amend law relative to transfer of	78	20	1	1
Real estate agents, license tax on, to amend law providing for	3461	49	1	5
Real Estate Title Insurance Company, to change name of	3960	49	2	5
Real estate belonging to, to authorize sale of certain	2378	48	2	5
Reform school in,				
Selection of new site for	39	42	2	3
Trustees of	3354	49	1	5
Reform school for girls, to incorporate	4030	49	2	5
Revised Statutes of, to amend	3685	49	2	5
Roads in,				
Purchase of toll-roads	*410	35	1	2
Do	1514	47	1	4
Rock Creek, to condemn land on, for park	3820	49	2	5
Safe burglary in office of district attorney	785	43	1	4
Saint Dominic's Church, to exempt from taxation parsonage lot	3738	49	2	5
School board, to create	2704	49	1	5
School,				
Building sites in, purchase and erection of	1445	46	2	4
Industrial, for girls, making appropriation to aid, in	1010	46	2	4
Sewerage in, to complete system of	1115	48	1	5
Slavery in, abolition of	691	24	1	1
Do	58	37	2	2
Small-pox in, to prevent spread of	215	20	1	1
Societies in, to amend law relative to incorporation of	1058	48	1	5
Steam boilers, inspection of, to amend act providing for	988	49	1	5
Streets, railroads, and pavements, construction of	3821	49	2	5
Street railroads in, to regulate carrying of passengers on	1884	47	2	4
Streets in,				
Commissioners to establish	4019	49	2	5
Light by gas	354	35	1	2
Meridian avenue, confirming order of District Commissioners for closing	279	48	1	5
Pennsylvania avenue, to macadamize from Capitol to White House	184	21	1	1
Do	291	22	1	1
Do	604	24	1	1
Vacate a certain part of Rock street, in Georgetown	605	47	1	4
Supreme court,				
Reporter for	3819	49	2	5
To regulate sessions and meetings of	3792	49	2	5
Tax sales in, advertising, to regulate	187	21	1	1
Do	3769	49	2	5
Taxes in,				
Arrears of, collection of	1779	47	1	4
Arrears of, interest on	3768	49	2	5
Assessment and collection of	813	47	1	4
Do	1202	47	1	4
Bank shares on	1523	48	1	5
Parsonages and rectories, to exempt from	1573	46	2	4
Sale of real estate for	2582	48	2	5
Do	3458	49	1	5
School property in, to declare meaning of act of 1870 for	980	48	1	5
Settlement of, with Baltimore and Ohio Railroad	1109	46	2	4
Washington Monument, railway for filling about the base of	3915	49	2	5
Washington Safe Deposit Company, to enlarge powers of	3794	49	2	5
Water supply in,				
To amend act for increasing	981	48	1	5
Extending time for claiming damages by increasing	2491	48	2	5
Windsor Hotel Company, to incorporate	3933	49	2	5
DIXON, JAMES, for relief	69	28	2	1
Do	89	29	1	1
Do	363	29	1	1
Do	497	30	1	1
Do	85	31	1	1
DONOVAN, DANIEL, for relief	1778	47	1	4
DOUGHERTY, REBECCA, for relief	1885	47	2	4
DULIN, JOHN (guardian), for relief	592	27	2	1
EASTERN BRANCH OF POTOMAC, bridges across	106	19	1	1
	137	29	1	1
Do	643	30	1	1

*And views of minority.

Subject.	Report.	Congress.	Session.	Volume.
EASTERN BRANCH OF POTOMAC, bridges across	257	43	1	4
Do	596	43	1	4
Do	2708	49	1	5
EDUCATION. (*See* SCHOOLS.)				
EGAN, MARY ANNA, for relief	3462	49	1	5
ELEVATORS in D. C., construction and operation of	3793	49	2	5
ELLIOTT, HENRY R. (trustee), for relief	1906	47	2	4
ELLIOTT, JONATHAN, for relief	57	16	1	1
ENGINEERING STEAM, in D. C., to regulate	2374	49	1	5
EVANS, THOMAS, for relief	582	47	1	4
EXECUTORS in D. C., bonds of, to amend law regulating	318	48	1	5
Do	1639	49	1	5
Do	2645	49	1	5
EXECUTORS, FOREIGN, to allow them to bring suits in D. C	2378	49	1	5
EYE, EAR, AND THROAT HOSPITAL in D. C., to incorporate	285	45	2	4
FIFTEENTH STREET RAILWAY in D. C., to incorporate	262	47	1	4
FINANCE of D. C., investigation of	1434	48	1	5
FIRE COMPANIES. (*See* VOLUNTEER FIRE COMPANIES.)				
FIRE DEPARTMENT in D. C., to organize	307	21	1	1
FIRE ESCAPES in D. C., requiring hotels and boarding houses to provide	1313	48	1	5
FIREMEN in D. C., providing relief for disability incurred in service	979	48	1	5
FIREMEN'S INSURANCE COMPANY OF WASHINGTON AND GEORGETOWN, extending charter of	4038	49	2	5
FIRES in D. C., for further protection against	3051	49	1	5
FISHING in D. C., defining season for	1275	47	1	4
Do	978	48	1	5
FITZHUGH, MARIA C., for relief	1270	47	1	4
FOREIGN EXECUTORS, to allow suits to be brought in District by	2378	49	1	5
FRANKLIN INSURANCE COMPANY of D. C., to extend charter of	231	45	2	4
FRENCH, THOMAS O., for relief	1774	47	1	4
GAMING in D. C., to suppress	1272	47	1	4
GARFIELD MEMORIAL HOSPITAL in D. C., to incorporate	7	47	1	4
GAS COMPANIES in D. C., organizations of	592	29	1	1
Do	233	45	2	4
GAS LIGHTS in D. C., for certain street in D. C	354	35	1	2
GEORGETOWN, D. C.,				
Canal debt, relief in payment of	269	24	1	1
Citizens of, memorial for removal of Long Bridge across the Potomac	108	24	1	1
Do	318	24	1	1
Corporation of, to reimburse, for money advanced for building bridges across the Potomac River	96	35	1	2
Do	462	36	1	2
Streets in,				
Lighting of	355	35	1	2
To vacate Rock	605	47	1	4
Tax sales, to amend charter regulating	187	21	1	1
GERMAN PROTESTANT ORPHAN ASYLUM ASSOCIATION of D. C., to change name of	162	47	1	4
GIBBONS, JAMES, for relief	1104	47	1	4
GRANT, ROBERT, memorial for furnishing gas to public buildings	6	27	1	1
GRAVES in D. C., to prevent desecration of	2257	48	2	5
Do	873	49	1	5
HAY in D. C., weighing of, at wholesale market	2034	47	2	4
HIGHWAYS in D. C., charters of	36	41	3	3
HORSEY, OUTERBRIDGE (assignee), for relief	745	48	1	5
HOUSE OF CORRECTION in D. C., selection of new site for	39	42	3	3
HOWARD INSTITUTION in D. C., for relief to the poor	16	28	1	1
HOWISON, WILLIAM G., for relief	143	33	1	1
HUTCHINSON, WILLIAM, for relief	582	36	1	2
IMPRISONMENT FOR DEBT in D. C., to abolish	732	24	1	1
IMPROVEMENT CERTIFICATES of D. C., funding of, in 8 per cent. bonds	207	46	3	4
INAUGURATION DAY in D. C., to declare a legal holiday	198	46	3	4
INDUSTRIAL SCHOOL FOR GIRLS in D. C., making appropriation for aid of	1010	46	2	4
INSPECTION OF WOOD in D. C., to repeal law for	1576	47	1	4
INSURANCE in D. C., to regulate	3426	49	1	5
INTEREST ON D. C. BONDS, to provide for	774	43	1	4
IRON PAVEMENT on Pennsylvania avenue, D. C., providing for	356	35	1	2
JAIL in D. C.:				
To erect new	211	35	2	2
Do	41	38	1	2
Exclusion of visitors from	11	37	2	2
JUSTICES OF PEACE in D. C., to extend jurisdiction of	242	47	1	4
KILBOURN, HALLET, investigation of, in connection with real estate pool	242	44	1	4
LAMPS in D. C., for erection of, in	836	27	2	1
LAND RECORDS in D. C., improved system of indexing	1777	47	1	4
LAND TITLES, in D. C.,				
To quiet	1271	47	1	4
Do	1775	47	1	4
LAND, United States, in D. C.,				
Retrocession of, to Virginia all south of Potomac River	325	29	1	1
Sale of	1012	46	2	4

Subject.	Report.	Congress.	Session.	Volume.
OHN, for relief	57	16	1	1
ENCE, RICHARD, *et al.*, for relief	923	25	2	1
of D. C., authorizing a code of	269	21	1	1
Do	96	22	2	1
Do	683	46	2	4
Do	8	47	1	4
, WILLIAM, for relief	272	31	1	1
COURT in D. C., reorganization of	721	29	1	1
SE TAX in D. C., assessment and collection of	813	47	1	4
Do	3461	49	1	5
MECHANICS', in D. C., amending law relative to	1666	48	1	5
RS (*see also* DISTILLED SPIRITS) manufacture and sale of, to regulate	2581	48	2	5
E FALLS, in D. C., bridge across Potomac River at, to reimburse the corpo-				
on of Georgetown, D. C., for	98	35	1	2
Do	462	36	1	2
BRIDGE across Potomac River, D. C.,				
noval of	108	34	1	1
Do	318	34	1	1
RY TICKETS in D. C.,				
posal of, to prohibit	48	16	2	1
Do	174	20	1	1
E HOME in D. C., to exempt from taxation	3050	49	1	5
NS, ISAIAH, for relief	225	27	3	1
ER STATUE ASSOCIATION of D. C., to incorporate	280	48	1	5
EET CROSS-TOWN RAILWAY of D. C., to incorporate	350	47	1	4
, OWEN, for relief	293	25	3	1
to furnish gas-lights for certain streets passing through	354	35	1	2
LAND, memorial of State, asking Congress to improve navigation of Potomac River	111	17	1	1
ANICS' LIENS. (*See* LIENS.)				
IAN AVENUE, confirming order of commissioners for closing	279	48	1	5
POLITAN GAS-LIGHT COMPANY, incorporation of	275	36	1	2
POLITAN POLICE, payment of	59	41	2	2
POLITAN RAILROAD,				
ending line of	127	46	3	4
rporation of	*565	36	1	2
S, protection of, in D. C	4017	49	2	5
AGES in D. C. on personal property, regulating	1907	47	2	4
WILLIAM B., for relief	163	47	1	4
Do	1790	48	1	5
IPAL GAS COMPANY, incorporation of	1108	46	2	4
AL FIRE INSURANCE COMPANY, charter of, to amend	361	48	1	5
MICHAEL, for relief	411	35	1	2
NAL SAFE DEPOSIT COMPANY, charter of, to amend	1775	48	1	5
Do	2705	49	1	5
enlistment of colored criminals of D. C. in	23	38	2	2
R, JAMES G., for relief	88	47	1	4
ES, sale of free negroes for court charges in D. C	43	19	2	1
Do	60	20	2	1
. W. (assignee), for relief	106	29	1	1
Do	594	30	1	1
Do	216	34	1	1
Do	217	34	1	1
Do	100	35	1	2
Do	117	35	1	2
Do	439	35	1	2
Do	405	36	1	2
Do	406	36	1	2
Do	407	36	1	2
Do	30	37	2	2
N ASYLUM OF ALEXANDRIA, granting charter and public lands to	35	28	1	1
Do	312	29	1	1
, MATHIAS, for relief	735	47	1	4
NAGES in D. C., taxing of	1573	46	2	4
AL, MARGARET L., petition for closing alley in Washington, D. C	1111	46	2	4
RSON, ELIZA W., for relief	246	48	1	5
ENTIARY in D. C., erection of	52	18	2	1
Do	41	38	1	2
YLVANIA AVENUE, D. C.,				
pavement, to lay	356	35	1	2
adamizing of	184	21	1	1
Do	291	22	1	1
Do	604	24	1	1
Do	8	27	1	1
NAL PROPERTY in D. C., bills of sale and mortgages on	1907	47	2	4
MACEUTICAL ASSOCIATION of D. C., to incorporate	116	35	1	2
MACY in D. C., to regulate practice of	351	45	2	4
CIANS TO THE POOR in D. C., compensation of	4039	49	2	5
, MELISSA G., for relief	1904	47	2	4
Do	181	48	1	5

*And views of minority.

Subject.	Report.	Congress.	Session.	Volume.
BARGY & VAN ALSTINE, for relief of assignee	106	29	1	1
Do	594	30	1	1
Do	216	34	1	1
Do	217	34	1	1
BENNETT, H. M., for relief	82	47	1	4
BENNING, WILLIAM, for relief	106	19	1	1
BILLS OF SALE. (*See* MORTGAGES.)				
BOARD OF FOREIGN MISSIONS, property in District, to hold	2697	49	1	5
BOARD OF PUBLIC WORKS, D. C., workmen under, payment of	1200	47	1	4
BOILERS. (*See* STEAM BOILERS.)				
BONDS, D. C.,				
Executors, amending law regulating	818	48	1	5
Do	1629	49	1	5
Do	2645	49	1	5
Interest on, payment of	774	43	1	4
BOTTLERS in D. C., to protect	987	49	1	5
BOWEN, WILLIAM, for relief	1190	47	1	4
Do	1954	48	1	5
BOYLE, CORNELIUS, for relief of heirs	1112	46	2	4
BRIDGES in D. C.,				
Across Eastern Branch,				
To make free	187	29	1	1
Do	643	30	1	1
To construct a new	106	19	1	1
Do	187	29	1	1
Do	643	30	1	1
Do	257	43	1	4
Do	596	42	1	4
Do	2703	49	1	5
Across Potomac River,				
Aqueduct, to purchase	1958	48	1	5
Do	2300	49	1	5
Long Bridge, purchase of	484	22	1	1
At Three Sisters, to construct	470	48	1	5
Do	1958	48	1	5
Do	2300	49	1	5
BROWN, B. PEYTON, *et al.*, petition against taxing church property in District.	1572	46	2	4
BURGLARY. (*See* SAFE BURGLARY.)				
BURROWS, JOSEPH, *et al.*, memorial for straightening F and G streets in Washington	318	22	1	1
CANALS in D. C., Tiber Creek, to provide for filling	690	47	1	4
CAPITOL, NORTH O STREET AND SOUTH WASHINGTON RAILROAD,				
To incorporate	129	46	3	4
To provide for extension of	1102	47	1	4
CARROLL, ANN C., for relief	1870	47	1	4
CARROLL, DANIEL, for relief of devisees	176	48	1	5
CASEY, STEPHEN, for relief	2007	47	2	4
CERTIFICATES, IMPROVEMENT, D. C., providing for funding of	207	46	3	4
CHESAPEAKE AND OHIO CANAL COMPANY, D. C., to amend act of incorporation	48	29	2	1
Do	126	30	1	1
CHILDREN in D. C., providing for protection of	1444	46	2	4
Do	1957	48	1	5
CHITTENDEN BROTHERS, contractors for building dam across Potomac River at Great Falls, claim for relief	3686	49	2	5
CHURCH OF THE ASCENSION in D. C., for relief	2580	48	2	5
CHURCHES in D. C., exempting from taxation	1573	46	2	4
Do	980	48	1	5
CLARK, E. B., for relief of heirs	1115	46	2	4
CLARKE, BAILEY L. and MASON E., for relief	515	23	1	1
CODE OF LAWS, D. C., providing for	269	21	1	1
Do	96	22	2	1
Do	683	46	2	4
Do	8	47	1	4
COGSWELL FOUNTAIN, acceptance of, by District	1372	47	1	4
COLLATERAL TRUST AND INDEMNITY COMPANY, D. C., to incorporate.	492	48	1	5
COLORED CRIMINALS. (*See* CRIMINALS IN D. C.)				
COLUMBIA TURNPIKE COMPANY, D. C., to forfeit charter of	36	41	3	2
COLUMBIA COLLEGE, D. C., memorial of president of board of trustees	290	21	1	1
Do	334	22	1	1
COLUMBIAN INSTITUTION FOR DEAF, DUMB, AND BLIND, D. C., for relief	60	35	1	2
CONNOLLY, JOHN, for relief	128	46	3	4
Do	1998	47	2	4
Do	928	48	1	5
CONTAGIOUS DISEASES in D. C., to prevent spread of	215	20	1	1
CONTRACTS in D. C., made by board of public works, defining liabilities under.	2121	48	1	5
CONVEYANCES in D. C., acknowledgments of	491	48	1	5
COOK, MATTHEW, for relief	1260	47	1	4
COOK, PATRICK, for relief	1992	47	2	4
Do	347	48	1	5

Subject.	Report.	Congress.	Session.	Volume.
ET GALLERY, to exempt from taxation	3049	49	1	5
ND PAUPERS. (*See also* ANATOMICAL SUBJECTS.)				
a D. C., enlistment of colored criminals in Army and Navy of States	22	38	2	2
GES in D. C., recovery of	2379	48	2	5
st. improvement certificates	307	46	3	4
to provide for	774	43	1	4
edit certain, on	3429	49	1	5
f	302	47	1	4
LLIAM H., for relief	183	35	2	2
Do	108	36	1	2
FREDERICK C., for relief	251	34	1	1
ANCIS, for relief	3646	49	1	5
Do	3459	49	1	5
D. C., to regulate practice of	2258	48	2	5
BONDS in D. C., to compel compliance with the law	2343	47	2	4
IRITS in D. C., to regulate manufacture and sale of	2681	48	2	5
TORNEY of D. C., safe burglary in office of	786	43	1	4
COLUMBIA,				
vestigation of	72	42	3	3
Do	7	42	3	3
Do	647	43	1	4
Do	793	44	1	4
Do	64	44	2	4
ge	1378	47	1	4
to close	430	47	1	4
in square 635	729	49	1	5
Do	1012	49	1	5
s	1196	48	1	5
ust Company to incorporate	4086	49	2	5
subjects in, to authorize delivery of dead bodies of criminals and s to colleges for	2257	48	2	5
Do	573	49	1	5
certificates, providing for redemption of outstanding	1105	47	1	4
Do	1371	47	1	4
Do	1778	47	1	4
in, to refund to certain citizens	1814	48	1	5
charter of	76	14	1	1
Do	56	16	1	1
Do	56	18	1	1
Do	4	27	1	1
Do	332	28	1	1
n, to amend law on personal property in	1907	47	2	4
est on	774	43	1	4
o protect	987	49	1	5
t, to purchase	470	48	1	5
Do	1958	48	1	5
Do	2300	49	1	5
Branch, to construct new	257	43	1	4
Do	596	43	1	4
Do	2703	49	1	5
Branch, to make free	137	29	1	1
Do	643	30	1	1
dge, to purchase	484	22	1	1
ters, to construct	470	48	1	5
Do	1958	48	1	5
Do	2300	49	1	5
ters, to build	470	48	1	5
Do	1958	48	1	5
Do	2300	49	1	5
filling Tiber Creek	690	47	1	4
l. Trust, and Indemnity Company in, to grant	492	48	1	5
Fire Insurance Company, to amend	361	48	1	5
Safe Deposit Company of, to amend	1775	48	1	5
Do	2705	49	1	5
et and Bladensburg Railroad, to grant	959	48	1	5
Maryland Railroad, to change	1712	49	1	5
tates Gas, Electric Light and Fuel Company in, to grant	1116	48	1	5
ton Traction Railway, to grant	2299	49	1	5
for protection of	1444	46	2	4
Do	1957	48	1	5
relative to taxation of	1573	46	2	4
Do	980	48	1	5
minal code, provide for	269	21	1	1
Do	96	22	2	1
iseases in, prevent spread of	215	20	1	1
board of public works, to define	2131	48	1	

Subject.	Report.	Congress.	Session.	Volume.
DISTRICT OF COLUMBIA—Continued.				
Conveyances in, acknowledgments of	481	48	1	5
Court, levy, reorganization of, in	721	29	1	1
Criminal code, to provide	2130	48	1	5
Criminals in, enlistment of colored, in Army and Navy of United States	23	35	2	2
Death damages, to provide for recovering	2279	48	2	5
Debt of, to fund bonded	774	43	1	4
Do	207	46	2	4
Do	362	47	1	4
Do	3439	49	1	5
Dentistry in, to regulate practice of	2286	48	2	5
Detectives in, to compel compliance with law	2048	47	2	4
District attorney, safe burglary in office of	785	43	1	4
Elevators in, authority to supervise and control construction and operation of	3798	49	2	5
Engineering, to regulate steam engineering in	2874	48	1	5
Executors in,				
To amend law relative to bonds of	318	48	1	5
Do	1629	49	1	5
Do	3045	49	1	5
Foreign, to allow suits by	2373	49	1	5
Financial affairs in, investigation of	1424	48	1	5
Firemen's Insurance Company of Washington and Georgetown, extending charter of	4088	49	2	5
Fire companies in, to organize and encourage	207	21	1	1
Fire escapes in, to require in hotels and boarding houses	1513	48	1	5
Firemen, to provide relief for those disabled in service in District	979	48	1	5
Fires in, protection against	3051	49	1	5
Fishing season in, to define	1975	47	1	4
Gaming in, to more effectually suppress	1272	47	1	4
Government of	337	22	1	1
Do	55	41	3	3
Highways in, to forfeit charters of	96	41	3	3
Imprisonment in, for debt, to abolish	732	24	1	1
Inspection of wood in, to repeal laws for	1576	47	1	4
Insurance in, to regulate	3426	49	1	5
Jail in, for the erection of	211	35	2	2
Do	41	36	1	2
Justices of peace, to extend jurisdiction of	242	47	1	4
Land records in, to improve system of indexing	1777	47	1	4
Land titles in,				
To certain United States property	1012	46	2	4
To quiet certain	1271	47	1	4
Do	1775	47	1	4
Do	4016	49	2	5
Quieting	1734	47	1	4
To amend law relative to	1953	48	1	5
Lands in,				
Retrocede to Virginia land allotted to	325	29	1	1
Subdivisions to be made by Commissioners of	4019	49	2	5
Laws, appointment of commission to provide code of	269	21	1	1
Do	96	22	2	1
Do	663	46	2	4
Do	8	47	1	4
Licenses tax in, assessment and collection of	813	47	1	4
Liquor in, to regulate manufacture and sale of	2561	48	2	5
Do	4014	49	2	5
Lottery tickets in, prohibiting sale of	174	20	1	1
Do	1631	49	1	5
Mechanics' liens in, to amend law relative to	1666	48	1	5
Minors in, protection of	4017	49	2	5
Mortgages in, to amend law relative to, on personal property	1967	47	2	4
National Guard in, to maintain order during competitive drill and parade of	3702	49	2	5
Negroes in, sale of, for court charges	43	19	2	1
Do	60	20	2	1
Physicians to the poor in, compensation of	4039	49	2	5
Police, metropolitan, in,				
Organization of	686	27	2	1
Increase of	4015	49	2	5
Payment of	59	41	2	2
Regulation of	1437	48	1	5
Relief for those disabled in service	979	48	1	5
Police court in,				
Lease of Unitarian church for	*418	45	2	4
To regulate service of process in	2301	49	1	5
Pool-selling in, to prohibit	1680	49	1	5
Poultry, undrawn, in, to prevent sale of	1263	49	1	5
Prisoners in, commitment of	815	45	2	4
Public buildings,				
Furnishing illuminating gas for	6	27	1	1
To repair roof of court-house in Alexandria, D. C	456	28	1	1

* And views of minority.

Subject.	Report.	Congress.	Session.	Volume.
DISTRICT OF COLUMBIA—Continued.				
Railroads in,				
Capitol, North O Street and South Washington, to incorporate	129	46	3	4
Fifteenth Street, to incorporate	352	47	1	4
M Street Cross-Town, to incorporate	350	47	1	4
Metropolitan, extending line of	127	46	3	4
Southern Maryland, amend act incorporating	1108	47	1	4
Southern Maryland, to extend	1712	48	1	5
Thirteenth Street, to incorporate	351	47	1	4
Washington and Atlantic, extension of	1512	47	1	4
Washington and Chesapeake, to extend their limits	197	46	3	4
Washington and Point Lookout, extension	1513	47	1	4
Real estate in, to amend law relative to transfer of	78	20	1	1
Real estate agents, license tax on, to amend law providing for	3461	49	1	5
Real Estate Title Insurance Company, to change name of	3960	49	2	5
Real estate belonging to, to authorize sale of certain	2378	48	2	5
Reform school in,				
Selection of new site for	39	42	2	3
Trustees of	3354	49	1	5
Reform school for girls, to incorporate	4030	49	2	5
Revised Statutes of, to amend	3685	49	2	5
Roads in,				
Purchase of toll-roads	*410	35	1	2
Do	1514	47	1	4
Rock Creek, to condemn land on, for park	3820	49	2	5
Safe burglary in office of district attorney	785	43	1	4
Saint Dominic's Church, to exempt from taxation parsonage lot	3738	49	2	5
School board, to create	2704	49	1	5
School,				
Building sites in, purchase and erection of	1445	46	2	4
Industrial, for girls, making appropriation to aid, in	1010	46	2	4
Sewerage in, to complete system of	1115	48	1	5
Slavery in, abolition of	691	24	1	1
Do	58	37	2	2
Small-pox in, to prevent spread of	215	20	1	1
Societies in, to amend law relative to incorporation of	1058	48	1	5
Steam boilers, inspection of, to amend act providing for	988	49	1	5
Streets, railroads, and pavements, construction of	3821	49	2	5
Street railroads in, to regulate carrying of passengers on	1884	47	2	4
Streets in,				
Commissioners to establish	4019	49	2	5
Light by gas	354	35	1	2
Meridian avenue, confirming order of District Commissioners for closing	279	48	1	5
Pennsylvania avenue, to macadamize from Capitol to White House	184	21	1	1
Do	291	22	1	1
Do	604	24	1	1
Vacate a certain part of Rock street, in Georgetown	605	47	1	4
Supreme court,				
Reporter for	3819	49	2	5
To regulate sessions and meetings of	3792	49	2	5
Tax sales in, advertising, to regulate	187	21	1	1
Do	3769	49	2	5
Taxes in,				
Arrears of, collection of	1779	47	1	4
Arrears of, interest on	3768	49	2	5
Assessment and collection of	813	47	1	4
Do	1202	47	1	4
Bank shares on	1523	48	1	5
Parsonages and rectories, to exempt from	1573	46	2	4
Sale of real estate for	2582	48	2	5
Do	3458	49	1	5
School property in, to declare meaning of act of 1870 for	980	48	1	5
Settlement of, with Baltimore and Ohio Railroad	1109	46	2	4
Washington Monument, railway for filling about the base of	3915	49	2	5
Washington Safe Deposit Company, to enlarge powers of	3794	49	2	5
Water supply in,				
To amend act for increasing	981	48	1	5
Extending time for claiming damages by increasing	2491	48	2	5
Windsor Hotel Company, to incorporate	3933	49	2	5
DIXON, JAMES, for relief	69	28	2	1
Do	89	29	1	1
Do	363	29	1	1
Do	497	30	1	1
Do	85	31	1	1
DONOVAN, DANIEL, for relief	1778	47	1	4
DOUGHERTY, REBECCA, for relief	1885	47	2	4
DULIN, JOHN (guardian), for relief	592	27	2	1
EASTERN BRANCH OF POTOMAC, bridges across	106	19	1	1
Do	137	29	1	1
Do	643	30	1	1

*And views of minority.

Subject.	Report.	Congress.	Session.	Volume.
EASTERN BRANCH OF POTOMAC, bridges across	257	43	1	4
Do	596	43	1	4
Do	2708	49	1	5
EDUCATION. (*See* SCHOOLS.)				
EGAN, MARY ANNA, for relief	3462	49	1	5
ELEVATORS in D. C., construction and operation of	2793	49	2	5
ELLIOTT, HENRY R. (trustee), for relief	1906	47	2	4
ELLIOTT, JONATHAN, for relief	57	16	1	1
ENGINEERING STEAM, in D. C., to regulate	2374	49	1	5
EVANS, THOMAS, for relief	582	47	1	4
EXECUTORS in D. C., bonds of, to amend law regulating	318	48	1	5
Do	1639	49	1	5
Do	2645	49	1	5
EXECUTORS, FOREIGN, to allow them to bring suits in D. C	2373	49	1	5
EYE, EAR, AND THROAT HOSPITAL in D. C., to incorporate	235	45	2	4
FIFTEENTH STREET RAILWAY in D. C., to incorporate	353	47	1	4
FINANCE of D. C., investigation of	1434	48	1	5
FIRE COMPANIES. (*See* VOLUNTEER FIRE COMPANIES.)				
FIRE DEPARTMENT in D. C., to organize	207	21	1	1
FIRE ESCAPES in D. C., requiring hotels and boarding houses to provide	1313	48	1	5
FIREMEN in D. C., providing relief for disability incurred in service	979	48	1	5
FIREMEN'S INSURANCE COMPANY OF WASHINGTON AND GEORGETOWN, extending charter of	4038	49	2	5
FIRES in D. C., for further protection against	3051	49	1	5
FISHING in D. C., defining season for	1275	47	1	4
Do	978	48	1	5
FITZHUGH, MARIA C., for relief	1370	47	1	4
FOREIGN EXECUTORS, to allow suits to be brought in District by	2373	49	1	5
FRANKLIN INSURANCE COMPANY of D. C., to extend charter of	231	45	2	4
FRENCH, THOMAS O., for relief	1774	47	1	4
GAMING in D. C., to suppress	1272	47	1	4
GARFIELD MEMORIAL HOSPITAL in D. C., to incorporate	7	47	1	4
GAS COMPANIES in D. C., organizations of	592	29	1	1
Do	233	45	2	4
GAS LIGHTS in D. C., for certain street in D. C	354	35	1	2
GEORGETOWN, D. C.,				
Canal debt, relief in payment of	269	24	1	1
Citizens of, memorial for removal of Long Bridge across the Potomac	108	34	1	1
Do	318	34	1	1
Corporation of, to reimburse, for money advanced for building bridges across the Potomac River	96	35	1	2
Do	463	36	1	2
Streets in,				
Lighting of	355	35	1	2
To vacate Rock	605	47	1	4
Tax sales, to amend charter regulating	187	21	1	1
GERMAN PROTESTANT ORPHAN ASYLUM ASSOCIATION of D. C., to change name of	162	47	1	4
GIBBONS, JAMES, for relief	1104	47	1	4
GRANT, ROBERT, memorial for furnishing gas to public buildings	6	27	1	1
GRAVES in D. C., to prevent desecration of	2257	48	2	5
Do	873	49	1	5
HAY in D. C., weighing of, at wholesale market	2034	47	2	4
HIGHWAYS in D. C., charters of	36	41	3	3
HORSEY, OUTERBRIDGE (assignee), for relief	745	48	1	5
HOUSE OF CORRECTION in D. C., selection of new site for	39	42	2	3
HOWARD INSTITUTION in D. C., for relief to the poor	16	28	1	1
HOWISON, WILLIAM G., for relief	143	33	1	1
HUTCHINSON, WILLIAM, for relief	582	36	1	2
IMPRISONMENT FOR DEBT in D. C., to abolish	732	24	1	1
IMPROVEMENT CERTIFICATES of D. C., funding of, in 8 per cent. bonds	207	46	3	4
INAUGURATION DAY in D. C., to declare a legal holiday	198	46	3	4
INDUSTRIAL SCHOOL FOR GIRLS in D. C., making appropriation for aid of	1010	46	2	4
INSPECTION OF WOOD in D. C., to repeal law for	1576	47	1	4
INSURANCE in D. C., to regulate	3426	49	1	5
INTEREST ON D. C. BONDS, to provide for	774	43	1	4
IRON PAVEMENT on Pennsylvania avenue, D. C., providing for	356	35	1	2
JAIL in D. C.:				
To erect new	211	35	2	2
Do	41	36	1	2
Exclusion of visitors from	11	37	2	2
JUSTICES OF PEACE in D. C., to extend jurisdiction of	242	47	1	4
KILBOURN, HALLET, investigation of, in connection with real estate pool	242	44	1	4
LAMPS in D. C., for erection of, in	836	27	2	1
LAND RECORDS in D. C., improved system of indexing	1777	47	1	4
LAND TITLES, in D. C.,				
To quiet	1271	47	1	4
Do	1775	47	1	4
LAND, United States, in D. C.,				
Retrocession of, to Virginia all south of Potomac River	325	49	1	1
Sale of	1012	46	2	4

Subject.	Report.	Congress.	Session.	Volume.
LAW, JOHN, for relief	57	16	1	2
LAWRENCE, RICHARD, *et al.*, for relief	228	25	2	1
LAWS of D. C., authorizing a code of	289	31	1	1
Do	85	32	2	1
Do	602	46	2	4
Do	8	47	1	4
LEACH, WILLIAM, for relief	372	31	1	1
LEVY COURT in D. C., reorganization of	721	29	1	1
LICENSE TAX in D. C., assessment and collection of	813	47	1	4
Do	2461	49	1	5
LIENS, MECHANICS', in D. C., amending law relative to	1958	48	1	5
LIQUORS (see also DISTILLED SPIRITS) manufacture and sale of, to regulate	2561	48	2	5
LITTLE FALLS, in D. C., bridge across Potomac River at, to reimburse the corporation of Georgetown, D. C., for	96	26	1	2
Do	462	28	1	2
LONG BRIDGE across Potomac River, D. C.,				
Removal of	108	34	1	1
Do	818	34	1	1
LOTTERY TICKETS in D. C.,				
Disposal of, to prohibit	48	16	2	1
Do	174	20	1	1
LOUISE HOME in D. C., to exempt from taxation	2059	49	1	5
LUKENS, ISAIAH, for relief	226	27	3	1
LUTHER STATUE ASSOCIATION of D. C., to incorporate	280	48	1	5
M STREET CROSS-TOWN RAILWAY of D. C., to incorporate	250	47	1	4
McCUE, OWEN, for relief	366	28	2	1
MALL, to furnish gas-lights for certain streets passing through	364	35	1	2
MARYLAND, memorial of State, asking Congress to improve navigation of Potomac River	111	17	1	1
MECHANICS' LIENS. (*See* LIENS.)				
MERIDIAN AVENUE, confirming order of commissioners for closing	279	48	1	5
METROPOLITAN GAS-LIGHT COMPANY, incorporation of	275	36	1	2
METROPOLITAN POLICE, payment of	60	41	2	2
METROPOLITAN RAILROAD,				
Extending line of	127	46	3	4
Incorporation of	*565	36	1	2
MINORS, protection of, in D. C	4017	49	2	5
MORTGAGES in D. C. on personal property, regulating	1907	47	2	4
MOSES, WILLIAM B., for relief	168	47	1	4
Do	1790	48	1	5
MUNICIPAL GAS COMPANY, incorporation of	1108	46	2	4
MUTUAL FIRE INSURANCE COMPANY, charter of, to amend	361	48	1	5
NASH, MICHAEL, for relief	411	35	1	2
NATIONAL SAFE DEPOSIT COMPANY, charter of, to amend	1775	48	1	5
Do	2705	49	1	5
NAVY, enlistment of colored criminals of D. C. in	23	38	2	2
NAYLOR, JAMES G., for relief	88	47	1	4
NEGROES, sale of free negroes for court charges in D. C	43	19	2	1
Do	60	20	2	1
NYE, J. W. (assignee), for relief	106	29	1	1
Do	594	30	1	1
Do	216	34	1	1
Do	217	34	1	1
Do	100	35	1	2
Do	117	35	1	2
Do	439	35	1	2
Do	405	36	1	2
Do	406	36	1	2
Do	407	36	1	2
Do	30	37	2	2
ORPHAN ASYLUM OF ALEXANDRIA, granting charter and public lands to	35	28	1	1
Do	312	29	1	1
PABST, MATHIAS, for relief	735	47	1	4
PARSONAGES in D. C., taxing of	1573	46	2	4
PASCHAL, MARGARET L., petition for closing alley in Washington, D. C	1111	46	2	4
PATTERSON, ELIZA W., for relief	246	48	1	5
PENITENTIARY in D. C., erection of	52	18	2	1
Do	41	38	1	2
PENNSYLVANIA AVENUE, D. C.,				
Iron pavement, to lay	356	35	1	2
Macadamizing of	184	21	1	1
Do	291	22	1	1
Do	604	24	1	1
Do	8	27	1	1
PERSONAL PROPERTY in D. C., bills of sale and mortgages on	1907	47	2	4
PHARMACEUTICAL ASSOCIATION of D. C., to incorporate	116	35	1	2
PHARMACY in D. C., to regulate practice of	351	45	2	4
PHYSICIANS TO THE POOR in D. C., compensation of	4039	49	2	5
POLER, MELISSA G., for relief	1904	47	2	4
Do	181	48	1	5

*And views of minority.

Subject.	Report.	Congress.	Session.	Volume.
POLICE in D. C.,				
Creating force of	836	27	2	1
Disabled, for relief of	979	48	1	5
Increase of	4015	49	2	5
Pay of, to regulate	59	41	2	2
Regulations for	1427	48	1	5
POLICE COURT,				
Lease of Unitarian church for	*418	45	2	4
Service of process in, regulating	2301	49	1	5
POOL-SELLING in D. C., prohibiting	1680	49	1	5
POTOMAC BRIDGE, repair of	7	27	1	1
Do	49	29	2	1
POTOMAC FLATS,				
Reclamation of, to provide for	83	47	1	4
Title to ownership of, to quiet	1775	47	1	4
United States interests in, providing for protection of	172	49	1	5
POTOMAC INSURANCE COMPANY, Georgetown, D. C., for relief	1114	46	2	4
POTOMAC RIVER,				
Bridge across, at Three Sisters, to purchase or build	470	48	1	5
Do	1958	48	1	5
Do	2300	49	1	5
Bridge across, to purchase or build, at Georgetown, D. C	470	48	1	5
Do	1958	48	1	5
Do	2360	49	1	5
Bridge over Eastern Branch,				
To make free	137	29	1	1
Do	643	30	1	1
To build new	257	43	1	4
Do	596	43	1	4
Do	2703	49	1	5
Fisheries in, to protect	978	48	1	5
Long Bridge, removal of	108	34	1	1
Do	318	34	1	1
Navigation of, Federal aid to improve	111	17	1	1
POULTRY in D. C., to prevent sale of undrawn	1383	49	1	5
PRISONERS in D. C., commitment of	815	45	2	4
PROVIDENT ASSOCIATION OF CLERKS, dissolution of	353	35	1	2
PUBLIC BUILDINGS in D. C.,				
Alexandria court-house, to repair	458	28	1	1
Gas for, to furnish	6	27	1	1
PUTNEY, TRUE, for relief	700	47	1	4
RAILROADS in D. C.,				
Capitol and North O Street and South Washington, to incorporate	129	46	3	4
Fifteenth Street Company, to incorporate	352	47	1	4
M Street Cross-Town Company, to incorporate	350	47	1	4
Metropolitan Railroad, to extend line of	127	46	3	4
Sixth Street and Bladensburg, to incorporate	959	48	1	5
Washington and Atlantic Railroad, to enter	1512	47	1	4
Washington and Chesapeake Railroad, to extend line	197	46	3	4
Washington and Point Lookout Railroad, to enter	1513	47	1	4
RANDALL, HENRY K., for relief of heirs	1906	47	2	4
RANDOLPH, CORNELIUS P., *et al.*, for relief	2741	49	1	5
REAL ESTATE in D. C.,				
Sale of certain, authorizing	2374	48	2	5
Do	2582	48	2	5
Transfer of, to amend law relative to	78	20	1	1
REAL ESTATE AGENTS in D. C., to amend license tax on	3461	49	1	5
REAL ESTATE POOL in D. C., investigation of	242	44	1	4
REAL ESTATE TITLE INSURANCE COMPANY of D. C., to change name of	3960	49	2	5
RECTORIES. (*See* PARSONAGES.)				
REDMOND, SARAH A., for relief	1905	47	2	4
Do	182	48	1	5
REFORM SCHOOL in D. C.,				
Site for, selection of	39	42	2	2
Trustees of, relative to	3354	49	1	5
REFORM SCHOOL FOR GIRLS, D. C., to incorporate	4030	49	2	5
RICHARDS, R. R., for relief	352	35	1	2
ROCK CREEK, D. C.,				
Park on, to condemn land for	3820	49	2	5
Stone bridge over, to erect	604	24	1	1
ROCK STREET, Georgetown, D. C., to vacate part of	605	47	1	4
RUPPERT, CHRISTIAN, and others (trustees), for relief	1198	47	1	4
SAFE BURGLARY in D. C., robbery in office of United States district attorney	785	43	1	4
SAINT DOMINIC'S CHURCH, D. C., to exempt from taxation parsonage lot	3788	49	2	5
SAINT LUKE'S CHURCH, D. C., for relief	977	48	1	5
SAINT MARK'S EPISCOPAL CHURCH in D. C., for relief	2579	48	2	5
Do	1137	49	1	5
SAINT PATRICK'S CHURCH, D. C., for relief	1136	49	1	5
SALOMON, JOHN C. FR., memorial for furnishing city of Washington, D. C., with water	174	33	1	1

* And views of minority.

Subject.	Report.	Congress.	Session.	Volume.
RD, D. C., to create	2704	49	1	5
ES in D. C.,				
upon taxation	980	48	1	5
sites for and erect	1445	46	2	4
USTRIAL, FOR GIRLS in D. C., appropriation to aid in estab-				
	1616	46	2	4
SE, D. C., relative to purchase of	813	45	3	4
YSTEM. (*See* DISTRICT OF COLUMBIA.)				
T AND BLADENSBURG RAILROAD, D. C., to incorporate	868	46	1	5
RAND BASIN in D. C., construction for supplying public build-				
ith water	281	21	1	1
Do	275	21	1	1
D. C., abolition of	691	24	1	1
Do	58	27	2	3
D. C., checking progress of	216	26	1	1
NCORPORATE in D. C., amending law relating to	1629	48	1	5
MON, for relief of heirs	582	27	3	1
ARYLAND RAILROAD COMPANY of D. C.,				
t of incorporation	1108	47	1	4
ad into District	1712	48	1	5
DISTRIBUTIVE AGENCY in D. C., to incorporate	222	45	2	4
ESSMENTS in D. C., to regulate	1271	47	1	4
RS in D. C., inspection of	968	49	1	5
NEERING in D. C., to regulate	2874	49	1	5
GH, for relief of assignee	106	29	1	1
Do	594	30	1	1
Do	216	34	1	1
Do	217	34	1	1
Do	160	35	1	2
ROADS in D. C., to regulate carrying of passengers on	1884	47	2	4
C.,				
are 224, to vacate	1106	46	1	5
are 635, to convey	729	46	1	5
Do	1012	46	2	5
n District, to change	1278	47	1	4
ges of streets passing through the "Mall"	394	28	1	2
enue, confirming order to vacate	279	48	1	6
., to close alley known as	430	47	1	4
avenue from Capitol to White House, to macadamize	184	21	1	1
Do	291	22	1	1
Do	604	24	1	1
in Georgetown, D. C., to vacate portion of	605	47	1	4
D. C., restricting right of	83	19	1	1
Do	24	28	2	1
URT of D. C.,				
	3819	49	2	5
meetings of, to regulate	3792	49	2	5
AL MUTUAL AND BENEVOLENT SOCIETY in D. C., to				
orate	224	45	2	4
,				
eneral taxes, collection of	1779	47	1	4
nterest on	3768	49	2	5
and collection of, providing for	813	47	1	4
Do	1202	47	1	4
Do	1779	47	1	4
and rectories, providing for	1578	44	2	4
rty, defining act of 1870 concerning	980	48	1	6
made by District Commissioners with Baltimore and Ohio Rail-				
o ratify	1109	46	3	4
D. C.,				
to amend charter of Georgetown relative to	187	21	1	1
	3769	49	2	5
WN ROAD in D. C., to make free	1514	47	1	4
STREET RAILWAY, D. C., to incorporate, in	851	47	1	4
AND in D. C., quieting	1271	47	1	4
Do	1734	47	1	4
DADS in D. C., purchasing toll-gates on	*410	35	1	2
ED BANKING ASSOCIATIONS. (*See* BANKS.)				
D. C., to change name to Anacostia	171	49	1	5
CHURCH PROPERTY in D. C., to lease for police court	*418	45	2	4
TES AGRICULTURAL SOCIETY of D. C., incorporation of	66	36	1	2
TES DISTRICT ATTORNEY. (*See* DISTRICT ATTORNEY.)				
TES GAS AND FUEL COMPANY of D. C., to incorporate	†1928	47	2	4
Do	1116	48	1	5
for relief	1113	46	2	4
State, asking Congress to improve navigation of Potomac River	111	17	1	1
of that portion of District of Columbia south of Potomac River to	325	29	1	1
FIRE COMPANIES in D. C., organization and encouragement of	207	21	1	1
H. D. and H. S., for relief	1197	47	1	4

*And views of minority. †Parts 1, 2.

Subject.	Report.	Congress.	Session.	Volume.
WASHINGTON AQUEDUCT, D. C., construction of	320	34	1	1
WASHINGTON BRIDGE, D. C., providing for sale of	484	22	1	1
WASHINGTON CABLE RAILWAY, D. C., to incorporate	2549	49	1	5
WASHINGTON COUNTY, D. C., asking for reorganization of levy court, by citizens of	721	29	1	1
WASHINGTON, D. C.,				
Assessment law of	83	19	1	1
F and G streets in city of, to straighten	318	22	1	1
Gas company in, to establish	592	29	1	1
Do	233	45	2	4
Grounds in, relative to low	814	45	2	4
Land in, relative to square 446	1110	46	2	4
Lamps in city of, to erect	836	27	2	1
Lotteries in, to regulate	48	16	2	1
Mall, to light with gas the streets passing through the	354	35	1	2
Market-house from Capitol Hill, to remove	1038	25	2	1
Park in, to purchase land for public	64	47	1	4
Public force in, to establish an efficient	836	27	2	1
Police improvements in	184	21	1	1
Do	291	22	1	1
Public lands in, to provide for sale of	91	28	1	1
Relief of corporation of	366	23	1	1
Do	269	24	1	1
Suffrage in city of, to extend right of	24	28	2	1
Title to land in, to quiet	4016	49	2	5
WASHINGTON, D. C., EYE, EAR, AND THROAT HOSPITAL, to incorporate	235	45	2	4
WASHINGTON, D. C., INFIRMARY, relative to management of	319	36	1	2
WASHINGTON, D. C., MARKET COMPANY,				
Charter of, to repeal	1011	46	2	4
Incorporation of, to amend act of	189	43	2	4
WASHINGTON MONUMENT,				
Completion of	48	42	2	3
Do	1107	46	2	4
Erection of	*567	36	1	2
Railway for filling about base of	3915	49	2	5
WASHINGTON (D. C.) SAFE DEPOSIT COMPANY, to enlarge powers of	3794	49	2	5
WASHINGTON AND ATLANTIC RAILROAD, to authorize extension of, within D. C	1512	47	1	4
WASHINGTON AND CHESAPEAKE RAILROAD, to extend their railroad into and within the limits of the D. C	197	46	3	4
WASHINGTON AND POINT LOOKOUT RAILROAD, to authorize extension of into and within D. C	1513	47	1	4
WASHINGTON (D. C.) AND ROCKVILLE TURNPIKE COMPANY, to forfeit charter of	36	41	3	2
WASHINGTON (D. C.) TRACTION RAILWAY, to incorporate	2299	49	1	5
WASHINGTON MONUMENTAL SOCIETY, memorial of officers and managers of	483	24	1	1
WATER SUPPLY, D. C.,				
To amend act for increasing	961	48	1	5
To extend time for claiming damages caused by increasing	2491	48	2	5
WATSON, GEORGE W., to quiet title to certain lands in district	317	48	1	5
WEBB, W. B. (trustee), for relief	1906	47	2	4
WELLS, THOMAS C., for relief	272	31	1	1
WHEATLY, WILLIAM, for relief	197	27	2	1
Do	94	33	1	1
WHOLESALE MARKET, D. C., to amend law relative to weighing hay at	2094	47	2	4
WILLIAMS, JAMES, for relief	682	29	1	1
WINDSOR HOTEL COMPANY, D. C., to incorporate	2933	49	2	5
WOOD in D. C., to repeal laws requiring inspection of	1576	47	1	4
YOUNG, JAMES, for relief	416	28	1	1
YOUNG MEN'S CHRISTIAN ASSOCIATION of D. C., to exempt property of, from taxation	1724	49	1	5
Do	3460	49	1	5
YOUNG WOMAN'S CHRISTIAN HOME, D. C., to incorporate	1726	49	1	5

*And views of minority.

REPORTS

OF THE

COMMITTEE ON EDUCATION,

HOUSE OF REPRESENTATIVES,

FROM THE ORGANIZATION OF THE COMMITTEE, MARCH 21, 1867, TO THE CLOSE OF THE FORTY-NINTH CONGRESS, 1887, INCLUSIVE,

IN ONE VOLUME.

COMPILED, UNDER THE DIRECTION OF THE JOINT COMMITTEE ON PRINTING,

BY

T. H. McKEE,

CLERK, DOCUMENT ROOM, UNITED STATES SENATE.

WASHINGTON:
GOVERNMENT PRINTING OFFICE.
1887.

9229

FORTY-NINTH CONGRESS, FIRST SESSION.

[PUBLIC RESOLUTION—No. 24.]

Joint resolution authorizing the preparation of a compilation of the reports o
mittees of the Senate and House of Representatives.

Resolved by the Senate and House of Representatives of the
States of America in Congress assembled, That there be prepared
the direction of the Joint Committee of Printing, a compilation
reports of the Senate and House of Representatives from the
teenth to the Forty-eighth Congress, inclusive, classified by comm
arranged, indexed, and bound in suitable volumes for the use
standing committees of the two Houses of Congress. And the s
seven thousand seven hundred and fifty dollars, or so much ther
may be found necessary, is hereby appropriated, out of any mo
the Treasury not otherwise appropriated, for the preparation o
work, which sum may be paid by the Secretary of the Treasury
the order of the chairman of said Joint Committee, as additional
compensation to any officer or employee of the United States.

Resolved further, That the Clerk of the House and Secretary
Senate be, and they are hereby directed, to procure and file, for t
of their respective Houses, copies of all reports made by each co
tee of all succeeding Congresses; and that the Clerk of the Hous
the Secretary of the Senate be, and they are hereby, authorize
directed at the close of each session of Congress, to cause said re
to be indexed and bound, one copy to be deposited in the libra
each House and one copy in the room of the committee from whi
reports emanated.

Approved, July 29, 1886.

COMPILER'S NOTICE.

This compilation embraces all the printed reports made by both Houses of Congress from the commencement of the Fourteenth to the close of the Forty-ninth Congress. They are classified by committees and arranged in numerical order. The collection for each committee is divided into volumes of suitable size. Each committee has a separate index, a copy being bound in each volume.

The SPECIAL and SELECT reports are all compiled in one collection having one index, a copy of which is bound in each volume.

The plan throughout the compilation is to place each report to the committee from which it was reported, without reference to the subject-matter.

The House and Senate reports are compiled separately. Care will be required in noticing the chronological order, as in some instances an entire session or Congress may not appear in certain volumes from the fact that during this period no reports were made by this committee.

T. H. McKEE.

INDEX

TO

REPORTS OF COMMITTEE ON EDUCATION,

HOUSE OF REPRESENTATIVES.

FROM 1867 TO 1887, INCLUSIVE.

Subject.	Report.	Congress.	Session.	Volume.
AGRICULTURAL COLLEGES,				
Financial management of	57	43	2	1
Land grants in aid of	57	43	2	1
Education at, cost of	57	43	2	1
AMERICAN MISSIONARY ASSOCIATION, payments made to, from Freedmen's Bureau	121	41	2	1
AMERICAN PRINTING HOUSE FOR THE BLIND, Government aid for	455	45	2	1
BEAUFORT, SOUTH CAROLINA, redemption and sale of school-farm lands held by United States in	1266	49	1	1
BLIND, American Printing House for Education of, aid to	455	45	2	1
BOARD OF EDUCATION, conveyance of certain lot and buildings at Harper's Ferry, W. Va., to	1353	48	1	1
BOUNTY TO COLORED SOLDIERS, unclaimed appropriation of, to be applied to the education of colored youth	518	46	2	1
BUREAU OF FREEDMEN, success of	121	41	2	1
CHINESE IMMIGRATION, restriction of	*1017	47	1	1
COLLEGES,				
William and Mary College, aid to	53	41	3	1
Do	9	42	2	1
Do	203	44	1	1
Do	12	45	2	1
National University, to establish	90	42	3	1
Agricultural, to establish	57	43	2	1
Iowa Agricultural, public lands in aid of	917	47	1	1
Protestant Episcopal Seminary in Virginia, relief of	91	45	2	1
Lands to aid in erection of	917	47	1	1
COLORED YOUTH, education of	518	46	2	1
COLORED RACE, education of	608	47	1	1
COMMON SCHOOLS, support of	1214	47	1	1
Do	495	48	1	1
DEPARTMENT OF EDUCATION, examination of	25	40	3	1
DISTRICT OF COLUMBIA,				
Free kindergarten in, establishment of	522	46	2	1
Kindergarten in Washington, for aid	522	46	2	1
EDUCATION, DEPARTMENT OF, to establish	25	40	3	1
EDUCATION IN THE SOUTH, North Carolina, to establish universities in	521	46	2	1
EDUCATION OF COLORED YOUTH, unclaimed appropriations for pay and bounties of colored soldiers to be applied to	518	46	2	1
EDUCATION OF THE COLORED RACE	608	47	1	1
EDUCATION OF THE BLIND, to promote	455	45	2	1
EIGHT-HOUR LAW, enforcement of	520	46	2	1
EMANCIPATION, British and French	121	41	2	1
FREEDMAN'S SAVINGS BANK, reimbursing depositors of	†1991	47	1	1
FREEDMEN, education of	121	41	2	1
Do	†608	47	1	1
FREEDMEN'S BUREAU,				
Origin of	121	41	2	1
Payments made by, to American Missionary Association	121	41	2	1

* And views of minority, Part 2. † And views of minority.

Subject.	Report.	Congress.	Session.	Volume.
FREE KINDERGARTEN, establishment of, in District of Columbia	522	46	2	1
HARPER'S FERRY, WEST VIRGINIA, conveyance of certain lot and buildings to board of education	1353	48	1	1
HOWARD, O. O., charges against	*121	41	2	1
HOWARD UNIVERSITY, purchase of land for	121	41	2	1
ILLITERACY,				
In the United States	1214	47	1	1
Facilitate removal of, in United States	*495	48	1	1
INTERSTATE EDUCATIONAL COMMISSION, views of, regarding education	*495	48	1	1
INVESTIGATION, charges against General O. O. Howard	*121	41	2	1
IOWA AGRICULTURAL COLLEGE, granting public lands to, for encouragement of agricultural and mechanical arts	917	47	1	1
KENTUCKY, education of the blind in	455	45	2	1
KINDERGARTEN, petition for the establishment of, in District of Columbia	522	46	2	1
LABOR,				
Condition of American	240	45	2	1
Six Chinese Companies, memorial of the, on Chinese immigration	240	45	2	1
Do	62	45	3	1
Do	519	46	2	1
Do	67	47	1	1
California senate on memorial of	240	45	2	1
Eight-hour law, enforcement of	520	46	2	1
LAND SCRIP,				
Investment of proceeds of sale of	57	43	2	1
Agricultural colleges, in aid of	57	43	2	1
MECHANICS AND ARTS, College of, sale of lands granted to	917	47	1	1
MORGANTON, NORTH CAROLINA, relief of certain churches at	1854	48	1	1
NATIONAL IRON-MOLDERS' UNION, incorporation of	364	45	2	1
NATIONAL UNIVERSITY, establishment of	90	42	3	1
NEW YORK, Union Home School in	95	42	2	1
NORTH CAROLINA,				
Universities in, to establish	521	46	2	1
Relief of certain churches at Morganton	1354	48	1	1
ORPHANS OF VOLUNTEER SOLDIERS AND SEAMEN, education of	95	42	2	1
ORTHOGRAPHY OF PUBLIC DOCUMENTS, commission on "Spelling Reform of the English Language"	1824	46	2	1
PHYSIOLOGY AND HYGIENE, study of, in public schools	1765	49	1	1
PROTESTANT EPISCOPAL SEMINARY AND HIGH SCHOOL OF VIRGINIA, relief of	91	45	2	1
PUBLIC SCHOOLS, study of physiology and hygiene in	1765	49	1	1
SCHOOL FARM LANDS, sale and redemption of, held by United States in Beaufort, S. C	1266	49	1	1
SIX CHINESE COMPANIES, memorial of	240	45	2	1
SPELLING REFORM OF THE ENGLISH LANGUAGE, commission on	1824	46	2	1
UNION HOME AND SCHOOL OF NEW YORK, aid of	95	42	2	1
VIRGINIA, William and Mary College, aid of	58	41	3	1
Do	9	42	2	1
Do	203	44	1	1
Do	12	45	2	1
VOLUNTEER SOLDIERS AND SEAMEN, orphans of, education, care, and maintenance of	95	42	2	1
WILLIAM AND MARY COLLEGE, petition for aid	58	41	3	1
Do	9	42	2	1
Do	203	44	1	1
Do	12	45	2	1

*And views of minority.

REPORTS

OF THE

COMMITTEE ON ELECTIONS,

HOUSE OF REPRESENTATIVES,

FROM THE FOURTEENTH CONGRESS, 1815, TO THE FORTY-NINTH CONGRESS, 1887, INCLUSIVE.

IN FIFTEEN VOLUMES.

COMPILED, UNDER THE DIRECTION OF THE JOINT COMMITTEE ON PRINTING,

BY

T. H. McKEE,

CLERK, DOCUMENT ROOM, UNITED STATES SENATE.

WASHINGTON:
GOVERNMENT PRINTING OFFICE.
1887.

9224 ELEC H

FORTY-NINTH CONGRESS, FIRST SESSION.

[PUBLIC RESOLUTION—No. 24.]

Joint resolution authorizing the preparation of a compilation of the reports o mittees of the Senate and House of Representatives.

Resolved by the Senate and House of Representatives of the l States of America in Congress assembled, That there be prepared ı the direction of the Joint Committee of Printing, a compilation c reports of the Senate and House of Representatives from the teenth to the Forty-eighth Congress, inclusive, classified by commi arranged, indexed, and bound in suitable volumes for the use c standing committees of the two Houses of Congress. And the sı seven thousand seven hundred and fifty dollars, or so much there may be found necessary, is hereby appropriated out of any moı the Treasury not otherwise appropriated, for the preparation oi work, which sum may be paid by the Secretary of the Treasury the order of the chairman of said Joint Committee, as additional ı compensation to any officer or employee of the United States.

Resolved further, That the Clerk of the House and Secretary c Senate be, and they are hereby directed, to procure and file, for th of their respective Houses, copies of all reports made by each coı tee of all succeeding Congresses; and that the Clerk of the Hous the Secretary of the Senate be, and they are hereby, authorizec directed at the close of each session of Congress, to cause said re to be indexed and bound, one copy to be deposited in the libr each House and one copy in the room of the committee from whic reports emanated.

Approved, July 29, 1886.

COMPILER'S NOTICE.

'his compilation embraces all the printed reports made by both ıses of Congress from the commencement of the Fourteenth to the ;e of the Forty-ninth Congress. They are classified by committees l arranged in numerical order. The collection for each committee is ided into volumes of suitable size. Each committee has a separate ex, a copy being bound in each volume.

:he SPECIAL and SELECT reports are all compiled in one collection ring one index, a copy of which is bound in each volume.

The plan throughout the compilation is to place each report to the nmittee from which it was reported, without reference to the subject-ıtter.

The House and Senate reports are compiled separately. Care will required in noticing the chronological order, as in some instances an tire session or Congress may not appear in certain volumes from the ct that during this period no reports were made by this committee.

T. H. McKEE.

INDEX

TO

PORTS OF THE COMMITTEE ON ELECTIONS,

HOUSE OF REPRESENTATIVES.

FROM 1815 TO 1887, INCLUSIVE.

xes to the reports upon contested election cases are arranged, first, by Congresses; sec- tates, each in numerical and alphabetical order; then followed by a general-subject index, h a partial digest of each case.]

CONTESTED CASES BY CONGRESSES.*

Subject.	Report.	Congress.	Session.	Volume.
NTH CONGRESS,				
Rufus, *vs.* Scott, John	22	14	2	1
Do	28	14	2	1
eld, Robert, *vs.* McCoy, William	54	14	1	1
thby, Westel, *vs.* Smith, William S	3	14	1	1
TH CONGRESS,				
Elias	31	15	1	1
nd, C., *vs.* Herrick S	30	15	1	1
Do	31	15	1	1
rd, George	37	15	1	1
TH CONGRESS,				
James, jr., *vs.* Sage, Ebenezer	39	16	1	1
, Rollin C., *vs.* Morrill, Orsamus C	27	16	1	1
ENTH CONGRESS,				
hillip, *vs.* Cosden, Jeremiah	64	17	1	1
NTH CONGRESS,				
Parmenio, *vs.* Wilson, Isaac	15	18	1	1
John, *vs.* Richard, Gabriel	27	18	1	1
electors of Massachusetts *vs.* Bailey, John, of Massachusetts	67	18	1	1
NTH CONGRESS,				
John, *vs.* Wing, Austin E	39	19	1	1
Do	69	19	1	1
l, Gabriel, *vs.* Wing, Austin E	39	19	1	1
Do	69	19	1	1
FIRST CONGRESS,				
Thomas D., *vs.* Lea, Pryor	32	21	1	1
George, *vs.* Newton, Thomas	213	21	1	1
rn, Reuel, *vs.* Ripley, James W	88	21	1	1
, Silas, jr., *vs.* Fisher, George	95	21	1	1
SECOND CONGRESS,				
Joseph, *vs.* Johnston, Charles C	444	22	1	1
THIRD CONGRESS,				
, Robert P., *vs.* Moore, Thomas P	†446	23	1	1
citizens and electors of Ohio, *vs.* Allen, William	110	23	1	2
FOURTH CONGRESS,				
d, David, *vs.* Graham, James	378	24	1	2
FIFTH CONGRESS,				
ne, John F. H	2	25	1	2
Do	379	25	2	2
ames D., *vs.* Jones, George W	7	25	3	2
, Samuel J	2	25	1	2
Do	379	25	2	2
ippi election case (Gholson and Claiborne)	2	25	1	2
Do	379	25	2	2

* For digest of cases see general index.

† Part 2.

Contested cases by Congresses—Continued.

Subject.	Report.	Congress.	Session.	Volume.
TWENTY-SIXTH CONGRESS,				
Ingersoll, C. J., *vs.* Naylor, Charles	588	26	1	4
New Jersey case	506	26	1	3
Do	541	26	1	3
TWENTY-SEVENTH CONGRESS,				
Florida, citizens of, *vs.* Levy, David	450	27	2	5
Lowell, Joshua A	285	27	2	5
TWENTY-EIGHTH CONGRESS,				
Botts, John M., *vs.* Jones, John W	492	28	1	5
Goggin, William L., *vs.* Gilmer, Thomas W	76	28	1	5
Members elected by general ticket	60	28	1	5
TWENTY-NINTH CONGRESS,				
Baker, Edward D	86	29	2	5
Brockenbrough, W. H., *vs.* Cabell, Edward C	35	29	1	5
Farlee, Isaac G., *vs.* Runk, John	310	29	1	5
Newton, Thomas W	86	29	2	5
THIRTIETH CONGRESS,				
Monroe, James, *vs.* Jackson, David S	403	30	1	6
Sibley, Henry H., of Wisconsin Territory	10	30	2	6
THIRTY-FIRST CONGRESS,				
Babbitt, Almon W., of Deseret	219	31	1	6
Little, John S., *vs.* Robbins, John, jr	488	31	1	6
Messervy, William S., of New Mexico	20	31	2	6
Miller, Daniel F., *vs.* Thompson, William	400	31	1	6
Perkins, Jared, *vs.* Morrison, George W	3	31	2	6
Smith, Hugh N., of New Mexico	220	31	1	6
THIRTY-SECOND CONGRESS,				
Wright, Hendrick B., *vs.* Fuller, Henry M	136	32	1	6
THIRTY-THIRD CONGRESS,				
Lane, William C., *vs.* Gallegos, José M	121	33	1	6
THIRTY-FOURTH CONGRESS,				
Archer, William B., *vs.* Allen, James C	8	34	1	
Do	*167	34	1	6
Bennett, Hiram P., *vs.* Chapman, Bird B	65	34	1	
Clark, R. S. B., *vs.* Hall, Augustus	78	34	3	6
Milliken, James A., *vs.* Fuller, Thomas J. D	44	34	1	
Otero, Miguel A., *vs.* Gallegos, José M	90	34	1	
Reeder, A. H., *vs.* Whitfield, J. W	3	34	1	
Do	275	34	1	
Do	186	34	3	
Turney, L. J. S., *vs.* Marshall, S. S	194	34	1	
THIRTY-FIFTH CONGRESS,				
Brooks, Henry P., *vs.* Davis, Henry Winter	105	35	1	
Cavanaugh, James M., of Minnesota	406	35	1	
Chapman, Bird B., *vs.* Ferguson, Fenner	65	34	1	
Do	51	35	1	7
Do	156	35	2	7
Fuller, Alpheus G., *vs.* Kingsbury, W. W	435	35	1	7
Phelps, W. W., of Minnesota	468	35	1	7
Vallandigham, C. L., *vs.* Campbell, Lewis D	50	35	1	7
Do	380	35	1	7
Whyte, W. Pinkney, *vs.* Harris, J. Morrison	538	35	1	7
THIRTY-SIXTH CONGRESS,				
Blair, Francis P., jr., *vs.* Barrett, J. Richard	568	36	1	7
Chrisman, James S., *vs.* Anderson, William C	627	36	1	7
Daily, S. G., *vs.* Easterbrook, E	446	36	1	7
Harrison, William G., *vs.* Davis, H. Winter	60	36	2	7
Howard, William A., *vs.* Cooper, George B	57	36	1	7
Do	445	36	1	7
Preston, William P., *vs.* Harris, J. Morrison	89	36	2	7
Williamson, Amor J., *vs.* Sickles, Daniel E	80	36	1	7
Do	61	36	2	7
THIRTY SEVENTH CONGRESS,				
Beach, S. Ferguson, of Virginia	49	37	2	8
Butler, John M., *vs.* Lehman, William E	6	37	2	8
Byington, Le Grand, *vs.* Vanderver, William	68	37	2	8
Clements, Andrew J., claim to seat from Fourth Congressional district of Tennessee, said State then being in rebellion	9	37	2	8
Flanders, Benjamin F	22	37	3	8
Foster, Charles H., of North Carolina	118	37	2	8
Graffin, C. L	43	37	3	8
Hahn, Michael	22	37	3	8
Hawkins, Alvin	46	37	3	8
Kline, John, *vs.* Verree, John P	40	37	2	8
Lowe, F. F., of California	79	37	2	8
McKenzie, Lewis, on petition for admission to seat in House from Virginia	33	37	3	8

* Views of minority.

Contested cases by Congresses—Continued.

Subject.	Report.	Congress.	Session.	Volume.
HIRTY-SEVENTH CONGRESS—Continued.				
Morton, J. Sterling, *vs.* Daily, Samuel G	3	37	1	8
Do	69	37	2	8
Pigott, Jennings, on claim to seat in House from North Carolina	41	37	3	8
Segar, Joseph, of Virginia	12	37	2	8
Do	70	37	2	8
Shiel, George K., *vs.* Thayer, Andrew J	4	37	1	8
Upton, Charles H., of Virginia	17	37	2	8
Wing, W. W., *vs.* McCloud, J. B	23	37	3	8
HIRTY-EIGHTH CONGRESS.				
Bonzano, M. F., of Louisiana	13	38	2	8
Bruce, John P., *vs.* Loan, Benjamin F	44	38	1	8
Carrigan, Charles W., *vs.* Thayer, M. Russell	126	38	1	8
Chandler, Lucius H., of Virginia	50	38	1	8
Field, A. P., of Louisiana	8	38	1	8
Do	16	38	1	8
Jacks, T. M., of Arkansas	18	38	2	8
Johnson, J. M., of Arkansas	18	38	2	8
Kline, John, *vs.* Myers, Leonard	127	38	1	8
Knox, Samuel, *vs.* Blair, F. P	66	38	1	8
Lindsay, James, *vs.* Scott, John G	117	38	1	8
McHenry, John H., *vs.* Yeaman, George H	70	38	1	8
McKenzie, Lewis, *vs.* Kitchen, B. M	14	38	1	8
Mann, W. D., of Louisiana	17	38	2	8
Sleeper, John S., *vs.* Rice, Alexander H	23	38	1	8
Todd, J. B. S., *vs.* Jayne, William	1	38	1	8
Do	99	38	1	8
HIRTY-NINTH CONGRESS.				
Baldwin, Augustus C., *vs.* Trowbridge, Rowland E	13	39	1	9
Boyd, S. H., *vs.* Kelso, John R	88	39	1	9
Coffroth, Alexander H., claim to seat from the Sixteenth Congressional district of Pennsylvania	12	39	1	9
Dodge, William E., *vs.* Brooks, James	41	39	1	9
Follett, Charles, *vs.* Delano, Columbus	59	39	1	9
Fuller, Smith, *vs.* Dawson, John L	83	39	1	9
Koontz, William H., claim to seat from the Sixteenth Congressional district of Pennsylvania	12	39	1	9
Koontz, William H., *vs.* Coffroth, Alexander H	92	39	1	9
Rodgers, John B., on petition for admission to seat from Tennessee	32	37	3	8
Thomas, Dorsey B., *vs.* Arnell, Samuel M	5	39	2	9
Washburn, Henry D., *vs.* Voorhees, Daniel W	18	39	1	9
FORTIETH CONGRESS.				
Blakeley, George D., *vs.* Golladay, J. S	1	40	2	9
Burch, James H., *vs.* Van Horn, Robert T	4	40	2	9
Butler, Roderick R., loyalty in question	18	40	2	9
Casement, J. S., of Wyoming Territory	30	40	3	9
Chaves, J. Francisco, *vs.* Clever, Charles P	18	40	3	9
Christy, John H., *vs.* Wimpy, John A	8	40	3	9
Delano, Columbus, *vs.* Morgan, George W	42	40	2	9
Hamilton, Thomas A., of Tennessee	28	40	3	9
Hogan, John, *vs.* Pile, William A	62	40	2	9
Hunt, Caleb S., *vs.* Menard, J. Willis	27	40	3	9
Jones, Simon, *vs.* Mann, James	27	40	3	9
Kentucky election	2	40	2	9
McGrorty, William, *vs.* Hooper, William H	79	40	2	9
McKee, Samuel, *vs.* Young, John D	29	40	2	9
Do	59	40	2	9
Do	49	49	2	9
Smith, Samuel E., *vs.* Brown, J. Young	11	40	2	9
Switzler, William F., *vs.* Anderson, George W	28	40	2	9
Do	7	43	3	9
Symes, G. G., *vs.* Trimble, Lawrence S	6	40	2	9
FORTY-FIRST CONGRESS.				
Barnes, Sidney M., *vs.* Adams, George M	74	41	2	10
Boyden, Nathaniel, *vs.* Shober, Francis E	17	41	3	10
Covode, John, *vs.* Foster, Henry D	15	41	2	10
Darrall, Chester B., *vs.* Bailey, Adolphe	63	41	2	10
Eggleston, Benjamin, *vs.* Strader, Peter W	78	41	2	10
Foster, Henry D., *vs.* Covode, John	2	41	1	10
Georgia cases	16	41	2	10
Hoge, S. L., *vs.* Reed, J. P	3	41	1	10
Do	6	41	1	10
Hunt, C. S., *vs.* Sheldon, L. A	4	41	1	10
Do	38	41	2	10
Morey, Frank, *vs.* McCranie, G. W	10	41	1	10
Do	62	41	2	10
Myers, Leonard, *vs.* Moffet, John	9	41	1	10
Newsham, J. P., *vs.* Ryan, Michael	61	41	2	10

Contested cases by Congresses—Continued.

Subject.	Report.	Congress.	Session.	Volume.
FORTY-FIRST CONGRESS—Continued.				
Reid, John S., *vs.* Julian, George W	116	41	2	10
Rodgers, John B., of Tennessee, claim for additional representative	12	41	1	10
Segar, Joseph, claim for additional representative	51	41	2	10
Sheafe, C. A., *vs.* Tillman, Lewis	3	41	2	10
Shields, James, *vs.* Van Horn, Robert T	122	41	2	10
Switzler, William F., *vs.* Dyer, David P	106	41	2	10
Sypher, J. H., *vs.* St. Martin, Louis	11	41	1	10
Do	60	41	2	10
Taylor, Caleb N., *vs.* Reading, John R	50	41	2	10
Tucker, George, *vs.* Booker, George W	41	41	2	10
Van Wyck, Charles H., *vs.* Greene, George W	22	41	2	10
Wallace, A. S., *vs.* Simpson, William D	5	41	1	10
Do	7	41	1	10
Do	17	41	2	10
Do	71	41	2	10
Whittlesey, Charles, *vs.* McKenzie, Lewis	75	41	2	10
Zeigler, J. L., *vs.* Rice, J. M	107	41	3	10
FORTY-SECOND CONGRESS,				
Boles, Thomas, *vs.* Edwards, John	3	42	2	11
Do	10	42	2	11
Bowen, Christopher C., *vs.* DeLarge, Robert C	87	42	3	11
Burleigh, W. A., *vs.* Armstrong, M. K	43	42	2	11
Cessna, John, *vs.* Meyers, Benjamin F	11	42	2	11
Clark, W. T., of Texas	2	42	2	11
Giddings, D. C., *vs.* Clark, W. T	2	42	2	11
Do	65	42	2	11
Gooding, David S., *vs.* Wilson, Jeremiah M	41	42	2	11
McKenzie, Lewis, *vs.* Braxton, Elliott M	4	42	2	11
McKissick, Isaac G., *vs.* Wallace, Alexander S	66	42	2	11
Niblack, Silas L., *vs.* Walls, Josiah T	41	42	3	11
Norris, B. W., *vs.* Handley, W. A	83	42	2	11
Spink, S. L., *vs.* Armstrong, M. K	43	42	2	11
Tennessee election, question of validity of an election held in the month of November	1	42	1	11
FORTY-THIRD CONGRESS,				
Bell, Marcus L., *vs.* Snyder, O. P	11	43	2	11
Bradley, John M., *vs.* Hynes, William J	646	43	1	11
Burns, John M., *vs.* Young, John D	385	43	1	11
Davis, John J., *vs.* Wilson, Benjamin	7	43	1	11
Gause, Lucien C., *vs.* Hodge, Asa	264	43	2	11
Gunter, Thomas M., *vs.* Wilshire, W. W	92	43	1	11
Do	631	43	1	11
Hagans, Marshall, *vs.* Martin, Benjamin F	7	43	1	11
Lawrence, Effingham, *vs.* Sypher, J. Hale	269	43	2	11
Maxwell, George R., *vs.* Cannon, George Q	484	43	1	11
Sheridan, George A., *vs.* Pinchback, P. B. S	597	43	1	11
Do	263	43	2	11
Sloan, Andrew, *vs.* Rawls, Morgan	216	43	1	11
FORTY-FOURTH CONGRESS,				
Abbott, Josiah G., *vs.* Frost, Rufus S	653	44	1	11
Bromberg, Frederick G., *vs.* Haralson, Jere	294	44	1	11
Buttz, C. W., *vs.* Mackey, E. W. M	758	44	1	11
Cox, E. St. Julien, *vs.* Strait, Horace B	391	44	1	11
Fenn, S. S., *vs.* Bennett, T. W	624	44	1	11
Finley, Jesse J., *vs.* Walls, Josiah T	295	44	1	11
Lee, Samuel, *vs.* Rainey, Joseph H	578	44	1	11
LeMoyne, John V., *vs.* Farwell, Charles B	383	44	1	11
Platt, James H., *vs.* Goode, jr., John	762	44	1	11
Spencer, William B., *vs.* Morey, Frank	442	44	1	11
FORTY-FIFTH CONGRESS,				
Acklen, Joseph H., *vs.* Darrall, Chester B	147	45	1	12
Dean, Benjamin, *vs.* Field, Walbridge A	239	45	2	12
Finley, Jesse J., *vs.* Bisbee, Horatio	95	45	3	12
Frost, R. Graham, *vs.* Metcalfe, Lyne S	118	45	3	12
Nutting, James L., *vs.* Reilly, James B	291	45	3	12
Patterson, Thomas M., *vs.* Belford, James B	14	45	2	12
Richardson, John S., *vs.* Rainey, Joseph H	806	45	2	12
Tillman, G. D., *vs.* Smalls, Robert	916	45	2	12
Wigginton, Peter D., *vs.* Pacheco, Romualdo	83	45	2	12
Do	118	45	2	12
FORTY-SIXTH CONGRESS,				
Bisbee, Horatio, jr., *vs.* Hull, Noble A	86	46	3	13
Boynton, E. Moody, *vs.* Loring, George B	18	46	3	13
Bradley, John M., *vs.* Siemens, William F	427	46	2	13
Curtin, Andrew G., *vs.* Yocum, Seth H	345	46	2	13
Donnelly, Ignatius, *vs.* Washburn, William D	1791	46	2	13
Duffy, Sebastian, *vs.* Mason, Joseph	1568	46	2	13

Contested cases by Congresses—Continued.

Subject.	Report.	Congress.	Session.	Volume.
FORTY-SIXTH CONGRESS—Continued.				
Herbert, Robert O., *vs.* Acklen, Joseph H	382	46	3	13
Iowa contested election cases (*see* HOLMES, J. C.; WILSON, JOHN J.)	19	46	3	13
McCabe, James, *vs.* Orth, Godlove S	260	46	3	13
Merchant, W. B., *vs.* Acklen, J. H	382	46	3	13
O'Hara, James E., *vs.* Kitchen, William H	268	46	3	13
Yeates, Jesse J., *vs.* Martin, Joseph J	123	46	3	13
FORTY-SEVENTH CONGRESS,				
Anderson, Samuel J., *vs.* Reed, Thomas B	1697	47	1	14
Ball, M. D., petition for admission to a seat in Congress as a Delegate from Alaska	500	47	1	14
Bayley, S. P., *vs.* Barbour, John S	1040	47	1	14
Bisbee, Horatio, jr., *vs.* Finley, Jesse J	1066	47	1	14
Buchanan, George M., *vs.* Manning, Van H	1890	47	2	14
Do	1891	47	2	14
Cannon, George Q., *vs.* Campbell, Allen G	559	47	1	14
Cook, John C., *vs.* Cutts, Marsena E	1961	47	2	14
Jones, John W., *vs.* Shelley, Charles M	1886	47	2	14
Lee, Samuel, *vs.* Richardson, John S	1983	47	2	14
Lowe, William M., *vs.* Wheeler, Joseph	1273	47	1	14
Lynch, John R., *vs.* Chalmers, James R	931	47	1	14
Mabson, Algernon A., *vs.* Oates, William C	938	47	1	14
Mackey, E. W. M., *vs.* O'Connor, M. P	989	47	1	14
Sessinghaus, Gustavus, *vs.* Frost, R. Graham	1409	47	1	14
Do	1959	47	2	14
Smalls, Robert, *vs.* Tillman, George D	1525	47	1	14
Smith, Alexander, *vs.* Robertson, E. W	631	47	1	14
Smith, James Q., *vs.* Shelley, Charles M	1522	47	1	14
Stolbrand, C. J., *vs.* Aiken, D. Wyatt	932	47	1	14
Stovall, John T., *vs.* Cabell, George C	1696	47	1	14
Strobach, Paul, *vs.* Herbert, Hillery A	1521	47	1	14
Witherspoon, George W., *vs.* Davidson, R. H. M	1278	47	1	14
FORTY-EIGHTH CONGRESS,				
Botkin, A. C., *vs.* Maginnis, Martin	2138	48	1	15
Campbell, James E., *vs.* Morey, Henry Z	*1845	48	1	15
Chalmers, J. R., *vs.* Manning, Van H	†283	48	1	15
Chalmers, James R., *vs.* Manning, Van H	‡1959	48	1	15
Craig, George H., *vs.* Shelley, Charles M	2137	48	1	15
English, William E., *vs.* Peelle, Stanton J	†1547	48	1	15
Frederick, Benjamin T., *vs.* Wilson, James	*2623	48	2	15
Garrison, George T., *vs.* Mayo, Robert M	286	48	1	15
Do	954	48	1	15
McLean, James H., *vs.* Broadhead, James O	†2613	48	2	15
Manzanares, Francisco A., *vs.* Luna, Tranquillino	667	48	1	15
Massey, John E., *vs.* Wise, John S	†2024	48	1	15
O'Ferrall, Charles T., *vs.* Paul, John	*1435	48	1	15
Poole, Charles C., *vs.* Skinner, Thomas G	‡727	48	1	15
Wallace, Jonathan H., *vs.* McKinley, William, jr	†1548	48	1	15
Wood, S. N., *vs.* Peters, S. R	†794	48	1	15
FORTY-NINTH CONGRESS,				
Campbell, Frank T., *vs.* Weaver, J. B	*1622	49	1	15
Hurd, Frank H., *vs.* Romeis, Jacob	‡1449	49	1	15
Kidd, Meredith H., *vs.* Steele, George W	4142	49	2	15
Page, Charles H., *vs.* Pirce, William A	*1623	49	1	15
Do	†3617	49	2	15

* Parts 1, 2. † And views of minority. ‡ Parts 1, 2, 3.

CONTESTED CASES BY STATES.*

Subject.	Report.	Congress.	Session.	Volume.
ALABAMA.				
First Congressional district,				
Bromberg, Frederick G., *vs.* Haralson, Jere	294	44	1	11
Second Congressional district,				
Strobach, Paul, *vs.* Herbert, Hillery A	1521	47	1	14
Third Congressional district,				
Mabson, A. G., *vs.* Oates, W. C	988	47	1	14
Morris, B. W., *vs.* Hendley, W. A	83	43	2	11
Fourth Congressional district,				
Craig, George H., *vs.* Shelley, Charles M	2137	48	1	15
Jones, John W., *vs.* Shelley, Charles M	1886	47	2	14
Smith, James Q., *vs.* Shelley, Charles M	1522	47	1	14
Eighth Congressional district,				
Lowe, W. M., *vs.* Wheeler, Joseph	1273	47	1	14
ALASKA TERRITORY.				
Delegate,				
Ball, M. D., petition for admission as Delegate from Alaska	560	47	1	14
ARKANSAS.				
First Congressional district,				
Gause, Lucien C., *vs.* Hodges, Asa	204	43	2	11
Jacks, T. M	18	38	2	8
Second Congressional district,				
Bell, Marcus L., *vs.* Snyder, O. P	[illegible]	43	2	11
Bradley, John M., *vs.* Slemons, William F	427	46	2	13
Third Congressional district,				
Boles, Thomas, *vs.* Edwards, John	3	42	2	11
Do	10	42	2	11
Gunter, Thomas M., *vs.* Wilshire, W. W	92	43		11
Do	631	43		11
Johnson, J. M	18	38		8
Representative at large,				
Bradley, John M., *vs.* Hynes, William J	646	43		11
Newton, Thomas W	86	29		5
CALIFORNIA.				
Relative to contested-election cases in	2338	49	1	15
Fourth Congressional district,				
Wigginton, Peter D., *vs.* Pacheco, Romualdo	88	45	2	12
Do	118	45	2	12
Representative at large,				
Lowe, F. F	79	37	2	8
COLORADO.				
Relating to election of Delegate from Territory of Colorado, to determine as to *prima facie* right to a seat	3	40	1	9
State at large,				
Patterson, Thomas M., *vs.* Belford, James B	14	45	2	12
DAKOTA TERRITORY.				
Delegate,				
Burleigh, W. A., *vs.* Armstrong, M. K	43	42	2	11
Spink, S. L., *vs.* Armstrong, M. K	43	42	2	11
Todd, J. B. S., *vs.* Jayne, William	1	38	1	8
Do	99	38	1	8
DESERET.				
Delegate.				
Babbitt, Almon W	219	31	1	6
FLORIDA.				
Citizens of, *vs.* Levy, David	10	27	1	5
Do	450	27	2	5
First Congressional district,				
Niblack, Silas L., *vs.* Walls, Josiah T	41	42	3	11
Witherspoon, George W., *vs.* Davidson, R. H. M	1278	47	1	14
Second Congressional district,				
Bisbee, Horatio, jr., *vs.* Finley, Jesse J	1066	47	1	14
Bisbee, Horatio, jr., *vs.* Hull, Noble A	86	46	3	13
Finley, Jesse J., *vs.* Bisbee, Horatio	95	45	3	12
Finley, Jesse J., *vs.* Walls, Josiah T	295	44	1	11
State at large,				
Brockenbrough, W. H., *vs.* Cabell, Edward C	35	29	1	5

* For digest of cases see general index.

Contested cases by States—Continued.

Subject.	Report.	Congress.	Session.	Volume.
ORGIA,				
Legality of the election of members to the Twenty-eighth Congress from	60	28	1	5
First Congressional district,				
Sloan, Andrew, *vs.* Rawls, Morgan	216	43	1	11
Sixth Congressional district,				
Christy, John H., *vs.* Wimpy, John A	8	40	3	9
General election,				
Members from Georgia claimed seats in two Congresses by virtue of a single election under an ordinance of constitutional convention. Claim held not to be valid	16	41	2	10
AHO TERRITORY,				
Delegate,				
Fenn, S. S., *vs.* Bennett, T. W	624	44	1	11
LINOIS,				
Baker, Edward D	86	29	2	5
Third Congressional district,				
Le Moyne, John V., *vs.* Farwell, Charles B	285	44	1	11
Seventh Congressional district,				
Archer, William B., *vs.* Allen, James C	8	34	1	6
Do	167	34	1	6
Ninth Congressional district,				
Turney, L. J. S., *vs.* Marshall, S. S	194	34	1	6
DIANA,				
Fourth Congressional district,				
Gooding, David S., *vs.* Wilson, Jeremiah M	41	42	2	11
Reid, John S., *vs.* Julian, George W	116	41	2	10
Seventh Congressional district,				
English, William E., *vs.* Peelle, Stanton J	*1547	48	1	15
Washburn, Henry D., *vs.* Voorhees, Daniel W	18	39	1	9
Ninth Congressional district,				
McCabe, James, *vs.* Orth, Godlove S	260	46	3	13
Eleventh Congressional district,				
Kidd, Meredith H., *vs.* Steele, George W	178	34	3	6
WA.				
First Congressional district,				
Clark, R. S. B., *vs.* Hall, Augustus	178	34	3	6
Miller, Daniel F., *vs.* Thompson, William	400	31	1	6
Second Congressional district,				
Byington, Le Grand, *vs.* Vandever, William	68	37	2	8
Fifth Congressional district,				
Frederick, Benjamin F., *vs.* Wilson, James	†2623	48	2	15
Sixth Congressional district,				
Campbell, Frank T., *vs.* Weaver, J. B	†1622	49	1	15
Cook, John C., *vs.* Cutts, Massena E	1961	47	2	14
Eighth Congressional district,				
Holmes, J. C., *vs.* Sapp, William F	19	46	3	13
Ninth Congressional district,				
Wilson, J. J., *vs.* Carpenter, C. C	19	46	3	13
ANSAS.				
Delegate,				
Reeder, A. H., *vs.* Whitfield, J. W	3	34	1	6
Do	275	34	1	6
Do	186	34	3	6
State at large,				
Wood, S. N., *vs.* Peters, S. R	*794	48	1	15
ENTUCKY.				
On credentials of James B. Beck, A. P. Grover, and others, claiming to be representatives from	6	40	1	9
Relative to the right to seats of certain persons as members from	2	40	2	9
First Congressional district,				
Symes, G. G., *vs.* Trimble, Lawrence S	6	40	2	9
Second Congressional district,				
McHenry, John H., *vs.* Yeaman, George H	70	38	1	8
Smith, Samuel E., *vs.* Brown, J. Young	11	40	2	9
Third Congressional district,				
Blakely, George D., *vs.* Golladay, J. S	1	40	2	9
Fourth Congressional district,				
Chrisman, James S., *vs.* Anderson, William C	627	36	1	7
Eighth Congressional district,				
Barnes, Sidney M., *vs.* Adams, George M	74	41	2	10
Ninth Congressional district,				
McKee, Samuel, *vs.* Young, John D	29	40	2	9
Do	59	40	2	9
Zeigler, J. L., *vs.* Rice, J. M	107	41	2	10
Tenth Congressional district,				
Burns, John M., *vs.* Young, John D	383	43	1	11

* And views of minority. † Parts 1, 2.

Contested cases by States—Continued.

Subject.	Report.	Congress.	Session.	Volume.
LOUISIANA.				
Representative at large,				
Sheridan, George A., *vs.* Pinchback, P. B. S	597	43	1	11
Do	263	43	2	11
Bonzano, M. F	13	38	2	8
Field, A. P	1	38	1	8
Do	16	38	1	8
Mann, W. D	17	38	2	8
First Congressional district,				
Flanders, Benjamin F	22	37	3	8
Lawrence, E., *vs.* Sypher, J. H	269	43	2	11
Sypher, J. H., *vs.* St. Martin, Louis	11	41	1	10
Do	60	41	2	10
Second Congressional district,				
Hahn, Michael	22	37	3	8
Hunt, Caleb S., *vs.* Menard, J. Willis	27	40	3	9
Hunt, C. S., *vs.* Sheldon, L. A	4	41	1	10
Do	38	41	2	10
Jones, Simon, *vs.* Mann, James	27	40	3	9
Third Congressional district,				
Acklen, Joseph H., *vs.* Darrall, Chester B	147	45	2	12
Darrall, Chester B., *vs.* Bailey, Adolphe	63	41	2	10
Hebert, R. O., *vs.* Acklen, J. H	363	46	3	13
Merchant, W. B., *vs.* Acklen, J. H	362	46	3	13
Fourth Congressional district,				
Newsham, J. P., *vs.* Hahn, Michael	61	41	2	10
Fifth Congressional district.				
Morey, Frank, *vs.* McCraine, G. W	10	41	1	10
Do	62	41	2	10
Spencer, William B., *vs.* Morey, Frank	442	44	1	11
Sixth Congressional district,				
Smith, Alexander, *vs.* Robertson, E. W	681	47	1	14
MAINE.				
First Congressional district,				
Anderson, Samuel J., *vs.* Reed, Thomas B	1697	47	1	14
Sixth Congressional district,				
Milliken, James A., *vs.* Fuller, Thomas J. D	44	34	1	6
Seventh Congressional district,				
Lowell, Joshua A	285	27	2	5
State at large,				
Washburn, Reuel, *vs.* Ripley, James W	88	21	1	1
MARYLAND.				
First Congressional district,				
Reed, Philip, *vs.* Cosden, Jeremiah	94	17	1	1
Third Congressional district.				
Preston, William P., *vs.* Harris, J. Morrison	80	36	2	7
Stewart, Joseph, *vs.* Phelps, Charles E	2	40	1	9
Whyte, W. Pinkney, *vs.* Harris, J. Morrison	538	35	1	7
Fourth Congressional district,				
Brooks, Henry P., *vs.* Davis, Henry Winter	105	35	1	7
Harrison, William G., *vs.* Davis, Henry Winter	60	36	2	7
MASSACHUSETTS.				
Norfolk district,				
Citizens of, *vs.* Bailey, John	67	18	1	1
Sundry electors of, *vs.* Bailey, John, of Massachusetts	67	18	1	1
Third Congressional district,				
Dean, Benjamin, *vs.* Field, Walbridge	289	45	2	12
Sleeper, John S., *vs.* Rice, Alexander H	23	38	1	8
Fourth Congressional district,				
Abbott, Josiah G., *vs.* Frost, Rufus S	653	44	1	11
Sixth Congressional district,				
Boynton, E. Moody, *vs.* Loring, George B	18	46	3	13
MICHIGAN,				
Delegate.				
Biddle, John, *vs.* Richard, Gabriel	27	18	1	1
Biddle, John, *vs.* Wing, Austin E	89	19	1	1
Do	69	19	1	1
Richard, Gabriel, *vs.* Wing, Austin E	89	19	1	1
Do	69	19	1	1
First Congressional district,				
Howard, William A., *vs.* Cooper, George B	87	36	1	7
Do	445	36	1	7
Fifth Congressional district,				
Baldwin, Augustus C., *vs.* Trowbridge, Rowland E	13	39	1	9
MINNESOTA,				
Delegate.				
Cavanaugh, James H	408	35	1	7
Phelps, W. W	408	35	1	7
Fuller, Alpheus G., *vs.* Kingsbury, W. W	485	35	1	7

Contested cases by States—Continued.

Subject.	Report.	Congress.	Session.	Volume.
MINNESOTA—Continued.				
Second Congressional district,				
Cox, E. St. Julian, *vs.* Strait, Horace B	391	44	1	11
Third Congressional district,				
Donnelly, Ignatius, *vs.* Washburn, William D	1791	46	2	13
MISSISSIPPI,				
Legality of the election of members to the Twenty-eighth Congress from	60	28	1	5
Second Congressional district,				
Buchanan, George M., *vs.* Manning, Van H	1890	47	2	14
Do	1891	47	2	14
Chalmers, J. R., *vs.* Manning, Van H	*283	48	1	15
Chalmers, James R., *vs.* Manning, Van H	†1959	48	1	15
Sixth Congressional district,				
Lynch, John R., *vs.* Chalmers, James R	931	47	1	14
State at large,				
Claiborne, John F. H	2	25	1	2
Do	379	25	2	2
Gholson, Samuel J	2	25	1	2
Do	379	25	2	2
MISSOURI,				
Relative to the legality of the election of members to the Twenty-eighth Congress from	60	28	1	5
Delegate,				
Easton, Rufus, *vs.* Scott, John	22	14	2	1
Do	28	14	2	1
First Congressional district,				
Blair, jr., Francis P., *vs.* Barrett, J. Richard	563	36	1	7
Hogan, John, *vs.* Pile, William A	62	40	2	9
Knox, Samuel, *vs.* Blair, F. P	66	38	1	8
Third Congressional district,				
Frost, R. Graham, *vs.* Metcalfe, Lyne S	118	45	3	12
Lindsay, James, *vs.* Scott, John G	117	38	1	8
Sessinghaus, Gustavus, *vs.* Frost, R. Graham	1409	47	1	14
Do	1959	47	2	14
Fourth Congressional district,				
Boyd, S. H., *vs.* Kelso, John R	88	39	1	9
Sixth Congressional district,				
Burch, James H., *vs.* Van Horn, Robert T	4	40	2	9
Shields, James, *vs.* Van Horn, Robert T	122	41	2	10
Seventh Congressional district,				
Bruce, John P., *vs.* Loan, Benjamin F	44	38	1	8
Ninth Congressional district,				
McLean, James H., *vs.* Broadhead, James O	*2613	48	2	15
Switzler, William F., *vs.* Anderson, George W	28	40	2	9
Do	7	40	3	9
Switzler, William F., *vs.* Dyer, David P	106	41	2	10
MONTANA,				
Delegate.				
Botkin, A. C., *vs.* Maginnis, Martin	2138	48	1	15
NEBRASKA,				
Delegate,				
Bennet, Hiram P., *vs.* Chapman, Bird B	65	34	1	6
Chapman, B. B., *vs.* Ferguson, F	65	34	1	6
Do	51	35	1	7
Do	156	35	2	7
Daily, S. G., *vs.* Easterbrook, E	446	36	1	7
Morton, J. Sterling, *vs.* Daily, Samuel G	3	37	1	8
Do	69	37	2	8
NEW HAMPSHIRE,				
Legality of the election of members to the Twenty-eighth Congress from	60	28	1	5
Third Congressional district,				
Perkins, Jared, *vs.* Morrison, George W	3	31	2	6
NEW JERSEY,				
Relative to contested election cases for Congressmen in 1840, from	541	26	1	3
State at large,				
Dickerson, Philemon, *et al.*, *vs.* Stratton, C. C., *et al.*	506	26	1	2
Third Congressional district,				
Farlee, Isaac G., *vs.* Runk, John	310	29	1	5
Nailor *vs.* Ingersoll	588	26	1	4
NEW MEXICO,				
Delegate,				
Chaves, J. Francisco, *vs.* Clever, Charles P	18	40	3	9
Lane, William C., *vs.* Gallegos, José M	121	33	1	6
Messervy, William S	20	31	2	6
Otero, Miguel A., *vs.* Gallegos, José M	90	34	1	6
Smith, Hugh N	220	31	1	6

* And views of minority. † Parts 1, 2, 3.

Contested cases by States—Continued.

Subject.	Report.	Congress.	Session.	Volume.
NEW YORK,				
First Congressional district,				
Guyon, James, jr., *vs.* Sage, Ebenezer	39	16	1	1
Third Congressional district,				
Williamson, Amor J., *vs.* Sickles, Daniel E	80	36	1	7
Do	61	36	2	7
Sixth Congressional district,				
Monroe, James, *vs.* Jackson, David S	408	30	1	6
Eighth Congressional district,				
Dodge, William E., *vs.* Brooks, James	41	39	1	9
Eleventh Congressional district,				
Van Wyck, Charles H., *vs.* Greene, George W	22	41	2	10
Seventeenth Congressional district,				
Willoughby, Westel, *vs.* Smith, William S	3	14	1	1
Twentieth Congressional district,				
Wright, Silas, jr., *vs.* Fisher, George	95	21	1	1
Twenty-fourth Congressional district,				
Duffy, Sebastian, *vs.* Mason, Joseph	1568	46	2	12
Twenty-ninth Congressional district,				
Adams, Parmenia, *vs.* Wilson, Isaac	15	18	1	1
NORTH CAROLINA,				
First Congressional district,				
Yeates, Jesse J., *vs.* Martin, Joseph J	123	46	3	13
Pool, Charles C., *vs.* Skinner, Thomas G	*727	48	1	15
Second Congressional district,				
Foster, Charles H	118	37	2	8
O'Hara, James E., *vs.* Kitchen, William H	263	46	3	13
Pigott, Jennings	41	37	3	8
Sixth Congressional district,				
Boyden, Nathaniel, *vs.* Shober, Francis E	17	41	3	10
Twelfth Congressional district,				
Newland, David, *vs.* Graham, James	378	24	1	2
OHIO,				
Relative to status of right of James S. Robinson to seat in Forty-eighth Congress	2079	48	2	15
Hammond, C., *vs.* Herrick S	30	15	1	1
Do	31	15	1	1
First Congressional district,				
Eggleston, Benjamin, *vs.* Strader, Peter W	73	41	2	10
Third Congressional district,				
Vallandigham, C. L., *vs.* Campbell, Lewis D	50	35	1	7
Do	380	35	1	7
Fourth Congressional district,				
Sundry citizens and electors of State, *vs.* Allen, William	†110	23	1	1
Seventh Congressional district,				
Campbell, James E., *vs.* Morey, Henry L	†1845	48	1	15
Tenth Congressional district,				
Hurd, Frank H., *vs.* Romeis, Jacob	‡1449	49	1	15
Thirteenth Congressional district,				
Delano, Columbus, *vs.* George W. Morgan	1	40	1	9
Do	42	40	2	9
Follett, Charles, *vs.* Delano, Columbus	59	39	1	9
Eighteenth Congressional district,				
Wallace, Jonathan H., *vs.* McKinley, William, jr	§1548	48	1	15
OREGON,				
State at large,				
Shiel, George K., *vs.* Thayer, Andrew J	4	37	1	8
PENNSYLVANIA,				
First Congressional district,				
Butler, John M., *vs.* Lehman, William E	6	37	2	8
Third Congressional district,				
Ingersoll, C. J., *vs.* Naylor, Charles	586	26	1	4
Kline, John, *vs.* Verree, John P	40	37	2	8
Myers, Leonard, *vs.* Moffet, John	9	41	1	10
Fourth Congressional district,				
Littel, John S., *vs.* Robbin, John, jr	488	31	1	6
Fifth Congressional district,				
Carrigan, Charles W., *vs.* Thayer M. Russell	117	38	1	8
Taylor, Caleb N., *vs.* Reading, John R	50	41	2	10
Twelfth Congressional district,				
Wright, Hendrick B., *vs.* Fuller, Henry M	136	32	1	6
Thirteenth Congressional district,				
Nutting, James L., *vs.* Reilly, James B	291	45	3	12
Sixteenth Congressional district,				
Cessna, John, *vs.* Meyers, Benjamin F	11	42	2	11
Coffroth, Alexander H	12	39	1	9
Koontz, William H., *vs.* Coffroth, Alexander H	92	39	1	9
Koontz, William H	13	39	1	9

*Parts 1, 2, 3. † Parts 1 and 2. ‡ Parts 1, 2, and 3. § And views of minority.

Contested cases by States—Continued.

Subject.	Report.	Congress.	Session.	Volume.
PENNSYLVANIA—Continued.				
Twentieth Congressional district,				
Curtin, Andrew G., *vs.* Yocum, Seth H	345	46	2	13
Kline, John, *vs.* Myers, Leonard	137	38	1	8
Twenty-first Congressional district,				
Covode, John, *vs.* Foster, Henry D	15	41	2	10
Foster, Henry D., *vs.* Covode, John	2	41	1	10
Fuller, Smith, *vs.* Dawson, John L	69	39	1	9
RHODE ISLAND,				
Second Congressional district,				
Page, Charles H., *vs.* Pirce, William A	*1683	49	1	15
Do	†2617	49	2	15
SOUTH CAROLINA,				
First Congressional district,				
Lee, Samuel, *vs.* Rainey, Joseph H	578	44	1	11
Lee, Samuel, *vs.* Richardson, John S	1962	47	2	14
Richardson, John S., *vs.* Rainey, Joseph H	806	45	2	12
Second Congressional district,				
Bowen, Christopher C., *vs.* De Large, Robert C	37	42	2	11
Butts, C. W., *vs.* Mackey, E. W. M	758	44	1	11
Mackey, E. W. M., *vs.* O'Connor, M. P	869	47	1	14
Third Congressional district,				
Hoge, S. L., *vs.* Reed, J. P	3	41	1	10
Do	6	41	1	10
Stolbrand, C. J., *vs.* Aiken, D. Wyatt	982	47	1	14
Fourth Congressional district,				
McKissick, Isaac G., *vs.* Wallace, Alexander S	46	42	2	11
Wallace, A. S., *vs.* Simpson, William D	5	41	1	10
Do	7	41	1	10
Do	17	41	2	10
Do	71	41	2	10
Fifth Congressional district,				
Smalls, Robert, *vs.* Tillman, George D	1525	47	1	14
Tillman, G. D., *vs.* Smalls, Robert	916	45	2	12
TENNESSEE,				
On claim of seat to Congress by J. B. Rodgers	33	37	3	8
State at large,				
Hamilton, Thomas A., claim as additional representative	28	40	3	9
Rodgers, John B., claim as additional representative	12	41	1	10
General election,				
Question as to validity of the election	1	42	1	11
First Congressional district,				
Butler, Roderick R	11	40	2	9
Second Congressional district,				
Arnold, Thomas D., *vs.* Lea, Pryor	32	21	1	1
Fourth Congressional district,				
Clements, Andrew J	9	37	2	8
Sheafe, C. A., *vs.* Tillman, Lewis	3	41	3	10
Sixth Congressional district,				
Thomas, Dorsey B., *vs.* Arnell, Samuel M	5	39	2	9
Ninth Congressional district,				
Hawkins, Alvin	46	37	3	8
TEXAS,				
Third Congressional district,				
Giddings, D. C., *vs.* Clark, W. T	2	42	2	11
Do	65	42	2	11
UTAH TERRITORY,				
Delegate,				
Cannon, George Q., *vs.* Campbell, Allen G	559	47	1	14
McGrorty, William, *vs.* Hooper, William H	79	40	2	9
Maxwell, George R., *vs.* Cannon, George Q	484	43	1	11
VERMONT,				
General election,				
Mallary, Rollin C., *vs.* Merrill, Orsamus C	27	16	1	1
VIRGINIA,				
On claim of seat to Congress by Lewis McKenzie, of	33	37	3	8
First Congressional district,				
Segar, Joseph	12	37	2	8
Do	70	37	2	8
Do	9	38	1	8
Garrison, George T., *vs.* Mayo, Robert M	286	48	1	15
Do	954	48	1	15
Second Congressional district,				
Chandler, Lucius H			1	8
Platt, James H., *vs.* Goode, John	50	38	1	11
Wing, W. W., *vs.* McCloud, J. B	783	34	3	8

* Parts 1, 2. † Views of minority.

Contested cases by States—Continued.

Subject.	Report.	Congress.	Session.	Volume.
VIRGINIA—Continued.				
Fourth Congressional district,				
Tucker, George, *vs.* Booker, George W	41	41	2	10
Fifth Congressional district,				
Goggin, William L., *vs.* Gilmer, Thomas W	76	28	1	5
Letcher, Robert P., *vs.* Moore, Thomas P	*446	23	1	1
Stovall, John T., *vs.* Cabell, George C	1696	47	1	14
Sixth Congressional district,				
Botts, John M., *vs.* Jones, John W	492	28	1	5
Seventh Congressional district,				
Beach, S. Ferguson	42	37	2	8
McKenzie, Lewis, *vs.* Kitchen, B. M	14	38	1	8
McKenzie, Lewis, *vs.* Braxton, Elliott M	4	42	2	11
O'Ferrall, Charles T., *vs.* Paul, John	†1435	48	1	15
Upton, Charles H	17	37	2	8
Whittlesey, Charles, *vs.* McKenzie, Lewis	75	41	2	10
Eighth Congressional district,				
Bayley, S. P., *vs.* Barbour, John S	1040	47	1	14
Graffin, C. L	43	37	3	8
Ninth Congressional district,				
Porterfield, Robert, *vs.* McCoy, William	54	14	1	1
Abingdon district,				
Draper, Joseph, *vs.* Johnston, Charles C	444	22	1	1
Norfolk district,				
Loyall, George, *vs.* Newton, Thomas	213	21	1	1
State at large,				
Segar, Joseph, claim for additional representative	51	41	2	10
Massey, John E., *vs.* Wise, John S	‡2024	48	1	15
WEST VIRGINIA,				
First Congressional district,				
Davis, John J., *vs.* Wilson, Benjamin	7	42	1	11
Second Congressional district,				
Hagans, Marshal, *vs.* Martin, Benjamin F	7	42	1	11
WISCONSIN,				
Delegate,				
Doty, James D., *vs.* Jones, George W	7	25	3	2
Sibley, Henry H	10	30	2	6
WYOMING TERRITORY,				
Casement, J. S., claim to seat as delegate	80	40	3	9

* Part 2. † Parts 1, 2. ‡ And views of minority.

Subject.	Report.	Congress.	Session.	Volume.
YTT vs. FROST, of Massachusetts. Fraud and conspiracy	602	44	1	11
RACT OF VOTES (see also VOTES) returned to the office of secretary of state, though not obtained within sixty days, can be used as documentary evidence (Vallandigham vs. Campbell)	50	35	1	7
LEN vs. DARRALL, of Louisiana. Charge of gross fraud and mismanagement on the part of the election officers and the returning board. Held, that where the poll was removed from the place fixed by law to another and unauthorized place, such poll must be rejected	147	45	3	12
LEN, JOSEPH H., of Louisiana (contestee)	352	46	3	12
MS vs. WILSON, of New York. Inspectors of elections to decide on the acceptance of a ballot where an erasure has been made. Duplicate or folded ballots being prohibited by law, are to be wholly rejected, and are not to be counted as single ballots	15	18	1	1
MS, GEORGE M., of Kentucky (contestee)	74	41	2	10
king to be paid his expenses in the contested-election case of Barnes vs. Adams	66	46	2	12
DAVITS,				
parte affidavits taken after case has been fully considered, not admissible (Blair vs. Barrett)	563	36	1	7
Aiken, D. Wyatt, of South Carolina (contestee)	322	47	1	14
KA TERRITORY,				
lative to the admission of M. D. Ball as a Delegate to Congress from	560	47	1	14
N, JAMES C., of Illinois (contestee)	8	34	1	6
Do	167	34	1	6
EN, WILLIAM, protest of citizens of Ohio as to election of, from Seventh district	110	38	1	8
ERSON vs. REED, of Maine. Alleged bribery of voters; illegal rejection of votes; fraud and intimidation	1697	47	1	14
ERSON, GEORGE W., of Missouri (contestee)	38	40	2	9
Do	7	43	3	9
ERSON, WILLIAM C., of Kentucky (contestee)	627	36	1	7
ORTIONMENT. Relative to suspending the operation of the second section of the act of June 25, 1842, relating to the apportionment of Representatives among the several States according to the sixth census	100	27	3	5
Do	60	28	1	5
HER vs. ALLEN, of Illinois. Contestant claimed that returns made by the returning officers were incorrect	8	34	1	6
Do	*167	34	1	6
ISTRONG, M. K., of Dakota Territory (contestee)	43	42	2	11
ELL, SAMUEL M., of Tennessee (contestee)	5	39	2	9
OLD vs. LEA, of Tennessee. Regarding the legal custody of the ballot-box. Gourd used instead of a box and tied, held not to invalidate the election	32	21	1	1
BITT, ALMON W., of Deseret. Held that a territorial government must be established before a Delegate is admitted	219	31	1	6
LEY, ADOLPHE, of Louisiana (contestee)	63	41	2	10
LEY, JOHN, of Massachusetts. Election contested on the grounds that he was not an inhabitant of the State. At the time of the election he was a clerk in the Department of State at Washington, and the House decided that he was not eligible	67	18	1	1
KER, EDWARD D., of Illinois (contestee), having accepted military appointment under the Government, held that the acceptance vacated the seat at once	86	29	2	5
LDWIN vs. TROWBRIDGE, of Michigan. Contest relative to fixing the places of election. Decided that where there is a conflict of authority between the constitution and legislature of the State in regard to fixing place of elections, the power of the legislature is paramount	13	39	1	9
LL, M. D., of Alaska Territory,				
Relative to petition for admission to a seat in Congress as Delegate from Alaska Territory of	560	47	1	14
Relative to payment of account claimed for expenses and compensation as Delegate or agent of the people of Alaska	1988	47	2	14
ALLOT. The voter (by ballot) cannot be deprived of his right of secrecy, and if it is done by judges of election, it tends to vitiate the entire proceedings (Otero vs. Gallegos)	90	34	1	6
ALLOT-BOXES,				
In regard to the legal custody of the	32	21	1	1
A gourd being used instead of a box and tied, held not to invalidate an election	32	21	1	1
Votes once placed in box cannot afterward be changed	88	21	1	1

*Minority.

Contested cases—general index—Continued.

Subject.	Report.	Congress.	Session.	Volume.
BALLOT-BOXES—Continued.				
Recount of votes not permitted to overturn original sworn statements (Klein *vs.* Verree)	40	37	2	8
Held that the removal of a ballot-box to a point distant from where the election is held gives an opportunity for fraud, and the returns should be excluded from the count (Spencer *vs.* Morey)	442	44	1	11
BALLOTS. Held that ballots cast for either candidate upon which the names were misspelled should be counted (Lee *vs.* Rainey)	578	44	1	11
BANK OF THE UNITED STATES, relative to prescribing a mode for taking the sense of the people on the question of the constitutionality of a	575	28	1	5
BANKS, relative to taking a sense of the people with respect to the constitutionality of banks under the authority of the States	575	23	1	5
BARBOUR, JOHN S., of Virginia (contestee)	1040	47	1	14
BARNES *vs.* ADAMS, of Kentucky. Allegations of fraud and violation of law	74	41	2	10
BARRETT, J. RICHARD, of Missouri (contestee)	563	36	1	7
BAYLEY *vs.* BARBOUR, of Virginia. Frauds and violence; alleged ineligibility and disqualification of contestee	940	47	1	14
BEACH, S. FERGUSON. District in possession of rebels so far as to prevent a fair election, and non-compliance with State laws owing to existence of rebellion, it was treated as a nullity	43	37	2	8
BECK, Hon. J. B., on credentials of	6	40	1	9
BECK, JAMES B., of Kentucky. Relation to eligibility to seat as a Representative	2	40	2	9
BELFORD, JAMES B., of Colorado (contestee)	14	45	2	12
BELL *vs.* SNYDER, of Arkansas. Irregularities by officers of election, and frauds	11	43		11
BENNETT *vs.* CHAPMAN, of Nebraska. Allegations of illegalities on both sides. Sitting Delegate retains seat	65	34		6
BENNETT, T. W., of Idaho Territory (contestee)	624	44		11
BIDDLE *vs.* RICHARD, of Michigan. Election contested on the ground that the contestee was an alien and had not been duly naturalized. Naturalization may be acquired on application to the county courts of the Territories of the United States	27	18		
BISBEE *vs.* FINLEY, of Florida. Illegal rejection of votes cast for contestant; ballot-box stuffing, &c	1066	47		14
BISBEE *vs.* HULL, of Florida. In this case the State canvassing board rejected the vote of a county on the ground that one precinct had made no returns	86	46		13
BISBEE, HORATIO, of Florida (contestee)	95	45		12
BLAIR, Jr., *vs.* BARRETT, of Missouri. Charges of fraud and irregularities. Contestant successful	563	36		
BLAIR, F. P., of Missouri (contestee)	66	38		
Relative to the military appointment of	110	38		
BLAKELY *vs.* GOLLADAY, of Kentucky. Contest of the validity of elections held at different times	1	40		
BOARD OF CANVASSERS (*See* CANVASSERS.)				
BOLES *vs.* EDWARDS, of Arkansas. Allegations of fraud. Application of contestee for extension of time rejected	3	42	2	11
Do	10	42	2	11
BONZANO, M. F., of Louisiana	13	38	2	8
BOOKER, GEORGE W., of Virginia (contestee)	41	41	2	10
BOTKIN *vs.* MAGINNIS, of Montana	2188	48	1	15
BOTTS *vs.* JONES, of Virginia. Contest to establish the right of the voter challenged. Held by the committee that every voter admitted by the regular officers shall be legally qualified unless the contrary be shown	492	28	1	5
BOWEN *vs.* DE LARGE, of South Carolina. Fraud and irregularities in the conduct of the election	37	42	3	11
BOYD *vs.* KELSO, of Missouri. Allegations of fraud. Sitting member retained the seat by a *nem. con.* vote	88	39	1	9
BOYDEN *vs.* SHOBER, of North Carolina. Fraud and intimidation	17	41	3	10
BOYNTON *vs.* LORING, of Massachusetts. Charge of illegal votes being cast for contestee, and that a number of ballots failed to designate the office for which the candidate was designed	18	46	3	13
BRADLEY *vs.* HYNES, of Arkansas. Alleged manipulation of returns, altering and suppression of votes, and the corrupt use of money	646	43	1	11
BRADLEY *vs.* SLEMONS, of Arkansas. Charge of corrupt conspiracy	427	46	2	13
BRADLEY, JOHN M., claiming additional allowance for expenses of contest in case of Bradley *vs.* Slemons	15	46	3	13
BRAXTON, ELLIOTT M., of Virginia (contestee)	4	42	2	11
BROADHEAD, JAMES O., of Missouri (contestee)	*2613	48	2	15
BROCKENBROUGH *vs.* CABELL, of Florida. Validity of returns not questioned	35	29	1	5
BROMBERG *vs.* HARALSON, of Alabama. Charges of illegal and fraudulent votes and the presence of United States troops at the polls	294	44	1	12
BROOKS *vs.* DAVIS, of Maryland. Contest upon grounds of alleged fraud, intimidation, and violence	105	35	1	7

*And views of minority.

Contested cases—general index—Continued.

Subject.	Report.	Congress.	Session.	Volume.
JAMES, of New York (contestee)	41	30	1	9
JOHN YOUNG, of Kentucky (contestee). As to eligibility to hold seat a member	2	42	2	9
Do	11	40	2	9
LOAN of Missouri. Grounds of contest were, interference with the election by the State militia	44	38	1	8
AN vs. MANNING, of Mississippi. There are thirteen grounds of contest set out in contestant's notice	1380	47	2	14
Do	1381	47	2	14
VAN HORN, of Missouri. Illegal action of officers of registration; fraudulent voting	4	40	2	9
vs. ARMSTRONG, of Dakota Territory. Alleged illegal votes received from non-residents and Indians	43	42	3	11
YOUNG, of Kentucky. Irregularity in count of vote. Sitting member retains seat	285	43	1	11
vs. LEHMAN, of Pennsylvania. Main contest as to who received the highest number of legal votes. Contestee successful	5	37	2	8
RODERICK R., of Tennessee. Alleged ineligibility to hold seat as Representative. Joint resolution passed relieving him from disabilities	18	40	2	9
MACKEY, of South Carolina. Charges of fraud, bribery, intimidation, and violence	759	44	1	11
ON vs. VANDEVER, of Iowa.				
…stee accepted office of colonel of volunteers, and sworn into military service. Seat vacated	68	37	2	8
…r office in the military service incompatible with occupying a seat in Congress	68	37	2	8
EDWARD C., of Florida (contestee)	25	29	1	5
GEORGE C., of Virginia (contestee)	1686	47	1	14
JOHN T. Relative to the application of same to be admitted as Delegate from Utah Territory	1865	47	1	14
LL vs. MOREY, of Ohio	*1845	48	1	15
LL vs. WEAVER, of Iowa	*1822	48	1	15
LL, ALLEN G., of Utah Territory (contestee)	559	47	1	14
LL, LEWIS D., of Ohio (contestee)	80	36	1	7
Do	280	36	1	7
vs. CAMPBELL, of Utah Territory. Contestant claims majority of votes cast	559	47	1	14
GEORGE Q., of Utah Territory (contestee)	484	43	1	11
…e to charges preferred against, and as to qualifications to sit as Delegate from Utah	106	43	2	11
…e to pay and mileage to be allowed to	1411	47	1	14
…ERS A board of canvassers can only ascertain and declare the result of the poll (Blakely vs. Golladay)	1	40	2	9
…N vs. THAYER, of Pennsylvania. Contest as to majority of legal votes	126	38	1	8
…N, CHARLES. (*See* FLORENCE, T. B.)				
…T, J. S., of Wyoming Territory. Claim to a seat as Delegate; Territory not organized	30	40	3	9
…UGH, JAMES H., of Minnesota. The election of members by a general ticket instead of by districts is not a bar to admission to seats in House. Minnesota constitution provided for the election of three members, while the act of admission fixed the number at two. But two members were returned. Held that the rights of the two members were not invalidated	408	35	1	7
…ical census too vague for a judicial decision (Ingersoll vs. Naylor)	588	26	1	4
…and act relative to making appointment of Representatives among the several States according to the sixth	100		3	5
Do	60		1	5
…icipal census *prima facie* evidence of facts it contains (Blair vs. Barrett)	563	27	1	7
…CATES OF ELECTION, examination of certain members'	66	34	1	1
vs. MEYERS, of Pennsylvania. Qualification of voters as to residence when temporarily employed in construction of a railroad; qualification as to paupers voting	11	42	2	11
…RS vs. MANNING, of Mississippi	†283	48	1	15
Do	‡1959	48	1	15
…RS, JAMES R., of Mississippi (contestee)	931	47	1	14
…ER, LUCIUS H., of Virginia. District within control of rebel authorities. Election regarded as a nullity	59	38	1	8
…N vs. FERGUSON, of Nebraska Territory. Allegations of fraud and irregularities	156	35	2	7
…N, BIRD B., of Nebraska (contestant)	65	34	1	6
Do	51	35	1	7
vs. CLEVER, of New Mexico. Allegations of fraud	18	40	3	9
AN vs. ANDERSON, of Kentucky. Alleged mistake in the returns discovered after the county boards had sent them	627	36	1	7
…Y vs. WIMPY, of Georgia. Allegations of disloyalty	8	40	3	9

* Parts 1, 2. † And views of minority. ‡ Parts 1, 2, 3.

Contested cases—general index—Continued.

Subject.	Report.	Congress.	Session.	Volume.
CIRCUIT COURTS OF THE UNITED STATES, relative to authorizing testimony in contested-election cases to be taken by commissioners of the	1145	47	1	14
CITIZEN AND CITIZENSHIP,				
Relative to the difference between citizen and inhabitant	67	18	1	1
Do	77	18	1	1
Do	450	27	2	5
Mexicans, inhabitants of United States Territory, under treaty stipulations elected to be Mexican citizens, and afterward voted for Delegate to Congress. Votes to be rejected (Otero *vs.* Gallegos)	90	34	1	6
CLAIBORNE, JOHN F. H., of Mississippi. Elected at a special election, under proclamation of governor for an extra session. Held that he was entitled to seat for an entire Congress. At subsequent session a contestant appeared who was chosen at the regular session. He was admitted, the House reversing its first decision	2	25	1	2
Do	379	25	2	2
CLARK *vs.* HALL, of Iowa. Allegations of informalities in the county abstract of votes	178	34	3	6
CLARK, R. L. B., for compensation and mileage as Representative to the Thirty-fourth Congress	157	35	1	7
CLARK, W. T., of Texas (contestee)	2	42	2	11
Do	65	42	2	11
CLEMENTS, ANDREW J., of Tennessee	9	37	2	8
CLEVER, CHARLES P., of New Mexico (contestee)	18	40	3	9
CLIFT, J. W., of Georgia	16	41	2	10
COFFROTH, ALEXANDER H., of Pennsylvania (contestee). This was a *prima facie* case where the governor omitted to declare any person elected. Pending the contest on the merits, the House gave the seat to Mr. Coffroth	12	39	1	9
Do	92	39	1	9
COMMISSIONERS OF UNITED STATES CIRCUIT COURTS, relative to authorizing testimony in contested-election cases to be taken by	1145	47	1	14
COMMITTEE ON ELECTIONS. (*See* ELECTIONS.)				
CONGRESS,				
Relative to the appointment of Representatives to Congress among the several States according to the sixth census	100	27	3	5
Do	60	28	1	5
Relative to the right of members to their seats (majority and minority)	60	28	1	5
To establish a uniform time for holding elections for members of the House of Representatives in	194	28	1	5
CONSTITUTION. Proposed amendment to the Constitution relating to the election of President and Vice-President	120	43	2	11
CONTESTED-ELECTION EXPENSES. Statement of expense accounts of parties to election contests, and amounts allowed to each party therein named	1385	47	1	14
Do	1410	47	1	14
Do	1974	47	2	14
CONVENTION. A constitutional convention cannot assume legislative functions in presence of the legislature (Beach)	42	37	2	8
CONWAY, M. F., fixing date when compensation as member shall commence	93	36	2	7
Do	71	37	2	8
COOK *vs.* CUTTS, of Iowa. Alleged disqualification of persons voting for contestee	1961	47	2	14
COOPER, GEORGE B., of Michigan (contestee)	87	36	1	7
COSDEN, JEREMIAH, of Maryland (contestee)	64	17	1	1
COUNTY, the act of a legislature does not organize a county. County officers must first be elected (Morton *vs.* Daily)		37	1	8
Do	69	37	2	8
COUNTY ABSTRACTS. (*See* VOTES.)				
COVODE *vs.* FOSTER, of Pennsylvania. Allegations of fraud and irregularities, on final merits	15	41	2	10
COVODE, JOHN, of Pennsylvania (contestee.)	2	41	1	10
COX *vs.* STRAIT, of Minnesota. Charges made that election districts had been illegally established	891	44	1	11
CRAIG *vs.* SHELLEY, of Alabama	2137	48	1	15
CREDENTIALS.				
Governor of Territory gives certificate to one candidate, and upon the alleged ground of discovered fraud revoked it and gave it to another. House approved proceeding (Morton *vs.* Daily)	3	37	1	
Refusal of a governor to grant a certificate does not prejudice right of claimant (Clements)	9	37	2	
CURTIN *vs.* YOCUM, of Pennsylvania. The principal question in this case is whether all the clauses in the new constitution and laws of Pennsylvania relating to "suffrage and elections" are mandatory and not to be deviated from, &c	345	46	2	13
CUTTS, M. E., of Iowa (contestee)	1961	47	2	14
DAILY *vs.* EASTERBROOK, of Nebraska	446	36	1	
DAILY, SAMUEL G., of Nebraska (contestee)	3	37	1	
Do	69	37	2	

Contested cases—general index—Continued.

Subject.	Report.	Congress.	Session.	Volume.
RALL *vs.* BAILEY, of Louisiana. Violence and intimidation	63	41	2	10
RALL, CHESTER B., of Louisiana (contestee)	147	45	2	12
IDSON, R. H. M., of Florida (contestee)	1278	47	1	14
IS *vs.* WILSON, of West Virginia. Contest relative to the date of holding elections in State for Representatives to Congress	7	43	1	11
IS, HENRY WINTER, of Maryland (contestee)	105	35	1	7
Do	90	35	2	7
'SON, JOHN L., of Pennsylvania (contestee)	38	39	1	9
N *vs.* FIELD, of Massachusetts. The contest in this case arises on account of the alleged errors of the ward officers of the city of Boston in making the count, which errors a committee of aldermen sought to correct in pursuance of an act of the legislature of Massachusetts	288	45	2	12
ANO *vs.* MORGAN, of Ohio. Allegations of fraud. Polls rejected. Votes of deserters rejected	42	40	2	9
ANO, COLUMBUS, of Ohio (contestee)	80	39	1	9
ANO, COLUMBUS (contestant), on memorial contesting right of seat of George W. Morgan from Thirteenth Congressional district of Ohio	1	40	1	9
LARGE, ROBERT C., of South Carolina (contestee)	37	42	2	11
EGATES.				
ight of Territory without State limits to send Delegates to Congress (Sibley; Fuller *vs.* Kingsbury)	10	30	2	6
Do	435	35	1	7
Held that Delegates to Congress from Territories are the creatures of statute, and that the legislative branch of the Government may abolish the office altogether (Cannon *vs.* Campbell)	569	47	1	14
ERTION. Held that desertion may disqualify from voting (under special enactment) without conviction of the offense in a court (Delano *vs.* Morgan)	42	40	2	9
KERSON, PHILEMON, *et al.*, *vs.* STRATTON, C. C., *et al.*, of New Jersey. The disqualification of an officer, to effect the legality of an election, must be co-existent with the election. That *prima facie* it is to be taken that none but qualified votes have been received	506	26	1	2
LOYALTY.				
charge of disloyalty against a member elect should be investigated previous to taking the seat (Kentucky election)	2	40	2	9
Expressed in a letter disqualifies from holding office under special Congressional enactment	11	40	2	9
GE *vs.* BROOKS, of New York. Allegations of fraud	41	39	1	9
ICILE. (*See also* RESIDENCE.) Domicile of the father is domicile of the son during his minority, while the son is under the control and direction of the father (Levy)	450	27	2	5
NELLY *vs.* WASHBURN, of Minnesota. Charges of bribery, and coercion, and intimidation of voters, and the counting of illegal votes by the canvassing officers	1791	46	2	13
Y *vs.* JONES, of Wisconsin Territory. The contestee, though elected in 1836, and taking his seat at that time, claimed the time did not legally commence till March 4, 1837, and, therefore, did not end till 1839. The seat was given to the contestant	7	25	3	2
PER *vs.* JOHNSTON, of Virginia. A freehold not acquired by obtaining a mere equitable interest in land. The law is not to be so construed as to give more than three days to the election	444	22	1	1
FY *vs.* MASON, of New York. Alleged fraud, the buying of votes, and other corrupt and illegal means on the part of contestee	1568	46	2	13
R, DAVID P., of Missouri (contestee)	106	41	2	10
LE, ELIAS, of South Carolina	31	15	1	1
TERBROOK, EXPERIENCE, of Nebraska (contestee)	446	36	1	7
TON *vs.* SCOTT, of Missouri. When the election is by ballot the voter cannot be compelled to disclose the name of the candidate for whom he voted. A law requiring votes to be "set down in writing" is sufficiently complied with if they be stated in figures	22	14	2	1
Do	28	14	2	1
ARDS, JOHN, of Arkansas (contestee)	3	42	2	11
Do	10	42	2	11
ARDS, W. P., of Georgia	16	41	2	10
ESTON *vs.* STRADER, of Ohio. Illegalities	73	41	2	10
TION CONTESTS. (*See* EXPENSE ACCOUNTS.)				
TION LAWS, relative to altering State	221	19	1	1
TIONS (*see also* JUDGES OF ELECTIONS).				
st of members declared entitled to seats in the House by the committee on	9	14	2	1
Do	22	17	1	1
elative to right of member to a seat for an entire Congress who was elected at a special election under proclamation of the governor for an extra session (Gholson and Claiborne)	2	25	1	2
Do	379	25	2	2
establish a uniform time for holding elections for members of the House of Representatives, and for electors of President and Vice-President	194	28	1	5
here the law or custom fixes the election at a particular place and it is held at another, the vote shall be rejected (Howard *vs.* Cooper)	87	36	1	7

Contested cases—general index—Continued.

Subject.	Report.	Congress.	Session.	Volume.
ELECTIONS—Continued.				
Members from Georgia claimed seats in two Congresses by virtue of a single election under an ordinance of constitutional convention. Claim held not to be valid	16	41	2	10
On proposed amendment to the Constitution relative to mode of electing the President and Vice-President of United States	120	43	2	11
ELECTIONS, CONTESTED.				
Relative to printing of evidence in election cases prior to convening of Congress.	1335	49	1	15
Relative to contested-election cases in Forty-ninth Congress from California.	2338	49	1	15
ELECTORS.				
Relative to establishing a uniform time for holding elections for electors of President and Vice-President of the United States	194	28	1	5
Inspectors of elections are judges of the qualifications of (Whyte *vs.* Harris)	538	35	1	7
ELIGIBILITY. (*See* INELIGIBILITY.)				
ENGLISH *vs.* PEELLE, of Indiana	*1547	48	1	15
Do	1547	48	1	15
EVIDENCE.				
Hearsay evidence inadmissible	506	26	1	2
Do	541	26	1	3
Do	588	26	1	4
Do	538	35	1	7
Do	116	41	2	10
The declaration of a voter as to any matter concerning his own vote is admissible,				
New Jersey case	506	26	1	2
Farlee *vs.* Runk	310	29	1	5
Monroe *vs.* Jackson	403	30	1	6
Vallandigham *vs.* Campbell	50	35	1	7
Poll lists not sufficient evidence that a person voted—parole evidence is necessary (New Jersey case; Vallandigham *vs.* Campbell)	506	26	1	2
Do	541	26	1	3
Do	50	35	1	7
The declaration of a voter as to any matter concerning his own vote is admissible (Farlee *vs.* Runk)	310	29	1	5
Ex parte affidavits, taken after case has been fully considered, not admissible (Blair *vs.* Barrett)	563	36	1	7
Census returns taken by municipal authorities are *prima facie* evidence of the facts they contain (Blair *vs.* Barrett)	563	36	1	7
Sworn muster-rolls of regiments admitted as evidence of the age of voters, and when made at the time of the election, of the number and names of the men composing the regiment	66	38	1	8
EXPENSE ACCOUNTS. Statement of expense accounts of parties to election contests, and amounts allowed to same therein named	1385	47	1	14
Do	1410	47	1	14
Do	1974	47	2	14
EXTRA SESSION. Relative to admission of persons as members who have been elected, at a call of the governor of a State, for an (Gholson *vs.* Claiborne)	2	25	1	3
Do	379	25	2	2
FARLEE *vs.* RUNK, of New Jersey. Contestant alleged that the contestee received a number of illegal votes, cast by college students. Held that the votes were legal	310	29	1	5
FARWELL, CHARLES B., of Illinois (contestee)	385	44	1	11
FENN *vs.* BENNETT, of Idaho Territory. Illegal action of board of canvassers	624	44	1	11
FERGUSON, FENNER, of Nebraska (contestee)	51	35	1	7
Do	156	35	2	7
FINLEY *vs.* BISBEE, of Florida. Charged the returns were forged and false	95	45	3	12
FINLEY *vs.* WALLS, of Florida. Charges of fraud, irregular conduct of election officers, and illegal count	295	44	1	11
FINLEY, JESSE J., of Florida (contestee)	1066	47	1	14
FIELD, A. P., of Louisiana. Irregularities and a partial election. District in rebellion treated as a nullity	1	38	1	8
Do	8	38	1	8
Do	16	38	2	8
FIELD, WALBRIDGE A., of Massachusetts (contestee)	239	45	2	12
FISHER, GEORGE, of New York (contestee)	95	21	1	1
FLANDERS, BENJAMIN. Relative to right of seat from First Louisiana district.	22	37	3	8
FLORENCE, THOMAS B., of Pennsylvania. Claim for expenses in election case against Freeman	264	46	3	13
FLORIDA, CITIZENS OF, *vs.* LEVY, of Florida. It was alleged that the Delegate was not a citizen of the United States	450	27	2	5
FOLLETT *vs.* DELANO, of Ohio. Contest that the poll-books were defective. Held that the tally-sheets being unimpeached, the stated results could not be set aside	59	39	1	9
FOREIGNERS. Where foreigners were naturalized contrary to United States and State laws, it was held that their votes shall be rejected (Van Wyck *vs.* Green)	22	41	2	10

* And views of minority.

Contested cases—general index—Continued.

Subject.	Report.	Congress.	Session.	Volume.
FORSYTH, JOHN, of Georgia. In this case it was decided that a citizen of the United States, residing as a public minister at a foreign court, does not lose his character of inhabitant of that State of which he is a citizen, so as to be disqualified for election to Congress	77	18	1	1
FOSTER *vs.* COVODE, of Pennsylvania. *Prima facie* case; allegations of fraud	2	41	1	10
FOSTER, CHARLES H., of North Carolina. District in rebellion, the election partial and treated as a nullity	118	37	2	8
FOSTER, HENRY D., of Pennsylvania (contestee)	15	41	2	10
FRAUDS.				
May be of such a character as to taint the entire poll, in which case only votes subsequently proved can be counted (Washburn *vs.* Voorhees)	15	39	1	9
When an election return is so tainted with fraud that the truth cannot be deduced therefrom, the same must be set aside (Dodge *vs.* Brooks)	41	39	1	9
The ballots cast at an election are not sufficient evidence of the result, when the question of fraud is raised (Reid *vs.* Julian)	118	41	2	10
FREDERICK *vs.* WILSON, of Iowa	*[illegible]	48	2	15
FROST *vs.* METCALFE, of Missouri. Bribery and corruption	118	45	2	12
FROST, R. GRAHAM, of Missouri (contestee)	1409	47	1	14
Do	1960	47	2	14
FROST, RUFUS S., of Massachusetts (contestee)	655	44	1	11
FULLER *vs.* DAWSON, of Pennsylvania. Allegations of illegalities on the part of return judges. Decided for contestee	68	39	1	9
FULLER *vs.* KINGSBURY, of Minnesota Territory. Claims to represent territory without the limits of the State of Minnesota	435	35	1	7
FULLER, THOMAS J. D., of Maine (contestee)	44	34	1	6
GALLEGOS, JOSÉ M., of New Mexico (contestee)	121	33	1	5
Do	90	34	1	6
GARRISON *vs.* MAYO, of Virginia	[illegible]	48	1	15
Do	954	48	1	15
GAUSE *vs.* HODGES, of Arkansas. Spurious and illegal votes counted; tampering with the ballot-boxes	204	43	2	11
GENERAL TICKET. Members elected by general ticket entitled to seats (Cavanaugh)	460	35	1	7
GEORGIA.				
Relative to the eligibility of John Forsyth to a seat as member from State of	87	18	1	1
Relative to the legality of the election of members to the Twenty-eighth Congress from	60	28	1	5
GHOLSON, SAMUEL J., of Mississippi. Elected at a special election, under proclamation of the governor for an extra session. Held that he was entitled to seat for an entire Congress. At a subsequent session a contestant appeared, who was chosen at the regular session. He was admitted, the House reversing its first decision	2	25	1	2
Do	379	25	2	2
GIBSON, RANDALL L., of Louisiana, relative to claim for contested-election expenses of	213	46	3	13
GIDDINGS *vs.* CLARK, of Texas.				
Prima facie case	2	42	2	11
Separate voting places within the limits of one election precinct, one for white men, the other for colored men, declared illegal	65	42	2	11
GOGGIN *vs.* GILMER, of Virginia. Contest arose from alleged illegal acts of the officers of election	76	28	1	5
GOLLADAY, J. S., of Kentucky (contestee)	1	40	2	9
GOODE, Jr., JOHN, of Virginia (contestee)	762	44	1	11
GOODING *vs.* WILSON, of Indiana. Alleged miscount of ballots; ineligibility of election officers who were not freeholders	41	42	2	11
GOURD. (*See* BALLOT-BOX.)				
GOVE, SAMUEL F., of Georgia	16	41	2	10
GRAFFLIN, C. L., of Virginia	43	37	3	8
GRAHAM, JAMES, of North Carolina (contestee)	378	24	1	2
GREENE, GEORGE W., of New York (contestee)	22	41	2	10
GROVER, Hon. A. P., on credentials of	6	40	1	9
GROVER, A. P., of Kentucky. As to eligibility to hold seat as member	2	40	2	9
GUNTER *vs.* WILSHIRE, of Arkansas.				
Prima facie right	92	43	1	11
Merits	631	43	1	11
GUTHRIE, ABELARD. For compensation and mileage as Delegate to Thirty-second Congress	257	34	1	6
Do	67	37	2	8
GUYON, Jr., *vs.* SAGE, of New York. A mistake in the inspector's return, omitting the word "junior" where it ought to have been inserted, may be corrected in the House	39	16	1	1
HAGANS *vs.* MARTIN, of West Virginia. Contest rests upon a construction of statute prescribing the time for electing Representatives to Congress	7	43	1	11
HAHN, MICHAEL, relative to right of seat from Second Louisiana district	22	37	3	8
HALL, AUGUSTUS, of Iowa (contestee)	178	34	3	6
HAMILTON, THOMAS A., of Tennessee. Claim as an additional member	28	40	3	9
HAMMOND *vs.* HERRICK, of Ohio	30	15	1	1
Do	31	15	1	1

* Parts 1, 2.

Contested cases—general index—Continued.

Subject.	Report.	Congress.	Session.	Volume.
HARALSON, JERE, of Alabama (contestee)	294	44	1	11
HARRIS, J. MORRISON, of Maryland (contestee)	538	35	1	7
Do	89	36	2	7
HARRISON *vs.* DAVIS, of Maryland. Alleged intimidation and violence; also that law of 1851 was not complied with. Case not reached	60	36	2	7
HAWKINS, ALVIN, of Tennessee	46	37	3	8
HEBERT *vs.* ACKLEN, of Louisiana	382	46	3	13
HENDLEY, W. A., of Alabama (contestee)	33	42	2	11
HERBERT, HILARY A., of Alabama (contestee)	1521	47	1	14
Claim for expenses incurred in contested-election case of Strobach *vs.* Herbert	1452	47	1	14
HERRICK, SAMUEL, of Ohio (contestee)	30	15	1	1
Do	31	15	1	1
HODGES, ASA, of Arkansas (contestee)	264	43	2	11
HOGAN *vs.* PILE, of Missouri. Allegations of fraud and illegal voting	62	40	2	9
HOGE *vs.* REED, of South Carolina. *Prima facie* case Second certificate issued.	3	41	1	10
Do	6	41	1	10
HOLMES, J. C., of Iowa. Claims seat from Eighth Congressional district of the State of Iowa	19	46	3	13
HOOPER, WILLIAM H., of Utah (contestee)	79	40	2	9
HOUSE OF REPRESENTATIVES. (*See* CONGRESS.)				
HOWARD *vs.* COOPER, of Michigan. Main contest upon allegations of illegal voting, rioting at the polls, &c. Contestant obtained the seat	87	36	1	7
Do	445	36	1	7
HULL, NOBLE A., of Florida (contestee)	86	46	3	13
HUNT *vs.* MENARD, of Louisiana. The State was redistricted subsequent to the regular election, and the election for the vacancy was substantially a new district. Held that it was not valid	27	40	3	9
HUNT *vs.* SHELDON, of Louisiana. Alegations of intimidations and violence.	4	41	1	10
Do	38	41	2	10
HURD *vs.* ROMEIS, of Ohio	*1449	49	1	15
HAYNES, WILLIAM J., of Arkansas (contestee)	646	43	1	11
INDIAN RESERVATIONS.				
Trespassers on same entitled to vote. House refused to sustain the committee (Bennett *vs.* Chapman)	65	34	1	6
Votes on Indian reservation in Nebraska Territory rejected (Morton *vs.* Daily)	3	37	1	8
Do	69	37	2	8
INELIGIBILITY,				
Of member elect gives no claim to candidate receiving next highest number of votes (Blakely *vs.* Golladay)	1	40	2	9
Disloyalty a bar to membership (Kentucky election)	2	40	2	9
Disloyalty expressed in a published letter a bar to membership	11	40	2	9
INGERSOLL *vs.* NAYLOR, of Pennsylvania. Allegations of fraud and irregularities. Held that where extensive frauds were alleged hearsay evidence should be refused. A political census taken considered too vague upon which to base a judicial decision	588	26	1	4
INGERSOLL, CHARLES J. Indemnity for expense incurred in prosecuting right to seat	249	31	1	6
Do	4	34	1	6
Do	5	35	1	7
INHABITANT,				
A person representing the United States at a foreign court does not cease to be an inhabitant of a State so as to be eligible to Congress	67	18	1	1
Do	77	18	1	1
Definition and meaning of the word, also the difference between citizen and	67	18	1	1
INSPECTOR OF ELECTIONS,				
A judge of an election cannot usurp the duties of an (Wright *vs.* Fuller)	136	32	1	6
Are judges of the qualifications of electors, and if they err without wrong intent the general result shall not be affected (Whyte *vs.* Harris)	538	35	1	7
The law requiring that board of inspectors shall consist of three persons, and but two officiated. The vote was rejected (Howard *vs.* Cooper)	87	36	1	7
INTIMIDATIONS. (*See* VIOLENCE.)				
IOWA CONTESTED-ELECTION CASES	19	46	3	13
JACKS, T. M., of Arkansas	18	38	2	8
JACKSON, DAVID S., of New York (contestee)	403	30	1	6
JAYNE, WILLIAM, of Dakota Territory (contestee)	1	38	1	8
Do	99	38	1	8
JOHNSON, J. M., of Arkansas	18	38	2	8
JOHNSTON, CHARLES C., of Virginia (contestee)	444	22	1	1
JONES *vs.* MANN, of Louisiana. Allegations of fraud and violence	27	40	3	9
JONES *vs.* SHELLEY, of Alabama. This case grows out of a special election held to fill a vacancy caused by the unseating of C. M. Shelley (*see* Smith *vs.* Shelley)	1866	47	2	14
JONES, GEORGE W., of Wisconsin (contestee)	7	25	3	2
JONES, JOHN W., of Virginia (contestee)	492	28	1	5
JONES, THOMAS L., of Kentucky. As to eligibility to hold seat as member	2	40	2	9

*Parts 1, 2, 3.

Contested cases—general index—Continued.

Subject.	Report.	Congress.	Session.	Volume.
Hon. THOMAS L., on credentials of	8	40	1	9
S OF ELECTION.				
s having been deposited in the wrong box by mistake, the judges corrected it. The House vacated the seat (Newland *vs.* Graham)	378	24	1	2
dge of an election cannot usurp the duties of an inspector (Wright *vs.* Fuller)	136	32	1	6
I, GEORGE W., of Indiana (contestee)	116	41	2	10
t. The omission of that word on ballots or left out in the inspector's return may be amended	3	14	1	1
Do	30	16	2	1
Do	95	21	1	1
v. STEELE, of Indiana. Unlawful use of money	4142	49	2	16
JOHN R., of Missouri (contestee)	88	39	1	9
BURY, W. W., of Minnesota Territory	435	35	1	7
EN, R. M., of Virginia (contestee)	14	38	1	8
EX, WILLIAM H., of North Carolina (contestee)	262	46	3	13
vs. MYERS, of Pennsylvania. Allegations of fraud and illegal voting	127	38	1	8
vs. VERREE, of Pennsylvania. Allegations of illegal voting and fraud; ballot-boxes opened but the recount not permitted to overturn the original return on the ground that they might have been tampered with	40	37	2	8
, Hon. J. PROCTOR, on credentials of	6	40	1	9
, J. PROCTOR, of Kentucky. As to eligibility to hold seat as member	2	40	2	9
vs. BLAIR, of Missouri. Allegations of fraud, illegal voting, and military interference. Contestant obtained the seat	66	38	1	8
Z *vs.* COFFROTH, of Pennsylvania. Allegations of fraudulent and illegal voting. Early in the session the House gave the seat, on a *prima facie* contest, to Mr. Coffroth, pending a contest on the merits. Second report decides in favor of contestant	92	39	1	9
Z, WILLIAM H., of Pennsylvania. This was a *prima facie* case where the governor omitted to declare any person elected. Pending the contest on the merits the House gave the seat to Mr. Coffroth; afterwards to Mr. Koontz, July 16, 1866	12	39	1	9
, FRANK, *in re* Sessinghaus *vs.* Frost, asking for an order to examine	1466	47	1	14
vs. GALLEGOS, of New Mexico. Charges of fraud and illegal practices not sustained	121	33	1	6
(See ELECTION LAWS.)				
NCE *vs.* SYPHER, of Louisiana. Conflicting returns of the election, and question raised as to which of the five boards constituted the legal returning board	269	43	2	11
RYOR, of Tennessee (contestee)	32	21	1	1
RAINEY, of South Carolina. Certain ballots cast and counted for contestee were misprinted, and it was urged by contestant that all such ballots shall be excluded from the count	578	44	1	11
RICHARDSON, of South Carolina. Alleged fraud, violence, and intimidation	1983	47	2	14
ATURE. (*See* STATE LEGISLATURE.)				
N, WILLIAM E., of Pennsylvania (contestee)	6	37	2	8
NE *vs.* FARWELL, of Illinois. Allegations of fraud committed, disregard of law by election officers, ballots improperly counted, paupers permitted to vote, and ballot-boxes tampered with	385	44	1	11
ER *vs.* MOORE, of Virginia. Irregularities of election	*446	23	1	1
DAVID, of Florida, protest against right of seat in House to	10	27	1	5
DAVID, of Florida (contestee)	450	27	2	5
Y *vs.* SCOTT, of Missouri. Allegations that disloyal men voted in contravention of State law	117	38	1	8
vs. ROBBINS, of Pennsylvania. Charges of fraud. Evidence held insufficient. Nothing but the most unequivocal evidence can destroy the credit of official returns	488	31	1	6
ENJAMIN F., of Missouri	44	38	1	8
, GEORGE B., of Massachusetts (contestee)	18	46	3	13
v. WHEELER, of Alabama. Illegal rejection of large number of votes cast for contestant	1273	47	1	14
. F., of California. Seat claimed as an additional representative under the eighth census	79	37	2	8
, JOSHUA A., of Maine) contestee)	285	27	2	5
vs. NEWTON, of Virginia. Relative to the right of suffrage and ballot in the State of Virginia	213	21	1	1
RANQUILINO, of New Mexico (contestee)	667	48	1	15
vs. CHALMERS, of Mississippi. Charges of fraud and violation of law on the part of the commissioners of election	931	47	1	14
vs. OATES, of Alabama. Alleged fraud and violence	938	47	1	14
vs. ORTH, of Indiana. Alleged bribery	200	46	3	13
D, J. B., of Virginia (contestee)	23	37	3	8
WILLIAM, of Virginia (contestee)	54	14	1	1
IE, G. W., of Louisiana (contestee	10	41	1	10
Do	62	41	2	10
TY *vs.* HOOPER, of Utah. Seven allegations in the contest (*see* CASE)	77	40	2	9

* Part 2.

Contested cases—general index—Continued.

Subject.	Report.	Congress.	Session.	Volume.
McHENRY *vs.* YEAMAN, of Kentucky, allegations of fraud and military interference	70	38	1	8
McKEE *vs.* YOUNG, J. D., of Kentucky. Allegations of disloyalty; also of illegalities	29	40	2	9
Do	59	40	2	9
Do	49	40	2	9
McKENZIE *vs.* BRAXTON, of Virginia. Allegations that imperfect ballots were erroneously counted for contestee; that the returns were not properly certified	4	42	2	11
McKENZIE *vs.* KITCHEN, of Virginia. District being in rebellion, the election partial and treated as a nullity	14	38	1	8
McKENZIE, LEWIS, of Virginia (contestant)	33	37	3	8
McKENZIE, LEWIS, of Virginia (contestee)	75	41	2	10
MACKEY *vs.* O'CONNOR, of South Carolina. Fraudulent action on part of commissioners of election; ballot-box violated and tampered with	989	47	1	14
MACKEY, E. W. M., of South Carolina (contestee)	758	44	1	11
McKINLEY, WILLIAM, Jr., of Ohio (contestee)	1548	48	1	15
Do	*1548	48	1	15
McKISSICK *vs.* WALLACE, of South Carolina. General irregularities in conduct of election; ballots uncounted for several days after the election was held	66	42	2	11
McLEAN *vs.* BROADHEAD, of Missouri	2613	48	2	15
Do	*2613	48	2	15
MAGINNIS, MARTIN, of Montana (contestee)	2138	48	1	15
MALLARY *vs.* MERRILL, of Vermont: If return of votes be required to be made under seal, and it be not so made, the votes are not, for that reason, and in the absence of fraud, to be rejected; a literal compliance with the forms is not required if the spirit of the law is not violated	27	16	1	1
MANN, JAMES, of Louisiana (contestee)	27	40	3	9
MANN, W. D., of Louisiana, relative to credentials of	17	38	2	8
MANNING, VAN H., of Mississippi (contestee)	1890	47	2	14
Do	1891	47	2	14
Do	†1959	45	1	15
MANNING, of Mississippi (contestee)	*283	48	1	15
MANZANARES *vs.* LUNA, of New Mexico	667	48	1	15
MARSHALL, S. S., of Illinois (contestee	194	34	1	6
MARTIN, BENJAMIN F., of West Virginia (contestee)	7	43	1	11
MARTIN, JOSEPH J., of North Carolina (contestee)	123	46	3	13
MASON, JOSEPH, of New York (contestee)	1568	46	2	13
MASSACHUSETTS, citizens of Norfolk district remonstrate against the return of John Bailey	67	18	1	1
MASSEY *vs.* WISE, of Virginia	*2024	48	1	15
MAXWELL *vs.* CANNON, of Utah Territory. Irregularities in conduct of election and making up of returns; also as to qualification of sitting member	484	43	1	11
MAYO, ROBERT M., of Virginia (contestee)	286	48	1	15
Do	954	48	1	15
MEMBER ELECT. (*See* INELIGIBILITY.)				
MENARD, J. WILLIS, of Louisiana (contestee)	27	40	3	9
MERCHANT *vs.* ACKLEN, of Louisiana	882	46	3	13
MERRILL, ORSAMUS C., of Vermont (contestee)	27	16	1	1
MESSERVY, WILLIAM S., of New Mexico, Territory not organized and election a nullity	20	31	2	6
METCALFE, LYNE S., of Missouri (contestee)	118	45	3	12
MEYERS, BENJAMIN F., of Pennsylvania (contestee)	11	42	2	11
MICHIGAN, relative to an election held in, for a delegate to represent the Territory of, in the Nineteenth Congress (*see* BIDDLE, RICHARDS, WINGS)	39	19	1	1
Do	69	19	1	1
MILITARY INTERFERENCE. (*See* BRUCE *vs.* LOAN.)				
MILITARY SERVICE, relative to the appointment of Hon. Francis P. Blair in the	110	38	1	8
MILLER *vs.* THOMPSON, of Iowa. Charges of illegal and fraudulent voting on both sides. House vacated the seat	400	31	1	6
MILLIKEN *vs.* FULLER, of Maine. Officers irregularly chosen	44	34	1	6
MINORITY. (*See* VOTERS.)				
MISPRINT. (*See* BALLOTS.)				
MISSISSIPPI, relative to the legality of the election of members to the Twenty-eighth Congress from	60	28	1	5
MISSOURI, relative to the legality of the election of members to the Twenty-eighth Congress from	60	28	1	5
MISSPELL. (*See* BALLOTS.)				
MOFFET, JOHN, of Pennsylvania (contestee)	9	41	1	10
MONROE *vs.* JACKSON of New York. Allegations of fraudulent voting on part of paupers, convicts, and others; also of fraudulent conduct on part of election officers	403	30	1	6

* Views of minority. † Parts 1, 2 and 3.

Contested cases—general index—Continued.

* Parts 1, 2. † Views of minority.

Contested cases—general index—Continued.

Subject.	Report.	Congress.	Session.	Volume.
PERKINS *vs.* MORRISON, of New Hampshire. The legislature redistricted the State, and upon the resignation of a member a new election was held under the new act, the other members of the delegation holding their seats under the old one. The new district included towns previously included in another. Thus the voters in these towns helped elect two members of the same Congress exercising their functions at the same time. It was held that the election was valid	3	31	2	6
PETERS, S. R., of Kansas (contestee)	*794	48	1	15
PHELPS, CHARLES E. (contestee), case of Joseph J. Stewart against	2	40	1	9
PHELPS, W. W., of Minnesota. (*See* CAVANAUGH, JAMES M.)				
PIGOTT, JENNINGS, of North Carolina	41	37	3	8
PILE, WILLIAM A., of Missouri (contestee)	62	40	2	9
PINCHBACK, P. B. S., of Louisiana (contestee)	597	43	1	11
Do	263	43	2	11
PIRCE, WILLIAM A., of Rhode Island (contestee)	†1623	49	1	15
PLATT, Jr., *vs.* GOODE, Jr., of Virginia. Charges of fraud, threats, violence, and intimidation	762	44	1	11
POLL BOOKS not certified to by any officer of election to be rejected (Chrisman *vs.* Anderson)	627	30	1	7
POLLS. Two separate voting places within the limits of one election precinct, one for white men, the other for colored men, declared illegal (Giddings *vs.* Clark)	65	42	2	11
POOL *vs.* SKINNER, of North Carolina	‡727	48	1	15
PORTERFIELD *vs.* McCOY, of Virginia. All votes recorded upon poll lists should be presumed good unless impeached by evidence. Certified copies of the commissioner's books, or land lists, are *prima facie* evidence of the qualification of voters whose name appears on them	54	14	1	1
PRESIDENT OF THE UNITED STATES,				
Relative to establishing a uniform time for holding elections in all the States for electors of	194	28	1	5
Relative to proposed amendment to the Constitution for election of	120	43	2	11
PRESTON *vs.* HARRIS, of Maryland. Contest that judges of election were not legally qualified. Alleged intimidation and violence	89	36	2	7
PRINCE, C. H., of Georgia	16	41	2	10
RAINEY, JOSEPH H., of South Carolina (contestee)	578	44	1	11
Do	808	45	2	12
RAWLS, MORGAN, of Georgia (contestee)	216	43	1	11
Respecting claim for expenses during contested election case	274	46	3	13
READING, JOHN R., of Pennsylvania (contestee)	50	41	2	10
RECOUNT. (*See* BALLOT-BOXES; VOTES.)				
REED *vs.* COSDEN, of Maryland	64	17	1	1
REED, J. P., of South Carolina (contestee)	3	41	1	10
REED, THOMAS B., of Maine (contestee)	1697	47	1	14
REEDER *vs.* WHITFIELD, of Kansas. Validity of the election denied on the ground that the legislature which established it was imposed upon the people of Kansas by force	3	34	1	6
Do	275	34	1	6
Do	186	34	3	8
REID *vs.* JULIAN, of Indiana. Allegations of fraud	116	41	2	10
REILLY, JAMES S., of Pennsylvania (contestee)	291	45	3	12
REPRESENTATIVES. (*See* CONGRESS.)				
RESIDENCE,				
To constitute residence there must be intention to remain. If the State law requires that the electors shall vote only in counties where they reside, and at designated places, votes given at other places should not be counted (Miller *vs.* Thompson)	400	31	1	6
The legal residence of a pauper is the place from which he entered the almshouse (Monroe *vs.* Jackson)	403	30	1	6
RETURNS (*see also* VOTES),				
Where secretary of state refused to count the returns, it was held that his duties were ministerial and not judicial (Switzler *vs.* Anderson)	28	40	2	9
Where returns have been tampered with, they must be thrown out (Delano *vs.* Morgan)	42	40	2	[illegible]
Where secretary of state refused to count the returns, it was held that his duties were ministerial and not judicial (Switzler *vs.* Dyer)	106	41	2	10
Cannot be rejected by a governor of a State (Sheafe *vs.* Tillman)	3	41	3	10
RICE, JOHN S., of Massachusetts (contestee)	23	38	1	8
RICE, JOHN M., of Kentucky (contestee)	107	41	2	10
RICHARD, GABRIEL, of Michigan (contestee)	27	18	1	1
RICHARDSON *vs.* RAINEY, of South Carolina. Charges of intimidation, violence, and military interference, and of irregularities and informalities at the polls	806	45	2	12
RICHARDSON, JOHN S., of South Carolina (contestee)	1983	47	2	14
RIPLEY, JAMES W., of Maine (contestee)	88	21	1	1
ROBBIN, JOHN, of Pennsylvania (contestee)	488	31	1	6
ROBERTSON, E. W., of Louisiana (contestee)	631	47	1	14
ROBINSON, JAMES S., of Ohio. Relative to status of right to seat in Forty-eighth Congress	2679	48	2	15

* And views of minority. † Parts 1, 2. ‡ Parts 1, 2, 3.

Contested cases—general index—Continued.

Subject.	Report.	Congress.	Session.	Volume.
RS, JOHN B., of Tennessee (contestant)	32	37	3	8
ES, JOHN B., of Tennessee. Claim for additional Representative	12	41	1	10
, JACOB, of Ohio (contestee)	*1440	49	1	15
OHN, of New Jersey (contestee)	310	29	1	5
IICHAEL, of Louisiana (contestee)	61	41	2	10
BENEZER, of New York (contestee)	39	16	1	1
TIN, LOUIS, of Louisiana (contestee)	11	41	1	10
Do	60	41	2	10
JOHN, of Missouri (contestee)	22	14	2	1
Do	28	14	2	1
JOHN G., of Missouri	117	38	1	8
JOSEPH, of Virginia. Owing to the rebellion, election partial and invalid	12	37	2	8
Do	70	37	2	8
Do	9	38	1	8
Do	51	41	2	10
HAUS *vs.* FROST, of Missouri. Alleged illegal action on part of the judges of election	1409	47	1	14
Do	1959	47	2	14
vs. TILLMAN, of Tennessee. Allegations of fraud. Contestee retained his seat	3	41	3	10
N, LIONEL A., of Louisiana (contestee)	4	41	1	10
Do	38	41	2	10
Y, CHARLES M., of Alabama (contestee)	1522	47	1	14
Do	1886	47	2	14
Do	2137	48	1	15
AN *vs.* PINCHBACK, of Louisiana. Two certificates issued. Question as to which of the State governments was legally in power	597	43	1	11
Do	263	43	2	11
F. Authority given to a sheriff to appoint writers and open polls, gives him power to appoint but one writer and open but one poll (Botts *vs.* Jones)	492	28	1	5
THAYER, of Oregon. Contest relative to the time legally fixed for holding election for Representative	4	37	1	8
S *vs.* VAN HORN, of Missouri. Allegations of fraud	122	41	2	10
, FRANCIS E., of North Carolina (contestee)	17	41	3	10
HENRY H., of Wisconsin Territory. Question as to right to seat as Delegate. Held that a territorial government is not merged in the State government, but has a legal existence over the people and Territory outside the State limits	10	30	2	6
S, DANIEL E., of New York (contestee)	80	36	1	7
Do	61	36	2	7
S, WILLIAM D., of South Carolina (contestee)	7	41	1	10
Do	17	41	2	10
Do	71	41	2	10
ENSUS. (*See* CENSUS.)				
R, THOMAS G., of North Carolina (contestee)	*727	48	1	15
R *vs.* RICE, of Massachusetts. Irregularity and inaccuracy of returns	23	38	1	8
S, WILLIAM F., of Arkansas (contestee)	427	46	2	13
RAWLS, of Georgia. Fraudulent and illegal practices, threatening and overawing election officers, and intimidation of voters	216	43	1	11
vs. TILLMAN, of South Carolina. Alleged violence and intimidation	1525	47	1	14
ROBERT, of South Carolina (contestee)	916	45	2	12
BROWN, of Kentucky. Alleged disloyalty	11	40	2	9
ROBERTSON, of Louisiana. Case dismissed without prejudice	631	47	1	14
SHELLEY, of Alabama. Contestant charges fraud, ballot-box stuffing, conspiracy, and illegal rejection of returns	1522	47	1	14
IUGH N., of New Mexico. Held that a territorial government must be established before a Delegate is admitted	220	31	1	6
WILLIAM S., of New York (contestee)	3	14	1	1
, O. P., of Arkansas (contestee)	11	43	2	11
S' VOTES. Held that the soldiers' vote should be rejected except in cases where said soldiers resided in the precinct at the time of enlistment, or remained for years after (Taylor *vs.* Reading)	50	41	2	10
ELECTIONS. Members elected under proclamation of governor for an extra session, at a special election, held their seats only till members were chosen at the regular election (Gholson and Claiborne)	2	25	1	2
Do	370	25	2	2
SESSION. (*See* EXTRA SESSION; GHOLSON; CLAIBORNE; MISSISSIPPI.)				
R *vs.* MOREY, of Louisiana. Irregularity in the conduct of election, and unlawful count of ballots by the commissioners of election	442	44	1	11
ARMSTRONG, of Dakota. Alleging illegal votes received from non-residents and Indians	43	42	2	11
BANKS. (*See* BANKS.)				
EGISLATURE. Its authority to regulate elections paramount to State constitution (Baldwin *vs.* Trowbridge)	13	39	1	9
RT, JOSEPH J. (contestant). On memorial contesting seat of Charles E. Phelps, from Third district of Maryland	2	40	1	9

*Parts 1, 2, 3.

Contested cases—general index—Continued.

Subject.	Report.	Congress.	Session.	Volume.
STOLBRAND *vs.* AIKEN, of South Carolina. Case dismissed. Grounds for contest do not appear in report	932	47	1	14
STOVALL *vs.* CABELL, of Virginia. Frauds, intimidation, and threats of proscription	1696	47	1	14
STRADER, PETER W., of Ohio (contestee)	78	41	2	10
STRAIT, HORACE B., of Minnesota (contestee)	391	44	1	11
STROBACH *vs.* HERBERT, of Alabama. Failure on part of proper officers to give notice of election in a certain county. Misspelling of name of contestee	1521	47	1	14
STROBACH, PAUL. Claim for expenses in contested election of Strobach *vs.* Herbert	1452	47	1	14
SUPPLEMENTARY RETURNS. (*See also* VOTES.) Where judges of an election discover a mistake after a recount, their supplementary return is entitled to be received (Archer *vs.* Allen)	8	34	1	6
SWITZLER *vs.* ANDERSON, of Missouri. In this case the secretary of state went behind the returns of the county clerks, and rejected the vote of a county. Held by the committee to be illegal	28	40	2	9
Do	7	40	3	9
SWITZLER *vs.* DYER, of Missouri. The secretary of state rejected the returns from two counties. Held to be illegal and improper	106	41	2	10
SYMES *vs.* TRIMBLE, of Kentucky. Alleged disloyalty against contestee	6	40	2	9
SYPHER *vs.* ST. MARTIN, of Louisiana. Allegations of fraud and violence	11	41	1	10
Do	60	41	2	10
SYPHER, J. HALE, of Louisiana (contestee),				
Relative to investigation of charges against	91	42	3	11
Do	269	43	2	11
Relative to claim for contested election expenses of	152	46	3	13
TAYLOR *vs.* READING, of Pennsylvania. Allegations of illegal and fraudulent voting; relative also to the soldiers' votes	50	41	2	1
TENNESSEE. Question as involved the validity of an election held for members of Congress in the month of November, and the construction of a State law relating to elections by the people to be held in August	1	42	1	11
TERRITORY,				
If the corporation of a Territory is dissolved the offices connected therewith expire (Doty *vs.* Jones)	7	25	3	2
A territorial government is not merged in the State government, but has a legal existence over the people and territory outside the State limits (Sibley)	10	30	2	6
Territorial government must be established before a Delegate is admitted (Babbitt, Smith, Messervy)	219	31	1	6
Do	220	31	1	6
Do	20	31	2	6
A State having been formed out of a Territory, the inhabitants not included within the State limits are not entitled to send a Delegate to Congress. This decision is later than contrary one in case of Sibley (Fuller *vs.* Kingsbury)	435	35	1	7
TESTIMONY (*see also* EVIDENCE),				
Testimony violating secrecy of the ballot inadmissible (Obero *vs* Gallegos)	90	34	1	6
Ex parte testimony taken after the sixty days incompetent (Todd *vs.* Jayne)	1	38	1	8
Do	97	38	1	8
Relative to authorizing commissioners of circuit courts of United States to take testimony in cases of contested election of members of the House of Representatives	1145	47	1	14
THAIN, R. S., of South Carolina. Claim for pay as member of the Forty-second Congress	2	46		13
THAYER, ANDREW J., of Oregon (contestee)	4	37		8
THAYER, M. RUSSELL, of Pennsylvania (contestee)	117	38		8
THOMAS *vs.* ARNELL, of Tennessee. Defective notice to contest	5	39		9
THOMPSON, WILLIAM, of Iowa (contestee)	400	31		6
TIFT, NELSON, of Georgia	16	41		10
TILLMAN *vs.* SMALLS, of South Carolina. Violence, intimidation, and fraud	916	45		13
TILLMAN, GEORGE D., of South Carolina (contestee)	1525	47		14
TILLMAN, LEWIS, of Tennessee (contestee)	3	41	3	10
TODD *vs.* JAYNE, of Dakota. Allegations of fraud and illegal voting. Contestant obtained the seat	1	38	1	8
Do	99	38	1	8
TRIMBLE, LAWRENCE S., of Kentucky (contestee), relative to eligibility to hold seat as member	2	40	2	9
Do	6	40	2	9
TROWBRIDGE, ROWLAND E., of Michigan (contestee)	13	39	1	9
TUCKER *vs.* BOOKER, of Virginia. Allegations of ineligibility	41	41	2	10
TURNEY *vs.* MARSHALL, of Illinois	194	34	1	6
UPTON, CHARLES H., of Virginia. Relative to eligibility to seat	17	37	2	8
UTAH TERRITORY. Relative to the application of John T. Caine to be admitted as Delegate from	1865	47	2	14
VALLANDIGHAM *vs.* CAMPBELL, of Ohio. Main contest upon alleged illegal voting. Contestant obtained seat	50	35	1	7
Do	380	35	1	7

Contested cases—general index—Continued.

Subject.	Report.	Congress.	Session.	Volume.
VANDEVER, WILLIAM, of Iowa (contestee)	68	37	2	8
VAN HORN, ROBERT T., of Missouri (contestee)	4	40	2	9
Do	122	41	3	10
VAN WYCK *vs.* GREENE, of New York. Allegations of fraud	23	41	2	10
VERREE, JOHN P., of Pennsylvania (contestee)	40	37	2	8
VICE-PRESIDENT OF THE UNITED STATES. Relative to establishing a uniform time for holding elections in all the States for electors of President and	194	28	1	5
VIOLENCE,				
Intimidation and violence in certain precincts do not invalidate the election in those which were peaceable (Hunt *vs.* Sheldon)	4	41	1	10
Do	38	41	2	10
Intimidation and violence a sufficient cause for the rejection of the whole vote of a parish (Hunt *vs.* Sheldon)	4	41	1	10
Do	38	41	2	10
VOORHEES, DANIEL W., of Indiana (contestee)	18	39	1	9
VOTERS,				
Every voter admitted by the proper officers must be considered legally qualified till the contrary is proved	492	28	1	5
Sworn muster-rolls of regiments admitted as evidence of the age of the voter	66	28	1	5
A minority of voters cannot elect a Representative (Blakely *vs.* Golladay)	1	40	2	9
VOTES (*see also* SUPPLEMENTARY RETURNS),				
Not to be changed after they are placed in the ballot-box	88	21	1	1
It is not sufficient to doubt the legality of a vote	506	26	1	2
Do	541	26	1	3
Return of votes when not made within time specified by law, under certain circumstances, may be counted (Brockenbrough *vs.* Cabell)	36	29	1	5
Where judges of election discover a mistake after a recount, their supplementary return is entitled to be received (Archer *vs.* Allen)	8	34	1	6
Do	167	34	1	6
Informality in county abstracts of votes held not sufficient cause for rejection (Clark *vs.* Hall)	178	34	2	6
Recount of votes not permitted to overturn original sworn statements (Kline *vs.* Verree)	40	37	2	8
WALLACE *vs.* SIMPSON, of South Carolina. *Prima facie* case. Second certificate issued	5	41	1	10
Do	7	41	1	10
Do	17	41	2	10
Do	71	41	2	10
WALLACE *vs.* McKINLEY, of Ohio	*1548	48	1	15
WALLACE, ALEXANDER S., of South Carolina (contestee)	66	42	2	11
WALLS, JOSIAH T., of Florida (contestee)	41	42	3	11
Do	295	44	1	11
WASHBURN *vs.* RIPLEY, of Maine. Votes placed in a ballot-box cannot afterwards be changed	88	21	1	1
WASHBURN *vs.* VOORHEES, of Indiana. Illegal voting, fraudulent tampering with ballot-boxes, and false returns. Contestant given the seat	18	39	1	9
WASHBURN, WILLIAM D., of Minnesota (contestee)	1791	46	2	13
WEAVER, JAMES B., of Iowa (contestee)	†1622	49	1	15
WEST VIRGINIA CONTESTED-ELECTIONS. (*See* Report 7, Forty-third Congress, first session, vol. 11.)				
WHEELER, JOSEPH, of Alabama (contestee)	1273	47	1	14
WHITFIELD, J. W., of Kansas (contestee)	3	34	1	6
Do	275	34	1	6
Do	186	34	3	6
WHITTLESEY *vs.* McKENZIE, of Virginia. Allegations of disloyalty	75	41	2	10
WHYTE *vs.* HARRIS, of Maryland. Allegations of violence at the polls and irregularities	538	35	1	7
WIGGINTON *vs.* PACHECO, of California. Irregularities and illegal practices	83	45	2	12
Do	118	45	2	12
WILLIAMSON *vs.* SICKLES, of New York. Notice not served upon contestee within the specified sixty days. Case not reached	80	36	1	7
Do	61	36	2	7
WILLOUGHBY, Jr., *vs.* SERRITT, of New York. Errors and omissions of inspectors and returning officers are to be corrected so as to do substantial justice to the parties. The omission in this case was of the word "junior," but was held upon the proof given not to vitiate the votes	3	14	1	1
WILSHIRE, W. W., of Arkansas (contestee)	92	43	1	11
Do	631	43	1	11
WILSON, BENJAMIN, of West Virginia (contestee)	7	43	1	11
WILSON, ISAAC, of New York (contestee)	15	18	1	1
WILSON, JAMES, of Iowa (contestee)	†2623	48	2	15
WILSON, JEREMIAH M., of Indiana (contestee)	41	42	2	11
WILSON, JOHN J., of Iowa. Claims seat from Ninth Congressional district of Iowa	19	46	3	13
WING *vs.* McCLOUD, of Virginia. Irregularity of voting and election laws not complied with	23	37	3	8

* And views of minority. † Parts 1, 2.

Contested cases—general index—Continued.

* And views of minority. † Parts 1, 2. ‡ Parts 1, 2, 3.

Contested cases—general index—Continued.

Subject.	Report.	Congress.	Session.	Volume.
RS, JOHN B., of Tennessee (contestant)	32	37	3	8
RS, JOHN B., of Tennessee. Claim for additional Representative	12	41	1	10
, JACOB, of Ohio (contestee)	*1449	49	1	15
OHN, of New Jersey (contestee)	310	29	1	5
MICHAEL, of Louisiana (contestee)	61	41	2	10
BENEZER, of New York (contestee)	39	16	1	1
RTIN, LOUIS, of Louisiana (contestee)	11	41	1	10
Do	60	41	2	10
JOHN, of Missouri (contestee)	22	14	2	1
Do	28	14	2	1
JOHN G., of Missouri	117	38	1	8
JOSEPH, of Virginia. Owing to the rebellion, election partial and invalid	12	37	2	8
Do	70	37	2	8
Do	9	38	1	8
Do	51	41	2	10
HAUS *vs.* FROST, of Missouri. Alleged illegal action on part of the judges of election	1409	47	1	14
Do	1959	47	2	14
vs. TILLMAN, of Tennessee. Allegations of fraud. Contestee retained his seat	3	41	3	10
N, LIONEL A., of Louisiana (contestee)	4	41	1	10
Do	38	41	2	10
Y, CHARLES M., of Alabama (contestee)	1522	47	1	14
Do	1886	47	2	14
Do	2137	48	1	15
AN *vs.* PINCHBACK, of Louisiana. Two certificates issued. Question as to which of the State governments was legally in power	597	43	1	11
Do	263	43	2	11
F. Authority given to a sheriff to appoint writers and open polls, gives him power to appoint but one writer and open but one poll (Botts *vs.* Jones)	492	28	1	5
. THAYER, of Oregon. Contest relative to the time legally fixed for holding election for Representative	4	37	1	8
S *vs.* VAN HORN, of Missouri. Allegations of fraud	122	41	2	10
FRANCIS E., of North Carolina (contestee)	17	41	3	10
HENRY H., of Wisconsin Territory. Question as to right to seat as Delegate. Held that a territorial government is not merged in the State government, but has a legal existence over the people and Territory outside the State limits	10	30	2	6
, DANIEL E., of New York (contestee)	80	36	1	7
Do	61	36	2	7
, WILLIAM D., of South Carolina (contestee)	7	41	1	10
Do	17	41	2	10
Do	71	41	2	10
ENSUS. (*See* CENSUS.)				
E, THOMAS G., of North Carolina (contestee)	*727	48	1	15
R *vs.* RICE, of Massachusetts. Irregularity and inaccuracy of returns	23	38	1	8
S, WILLIAM F., of Arkansas (contestee)	427	46	2	13
. RAWLS, of Georgia. Fraudulent and illegal practices, threatening and overawing election officers, and intimidation of voters	216	43	1	11
vs. TILLMAN, of South Carolina. Alleged violence and intimidation	1525	47	1	14
ROBERT, of South Carolina (contestee)	916	45	2	12
. BROWN, of Kentucky. Alleged disloyalty	11	40	2	9
. ROBERTSON, of Louisiana. Case dismissed without prejudice	631	47	1	14
SHELLEY, of Alabama. Contestant charges fraud, ballot box stuffing, conspiracy, and illegal rejection of returns	1522	47	1	14
UGH N., of New Mexico. Held that a territorial government must be established before a Delegate is admitted	220	31	1	6
WILLIAM S., of New York (contestee)	3	14	1	1
, O. P., of Arkansas (contestee)	11	43	2	11
S' VOTES. Held that the soldiers' vote should be rejected except in cases where said soldiers resided in the precinct at the time of enlistment, or remained for years after (Taylor *vs.* Reading)	50	41	2	10
. ELECTIONS. Members elected under proclamation of governor for an extra session, at a special election, held their seats only till members were chosen at the regular election (Gholson and Claiborne)	2	25	1	2
Do	379	25	2	2
. SESSION. (*See* EXTRA SESSION; GHOLSON; CLAIBORNE; MISSISSIPPI.)				
R *vs.* MOREY, of Louisiana. Irregularity in the conduct of election, and unlawful count of ballots by the commissioners of election	442		1	11
. ARMSTRONG, of Dakota. Alleging illegal votes received from non-residents and Indians	43	44 42	2	11
ANKS. (*See* BANKS.)				
EGISLATURE. Its authority to regulate elections paramount to State constitution (Baldwin *vs.* Trowbridge)	13		1	9
T, JOSEPH J. (contestant). On memorial contesting seat of Charles E. Phelps, from Third district of Maryland	2	39 40	1	9

*Parts 1, 2, 3.

FORTY-NINTH CONGRESS, FIRST SESSION.

[PUBLIC RESOLUTION—No. 24.]

Joint resolution authorizing the preparation of a compilation of the reports of committees of the Senate and House of Representatives.

Resolved by the Senate and House of Representatives of the United States of America in Congress assembled, That there be prepared under the direction of the Joint Committee of Printing, a compilation of the reports of the Senate and House of Representatives from the Fourteenth to the Forty-eighth Congress, inclusive, classified by committees, arranged, indexed, and bound in suitable volumes for the use of the standing committees of the two Houses of Congress. And the sum of seven thousand seven hundred and fifty dollars, or so much thereof as may be found necessary, is hereby appropriated out of any money in the Treasury not otherwise appropriated, for the preparation of said work, which sum may be paid by the Secretary of the Treasury upon the order of the chairman of said Joint Committee, as additional pay or compensation to any officer or employee of the United States.

Resolved, further, That the Clerk of the House and Secretary of the Senate be, and they are hereby directed, to procure and file, for the use of their respective Houses, copies of all reports made by each committee of all succeeding Congresses; and that the Clerk of the House and the Secretary of the Senate be, and they are hereby, authorized and directed at the close of each session of Congress, to cause said reports to be indexed and bound, one copy to be deposited in the library of each House and one copy in the room of the committee from which the reports emanated.

Approved, July 29, 1886.

COMPILER'S NOTICE.

This compilation embraces all the printed reports made by both Houses of Congress from the commencement of the Fourteenth to the close of the Forty-ninth Congress. They are classified by committees and arranged in numerical order. The collection for each committee is divided into volumes of suitable size. Each committee has a separate index, a copy being bound in each volume.

The SPECIAL and SELECT reports are all compiled in one collection having one index, a copy of which is bound in each volume.

The plan throughout the compilation is to place each report to the committee from which it was reported, without reference to the subject-matter.

The House and Senate reports are compiled separately. Care will be required in noticing the chronological order, as in some instances an entire session or Congress may not appear in certain volumes from the fact that during this period no reports were made by this committee.

T. H. McKEE.

INDEX

TO

REPORTS OF COMMITTEE ON ELECTION OF PRESIDENT AND VICE-PRESIDENT,

HOUSE OF REPRESENTATIVES.

FROM 1815 TO 1887, INCLUSIVE.

Subject.	Report.	Congress.	Session.	Volume.
CONSTITUTION OF UNITED STATES,				
To amend Article II and Article XII	*819	45	2	1
To amend, creating, and defining office of Second Vice-President	*2493	49	1	1
DALLAS, Hon. GEORGE M., notification of his election as Vice-President	142	28	2	1
ELECTION OF PRESIDENT AND VICE-PRESIDENT, to amend Article II and Article XII of Constitution of United States	*819	45	2	1
Do	1207	47	1	1
ELECTORAL VOTE,				
Comparing popular vote with	347	46	2	1
Counting of, to provide for	1117	48	1	1
Counting of, to amend law regulating	347	46	2	1
Do	1207	47	1	1
Mode of examining	106	28	2	1
ELECTORS, to fix day for meeting, and to regulate counting votes of, for President and Vice-President	†1638	49	1	1
HOUSE OF REPRESENTATIVES,				
Mode of examining votes for President and Vice-President of United States	106	28	2	1
Rules to be observed in choosing President and Vice-President of United States by	41	18	2	1
POLK, Hon. JAMES K., notification of his election as President	142	28	2	1
POPULAR VOTE,				
To provide for election of President and Vice-President of United States by	347	46	2	1
Comparison of electoral vote with	347	46	2	1
PRESIDENT OF UNITED STATES,				
Article II and Article XII of Constitution of United States, to amend	*819	45	2	1
Counting electoral votes for, to amend law relating to	347	46	2	1
Do	1207	47	1	1
Do	1638	49	1	1
Electors of, to fix day for meeting of	1117	48	1	1
Mode of examining votes for	106	28	2	1
Performance of duties of, in case of removal, death, resignation, or inability	1323	48	1	1
Rules to be observed by House of Representatives in choosing	41	18	2	1
Succession of, to amend law regulating	26	49	1	1
PRESIDENTIAL SUCCESSION, to amend law relating to	26	49	1	1
RULES, to be observed in choosing President and Vice-President of United States	41	18	2	1
SECRETARY OF STATE, regulating succession of, to office of President of United States	26	49	1	1
SECOND VICE-PRESIDENT OF UNITED STATES, to amend Constitution of United States creating and defining office of	*2493	49	1	1
STATES, popular comparison of vote of	347	46	2	1
VICE-PRESIDENT OF UNITED STATES,				
Article II and Article XII of Constitution of United States, to amend	*819	45	2	1
Counting electoral votes for, to amend law relating to	347	46	2	1
Do	1207	47	1	1
Do	1638	49	1	1
Electors of, to fix day for meeting of	1117	48	1	1
Do	1638	49	1	1
Performance of duties in case of removal, death, resignation, or inability	1323	48	1	1
Second, creating the office of	*2493	49	1	1
Succession of, to amend law regulating	26	49	1	1
Prescribing mode of examining votes for	106	28	2	1
Rules to be observed by House of Representatives in choosing	41	18	2	1

* And views of minority. † Parts 1, 2.

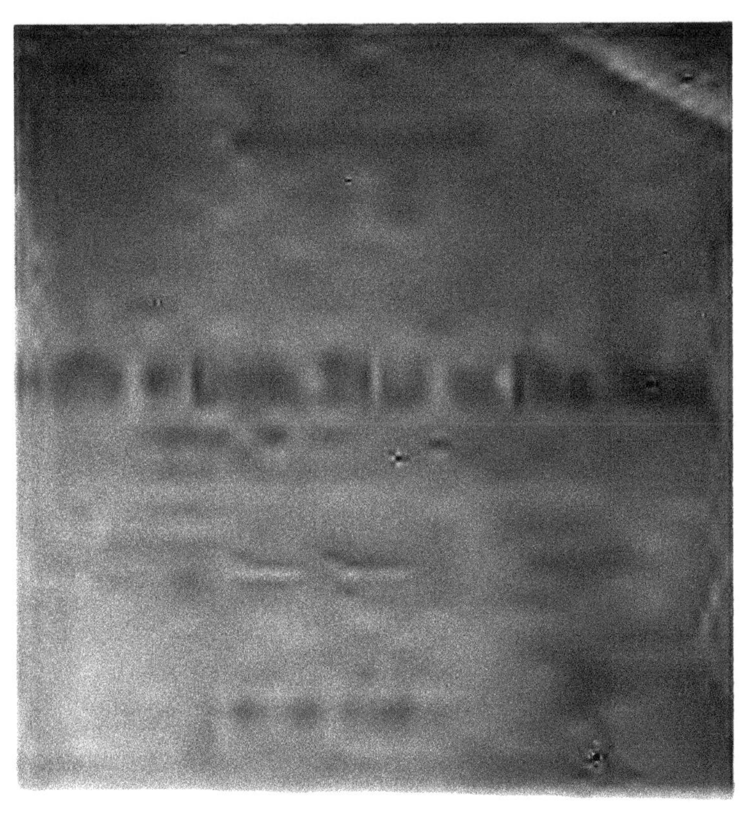

COMPILED, UNDER THE DIRECTION OF THE JOINT COMMITTEE ON PRINTING,

BY

T. H. McKEE,

CLERK, DOCUMENT ROOM, UNITED STATES SENATE.

WASHINGTON:
GOVERNMENT PRINTING OFFICE.
1887.

9271

FORTY-NINTH CONGRESS, FIRST SESSION.

[PUBLIC RESOLUTION—No. 24.]

Joint resolution authorizing the preparation of a compilation of the reports of committees of the Senate and House of Representatives.

Resolved by the Senate and House of Representatives of the United States of America in Congress assembled, That there be prepared under the direction of the Joint Committee of Printing, a compilation of the reports of the Senate and House of Representatives from the Fourteenth to the Forty-eighth Congress, inclusive, classified by committees, arranged, indexed, and bound in suitable volumes for the use of the standing committees of the two Houses of Congress. And the sum of seven thousand seven hundred and fifty dollars, or so much thereof as may be found necessary, is hereby appropriated out of any money in the Treasury not otherwise appropriated, for the preparation of said work, which sum may be paid by the Secretary of the Treasury upon the order of the chairman of said Joint Committee, as additional pay or compensation to any officer or employee of the United States.

Resolved further, That the Clerk of the House and Secretary of the Senate be, and they are hereby directed, to procure and file, for the use of their respective Houses, copies of all reports made by each committee of all succeeding Congresses; and that the Clerk of the House and the Secretary of the Senate be, and they are hereby, authorized and directed at the close of each session of Congress, to cause said reports to be indexed and bound, one copy to be deposited in the library of each House and one copy in the room of the committee from which the reports emanated.

Approved, July 29, 1886.

2

COMPILER'S NOTICE.

This compilation embraces all the printed reports made by both Houses of Congress from the commencement of the Fourteenth to the close of the Forty-ninth Congress. They are classified by committees and arranged in numerical order. The collection for each committee is divided into volumes of suitable size. Each committee has a separate index, a copy being bound in each volume.

The SPECIAL and SELECT reports are all compiled in one collection having one index, a copy of which is bound in each volume.

The plan throughout the compilation is to place each report to the committee from which it was reported, without reference to the subject-matter.

The House and Senate reports are compiled separately. Care will be required in noticing the chronological order, as in some instances an entire session or Congress may not appear in certain volumes from the fact that during this period no reports were made by this committee.

T. H. McKEE.

INDEX

TO

RTS OF COMMITTEE ON EPIDEMIC DISEASES AND PUBLIC HEALTH,

HOUSE OF REPRESENTATIVES.

FROM 1879 TO 1887, INCLUSIVE.

Subject.	Report.	Congress.	Session.	Volume.
RA, international sanitary conference for purpose of suppressing	620	46	2	1
ommission to examine into and report upon adulteration of	199	46	3	1
NATIONAL SANITARY CONFERENCE, authorizing President of United States to call	620	46	2	1
NAL BOARD OF HEALTH,				
crease efficiency of	619	46	2	1
ibution of pure vaccine virus by	607	47	1	1
s to pay expenses of existence of	1678	48	1	1
ENT OF THE UNITED STATES,				
orizing him to appoint a commission to examine into and report upon adulteration of food in United States	199	46	3	1
orizing him to call an international sanitary conference	620	46	2	1
RY CONFERENCE. (*See* INTERNATIONAL SANITARY CONFERENCE.)				
E VIRUS, distribution of, by National Board of Health	607	47	1	1
Y FEVER, international sanitary conference for the purpose of suppressing	620	46	2	1

O

REPORTS

OF THE

COMMITTEE ON EXPENDITURES IN INTERIOR DEPARTMENT,

HOUSE OF REPRESENTATIVES,

FROM THE ORGANISATION OF THE COMMITTEE, MARCH 16, 1860, TO THE CLOSE OF THE FORTY-NINTH CONGRESS, 1887, INCLUSIVE.

IN ONE VOLUME.

COMPILED, UNDER THE DIRECTION OF THE JOINT COMMITTEE ON PRINTING,

BY

T. H. McKEE,

CLERK, DOCUMENT ROOM, UNITED STATES SENATE.

WASHINGTON:
GOVERNMENT PRINTING OFFICE.
1887.

9264

[PUBLIC RESOLUTION—No. 24.]

Joint resolution authorizing the preparation of a compilation of the reports of committees of the Senate and House of Representatives.

Resolved by the Senate and House of Representatives of the United States of America in Congress assembled, That there be prepared under the direction of the Joint Committee of Printing, a compilation of the reports of the Senate and House of Representatives from the Fourteenth to the Forty-eighth Congress, inclusive, classified by committees, arranged, indexed, and bound in suitable volumes for the use of the standing committees of the two Houses of Congress. And the sum of seven thousand seven hundred and fifty dollars, or so much thereof as may be found necessary, is hereby appropriated out of any money in the Treasury not otherwise appropriated, for the preparation of said work, which sum may be paid by the Secretary of the Treasury upon the order of the chairman of said Joint Committee, as additional pay or compensation to any officer or employee of the United States.

Resolved further, That the Clerk of the House and Secretary of the Senate be, and they are hereby directed, to procure and file, for the use of their respective Houses, copies of all reports made by each committee of all succeeding Congresses; and that the Clerk of the House and the Secretary of the Senate be, and they are hereby, authorized and directed at the close of each session of Congress, to cause said reports to be indexed and bound, one copy to be deposited in the library of each House and one copy in the room of the committee from which the reports emanated.

Approved, July 29, 1886.

COMPILER'S NOTICE.

This compilation embraces all the printed reports made by both Houses of Congress from the commencement of the Fourteenth to the close of the Forty-ninth Congress. They are classified by committees and arranged in numerical order. The collection for each committee is divided into volumes of suitable size. Each committee has a separate index, a copy being bound in each volume.

The SPECIAL and SELECT reports are all compiled in one collection, having one index, a copy of which is bound in each volume.

The plan throughout the compilation is to place each report to the committee from which it was reported, without reference to the subject-matter.

The House and Senate reports are compiled separately. Care will be required in noticing the chronological order, as in some instances an entire session or Congress may not appear in certain volumes from the fact that during this period no reports were made by this committee.

T. H. McKEE.

INDEX

TO

[TS OF COMMITTEE ON EXPENDITURES IN THE INTERIOR DEPARTMENT,

HOUSE OF REPRESENTATIVES.

FROM 1860 TO 1887, INCLUSIVE.

Subject.	Report.	Congress.	Session.	Volume.
S, investigation of Hot Springs Reservation in	1846	48	1	1
OF PENSION BILL, testimony in relation to	189	45	3	1
YS IN PENSION CASES	189	45	3	1
OF COLUMBIA, investigation of management of Government Hospital for Insane in	793	44	1	1
LAND OFFICE, to promote efficiency of	4001	49	2	1
ENT HOSPITAL FOR INSANE, to investigate management of	793	44	1	1
NGS, ARKANSAS, investigation of Government property on reser-tion at	1846	48	1	1
overnment hospital for, to investigate management of	793	44	1	1
DEPARTMENT,				
itures in	793	44	1	1
Do	189	45	3	1
ation of management	861	49	1	1
ATION,				
nent Hospital for Insane, to investigate management of	793	44	1	1
ng Territory, to investigate abuses in awarding contracts for survey public lands in	794	44	1	1
Department, to investigate expenditures in	189	45	3	1
ings Reservation, to investigate certain things connected with Gov-nment property on	1846	48	1	1
Bureau	861	49	1	1
ICE, to promote efficiency of	4001	49	2	1
CHARLES H., investigation of management of Government Hospital r Insane	793	44	1	1
GAZETTE, testimony in relation to	189	45	3	1
FFICE, testimony in relation to	189	45	3	1
ATTORNEYS, testimony in relation to	189	45	3	1
BUREAU, investigation of	861	49	1	1
OFFICE, testimony in relation to	189	45	3	1
ANDS, Wyoming Territory, to investigate abuses in awarding con-acts for survey of	794	44	1	1
Y,				
nent Hospital for Insane, relative to management of	793	44	1	1
ng Territory, relative to certain abuses in awarding contracts for Gov-nment surveys in	794	44	1	1
Department, relative to expenditures in	189	45	3	1
TERRITORY, to investigate abuses in awarding contracts for sur-y of public lands by surveyor-general of	494	44	1	1

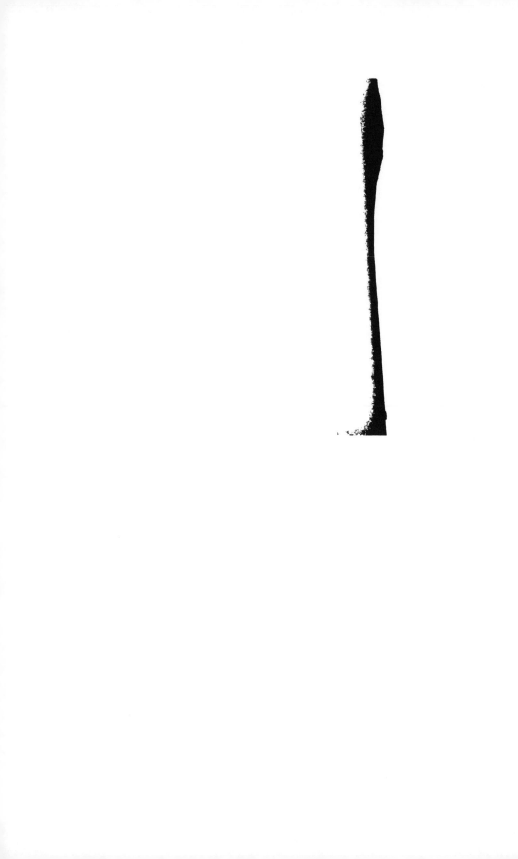

'RTS

OF THE

ON EXPENDITURES

HOUSE OF REPRESENTATIVES,

FROM THE ORGANIZATI
CLOSE OF THE

IN THREE VOLUMES.

COMPILED, UNDER THE DIRECTION OF THE JOINT COMMITTEE ON PRINTING,

BY

T. H. McKEE,

CLERK, DOCUMENT ROOM, UNITED STATES SENATE.

WASHINGTON:
GOVERNMENT PRINTING OFFICE.
1887.

9259

FORTY-NINTH CONGRESS, FIRST SESSION.

[PUBLIC RESOLUTION—No. 24.]

Joint resolution authorizing the preparation of a compilation of the reports of committees of the Senate and House of Representatives.

Resolved by the Senate and House of Representatives of the United States of America in Congress assembled, That there be prepared under the direction of the Joint Committee of Printing, a compilation of the reports of the Senate and House of Representatives from the Fourteenth to the Forty-eighth Congress, inclusive, classified by committees, arranged, indexed, and bound in suitable volumes for the use of the standing committees of the two Houses of Congress. And the sum of seven thousand seven hundred and fifty dollars, or so much thereof as may be found necessary, is hereby appropriated out of any money in the Treasury not otherwise appropriated, for the preparation of said work, which sum may be paid by the Secretary of the Treasury upon the order of the chairman of said Joint Committee, as additional pay or compensation to any officer or employee of the United States.

Resolved further, That the Clerk of the House and Secretary of the Senate be, and they are hereby directed, to procure and file, for the use of their respective Houses, copies of all reports made by each committee of all succeeding Congresses; and that the Clerk of the House and the Secretary of the Senate be, and they are hereby, authorized and directed at the close of each session of Congress, to cause said reports to be indexed and bound, one copy to e deposited in the library of each House and one copy in the room of the committee from which the reports emanated.

Approved, July 29, 1886.

COMPILER'S NOTICE.

This compilation embraces all the printed reports made by both Houses of Congress from the commencement of the Fourteenth to the close of the Forty-ninth Congress. They are classified by committees and arranged in numerical order. The collection for each committee is divided into volumes of suitable size. Each committee has a separate index, a copy being bound in each volume.

The SPECIAL and SELECT reports are all compiled in one collection having one index, a copy of which is bound in each volume.

The plan throughout the compilation is to place each report to the committee from which it was reported, without reference to the subject-matter.

The House and Senate reports are compiled separately. Care will be required in noticing the chronological order, as in some instances an entire session or Congress may not appear in certain volumes from the fact that during this period no reports were made by this committee.

T. H. McKEE.

INDEX

TO

REPORTS OF COMMITTEE ON EXPENDITURES IN DEPARTMENT OF JUSTICE,

HOUSE OF REPRESENTATIVES.

FROM 1874 TO 1887, INCLUSIVE.

Subject.	Report.	Congress.	Session.	Volume.
ACCOUNTS, unsettled, in accounting office of United States Treasury	2645	48	2	3
ALABAMA, clerk of middle district of, to investigate delinquency	611	43	1	1
ARKANSAS, western judicial district of, inquiring into expenses, disbursements, and general management	626	43	1	1
ATTORNEYS, employment of, and fees paid to	298	44	1	1
BALANCES DUE UNITED STATES, from defalcation	2645	48	2	3
BARKER, J. J., charges against Judge William Lawrence, made by, investigation of	2675	48	2	3
BELL TELEPHONE COMPANY. (*See* TELEPHONES.)				
BLAKE, E. V. C., delinquency of, as clerk middle judicial district of Alabama, (Parts 1 and 2)	611	43	1	1
BOWEN, GEORGE P., clerk of southern judicial district of Illinois, to investigate official conduct of	155	43	2	1
COMPENSATION OF COURT OFFICIALS, President's message relating to	1779	48	1	3
CONTINGENT FUND OF DEPARTMENT OF JUSTICE, rule of House requiring examination into	610	43	1	1
COURT OFFICIALS, compensation of, to regulate	2509	48	2	3
Do	1132	49	1	3
COURTS OF UNITED STATES,				
Alabama, to investigate delinquency of clerk of middle district of	*611	43	1	1
Arkansas, expenses, disbursements, and general management of western judicial district of	626	43	1	1
Fees.				
Regulating, of United States district attorneys and marshals	1779	48	1	3
Do	2509	48	2	3
Do	1132	49	1	3
To abolish fee system in	†2164	48	1	3
Georgia, southern judicial district of, receipts of	480	43	1	1
Illinois, investigation of official conduct of George P. Bowen as clerk of southern judicial district of	155	43	2	1
Michigan, payment of certain expenses of district judge of western district of	27	46	2	2
Nebraska, expenses of	104	43	2	1
North Carolina, expenditures in western district of	275	43	2	1
DEFALCATIONS, list of, in accounting office of United States Treasury	2645	48	2	3
DEPARTMENT OF JUSTICE,				
Accounts pertaining to, alleged improper allowances	2675	48	2	3
Contingent fund of, examination into	610	43	1	1
Expenditures in, to investigate	†800	44	1	2
Do	†2164	48	1	3
Do	2509	48	2	3
Expenditures in, to regulate	1132	49	1	3
History of committee and labor of	278	43	2	1
President's message relating to expenditures in	1779	48	1	3
Special counsel, expenses incurred in employment of	298	44	1	1
Star route correspondence between Post-Office Department and, to furnish copies of	372	48	1	3
Star route frauds, to investigate expenditures in connection with	†2165	48	1	3

* Parts 1, 2. † And views of minority.

Subject.	Report.	Congress.	Session.	Volume.
DICKERSON, JOHN S., to investigate income tax case of United States against	109	46	3	2
DISBURSEMENTS, to investigate, under registration act	*800	44	1	2
DISTRICT ATTORNEYS OF UNITED STATES (*see also* UNITED STATES DISTRICT ATTORNEYS),				
Compensation of, to regulate	2509	48	2	3
Salaries to, payment of, in lieu of payment by fees	1779	48	1	3
Do	2509	48	2	3
Do	1132	49	1	3
ELECTIONS, supervisors of, to repeal all laws for appointment and pay of	120	45	3	2
EXPENDITURES, DEPARTMENT OF JUSTICE,				
To investigate	*2164	48	1	3
Western district of North Carolina, public funds in	275	43	2	1
EXPENSES IN DEPARTMENT OF JUSTICE, investigation of	610	48	1	1
FEE BOOKS, to regulate manner of keeping by United States marshals	584	46	2	2
FIRST COMPTROLLER OF TREASURY, to investigate charges made against	2675	48	2	3
FRAUDS IN STAR ROUTES. (*See* STAR ROUTE MAIL SERVICE.)				
GEORGIA, southern judicial district of, receipts of office of	480	43	1	1
ILLINOIS, investigation of official conduct of George P. Bowen as clerk of southern judicial district of	155	43	2	1
INVESTIGATIONS,				
E. V. C. Blake, official conduct of, as clerk of middle judicial district of Alabama	*611	43		1
Department of Justice, expenditures in	†2164	48	1	4
Lot Wright, charges against as United States marshal for southern district of Ohio	*2681	48	2	3
Arkansas, inquiring into expenses, disbursements, and general management of western judical district of	626	43	1	1
Department of Justice:				
To investigate expenditure of contingent fund	610	48	1	1
To inqnire into employment of special counsel by	298	44	1	1
Star route frauds	*2165	48	1	3
First Comptroller of Treasury, charges against	2675	48	2	3
Nebraska, inquiring into expenses of United States courts in State of	104	43	2	1
North Carolina, inquiring into expenditures in western district of	275	43	2	1
Star-rontes, frauds in connection with	*2165	48	1	3
Telephones, expenditures in contest relative to patents on	521	49	1	2
JUDICIAL DISTRICTS. (*See* COURTS OF UNITED STATES.)				
JUSTICE. (*See* DEPARTMENT OF JUSTICE.)				
LAWRENCE, Judge WILLIAM, investigation of charges made by J. J. Barker against	2675	48	2	3
McPHERSON, JAMES, requiring him to produce books showing receipts of his office	480	43	1	1
MARQUETTE, MICHIGAN, providing for certain expenses of United States district judge at	27	46	2	2
MARSHALS (*see also* UNITED STATES MARSHALS), salaries of, to be paid in lieu of fees	1779	48	1	3
Do	2509	48	2	3
Do	1132	49	1	3
MICHIGAN, district judge of western judicial district of, expenses of	27	46	2	2
MILEAGE, marshals, regulating amount paid United States for	584	46	2	2
NEBRASKA, inquiring into expenses of United States courts in State of	104	43	2	1
NON-RESIDENT MARSHALS, appointment and arming of, in Ohio by Lot Wright, United States marshal for southern district of Ohio	*2681	48	2	3
NORTH CAROLINA, inquiring into expenditures in western district of	275	43	2	1
OCTOBER ELECTION IN OHIO. (*See* OHIO.)				
OHIO, Lot Wright, to investigate charges against, as United States marshal for southern district of	*2681	48	2	3
PAN-ELECTRIC TELEPHONE COMPANY. (*See* TELEPHONES.)				
PATENTS, to investigate expenditures in contest relative to patents on telephones	521	49	1	2
POSTMASTER-GENERAL, requesting him to furnish copies of correspondence between the Post-Office Department and Department of Justice relative to star routes	872	48	1	3
POST-OFFICE DEPARTMENT, requesting Postmaster-General to furnish copies of star route correspondence between Department of Justice and	872	48	1	3
PUBLIC DEFALCATIONS. (*See* DEFALCATIONS.)				
REGISTRATION ACT, to investigate disbursements under	*800	44	1	2
REVISED STATUTES, to amend section 554 relative to salaries of United States district judges	27	46	2	2
SECRET-SERVICE FUND, to investigate expenditures of	*800	44	1	2
SECRETARY OF TREASURY, requesting him to furnish the Department of Justice with names of all United States officials whose accounts remain unadjusted	2645	48	2	
SPECIAL COUNSEL (*see also* ATTORNEYS), inquiring into employment of and fees paid to	298	44	1	
SPECIAL MARSHALS, to repeal all laws for appointment and pay of	120	45	3	
STAR-ROUTE CORRESPONDENCE, requesting Postmaster-General to furnish copies of	872	48	1	
STAR-ROUTE MAIL SERVICE, to investigate frauds of certain contractors in	*2165	48	1	
SUPERVISORS OF ELECTIONS, to repeal all laws for appointment and pay of	120	45	3	

*And views of minority. †Parts 1, 2.

Subject.	Report.	Congress.	Session.	Volume.
ELEPHONES, to investigate expenditures in contest relative to patents on.....	521	49	1	3
ESTIMONY,				
On alleged improper allowances by First Comptroller of Treasury	2675	48	2	3
On testimony before Committee on Expenditures in Department of Justice, relating to October election in Ohio...........................	*2681	48	2	3
REASURY DEPARTMENT, investigation of charges against First Comptroller of..	2675	48	2	3
NITED STATES DISTRICT ATTORNEYS, inquiring into amount of extra fees paid to..	296	44	1	1
NITED STATES MARSHALS,				
Regulating fees for mileage paid to..	584	46	2	2
Lot Wright, to investigate charges against, as United States marshal for southern district of Ohio	*2681	48	2	3
NSETTLED ACCOUNTS. (*See* ACCOUNTS.)				
ESTERN JUDICIAL DISTRICT OF ARKANSAS. (*See* ARKANSAS.)				
OLROTH, FRED, on memorial of, to investigate income tax case of United States against John S. Dickerson	109	46	3	2
RIGHT, LOT, to investigate certain charges against, as United States marshal for southern district of Ohio..	*3681	48	2	3

* And views of minority.

REPORTS

OF THE

OMMITTEE ON EXPENDITURES IN NAVY DEPARTMENT,

HOUSE OF REPRESENTATIVES,

FROM THE FOURTEENTH CONGRESS, 1816, TO THE FORTY-NINTH CONGRESS, 1887, INCLUSIVE.

IN ONE VOLUME.

COMPILED, UNDER THE DIRECTION OF THE JOINT COMMITTEE ON PRINTING,

BY

T. H. McKEE,
CLERK, DOCUMENT ROOM, UNITED STATES SENATE.

WASHINGTON:
GOVERNMENT PRINTING OFFICE.
1887.

9261

FORTY-NINTH CONGRESS, FIRST SESSION.

[PUBLIC RESOLUTION—No. 24.]

Joint resolution authorizing the preparation of a compilation of the reports of committees of the Senate and House of Representatives.

Resolved by the Senate and House of Representatives of the United States of America in Congress assembled, That there be prepared under the direction of the Joint Committee of Printing, a compilation of the reports of the Senate and House of Representatives from the Fourteenth to the Forty-eighth Congress, inclusive, classified by committees, arranged, indexed, and bound in suitable volumes for the use of the standing committees of the two Houses of Congress. And the sum of seven thousand seven hundred and fifty dollars, or so much thereof as may be found necessary, is hereby appropriated out of any money in the Treasury not otherwise appropriated, for the preparation of said work, which sum may be paid by the Secretary of the Treasury upon the order of the chairman of said Joint Committee, as additional pay or compensation to any officer or employee of the United States.

Resolved further, That the Clerk of the House and Secretary of the Senate be, and they are hereby directed, to procure and file, for the use of their respective Houses, copies of all reports made by each committee of all succeeding Congresses; and that the Clerk of the House and the Secretary of the Senate be, and they are hereby, authorized and directed at the close of each session of Congress, to cause said reports to be indexed and bound, one copy to be deposited in the library of each House and one copy in the room of the committee from which the reports emanated.

Approved, July 29, 1886.

COMPILER'S NOTICE.

This compilation embraces all the printed reports made by both Houses of Congress from the commencement of the Fourteenth to the close of the Forty-ninth Congress. They are classified by committees and arranged in numerical order. The collection for each committee is divided into volumes of suitable size. Each committee has a separate index, a copy being bound in each volume.

The SPECIAL and SELECT reports are all compiled in one collection having one index, a copy of which is bound in each volume.

The plan throughout the compilation is to place each report to the committee from which it was reported, without reference to the subject-matter.

The House and Senate reports are compiled separately. Care will be required in noticing the chronological order, as in some instances an entire session or Congress may not appear in certain volumes from the fact that during this period no reports were made by this committee.

T. H. McKEE.

INDEX

TO

)RTS OF COMMITTEE ON EXPENDITURES IN THE NAVY DEPARTMENT,

HOUSE OF REPRESENTATIVES.

FROM 1816 TO 1887, INCLUSIVE.

Subject.	Report.	Congress.	Session.	Volume.
:S IN NAVY DEPARTMENT, investigation of	621	36	1	1
:S (United States sloop), claim for extra work done on	*787	45	2	1
ITRITE (iron-clad), investigation of contract for work on	*787	45	2	1
KLYN NAVY-YARD, investigation of alleged corrupt practices in	621	36	1	1
AU OF PROVISIONS AND CLOTHING, investigation as to indebtedness of	*787	45	2	1
AGENT, investigation of appointment of, by Secretary of Navy	621	36	1	1
INGENT EXPENDITURES, investigation of, in Navy Department	45	18	2	1
Do	93	21	2	1
Do	119	22	2	1
Do	513	23	1	1
RPRISE (United States sloop), in regard to claim for extra work done on	*787	45	2	1
X (United States sloop), claim for extra work done on	*787	45	2	1
NDITURES, to investigate, in Navy Department	67	16	2	1
Do	393	21	1	1
Do	787	45	2	1
BER, GILES B., for relief	3205	49	1	1
STIGATION,				
avy Department expenditures	67	16	2	1
Do	45	18	2	1
Do	93	21	2	1
Do	393	21	1	1
Do	119	22	2	1
Do	513	23	1	1
Do	621	36	1	1
Do	*787	45	2	1
ive-oak, contract with James C. Zabriskie	195	28	2	1
BERLY BROTHERS, for relief	578	46	2	1
E-SAVING BOATS, investigation as to cost and utility of	*787	45	2	1
E-OAK CONTRACTS, investigation of	621	36	1	1
E-OAK TIMBER, investigation of contract with James C. Zabriskie, for furnishing	195	28	2	1
CHINERY CONTRACTS, investigation of awards of	621	36	1	1
RINE CORPS,				
Distribution and strength of	67	16	2	1
To pay Kimberly Brothers for rations supplied to	578	46	2	1
ARTIN, DANIEL B., investigation of appointment as member of board of engineers	621	36	1	1
ANTONOMOH (iron-clad), investigation of contract for work on	*787	45	2	1
ONADNOCK (iron-clad), investigation of contract for work on	*787	45	2	1
ORAN, WILLIAM P., for relief	1390	46	2	1
AVY DEPARTMENT,				
Abuses in, investigation of	621	36	1	1
Expenditures in, investigation of	67	16	2	1
Do	45	18	2	1
Do	93	21	2	1
Do	393	21	1	1
Do	119	22	2	1
Do	513	23	1	1
Do	*787	45	2	1

* And views of minority.

Subject.	Report.	Congress.	Session.	Volume.
NAVY-YARD PATRONAGE, distribution by Secretary of Navy, among members of Congress	621	36	1	1
PURITAN (iron-clad), investigation of contract for work on	*787	45	2	1
SCHEUTZE, WILLIAM H., for relief	3205	49	1	1
SECRETARY OF NAVY, appointment of coal agent by	621	36	1	1
SUSPENDED CONTRACTS, testimony in regard to contracts for iron-clads and boilers	*787	45	2	1
SUSPENDED TIMBER ORDERS, testimony in regard to	*787	45	2	1
SWIFT, WILLIAM C. N., investigation of contract of Secretary of Navy for furnishing live-oak timber	621	36	1	1
TERROR (iron-clad), investigation of contract for work on	*787	45	2	1
TILTON, WHEELWRIGHT & CO., allowance of claim	*788	44	1	1
WOOD, DIALOGUE & CO., for payment of indebtedness claimed by	*787	45	2	1
ZABRISKIE, JAMES C., investigation of contract for furnishing live-oak timber to Navy Department	195	28	2	1

* And views of minority.

REPORTS

OF THE

)MMITTEE ON EXPENDITURES IN POST-OFFICE DEPARTMENT,

HOUSE OF REPRESENTATIVES,

FROM THE FOURTEENTH CONGRESS, 1815, TO THE FORTY-NINTH CONGRESS, 1887, INCLUSIVE.

IN ONE VOLUME.

COMPILED, UNDER THE DIRECTION OF THE JOINT COMMITTEE ON PRINTING,

BY

T. H. McKEE,

CLERK, DOCUMENT ROOM, UNITED STATES SENATE.

WASHINGTON:
GOVERNMENT PRINTING OFFICE.
1887.

9262

FORTY-NINTH CONGRESS, FIRST SESSION.

[PUBLIC RESOLUTION—No. 24.]

Joint resolution authorizing the preparation of a compilation of the reports of committees of the Senate and House of Representatives.

Resolved by the Senate and House of Representtives of the United States of America in Congress assembled, That there be prepared under the direction of the Joint Committee of Printing, a compilation of the reports of the Senate and House of Representatives from the Fourteenth to the Forty-eighth Congress, inclusive, classified by committees, arranged, indexed, and bound in suitable volumes for the use of the standing committees of the two Houses of Congress. And the sum of seven thousand seven hundred and fifty dollars, or so much thereof as may be found necessary, is hereby appropriated out of any money in the Treasury not otherwise appropriated, for the preparation of said work, which sum may be paid by the Secretary of the Treasury upon the order of the chairman of said Joint Committee, as additional pay or compensation to any officer or employee of the United States.

Resolved further, That the Clerk of the House and Secretary of the Senate be, and they are hereby directed, to procure and file, for the use of their respective Houses, copies of all reports made by each committee of all succeeding Congresses; and that the Clerk of the House and the Secretary of the Senate be, and they are hereby, authorized and directed at the close of each session of Congress, to cause said reports to be indexed and bound, one copy to be deposited in the library of each House and one copy in the room of the committee from which the reports emanated.

Approved, July 29, 1886.

COMPILER'S NOTICE.

This compilation embraces all the printed reports made by both Houses of Congress from the commencement of the Fourteenth to the close of the Forty-ninth Congress. They are classified by committees and arranged in numerical order. The collection for each committee is divided into volumes of suitable size. Each committee has a separate index, a copy being bound in each volume.

The SPECIAL and SELECT reports are all compiled in one collection having one index, a copy of which is bound in each volume.

The plan throughout the compilation is to place each report to the committee from which it was reported, without reference to the subject-matter.

The House and Senate reports are compiled separately. Care will be required in noticing the chronological order, as in some instances an entire session or Congress may not appear in certain volumes from the fact that during this period no reports were made by this committee.

T. H. McKEE.

INDEX

TO

RTS OF COMMITTEE ON EXPENDITURES IN POST-OFFICE DEPARTMENT,

HOUSE OF REPRESENTATIVES.

FROM 1816 TO 1887, INCLUSIVE.

Subject.	Report.	Congress.	Session.	Volume.
Y, ABRAHAM, Jr., investigation of charges against, as Assistant Postmaster-General	77	14	1	1
GENT EXPENSES, statement showing, of Post-Office Department from October 1, 1829, to December 31, 1830	118	21	2	1
ITURES, investigation of, in Post-Office Department	140	15	2	1
Do	198	28	2	1
GATION, POST-OFFICE DEPARTMENT.				
gent expenses	118	21	2	1
ditures of	140	15	2	1
Do	198	28	2	1
Do	77	14	1	1
NY relative to general management of Post-Office Department	77	14	1	1

REPORTS

OF THE

[COM]MITTEE ON EXPENDITURES ON PUBLIC BUILDINGS

HOUSE OF REPRESENTATIVES,

FROM THE FOURTEENTH CONGRESS, 1816, TO THE FORTY-NINTH CONGRESS, 1887, INCLUSIVE.

IN ONE VOLUME.

COMPILED, UNDER THE DIRECTION OF THE JOINT COMMITTEE ON PRINTING,

BY

T. H. McKEE,

CLERK, DOCUMENT ROOM, UNITED STATES SENATE.

WASHINGTON:
GOVERNMENT PRINTING OFFICE.
1887.

9265

FORTY-NINTH CONGRESS, FIRST SESSION.

[PUBLIC RESOLUTION—No. 24.]

Joint resolution authorizing the preparation of a compilation of the reports of committees of the Senate and House of Representatives.

Resolved by the Senate and House of Representatives of the United States of America in Congress assembled, That there be prepared under the direction of the Joint Committee of Printing, a compilation of the reports of the Senate and House of Representatives from the Fourteenth to the Forty-eighth Congress, inclusive, classified by committees, arranged, indexed, and bound in suitable volumes for the use of the standing committees of the two Houses of Congress. And the sum of seven thousand seven hundred and fifty dollars, or so much thereof as may be found necessary, is hereby appropriated out of any money in the Treasury not otherwise appropriated, for the preparation of said work, which sum may be paid by the Secretary of the Treasury upon the order of the chairman of said Joint Committee, as additional pay or compensation to any officer or employee of the United States.

Resolved further, That the Clerk of the House and Secretary of the Senate be, and they are hereby directed, to procure and file, for the use of their respective Houses, copies of all reports made by each committee of all succeeding Congresses; and that the Clerk of the House and the Secretary of the Senate be, and they are hereby, authorized directed at the close of each session of Congress, to cause said to be indexed and bound, one copy to be deposited in the library of each House and one copy in the room of the committee from which the reports emanated.

Approved, July 29, 1886.

COMPILER'S NOTICE.

compilation embraces all the printed reports made by both s of Congress from the commencement of the Fourteenth to the f the Forty-ninth Congress. They are classified by committees ranged in numerical order. The collection for each committee is l into volumes of suitable size. Each committee has a separate a copy being bound in each volume.

SPECIAL and SELECT reports are all compiled in one collection one index, a copy of which is bound in each volume.

plan throughout the compilation is to place each report to the ttee from which it was reported, without reference to the subject-.

House and Senate reports are compiled separately. Care will ired in noticing the chronological order, as in some instances an session or Congress may not appear in certain volumes from the at during this period no reports were made by this committee.

T. H. McKEE.

INDEX

TO

TS OF COMMITTEE ON EXPENDITURES ON PUBLIC BUILDINGS,

HOUSE OF REPRESENTATIVES.

FROM 1816 TO 1887, INCLUSIVE.

[See in addition volumes of Reports made by Committee on Public Expenditures.]

Subject.	Report.	Congress.	Session.	Volume.
DRIA, VIRGINIA,				
house building in	649	26	1	1
	84	19	2	1
Do	258	20	1	1
ECT OF PUBLIC BUILDINGS, to investigate management and conduct of	480	27	2	1
EY-GENERAL, rents paid by, for buildings in use by Department of Justice	1730	46	2	1
, CHARLES A., for relief	57	19	2	1
, (National), removal of	*52	41	3	1
BUILDING (Washington, D. C.),				
rior to destruction by the British in August, 1814	184	15	1	1
ditures upon	184	15	1	1
Do	79	17	1	1
Do	86	17	1	1
Do	93	17	2	1
Do	106	18	1	1
Do	38	18	2	1
Do	134	19	1	1
Do	84	19	2	1
Do	258	20	1	1
Do	350	24	1	1
Do	312	24	2	1
Do	772	25	2	1
Do	308	25	3	1
Do	649	26	1	1
igation of expenditures and manner of executing design and work on extension (testimony)	137	37	2	1
TTE, NORTH CAROLINA, expenditures on branch mint at	18	26	2	1
money advanced for ornament for clock for use of Senate	106	18	1	1
SIONER OF PUBLIC BUILDINGS,				
nts of	184	15	1	1
Do	79	17	1	1
Do	86	17	1	1
Do	93	17	2	1
Do	106	18	1	1
Do	38	18	2	1
Do	134	19	1	1
Do	84	19	2	1
Do	258	20	1	1
Do	350	24	1	1
Do	312	24	2	1
Do	772	25	2	1
Do	308	25	3	1
Do	649	26	1	1

* And views of minority.

Subject.	Report.	Congress.	Session.	Volume.
COMMISSIONER OF PUBLIC BUILDINGS—Continued.				
Accounts of	775	29	1	1
Do	776	29	1	1
To fix salary of	186	15	1	1
CONSTRUCTION BUREAU, qualification of members for discharge of duties connected with extensions of Treasury and Capitol buildings	137	37	2	1
CONTRACTS IN TREASURY DEPARTMENT, investigation of	51	41	3	1
COURT-HOUSES AT ALEXANDRIA, VA., expenditure upon building	649	26	1	1
COURTS OF UNITED STATES,				
Circuit court, providing permanent apartments in City Hall for Washington County, D. C	106	18	1	1
Do	38	18	2	1
Do	258	20	1	1
Washington County, D. C., providing permanent apartments in City Hall for county circuit court in	106	18	1	1
Do	38	18	2	1
Do	258	20	1	1
DEPARTMENT OF INTERIOR, rents paid for buildings occupied by	1730	46	2	1
DEPARTMENT OF JUSTICE, rents paid for buildings in use by Attorney-General's Department	1730	46	2	1
DEPARTMENT OF TREASURY, investigation of contracts in	51	41	3	1
DISTRICT OF COLUMBIA,				
Expenditures upon public buildings in	184	15	1	1
Do	79	17	1	1
Do	86	17	1	1
Do	93	17	2	1
Do	106	18	1	1
Do	38	18	2	1
Do	134	19	1	1
Do	84	19	2	1
Do	258	20	1	1
Do	350	24	1	1
Do	312	24	2	1
Do	772	25	2	1
Do	308	25	3	1
Do	649	26	1	1
Do	775	29	1	1
Do	776	29	1	1
Investigation of expenditures upon Capitol and Treasury extensions, under Bureau of Construction in	137	37	2	1
EXECUTIVE MANSION,				
Cost prior to destruction by British in August, 1814	184	15	1	1
Expenditures upon	186	15	1	1
Do	79	17	1	1
Do	86	17	1	1
Do	93	17	2	1
Do	106	18	1	1
Do	38	18	2	1
Do	134	19	1	1
Do	84	19	2	1
Do	258	20	1	1
Do	350	24	1	1
Do	312	24	2	1
Do	772	25	2	1
Do	308	25	3	1
Do	649	26	1	1
Expenditure for furniture in	552	27	3	1
GERRY, ELBRIDGE, to erect monument over tomb of	106	18	1	1
INTERIOR DEPARTMENT, rents paid for buildings occupied by	1730	46	2	1
INVESTIGATION, contracts made with Treasury Department	51	41	3	1
JAIL,				
Alexandria, Va	84	19	2	1
Do	258	20	1	1
Washington, D. C	84	19	2	1
Do	258	20	1	1
Do	649	26	1	1
KENNEDY, JOSEPH C. G., claim for relief	77	23	2	1
MADDOX, WILLIAM R., claim for relief	16	19	2	1
Do	172	20	1	1
MINTS, expenditure upon branch mint at Charlotte, N. C	18	26	2	1
NATIONAL CAPITAL, removal of, to the Mississippi Valley	52	41	3	1
NAVY DEPARTMENT, rents paid for buildings occupied by	1730	46	2	1
NEW YORK (city), investigation of expenditures in construction of post-office building in	761	44	1	1
PATENT OFFICE BUILDING, expenditures upon	312	24	2	1
Do	772	25	2	1
Do	308	25	3	1
Do	649	26	1	1
Do	775	29	1	1
Do	776	29	1	1

Subject.	Report.	Congress.	Session.	Volume.
PENITENTIARY, expenditures upon penitentiary in Washington, D. C	84	19	2	1
Do	258	20	1	1
POST-OFFICE DEPARTMENT, rents paid for buildings used by	1730	46	2	1
POST-OFFICE DEPARTMENT BUILDING, expenditures upon	649	26	1	1
PRESIDENT'S HOUSE. (*See* EXECUTIVE MANSION.)				
PUBLIC BUILDINGS,				
Alexandria, Va.,				
Expenditures upon jail in	84	19	2	1
Do	258	20	1	1
Expenditures upon court-house at	649	26	1	1
Architect and superintendent, investigation of management by	460	27	2	1
Charlotte, N. C., expenditures upon branch mint at	18	26	2	1
Cost, prior to destruction by enemy in August, 1814	184	15	1	1
New York City, upon post-office building in	761	44	1	1
Rents, investigation of amounts paid for use of public buildings	1730	46	2	1
Washington, D. C., expenditures upon jail in	84	19	2	1
Do	258	20	1	1
Do	649	26	1	1
SENATE, expenditure for ornament to clock in Senate	106	18	1	1
TREASURY BUILDING,				
Cost of, prior to destruction by enemy in August, 1814	184	15	1	1
Expenditures upon	184	15	1	1
Do	86	17	1	1
Do	312	24	2	1
Do	772	25	2	1
Do	308	25	3	1
Do	649	26	1	1
Do	775	29	1	1
Do	776	29	1	1
Investigation of expenses and manner of executing design of extension to	137	37	2	1
TREASURY DEPARTMENT,				
Contracts in, investigation of	51	41	3	1
Rents paid for buildings occupied by	1730	46	2	1
WAR DEPARTMENT, rents paid for buildings occupied by	1730	46	2	1
WAR OFFICE BUILDING,				
Cost of, prior to destruction by enemy in August, 1814	184	15	1	1
Expenditures upon	184	15	1	1
Do	86	17	1	1
Do	258	20	1	1
WASHINGTON CITY. (*See* DISTRICT OF COLUMBIA.)				
WHITE HOUSE. (*See* EXECUTIVE MANSION.)				

REPORTS

OF THE

COMMITTEE ON EXPENDITURES IN DEPARTMENT OF STATE,

HOUSE OF REPRESENTATIVES,

FROM THE FOURTEENTH CONGRESS, 1815, TO THE FORTY-NINTH CONGRESS, 1887, INCLUSIVE.

IN ONE VOLUME.

COMPILED, UNDER THE DIRECTION OF THE JOINT COMMITTEE ON PRINTING,

BY

T. H. McKEE,

CLERK, DOCUMENT ROOM, UNITED STATES SENATE.

WASHINGTON:
GOVERNMENT PRINTING OFFICE.
1887.

9270

FORTY-NINTH CONGRESS, FIRST SESSION.

[PUBLIC RESOLUTION—No. 24.]

Joint resolution authorizing the preparation of a compilation of the reports of committees of the Senate and House of Representatives.

Resolved by the Senate and House of Representatives of the United States of America in Congress assembled, That there be prepared under the direction of the Joint Committee of Printing, a compilation of the reports of the Senate and House of Representatives from the Fourteenth to the Forty-eighth Congress, inclusive, classified by committees, arranged, indexed, and bound in suitable volumes for the use of the standing committees of the two Houses of Congress. And the sum of seven thousand seven hundred and fifty dollars, or so much thereof as may be found necessary, is hereby appropriated out of any money in the Treasury not otherwise appropriated, for the preparation of said work, which sum may be paid by the Secretary of the Treasury upon the order of the chairman of said Joint Committee, as additional pay or compensation to any officer or employee of the United States.

Resolved further, That the Clerk of the House and Secretary of the Senate be, and they are hereby directed, to procure and file, for the use of their respective Houses, copies of all reports made by each committee of all succeeding Congresses; and that the Clerk of the House and the Secretary of the Senate be, and they are hereby, authorized and directed at the close of each session of Congress, to cause said reports to be indexed and bound, one copy to be deposited in the library of each House and one copy in the room of the committee from which the reports emanated.

Approved, July 29, 1886.

COMPILER'S NOTICE.

This compilation embraces all the printed reports made by both Houses of Congress from the commencement of the Fourteenth to the close of the Forty-ninth Congress. They are classified by committees and arranged in numerical order. The collection for each committee is divided into volumes of suitable size. Each committee has a separate index, a copy being bound in each volume.

The SPECIAL and SELECT reports are all compiled in one collection having one index, a copy of which is bound in each volume.

The plan throughout the compilation is to place each report to the committee from which it was reported, without reference to the subject-matter.

The House and Senate reports are compiled separately. Care will be required in noticing the chronological order, as in some instances an entire session or Congress may not appear in certain volumes from the fact that during this period no reports were made by this committee.

T. H. McKEE.

INDEX

TO

REPORTS OF COMMITTEE ON EXPENDITURES IN DEPARTMENT OF STATE,

HOUSE OF REPRESENTATIVES.

FROM 1816 TO 1867, INCLUSIVE.

Subject.	Report.	Congress.	Session.	Volume.
ADAMS, JOHN QUINCY, communication from, showing expenditures in Department of State	106	17	1	1
CLAY, HENRY, communication from, showing expenditures in Department of State	226	20	1	1
BRADFORD, OLIVER B., impeachment, as late vice-consul-general at Shanghai, China	818	45	2	1
BRIDGLAND, JOHN A., investigation of charges against	760	44	1	1
BROWNE, WILLIAM, disbursements made by	226	20	1	1
CHINA, George F. Seward, investigation of official conduct as minister to	*117	45	3	1
Do	*134	45	3	1
CLAIMS SATISFIED BY DEPARTMENT OF STATE, inquiry as to vouchers in support of	226	20	1	1
CONSULAR AND DIPLOMATIC SERVICE,				
Statement of expenses	931	25	2	1
Expenses of	88	42	3	1
CONSULATES GENERAL, salaries of, act of Congress authorizing	88	42	3	1
CONTINGENT EXPENSES DEPARTMENT OF STATE,				
For years 1823 and 1824	57	18	2	1
For years 1825, 1826, and 1827	226	20	1	1
From July 1, 1843, to December 1, 1843	484	28	1	1
Balances on March 4, 1841, and on December 1, 1843	484	28	1	1
DEFAULTERS, payment of moneys by, due United States by	226	20	1	1
DEPARTMENT OF STATE,				
Investigation of expenditures in	106	17	1	1
Do	57	18	2	1
Do	226	20	1	1
Pay and emoluments of offices in	88	42	3	1
DESTITUTE SEAMEN, consuls' duty under appropriation for relief of	88	42	3	1
DIMON, THEODORE W., abstract of disbursements by	88	42	3	1
FOREIGN INTERCOURSE, contingent expenses of	226	20	1	1
Do	384	21	1	1
FOREIGN MISSIONS, contingent expenses of	226	20	1	1
IMPEACHMENT, Bradford, Oliver B., as late vice-consul-general at Shanghai, China	818	45	2	1
INVESTIGATION,				
Bridgland, John A., charges against	760	44	1	1
Department of State, expenditures in	106	17	1	1
Seward, George F., official conduct of, as minister to China	*117	45	3	1
Do	*134	45	3	1
LAWS OF UNITED STATES,				
Appropriation made for publication of	88	42	3	1
Contingent expenses for publication of	931	25	2	1
MOORE, W. BOWEN, testimony of, on conduct of John A. Bridgland	760	44	1	1
PATENT OFFICE, receipts and expenditures in	86	17	2	1
PLEASANTON, S., communication of, to Hon. Henry Clay, relative to expenditures in Department of State	226	20	1	1

*And views of minority.

Subject.	Report.	Congress.	Session.	Volume.
RETRENCHMENT in Department of State	226	20	1	1
SEWARD, GEORGE F., investigation of official conduct, as minister to China	*117	46	3	1
Do	*134	46	3	1
SHANGHAI, CHINA, Bradford, Oliver B., impeachment of, as late vice-consul-general at	818	45	2	1
TREATY OF GHENT, expenses of	384	21	1	1
UNITED STATES CONSULATE, Dimon, Theodore W. disbursements of, as agent for	88	42	3	1

*And views of minority.

O

HOUSE OF REPRESENTATIVES,

FROM THE FOURTEENTH CONGRESS, 1816, TO THE FORTY-NINTH CONGRESS, 1887, INCLUSIVE.

IN ONE VOLUME.

COMPILED, UNDER THE DIRECTION OF THE JOINT COMMITTEE ON PRINTING

BY

T. H. McKEE,

CLERK, DOCUMENT ROOM, UNITED STATES SENATE.

WASHINGTON:

GOVERNMENT PRINTING OFFICE.

1887.

9263

FORTY-NINTH CONGRESS, FIRST SESSION.

[PUBLIC RESOLUTION—No. 24.]

Joint resolution authorizing the preparation of a compilation of the reports of committees of the Senate and House of Representatives.

Resolved by the Senate and House of Representatives of the United States of America in Congress assembled, That there be prepared under the direction of the Joint Committee of Printing, a compilation of the reports of the Senate and House of Representatives from the Fourteenth to the Forty-eighth Congress, inclusive, classified by committees, arranged, indexed, and bound in suitable volumes for the use of the standing committees of the two Houses of Congress. And the sum of seven thousand seven hundred and fifty dollars, or so much thereof as may be found necessary, is hereby appropriated out of any money in the Treasury not otherwise appropriated, for the preparation of said work, which sum may be paid by the Secretary of the Treasury upon the order of the chairman of said Joint Committee, as additional pay or compensation to any officer or employee of the United States.

Resolved further, That the Clerk of the House and Secretary of the Senate be, and they are hereby directed, to procure and file, for the use of their respective Houses, copies of all reports made by each committee of all succeeding Congresses; and that the Clerk of the House and the Secretary of the Senate be, and they are hereby, authorized and directed at the close of each session of Congress, to cause said reports to be indexed and bound, one copy to be deposited in the library of each House and one copy in the room of the committee from which the reports emanated.

Approved, July 29, 1886.

COMPILER'S NOTICE.

compilation embraces all the printed reports made by both of Congress from the commencement of the Fourteenth to the the Forty-ninth Congress. They are classified by committees anged in numerical order. The collection for each committee is into volumes of suitable size. Each committee has a separate copy being bound in each volume.

PECIAL and SELECT reports are all compiled in one collection one index, a copy of which is bound in each volume.

lan throughout the compilation is to place each report to the tee from which it was reported, without reference to the subject-

Iouse and Senate reports are compiled separately. Care will ired in noticing the chronological order, as in some instances an ession or Congress may not appear in certain volumes from the t during this period no reports were made by this committee.

T. H. McKEE.

INDEX

TO

'S OF COMMITTEE ON EXPENDITURES IN TREASURY DEPARTMENT,

HOUSE OF REPRESENTATIVES.

FROM 1816 TO 1887, INCLUSIVE.

Subject.	Report.	Congress.	Session.	Volume.
: OF PAYMENTS, on account of contingent expenses of Treasury partment	108	21	2	1
:URES, investigation of, in Treasury Department	346	21	1	1
Do	108	21	2	1
ATION,				
tures in Treasury Department	346	21	1	1
Do	108	21	2	1
sick and disabled, fund for relief of	655	36	1	1
:R, RICHARD D., recovery of judgment for $25,000	3215	49	1	1
Do	3753	49	2	1
Y OF TREASURY, letter from, transmitting an abstract of contin- it expenditures of Treasury Department for 1830	108	21	2	
DISABLED SEAMEN, fund for, investigation of use of	655	36	1	1
: DEPARTMENT, investigation of	346	21	1	1
Do	108	21	2	1

REPORTS

OF THE

MITTEE ON EXPENDITURES IN WAR DEPARTMENT,

HOUSE OF REPRESENTATIVES,

FROM THE FOURTEENTH CONGRESS, 1815, TO THE FORTY-NINTH CONGRESS, 1887, INCLUSIVE.

IN TWO VOLUMES.

MPILED, UNDER THE DIRECTION OF THE JOINT COMMITTEE ON PRINTING,

BY

T. H. McKEE,

CLERK, DOCUMENT ROOM, UNITED STATES SENATE.

WASHINGTON:
GOVERNMENT PRINTING OFFICE.
1887.

9260

FORTY-NINTH CONGRESS, FIRST SESSION.

[PUBLIC RESOLUTION—NO. 24.]

Joint resolution authorizing the preparation of a compilation of the reports of committees of the Senate and House of Representatives.

Resolved by the Senate and House of Representatives of the United States of America in Congress assembled, That there be prepared under the direction of the Joint Committee of Printing, a compilation of the reports of the Senate and House of Representatives from the Fourteenth to the Forty-eighth Congress, inclusive, classified by committees, arranged, indexed, and bound in suitable volumes for the use of the standing committees of the two Houses of Congress. And the sum of seven thousand seven hundred and fifty dollars, or so much thereof as may be found necessary, is hereby appropriated out of any money in the Treasury not otherwise appropriated, for the preparation of said work, which sum may be paid by the Secretary of the Treasury upon the order of the chairman of said Joint Committee, as additional pay or compensation to any officer or employee of the United States.

Resolved further, That the Clerk of the House and Secretary of the Senate be, and they are hereby directed, to procure and file, for the use of their respective Houses, copies of all reports made by each committee of all succeeding Congresses; and that the Clerk of the House and the Secretary of the Senate be, and they are hereby, authorized and directed at the close of each session of Congress, to cause said reports to be indexed and bound, one copy to be deposited in the library of each House and one copy in the room of the committee from which the reports emanated.

Approved, July 29, 1886.

COMPILER'S NOTICE.

compilation embraces all the printed reports made by both of Congress from the commencement of the Fourteenth to the ' the Forty-ninth Congress. They are classified by committees anged in numerical order. The collection for each committee is into volumes of suitable size. Each committee has a separate copy being bound in each volume.

SPECIAL and SELECT reports are all compiled in one collection one index, a copy of which is bound in each volume.

lan throughout the compilation is to place each report to the tee from which it was reported, without reference to the subject-

House and Senate reports are compiled separately. Care will ired in noticing the chronological order, as in some instances an ession or Congress may not appear in certain volumes from the t during this period no reports were made by this committee.

T. H. McKEE.

INDEX

TO

TS OF THE COMMITTEE ON EXPENDITURES IN WAR DEPARTMENT.

HOUSE OF REPRESENTATIVES.

FROM 1816 TO 1887.

Subject.	Report.	Congress.	Session.	Volume.
l. Elias Earle, to investigate furnishing of, by	101	14	2	1
Do	43	15	1	1
penditures for investigation of	507	22	1	1
, O. E., testimony relating to charges against	*799	44	1	2
', WILLIAM W., impeachment of, as Secretary of War	186	44	1	1
. HON. B. H., statement before Committee on Expenditures in War 'epartment	*799	44	1	2
marble columns for extension of, investigation of contract by Rice, aird & Heebner, for furnishing	*566	36	1	1
E HIRE, cost of, for War Department from March 4, 1869, to March 1, 376	*799	44	1	2
investigation of, allowed in offices of Quartermaster-General, Commis-ary-General, and Third Auditor	2002	47	2	2
ARY-GENERAL, investigation of claims allowed in office of	2002	47	2	2
& BREGA, testimony relative to contracts with, for extermination of oths in Army clothing	*799	44	1	2
OL. ELIAS, investigation of, furnishing arms to United States	101	14	2	1
Do	43	15	1	1
TURES WAR DEPARTMENT, investigation of	105	17	1	1
Do	507	22	1	1
Do	87	42	3	1
Do	*799	44	1	2
Do	*138	45	3	2
ATIONS, investigation of expenditures for	507	22	1	1
PRUSSIAN WAR, to investigate sales of ordnance stores made by nited States Government during	*46	42	2	1
DEPARTMENT, Investigation of expenditures in	507	22	1	1
GATION,				
Michael C., of charges against	654	44	1	1
ice stores, to investigate sales of, during Franco-Prussian war, by United States Government	*46	42	2	1
Service, to investigate alleged unlawful expenditures by Chief of	2023	49	1	2
epartment, expenditures in	105	17	1	1
Do	507	22	1	1
Do	*799	44	1	2
Do	*138	45	3	2
KY CENTRAL RAILROAD, testimony relating to claim of	*799	44	1	2
ICHAEL C., investigation of charges against	654	44	1	1
Do	*799	44	1	2
DWARD, to investigate payment for services of his father	170	25	3	1
AMUEL, inquiry as to payment for services of minor son	170	25	3	1
CE STORES, to investigate sales of, to France and Germany by United States Government	*46	42	2	1
D EMOLUMENTS, War Department, of officers in	87	42	3	1
ADERSHIPS, testimony before Committee on Expenditures in War Department	*799	44	1	2
RMASTER-GENERAL, investigation of claims allowed in office of	2002	47	2	2

* Views of the minority.

Subject.	Report.	Congress.	Session.	Volume.
RICE, BAIRD & HEEBNER, investigation of contract for furnishing marble columns for extension of Capitol	*566	36	1	1
SECRETARY OF WAR,				
Investigation of expenditures in office of	507	22	1	1
Ordnance stores, to investigate sale of, during Franco-Prussian war, made by	*46	42	2	1
William W. Belknap, impeachment of	186	44	1	1
SIGNAL SERVICE, to investigate alleged unlawful expenditures by Chief of	2023	49	1	2
SIOUX RESERVATION, enlargment of, in Dakota	*799	44	1	2
TESTIMONY,				
Babcock, O. E., charges against	*799	44	1	2
Belknap, William W., impeachment of	186	44	1	1
Commissary-General, claims allowed in office of	2002	47	2	2
Cowles & Brega, contracts with, for extermination of moths in Army clothing	*799	44	1	2
Kerr, Michael C., investigation of charges against	654	44	1	1
Do	799	44	1	1
Kentucky Central Railroad, claim of	*799	44	1	2
Post traderships, before Committee on Expenditures in War Department relative to sale of	*799	44	1	1
Quartermaster-General, relative to claims allowed in offices of	2002	44	2	2
Secretary of War and others, relative to sale of ordnance stores by United States Government during Franco-Prussian war	*46	42	2	1
Third Auditor, claims allowed by	2002	47	2	2
THIRD AUDITOR, investigation of claims allowed in office of	2002	47	2	2
UNLAWFUL EXPENDITURES IN SIGNAL OFFICE, to investigate	2023	49	1	2
WAR DEPARTMENT,				
Carriage-hire, cost of, from March 4, 1869, to March 1, 1876	*799	44	1	2
Investigation of expenditures in	105	17	1	1
Do	507	22	1	1
Do	87	42	3	1
Do	*799	44	1	2
Do	*138	45	3	1

* Views of minority.

○

FROM THE ORGANIZATION OF THE COMMITTEE, MARCH 13, 1822, TO THE CLOSE OF THE FORTY-NINTH CONGRESS, 1887, INCLUSIVE.

IN TWELVE VOLUMES.

COMPILED, UNDER THE DIRECTION OF THE JOINT COMMITTEE ON PRINTING,

BY

T. H. McKEE,

CLERK, DOCUMENT ROOM, UNITED STATES SENATE.

WASHINGTON:
GOVERNMENT PRINTING OFFICE.
1887.

9242 F A H

FORTY-NI TH CONGRESS, FIRST SESSION.

[PUBLIC RESOLUTION—No. 24.]

Joint resolution authorizing the preparation of a compilation of the reports of committees of the Senate and House of Representatives.

Resolved by the Senate and House of Representatives of the United States of America in Congress assembled, That there be prepared under the direction of the Joint Committee of Printing, a compilation of the reports of the Senate and House of Representatives from the Fourteenth to the Forty-eighth Congress, inclusive, classified by committees, arranged, indexed, and bound in suitable volumes for the use of the standing committees of the two Houses of Congress. And the sum of seven thousand seven hundred and fifty dollars, or so much thereof as may be found necessary, is hereby appropriated out of any money in the Treasury not otherwise appropriated, for the preparation of said work, which sum may be paid by the Secretary of the Treasury upon the order of the chairman of said Joint Committee, as additional pay or compensation to any officer or employee of the United States.

Resolved further, That the Clerk of the House and Secretary of the Senate be, and they are hereby directed, to procure and file, for the use of their respective Houses, copies of all reports made by each committee of all succeeding Congresses; and that the Clerk of the House and the Secretary of the Senate be, and they are hereby, authorized and directed at the close of each session of Congress, to cause said reports to be indexed and bound, one copy to be deposited in the library of each House and one copy in the room of the committee from which the reports emanated.

Approved, July 29, 1886.

COMPILER'S NOTICE.

compilation embraces all tne printed reports made by both ɩ of Congress from the commencement of the Fourteenth to the f the Forty-ninth Congress. They are classified by committees ranged in numerical order. The collection for each committee is l into volumes of suitable size. Each committee has a separate a copy being bound in each volume.

SPECIAL and SELECT reports are all compiled in one collection ; one index, a copy of which is bound in each volume.

plan throughout the compilation is to place each report to the ttee from which it was reported, without reference to the subject- .

House and Senate reports are compiled separately. Care will ıired in noticing the chronological order, as in some instances an session or Congress may not appear in certain volumes from the at during this period no reports were made by this committee.

T. H. McKEE.

INDEX

TO

[illegible]PORTS OF THE COMMITTEE ON FOREIGN AFFAIRS,

HOUSE OF REPRESENTATIVES.

FROM MARCH 13, 1822, TO MARCH 3, 1887, INCLUSIVE.

Subject.	Report.	Congress.	Session.	Volume.
BAKER, JOHN M., claim for diplomatic services	276	26	1	3
Do	335	24	1	3
BARRON, EUSTACE, claim for relief	16	31	1	4
BARRY, JAMES (executors of), claim under treaty of 1819 with Spain for loss of property	262	20	1	1
BARTHOLDI STATUE OF LIBERTY, expense of inaugurating	2899	49	1	12
BARTLETT, EDWIN, claim for diplomatic services	744	27	2	4
BARTON, THOMAS P., compensation for diplomatic services	294	24	1	3
BEAUBOUCHER, VICTOR, claim for relief	325	48	1	12
Do	28	49	1	12
BEAUMARCHAIS, CARON DE, claim of heirs, to adjudicate	217	19	1	1
Do	220	20	1	1
BEELEN, FREDERICK A., claim for difference in salary	41	37	2	6
Do	34	38	1	6
BELGIUM, tonnage duties on vessels from	333	24	1	3
BELL, H. S., claim against Mexico for rehearing of	115	45	2	[illegible]
BELLIGERENT RIGHTS, according to Cubans	80	41	2	7
BESSOM, PHILIP, claim for relief	92	23	1	2
BEYER, G. T., claim for property seized by British forces	25	20	2	1
Do	529	24	1	3
BETSY (schooner), indemnity to owners of	53	26	2	3
BILLS OF EXCHANGE, rate at which they have been negotiated prior to January 1, 1829	466	22	1	2
BISCOE, GEORGE W., indemnity for loss of property	533	25	2	3
BLACK, JOHN, compensation for diplomatic service	443	30	1	4
Do	31	41	3	7
Do	55	42	2	7
BLACKFORD, WILLIAM M., claim for additional pay	336	30	1	4
BLAKE, ALPHONSA F. A., claim for relief	634	26	1	3
BLENKINSHIP, GEORGE, claim for relief	264	20	1	1
BLISS, PORTER C., imprisonment by Paraguayan Government of	65	41	3	7
BOARD OF ARBITRATION. (*See* ARBITRAMENT.)				
BOGERT & KNEELAND *et al.*, claim for relief against Venezuela	18	33	1	5
BONNEFIT, PETER, claim for relief under treaty of 1819 with Spain	284	21	1	2
BOUNDARY LINES,				
British America, to determine and establish, between United States and	1	42	2	7
Mexico, to define	151	28	1	4
Do	70	29	2	4
Northwestern, President authorized to appoint commission on	19	41	3	7
Texas and Mexico, to establish, between United States	151	28	1	4
BOWIE & KURTZ *et al.*, claim for relief	75	20	2	1
Do	100	21	1	2
BRADFORD, DUNSCOMB, claim for diplomatic services	924	25	2	3
BRADFORD, ROBERT B., claim for relief	63	37	2	6
BRAZIL, commercial relations with, to advance closer	1647	49	1	12
BREMEN, salary of consul at, to increase	564	30	1	4
BRENT, THOMAS L. L., claim for diplomatic services	675	24	1	3
Do	742	27	2	4
Do	957	27	2	4
Do	236	35	1	6
BRIDGES. (*See* RIVERS AND HARBORS; also name of stream over which proposed to be built.)				
BRITISH NORTH AMERICA,				
American vessels against unlawful discriminations in ports of, protection of	4067	49	2	11
Boundary line, to establish, between United States and	1	42	2	7
BRITISH PROVINCES,				
Commercial intercourse between certain	801	23	2	2
Reciprocity treaty with	1127	46	2	10
BROMBERY, SAMUEL, compensation for diplomatic services	51	43	3	7
BROWN, JOHN P.,				
Claim for additional pay	169	35	1	6
Do	30	38	2	6
Claim for relief of widow	40	42	3	7
BROWN, JOSEPH J., claim for damages for property destroyed by United States troops	281	43	1	7
BROWNE, J. ROSS, claim for relief	54	42	3	7
BUENOS AYRES. (*See* SPANISH PROVINCES.)				
BURNETT, JOSEPH, claim for loss of property under treaty of Ghent	198	20	1	1
BURNHAM, JOHN, claim for relief	102	20	2	1
Do	19	21	1	[illegible]
Do	45	21	2	[illegible]
BUTTERFIELD, CARLOS,				
Certified copies of papers in claim of	100	45	3	[illegible]
Claim for relief	672	45	2	[illegible]
CALDERA (bark), relief of certain insurance companies by destruction in foreign waters of	264	44	1	[illegible]
CALDERA CLAIMS, to supplement act of 1878 for adjudication of	970	48	1	12
CANADA (*see also* BRITISH NORTH AMERICA),				
Arrest and imprisonment of United States citizens by authorities of, in 1866	7	40	2	7
Importation of goods from United States into, act of Parliament of Great Britain (August, 1822) regulating	96	17	2	1
Renewal of reciprocity treaty of 1854 with	2149	48	1	12

Subject.	Report.	Congress.	Session.	Volume.
Y, JOHN, claim against Egyptian Government	1458	47	1	11
IAEL, WILLIAM, claim for relief of heirs	634	26	1	3
E (steamboat), burning of, inquiry into	162	26	2	3
Y, Z. B., compensation for extra diplomatic service	35	37	2	6
L AMERICA,				
ercial relations with, to advance closer	1647	49	1	12
ission on trade with, to appoint	1445	48	1	12
, LOUIS P. DI, claim for relief	202	46	2	10
Do	279	46	2	10
(ship), for relief of owners	671	46	2	10
Do	475	47	1	11
d PERU, alleged corrupt connection of United States officials with ffairs of	*1790	47	1	11
ercial and political relations with	93	27	3	4
with, to execute	3691	49	2	12
UTUAL INSURANCE COMPANY, claim for relief (Caldera claims)	264	44	1	8
IMMIGRATION,				
trict	111	45	3	9
end act of 1882 governing	†614	48	1	12
Do	2043	49	1	12
INDEMNITY CLAIMS. (*See* CHINESE SUBJECTS.)				
INDEMNITY FUND, to restore, to China	970	48	1	12
SUBJECTS, to indemnify, for losses sustained within United States	2044	49	1	12
A. (*See* EPIDEMIC DISEASES.)				
S. (*See* AMERICAN CITIZENS.)				
SHIP, to allow citizens who have become naturalized subjects of Great Britain to be restored to	670	46	2	10
Do	122	47	1	11
spoliation, from 1793 to 1800, to adjust	32	17	1	1
Do	94	18	1	1
, to adjudicate claims of, arising from treaty of August, 1842	366	35	1	6
chusetts, to adjudicate claims of, arising under treaty of August, 1842	366	35	1	6
, private claims against	320	23	3	3
aela, claims of American citizens against	79	41	2	7
Do	29	42	2	7
Do	4	42	3	7
JOHN, claim for relief of assignee	609	43	1	7
RANDOLPH, claim for additional pay	212	24	1	3
Do	534	25	2	3
Do	21	27	3	4
Do	260	36	1	6
N-BULWER TREATY, abrogation of	1121	46	2	10
Do	224	46	3	10
OF COMMITTEES. (*See* COMMITTEE CLERKS.)				
orem duty on Java, to repeal part of act of August 30, 1842, making	428	29	1	4
minating duty on, from the Netherlands	534	28	1	4
J. J., claim for relief	939	47	1	11
A, SOUTH AMERICA (*see also* SPANISH PROVINCES), acceptance by President of United States of medal from the President Liberator of	170	21	1	2
ATION,				
in Africa for free negroes, to establish	277	22	1	2
Do	469	28	1	4
or voluntary, to purchase	134	46	3	10
PEOPLE. (*See* COLONIZATION; FREEDMEN.)				
A RIVER, protection of citizens of United States trading on, providing for	101	25	3	3
CE,				
s upon, to protect United States from	124	18	1	1
committed by Spanish privateers on American	47	18	2	1
CIAL INTERCOURSE (*see also* CONSULAR AND DIPLOMATIC SERVICE),				
ine Republic, to extend, between United States and	1120	46	2	10
to cultivate and improve, with	93	27	3	4
to extend, between United States and	428	28	1	4
cotia and New Brunswick, to open to United States free, with	301	25	3	3
Do	650	27	2	4
ich Islands, to cultivate and improve, with	93	27	3	4
America, to appoint commissioner to promote, with	1457	47	1	11
Do	1445	48	1	12
CIAL RELATIONS WITH CANADA, renewal of reciprocity treaty f 1854	2149	48	1	12
IONS, President to appoint, on northwestern boundary	19	41	3	7
TEE CLERKS, employment and duties of	40	39	1	6
NIE GÉNÉRALE TRANSATLANTIQUE, referring claim of, to Court f Claims	3476	49	2	12
HENRY, claim for relief	33	46	1	10
EDWARD O'MEAGHER, imprisonment by authorities of Great Britain of	342	43	1	7

* Parts 1, 2. † And views of minority.

Subject.	Report.	Congress.	Session.	Volume.
FOREST BELLE (ship), claim for relief of owners of	112	45	3	9
Do	1124	46	2	10
FRANCE,				
Extension of time allowed for discharge of the duties of the commissioners for carrying into effect the convention with	293	23	1	2
Line of steamers between New York and Havre jointly with Government of France	944	27	2	4
Political relations with	183	22	2	2
Seizure of bark Adriatic, by Government of	539	35	1	6
Do	261	36	1	6
FRANKLIN ASSOCIATION OF MINISTERS, memorial for adjustment of national controversies by arbitration	194	25	3	3
FRAUDULENT CLAIMS, to punish prosecution of, against foreign government	2391	48	2	12
FREEDMEN, purchase of land in Mexico or Central America for voluntary colonization of	134	46	3	10
FRENCH ATLANTIC CABLE COMPANY (*see also* OCEAN TELEGRAPH), concessions granted to	35	41	2	7
FRENCH CONVENTION. (*See* FRANCE.)				
FRENCH INDUSTRIAL EXHIBITION. (*See* PARIS EXPOSITION.)				
FRENCH SPOLIATION CLAIMS (*see also* CLAIMS),				
Adjudication of, prior to 1800	82	20	2	1
Do	121	23	2	2
Do	343	26	1	3
Do	254	36	1	6
Ascertainment and settling of, providing for	355	31	1	4
Do	1067	47	1	11
Do	109	48	1	12
Extension of time for entering	293	23	1	2
Schedule of claims on foreign governments	87	19	2	1
Schedule of claims of citizens of New York	87	19	2	1
Schedule of memorialists to Congress during 19th, 20th, 21st, 22d, 23d, 24th, 25th, and 26th Congresses on account	445	25	2	3
Do	343	26	1	3
Do	16	27	2	4
Memorials for payment of claims from,				
Alexandria, Va., citizens of	94	18	1	1
Maine, citizens of	94	18	1	1
Do	87	19	2	1
Maryland, citizens of	127	18	1	1
Do	87	19	2	1
Massachusetts, citizens of	94	18	1	1
Do	202	19	1	1
New Hampshire, citizens of	87	19	2	1
New York, citizens of	87	19	2	1
North Carolina, citizens of	94	18	1	1
Pennsylvania, merchants of	87	19	2	1
Do	127	18	1	1
FRIAS, ANTONIO DE, claim for relief	209	24	1	3
FRONTIER, defense of northern	7	39	2	6
FRY, BENJAMIN, indemnity for losses sustained	87	19	2	1
FRYE, JED, claim for relief	142	30	2	4
GENERAL ARMSTRONG (brig), for relief of owners and crew	159	33	1	5
Do	1014	46	2	10
Do	207	47	1	11
GERMANY,				
Discriminating duties against, adopting	2682	48	2	12
Treaty of naturalization to negotiate with	1898	47	2	11
Treaty with, notice for termination of	96	44	1	8
Treaty of 1868, termination of, with	2590	48	2	12
GHENT, TREATY OF. (*See* TREATIES.)				
GIBSON, WALTER M., arrest and imprisonment of, by Government of Holland	307	34	1	5
Do	511	35	1	6
GILMORE, ROBERT, indemnity for loss of property	290	24	2	3
GLOVER, WILLIAM R., claim for relief	126	33	2	5
GOLDSBURY, SAMUEL, indemnity for loss of property	799	25	2	3
GRACIE, ARCHIBALD, and others, claim for relief	127	18	1	1
GREAT BRITAIN,				
Act of August, 1882, passed by Parliament respecting importation of goods	96	17	2	1
Arrests of American citizens in	44	40	3	7
Citizenship of such citizens of United States as have become naturalized subjects of, providing for restoration to	670	46	2	10
Do	22	47	1	11
Destruction of Houses of Parliament and other public buildings in London, attempted	2600	48	2	12
Mail service between United States and, to establish	311	24	2	3
Northwest boundary line between United States and		42	2	7
Terminating convention of 1818 between United States and	34	29		4
Trade with British possessions in West Indies	650	27	2	4
Treaty between United States and, relating to fisheries, to carry into effect	52	42	3	
Treaty of 1871 relative to fisheries, to terminate certain provisions in	235	47	1	1

Subject.	Report.	Congress.	Session.	Volume.
HN, claim for relief	482	43	1	7
SEPH, claim for diplomatic services	147	34	3	5
EXPORTATIONS.)				
JAMIN E., claim for diplomatic services	90	26	2	4
es at, investigation of	281	36	1	6
n of authorities of, over Punta Arenas	221	36	1	6
OBERT E., *et al.*, claim under treaty with Spain of 1819 for losses red	201	19	1	1
ULIUS, remission of duties on gifts tendered	96	45	3	9
KELLEY, claimants on France for spoliations	268	20	1	1
NDS, laws relative to, suspension of	282	48	1	12
XICO, piracy in, to suppress	124	18	1	1
ATHANIEL, claim for prize money	380	25	2	3
S., claim for relief	298	21	1	2
OHN P., claim for relief	2807	49	2	12
IAM J., claim for relief	2689	48	2	12
SHERIES COMMISSION, alleged frauds in proofs before	329	46	3	10
NIUS, claim for relief	453	22	1	2
RAHAM S., indemnity for property destroyed by Spanish priva- Fortune	22	18	1	1
MERICAN PACKET COMPANY, tonnage duties to, refund of	17	46	1	10
ROBERT M., claim for diplomatic services	292	34	1	5
ALEXANDER, claim for diplomatic services	820	24	1	3
Do	566	25	2	3
Do	342	26	1	3
OHN and P. R., claim of Maine for advances made to	249	24	2	3
ICHARD, claim for diplomatic services	265	23	2	2
Do	861	[illegible]	2	2
OBERT, *et al.*, indemnity for losses sustained	814	43	1	7
VILLIAM H., claim for additional pay	378	21	1	2
WELL, claim for relief of administration	16	27	2	4
of steamers jointly with Government of France between New and Havre, to establish	944	27	2	4
ISLANDS, treaty of 1875 with, to terminate	*1860	47	2	11
T INDIES,				
l intercourse with, to extend	428	26	1	4
d diplomatic relations with, to establish	426	26	1	4
Y. (*See* IMMIGRATION.)				
, FRANCIS, to adjudicate claims of	183	20	1	1
nish brig), claim of owners of	65	16	1	1
Do	100	21	2	2
NJAMIN, indemnity for loss of slave	415	23	1	2
Do	500	24	1	3
Do	261	25	2	3
RY YOULE, charges against Halifax Fisheries Commission by	329	46	3	10
NJAMIN (widow of), indemnity for loss of slave	241	24	2	3
Do	262	25	2	3
Do	767	29	1	4
Do	81	30	1	4
HAEL, claim for diplomatic services	105	22	2	2
S, T. H., claim for relief	56	42	2	7
imprisonment of Walter M. Gibson by Government of	307	34	1	5
claims against, to adjust	87	19	2	1
IAM (administrator), indemnity for injuries received	218	19	1	1
IAM H., to allow him to accept medal from Emperor of Russia	482	48	1	12
ORT CHARGES, copies of, to purchase	2716	49	1	12
LLIAM, claim for additional pay	140	34	1	5
Do	479	35	1	6
N, J. P., claim for expenses incurred in diplomatic service	115	24	2	3
Do	749	25	2	3
N, HENRY, claim for relief	265	20	1	1
B, claim for relief against Venezuela	18	33	1	5
ON (*see also* EMIGRATION),				
restrict	111	45	3	9
aty stipulations, to amend act of May, 1882, making	614	48	1	12
S, regulating vessels carrying, and providing for care on landing of.	1	46	2	10
IES,				
Netherlands, imposed by tariff act of 1842	534	28	1	4
ing duties against Germany, to adopt	2682	48	2	12
Portugal, imposed by tariff act of 1842	124	28	1	4
Do	107	31	2	4
N, plaster to United States from British possessions in North ica and West India Islands prohibited	83	14	1	1
T, American seamen, right of, against	13	40	2	7
FUND,				
return of balance of	113	45	3	9
Do	1124	46	2	10
Do	970	48	1	12

* Parts 1, 2.

Subject.	Report.	Congress.	Session.	Volume.
INDEMNITY FUND—Continued.				
Japanese, distribution of	79	43	2	7
Do	153	43	2	7
Disposal of balance of	913	45	2	9
Do	669	46	2	10
Return balance of	138	47	1	11
INTERNATIONAL AMERICAN CONGRESS.				
President of United States authorized to invite foreign governments to send delegates to	1646	49	1	12
For international conference on arbitration and commerce with South American States	*1648	49	1	12
INTERNATIONAL ARBITRATION, international conference, to provide for, on	*1648	49	1	12
INTERNATIONAL FISHERIES EXHIBITION, providing for United States to attend and take part in	1413	47	1	11
INTERNATIONAL LAWS, congress of nations to prepare code of	671	29	1	4
INTERNATIONAL PRISON CONGRESS, President to appoint a commission to	1289	48	1	12
INTEROCEANIC CANALS (*see also* CLAYTON-BULWER TREATY),				
Monroe doctrine as applied to construction of, to enforce	224	46	3	10
Nicaragua Maritime Canal Company, to incorporate	†1696	47	1	11
INVASION, defense of United States against, additional powers to President for the	314	25	3	3
INVESTIGATION, Emma Mine Company, connection of General Robert C. Schenck, United States minister to Court of St. James, with the	579	44	1	8
IRELAND,				
National aid for the suffering poor of	116	37	2	6
Do	465	46	2	10
Struggle of, for independence, resolutions on	100	39	1	6
IRISH, JOSEPH, to accept decoration from Spanish Government	97	45	3	9
IRWIN, W. W., claim for relief of widow	99	35	2	6
ITALY, minister plenipotentiary to, to establish full mission by	80	30	1	4
JACOBS, ENOCH, compensation for diplomatic services	560	43	1	7
JAMES LAWRENCE (brig), to indemnify owners of	247	20	1	1
JAPANESE INDEMNITY FUND. (*See* INDEMNITY FUND.)				
JARERO, JOSE MARIA, claim for relief	317	33	1	5
JENNINGS, W. K., and others, indemnity for loss of property	148	34	3	5
JOHNSTON, JOHN and ALEXANDER, indemnity for losses sustained	87	19	2	1
JONES, EMANUEL, claim for relief of widow	932	47	1	11
JONES, RICHARD B., additional compensation for diplomatic services	60	37	2	6
JONES, THOS. AP CATESBY, claim for diplomatic services	920	25	2	3
Do	92	28	2	4
Do	108	29	1	4
JONES, WILLIAM D., claim for diplomatic services	633	26	1	3
JORDAN, JOSIAH, and others, indemnity under Florida treaty for property captured	90	18	1	1
JOSEPH (schooner), claim for relief of owners	873	25	2	3
KEENAN, JAMES, claim for relief	49	38	1	6
KENOFSKY, MARTIN, claim for relief	1569	48	1	12
KENT, J. F., to accept testimonial from governor-general of Canada	401	47	1	11
KEY, RICHARD, and others, claimants under treaty of 1819 with Spain	201	19	1	1
KING, RALPH, claim for diplomatic services	186	34	3	5
Do	507	36	1	6
Do	29	37	2	6
Do	49	42	2	7
Do	776	43	1	7
Do	528	44	1	8
Do	1780	48	1	12
KRITTMAN, JOSEPH, claim for injuries received from the Government of Hamburg	39	20	2	1
LA ABRA MINING COMPANY (*see also* MEXICAN AWARDS),				
Claims of, to suspend payment of	27	45	2	9
Do	1702	46	2	10
Distribution of award to, to amend act of 1878 for	3474	49	1	12
LAFFITTE & CO., claim for relief	918	27	2	4
LANDREAU, JOHN C., claim of, against Peru Government	114	45	3	9
LA REINTRIE, HENRY, claim for extra compensation	122	31	1	4
Do	123	31	1	4
LASKER, EDWARD, resolutions in House Representatives on the death of	968	48	1	12
LAVALLETTE, E. A. F., claim for relief	98	33	1	5
LEDYARD, HENRY, claim for diplomatic services	26	28	2	4
LEIPSKER, MATILDA, claim for relief	251	43	2	7
LEPAPE, LEONARD, indemnity for property destroyed by Mexicans	43	35	1	6
LEVY, JONAS P., claim of, to adjudicate	317	33	1	5
Do	610	35	1	6
Do	98	35	2	6
Do	110	45	3	9
Do	1128	46	2	10
Do	1548	47	1	11
LEWIS, REBECCA, claim for relief	939	47	1	11

*And views of minority. †Parts 1, 2, 3.

Subject.	Report.	Congress.	Session.	Volume.
TY ENLIGHTENING THE WORLD. (*See* BARTHOLDI STATUE OF LIBERTY.)				
RY, purchase of General Washington's	381	23	1	2
T, GEORGE W., compensation for diplomatic services	143	34	1	5
Do	508	35	1	6
STON, JOSEPH W., claim for relief of widow	96	45	3	9
Do	86	46	2	10
N (*see also* GREAT BRITAIN).				
rican consul at, increase of allowance to	7	23	2	2
Do	119	24	1	3
rican Exposition to be held May, 1886, at, resolution in House on	377	40	1	12
HARLES CHAILTE, claim for relief	2261	48	2	12
TUDE, international convention to establish a prime meridian	1519	47	1	11
ELSON (British schooner), relief of owners of	3743	49	2	12
INE, Sir LAMBTON, thanks of Congress to	781	43	1	7
ELIPHALET, claim for relief	25	19	1	1
LEY, D. S., relief of widow of	95	33	1	5
Do	336	34	1	5
Do	81	37	2	6
JAMES, indemnity for loss of property destroyed by the French	978	25	2	3
GAN, JOHN, indemnity for loss of property and imprisonment by British Government	478	23	1	2
D, ALEXANDER, imprisonment of	162	26	2	3
ION, Rev. JOHN, imprisonment for life by Canadian authorities, investigation of	7	40	2	7
ER, ALEXANDER, indemnity for acts of violence by French Government	32	17	1	1
ORE, MOROCCO, consulariship at, to establish	170	15	1	1
ERVICE, establishment of, between Great Britain and United States	311	24	2	3
ns of, to adjudicate, under treaty with Great Britain of August, 1842	366	35	1	6
urbances upon Aroostook River in	314	25	3	3
ch spoliation claims of citizens of, to adjudicate	87	19	2	1
eys paid to John and Phineas R. Harford, to reimburse for	249	24	2	3
consul at, fixing salary of	564	36	1	6
A. DUDLEY, compensation for diplomatic services	254	35	2	6
NG, CORNELIUS, indemnity for loss of slave taken by the British	291	24	2	3
Do	263	25	2	3
Do	706	29	1	4
Do	82	30	1	4
IME CANAL COMPANY OF NICARAGUA, to incorporate	*1698	47	1	11
GEORGE P., compensation for judicial services under act of August 11, 1848, while minister resident to Ottoman Porte	166	34	1	5
Do	168	35	1	6
Do	350	36	1	6
N, J. E., claim for additional compensation as acting chargé d'affaires at Lisbon	115	37	2	6
Do	47	39	1	6
Do	8	42	2	7
N, JACOB L., compensation for diplomatic services	516	30	1	4
ship), claim of owners for relief	1041	25	2	3
AND, claim of merchants, against France for spoliations committed since 1806	127	18	1	1
Do	87	19	2	1
CHUSETTS,				
s of merchants of, against France for spoliations committed since 1806	94	18	1	1
s of State, to adjudicate under treaty with Great Britain of August, 1842	366	35	1	6
RMAN, GEORGE F., imprisonment by Paraguayan authorities of	65	41	2	7
R, THOMAS W., claim for relief	126	33	2	5
RICHARD W., indemnity under treaty of February 22, 1819, with Spain	174	19	1	1
Do	58	20	1	1
Do	316	22	1	2
Do	167	23	1	2
Do	457	27	2	4
Do	94	30	1	4
Do	5	33	1	5
acceptance of, by President of United States presented by President of Colombia	170	21	1	2
NTILE MUTUAL INSURANCE COMPANY, claim for relief (Caldera claims)	264	44	1	8
AN AWARDS,				
ibution of, to amend act of 1878 for	3428	49	1	12
Do	3474	49	1	12
nding payment of claims under	27	45	2	9
Do	1702	46	2	10
AN BORDER,				
ction of, in Texas along Rio Grande River	701	45	2	9
tigation of troubles in Texas along	701	45	2	9

* Parts 1, 2, 3.

Subject.	Report.	Congress.	Session.	Volume.
MEXICAN CLAIMS COMMISSION (*see also* MEXICAN AWARDS).				
Appropriation made for, distribution of	614	44	1	8
La Abra Silver Mining Company, and of Benjamin Weil on the American docket of the late, suspending payment of claims of	27	45	2	9
Do	1702	46	2	10
Organization of, providing for	505	28	1	3
Private claims by United States citizens upon Mexico to be referred to	320	25	3	3
MEXICAN GOVERNMENT, thanks of Congress to, tendering	1015	46	2	10
MEXICAN WAR. (*See* WAR WITH MEXICO.)				
MEXICO,				
Adjustment of claims against	1096	27	2	4
Boundary line between United States and Texas and, defining	151	28	1	4
Do	70	29	2	4
Commercial relations with, to advance closer	1647	49	1	12
Convention between United States and, continuation of	614	44	1	8
Diplomatic relations between United States and	129	38	1	6
Political relations between United States and	281	24	2	3
Do	1056	25	2	3
Private claims by citizens of United States upon, to be referred to Mexican Claims Commission	320	25	3	3
Treaty with, to establish further	108	45	3	9
MICHEL, COLIN (executor), claim for relief	209	24	1	3
MICKLE, CALVIN (executor), claim for relief	209	24	1	3
MIDDLETON, ARTHUR, compensation for diplomatic services	993	27	2	4
MILITARY and NAVAL ATTACHÉS, Army and Navy officers, assignment of, as	3145	49	1	12
MINISTERS PLENIPOTENTIARY (*see also* CONSULAR AND DIPLOMATIC SERVICE), number of, reduction in	180	22	1	2
MISDEMEANOR, fitting out and equipping vessels of war for foreign countries.	80	41	2	7
MONROE DOCTRINE. (*See* INTEROCEANIC CANALS; CLAYTON-BULWER TREATY.)				
MOORE, FREDERICK G., present from foreign government, acceptance of, by	60	44	2	8
MOORHEAD, WILLIAM G., claim for diplomatic services	368	35	1	6
MORGAN, JOHN, and others, claim for relief	53	26	2	3
MOROCCO, consulship at Magadore in, to establish	170	15	1	1
MORROW, JAMES, claim for relief	171	34	1	5
MORSE, ISAAC E., claim for relief of widow	57	42	2	7
MULLIGAN, JANE, claim for relief	1113	47	1	11
MULLOWNY, JOHN, claim for relief of estate	460	23	1	2
MURAD, G. S., claim for relief	168	35	2	6
NAGLE, DAVID, claim for relief of heir	209	24	1	3
NAPLES,				
Chargés d'affaires, to abolish mission of, to	80	30	1	4
Claims against, for spoliations on American commerce, to adjudicate	87	19	2	1
NATIONAL PEACE CONGRESS, establishment of, for settlement of national disputes	979	25	2	3
NATURALIZATION. (*See* CITIZENSHIP.)				
NATURALIZATION TREATY (*see also* GERMANY), to negotiate, with Germany.	[illegible]	47	2	11
NAVIGATION,				
Amazon River,				
Negotiation for free, of	95	33	2	5
Light-houses, buoys, &c., on Bahama Banks for benefit of, erection of	29	18	2	1
Saint Lawrence River, measures for securing free, of	295	31	1	4
NAVY, officers of, assignment as naval attachés to foreign legations of	3145	49	1	12
NETH, LEWIS, claim for relief under Florida treaty	55	20	2	1
NETHERLANDS, duty on coffee imported from the	534	28	1	4
Do	511	35	1	6
NEUTRAL RELATIONS, amending Revised Statutes to effectually preserve, with foreign countries	169	30	1	6
NEW BRUNSWICK, commercial intercourse with	301	25	3	3
NEW GRENADA. (*See* SPANISH PROVINCES.)				
NEWBURYPORT, MASSACHUSETTS, claim of citizens of, for payment of French spoliation claims	202	19		
NEW HAMPSHIRE,				
Accounts of State, providing for settlement of	176	25		
Claims of citizens of, payment of, for damages under French spoliation measure.	87	19		
NEW YORK, claim of citizens of, payment of, for damages under French spoliation measure	87	19		
NEW YORK MUTUAL INSURANCE COMPANY, claim for relief (Caldera claims)	264	44		
NICARAGUA ACCESSORY TRANSIT COMPANY, claim for damages to property at Greytown	281	36		
NICARAGUA CANAL. (*See* MARITIME CANAL COMPANY).				
NICARAGUA SHIP-CANAL, construction of	1698	47		11
NICARAGUAN CLAIMS, to adjudicate	396	46	3	10
Do	255	47		11
NORTHEASTERN FRONTIER. (*See* FRONTIER.)				
NORTH GERMAN CONFEDERATION. (*See* GERMAN.)				
NORTH GERMAN LLOYD STEAMSHIP COMPANY, tonnage duties to, refunding of	17	46		10
NORTHWESTERN BOUNDARY COMMISSION, appointment of	19	41	3	

Subject.	Report.	Congress.	Session.	Volume.
TIA, commercial intercourse with	301	23	2	3
LEGRAPH CABLES, concessions granted certain companies to lay..	35	41	2	7
Do	1	41	3	7
AFFIC, execution of treaty with China respecting	3801	49	2	12
y line of, defining	34	20	1	4
on of citizens of United States residing in, providing for	101	25	2	3
y of, matters affecting	69	22	1	4
October, 1818, with Great Britain affecting, to abrogate	34	20	1	4
ES L., claim for relief of widow	823	43	1	7
rig), indemnity to owners of, for seizure of property by Portuguese vernment	24	20	2	1
ORGE H., claim for relief	4039	49	2	12
VANNI, claim for relief	329	48	1	12
Congress of, invitation to United States to participate in	137	19	1	1
XA, MICHAEL, claim for relief	210	35	1	6
Y.				
ies between United States and Republic of, to adjust	365	35	1	6
ment of certain American citizens by authorities of	65	41	2	7
POSITION, invitation of France to United States Government to participate in the International Industrial Exhibition (1878)	3	45	1	9
ILLIAM C., claim for prize money	297	24	2	3
Do	369	25	2	3
ETER, compensation for diplomatic services	516	30	1	4
Do	141	34	1	5
S, reduction of fees on	4046	49	2	12
, HIRAM, claim for relief	63	30	1	6
NGRESS. (*See also* ARBITRATION.)				
NGRESS, to establish National	879	23	2	3
RY E., claim for relief	28	39	2	6
R, ANTONIO, claim for indemnity from Hayti	51	45	2	9
N, JOHN S., compensation for extra diplomatic service	1	34	1	5
VANIA, merchants of, for payment of French spoliation claims	127	18	1	1
Do	87	19	2	1
L. and TRAUTMAN, compensation for loss of property	266	43	2	7
plomatic relations with, to establish	1648	47	1	11
e CHILI AND PERU.)				
HADDEUS (executor of), claim for relief against Venezuela	18	33	1	5
N, compensation for diplomatic services	168	34	1	5
J. T., claim for relief	474	47	1	11
Do	121	48	1	12
JAMES C., compensation for diplomatic services	49	35	1	6
SOMERVILLE (administrator), claim for indemnity under Florida aty	235	24	1	3
Do	503	25	2	3
Do	948	27	2	4
ed by Spanish privateers on American commerce	47	18	2	1
ion of, in neighborhood of Cuba and Porto Rico	124	18	1	1
prohibiting exportation of or importation of, to or from British possions, except in American vessels	83	14	1	1
RGES. (*See* HUNTER'S PORT CHARGES.)				
ALEXIS, indemnity for loss of tobacco	104	31	2	4
. D., claim for relief	97	33	1	5
ANTON L. C., claim for additional pay	351	36	1	6
, import duties on wines from	124	28	1	4
Do	107	31	2	4
IN, claim for relief	1467	49	1	12
acceptance by United States agents or consuls from foreign Governnts of	107	21	2	2
Do	302	23	1	2
T OF UNITED STATES,				
ce of medal from President Liberator of Colombia by	170	21	1	2
al powers for defense of United States against invasion to, giving	314	25	3	3
ed to protect rights of American fisheries	4087	49	2	12
tional duty and powers of, connected with diplomatic negotiations	129	38	1	6
RIDIAN. (*See* LONGITUDE.)				
MES B. L., claim against Mexican Government, for rehearing of	115	45	3	9
, Americans confined as, at Van Dieman's Land	85	28	2	4
D BILLS, number and amount of each bill drawn by foreign agents United States on Navy Department since January 1, 1829	466	22	1	2
NISTERS, revision of laws relating to direct and contingent exses of	220	21	1	2
Do	333	22	1	2
ENAS, jurisdiction of authorities of Greytown over	251	36	1	6
ARCUS, claim for relief	61	44	2	8
ONDY, libellous article against, investigation of	212	20	1	1
e FENIAN RAID.)				
H. T. A., claim for relief	166	35	2	6
EXCHANGE, rate at which bills drawn by United States foreign nts have been negotiated prior to and since January, 1829	466	23	1	

Subject.	Report.	Congress.	Session.	Volume.
RAY, JAMES, claim for relief	247	20	1	1
REA, JAMES, claim for relief	109	43	1	7
Do	816	47	1	11
RECIPROCITY TREATIES. (*See* TREATIES.)				
REGIE CONTRACTS. (*See* TOBACCO.)				
REID, SAM. C., claim for relief	2194	48	2	12
REINTRIE, HENRY LA, extra compensation for services	122	31	1	4
Do	123	31	1	4
REVISED STATUTES,				
Amending statutes affecting neutrality laws	100	39	1	6
To amend and repeal,				
Section 1742, pay of diplomatic and consular officers	466	46	2	10
Section 2931, tonnage duties	124	45	2	9
REYNOLDS, L. K., foreign decoration, authorized to accept	1792	47	1	11
RICE, E. E., claim for relief	90	45	3	9
RICH, WILLIAM, compensation for diplomatic services	209	24	2	5
Do	170	25	1	3
RIDGELY, CHARLES G., claim for expenses incurred in diplomatic service	118	24	2	3
Do	489	25	2	3
Do	498	26	1	3
Do	191	30	1	4
RIGHT OF EXPATRIATION. (*See* EXPATRIATION.)				
RIGHT OF SEARCH, question of	13	40	2	7
RIGHTS OF UNITED STATES CITIZENS, protection of	210	31	1	4
RILEY, JAMES, *et al.*, claim on France for spoliations	263	20	1	1
RIO GRANDE BORDER. (*See* TEXAS; MEXICAN BORDER.)				
RIVERS AND HARBORS,				
Amazon River, free navigation of	95	33	2	5
Columbia River, providing for protection of citizens of United States trading on	101	25	3	3
Saint Francis River, international bridge over	226	46	3	10
Do	234	47		11
Saint John River, international bridge over	226	46	3	10
Do	234	47	1	11
Saint Lawrence River, free navigation of	295	31		4
ROBERTS, EDMUND, claim for additional pay	25	23		2
Do	317	25		3
ROBERTS, ROBERT, claim for loss of property under Spanish treaty of 1819	874	25	2	3
ROBINSON, GEORGE F., claim for relief	33	41	3	7
ROGERS, H. GOLD, extra compensation for diplomatic services	308	29	1	4
Do	20	44	1	8
ROSARIO AND CARMEN MINING COMPANY, rehearing claim of, against Mexico	700	45	2	9
RUGER, EMIL, claim against Government of Denmark	20	41	2	7
RUSH, BENJAMIN, extra compensation for diplomatic services	291	31	1	4
RUSSIA, treaty with, consideration of, upon purchase of Russian America	37	40	2	7
RYDER, HENRY B., claim for relief	259	43	2	7
SAINT FRANCIS RIVER, construction of international bridge over	226	46	3	10
Do	234	47	1	11
SAINT JOHN RIVER, construction of international bridge over	226	46	3	10
Do	234	47	1	11
SAINT LAWRENCE RIVER, free navigation of	295	31	1	4
SAINT MICHAEL, consulate at, to establish	29	43	1	7
SALARIES (*see also* CONSULAR AND DIPLOMATIC SERVICE), consular and diplomatic officers, regulating pay of	466	46	2	10
SANDS, J. R., claim for relief	96	33	1	5
SANDWICH ISLANDS,				
Commercial and political intercourse with	93	27	3	4
Commissioner to, increasing salary of	285	29		4
SARDINIA, chargés d'affaires to, abolishing of mission by	80	30		4
SAVAGE, HENRY, claim for diplomatic services	60	43		7
SCHENCK, Hon. ROBERT M., connection of, with the Emma mine and Machado claim	123	44		8
SCHIEFFELIN, JACOB and HENRY, claim for relief	85	17	1	1
Do	37	17	2	1
SCHUCHARDT, WILLIAM, compensation for extra services	101	45	3	9
Do	1703	46	2	10
Do	356	47	1	11
SCOTT, ALEXANDER, claim for relief	182	20	1	1
Do	72	20	2	1
Do	20	21	1	2
Do	427	23		2
Do	550	24		3
Do	518	25		3
Do	201	26	2	3
SEAMEN, impressment of American	13	40	2	7
SEYS, JOHN, claim for relief	83	41	3	7
SHAW, Lieutenant, U. S. A., acceptance by, of portraits of governors-general of Canada	401	47	1	11
SHEPARD, CHARLES O., claim for diplomatic services	262	43	2	7
SHIP-CANALS (*see also* CANALS), construction of Nicaraguan Canal	1698	47	1	11

Subject.	Report.	Congress.	Session.	Volume.
...GREAVES, SAMUEL, accounts of, to settle and close	54	20	2	1
Do	106	21	1	1
...ADE, ELIZA A., claim for relief	[illegible]	27	2	4
...DAT, JOHN D., claim for relief	471	22	1	2
...H, JOHN ADAMS, claim for diplomatic services	541	24	1	3
Do	[illegible]	25	2	3
Do	748	27	2	4
SMITH, JONATHAN S., indemnity for property lost in Algiers	95	18	1	1
Do	[illegible]	20	1	1
SOUTH AMERICA, commission for promoting commercial intercourse with, to appoint	1457	47	1	11
Do	1445	48	1	12
Do	1846	49	1	12
Do	1847	49	1	12
SPAIN,				
Claim of citizens of Florida under treaty of 1819, to pay	112	19	1	1
Do	99	20	2	1
Do	[illegible]	22	1	2
Do	[illegible]	23	1	2
Do	1206	47	1	11
Contest between Cuba and	80	41	2	7
Differences with Government of, to adjudicate unadjusted	[illegible]	25	2	3
SPALDING, BASIL, relief of representatives of	69	28	2	[illegible]
SPANISH PRIVATEERS, piracy and outrages on American commerce by	47	18	2	1
SPANISH PROVINCES, recognition of late provinces in America	73	17	1	1
SPANISH VESSELS, tonnage duties on	692	26	1	3
Do	42	27	2	4
Do	82	27	3	4
Do	428	29	1	4
...RAGUE, HORATIO, claim for relief	205	[illegible]	1	4
...IER, E. GEORGE, compensation for diplomatic service	[illegible]	26	1	6
Do	[illegible]	26	1	6
...ATE DEPARTMENT. (*See* DEPARTMENT OF STATE.)				
...ATE, SECRETARY OF. (*See* SECRETARY OF STATE.)				
...AMERS. (*See* VESSELS.)				
...WART, ARCHIBALD, claim for relief	32	17	1	1
...HAM, A. S., acceptance of medal from British Government by	1707	47	1	12
...MARINE CABLES, protection of, providing for	3198	49	1	12
SUBSIDY, line of steamers, jointly with France, between New York and Havre, Government aid to establish	944	27	2	4
SUN MUTUAL INSURANCE COMPANY, claim for relief (Caldera claims)	264	44	1	8
SWAN, BENJ. L., claim for relief against Venezuela	18	33	1	5
SWATOW, consul at, fixing salary of	564	36	1	6
SWEETZER, SETH, compensation for diplomatic services	131	27	3	4
Do	37	28	1	4
Do	36	29	1	4
TAYLOR, GEORGE, indemnity for spoliations prior to 1800	82	20	2	1
TELEGRAPH LINES,				
Concessions granted companies to lay submarine	1	41	3	7
Protection of submarine	3198	49	1	12
TELLER, WOOLSEY, claim against Nicaragua for personal injuries received	96	45	3	9
Do	86	46	2	10
TEN BROOK, ANDREW, claim for additional pay	50	42	2	7
Do	137	43	2	7
TEXAS,				
Boundary line between United States, Mexico, and	151	28	1	4
Recognition of the independence of	854	24	1	3
Do	240	24	2	3
Rio Grande border in, protection of	701	45	2	9
THANKS OF CONGRESS,				
Tendering to,				
Lorraine, Sir Lampton	781	48	1	7
Mexican Government	1015	46	2	10
THOMSON, ALEXANDER, claim for relief	108	43	1	7
THORNDIKE, ISRAEL, indemnity for loss of vessel	25	19	1	1
TOBACCO, to open negotiations with certain foreign Governments relative to importation of tobacco into their dominions	1259	46	2	10
TONNAGE DUTIES,				
Compagnie Générale Transatlantique, claim for alleged illegal exaction of	3476	49	2	12
Foreign vessels, to amend rates on	333	24	1	3
North German Lloyd Steamship Company and Hamburg-American Packet Company, to refund to	17	46	1	10
Repayment of, amending section 2931 Revised Statutes, authorizing	124	45	2	9
Spanish vessels, duties levied upon, in ports of United States	692	26	1	3
Do	42	27	2	4
Do	82	27	3	4
Do	428	29	1	4
TREATIES,				
British provinces, appointment of commissioners to ascertain and report basis for reciprocity treaty with	1127	46	2	10
China, to execute, with, on importation of opium	2091	49	2	12

Subject.	Report.	Congress.	Session.	Volume.
TREATIES—Continued.				
Enforcement of certain provisions of, made with United States and foreign countries	422	29	1	4
France, to execute treaty of July 4, 1831, made	133	22	2	2
Germany, termination of, made with	96	44	1	8
Great Britain,				
To carry into effect treaty relating to fish and fisheries made with	52	42	3	7
To terminate certain articles of treaty of Washington upon fisheries made with	1275	46	2	10
Do	1746	46	2	10
Hawaiian Islands, to terminate treaty of 1875 with	1860	47	2	11
Mexico, establishing further provisions of, made with	108	45	3	9
Russia, consideration of purchase of Alaska under treaty with	37	40	2	7
Spain, payment of claims of citizens of Florida under treaty of 1819, with	112	19	1	1
Do	90	20	2	1
Do	223	22	1	2
Do	306	23	1	2
Do	227	46	3	10
Do	1866	47	1	11
TREATY-MAKING POWER, defining authority, duties, and extent of	225	46	3	10
TREATY OF GHENT, relief of claimants under the first article of	79	20	2	1
TREATY OF WASHINGTON. (*See* TREATIES.)				
TRESCOTT, WILLIAM H. (*See* CHILI AND PERU.)				
TUDOR, WILLIAM, Jr., relief of representatives of	290	24	2	3
Do	204	25	2	3
UNITED STATES, mail service between Great Britain and, to establish	311	24	2	3
URRIZA, FRANCISCO LOPEZ, claim for relief	227	35	1	6
VAIL, AARON, relief of estate	23	18	2	1
Do	687	25	2	3
VALVERDE, YSABEL OSORNO DE, indemnity under treaty of 1819 with Spain for loss of property	49	20	1	1
VAN DIEMAN'S LAND, American prisoners confined at	85	28	2	4
VAN NESS, CORNELIUS P., salary of, to refund part of	929	27	2	4
VENABLE, JANE, claim for relief	315	36	1	6
Do	328	46	3	10
Do	1814	48	1	12
VENEZUELA (*see also* SPANISH PROVINCES),				
Claims of American citizens against, to adjust	79	41	2	7
Do	29	42	2	7
Arrest and imprisonment of John E. Wheelock, claim against, for	1238	48	1	12
VENEZUELA AWARDS, commission on, to appoint new	1758	47	1	11
Do	2610	48	2	12
VENEZUELA CLAIMS,				
Adjudication and settlement of	4	42	3	7
Commission on, appointment of	327	46	3	10
VENEZUELAN MIXED COMMISSION,				
Appointment of a new	327	46	3	10
Awards made by, investigation of	787	44	1	8
Do	702	45	2	9
Do	805	45	3	9
VESSELS,				
Line of steamers between Havre and New York, to establish	944	27	2	4
List of American vessels seized, detained, or warned off from Canadian ports	4067	49	2	13
Tonnage duties,				
To amend rates of, on foreign	333	24	1	3
Levied on Spanish vessels in American ports	632	26	1	3
Do	42	27	2	4
Do	82	27	3	4
Do	428	29	1	4
VIGNAUD, HENRY, to permit him to receive foreign decoration	1708	47	1	11
Do	2656	48	2	12
VIRGINIA, claim citizens, under first article of treaty of Ghent	79	20	2	1
WAGGONER, HENRY O., claim of creditors for relief	745	47	1	11
WALKER, WILLIAM, claim for diplomatic services	483	43	1	7
WALSH, CHARLES S., claim for diplomatic services	639	25	2	3
WALSH, ROBERT M., claim for diplomatic services	106	31	2	4
WAR WITH MEXICO,				
Declaration of	752	29	1	4
President's message on	70	29	2	4
WARD, THOMAS W., claim for relief	100	35	2	6
WASHINGTON, General GEORGE, library and papers belonging to, purchase of	381	23	1	2
WASHINGTON TREATY. (*See* TREATIES.)				
WATER-WITCH (United States steamship), attack by Paraguayan forces upon	365	35	1	6
WATSON, AUGUSTUS, survey of railroad in Liberia	349	45	2	9
WEBSTER, WILLIAM, claim for relief	1787	46	2	10
Do	1543	48	1	12
WEEMS, STEPHEN H., compensation for diplomatic services	142	34		5
Do	226	35		6
WEIL, BENJAMIN, claim against Mexico	27	45		9
Do	1702	46	2	10
Do	3428	49	1	13

Subject.	Report.	Congress.	Session.	Volume.
JOHN, *et al.*, indemnity under French spoliation prior to 1800	16	27	2	4
FARGO & CO., claim for relief	2654	48	2	12
INDIES, piracy in, to suppress	124	18	1	1
WILLIAM B., claim for relief	406	42	1	7
TON'S DIGEST OF INTERNATIONAL LAW, printing of, to authorise	2518	49	1	12
TON, HENRY, claim for relief	213	24	1	3
LER, JOHN H., claim for relief	206	35	1	6
LOCK, JOHN E., arrest and imprisonment in Venezuela of	1328	48	1	12
AMS, JAMES, claimant for indemnity under Florida treaty	235	24	1	3
Do	503	25	2	3
MS, S. WELLS, for services as interpreter	57	34	1	5
, import duties on wines from Portugal	124	28	1	4
Do	107	31	2	4
J. and W. R., claim for relief	409	43	1	7
JOHN, *et al.*, claim for relief	873	26	2	3
HOUSE, H. E., rehearing of claim against Mexico	115	45	3	9

REPORTS

OF THE

[C]OMMITTEE ON INDIAN AFFAIRS,

HOUSE OF REPRESENTATIVES,

FROM THE ORGANIZATION OF THE COMMITTEE, DECEMBER 17, 1821, TO THE CLOSE OF THE FORTY-NINTH CONGRESS, 1887, INCLUSIVE.

IN TEN VOLUMES.

COMPILED, UNDER THE DIRECTION OF THE JOINT COMMITTEE ON PRINTING,

BY

T. H. McKEE,

CLERK, DOCUMENT ROOM, UNITED STATES SENATE.

WASHINGTON:
GOVERNMENT PRINTING OFFICE.
1887.

9220 IND H

FORTY-NINTH CONGRESS, FIRST SESSION.

[PUBLIC RESOLUTION—No. 24.]

Joint resolution authorizing the preparation of a compilation of the reports of committees of the Senate and House of Representatives.

Resolved by the Senate and House of Representatives of the United States of America in Congress assembled, That there be prepared under the direction of the Joint Committee of Printing, a compilation of the reports of the Senate and House of Representatives from the Fourteenth to the Forty-eighth Congress, inclusive, classified by committees, arranged, indexed, and bound in suitable volumes for the use of the standing committees of the two Houses of Congress. And the sum of seven thousand seven hundred and fifty dollars, or so much thereof as may be found necessary, is hereby appropriated out of any money in the Treasury not otherwise appropriated, for the preparation of said work, which sum may be paid by the Secretary of the Treasury upon the order of the chairman of said Joint Committee, as additional pay or compensation to any officer or employee of the United States.

Resolved further, That the Clerk of the House and Secretary of the Senate be, and they are hereby directed, to procure and file, for the use of their respective Houses, copies of all reports made by each committee of all succeeding Congresses; and that the Clerk of the House and the Secretary of the Senate be, and they are hereby, authorized and directed at the close of each session of Congress, to cause said reports to be indexed and bound, one copy to be deposited in the library of each House and one copy in the room of the committee from which the reports emanated.

Approved, July 29, 1886.

2

COMPILER'S NOTICE.

This compilation embraces all the printed reports made by both Houses of Congress from the commencement of the Fourteenth to the close of the Forty-ninth Congress. They are classified by committees and arranged in numerical order. The collection for each committee is divided into volumes of suitable size. Each committee has a separate index, a copy being bound in each volume.

The SPECIAL and SELECT reports are all compiled in one collection having one index, a copy of which is bound in each volume.

The plan throughout the compilation is to place each report to the committee from which it was reported, without reference to the subject-matter.

The House and Senate reports are compiled separately. Care will be required in noticing the chronological order, as in some instances an entire session or Congress may not appear in certain volumes from the fact that during this period no reports were made by this committee.

T. H. McKEE.

INDEX

TO

REPORTS OF COMMITTEE ON INDIAN AFFAIRS,

HOUSE OF REPRESENTATIVES,

FROM DECEMBER 17, 1821, TO MARCH 4, 1887, INCLUSIVE.

Subject.	Report.	Congress.	Session.	Volume.
ABELL, G. B., & CO., claim for relief	287	20	1	3
ABSENTEE SHAWNEE LANDS, relief of settlers in Kansas upon	433	46	2	9
ABUSES, Indian affairs, investigation of, in	98	42	3	7
ADAMS, REBECCA, claim for relief	2129	48	1	10
Do	3679	49	2	10
AGENCIES, appropriation for 1827 as relates to certain Indian, estimate of	86	19	2	1
AGENTS,				
Disbursements of money by	409	47	1	9
Indian, to dispense with	2	46	2	9
Sale of timber at Green Bay by, to confirm action of	448	47	1	9
ALABAMA, claims of State for losses in Creek war, to audit	177	35	1	5
ALCOTT, SAMUEL, claim for relief	287	20	1	3
ALEXANDER, JAMES, claim for relief	131	24	1	2
ALLEGANY INDIANS OF NEW YORK, lease of lands, authorized to grant, and quiet title to	478	43	1	8
ALLEN, EUGENE B., claim for relief	490	47	1	9
ALLEN, GEORGE G., claim for relief	113	25	3	2
ALLEN, JOHN L., claim for relief	760	25	2	2
AL-LO-LAH (Miami chief), claim for relief	277	31	1	4
ALLOTMENT OF LANDS IN SEVERALTY. (*See* INDIANS.)				
ALSBURY, THOMAS J., claim for relief	291	35	1	5
AMERICAN INDIAN MISSION ASSOCIATION, spiritual and temporal interests of Indians, memorial on, by	751	29	1	3
ANDERSON, WILLIAM, claim for relief of representatives of	252	24	1	2
Do	284	25	3	2
ANNUITIES, distribution of, investigation of	98	42	3	7
APPALACHICOLA INDIANS, claim for relief under treaty of 1823 with Florida Indians	746	27	2	2
APPEL, DANIEL M., claim for relief	797	47	1	9
APPROPRIATIONS, estimate for Indian service (1827)	86	19	2	1
ARGENTI, FELIX, claim for relief	127	33	2	4
ARIZONA, Indian school at Yuma in, to establish	1731	48	1	10
ARIZONA NARROW-GAUGE RAILROAD COMPANY, right of way through White Mountain Indian Reservation to	4170	49	2	10
ARMBRISTER, MICHAEL, claim for relief	888	25	2	2
ARMSTRONG, WILLIAM, claim for relief	771	30	1	3
Do	17	31	2	4
ASSISTANT COMMISSIONER OF INDIAN AFFAIRS, office of, to create	1763	49	1	10
ATWATER, CALEB, claim for relief	151	27	3	2
BABBITT, ALMON W., claim for relief of heirs	131	35	2	5
Do	346	36	1	5
BABCOCK, CHARLES P., accounts of, to audit	7	34	1	4
BAINTER, JAMES, claim for relief	3193	49	1	10
BAKER, ROBERT, claim for relief	87	31	2	4
BANNOCK INDIANS, sale of lands by, to ratify	658	47	1	9
Do	659	47	1	9
BAPTIST MISSIONARY CONVENTION, settlement west of Mississippi River by, formation of	219	20	1	1
Do	247	21	1	1
BARROW, PORTER & CO., claim for relief	106	36	2	5
BEAUGRAND, JOHN B., claim for relief of heirs	514	35	1	5
BECK, JAMES P. (administrator), claim for relief	95	43	1	8
BEDDO, WILLIAM, *et al.*, claim for relief	1135	48	1	10
BEEBE, ELIJAH, claim for relief of widow and heirs	2	34	1	4
BEERS, CYRENUS, claim for relief	1346	48	1	10
Do	4152	49	2	10
BELL, SAMUEL W., claim for relief	80	20	2	3
BENT, ST. VRAIN & CO., Indian depredation claim	194	28	2	3

Subject.	Report.	Congress.	Session.	Volume.
BENT, W. W., claim for relief	151	25	2	5
BETTON, SOLOMON, accounts of, to audit	430	22	1	1
BEVERIDGE, BENJAMIN F., claim for relief	644	44	1	8
BILLINGS, CLARK'S FORK AND COOKE CITY RAILROAD, right of way through Crow Indian Reservation in Montana to	3605	49	2	10
Do	4132	49	2	10
BINGHAM, BENJAMIN F., claim for relief	123	46	2	9
BLACK BOB INDIANS, sale of lands to actual settlers only belonging to	*118	41	2	5
BLACK HAWK WAR. (*See* INDIAN WARS.)				
BLACK, JOHN, claim for relief	1419	46	2	9
Do	491	47	1	9
BODDY, LOUISA, claim for relief	1896	47	2	9
Do	9	48	1	10
BOGARDUS, JOHN L., claim for relief	312	24	1	2
BOGGS, JOSEPH, claim for relief	91	22	2	1
BONDS, payment of Indian war	86	45	3	9
Do	123	46	2	9
BOUNTIES, investigation of, paid under treaties and laws of Congress to all Indians	98	42	3	7
BOWERS & RICHARDS, claim for relief	1515	46	2	9
BOYER, CECILLE, claim for relief	127	20	1	1
BRANNIN, RICHARD, claim for relief	91	22	2	1
BRASHEARS, ZADOCK, *et al.*, claim for relief	479	26	1	2
BREARLEY, DAVID, claim for relief	125	22	2	1
BROTHERTON INDIANS, reservation in Wisconsin belonging to, partition off	445	44	1	8
Do	37	45	2	9
BROWN, BASIL, claim for relief	605	24	1	2
Do	524	25	2	2
BROWN, G. H., claim for relief	287	29	1	3
BROWN, H. M. C., claim for relief	532	36	1	5
Do	56	37	2	5
BROWN, JAMES, claim for relief	73	22	2	1
Do	122	24	1	2
Do	288	24	1	2
Do	685	25	2	2
BROWN, JOHN, claim for relief	73	22	2	1
Do	122	24	1	2
Do	288	24	1	2
BROWN, JOSEPH, claim for relief	311	22	1	1
Do	175	23	1	1
BROWN, LOYOL P., claim for relief	87	45	2	9
BROWN, MARGARET C., claim for relief	446	29	1	3
BROWNING, WILLIAM W., claim for relief	36	28	1	3
BRUQUIER, THEOPHILE, claim for relief	11	35	2	5
BRYAN, JOHN A., claim for relief	359	26	1	3
Do	700	29	1	3
Do	93	30	1	4
BUCKNER, SIMEON, claim for relief of widow	222	33	1	4
BUFFALO CREEK TREATY OF 1838, settlement with Indians under	2001	47	2	9
BULKLEY, F. C., claim for relief	1296	48	1	10
Do	2885	49	1	10
BUNCH, SAMUEL H., claim for relief of sureties of	98	31	1	4
Do	15	31	2	4
BURCHARD, J. L., claim for relief	1150	47	1	9
Do	1055	48	1	10
BUREAU OF INDIAN AFFAIRS,				
Accounts in, to audit unpaid	753	46	2	9
Do	812	47	1	9
Administration of, investigation of	778	43	1	8
Transfer to War Department of	240	44	1	8
Do	241	45	2	9
Do	92	45	3	9
Do	193	45	3	9
Do	1393	46	2	9
BURNHAM, GEORGE, claim for relief	1347	48	1	10
Do	2917	49	1	10
BUTLER, THAD., accounts of, to audit	1080	47	1	9
CADDO INDIANS, treaty with, frauds connected with	1035	27	2	3
CALIFORNIA,				
Indian war bonds of, payment of	86	45		
Do	123	46		
Mission Indians in, relief of	2559	49		10
CARRIER, ARTHUR J., claim for relief	231	46		
CATTARAUGUS INDIANS, lease of lands, authorized to grant, and quiet title to	473	43		
CEMETERY PURPOSES, title of lands for	1709	46		
CENSUS. (*See* INDIANS; STATISTICS.)				
CHAPMAN, THOMAS J., claim for relief	594	29		
CHASE, SILL & CO., claim for relief	287	29		
CHEATHAM, L. P., claim for relief	734	29		

* Parts 1, 2. † Joint report.

Subject.	Report.	Congress.	Session.	Volume.
CHENERY, RICHARD, claim for relief	150	25	2	5
Do	510	26	1	5
Do	3	27	3	5
CHEROKEE COMMISSIONERS, abstract of report of	391	28	1	3
CHEROKEE INDIANS (see also under title INDIANS),				
Citizenship of, commission on claims to	1307	48	1	10
Claims arising under treaty of 1828 with, to adjudicate	834	25	2	2
Claims arising under treaty of 1835–'36 with, to adjudicate	391	26	1	3
Condition of,				
Report of Colonel Hitchcock	960	27	2	3
Memorial from Massachusetts on	245	21	1	1
Domestic strife among, to protect from	683	29	1	3
Eastern band, to prosecute suits in Court of Claims	647	44	1	8
Do	486	45	2	9
Frauds committed upon, message of President on	271	27	3	3
Georgia,				
Claim of State for lands belonging to	397	21	1	1
To extinguish Indian title to land in, by purchase from	77	18	2	1
Government by, organization of independent system of	67	20	1	1
Intercourse with, against extending benefit of act to citizens of Texas on subject of	37	31	2	4
North Carolina,				
To refund to, moneys paid for land to	92	20	1	1
To audit claims of, residing in	633	30	1	3
Pension laws for benefit of	252	34	3	4
Removal of,				
Citizens of Pennsylvania on	236	21	1	1
Do	291	21	1	1
Delegation of nation on	311	21	1	1
Removal west of Mississippi River, contract for	1098	27	2	2
Do	288	27	3	2
Salt Springs in Indian Territory, to authorise them to lease	1545	47	1	9
Treaties of 1817 and 1819 with, to execute, by making provisions for the reservations under same	204	34	3	4
Do	290	35	1	5
Do	534	36	1	5
Treaties of 1835 and 1846, claim for payment of moneys due under, by those living east of Mississippi River	128	33	1	4
Western band of, claim for relief	390	45	2	9
Do	1603	47	1	9
CHEROKEE LANDS, North Carolina, moneys paid for, to refund to	92	20	1	1
CHEROKEE NATION, payments under act of 1883 to tribes in, to equalize	2614	49	1	10
CHEROKEE NEUTRAL LANDS OF KANSAS,				
Arguments presented by attorneys upon	53	41	2	5
Disposal of, to actual settlers only	5	41	3	5
Do	12	41	3	5
CHESUM, JOHN S., claim for relief	1343	48	1	10
CHICAGO, ILLINOIS, Indian trading post established at	66	14	2	1
CHICAGO, KANSAS AND NEBRASKA RAILROAD, right of way through Indian Territory to	2247	49	1	10
CHICAGO, MILWAUKEE AND SAINT PAUL RAILROAD, right of way through Sioux reservation	829	48	1	10
CHICKASAW INDIANS (see also under title INDIANS),				
Arrears of interest due, payment of	354	45	2	9
Do	808	45	2	9
Citizenship of, for commission on claims to	1307	48	1	10
Lands from, purchase of, to attach to Monroe County, Mississippi	135	20	1	1
Stocks held in trust for, sale of	1	40	3	5
Treaty of May 24, 1834, with, to fulfill	113	25	3	2
CHICKASAW BLUFFS, MISSISSIPPI, established as an Indian trading post	66	14	2	1
CHIPPEWA INDIANS (see also under title INDIANS),				
Annuities due,				
Payment of	18	37	3	5
Payment to certain band in Michigan	8	36	2	5
Do	19	38	1	5
Bad River band of, relief of	166	45	3	9
Do	175	46	2	9
Claims of citizens of Michigan and Indiana against, to adjudicate	442	30	1	3
Lac Court Oreilles band of, relief of	166	45	3	9
Do	175	46	2	9
Lac Flambeau band of, relief of	166	45	3	9
Do	175	46	2	9
Lake Superior and Mississippi bands of, to fulfill treaty stipulations with	50	46	3	9
L'Anse and Vieux De Sert bands of, relief of	396	43	1	8
Removal of	562	43	1	8
Title to lands of, to extinguish	2	46	2	9
Treaty with, authorised to be held	519	28	1	3
Treaties of 1837 and 1838 made with, to fulfill	27	28	1	3
Turtle Mountain band of, support and civilization of	1144	47	1	9
CHOCTAW ACADEMY, conduct of affairs at, investigation of	193	28	2	

Subject.	Report.	Congress.	Session.	Volume.
CHOCTAW INDIANS (*see also* under title INDIANS),				
Action in Court of Claims for recovery of balance of moneys due	251	45	2	9
Citizenship of, for commission on claims to	1307	48	1	10
Claims of, under 14th article of treaty of 1830	479	24	1	2
Do	663	24	1	2
Do	294	25	3	3
Heads of families, claims of	430	24	1	2
Lands ceded in 1830, settlement of claim for	499	44	1	8
Net proceeds claim of, payment of balance	80	42	3	6
Do	599	43	1	8
To ascertain amount due on	4	46	1	9
Removal of, from State of Louisiana	276	31	1	4
Treaty stipulations with, to carry into effect	77	40	2	5
Trust funds of, sale of	*1	40	3	5
CHORPENNING, GEORGE, claim for relief	133	35	1	5
Do	87	37	3	5
Do	61	37	3	5
Do	55	39	1	5
CHRISTY, CHARLES, claim for relief	279	33	1	4
CITIZENSHIP (*see also* under title INDIANS), commission to settle claims of certain Indians to	1307	48	1	10
CIVILIZATION OF INDIANS, repeal of act of March 3, 1819, making provision for	92	18	1	1
Do	854	27	2	2
CLAIMS (*see also* DEPREDATION CLAIMS),				
Cherokee Indians under treaty of May 6, 1828	824	25	2	3
Cherokee treaty of 1835–'36, to adjudicate same arising under	391	28	1	3
"Choctaw head of family," regulating claim of	430	24	1	2
Choctaw treaty of 1830, to lands under	479	24	1	2
Do	663	24	1	2
Do	294	25	3	3
Indiana and Michigan against Ottawa, Chippewa, and Pottawatomie Indians, to adjudicate claims of citizens of	442	30	1	3
COGSWELL, E. B., claim for relief	618	30	1	3
COLBY, A., claim for relief	489	43	1	8
COLLINS, S. L., & CO., claim for relief	287	29	1	3
COLONIAL AND STATE GOVERNMENTS, laws relating to Indians under	319	21	1	1
COMANCHE INDIANS, resolution of the legislature of Illinois in regard to	82	18	2	1
COMMAGER, HENRY S., claim for relief	424	28	1	3
COMMISSIONER OF INDIAN AFFAIRS,				
Contracts by, investigation of, award of	10	39	2	5
Salary of, increase of	688	47	1	9
COMPARE, CECILE, permission to sell her Kansas half-breed lands	134	35	1	5
COMPARET, FRANCIS, claim for relief	38	21	1	1
COMSTOCK, GEORGE S.,				
Claim for relief	1574	48	1	10
Do	3194	49	1	10
CONGRESS,				
Delegate from Indian Territory to, authorizing election of	95	45	2	9
Do	807	45	2	9
Do	1002	45	2	9
Right of the President to withhold papers when called to furnish by	271	27	3	3
CONVEYANCES OF LAND, to confirm, executed by guardians appointed by courts of Kansas	5	43	3	9
COODY, SUSAN, and others, claim for relief	367	33	1	4
COOK, JOHN, claim for relief	1133	48	1	10
COTTLE, IRA, claim for relief	91	22	2	1
COUNSEL FEES, payment of, in Osage ceded land suits	377	45	2	9
COURT OF CAIMS,				
Eastern band of Cherokee Indians to prosecute suits in the	647	44		
Do	231	45		
Do	466	45		
Jurisdiction of, to Indian treaties, extending	1001	45		
CREEK INDIANS (*see also* under title INDIANS),				
Citizenship of, for commission on claims to	1307	48		10
Depredations committed in Mississippi by, claim for	38	14		
Georgia, to extinguish Indian title to land in, purchased from	77	18		
To adjudicate claims of citizens of	128	20		
Do	115	21		
Do	15	22		
Do	140	23		
Do	177	25		
Indemnity for property destroyed by citizens of Georgia	109	21		
Indemnity for property destroyed belonging to friendly	127	22		
Lands purchased from, to pay for	609	47		
Memorial of	169	21		
Moneys due, payment of balance of	826	30		
Orphan fund of, to reimburse	905	45		
Do	310	47		
CREEK ORPHAN FUND. (*See* ORPHAN FUND.)				

* And views of minority.

Subject.	Report.	Congress.	Session.	Volume.
, trial of Indians for committing	3622	49	2	10
NDIANS (*see also* under title INDIANS), agreement to sell portion of reservation, to ratify	216	46	3	9
Do	311	47	1	9
Do	582	47	1	9
LL, JOHN, claim for relief of representatives	144	30	2	3
ENDEN, JOEL, claim for relief	278	31	1	4
R, F. B., claim for relief	642	44	1	8
Do	228	45	2	9
NGS, GEORGE W., and others, indemnity for damages under the Winnebago treaty	513	35	1	5
, T. R., claim for relief	60	42	2	6
, ANGELIA, claim for relief	127	20	1	1
A, Sioux Reservation in, to divide	1724	46	1	10
Do	1227	49	1	10
A CENTRAL RAILROAD, right of way through Sioux Reservation	830	48	1	10
A INDIANS, removal of	13	37	3	5
ANSON, claim for relief	5	34	1	4
Do	125	34	3	4
Do	52	35	2	5
Do	1	36	1	5
JOSEPH, claim for relief	200	35	2	5
SILOMA, claim for relief	96	43	1	8
ATE. (*See* CONGRESS.)				
'ARE INDIANS (*see also* under INDIANS),				
k, indemnity for loss of	739	43	1	8
Do	1348	48	1	10
Do	1349	48	1	10
ty stipulations with, to fulfill	537	47	1	9
Do	580	47	1	9
Do	1348	48	1	10
N AND WASHITA VALLEY RAILROAD, right of way through Indian Territory	769	49	1	10
Do	2488	49	1	10
VANTINE & CO., claim for relief	149	33	2	4
Do	183	35	1	5
Do	78	40	2	5
TMENT OF INDIAN AFFAIRS,				
ses and irregularities in, investigation of	853	24	1	2
ursements for the years of 1824 and 1825 made in	226	19	1	1
nization of	474	23	1	1
ganization of, and amendment of act of 1834	53	29	2	3
TMENT OF WAR, Indian Bureau, transfer of, to	240	44	1	8
Do	241	45	2	9
Do	92	45	3	9
Do	*93	45	3	9
Do	1303	46	2	9
DATION CLAIMS. (*See also* INDIAN WARS.)				
DATION CLAIMS,				
k Hawk war of 1832, to settle claims of citizens arising from	179	33	1	4
gia, to indemnify, for property destroyed by Indians	128	20	1	1
Do	115	21	1	1
Do	65	22	1	1
Do	317	22	1	1
Do	140	23	1	1
Do	37	31	2	4
Do	177	35	1	5
esota, to adjudicate Indian war claims of, committed by Sioux in 1862	42	38	1	5
Do	883	45	2	9
ouri, to indemnify citizens for depredations committed by Sacs, Fox, and Iowa Indians	51	19	2	1
Mexico, indemnity to citizens of, for property destroyed by Indians	122	36	1	5
Do	30	44	2	8
awatomie Indians, claim for property destroyed by other Indians	433	45	2	9
as, to adjust losses to citizens by Comanche Indians	151	33	2	4
Do	255	35	2	5
Do	535	36	1	5
Do	395	43	1	8
RMÁN, A. L., *et al.*, claim for relief	2688	48	2	10
ELIJAH W., claim for relief	439	48	1	10
BROWN & CO., claim for relief	73	46	3	9
IAN, GEORGE D., claim for relief	256	34	1	4
Do	536	36	1	5
IET, SAMUEL, *et al.*, claim for relief	1067	25	2	2
Do	803	29	1	3
VALLEY RESERVATION, NEVADA, settlers on, to pay for improvement on	1460	47	1	9
Do	1295	48	1	10
, JOSEPH, claim for relief	719	25	2	2

*Joint report.

Subject.	Report.	Congress.	Session.
DULUTH AND WINNIPEG RAILROAD COMPANY, right of way through Red Lake and Pembina Reservations to	1820	46	2
DUNLAP, JOSEPH, claim for relief	52	43	2
DURHAM, GEORGE G., claim for relief	278	36	1
DUVAL, GEORGE, *et al.*, claim for relief	824	23	2
EASTERN BAND OF CHEROKEE INDIANS. (*See* INDIANS.)			
ECOUCHATIMICO (Indian chief), claim for relief	83	28	2
EDUCATION (*see also* SCHOOLS; INDIANS),			
California, to establish Indian schools in	207	33	1
Indian youths, additional schools for	446	47	1
EGNEW, NANCY, claim for relief	59	30	2
ELLIOTT, GEORGE, claim for relief	88	22	1
ELLIOTT, THEODORE E., claim for relief	842	33	1
EVANS, LEWIS, claim for relief	519	25	2
Do	760	27	2
EVANS, MARK, claim for relief	287	29	1
EVANS, NICHOLS & CO., claim for relief	488	47	1
EWING & JOHNSON, claim for relief	35	37	2
FACTOR, WILLIAM SENNA, claim for relief	140	33	1
FELL, JOHN G., claim for relief	1347	48	1
Do	2917	49	1
FINDLEY, CHARLES, *et al*, claim for relief	507	30	1
FISH, E. N., & CO., claim for relief	1517	46	2
FISHER, A. D., claim for relief	6	45	2
FISHER, GEORGE,			
Claim for relief	484	25	2
Claims of legal representatives of, to audit	467	35	1
Do	345	36	1
Do		36	2
FISHER, SILAS D., claim for relief	191	23	1
FLANDRAU, CHARLES E., claim for relief	68	36	2
Do	28	37	2
Do	7	38	1
FLETCHER, JOHN, claim for relief	*780	43	1
Do	498	47	1
Do	1344	48	1
Do	3624	49	2
FLORIDA,			
Indians in State of, condition of	97	17	2
Indian hostilities, to reimburse citizens of, for losses sustained in	37	31	2
FORSYTH, J. H., claim for relief	287	29	1
FORSYTH, R. A., claim for relief	287	29	1
FORSYTH & HULL, claim for relief	287	29	1
FORT CONFEDERATION, Indian trading post established at	66	14	2
FORT HALL, right of way to Utah and Northern Railroad through reservation at	2767	49	1
FORT MITCHELL, GEORGIA, Indian trading post established at	66	14	2
FORT OSAGE, Indian trading post established at, on Missouri River	66	14	2
FORT WORTH AND DENVER RAILROAD, right of way through Indian Territory to	475	48	1
Do	849	49	1
FOWLER, WILLIAM, & CO., claim for relief	287	29	1
FRANCE, PRYOR, claim of George G. Allen against	113	25	3
FRANCIS, JOSEPH, pension and bounty land to heirs of	130	35	1
FRAUDS, investigation of, committed against Indians	98	42	3
FRAZIER, HENRY C., claim for relief	694	48	1
FREMONT, JOHN CHARLES, claim for relief	289	33	1
FRONTIERS, laws to preserve peace on	474	23	1
Do	37	31	2
GEE, N., & CO., claim for relief	287	29	1
GENERAL BRADY (steamboat), claim for relief of owners	287	29	1
GENTRY, REUBEN, claim for relief	266	24	
Do	212	25	
GERRY, ELBRIDGE, claim for relief	63	42	
GEORGIA,			
Creek Indians for property destroyed by citizens of, claim of	109	21	2
Defense against Indians from 1795 to 1818, to refund money expended by, for	230	46	2
Depredations committed in 1826–'30, indemnity to citizens of, for	317	22	
Do	177	35	
Depredations committed by Creek Indians prior to 1802, claim of citizens for	128	20	
Do	115	21	
Do	65	22	
Do	140	23	
Indian title to land in, to extinguish	77	18	2
Do	397	21	1
GILSCHRIST, WYATT, claim for relief	405	47	
Do	1452	48	1
GONZALES, JOSÉ MARIA, claim for relief	650	44	1
GOODHUE & CO., claim for relief	287	29	1
GRAHAM, ALEXANDER, claim for relief	1748	46	2

* Parts 1. 2.

Subject.	Report.	Congress.	
INDIAN RESERVATIONS—Continued.			
Cœur d'Alene, right of way to Spokane and Palouse Railway Company across.	3836	49	
Do	4134	49	
Right of way to Washington and Idaho Railroad Company through	4133	49	
Devil's Lake, right of way to Jamestown and Northern Railroad Company	3623	49	
Indians on, from going into Texas, to prohibit	432	46	
Miami, to carry out provisions of treaty of 1854	4109	49	
New York Indian lands in Kansas, regulating price for	4179	49	
Nez Percé Reservation, purchase of lands in Idaho for	63	43	
Number of, reduction of	2	46	
Pembina right of way to Duluth and Winnipeg Railroad Company through	1520	46	
Police regulations for	430	46	
Pottawatomie, creditors of	3978	49	
Railroads in Northern Montana, right of way through, to	2336	49	
Red Lake, right of way to Duluth and Winnipeg Railroad through	1520	46	
Religious denominations in the, equal rights to all	167	45	
Do	32	46	
Timber on, sale of dead	748	47	
Uncompahgre and Uintah, right of way to Utah	3977	49	
Do	4135	49	
White Mountain, right of way to Arizona Narrow-Gauge Railroad Company through	4170	49	
Yakama, right of way to Northern Pacific Railroad across	4138	49	
Yankton, Dakota, right of way to Yankton and Missouri Railroad Company through	4137	49	
INDIAN TERRITORY,			
Chicago, Kansas and Nebraska Railroad through, right of way to	2247	49	
Citizenship in, for commission on claims of Indians to	1307	48	
Delegate to Congress from	95	43	
Do	507	45	
Do	1002	45	
Indian lands in, House committee directed to investigate leasing	1345	48	1
Denison and Washita Valley Railroad, right of way through	769	49	1
Do	2488	49	1
Fort Worth and Denver Railroad through, right of way to	475	48	1
Do	849	49	1
Gulf, Colorado and Santa Fé Railroad through, right of way to	110	48	1
Kansas and Arkansas Valley Railroad, right of way through	768	49	1
Do	2343	49	1
Kansas City, Fort Scott and Gulf Railroad through lands of, right of way to.	1723	48	1
Do	840	49	1
Do	2302	49	1
Mississippi, Albuquerque and Interocean Railroad Company through, right of way to	1933	47	2
Pacific and Great Eastern Railroad through, right of way to	1474	49	1
Quapaw reservation for settlement in	13	46	1
Railroads in, to provide for granting rights of way for	1356	49	1
Saint Louis and San Francisco Railroad through, right of way to	934	47	1
Do	2260	48	1
Do	182	49	1
Do	1091	49	1
Salt Springs in, authorizing Cherokee Nation to lease	1545	47	1
Southern Kansas Railroad through, right of way to	211	48	1
Do	1451	48	1
Territorial government in, to organize	736	30	1
Do	151	43	2
Do	299	44	1
Wichita and Arkansas Valley Railroad right of way through	1473	49	1
INDIAN SCHOOLS. (*See* SCHOOLS.)			
INDIAN TRADE. (*See* TRADE.)			
INDIAN TRADERS, prohibiting others than Indians to engage as	3534	49	2
INDIAN TRADING POSTS. (*See* TRADING POSTS; INDIANS.)			
INDIAN TRAINING SCHOOLS, OREGON, purchase of land for use of	3534	49	2
INDIAN TREATIES. (*See* TREATIES.)			
INDIAN TRUST FUNDS (*see also* TRUST FUNDS), sale of Choctaw	*12	40	3
INDIAN WAR BONDS, payment of certain California	86	45	3
Do	123	46	2
INDIAN WARS (*see also* DEPREDATION CLAIMS; INDIANS),			
Claims arising from Indian depredations in Black Hawk war of 1832, settlement of	179	33	[illegible]
Georgia,			
For property destroyed by Indians at different periods, to indemnify citizens of	128	20	1
Do	115	21	1
Do	65	22	1
Do	317	22	1
Do	140	23	1
Do	37	31	2
Do	117	35	1
For expenditures in, to reimburse	230	46	3

* Views of minority.

Subject.	Report.	Congress.	Session.	Volume.
IAN WARS—Continued.				
Minnesota, to adjust losses of citizens in, committed by the Sioux Indians in 1862	42	38	1	5
New Mexico, to adjust losses of citizens in, from Indian depredations	123	36	1	6
Do	20	44	2	8
Nez Percé and Bannock wars, relief of volunteers in	249	48	1	10
Sioux Indians who served in Army during Sioux war of 1862, to restore annuities and money to	95	46	3	9
Texas,				
For losses arising from depredations committed by Comanche and other Indians, to indemnify citizens of	151	33	2	4
Do	235	35	2	5
Do	535	36	1	5
Adjust losses of citizens of, arising from Indian depredations	285	42	1	8
ANA, to adjudicate claims of citizens of, against Ottawa, Chippewa, and Pottawatomie Indians	391	21	1	1
Do	442	30	1	3
ANS,				
Allotment of lands to, providing for	165	45	3	9
Do	1576	46	2	9
Do	2247	48	2	10
Do	1536	49	1	10
Appropriation, annual, for 1887–'88	3490	49	2	10
Appropriations for, providing	835	49	1	10
Census, tabular statement of statistics and	53	28	2	3
Citizenship of, for commission to settle claims of Indians relative to	1307	48	1	10
Civilization of, repeal act of March 3, 1819, making provision for	*92	18	1	1
Do	854	27	2	2
Condition under colonial and State laws	319	21	1	1
Consolidation of certain bands of, in Washington Territory	296	33	2	4
Duck Valley reservation, relief of settlers on	1469	47	1	9
Do	1295	48	1	10
Frauds and wrongs committed against all tribes or individual Indians, investigation of	98	42	3	7
Intercourse with, to amend laws regulating trading and	66	14	2	1
Do	229	19	1	1
Do	474	23	1	1
Do	37	31	2	4
Removal of, memorials for and against	56	20	1	1
Do	130	20	1	1
Do	87	20	2	1
Do	209	21	1	1
Do	227	21	1	1
Do	233	21	1	1
Schools for,				
List of	92	18	1	1
Do	226	19	1	1
Establishment in California of	207	33	1	4
Providing for additional	446	47	1	9
To establish at Yuma, Ariz	1731	48	1	10
To complete school at Lawrence, Kans	1315	49	1	10
Shoshone and Bannocks, to negotiate railroad right of way with, through Fort Hall Indian Reservation	4131	49	2	10
Trial of, for crimes committed, the same as other persons	3622	49	2	10
Texas, to prohibit all Indians on reservations from going into	432	46	2	9
Trading with,				
To amend laws relative to	66	14	2	1
Do	1655	47	1	9
To regulate intercourse and	474	23	1	1
Do	37	31	2	4
Treaties with, defining terms on which treaties shall hereafter be made with certain tribes	133	33	1	4
Tribes of,				
Allegany, to authorize lease of lands and quiet title to same by	473	43	1	8
Apalachicola, claim for relief under treaty of 1823 by the	746	27	2	2
Bannocks, to ratify agreement for sale of lands	658	47	1	9
Do	659	47	1	9
Brotherton, reservation of the	445	44	1	8
Do	37	45	2	9
Caddos, frauds connected with treaty made with	1035	27	2	2
Cattaraugus, to authorize lease of lands and quiet title to same by	473	43	1	8
Cherokee,				
To extinguish title to land in Georgia by purchase from	77	18	2	1
Organization of an independent government by	67	20	1	1
To refund to North Carolina certain moneys paid for land to	92	20	1	1
Memorial of citizens of Pennsylvania relative to removal of	235	21	1	1
Do	261	21	1	1
Memorial from, relative to their removal	311	21	1	1
Claim of Georgia for lands belonging to	397	21	1	1
Claims under treaty of May 6, 1828	824	25	2	2

* Parts 1, 2.

*Parts 1, 2.

Subject.	Report.	Congress.	Session.	Volume.
INDIANS—Continued.				
Tribes of—Continued.				
Delaware—Continued.				
To fulfill treaty stipulations with	557	47	1	9
Do	560	47	1	9
Do	1248	48	1	10
Iowas, to sell reservation in Kansas and Nebraska belonging to	828	48	1	10
Kansas,				
To pay for advertising sale of reservation	667	47	1	9
To provide for payment of Kansas Indian scrip	1846	48	1	10
Kickapoo,				
To sell part of reservation in	1808	47	1	9
Do	785	48	1	10
Do	842	48	1	10
To settle estates of deceased	673	49	1	10
Do	1998	49	1	10
Klamath reservation, to restore to public domain	1354	46	2	9
Do	1148	47	1	9
Do	2134	48	1	10
Menomonee,				
Extinguishment of land title in Wisconsin held by the	90	29	1	3
Sale of timber cut on reservation	34	47	1	9
Do	1895	47	1	9
Miami,				
Provisions of treaties of 1834, 1838, and 1840 made with the	498	28	1	3
Relating to those located in Indiana	480	29	1	3
Do	42	33	1	5
Claim for moneys due by	620	30	1	3
Intruders on reservation in Kansas of the	256	36	1	5
To allot lands in severalty to	1319	46	2	9
To provide for sale of lands in Kansas belonging to	22	47	1	9
Mission, relief of	2356	48	1	10
Navajo, relinquishment of portion of reservation by the	628	42	1	8
New York, to sell lands in Kansas belonging to	751	46	2	9
Do	*449	47	1	9
Do	673	48	1	10
Nez Percé,				
Establishing a reservation in Idaho for the	63	43	1	8
For relief of volunteers in wars with	386	48	1	10
Omaha, to sell part of reservation belonging to	1530	47	1	9
Oneida,				
Claim for balance of moneys due	18	31	2	4
Claim for payment of interest by	61	33	1	4
Osage,				
Provisions of the treaty made with	63	40	2	5
Resolution from the national council of	186	44	2	8
Do	914	45	2	9
Do	1319	46	2	9
To carry into effect the second and sixteenth articles of treaty of 1867 with the Great and Little	106	45	3	9
Do	1395	46	2	9
Payment of counsel fees in ceded land suits of the	377	45	2	9
Otoe and Missouria,				
Authorized to sell part of reservation	31	46	3	9
Do	1305	47	1	9
To extend payments of purchasers of reservation	1683	49	1	10
Ottawas,				
Removal of	519	28	1	3
Payment of certain claims against	287	29	1	3
Claims of citizens of Michigan and Indiana against	442	30	1	3
Relief of certain	8	36	2	5
Do	19	38	1	5
Papago, right of way to Arizona Southern Railroad through reservation of	1424	47	1	9
Pawnee, removal of tribe and sale of the reservation in Nebraska	140	43	2	8
Do	241	44	1	8
Peorias,				
To allot lands in severalty to	1319	46	2	9
Do	1682	49	1	10
To adjudicate claims of	1006	48	1	10
Poncas, relief of	107	45	3	9
Pottawatomies,				
Removal of	519	28	1	3
Do	562	43	1	8
To adjudicate claims of citizens of Michigan and Indiana against	442	30	1	3
Do	18	37	3	5
Relief of certain	8	36	2	5
Do	19	38	1	5
Claim for balance of moneys due under various treaties to	819	43	2	8
Indemnity for depredations committed by others upon stock of the	70	44	1	8
Do	433	45	2	9

* Parts 1, 2.

Subject.	Report.	Congress.	Session.	Volume.
INDIANS—Continued.				
Tribes of—Continued.				
Pottawatomies—Continued.				
Payments to	291	44	1	8
To fulfill treaty stipulations with	1149	47	1	9
Do	1404	47	1	9
To authorize final settlement with	210	48	1	10
Do	1956	48	1	10
Do	1476	49	1	10
To sell lands in Kansas of Prairie band	2139	48	1	10
Red Lake reservation, relative to	183	48	1	10
Quapaw, to open for settlement reservation of the	13	46	1	9
Do	176	49	1	10
Sac and Fox,				
Indemnity for property destroyed in Kansas belonging to	88	37	2	5
Purchase of land from the	902	27	2	2
Sac and Fox reservation, to provide for sale of, in Kansas and Nebraska.	1306	48	1	10
Do	850	49	1	10
Seminole, pay for lands purchased from	609	47	1	9
Senecas,				
Treaty with	209	19	1	1
To authorize lease of lands and quiet title to same by certain bands of.	478	43	1	8
Authorized to convey certain lands for cemetery purposes	1709	46	2	9
Do	347	47	1	9
To allot lands to	2344	49	1	10
Shawnee,				
Balance of fund due	541	28	1	8
Indemnity for destruction of property in Kansas belonging to	300	36	1	5
To confirm certain conveyances executed by the guardian for any incompetent member of the	6	45	3	9
Sheepeaters, to ratify agreement for sale of lands	658	47	1	9
Shoshones,				
To ratify their agreement for sale of lands	658	47	1	9
Do	659	47	1	9
Compensation to settlers on reservation in Duck Valley	1460	47	1	9
Sioux,				
Annuities to half and quarter breed of	60	30	2	4
Apportionment and cession of reservation in Minnesota belonging to	138	33	1	4
Removal from Minnesota of	13	37	3	5
To discharge certain obligations of the United States to the creditors of the upper and lower bands of	75	43	1	8
To ascertain amounts due to parties for supplies furnished to	81	44	2	8
Do	833	45	2	9
Do	1420	46	2	9
Do	406	47	1	9
Do	209	48	1	10
Do	1350	48	1	10
For relief of those who served in United States Army	93	46	3	9
Right of way to Chicago, Milwaukee and Saint Paul Railroad through lands of	829	48	1	10
Right of way to Dakota Central Railroad through lands of	830	48	1	10
To survey reservation of	581	47	1	9
To negotiate for apportionment and cession of reservation	1536	47	1	9
To provide permanent reservations for various tribes of, in Northern Montana	2048	48	2	10
Sioux reservation,				
To divide into separate reservations	1724	48	1	10
Do	1227	49	1	10
Stockbridge, relief of	447	29	1	3
Do	813	44	1	8
Do	1950	47	2	9
Do	1054	48	1	10
Umatilla,				
To extinguish title to lands of	2	46	2	9
To sell lands belonging to	447	47	1	9
To allot lands in severalty to	1654	47	1	9
Do	387	48	1	10
Ute				
To extinguish title to lands of	2	46	2	9
To ratify agreement to sell reservation	1401	46	2	9
To open reservation to settlement	1404	47	1	9
For payment of claims for depredations by, at White River massacre	693	48	1	10
Warm Springs, to extinguish title to lands of	2	46	2	9
Winnebago,				
Removal from the "neutral ground"	640	27	2	2
Do	363	28	1	3
Do	324	29	1	3
To refund certain moneys to	279	31	1	3
Indemnity to claimants for damages sustained under treaty with	513	35	1	5
Contract for removal from Iowa and Wisconsin to Minnesota of the	501	31	1	4
Do	562	43	1	8

Subject.	Report.	Congress.	Session.	Volume.
INTERCOURSE, to regulate, with the Indians	[illegible]	19	1	1
Do	474	22	1	1
Do	87	31	2	4
INVESTIGATION, frauds and wrongs committed against the Indians	98	42	3	7
Do	778	43	1	8
IOWA, legislative assembly of, relating to removal of Winnebago Indians from their location on the "neutral ground"	690	27	2	2
Do	563	28	1	3
IOWA INDIANS, to sell reservation in Kansas and Nebraska	828	48	1	10
JACKSON, ALVERNUS, and others, claim for relief	46	34	1	4
JACKSON, HENRY W., claim for relief	518	35	1	5
JACKSON, JOHN, claim for relief	665	44	1	8
JAMESTOWN AND NORTHERN RAILROAD COMPANY, right of way across Devil's Lake Indian Reservation	3623	49	2	10
JAMISON, MARY, claim for relief of heirs	108	33	2	4
Do	176	34	1	4
Do	60	35	1	5
Do	234	36	1	5
JESSUP, A., claim for relief	297	29	1	3
JOHNSON, GEORGE C., claim for relief	744	25	2	2
Do	34	27	3	2
Do	85	27	3	3
JOHNSON, ISRAEL, claim for relief	163	28	2	3
Do	565	30	1	3
Do	87	31	1	4
Do	133	35	2	5
Do	116	36	1	5
JOHNSON, JAMES L., claim for relief	94	42	1	8
JOHNSON, JOHN, claim for relief	179	33	1	4
Do	122	35	2	5
Do	45	36	1	5
JOHNSON, ROBERT (administrator), claim for relief	184	25	3	2
JONES, A. H., claim for relief	562	36	1	5
Do	56	37	2	5
JONES, JOHN T., claim for relief	136	37	2	5
Do	102	39	1	6
JONES, ROBERT A., claim for relief	47	34	1	4
JOSLYN, ERASTUS S., claim for relief	419	36	1	5
Do	62	42	2	6
KANSAS,				
Kickapoo Indians in,				
To settle estate of deceased	673	49	1	10
Do	1992	49	1	10
To sell lands of	765	48	1	10
Do	642	49	1	10
Iowa Indians in, sale of reservation of	828	48	1	10
New York Indian lands in, regulating price for	4179	49	2	10
Otoe and Missouria Indian lands in State, to extend payments of purchasers of.	1683	49	1	10
Prairie band of Pottawatomie Indians in, to sell lands of	2139	48	1	10
Pottawatomie Indians of, final settlement of	1956	48	1	10
Do	1476	49	1	10
Sac and Fox Indian Reservation in, sale of	1306	48	1	10
Do	850	49	1	10
KANSAS AND ARKANSAS VALLEY RAILROAD, right of way through Indian Territory	768	49	1	10
Do	2843	49	1	10
KANSAS CITY, FORT SCOTT AND GULF RAILROAD, right of way through Indian Territory to	840	49	1	10
Do	1723	49	1	10
Do	2802	49	1	10
KANSAS INDIAN SCRIP, providing for payment of	1308	48	1	10
KANSAS INDIANS, to pay for advertising sale of reservation	657	47	1	9
KAULA, JOHN, claim for relief	1132	48	1	10
KAW SCRIP, payment of	1308	48	1	10
KELSEY, PORTER, claim for relief	287	29	1	3
KENNEDY, JOSHUA, claim for relief of legal representatives	79	33	1	4
KENNEDY, WILLIAM, claim for relief	139	37	2	5
KENTUCKY, Choctaw Academy, investigation of affairs of	198	28	2	3
KENZIE, JOHN H., claim for relief	567	27	2	2
KERR, BRIERLY & CO., claim for relief	471	35	1	5
Do	197	36	1	5
KETCHUM, ISAAC S., claim for relief	421	28	1	3
Do	422	28	1	3
KICKAPOO INDIANS (*see also* INDIANS),				
Estates of deceased, to settle	673	49	1	10
Do	1992	49	1	10
Reservation of, sale of	1303	47	1	9
Do	765	48	1	10
Do	642	49	1	10
KINNEY, JAMES, claim for relief	287	29	1	3

Subject.	Report.	Congress.	Session.	Volume.
KLAMATH INDIANS, to restore reservation to public domain	1354	46	2	9
Do	1148	47	1	9
Do	2124	48	1	10
LADD, MOSES, claim for relief	646	44	1	8
LAND CLAIMS. (*See* CLAIMS.)				
LAND SUITS, counsel fees in Osage ceded, payment of	377	45	2	9
LAND TITLES,				
Indian title to land in Georgia, extinguishment of	77	18	2	1
Indian title to certain land in Missouri, extinguishment of	379	24	1	2
Seneca Indians, to authorize certain bands of, to quiet their	473	43	1	8
Title of lands belonging to Indian tribes, to extinguish	2	44	2	9
Wisconsin, extinguishment of Indian title to land in	90	28	1	3
LANDS,				
Kansas upon the Absentee Shawnee, relief of settlers in	433	44		9
Secretary of the Interior authorized to issue lands to Indians in severalty	165	45		9
Do	1576	46		9
Seneca Indians in New York to grant title to lands for cemetery purposes	1709	46		9
LAWRENCE, KANSAS, to complete Indian school at	1315	48		10
LAWS, enacted by Colonial and State governments for treatment of Indians	319	21		1
LEACH, HENDERSON C., claim for relief	507	48		10
LEE, ABEL, claim for relief of heirs	378	45		9
LIVINGSTON, KINCAID & CO., claim for relief	466	35		5
Do	36	36		5
LOCKWOOD, BELVA A., claim for relief	2127	48	1	10
LOCKWOOD, MYRON M., claim for relief	804	45	2	9
LOUISIANA, removal of Choctaws from State of	276	31	1	4
LOVE, OVERTON, claim for relief	405	47	1	9
Do	1452	48	1	10
LOWER DUBLIN, PENNSYVANIA, memorial from citizens relative to condition of Indians	254	21	1	1
LOWRY, JOHN, claim for relief	916	25	2	4
McCANN, DWIGHT J., claim for relief	417	43	1	8
McCARTNEY, JOHN, claim for relief	74	19	1	1
McCLENAHAN, JOHN, claim for relief	31	22	2	1
Do	78	23	1	1
Do	222	25	3	2
McCOLLUM, V. B., claim for relief	439	43	1	8
McCORMICK, TIMOTHY, claim for relief	1134	48	1	10
McDANIEL, JAMES, claim for relief of heirs of	533	36		5
McDOUGALL, DANIEL S., claim for relief	750	40		9
McGREGOR, JAMES, claim for relief	220	45		9
McKAY, GEORGE, claim for relief	257	29		3
McKEE, REDICK, claim for relief	202	44		8
McKITTRICK, FELIX, claim for relief	1419	48		10
McLEAN, NATHANIEL, claim for relief	68	36		5
Do	28	37		5
Do		38		5
MAGILL, DAVID, claim for relief	91	22		1
MAGUIRE, GEORGE, claim for relief	544	30		3
MAHER, BRIDGET, claim for relief	128	31		4
MARBLE, SUSANA, *et al.*, claim for relief	378	45		9
MARK, ELISHA, claim for relief	287	29		3
MARMADUKE, M. M., and others, claim for relief	293	35		5
Do	420	36		5
MARSHALL, S. T., claim for relief	257	44		8
Do	467	45	2	9
MARTIN, R. C., claim for relief	495	36	1	5
MASSACHUSETTS, memorial of State in relation to Cherokee Indians	245	21	1	1
Do	310	21	1	1
MATHIS, WILLIAM, claim for relief	286	29	1	3
MAXWELL, GEORGE, claim for relief	1071	48		10
Do	287	29		
MEAD, AARON B., *et al.*, claim for relief	287	29		
MEAD, JAMES R., claim for relief	93	43		
Do	738	43		
Do	741	44		
Do	376	45		
Do	50	46		
Do	309	47		
MEAD, MARSTON, claim for relief	144	23		
MENOMONEE INDIANS,				
Timber cut on reservation, sale of	84	47	1	9
Do	1896	47	2	9
Title to lands in Wisconsin held by, extinguishment of Indian	90	29	1	3
MEXICO, ascertainment of extent of depredations committed upon inhabitants of Texas by Indians residing in, and by citizens of	535	36	1	5
MIAMI INDIANS,				
Indiana made by portion of, on petition to remain in	480	29	1	3
Do	42	39	1	5
Intruders on reservation in Kansas of	256	36	1	5
Lands in Kansas belonging, to provide for sale of	22	47	1	9

Subject.	Report.	Congress.	Session.	Volume.
INDIANS—Continued.				
s in severalty, to allot	1316	46	2	9
...fine, claim for	620	30	1	[illegible]
...ties 1836, 1838, and 1846 made with the,				
provisions of	466	27	1	3
...[illegible]	4149	48	2	10
AN, claims of citizens against Ottawa, Chippewa, and Pottawatomie Indians	442	30	1	3
Y, WILLIAM, claim for relief	3182	48	1	10
(Indian woman), claim for relief	874	27	2	2
Do	149	28	1	3
OTA.				
predations committed by Sioux Indians in 1862 in	42	38	1	5
Lake Indian reservation in	176	49	1	10
ties furnished Sioux Indians in payment for	1269	49	1	10
F INDIANS, relief of	2958	49	1	10
ARY SYSTEM. (*See* CIVILIZATION; EDUCATION; SCHOOLS.)				
IPPI, to attach part of Chickasaw country to Monroe County, Mississippi.	123	30	1	1
IPPI, ALBUQUERQUE AND INTER-OCEAN RAILROAD COMPANY, right of way through Indian Territory to	1000	47	2	9
RI.				
predations committed by Sacs, Fox, and Iowa Indians, indemnity to citizens for	*81	19	2	1
n title to piece of land between western boundary of, and Missouri River, to extinguish	379	34	1	2
ELL, R. H., claim for relief	135	30	2	3
Do	737	30	1	3
S, WILLIAM, *et al.*, claim for relief	366	34	1	2
NA.				
Percé and Bannock Indian wars, relief of citizens for service in	596	48	1	10
rvations for various tribes of Indians in northern part of State, to provide for	3648	49	2	10
t of way through Indian reservations in Northern, to railroads	2396	49	1	10
ITH, JOHN H. (deceased), accounts of, to audit	19	48	1	10
OMERY COUNTY, PENNSYLVANIA, condition of Cherokee and other Indians, memorial on	295	21	1	1
Do	261	21	1	1
OUSE, JACOB, claim for relief	524	35	1	5
ON, JESSE, claim for relief	292	35	1	5
ON, WILLIAM, claim for relief	130	19	1	1
ON, WILLIAM M., claim for relief	315	44	1	8
Do	2589	48	2	10
, MALACHIAH, claim for relief of heir	803	29	1	3
Y, JOHN, claim for relief of heirs	547	29	1	3
S, JOHN, relief of	36	28	1	3
Y, BENJAMIN, claim for relief	162	24	1	2
Do	549	25	2	2
Do	307	28	1	3
Y, ELLA P., claim for relief	632	43	1	8
Do	65	45	2	9
Y, RICHARD G., claim for relief	68	36	2	5
Do	28	37	2	5
Do	7	38	1	5
Y, THOMAS, Jr., claim for relief of widow	696	25	2	2
Do	137	27	3	2
Do	446	29	1	8
RA, claim for relief	181	24	1	2
TOCHES, Indian trading post established near	66	14	2	1
INDIANS, relinquishment of part of reservation by	638	43	1	8
KA.				
Indians in State of, sale of reservation of	828	48	1	10
oe and Missouria Indian lands in, to extend payments of purchasers of	1683	49	1	10
c and Fox Indian Reservation in, sale of reservation of	1306	48	1	10
Do	850	49	1	10
AL GROUND, removal of Winnebago Indians from location on	680	27	2	2
Do	363	28	1	3
A, relief of settlers in Duck Valley Indian Reservation	1460	47	1	9
L, RUSSELL S., Indian depredation claim	3678	49	2	10
RSEY, condition of Southern Indians, memorial from citizens on	256	21	1	1
N, H. L., claim for relief	2883	49	1	10
EXICO, Indian depredations, to audit claims of citizens for	122	36	1	5
Do	30	44	2	8
ORK (State), allotment of lands to Seneca Indians in	2344	49	1	10
ORK BAPTIST MISSION, condition of Indians, memorial from, on	247	21	1	1
ORK INDIANS, to sell lands in Kansas belonging to	*751	46	2	9
Do	*449	47	1	9
Do	673	48	1	10
Do	4179	49	2	10
RCÉ INDIANS, purchase of lands in Idaho for reservation for	03	43	1	8

*Parts 1, 2.

Subject.	Report.	Congress.	Session.	Volume.
NEZ PERCÉ WAR, relief of volunteers in	386	48	1	19
NORRIS, SAMUEL, claim for relief	11	38	2	5
NORTH CAROLINA,				
Bonds with, to exchange	*672	48	1	19
Cherokee Indians residing in, claim of	632	30	1	3
Eastern band of Cherokee Indians in, sale of lands of	627	48	1	19
Moneys paid to Cherokee Indians for land by, to refund	92	29	1	1
NORTHERN PACIFIC RAILROAD COMPANY, right of way through Yakhma Indian Reservation to	4128	49	2	19
ODELL, ELIZABETH, claim for relief	19	31	2	4
Do	8	34	3	4
Do	657	36	1	5
Do	27	37	2	5
OHIO,				
Indians to Western Reservation, memorial of citizens of Miami County, for removal of	302	21	1	1
Southern Indians, memorial of citizens for relief of	268	21	1	1
OKLAHOMA. (See INDIAN TERRITORY.)				
OLD SETTLER OR WESTERN CHEROKEES. (See INDIANS.)				
OMAHA, to sell part of reservation at	1530	47	1	9
ONEIDA INDIANS,				
Claim for balance of moneys due	18	31	2	4
Claim for payment of interest to	61	33	1	4
OREGON,				
Indian training school, purchase of land for use of	3534	49	2	10
To lands in severalty to Umatilla Indians in State, to allot	387	48	1	19
Nez Percé and Bannock Indian wars, relief of citizens who served in	386	48	1	19
ORPHAN FUND, distribution of	640	43	1	8
Do	214	44	2	8
Do	905	45	2	9
Do	431	46	2	9
Do	310	47	1	9
OSAGE INDIANS (see also INDIANS),				
Counsel fees in ceded land suits of, payment of	877	45	2	9
Execution of resolution of national council of, to authorize	186	44	2	8
Do	914	45	2	9
Do	1519	46	2	9
Treaty of 1867 with the Great and Little, to carry into effect second and sixteenth articles of	106	45	2	9
Do	1395	46	2	9
Treaty with, to fulfill	63	40	2	5
OTOE AND MISSOURIA INDIANS,				
Reservation, sale of	31	46	3	9
Do	1305	47	1	9
Extending time of payments of purchasers of	1682	49	1	19
OTTAWA INDIANS (see also INDIANS), claims against, payment of	287	29	1	3
Do	442	30	1	3
Relief of certain	8	36	2	5
Do	19	38	1	5
Removal of	519	28	1	3
PACIFIC AND GREAT EASTERN RAILROAD, to right of way through Indian Territory to	1474	49	1	10
PAPAGO INDIANS, right of way to Arizona Southern Railroad through reservation of	1494	47	1	9
PARIS, RICHARD S., claim for relief	466	28	1	4
PATRICK, JOHN, claim for relief	287	29	1	3
PAWNEE INDIANS, removal from Nebraska and sale of reservation	140	43	2	8
PEASE, L. T., claim for relief	191	28	2	3
Do	88	29	1	3
PENNSYLVANIA, condition of Indians, memorial from citizens of	253	21	1	1
Do	254	21	1	1
Do	261	21	1	1
Do	264	21	1	1
PENSION LAWS,				
Benefit to Cherokee Indians, execution of, for	252	34	3	4
Pensions paid under treaties or laws of Congress to all tribes or individual Indians	98	43	2	7
PEORIA INDIANS,				
Claims of, to settle	1006	48	1	19
Lands in severalty, to allot	1319	46	2	9
Do	1682	49	1	19
PERPALL, GABRIEL W., claim for relief	210	19	1	1
PERRY, JOSEPH, claim for relief	129	30	1	3
PETTIGREW, GEORGE H., claim for relief	2844	49	1	19
PETTIGREW, JOHN, claim for relief of heirs	406	29	1	3
PETTIGREW, ROBERT A., claim for relief	368	21	1	1
PETTIGREW, TIMOTHY D., claim for relief	368	21	1	1
PHILLIPS, FRED., claim for relief	1081	47	1	9
Do	1450	48	1	19

*Parts 1, 2.

Subject.	Report.	Congress.	Session.	Volume.
PHILLIPS, JOHN, claim for relief	642	44	1	8
PICKERING, JOHN H., claim for relief	32	44	1	8
PICKRELL, ELIZA, claim for relief	269	22	1	2
PIERCE, JOSHUA, claim for relief	230	24	1	2
POLICE REGULATIONS, authorizing the President to prepare suitable, for Indian reservations	486	46	2	9
PONCA INDIANS, relief of	107	45	3	9
POST-TRADERSHIPS. (See TRADE.)				
POTTAWATOMIE INDIANS (see also INDIANS),				
Claims of citizens of Michigan and Indiana against, to adjudicate	643	30	1	3
Creditors of	3072	49	2	10
Indemnity for depredations committed upon stock of	70	44	1	8
Do	453	45	2	9
Payment of funds under various treaties to	319	43	2	8
Do	201	44	1	8
Prairie band of, to sell lands in Kansas of	2132	48	1	10
Relief of certain	8	33	2	5
Do	19	33	1	5
Removal of	519	26	1	3
Do	562	43	1	8
Treaty stipulations with, to fulfill	1140	47	1	9
Do	1604	47	1	9
Do	310	48	1	10
Do	1956	48	1	10
Do	1476	49	1	10
POWERS, D. and E., claim for relief	7	46	2	9
Do	407	47	1	9
POWERS & NEWMAN, claim for relief	7	46	2	9
Do	407	47	1	9
PRAIRIE DU CHIEN, Indian trading post established on Mississippi River at	66	14	2	1
PRAY, WELCOME, claim for relief	287	29	1	3
PRESCOTT, P., additional compensation as interpreter	220	29	1	3
PRESIDENT OF UNITED STATES,				
Police regulations for Indian reservations, authorized to prepare	480	46	2	9
Power of, to withhold papers when called for by Congress	271	27	3	2
PRIMEAN & CHAPMAN, claim for relief	586	29	1	3
PUBLIC LANDS (see also LANDS), claim of Georgia for lands belonging to Cherokee Indians	207	21	1	1
PULAH, FRANCIS, claim for relief	287	29	1	3
QUAPAW INDIANS, to open for settlement lands in reservation of	13	46	1	9
RACE, JOHN, claim for relief	287	29	1	3
RAILROADS. (See also INDIANS; RIGHT OF WAY, and under names of respective roads.)				
RANDON, JOHN, claim for relief of heir	16	31	2	4
RAWLINGS, JAMES E., claim for relief	481	29	1	3
RAY, ALEXANDER (guardian), claim for relief	14	31	2	4
RED LAKE RESERVATION (see also INDIANS), disposition of	183	48	1	10
Do	176	49	1	10
REDUS, WILLIAM, claim for relief	255	46	2	9
REEVES, ROLLIN J., claim for relief	85	45	3	9
RELIGIOUS DENOMINATIONS, equal rights and privileges in the Indian reservations to all	167	45	3	9
Do	32	46	1	9
REMOVAL OF INDIANS. (See also INDIANS; also under names of respective tribes.)				
RESERVATIONS. (See INDIAN RESERVATIONS.)				
REVISED STATUTES, to amend or repeal section 2133, Indian traders	4180	49	2	10
ROCKY FORK AND COOKE CITY RAILWAY COMPANY, right of way through Crow Indian Reservation, Montana	4008	49	2	10
RHODES, THOMAS J., claim for relief	1131	48	1	10
RICE, HENRY M., contract for removal of Winnebagoes made with	501	31	1	4
RICHMOND, J. H., claim for relief	60	42	2	6
RIGHT OF WAY (see also STATE OR TERRITORY; INDIANS, and under name of respective railroads),				
Arizona Southern Railroad through Papago Indian Reservation	1424	47	1	9
Saint Louis and San Francisco Railroad through Indian Territory	934	47	1	9
Duluth and Winnipeg Railroad Company through Red Lake and Pembina reservations	1520	46	2	9
RILEY, DAYTON, claim for relief	287	29	1	3
RIVAR, FRANCES, claim for relief	225	25	3	2
ROBB, DAVID, claim for relief	533	28	1	3
Do	117	30	1	3
ROBERTS, LEWIS, claim for relief	64	38	1	5
ROBERTSON, JAMES O., claim for relief	84	45	3	9
ROBINSON, JOHN, claim for relief	625	29	1	3
ROBISON, ALEXANDER J., compensation for medical services	30	22	2	1
Do	172	23	1	1
ROBY, CHARLES C., claim for relief	103	29	1	3
ROBY & UTLEY, claim for relief	103	29	1	3
ROCKWELL, SAMUEL, claim for relief of legal representatives of	42	36	1	5
RODGERS, JAMES, claim for relief	464	22	1	1

Subject.	Report.	Congress.	Session.	Volume.
SMITH, NEAL (administrator), claim for relief	282	34	1	4
SOUTHERN KANSAS RAILROAD, right of way through Indian Territory	211	48	1	10
Do	1451	48	1	10
SPEARS & HUTCHINSON, claim for relief	287	29	1	3
SPENCER, JUAN, claim for relief	88	43	1	8
Do	736	43	1	8
Do	741	44	1	8
Do	276	46	2	9
Do	72	46	3	9
Do	309	47	1	9
SPOKANE AND PALOUSE RAILWAY COMPANY, right of way through Coeur d'Alene Indian Reservation, Idaho	3536	49	2	10
Do	4134	49	2	10
STATES, laws governing Indians issued by	319	21	1	1
STATISTICS, Indian tribes, to obtain additional, of	86	29	2	3
STEPHENS, WILLIS, claim for relief	220	28	2	3
Do	162	29	1	3
STEUBENVILLE, OHIO, forcible removal of Indians from limits of United States, memorial from citizens on	209	21	1	1
STEVENS, MARGARET L., claim for relief	11	33	1	5
STEWART, ALFRED, claim for relief	363	23	1	1
STOCKBRIDGE INDIANS, claim for relief by	961	27	2	2
Do	447	29	1	3
Do	812	44	1	8
Do	1999	47	2	9
Do	1004	48	1	10
STOKES, GEORGE, claim for relief	699	47	1	9
Do	695	48	1	10
SUBLETTE CUT-OFF MASSACRE, relief of survivors of	290	36	1	5
SUITS. (See LAND SUITS.)				
SUTTON, JESSE, claim for relief	519	30	1	3
Do	15	31	1	4
SWAGGER, DRUSILLA H., claim for relief	229	46	3	9
Do	348	47	1	9
TALBOT, THOMAS, *et al.*, claim for relief	570	28	1	3
Do	290	30	1	3
TALIAFERRO, LAWRENCE, claim for relief	265	28	1	3
TARVIN, RICHARD, claim for relief of heirs	40	35	1	5
TATUM, LAWRIE, claim for relief	1983	47	2	9
TAYLOR, Mrs., claim for relief	287	29	1	3
TAYLOR, NATHANIEL, claim for relief	92	25	3	2
TEXAS,				
Indian depredations, to ascertain and adjust losses by, to citizens of	151	33	2	4
Do	255	35	2	5
Do	535	36	1	5
Do	395	43	1	8
Indian intercourse, extending benefits of act on subject of, to citizens of	37	31	2	4
Indians on reservations from going into, to prohibit all	432	46	2	9
Indian and Mexican depredations of frontier of, to provide for protection from	61	43	1	8
THACHER & WHITING, claim for relief	287	29	1	3
THOMAS, JACOB, claim for relief	470	35	1	5
THOMAS, PHINEAS, claim for relief	486	28	1	4
TIMBER, cutting and sale on Indian reservations of dead and damaged	748	47	1	9
TITLES. (See LAND TITLES.)				
TOD, ELISHA, claim for relief	91	22	2	1
TRACY, CHARLES F., claim for relief	25	42	2	6
TRADE, appropriation for, with Indians	59	15	1	1
TRADING POSTS,				
Abolishment of Indian	129	18	1	1
Appropriation for certain	86	19	2	1
List of Indian, as established in 1817	66	14	2	1
Trade and intercourse with Indian tribes by establishment of, to regulate	66	14	2	1
Do	91	15	2	1
TREATIES,				
Appropriation for holding one with Seneca or Six Nations of Indians	209		1	1
Buffalo Creek treaty of 1838, to provide for settlement with Indians included in	2001		2	9
Caddo Indians, frauds connected with treaty with	1035		2	2
Cherokee Indians, reservations under the treaties of 1817 and 1819 with the	290		1	5
Do	534		1	5
Cherokee treaty of 1835-'36 to adjudicate claims arising under the	391	19	1	3
Cherokee Indians under treaty of May 6, 1828, claims by	824	[illegible]	2	2
Cherokees of December 29, 1835, amount appropriated and expended under treaty with the	288	27	3	2
Chickasaw Indians, giving provisions of the treaty of May 24, 1834, with the	113	25	3	2
Choctaw, to carry into effect certain stipulations of the	77	40	2	5
Choctaw, claims to reservations under the	479	24	1	2
Do	663	24	1	2
Do	204	25	3	2
Court of Claims to Indian, extending jurisdiction of the	1001	45	2	9
Indians, terms of same hereafter to be made with certain tribes of	133	33	1	6

Subject.	Report.	Congress.	Session.	Volume.
TREATIES—Continued.				
Guadalupe Hidalgo, to carry out the treaty of	280	31	1	4
Miami Indians.				
Setting forth the provisions made with, in 1834, 1838, and 1840	486	28	1	3
To carry out provisions of treaty of 1854	4109	49	2	10
Missouri, western boundary of, title to land between the, and Missouri River	379	24	1	2
Osage, provisions of the	63	40	2	5
Winnebago Indians, to adjust damages to claimants under the	513	35	1	5
TRIBES. (*See* INDIANS, and alphabetical list under same, also under special name of tribe.)				
TRIPLETT, THOMAS T., claim for relief	116	22	2	1
Do	567	24	1	2
Do	211	25	2	2
TRISSARRE, MARIANA, claim for relief	649	44	1	8
TROTTER, WILLIAM B., claim for relief	251	34	3	4
TRUST FUNDS (*see also* INDIAN TRUST FUNDS),				
Choctaw and Chickasaw Indians, sale of certain stocks held in trust for the	12	40	3	5
Investment and disposition of moneys appropriated for use of Indians	892	25	2	2
Shawnee Indians, balance due the	541	28	1	3
Stocks held in trust for Indians and Indian tribes, statement of	892	25	2	2
TURNER, CYRUS, claim for relief of heirs	557	29	1	3
UMATILLA INDIANS (*see also* INDIANS),				
Lands belonging to, to sell	447	47	1	9
Lands in severalty, to allot	1654	47	1	9
Title to lands of, to extinguish	2	46	2	9
UNDERWOOD, W. H., claim for relief of heirs of	42	36	1	5
UNITED STATES INDIAN TRADE ESTABLISHMENT, statement made by agents appointed to wind up the	129	18	1	1
US-SE-YOHOLO, claim for relief	588	24	1	2
UTAH MIDLAND RAILWAY COMPANY, right of way through Uncompahgre and Uintah reservations	3977	49	2	10
Do	4135	49	2	10
UTAH AND NORTHERN RAILROAD, right of way through Fort Hall reservation to	2767	49	1	10
UTE INDIANS (*see also* INDIANS),				
Reservation to settlement, to open	1401	46	2	9
Do	1304	47	1	9
Title to lands of, to extinguish	2	46	2	9
VAIL & ROBINSON, claim for relief of representatives	1346	48	1	10
VANDRUFF, JOSHUA, claim for relief	196	33	1	4
WAIDE, J. M., claim for relief	2125	48	1	10
WALKER, THIGH, claim for relief	333	25	2	2
WALLIS, GEORGE, claim for relief	150	28	1	3
WALNUT GROVE MINING COMPANY, claim for relief	1347	48	1	10
WAR BONDS. (*See* INDIAN WAR BONDS.)				
WAR DEPARTMENT. (*See* DEPARTMENT OF WAR.)				
WARD, JOSEPH, claim for relief	529	28	1	3
Do	318	29	1	3
Do	73	30	1	3
WARD, LINDSAY, claim for relief	529	28	1	3
Do	318	29	1	3
Do	73	30	1	3
WARM SPRINGS INDIANS, to extinguish title to lands of	2	46	2	9
WARREN, HENRY, claim for relief	683	43	1	8
Do	227	45	2	9
Do	256	46	2	9
WARS. (*See* INDIAN WARS.)				
WASHINGTON AND IDAHO RAILROAD COMPANY, right of way through Cœur d'Alene Indian Reservation	4133	49	2	10
WASHINGTON TERRITORY,				
Consolidation of certain bands or tribes of Indians in	296	43	2	4
Indian school building, to change site for	4136	49	2	10
Nez Percé and Bannock Indian wars, for relief of citizens of, who served in	386	48	1	10
WATSON, JAMES C., claim for relief	558	27	2	2
WATSON JOSEPH, claim for relief of representatives	198	33	1	4
WEBSTER, H. A., claim for relief	439	43	1	8
WESTERN CHEROKEE INDIANS. (*See* INDIANS.)				
WESTERN TERRITORY,				
Establishment of the	474	23	1	1
Indian title to certain lands bordering on the Missouri line and to extinguish	379	24	1	2
WESTWARD, removing Indians	56	20	1	1
Do	130	20	1	1
Do	87	20	2	1
Do	227	21	1	1
WHITE, JAMES, claim for relief	199	25	3	2
WHITEMAN, ISAAC, claim for relief	486	28	1	4
WICHITA AND ARKANSAS VALLEY RAILROAD, right of way through Indian Territory	1473	49	1	10
WILDER, CHARLES S., claim for relief	750	46	2	9
WILLIAMS, ELEAZER, claim for relief	459	35	1	5
WILLIAMS, GIDEON, claim for relief	534	35	1	5

Subject.	Report.	Congress.	Session.	Volume.
LIAMS, JOHN L., claim for relief	646	44	1	8
LIAMS, LOWRY, claim for relief	644	30	1	3
LIAMS, MARY ANN, claim for relief	89	31	2	4
LIAMS, O., & CO., claim for relief	257	30	1	3
D RIVER VALLEY, WYOMING TERRITORY, for relief of certain settlers in	740	44	1	8
Do	585	45	2	9
Do	36	46	3	9
Do	1101	47	1	9
NEBAGO INDIANS (*see also* INDIANS),				
damages to claimants under treaty with the, to adjust	513	35	1	5
moneys to, refund of	279	31	1	4
removal of	680	27	2	2
Do	368	28	1	3
Do	334	30	1	3
Do	13	37	3	5
Do	562	42	1	8
removal from Iowa and Wisconsin to Minnesota of the, contract made with Henry M. Rice	501	31	1	4
CONSIN, title to lands held by the Menomonee Indians in extinguishment of	90	30	1	3
COTT, JAMES, and wife, claim for relief	36	19	1	1
D, FLEMING, claim for relief	120	28	2	3
Do	88	31	2	4
D, S. N., claim for relief	786	43	1	10
DBURY, MARY, claim for relief	19	31	2	4
Do	3	34	3	4
Do	867	36	1	5
Do	27	37	2	5
DWARD, ELIZABETH, claim for relief	123	35	1	5
Do	61	37	3	5
Do	139	36	1	5
GHT, JOHN W., and others, investigation of alleged frauds against First, Second, and Third Regiments of Indian Home Guards committed by	96	42	2	8
GHT, REUBEN, claim for relief	356	44	1	8
MING TERRITORY, relief of settlers in Wind River Valley	740	44	1	8
Do	585	45	2	9
Do	36	46	3	9
Do	1101	47	1	9
KTON AND MISSOURI VALLEY RAILWAY COMPANY, right of way through Yankton Indian Reservation in Dakota	4137	49	2	10
ES, FRANK D., *et al.*, claim for relief	1637	46	2	9
ES, MILLEY, claim for relief	447	24	1	2
Do	146	25	2	2
NG, BRIGHAM, to audit and settle accounts of ex-Governor	62	37	3	5
Do	21	38	1	5
NG, WILLIAM, claim for relief	389	22	1	1

REPORTS

OF THE

COMMITTEE ON INTERNAL IMPROVEMENTS,

HOUSE OF REPRESENTATIVES,

FROM THE TWENTIETH CONGRESS, 1828, TO THE TWENTY-SECOND CONGRESS, 1832, INCLUSIVE.

IN ONE VOLUME.

COMPILED, UNDER THE DIRECTION OF THE JOINT COMMITTEE ON PRINTING,

BY

T. H. McKEE,

CLERK, DOCUMENT ROOM, UNITED STATES SENATE.

WASHINGTON:
GOVERNMENT PRINTING OFFICE.
1887.

9273

FORTY-NINTH CONGRESS, FIRST SESSION.

[PUBLIC RESOLUTION—No. 24.]

Joint resolution authorizing the preparation of a compilation of the reports of committees of the Senate and House of Representatives.

Resolved by the Senate and House of Representatives of the United States of America in Congress assembled, That there be prepared under the direction of the Joint Committee of Printing, a compilation of the reports of the Senate and House of Representatives from the Fourteenth to the Forty-eighth Congress, inclusive, classified by committees, arranged, indexed, and bound in suitable volumes for the use of the standing committees of the two Houses of Congress. And the sum of seven thousand seven hundred and fifty dollars, or so much thereof as may be found necessary, is hereby appropriated out of any money in the Treasury not otherwise appropriated, for the preparation of said work, which sum may be paid by the Secretary of the Treasury upon the order of the chairman of said Joint Committee, as additional pay or compensation to any officer or employee of the United States.

Resolved further, That the Clerk of the House and Secretary of the Senate be, and they are hereby directed, to procure and file, for the use of their respective Houses, copies of all reports made by each committee of all succeeding Congresses; and that the Clerk of the House and the Secretary of the Senate be, and they are hereby, authorized and directed at the close of each session of Congress, to cause said reports to be indexed and bound, one copy to be deposited in the library of each House and one copy in the room of the committee from which the reports emanated.

Approved, July 29, 1886.

2

COMPILER'S NOTICE.

This compilation embraces all the printed reports made by both Houses of Congress from the commencement of the Fourteenth to the close of the Forty-ninth Congress. They are classified by committees and arranged in numerical order. The collection for each committee is divided into volumes of suitable size. Each committee has a separate index, a copy being bound in each volume.

The SPECIAL and SELECT reports are all compiled in one collection having one index, a copy of which is bound in each volume.

The plan throughout the compilation is to place each report to the committee from which it was reported, without reference to the subject-matter.

The House and Senate reports are compiled separately. Care will be required in noticing the chronological order, as in some instances an entire session or Congress may not appear in certain volumes from the fact that during this period no reports were made by this committee.

T. H. McKEE.

INDEX

TO

)RTS OF COMMITTEE ON INTERNAL IMPROVEMENTS,

HOUSE OF REPRESENTATIVES.

FROM 1828 TO 1832, INCLUSIVE.

Subject.	Report.	Congress.	Session.	Volume.
IATION, for internal improvement	257	20	1	1
)RIA CANAL COMPANY, subscription to capital stock of	419	22	1	1
:T BRIDGE, DISTRICT OF COLUMBIA, estimate cost of	71	21	2	1
RE AND OHIO RAILROAD COMPANY,				
with Chesapeake and Ohio Canal	211	21	1	1
t Government aid to	211	21	1	1
dria, subscription by the Government to the capital stock of	280	21	1	1
:ARRE, LOUISIANA,				
, Government aid to maintain	63	21	2	1
dria, to grant land to aid in construction of	71	21	2	1
dria, subscription by the Government to capital stock of	419	22	1	1
;ake and Ohio, to grant Government aid to	280	21	1	1
and Michigan, Government aid to construct	446	22	1	1
see and Coosa River, to grant land in construction of	180	21	1	1
AKE AND OHIO CANAL,				
with the Baltimore and Ohio Railroad	211	21	1	1
t Government aid in construction of	280	21	1	1
ICUT RIVER, survey of route for canal or railroad along, from the				
ound to the Canada line	294	21	1	1
.AND RIVER, removal of obstructions in, at Harpeth Shoals	181	21	1	1
.AND (OR NATIONAL) ROAD,				
on, at Wheeling	399	21	1	1
through Dayton and Eaton, Ohio	410	21	1	1
OF COLUMBIA, Aqueduct Bridge, estimate cost of	71	21	2	1
ON,				
ution of surplus money among the States to promote	77	21	2	1
'unds from sales of public lands	446	22	1	1
CUMBERLAND RIVER, removal of obstructions at	181	21	1	1
TON AND HAMPSHIRE CANAL COMPANY, survey along Con-				
necticut River, as affecting	341	21	1	1
RE AND HAMPDEN CANAL COMPANY, survey along Connecti-				
ut River, as affecting	341	21	1	1
I SHOALS, removal of obstructions in Cumberland River at	181	21	1	1
N CANAL, construction of	446	22	1	1
AND MICHIGAN CANAL, to grant Government aid to construct	446	22	1	1
L IMPROVEMENTS,				
nce Committee report on bill for	257	20	1	1
utional authority for, by the General Government	77	21	2	1
s and estimates for	416	22	1	1
LE, TENNESSEE, survey and estimate of improvements from the Suck				
Tennessee to	64	21	2	1
ANT,				
dria Canal, to aid in construction of	71	21	2	1
Do	419	22	1	1
see and Coosa River Canal, to aid in construction of	180	21	1	1
I, improvement of Ohio River	97	21	2	1
.L ROAD,				
for construction of	196	21	1	1
ng and Belmont Bridge, Government aid in construction of	399	21	1	1
through Dayton and Eaton, Ohio	410	21	1	1

Subject.	Report.	Congress.	Session.	Volume.
NORTH CAROLINA, survey and improvement of Roanoke Inlet in	417	22	1	1
OHIO RIVER, improving channel of	97	21	1	1
PITTSBURGH, PENNSYLVANIA, survey of National Road from Uniontown to	196	21	1	1
PRESQUE ISLE, PENNSYLVANIA, survey of National Road from Uniontown to	196	21	1	1
PUBLIC IMPROVEMENTS, expenditure for, from 1792 to 1829	77	21	2	1
RAILROAD,				
Baltimore and Ohio, to grant Government aid to	211	21	1	1
Do	280	21	1	1
Construction of, from Illinois River to Lake Michigan	446	22	1	1
Survey of route along Connecticut River from Sound to Canada line, for	294	21	1	1
Do	341	21	1	1
RIVERS AND HARBORS, improvement of	491	22	1	1
ROADS, CANALS, &c., report on those for which surveys and estimates have been made	416	22	1	1
ROANOKE INLET, survey and improvement of	417	22	1	1
SANDY AND BEAVER CANAL, survey and estimates for improvement of	357	21	1	1
SKINNER'S GRAND CENTRAL BASIN, DISTRICT OF COLUMBIA, survey of	376	21	1	1
SUCK ON TENNESSEE RIVER, survey and estimate of improvements from Knoxville, Tenn., to	64	21	2	1
TENNESSEE AND COOSA RIVER CANAL, to grant lands to aid in construction of	180	21	1	1
TENNESSEE and HOLSTON RIVERS, survey and estimate of improvements from the Suck on the Tennessee to Knoxville, Tenn	64	21	2	1
TREASURY, UNITED STATES, surplus in, distribution of among the States	77	21	2	1
UNIONTOWN, PENNSYLVANIA, survey of National Road from, to Pittsburgh	196	21	1	1
UNITED STATES TREASURY, surplus in, distribution of, among the States	77	21	2	1
WASHINGTON CITY, DISTRICT OF COLUMBIA, survey of Skinner's Grand Central Basin	376	21	1	1
WHEELING AND BELMONT BRIDGE, Government aid in construction of	399	21	1	1

○

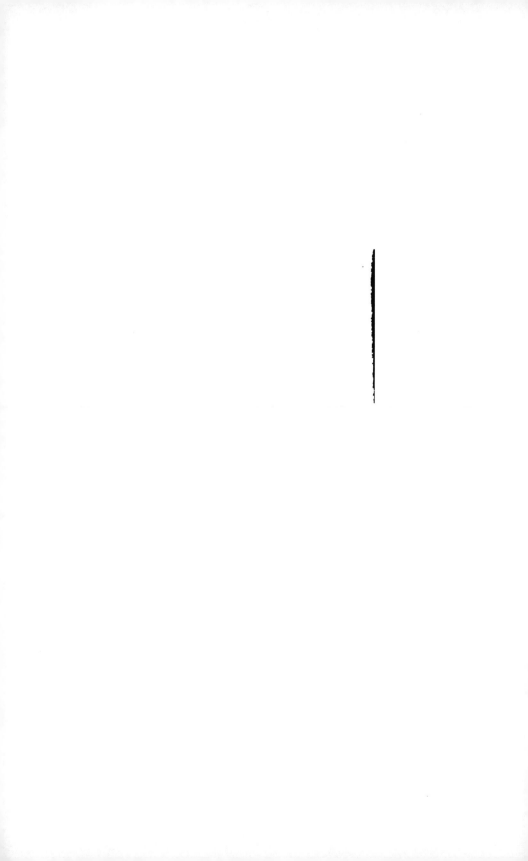

REPORTS

OF THE

COMMITTEE ON INVALID PENSIONS,

HOUSE OF REPRESENTATIVES,

FROM THE ORGANIZATION OF THE COMMITTEE, JANUARY 10, 1831, TO THE CLOSE OF THE FORTY-NINTH CONGRESS, 1887, INCLUSIVE,

IN TWENTY-TWO VOLUMES.

COMPILED, UNDER THE DIRECTION OF THE JOINT COMMITTEE ON PRINTING,

BY

T. H. McKEE,

Clerk Document Room, United States Senate.

WASHINGTON:
GOVERNMENT PRINTING OFFICE.
1887.

9196 PEN H

FORTY-NINTH CONGRESS, FIRST SESSION.

[PUBLIC RESOLUTION—No. 24.]

Joint resolution authorizing the preparation of a compilation of the reports of committees of the Senate and House of Representatives.

Resolved by the Senate and House of Representatives of the United States of America in Congress assembled, That there be prepared under the direction of the Joint Committee of Printing, a compilation of the reports of the Senate and House of Representatives from the Fourteenth to the Forty-eighth Congress, inclusive, classified by committees, arranged, indexed, and bound in suitable volumes for the use of the standing committees of the two Houses of Congress. And the sum of seven thousand seven hundred and fifty dollars, or so much thereof as may be found necessary, is hereby appropriated out of any money in the Treasury not otherwise appropriated, for the preparation of said work, which sum may be paid by the Secretary of the Treasury upon the order of the chairman of said Joint Committee, as additional pay or compensation to any officer or employé of the United States.

Resolved further, That the Clerk of the House and Secretary of the Senate be, and they are hereby directed, to procure and file, for the use of their respective Houses, copies of all reports made by each committee of all succeeding Congresses; and that the Clerk of the House and the Secretary of the Senate be, and they are hereby, authorized and directed at the close of each session of Congress, to cause said reports to be indexed and bound, one copy to be deposited in the library of each House and one copy in the room of the committee from which the reports emanated.

Approved, July 29, 1886.

COMPILER'S NOTICE.

This compilation embraces all the printed reports made by both Houses of Congress from the commencement of the Fourteenth to the close of the Forty-ninth Congress. They are classified by committees and arranged in numerical order. The collection for each committee is divided into volumes of suitable size. Each committee has a separate index, a copy being bound in each volume.

The SPECIAL and SELECT reports are all compiled in one collection having one index, a copy of which is bound in each volume.

The plan throughout the compilation is to place each report to the committee from which it was reported, without reference to the subject-matter.

The House and Senate reports are compiled separately. Care will be required in noticing the chronological order, as in some instances an entire session or Congress may not appear in certain volumes from the fact that during this period no reports were made by this committee.

T. H. McKEE.

INDEX

TO

?ORTS OF COMMITTEE ON INVALID PENSIONS.

Reports from this committee are classified under two titles, the first referring to general legis-
apon laws relating to pensions, the second to reports upon bills and petitions of a personal
ter. Other reports relative to pension laws will be found in the volumes of reports made by
mmittee on Pensions and the Select Committee on Payment of Pensions, Bounty, and Back

GENERAL LEGISLATION.

Subject.	Report.	Congress.	Session.	Volume.
'S. (*See* PENSION AGENTS.)				
)MENTS TO PENSION LAWS. (*See* PENSIONS.)				
TIES FOR LIFE, to officers of the war of the Revolution	164	27	3	3
equalization of pensions in	177	34	3	6
Do	242	35	1	6
RS OF PENSIONS. (*See* PENSIONS.)				
HAWK WAR. (*See* INDIAN WARS.)				
Y LAND, granting, to soldiers of the Mexican war	392	31	1	5
ALIA (Mo.), pensioning dependents of soldiers killed in massacre at	477	43	1	8
SSIONER OF PENSIONS, to fix salary of	1352	46	2	12
NSATION. (*See* SALARY.)				
DERATE ARMY, removing disability of those who served in, and have since enlisted in the Army of the United States (amend section 4716 Revised Statutes)	3628	49	2	22
. WAR. (*See* INDIAN WARS.)				
IOOR (England), granting compensation and bounty lands to American seamen confined in prison at	344	33	1	5
E OF DISABILITY, allowing the pension officers to determine and fix, in all pension cases, the	1734	48	1	16
DENT RELATIVES, increasing rate of pension to	605	48	1	14
Do	48	49	1	18
Do	1871	49	1	19
Do	4126	49	2	22
DENT SOLDIERS AND SAILORS, granting a pension of $8 per month to all	4126	49	2	22
IZATION OF PENSIONS. (*See* ARMY, NAVY, MARINE.)				
NCE IN PENSION CASES, regulating the proof required	395	48	1	14
Do.	1874	48	1	16
)A WAR. (*See* INDIAN WARS.)				
FOR DISABLED VOLUNTEERS (*see also* SOLDIERS' HOMES), establishing	28	38	2	7
ASE OF PENSIONS. (*See* PENSIONS.)				
IA, resolutions of legislature asking for extra pay, bounty lands, and pensions to soldiers for service in Mexican war	392	31	1	5
WARS (Black Hawk war), to pension soldiers of	117	44	1	9
Do	64	45	2	10
Do	127	46	2	11
k war, to pension soldiers of	64	45	2	10
Do	127	46	2	11
ida war, to pension soldiers of	117	44	1	9
Do	64	45	2	10
Do	127	46	2	11
inole war, to pension soldiers of	117	44	1	9
Do	64	45	2	10
to amend the laws for pensions to special class of disabled soldiers	1686	48	1	16
F PENSIONERS who have lost both hands	3637	49	2	22

General legislation—Continued.

Subject.	Report.	Congress.	Session.	Volume.
LOSS OF BOTH HANDS, increase of pension for	3627	49	2	22
MAJOR GENERALS, list of those killed or who died during the war of rebellion.	3858	49	2	22
MARINES, to equalize pensions to	177	34	3	6
Do	242	35	1	6
MASSACRE, pensions to dependents of soldiers killed at Centralia, Mo	477	43	1	8
Pensions to dependents of soldiers killed at New Ulm, Minn	1657	46	2	12
MEXICAN WAR. (*See* WAR WITH MEXICO.)				
MILITIA				
To pension (amend section 4693 Revised Statutes)	1657	46	2	12
To pension, not mustered in United States service, who have been wounded in service	550	49	1	18
MINNESOTA, to pension militia men who fought at New Ulm	1657	46	2	12
MISSOURI, pensioning dependents of soldiers killed at Centralia massacre in	477	43	1	8
MITCHELL RAIDERS, to pension the	413	47	1	13
Do	3892	49	2	22
MUSTER, fact of muster in evidence of soundness at time of	1874	48	1	16
NATIONAL SOLDIERS' HOME, fines imposed upon beneficiaries of	654	43	1	8
NAVY, equalization of pensions in	177	34	3	6
Do	242	35	1	6
NEW ULM (Minn.), to extend pension laws to militia in battle of	1657	46	2	12
NEW YORK,				
Memorial of citizens from State asking for pension for services rendered in war of 1812	317	34	1	6
Do	78	35	1	6
Resolutions of legislature relative to granting pensions commencing at date of disability	99	36	2	7
ORDER OF BUSINESS, HOUSE OF REPRESENTATIVES, fixing date for consideration of bills from Committee on Pensions	2446	49	1	20
ORPHANS,				
Amend section 4706, Revised Statutes, relative to pensions to	174	46	3	12
Arrears of pensions to	488	46	2	11
Half-pay pensions to	312	35	1	6
Mothers of, to receive pension of	1342	47	1	13
Payment of pensions to	101	33	1	5
PENSION AGENTS, compensation of	43	34	1	6
Compensation and expenses of	780	46		11
PENSION BUREAU,				
Additional clerks in	20	46		11
Cases pending in, effect of special acts upon	2640	49		22
Delay of business in	352	45		10
PENSION LAWS, to amend	2744	49		21
PENSIONS,				
Act of July, 1861, amending	30	37		7
Army, equalization of pensions in	177	34		6
Do	242	35		6
Arrears of, applications filed prior to January 1, 1875, shall commence from date of death or discharge	340	43	2	8
To amend laws granting	99	36		7
Do	88	33		7
Do	293	41		9
Extending limitation of act granting	1606	48		15
Do	783	47		19
Allowing arrears to widows and heirs	483	45	2	11
Black Hawk war, to pension soldiers who served in	117	44		9
Do	127	46		11
Centralia, Mo., to pension dependent relatives of soldiers killed in massacre at.	477	43		8
Commissioner of Pensions, to regulate salary of	1332	46		13
Confederate soldiers, who have enlisted in United States Army (amend section 4716, Revised Statutes)	2628	49	2	22
Creek war, to pension soldiers of	127	46		11
Dependent relatives, increasing rates to	603	48		14
Do	48	49		18
Do	1371	49		19
Do	4120	49		22
Dependent sailors and soldiers, granting to	4120	49		22
Equalizations of, in Army, Navy, and Marine Corps	177	34		6
Do	242	35		6
Florida war, to pension soldiers of	117	44		9
Do	127	46	2	11
Granted by special acts of Congress	1734	48	1	16
Increase of,				
For loss of hand or foot	201	45	3	10
For loss of arm or leg	201	45	3	10
For disability equivalent to loss of both feet	219	45	3	10
For loss of both hands	3627	49	2	22
For disability equivalent to loss of both hands	219	45	3	10
For loss of both eyes	219	45	3	10
Invalid, granting	28	38		7

General legislation—Continued.

Subject.	Report.	Congress.	Session.	Volume.
PENSIONS—Continued.				
Laws for, amending	127	46	2	11
Marine Corps, equalization of pensions to enlisted men in	177	34	3	6
Do	242	35	1	6
Mexican war, granting pension to survivors of	247	43	2	8
Do	117	44	1	9
Do	127	46	2	11
Militia, to amend section 4693 Revised Statutes, relating to pensions to	1657	46	2	12
Mode of payment, to change	43	34	1	6
Navy, equalization of pensions in	177	34	3	6
Do	242	35	1	6
New Ulm, Minn., pension to militia engaged in battle of	1657	46	2	12
Orphans, to amend section 4706 Revised Statutes, relating to pensions of	174	46	3	12
Do	1342	47	1	13
Pension agents, compensation of	43	34	1	6
Do	780	46	2	11
Pilots, establishing rate of pension for	2551	48	2	17
Prisoners of war, to pension	344	33	1	5
Do	*1438	48	1	15
Do	1868	49	1	20
Rates of,				
Regulating time of commencement of	263	33	1	5
To increase, for total disability	252	43	1	8
To increase, from $31.25 to $50 per month for total disability	252	43	1	8
To increase, for loss of arm	253	43	1	8
Increasing, for loss of arm above elbow and leg above knee	431	45	2	10
Do	201	45	3	10
Do	489	46	2	11
For loss of one foot and one hand	802	45	2	10
For loss of leg below knee	431	45	2	10
For loss of arm below elbow	431	45	2	10
To increase, for total disability from $50 to $72 per month	499	46	2	11
To increase, for loss of arm at shoulder-joint	498	46	2	11
Do	1514	49	1	19
To increase, in cases of more than one disability	551	47	1	13
Increasing, to dependent relatives	605	48	1	14
Do	48	49	1	18
Do	1371	49	1	19
For deafness, fixing	593	49	1	18
To increase, for loss of sight of an eye	1525	49	1	19
To increase, for loss of arm below elbow and loss of leg at knee-joint	1525	49	1	19
To increase, for loss of arm or leg	2744	49	1	21
Increasing, for loss of both hands	3627	49	2	22
Relinquished pensions, to restore to Revolutionary pensioners	152	27	2	3
Revenue service, to pension widows of persons in	87	38	1	7
Revolutionary war,				
To amend act providing pensions for soldiers of	152	27	2	3
Annuities to be discontinued on payment of five years' full pay	164	27	3	3
Sick leave, defining law granting pension to enlisted men on	2560	49	1	21
Special acts granting, effect of, upon cases pending in the Pension Bureau	3640	49	2	22
Teamsters, granting pension to, for service during war of rebellion	86	38	1	7
Total disability,				
Continuing pension to widows and children of parties pensioned for	179	43	2	8
To increase rate from $31.25 to $50 per month for	252	43	1	8
To increase rate from $50 to $72 per month for	499	46	2	11
Fixing rate of pension for	2830	49	1	21
War of 1812, to grant pensions to soldiers of	317	34	1	6
Do	262	34	3	6
Do	652	36	1	7
Do	6	39	2	7
Widows and orphans,				
To amend law regulating payment of	101	33	1	5
Do	174	46	3	12
To extend time of half-pay pension	312	35	1	6
To grant pensions to	1342	47	1	13
Widows and dependent relatives, Increasing rate of pension to	605	48	1	14
PILOTS, granting pensions to, serving in war of rebellion	2251	48	2	17
PRESIDENTIAL VETOES. (*See* title VETO CASES, and also under names of respective parties.)				
PRISONERS OF WAR.				
To pension seamen taken as	344	33	1	5
To pension, and their widows	*1438	48	1	15
Do	1868	49	1	20
PROOF, regulating evidence required in certain pension cases	1874	48	1	16
RATES OF PENSION. (*See* PENSIONS.)				
REVISED STATUTES, amending				
Section 4693, to pension militia	1657	46	2	12
Section 4 :93, to pension persons serving in Army but not regularly mustered	550	49	1	18

* Views of minority.

General legislation—Continued.

Subject.	Report.
REVISED STATUTES, amending—Continued.	
Section 4700, pensioning officers and enlisted men on sick-leave	
Section 4706, to amend act relative to pensions to orphans and widows	
Section 4716, granting pensions to Confederate soldiers who have enlisted in the United States Army	
REVENUE SERVICE, to pension widows of persons engaged in	
REVOLUTIONARY WAR. (*See* WAR OF THE REVOLUTION.)	
SALARY,	
To pension agents	
Do	
Of Commissioner of Pensions	
SEAMEN, to pension, as prisoners of war	
SEMINOLE WAR, to pension soldiers of	
SICK-LEAVE. (*See* PENSIONS).	
SIOUX INDIAN MASSACRE, to pension militia engaged in battle of New [illegible]	
SOLDIERS' HOMES (*see also* HOMES FOR DISABLED VOLUNTEERS), establishi[illegible]	
SPECIAL ACTS, effect of granting pensions by	
TEAMSTERS, granting pensions to	
VETO CASES,	
Elderkin, David T	
Farris, John W	
Harden, Simmons W	
Hunter, Maria	
Luce, Elizabeth	
McCarty, Catharine	
Norman, Mary	
Romiser, Joseph	
Tiller, Carter W	
Wilson, Andrew J	
Dependent parents	
Hopkins, Thomas	
WAR OF REBELLION (*see also* PENSIONS).	
Pensions to all for service in	
To amend law granting pension to certain class of disabled sol[illegible]	
Prisoners of war, to pension those confined in Confederate [illegible] during	
WAR OF THE REVOLUTION,	
Annuities to officers of the	
Pensions for soldiers of	
Restoring relinquished pensions to soldiers of the	
WAR WITH GREAT BRITAIN (1812),	
List of pensioners living in 1860	
New York citizens for pensions for services during	
Do	
Pensioning soldiers of	
Do	
Do	
Do	
Do	
WAR WITH INDIANS. (*See* INDIAN WARS.)	
WAR WITH MEXICO,	
Bounty land to soldiers who served in	
Pensions to soldiers of	
Do	
Do	
Do	
WEST VIRGINIA VOLUNTEERS, granting [illegible]	
WIDOWS,	
Arrears of pensions to	
Do	
Half-pay pensions, to extend time of	
List of, who have been placed upon the p[illegible]	
Pensions to, amend section 4706 Revised [illegible]	
Pensions, payment of	
Rates of pension, to increase	
Do	

PRIVATE LEGISLATION.

REPORTS ON PERSONAL BILLS AND PETITIONS FOR PENSIONS.

Subject.	Report.	Congress.	Session.	Volume.
S, JAMES	67	46	2	11
Do	1157	48	1	15
S, WILLIAM JAMES	16	24	2	4
Do	94	25	2	4
HORACE B	250	26	1	2
Do	626	27	2	3
Do	196	27	3	3
MINERVA	2566	49	2	21
T, CYNTHIA H	566	44	1	9
T, HARRIET N	1420	47	1	13
T, MARY	2116	48	2	17
T, NANCY	356	43	1	6
T, WILLIAM N	2542	49	1	21
LOUIS	264	49	1	18
MARY P	89	44	1	9
Do	319	46	2	11
Do	796	48	1	14
ROTH, WILLIAM	697	44	1	9
Do	913	45	2	10
CALES	796	48	1	14
DI, MARY SCALES	50	36	1	7
DI, SALVADOR	66	33	2	5
Do	551	36	1	7
THOMAS I	70	38	2	8
WILLIAM D	1786	49	1	20
AARON	665	26	1	2
ADELAIDE	50	36	1	7
Do	247	38	1	8
DANIEL W	1818	48	1	16
FRANKLIN C	3870	49	2	22
GEORGE (widow of)	223	35	2	6
Do	50	36	1	7
JAMES H	1200	48	1	15
JEROME B	1421	47	1	13
JOHN	1087	47	1	13
Do	2262	49	1	20
JOSEPH H	1542	46	2	12
Do	961	48	1	14
Do	3263	49	1	21
MARY H	1974	49	1	20
PETER	2083	49	1	20
SAMUEL V	866	45	2	10
Do	1192	48	1	15
RUTH	2458	49	1	20
S, THEO	1215	48	1	15
JULIA	280	33	1	5
MARY F	1431	46	2	12
GRACE	767	45	2	10
E, NELSON	541	44	1	9
JAMES M	1175	46	2	12
Do	827	47	1	13
T, DAVID	801	27	2	3
Do	297	28	1	3
T, LEONARD (heirs)	834	46	2	11
CHT, JOHN	3729	49	2	22
D, MARY ANN	101	35	2	6
GHT, ELIZABETH	847	46	2	12
CHARLES L	2521	48	2	17
HANNAH E	1583	47	1	13
HENRY	1208	48	1	15
CH, CAROLINE	1012	48	1	14
NDER, JAMES	231	36	1	7
NDER, JOHN	659	24	1	1
NDER, ROBERT	212	22	1	1
S, B	415	40	1	18
D, LINA	1766	49	1	20
Y, A. H	2656	49	1	21
SUSAN E	4062	49	2	22
R, CHARLOTTE	1272	49	1	19
JOHN	1476	48	1	15
CE, SAMUEL	1021	46	2	11

Private legislation—Continued.

Subject.	Report.	Congress.	Session.	Volume.
ALLCOCK, THOMAS	237	34	1	6
Do	83	35		6
Do	221	43		8
Do	1350	46		12
Do	1287	43	1	10
ALLEE, JOHN	1111	48	1	14
ALLEN, ALBERT L	416	40	1	10
ALLEN, AMANDA	2400	48	2	17
ALLEN, ANNA H	462	30	1	4
ALLEN, BENJAMIN	42	23	2	3
Do	473	23	1	4
Do	250	34	1	6
Do	106	35	2	6
ALLEN, CHARLES	17	31	1	3
ALLEN, CHARLES L	172	44	1	9
ALLEN, CHARLOTTE	1159	46	2	12
ALLEN, GEORGE W	614	30	1	7
ALLEN, ISAAC	622	26	1	2
Do	203	27	2	2
Do	10	28	2	3
Do	21	33	2	5
Do	485	33	1	6
Do	382	30	1	7
ALLEN, JAMES	287	25	2	2
ALLEN, JOHN	113	22	2	1
Do	965	27	2	3
ALLEN, JOHN L	80	29	1	4
ALLEN, JOHN M	726	43	1	8
ALLEN, MAJOR F	1145	46	2	12
ALLEN, MARY	462	48	1	14
ALLEN, MARY A	289	44	1	9
Do	718	45	2	10
ALLEN, PETER L	200	24	1	1
Do	465	29	1	4
ALLEN, REBECCA	1714	49	1	20
ALLEN, REBECCA S	82	40	2	11
ALLEN, THOMAS G	2235	48	2	17
ALLEN, WILLIAM	284	28	1	3
Do	44	28	2	3
Do	297	35	1	6
ALLISON, JAMES M	962	45	2	10
Do	151	46	2	11
ALLISON, JOHN	678	25	2	2
Do	219	26	1	2
ALMIER, CHRISTIANA	1884	48	1	16
ALMY, BENJAMIN	24	33	2	6
ALSTEAD, ABRAHAM	181	45	2	10
Do	1681	46	2	13
ALTENBURG, ISAIAH	1217	46	2	13
ALWAY, ISAAC	290	31	1	3
ALYEA, JOHN W	1409	49	1	22
AMANN, KATE	633	43	1	24
Do	401	49	1	26
AMBLER, ALMIRA	3074	49	1	24
Do	3076	49	1	25
AMBLER, PETER	291	26	1	2
AMBRESTER, MARY E	1469	47	1	13
AMES, DAVID A	426	23	1	1
Do	1	23	1	1
AMMERMAN, WILLIAM M	1485	48	1	15
AMMONS, RUFUS G	2251	49	1	20
AMOS, BENJAMIN F	1533	48	1	15
ANCRUM, SALLIE	1792	49	1	20
ANDERSON, ELIAS	777	44	1	9
ANDERSON, ELIZA BAYARD	533	45	2	10
ANDERSON, HIRAM	76	26	2	7
ANDERSON, JAMES	1587	49	1	19
ANDERSON, JAMES A	56	40	2	7
ANDERSON, JOHN W	1103	46	2	11
ANDERSON, LEVI	94	47	1	13
Do	137	48	1	14
ANDERSON, LUCY E	3255	49	1	24
ANDERSON, MARY	2056	49	1	20
Do	3430	49	1	24
ANDERSON, MILLEY	777	45	2	10
ANDERSON, MISSOURI	1355	46	2	12
Do	2050	49	1	20
ANDERSON, OTIS B	38	44	1	6
Do	533	45	2	10

***Private legislation*—Continued.**

Subject.	Report.	Congress.	Session.	Volume.
SON, PETER	87	30	1	7
SON, SAMUEL	2894	49	1	21
SON, SYVERT A	636	45	2	10
Do	824	47	1	13
SON, WILLIAM H. H	93	44	1	9
Do	863	47	1	13
TON, WILLIAM	314	44	1	9
SS, THOMAS	1940	48	1	16
WS, COLLINS	479	31	1	5
WS, GEORGE	583	45	2	10
Do	596	46	2	11
Do	219	47	1	13
WS, WILLIAM W	842	48	1	14
Do	122	49	1	18
S, CEPHAS E	1174	47	1	13
L, MARTHA	1906	48	1	16
ANNE W	159	33	1	5
Do	58	34	1	6
HENRY	674	49	1	18
Y, PETER D	307	36	1	7
ANN	598	44	1	9
CH, PHILLIP	222	26	2	2
WILLIAM	1210	49	1	19
NY, CHARLES H	1774	49	1	20
NE, JOHN	2567	48	2	17
LY, WILLIAM	1061	49	1	19
SON, REUBEN	232	35	1	6
BY, STEPHEN	648	25	2	2
Do	133	25	3	2
Do	181	26	1	2
GATE, WILLIAM P	1804	49	1	20
TON, CHARLES	226	36	1	7
R, MARY RINGGOLD	145	49	1	18
R, MOSES	570	25	1	2
Do	228	26	2	3
BALD, WILLIAM	944	48	1	14
RUST, JOHN D. M.	2170	49	1	20
RONG, AMOS	813	29	1	4
Do	553	30	1	4
Do	341	31	1	6
RONG, BURTON	358	47	1	13
RONG, ELIJAH	100	31	1	5
RONG, FRANCIS	67	43	2	8
RONG, FRANKLIN W	288	34	1	6
RONG, GEORGE	473	26	1	2
Do	266	27	3	3
Do	180	28	1	3
RONG, HARRIET	2265	48	2	17
RONG, HENRY A	2072	48	1	16
RONG, JOSHUA	2593	49	1	21
RONG, MRS. WILLIE	1584	49	1	19
, CHRISTIAN	2524	48	2	17
, PHILIP	1496	49	1	19
D, ABBY P	2280	48	2	17
D, ANDREW J	1554	46	2	12
D, GEORGE L	1365	49	1	19
D, JOSEPH C	1362	48	1	15
NGTON, SUSANNAH	2071	49	1	21
R, CORNELIA M.	717	43	1	8
R, JOHN	1368	49	1	19
, THEODORE	742	45	2	10
Do	531	46	2	11
Y, SAMUEL M	388	23	1	1
Do	558	24	1	1
Do	297	25	2	2
Do	76	25	3	2
Do	176	26	1	2
Do	236	27	2	3
Do	420	27	2	3
, NATHAN	78	29	1	4
FELTER, EMMA M	835	44	1	9
Y, ELIZA K	101	46	3	11
, JOHN	422	23	1	1
Y, THOMAS	247	49	1	18
, ISAAC	2834	49	1	21
, JOHN	225	26	2	2
Do	291	29	1	4
SON, JOHN H	563	49	1	18

Private legislation—Continued.

Subject.	Report.	Congress.	Session.	Volume.
ATTLETON, CLARA L.	720	44	1	6
ATTWATER, SUSAN Y.	1631	[illegible]	1	15
ATWOOD, ANNA M	771	44	1	9
Do	[illegible]	45	2	10
AULTS, ELIZABETH	84	[illegible]	2	11
AURAND, ELIZABETH	[illegible]	[illegible]	2	17
Do	[illegible]	[illegible]	2	17
AUSMAN, ABRAHAM	471	[illegible]	1	4
Do	[illegible]	[illegible]	2	4
Do	165	[illegible]	1	5
AUSTIN, JOSEPH	[illegible]	[illegible]	2	11
Do	[illegible]	[illegible]	1	14
AUSTIN, LORENSO D	[illegible]	[illegible]	1	15
AUSTIN, SOPHRONIA	175	[illegible]	1	6
AVERILL, CAMFIELD	[illegible]	[illegible]	1	4
Do	61	31	1	5
AXLINE, MARY C	[illegible]	44	1	9
Do	[illegible]	[illegible]	1	16
AXMAKER, AUGUSTUS	[illegible]	[illegible]	1	15
AXTELL, LAFAYETTE	[illegible]	[illegible]	1	13
AYER, ZEBA S	[illegible]	[illegible]	1	15
AYERS, EDWARD	[illegible]	[illegible]	1	20
AYERS, LEWIS W	[illegible]	[illegible]	1	16
AYERS, WILLIAM E	[illegible]	[illegible]	2	17
AYRES, JOHN E	[illegible]	44	1	9
AYRES, WILLIAM E	[illegible]	[illegible]	3	12
BABB, JOHN H	[illegible]	[illegible]	1	6
BABB, JOSIE H	[illegible]	[illegible]	1	19
BABB, LIBEAS H	[illegible]	[illegible]	1	3
BABBET, ELIJAH C	[illegible]	[illegible]	1	3
Do	[illegible]	[illegible]	1	4
BABCOCK, CATHERINE E	[illegible]	[illegible]	3	22
BABSON, EMELINE J	[illegible]	[illegible]	1	20
BACHE, MARIA B. C	[illegible]	[illegible]	1	8
BACON, SARAH	714	[illegible]	1	8
BACON, SARAH W	713	[illegible]	1	8
BADEN, WILLIAM	[illegible]	[illegible]	1	1
BADGER, NEHEMIAH M	[illegible]	[illegible]	1	1
BADGER, THOMAS	[illegible]	[illegible]	1	4
BAGLEY, ANNIE	[illegible]	[illegible]	2	17
Do	[illegible]	[illegible]	1	15
BAGLEY, DAVID W	[illegible]	[illegible]	1	20
BAGLEY, LETTA	[illegible]	[illegible]	1	8
BAGLEY, MARY	1621	[illegible]	1	20
BAILEY, ANNIE E	[illegible]	[illegible]	2	17
BAILEY, MRS. C. A	[illegible]	[illegible]	1	20
BAILEY, CHRISTIANA	[illegible]	[illegible]	1	8
BAILEY, HARRIET M	[illegible]	[illegible]	2	17
BAILEY, JAMES	[illegible]	[illegible]	2	2
Do	[illegible]	[illegible]	1	3
Do	[illegible]	[illegible]	3	3
BAILEY, JAMES M	[illegible]	[illegible]	1	9
BAILEY, JOSEPH	144	[illegible]	3	6
BAILEY, LIZZIE	[illegible]	[illegible]	2	13
BAILEY, MARY	[illegible]	[illegible]	2	6
BAILEY, MICHAEL L	[illegible]	[illegible]	1	7
BAILEY, WILLIAM F. D	[illegible]	[illegible]	1	20
BAINBRIDGE, HENRY (widow)	37	[illegible]	1	5
BAIRD, WILLIAM	[illegible]	[illegible]	1	6
BAIRD, RICHARDSON K	[illegible]	[illegible]	3	11
BAKER, BARTON R	[illegible]	[illegible]	1	9
BAKER, DANIEL	[illegible]	[illegible]	1	2
BAKER, EMILY B	[illegible]	[illegible]	1	[illegible]
BAKER, HARVEY D	[illegible]	[illegible]	3	12
BAKER, HUGH	[illegible]	[illegible]	1	7
BAKER, IRENE	[illegible]	[illegible]	1	14
BAKER, JACOB	348	[illegible]	1	8
Do	[illegible]	[illegible]	1	20
BAKER, JAMES A	[illegible]	[illegible]	3	12
BAKER, JOHN	[illegible]	[illegible]	3	8
Do	198	[illegible]	1	9
Do	[illegible]	[illegible]	1	9
BAKER, JOSIAH C	3684	[illegible]	2	[illegible]
BAKER, MARY E	3513	[illegible]	2	[illegible]
BAKER, NEWTON O	2203	[illegible]	2	[illegible]
Do	[illegible]	[illegible]	1	[illegible]
BAKER, RICHARD M	151	[illegible]	1	[illegible]
BAKER, SAMUEL	[illegible]	[illegible]	2	[illegible]

Private legislation—Continued.

Subject.	Report.	Congress.	Session.	Volume.
OMAS F	1891	47	1	13
ILLIAM	411	26	1	2
ILLIAM B	1142	48	1	14
	2656	49	1	21
N R	138	27	3	3
ALFRED	278	22	1	1
	122	23	1	1
ALGER J	1247	47	1	13
AMELIA	306	29	1	4
ANDREW J	218	43	1	8
CHARLES W	513	46	2	11
	2093	48	1	16
DAVID A	218	26	1	2
	41	26	2	2
ELECTA L	351	46	2	11
	1117	47	1	13
HERMAN	38	46	2	11
WILLIAM G	2060	48	1	16
RY	287	26	1	2
RGE	1013	48	1	14
	92	43	2	8
MAS	298	23	1	1
THA	1868	46	2	12
LIAM	558	26	1	2
WILLIAM	78	44	2	9
	298	48	1	14
R, HENRY	1203	48	1	15
R, HENRY G	1779	49	1	20
BR, JOSEPH	1718	46	2	12
, ELEANOR C	70	49	1	18
HN G	270	48	1	14
VERS	1494	48	1	15
WILLIAM H	1457	48	1	15
MICHAEL	456	43	1	8
	1834	49	1	20
EORGE N. (heirs of)	1646	46	2	12
ILES	360	45	2	10
	2572	48	2	17
HODA L	1141	46	2	12
ELIZABETH A	889	48	1	14
	1498	48	1	15
RY CLARKE	152	44	2	9
VILLIAM	2796	49	1	21
NN G	146	36	1	7
ARTON R	833	44	1	9
LIZABETH	2050	49	1	20
SAAC	402	28	1	3
	46	29	1	4
VILLIAM J	400	48	1	14
	2061	49	1	20
GEORGE	733	24	1	1
	190	25	2	2
	353	26	1	2
HULDA L	312	46	2	11
SAMUEL	1198	48	1	15
ORNELIA A	701	48	1	14
ENTON C	318	46	2	11
ATHARINE	502	44	1	9
ORDON B	148	44	1	9
	731	45	2	10
IARY T	295	48	1	14
ICHARD W	714	48	1	14
	2085	48	1	16
VILLIAM B	3094	49	1	21
	3741	49	2	22
NICHOLAS W	416	47	1	13
	59	49	1	18
HARRIET	174	28	1	3
	19	30	1	4
LOUIS	283	36	1	2
	231	27	2	3
D, WILLIAM	1204	46	2	12
T, JACOB	67	46	3	12
NRY	883	49	1	19
MES	272	28	1	3
RAH	2502	49	1	20
ANNAH	1590	48	1	15
, DWIGHT A	183	43	2	8
	18	45	2	10

Private legislation—Continued.

Subject.	Report.	Congress.
BARRETT, GEORGE	53	49
BARRETT, LUCINDA	845	45
Do	2954	49
BARRY, JOHN H	322	49
BARRY, SUSAN E	3240	49
BARTHOLOMEW, BETSY	1996	49
BARTHOLOMEW, EDWARD	2089	48
BARTIS, ETHEL	809	30
BARTLETT, ADON	187	25
Do	262	27
BARTLETT, DAVID	186	25
Do	292	26
Do	424	27
BARTLETT, MARY U	820	46
BARTLETT, SAMUEL M	1921	48
BARTLETT, WILLIAM P	168	43
BARTLEY, JOHN L	234	44
Do	811	46
BARTON, HENRY	679	25
Do	3272	49
BARTON, HESTER S	180	35
Do	309	36
BARTON, JOB	227	23
BARTON, THOMAS G	328	49
BARTON, WILLIAM	164	27
BARTOW, JOHN	325	46
BASHFORD, FRANCIS	148	24
BASS, ELIZA M	1239	47
BASS, OBEDIAH	666	29
BASSETT, SARAH E	1972	49
BASTIN, MARTHA	2055	48
BATCHELDOR, WILLIAM	19	32
BATDORFF, DANIEL	2660	49
BATES, GEORGE W	285	44
BATES, JAMES C	330	44
Do	595	45
BATTORFF, NANCY	1768	49
BAUER, ELIZABETH	78	46
Do	505	47
Do	676	48
BAUM, GEORGE A. R	1220	46
BAUMAN, CHRISTIAN	1797	48
BAUMAN, FREDERICK	752	49
BAUMHAGER, HERMAN	2782	49
BAXTER, ROBERT	401	49
BAXTER, WILLIAM Q	729	45
BAYARD, ANTHONY WALTON	333	29
Do	21	30
Do	141	31
Do	88	32
Do	51	33
Do	239	34
Do	31	35
Do	73	36
BAYLESS, ISRAEL	451	30
BAYLOR, JAMES R	2417	42
BEALL, ELIZABETH T	204	41
BEAN, ALEXANDER S	310	35
BEAN, GEORGE W	484	35
BEAN, JAMES O	142	34
BEAN, JONATHAN	177	22
Do	7	22
Do	148	26
Do	158	27
Do	13	28
BEAN, LYDA	828	29
BEARD, ROBERT	1211	49
BEARD, WILLIAM C	73	23
Do	330	24
BEARDSLEY, PHILO	2201	48
BEASLEY, EPHRAIM	563	26
BEATLEY, HECTOR ST. JOHN	81	35
Do	820	36
BEAUMENT, FANNIE C	803	48
BECK, ANNA	1146	48
BECK, JOHN	1582	48
BECK, WILLIAM H	2090	49
BECKTEL, SARAH A	896	48

Subject.	Report.	Congress.	Session.	Volume.
AMES, SR	2515	48	2	17
PAUL C	77	46	3	12
TSEY	1008	27	2	3
USTUS	329	46	2	11
	1026	47	1	13
THEOPHILUS E	120	24	1	1
ARGARETT	588	43	1	8
OPHIA	2508	48	2	17
	2102	49	1	20
ER, MARTHA A	1211	46	2	12
	802	47	1	13
HECTOR ST. JOHN	82	20	1	4
LOUISA C	1692	49	1	20
IDA P	2406	48	2	17
OLLY	801	49	1	19
OKSEY	112	32	1	5
A J	3511	49	2	22
ABETH B	1336	49	1	19
NK, CAPT	3955	49	2	22
N H	222	43	2	8
PH	183	20	1	4
	1614	48	1	15
IE	1909	48	1	16
WELLYN	361	43	1	8
GARET C	143	44	1	9
IA C	356	20	1	2
AH A	528	45	2	10
TH	370	44	1	9
E, JOHN Q	1604	48	1	15
SOLOMON R	2555	48	2	17
NE, JOSEPH R	666	47	1	13
B. B	99	32	1	5
, CHARLES (widow of)	35	35	1	6
	152	36	1	7
, GILMON	103	43	1	8
, J. W	412	49	1	18
, JAMES	1508	47	1	13
JOHN	246	24	1	1
, MARY	152	26	1	7
	96	38	1	7
, ROBERT K	2520	49	1	20
, SUSAN	238	43	1	8
, W. H	1942	48	1	16
ALICE J	1778	46	2	12
	1387	47	1	13
EDERICK	2614	48	2	17
ER, WILLIAM	413	47	1	13
C. M	1384	48	1	15
JOHN	2276	48	2	17
	241	49	1	18
THOMAS	3573	49	2	22
BOTT B. J	894	49	1	19
	1796	49	1	20
LLY B	2544	49	1	21
Y, GEORGE M	128	33	1	5
	20	33	2	5
Y, HECTER ST. JOHN	82	20	1	4
Y, WATSON S	787	46	2	11
	1024	48	1	15
, CATHARINE L	782	47	1	13
	440	49	1	18
, HENRY B	644	43	1	8
GHAM, JAMES	871	45	2	10
D, ALLEN G	43	46	3	12
D, ALEXANDER ST	3	44	1	9
D, FRANCIS	23	43	1	8
o	62	44	1	9
D, WILLIAM G	451	30	1	7
RT, CATHARINE	2503	49	1	20
L, LEVINA	244	43	2	8
ELIZA E	1716	49	1	20
HENRY	1746	49	1	20
MARGARET A	2048	48	1	16
THOMAS	140	34	3	6
o	492	35	1	6
o	225	36	1	7
MAN, SARAH F	121	37	2	7
LF, JANE	125	44	1	9

Private legislation—Continued.

Subject.	Report.	Congress.	Session.	Volume.
BERTRAM, ELIZABETH	367	47	1	13
BETTS, MARIAH	1528	48	2	12
BETHUSEN, WILLIAM	2300	49	1	20
BEWLEY, WILLIAM S.	3563	49	2	22
BEYER, ANTHONY	2222	48	2	17
BEYLAND, JOHN C. F	1875	48	1	16
BEYMER, MARGARET	167	46	3	12
BICKER, EBENEZER	42	25	2	6
BICKERDYKE, MARY A	1088	49	1	19
BICKFORD, JOHN N	2657	49	1	21
BICKNELL, LYDA S	1004	44	2	11
BIDDLE, JACOB S	2626	49	1	21
BIDDLE, JESSE	84	29	1	4
BIEDERBICK, HENRY	2460	48	2	17
BIGELOW, HOPESTILL	405	26	1	2
Do	814	27	2	3
Do	516	33	1	6
BIGELOW, JONAS A	465	44	1	9
BIGGS, JOHN	81	32	1	7
BILHARTEY, FRANCIS W	341	46	3	12
BILLINGS, ANDREW W	1571	49	1	19
BILLINGS, JOHN S	861	26	1	2
BINFORD, J. D	345	45	2	10
BINGHAM, SAMUEL S. (widow of)	555	36	1	7
BINGMAN, DANIEL J	2606	49	1	20
BINNAMON, HENRY	101	46	2	12
Do	362	47	1	13
BIRCHMORE, JULIANA	172	28	1	3
Do	41	29	1	4
BIRD, ANN	1519	49	1	19
BIRD, FRANCIS H	97	46	2	11
BIRD, MARGARET J	1811	47	1	12
BIRNEY, ANTIONETTE	1712	49	1	20
BISCHER, FREDERICK	3962	49	2	22
BISER, NANCY	1377	48	1	16
BISHOP, E. S	3648	49	2	22
BISHOP, WILLIAM	1904	49	1	20
BIXBY, SOPHIA F.	1030	49	1	19
BLACK, EMILLIA O	168	45	2	8
BLACK, JOHN H	36	46	2	11
BLACK, JOSHUA W	281	44	1	9
BLACK, MARY F	2482	49	1	20
BLACK, MARY M	3636	49	1	20
BLACK, WILLIAM	347	45	2	10
BLACKBURN, CYRENUS C	64	36	1	7
BLACKBURN, HESTER V	[illegible]	49	1	21
BLACKMAN, CORNELIA V	[illegible]	48	2	17
BLACKMAN, CORNELIUS C	528	35	1	6
BLACKMAN, GEORGE H	318	46	2	11
Do	419	47	1	13
BLACKNALL, NANCY H	278	44	1	9
BLACKWELL, SARAH	28	35	2	6
Do	147	36	1	7
BLAIR, APOLLINE A	*767	48	1	16
Do	3626	49	2	22
BLAIR, LEWIS J	2046	49	1	20
BLAIR, WILLIAM H	566	43	1	8
BLAISDELL, ENOCH	321	28	1	3
Do	46	29	1	4
BLAISDELL, WILLIAM	135	46	2	12
BLAKE, CHARLES	404	26	1	2
BLAKE, CHARLES E	2263	49	1	20
BLAKE, DANIEL W	1222	47	1	12
BLAKE, HARRIET P	2481	48	2	17
BLAKE, JOHN W	1747	49	1	20
BLAKE, MARY F	2293	48	2	17
BLAKE, MARGARET A.	447	48	1	15
BLAKE, MARY F.	2306	49	1	20
BLAKE, W. H	372	48	1	14
Do	118	48	1	13
BLAKE, WILLIAM	186	28	1	3
Do	16	29	1	4
BLANCHARD, WILLIAM	1421	49	1	19
BLATTENBERGER, JOHN (widow of)	147	36	1	7
Do	46	36	2	7
BLATTNER, CONRAD	75	46	2	12
BLAZE, ELIZA A	369	34	1	6

* Views of minority.

Private legislation—Continued.

Subject.	Report.	Congress.	Session.	Volume.
EORGE	2730	49	1	22
T, ELIJAH	84	22	2	1
Do	573	23	2	1
Do	74	25	3	2
Do	178	26	1	2
Do	446	27	2	3
Do	229	28	1	3
Do	11	28	2	3
Do	45	29	1	4
T, HENRY	233	22	1	1
T, SYLVANUS	779	30	1	4
Do	305	31	1	5
Do	12	32	1	5
JAMES H	2939	49	1	21
MARY J	123	43	1	8
ROBERT AND HENRY	833	30	1	4
Do	105	32	1	5
S, MARY	508	46	2	11
Do	205	47	1	13
OHN (widow of)	149	31	1	5
, ELIZA JANE	145	44	1	9
K, LEWIS	292	46	2	11
Do	946	47	1	13
JOHN C	1196	46	2	12
JAMES V	4117	49	2	22
JOSEPH H	326	46	2	11
, ABRAM D. W	487	26	1	2
Do	299	28	1	3
ELLEN M	1762	46	2	12
ROBERT P	733	45	2	10
Do	784	46	2	11
LYDIA	75	46	3	12
SAMUEL	1047	49	1	19
ANDREW J	2088	48	1	16
, ALFRED	190	43	1	8
AROLINE	61	46	2	12
CHARLES E	1031	49	1	19
GER, H G	3086	49	1	21
N HENRY	1743	49	1	20
, ABIJAH T	100	30	2	4
Do	68	31	1	5
CAROLINE P	2920	49	1	21
EORGE	155	34	1	6
RK, WILLIAM	943	48	1	14
, JOHN	341	35	1	6
AN, GEORGE W	1908	48	1	16
SKA, VOUCHER	335	35	1	6
HUBERT H	556	30	1	4
Do	221	31	1	5
LARK	2123	49	1	20
DANIEL	472	31	1	5
SAMUEL M	1586	46	2	12
WILLIAM	367	46	3	12
Do	1244	47	1	13
Do	1695	48	1	16
Do	771	49	1	19
THOMAS	431	36	1	7
S, JOHN	956	45	2	10
MARGARET	226	27	3	3
AND JAMES M	66	46	3	11
RT, HENRY M	2659	49	1	21
RT, WILHELMINA	236	43	2	8
TER, JOHN	1496	48	1	15
S, JOSEPH	3004	49	1	21
VICK, JUDSON	2079	48	1	16
ORTH, JOHN	7	24	2	1
Do	183	25	2	2
SER, DOROTHEA	1664	46	2	12
Do	571	48	1	14
GER, JOHN J	454	43	1	8
S, WYATT	301	46	2	11
JER, FREDERICK	116	49	1	18
HER, MINNIE C	3016	49	1	21
HTON, HAMILTON	1687	46	2	12
TER, SARAH E	3261	49	1	21
TWELL, ABRAHAM E	544	23	1	1
TWELL, DANIEL W	1425	49	1	19
TWELL, NEWTON	948	47	1	13

Private legislation—Continued.

Subject.	Report.	Congress.	Session.	Volume.
BOWERS, HENRY F	34	35	2	6
Do	367	36	1	7
BOWERS, JEFFERSON	85	44	1	9
BOWERS, JOSEPH	321	46	2	11
Do	369	48	1	14
BOWIE, ELLEN	393	36	1	7
BOWKER, LOVINA ADELINE	334	44	1	9
BOWLEN, JOSEPH	228	27	2	3
Do	115	27	3	3
Do	12	28	2	3
BOWLING, SAMUEL W	1652	48	1	16
Do	1590	49	1	19
BOWMAN, HARRIET L	200	43	2	8
Do	373	44	2	9
BOWMAN, MILO	3842	49	2	22
BOWMAN, WILLIAM	130	24	2	1
Do	223	25	2	2
Do	216	26	1	2
Do	51	46	2	11
BOWMAN, WILLIAM C. H	1086	48	1	14
Do	126	49	1	18
BOYD, ELIZA	2814	49	1	21
BOYD, ISAAC	300	25	2	2
Do	85	25	3	2
Do	215	26	1	2
Do	620	27	2	3
BOYD, ROBERT	3990	49	2	22
BOYD, WILLIAM D	119	43	1	8
BOYDSTON, ELIZABETH	3269	49	1	21
BOYLE, JOHN	1183	46	2	12
Do	1139	48	1	14
BOYLE, MARY	104	35	1	6
BOYNTON, SAMUEL	536	35	1	6
BRACKEN, JANE	778	45	1	14
BRACKETT, ANN M	125	43	1	8
BRACKETT, HEARD	217	22	1	1
Do	7	22	2	1
Do	1	23	1	1
BRACKETT, WILLIAM	425	22	1	1
Do	1	23	1	1
BRADBURY, AUGUSTUS	3635	49	2	22
BRADBURY, P. W	886	48	1	14
BRADFORD, JAMES	960	48	1	14
BRADFORD, JAMES H	227	25	2	2
Do	367	36	1	7
BRADFORD, SARAH H	875	45	2	10
Do	189	46	3	12
BRADLEY, SALLY ANN	1605	48	1	15
Do	778	49	1	19
Do	3420	49	1	21
BRADLEY, PETER	426	22	1	1
BRADY, BERNARD	107	46	2	11
Do	1717	46	2	12
Do	594	47	1	13
BRADY, ELIZABETH	206	43	1	8
BRADY, JOHN	602	44	1	9
BRADY, JOHN N	237	45	3	10
BRADY, MARY	2945	49	1	21
BRADY, ROBERT	570	44	1	9
BRADY, SAMUEL W	31	33	1	5
BRADY, WILLIAM P	199	30	1	4
BRAGG, SARAH L	643	48	1	14
Do	140	49	1	18
BRAIN, ELIZABETH	1078	48	1	15
BRAIN, STEPHEN	664	29	1	4
BRAKE, JOHN T	1709	48	1	16
BRAMFORD, ROBERT C	597	45	2	10
BRANCH, DUDLEY B	2055	49	1	20
BRANCH, PALMER	284	26	1	2
Do	224	26	2	2
Do	161	27	2	3
Do	503	29	1	4
Do	85	30	1	4
BRANHAM, BENJAMIN O	76	33	1	5
BRANT, ALBERT	937	48	1	14
BRANT, GEORGE W	3142	49	1	20
BRARY, NATHANIEL	3268	49	1	21
BRASEL, ANNA	363	43	1	8
Do	374	44	1	9

Private legislation—Continued.

Subject.		Congress.	Session.	Volume.
...ER, DANIEL F	1843	47	1	13
...RS, SCIOTHA	969	43	1	8
..., JOSEPH	790	45	2	10
..., ELIZABETH	553	43	1	8
...ALD, FREDERICK	1218	48	1	15
...IZABETH	945	47	1	13
...RD, SAMUEL D	257	26	1	2
... RICHARD	151	36	1	7
...OSEPH	70	30	2	4
...LIVER S	160	43	1	8
...S, ELIZABETH	114	35	1	6
...R, SARAH J	375	46	2	11
...	1286	48	1	15
..., CATHARINE	85	44	2	9
...	296	45	2	10
...GER, JACOB	1913	49	1	20
...IO, WILLIAM	2966	49	1	21
...OHN	505	35	1	6
...T, ABRAHAM N	250	26	1	2
...ELIZABETH	550	43	1	8
... HENRY	308	36	1	7
... JACKSON A. (heirs of)	555	43	1	8
... REBECCA	74	36	2	7
...ER, MARGARET	457	46	2	11
...ER, VICTORIA L	693	43	1	8
...	155	45	2	10
...KER, DIANA	209	44	1	9
...TEPHEN	684	29	1	4
...DIKE, M. A	9	49	1	18
... CARLISLE	338	44	1	9
... ELIZABETH	2484	49	1	20
... JOHN D	1466	48	1	15
... JOHN S	2822	49	1	20
... SARAH F	3675	49	2	22
... WILLIAM	608	42	1	18
...EHOSHAPHAT	225	26	1	2
...	256	27	2	3
...LAFAYETTE	166	43	2	8
...VELL, ALEXANDER	162	27	2	3
..., JOSIAH	202	43	1	8
...R, JOHN P	575	49	1	18
...LL, SYLVANUS	1769	48	1	16
...LL, GEORGE W	1426	46	2	12
...ALL, GEORGE	177	44	1	9
...E, HARRIETT S	1287	48	1	15
... LYMAN	199	26	1	2
...N, JOHN H	774	44	1	9
..., DAVID	119	44	1	9
..., JOHN L	288	44	1	9
... MARTHA E	171	43	1	8
...CS, P. E	2334	48	2	17
...	65	49	1	18
...US, WILLIAM T	31	35	2	6
...RICK, JACOB	552	26	1	2
...TT, THOMAS	2227	48	2	17
...	135	49	1	18
...CK, ANNIE M	4120	49	2	22
...HIN, ANGELINE	248	49	1	18
...GH, THOMAS	77	28	2	3
...	163	33	1	5
... CHARLES W	131	36	1	7
... EDWARD	1068	27	2	3
... HENRY	1531	49	1	19
... NANCY	289	43	1	8
... SARAH	1744	49	1	20
...HIRE, NOAH B	610	49	1	18
... CHARA	113	44	1	9
...TON, HAMILTON	2202	48	2	17
... ABBIE R	4068	49	2	22
... AMASA	482	28	1	3
... ANN ELIZA	728	43	1	8
...ELIPHAS C	559	30	1	4
...	52	31	1	5
...FIELDING G	276	28	1	3
...	663	29	1	4
...	628	30	1	4
...	238	31	1	5
...GEORGE	70	30	2	4

Private legislation—Continued.

Subject.	Report.	Congress.	Session.	Volume.
BROWN, HENRY	187	44	1	9
Do	849	45	2	10
BROWN, JAMES	2062	46	1	16
Do	2278	46	2	17
BROWN, JAMES W.	1627	48	1	16
BROWN, JOHN	777	25	2	2
Do	229	26	1	2
BROWN, JOSEPH	294	26	1	2
Do	941	27	2	3
Do	583	28	1	4
BROWN, JOSIAH H	304	22	1	1
Do	46	24	1	1
BROWN, LEVI	295	22	1	1
Do	59	23	1	1
Do	232	26	1	2
BROWN, LIZZIE	3253	46	1	21
BROWN, MAHALA	2986	49	1	21
BROWN, MARTHA J	383	44	1	9
BROWN, NANCY R	1715	49	1	20
BROWN, OLIVER	154	33	1	5
BROWN, OWEN M	796	46	2	11
BROWN, PAMELA	402	25	2	2
Do	201	26	1	2
Do	42	33	1	5
BROWN, PENELOPE C	170	42	1	8
Do	157	44	1	9
BROWN, RUTH B	207	43	2	8
BROWN, SAMPSON	84	27	3	3
Do	111	28	1	3
Do	152	29	1	4
BROWN, SAMUEL	810	24	1	1
Do	184	25	2	2
Do	213	26	1	2
Do	159	27	2	3
BROWN, SAMUEL J	1286	49	1	20
BROWN, SARAH	531	35	1	6
BROWN, SHADRACH	3561	49	2	22
BROWN, THOMAS	2418	48	1	20
BROWN, THOMAS H	265	28	1	3
Do	47	29	1	4
BROWN, THOMAS W	666	44	1	9
Do	168	45	2	10
BROWN, WILLIAM	15	33	2	5
Do	231	35	2	6
Do	2853	49	1	20
BROWN, WILLIAM T	1293	47	1	13
BROWN, WILSON W., AND OTHERS	413	47	1	13
Do	2150	48	1	16
BROWNE, WILLIAM R	769	45	2	10
Do	852	48	1	14
BROWNELL, EDWARD T	80	46	2	11
BROWNELL, HORACE W	3578	49	2	22
BROWNELL, KADY	1876	48	1	16
Do	1880	48	1	16
BROWNING, GEORGE W	760	45	2	10
BRUCE, JOHN L	2088	49	1	20
BRUCKNER, HENRY	210	43	1	8
BRUMFIELD, RICHARD B	198	27	3	3
BRUMSEY, MALACHI J., (widow of)	215	47	1	12
BRUNER, F. M	337	44	1	9
BRUNER, FREDERICK R	554	45	2	10
BRUNER, J. F	55	46	1	
BRUNER, THOMAS R	1636	48	1	
Do	3348	49	2	
BRUNT, WILLIAM	286	43	1	
BRUSH, JOSHUA	59	35	1	
BRUTCHIE, CARL	247	42	2	
BRUTSCH, CHARLES	1803	48	1	
BRYAN, DAVID	2417	46	2	
BRYANT, ABEL M	474	35	2	
BRYANT, JOHN	27	36	[illegible]	
BRYANT, ROBERT	1551	48	1	
BRYANT, SAMUEL E	1717	49	1	
BRYANT, SARAH A	871	46	1	
BRYANT, WILLIAM	93	46	1	
BRYSON, MARY ANN	1922	49	1	
BUCHANAN, AARON	110	44	1	
Do	1874	47	1	

Private legislation—Continued.

Subject.	Report.	Congress.	Session.	Volume.
AN, ELIJAH	73	30	1	4
AN, JAMES	762	45	2	10
	1621	47	1	13
	1690	48	1	14
AN, JOHN	2896	49	1	21
AN, RICHARD	178	30	1	4
AN, SALLY MURRAY	75	46	2	11
AN, WILLIAM	374	44	1	9
ARLOTTE	571	45	2	10
	1636	49	1	19
SSE C	1698	49	1	19
ILLIAM G	1364	49	2	20
ILLIAM H. H	709	42	1	6
	2129	49	1	21
HAM, JARED	141	22	1	1
	30	23	2	1
	46	24	1	1
, WILLIAM	587	44	1	9
	645	45	2	10
R, HARVEY P	587	48	1	14
R, WILLIAM	1722	48	1	16
TON, EDWARD J	2637	49	2	22
ARTIN	251	46	2	11
ARAH	282	44	1	9
CHARLES H	219	43	2	8
	272	44	1	9
	581	45	2	10
, MABELLE R	1084	49	1	19
IOS	872	26	1	2
	628	29	1	4
	562	30	1	4
HN	159	27	3	3
	21	28	1	3
SES	872	28	1	3
RMAN S	357	49	1	19
, CATHARINE	688	48	1	14
, WILLIAM	162	45	2	10
, ISABELLA	2089	49	1	21
, JAMES P	330	35	1	6
, WILLIAM	64	33	2	5
	314	35	1	6
	232	36	1	7
SAMUEL	2551	49	1	21
H, JAMES	22	29	1	4
MUEL	176	29	1	4
G. W	1936	49	1	20
ISAIAH W	42	46	2	11
	1745	49	1	20
L, STEPHEN	30	35	1	6
	139	36	1	7
K, ABBY L	461	49	1	18
K, HORACE H	2203	48	2	17
OSEPH W	445	49	1	18
TT, BENJAMIN	1522	48	1	15
ELD, SARAH A	1927	48	1	16
, ELNATHAN	89	38	1	7
, MRS. LYDIA	3984	49	2	22
L. BURNETT	289	25	3	2
	527	26	1	2
	23	27	2	3
FRANKLIN P	2058	48	1	16
ARVEY	324	44	1	9
	83	46	2	11
UCINDA	3733	49	2	22
LISE	2000	49	1	20
JOHN	260	34	1	6
AME, BENJAMIN	186	22	2	1
	7	22	2	1
	1	23	1	1
N, JOHN	103	28	1	3
, HATTIE A	2151	49	1	20
, WARD B	485	46	2	11
M, EZEKIEL	82	24	2	1
M, SYLVANUS	38	35	1	6
	133	36	1	7
	45	37	2	7
IENRIETTE	2405	49	1	20
AMES	358	30	1	4

Private legislation—Continued.

Subject.	Report.	Congress.	Session.	Volume.
BURNS, PETER	1747	48	1	16
BURNS, SARAH	466	43	1	8
BURNS, WILLIAM	486	35	1	6
Do	226	36	1	7
Do	52	38	1	7
BUROUGHS, THOMAS	333	45	2	10
BURRILL, ANDREW J	2823	49	1	21
BURRILL, JOHN G	1343	49	1	19
BURRIS, JAMES	697	43	1	8
BURRIS, NEWTON J	2517	48	2	17
BURRITT, LOREN	2019	49	1	20
BURTZ, AMBROSE	425	49	1	18
BURWELL, SAMUEL	1668	46	2	12
Do	69	47		11
BUSH, WILLIAM W	2553	48		17
BUSHY, REBECCA E	3282	49		21
BUSTER, FELIX R	1593	49		19
BUTLER, ARETUS N	2081	49		20
BUTLER, CHARLOTTE	32	35		6
BUTLER, JAMES	379	31		[illegible]
Do	157	33		5
Do	271	49		19
Do	2133	49		20
BUTLER, JAMES H	2307	49		20
BUTLER, JOHN	1798	49		20
BUTLER, JOHN (widow of)	374	30	1	[illegible]
BUTLER, M. LOUISE	3564	49	2	22
BUTLER, MARGARET	770	49		20
BUTLER, ROBERT	526	45		10
BUTLER, SAMUEL	400	26		2
Do	674	27		3
Do	221	28		3
Do	87	30	2	4
BUTLER, WILLIAM	278	30	1	4
BUTTERFIELD, MRS. ANNA	3871	49	2	22
BUTTERFIELD, ASA	22	30	2	[illegible]
BUTTERFIELD, WILLIAM	209	26	1	2
Do	159	26	2	2
Do	163	27	2	3
Do	57	28	1	3
BYERS, ELIZA M	2397	48	2	17
BYERS, MARY	2354	49	1	20
BYNUM, JOHN W	1909	49	1	20
BYRNE, LOUISA ABERT	46	37	2	7
BYRNES, DANIEL J	1035	49	1	19
CADDIS, ADELINE	148	36	1	[illegible]
CADDY, CHARLES B	854	48	1	14
CADY, JOEL E	2327	48	2	17
CAINE, THOMAS	1471	47	1	13
Do	482	48	1	14
CALDWELL, DAVID B	3385	49	1	21
CALDWELL, ISAAC R. H	1535	48	1	15
Do	2987	49	1	21
CALDWELL, JOSEPH T	270	48	1	14
CALDWELL, JUDSON W	775	44	1	9
CALHOUN, BENJAMIN	426	22	1	1
CALHOUN, GEORGE W	172	44		9
CALKENS, ELENOR	821	27	2	3
CALKINS, NEWTON A	2152	49		20
CALL, IRA	230	33		[illegible]
CALL, RUFUS JR	299	36		[illegible]
CALLAHAN, GEORGE	822	27	2	3
CALLANAN, MARGARET	456	48	1	14
Do	429	49	1	18
CALLANAN, PATRICK A	2068	49	1	20
CALLISON, CLAIBORN	3273	49	1	21
CALLUM, ANDREW S	2355	49	1	20
CALVIN, JACOB	433	28	1	3
CALVIN, JAMES	93	23	2	1
Do	46	24		1
CAMERON, JOHN W	77	33		5
CAMERON, SARAH J	1595	47		13
CAMMACK, JOHN	296	25		2
CAMP, JOHN	105	35		6
CAMPBELL, ELI W	2273	48		17
Do	64	49	1	18
Do	1602	49	1	20
CAMPBELL, GEORGE H	816	49		18

Private legislation—Continued.

Subject.	Report.	Congress.	Session.	Volume.
, ISABEL	674	48	1	14
, JAMES	554	26	1	2
	936	27	2	3
	307	29	1	4
, JESSE	662	29	1	4
	2663	49	1	21
, JOHN	425	27	2	3
	469	29	1	4
	289	30	1	4
	482	31	1	5
	161	34	1	6
	146	35	1	6
	3854	49	2	22
, MARGARET S	2084	48	1	16
, NICHOLAS I	2213	48	2	17
, PETER	696	43	1	8
	564	44	1	9
, PHILIP D	10	49	1	18
, PHŒBE	2598	49	1	21
, WILLIAM F	2902	49	1	21
, WILLIAM S	2109	49	1	20
, LIZUR B	286	30	1	4
ICHAEL	1221	48	1	15
UGH	668	26	1	2
VILLIAM	582	49	1	18
ENRY	3387	49	1	21
, CHARLES E	2887	49	1	21
, ELIAS	185	28	1	3
ELSON	1824	48	1	16
LLIAM M	514	48	1	14
BAGAIL H	1370	49	1	19
CHIBALD A	187	46	3	12
	808	47	1	13
THER M	1590	47	1	13
MES	58	42	3	7
CHARLES C	35	30	2	4
, ISAAC	1098	49	1	19
, WILLIAM P	1776	49	1	20
ERNARD	60	49	1	18
AMES	2684	49	1	21
ARY B	341	49	1	18
ANNIE	3289	49	1	21
EL, SUSANNAH	324	49	1	18
N, ABIGAIL	1596	49	1	20
R, ANSON G	2594	49	1	21
R, ELIAS	83	29	1	4
R, ISAAC	79	35	1	6
	137	36	1	7
R, RICHARD	1428	46	2	12
	851	47	1	13
R, THOMAS	812	27	2	3
RLES H	543	48	1	14
E	2315	49	1	20
N W	1767	48	1	16
ITIA	460	43	1	8
	2602	49	1	21
RY	2455	49	1	20
RY C., AND OTHERS	53	36	1	7
RY M	330	35	1	6
	2597	49	1	21
PHILANDA	2478	48	2	17
RANKLIN	1179	48	1	15
AMES	698	49	1	18
HAMILTON	237	31	1	5
SARAH M	2309	49	1	20
LLEN W. P	363	46	2	11
	1810	47	1	13
SAAC	447	23	1	1
	46	24	1	1
OEL R	1652	46	2	12
	663	47	1	13
ULIA ANN	740	45	2	10
ANDOLPH	229	25	2	2
	292	25	3	2
	94	26	2	2
	131	27	2	3
ENRY I	2016	49	1	20
HT, JOSEPH	300	46	2	11

Private legislation—Continued.

Subject.	Report.	Congress.	Session.	Volume.
CARTWRIGHT, JOSEPH V	683	43	1	8
CARTY, DENNIS	696	49	1	18
CARVER, FRANCIS	318	35	1	6
CARY, BARNABAS	430	27	2	3
CARY, ROBERT	197	45	3	10
Do	1532	47	1	13
Do	2237	48	2	17
CASE, JACOB	2585	49	1	21
CASE, MRS. MARY JANE	4061	49	2	22
CASE, SOLOMON	80	23	2	1
CASEY, FLORIDA G	1390	47	1	13
CASEY, JOHN	282	23	1	1
Do	330	24	1	1
Do	461	25	2	2
CASEY, JULIA	843	46	2	11
CASEY, ROBERT	318	25	2	2
CASHIN, MARGARET	3386	49	1	21
CASKEY, ALEXANDER	754	49	1	19
CASKEY, JAMES T	77	49	1	18
CASSADAY, GEORGE	412	26	1	2
Do	440	27	2	3
Do	577	30	1	4
Do	47	31	1	5
Do	85	32	1	5
Do	241	34	1	6
CASSADY, JANE	343	48	1	14
CASSIDY, ISABELLA	100	44	2	9
Do	172	45	2	10
CASTEEL, SARAH	1702	49	1	20
CASTERWELLER, MARY A	376	44	1	9
Do	289	46	2	11
CASTLE, ANTHONY (alias Casloa)	108	35	2	6
CASTLE, F. M	1721	48	1	16
CASWELL, MARGARET A	258	48	1	14
Do	463	49	1	18
CASWELL, RICHARD G	392	31	1	5
CASWELL, SIMEON	234	27	2	3
Do	98	28	1	3
Do	509	29	1	4
CATON, NOAH	47	46	2	11
Do	509	47	1	13
Do	1154	48	1	15
CAULK, ROBERT W	66	34	3	6
Do	343	35	1	6
CAUSEY, WILLIAM	657	29	1	4
CAUSIN, ELIZA	801	24	1	1
Do	458	25	2	2
CAVAN, TIMOTHY	52	36	1	7
CAVANAUGH, ROBERT	206	43	2	8
Do	81	44	1	9
CEVILLE, ELIZA	530	45	2	10
CHABOT, HELEN	2282	48	2	17
CHADBOURNE, ADELINE E	2244	48	2	17
CHADDOCK, ALONZO A	2981	49	1	21
CHADDOCK, JARED	704	48	1	14
CHALFANT, JOSEPH	753	49	1	19
CHALLER, HENRY	680	25	2	2
CHAMBERLAIN, JABEZ	2230	48	2	17
Do	133	49	1	18
CHAMBERLAIN, JOSEPH	229	22	1	1
Do	7	22	2	1
Do	69	23	1	1
CHAMBERLAIN, SARAH A. M	495	46	2	11
CHAMBERLIN, JOSIAH B	309	45	2	10
CHAMBERLIN, SIMON C	242	45	3	10
CHAMBERS, GEORGE	1736	49	1	[illegible]
CHAMBERS, GREEN	1925	49	1	[illegible]
CHAMBERS, HORACE A. (heirs)	751	45	2	10
Do	81	46	2	11
CHAMBERS, JULIA A	173	46	3	12
Do	633	48	1	14
CHAMBERS, SOPHIA	2607	49	1	22
CHAMPION, SILAS	7	22	1	1
Do	67	23	1	1
CHAMPLAIN, PRENTIS	432	36	1	7
CHANDLER, ELLEN M	333	49	1	[illegible]
CHANDLER, JAMES C	2052	49	1	[illegible]
CHANDLER, LARKIN	2312	49	1	[illegible]

Private legislation—Continued.

Subject.	Report.	Congress.	Session.	Volume.
ER, MARTIN D	711	48	1	[illegible]
Y, MARGARET A	484	48	1	[illegible]
MYRON	381	25	2	[illegible]
	79	25	3	[illegible]
	127	25	1	[illegible]
N, ALICE	2561	49	1	20
K, DANIEL S	230	25	1	6
N, HANNAH M	226	49	1	16
CAROLINE	307	47	1	13
CHARLES A	1197	48	1	15
	2972	49	1	21
DANIEL	145	26	2	2
	143	27	2	3
JOHN F	520	45	2	10
	319	47	1	12
	1878	48	1	16
	776	46	1	15
	1582	49	1	19
NATHANIEL D	2271	49	2	22
HOVE	159	34	2	8
	327	35	1	6
SUSAN A	587	44	1	9
LD, ALONZO B	1145	48	1	14
	1461	48	1	15
	6166	49	2	22
LD, SILAS	712	29	1	4
	684	30	1	4
S, GRIFFITH	136	44	1	9
Y, BARBARA A	1982	48	1	16
FIDELIA A	551	49	1	18
ETH, ISAAC	115	49	1	18
NG, REUBEN J	69	44	2	9
	24	45	2	10
E, THOMAS	401	48	1	14
NG, REUBEN J	69	44	2	9
	24	45	2	10
	1740	48	1	16
EMMA K	1320	47	1	13
HENRY	710	30	1	4
N, SARAH J	245	45	3	10
	1100	46	2	11
	713	48	1	14
DEN, HERMAN	292	33	1	5
DEN, NOAH	228	23	1	1
	497	25	2	2
HIRAM K	1402	48	1	15
	1978	49	1	20
AN, JAMES T	198	45	3	10
	783	46	2	11
E, EUNICE	585	43	1	8
E, LEWIS	1010	48	1	16
E, WILLIAM	2206	48	2	17
	653	49	1	18
TER, LEWIS	2483	49	1	20
DANIEL W	669	26	1	2
	57	26	2	2
	436	28	1	3
WILLIAM	150	46	2	11
	3254	49	1	21
ILL, POLLY	565	26	1	2
MAN, HENRY J	792	46	2	11
WELL, JOHN W	304	46	2	11
MARY A	164	43	1	8
C. A	715	48	1	14
JONATHAN	2149	34	1	6
NIRIUS	2948	49	1	21
ON, AUSLEM	30	35	2	6
o	228	36	1	7
ELL, JUDSON W	775	44	1	9
ENS, PETER	852	46	2	11
N, GEORGE S	707	30	1	4
o	293	31	1	5
o	27	33	1	5
AVID	204	22	1	1
EMMA L	1341	40	1	19
ANNA M	2250	49	1	20
CAREY	213	22	1	1
CAROLINE E	858	36	1	7
o	94	37	2	7

Private legislation—Continued.

Subject.	Report.	Congress.	Session.	Volume.
CLARK, CATHARINE	706	[illegible]	1	[illegible]
Do	480	31	1	5
Do	82	32	1	[illegible]
CLARK, CHARLOTTE T	1174	46	2	[illegible]
CLARK, DANIEL B	19	[illegible]	1	[illegible]
CLARK, DAVID S	1046	[illegible]	1	[illegible]
CLARK, ELIZABETH	359	43	1	[illegible]
CLARK, EUNICE E	1539	49	1	[illegible]
CLARK, GEORGE W	2842	48	2	17
CLARK, HENRIETTA S	82	35	1	6
CLARK, JAMES	841	48	1	14
CLARK, JOHN	750	24	1	1
Do	185	25	2	2
CLARK, JOHN C	2237	46	2	17
Do	51	46	1	14
CLARK, JOHN D	260	46	1	14
CLARK, LIVINGSTON	2934	49	1	21
CLARK, MARION	657	48	1	14
CLARK, MARY ANN	149	34	1	6
CLARK, MICHAEL R	108	35	2	6
Do	145	36	1	7
CLARK, NOAH D	703	45	1	14
CLARK, OVID H	813	45	2	10
CLARK, PHILA	2937	49	1	21
CLARK, SUSAN C	243	43	2	8
CLARK, WILLIAM L	1970	49	1	[illegible]
CLARY, DANIEL	529	44	1	9
Do	139	45	2	10
CLAY, CECIL	818	47	1	13
CLAY, M. S.	557	48	1	14
CLEMENTS, MILTON H	1631	47	1	13
Do	273	48	1	14
CLICK, HENRY	263	22	1	1
Do	7	22	2	1
Do	706	29	1	4
Do	146	31	1	5
Do	96	32	1	3
CLIFT, WILLIAM N	1197	46	2	12
CLIPPENGER, ANNA M	339	45	2	10
CLOSE, ELIJAH	42	32	1	3
Do	338	34	1	6
Do	307	35	1	6
CLOUD, GEORGE C	800	46	2	12
CLUNE, ELIZABETH	1193	49	1	13
CLUNE, MARGARET R	68	43	2	6
Do	2538	49	1	21
COATS, THOMAS	147	31	1	5
COBAUGH, WILLIAM D	32	44	1	7
Do	649	45	2	10
COBB, EUNICE	224	36	1	[illegible]
Do	55	37	2	[illegible]
COBB, JUSTUS	66	23	2	1
COBB, SURRANUS	466	29	1	4
Do	55	37	2	[illegible]
COBB, URSULA E	147	34	1	6
COBBS, ELIZABETH S	801	30	1	4
COBERLY, JOSEPH	632	27	2	3
Do	167	27	3	3
Do	33	30	1	4
COBURN, HARVEY	2810	[illegible]	1	[illegible]
COCHRAN, JAMES	37	[illegible]	2	4
COCHRAN, MARGARET E	[illegible]	[illegible]	1	13
COCHRAN, SAMUEL	81	[illegible]	1	[illegible]
COCKRUM, ALBERTINE	1977	[illegible]	1	[illegible]
Do	[illegible]	[illegible]	1	[illegible]
CODDINGTON, MRS. ARABELLA	4067	[illegible]	2	[illegible]
COE, JAMES	[illegible]	[illegible]	1	4
COFER, THOMAS J	384	47	1	13
COFFEE, MARGARET	[illegible]	[illegible]	1	[illegible]
COFFEY, WILLIAM M	[illegible]	[illegible]	2	13
COFFIELD, PATRICK	[illegible]	[illegible]	1	[illegible]
COFFIN, CATHARINE E	2113	[illegible]	1	[illegible]
COFFIN, CHARLES	[illegible]	[illegible]	2	1
Do	[illegible]	[illegible]	2	[illegible]
COFFIN, NATHANIEL JOHNSON	78	44	2	[illegible]
Do	[illegible]	[illegible]	1	13
COGBURN, MARGARET E	[illegible]	[illegible]	1	[illegible]
COGLEY, THOMAS S	[illegible]	[illegible]	2	12

***Private legislation*—Continued.**

Subject.	Report.	Congress.	Session.	Volume.
WILLIAM	560	45	2	10
RY S.	665	49	1	18
MARGARET	1099	49	1	20
LIZABETH J.	796	46	2	11
	1002	46	1	14
RA	2514	49	2	22
RY G.	288	49	1	18
AIN	474	22	1	1
	58	22	2	1
ARD	705	30	1	4
KE	498	36	1	7
.	612	27	2	3
IER	367	34	1	6
JEL	356	24	1	1
SSA B.	651	48	1	8
EDWARD	2628	49	1	21
HESTER	549	43	1	8
WILLIAM H. H.	1936	48	1	16
RANCIS	88	38	1	7
NDERSON	423	49	1	15
BRAM	1340	47	1	13
	884	48	1	14
OLEMAN A.	329	24	1	1
NDREWS	479	31	1	5
BRIDGET	730	43	1	8
	684	44	1	9
ATHERINE	99	49	1	18
LIZABETH	2136	49	1	20
ANNY	849	49	1	18
ERIAH	1479	48	1	15
	2098	49	1	20
OEL	63	28	2	5
IADISON	675	26	1	2
SCAR S.	418	44	1	9
HOMAS	98	24	2	1
	181	25	2	2
	75	25	3	2
	179	26	1	2
	21	26	2	2
	129	27	2	3
ILLIAM	60	23	1	1
	48	24	2	1
	498	25	2	2
IAH	831	46	2	11
VI	645	25	2	2
	239	25	3	2
	220	26	1	2
	77	26	2	2
	138	27	3	3
	96	28	1	3
	456	30	1	4
MARGARET R.	712	44	1	9
	131	45	2	10
	299	46	2	11
	821	47	1	13
JAMES W.	805	49	1	19
LIE	37	23	1	1
R, HANNAH S.	178	46	3	12
R, AGNES	348	46	3	12
THOMAS M.	18	49	1	18
T, DAVID	2323	48	2	17
DANIEL	145	45	2	10
ABEL	2121	49	1	20
NORMAN	604	44	1	9
RTEMUS	279	30	1	4
	15	32	1	5
ILLIAM	277	49	1	18
RTHUR	514	46	2	11
RN G.	359	46	2	11
MUEL	296	29	1	4
	197	30	1	4
IARY A.	491	46	2	11
	711	47	1	13
OHN	309	23	1	1
	316	24	1	1
	22	32	1	5
AAC	984	25	2	2

Private legislation—Continued.

Subject.	Report.	Congress.	Session.	Volume.
CONN, THOMAS K	91	38	1	7
Do	133	38	1	7
CONNELLY, JULIA	1273	49	1	19
CONNER, CHARLES	62	33	2	5
CONNER, LABAN	1190	46	2	12
Do	1028	47	1	13
CONNER, NANCY	2481	49	1	20
CONNER, NOAH	247	28	1	2
CONNER, WILLIAM	2419	49	1	20
CONNOLLY, DANIEL	272	46	2	12
Do	109	49	1	18
CONNOLLY, JOHN	152	34	1	6
CONNOR, MORRIS O	1766	48	1	16
CONNOR, SARAH	50	33	2	5
CONRAD, JESSE	1099	46	2	11
CONRAD, MARY JANE	786	49	1	19
CONROY, JANE	399	44	1	9
CONWELL, ANN J	458	49	1	19
COOK, ANNA E	164	33	1	5
COOK, HOLDEN	1472	48	1	15
Do	2270	48	2	17
Do	13	49	1	18
COOK, JAMES H	879	45	2	10
COOK, JOHN H	1010	48	1	14
COOK, JEFFERSON W	387	31	1	5
COOK, LEWIS B	951	47	1	12
COOK, LYMAN N	208	26	1	2
Do	158	26	2	2
Do	805	27	2	3
Do	375	28	1	3
Do	44	33	1	5
Do	151	34	1	6
Do	27	35	2	6
COOK, MAGDALENA	779	48	1	14
COOK, MARSHALL N	1505	48	1	15
COOK, MEDAD	198	26	1	2
COOK, PETER	221	24	1	1
COOK, ROBERT	1599	47	1	13
COOKE, DANIEL	217	27	2	3
COOKSEY, HEILA C	196	43	2	8
Do	151	44	1	9
COOLEY, ABRAM	1340	47	1	13
COOLEY, ELI W	3246	49	1	21
COOLEY, ORIN P	2959	49	1	21
COOMER, PIUS A	494	46	2	11
COON, FARLEY F	537	35	1	6
COON, TOBIAS M	548	49	1	19
COONEY, ANN E	1505	49	1	19
COONEY, BETSEY	3257	49	1	21
COONEY, LIZZIE E	224	49	1	18
COOPER, ALONZO	1163	48	1	13
COOPER, ELVIRA	4158	49	2	22
COOPER, GILBERT	121	35	2	6
COOPER, JOHN	625	27	2	3
COOPER, SAMUEL Z	76	43	2	8
Do	1216	48	1	15
COOPER, SARAH S	718	43	1	8
COPELAND, ELIZABETH	178	43	1	8
CORBETT, MARY	2925	49	1	21
CORBIN, ANN	1087	48	1	14
CORCORAN, ELLEN	2297	49	1	20
CORDOVA, JOHN	285	46	2	12
COREY, LEANDER W	1117	49	1	19
CORFE, FREDERICK	1685	48	1	16
CORL, MICHAEL S	723	45	2	10
CORLETT, JOHN S	578	43	1	8
Do	573	45	2	10
Do	1106	46	2	11
CORNELL, F. C	1222	46	2	12
CORNELL, GEORGE (widow of)	83	36	2	7
CORNELL, MARY ANN	176	44	1	9
CORNELL, SCOTT	218	48	1	14
CORNING, EDWARD	2314	42	1	[illegible]
Do	3018	49	1	21
CORNWELL, ALONZO	1865	48	1	16
CORNWELL, DANIEL	1104	46	2	11
Do	2402	48	2	17
CORRIGON, MARGARET	2530	48	2	17

Private legislation—Continued.

Subject.	Report.	Congress.	Session.	Volume.
ETTA	3712	49	2	22
RIET A. B	2408	48	2	17
CHARLES	342	29	1	4
HEN A	718	30	1	4
	304	31	2	5
ILAS	1641	49	1	19
JOHN B	978	45	2	10
NED	180	45	2	10
	1707	48	1	20
	1910	48	1	20
ATHANIEL W	1214	46	2	12
IAS B	3709	49	2	22
W	1911	48	1	20
RICHARD	650	24	1	1
	57	26	2	2
N	1	22	1	1
RAHAM	1287	48	1	15
STER	34	30	1	4
N	1783	49	1	20
HN	380	46	2	12
HARLOTTE M	113	46	2	11
	217	48	1	14
HOMAS	383	36	1	7
	550	36	1	7
STUS C	222	36	1	7
M P	1701	48	1	15
CIS M	1216	47	1	13
GE W	1503	49	1	19
S	285	26	1	2
C	104	42	3	8
W	583	22	1	1
	779	25	2	2
	475	26	1	2
	184	34	2	6
H W	607	27	2	3
EL	727	44	1	9
TRICK	1219	46	1	15
ELEN	763	45	2	10
LITTLETON	290	29	1	4
INDA	700	43	1	8
RIA B	176	45	2	10
LIAM	240	34	1	6
S, JOSEPH	74	28	2	3
	184	20	1	4
EON	1538	48	1	15
MEON	1317	47	1	13
RRILL H	229	45	3	10
	1219	46	2	12
T, GEORGE W	1102	49	1	19
IARY	1243	47	1	13
OAH S	3096	49	1	21
, GEORGE W	420	48	1	14
JOHN (widow of)	935	27	2	3
N	161	43	1	8
ARLOTTE	115	43	1	8
RRILL H	229	45	3	10
	1219	46	2	12
TRICK	964	47	1	13
, MARY	213	43	2	8
AMUEL	40	35	2	6
PETER J	241	43	1	8
MARIE LOUISE	2465	48	2	17
	2479	48	2	17
A. M. (widow of)	2117	40	1	20
JOSEPH R.	1017	49	1	19
D, EMELINE	679	49	1	18
D, J. G	1468	48	1	15
D, RICHARD B	52	42	2	7
D, THOMAS	241	36	1	7
	270	44	1	9
	26	45	2	10
ANUEL	294	22	1	1
	69	23	1	1
REVLIN C	3012	49	1	21
ON, ELIZABETH W	2196	48	2	17
S, MOSES	474	22	1	1
BENJAMIN	266	34	1	6
ENJAMIN R	737	43	1	8

Private legislation—Continued.

Subject.	Report.	Congress.	Session.	Volume.
CRINIAN, JOHN	75	[illegible]	1	8
CRITES, ROBERT A	[illegible]	[illegible]	1	18
CRITTEN, JACOB R	[illegible]	[illegible]	2	22
CROAN, WARREN	2071	[illegible]	1	18
CROCKER, CHARLOTTE D	[illegible]	[illegible]	1	[illegible]
CROCKETT, DANIEL H	576	[illegible]	2	3
CROMAN, JACOB G	[illegible]	[illegible]	2	10
CRONK, SARAH M	1427	[illegible]	1	19
CRONKHITE, LEWIS A	[illegible]	[illegible]	1	21
CRASLY, JACOB	[illegible]	[illegible]	2	22
CROSBY, ORRIS	154	[illegible]	1	4
CROSBY, SARAH ANN	75	[illegible]	2	3
CROSBY, THOMPSON H	221	36	3	6
Do	57	[illegible]	1	6
CROSS, MARY BRADLEY	573	[illegible]	2	10
CROSS, THOMAS R	762	[illegible]	2	10
CROUCH, MARTIN V	1062	[illegible]	1	19
CROUNSE, A	2857	[illegible]	1	21
CROW, JOSEPH H	1059	[illegible]	2	22
Do	[illegible]	47	1	23
CROW, WALTER H	657	[illegible]	1	24
CROWLEY, ELIZABETH	[illegible]	[illegible]	1	23
CROWLEY, JAMES W	873	[illegible]	2	16
CROZIER, JOHN A	[illegible]	[illegible]	1	24
CRUBAUGH, REPHENIAH	[illegible]	45	2	19
CRUM, ABRAHAM	[illegible]	35	1	6
Do	71	[illegible]	1	7
CRUM, ALEXANDER M	421	[illegible]	1	14
CRUTE, JOHN	164	27	3	3
CRYMBLE, ELLEN	795	[illegible]	1	18
CULLEN, BRIDGET M	[illegible]	[illegible]	1	19
CULLEN, JAMES F	[illegible]	47	1	13
Do	2901	[illegible]	1	24
CULLINS, JOHN	[illegible]	23	1	1
CULLISON, RACHEL A	[illegible]	44	1	9
CULVER, ORLANDO	[illegible]	[illegible]	1	14
CUMMINGS, JAMES	[illegible]	[illegible]	1	2
CUMMINGS, LAURINDA G	1056	47	1	13
Do	2562	[illegible]	2	17
Do	[illegible]	[illegible]	2	22
CUMMINGS, LUCY ANN	340	[illegible]	1	8
CUMMINS, BENJAMIN	22	[illegible]	2	6
CUMMINS, JOHN W	201	[illegible]	1	15
CUNNINGHAM, CRISTOPHER	[illegible]	[illegible]	1	4
CUNNINGHAM, JESSE	[illegible]	[illegible]	1	1
Do	7	[illegible]	2	1
Do	[illegible]	[illegible]	1	1
Do	[illegible]	[illegible]	1	2
CUNNINGHAM, JOHN	116	[illegible]	2	6
Do	[illegible]	37	2	7
CUNNINGHAM, MARIA	1816	49	1	[illegible]
CUNNINGHAM, MARY	[illegible]	[illegible]	2	5
CUNNINGHAM, ROBERT	[illegible]	[illegible]	2	6
Do	[illegible]	[illegible]	2	6
Do	[illegible]	[illegible]	1	7
CUPPY, MARY	1198	[illegible]	2	12
CURBY, ABRAHAM	[illegible]	[illegible]	2	[illegible]
CURETON, JOHN (*heirs of*)	[illegible]	[illegible]	1	6
CURRAN, FRANCIS	[illegible]	[illegible]	1	9
Do	[illegible]	[illegible]	1	[illegible]
CURRIE, HANNAH E	[illegible]	[illegible]	1	[illegible]
CURRY, MARTIN V	[illegible]	[illegible]	1	[illegible]
CURRY, NANCY	[illegible]	[illegible]	1	[illegible]
CURTIN, PATRICK	[illegible]	[illegible]	1	[illegible]
CURTIS, BELINDA	610	[illegible]	2	11
CURTIS, KELSEY	510	[illegible]	1	16
CUSHING, KATE L	[illegible]	[illegible]	1	[illegible]
CUSHMAN, NANNIE	[illegible]	[illegible]	1	[illegible]
CUSIC, DANIEL	[illegible]	[illegible]	1	[illegible]
CUTBUSH, JAMES S	[illegible]	[illegible]	1	[illegible]
CUTLER, GEORGE W	[illegible]	[illegible]	1	[illegible]
CUTTER, AMANDA	[illegible]	[illegible]	1	[illegible]
DADE, AMANDA M	[illegible]	[illegible]	1	[illegible]
DAGGETT, JAMES C	[illegible]	[illegible]	2	[illegible]
DAGLEY, STOKELY D	[illegible]	[illegible]	1	[illegible]
DAIL, JAMES I	[illegible]	[illegible]	1	[illegible]
DAILEY, ELIJAH	[illegible]	[illegible]	[illegible]	[illegible]
DAILY, DANIEL	[illegible]	[illegible]	1	[illegible]

Subject.	Report.	Congress.	Session.	Volume.
IARGARET	851	48	1	14
VILLIAM	102	35	2	6
VILLIAM (heirs of)	96	46	2	11
)SEPH (heirs of)	24	38	2	5
HANNAH M	330	43	2	8
MARY B	117	43	1	8
	74	46	2	11
ICHAEL	1598	48	1	15
	2072	49	1	20
, JAMES E. B	1367	49	1	19
IARRIET P	1610	48	1	15
EROME	559	48	1	14
ARY E	1191	46	2	12
HODA	7	49	1	18
JOHN M	380	46	2	11
, AMOS	282	28	1	3
, FRANCIS	2207	48	2	17
, JOHN	870	45	2	10
JOHN W	685	43	1	8
, DAVID	1315	47	1	13
, ELI	28	34	3	6
, EZEKIEL	130	38	1	7
, JAMES D	1904	49	1	20
, NATHAN H	172	32	1	5
L, HIRAM A	3944	49	2	22
, CHANCEY G	2568	48	2	17
. JAMES S	1647	48	1	16
RTY, CREET H	2052	48	1	16
ORT, JOHN	115	32	1	5
ORT, LEVI C	586	45	2	10
ORT, PATSEY	14	46	2	11
RITCHIE (widow of)	307	44	1	9
)N, CHRISTOPHER P	297	48	1	14
)N, CLARA B	2943	49	1	21
)N, JAMES	144	28	2	3
)	16	29	1	4
)N, JOHN W	4157	49	2	22
)N, SAMUEL	1826	48	1	16
ADELINE	88	44	2	9
ANDERSON	190	43	2	8
ASA	800	27	2	3
)	435	28	1	3
BELFORD E	3947	49	2	22
ELIZABETH	734	45	2	10
)	1213	46	2	12
)	593	47	1	13
)	1961	48	1	16
HENRY	1865	48	1	16
EFFERSON W	111	43	1	8
OHN	552	48	1	14
OHN M	512	46	2	11
OHN P	16	49	1	18
ONATHAN E. (widow of)	2003	49	1	20
A	2277	48	2	17
OT	365	33	1	5
OUIS	235	27	2	3
)	1363	49	1	19
MARQUIS D	1096	48	1	14
MARY A	781	47	1	13
MOSES	231	28	1	3
o.	533	29	1	4
NATHANIEL	298	25	2	2
o.	81	25	3	2
o.	186	26	1	2
o.	227	26	2	2
o.	230	27	2	3
NATHANIEL W	294	45	1	18
RACHEL A	768	45	2	10
SAMUEL	448	48	1	14
THEODORUS	461	30	1	4
VERLINDA	357	46	3	12
W.C	1115	49	1	19
WILLIAM B	3013	49	1	21
WILLIAM C	701	43	1	8
WILLIAM S	87	45	2	10
ON, PEYTON	1821	48	1	16
GEORGE	785	48	1	14
SY, ABIGAIL S	377	44	1	9

Private legislation—Continued.

Subject.	Report.	Congress.	Session.	Volume.
DAY, CHARLES H	173	45	2	16
Do	1175	47	1	13
DAY, CHARLOTTE E	281	46	[illegible]	[illegible]
DAY, HARMON	3572	49	[illegible]	[illegible]
DAY, MARTIN V	86	44	[illegible]	[illegible]
DAY, MARY E	594	44	[illegible]	[illegible]
DAY, NEWTON	737	48	1	[illegible]
DAY, WILLIAM L	279	46	[illegible]	[illegible]
DAY, WILLIAM W	344	48	1	[illegible]
DAYSPRING, GEORGE	296	42	[illegible]	[illegible]
DAYTON, SARAH	138	46	[illegible]	[illegible]
DEAN, JOHN	250	32	[illegible]	[illegible]
DEAN, JOHN A	648	46	[illegible]	[illegible]
DEANY, MARY	82	33	1	[illegible]
DEARTH, FREDERICK P	1990	48	[illegible]	[illegible]
DEATS, ALFRED C	1238	47	[illegible]	[illegible]
DEAVENPORT, MICHAEL A	311	35	[illegible]	[illegible]
DE BELLEVUE, F. B	313	27	[illegible]	[illegible]
DECKER, ELLEN	1800	48	[illegible]	[illegible]
DECKER, ELMER	1806	48	[illegible]	[illegible]
DECKER, LAFAYETTE	389	44	[illegible]	[illegible]
DECKER, MARY BELL	164	44	[illegible]	[illegible]
DECKER, SELAR B	759	43	[illegible]	[illegible]
DEERY, WILLIAM H	357	45	[illegible]	[illegible]
DEFENBAUGH, JOHN	67	49	[illegible]	[illegible]
DE GARMO, PAUL	819	29	1	[illegible]
DE GROFFT, HIRAM H	1382	47	[illegible]	[illegible]
DE HAVEN, MARY N	972	45	2	[illegible]
Do	216	45	[illegible]	[illegible]
DEICHER, FRANK	289	45	[illegible]	[illegible]
DE KILPATRICK, LOUISA V	262	48	[illegible]	[illegible]
DELANE, JAMES	1042	48	1	[illegible]
DELAY, JOHN W	1149	46	[illegible]	[illegible]
DELOACH, SIMON	206	22	[illegible]	[illegible]
Do	37	23	1	[illegible]
DELP, JOHN W	2155	49	1	[illegible]
DELPH, LARKIN	2077	49	1	[illegible]
DEMARANVILLE, ISAAC	461	48	1	[illegible]
DE MAY, EFFISIA C	297	36	1	[illegible]
DEMING, ELISHA	245	29	1	[illegible]
DEMING, FRANCIS	1503	49	1	[illegible]
DEMMICK, RUSSEL H	1890	48	1	[illegible]
DE MOTTE, GEORGE W	3517	49	2	[illegible]
DEMPSEY, CATHERINE	1685	46	2	[illegible]
DEMPSEY, EDWARD	271	44	1	[illegible]
DEMPSEY, JOSEPH	1662	46	2	[illegible]
DENENE, WILLIAM	580	45	2	[illegible]
DENHAM, WASHINGTON	398	31	1	[illegible]
DENIO, FREDERICK	171	37	[illegible]	[illegible]
DENNEY, GEORGE	877	45	2	[illegible]
DENNIN, SIMEON	156	38	1	[illegible]
DENNIS, MRS. G. A	91	44	2	[illegible]
DENNIS, J. M	1979	49	1	[illegible]
DENNIS, WILLIAM W	1991	48	1	[illegible]
DENNY, ALFRED	2122	49	1	[illegible]
DENNY, D. H	1987	48	1	[illegible]
DENNY, JAMES	104	35	2	[illegible]
Do	301	36	1	[illegible]
DENSLOW, OLIVER C	177	43	1	[illegible]
DENSON, BENNETT J	103	46	[illegible]	[illegible]
DENTON, ELIZABETH N	108	33	[illegible]	[illegible]
DENTON, SIDNEY	2806	49	1	21
DE QUINDRE, JULIA	3567	49	[illegible]	[illegible]
DEREMER, PHILIP	675	49	1	[illegible]
DERMODY, WILLIAM	431	49	1	[illegible]
DETTWEILER, GERMAIN	187	43	[illegible]	[illegible]
DEUTSCHER, ELIZABETH C	2208	47	[illegible]	17
DEVALL, JAMES M	3891	49	[illegible]	[illegible]
DEVAUL, CONRAD	394	36	[illegible]	[illegible]
DEVEREUX, JANE W	550	49	1	[illegible]
DEVINE, DAVID D	1193	46	[illegible]	[illegible]
DEVITT, RICHARD	1641	48	[illegible]	[illegible]
Do	801	47	1	[illegible]
Do	511	46	1	[illegible]
DEVOL, E	2817	49	1	21
DE WITT, AMY L	1986	48	1	[illegible]
DE WITT, HANNAH C	3711	49	2	[illegible]
Do	3713	49	2	[illegible]

COMMITTEE ON INVALID PENSIONS, HOUSE.

Private legislation—Continued.

Subject.	Report.	Congress.	Session.	Volume.
P. I. CLINTON	392	45	3	10
, HENRY H. (parents of)	3796	49	2	22
AMUEL	1601	48	1	16
Do	3780	49	1	21
ATHERINE	1679	48	1	16
S, WILLIAM	2882	49	1	21
SON, NATHANIEL	387	36	1	6
N, ABNER	158	35	1	6
N, FREDERICK	618	27	2	3
N, J. T	3276	49	1	21
N, MARY ELIZA	306	45	3	14
N, SAMUEL	257	30	1	4
N, WALTER	555	46	1	14
AMUEL	181	28	2	2
Do	160	27	2	2
WILLIAM W	158	34	1	6
Do	363	36	1	7
NG, FREDERICK	3641	49	2	22
CH, C. A	1158	46	2	12
Do	421	47	1	13
CH, LOTTIE E	2292	49	1	20
R, THEODORE	2068	49	1	21
BBY A	727	43	1	8
ELISHA	89	33	1	7
DANIEL M	2200	48	2	17
GER, JOHN	860	45	2	10
, GEORGE D	344	35	1	6
, RICHARD	1661	46	2	12
Do	1794	48	1	16
, WILLIAM B	602	45	3	10
ELIZABETH E	3286	49	1	21
S, JOHN	2148	49	1	20
D, HANNAH	1506	49	1	19
LE, GEORGE (heirs of)	848	29	1	4
ILLMAN E	147	44	2	9
JOHN	104	27	3	3
Do	183	28	1	3
Do	293	29	1	4
JOSEPH	939	27	2	3
NANCY	81	44	1	9
JOSEPH F. (heirs of)	26	43	1	8
. JESSE	91	31	1	5
S, CUTLER S	44	46	3	12
Do	1817	48	1	16
WILLIAM	2078	49	1	20
, BENJ. F	623	47	1	13
S, ENOCH	175	29	1	4
Do	475	31	1	5
MAGDALENA	242	43	1	8
H. H	3239	49	1	21
JOSEPH R	2399	48	2	17
, FRANCIS	84	28	2	3
, LEVI	2079	48	1	16
, RICHARD	357	49	1	18
N, BIGSBY E	365	43	1	8
Do	561	45	2	10
TT, JOHN E	2346	49	1	20
MARGARET	478	36	1	7
D, DANIEL	377	36	1	7
OFER, MICHAEL	3207	49	1	21
ER, HENRY	882	49	1	19
Do	2528	49	1	20
OWER, JOHN F	556	49	1	18
AY, JAMES	233	28	1	3
ICE, BERNARD	1580	48	1	15
LDSON, WALTER A	2932	49	1	21
ELLY, DANIEL	585	45	2	10
ROBERT M	1520	48	1	15
AN, JOHANNA	229	49	1	18
IS, GUSTINE	840	44	1	9
ETT, OLIVER	610	25	2	2
EY, DANIEL A	413	47	1	13
, DE FOREST T	504	45	2	10
LE, W. H. L	1453	48	1	15
ERTY, ELIZABETH	63	46	2	11
HERTY, HUGH	1199	48	1	15
HERTY, MARY ANN	4085	49	2	22
HERTY, ROSE	1501	48	1	15

Private legislation—Continued.

Subject.	Report.	Congress.	Session.	Volume.
DOUGHERTY, SANFORD M	3005	49	1	21
DOUGHTY, JAMES A	785	46	2	11
DOUGHTY, RICHARD	784	24	1	1
DOUGHTY, ROBERT N	2996	49	1	22
DOUGLAS, CHARLES	1787	48	1	20
DOUGLAS, MARY S	749	49	1	19
DOUGLASS, ELEANOR	403	44	1	9
DOUGLASS, MARTHA JANE	347	46	2	11
Do	1620	47	1	12
DOUGLASS, MARTIN	1223	48	1	15
DOULL, ELIZABETH MARIA	1019	46	2	11
DOUTHART, IRA	467	43	1	8
DOW, BENJAMIN	232	22	1	1
Do	7	22	2	1
DOW, JENNETTE	2535	49	1	21
DOWD, BENJAMIN B	803	25	2	2
DOWD, BRIDGET	861	48	1	14
DOWELL, GEORGE M	3725	49	2	22
DOWNEY, JOHN	458	43	1	8
DOWNING, JOHN H	2058	49	1	20
DOWNS, DAVENPORT	560	43	1	8
DOWNS, MARTHA	1538	48	1	19
DOWNS, ISAAC	712	30	1	4
Do	301	31	1	5
DOWNS, JOHN	494	29	1	4
DOWNS, WILLIAM	483	46	2	11
Do	157	47	1	13
DOXSIE, PHŒBE C	1990	47	1	13
DOYLE, CATHERINE	2283	49	1	20
DOYLE, DENNIS	1007	27	2	3
Do	274	28	1	3
DOYLE, ELLEN N	544	43	1	8
DOYLE, MARY A	121	44	1	9
DOYLE, PATRICK	253	43	1	8
DRAHER, CHARLES A	181	42	2	8
DRAIN, DANIEL	67	34	2	6
DRAKE, CLARA W	880	46	1	14
DRAKE, JOSEPH	221	35	1	6
DRAKE, LYDIA A	190	46	2	12
DRAKE, WILLIAM J	112	44	1	9
DRAKE, WILLIAM M	648	43	1	8
Do	173	44	1	9
DRAYER, GODFREY	501	47	1	13
DREESEN, B. J	1918	48	1	16
Do	2573	48	2	17
Do	57	49	1	19
DRESSER, ELISHA	544	48	1	14
DRESSER, GEORGE F	260	48	1	14
DRESSER, THOMAS	244	29	1	4
DREW, LUCY ANN	1348	48	1	15
DREW, SAMUEL	190	28	1	3
DREWRY, THOMAS W	155	27	3	3
DRINKWATER, MAXIM	159	46	2	12
DRISCOLL, MARGARET M	3100	49	1	22
DRISCOLL, TIMOTHY	800	49	1	19
DRONEY, PATRICK	366	46	2	12
Do	1613	47	1	13
Do	346	48	1	14
DROUT, JOHN	286	34	1	6
DRUMMOND, GRIEVE	154	22	1	1
DRUMWRIGHT, CHARLES T	131	43	1	8
DRURY, EMILY H	1090	47	1	13
DUBACH, BENJAMIN	851	49	1	19
DUBBS, CYRUS	2311	49	1	20
DUBOIS, ELIZABETH T	401	44	1	9
Do	248	45	2	10
Do	1360	46	2	11
Do	1056	47	1	12
DUBOISE, HANNAH	482	28	1	3
Do	40	28	2	3
DUCHANOIS, FERDINAND	1586	47	1	13
DUCOING, FRANÇOIS	157	23	1	1
Do	69	23	1	1
Do	235	23	1	1
DUDLEY, DAVID C	1901	48	2	16
DUDLEY, THOMAS P	84	33	1	5
Do	271	34	1	6
DUFFY, FRANCIS	1624	47	1	13

Subject.	Report.	Congress.	Session.	Volume.
OHN	2890	49	1	21
DANIEL	434	27	2	3
R	2124	49	1	20
ERAPHINA E	2997	49	1	21
T, JANE	297	43	1	8
	65	44	1	9
	826	47	1	13
I. JOHN M	1827	48	1	16
ISABELL	290	45	2	10
JAMES	798	49	1	19
MARIA G	2644	48	2	17
CAROLINE	463	43	1	8
CHARLES D	453	48	1	14
ELIZA	1759	46	2	12
JOHN	176	35	1	6
R. W	1008	48	1	15
SUSAN A	2407	49	1	20
	3724	49	2	22
WILLIAM R	71	43	2	8
	33	44	1	9
, CHRISTOPHER T. (heirs of)	919	47	1	13
, DANIEL	33	23	2	1
	8	27	3	3
	157	28	1	3
, HARRIET C	320	44	1	9
, SARAH E	1170	46	2	12
MARGARET	3017	49	1	21
ZELICA T	712	48	1	14
E, THEODORE	2749	49	1	21
BRAANNA L	172	43	2	8
ANE BROWN	4000	49	2	22
ARAH M	1279	49	1	19
G, JAMES	234	36	1	7
RE, FRANKLIN R	2979	49	1	21
, ALECIA	1383	48	1	15
, JOHN	1758½	46	2	12
LAWRENCE A	1822	48	1	16
ANDREW J	2456	49	1	20
T, ALICIA	567	48	1	14
ERY, MARY B	315	34	1	6
	174	35	1	6
, JOSEPH	470	29	1	4
R, LUCY G	2158	49	1	20
EDGAR L	2516	48	2	17
JONAS	578	30	1	4
CONRAD	495	35	1	6
THOMAS S	2623	49	1	21
Y, WILLIAM	87	32	1	5
, MORRIS	57	44	1	9
JOHN	1472	47	1	13
	1600	48	1	15
A	1579	48	1	15
MES	15	49	1	18
	2272	48	2	17
	2569	48	2	17
INS S	1534	46	2	12
HUA S	667	47	1	13
LIZABETH B	36	44	1	9
OHN W	2011	49	1	20
OBERT HENRY	114	32	1	5
ALTER	408	24	1	1
, DENNIS	361	26	1	2
	254	27	2	3
	110	28	1	3
	77	29	1	4
RACE F	2729	49	1	21
JAMES (heirs of)	495	46	2	11
	830	47	1	13
GEORGE W	2321	48	2	17
LOUISA	1167	48	1	15
GEORGE G	2532	49	1	21
T, WILLIAM	2600	48	2	17
IOMAS B	1424	49	1	19
N, EDMUND	53	46	2	11
	508	47	1	13
N, ELI	70	24	2	1
NN	362	46	2	12
ORLANDO W	1643	48	1	16

Private legislation—Continued.

Subject.	Report.	Congress.	Session.	Volume.
EATON, ALANSON W	1101	46	[illegible]	11
EATON, BETSEY A	158	43	[illegible]	[illegible]
EATON, CLEMMONS	106	32	1	[illegible]
EATON, HANNAH B	282	43	1	[illegible]
EATON, MARY ANN	724	42	1	[illegible]
EATON, MARY K. S	2346	48	2	17
Do	2351	48	2	17
EATON, ORIGEN	512	22	1	[illegible]
Do	46	24	1	[illegible]
EBBERMAN, REUBEN J	1623	48	1	15
EBERLEIN, ANTON	2284	49	1	19
ECKRIGHT, ISAAC	70	23	2	[illegible]
Do	753	24	1	[illegible]
EDDY, EDWARD F	317	44	1	[illegible]
EDDY, WILLIAM	235	36	1	7
EDENS, HENRY W	1803	48	1	16
EDINGER, JACOB	95	38	1	7
EDMISTON, ELLEN	1931	48	1	16
EDMONDS, SAMUEL T	1044	48	1	16
EDMONDSON, CATHARINE S	970	43	2	10
Do	1455	48	1	15
EDMONDSON, WILLIAM C	246	43	2	8
EDWARDS, DAVID D	388	46	2	11
Do	720	47	1	13
EDWARDS, GREEN	328	44	1	9
EDWARDS, HARRIET E	302	45	2	10
Do	165	47	3	12
EDWARDS, JAMES M	129	24	2	1
Do	216	25	2	1
EDWARDS, MARGARET	31	43	1	8
EDWARDS, WILLIAM B	115	30	1	4
Do	306	31	1	5
Do	47	33	1	5
EDWARDS, WILLIAM H	127	43	1	8
Do	764	45	2	10
EGBERT, CAROLINE M	793	45	2	10
EGBERT, MARION D	1813	48	1	16
EGGLESTON, SPEDIE B	164	46	3	12
Do	822	47	1	13
EHLE, HERMAN J	430	36	1	7
Do	90	37	2	7
EICHHOLTZ, HUGO	1124	47	1	13
EICHMAN, ANNA D. W	66	49	1	18
EIGHMY, S. S	2206	48	2	17
EILBER, CHARLES F	846	49	1	19
EITAPENCE, ANTHON	2838	49	1	21
EKENGREN, C. W	2412	49	1	20
ELDERKIN, DAVID T	1099	49	1	19
Do	3217	49	1	21
ELDRED, MOSES	650	25	2	2
ELDRIDGE, REBECCA	330	49	1	18
ELLERY, JOSEPH	1005	27	2	3
ELLINGTON, ROBERT	3953	49	2	22
ELLIOTT, FRANCES C	34	44	1	9
ELLIOTT, GEORGE	245	24	1	1
Do	260	33	1	5
ELLIOTT, JAMES S	33	43	1	8
ELLIOTT, THOMAS R	2982	49	1	21
ELLIS, CORNELIA W	779	49	1	19
ELLIS, ELIZABETH J	181	46	2	12
ELLIS, JESSE	49	29	1	4
ELLIS, JOHN F	563	45	2	10
Do	1177	47	1	13
ELLIS, NANCY	136	48	1	15
ELLIS, ROBERT	845	29	1	4
ELLIS, THOMAS	161	33	1	5
ELLIS, WILLIAM	82	30	2	4
ELLSWORTH, CATHERINE F	4075	49	2	22
ELTON, N	232	28	1	3
ELY, ELIZA	284	46	3	12
EMERSON, SOLOMON	804	27	2	3
EMMONS, SARAH	231	44	1	9
EMPSON, DOLLY	113	29	2	4
Do	150	31	1	5
ENGLAND, DAVID B	3001	49	1	21
ENGLISH, ELKANAH	223	24	2	1
ENGLISH, JOHN	397	31	1	5
ENLIND, JOHANNA SOFIA	3262	49	1	[illegible]

Private legislation—Continued.

Subject.	Report.	Congress.	Session.	Volume.
JACOB E	540	42	1	[illegible]
BERGER, ADAM	1366	48	2	12
A, SUSANNA	543	49	1	[illegible]
HOOK, S. ANNIE	1467	47	1	[illegible]
LOUISA A	2297	48	2	17
ALEXANDER	761	34	1	1
CHARLES J	2458	49	1	20
Do.	2457	49	1	20
JAMES M	576	48	1	14
JOHN	98	44	2	[illegible]
JADUS	256	35	3	[illegible]
Do.	311	[illegible]	1	[illegible]
Do.	41	[illegible]	2	[illegible]
Do.	124	37	2	3
WILLIAM	1695	48	1	15
ALEXANDER	129	49	1	18
ANN	462	29	1	1
ANNIE	2245	49	1	20
EVAN	700	48	1	14
FANNIE E	566	49	1	15
HENRY F	46	[illegible]	1	5
ISABEL L	667	46	2	10
Do.	1090	46	2	11
ISABEL M	1026	46	2	11
JOHN H. (heirs of)	697	[illegible]	[illegible]	[illegible]
JULIA S. W	298	[illegible]	2	10
SAMUEL P	72	43	2	[illegible]
WILLIAM (heirs of)	764	27	3	[illegible]
Do.	776	[illegible]	3	[illegible]
Do.	55	[illegible]	1	4
Do.	196	[illegible]	1	4
ELVIRA W	1164	46	2	12
ILLIAM B	2967	49	1	21
ART, OLIVER T	[illegible]	44	1	9
CHARLES	275	[illegible]	1	2
ELIZABETH J	588	43	1	8
FRANKLIN R	3290	49	1	21
SARAH J	2169	49	1	20
THOMAS	1640	48	1	16
MARGARET S	2584	49	1	21
ILDS, STEPHEN	1022	46	2	11
AGNES	134	45	2	10
Do.	850	47	1	15
ER, PETER	1799	48	1	16
Do.	1056	49	1	19
SAMUEL D	372	44	1	9
ER, IRA	560	26	1	2
ANNIE	171	43	2	8
Do.	41	43	1	8
Do.	554	45	2	10
BENJAMIN	354	43	1	8
MILES B	139	48	1	14
AM, JOHN	321	27	2	3
Do.	94	28	1	3
Do.	101	29	1	4
Do.	562	30	1	4
AM, JOHN C	162	44	1	8
VORTH, ALMIRA	352	46	2	11
Do.	149	47	1	13
VORTH, WILLIAM D	2565	48	2	17
M, REUBEN	2400	49	1	20
IAR, MARY HOWARD	1744	48	1	16
EDWARD	350	46	3	12
Do.	1123	47	1	13
R, ABRAM F	331	46	2	11
R, JOSEPH	264	26	1	2
R, NELSON M	551	45	2	10
GTON, MARCH	627	27	2	3
Do.	81	27	3	3
Do.	179	28	1	3
Do.	38	28	2	3
Do.	502	29	1	4
Do.	722	30	1	4
Do.	69	31	1	5
JOHN W	1484	49	1	19
Do.	3216	49	1	21
W, WILLIAM L	353	46	2	11
GEORGE	2062	49	1	21

Private legislation—Continued.

Subject.	Report.	Congress.	Session.	Volume.
FAULK, JOHN H	[illegible]	[illegible]	1	[illegible]
FAULKNER, JESSE R	[illegible]	[illegible]	1	[illegible]
FAUST, AUGUST	[illegible]	[illegible]	1	[illegible]
FEATHERS, JOSEPH M	[illegible]	[illegible]	1	[illegible]
FEBRUARY, JOSEPH H	[illegible]	[illegible]	[illegible]	[illegible]
FECHTELS, HELENA	[illegible]	[illegible]	1	[illegible]
Do	[illegible]	[illegible]	2	[illegible]
Do	[illegible]	[illegible]	2	[illegible]
FEDLER, HENRY	[illegible]	[illegible]	1	[illegible]
FEGAN, CHRISTOPHER	[illegible]	[illegible]	2	[illegible]
FEHLHABER, FREDERICK	[illegible]	[illegible]	1	[illegible]
FEHRENBACH, WILLIAM E	[illegible]	[illegible]	1	[illegible]
FELKER, DAVID	[illegible]	[illegible]	2	[illegible]
FELLOWS, MYRON	[illegible]	[illegible]	1	[illegible]
FELLOWS, STEPHEN	[illegible]	[illegible]	1	[illegible]
FELTNER, ADAM	[illegible]	[illegible]	1	[illegible]
FELTON, SKELTON	[illegible]	[illegible]	1	[illegible]
Do	56	[illegible]	1	[illegible]
FENSCKE, JOHN C	87	44	1	[illegible]
Do	1705	47	1	[illegible]
Do	1738	48	1	[illegible]
FENTON, JOSEPH H	1638	48	1	[illegible]
FERGUSON, ANDREW	39	[illegible]	1	[illegible]
FERGUSON, DANIEL T	332	[illegible]	1	[illegible]
FERGUSON, MRS. M. E. A	866	[illegible]	1	[illegible]
FERGUSON, RUSSEL	1641	48	1	[illegible]
FERGUSON, THOMAS	1656	46	2	[illegible]
Do	1815	48	1	[illegible]
Do	545	49	1	[illegible]
FERGUSON, WILLIAM	383	31	1	[illegible]
FERNALD, GEORGE E	1756	48	1	[illegible]
FERRELL, JOHN H	846	45	2	[illegible]
Do	805	46	2	[illegible]
FERRIS, JAMES J	147	46	2	[illegible]
FERRY, CATHARINE	216	43	2	[illegible]
Do	568	44	1	[illegible]
FICKLIN, JOHN	17	[illegible]	2	[illegible]
Do	53	[illegible]	1	[illegible]
FIELD, ELIZABETH E. V	90	[illegible]	1	[illegible]
Do	95	[illegible]	2	[illegible]
Do	28	35	1	[illegible]
FIELD, GEORGE	346	[illegible]	1	[illegible]
Do	7	[illegible]	2	[illegible]
FIELD, WILLIAM	1337	[illegible]	1	[illegible]
FIELDING, DANIEL	350	[illegible]	1	[illegible]
Do	441	27	2	[illegible]
FIELDS, GEORGE	557	24	1	[illegible]
FIELDS, GREEN	2922	[illegible]	1	[illegible]
FIFE, HENRY M	169	[illegible]	[illegible]	[illegible]
FIFIELD, ALFRED G	1538	[illegible]	[illegible]	[illegible]
Do	1048	[illegible]	[illegible]	[illegible]
FILES, JOSEPH	121	[illegible]	[illegible]	[illegible]
Do	154	[illegible]	1	7
FILLEBROWN, MARY E	2345	[illegible]	[illegible]	[illegible]
FILLIS, ELEANOR K	1663	[illegible]	[illegible]	[illegible]
Do	1092	[illegible]	1	[illegible]
FINCHER, JOHN D	3081	[illegible]	1	[illegible]
FINE, WILLIAM C	1658	[illegible]	[illegible]	[illegible]
FINK, ALANSON	512	[illegible]	[illegible]	[illegible]
FINK, JOHN	721	[illegible]	1	[illegible]
FINK, WILLIS W	404	[illegible]	1	[illegible]
FINLEY, ELIZABETH S. M	214	[illegible]	1	[illegible]
FINN, MASACH	153	[illegible]	[illegible]	[illegible]
FINNEY, LEWIS H	19	[illegible]	[illegible]	[illegible]
FISH, DUDLEY A	169	[illegible]	[illegible]	[illegible]
FISH, GILBERT SPRAGUE	126	[illegible]	[illegible]	[illegible]
Do	221	[illegible]	[illegible]	[illegible]
Do	136	[illegible]	[illegible]	[illegible]
FISHBURNE, HENRY	778	[illegible]	[illegible]	[illegible]
FISHER, BENJAMIN	3706	[illegible]	[illegible]	[illegible]
FISHER, ELIZA A	1032	[illegible]	1	[illegible]
FISHER, ELIZA G	25	[illegible]	[illegible]	[illegible]
FISHER, FRANK	17-0	[illegible]	1	[illegible]
FISHER, HENRIETTA	684	[illegible]	[illegible]	[illegible]
FISHER, HENRY H	46	[illegible]	[illegible]	[illegible]
FISHER, JOHN (guardian)	96	[illegible]	[illegible]	[illegible]
FISHER, JOHN A	33	[illegible]	[illegible]	[illegible]
FISHER, JOSEPH	500	[illegible]	1	[illegible]

Private legislation—Continued.

Subject.	Report.	Congress.	Session.	Volume.
LEWIS	254	26	1	2
D	216	27	2	3
SAMUEL C	1014	49	1	19
WILLIAM E	2868	49	2	22
LIJAH	290	23	1	1
BENJAMIN	349	22	1	1
BUTLER	211	44	1	9
EMELINE L	2320	48	2	17
HORATIO	837	30	1	4
HORATIO S	177	28	1	3
MARY ANN	177	28	1	3
THOMAS D	2344	48	2	17
TT, CHARLES	179	48	1	8
JEREMIAH M	1097	49	1	19
FRANK F	481	48	1	14
EUBEN H	373	46	3	12
D	1209	48	1	16
ALD, CORNELIUS	1250	47	1	13
D	413	48	1	14
TRICK, MICHAEL	2631	49	1	21
TER, JONATHAN	198	30	1	4
ROBERT M	143	48	1	14
ALGERNON S	1191	49	1	19
ELLEN M	396	48	1	14
TY, MARGARET	2529	48	2	17
D	17	49	1	18
F, ROSANNA	1018	49	1	19
AN, JOHN	230	27	2	3
AN, THOMAS	302	30	1	4
D	327	31	1	5
AN, ANDREW	863	30	1	4
B, A. W	245	26	1	7
B, JAMES	277	25	2	2
D	77	25	3	2
D	175	26	1	2
GEORGE W	651	49	1	18
HERMAN	320	45	2	10
JOHN	647	26	1	2
D	17	27	2	3
MARTHA	721	30	1	4
PHILIP	207	45	3	10
THOMAS	239	35	1	6
D	224	35	2	6
D	149	36	1	7
GEORGE H	1066	48	1	14
JAMES	1590	48	1	15
DAVID	1749	46	2	12
JOHN	45	45	2	10
STEPHEN	1786	49	1	20
JOSIAH	1274	49	1	19
PATRICK	869	48	1	14
JOHN	275	43	1	8
SBEE, JULIA	211	45	3	10
D	503	46	2	11
ENOCH L	92	44	2	9
JAMES B	81	23	1	1
D	46	24	1	1
WILLIAM S	776	45	2	10
Y, MILTON WALLACE	2509	49	1	20
NICHOLAS	345	35	1	6
ALMIRA	688	44	1	9
DUNCAN	2160	49	1	20
MAZIAH	101	31	1	5
ALPH P	1756	46	2	12
D	1170	47	1	13
ETH L	1178	46	2	12
RIGHT	316	35	1	6
N, CHARLES	1517	49	1	19
N, ELIZABETH	18	33	2	5
N, RICHARD	2935	49	1	21
JOHN	73	31	1	5
, ELIZABETH	3548	49	2	22
JAMES A	105	43	2	8
T, JOHN	836	30	1	4
ABRAHAM	744	45	2	10
H, ALEXANDER	1116	49	1	19
H, ROBERT M	2279	48	2	17
Do	58	49	1	18

Private legislation—Continued.

Subject.	Report.	Congress.	Session.	Volume.
FOSSETT, ISAAC	2084	49	1	20
FOSTER, ANNA J	1369	48	1	15
FOSTER, ELISHA	38	29	1	4
FOSTER, ELLEN B	336	45	2	10
FOSTER, EZRA B	240	43	1	8
FOSTER, GEORGE	231	45		10
Do	368	46	2	11
FOSTER, GRIGSBY	1636	48		16
FOSTER, LATHROP	216	27	3	3
Do	265	28		3
FOSTER, MARY A	266	49		18
FOSTER, PETHUEL	824	27		3
FOSTER SAMUEL	1415	49		19
FOUGHT, SIMON J	210	47		13
Do	1057	49	1	19
FOUKE, WILLIS	470	31	1	5
FOUST, ELEANOR	787	49	1	19
FOUST, HENRIETTA J	336	44	1	9
FOWLER, ABRAHAM C. (widow of)	21	36	2	7
FOWLER, ELIZABETH	452	48	1	14
FOX, AUGUSTUS C	223	36	1	7
FOX, CHARLES H	244	43	3	10
Do	1172	46	2	12
FOX, THOMAS J	406	44		
FRAILEY, ELIZA H	858	45	2	10
FRALEY, GEORGE W	75	49		12
FRAME, JAMES	17	30	2	
FRANCESCO, ELIZA	1006	49		15
FRANCIS, ELI C	200	45		10
FRANCIS, MILLER	677	25		2
FRANK, CHARLES H	1540	46		12
Do	511	47		13
FRANK, MARY M. J	1091	47	1	13
FRANKLIN, BENJAMIN	132	27	2	3
Do	210	45	3	10
Do	1557	46	2	12
FRANKLIN, NANCY	1793	49	1	20
FRANKLIN, REBECCA	93	44	2	9
FRASER, THOMAS	29	32	1	5
FRASNER, ALTHEA A	1186	49	1	19
FRAZEE, MARY	648	45	2	10
FRAZER, FRANCES	850	46	2	11
FRAZER, THOMAS	423	25	2	2
FRAZIER, JAMES	1537	48	1	15
FRAZIER, ROBERT	840	24	1	1
Do	320	25	2	2
Do	196	26	1	2
FREELS, NANCY J	218	49	1	18
FREEMAN, EDGAR	207	22	1	1
FREEMAN, MATILDA	2353	48	2	17
FREES, JOHN C	280	49	1	17
FREET, OLIVER	1510	49		19
FREIL, LEVI J	515	43	2	10
FRENCH, CALVIN H	1677	40	2	12
Do	850	43		14
FRENCH, CAROLINE R	1714	47		13
FRENCH, ELIZABETH	3007	49		21
FRENCH, JAMES M	835	30		[illegible]
Do	235	31		4
FRENCH, JESSE	109	33		[illegible]
FRENCH, LUTHER C	80	43		[illegible]
FRENCH, MARY H	1146	40		12
FRENCH, THOMAS D	3293	49		21
FREY, JOHN	586	44		9
Do	359	45		10
FRICK, ELIZA M	54	46		11
FRIED, DAVID	2047	48		16
FRINK, AUSTIN L	711	48		14
Do	1039	49		19
FRISBEE, JOSEPH	3000	49		21
FRITTERS, TRAVIES	603	24		[illegible]
FRITZ, FERDINAND	3280	49	1	21
FRITZ, GEORGE	691	44	1	9
Do	620	45	2	10
FROGGE, ARTHUR R	93	28	1	3
Do	18	28		3
Do	55	29		4
FROST, NATHANIEL G	1039	49	1	19

Private legislation—Continued.

Subject.	Report.	Congress.	Session.	Volume.
...TER	328	31	1	5
...MUEL	611	49	1	19
...BY ANN	60	44	2	9
...OB	208	45	3	10
...EDS, GENERAL	4905	49	2	22
...ER, WILLIAM W	1137	[illegible]	1	14
...ARBARA	1621	49	1	19
JAMES	284	30	1	4
	215	35	1	6
...LIZABETH	50	44	2	9
	860	45	3	10
	840	47	1	13
ANDREW J	381	49	1	18
CHARLES A	1875	48	1	15
CHAUNCY W	144	26	2	7
DANIEL	347	23	1	1
	7	22	2	1
	1	23	1	1
JAMES	1	18	1	1
	435	27	2	3
	222	35	1	6
JOHN B	3040	49	2	22
SILAS	627	27	2	3
ZACHEUS	736	48	2	16
...ARY E. S	445	46	2	11
...ON, ALLEN	583	27	2	3
..., PATRICK	2548	48	2	17
JAMES B	288	45	2	10
	294	46	2	11
JAMES S	3041	49	2	21
ALEXANDER	280	25	2	3
...THOMAS B. (guardian)	565	42	2	5
MARCEL	2597	49	1	21
...ESSE H	1015	48	1	18
R. L.	963	35	1	6
...TH, ROSE ANN	875	48	1	14
...RDELIA	2175	48	2	17
...EDERICK	2554	48	2	17
...AAC	588	25	2	2
...HN R. (widow of)	215	47	1	13
CHARLES G	327	45	2	10
...IER, CATHARINE H	725	43	1	8
	828	44	1	9
	356	45	3	10
...IER, E. K. (widow of)	710	49	1	19
...IER, SARAH	1007	48	1	14
	1188	48	1	15
...AN, MARY M	407	49	1	18
WILLIAM	206	22	1	1
..., JOHN	708	48	1	14
...AY, THOMAS	408	44	1	9
..., ROBINSON	160	34	1	6
	319	35	1	6
...S, NELSON	1409	48	1	15
...HINEAS	298	46	2	11
...ILLIAM	105	35	2	6
...TY, ELIZABETH	2798	49	1	21
...SIN M	2409	49	1	20
...ER, JOHN O	2000	48	1	20
...R, ADAM D	112	34	3	6
...R, STEPHEN	166	46	3	12
	218	47	1	13
	457	49	1	18
...R, WILLIAM A	349	46	3	12
	318	47	1	13
...R, WYLEY	1016	46	2	11
...ARON	2589	49	1	21
..., FREDERICK A	102	46	3	12
	1318	47	1	13
..., ADAM	138	36	1	7
THOMAS	418	27	2	3
...D, LETITIA J	2134	49	1	20
...I, DAVID J	64	44	1	9
...T, IRENE	148	44	2	9
...T, SAMUEL F	465	49	1	18
...T, WILLIAM H	720	45	2	10
...N, JAMES C	1202	49	1	19
...N, JOHN H	129	44	1	9

Private legislation—Continued.

Subject.	Report.	Congress.	Session.	Volume.
GARRITY, CATHARINE J	789	46		11
GARTHOEFFNER, ANTON	1416	48		15
GASSAWAY, JOHN	265	26		2
GASTON, ADAM	1185	49		18
GATES, H. LOUISE	878	45		10
GATES, HORACE	128	25		1
GATES, JACOB	623	26		1
Do	133	27		1
GATES, SARAH M	518	25		1
GATLIN, STEPHEN	241	21		1
GATTIE, CATHERINE	1707	48		16
GATLIN, EDMOND	1746	48		16
GAUSE, JOHN H	2414	49		20
GAVIN, CHRISTINA	1177	43		11
GAVIN, JOHN	867	45		10
GAVITT, ELIZABETH	404	26		2
GAWNEY, JOHN	810½	30		
GAYLORD, JOHN W	1103	40		12
GEAR, RICHARD	435	49		15
GEE, JAMES	403	26		
Do	376	28		
Do	331	29		
GEIBEL, JOHN	1751	48		16
GELWICKS, JACOB	286	45		11
GEMMILL, CATHARINE	778	45	2	10
GENTRY, DAVID	3851	49	2	23
GEORGE, DANIEL G	1418	47		11
GEORGE, ESTHER A	529	45	2	10
GEORGE, JAMES K	84	20	2	
GEORGE, STEPHEN L	577	45	2	10
GERODELLE, JOHN	448	23		
GERRISH, CAROLINE P	165	43		
GERST, ANNA M	92	47	1	11
GERSTRUNG, JOHN S	1800	48	1	16
GETTIS, SARAH A	552	49		17
GEURRANT, DANIEL	427	27	2	3
GIBBONS, WILLIAM	1620	48	1	15
GIBBS, LEEMAN	99	33		
Do	264	34	1	
GIBBS, REUBEN W	221	29	2	
GIBBS, SAMUEL	418	30	1	
GIBSON, ARCHIBALD A	529	35	1	
GIBSON, ELLA E	1493	49	1	17
GIBSON, GEORGE W	63	33	1	5
GIBSON, JAMES C	827	46	2	11
GIBSON, NARCISSA	1558	46	2	12
GIBSON, WILLIAM	779	45	2	10
GIFFORD, ISAAC H	416	27	2	3
GIFFORD, W. H.	1063	48	1	14
GIFFORD, WILLIAM H	2153	49	1	20
GILBERT, CHARLES	1192	46	2	12
GILBERT, EPHRAIM F	444	23	1	1
Do	353	24	1	1
GILBERT, JOHN	460	30	1	4
GILBERT, MARY J	3893	49	2	22
GILES, SUSAN	199	43	2	8
GILL, AMELIA J	2687	48	2	17
Do	1029	49	1	19
GILLAM, JOHN R	1478	48	1	15
GILLEM, MARGARET A	146	44	2	9
GILLESPIE, ELLEN	87	46	2	10
Do	1086	47	1	13
GILLESPIE, JAMES B	604	44	1	9
Do	142	45	2	10
GILLESPIE, JOHN B	796	45		10
GILLESPIE, ROBRET J	1666	47		13
Do	1207	48		15
Do	131	49		18
GILLESPIE, WILLIAM H. H	384	41		9
Do	879	42		13
GILLETT, CYPHERT P	77	43		8
GILLETTE, ORINEL	1614	47		13
GILLEY, WILLIAM H. H	2593	48		17
GILLHAM, JAMES G	1650	48		16
GILLHAM, MARY M	2533	49		21
GILMAN, SUSAN	1420	47	1	13
GINDER, JACOB	62	46		11
GING, JACOB	1022	43		15

Private legislation—Continued.

Subject.	Report.	Congress.	Session.	Volume.
ANNA	2852	48	2	17
, JAMES W	775	46	2	11
IN, PATRICK	298	43	2	8
Do	11	44	1	9
Do	842	45	2	10
ING, JAMES A	242	34	1	6
RENER, ELIZABETH AND MARY	2556	49	2	22
IOW, THOMAS	585	35	1	6
Do	243	36	1	7
STTER, FRIDOLINE	2067	49	1	21
ER, ASA	46	28	1	3
ON, THOMAS	2009	49	1	20
, JOHN	1873	47	1	13
NG, WILLIAM	1788	46	2	12
CATHERINE H	1261	48	1	15
EN, SARAH J	254	49	1	18
R, WILLIAM	6	24	2	1
Do	355	25	2	2
Do	221	26	1	2
Do	315	27	2	3
Do	15	28	1	3
RD, LAURA J	670	48	1	14
EY, ELLEN M	1233	47	1	13
EY, JOHN	644	26	1	2
KEY, JOHN A	115	44	1	9
ANFORD	562	49	1	18
DANIEL W	262	24	2	1
Do	426	25	2	2
Do	182	26	1	2
N, TEMPLE	646	48	1	14
RMAN, SARAH C	1320	47	1	13
Do	1429	47	1	13
OROUGH, ELIZABETH WIRT	214	46	2	12
Do	212	47	1	13
LE, LEFFIE E	690	48	1	14
LL, ROBERT S	99	46	2	11
ROBERT F. H	264	49	1	18
, JOHN B	1998	48	1	16
, MRS. S. C	3981	49	2	22
NG, ANDREW A	519	45	2	10
NG, JAMES W	2397	49	1	20
OW, ARMSTEAD	1782	46	2	12
IGHT, HENRY W	4121	49	2	22
ICH, BENJAMIN	426	22	1	1
Do	7	22	2	1
ICH, DAVID	271	46	3	12
ICH, JERUSHA A	171	44	1	9
ICH, MARIA	351	46	3	12
ICH, SAMUEL, JR	138	34	3	6
Do	34	35	1	6
Do	136	36	1	7
Do	105	37	2	7
PEED, CHARLES	296	36	1	7
Do	104	37	2	7
VIN, AMAZIAH	855	26	1	2
Do	150	27	2	3
VIN, ASA A	3714	49	2	22
VIN, AQUILLA	316	72	2	3
Do	474	20	1	4
Do	304	30	1	4
VIN, PHINEAS	284	49	1	18
NS, IRENE	2947	40	1	21
DAVID L	1929	48	1	16
BY, JOHN H	4	30	2	4
ON, JAMES R	771	45	2	10
Do	296	46	2	11
Do	1173	47	1	13
ON, JOHN	80	30	2	4
ON, LOUIS	622	27	2	3
Do	140	27	3	3
ON, MARY VAN	1680	46	2	12
ON, MORGAN	2778	49	1	21
ON, WILLIAM	1270	49	1	19
AM, W. H. H	1162	46	2	12
ER, MARY J	767	46	2	11
ENOCH	738	49	1	19
RUSSELL	29	30	1	4
SARAH J	379	44	1	9
Do	555	45	2	10
Do	809	40	2	11

Private legislation—Continued.

Subject.	Report.	Congress.	Session.	Volume.
GOSSAGE, JARED	399	23	1	1
Do	79	26	2	2
Do	130	27	2	3
Do	495	29	1	4
GOSSETT, MARY	339	46	2	11
GOTT, JAMES E	1118	47	1	13
Do	3867	49	2	22
GOTT, WILLIAM	564	30	1	4
GOULD, GEORGE	176	46	3	12
GOULD, LUCINDA	852	49	1	16
GOULD, THEODORE	59	28	1	3
GOULD, WILLIAM H	337	45	2	10
GOVE, WILLIAM	293	33	1	5
GOWERY, JOHN	846	29	1	4
GOYIN, RICHARD	1753	48	1	16
Do	1762	48	1	16
GRACY, WILLIAM	463	30	1	4
GRAFFAM, FREDERICK O	3631	49	2	22
GRAHAM, FRENCH	288	45	3	10
GRAHAM, ISAAC	392	31	1	5
GRAHAM, WILLIAM A	2577	48	2	17
GRANT, ISAAC M	129	43	1	8
GRATTAN, PETER	162	46	3	12
GRAVES, ALMON P	205	43	1	8
Do	162	44	1	9
GRAVES, ANTHONY B	1584	47	1	13
GRAVES, ELIZABETH	517	46	2	11
GRAVES, D. S	1307	49	1	19
GRAVES, DANIEL S	555	49	1	18
GRAVES, JOSHUA H	1428	49	1	19
GRAVES, SAMUEL	618	36	1	7
GRAVES, SARAH E	1395	48	1	15
GRAVES, SETH	1383	48	1	15
GRAY, AARON P	2339	49	1	21
GRAY, FRANK	1882	48	1	16
GRAY, FRANK N	1339	49	1	19
GRAY, JAMES	41	27	2	3
Do	33	27	3	3
GRAY, MARTHA	4082	49	2	22
GRAY, ROBERT	1742	49	1	20
GRAY, SAMUEL	285	30	1	4
GRAY, SPENCER D. (widow of)	215	47	1	13
GRAY WILSON G	134	49	1	18
GREELAUD, RUTH ELLEN	31	44	1	9
GREEN, AMELIA M	806	49	1	19
GREEN, CHARLES W	2467	48	2	17
GREEN, DUANE M	1344	47	1	13
GREEN, FRANCIS	1006	27	2	3
GREEN, FRANCIS M	377	46	2	11
GREEN, HENRY H	228	49	1	18
GREEN, ISAIAH W	220	34	3	[illegible]
Do	520	35	1	[illegible]
GREEN, JAMES F	299	31	[illegible]	[illegible]
Do	28	33	[illegible]	5
GREEN, SOPHIA	178	43	[illegible]	[illegible]
GREENFIELD, PEITER	1935	49	[illegible]	[illegible]
GREENLEE, MARY S	153	44	[illegible]	[illegible]
GREENOUGH, SYLVESTER	2221	48	2	17
GREER, NATHANIEL S	290	43	[illegible]	8
GREGG, SARAH	1542	47	[illegible]	[illegible]
GREGARY, JACOB R	3838	49	[illegible]	[illegible]
GREGORY, LUTHER	828	27	2	3
GREGORY, WILLIAM M	1639	48	[illegible]	[illegible]
GRELAND, BUTH ELLEN	197	43	[illegible]	[illegible]
GRENNON, MARY A	2210	48	[illegible]	[illegible]
GREWELL, HENRY D	1913	48	[illegible]	16
Do	63	49	[illegible]	18
GREYBIG, CATHARINE	91	44	[illegible]	9
Do	1158	46	[illegible]	12
Do	718	47	[illegible]	12
GRIDLEY, ANN E	2263	48	[illegible]	17
GRIFFIN, ISRAEL	98	30	[illegible]	4
GRIFFIN, H. F. (widow of)	254	43	[illegible]	[illegible]
GRIFFIN, JEANIE H	2219	48	[illegible]	17
GRIFFIN, ROSS	1335	47	[illegible]	[illegible]
GRIFFITH, FRANCIS	64	20	[illegible]	[illegible]
Do	826	27	[illegible]	3
GRIFFITH, JOHN	2406	49	[illegible]	[illegible]

Private legislation—Continued.

Subject.	Report.	Congress.	Session.	Volume.
MARY A	878	46	1	14
PRISCILLA	64	42	2	8
SAMUEL	612	37	2	3
WYATT	22	33	2	5
	327	35	1	6
BRAHAM P	2548	49	1	21
SMUEL (widow of)	216	47	1	13
ROBERT	905	27	3	3
JOSEPH	808	46	2	11
ANDON B	1504	47	1	13
ARY	[illegible]	49	1	21
ELIZABETH C	4050	49	2	22
SOLOMON J	962	47	1	13
	2009	49	1	16
	1781	49	1	20
, CHESTER	564	29	1	3
COB M	540	45	2	10
HENRY C	113	46	2	11
OSES	120	35	2	6
	360	36	1	7
JOHN	223	44	1	9
ACOB	468	43	1	8
WRENCE	128	44	1	9
A	3002	49	1	21
, HENRY	719	45	2	10
ORGE	780	44	1	9
	343	45	2	10
NDREW J. (heirs of)	2218	48	2	17
ENJAMIN	314	22	1	1
	87	23	1	1
AN, LOUIS	592	46	2	11
JOHN	865	45	2	10
CHARLES	106	35	2	6
, FRANK M	1743	48	1	16
LLEY	630	27	2	3
	171	28	1	3
NDROS	129	47	1	13
LIAM	16	28	2	3
	426	29	1	4
RY N	1171	47	1	13
NANCY	2820	49	1	21
TEPHEN M	368	46	3	12
WILLIAM	482	46	2	11
GEORGE D	1358	48	1	15
LOUISA J., AND OTHERS	141	45	2	10
PH	1905	49	1	20
ORGE W	444	49	1	18
MIRAD	578	49	1	18
AN, ELIZABETH	207	43	1	8
CHARD M	286	36	1	7
IENRY	531	45	2	10
, JOHN G	2557	48	2	17
. WILLIAM	110	43	1	8
	107	45	2	10
ATHARINE	542	44	1	9
ANIEL, JR	116	32	1	5
N, MARY J	2082	49	1	21
HENRY H	3586	49	2	22
PETER M	2147	48	1	16
RAH	1423	49	1	19
N, CHARLES	2923	49	1	21
HARLES C	719	43	1	8
RY C	600	45	2	10
	511	46	2	11
LAS K	2156	49	1	20
ES N	801	49	1	19
NATHANIEL	963	45	2	10
ENVILLE R	1187	49	1	19
RDECAI	164	27	3	3
WELL	209	29	1	4
HN	229	44	1	9
	402	44	1	9
	652	45	2	10
	667	29	1	4
ZABETH	735	43	2	10
EMAN N	374	46	3	12
MES S	58	26	2	2
N S	134	44	1	9
	130	45	2	10

Private legislation—Continued.

Subject.	Report.	Congress.	Session.	Volume.
HALL, JOSEPH	408	28	1	2
HALL, JULIET E	116	43	1	6
HALL, MARY F	284	44	1	9
Do	819	46	2	11
HALL, POLLY	432	49		18
HALL, REBECCA	1755	46	2	12
Do	1407	48	1	15
HALL, RICHARD	937	24		1
Do	279	25	2	2
Do	293	26		2
HALL, SARAH C	2073	48		16
HALL, SAMUEL S	1215	49		19
HALL, THOMAS	265	46		12
HALLAM, HANNAH	745	45	2	10
HALLOCK, JAMES C	529	26	1	2
Do	187	27	2	3
Do	38	28	1	3
HALLOWELL, ANNA E	81	46	2	11
HALPINE ANTHONY	509	46	2	11
HALPINE, MARGARET G	1893	47	1	13
Do	1502	48		15
HALSTEAD, CALVIN	789	45		10
HALSTEAD, HENRY N	39	28		
Do	560	30		
Do	20	33		
HAM, GEORGE	3241	49		21
HAM, JOHN D	2069	49		21
HAM, ROBERT	78	33		
HAMBOUGH, GEORGE W	1908	49		19
HEMER, KATHARINE M	481	35		6
HAMILL, WILLIAM	224	45		10
Do	152	46		11
HAMILTON, ALEXANDER	1388	48		15
HAMILTON, BRIDGET	1627	47		13
HAMILTON, CHARLES M	1737	49		19
HAMILTON, CHARLES N	562	48		15
HAMILTON, DAVID W	2051	49	1	19
HAMILTON, EMPSON	966	27	2	3
Do	192	27	3	3
Do	18	28	1	3
HAMILTON, HANNAH	26	28	1	3
HAMILTON, JOHN	508	44	1	9
HAMILTON, MARCUS A	457	48	1	14
Do	348	49	1	18
HAMILTON, MARY C	313	35	1	6
HAMILTON, MARY L. P	879	44	1	14
HAMILTON, SAMUEL	158	35	1	6
Do	238	36	1	7
HAMILTON, SARAH	565	45	2	10
Do	3266	49	1	21
HAMILTON, SIDNEY B	1654	46	2	12
HAMILTON, ZENAS	1711	48	1	16
HAMLIN, DECATUR	709	48	1	16
HAMLINK, DERRICK F	660	45	2	10
Do	2475	48	2	17
HAMMER, CATHARINE	2411	48	2	17
HAMMER, MARIA L	804	48	1	16
HAMMILL, GEORGE	201	26	1	2
Do	150	26	2	2
Do	314	27	2	3
HAMMOCK, JOSEPH H	171	46	2	12
HAMMOND, ANGELICA	201	43	1	8
HAMMOND, BENJAMIN	22	23	1	1
HAMMOND, NANCY A	323	44	1	9
HANCOCK, ALMIRA RUSSELL	1023	49	1	19
HANCOCK, SAMUEL O	3588	49	2	22
HANDY, WHIPPLE	3274	49	1	21
HANLEY, EDWARD	231	43	2	8
HANLY, EDWARD	799	47	1	13
HANNAFORD, MARY J	1507	47	1	13
HANSON, SAMUEL	1907	48	1	16
Do	403	49	1	18
HANSON, MARGARET C., AND OTHERS	313	35	1	6
HANSON, MICHAEL	224	34	3	6
Do	29	35	2	6
Do	153	36	1	7
HARBAUGH, SARAH	1920	49	1	19
HARBERT, EDWARD	1978	48	1	16

Subject.	Report.	Congress.	Session.	Volume.
ON, WILLIAM	1152	48	1	15
N, SIMMONS W	329	49	1	18
o	3204	49	1	21
STY, EDWARD	381	36	1	7
IAN, PATRICK	822	46	2	11
I. MOSES B	714	43	1	8
IG, ELIZABETH	554	43	1	8
IG, SAMUEL P	2333	48	2	17
ICK, THOMAS R	37	43	1	8
, WILLIAM E	617	49	1	18
ELIZABETH B. C	361	45	2	10
. JOHN	86	32	1	5
. SARAH	254	26	1	2
ESS, AGNES	2357	49	1	20
N, W. B	233	43	2	8
N, HENRIETTA	1748	49	1	20
N, MINNIE	90	46	3	12
lo	717	47	1	13
N, RICHARD P	1390	48	1	15
N, WILLIAM F	2518	49	2	22
Y, FRANK W	493	46	2	11
Y, HEZEKIAH	3277	49	1	21
NDING, HIRAM G. (heirs of)	855	45	2	10
R, ALBERT	2519	48	2	17
R, ALEXANDER	1620	48	1	15
o	49	49	1	18
R, J. L	386	36	1	7
R, SAMUEL D	2229	48	2	17
AM, JEREMIAH	572	30	1	4
LL, NANCY	208	43	2	8
T, BARNEY	174	28	1	3
AN, JOHN	841	30	1	4
AN, SAMANTHA	1138	48	1	14
IGTON, EDWARD M	1271	49	1	19
IGTON, HARRIETT R	1196	49	1	19
IGTON, HARRY B., AND GRACE A	255	49	1	18
IGTON, JAMES	439	23	1	1
IGTON, MARTIN	1997	48	1	16
, CATHARINE	540	45	2	10
, ISAAC	736	43	1	8
, JANE A	37	44	1	9
o	546	45	2	10
, LEVI H	541	43	1	8
, MARY G	294	43	1	8
o	545	45	2	10
, MERLIN C	368	48	1	14
, WAITIE F	2769	49	1	21
, WILLIAM	1892	48	1	16
ON, ADA L	779	44	1	9
ON, CARRIE G	1023	46	2	11
ON, GEORGE A	981	45	2	10
ON, HELEN M	407	48	1	14
ON, JAMES FORSYTH	95	46	2	11
ON, JONATHAN C	2536	48	2	17
ON, REBECCA S	584	44	1	9
ON, THOMAS	796	25	2	2
o	319	27	2	3
o	52	28	1	3
ON, WILLIAM H	165	44	1	9
L, ANTHONY	746	49	1	19
CHARLES F	546	48	1	14
OZIAS	118	33	2	5
NGER, CLEMENTINE	3510	49	2	22
EY, JOHN	93	30	2	4
ELL, BETSEY H	352	26	1	2
Y, RUFUS L	663	36	1	7
Do	103	37	2	7
Y, RUSSEL	1989	48	1	16
Do	3284	49	1	21
Y, SARAH L	417	48	1	14
Do	3585	49	2	22
LL, BAILEY	1527	49	1	19
ZAHL, FRANCES	874	48	1	14
LL, FLAVIA A	2160	48	1	16
NS, ADALINE G	965	47	1	13
NS, LAURA C. P	408	48	1	14
NS, REBECCA E	2065	49	1	20
LL, JOHN A	568	48	1	14

Private legislation—Continued.

Subject.	Report.	Congress.	Session.	Volume.
HASTINGS, ASA	624	30	1	[illegible]
HASTINGS, LEWIS	332	29	1	[illegible]
Do	291	30	1	[illegible]
Do	50	31	1	[illegible]
HASTINGS, MARY	701	49	1	[illegible]
HATCH, MARIA B	3673	49	2	[illegible]
HATFIELD, DANIEL B	333	46	2	11
HATHAWAY, S J. (guardian)	1649	46	2	[illegible]
HATTER, NICHOLAS	1454	48	1	[illegible]
HAUG, GODFREID	2326	48	2	17
HAUKS, THERON W	680	43	1	[illegible]
HAUP, JOHN	631	30	1	[illegible]
HAVELY, W. D	2396	49	1	[illegible]
HAVENS, HENRY B	234	43	1	[illegible]
Do	1569	49	1	[illegible]
HAVILAND, ABBY C	853	45	[illegible]	[illegible]
HAWES, SUSAN	2347	49	1	[illegible]
HAWK, MARY G	1901	47	1	[illegible]
Do	460	48	1	[illegible]
HAWKE, MARY	2049	49	1	[illegible]
HAWKINS, DARIUS	267	26	1	[illegible]
Do	438	27	2	[illegible]
Do	30	27	3	[illegible]
Do	112	28	[illegible]	[illegible]
HAWKINS ISAAC N	1698	49		[illegible]
HAWKINS, JAMES	1098	46		[illegible]
HAWKINS, MARTIN	413	47		[illegible]
HAWKINS, THEODORE C	376	46	2	11
Do	300	48		[illegible]
HAWKS, MICAJAH	227	35		[illegible]
Do	51	36		7
HAWLEY, CAROLINE	592	45		[illegible]
HAWLEY, GEORGE S	2442	48		17
Do	1106	49		[illegible]
HAWLEY, GILES C	278	49		[illegible]
HAWLEY, JOSEPHUS	172	47		[illegible]
HAWORTH, JAMES D	2306	49		[illegible]
HAWTHORNE, JAMES	709	47	1	[illegible]
HAY, ABBIE M	3570	49	2	[illegible]
HAY, BARNARD	29	27		3
HAYDEN, JOHN	2506	49	1	[illegible]
HAYES, JAMES H	722	45	2	10
HAYES, THOMAS J	3581	49	2	[illegible]
HAYES, W. A	2354	48	2	17
HAYFORD, GILBERT	404	48	1	[illegible]
HAYNES, WALTER S	561	49	1	[illegible]
HAYNIE, GEORGE C	144	49	1	[illegible]
HAYS, ANNIE A	526	46	[illegible]	11
Do	61	47	1	13
HAYS, JOHN B	351	49	[illegible]	[illegible]
HAYS, SAMUEL	371	46	[illegible]	[illegible]
HAYWARD, LEVI D	331	44	1	[illegible]
HAZEL, SAMUEL	785	46	2	11
Do	1630	46	[illegible]	[illegible]
HAZELIT, WILLIAM	1334	47	1	[illegible]
HAZELWOOD, JOHN	1880	48	1	[illegible]
HAZEN, JOHN	375	31	1	[illegible]
HAZENZAHL, FRANCES	793	49	1	[illegible]
HAZLE, WILLIAM	2266	48	2	[illegible]
HAZLEWOOD, JOHN	1593	47	1	[illegible]
HAZZARD, HANNA	293	[illegible]	1	[illegible]
HEADERICK, JACOB	552	26	1	[illegible]
HEALD, PENELOPE T	30	43	1	[illegible]
HEATH, ABBIE B	2826	49	1	[illegible]
HEATH, JAMES C	2681	49	1	[illegible]
HEATH, LAVISA	2306	48	2	[illegible]
HEBNER, NICHOLAS	84	38	1	[illegible]
HECKING, HENRY	1401	48	1	[illegible]
HEDDINGER, JOHN	461	43	1	[illegible]
HEDRICK, MARY E	2021	49	1	[illegible]
HEENAN, DANIEL	624	46	2	[illegible]
HEINE, FREDERICK	1693	49	1	[illegible]
HEINEMAN, ROSINA	780	48	1	[illegible]
Do	701	49	1	[illegible]
HEINRICI, ANN	247	45	[illegible]	[illegible]
HEINTZELMAN, MARGARET S	1645	46	[illegible]	[illegible]
HEINZEL, EDWARD	735	43	1	[illegible]
Do	82	44	1	[illegible]
Do	208	45	[illegible]	[illegible]

Private legislation—Continued.

Subject.	Report.	Congress.	Session.	Volume.
P. A	78	38	2	6
ABLES	854	45	2	10
, JOSEPHINE D	1383	48	1	15
	732	49	1	19
HARDIE HOGAN	1628	49	1	19
AY, STEPHEN F	178	38	1	6
R, CHRISTIAN	142	44	1	9
R, JEPTHA L	384	38	1	6
ON, GEORGE	3672	49	1	21
	3832	49	2	22
ON, HIRAM C	378	46	2	11
	1465	48	1	15
ON, SAMUEL	534	45	1	8
ON, WILLIAM	375	36	1	2
ON, WILLIAM A	92	44	1	9
, PERNETTA	194	44	1	9
KS, FRANCES E	464	48	1	14
KSON, JULIETT A	323	44	1	9
, JOHN	414	43	1	8
, CHARLES	1796	48	1	16
SAMUEL T	1525	47	1	13
BY, AUGUSTINE	908	45	2	10
ATHARINE	494	46	2	11
	708	48	1	14
	774	48	1	14
ELIZABETH VERNOR	352	46	2	12
	562	47	1	13
ASPER J	1960	48	1	16
ARY A	1469	48	1	15
ARY ANN	171	35	1	6
	69	36	1	7
PHILIP	843	45	2	10
RUFUS	82	38	2	3
SAMUEL	2094	48	1	16
	11	49	1	18
SARAH E	2119	49	1	20
SEREPTA M. I	250	46	3	10
, ELIZAH P	800	49	1	19
LAURA	507	47	1	13
T, CHARLES	295	43	1	8
F	2510	49	1	20
N, GOTTLIEB	1591	48	1	15
MANUEL B	168	44	1	9
, JOHN	234	23	1	1
	461	24	1	1
K, OLIVER	426	22	1	1
o	7	22	2	1
o	377	28	1	3
o	507	29	1	4
AN, J. V	2010	49	1	20
G, GARDNER	715	30	1	4
o	303	31	1	5
o	6	32	1	5
G, WILLIAM	1691	48	1	16
, FANNIE M	211	43	2	8
, GARDNER	818	27	2	3
S, JOHN R	3731	49	2	22
S, REBECCA S	1475	47	1	13
ANNA	1460	48	1	15
CK, JOHN S	1060	49	1	19
ALVIN	649	43	1	8
WILLIAM J	2086	48	1	16
, ANNA	1399	48	1	15
K, JAMES W	3847	49	2	22
ED, WELLINGTON V	328	46	2	11
Do	1321	47	1	13
, HENRY	1201	49	1	19
, GEORGE R. T	245	26	1	2
T, CHARLES	605	45	2	10
T, ELBERT	2341	48	2	17
T, PORTER B	1619	48	1	15
Do	121	49	1	18
T, THOMAS W	535	44	1	9
Do	511	45	2	10
N, HENRY	77	36	2	7
ES, MARY	723	44	1	9
Do	319	45	2	10

Private legislation—Continued.

Subject.	Report.	Congress.	Session.	Volume.
GARRITY, CATHARINE J	789	46	2	11
GARTHOEFFNER, ANTON	1416	49	1	19
GASSAWAY, JOHN	265	30	1	2
GASTON, ADAM	1185	49	1	19
GATES, H. LOUISE	878	45	2	10
GATES, HORACE	128	35	1	
GATES, JACOB	623	36	1	
Do	122	37	2	
GATES, SARAH M	518	35	1	
GATLIN, STEPHEN	241	23	1	
GATTIE, CATHERINE	1707	48	1	16
GATLIN, EDMOND	1746	48	1	16
GAUSE, JOHN H	2414	49	1	21
GAVIN, CHRISTINA	1177	46	1	13
GAVIN, JOHN	867	45	2	10
GAVITT, ELIZABETH	404	26	1	2
GAWNEY, JOHN	810½	30	1	
GAYLORD, JOHN W	1103	49	1	19
GEAR, RICHARD	435	49	1	18
GEE, JAMES	403	26	1	2
Do	376	28	1	
Do	331	29	1	4
GEIBEL, JOHN	1751	48	1	16
GELWICKS, JACOB	286	46	2	11
GEMMILL, CATHARINE	778	45	2	10
GENTRY, DAVID	3851	49	2	22
GEORGE, DANIEL G	1418	47	1	13
GEORGE, ESTHER A	529	45	2	10
GEORGE, JAMES K	84	26	2	
GEORGE, STEPHEN L	577	45	2	10
GERODELLE, JOHN	448	23	1	
GERRISH, CAROLINE P	165	43	1	
GERST, ANNA M	92	47	1	13
GERSTRUNG, JOHN S	1800	48	1	16
GETTIS, SARAH A	552	49	1	18
GEURRANT, DANIEL	427	27	2	
GIBBONS, WILLIAM	1626	48	1	15
GIBBS, LEEMAN	90	33	1	5
Do	264	34	1	6
GIBBS, REUBEN W	221	27	2	2
GIBBS, SAMUEL	448	36	1	7
GIBSON, ARCHIBALD A	529	35	1	6
GIBSON, ELLA E	1493	49	1	19
GIBSON, GEORGE W	63	33	1	5
GIBSON, JAMES C	327	46	2	11
GIBSON, NARCISSA	1553	46	2	12
GIBSON, WILLIAM	779	45	2	10
GIFFORD, ISAAC H	416	27	2	3
GIFFORD, W. H	1083	48	1	14
GIFFORD, WILLIAM H	2153	49	1	20
GILBERT, CHARLES	1192	46	2	12
GILBERT, EPHRAIM F	444	23	1	1
Do	353	24	1	1
GILBERT, JOHN	460	30	1	4
GILBERT, MARY J	3893	49	2	22
GILES, SUSAN	190	43	2	8
GILL, AMELIA J	2687	48	2	17
Do	1029	49	1	19
GILLAM, JOHN R	1473	48	1	15
GILLEM, MARGARET A	146	44	2	8
GILLESPIE, ELLEN	87	46	2	10
Do	1086	47	1	13
GILLESPIE, JAMES B	604	44	1	9
Do	142	45	2	10
GILLESPIE, JOHN B	796	45	2	10
GILLESPIE, ROBRET J	1666	47	1	13
Do	1207	48	1	15
Do	131	49	1	18
GILLESPIE, WILLIAM H. H	884	44	1	9
Do	879	49	1	19
GILLETT, CYPHERT P	77	43	2	8
GILLETTE, ORINEL	1614	47	1	13
GILLEY, WILLIAM H. H	2583	48	2	17
GILLHAM, JAMES G	1650	48	1	16
GILLHAM, MARY M	2533	49	1	21
GILMAN, SUSAN	1420	49	1	19
GINDER, JACOB	62	46	2	11
GING, JACOB	1022	49	1	19

Private legislation—Continued.

Subject.	Report.	Congress.	Session.	Volume.
ANNA	2352	48	2	17
, JAMES W	775	46	2	11
IN, PATRICK	208	42	2	8
Do	11	44	1	9
Do	842	45	2	10
ING, JAMES A	243	34	1	6
BENER, ELIZABETH AND MARY	2556	49	2	22
OW, THOMAS	585	35	1	6
Do	242	36	1	7
TTER, FRIDOLINE	2067	49	1	21
R, ASA	46	28	1	3
N, THOMAS	2009	49	1	20
JOHN	1872	47	1	13
G, WILLIAM	1782	46	2	12
CATHERINE H	1361	48	1	15
N, SARAH J	354	49	1	18
, WILLIAM	6	24	2	1
Do	356	25	2	2
Do	221	26	1	2
Do	315	27	2	3
Do	15	28	1	3
RD, LAURA J	870	48	1	14
EY, ELLEN M	1838	47	1	13
SY, JOHN	644	26	1	2
REY, JOHN A	115	44	1	9
ANFORD	802	49	1	18
DANIEL W	298	24	2	1
Do	426	25	2	2
Do	182	26	1	2
, TEMPLE	646	48	1	14
RMAN, SARAH C	1336	47	1	13
Do	1429	47	1	13
OROUGH, ELIZABETH WIRT	214	46	2	12
Do	212	47	1	13
LE, LEFFIE E	899	48	1	14
LL, ROBERT S	99	46	2	11
ROBERT F. H	264	49	1	18
, JOHN B	1998	48	1	16
, MRS. S. C	3981	49	2	22
G, ANDREW A	519	45	2	10
G, JAMES W	2397	49	1	20
OW, ARMSTEAD	1782	46	2	12
GHT, HENRY W	4121	49	2	22
ICH, BENJAMIN	426	22	1	1
Do	7	22	2	1
ICH, DAVID	271	46	3	12
CH, JERUSHA A	171	44	1	9
CH, MARIA	351	46	3	12
ICH, SAMUEL, Jr	138	34	3	6
Do	34	35	1	6
Do	136	36	1	7
Do	105	37	2	7
EED, CHARLES	296	36	1	7
Do	104	37	2	7
IN, AMAZIAH	355	26	1	2
Do	150	27	2	3
IN, ASA A	3714	49	2	22
IN, AQUILLA	316	72	2	3
Do	474	20	1	4
Do	304	30	1	4
IN, PHINEAS	284	49	1	18
SS, IRENE	2047	40	1	21
DAVID L	1929	48	1	16
BY, JOHN H	4	30	2	4
N, JAMES R	771	45	2	10
Do	296	46	2	11
Do	1173	47	1	13
N, JOHN	80	30	2	4
N, LOUIS	622	27	2	3
Do	140	27	3	3
N, MARY VAN	1680	46	2	12
N, MORGAN	2778	49	1	21
N, WILLIAM	1270	49	1	19
AM, W. H. H	1162	46	2	12
E, MARY J	767	46	2	11
ENOCH	738	49	1	19
RUSSELL	29	30	1	4
SARAH J	379	44	1	9
Do	555	45	2	10
Do	809	40	2	11

Private legislation—Continued.

Subject.	Report.	Congress.	Session.	Volume.
GOSSAGE, JARED	399	23	1	1
Do	79	26	2	2
Do	130	27	2	3
Do	495	29	1	4
GOSSETT, MARY	339	46	2	11
GOTT, JAMES E	1118	47	1	13
Do	3887	49	2	22
GOTT, WILLIAM	564	30	1	4
GOULD, GEORGE	176	46	3	12
GOULD, LUCINDA	352	49	1	18
GOULD, THEODORE	59	28	1	3
GOULD, WILLIAM H	337	45	2	10
GOVE, WILLIAM	293	33	1	5
GOWERY, JOHN	848	29	1	4
GOYIN, RICHARD	1753	48	1	16
Do	1762	48	1	16
GRACY, WILLIAM	463	29	1	4
GRAFFAM, FREDERICK O	3631	49	2	22
GRAHAM, FRENCH	288	45	3	10
GRAHAM, ISAAC	392	31	1	5
GRAHAM, WILLIAM A	2577	48	2	17
GRANT, ISAAC M	129	43	1	8
GRATTAN, PETER	162	46	3	13
GRAVES, ALMON P	205	43	1	8
Do	162	44	1	9
GRAVES, ANTHONY B	1584	47	1	13
GRAVES, ELIZABETH	517	46	2	11
GRAVES, D. S	1307	49	1	19
GRAVES, DANIEL S	555	49	1	18
GRAVES, JOSHUA H	1428	49	1	19
GRAVES, SAMUEL	618	36	1	7
GRAVES, SARAH E	1395	48	1	15
GRAVES, SETH	1385	48	1	15
GRAY, AARON P	2539	49	1	21
GRAY, FRANK	1682	48	1	16
GRAY, FRANK N	1339	49	1	19
GRAY, JAMES	414	27	2	3
Do	33	27	3	3
GRAY, MARTHA	4082	49	2	22
GRAY, ROBERT	1742	49	1	20
GRAY, SAMUEL	285	30	1	4
GRAY, SPENCER D. (widow of)	215	47	1	13
GRAY WILSON G	134	49	1	18
GREELAUD, RUTH ELLEN	31	44	1	9
GREEN, AMELIA M	806	49	1	19
GREEN, CHARLES W	2467	48	2	17
GREEN, DUANE M	1344	47	1	13
GREEN, FRANCIS	1006	27		3
GREEN, FRANCIS M	377	46		11
GREEN, HENRY H	228	49		19
GREEN, ISAIAH W	220	34		
Do	520	35		
GREEN, JAMES F	299	31		
Do	28	33		5
GREEN, SOPHIA	178	43		8
GREENFIELD, PEITER	1935	49		19
GREENLEE, MARY S	153	44		9
GREENOUGH, SYLVESTER	2221	48	2	17
GREER, NATHANIEL S	290	43		8
GREGG, SARAH	1542	49	1	19
GREGARY, JACOB R	3838	49	2	23
GREGORY, LUTHER	828	27	2	3
GREGORY, WILLIAM M	1639	48	1	16
GRELAND, BUTH ELLEN	107	43	2	8
GRENNON, MARY A	2210	48	2	17
GREWELL, HENRY D	1913	48		17
Do	63	49		19
GREYBIG, CATHARINE	91	44		9
Do	1158	46		11
Do	718	47		12
GRIDLEY, ANN E	2263	48		17
GRIFFIN, ISRAEL	98	30		4
GRIFFIN, H. F. (widow of)	254	43		8
GRIFFIN, JEANIE H	2219	48		17
GRIFFIN, ROSS	1335	47	1	13
GRIFFITH, FRANCIS	64	26		[illegible]
Do	826	27		[illegible]
GRIFFITH, JOHN	2406	48		[illegible]

Private legislation—Continued.

Subject.	Report.	Congress.	Session.	Volume.
H, MARY A	578	46	1	14
H, PRISCILLA	94	42	2	8
H, SAMUEL	613	37	2	3
H, WYATT	23	26	2	5
	317	26	1	6
ABRAHAM P	2846	49	1	21
LEMUEL (widow of)	216	47	1	13
, ROBERT	90	27	2	3
, JOSEPH	808	46	2	11
LANDON B	1594	47	1	12
MARY	[illegible]	49	1	21
, ELIZABETH C	4090	49	2	22
, SOLOMON J	969	47	1	13
	2878	48	1	16
	1701	48	1	20
D, CHESTER	564	26	1	3
JACOB M	549	45	2	10
, HENRY C	112	44	2	11
MOSES	120	35	2	6
	360	26	1	7
, JOHN	212	44	1	9
JACOB	463	43	1	8
AWRENCE	138	44	1	9
A	3092	49	1	21
AN, HENRY	719	45	2	10
GEORGE	726	44	1	9
	242	46	2	10
ANDREW J. (heirs of)	2218	48	2	17
BENJAMIN	214	22	1	1
	37	22	1	1
MAN, LOUIS	592	46	2	11
S, JOHN	865	45	2	10
CHARLES	168	33	2	6
Y, FRANK M	1748	48	1	16
OLLEY	630	27	2	3
	171	28	1	3
ANDROS	129	47	1	13
ILLIAM	16	28	2	3
	426	29	1	4
ENRY N	1171	47	1	13
ES, NANCY	2820	49	1	21
STEPHEN M	368	46	3	12
WILLIAM	482	46	2	11
Y, GEORGE D	1358	48	1	15
, LOUISA J., AND OTHERS.	141	45	2	10
EPH	1905	49	1	20
GEORGE W	444	49	1	18
, MIRAD	578	49	1	18
MAN, ELIZABETH	207	43	1	8
RICHARD M	286	36	1	7
HENRY	581	45	2	10
ES, JOHN G	2557	48	2	17
DS, WILLIAM	110	43	1	8
	167	45	2	10
CATHARINE	542	44	1	9
DANIEL, Jr	116	32	1	5
AN, MARY J	2062	49	1	21
D HENRY H	3586	49	2	23
PETER M	2147	48	1	16
SARAH	1423	49	1	19
IAN, CHARLES	2923	49	1	21
CHARLES C	719	43	1	8
MARY C	600	45	2	10
	511	46	2	11
SILAS K	2156	49	1	20
AMES N	891	49	1	19
T, NATHANIEL	963	45	2	10
REENVILLE R	1187	49	1	19
ORDECAI	164	27	3	3
OSWELL	209	29	1	4
JOHN	229	44	1	9
	402	44	1	9
	652	45	2	10
SA	667	29	1	4
LIZABETH	735	45	2	10
REEMAN N	374	46	3	12
AMES S	58	26	2	2
OHN S	134	44	1	9
	130	45	2	10

Private legislation—Continued.

Subject.	Report.	Congress.	Session.	Volume.
HALL, JOSEPH	408	26	1	2
HALL, JULIET E.	116	43	1	5
HALL, MARY F	284	44	1	9
Do	819	46	2	11
HALL, POLLY	452	49	1	18
HALL, REBECCA	1755	46	2	12
Do	1467	48	1	15
HALL, RICHARD	837	24	1	1
Do	279	25	2	2
Do	295	26	1	2
HALL, SARAH C	2078	48	1	16
HALL, SAMUEL S	1215	49	1	19
HALL, THOMAS	365	46	3	12
HALLAM, HANNAH	745	45	2	10
HALLOCK, JAMES C	529	26	1	2
Do	137	27	2	3
Do	38	28	1	3
HALLOWELL, ANNA E	81	46	2	11
HALPINE ANTHONY	509	46	2	11
HALPINE, MARGARET G	1393	47	1	13
Do	1502	48	1	15
HALSTEAD, CALVIN	789	45	2	10
HALSTEAD, HENRY N	39	28	2	3
Do	560	30	1	4
Do	20	33	1	5
HAM, GEORGE	3241	49	1	21
HAM, JOHN D	2069	49	1	20
HAM, ROBERT	78	33	1	5
HAMBOUGH, GEORGE W	1908	49	1	20
HEMER, KATHARINE M	481	35	1	6
HAMILL, WILLIAM	224	45	3	10
Do	152	46	2	11
HAMILTON, ALEXANDER	1388	48	1	15
HAMILTON, BRIDGET	1627	47	1	13
HAMILTON, CHARLES M	1737	49	1	20
HAMILTON, CHARLES N	562	48	1	14
HAMILTON, DAVID W	2051	49	1	20
HAMILTON, EMPSON	966	27	2	3
Do	192	27	3	3
Do	18	28	1	3
HAMILTON, HANNAH	26	28	1	3
HAMILTON, JOHN	508	41	1	9
HAMILTON, MARCUS A	457	48	1	14
Do	348	48	1	14
HAMILTON, MARY C	813	35	1	6
HAMILTON, MARY L. P	879	48	1	14
HAMILTON, SAMUEL	153	35	1	6
Do	238	36	1	7
HAMILTON, SARAH	565	45	2	10
Do	3266	49	1	21
HAMILTON, SIDNEY B	1654	46	2	12
HAMILTON, ZENAS	1711	48	1	15
HAMLIN, DECATUR	709	48	1	14
HAMLINK, DERRICK F	660	45	2	10
Do	2475	48	2	17
HAMMER, CATHARINE	2411	48	2	17
HAMMER, MARIA L	864	48	1	14
HAMMILL, GEORGE	201	[illegible]	1	2
Do	150	25	2	2
Do	314	[illegible]	2	3
HAMMOCK, JOSEPH H	171	46	3	12
HAMMOND, ANGELICA	201	[illegible]	1	6
HAMMOND, BENJAMIN	22	[illegible]	1	8
HAMMOND, NANCY A	323	[illegible]	1	9
HANCOCK, ALMIRA RUSSELL	1023	[illegible]	1	10
HANCOCK, SAMUEL O	3588	[illegible]	2	22
HANDY, WHIPPLE	3274	[illegible]	1	21
HANLEY, EDWARD	231	[illegible]	2	8
HANLY, EDWARD	799	[illegible]	1	13
HANNAFORD, MARY J	1597	47	1	13
HANSON, SAMUEL	1907	[illegible]	1	19
Do	402	[illegible]	1	15
HANSON, MARGARET C., AND OTHERS	312	[illegible]	1	6
HANSON, MICHAEL	224	[illegible]	3	6
Do	29	[illegible]	2	6
Do	153	[illegible]	1	7
HARBAUGH, SARAH	1920	[illegible]	1	20
HARBERT, EDWARD	1976	[illegible]	1	20

Private legislation—Continued.

Subject.	Report.	Congress.	Session.	Volume.
ON, WILLIAM	1182	48	1	15
, SIMMONS W	329	49	1	18
....	3204	49	1	21
TY, EDWARD	881	36	1	7
AN, PATRICK	822	46	2	11
MOSES B	714	43	1	8
3, ELIZABETH	554	43	1	8
, SAMUEL P	2838	48	2	17
CK, THOMAS B	37	43	1	8
WILLIAM E	617	48	1	16
LIZABETH B. C	861	45	2	10
JOHN	88	32	1	5
SARAH	204	26	1	2
SS, AGNES	2357	49	1	20
, W. B	222	43	2	8
, HENRIETTA	1748	49	1	20
, MINNIE	88	46	2	12
....	717	47	1	13
, RICHARD P	1690	48	1	15
, WILLIAM F	2518	49	2	22
, FRANK W	493	46	2	11
, HEZEKIAH	3277	49	1	21
DING, HIRAM G. (heirs of)	855	46	2	10
, ALBERT	2519	48	2	17
, ALEXANDER	1620	48	1	15
....	48	49	1	18
, J. L	288	38	1	7
, SAMUEL D	2229	48	2	17
M, JEREMIAH	572	30	1	4
L, NANCY	308	43	2	8
T, BARNEY	174	22	1	2
AN, JOHN	841	30	1	4
AN, SAMANTHA	1138	48	1	16
GTON, EDWARD M	1271	49	1	19
GTON, HARRIETT R	1198	49	1	19
GTON, HARRY B., AND GRACE A	255	49	1	18
GTON, JAMES	439	23	1	1
GTON, MARTIN	1907	48	1	16
CATHARINE	540	45	2	10
ISAAC	736	43	1	8
JANE A	37	44	1	9
....	546	45	2	10
LEVI H	541	43	1	8
MARY G	294	43	1	8
....	545	45	2	10
MERLIN C	368	48	1	14
WAITIE F	2769	49	1	21
WILLIAM	1802	48	1	16
ON, ADA L	779	44	1	9
ON, CARRIE G	1023	46	2	11
ON, GEORGE A	981	45	2	10
ON, HELEN M	407	48	1	14
ON, JAMES FORSYTH	95	46	2	11
ON, JONATHAN C	2536	48	2	17
ON, REBECCA S	584	44	1	9
ON, THOMAS	798	25	2	2
....	319	27	2	3
....	52	28	1	3
ON, WILLIAM H	165	44	1	9
ANTHONY	746	49	1	19
HARLES F	546	48	1	14
ZIAS	118	33	2	5
GER, CLEMENTINE	3510	49	2	22
Y, JOHN	93	30	2	4
ELL, BETSEY H	352	26	1	2
, RUFUS L	663	36	1	7
....	103	37	2	7
, RUSSEL	1989	48	1	16
....	3284	49	1	21
, SARAH L	417	48	1	14
....	3585	49	2	22
L, BAILEY	1527	49	1	19
AHL, FRANCES	874	48	1	14
L, FLAVIA A	2160	48	1	16
IS, ADALINE G	965	47	1	13
IS, LAURA C. P	408	48	1	14
IS, REBECCA E	2065	49	1	20
L, JOHN A	568	48	1	14

Private legislation—Continued.

Subject.	Report.	Congress.	Session.	Volume.
HASTINGS, ASA	624	36	1	7
HASTINGS, LEWIS	332	29	1	[illegible]
Do	291	30	1	[illegible]
Do	50	31	1	[illegible]
HASTINGS, MARY	701	49	1	[illegible]
HATCH, MARIA B	3872	49	2	[illegible]
HATFIELD, DANIEL B	333	49	2	[illegible]
HATHAWAY, S J. (guardian)	1649	46	2	[illegible]
HATTER, NICHOLAS	1454	48	1	[illegible]
HAUG, GODFREID	2326	48	2	[illegible]
HAUKS, THERON W	689	43	1	[illegible]
HAUP, JOHN	631	[illegible]	1	4
HAVELY, W. D	2896	49	1	[illegible]
HAVENS, HENRY B	234	43	1	8
Do	1589	49	1	[illegible]
HAVILAND, ABBY C	858	45	2	[illegible]
HAWES, SUSAN	2347	49	1	[illegible]
HAWK, MARY G	1901	47	1	[illegible]
Do	460	48	1	[illegible]
HAWKE, MARY	2049	49	1	[illegible]
HAWKINS, DARIUS	267	26	1	2
Do	438	27	2	3
Do	30	27	3	3
Do	112	28	1	3
HAWKINS ISAAC N	1698	49	1	20
HAWKINS, JAMES	1098	48	1	14
HAWKINS, MARTIN	413	47	1	13
HAWKINS, THEODORE C	376	46	2	11
Do	300	48	1	15
HAWKS, MICAJAH	227	35	2	6
Do	51	36	1	7
HAWLEY, CAROLINE	593	45	2	10
HAWLEY, GEORGE S	2442	48	2	17
Do	1106	49	1	19
HAWLEY, GILES C	278	49	1	18
HAWLEY, JOSEPHUS	172	47	1	13
HAWORTH, JAMES D	2306	49	1	20
HAWTHORNE, JAMES	709	47	1	13
HAY, ABBIE M	3570	49	2	22
HAY, BARNARD	29	27	3	3
HAYDEN, JOHN	2506	49	1	20
HAYES, JAMES H	722	45	2	10
HAYES, THOMAS J	3581	49	2	22
HAYES, W. A	2354	48	2	17
HAYFORD, GILBERT	404	48	1	14
HAYNES, WALTER S	761	49	1	18
HAYNIE, GEORGE C	144	49	1	18
HAYS, ANNIE A	526	46	2	11
Do	61	47	1	13
HAYS, JOHN B	3516	49	2	22
HAYS, SAMUEL	371	46	2	11
HAYWARD, LEVI D	331	44	1	9
HAZEL, SAMUEL	785	46	2	11
Do	1630	48	1	16
HAZELIT, WILLIAM	1334	47	1	13
HAZELWOOD, JOHN	1886	48	1	16
HAZEN, JOHN	375	31	1	5
HAZENZAHL, FRANCES	793	49	1	18
HAZLE, WILLIAM	2266	48	2	17
HAZLEWOOD, JOHN	1593	47	1	13
HAZZARD, HANNA	203	26	1	2
HEADERICK, JACOB	552	26	1	2
HEALD, PENELOPE T	30	43	1	8
HEATH, ABBIE B	2826	49	1	21
HEATH, JAMES C	2681	49	1	21
HEATH, LAVISA	2396	48	2	17
HEBNER, NICHOLAS	84	38	1	7
HECKING, HENRY	1401	48	1	15
HEDDINGER, JOHN	401	43	1	8
HEDRICK, MARY E	2021	49	1	21
HEENAN, DANIEL	824	46	2	11
HEINE, FREDERICK	1003	49	1	19
HEINEMAN, ROSINA	780	48	1	14
Do	791	49	1	19
HEINRICI, ANN	247	45	3	10
HEINTZELMAN, MARGARET S	1645	46	2	12
HEINZEL, EDWARD	735	43	1	8
Do	82	44	1	9
Do	208	45	3	10

Private legislation—Continued.

Subject.	Report.	Congress.	Session.	Volume.
F. A	78	28	2	3
RLES	804	45	2	10
JOSEPHINE D	1382	48	1	15
	782	49	1	19
LARDIE HOGAN	1032	48	1	16
Y, STEPHEN F	178	26	1	2
, CHRISTIAN	142	44	1	9
, JEPTHA L	804	32	1	5
N, GEORGE	2973	49	1	21
	3632	49	2	22
N, HIRAM C	373	46	2	11
	1465	48	1	15
N, SAMUEL	594	43	1	8
N, WILLIAM	275	29	1	4
N, WILLIAM A	93	44	1	9
PERNETTA	184	44	1	9
S, FRANCES E	404	48	1	14
SON, JULIETT A	523	44	1	9
JOHN	414	43	1	8
CHARLES	1796	48	1	16
AMUEL T	1366	47	1	13
Y, AUGUSTINE	968	45	2	10
ATHARINE	484	46	2	11
	762	48	1	14
	774	48	1	14
IZABETH VERNOR	882	46	2	12
	882	47	1	12
SPER J	1960	48	1	16
ARY A	1469	48	1	15
ARY ANN	171	35	1	6
	80	36	1	7
HILIP	342	45	2	10
UFUS	83	26	2	2
AMUEL	2004	48	1	16
	11	48	1	13
ARAH E	2119	49	1	20
REPTA M. I	250	45	3	10
ELIZAH P	800	49	1	19
ACRA	507	47	1	13
CHARLES	205	43	1	8
	2510	49	1	20
, GOTTLIEB	1591	48	1	15
ANUEL B	168	44	1	9
JOHN	234	23	1	1
	461	24	1	1
OLIVER	426	22	1	1
	7	22	2	1
	377	28	1	3
	507	29	1	4
, J. V	2010	49	1	20
GARDNER	715	30	1	4
	303	31	1	5
	6	32	1	5
WILLIAM	1691	48	1	16
ANNIE M	211	43	2	8
GARDNER	818	27	2	3
OHN R	3731	49	2	22
EBECCA S	1475	47	1	13
NNA	1460	48	1	15
JOHN S	1060	49	1	19
VIN	649	43	1	8
LIAM J	2086	48	1	16
NNA	1399	48	1	15
JAMES W	3847	49	2	23
, WELLINGTON V	323	46	2	11
	1321	47	1	13
ENRY	1201	49	1	19
EORGE R. T	245	26	1	2
CHARLES	605	45	2	10
ELBERT	2341	48	2	17
PORTER B	1619	48	1	15
	121	49	1	18
THOMAS W	585	44	1	9
	511	45	2	10
, HENRY	77	36	2	7
, MARY	723	44	1	9
	819	45	2	10

Private legislation—Continued.

Subject.	Report.	Congress.	Session.	Volume.
HEYMES, MATILDA	723	44	1	9
Do	319	45	2	[illegible]
HIAR, ROYAL J	2077	49	1	[illegible]
HIBBERT, JOHN	279	26	1	[illegible]
Do	267	30	1	[illegible]
HIBBERT, ROSELLA E	2774	49	1	[illegible]
HIBNER, NICHOLAS	1178	47	1	[illegible]
HICKEY, BENJAMIN	412	44	1	[illegible]
HICKEY, PATRICK	212	42	1	[illegible]
HICKOX, EBENEZER	300	24	1	[illegible]
HICKS, ALVAH W	212	42	2	[illegible]
HICKS, ELIZA	1477	46	1	[illegible]
HICKS, JOHN	146	26	2	[illegible]
Do	808	27	2	[illegible]
HICKS, JOHN H	158	33	1	[illegible]
HICKS, SARAH A	2014	49	1	[illegible]
HICKS, WILLIAM	2147	49	1	[illegible]
HIGGERSON, CAROLINE	2148	48	1	[illegible]
HIGGINS, ANDREW F	842	45	2	[illegible]
HIGGINS, W. H	1755	48	1	[illegible]
HIGH, WILLIAM	3683	49	2	[illegible]
HIGLE, JACOB	261	26	1	[illegible]
HIGLEY, ELAM	877	25	2	[illegible]
HIGLEY, HENRY W	319	44	1	[illegible]
Do	650	44	2	[illegible]
HILDABRANT, NATHAN	347	49	2	[illegible]
HILDRETH, CHARLES F	1534	49	1	[illegible]
HILDRETH, EDNA M	3874	49	2	[illegible]
HILDRETH, SARAH	528	26	1	[illegible]
Do	10	27	3	[illegible]
Do	194	30	1	[illegible]
Do	234	34	1	[illegible]
Do	118	35	2	[illegible]
Do	594	36	1	[illegible]
HILGEMANN, CAROLINE	1157	46	2	[illegible]
Do	153	47	1	[illegible]
HILL, ALFRED J	2451	49	1	[illegible]
HILL, ANDREW J	287	49	1	[illegible]
HILL, CHARLES C	3264	49	1	[illegible]
HILL, EDWARD L	676	49	1	[illegible]
HILL, HENRY O	1419	49	1	19
HILL, MARY E	1389	48	1	15
Do	1028	49	1	19
HILL, WILLIAM H	708	47	1	13
HILLARD, FRANK S	1925	48	1	16
Do	1926	48	1	16
HILLBERG, ANDREW J	1921	49	1	20
HILLIKER, BENJAMIN F	3983	49	2	22
HILLMAN, BENJAMIN	2070	49	1	21
HILTON, CATHARINE	2626	48	2	17
HILTON, JANE	1084	48	1	14
HINCHMAN, DALTON	534	44	1	9
Do	717	45	2	10
Do	146	46	2	11
Do	3846	49	2	22
HINCKLEY, BENJAMIN	281	26	1	1
HINELEY, LEWIS	241	43	1	8
HINES, HULDA	1907	49	1	20
HINKLE, CHARLES	382	31	1	5
HIPPLE, HENRY, JR	1501	49	1	19
HIPSLEY, REBECCA R	238	46	2	12
HISELER, SAMUEL	2813	49	1	21
HITCHCOCK, APPOLLOS	392	31	1	5
HITCHCOCK, EBENEZER	326	35	1	6
Do	370	36	1	7
HIXON, LLOYD W	1922	48	1	16
HIXSON, AMOS	184	45	2	10
HOBBS, H. D	3806	49	2	22
HOBBS, MARMADUKE, M. C	57	42	3	7
HOCH, FREDERICK	128	44	1	9
HODGE, JOHN O	107	32	1	5
HOERTH, JACOB	1532	48	1	15
HOEY, CATHERINE	1402	46	2	12
HOFELD, PHILIP	2601	48	1	[illegible]
HOFF, LOUISA BAINBRIDGE	215	46	2	[illegible]
Do	1025	47	1	[illegible]
Do	1338	47	1	[illegible]
HOFF, MARY	248	49	1	[illegible]

Private legislation—Continued.

Subject.	Report.	Congress.	Session.	Volume.
AN, CATHERINE	[illegible]	49	2	22
N, AUGUSTUS	[illegible]	48	1	14
CATHARINE	565	30	2	4
CHARLES	1797	48	1	16
JOHN	52	24	2	1
NOAH	676	48	1	12
PETER P	2007	46	1	[illegible]
PHILIP	55	49	1	18
EDWARD	2281	48	2	17
UEL	[illegible]	27	2	3
ANNA	373	35	1	4
ALIUS S	105	46	1	12
AMASA	93	35	1	7
JAMES L	1185	48	1	15
MOSES	246	39	1	3
JACOB	3060	49	2	20
BENJAMIN	94	[illegible]	2	1
	[illegible]	30	1	4
	[illegible]	30	1	4
	15	33	1	5
JOHN	560	34	1	6
	404	35	1	6
ROBERT	[illegible]	49	1	22
SAMUEL V	[illegible]	48	1	13
SUSAN M	1246	47	1	12
S, MARIA	1060	49	1	19
ANNA	741	49	1	19
WORTH, BENJAMIN	756	49	1	19
THNIEL P	346	46	2	10
Y, EMMA J	[illegible]	49	1	
Y, WASHINGTON A	729	48	1	
LD, L. V	3385	46	2	17
	4115	49	2	22
ABTLETT	226	28	1	3
EORGE	121	43	1	8
ANE.	3890	49	2	22
IALINDA A	238	49	1	18
IARY B	678½	49	1	18
OBERT	2093	49	1	20
RLES H	842	48	1	14
	240	49	1	18
VARD B	3875	49	2	22
S	147	49	1	18
OMON	2107	49	1	20
IEL	193	24	1	1
RANCIS M	450	30	1	4
DIA	1765	48	1	16
OKE, JOHN	379	23	1	1
AD, SETH W	162	44	1	
	1939	48	1	16
GEORGE	955	25	2	2
	210	26	1	2
	151	26	2	2
	314	27	2	3
BIGAIL	1962	48	1	16
	1900	48	1	16
RICHARD	1735	49	1	20
AMANDA	482	49	1	18
ZABETH	1373	48	1	15
LIE	46	33	1	5
	593	45	2	10
RY B	144	44	1	9
	1417	49	1	19
RS. ANNA ETHERIDGE	3763	49	2	22
ARTON	710	24	1	1
o	490	25	2	2
o	181	25	3	2
o	193	26	1	2
GEORGE R	3568	49	2	22
SARAH A	283	47	1	13
o	538	48	1	14
o	2845	49	1	21
ABNER	71	46	2	11
DAVID T	2534	48	2	17
, ABRAM C	882	48	1	14
, THOMAS S	620	47	1	13
Do	2546	49	1	21
Do	2547	49	1	21
Do	4175	49	2	22

Private legislation—**Continued.**

Subject.	Report.	Congress.	Session.	Volume.
HOPPER, BRIDGET T	278	44	1	9
Do	21	45	2	10
HOPPER, CHRISTOPHER	370	46	2	11
HOPPER, FRANCIS J	576	49	1	18
HOPPER, JOHN	1684	46	2	12
HOPPER, JONAS B	346	46	3	12
HOPPERTON, MARY	2062	48	1	16
HORAN, PATRICK	1551	47	1	13
Do	459	48	1	14
HORD, GEORGE W	1207	46	2	12
HORGAN, ELLEN	398	48	1	14
HORN, MARY	1362	49	1	19
HORNADAY, COLBY	108	46	2	11
HORNBECK, JEPTHA	113	49	1	15
HORNER, SAMUEL	1241	47	1	13
HORNER, WILLIAM	961	45	2	10
HOROBIN, LUKE	2810	49	1	21
HORTON, ANDREW J	1128	47	1	13
HORTON, JAMES H	2295	48	2	17
HORTON, JONATHAN F	810	27	2	3
HOSKINS, LEVI	2507	49	1	20
HOSKINS, THOMAS	3011	49	1	21
HOUGH, AMY A	252	43	1	8
HOUGH, MARY A	276	44	1	9
HOUGHTELIN, ANNA	554	49	1	15
HOUSENER, ELIZABETH	24	37	3	7
HOUSER, ANDREW	237	49	1	15
HOUSER, JOHN	291	34	1	5
Do	226	35	2	6
HOUSTON, SARAH	795	45	2	10
HOUSTON, WILLIAM A	665	26	1	2
Do	80	26	2	2
HOWARD, ABRAHAM	1531	46	2	12
Do	1159	48	1	15
Do	1799	49	1	20
HOWARD, AXEF S	66	43	2	8
HOWARD, EDWARD	497	46	2	11
HOWARD, GEORGE W. (widow of)	286	26	1	2
HOWARD, HIRAM M	1824	47	1	12
Do	463	48	1	14
HOWARD, LEWIS	274	26	1	2
HOWARD, MARY	3010	49	1	21
HOWARD, THOMAS	377	31	1	4
HOWARD, WILLIAM H	828	47	1	13
HOWE, MARY S	279	43	1	8
HOWE, SARAH B	213	43	2	8
HOWE, W. B	1215	46	2	12
HOWEL, JOHN W	20	30	2	4
HOWELL, WILLIAM	308	35	1	6
HOWLAND, EVALINA	358	49	1	15
HOWREN, EMILINE	282	46	2	11
HOY, BERNARD	29	27	3	3
HOYLE, HENRY	175	43	2	8
HOYT, AMANDA E	449	48	1	14
HOYT, ASA	208	22	1	1
HOYT, BIRNEY	357	46	2	11
HOYT, CHAUNCEY	230	35	1	7
HOYT, JONATHAN	771	29	1	4
HUBBARD, THADEUS	432	27	2	3
HUBBELL, GILBERT W	564	48	1	14
HUBBERT, JOHN W	3271	49	1	22
HUDSON, ELIZA	773	46	2	11
Do	949	47	1	13
HUDSON, ESTHER	1837	48	1	16
HUDSON, JOHN MORLEY	358	46	3	12
HUDSON, LEMUEL	*25	33	1	5
HUDSON, MELVILLE H	160	44	1	9
HUDSON, WILLIAM J	1190	48	1	15
HUESTED, WELLINGTON	1311	48	1	[illegible]
HUFF, CALVIN D	1655	46	2	[illegible]
HUFF, JAMES W	62	43	2	[illegible]
HUGGINS, GEORGE	246	[illegible]	2	[illegible]
HUGGINS, HENRY N	2409	48	2	[illegible]
Do	1801	49	1	[illegible]
HUGGINS, JENNIE	881	[illegible]	1	19
HUGHART, THOMAS	606	37	1	[illegible]
HUGHES, AARON B	698	48	1	[illegible]

Private legislation—Continued.

Subject.	Report.	Congress.	Session.	Volume.
C. K	1524	46	2	13
	513	47	1	13
	2166	48	1	20
CORNELIUS	871	30	1	4
	86	30	2	4
	451	31	1	5
	35	32	1	5
JAMES	797	46	2	11
JOHN C	419	48	1	14
ROBERT R	545	48	1	14
	14	49	1	18
WILLIAM	157	26	1	2
	610	27	2	2
	221	45	2	10
MUEL B	782	24	1	1
	122	24	2	1
	217	26	2	2
	168	25	3	2
	191	26	1	2
	147	26	2	2
	130	27	2	3
, GEORGE	320	46	2	11
. GEORGE	1387	47	1	12
IZABETH	166	43	2	8
IZABETH P	536	43	1	8
IZABETH R	69	44	1	9
	512	45	2	10
COB	1071	48	1	14
JACOB	1046	47	1	13
LIZA	1196	49	1	19
USAN	608	46	2	10
EYS, ANN	269	43	1	8
EYS, REBECCA HOLLINGSWORTH	2779	49	1	21
NJAMIN	154	26	2	2
	136	27	2	2
	100	29	1	4
ARINDA	2535	48	2	17
THARINE D	331	45	2	10
RANT F	1204	48	1	15
NRY	946	48	1	14
SIAH	85	26	2	2
WIS (widow and minor children of)	2094	49	1	20
OSES N	471	31	1	5
OSWELL	238	22	1	1
	7	22	2	1
MUEL	215	23	1	1
	203	24	1	1
ANN	1439	48	1	15
CATHERINE	135	48	1	14
JAMES (widow of)	178	24	2	1
	611	25	2	2
	33	25	3	2
	172	26	1	2
JAMES P	302	49	2	11
JOHN	804	49	1	19
JOHN F	228	35	2	6
	76	36	1	7
JOHN H	2085	49	1	20
JOHN L	688	49	1	18
MARIA	1522	49	1	19
	3214	49	1	21
	4066	49	2	22
MARY	1181	48	1	15
W. GODFREY	73	43	2	8
GTON, ASHER	264	22	1	1
	7	22	2	1
LBERT	1941	48	1	16
RT, GEORGE	1387	47	1	13
T, JOHN R	1741	48	1	16
T, TIMOTHY J	70	44	2	9
	758	45	2	10
T, WRIGHT	591	25	2	2
	137	25	3	2
AMY A	117	49	1	18
JOSEPH S	2601	48	2	17
MARY ANN	878	48	1	14
D, MARY MORRIS	1136	48	1	14
AMES H	2970	49	1	21

Private legislation—Continued.

Subject.	Report.	Congress.	Session.	Volume.
HUSTED, E. L	177	46		12
Do	504	47		13
HUSTON, FREELAND	1714	46		12
HUSTON, GEORGE	154	45		10
HUSTON, PETER	212	26		2
HUTCHINGS, ELIAKIM W	816	27		3
HUTCHINGS, LIDIA O	2075	49		20
HUTCHINS, ALPHEUS	356	24		1
HUTCHINS, ERASTUS	499	35		6
Do	221	36		7
HUTCHINS, HANNAH BABB	1058	49		19
HUTCHINSON, CAROLINE M	518	35		6
HUTCHINSON, DAVID G	1541	46		12
Do	661	47		13
HUTCHISON, SAMUEL B	64	46		11
HUTSON, HALL	118	32		5
HUTTEN, FREDERICK	2051	48		16
HYATT, BRUNER D	691	49		18
HYDER, WILLIAM F. M	798	46	2	11
INGALLS, WILLIAM W	1342	49	1	19
INGERSOLL, N. J	2092	48	1	16
INGHAM, SALLIE	941	48	1	14
INGHRAM, ELIZABETH H	2256	49	1	20
INGLE, MELVINA	285	44	1	9
Do	959	45	2	10
INGRAHAM, JOHN	501	29	1	4
INNES, JOHN A	230	45	3	10
Do	205	46	2	11
Do	617	47	1	13
IRELAND, DAVID A	3557	49	2	22
IRELAND, JEREMIAH	86	31	2	4
IRONS, OLIVER H	552	44	1	9
Do	646	45	2	10
IRVING, ARTHUR W	532	44	1	9
Do	572	45	2	10
Do	1547	46	2	12
Do	958	47	1	13
IRVING, WILLIAM	1609	48	1	15
IRWIN, JAMES T	2017	49	1	20
IRWIN, ROBERT	420	27	2	3
ISENBERG, ATHA L	2090	49	1	21
ISREAL, WILLIAM	330	35	1	6
IVERS, JOHN H. (alias John H. Wilson)	1306	48	1	15
IVORY, JAMES	815	27	2	3
JACK, ALBERT L	111	46	2	11
JACKS, DANIEL	781	49	1	19
JACKSON, ADDISON A	2824	49	1	21
JACKSON, ALEXANDER S	270	28	1	3
Do	37	29	1	4
JACKSON, ANDREW	554	44	1	9
JACKSON, DAVID C	1166	46	2	12
JACKSON, HARLAN	1905	48	1	16
JACKSON, JACOB	45	26	2	2
Do	255	27	2	3
JACKSON, JANE	2108	49	1	20
JACKSON, JESSE WASHINGTON	283	35	1	6
JACKSON, JOHN	289	36	1	7
JACKSON, JOHN H	853	46	2	11
Do	669	47	1	13
JACKSON, LEMUEL	606	27	2	3
JACKSON, MICHAEL	544	45	2	10
JACKSON, PATSEY	226	49	1	18
JACKSON, SARAH B	1170	48	1	15
Do	464	49	1	18
JACKSON, SUSAN J	40	28	1	3
JACKSON, SYLVADOR	1650	46	2	12
Do	212	47	1	13
JACKSON, THOMAS J	84	46	2	11
JACKSON, WILLIAM	259	27	2	3
JACOBS, ENOCH	650	43	1	8
JACOBS, FRANCIS	293	22	1	1
Do	122	23	1	1
JACOBS, JOHN L	2350	49	1	20
Do	2360	49	1	20
JACOBS, JUSTIN	41	28	2	3
Do	467	29	1	4
JACOBS, PHILIP	273	48	1	15
JACOBS, WILLIAM B	244	49	1	19

Private legislation—Continued.

Subject.	Report.	Congress.	Session.	Volume.
MARGARET A.	[illegible]	49	1	19
MARTIN	1682	49	1	19
HENRY	418	27	2	3
JOHN D	406	49	1	19
SILAS	875	49	1	19
, SAMUEL	819	33	1	6
Do.	239	33	1	7
, ISAAC	305	23	1	1
JOHN	320	27	2	3
GEORGE W	2071	49	1	20
S, SUSAN	789	47	1	13
S, MARY E	879	44	2	11
S, BENJAMIN	1981	48	1	16
S, THOMAS	2484	48	1	15
ALBERT	1698	48	1	16
JAMES S	641	48	1	14
, REUBEN	2477	48	2	17
ISABELLA	2852	49	1	21
, JOHN M	131	24	2	1
Do.	425	25	2	2
, PLINY	377	46	2	12
BRADLEY TRUE	389	24	1	1
Do.	185	26	2	3
RICHARD	1287	47	1	13
Do.	1326	48	1	15
, AARON C.	436	49	1	18
, CATHARINE	167	44	1	9
Do.	1482	49	1	19
, CATHARINE H. T	183	27	3	3
Do.	106	28	1	3
, DANIEL	1845	49	2	19
, ELIZABETH	3903	49	1	20
, EMMA	1206	46	2	12
Do.	714	47	1	13
, FREDERICK	651	46	2	11
, FREEMAN	815	46	2	11
, HEZEKIAH	73	33	1	5
, HIRAM	204	45	3	10
Do.	1316	47	1	13
, HUGH	442	27	2	3
, JACKSON T	3250	49	1	21
, JAMES	1612	47	1	13
, JAMES P	1871	48	1	16
, JENET L	799	49	1	19
, JENNIE E	2081	48	1	16
, JOHN	672	26	1	2
Do.	226	26	2	2
Do.	1490	48	1	15
, JOHN H	1531	48	1	15
, JOSEPH	182	29	1	4
, LEWIS	1715	46	2	12
, LYDIA	87	44	1	9
, LYDIA S	2145	49	1	20
, MARY E	1065	49	1	19
, NICHOLAS W	778	44	1	9
, OXLEY	4118	49	2	22
, PERRY	439	49	1	18
, RACHEL ANN	2476	48	2	17
, ROBERT	2091	48	1	16
, SALLY R.	86	30	2	4
, SAMUEL H	213	45	3	10
, SUSAN R	527	46	2	11
Do.	60	47	1	13
, WILLIAM	333	35	1	6
, WILLIAM A	185	36	1	7
, WILLIAM F	1067	46	2	12
, WILLIAM H	772	43	1	8
, ZACHARIAH (widow of)	615	36	1	7
ON, JAMES	3965	49	2	22
Do.	450	44	1	9
Do.	868	45	2	10
ON, JOSEPH	142	31	1	5
Do.	10	32	1	5
ON, LEVI	592	25	2	2
Do.	192	26	1	2
MARY V. B.	546	43	1	8
LEONARD	296	24	2	1
Do.	316	27	2	3
Do.	28	27	3	3

Private legislation—Continued.

Subject.	Report.	Congress.	Session.	Volume.
JONES, ALEXANDER	332	35	1	[illegible]
JONES, ANN	226	42	2	[illegible]
JONES, EDWARD B	529	33	1	[illegible]
JONES, EDWIN W	455	36	1	[illegible]
Do	62	37	2	[illegible]
JONES, ELIHU	2256	49	1	[illegible]
JONES, EZEKIEL	288	25	2	[illegible]
Do	117	25	2	[illegible]
Do	156	36	1	[illegible]
JONES, HARVEY	206	30	1	[illegible]
JONES, ISHMAEL	698	43	1	[illegible]
JONES, JEROME B	3291	49	1	[illegible]
JONES, JOHN	208	35	1	[illegible]
JONES, JOHN D	3954	49	2	[illegible]
JONES, JOSEPH	2965	49	1	[illegible]
JONES, LANSON	370	34	1	[illegible]
JONES, LEVI	1752	49	1	[illegible]
JONES, LUCINDA	376	43	1	[illegible]
JONES, MARTHA A	196	45	2	[illegible]
JONES, MARY A. M	190	33	1	[illegible]
Do	173	35	1	[illegible]
JONES, MARY C	447	46	1	[illegible]
JONES, RICHARD D	79	30	2	[illegible]
JONES, RICHARD L	18	33	1	5
JONES, ROBERT	239	35	1	6
JONES, ROBERT D	586	43	1	8
JONES, SAMUEL	1546	46	2	12
Do	1220	47	1	13
JONES, SARAH A	2969	49	1	21
JONES, WESLEY	287	45	3	10
JONES, WILLIAM H	572	46	1	11
JORDAN, ANDREW M	3949	49	2	22
JORDAN, JAMES L	772	46	2	11
JORDAN, JOHN (heirs of)	443	37	2	7
JORDAN, MARTIN V	1228	46	2	12
JORDEN, JOHN	521	36	1	7
Do	148	37	2	8
JOSEPHS, PETER	9	38	2	7
JOYCE, MARY	209	45	3	10
Do	814	46	2	11
Do	156	47	1	13
JOYNES, WILLIAM R	651	25	2	3
Do	143	26	2	3
Do	619	27	2	3
Do	298	28	1	3
JULIUS, PETER	106	46	2	11
JUSTICE, HANNAH	1758	46	2	12
JUSTICE, ISAAC	322	26	2	[illegible]
Do	83	25	3	[illegible]
Do	194	28	1	[illegible]
Do	90	28	2	[illegible]
Do	151	27	2	[illegible]
Do	90	25	1	[illegible]
JUSTICE, JOSHUA F	1811	48	1	16
KABERLA, ANNA	1057	47	1	13
KABERLA, JOHANNA PAUL	1057	47	1	13
KAHN, MOHOMMED	832	46	2	11
KAIME, JOHN	230	32	1	7
KAIN, DANIEL	782	49	1	19
KAISER, HENRY L	210	43	2	8
Do	282	44	1	9
KALER, ALMIRA B	1594	45	1	15
KALER, ELIZABETH	1690	48	1	16
Do	137	49	1	18
KAMPF, SOPHIE F	1750	48	1	16
KANE, JOHN	1205	48	1	15
KARBELLA, ANNA	252	49	1	18
KARSTETTER, MARY	1407	49	1	19
KASSON, JAMES L	405	49	1	18
KAUBLE, SOLOMON T	774	46	2	11
KAYLOR, MARY	2057	49	1	21
KEAN, ROBERT	215	32	1	7
KEARNS, MARGARET	1180	46	2	12
Do	1052	47	1	13
Do	775	48	1	14
Do	762	49	1	18
KECK, THOMAS	1885	48	1	16
KEEFER, HENRY	147	24	1	1

Private legislation—Continued.

Subject.	Report.	Congress.	Session.	Volume.
ERS, JACOBINA	41	35	2	6
, E. (guardian)	367	46	2	10
, JOHN	876	25	2	3
	162	25	3	2
	173	26	1	2
MARGARET	146	45	2	10
IS, JAMES POLK	367	46	2	11
ARY A	[illegible]	48	2	17
IVER	970	27	2	3
ILLIAM B	590	48	1	14
	8	49	1	18
WILLIAM	969	27	2	3
GEORGE	144	31	1	5
HENRY	1878	49	1	19
WILLIAM	315	24	1	1
	184	28	1	3
ALBERT C	2795	49	1	21
ALICE	3780	49	2	22
HONORA	1836	47	1	13
	458	48	1	14
JOSEPH	561	30	1	4
TRUMAN	806	25	2	3
ENJAMIN F	2975	49	1	21
RIFFIN	189	29	1	3
	472	30	1	4
ARTIN	1632	48	1	16
ICHARD	307	29	1	4
OBERT E	23	28	1	3
HOMAS	567	45	2	10
ILLIAM	1590	46	2	12
SOLOMON T	774	46	2	11
MUEL P	462	43	1	8
, SIDNEY	[illegible]	49	1	21
WILLIAM F	169	46	3	12
ER, LIZZIE	406	49	1	18
Y, MARY	738	45	2	10
, ARIOUS	236	43	1	8
, CATHARINE	1200	49	1	19
, ERASTUS	2304	49	1	20
, M. L	1612	48	1	15
, MICHAEL L	1544	46	2	12
, PATRICK W	1019	49	1	19
, SARAH	2289	48	2	17
, WILLIAM	805	30	1	4
ANDREW	723	47	1	13
MARY B	2404	49	1	20
, MIRIAM V	317	45	2	10
, BRITANNIA W	828	46	2	11
ONZO HAYWARD	3283	49	1	21
BENEZER	214	27	2	3
NNETTE S	1492	49	1	19
HINEAS M	111	33	2	5
, BRITANNIA W	822	46	2	11
, SIMON	187	27	3	3
GH, JOHN	77	30	2	4
	38	32	1	5
BENJAMIN	306	29	1	4
WILLIAMS	356	26	1	2
NNA B	3764	49	2	22
ARY	884	49	1	19
ER, ANN	2047	49	1	20
M. SINGLETON	667	24	1	1
M, JOHN	151	35	1	6
JEREMIAH	1	23	1	1
LVIRA	201	43	2	8
o	539	44	1	9
o	972	47	1	13
o	974	47	1	13
N, HARVEY B	126	44	1	9
RNE, LUCIEN	832	47	1	13
AMES	547	43	1	8
o	692	44	1	9
ARIA	1605	49	1	20
AN, DANIEL	2390	49	1	20
RICK, JUDSON (widow of)	262	48	1	14
L, JEREMIAH	318	27	2	3
o	46	27	3	3
o	105	28	1	

Private legislation—Continued.

Subject.	Report.	Congress.	Session.
KIMBALL, ROXANA	251	34	1
KIMMERLING, JOHN	2201	46	2
KINCADE, CATHARINE	112	35	2
KINCAID, ALEXANDER	861	45	2
KINCAID, GEORGE W	4059	49	2
KINCAID, JOHN	1	23	1
KINCAID, SAMUEL	222	34	1
Do	244	36	1
KINCHELOE, PHILIP	4122	49	2
KINDER, JEFFERSON	741	45	2
KING, DAVID	474	22	1
KING, ELIZABETH J	287	43	1
KING, ELIZABETH M	3097	49	1
KING, EZRA (widow of)	478	36	1
KING, JAMES	782	46	2
Do	1218	47	1
Do	414	48	1
Do	2151	48	1
KING, JAMES H	3449	49	1
KING, JOHN S	63	33	1
KING, LEONARD	1494	48	1
Do	594	49	1
KING, MATILDA	205	44	1
KING, SARAH J	215	44	1
KING, THOMAS	47	24	2
Do	332	25	2
KING, THOMAS	1032	27	2
KING, WILLIAM	270	28	1
KINGSBURY, GOULD	2116	49	1
KINGSBURY, WILLIAM	253	24	1
Do	40	35	2
KINGSLEY, ABRAHAM H	329	25	2
KINGSLEY, LUCINA	252	26	1
KINGSLEY, THOMAS G	567	44	1
KINMAN, WILLIAM H	1904	48	1
KINNEALLY, MARY	738	45	2
KINNEY, ANN	2296	49	1
KINNEY, JESSE (heirs of)	113	35	2
KINNEY, MIRIAM V	1670	45	2
KINSELLA, PATRICK	856	45	2
KIRBY, TARRANCE	285	24	1
Do	330	25	1
Do	85	36	1
KIRCHNER, ERDMUTHE	4803	49	1
KIRK, ALEXANDER	2829	48	2
KIRK, JAMES D	1720	48	1
KIRK, MARTIN	410	49	1
KIRK, WILLIAM T	1345	47	1
KIRKHART, JOSEPH F	2889	49	1
KIRKPATRICK, JOHN S	2402	49	1
KIRKPATRICK, ROBERT B	2080	48	1
KIRMAYER, FRANCIS H	340	49	1
KISER, GEORGE W	942	48	1
KISER, MARY	1483	49	1
KITCHEN, JAMES	103	46	2
Do	1519	48	1
KITTERIDGE, ALANSON	377	44	1
KITTS, DAVID	1167	46	2
KITZMILLER, FRANK	631	47	1
KITZMILLER, SAMUEL	1498	48	1
KLEIN, HENRY	706	48	1
KLINE, JOHN	565	39	1
KLINEDINST, MARGARET	1275	49	1
KNAPP, AMOS	477	31	1
Do	14	32	1
KNAPP, ELISHA B	220	42	2
KNAPP, SHEPHERD	169	34	1
KNAPP, ZEPANIAH	132	37	2
KNICK, CALVIN L	1061	48	2
KNIERIM, CATHERINE	237	43	2
KNIGHT, JOHN	391	30	1
KNIGHT, JOSEPH	173	[illegible]	1
Do	8	[illegible]	[illegible]
KNIGHT, SIMEON	646	[illegible]	[illegible]
Do	227	[illegible]	[illegible]
KNILL, DELILAH	547	49	[illegible]
KNIPE, J. W.	897	[illegible]	[illegible]
KNIPE, JOSEPH W	459	[illegible]	[illegible]
Do	206	[illegible]	[illegible]

Private legislation—Continued.

Subject.	Report.	Congress.	Session.	Volume.
MALACHI	2789	49	2	22
H, PHILIP	3090	49	1	21
DER, GEORGE	1752	46	2	12
OHN R	156	27	3	3
WILFRED (Wilford)	649	24	1	1
	649	25	2	2
	280	26	2	2
	344	28	2	3
	658	33	1	4
	464	30	1	4
R, MARY A	1197	48	1	15
, THOMAS J	225	49	1	18
NALD	844	48	1	15
NRY J	1606	48	1	15
, FERDINAND	1582	49	1	19
R, ANNA	776	44	1	9
	626	45	2	10
OHN	648	45	2	10
CHOLAS	88	46	3	12
ANDREW J	1217	48	1	15
LEVI	290	49	1	18
ENDERICK	1396	49	1	20
N, JACOB	1815	48	1	16
R, EDWARD	2504	48	2	17
ETER	1120	48	1	15
HERMAN	2062	48	2	17
WILLIAM H	3090	49	1	21
L, JOHN D	1283	49	1	19
ADA O	282	49	1	18
R. SUSANNA	1179	46	2	12
WENDELIN	1597	49	2	20
MAGDALENA	425	49	1	18
N, JOHANNA	596	46	2	11
UGUSTUS J	77	35	1	5
, CHARLES D	1718	48	1	16
EBECCA	1901	48	1	15
I. L	1369	49	1	19
N, MARTHA ALLEN	1251	47	1	13
MES	222	35	2	6
	62	36	1	7
VID	243	29	1	4
NDERSON	805	46	2	11
TY, JACOB	1147	48	1	14
MARTIN	270	48	1	8
, HENRY	2980	49	1	21
ETT, SOLOMON	17	33	2	5
T, JANE	120	43	1	8
LEWIS	425	29	1	4
IDRON C	2144	49	1	20
, JOSEPH	459	43	1	8
ALEB A	355	43	1	8
RT, CHRISTOPHER	419	27	2	3
Do	190	27	3	3
RT, FRANCES M	3015	49	1	12
G, ANNE E (Lamburg)	2780	49	1	21
RN, COFFIN	231	26	2	2
Y, REESE	724	44	1	9
TE, SUSAN B	1093	48	1	14
ENE, STACY	185	29	1	4
IER, EDGAR B	1327	47	1	13
, AUGUSTUS	825	46	2	11
MARY A	1173	46	2	12
Do	1629	48	1	16
RS, SARAH	835	46	2	11
UM, LAWRENCE P. N	149	44	2	9
JOHN	99	36	2	7
Do	101	37	2	7
JOHN F	1194	46	2	12
JOSEPH B	158	44	1	9
MICHAEL	2459	48	2	17
JAMES	182	49	1	18
ROBERT	421	27	2	3
ON, HANNAH R	4071	49	2	22
ORD, ANDERSON	530	46	2	11
AND, JOHN	690	44	1	9
Do	324	45	2	10
EY, ISAAC	248	34	1	9
Do	516	35	1	6

***Private legislation*—Continued.**

Subject.	Report.	Congress.	Session.	Volume.
LANGLEY, JANE M	759	45	1	16
LANGREEN, SUSANNA	191	32	1	3
Do	363	33	1	4
LANGSTON, EMMETT	159	46	2	8
Do	225	46	3	10
Do	225	48	2	11
LANGWORTHY, ANNIE L	885	49	1	19
LANGWORTHY, GEORGE I	1506	49	1	19
LANIGAN, CATHARINE	2696	49	1	21
LANMAN, ANN CORNELIA	798	45	2	16
Do	890	46	1	14
LANNAN, DANIEL	2081	49	1	21
LANNING, DR. A	2559	49	2	22
LANNING, ELIZABETH	194	43	2	8
LANSDOWNS, NATHANIEL	374	36	1	4
LANSING, EDWARD B	2154	49	1	20
LANSING, EDWARD D	874	46	1	14
LANTIER, MICHAEL	167	35	2	6
LANTY, FREDERICK	215	27	2	3
LAPHAM, SAMANTHA R	1943	48	1	16
Do	1942	49	1	19
LA POINTE, G. W	161	45	2	8
Do	15	44	1	9
LAPPERT, JOHN	299	48	2	23
Do	282	47	1	12
LARDNER, ELLEN	1468	47	1	12
LARRABEE, CHARLES	656	35	2	2
Do	262	36	1	2
Do	436	37	2	3
Do	22	38	2	2
LARRABEE, HARRIET M	694	48	1	13
LARRO, JAMES	1146	48	2	12
LARWOOD, JACOB	2100	49	1	20
LASH, JOHN H	2410	49	1	20
LASHELS, MARY	272	36	1	3
LATHAM, CORNELIUS H	30	33	1	5
Do	245	34	1	6
Do	217	35	1	6
LATHERMAN, GRANT, E. Q	3382	49	1	21
LATHROP, MRS. MARY	2854	46	2	23
LAUFFER, CAROLINE	256	46	2	13
Do	454	48	1	13
LAUFMAN, ALBERT O	409	48	1	14
LAUTER, JUDITH	250	48	1	14
LAW, JOHN S	2080	48	2	17
LAWLER, ELIZABETH H	1960	48	1	16
LAWRENCE, GEORGE	787	45	2	20
LAWRENCE, GEORGE H	2214	48	2	17
Do	2150	49	1	20
LAWRENCE, JANE MARY	216	32	1	1
LAWRENCE, R. D	1587	48	1	18
LAWRENCE, LEMUEL L	590	44	1	9
Do	140	45	2	10
LAWRENCE, THOMAS	1896	48	1	18
LAWRENCE, WILLIAM	342	32	1	1
Do	196	34	1	1
LAWS, ANTHONY A	225	43	2	8
LAWSON, MARTHA	1594	47	1	15
LAWTON, ORRIN	2046	50	1	20
LAWYER, ISAAC	825	37	2	3
LEACH, ASA	230	33	1	4
LEACH, NANCY B	2071	48	2	17
Do	2666	49	2	23
LEACH, THOMAS	136	44	1	8
LEAFFY, BRIDGET	74	46	2	8
Do	974	46	2	10
LEAMY, GEORGE W	295	43	2	8
Do	126	44	1	9
Do	792	46	2	10
Do	24	48	2	12
LEAVENWORTH, HARRIETT	35	37	1	5
LEBA, MARGARET	3000	49	1	21
LEBOW, MARY J	715	45	1	[illegible]
Do	549	46	2	[illegible]
LECKNER, MATTHIAS	119	44	1	[illegible]
LEDDY, ANN	798	45	1	[illegible]
Do	2005	49	1	[illegible]
LEDMAN, WILLIAM	7	48	2	[illegible]

Private legislation—Continued.

Subject.	Report.	Congress.	Session.	Volume.
…HUR M.	799	43	1	8
…IARINE	794	43	1	8
…IERINE M	4065	49	2	22
…ARD	394	36	1	7
…ES A	308	46	3	12
…I	214	36	1	6
…IA L	14	46	3	12
…	687	48	1	14
…G	456	28	1	3
…IE T	177	43	2	8
…LIAM H	337	45	2	10
…LIAM J	395	46	2	11
…	217	47	1	13
…	141	48	1	14
…, ELIZABETH	1580	46	2	12
…	1949	47	1	13
…LEVI	41	46	3	11
…LIAM J	1589	49	1	20
…ED. J	1026	49	1	19
…RAH BRYAN	267	44	1	14
…, MARY	217	46	2	11
…JACOB	890	29	1	4
…ILIP	909	27	2	3
…RTS, FRANCIS A	1490	49	1	19
…G, OTTO	1505	48	1	15
…. (widow of)	556	26	1	3
…GUSTUS	145	47	1	13
…PETER	1160	48	1	15
…NATHAN	2150	49	1	20
…ERNER	1453	48	1	15
…, HARRIET	562	43	1	8
…	182	45	3	10
…, NANCY	1139	47	1	13
…FREDERICK A	1011	48	1	14
…	2575	48	2	17
…ENJAMIN	410	28	1	1
…ANIEL	2415	49	1	20
…MARY P. B	112	33	2	5
…THEODORE	1816	48	1	16
…EL J	1368	48	1	15
…	1040	49	1	19
…MY A	2069	48	1	16
…	71	49	1	18
…TSIE	128	43	1	8
…ROLINE	1810	48	1	16
…WIN F	166	45	2	10
…	778	46	2	11
…NRIETTA A	2290	48	2	17
…MES M	575	30	1	4
…	109	33	1	5
…SEPH J	3840	49	2	22
…WIS	1050	47	1	13
…	411	48	1	14
…ARTHA A	1142	46	2	12
…	59	47	1	13
…	1783	49	1	20
…ERRITT	355	46	2	11
…	1027	47	1	13
…	269	48	1	14
…	3889	49	1	21
…RAH	710	47	1	13
…MON E	1634	48	1	16
…D, JACOB	277	28	1	3
…HENRY	635	49	1	18
…VARD H	215	45	3	10
…	92	46	3	11
…CE, ESTHER E	955	45	2	10
…	374	46	2	11
…OT, WILLIAM	249	26	1	2
…R, FRANK	282	49	1	18
…JOSEPHINE O	234	43	2	8
…LEONARD	23	34	3	6
…, EZEKIEL	175	28	1	3
…, JOHN H	771	25	2	2
…	255	25	3	2
…	184	26	1	2
…	138	27	3	3
…, JOHN	2061	48	1	16

Private legislation—Continued.

Subject.	Report.	Congress.	Session.	Volume.
LINGENFELTER, MICHAEL	45	[illegible]	[illegible]	[illegible]
LINN, JOSEPH	474	[illegible]	1	[illegible]
Do	7	[illegible]	[illegible]	[illegible]
LIPPE, GEORGE ANNA	[illegible]	[illegible]	1	[illegible]
LISLE, ROSALIE C. P	[illegible]	[illegible]	1	[illegible]
LITT, WILLIAM	1150	[illegible]	2	[illegible]
LITTLE, ANN	[illegible]	[illegible]	[illegible]	[illegible]
Do	774	[illegible]	1	[illegible]
LITTLE, FRANCIS	[illegible]	[illegible]	[illegible]	[illegible]
LITTLE, JOHN E	[illegible]	[illegible]	[illegible]	[illegible]
LITTLE, MARY A	[illegible]	[illegible]	1	[illegible]
LIVERMORE, JOHN S	[illegible]	[illegible]	[illegible]	[illegible]
LIVINGSTON, ROBERT W	815	[illegible]	[illegible]	[illegible]
Do	[illegible]	[illegible]	[illegible]	[illegible]
LOCEY, T. J	[illegible]	[illegible]	[illegible]	[illegible]
LOCKE, JOHN H	[illegible]	[illegible]	[illegible]	[illegible]
LOCKMAN, ISAAC P	1779	[illegible]	[illegible]	[illegible]
Do	[illegible]	[illegible]	1	[illegible]
LOE, LOUIS	[illegible]	[illegible]	1	[illegible]
LOEB, HENRIETTA	[illegible]	[illegible]	1	[illegible]
LOGAN, JOHN	[illegible]	[illegible]	1	[illegible]
LOGAN, JOHN W	650	[illegible]	[illegible]	[illegible]
LOGAN, MARY S	*3858	[illegible]	[illegible]	[illegible]
LOGSDON, FRANK	[illegible]	[illegible]	[illegible]	[illegible]
LOGSDON, MARY	[illegible]	[illegible]	1	[illegible]
LONDON, JOHN A	[illegible]	[illegible]	[illegible]	[illegible]
LONG, ABNER	[illegible]	[illegible]	1	[illegible]
LONG, ALBERT	[illegible]	[illegible]	1	[illegible]
LONG, DANIEL D	48	[illegible]	[illegible]	11
Do	[illegible]	[illegible]	1	12
LONG, GEORGE R	[illegible]	[illegible]	1	[illegible]
LONG, JACOB	[illegible]	[illegible]	[illegible]	[illegible]
LONG, JAMES	[illegible]	[illegible]	1	[illegible]
LONG, WILLIAM	[illegible]	[illegible]	1	[illegible]
LONGABAUGH, ANDREW	102	[illegible]	1	[illegible]
LONGBOTTOM, JOHN H	[illegible]	[illegible]	1	[illegible]
LOOBY, JOHN H	[illegible]	[illegible]	[illegible]	[illegible]
LOOKINGBILL, DANIEL	[illegible]	[illegible]	1	[illegible]
LOOMIS, ARETUS F	1574	[illegible]	1	[illegible]
LOOMIS, GEORGE W	[illegible]	[illegible]	1	[illegible]
LOOMIS, LEONARD	181	[illegible]	[illegible]	[illegible]
Do	[illegible]	[illegible]	[illegible]	[illegible]
Do	[illegible]	[illegible]	[illegible]	[illegible]
LOOMIS, MARY A. S	[illegible]	[illegible]	1	[illegible]
LOONEY, JOHN	[illegible]	[illegible]	[illegible]	[illegible]
LORD, MARY A	[illegible]	[illegible]	[illegible]	[illegible]
LOSE, CATHERINE	[illegible]	[illegible]	2	[illegible]
LOTZ, PHILIP	[illegible]	[illegible]	1	[illegible]
LOUDON, DAVID S	[illegible]	[illegible]	2	[illegible]
LOUDON, GILES	714	[illegible]	1	[illegible]
LOUIS, ROSALIE	[illegible]	[illegible]	[illegible]	[illegible]
LOVE, ISAIAH A	[illegible]	[illegible]	[illegible]	[illegible]
LOVEJOY, EVELYN M	[illegible]	[illegible]	[illegible]	[illegible]
LOVELAND, SAMUEL W	[illegible]	[illegible]	[illegible]	[illegible]
LOVELL, HARRIS B	[illegible]	[illegible]	[illegible]	[illegible]
LOVELL, MARGARET I	[illegible]	[illegible]	[illegible]	[illegible]
LOVELL, SARAH A	[illegible]	[illegible]	[illegible]	[illegible]
LOWE, MARY A	[illegible]	[illegible]	[illegible]	[illegible]
LOWELL, BENJAMIN V	[illegible]	[illegible]	[illegible]	[illegible]
LOWERY, CHARLES L	[illegible]	[illegible]	[illegible]	[illegible]
LOWERY, REBECCA J. (guardian)	[illegible]	[illegible]	[illegible]	[illegible]
Do	[illegible]	[illegible]	[illegible]	[illegible]
LOWRY, THOMAS	[illegible]	[illegible]	[illegible]	[illegible]
Do	[illegible]	[illegible]	[illegible]	[illegible]
LOWRY, WILLIAM P	[illegible]	[illegible]	[illegible]	[illegible]
LOWTHIAM, NICHOLAS J	[illegible]	[illegible]	[illegible]	[illegible]
Do	715	[illegible]	[illegible]	[illegible]
LOY, ADALINE P	[illegible]	[illegible]	[illegible]	[illegible]
Do	[illegible]	[illegible]	[illegible]	[illegible]
Do	[illegible]	[illegible]	[illegible]	[illegible]
LOYD, JAMES L	[illegible]	[illegible]	[illegible]	[illegible]
LUBY, JAMES B	[illegible]	[illegible]	[illegible]	[illegible]
LUCAS, BENJAMIN	[illegible]	[illegible]	[illegible]	[illegible]
LUCAS, DANIEL	[illegible]	[illegible]	[illegible]	[illegible]
Do	[illegible]	[illegible]	[illegible]	[illegible]
LUCAS, MARGARET	[illegible]	[illegible]	[illegible]	[illegible]

* Views of minority.

Private legislation—Continued.

Subject.	Report.	Congress.	Session.	Volume.
ROBERT	555	23	1	1
[illegible]	463	24	1	2
[illegible]	75	24	2	1
[illegible]	[illegible]	25	2	2
[illegible]	[illegible]	26	1	3
ELIZABETH	1100	43	1	13
[illegible]	[illegible]	49	1	21
[illegible]	*[illegible]	49	1	22
MARGARET	[illegible]	48	1	[illegible]
Y, ANN	[illegible]	44	1	15
HN	[illegible]	31	1	6
MUEL	455	32	1	8
JACOB	[illegible]	46	2	12
[illegible]	737	[illegible]	1	13
EMILY	3673	49	1	21
EMILY H	155	45	2	10
WILLIAM (widow of)	177	[illegible]	1	3
EMBREY	[illegible]	29	1	4
ANTONIA B	[illegible]	48	1	[illegible]
AUSTIN B	[illegible]	46	1	15
[illegible]	3778	49	2	22
CHARLES	256	[illegible]	1	5
GEORGE	104	30	1	3
[illegible]	[illegible]	[illegible]	1	[illegible]
GREENBURY	[illegible]	46	1	[illegible]
MARGARET	[illegible]	49	1	21
WILLIAM	[illegible]	30	1	4
[illegible]	[illegible]	31	1	5
[illegible]	[illegible]	32	1	6
ISAAC H	[illegible]	46	1	[illegible]
ABRAHAM	[illegible]	27	2	3
EMILY A	51	[illegible]	1	7
WILLIAM	187	43	2	8
S, SAMUEL C	[illegible]	31	1	5
MRS. ELIZABETH L	[illegible]	49	2	22
MS, SARAH	716	43	1	8
XANDER, ROBERT J	544	49	1	18
Y, JAMES	*72	48	1	14
Do	269	49	1	18
HUR, W. H. H	3093	49	1	21
YER, JOHN H	104	46	2	11
Do	847	45	2	10
DE, FORRESTER H	3740	49	2	22
DE, JAMES W	504	46	2	11
DE, ROBERT	749	24	1	1
Do	219	25	2	2
YER, JOHN H	847	45	2	10
Do	104	46	2	11
L, WILLIAM I	700	49	1	18
LA, THEODORE H	965	45	2	10
EB, SARAH E	4084	49	2	22
DLESS, ROBERT	90	38	1	7
SN, STEPHEN S	1098	46	2	11
RNEY, ANN	568	48	1	14
RROL, MARY ANN	55	46	2	11
RTHY, ANNIE	1381	48	1	15
RTHY, DENNIS	284	43	1	8
RTHY, HONORA	2282	48	2	17
RTHY, MARIA	74	46	3	12
RTHY, MARY	1340	49	1	19
RTY, CATHERINE	1084	48	1	16
Do	744	49	1	19
Do	*3207	49	1	21
Do	3207	49	1	21
RTY, CHARLES	173	43	1	8
Do	1543	46	2	12
RTY, MARGARET	1962	48	1	16
SLIN, FLORA C	498	47	1	13
ULEY, WILLIAM	450	28	1	3
Do	52	29	1	4
USLAND, ROBERT	345	22	1	1
Do	7	22	2	1
WLEY, MARY T	498	47	1	13
ESNEY, THOMAS M	2625	48	2	17
AIN, THOMAS	1578	47	1	13
AREN, JAMES L	466	49	1	18
ELLAND, CHARLES	1307	48	1	15

* Views of minority, Part 2.

Private legislation—Continued.

Subject.	Report.
McCLELLAND, JOHN H	1101
McCLELLAND, NANCY E	617
McCLENAHAN, JOHN	984
McCLOUD, JOHN	662
McCLUNEY, ELIZABETH	298
Do	269
McCLURE, SAMUEL	2515
McCLURE, T. N	4123
McCLURE, WILLIAM	1480
McCOLLY, GEORGE	446
McCOMB, DAVID	220
Do	747
McCONELL, ARTHUR I	1158
McCONNELL, ARTHUR	52
McCONNELL, ELIZA	598
Do	70
Do	2500
McCORMICK, MARGARET	414
Do	1374
McCOVEY, SARAH	452
McCOWLEY, JAMES	485
McCOWN, NICK S	1094
McCOY, DR. GEORGE	19
McCOY, MARY	3285
McCOY, WILLIAM T	50
Do	618
Do	1156
McCRACKEN, ELIZABETH R	236
McCRAY, MICHAEL	422
McCULLACH, MARTHA M. B	263
McCULLOCK, BENJAMIN	72
Do	540
Do	217
McCULLOUGH, J. LYLE	228
McDANIEL, ENOCH	54
McDERMOTT, DAVID L	1583
McDONALD, ADE H	364
McDONALD, ALEXANDER	557
Do	305
McDONALD, BELINDA	1675
McDONALD, DAVID	166
McDONALD, H. W	438
McDONALD, HELENA	217
McDONALD, JOHN P	2395
McDONALD, MARY ANN	191
Do	83
McDONALD, ROBERT A	980
McDONALD, WILLIAM O	3637
McDONNELL, MATHEW	227
Do	1171
Do	1095
McDONOUGH, THOMAS	291
McDOWELL, AMOS	2269
McDOWELL, HANNAH	54
McDOWELL, ISABEL	141
Do	612
McELROY, FOREST W	766
McELROY, JOHN P	2664
McEWEN, ALEXANDER	306
Do	800
McFADDEN, AMANDA J	809
McFADDEN, ELI A	103
McFADDEN, GEORGE	722
Do	224
Do	290
McFADDEN, HENRY	829
McFADDEN, WILLIAM	2978
McFALLS, LOU GOBRIGHT	2291
Do	2349
Do	2394
McFARLAND, JAMES	477
Do	276
McFARLAND, LOUISA J	568
McFARLIN, HEWLITT P	748
McFARREN, JACOB R	1781
Do	980
Do	1202
McFEE, GILBERT (widow of)	410

Private legislation—Continued.

Subject.	Report.	Congress.	Session.	Volume.
ARGARET A	2513	49	1	20
, JAMES (widow of)	18	38	2	7
	1361	49	1	19
OMAS	2400	48	2	17
, AUSTIN M	1339	47	1	15
DENNIS	794	45	2	10
	141	46	2	11
	1150	48	1	14
JOHN	96	37	2	7
ICHAEL	746	45	2	10
	1660	46	2	12
, BARBARA	10	42	1	8
JAMES	2686	49	[illegible]	21
, HUGH	158	44	2	9
HUGH R	1356	46	2	12
JOHN	1696	49	1	20
OHN	396	46	2	12
	551	48	1	14
, MICHAEL	256	48	2	17
	1391	47	1	15
	1767	49	1	20
EORGE R., LIEUT. (minor children of)	4156	49	2	22
IARGARET	516	35	1	6
JOSEPH	149	44	1	9
	1674	46	2	12
, HARVEY	612	49	1	19
MARTHA	2312	49	1	20
JAMES	16	38	2	5
JOHN	161	44	1	9
THOMAS J	126	43	1	8
JOHN	1	39	2	4
	40	33	1	5
JOSEPH	888	48	1	14
NIMROD	351	46	2	11
, BYRON R	3419	49	1	21
, JOHN	657	45	2	10
, MARY D	80	45	2	10
EXANDER	2115	49	1	20
NIEL F	1739	49	1	20
CHAEL	940	48	1	14
IATTIE D	10	44	1	9
LIZABETH	1285	49	1	19
OSETTA L	813	46	2	11
	350	47	1	13
ILLIAM	156	44	1	9
PATRICK	1586	49	1	19
WILLIAM	396	48	1	14
	2414	48	2	17
ARISSA	255	48	1	14
NE	852	45	2	10
NE W	1643	46	2	12
BERT C	1688	48	1	16
	740	49	1	19
ILLIAM R. (widow of)	540	36	1	7
R, MARY F	591	44	1	9
	521	45	2	10
	664	47	1	13
, ALEXANDER	3716	49	2	22
, CECILIA C	2313	49	1	20
, JAMES O	184	46	3	12
	2082	48	1	16
, JOHN	289	36	1	2
Y, CHARLES O	300	46	3	12
	648	48	1	14
Y, SUSAN J. (widow)	649	48	1	14
, WILLIAM	119	35	2	6
AN, MARGARET	1556	46	2	12
ANNE JANE	1672	46	2	12
	1077	48	1	14
SARAH	209	43	2	8
Y, ROBERT	1637	48	1	16
Y, JOHN	225	43	2	8
Y, JAMES B	384	46	2	11
, MARGARET J	768	46	2	11
ER, THOMAS	288	43	1	8
	496	46	2	11
M, MATTHEW	596	30	1	4
	19	30	2	4

Private legislation—Continued.

Subject.	Report.	Congress.	Session.	Volume.
McKNIGHT, SAMUEL	126	33	1	6
McLAIN, MARY	9	30	1	7
Do	271	44	1	9
McLANE, WILLIAM	983	27	2	8
McLAUGHLIN, ANN	1181	48	2	12
Do	[illegible]	43	1	[illegible]
McLAUGHLIN, LOUIS A	[illegible]	44	1	9
McLAUGHLIN, MARY	256	46	1	[illegible]
McLAY, WILLIAM	881	44	1	9
McLEAN, ALEXANDER	579	30	1	6
McLELLAND, JENNETTA	178	44	1	9
McLEMORE, MARTHA E	542	35	2	9
McLENNAN, DANIEL	1474	48	1	[illegible]
McLOUD, JOHN	682	36	1	9
McMAHON, ALICE	1058	47	1	[illegible]
McMAHON, MARY	2771	49	1	[illegible]
McMAHON, WILLIAM H	1795	48	2	[illegible]
McMANUS, JAMES	767	45	1	[illegible]
McMANUS, ROSE A	1135	49	1	[illegible]
McMANNUS, THOMAS	1046	47	1	[illegible]
McMILLAN, CONDACE	232	43	2	[illegible]
McMILLAN, JOSEPH	1281	49	1	[illegible]
McMILLAN, RACHEL	252	34	1	[illegible]
Do	181	35	2	6
Do	283	36	1	7
McMINN, JOSEPH	319	33	1	[illegible]
McMULLEN, JAMES	529	46	2	11
Do	245	49	1	[illegible]
McNAIR, CAROLINE C	2808	49	1	[illegible]
NcNAIR, IRA	1088	48	1	[illegible]
MoNALLY, ANTHONY	553	48	1	[illegible]
McNAMARA, FRANCIS B	524	45	2	[illegible]
Do	142	46	2	11
McNAMARA, MARY	148	45	2	[illegible]
McNEELEY, GEORGE	545	43	1	[illegible]
McNICHOLAS, PATRICK	554	48	1	[illegible]
McNUTT, JAMES H	1396	47	1	[illegible]
MACOMBER, ADDIE L	289	49	1	[illegible]
McPHERSON, MARIA C	848	48	1	[illegible]
Do	4076	49	2	[illegible]
McPHERSON, WILLIAM I	947	45	1	[illegible]
McQUAIDE, JANE R	2652	49	1	[illegible]
McQUIRE, JOSEPH A	2111	49	1	[illegible]
McREYNOLDS, JOSEPH	21	35	2	[illegible]
McROBERTSON, ANTHONY	2522	49	1	[illegible]
McTAGGART, MATTIE	341	45	2	[illegible]
McWETHY, C. H	3927	40	2	[illegible]
McWILLIAMS, JOHN	288	26	1	[illegible]
McWILLIAMS, PETER	226	27	3	[illegible]
MADDEN, JOHN	63	36	1	[illegible]
Do	53	40	2	7
MADDEN, MARGARET	876	48	1	[illegible]
Do	1740	42	1	[illegible]
MADDOX, MARY J.	37	35	2	[illegible]
Do	143	36	1	7
MADISON, J R	1071	46	2	12
MADISON, WILLIAM O	694	43	1	[illegible]
MAGGART, HENRY	711	24	1	[illegible]
MAGILL, NANCY	149	35	1	[illegible]
MAGINNIS, BRYAN	885	48	1	[illegible]
MAGNUS, LOUIS	1685	46	2	[illegible]
Do	1578	48	1	[illegible]
MAGOFFIN, ALBERT E	1406	48	1	[illegible]
Do	54	49	1	[illegible]
MAGOON, MARY JANE	3256	49	1	[illegible]
MAGOON, NATHAN	1849	46	1	[illegible]
MAGUIRE, BARTHOLOMEW	264	28	1	[illegible]
MAGUIRE, MARGARET A	1835	48	1	[illegible]
MAHAN, CHARLES P	871	48	1	[illegible]
MAHAN, MARY HELENA	1191	48	1	[illegible]
MAHER, ANN	1396	48	1	[illegible]
MAHEW, JAMES	791	43	2	[illegible]
MAHLER, HENRY	175	46	3	[illegible]
MAHONEY, JAMES	216	48	1	[illegible]
MAHONEY, JOSIAH	2624	49	1	[illegible]
MAIES, CLARISSA T	607	48	1	[illegible]
MAIN, LEMUEL	2511	49	1	[illegible]
MAIN, OLIVER	390	35	1	[illegible]

Private legislation—Continued.

Subject.	Report.	Congress.	Session.	Volume.
CLARK G	1577	46	1	15
JAMES	636	27	2	3
Do	317	27	3	3
Do	44	29	1	4
Do	390	31	1	5
HUGH B	146	45	2	10
E, GEORGE W	613	38	1	7
E, SUSAN	1794	49	1	20
EY, HONORAH	1344	49	1	20
EY, LAWRENCE	110	35	2	6
EY, JOHN	1867	48	1	15
ESTER, STEPHEN	3679	49	2	22
VILLE, SUSAN C	270	49	1	18
MARY	1784	49	1	20
ERT, FRANK	1108	49	1	19
, EDWARD	1894	48	1	16
UF, B. H	570	28	1	3
E, JOSEPH	243	45	3	10
NG, GEORGE W	2236	48	2	17
NG, MICHAEL	3715	49	2	22
N, JOHN K	1140	48	1	14
E, ANDREW	2412	48	2	17
SARAH	731	48	1	14
Do	1280	48	1	15
Do	792	49	1	19
E, MARTHA A	780	49	1	19
AND, MARGARET D	97	46	3	12
Do	736	49	1	18
Do	2568	49	1	21
ANT, REBECCA	1214	49	1	19
M, JULIA A	1786	48	1	16
N, EBENEZER K	2396	48	2	17
N, FREDERICK	1495	49	1	19
N, MICHAEL	284	46	3	12
Do	962	47	1	13
RAF, LOUISA	283	43	1	8
TTE, NANCY C	130	43	1	8
ARDT, BARBARA	1588	47	1	13
. FRANK S	1151	46	2	12
Do	1206	48	1	15
, MARY	2130	49	1	20
, MARY B	151	44	2	9
ALL, ANDREW E	77	36	1	7
ALL, ANDREW J	808	46	2	11
ALL, ANNA M	289	47	1	13
Do	2961	47	1	13
ALL, ELIZABETH	3888	49	2	22
ALL, FREDERICK	2105	49	1	20
ALL, JOHN T	347	48	1	14
ALL, REUBEN	1625	47	1	13
Do	274	48	1	14
ALL, ROBERT	562	26	1	2
Do	238	26	2	2
Do	617	27	2	3
Do	1067	27	2	3
ALL, SAMUEL W	489	27	2	3
Do	20	28	1	3
ALL, SUSAN W	132	43	1	8
Do	608	44	1	9
Do	588	45	2	10
AND, ELIZABETH	569	44	1	9
ON, ADELINE	353	49	1	18
. RUDOLPH J	319	48	1	14
N, CYNTHIA	1323	47	1	13
Do	2505	48	2	17
N, DANIEL W	138	45	2	10
N, FREDERICK B. F	268	34	1	6
N, GEORGE W	3845	49	2	22
N, JOEL B	1891	48	1	16
N, JOHN	304	28	1	3
Do	82	28	2	3
Do	69	29	1	4
N, JOSEPH S	144	27	2	3
N, MARY	171	45	2	10
Do	3735	49	2	22
N, MARY L	202	49	1	18
N, PHEBE	225	49	1	18
N, THOMAS	823	47	1	13

Private legislation—Continued.

Subject.	Report.	Congress.	Session.	Volume.
MARTIN, THOMAS H.	318	44	1	9
MARTIN, WILLIAM G.	3636	49	2	12
MARTZ, GEORGE	583	44	1	9
MASON, ELIHU A.	413	47	1	13
MASON, JAMES G.	303	45	2	10
MASON, JOSEPH	1896	46	1	14
MASON, NANCY	2797	49	1	21
MASSIE, SUSAN MARSHALL	497	47	1	13
MASTEN, CHARLES H	1915	49	1	20
MASTERS, NATHANIEL	553	26	1	2
MATHERLY, HARTFORD	3003	49	1	21
MATHES, JAMES G.	3082	49	1	21
MATHEWS, ARCHIBALD	1711	49	1	20
MATHEWSON, CHRISTOPHER H	2508	49	1	20
Do.	2988	49	1	21
MATTHEWS, JOSEPH P.	1882	47	1	13
MATTHEWS, MARY E.	171	47	1	13
MATTINGLY, JOHN M	1540	49	1	19
MATZANBAUGH, DANIEL	474	31	1	5
MAXHAM, ELIZA A.	24	43	1	8
MAXWELL, JEMIMA	465	43	1	8
MAXWELL, MARIA L	651	45	2	10
MAXWELL, REBECCA C	20	45	2	10
Do	737	44	1	9
MAY, ANNA M	772	44	1	9
MAY, MARGARET	286	44	1	9
MAY, MARY ANN	1678	46	2	12
MAY, WILLIAM, Sr	245	43	1	8
MAYER, FREDERICK	1456	48	1	15
MAYER, JACOB	1076	48	1	14
MAYFIELD, GEORGE	360	26	1	2
Do	147	27	2	3
MAYFIELD, SUTHERLAND	409	26	1	2
Do	71	27	2	3
Do	73	30	2	4
MAYHAM, MARGARET	1346	49	1	18
MAYNARD, ALONZO	459	49	1	18
MAYNARD, SARAH	184	43	2	8
MAYO, ISAIAH G	3029	49	2	22
MAYO, WILLIAM	110	33	1	5
MAYS, JOSEPH	2828	49	1	21
MAZELL, ELIZABETH	1527	46	2	12
MEAD, DAVID	539	43	1	8
MEAD, JOSEPH	404	23	1	1
MEAD, LARKIN G.	1573	49	1	19
MEAGHER, ELIZABETH M. J	3571	49	2	22
MEAL, CHARLES	1182	48	1	15
MEANS, CALVIN	220	49	1	18
MEECH, PHOEBE	314	46	2	11
MEEHAN, JOHANNA	109	46	2	11
MEEK, ISRAEL R	831	29	1	4
MEENAN, DANIEL	824	46	2	11
MEENAN, MICHAEL	290	46	2	11
MEHAN, CATHERINE	4124	49	2	22
MEIGHAN, MARY	542	45	2	10
Do	76	46	2	11
MEINKEN, HENRY	525	46	2	11
MEIS, CATHERINE	1162	48	1	15
MEIXSELL, ANNA M	774	45	2	10
MELCHER, LOUIS	2066	49	1	20
MELCHER, VALENTINE	1195	46	2	12
MELINE, MARY E.	320	43	2	8
Do	293	46	3	12
MELLACH, ANNE S	2471	48	2	17
MELLON, AUGUST	647	45	2	10
MELLON, ELIZA A	447	30	1	4
MELSON, SOPHIA A	285	46	2	11
MELVIN, DELINUS L	1147	46	2	12
MERCER, MARY F.	178	43	2	8
Do	722	44	1	9
MERCER, S. F. F.	383	46	2	11
MERCER, SAMUEL	173	43	2	8
Do	723	44	1	9
MERCER, SAMUEL AND MARY F	173	43	2	8
Do	722	44	1	9
Do	178	45	2	10
MERCHANT, CHARLES G. (widow of)	504	33	1	5
MERCHANT, SARAH LUMPKIN	41	46	3	12
Do	286	47	1	13

Subject.	Report.	Congress.	Session.	Volume.
EREDITH, WILLIAM C. (guardian)	2353	48	2	17
EREDITH, WILLIAM M	1047	47	1	13
ERICLE, HENRY	3383	49	1	21
ERRILL, ABNER	1	23	1	1
Do	66	33	2	5
ERRILL, LOUIS	402	48	1	14
ERRILL, MARY	887	49	1	19
ERRILL, STEVENS W	1212	49	1	19
ERRILL, SUSAN	402	26	1	2
ERRILL, WILLIAM S	357	26	1	2
ERRYMAN, ARCHIBALD	357	36	1	7
ESSICK, GEORGE	1400	48	1	15
ETCALF, ISAAC H	73	36	2	7
EYNELL, HENRY	276	43	2	8
IBORD, MARIA	227	49	1	18
ICKAL, PHILIP	1183	48	1	15
ICH, JOHN	652	43	1	8
IDDLETON, ASAHEL	258	49	1	18
IDDOUGH, DANIEL	761	45	2	10
IDWINTER, JOHN	39	24	2	1
Do	280	25	2	2
ILBURN, G. W	3245	49	1	21
ILES, JOHN	575	24	1	1
ILES, MRS. M. C	2794	49	1	21
ILES, PATRICK C	59	33	2	5
ILK, CHARLES	2049	48	1	16
ILKEY, HENRY	1795	48	1	16
MILLAR, JOHN	295	46	3	12
MILLARD, CORYDON	1736	48	1	16
MILLER, AARON H	404	44	1	9
Do	574	45	2	10
MILLER, ABRAM V	136	45	2	10
MILLER, ALBERT O	297	46	2	11
Do	1021	47	1	13
MILLER, GEORGE	237	26	2	2
Do	633	27	2	3
Do	832	29	1	4
MILLER, GEORGE Y	1426	49	1	19
MILLER, HENRY	91	32	1	5
Do	91½	32	1	5
Do	172	35	1	6
Do	389	36	1	7
MILLER, IRA	3565	49	2	22
MILLER, JACOB	220	26	2	2
Do	895	48	1	14
MILLER, JAMES S	2087	49	1	20
MILLER, JOHN	203	22	1	1
Do	292	46	3	12
Do	2587	49	1	21
MILLER, JOHN B	239	43	1	8
MILLER, KATE	268	49	1	18
MILLER, KUNIGUNDA A. (heirs of)	834	46	2	11
Do	955	47	1	13
MILLER, MAGDALENA	1379	48	1	15
MILLER, MARY ANN	780	49	1	19
MILLER, N. M	409	49	1	18
MILLER, NANCY	1011	48	1	14
MILLER, NOAH	155	22	1	1
Do	43	23	2	1
Do	354	24	1	1
MILLER, PHILIP	557	30	1	4
Do	8	32	1	5
MILLER, ROBERT H	1649	48	1	16
MILLER, ROSE	208	44	1	9
Do	296	45	2	10
MILLER, SAMUEL	2018	49	1	20
MILLER, WILLIAM	626	30	1	4
MILLER, WILLIAM A	163	45	2	10
MILLER, WILLIAM F	1475	48	1	15
Do	1110	49	1	19
MILLER, WILLIAM R	592	47	1	13
Do	1497	48	1	15
MILLIGAN, ROBERT	1	23	1	1
Do	426	27	2	3
Do	813	27	2	3
Do	640	30	1	4
Do	11	32	1	5
MILLIKIN, PAULINE E	1739	48	1	16

Private legislation—Continued.

Subject.	Report.	Congress.	Session.	Volume.
MILLS, ALMON F	375	44	1	9
MILLS, GEORGE W	2284	48	2	17
MILLS, HENRY	303	46	2	11
MILLS, HENRY C	716	43	1	8
MILLS, MARGARET	358	46	2	11
MILLSAPS, MARION	586	45	2	10
MILTON, JOHN M	149	49	1	19
MINER, JOHN	957	45	2	10
MINCER, SARAH E	642	48	1	16
MINET, PLEASANT	1864	48	1	16
MINIX, CHARLES W	74	49	1	18
MINOR, O. W	1224	48	1	15
MINSHALL, ISAAC N	1512	49	1	19
MISHLER, ABEL	2627	49	1	21
MITCHEL, LOUISE	1188	46	2	12
MITCHELL, EDMUND	155	33	1	5
Do	60	34	1	6
MITCHELL, EDWARD H	293	46	2	11
MITCHELL, ELLEN M	331	49	1	18
MITCHELL, HARRISON	590	43	1	8
Do	88	44	1	9
Do	155	44	2	9
Do	2050	48	1	16
MITCHELL, ISAIAH H	1504	49	1	19
MITCHELL, JENNIE S	1416	47	1	13
MITCHELL, JOHN	83	30	1	4
MITCHELL, LIZZIE M	481	46	2	11
Do	1248	47	1	13
MITCHELL, LUCY J	805	45	2	10
Do	223	49	1	18
MITCHELL, MARY	365	46	2	11
MITCHELL, PETER	1754	48	1	16
MITCHELL, PETER JR	1756	48	1	16
MITCHELL, THOMAS	69	23	1	1
MIX, RANSOM	186	24	2	1
MIZELLE, CYNTHIA A	84	44	2	9
Do	514	45	2	10
MOBLEY, RICHARD G	182	42	2	3
MODDRELL, ANDREW	73	29	1	4
MODDRELL, JOHN	73	29	1	4
MOINS, JAMES	283	28	1	3
MONAGHAN, JAMES	774	29	1	4
MONAHAN, ROBERT	1041	49	1	18
MONOHAN, JAMES	2775	49	1	21
MONROE, MRS. ALDANA B	3638	49	2	22
MONROE, ELIZABETH	96	34	3	6
MONROE, JAMES	105	35	2	6
MONROE, JOEL D	693	49	1	18
MONROE, JOHN H	817	29	1	4
MONROE, NELSON	1694	49	1	20
MONROE, ROBERT	430	35	1	6
MONROE, STEPHEN C	845	48	1	14
Do	421	49	1	18
MONTGOMERY, JAMES	2018	48	1	16
MONTI, FERDINAND	170	43	2	8
MONTIS, LIBBIE C	2605	49	1	21
MOODY, JOHN	1	23	1	1
MOON, EDWIN	1064	49	1	19
MOONYHAN, ELANDER M	1734	49	1	20
MOOR, ANNA L	244	35	2	6
MOORE, CHARLES S	2233	48	2	17
MOORE, ENOCH S	388	36	1	7
MOORE, FLORENCE V	314	45	3	10
MOORE, FRANCIS M	788	49	1	19
MOORE, HARRISON W	1207	49	1	19
MOORE, ISAAC	143	49	1	18
MOORE, JOHN	14	23	2	1
Do	4167	49	2	22
MOORE, JOSEPH	1808	48	1	16
MOORE, MARGARET	1586	48	1	15
MOORE, MARY	683	44	1	9
MOORE, MARY H	152	45	2	10
MOORE, MARY S	237	43	1	8
MOORE, WILLIAM H	2085	49	1	20
MOORELAND, JAMES	770	45	2	10
Do	794	46	2	11
MORAIN, WILLIAM	271	26	1	2
MORAN, JOHN	2882	49	1	21

Private legislation—Continued.

Subject.	Report.	Congress.	Session.	Volume.
, ROBERT	495	46	1	16
, THOMAS	461	26	1	2
AGRANGE F	1095	46	2	12
AD, ABNER	2048	49	1	20
AND, JAMES	770	48	2	20
Do	794	46	2	11
SAVIL	248	28	1	4
PARTEN H	2199	48	2	17
D, POLLY	191	46	2	12
D, WESLEY	1065	46	1	16
, BEN	996	48	1	14
, GIDEON	409	23	1	1
Do	166	24	1	1
, HENRY S	135	46	2	12
Do	281	46	1	13
, JAMES	189	49	1	16
Do	1113	49	1	16
, JOHN	211	27	2	2
, JOHN W	1298	48	1	15
Do	1281	49	1	16
, SOPHIA A	1099	46	2	12
Do	2419	48	2	17
, THOMAS	416	26	1	2
Do	812	32	1	4
, WILLIAM O	1552	46	2	12
, THEILMAN	2413	48	2	17
, DAVID M	1916	46	2	12
GSTAR, JACOB J	1148	46	1	14
, ADDISON	2678	48	2	17
, SIMON S	18	28	2	1
Do	262	27	2	2
, BYRON S	778	45	2	10
, EMILY	17	28	1	7
, HARRIET	17	24	1	7
, JOHN A	597	46	2	12
, JOHN F	2777	49	1	21
, JOSHUA L	745	49	1	19
, NANCY E	120	49	1	18
, REBECCA	2946	49	1	21
, LYDIA A	58	44	1	9
Do	516	45	2	10
ON, ANDREW J	826	45	2	10
Do	311	46	2	11
Do	155	47	1	13
ON, JOHN	223	30	1	4
Do	292	34	1	6
ON, JOSEPH	302	31	1	5
ON, LUCY	111	32	1	5
ON, MARY T	176	43	2	8
ON, THOMAS D	516	35	1	6
ON, WILLIAM D	138	43	1	8
W, ALEXANDER S	529	35	1	6
W, ELLEN	245	43	2	8
Do	322	44	1	9
ASA	770	44	1	9
Do	841	45	2	10
DANIEL	260	26	1	2
Do	496	29	1	4
Do	229	32	1	5
Do	330	35	1	6
JACOB W	302	36	1	7
N, JAMES	3265	49	1	21
N, SETH	339	30	1	4
N, THOMAS	499	23	1	1
N, TRUMAN A	2184	48	2	17
R, FRANCES	2138	47	1	20
AMES	647	49	1	18
VICTORINE	964	45	2	10
ON, MARY A	354	49	1	18
R, JAMES	205	35	2	6
R, BETSEY A	1156	46	2	12
Do	888	48	1	14
Do	2816	49	1	21
L, ELIZABETH	540	48	1	14
ETT, CHARLES E	3515	49	2	22
OLLAND, HUGH	1111	49	1	19
OLLAND, MARY	1883	48	1	15

Private legislation—Continued.

Subject.	Report.	Congress.	Session.	Volume.
MULHOLLAND, ST. CLAIR A	784	46	2	11
Do	788	47		12
Do	952	47	1	12
MULLALLY, ALICE	69	43	2	8
MULLEGAN, R	516	35		6
MULLIGAN, MARIAN A	1386	47		12
MULLIGAN, SALLY C	1429	46		12
Do	510	47		12
Do	2200	48	2	17
MULLINAX, ELBERT	111	35	2	6
MULLOY, HUGH	214	26	2	1
MULVEY, ANN W	257	48		14
MUMFORD, JANE D	2728	49	1	21
MUMFORD, WILLIAM	1664	47		13
MUMIAN, WILLIAM	1079	48	1	14
MUNDIN, I. (widow of)	215	47	1	12
MUNION, HENRY M	1190	48	1	15
MUNION, WILLIAM	1081	48	1	14
MUNROE, ALICE B	860	45	2	10
MUNROE, CHARLES	416	48	1	14
MUNSON, R. L	3630	49	2	22
MURPHY, DAVID	810	29		4
Do	716	30		4
Do	89	32		5
MURPHY, JOHN	316	45		10
Do	308	46		11
MURPHY, MARY	582	45		10
Do	148	49		18
MURPHY, MARY ANN	1640	46		12
Do	560	49		18
MURPHY, MARY E	298	43		8
MURPHY, MATTHEW	1806	48	1	16
MURPHY, PATRICK	1889	48	1	16
Do	2112	49	1	20
MURPHY, PLEASANT	516	35	1	6
MURPHY, SARAH ANN	686	49	1	18
MURPHY, THOMAS	510	45	2	10
Do	243	49	1	18
MURRAY, ANTHONY	426	22	1	1
MURRAY, BETSEY M	1036	49	1	19
MURRAY, ELISA A	816	46	3	11
Do	1019	47	1	12
MURRAY, FLORENCE	1422	49	1	19
Do	1537	49	1	19
MURRAY, JOHN G	1020	49	1	19
MURRAY, MARY C	839	46	2	11
Do	595	47	1	12
MURRAY, MARY E	240	46	3	11
Do	514	47	1	12
Do	265	48	1	14
MURRAY, RICHARD J	159	34	1	5
MURRY, THOMAS	1217	47	1	12
MUSGROVE, ELIJAH	279	46	2	12
MYERS, CHARLOTTE E	286	45	2	10
MYERS, EDWARD	188	28	1	3
MYERS, JAMES C	285	36	1	7
MYERS, JESSE T	291	46	2	11
MYERS, PETER	799	30	1	4
MYERS, PETER A	169	28	1	3
MYERS, SARAH E	2815	49	1	21
MYKINS, MARY A	2929	49	1	21
Do	2081	49	1	21
NAGLE, DAVID M	1176	48	1	15
NAIF, JONATHAN	76	30	1	4
NAIL, JOHN	170	46	2	12
NALLY, MARY	3850	49	2	22
NAPPERTANDY, JOHN	21	28	1	3
NARON, LEVI H	2411	49	1	20
NASH, SYLVESTER AND BETSEY	644	25	[illegible]	[illegible]
Do	131	25	[illegible]	[illegible]
Do	676	26	[illegible]	[illegible]
Do	432	27	[illegible]	[illegible]
Do	160	33	[illegible]	[illegible]
Do	59	34	[illegible]	[illegible]
NAVARRE, PETER	77	36	[illegible]	[illegible]
Do	54	38	[illegible]	[illegible]
NAYLOR, MARY E	412	43	[illegible]	[illegible]

Subject.		Congress.	Session.	Volume.
R, RUTH ISABELLE	169	43	2	8
Do	13	44	1	9
Do	137	45	2	10
JOHN T	397	44	1	9
Do	310	46	2	11
Y, JOSEPH L	198	43	2	8
SAMUEL	63	26	2	2
Do	802	27	2	3
Do	517	28	1	3
ALLEN O	1329	47	1	13
EZRA	2361	49	1	20
NG, ELIZABETH A	223	43	2	8
Do	16	44	1	9
Do	1576	49	1	19
IARTHA	94	46	2	11
NTONE	380	44	1	9
Y, ALTON	66	33	1	5
Y, FREDERICK	1471	47	1	13
Do	482	48	1	14
Y, LYDIA A	290	49	1	18
Y, NOAH	1488	49	1	19
Y, ROBERT	2212	48	2	17
Y, RUHANNA	1673	46	2	12
Y, WILLIAM H	125	49	1	18
EFIELD, HERMAN	162	43	2	8
Do	332	44	1	9
Do	836	45	2	10
WILLIAM H	1027	49	1	19
RGER, JACOB	1387	48	1	15
RRY, JAMES	1526	46	2	12
Do	516	47	1	13
RRY, NORTON L	1172	47	1	13
Do	2363	49	1	20
T, JENNY	413	26	1	2
OMB, FANNY	455	43	1	8
LL, DANIEL	429	27	2	3
Do	27	27	3	3
ALL, OCTAVIA A	887	48	1	14
AND, JOHN	820	27	2	3
AND, JOHN H	269	26	1	2
IAN, ELIZA	2062	49	1	20
IAN, THOMAS G	462	49	1	18
TON, GEORGE	135	27	2	3
Do	497	29	1	4
Do	20	30	1	4
TON, WILLIAM	234	26	2	2
Do	220	27	2	3
Do	273	28	1	3
OLAS, EDWARD	539	23	1	1
Do	46	24	1	1
IOLAS, JOHN G	2403	49	1	20
IOLS, EUNICE S	339	49	1	18
IOLS, H. C	468	49	1	18
EL, DANIEL	116	33	2	5
ELL, RACHEL	73	49	1	18
ERT, KATHARINA	2004	49	1	20
LING, ELIZABETH A	288	46	3	12
DS, HENRY CLAY (heirs of)	2362	49	1	20
ITINGALE, ELLEN	4077	49	2	22
ITINGALE, MARGERY	1623	47	1	13
BLETT, JOSEPH	523	26	1	2
Do	149	27	2	3
ST, JENNET H	277	43	1	8
JACOB	1630	47	1	13
Do	2140	49	1	20
N, ALBON H	1045	47	1	13
LE, ROWLAND	3278	49	1	21
ES, DANIEL G. (children of)	967	45	2	10
ES, GEORGE W	1204	49	1	19
ES, MAGGIE A	544	44	1	9
AN, PHILOMENA E	320	49	1	18
AND, LOUISA	127	49	1	18
TE, WILHELM	1933	49	1	20
ES, ANNA H	177	45	2	10
MAN, MARY	1107	49	1	19
Do	*3203	49	1	21
MAN, WILLIAM	23	28	2	3

* Views of minority, Part 2.

Private legislation—Continued.

Subject.	Report.	Congress.	Session.	Volume.
NORRIS, ELIZA J	1716	[illegible]	1	[illegible]
NORRIS, JAMES	83	[illegible]	2	[illegible]
NORTHEN, MARGARET A	325	44	1	[illegible]
NORTHUP, MARTHA E	112	[illegible]	1	[illegible]
NORTON, F. M. (widow)	2570	[illegible]	[illegible]	[illegible]
NORTON, SARAH E	3512	[illegible]	[illegible]	[illegible]
NORWOOD, GEORGE	1193	[illegible]	1	[illegible]
NOTT, JOHN (widow of)	361	[illegible]	1	[illegible]
NOTT, JUDITH	322	[illegible]	1	[illegible]
NOTT, OSCAR B	797	[illegible]	[illegible]	[illegible]
NOTTAGE, MARY J	2132	[illegible]	1	[illegible]
NOWELL, MARIAH E. A. B	1971	[illegible]	1	[illegible]
NOYES, JAMES	3887	[illegible]	2	[illegible]
NOYES, PETER	579	[illegible]	1	[illegible]
NUTALL, EWIN J	575	[illegible]	[illegible]	[illegible]
NUTT, ROBERT	140	46	1	[illegible]
NYE, EZRA O	552	[illegible]	[illegible]	[illegible]
NYE, FREDERICK W	581	[illegible]	1	[illegible]
OAKLEY, MERIT M	1493	[illegible]	1	[illegible]
OATLY, SALLY	172	[illegible]	1	[illegible]
O'BANNON, GEORGE	1872	[illegible]	1	[illegible]
OBEKIAH, BENJAMIN	2858	[illegible]	1	[illegible]
O'BRIEN, AGATHA	517	[illegible]	3	[illegible]
O'BRIEN, BRIDGET	262	[illegible]	1	[illegible]
O'BRIEN, ELLEN	1178	[illegible]	1	[illegible]
O'BRIEN, JOHN H	2473	[illegible]	3	17
O'BRIEN, KENNEDY	27	33	2	5
Do	209	35	1	6
O'BRIEN, MICHAEL	538	35	1	6
Do	189	44	1	9
Do	725	45	2	[illegible]
Do	1548	46	2	[illegible]
O'BRIEN, SARAH	2731	49	1	[illegible]
O'BRYAN, LUCY	50	29	1	4
OCHNER, LEWIS (widow of)	1159	46	2	[illegible]
O'CONNELL, NANCY	3877	49	2	[illegible]
O'CONNOR, JAMES	1140	46	3	[illegible]
Do	91	47	1	[illegible]
O'CONNOR, LAWRENCE	3639	49	2	[illegible]
O'CONNOR, MARGARET	2167	[illegible]	1	[illegible]
ODELL, CHARLES G	1997	[illegible]	1	[illegible]
ODELL, JOSEPH	597	44	1	[illegible]
Do	718	46	2	[illegible]
O'DRISCOLL, EDWARD	271	[illegible]	1	[illegible]
OGDEN, ELIZA W	857	45	2	[illegible]
OGLINE, GEORGE	1530	46	2	[illegible]
O'HANLAN, JAMES	960	47	1	[illegible]
O'HARA, ARMSTRONG	551	43	1	[illegible]
O'HARA, PATRICK	62	38	2	[illegible]
O'HEA, JOHN	275	44	1	[illegible]
O'KEEFFEE, TIMOTHY L	86	35	1	[illegible]
OLDHAM, JESSE D	671	28	1	[illegible]
O'LEARY, FRANCIS	1489	49	1	[illegible]
O'LEARY, JOHN	35	35	[illegible]	[illegible]
Do	552	36	[illegible]	[illegible]
OLIVER, EDWARD D	419	36	[illegible]	[illegible]
Do	988	37	[illegible]	[illegible]
OLIVER, HANNAH	340	46	[illegible]	[illegible]
OLIVER, RICHARD	614	27	[illegible]	[illegible]
OLIVER, WILLIAM L	387	34	[illegible]	[illegible]
OLIVER, WILLIS	3862	49	[illegible]	[illegible]
OLMSTEAD, MOSES	104	33	[illegible]	[illegible]
Do	40	35	[illegible]	[illegible]
O'NEAL, CHARLOTTE	3912	49	[illegible]	[illegible]
O'NEAL, HENRY	2499	49	[illegible]	[illegible]
O'NEAL, JOHN	474	23	[illegible]	[illegible]
O'NEAL, TEMPERANCE J	1600	47	[illegible]	[illegible]
O'NEIL, HUGH	661	46	[illegible]	[illegible]
O'NEILL, JOHN O	789	47	[illegible]	[illegible]
Do	1345	47	[illegible]	[illegible]
O'NEILL, MARGARET	2689	49	[illegible]	[illegible]
ONKST, JORIAL	[illegible]	[illegible]	[illegible]	[illegible]
Do	[illegible]	47	[illegible]	[illegible]
OOTHOUT, RICHARD	[illegible]	[illegible]	[illegible]	[illegible]
ORD, MARY M	[illegible]	48	[illegible]	[illegible]
Do	[illegible]	45	[illegible]	[illegible]
ORDWAY, CHARLES H	[illegible]	45	[illegible]	[illegible]
Do	1290	46	[illegible]	[illegible]

Private legislation—Continued.

Subject.	Report.	Congress.	Session.	Volume.
Y, CHARLES H	416	47	1	13
Do	2379	49	2	22
DRFF, JOHN A	1218	48	1	15
ALBERT S	1504	48	1	15
E, ANNA W	65	43	2	8
Do	291	45	2	10
Do	1029	47	1	13
T, FREDERICK	2106	49	1	20
JOSEPH H	141	29	1	3
JAMES E	2494	49	1	20
DOUT, NEWELL F	1329	47	1	13
Do	2672	49	2	17
IVAN, EUGENE	595	44	1	9
WASHINGTON T	1786	49	1	20
OHN	2226	48	2	17
ELT, CHARLES A	37	43	2	8
Y, HENRY	665	25	1	2
AN, SAMUEL W	226	46	2	11
IKE, GEORGE	289	46	1	14
T, JOHN S	2297	48	2	17
ANNIE C	2571	49	1	20
EZRA C	726	43	1	8
JAMES P	156	44	1	9
JOHN	121	27	3	3
Do	107	28	1	3
Do	177	30	1	4
MARY E	307	46	2	12
DENNIS (heirs of)	2023	49	1	21
JOHN	1192	47	1	13
THOMAS S	413	46	1	12
RD, SARAH A	3579	49	2	22
WILLIAM	457	30	1	4
Do	8	31	1	5
SAMUEL	98	30	2	4
TIMOTHY	134	43	1	8
Do	139	49	1	18
SAMUEL L	186	45	2	10
ER, MRS. HETTIE K	4114	49	2	22
S, SIDNEY	500	48	1	14
ER, DANIEL	235	22	1	1
Do	160	23	1	1
Do	967	27	2	3
Do	392	31	1	5
Do	468	31	1	5
IER, ISABELLA	1536	48	1	15
IER, JULIET H	1871	48	1	15
IER, SARAH C	159	45	2	10
IER, STAFFORD	369	46	3	12
Do	360	47	1	13
IER, WILLIAM F. (widow of)	472	36	1	7
GBURN, JOHN	345	35	1	6
IS, CHARLES F	1116	47	1	13
Do	1356	48	1	15
IS, CHARLES G	3520	49	2	22
ISH, CHARLES	314	34	1	6
ISH, LEVI H	392	28	1	3
KER, ALMIRA K	2340	48	2	17
KER, CHARLES W	685	44	1	9
KER, ELI B	1280	49	1	19
KER, GEORGIANA	274	48	2	8
KER, ISAIAH	264	24	2	1
Do	187	25	2	2
Do	83	25	3	2
Do	159	29	1	4
KER, JAMES	351	29	1	4
KER, LEMUEL	584	30	1	4
KER, MARIA N	3855	49	2	22
KER, MARTIN	424	22	1	1
Do	69	22	1	1
KER, MARY F	531	35	1	6
Do	293	36	1	7
Do	239	44	1	9
KER, NEWCOMB	2365	49	1	20
KER, OLIVE W	2066	48	1	16
KER, S. G	1919	48	1	16
KER, SOPHIA	1338	46	2	12
KER, WILLIAM (Seneca Indian)	445	27	2	3
Do	239	26	2	2
Do	295	33	1	5

Private legislation—Continued.

Subject.	Report.	Congress.	Session.	Volume.
PARKER, WILLIAM C	145	46	2	11
PARKER, WILLIAM H	179	45	2	10
PARKHURST, NANCY	170	43	1	8
PARKHURST, SAMUEL	1771	49	1	20
PARKINSON, THOMAS M	3083	49	1	21
PARKS, EDWIN R	2059	49	1	20
PARKS, GEORGE W	2398	49	1	20
PARKS, JENNIE M	3069	49	1	21
PARKS, LEVI	598	36	1	7
Do	591	43	1	8
PARMER, A. J	3251	49	1	21
PARNELL, JOHN	414	26	1	3
PARR, JOHN G	358	43	1	8
Do	14	44	1	9
PARR, LUCY	2523	48	2	17
PARRIS, GEORGE W	506	46	2	11
PARROTT, JACOB	469	43	1	8
Do	727	45	2	10
Do	413	47	1	13
PARROTT, JOHN	631	27	2	3
PARROTT, MARY	2924	49	1	21
PARRY, SARAH	2339	48	2	17
PARSHALL, CHARLES	1784	46	2	12
PARSONS, AMELIA S	147	44	1	9
PARSONS, CHARLOTTE C	2541	49	1	21
PARSONS, MARRILLA	2076	49	1	20
PARSONS, MEREDITH	1488	48	1	15
PARSONS, SPARHAWK	456	36	1	7
PARTILLO, JOHN J	326	44	1	9
PATRIDGE, MARY S	3717	49	2	22
PATTEE, WALLIS	2651	49	1	21
PATTERSON, AMERICUS D	398	44	1	9
PATTERSON, DAVID	1979	48	1	16
PATTERSON, B. FRANK	2590	49	1	21
PATTERSON, ROBERT	1218	46	2	12
Do	1937	48	1	16
PATTERSON, WILLIAM	85	27	3	3
Do	477	36	1	7
PATTI, BARBARA	204	43	2	8
PATTI, GREGORY	36	35	2	6
Do	308	36	1	7
PATTISON, MARGARET	193	43	2	8
PATTON, JOHN	258	26	1	2
Do	300	29	1	4
Do	2350	49	1	20
PATTON, MARY K	150	44	2	9
PATTON, NANCY	118	42	1	8
PATTON, THOMAS	1582	48	1	15
PAUGH, WILLIAM	1934	48	1	16
Do	448	49	1	18
PAUL, JOHANNA	252	49	1	18
PAUL, LOUISE	2773	49	1	21
PAULDING, ANN M	290	45	2	10
Do	330	46	2	11
PAYNE, ADAMS	178	28	2	3
PAYNE, B. O	31	30	2	4
PAYNE, EDGAR	219	49	1	18
PAYNE, JOHN N	354	46	3	12
PAYTON, JOHN W	2521	49	1	21
PEAK, HARRIET	2062	49	1	20
PEAK, JOHN	922	27	2	3
PEARL, JOHN	486	31	1	5
Do	294	33	1	5
PEARSE, JONATHAN	294	23	1	5
PEARSON, DAVID	474	22	1	1
Do	545	23	1	1
PEARSON, PHINEAS G	321	35	1	6
Do	323	36	1	7
PEASE, BARTLETT	359	30	1	4
PECK, ANN	1169	46	3	12
PECK, CLARISSA	23	36	2	7
PECK, SAMUEL C, JR	350	49	1	18
PEGG, ROSELLA	1603	48	1	15
PELKEY, ROBERT	662	47	1	13
PENDEGRAST, JEREMIAH	99	37	2	7
PENDERGRAST, EDWARD	892	49	1	20
PENDLETON, GEORGE	127	44	1	9
PENHALLOW, DANIEL	638	27	2	3
Do	962	27	2	3

Subject.	Report.	Congress.	Session.	Volume.
,AND, NOBLE A	83	28	2	3
Do	294	29	1	4
TELL, ANDREW J	172	46	3	12
TELL, EMERY C	441	49	1	18
IINGTON, JOHN	687	49	1	18
IINGTON, JOHN T	779	46	2	11
Do	1710	48	1	16
Do	1049	49	1	19
IY, ELIJAH	361	47	1	13
IYCOUGH, JAMES	329	45	2	10
IOSE, VALERIA C	874	45	2	10
VELL, JOHN N	3728	49	2	22
IY, ELIZABETH	828	46	2	11
Do	833	47	1	13
DUE, WILLIAM R	154	47	1	13
Do	1126	47	1	13
IAM, JOHN	46	24	2	1
Do	474	25	2	2
Do	282	26	1	2
Do	955	27	2	3
IAM, JOHN, JR	405	28	1	3
KINS, BENJAMIN G	453	30	1	4
KINS, DANIEL B	89	24	2	1
Do	354	25	2	2
Do	248	26	1	2
KINS, GEORGE H	234	49	1	18
KINS, HECTOR	707	30	1	4
KINS, JOSEPH	306	36	1	7
Do	1916	49	1	20
KINS, MARY ANN	2944	49	1	21
KINS, WEALTHY	781	45	2	10
IIGO, FREDERICK (widow of)	133	27	2	3
Do	106	32	1	5
Do	108	35	2	6
Do	453	36	1	7
Do	570	30	1	4
RY, ADELIZA	3071	49	1	21
RY, GIDEON A	217	26	2	2
Do	806	27	2	3
Do	334	29	1	4
Do	627	30	1	4
RY, JOHN	325	35	1	6
RY, LUCRETIA M	75	38	1	7
RY, RICHARD	55	26	2	2
RY, SHERMAN C	1171	48	1	15
RY, WILLIAM	673	26	1	2
SONS, ELI	579	43	1	8
'ERSON, ANTHONY	826	46	2	11
'ERSON, R. G	590	45	2	10
'ERSON, THOMAS S	310	45	2	10
TTIBONE, CHAUNCEY S	2348	48	2	17
TTIJOHN, THOMAS	252	45	2	10
Do	1212	46	2	12
TRY, ADAM	104	46	3	12
TTY, LOUIS D	1097	48	1	14
EIFFER, MARY A	3956	49	2	22
IARES, JESSE F	1051	47	1	13
IELPS, EDWARD D	3084	49	1	21
IELPS, ELNATHAN	392	31	1	5
IELPS, THOMAS W	325	36	1	7
HELPS, VINCENT	2401	48	2	17
HEMESTER, JOHN (heirs of)	1649	46	2	12
HILBRICK, FRANKLIN	1622	48	1	15
'HILLIPS, GILBERT A	1644	46	2	12
Do	1211	48	1	15
Do	1058	49	1	19
PHILLIPS, C. C	2332	48	2	17
PHILLIPS, CHARLES H	1500	48	1	15
PHILLIPS, EMILY	588	43	1	8
PHILLIPS, LOUISA A	2523	49	1	20
PHILLIPS, MARY H	2928	49	1	21
PHILLIPS, RACHEL W	577	43	1	8
PHILLIPS, RAY	3279	49	1	21
PHILLIPS, RICHARD	282	34	1	6
PHILLIPS, RUTH B	261	34	1	6
PHILLIPS, THOMAS	7	22	2	1
PHILLIPS, WALTER A	1104	49	1	19
PHILLIPS, WILLIAM	50	33	2	5

Private legislation—Continued.

Subject.	Report.	Congress.	Session.	Volume.
PHINNEY, CAROLINE	784	47	1	16
PIATT, FRANCES L	486	26	1	[illegible]
PICKELSIMER, ALFRED	1347	49	1	19
PICKETT, MANHATTAN	1797	49	1	20
PIDGEON, JOSEPH	1224	46	2	13
PIER, ANDULOTIA	22	35	2	6
Do	100	37	2	7
PIERCE, EBENEZER	61	26	2	2
PIERCE, ELIZABETH H	240	45	3	16
PIERCE, GARETTA H	2686	48	2	17
PIERCE, HENRY A	3728	49	2	22
PIERCE, MELVIN	480	48	1	14
PIERCE, PLINY	186	29	1	4
PIERCE, REBECCA J	412	48	1	14
PIERCE, SHERMAN	372	28	1	3
PIERCY, WILLIAM	246	36	1	7
PIERPONT, RACHEL ANN	2800	49	1	21
PIERSON CHARLES	1195	48	1	15
PIGEON, JOSEPH	1742	48	1	16
PIKE, JAMES M	1175	48	1	15
PIKE, JOSEPH	457	35	1	7
Do	131	36	1	7
PIKE, MARY	3880	49	2	22
PISE, FRANKLIN	1525	46	2	13
PILLARD, THEODORE	689	44	1	9
PINK, EMELINE	1053	47	1	12
PIPER, JOHN	170	26	1	2
Do	153	26	2	2
Do	422	27	2	3
Do	489	35	1	6
Do	140	36	1	7
PITCH, HORATIO	827	30	1	4
PITMAN, WILLIAM	711	30	1	4
PITTENGER, MARGARET A	707	43	1	8
PITTINGER, WILLIAM	413	47	1	13
PITTMAN, JOSEPH	2325	48	2	17
PITTMAN, JOSHUA	289	29	1	4
PITTS, L. W	2364	48	2	17
PLACE, CHARLES W. (widow of)	452	36	1	7
PLAISTED, JAMES W.	3718	49	2	22
PLATT, ANN ELIZA	56	35	2	7
PLATT, FRANCES L	486	26	1	2
PLATT, JONAS D	498	29	1	4
Do	228	31	1	5
Do	93	32	1	5
PLOWDEN, WALTER D	39	46	2	12
Do	751	49	1	19
PLOWDEN, WALTER J	509	48	1	14
PLUMB, ELISHA	236	26	2	2
PLUMMER, FRANCES H	11	37	3	7
PLUMMER, ISAAC	851	26	1	2
Do	317	27	2	3
Do	12	28	1	3
Do	506	29	1	4
Do	469	31	1	5
PLUMMER, JUDITH	3451	49	1	21
PLUNKETT, HELEN	3569	49	2	22
PLYMPTON, ELIZA M	24	36	2	7
PODESTER, ANNIE	835	46	1	11
POE, JOHN R	2254	49	1	20
POERTNER, ADAM	378	46	2	12
POINDEXTER, ROBERT	947	27	2	3
Do	47	28	1	3
POINTER, CHARLES H	41	32	1	5
Do	115	33	2	5
POINTS, ABRAHAM	2536	49	1	21
POLAND, MARGARET A	589	49	1	18
POLLARD, MARY ANN	802	30	1	4
POLLARD, SAMANTHA J	1916	48	1	16
POLLEY, THOMAS G	2064	48	1	17
POLLOCK, SAMUEL	719	47	1	12
POMEROY, EDWARD N	3719	49	2	22
POMEROY, GEORGE W	471	48	1	14
POMPILLY, BARNARD	149	34	1	[illegible]
PONTIONS, WILSON	1163	46	2	12
POOL, ALANSON	286	31	1	5
POOL, SIDNEY P	304	33	1	5
POOL, WILLIAM	185	30	1	4

Private legislation—Continued.

Subject.	Report.	Congress.	Session.	Volume.
EORGE	116	[illegible]	3	[illegible]
ILLIAM	[illegible]	[illegible]	[illegible]	[illegible]
	[illegible]	[illegible]	[illegible]	[illegible]
	[illegible]	[illegible]	[illegible]	[illegible]
	[illegible]	[illegible]	[illegible]	[illegible]
	[illegible]	[illegible]	[illegible]	[illegible]
	[illegible]	[illegible]	[illegible]	[illegible]
NIEL	770	48	[illegible]	11
IN	99	44	1	9
MMA A	1712	46	[illegible]	12
	947	[illegible]	1	[illegible]
	844	[illegible]	1	[illegible]
ALBERT	[illegible]	46	[illegible]	17
	[illegible]	49	1	18
B	122	[illegible]	1	[illegible]
CUMMINS	1791	48	1	[illegible]
ELIZA F	1512	47	1	13
ELIZABETH ANN	[illegible]	45	2	10
	[illegible]	45	3	10
EVELINA	[illegible]	[illegible]	1	5
	61	34	1	6
	311	[illegible]	1	6
JAMES P. H	[illegible]	[illegible]	1	4
JAMES R	[illegible]	[illegible]	2	8
	[illegible]	[illegible]	2	11
	[illegible]	[illegible]	1	15
JOHN	157	[illegible]	1	4
JOHN R	419	47	1	13
JOSEPH A	1407	48	1	15
	418	49	1	18
MARTHA J	139	[illegible]	2	11
THOMAS	104	[illegible]	1	6
VERLY	846	46	1	14
RAH	472	[illegible]	1	7
ANSYL	[illegible]	49	1	18
JOSEPH M	2854	49	1	21
OSEPH H	111	49	1	18
OBERT	2670	49	1	21
WILLIAM	2126	49	1	20
ACOB B	94	44	2	9
ANGELINA	725	44	1	9
THOMAS B	599	44	1	9
WOODSON	202	43	2	8
INTON	1648	48	1	16
	259	49	1	18
SARAH J	333	49	1	18
ASA	476	36	1	7
ALVIN E	888	45	2	10
CAROLINE E	2888	49	1	21
DANIEL	526	26	1	2
	109	28	1	3
	468	29	1	4
FERNANDO G	2891	49	2	22
FIELDING	68	24	2	1
	182	25	2	2
	34	25	3	2
	174	26	1	2
	149	26	2	2
	218	27	2	3
	265	27	3	3
ISAAC	2601	49	1	21
JOHN	235	45	3	10
HIRAM W	207	44	1	9
SARAH	168	27	3	3
BRAHAM	508	26	1	2
S, SUSANNA	777	30	1	4
TT, JOSEPH	112	22	2	1
Do	1	23	1	1
ON, JAMES	1748	48	1	16
MAN, GEORGE H	2077	48	1	16
MAN, MARY	24	32	1	5
S, CLARA L	2620	49	1	21
TT, JOHN	114	49	1	18
SARAH E	1466	48	1	15
WILLIAM H. H	3519	49	2	22
WILLIAM S. (heirs of)	656	45	2	10
E, GEORGE	190	43	3	10
Do	1581	48	1	15

Private legislation—Continued.

Subject.	Report.	Congress.	Session.	Volume.
PRINCE, MARY S.	122	43	1	8
PRINCE, W. E	22	43	1	8
PRINDLE, ELIZABETH	[illegible]	43	1	8
PRINDLE, SOLOMON	841	46	2	11
PRINTZ, WILLIAM	[illegible]	48	1	16
PRIOR, H. D	1562	48	1	15
PROBERT, ANNA H	1523	46	2	12
Do	417	47	1	13
Do	2079	49	1	[illegible]
Do	[illegible]	49	1	[illegible]
PROCTOR, ALEXANDER M	2060	48	1	18
PROST, JOSEPH	807	49	1	19
PROVOST, ELIZABETH	[illegible]	47	1	13
PRUIM, EUNO J	334	46	2	11
PRUITT, JAMES MADISON	1748	49	1	[illegible]
PRY, ADAM	4025	49	2	[illegible]
PUGH, C. W. F	221	49	1	18
PUGH, DAVID C	1586	49	1	[illegible]
PULCIFER, JOSEPH	560	26	1	2
Do	435	27	2	3
Do	174	29	1	4
PULLING, THOMAS	410	44	1	9
Do	228	45	2	10
PURCELL, JOHN	452	35	1	6
Do	334	36	1	7
PURCELL, MICHAEL	1801	48	1	16
PURCELL, SAMUEL	241	43	2	8
PURINGTON, JOSEPH E	2632	49	2	[illegible]
PURMAN, J. JACKSON	57	46	2	11
PURVIS, PHILEMON B	1070	46	1	14
Do	2255	49	1	[illegible]
PUSEY, MRS. LAURA F	3682	49	2	[illegible]
PUTNAM, ADALINE M	1418	49	1	19
PUTNAM, ANDREW J	261	49	1	18
PUTNAM, DANIEL C	801	45	2	10
PUTNEY, ELIJAH W	876	49	1	[illegible]
PYLE, MARY JANE	736	45	2	10
QUARRELL, GEORGE	865	45	2	14
Do	352	46	3	12
Do	1006	47	1	13
QUARRY, MICHAEL	722	43	1	8
QUEEN, RACHEL	2306	48	2	17
QUENTIN, REGINA	304	45	2	10
QUENTIN, WILLIAM	721	44	1	9
QUESADO, FRANCISCO	122	44	1	9
QUIGLEY, AARON	291	36	1	7
QUIGLEY, JAMES	273	43	1	8
QUILLIGAN, KATE	1713	47	1	13
QUINCY, EDWIN G	815	46	2	11
QUINLAN, JAMES A	945	48	1	14
QUINN, ALFRED A	513	48	1	14
QUINN, EDWARD	[illegible]	[illegible]	1	5
QUINN, EDWARD P	2197	[illegible]	2	17
QUINN, ROSANNA	[illegible]	[illegible]	1	8
RABERLE, JOHANNA	1768	[illegible]	1	16
RAFF, MARTIN	[illegible]	[illegible]	2	16
RAGAN, ELIZABETH	191	[illegible]	1	8
RAHM, CHARLES AND OTHERS	78	[illegible]	2	[illegible]
RAIBLE, JOSEPH	1057	[illegible]	1	[illegible]
RAIGER, P. E	1464	[illegible]	1	[illegible]
RAINES, GEORGE	166	[illegible]	2	[illegible]
Do	[illegible]	[illegible]	2	[illegible]
REAINS, MARTHA L.	[illegible]	[illegible]	1	[illegible]
RALLSTON, GEORGE J.	212	[illegible]	1	[illegible]
RAMSDELL, ISABELLA J.	1160	[illegible]	2	[illegible]
Do	1575	[illegible]	1	[illegible]
RAMSEY, EMMA A	[illegible]	[illegible]	2	[illegible]
Do	1297	[illegible]	1	[illegible]
RAMSEY, ROBERT	[illegible]	[illegible]	1	[illegible]
Do	[illegible]	[illegible]	1	[illegible]
RAMSEY, SARAH M.	[illegible]	[illegible]	1	[illegible]
RAMSEY, THOMAS C	[illegible]	[illegible]	2	[illegible]
RANDALL, DANIEL B	[illegible]	44	2	[illegible]
Do	[illegible]	[illegible]	1	[illegible]
RANDALL, ELIZABETH A	[illegible]	48	2	[illegible]
Do	[illegible]	[illegible]	1	[illegible]
RANDALL, JAMES B. F	[illegible]	[illegible]	2	[illegible]
Do	[illegible]	[illegible]	1	[illegible]

Pri -Continued.

Subject.	Report.	Congress.	Session.	Volume.
N A	3048	49	2	22
THAN	500	35	1	6
	142	36	1	7
ANKFUL	89	23	2	1
	97	24	1	1
	213	27	2	3
GINIA TAYLOR	2561	49	1	21
LLIAM	595	49	1	18
AH	2086	49	1	21
LACHI F	299	35	1	6
LLIAM F	2216	48	2	17
	3986	49	2	22
I J	180	46	3	12
D A	2059	48	1	16
Y C	393	48	1	14
SSA	600	43	1	8
M M	1926	49	1	20
OR C	3894	49	2	22
C	2827	49	1	21
DORE	1193	48	1	15
IN R	211	22	1	1
LLIAM W	1184	46	2	12
EL	292	24	2	1
	186	25	2	2
N C	323	35	1	6
RL L	1155	46	2	12
	1125	47	1	13
DORE	1596	47	1	13
NA F	296	33	1	5
	2444	43	1	8
	46	23	2	1
	46	24	1	1
TH J	3950	49	2	22
	3589	49	2	22
S	1928	48	1	16
	2141	49	1	20
ONZO	2805	49	1	21
Y C	161	46	3	12
RY J	584	43	1	8
RREN	555	30	1	4
	148	31	1	5
	262	33	1	5
VARD	815	29	1	4
NDER	48	28	1	3
E	76	35	1	6
B	648	24	1	1
R W	768	48	1	14
G	1593	48	1	15
IA L	683	44	1	9
AH P	189	43	2	8
ES T	1025	49	1	19
GER L. (widow of)	33	46	2	11
V	141	34	3	6
	487	35	1	6
NIE E	83	43	2	8
	63	44	1	9
	86	45	2	10
ON	1809	48	1	16
LIAM	3892	49	2	22
ES	265	34	1	6
NCY A	1184	48	1	15
T	133	44	1	9
P	2968	49	1	21
	636	48	1	14
	3844	49	2	22
B	2799	49	1	21
	426	22	1	1
	7	22	2	1
	170	28	1	3
	287	44	1	9
	335	45	2	10
S	349	29	1	4
ICE	2546	49	1	21
BENJAMIN	449	30	1	4
Y	848	46	2	11
	665	47	1	18
BETH	362	45	2	10
	1231	47	1	18

Private legislation—Continued.

Subject.	Report.	Congress.	Session.
REEVE, JAMES H	12	46	
REEVES, C. MELVILLE	331	35	
Do	371	36	
REEVES, CORNELIUS N	169	28	
REEVES, ELIZA	243	36	
REEVES, MARION	2517	49	
REGAN, MARGARET	2217	48	
REGAN, MATHUR O	558	48	
Do	770	48	
REGAN, THOMAS	1825	48	
REHKOPF, H. B	265	49	
REICH, REBECCA C	550	45	
REICHERT, FRANCIS	8270	46	
Do	499	47	
REID, JAMES	55	28	
RIEGHTER, MARGARET J	1500	49	
REILEY, GEORGE	176	28	
REILY, JOHN H	547	45	
REIMAN, MARY C	2596	48	
REINHARDT, WILLIAM	1085	48	
Do	1900	48	
REISINGER, CATHARINE	2265	49	
REIVING, HENRY	46	45	
RENDLEBURG, ISAAC	547	48	
RENFRO, MARY	2625	49	
RENNER, W. H	542	48	
RENNOE, DAVID M	2348	49	
RENNY, ELIJAH W	3248	49	
RENOIS, BARTHOLOMEW CLOVIS	840	35	
RENZ, AGNES	704	49	
RESSLER, ANNA MARIA	1153	48	
REUSS, P. F	577	44	
Do	300	45	
Do	845	46	
REVES, MRS. LAVINIA	3861	49	
REYNOLDS, DANIEL	469	36	
REYNOLDS, ELISHA E	1486	48	
REYNOLDS, ESTHER A	2168	49	
REYNOLDS, GEORGE H	470	43	1
REYNOLDS, HARVEY	283	23	1
Do	770	25	2
Do	130	25	2
Do	708	29	1
REYNOLDS, HAYDEN	1633	48	1
REYNOLDS, JOHN W	4073	49	2
REYNOLDS, JULIA M	1378	42	1
REYNOLDS, MARGARET	328	24	1
Do	825	27	2
Do	553	36	1
REYNOLDS, MARTIN J	1708	49	1
REYNOLDS, MARY A	1069	48	1
REYNOLDS, REBECCA	1750	48	2
Do	364	47	1
REYNOLDS, RICHARD	25	28	1
Do	260	30	1
Do	94	30	2
REYNOLDS, WILLIAM	682	44	1
Do	724	45	2
Do	2401	49	1
RHEA, JOSEPH M	47	26	2
Do	268	27	3
Do	634	27	2
Do	56	29	1
RHINEHART, JOSEPH V	2118	49	1
RIANS, RICHARD B	3433	49	1
RIBBLE, NANCY L	47	49	1
RICE, ASHLEY C	2926	49	1
RICE, ELIZABETH F	953	47	1
RICE, MARY B	391	31	1
RICE, SALLY W	3238	49	1
RICE, SHADRACH	39	34	2
RICE, STEPHEN	2252	49	1
RICE, WARREN L	2513	49	1
RICH, ADRIENE	287	36	1
RICH, FREDERICK S	2065	48	1
RICHARD, BAKER M	151	47	1
RICHARDS, ABIGAIL	3683	49	1
RICHARDS, ABRAHAM	472	36	1

Private legislation—Continued.

Subject.	Report.	Congress.	Session.	Volume.
NZO V	743	49	1	19
USTA M	460	49	1	18
NANIAS O	19	33	2	5
URELIA C	2550	49	1	21
LIZA J	1870	48	1	16
TEPHEN	571	26	1	2
ILLIAM H	785	47	1	13
AM	611	27	2	3
DERICK	3098	49	1	21
N	31	35	1	6
	1983	48	1	16
	147	47	1	13
N D	645	48	1	14
LIAM	1020	47	1	13
	2501	49	1	20
ZER	42	35	2	6
JAH	692	24	1	1
	532	35	1	6
	505	46	2	11
IE E	83	43	2	8
ES	2621	49	1	21
	138	30	1	4
TON C	1422	47	1	13
	479	48	1	14
T M	2001	49	1	20
	223	26	1	2
L S	28	33	2	5
I	3730	49	2	22
S	1165	48	1	15
T	842	46	2	11
TH	339	34	1	6
L	387	46	2	11
	1703	48	1	16
	111	44	1	9
	752	45	2	10
A	2405	48	2	17
	77	46	2	11
I M. S	454	36	1	7
	252	23	1	1
RGARET A	1836	48	1	16
TIA G	2566	48	2	17
A	586	49	1	18
ES	616	25	2	2
	182	25	3	2
	200	26	1	2
US W	2975	49	1	21
(widow of)	367	44	1	9
ES	294	46	3	12
K	785	49	1	19
	174	43	1	8
S	1394	47	1	13
GE W	2821	49	1	21
	1474	47	1	13
IA F	351	49	1	18
BETH A	1805	49	1	20
L	1704	49	1	20
OINE	157	34	1	6
	893	48	1	14
Y	2983	49	1	21
	250	49	1	18
S	338	30	1	4
BETH S	591	45	2	10
NE	1208	49	1	19
GE A	249	49	1	18
HAN	175	44	1	9
	576	45	2	10
N F	1702	48	1	16
I	571	25	2	2
	84	25	3	2
	147	25	3	2
	207	26	1	2
	156	26	2	3
	226	27	2	3
	239	28	1	3
	2	30	2	4
	144	48	1	14
Y P	844	45	2	10
CA	2364	49	1	20

Private legislation—Continued.

Subject.	Report.	Congress.
ROBERTS, WILLIAM	580	30
Do	593	36
ROBERTSON, FREDERICK	2388	49
ROBERTSON, SAMUEL B	164	45
ROBIDEAUX, ANTOINE	378	36
ROBINS MICHAEL	295	29
ROBINSON, CASSIUS H	2148	49
ROBINSON, CHARLES	2351	49
ROBINSON, DELOS	2578	48
ROBINSON, DILENO	145	48
Do	1194	49
ROBINSON, JAMES	2250	49
ROBINSON, JERRY	601	45
ROBINSON, JOHN W	376	31
Do	5	32
ROBINSON, MARTHA J	693	44
Do	645	45
Do	15	46
ROBINSON, MARTHA R	582	43
Do	230	44
ROBINSON, RICHARD	476	31
ROBINSON, SAMUEL W	3088	49
ROBINSON, WILLIAM	641	48
ROBSON, JOHN W	1938	48
Do	549	49
ROCKWELL, F. L	3091	49
RODEN, JAMES	938	48
RODENBACK, HENRY	1597	48
RODMAN, CHARLES G	112	49
RODMAN, SALLY	2404	48
ROGERS, CLAYTON E	1771	48
Do	690	49
ROGERS, HENRY	301	45
ROGERS, HUGH	4064	49
ROGERS, JOHN	25	36
ROGERS, MARY	691	44
ROGERS, WILLIAM H	290	36
ROGERS, WILLIAM R	168	46
ROHRER, ISADOR	1164	46
Do	1044	47
ROLLINS, AARON	45	28
Do	43	29
ROLLINS, DAVID	572	25
Do	133	25
ROLLINS, JOHN E	2686	49
ROMAHN, MICHAEL	2127	49
ROMISER, JOSEPH	2163	49
Do	3213	49
ROONEY, BRIDGET	400	44
ROOSA, TUNIS J	1486	49
ROOT, MARY JANE	1393	48
ROOT, SYLVESTER	1838	49
ROPER, ALICE	708	43
ROSCOE, HENRY	2531	49
ROSE, DANIEL W	501	46
ROSE, JAMES F	1676	46
Do	288	47
ROSE, JESSE	82	29
ROSE, JOHN W	1194	48
Do	433	49
ROSE, SENFORD	256	49
ROSE, MARY	359	45
ROSE, ROBERT	101	30
Do	71	31
ROSE, SALEM P	587	43
ROSEBURY, JOHN M	143	31
ROSHON, ISAAC	289	46
ROSS, ANN	462	25
Do	139	25
ROSS, DANIEL H	1697	48
Do	739	49
Do	2768	49
ROSS, JOHN B	581	49
ROSS, JOSEPH W	418	26
ROSS, JULIA A	1712	46
Do	395	47
ROSS, SUSAN	148	43
ROSSON, HATTIE J	243	45

Private legislation—Continued.

Subject.	Report.	Congress.	Session.	Volume.
R, FRANZ	3078	49	1	21
THOMAS U	516	46	2	11
	1022	47	1	13
IA	3069	49	1	21
JAMES	84	43	2	8
MARIA A	286	44	1	9
	1185	46	2	12
I, BENJAMIN E	2458	48	2	17
AMIN	227	27	2	3
	530	30	1	4
	45	32	1	5
	1905	49	1	20
EXANDER W	371	46	3	12
	721	47	1	13
AMES S	379	36	1	7
RAM S	2347	48	2	17
OXANA V., AND SON	888	49	1	19
OMAS A	2164	49	1	20
LEY	46	24	1	1
OUISE	447	44	1	9
	123	45	2	10
Y	1692	48	1	16
ES B	3079	49	1	21
WILLIAM	297	45	2	10
PTHA	730	45	2	10
ER J	578	48	1	14
LES L	606	44	1	9
GE W	1737	48	1	16
OLOMON K	1719	48	1	16
MIN	2984	49	1	21
AAC	503	24	1	1
OWARD	243	34	1	6
	310	35	1	7
ANNIE D	396	44	1	9
AAC	237	27	2	3
OHN A	3566	49	2	22
BRIDGET	3579	49	2	22
	105	46	2	11
AVID F	1202	46	2	12
J. (widow of)	971	45	2	10
EORGE W	2381	48	2	17
AMES B	880	49	1	19
ATHARINE K	61	34	3	6
	29	35	1	6
	292	36	1	7
OHN	258	34	1	6
HOMAS	109	32	1	5
OR F	655	45	2	10
RD, MARY	261	33	1	5
JAMINE S	560	45	2	10
GET	1772	49	1	20
H	939	48	1	14
S	218	45	3	10
	807	46	2	11
	2382	49	1	20
Y E	954	45	2	10
	1602	47	1	18
NRY B	134	43	1	8
ILTON	358	45	2	10
UCIUS	312	45	2	10
LOUIS J	829	47	1	13
LLEN	2085	49	1	21
PETER T	825	47	1	13
JOSEPH	460	25	2	2
ERNARD	605	43	1	8
IZABETH	3762	49	2	22
ACOB	30	35	2	6
RD, ALEXANDER	3	44	1	9
	640	48	1	14
RANCIS F	277	24	1	1
, DAVID	218	43	2	8
CHEL	356	30	1	4
JAMES F	2622	49	1	21
FREDRICK	525	25	2	2
SARAH S	2285	48	2	17
ON B	773	44	1	9
	536	48	1	14
	141	49	1	18

Private legislation—Continued.

Subject.	Report.	Congress.	Session.
SAMS, JAMES A	2953	49	
SAMS, NANCY E	2951	49	
SAMUELS, MARY A	2210	48	
SAMUELS, THEODORE J	1049	47	
Do	1404	48	
SANBORN, CHARLES W	3863	49	
SANBORN, COFFIN	647	25	
SANBORN, MARY H	1977	49	
SANDERS, BENJAMIN	840	45	
SANDERS, HENRY C	1471	47	
Do	482	48	
SANDERS, ISAAC D	621	27	
SANDERS, JOHN	390	23	
Do	75	36	
SANDERS, MARIA W	75	36	
Do	229	42	
SANDERS, MARY A	1473	47	
SANDERS, R	1471	47	
SANDERS, SIDNEY	818	46	
SANDERSON, MARTHA	283	36	
SANDHOVEL, HENRY	1820	48	
SANDS, HENRIETTA M	1143	48	
Do	2482	48	
SANFORD, HENRY	62	34	
Do	359	36	
SANFORD, JAMES W	778	49	
SANGSTON, WILLIAM J	561	48	
Do	2007	49	
SANSOM, JOSEPH	2537	48	
SARGEANT, JOHN	213	23	
SARGENT, MARIA H	1781	48	
SATTERLEE, THOMAS	372	36	
SATTLER, CATHERINE	2149	49	
SAUER, STEPHEN	2222	48	
Do	2297	48	
Do	794	49	
Do	2669	49	
SAUL, HIRAM	205	24	
Do	590	25	
Do	183	26	
SAULE, JEHIEL	751	24	
SAUNDERS, PHŒBE	146	49	
SAUNDERS, SIDNEY	239	45	
SAUNDERS, THOMAS R	778	30	
Do	145	31	
SAVAGE, ELBRIDGE G	876	46	1
SAVAGE, JOHN	229	27	1
Do	455	30	1
SAVERCOOL, JAMES	2583	49	1
SAWYER, JOHN I	1277	48	1
SAWYER, LUCINDA	2128	49	1
SAWYER, MARY E	291	49	1
SAWYER, PHYLENA	1143	46	2
SAWYER, SAMUEL	2726	49	1
SAWYER, WILLIAM J	865	45	1
SAYER, JAMES P	65	46	2
SCARCE, W. W	1878	48	1
SCATTERGOOD, MERCY E	224	43	2
SCHAEFER, GEORGE	1066	49	1
SCHAUM, FREDERICK	456	36	1
SCHELL, MRS. EMMA	1328	47	1
SCHENCK, CORNELIA R	2073	49	1
SCHENCK, ESTHER K	561	45	2
SCHIER, ANNA	2669	49	1
SCHINDLER, AUGUST	1614	48	1
Do	50	49	1
Do	2524	49	1
SCHLEYER, THERESA	2788	49	1
SCHMUCK, ELLEN AHERN	335	34	1
Do	230	35	2
SCHMUCK, JACOB (widow of)	230	35	2
SCHNEIDER, LEOPOLD	383	36	1
Do	142	37	2
SCHNETBERG, HENRY	12	46	1
SCHOOLS, CATHARINE	2407	48	2
SCHOONOVER, JAMES	383	33	1
SCHOONOVER, JONAS	2604	49	1
SCHOONOVER, WILLIAM G	408	49	1

Private legislation—Continued.

Subject.	Report.	Congress.	Session.	Volume.
UEL C	212	45	2	10
	69	46	2	11
ORGE A	601	42	1	8
NRAD	309	35	1	6
EDERICK	239	49	1	16
RAPHIM	1808	48	1	16
USTAV	1872	49	1	19
B	1738	48	1	18
RLES	1696	49	1	20
PH	1049	48	1	14
UEL	1280	49	1	19
ANIEL	2740	49	1	21
RMAN J	1807	46	2	12
NO	1775	49	1	20
ELIA A	150	47	1	12
	204	48	1	14
R	1127	48	1	15
A	219	44	1	9
IN P	183	27	2	3
	14	28	1	3
ILY	210	44	1	9
S	1489	48	1	15
	418	26	1	2
	297	22	1	1
	603	24	1	1
	168	46	2	12
	324	45	2	11
	286	46	2	11
	2294	48	2	17
A T	60	26	1	2
	363	45	2	10
A	650	48	1	14
M	359	26	1	2
	142	27	2	3
	72	27	2	3
	303	28	1	3
	1278	49	1	19
LIAM H	251	45	3	10
	149	46	2	11
ESLEY	575	48	1	14
E B	346	49	1	18
A	2006	49	1	20
Y A	100	46	2	11
US M	1225	46	2	12
	889	49	1	19
R F	1458	48	1	15
	553	49	1	18
OLPH	1606	49	1	20
WELL	1705	48	1	16
N, JR	281	46	3	12
LIAM	1410	48	1	15
IAM	2462	48	2	17
H	977	45	2	10
	2520	48	2	17
	3244	49	1	21
W	1777	49	1	20
GE C	26	23	2	1
THY H	1924	48	1	16
ARLES N	2131	49	1	20
LES	1205	49	1	19
A	834	44	1	9
BETH S	1024	47	1	13
GE	777	49	1	19
H W	332	46	2	11
	805	47	1	13
H E. E	849	48	1	14
E	2781	49	1	21
ERICK	1577	49	1	19
B	3841	49	2	22
	2076	49	1	21
PH B	1872	47	1	13
	134	48	1	14
S Y	182	45	2	10
A	650	49	1	18
Y	36	35	1	6
HN	213	23	1	1
ENT	164	27	3	3
RY J	2054	48	1	16

Private legislation—Continued.

Subject.	Report.	Congress.	Session.	Volume.
SEYMOUR, ISAAC	483	31	1	5
Do	516	25	1	6
SEYMOUR, MARY E	1164	48	1	15
SEYMOUR, WILLIAM N	1141	48	1	14
SHAAHAN, JAMES	565	48	1	14
SHACKELFORD, SARAH	180	43	1	8
SHACKLETT, JOHN C	1693	48	1	16
SHADDY, JACKSON	1689	48	1	16
SHADE, JACOB	316	24	2	1
Do	222	25	2	2
Do	525	26	1	2
Do	444	27	2	3
Do	665	28	1	4
SHADE, JACOB, Jr	83	32	1	5
SHAFER, BALDWIN B	2236	48	2	17
SHAFTOE, WILLIAM	3075	49	1	21
SHAGGS, SYDNEY L	2525	48	2	17
SHALER, EPHRAIM	1	23	1	1
Do	832	24	1	1
SHANE, ELIZABETH	213	26	2	2
SHANER, ADAM J	124	49	1	18
SHANNON, MARY A	1575	49	1	19
SHANNON, NEIL	739	25	2	3
Do	260	25	3	3
Do	177	26	1	3
Do	155	26	2	3
Do	415	27	2	3
Do	81	29	1	4
SHANNON, PRESTON M	539	48	1	14
SHANNON, THOMAS	30	44	1	8
Do	186	46	2	12
Do	1094	47	1	13
Do	1186	48	1	15
SHARER, ELIZA ANN	2563	48	2	17
SHARP, EPHRAIM	224	35	1	6
Do	334	35	1	6
SHARP, LINCHFIELD	568	30	1	4
SHARP NATHAN J	1577	48	1	15
SHARP, RICHARD G	861	48	1	14
SHATTUCK, ALFRED	3720	49	2	22
SHATTUCK, ALICE DE KALB	802	46	2	11
Do	1176	47	1	13
SHAW, CYNTHIA	1174	48	1	15
SHAW, GILMAN B		23	1	1
SHAW, HENRY B	4105	49	2	22
SHAW, HILLYARD	934	27	2	3
SHAW, JOANNA L	1219	47	1	13
SHAW, JOHN	521	35	1	6
SHAW, MARY	1177	46	2	12
Do	670	47	1	13
SHAW, PHILIP J	159	44	1	9
SHAWBELL, JOHN G	2336	48	2	17
Do	1048	49	1	19
SHAY, MARY	1201	46	2	12
SHEA, ELLEN	4013	49	2	22
SHEADS, ELIAS	709	49	1	18
SHEAFFER, SAMUEL	219	43	2	8
Do	411	44	1	9
SHEALEY, ELIZA A	1371	48	1	15
SHEARER, SARAH M	712	49	1	19
SHEDD, CAROLINE L	3042	49	2	20
SHEETS, CATHARINE	308	45	2	10
SHEFFIELD, ANN	1361	46	2	12
Do	1214	48	1	15
SHEFFIELD, WILLIAM H	654	49	1	18
SHEFFLER, GEORGE	128	27	2	3
SHEIBER, JOHN	85	45	2	10
Do	1549	46	2	12
SHELDON, ELVIRA BLISS	2820	49	1	21
SHELDON, GIDEON	207	24	2	1
Do	409	25	2	2
Do	86	25	3	2
Do	195	26	1	2
SHELLHORN, BALTZER H	283	27	2	3
SHELMERDINE, SAMUEL	430	29	1	4
SHELTON, WILLIAM P	2139	49	1	20
SHEMONECK, WILLIAM C	540	34	1	6
SHEPHARD, JOSHUA	1478	48	1	15

Private legislation—Continued.

Subject.	Report.	Congress.	Session.	Volume.
MES	2349	49	1	21
FRANK	1109	49	1	19
RON A. (heirs of)	1669	48	2	[illegible]
	506	47	1	13
EDERICK	136	36	1	7
IDGET	148	46	2	11
	294	48	1	14
	843	49	1	18
ICE T	853	48	1	14
DNEY	129	49	1	18
ESLEY H	1691	49	1	20
RLES, Jr	1566	48	1	15
ROLINE	221	48	1	14
CS	580	45	2	10
AEL	11	43	1	8
	1166	48	1	15
THANIEL	157	29	1	4
	290	30	1	4
M	797	49	1	19
	2526	49	1	20
IN (widow of)	491	35	1	6
	240	36	1	7
	50	35	1	7
W	664	43	1	8
RY A	2022	49	1	20
EBA ANN	155	36	1	7
ANDOLPH J	468	35	1	7
TON	148	35	1	6
TN	1917	49	1	20
W	257	25	3	2
	224	26	1	2
	70	27	3	3
TAN B	2666	49	1	21
SEPH	49	40	3	11
ZA	4063	49	2	22
UAL	46	26	2	2
	220	28	1	3
IN A	840	48	1	14
BETH	810	49	1	19
I.	2307	49	1	20
	1666	46	2	12
IAM H	170	45	2	10
ELIA A	150	47	1	13
R	801	46	2	11
RGE G (children of)	1993	48	1	16
ILES	1789	49	1	20
AS	791	46	2	11
M	231	33	1	5
	217	28	1	1
HA A	417	49	1	18
Y	95	30	2	4
GE	334	45	2	10
RINE	844	46	2	11
	622	47	1	13
SLEY	349	46	2	11
ERT D	2288	48	2	17
	467	49	1	18
Y A	140	46	2	11
Y E	241	45	3	10
RICE R	470	36	1	7
ELIA E	788	46	2	11
	217	47	1	13
LIAM H	1914	48	1	16
IARIAH	330	29	1	4
AN	192	43	2	8
AM T	84	43	2	8
	61	44	1	9
N L	1440	48	1	15
E R	558	30	1	4
	307	31	1	5
	100	32	1	5
	470	36	1	7
IAS	88	23	2	1
	2053	48	1	16
	546	49	1	18
LIAM	2514	49	1	20
I	210	26	2	2
	423	27	2	3

Private legislation—Continued.

Subject.	Report.	Congress.	Session.	Volume.
SINFIELD, SARAH	776	48	1	14
SINGER, JAMES M	771	46	2	11
SIPE, LEVI	1160	46	2	12
SKAGGS, JOHN B	3564	49	2	22
SKAGGS, MARTHA JANE	36	35	1	[illegible]
SKINNER, BENJAMIN C	351	43	1	8
SKINNER, HENRY T	854	46	2	11
SKINNER, JEDEDIAH	407	26	1	2
SKY, PETER (Onondaga Indian)	86	26	2	[illegible]
Do	18	27	2	3
SLACK, GEORGE	78	49	1	18
SLAMM, JANE E	1284	49	1	19
SLAUGHTER, EMILY L	248	43	1	8
SLAVIN, PARMELIA	269	28	1	3
Do	393	30	1	4
Do	149	31	1	5
Do	64	33	1	5
SLAVENS, RACHAEL	413	47	1	13
SLAYTON, THOMAS J	1533	49	1	19
SLEIGH, MARY	61	43	2	8
SLENBAKER, ELIZABETH	2166	49	1	20
SLEVIN, JOHN	1874	47	1	13
SLIVER, HENRY	345	29	1	[illegible]
Do	95	30	2	4
Do	135	38	1	7
SLOAN, WILLIAM	648	25	2	2
Do	134	25	3	2
Do	204	26	1	2
SLOAN, WILLIAM L	403	48	1	14
Do	406	48	1	14
Do	446	49	1	18
SLOCUM, ABBY S	2281	48	2	17
SLOCUM, WILLIAM	380	23	1	1
Do	311	27	2	3
Do	24	28	1	3
Do	3	30	2	4
Do	53	31	1	5
SLYTER, JONATHAN	394	30	1	4
SMALL, ELLA I	3721	49	2	22
SMALL, PRISCILLA J	2075	48	1	16
SMALL, WILLIAM H	75	43	2	8
SMALLEY, EUGENIA A	1518	49	1	19
SMALLWOOD, JAMES	415	26	1	2
SMART, ANN	1688	46	2	12
Do	1082	48	1	14
SMARZO, CHRISTIAN	437	49	1	18
SMILEY, G. S	1471	48	1	15
SMILEY, MARTIN	3727	49	2	22
SMITH, ABIGAIL	318	49	1	18
SMITH, ALBERT H	550	48	1	14
SMITH, ALLEN	143	34	2	6
Do	328	35	1	6
SMITH, ANN	2004	49	1	20
SMITH, ANNIE M	3818	49	2	22
SMITH, BENJAMIN P	81	30	2	4
Do	48	31	1	5
SMITH, BARBARA A	1151	48	1	14
SMITH, BRIDGET	699	49	1	18
SMITH, CATHERINE	1185	48	1	15
SMITH, CLINTON D	1906	47	1	13
SMITH, CYRENIUS W	1937	49	1	20
SMITH, DENNIS	322	46	2	11
Do	1028	47	1	13
SMITH, ELBRIDGE	3077	48	1	21
SMITH, ELIZABETH	1793	45	1	16
Do	2474	48	2	17
SMITH, EUGENE	413	43	1	8
SMITH, EUPHEMIA R	1114	49	1	19
SMITH, FRANCIS (widow of)	493	35	1	6
SMITH, FREDRICK	320	35	1	6
SMITH, FRED W	606	44	1	9
Do	579	45	2	10
SMITH, GEORGE W	680	49	1	18
SMITH, GILMAN	173	32	1	5
SMITH, HENRY	4083	49	2	22
SMITH, H. C. (widow of)	277	46	3	12
SMITH, ISAAC	3253	49	1	21
SMITH, JACOB	3705	49	2	22

Private legislation—Continued.

Subject.	Report.	Congress.	Session.	Volume.
J	48	46	2	11
	424	25	2	2
	208	26	1	2
TE. B	1515	49	1	19
	218	24	1	1
	457	43	1	8
	417	26	1	2
	288	36	1	7
	110	46	2	11
	1240	47	1	13
	1819	48	1	16
	1829	48	1	16
A	353	43	1	8
NCE W	228	45	3	10
	2199	48	2	17
RET	2097	49	1	20
N	234	22	1	1
	7	22	2	1
B	443	49	1	18
GRACE	1795	49	1	20
KIRBY	233	34	1	6
A	500	47	1	13
	206	26	1	2
C	2889	49	1	21
M	1202	48	1	15
NIEL (heirs of)	53	36	1	7
	506	35	1	6
IA	90	45	2	10
NS	46	24	1	1
CK	55	40	2	7
L	2074	48	1	16
L	543	43	1	8
E	238	45	3	10
THA A	1701	49	1	20
L	473	31	1	5
L J	51	24	2	1
	218	25	2	2
	23	32	1	5
	134	38	1	7
	81	26	2	2
	250	34	1	6
	516	35	1	6
	115	35	2	6
	585	36	1	7
EN D	1331	47	1	13
	3260	49	1	21
EN R	2099	49	1	20
	2303	49	1	20
S	453	44	1	9
EN S	2558	48	2	17
AM B	716	48	1	14
OMAS	4	35	1	6
OMAS T	279	49	1	18
JAMES	2463	48	2	17
	2942	49	1	21
I	206	44	1	9
Y	497	35	1	6
ARY E	1581	49	1	19
OB	2064	48	1	16
	61	49	1	18
W	1646	48	1	16
J	23	33	1	5
E	442	49	1	18
RINE D	352	26	1	2
ON	532	46	2	11
	1535	47	1	13
IS L	1203	49	1	19
NK	851	45	2	10
ES A	1914	49	1	20
RY	100	36	2	7
	2532	48	2	17
	2008	49	1	20
H	1753	48	1	16
	1206	49	1	13
HEOPHILUS	665	26	1	2
	119	28	1	3
	48	29	1	4
HEW	150	44	1	9
	559	45	2	10

Private legislation—Continued.

Subject.	Report.	Congress.	Session.	Volume.
SOMES, RINALDO R	776	49	1	19
SONDLES, JOHN	70	38	1	7
SOPER, J. R	2330	48	2	17
SOULE, JEHILE	751	24	1	1
SOWERS, FRANK S	1043	47	1	13
SOWLE, ORLANDO T	1044	49	1	19
SPAFFORD, ELIPHALET	384	25	2	2
Do	138	25	3	2
SPANGLER, MATILDA	1579	49	1	19
SPARKS, LEWIS M	868	49	1	19
SPARKS, SIMPSON	3275	49	1	21
SPARKS, WHITFIELD	790	49	1	19
SPARKS, WILLIAM	147	30	1	4
Do	294	31	1	5
SPARR, JOHN	2183	48		17
SPALDING, SAMUEL	665	26		3
Do	386	31		5
SPAULDING, LISETTA W	2260	49		20
SPAULDING, STILLMAN C	712	43		8
SPAWRS, VALENTINE	466	36		6
SPEAR, HORACE S	515	47		13
SPEARS, JOHN	228	29		2
Do	437	27		3
SPELLEN, MARIA	2225	48		17
SPENCER, ALEXANDER	1823	48		16
SPENCER, EDGAR L	209	43		8
SPENCER, ELMINA P	2182	48		17
SPENCER, JONATHAN R	589	42		8
SPENCER, LUTHER	2211	48		17
SPICER, EMILY LOUIS. A	775	49		19
SPOONER, HENRY B	1222	48		15
SPOOR, EPHRAIM	639	30		4
SPRADLIN, CYNTHIA	754	45		10
SPRAGUE, BELA	466	31		5
SPRAGUE, CHARLES	1210	46		12
SPRAGUE, DANIEL	374	28		3
SPRAGUE, HENRY	44	45		10
SPRAGUE, MARY	2530	49		20
SPRAIN, SOPHIA	2833	49		21
SPRATT, WILLIAM S	2441	48		17
SPRIGGS, JOHN F	1897	48		16
SPRINGSTEED, ELIZABETH A	1168	48		15
SPROUSE, SAMUEL C	847	48	1	14
SQUIBB, URIAL L	804	48	2	11
SQUIRES, WILLIAM P	326	49		18
Do	2096	49	1	20
SROFE, EMANUEL	220	25	2	2
Do	254	25	2	2
Do	214	26	1	3
STACK, JAMES	1482	48	1	15
STAFFORD, AARON	780	30	1	4
Do	41	31	3	5
Do	86	32	1	5
Do	72	33	1	5
STAFFORD, ETHELRED	586	36	1	7
STAFFORD, OTIS S	2518	49	1	20
STANCLIFF, MERTON	1209	46	2	12
Do	713	47	1	13
STANERT, JOHN	465	30	1	4
STANNARD, EMILY C	3577	49	2	21
STANNARD, EMILY J	3259	49	1	21
STANNARD, GEORGE J	680	48	1	14
STANSBERRY, WILLIAM	2522	48	2	17
STANSBURY, HELEN M	113	43	1	8
Do	145	44	2	9
STAPLES, CHARLES	97	32	1	5
Do	24	33	1	5
STAPLES, MILLIA	418	48	1	14
STAPLETON, GEORGE	867	48	1	14
STAPLETON, ROBERT H	118	49	1	19
STAPLIN, GEORGE W	766	45	2	10
Do	1487	48	1	15
STARIN, WILLIAM H	783	48	1	14
STARLING, SARAH E	4116	49	2	22
STARNE, LEVI M	113	49	1	19
STARNES, LUCINDA	335	44	1	9
STARR, WILLIAM H	1733	49	1	20
STARTZMAN, ELIZA	1580	49	1	19

Private legislation—Continued.

Subject.	Report.	Congress.	Session.	Volume.
ARY J	647	48	1	14
LINA J	2528	48	2	17
EMANUAL P	75	33	1	5
	203	34	1	6
ARY A	143	46	2	11
	93	47	1	13
I, JAMES B. (widow of)	415	48	1	14
EBSTER S	55	36	1	7
OHN	250	33	1	5
OHN	235	26	2	2
ROLINE	953	45	2	10
ER, CHRISTIAN H	1760	46	2	12
	548	48	1	14
, ROBERT E	1016	49	1	19
ON, WILLIAM W	599	45	2	10
AARON	4119	49	2	22
AUGUSTUS FIELD	2366	49	1	20
CATHERINE	1975	49	1	20
DAN	154	27	3	3
GEORGE W	3884	49	2	22
HARRIET L	1735	48	1	16
ISAAC	273	43	1	8
JAMES	262	24	1	1
JAMES H	1682	46	2	12
JOHN	1073	48	1	14
JOSHUA N	602	49	1	19
MARGARET L	34	37	3	7
ROBERT H	114	33	2	5
	246	34	1	6
SILAS	212	35	1	6
	373	36	1	7
JACKSON	2082	49	1	20
DANIEL M	1587	48	1	15
ELIZABETH	640	49	1	18
HENRY	247	34	1	6
JACOB	83	23	2	1
JOHN	78	30	2	4
JOHN A	59	44	1	9
	711	49	1	19
MARY E	705	43	1	8
PHILIP	164	27	3	3
SAMUEL B.	2319	49	1	20
SUSAN ELLEN	340	44	1	9
THADDEUS S	556	44	1	9
ADELBERT	1588	48	1	15
HELEN M	1536	49	1	19
OLINE	806	46	2	11
MUEL D	1647	46	2	12
	502	47	1	13
ORER E	1731	49	1	20
	1754	46	2	12
	1613	48	1	15
ULIA A	1339	47	1	13
ADAM S	84	45	2	10
AMUEL, Jr.	294	45	2	10
, JAMES	1932	40	1	20
SABIN	3734	49	2	22
, JAMES	1868	48	1	16
, RICHARD W	330	35	1	6
, AVERY	336	35	1	6
, DANIEL	209	22	1	1
	126	23	2	1
ISS AMANDA	1822	47	1	13
COB	1894	48	1	16
IN	1366	49	1	19
LA	856	48	1	14
HFORD A	2103	49	1	20
DBERT	558	49	1	18
IZABETH D	543	44	1	9
	23	45	2	10
	616	45	2	10
ILY	304	31	1	5
MES	591	49	1	18
HN	21	28	2	3
	42	29	1	4
HN (heir of)	458	25	2	2
HN B	1357	46	2	12
ARY J	21	40	3	7

Private legislation—Continued.

Subject.	Report.	Congress.	Session.	Volume.
STONE, SALLY A	2420	49	1	20
STONECYPHER, DAVID	2238	48	2	17
Do	420	49	1	18
STONER, FRANKLIN	357	43	1	8
STOREY, PLINEY	390	35	1	6
STORM, CHAUNCEY G	623	27	2	[illegible]
Do	269	27	3	[illegible]
STORRS, MARY	25	43	1	[illegible]
STOUFFER, SAMUEL	108	35	2	6
STOUGH, ELENOR	451	46	1	14
STOUGH, ISRAEL	1696	48	1	16
Do	2056	48	1	16
STOUT, GEORGE W	1054	49	1	19
STOUT, JANE	288	46	2	11
STOUT, MICAJAH	240	43	2	[illegible]
STOUT, ZEPHANIAH	2110	49	1	20
STOVER, CATHARINE	1382	47	1	13
Do	2505	48	2	17
STOVER, MARY J	850	45	2	10
Do	152	47	1	13
STRANSBURY, HELEN M	145	44	2	9
STRATTAN, RUTH	1359	48	1	15
STRATTON, GEORGIE E	91	46	2	11
STRAWBRIDGE, HENRY	961	47	1	12
STREET, SOLOMON	720	30	1	4
STRIBLING, MARTHA H	894	48	1	14
STRIBLING, MARTHA P	276	46	3	12
STRICKLAND, JESSE H	3809	49	2	22
STRINGHAM, HENRIETTA	150	45	2	10
STRITE, NICHOLAS	170	44	1	9
STROH, AMOS	1935	48	1	16
STRONG, JOSIAH	478	24	1	[illegible]
Do	302	25	2	[illegible]
Do	222	26	1	[illegible]
STRONG, LEVI	348	22	1	[illegible]
Do	37	22	1	[illegible]
STRONG, LEWIS M	3710	49	2	22
STRONG, MARIA L	3538	49	2	22
STRUNK, DAVID	1199	48	2	15
STRUNK, JASPER A	452	43	1	8
STRUNK, WILLIAM R	452	43	1	8
STUCKER, JOHN H	3465	49	1	21
STUCKEY, JOHN	3247	49	1	21
STUCKEY, JOHN F	710	48	1	14
STUGO, ASLANG O	1523	49	1	19
STURGIS, JOHN	1718	49	1	20
STURTEVANT, ELLEN M	3549	49	2	22
STURTZ, CAROLINE	1024	49	1	19
STUTER, JOHN M	849	45	2	10
Do	1161	46	2	12
STUTSMAN, HENRY H	72	49	1	18
Do	2529	49	1	20
STYLES, WILLIAM H	712	47	1	12
SUELL, JOSIAH B	286	49	1	18
SUFFALL, WILLIAM J	772	49	1	19
SUGG, CHARLES A	1365	48	1	15
SULLIVAN, DENNIS	875	46	2	12
Do	621	47	1	12
SULLIVAN, ELIZABETH	821	49	1	19
SULLIVAN, MARY	2157	49	1	20
SULLIVAN, PATRICK	957	47	1	12
SULSGROVE, EMANUEL	1089	48	1	14
SUMMERAUER, FRANCIS	298	28	[illegible]	[illegible]
Do	81	28	[illegible]	[illegible]
SUMMERS, HECTOR W	2076	48	[illegible]	16
SUMMERVILLE, SARAH	211	43	[illegible]	[illegible]
SUMNER, HANNAH W	233	44	[illegible]	[illegible]
SUPPLE, JAMES	866	48	[illegible]	14
SUTHERLAND, R. W	1208	46	[illegible]	12
SUTTON, A. SCHUYLER	79	46	[illegible]	12
Do	1476	47	[illegible]	13
Do	1212	48	[illegible]	15
Do	877	49	[illegible]	19
SUTTON, WILLIAM	154	35	1	[illegible]
Do	447	36	1	[illegible]
SUTZ, WILLIAM	219	34	3	[illegible]
Do	109	23	2	[illegible]
SWAIN, CLARISSA D	166	43	1	[illegible]

Private legislation—Continued.

Subject.	Report.	Congress.	Session.	Volume.
LARNARD	28	23	2	1
LEONARD	458	28	1	3
SAMUEL	412	27	2	3
ORAH A	278	43	1	8
N	240	27	2	3
Y F	289	34	1	6
VILLIAM	32	43	1	8
ILLIAM M	1501	46	1	10
D, JOSEPH	842	23	1	1
EREMIAH	1908	48	1	16
JOHN	320	48	1	14
E. B	449	49	1	18
JOHN	2287	44	2	17
ANKLIN	2819	49	1	21
BUS	1780	46	2	12
	1169	48	1	15
, JAMES	903	27	2	3
	566	36	1	7
LY M	3070	49	1	21
ATHAN WILLIAMS	496	35	1	6
	296	36	1	7
ON, ANNA	280	26	1	2
	56	26	2	3
RISSA	1169	49	1	19
RY	54	49	2	7
PELEG	222	26	2	2
RKIN	36	36	2	7
RAH	23	28	1	3
REBECCA	139	46	2	12
	892	47	1	13
L, CLARA M	3284	49	1	21
L, WILLIAM N	728	45	2	10
NES S	1102	46	2	11
GE	1886	48	1	16
MARY	1686	46	2	12
	1172	48	1	15
	2038	49	1	21
OHN	529	35	1	6
OMAS M	2776	49	1	21
ARON	174	48	2	8
LANTA T	2086	49	1	20
NJAMIN F	2286	49	1	20
ARLES	634	30	1	4
OWARD	554	30	1	4
	385	31	1	5
RA	34	43	1	8
EDERICK	587	30	1	4
EORGE	302	29	1	4
	1127	47	1	13
ENRY	137	34	3	6
	33	35	1	6
	141	36	1	7
AMES H	3583	49	2	22
OHN	231	22	1	1
	7	22	2	1
	316	46	2	1
	628	47	1	13
	1912	48	1	16
	703	49	1	18
OHN S	876	45	2	10
OHN P	2963	49	1	21
OSEPH	219	27	2	3
	579	30	1	4
	629	30	1	4
ARTIN	1200	49	1	19
ARY E	1382	47	1	13
ARY J	1491	49	1	19
MARY K	3287	49	1	21
MARY M	2836	49	1	21
ATHANIEL	79	49	1	18
ICHARD P	304	46	2	11
AMUEL	535	43	1	8
USAN	373	46	2	11
VILLIAM	411	49	1	18
T, CATHARINE A	2561	48	2	17
EN, ELIZABETH	323	45	2	10
ARREN	305	36	1	7
VID	3945	49	2	22

Private legislation—Continued.

Subject.	Report.	Congress.	Session.	Volume.
TEETER, MILTON	4074	49	2	22
TEGAN, THOMAS	1998	49	1	20
TEITS, JACOB	3095	49	1	21
TEMPLETON, ANDREW	247	35	2	6
Do	229	36	1	7
Do	102	37	2	7
TEMILLE, WILLIAM A	185	22	1	1
TERRELL, DOROTHY	156	29	1	4
TERRY, CATHERINE	772	48	1	14
TETER, GEORGE W	765	46	2	11
TEVIS, REZIN	808	30	1	4
THACKER, JOEL	811	29	1	4
Do	370	30	1	4
THAYER, ANSEL	205	43	2	4
THAYER, HELEN M	1864	47	1	13
THEADGILL, EMILY	1621	47	1	13
THENN, CATHERINE	1780	49	1	20
THEW, JAMES H	532	45	2	10
Do	1017	46	2	11
Do	716	47	1	13
THEYE, JOHN	1470	48	1	15
THEYSOHN, HENRY	174	45	2	10
THOMAS, ANNA M	1075	48	1	14
THOMAS, CAROLINE E	167	43	1	3
THOMAS, DE WITT C	328	46	2	11
Do	404	47	1	13
THOMAS, EDWIN	1376	48	1	15
THOMAS, ELIZABETH	180	43	2	4
THOMAS, ELIZABETH B	114	44	1	8
THOMAS, GEORGE C	302	31	1	5
THOMAS, GEORGINE	739	45	2	10
THOMAS, ISAAC	212	27	2	3
THOMAS, ISRAEL	923	27	2	3
THOMAS, JESSE	268	48	1	14
THOMAS, JOSEPHINE D	411	43	1	8
THOMAS, JOSEPHINE DA C	180	45	2	10
Do	330	45	2	10
THOMAS, JUDITH	156	22	1	1
Do	160	23	1	1
THOMAS, LINZA	666	26	1	2
THOMAS, LOUISA	687	43	1	8
THOMAS, MARY A	1713	49	1	20
THOMAS, SARAH A	2120	49	1	20
THOMAS, SARAH C	1713	48	1	16
THOMAS, SENECA	246	29	1	4
THOMAS, WILLIAM	327	44	1	8
Do	495	47	1	13
THOMPSON, CLARA A	345	46	2	12
THOMPSON, DIANTHA	218	26	2	2
THOMPSON, ELIZABETH F	360	43	1	8
THOMPSON, FRANKLIN (*see* Seelye, Sarah E. E)	849	48	1	14
THOMPSON, JAMES W	88	44	1	8
Do	525	45	2	10
Do	126	46	2	12
THOMPSON, JOHN	600	44	1	8
Do	280	46	2	12
THOMPSON, LOUISA J	855	48	1	14
THOMPSON, MARY	150	35	1	6
THOMPSON, MARY M	3291	49	1	21
THOMPSON, MARY P	528	46	2	11
Do	365	47	1	13
Do	294	48	1	14
THOMPSON, MARY T	306	45	2	10
THOMPSON, MARY W	630	30	1	4
Do	235	31	1	5
Do	97	34	3	6
Do	84	35	1	6
THOMPSON, MATTHEW	818	29	1	4
THOMPSON, MINERVA T	784	49	1	19
THOMPSON, RUTHA C	143	45	2	10
THOMPSON, STEPHEN W	1587	46	2	12
THOMPSON, THOMAS	582	30	1	4
THOMPSON, WILLIAM	222	34	1	6
THOMPSON, WILLIAM G	307	46	2	12
THOMPSON, WILLIAM R	1509	49	1	19
THOMPSON, WILSON M	1781	46	2	12
THON, PHILLIP	755	45	2	10
THOPKINS, ABRAN C	882	48	1	14

Private legislation—Continued.

Subject.	Report.	Congress.	Session.	Volume.
RRY, JOSEPH H	2091	49	1	20
RS, J. H.	3680	49	1	21
RY, LEWIS A	78	49	1	18
N, GEORGE M. D	274	44	1	8
N, J. W	316	44	1	9
N, JOHN W	652	46	1	13
ILL, EMILY	2972	49	1	21
R, JOHN	3663	49	2	22
N, WILLIAM	2953	49	1	21
, JOHN B	1917	48	1	16
	2162	49	1	20
, MARY A.	1769	49	1	20
, ESWELL F	1228	48	1	15
ANUEL	2416	48	2	17
NN, LOUIS CHRISTOPHER	975	45	2	10
, SYLVESTER	88	24	2	1
	321	26	2	2
	288	25	3	2
	202	26	1	2
MASA A	374	22	1	1
ARTER W	652	46	1	13
	3200	49	1	21
, HEZEKIAH	1782	49	1	20
JONATHAN R	716	44	1	9
	161	45	2	10
ABAGAIL S	1060	47	1	12
, SARAH A	472	43	1	8
ALMIRA	785	45	2	10
ALFRED M	182	45	2	10
ELIZABETH	387	43	1	8
NANCY	342	43	2	8
	152	44	1	9
	1027	46	2	11
SIAH	399	26	1	2
ICHAEL	275	48	1	14
ORGE	2067	49	1	20
MES P. F	2067	48	1	16
DREW J	3849	49	2	22
THARINE S	1741	49	1	20
CHAEL	2855	49	1	21
ROBERT S	329	44	1	9
NAS	283	49	1	18
	1921	49	1	20
ELLEN S	319	49	1	18
S, WILLIAM B	483	35	1	6
S, ZEBULON S	2591	49	1	21
, JOHN	280	46	3	12
EBERT	2224	48	2	17
LEVI L	2060	49	1	20
S, G. W	156	33	1	3
AUDELOUPE	292	43	1	8
ELIZABETH	175	45	2	10
JULIA H	555	44	1	9
	158	45	2	10
PETER	274	49	1	18
DAVID	504	29	1	4
	709	30	1	4
	78	31	2	5
	108	32	1	5
FRON S	414	49	1	18
ND, EUGENE L	1149	48	1	14
ND, MARY	251	49	1	18
ND, THOMAS F	3817	49	2	22
RY C	80	43	2	8
WILLIAM	1	23	1	1
EORGE C	833	46	2	11
	1224	47	1	13
AMUEL E	2770	40	1	21
AMUEL W	1866	48	1	16
LL, MINNIE	3270	49	1	21
HORACE	1037	49	1	19
S, ALICE E	2057	49	1	20
R, FRANCIS	2560	48	2	17
ELL, JAMES B	531	44	1	9
	325	45	2	10
N, ELIZA	3707	49	2	22
L, CAROLINE	2271	48	2	17
R, JOSEPH (heirs of)	340	35	1	6

Private legislation—Continued.

Subject.	Report.	Congress.	Session.
TRENT, ALBIRA, AND CHILDREN	810	46	2
TREVITT, ROBERT	389	21	1
TRIBBLE, ELIZABETH	1992	48	1
TRIBEAU, FRANCIS	36	32	1
TRIBON, FRANCIS	704	30	1
Do	79	31	2
TRIMBLE, ALEXANDER	2812	49	1
TRIMBLE, JOSEPH	292	22	1
Do	69	23	1
TRIPLETT, MARY B	214	45	1
TRIPLETT, MOSES	2050	49	1
TRIPP ALBRA	9	22	1
Do	115	33	1
Do	148	34	1
Do	38	35	2
TROUT, JEREMIAH	217	27	2
TROWBRIDGE, JOHN	278	26	1
TROXELL, DAVID	110	32	1
TRUE, NANCY	260	44	1
TRUETT, WILLIAM	185	45	2
TRYON, SPENCER W	415	47	1
Do	1906	49	1
TUBERSING, FRANK W	8865	49	2
TUCKER, AARON	574	25	2
Do	196	30	1
TUCKER, JOHN B	157	45	2
Do	1987	47	1
TUCKER, JOHN R	152	35	1
Do	876	36	1
TUCKER, RALPH H	1912	49	1
TUCKER, SARAH A	2349	49	1
TUDER, DANIEL F	3009	49	1
TULLAR, SIDNEY B	771	48	1
Do	2070	49	1
TUPPER, JONATHAN J	1700	48	1
TURK, ANDREW J	869	38	1
TURMAN, WILLIAM	490	46	2
TURNER, ADELINA A	234	45	2
Do	870	46	2
Do	1419	47	1
Do	1015	48	1
TURNER, ANN	801	24	1
TURNER, ISABELLA	2581	48	2
TURNER, LAURA A	1788	49	1
TURNER, LEWIS	82	38	1
TURNEY, IRA J. J	1745	48	1
Do	1760	48	1
Do	1772	48	1
TURNEY, MARTHA E	110	49	1
TURNEY, WILLIAM	451	28	1
Do	347	29	1
TURVILLE, WILLIAM	611	49	1
TUTT, BENJAMIN	160	46	2
TUTTLE, CHARLES H	141	44	1
TUTTLE, JEHIEL	940	27	2
TUTTLE, JOSEPH	1529	49	1
TWITCHELL, LEANDER C	747	49	1
TROOMBLY, CAROLINE	1223	47	1
TYLER, ANDREW F	165	27	2
TYLER, SARAH	1902	48	1
TYSON, MARY A	1459	48	1
UDELL, NATHAN	564	45	2
Do	790	45	2
UEBER, LUDWIG	541	45	2
UHLER, WILLIAM J	274	43	1
ULERY, MARY	385	46	2
Do	450	45	1
UNDERWOOD, JAMES A	233	49	1
UNDERWOOD, JEMIMA	1996	48	1
UPRIGHT, ELIZABETH	515	46	2
URBANSKY, DAVID	1798	48	1
USHER, KATE L	1168	46	1
Do	216	47	1
VALLANDINGHAM, JOHN O	757	45	1
Do	1995	48	1
VALLE, FRANÇOIS	827	29	1
VAN ARSDEL, JOSEPH	742	49	1
VAN ASSUM, ABRAHAM	1503	48	1

Private legislation—Continued.

Subject.	Report.	Congress.	Session.	Volume.
ARD, OLIVER	372	49	1	18
N, BARNET S.	3030	49	1	21
LEO, WILLIAM	71	22	2	1
LEN A.	1787	48	1	16
YBERRY	1912	48	1	20
DER, DELILIAH	3538	49	2	22
, O. G	731	43	1	8
, MARY ANN	2146	49	1	20
EN, MARY	1680	46	2	12
EN, WILLIAM P	397	48	1	14
JOSEPH	2864	49	1	20
JOSEPH E	1784	46	2	12
, JOSEPH E.	867	46	1	19
, MARY A.	2540	49	1	21
EN, SAMUEL C	492	46	2	11
MARK SPENCER	2408	49	2	17
, JEROME J	580	45	2	10
ON, CAROLINE	777	48	1	14
, ANDREW J	2855	49	1	21
JAMES	221	35	2	6
	302	36	1	7
ELEAR, SOLOMON (heirs of)	290	34	1	6
, JOHN	90	30	2	2
	772	29	1	4
, HARRY E	1626	47	1	13
	271	42	1	14
ENBURG, LAMBERT L.	67	29	2	1
Y ANN	3450	49	1	21
CHARLES	681	35	2	3
CATHARINE	738	50	2	20
	861	44	2	11
JOB	1615	48	1	16
MARY J	1563	48	1	16
	1565	48	1	16
LAIBORN	154	24	1	6
ARAH A	1700	49	1	20
THOMAS H	39	46	3	11
LAMANDER	114	35	2	6
AMES D	236	49	1	18
RY B	3857	49	2	22
INDA	3889	49	2	22
EREMIAH (legal representatives of)	111	37	2	7
OHN	2596	49	1	21
ROBERT	563	48	1	14
HARIET R. F	222	36	1	7
EDERICK	537	43	1	8
	819	47	1	13
ROLINE	218	44	1	9
ICORN, HENRY	2274	48	2	17
ANN R	249	43	1	8
	40	46	3	12
	1332	47	1	13
, JAMES	2319	48	2	17
LUKE	407	23	1	1
	278	24	1	1
MARTHA A	2161	49	1	20
	280	43	1	8
LIAM	41	28	1	3
DOLPH (widow of)	749	45	2	10
ANNA	192	46	3	12
LOR	325	49	1	18
, G. W	283	46	3	12
GEORGE	809	27	2	3
ORGE	809	29	1	4
RY	596	45	2	10
	56	46	2	11
	627	47	1	13
BULON	205	22	1	1
	7	22	2	1
, HENRY	420	27	2	3
AURENA	1051	49	1	19
MELISSA	850	45	2	10
	50	46	2	11
PHILIP	327	49	1	18
RAM L	263	49	1	18
ILLIAM C	3808	49	2	22
, REBECCA	891	48	1	14
JOSEPH	1226	46	2	12

Private legislation—Continued.

Subject.	Report.	Congress.	Session.	Volume.
WALDO, MOLLIE B	65	46	3	12
WALES, FREDERICK	1770	48	1	18
WALFORD, CHARLES H	1710	49	1	20
WALKER, ALEXANDER W	1757	46	2	12
WALKER, ALVIN	1187	46	2	12
Do	1568	47	1	13
Do	1072	48	1	14
WALKER, ANDREW G	377	48	1	14
WALKER, BARBARA (heirs of)	623	36	1	7
Do	91	37	2	7
WALKER, CALVIN	367	48	1	14
Do	1187	48	1	15
WALKER, GEORGE W	[illegible]	46	2	12
WALKER, DR. MARY E	[illegible]	45	2	10
WALKER, MARY L. AND ELLA	887	48	1	14
Do	[illegible]	48	1	15
WALKER, PAUL	44	46	2	11
WALKER, ROBERT P	716	45	2	10
Do	2851	46	2	13
Do	[illegible]	46	3	13
Do	[illegible]	47	1	13
WALKER, SALOME ANN	720	48	1	14
WALKER, SAMUEL C	516	33	1	6
WALKER, TANDY	376	25	2	3
WALKER, THOMAS J	[illegible]	48	1	16
WALKER, WALKER (heirs of)	91	37	2	7
WALKER, WILLIAM	[illegible]	26	1	2
Do	[illegible]	44	1	8
WALKER, WILLIAM H	[illegible]	45	2	10
Do	102	46	2	11
WALL, BURGESS	42	28	1	3
WALLACE, HUGH	216	43	1	8
WALLACE, JOHN	[illegible]	46	2	12
WALLACE, JOHN R	278	46	3	13
Do	567	48	1	14
WALLACE, WILLIAM	164	27	3	3
Do	127	23	1	5
Do	136	38	1	7
Do	5	39	1	7
WALLER, WALTER	1	23	1	1
WALLER, WILLIAM G	317	27	2	3
WALSH, JAMES	111	23	1	3
Do	[illegible]	38	1	7
WALSH, THOMAS	[illegible]	49	1	22
WALSH, THOMAS B	2187	49	1	20
WALSWORTH, CHARLES	[illegible]	29	1	4
WALTERS, JOHN H	[illegible]	49	1	20
WALTERS, JOSEPH B	[illegible]	49	1	[illegible]
WALTERS, WILLIAM	[illegible]	48	2	17
WALTON, WILLIAM	[illegible]	24	1	5
Do	[illegible]	28	1	3
WALZELL, JAMES E. B	[illegible]	49	1	[illegible]
WARD, CHARLES F	[illegible]	49	1	[illegible]
WARD, ELIZABETH	[illegible]	49	2	[illegible]
WARD, GEORGE E	[illegible]	46	2	[illegible]
Do	[illegible]	45	1	[illegible]
WARD, GEORGE P	[illegible]	49	2	[illegible]
WARD, HUGH	[illegible]	48	1	[illegible]
WARD, JOHN	772	45	2	[illegible]
WARD, JOSEPH	[illegible]	45	2	[illegible]
Do	[illegible]	47	1	[illegible]
WARD, JOSEPH D	[illegible]	30	1	[illegible]
Do	[illegible]	31	1	[illegible]
WARD, MARGARET A	[illegible]	45	2	[illegible]
WARD, MARY ANN	[illegible]	[illegible]	2	[illegible]
WARD, NEHEMIAH	1	23	1	[illegible]
Do	[illegible]	34	1	[illegible]
WARD, ROWLAND	[illegible]	47	1	[illegible]
Do	[illegible]	[illegible]	[illegible]	[illegible]
WARD, SALLIE T	[illegible]	[illegible]	[illegible]	[illegible]
WARD, SAMUEL	[illegible]	[illegible]	[illegible]	[illegible]
WARD, THOMAS	[illegible]	[illegible]	[illegible]	[illegible]
Do	[illegible]	[illegible]	[illegible]	[illegible]
WARD, WILLIAM E	[illegible]	[illegible]	[illegible]	[illegible]
Do	[illegible]	[illegible]	[illegible]	[illegible]
WARD, WILLIE F	[illegible]	[illegible]	[illegible]	[illegible]
WARDEN, WILLIAM	[illegible]	[illegible]	[illegible]	[illegible]
WARDWELL, CYRUS T	[illegible]	[illegible]	[illegible]	[illegible]

Private legislation—Continued.

Subject.	Report.	Congress.	Session.	Volume.
LEONARD	676	26	1	2
	436	27	2	3
IZABETH	878	48	1	16
MUEL J	1899	47	1	13
A	1962	48	1	16
NIEL H	76	29	2	3
	210	29	1	4
	288	30	1	6
ORGE A	2937	49	1	21
NERAL G. K. (widow of)	1890	47	1	13
RAEL	363	46	2	12
HN G	2807	49	1	21
ARGARET E	1014	48	1	14
IAH	555	28	1	2
N, KATESBURY R	2330	49	1	20
CORNELIA A	306	43	1	8
DARWIN E	3728	49	2	22
GEORGE A	2376	49	2	17
ISAAC P	236	34	1	6
LUCY A	2773	49	1	21
SILAS	34	27	3	3
	153	28	1	4
	72	29	2	4
	65	30	1	4
THARINE	3039	49	1	21
LI D	1154	46	2	12
Do	211	47	1	13
ULIA	329	44	1	9
	149	45	2	10
VID	272	34	1	6
	329	35	1	6
MES	1708	49	1	20
HN	1588	46	2	12
	668	47	1	13
	1915	48	1	16
	1773	49	1	20
SEPH	581	27	2	3
	97	28	1	3
	93	28	2	3
	54	29	1	4
SEPH J	585	30	1	4
LETITIA	239	46	3	12
SAN L	183	45	2	10
C	717	44	1	9
NCIS	223	45	3	10
	847	46	2	11
RGARETTE	449	36	1	7
ICHABOD	39	32	1	5
OLPH	1161	48	1	15
EE, LYDIA	2415	24	2	17
OW, STEPHEN	682	43	1	8
RASTUS C	766	48	1	14
EORGE	344	35	1	6
ENRY	2505	49	1	20
OHN	733	24	1	1
	190	25	2	2
	853	26	1	2
OHN H	42	46	3	12
ILLIAM H	2654	49	1	21
AS	2334	49	1	21
FORD	733	43	1	8
RGE J	956	47	1	13
PH	1	23	1	1
	238	33	1	5
	153	35	1	6
RISTIAN	1511	49	1	19
ONHARD	1121	47	1	13
BENJAMIN C	449	44	1	9
	22	45	2	10
E CAROLINE	233	43	1	8
MARY S	780	45	2	10
	790	46	2	11
	773	49	1	19
WILLIAM	1516	49	1	19
WILLIAM B	285	49	1	18
FIELD, WILLIAM	1155	48	1	15
	809	49	1	19
ANN JANE	202	45	3	10

Private legislation—Continued.

Subject.	Report.	Congress.	Session.	Volume.
WEEDEN, AMOS C	1785	49	1	20
WEEKLEY, THOMAS	2949	49	1	21
WEEKS, LOIS L	1221	47	1	13
WEHE, ANNA	604	45	2	10
Do	98	46	2	11
WEHE, ANNA M	798	47	1	12
Do	675	48	1	[illegible]
WEHRHEIM, VALENTINE G	40	35	1	[illegible]
WEIDE, ALEXANDER	2503	48	2	[illegible]
WEIDE, AUGUST	56	49	1	[illegible]
WEIGHTMAN, WILLIAM	2071	49	1	[illegible]
WEIMER, WILLIAM R	35	48	2	[illegible]
Do	656	49	1	[illegible]
WEINER, JACOB	2400	48	2	[illegible]
WEINSTEIN, ELIZABETH	1610	47	1	[illegible]
WEIR, HENRY CARY	2470	48	2	[illegible]
WEISS, EMILY E	407	44	1	[illegible]
WEISSE, MICHAEL (heirs of)	114	43	1	[illegible]
WEITZEL, LOUISA	587	49	1	[illegible]
WELCH, ANDREW J	182	46	2	[illegible]
WELCH, ELLEN J	2114	49	1	[illegible]
WELCH, HARRIET	2074	49	1	[illegible]
WELCH, ISAAC	62	49	1	[illegible]
WELCH, JAMES	516	35	1	[illegible]
WELCH, JAMES K	102	28	1	[illegible]
WELDING, CATHARINE	392	36	1	[illegible]
WELDY, SETH	3388	49	1	[illegible]
WELLS, ASA	245	35	2	[illegible]
Do	227	36	1	[illegible]
WELLS, GEORGE	689	49	1	[illegible]
WELLS, HENRY	530	26	1	[illegible]
Do	146	27	2	[illegible]
WELLS, MARY L	862	45	1	[illegible]
WELLS, WILLIAM	223	35	1	[illegible]
WELSCHBILLIG, PETER J	1651	46	2	[illegible]
Do	820	47	1	[illegible]
WELTON, CHARLOTTA A	1694	48	1	[illegible]
WEMS, ELIZABETH J	952	45	2	[illegible]
WENDELL, ANN JANE	202	45	3	[illegible]
WERTZ, AMOS C	1302	49	1	[illegible]
WESLEY, BENJAMIN F	49	24	2	1
Do	427	25	2	[illegible]
Do	148	25	3	[illegible]
Do	273	26	1	[illegible]
Do	49	31	1	[illegible]
WESNER, MARY ANN	658	49	1	[illegible]
WESSELS, CORNELIUS	1596	48	1	[illegible]
WEST, CALLIE	1697	49	1	[illegible]
WEST, ELI	433	29	1	[illegible]
WEST, GEORGE	814	29	1	[illegible]
WEST, GEORGE F	2350	48	2	17
WEST, JOHN C	105	30	2	7
WEST, MARGART E	201	42	1	[illegible]
Do	35	44	1	[illegible]
Do	73	46	2	11
WEST, MARY J	1142	47	1	13
WEST, NANCY A.	500	46	2	11
WEST, WILLIAM A	1018	46	2	11
WESTCOTT, CHARLOTTE S	162	35	1	[illegible]
WESTERHOUSE, JOHN H	1705	49	1	20
WESTERVELT, MARTHA	378	44	1	9
Do	318	45	2	10
Do	1396	46	2	12
Do	1054	47	1	13
WESTFALL, ABRAHAM	3243	49	1	21
WESTLAKE, JOSIAH	286	23	1	[illegible]
Do	407	24	1	[illegible]
Do	189	25	2	[illegible]
Do	140	25	3	[illegible]
Do	157	26	2	[illegible]
Do	924	27	2	[illegible]
WESTON, CYRUS	262	34	1	[illegible]
WESTON, CYRA L	2671	49	1	[illegible]
WETHERELL, GEORGE W	1297	49	1	[illegible]
WETHERELL, HORACE	946	27	2	[illegible]
WETMORE, ALPHONSO	192	28	1	[illegible]
WETMORE, HENRY STANLEY	773	46	2	11
WETTER, SARAH L	2317	49	1	20

Private legislation—Continued.

Subject.	Report.	Congress.	Session.	Volume.
ICHAEL	1827	48	1	20
H, ICHABOD	578	31	1	5
HENRY H	316	44	1	9
, NATHAN	629	38	1	7
, JOHN	1220	48	1	15
, JULIA J	888	45	2	16
WILLIAM H	2104	49	1	20
WILLIAM W	2883	49	1	21
K, EDWARD C	89	44	1	9
K, EMILY E	43	45	2	16
K, JARED D	1751	49	1	20
WILLIAM	793	36	1	4
	88	31	1	5
THOMAS	43	22	1	5
CHLOE A	3088	44	1	18
WILLIAM H	348	49	2	11
ER, JOHN H. (guardian)	2574	48	2	17
	584	49	1	18
S, ASHAEL D	2097	45	1	16
S, WILLIAM H	773	48	1	14
ARTLETT E	1976	49	1	20
ATHERINE	314	45	3	10
HARLES R	2460	48	2	17
	2461	48	2	17
HRISTOPHER C	2188	49	1	20
ORNELIA F	1470	47	1	13
MIRA	216	25	1	6
VALINE A	1190	49	1	19
ANNIE B	13	42	1	8
ANNIE S	124	44	1	9
EORGE	723	24	1	1
AMES B	817	46	3	11
	968	47	1	12
OHN C	580	49	1	16
OHN Q	1648	48	2	19
EWIS (widow of)	215	47	1	13
ICHAEL	393	31	1	5
OSES	164	27	3	3
OBERT	954	27	2	3
	164	27	3	3
LAS S	2464	48	2	17
	577	49	1	18
EPHEN	1524	49	1	19
HOMAS R. (widow of)	71	34	3	6
	74	36	1	7
ILLIAM	678	43	1	8
RD, MARY L	1182	46	2	12
AD, GEORGE R	553	45	2	10
AD, MARGARET	87	35	1	6
	298	36	1	7
L, CATHARINE	1499	49	1	19
, GEORGE J	1221	46	2	12
, JAMES	1645	48	1	16
, NATHAN	429	36	1	7
, RICHARD L	355	46	2	12
, WALT	3856	49	2	22
E, JOHN	355	30	1	4
E, LOUIS K	837	46	2	11
, EDMUND W	373	46	3	12
, S. S	578	45	2	10
T, JAMES	141	23	1	1
ER, MATTHEW B	718	43	1	8
, GEORGE	218	27	3	3
, GEORGE W	117	33	2	5
	241	34	1	6
	347	35	1	6
, ROBERT	299	25	2	2
	78	25	3	2
	205	26	1	2
	59	26	2	2
	258	27	2	3
	550	30	1	4
GTON, DAVID	1869	48	1	16
GTON, MARY	1176	46	2	12
, JASPER M	602	44	1	9
Y, LOUIS	1495	49	1	19
LARA	1916	47	1	13
M. ROBERT	26	35	2	6

Private legislation—Continued.

Subject.	Report.	Congress.	Session.	Volume.
WICKWIRE, GEORGE W	88	45	2	
Do	863	48	1	
WIDNEY, ROBERT M	160	45	2	
WIDTMEYER, PHILIP J	1122	47	1	
WIGGIN, JOSEPH	106	38	1	
WIGGINS, MARGARET	1468	48	1	
WIGGINS, PHILIP	836	48	1	
WIGGINS, V. L	427	49	1	
WILBORNE, SAMUEL A	726	44	1	
WILBOURN, NATHANIEL	23	35	2	
Do	375	36	1	
WILCOX, EDWARD	1928	48	1	
WILDE JAMES B	1487	49	1	
WILDER, TABITHA	37	30	2	
WILDES, THOMAS F	409	44	1	
WILEY, JOHN F	361	23	1	
Do	269	24	1	
Do	228	25	2	
Do	96	25	3	
Do	238	27	2	
Do	807	27	2	
Do	384	23	1	
WILGES, WILLIAM	959	48	1	1
WILHELM, FREDERICK	1152	46	2	1
WILHORLITZ KATE	954	47	1	1
Do	1213	48	1	1
Do	2034	45	2	1
WILKERSON, ISOM	522	42	2	1
WILKES, MARY	453	43	1	
WILKINS, CORDELIA	1920	48	1	1
WILKINS, EDWARD M. (widow of)	2803	49	1	2
WILKINS, ELIZA	1764	48	1	1
WILKINSON, CHARLES	79	46	2	1
WILKINSON, FRANCES M	698	43	1	
WILKINSON, HARRIET W	163	43	2	
WILKINSON, JAMES	140	44	1	
WILLARD, JANE N	969	45	2	1
WILLCOX, CATHERINE S	249	45	3	1
WILLETS, I. HOWARD	738	48	1	1
WILLEY, ROBERT L	645	26	1	
WILLEY, SETH	169	44	1	
WILLHOIT, DANIEL	1052	49	1	1
WILLHOITE, SANFORD C	1717	48	1	1
WILLIAMS, ANN J	2316	49	1	2
Do	53	38	1	
WILLIAMS, EDWARD	72	46	2	1
WILLIAMS, HARRY E	783	47	1	1
Do	830	46	2	1
WILLIAMS, HENRY C	2275	48	2	1
Do	426	49	1	1
Do	557	45	2	1
WILLIAMS, JAMES G	806	46	2	1
Do	557	36	1	
WILLIAMS, JAMES L	554	36	1	
WILLIAMS, JOEL	40	46	2	1
WILLIAMS, JOHN L	2089	49	1	2
WILLIAMS, JOHN S	3087	49	1	2
WILLIAMS, JOHN W	1812	48	1	1
WILLIAMS, JOSEPH	142	49	1	1
Do	255	26	1	
WILLIAMS, LABAN	776	46	2	1
WILLIAMS, M. D	1196	48	1	1
WILLIAMS, MAJ. D	1580	48	1	1
Do	777	46	2	1
WILLIAMS, MARTHA A	311	45	2	1
WILLIAMS, MARY D	3961	49	2	2
WILLIAMS, MARY L	603	44	1	
WILLIAMS, MINERVA	3985	49	2	2
WILLIAMS, MOSES	3547	49	2	2
WILLIAMS, RHODA	1730	49	1	2
WILLIAMS, SARAH ANN	136	49	1	2
WILLIAMS, THOMAS	1165	46	2	2
WILLIAMS, WILLIAM	166	34	3	
WILLIAMS, ZINA	47	35	1	
Do	135	36	1	
Do	92	37	2	
Do	1621	48	1	1
WILLIAMSON, AMOS				

Private legislation—Continued.

Subject.	Report.	Congress.	Session.	Volume.
SON, MARTHA A	724	44	1	9
	721	45	2	10
	717	46	2	11
	707	47	1	12
DWARD	3057	49	2	22
HN W	3562	49	2	22
THANIEL H	119	33	1	5
HOMAS	65	43	2	8
SAMUEL J	979	45	2	10
. M	1630	48	1	14
LEXANDER	839	29	1	4
MANDA F	2318	49	1	20
MELIA ANN	1425	46	2	12
NDREW J	1528	49	1	19
	3301	49	1	21
RTHUR	452	30	1	4
ANIEL	84	30	2	4
AVID	236	25	2	2
	212	26	1	2
EDWARD	887	44	1	9
LIZABETH C	2595	49	1	21
LLEN	12	43	1	8
UNICE	706	43	1	8
EORGE W	964	46	2	12
EORGE W. (widow of)	215	47	1	12
AMES	166	27	2	3
OHN	549	30	1	4
OHN A	413	47	1	13
OHN H. (*see* John H. Ivers)	1366	48	1	15
OSEPH F	1615	47	1	13
MARCELLUS	698	46	2	10
OWEN P	2974	49	1	21
AMUEL	222	45	2	10
THOMAS	291	25	2	2
	190	26	1	2
	48	26	2	2
	1426	47	1	13
HOMAS E	410	48	1	14
WILLIAM H	640	26	1	2
	500	29	1	4
	551	30	1	4
	94	38	1	7
Y, ROBERT S	156	34	1	6
LEWIS E	737	45	2	10
HN	2804	49	1	21
AH	183	46	3	12
LUTHER	616	36	1	7
LD, WILLIAM, JR	431	27	2	3
. M. V. B	1607	48	1	15
JEREMIAH A	256	26	1	2
MARY B	146	34	1	6
, CATHARINE A	686	43	1	8
	710	44	1	9
, JARED	878	25	2	2
	80	25	3	2
	185	26	1	2
, SAMUEL T	71	24	2	1
	260	27	2	3
	561	29	1	4
	70	31	1	5
JACOB	810	27	2	3
, ELIZABETH	513	45	2	10
	100	46	3	12
, NATHAN A	679	43	1	8
	750	45	2	10
ARLES V	80	49	1	18
CHARLES H	849	48	2	11
, REBECCA	2727	49	1	21
, NICHOLAS	2456	48	2	17
, SOPHRONIA	1530	49	1	19
NIEL	844	29	1	4
ARTHA	680	43	1	8
IZABETH	367	43	1	8
ORGE	732	45	2	10
HN B	3943	49	2	22
AMES	1513	49	1	19
, S. A. (heirs of)	804	30	1	4
WEBER, LOUIS A	2015	49	1	20

Private legislation—Continued.

Subject.	Report.	Congress.	Session.	Volume.
WOLVERTON, BENJAMIN S	677	49	1	18
WONDRAK, MATHIAS	243	46	2	12
Do	806	47	1	13
WOOD, BENJAMIN	629	27	2	3
WOOD, CALEB (heirs of)	560	30	1	7
WOOD, EMMA A	72	36	1	7
WOOD, GEORGE W. T. (widow of)	490	35	1	6
Do	73	36	1	7
WOOD, HANNAH A	451	44	1	9
WOOD, JAMES RUFFIN	362	44	1	9
Do	976	45	2	10
WOOD, JOB	434	22	1	1
Do	232	23	1	1
Do	244	24	1	1
Do	171	26	1	2
Do	261	27	2	3
Do	141	27	3	3
WOOD, MARY	2941	49	1	21
WOOD, MICHAEL	1391	48	1	15
WOOD, NELSON F	360	46	2	11
WOOD, PRISCILLA	1749	48	1	16
Do	1761	48	1	16
Do	2012	49	1	20
WOOD, ROSE M	1341	47	1	13
WOOD, SARAH	625	30	1	4
WOOD, SIDNEY J	165	43		
WOOD, SILAS M	411	27		3
WOOD, W. J	2416	49		20
WOOD, WALTER H	1074	48		14
WOOD, WARREN F	279	44		9
Do	336	45		10
Do	2548	49		21
WOODALL, SARAH	570	45		10
WOODARD, JAMES	1807	48		16
WOODBURY, MRS. D. P	1706	48		16
Do	2008	49		21
WOODGILL, ELIZABETH	2519	49	1	20
WOODRUFF, FRANK M	569	48	1	14
WOODRUFF, HARRIETTE A	410	45	1	8
WOODRUM, MARTHA F	1545	46	2	12
Do	4078	49	2	23
WOODS, MRS. M. E	3742	49	2	22
WOODSON, MARY S	1706	49	1	20
WOODWARD, GEORGE W	78	46	2	11
WOODWARD, HENRY S	1395	47	1	13
WOODWARD, JONAH	298	46	3	12
WOODWORTH, SARAH A	107	43	2	9
WOODY, WILEY G	217	44	1	9
WOOLFORD, DANIEL	234	28	1	3
WOOLLEY, SUSAN	2518	48	2	17
Do	469	49	1	18
WOOLSEY, JAMES	132	44	1	9
Do	938	45	2	10
WOOLSEY, WILLIAM	225	35	1	6
WORDEN, JAMES	113	34	1	6
WORMLEY, HUGH WALLACE	152	26	2	2
Do	145	27	3	3
Do	72	27	3	3
Do	53	28	1	3
Do	478	31	1	3
Do	17	32	1	3
WORNOM, CHARLES T	2811	49	1	21
WORRELL, BENJAMIN F	144	46	2	11
WORTH, SUSAN	10	31	1	5
WORTHINGTON, MARIA C	1535	46	2	12
Do	420	47	1	13
WORTHINGTON, THOMAS	1450	46	2	12
WRIGHT, ANNA	3046	49	2	22
WRIGHT, BERIAH	76	26	2	2
Do	613	27	2	3
Do	508	29	1	4
Do	454	30	1	4
Do	213	35	1	6
Do	134	36	1	7
WRIGHT, CRAFTS J	781	46	2	11
WRIGHT, DANIEL K	1985	48	1	16
Do	267	49	1	18
WRIGHT, GILES	2856	49	1	21

Private legislation—Continued.

Subject.	Report.	Congress.	Session.	Volume.
., HANNAH M	1839	46	2	12
Do	812	47	1	12
., IRA	178	22	1	3
., JAMES J	474	26	1	2
Do	37	22	1	6
Do	227	22	1	3
., JAMES S	1617	48	1	16
., JEREMIAH	222	25	2	2
Do	675	27	2	3
Do	236	27	3	3
Do	175	35	1	6
., JOHN E	290	25	2	2
Do	180	26	1	2
Do	80	26	2	2
Do	312	27	2	3
Do	79	28	2	3
., JOHN W	296	43	1	8
Do	2334	48	2	17
., LAURA A	4079	49	2	22
., MARY	30	32	1	5
., MARY F	2256	49	1	20
., MOSES	846	29	1	4
., SAMUEL C	345	48	1	14
., SARAH C	2825	49	1	21
., WILLIAM	584	35	1	6
RLIN, JOHN E	84	44	1	9
, KATHARINA T	837	48	1	14
Do	1461	48	1	15
, CHARLES	895	49	1	19
, ALFRED H (heirs at law)	885	46	2	11
FF, JOHN W	251	26	1	2
F, SOLOMON	804	47	1	13
, JOHN F	228	25	2	2
., JAMES	927	25	2	2
Do	51	29	1	4
., HARRIET S	326	36	1	7
OLIVER	523	45	2	10
LL, ELIZA J	1119	47	1	13
LL, PETER	792	45	2	10
BENJAMIN	530	35	1	6
JANE	284	36	1	7
Do	187	38	1	7
., AUGUSTUS S	200	43	1	8
., AMOS A	780	44	1	9
ER, MARY R	1751	46	2	12
N, RICHARD R	2002	48	1	16
L, SOLOMON	861	46	3	12
CATHARINE	508	47	1	13
ILLIAM (heir of)	290	33	1	5
UGUSTA	696	48	1	14
ANDERSON W	2952	49	1	21
ANSON K	588	44	1	9
Do	206	45	3	10
Do	222	45	3	10
Do	1558	46	2	12
CHARLES	271	28	1	3
F	160	43	2	8
FREEMORTON	3006	49	1	21
GEORGE, AND OTHERS	79	43	2	8
HARRISON D. F	1611	48	1	15
, JACOB	354	46	2	11
JAMES H	3072	49	1	21
JANE	782	48	1	14
, JESSE	84	30	1	4
, JOHN M	3560	49	2	22
, JONATHAN D	3732	49	2	22
, JOSEPH L	321	45	2	10
, ORSON	548	43	1	8
, SARAH	2919	49	1	21
, SUSAN V	2391	49	1	20
, SUTTON M	229	35	2	6
Do	182	36	1	7
., THOMAS C	864	45	2	10
., WILLIAM WALLACE	4165	49	2	22
BLUE, FREDERICK	131	44	1	9
ER, JOHN W	3252	49	1	21
S, WILLIAM	33	35	2	6
ADAM	419	49	1	18

Private legislation—Continued.

Subject.	Report.	Congress.	Session.	Volume.
ZEIGLER, EMMA O	1794	48	1	16
ZEILER, THOMAS	146	44	1	9
ZEILIN, VIRGINIA	1372	48	1	15
ZEIS, HENRY	586	44	1	9
ZETTERMAN, GARRET D	2818	49	1	21
ZIEFLE, GEORGE	1099	48	1	14
ZIMMERMAN, JACOB	92	31	1	4
ZIMMERMAN, JOHN	2413	49	1	20
ZOLLER, KEZIA	217	43	2	8

REPORTS

OF THE

MMITTEE ON THE

HOUSE OF REPRESENTA

FROM THE FOURTEENTH CONGRES 18
FORTY-NINTH CONGRESS, 1887,

IN ELEVEN VOLUMES.

MPILED, UNDER THE DIRECTION OF THE JOINT COMMITTEE ON PRINTING,

BY

T. H. McKEE,
CLERK, DOCUMENT ROOM, UNITED STATES SENATE.

WASHINGTON:
GOVERNMENT PRINTING OFFICE.
1887.

9269 J 11

FORTY-NINTH CONGRESS, FIRST SESSION.

[PUBLIC RESOLUTION—No. 24.]

Joint resolution authorizing the preparation of a compilation of the reports of mittees of the Senate and House of Representatives.

Resolved by the Senate and House of Representatives of the U States of America in Congress assembled, That there be prepared u the direction of the Joint Committee of Printing, a compilation of reports of the Senate and House of Representatives from the I teenth to the Forty-eighth Congress, inclusive, classified by commit arranged, indexed, and bound in suitable volumes for the use of standing committees of the two Houses of Congress. And the su seven thousand seven hundred and fifty dollars, or so much there may be found necessary, is hereby appropriated out of any mon the Treasury not otherwise appropriated, for the preparation of work, which sum may be paid by the Secretary of the Treasury the order of the chairman of said Joint Committee, as additional p compensation to any officer or employee of the United States.

Resolved further, That the Clerk of the House and Secretary o Senate be, and they are hereby directed, to procure and file, for th of their respective Houses, copies of all reports made by each com tee of all succeeding Congresses; and that the Clerk of the Hous the Secretary of the Senate be, and they are hereby, authorized directed at the close of each session of Congress, to cause said re to be indexed and bound, one copy to be deposited in the libra each House and one copy in the room of the committee from which reports emanated.

Approved, July 29, 1886.

COMPILER'S NOTICE.

This compilation embraces all the printed reports made by both Houses of Congress from the commencement of the Fourteenth to the close of the Forty-ninth Congress. They are classified by committees and arranged in numerical order. The collection for each committee is divided into volumes of suitable size. Each committee has a separate index, a copy being bound in each volume.

The SPECIAL and SELECT reports are all compiled in one collection having one index, a copy of which is bound in each volume.

The plan throughout the compilation is to place each report to the committee from which it was reported, without reference to the subject-matter.

The House and Senate reports are compiled separately. Care will be required in noticing the chronological order, as in some instances an entire session or Congress may not appear in certain volumes from the fact that during this period no reports were made by this committee.

T. H. McKEE.

INDEX

TO

REPORTS OF COMMITTEE ON THE JUDICIARY,

HOUSE OF REPRESENTATIVES.

FROM 1815 TO 1887, INCLUSIVE.

Subject.	Report.	Congress.	Session.	Volume.
ED PROPERTY IN THE INSURRECTIONARY STATES, collec- n of, act of March 12, 1863, right of the President to sign after the ournment of Congress	108	38	1	8
)F MEMBERS OF CONGRESS, deduction of pay of members for..	37	41	2	8
ES TO CRIMINAL ACTS, to amend laws relative to trial of, after fact, before conviction of principal	1267	47	1	10
United States and State of Mississippi	35	34	1	3
United States courts in Oregon and Washington Territories	67	36	2	7
ndiana, and Ohio claims, of 2 per cent., settlement	40	41	3	8
Do	21	42	2	8
Do	47	42	2	8
and other officers, action of accounting officers of the Treasury in tlement of	3797	49	2	11
companies, settlement of	909	45	2	9
NG OFFICERS OF THE TREASURY, right of Attorney-General overrule, in settlement of accounts of marshals and other officers	3797	49	2	11
lon. J. H., charges against, inquiry into	1582	46	2	9
EDGMENT OF GOD and the Christian religion in the Constitu-	148	43	1	8
ARCH 12, 1863, providing for collection of abandoned property, rela- e to Executive approval of, after the adjournment of Congress	108	38	1	8
ULY 1, 1862, &c., concerning the Union Pacific Railroad Company	615	43	1	8
D., surety on bond of S. A. Blaine, Indian agent, relief	3925	49	2	11
ATION OF FOOD. (*See* FOOD ADULTERATION.)				
n. D. WYATT (a Representative from South Carolina), right of, to e the oath of office at his home in South Carolina, on account of sick- s	3745	49	2	11
ation of certain physicians for services rendered by order of district rt in	613	48	1	11
r southern judicial district of, to appoint	194	49	1	11
Do	3404	49	1	11
old in, exempt from tax for five years, to relieve State from bur- n of	26	17	1	1
ate writs of error in middle district of	114	29	1	3
CLAIMS,				
f the Geneva arbitration	*628	43	1	8
tion of award	628	42	3	8
Do	663	45	2	9
tion of unappropriated moneys	†243	44	1	9
tion of law distributing award	‡47	42	3	8
time for filing claims	5	44	1	9
CLAIMS COURT,				
act establishing	307	47	1	10
Do	*1032	48	1	11
business of	945	49	1	11
duration of	190	48	1	11
IC LIQUOR TRAFFIC, power of Congress to regulate	250	43	1	8

* And views of minority. † Part 2. ‡ Parts 1, 2.

* And views of minority.

Subject.	Report.	Congress.	Session.	Volume.
MANUEL DEL, slave claim	81	21	1	1
, **JACOB**, estate of, relief	140	22	2	2
, **E. W.**, recusant witness	99	44	2	9
, **JOHN**, forfeiture, claim under act January 8, 1808	435	27	2	2
, **S.**, removal of political disability	3406	69	1	11
, **SETH M.**, removal of political disability	2890	49	1	11
SBY, WILLIAM, cotton claim	482	46	2	9
Y, MICHIGAN, to hold terms of United States courts at	1508	48	1	11
Do	1318	49	1	11
Do	2909	49	1	11
D, JAMES B., seat as Representative from Colorado	67	44	2	9
F, W. W., impeachment of	222	44	1	9
Do	245	44	1	9
, **EDMUND**, military land warrant	308	32	1	3
. (*See* POLYGAMY.)				
F LADING, to make them conclusive evidence in certain cases	1299	48	1	11
Do	*901	49	1	11
M, H. H., additional compensation	801	47	1	10
T, R. T. (assignee of Thomas H. Duvall), claim for fees as clerk Territorial court of Florida	278	34	1	3
Do	296	34	3	3
Do	198	35	1	3
, JOHN E., representative of, claim	89	28	1	2
, Lieut. JOHN F., seizure of Malaga, relief from prosecution of owners of	50	30	2	2
RANGE M., army contract	219	46	3	9
T, Hon. HENRY W., investigation of charges against	142	46	3	9
T, REBECCA, title to certain real estate	157	20	1	1
ICHARD, and others, passing counterfeit coin	482	39	1	6
SEPH, and others (heirs of Joseph Piacy), claim for relief	238	28	1	2
(*See* DEBT OF UNITED STATES.)				
MASSACHUSETTS,				
...wealth Bank of, claims of United States against	207	28	1	2
National Bank of	682	48	2	8
T, ELIAS C., tax upon tobacco raised in the Indian Territory	52	41	2	8
Do	39	41	3	8
Do	6	42	2	8
Do	939	45	2	9
Do	120	46	3	9
Y, J. E. (heirs of), land claim	37	46	3	9
RY OF				
a and Georgia, to establish	204	20	1	1
Do	191	21	1	1
ska, northern boundary of, to establish	253	46	3	9
and Indian Territory, to define	1282	47	1	10
Y,				
ors, to punish	1269	47	1	10
nesses, to punish	1268	47	1	10
River into Kentucky	387	21	1	1
River at Wheeling, Va	167	32	1	3
ETT, RICHARD J. (assignee), (*see* THOMAS H. DUVAL)	276	34	1	3
Do	256	34	3	3
Do	198	35	1	3
N, ABRAHAM, forfeiture under internal-revenue law, relief	964	48	1	11
GEORGE (sureties of), liability on bond	250	21	1	1
HARVEY, quartermaster, United States Army, civil action against, relief	74	22	1	1
NOAH, claim for the loss of the brig Warrior	122	15	1	1
RETURN B. (captain, United States Army) settlement of accounts	739	24	1	2
Do	376	25	2	2
GTON, IOWA, to remove United States court from Keokuk, Iowa, to	611	48	1	11
GTON AND DES MOINES TRANSPORTATION COMPANY, claim for relief	435	26	1	2
, SIDNEY C. (widow of) claim for relief	65	36	2	7
D, Judge RICHARD, impeachment of	773	43	1	8
, AMOS, claim for printing	250	21	1	1
, EDWARD G. W., removal of political disabilities	33	49	1	11
WORTH, SAMUEL F., surety on postmaster's bond, relief	528	36	1	7
ELL, ALEXANDER, recognizance bond, relief	205	28	1	2
RNIA.				
...ial districts, to establish southern	374	48	1	11
Do	313	49	1	11
s in, title to	634	46	2	9
s of the San Buenaventura Missions in, ownership of	614	43	1	8
...ary reservation at Point San José, in	527	43	1	8
Do	922	43	2	9
...te land claims in Napa County, settlement of	70	33	1	3
JOHN G., settlement of accounts	62	35	1	3

* And views of minority.

Subject.	Report.	Congress.	Session.	Volume.
…PEARSON, settlement of accounts	396	26	1	2
…ARD, Jr., to release from liability as surety	328	27	2	2
…MES L., funds stolen from United States depository, Santa Fé, …	104	43	1	8
…ion of clerks of United States courts in	648	47	1	10
… a Representative in Congress	767	44	2	9
…ies courts in, to regulate terms of	571	49	1	11
…ER OF GENERAL LAND OFFICE, conduct of, under resolution …arch 17, 1832	449	22	1	1
…ER OF INTERNAL REVENUE, to authorize, to refund taxes …lly collected	3068	49	2	11
…ON THE JUDICIARY. (*See* JUDICIARY COMMITTEE.)				
…ALTH BANK OF BOSTON, claims of United States against	257	25	1	2
…ION,				
…f Congress appointed or elected to fill a vacancy, to regulate	3795	49	2	11
…f Congress, to fix	269	34	3	3
…s and special deputy marshals at elections	609	46	2	9
…tes district attorneys, to fix	1137	47	1	10
…LAWS OF DAKOTA TERRITORY, funds for	142	43	1	8
…NT OF CERTAIN CRIMES, to amend law relative to	1270	47	1	10
…ON, prohibiting confiscation of property beyond the natural term …	1	39	1	8
…ON OF REAL ESTATE, under act of July 17, 1863	1	39	2	8
…nent of Representatives under ninth census	25	42	2	8
…f, compensation, to fix	269	34	3	3
Do	27	41	2	8
…f, compensation, when appointed or elected to fill a vacancy	3795	49	2	11
…xempt from arrest, except in certain cases, while in attendance at …m of	3	39	2	8
…to regulate the liquor traffic	250	42	1	7
…Judge ALFRED, charges against	342	21	1	1
Do	244	25	2	2
Do	168	26	2	2
…HN, claim for relief	328	21	1	1
…IONAL CENTENNIAL COMMISSION OF PHILADELPHIA, …missioners of the United States to aid the	4032	49	2	11
…ON OF THE UNITED STATES, proposed amendments to,				
…tion bills, to give President power to veto separate items in	1879	49	1	11
… United States Senators by the people	3796	49	2	11
… prohibiting	2568	49	1	11
…reed, to give expression in Constitution to	143	43	1	8
…ative to payment for emancipation of	33	39	1	8
…hat shall not be abridged on account of nativity	1674	48	1	11
…ffrage, to enforce	*1330	48	1	11
…ONAL QUESTIONS, to be decided by Supreme Court	34	20	2	1
…ELECTIONS (*see also* ELECTIONS, CONTESTED), to regulate expenses …	179	48	1	11
…, CONDITIONAL, for purchase of sites for public building in …more, Md	257	34	3	3
…ID, claim for relief	223	27	3	2
Do	249	28	1	2
…N K., removal of political disabilities	1729	48	1	11
…ARLES, and other laborers on improvement Des Moines Rapids, …ent of, by United States after failure of contractors	30	41	2	8
…THOMAS, to have refunded fine for libel	16	19	1	1
Do	149	21	1	1
Do	244	22	1	1
Do	473	23	1	1
Do	302	24	1	2
Do	343	25	2	2
Do	37	29	1	3
Do	11	31	1	3
…S				
… the period of limitation and renewal of	8	21	2	1
Do	1052	25	2	3
…o foreigners	189	48	1	11
…VI H., calendar copyright	613	30	1	3
…ITING foreign securities, to fix penalty for	1885	47	2	10
Do	2329	48	1	11
…LAIMS,				
…ry of the act establishing a	513	36	1	7
… section 3220, in relation to payment of judgment	383	46	3	9
Do	1636	47	1	10
…ng court to investigate claims against the Government	*34	37	2	7
…a judgment of	387	47	1	11
Do	195	48	1	11
Do	6	49	1	11
…n of causes to the docket of	69	46	3	9

* And views of minority.

Subject.	Report.	Congress.	Session.	Volume.
COURT OF CLAIMS—Continued.				
Restoration of causes to the docket of	1073	47	1	10
Right of action in	1642	49	1	11
COURT OF COMMISSIONERS OF ALABAMA CLAIMS.				
To revive	307	47	1	10
To extend duration of	190	48	1	11
COURTS OF UNITED STATES,				
Alabama, to appoint judges for southern district of	194	49	1	11
Do	3404	49	1	11
Amending laws for	105	17	2	3
Amend judicial system of	429	23	1	1
Appeals, to amend law regulating bonds in	500	48	1	11
Arkansas,				
To divide eastern judicial district into two divisions	101	49		11
To hold courts at Texarkana	2637	49		11
To amend judicial districts in	1391	49		11
Attachments in, issuing	1268	46		9
California, to establish southern judicial district in	318	49		11
Circuit,				
Second, for an additional judge in	2290	49		11
Fourth, fixing time for holding terms of	1774	46		9
Clerks,				
Accounts of clerks in Oregon and Washington Territories	67	36		7
Fees of	1319	49		11
Do	3158	49		11
Salary of, to increase	170	34	1	3
Colorado,				
To regulate terms of United States courts in	571	49	1	11
Fees of clerks of United States circuit and district courts in	648	47	1	10
Cost and expenses, payment of, in certain judicial proceedings	153	46	2	9
Creditors, judgment against, in	225	45	2	9
Criminal cases, to regulate proceedings	3924	49	2	11
Criminal procedure, to simplify	2884	49	1	11
Dakota,				
Additional justice for supreme court in	1657	47	2	10
Do	753	48	1	11
Increasing jurisdiction of probate courts in	2637	48	2	11
District attorneys, to fix compensation of	86	36	2	7
District judges, salaries of	118	29	1	2
Duluth, Minn., providing for holding terms of, at	3690	49	2	11
Establishment of, repeal of act of September 14, 1789	43	21	2	1
Fees,				
Of certain officers	50	32	1	3
Do	606	46	2	9
To repeal double allowance of clerk fees in Nevada, California, and Oregon	1088	48	1	11
Florida,				
Appeal to writs in	50	21	1	1
To investigate official conduct of judges of the district courts of	87	18	2	1
To alter time of holding courts in southern district	715	49	1	11
Georgia,				
Separate courts for northern and southern districts of	13	47	1	10
Creating two southern judicial districts	388	47	1	10
To change time of holding	593	48	1	11
Illinois,				
To divide into three judicial districts	729	48	1	11
To amend judicial districts in	344	49	1	11
Indiana,				
United States court at Fort Wayne	626	46	2	9
Salary of district judge in	632	47	1	10
Indian Territory,				
To establish a judicial district at Oklahoma, in	122	43		8
Conferring civil jurisdiction on United States courts in	388	49		11
Iowa,				
Circuit courts, where to be held	625	46		9
Dividing State into two judicial districts	251	47		10
Removal to Burlington of	123	43		8
Do	611	48		11
Time of holding terms in northern district of	3999	49		11
Judges,				
Providing for an additional judge for Nevada	1143	47		10
Retirement of	3919	49		11
Salaries of	*499	48		11
Do	1761	49		11
Judgments,				
To amend law relative to interest on	6	49		11
To regulate effect of	1555	48		11
Do	199	49		11
Judicial terms, to increase number, in New York	855	21		1
Judiciary, reorganization of	45	44		9

* And views of minority.

Subject.	Report.	Congress.	Session.	Volume.
)F UNITED STATES—Continued.				
ry system, amendment of	307	19	1	1
Do	184	20	1	1
Do	43	21	2	2
district and circuit, to be used interchangeably when sitting at same				
ne and place	3606	49	2	11
rge to be delivered in writing to	315	49	1	11
sion,				
istrict courts in Territories, under the bankrupt act of 1841	681	27	2	2
xtend, throughout the United States	72	31	1	3
mend act of March 3, 1875, regulating circuit courts	660	47	2	10
r State officers	1864	48	1	11
define, in suits against officers of United States	2634	48	2	11
ing pay of	40	21	1	1
scribing time of service of	1571	47	1	10
rict court at Wichita	122	46	2	9
Do	545	47	1	10
divide into two judicial districts	1676	48	1	11
ky, to establish judicial district in	141	43	1	8
na, dividing State into two judicial districts	328	46	2	9
Do	361	46	2	9
ls, to fix compensation of	86	36	2	7
n.				
livide into two judicial districts	482	39	1	3
Do	272	35	1	6
hold terms at Bay City	1569	48	1	11
Do	1313	49	1	11
Do	2906	49	1	11
ota, to hold term of circuit court at Minneapolis	2639	48	1	11
ppi,				
icial districts in	2714	49	1	11
ssissippi City, providing for holding terms of, at	3482	49	2	11
ksburg, providing for holding terms of, at	1317	49	1	11
reate additional courts in	1877	49	1	11
,				
icial districts in	370	49	1	11
livide the eastern judicial district of	1285	47	1	10
, supreme court of	1454	49	1	11
Do	2910	49	1	11
a, to regulate terms in	1320	49	1	11
rsey, Newark, providing for holding terms of, at	3826	49	2	11
xico, additional justice in supreme court of	2908	49	1	11
rk,				
charged by officers in southern district of	195	15	1	1
thern judicial districts in, fixing terms of	389	47	1	10
Do	200	49	1	11
olution of inquiry as to use of funds by	138	15	1	1
'arolina,				
give circuit jurisdiction to district court in eastern district of	790	48	1	11
mington, providing for holding terms of, at	799	48	1	11
Do	4	49	1	11
livide into two judicial districts	838	29	1	3
ension of jurisdiction of the United States in	72	31	1	3
ng time of holding courts in northern district of	182	47	1	10
vania, additional judicial district in	20	42	3	8
Do	1867	49	1	11
ns, to compensate for services rendered by order of district courts	613	48	1	11
in, regulating	67	31	2	3
Do	610	46	2	9
s, serving of	71	19	1	1
Do	222	19	1	1
Do	611	36	1	7
ions,				
rges to jury	315	49	1	11
criminal proceedure	373	48	1	11
Do	754	48	1	11
Do	631	49	1	11
l of causes	196	48	1	11
Do	367	48	1	11
Do	1078	49	1	11
Do	1305	49	1	11
Do	3775	49	2	11
nization of judiciary	45	44	1	9
, to increase, of district judges of United States	355	21	1	1
land in Texas by order of, to set aside conveyance by	3649	49	2	11
'arolina, terms of, in, to regulate	3776	49	2	11
see, to establish United States court at Chattanooga	1206	46	2	9

* View of minority.

Subject.	Report.	Congress.	Session.	Volume.
NCIA, JOSEPH, arms furnished United States, claim for	78	29	2	3
Do	667	30	1	3
, account for money expended during war of 1812	1676	48	1	11
IN CONGRESS, disqualifying polygamists from being admitted as	386	47	1	10
. H., executor of Dr. Thomas Cooper, deceased	11	31	1	3
NT OF JUSTICE,				
Attorney-General for Post-Office Department in, defining duties	554	47	1	10
tion of United States district attorneys	1137	47	1	10
NTS, EXECUTIVE, regulating appointment of clerks in	9	29	1	3
ARSHALS, pay of special, at elections	609	46	2	9
ICHIGAN, right of United States to certain lands in	2248	48	2	11
ONY, claim for invention for breaking and cleaning hemp, &c	102	17	1	1
EORGE B., surety on bond	69	29	2	3
Do	107	30	1	3
X,				
time for the redemption of lands sold under the, of 1823	6	19	1	1
inst States for, used as offsets	*35	49	1	11
TTORNEYS, compensation of United States	1137	47	1	10
OURTS. (See COURTS OF UNITED STATES.)				
UDGES, expenses of	226	44	1	9
F COLUMBIA,				
regulate appeals from	1260	48	1	11
mages, to provide for the recovery of	1785	48	1	11
tions between the United States and the	627	43	1	8
n	280	43	2	8
relief	609	48	1	11
, relative to	2	39	1	8
See MARRIAGE AND DIVORCE.)				
COURT OF CLAIMS, restoration of causes to	69	46	3	9
OHN, loss of vessel	206	21	1	1
(schooner), claim for	439	45	2	9
HN E., contract for naval supplies	96	19	1	1
NA, to allow slaves in Cuba to enter United States, property of	70	20	1	1
NNESOTA, providing for holding terms of United States court at	3690	49	2	11
ILLIAM L. (trustee), title to land in District of Columbia	1334	49	1	11
CHECKS, issuance of certain, by superintendent San Francisco				
, ratifying	248	47	1	10
dge E. H., impeachment of	96	42	3	8
Do	732	43	1	8
act of March 2, 1833	86	36	1	7
ed merchandise, to regulate	†35	46	1	9
OMAS H., clerk of Territorial superior court of middle district of				
ida	276	34	1	3
Do	256	34	3	3
Do	198	35	1	3
) PHŒNIX MANUFACTURING COMPANY OF COLUMBUS,				
ORGIA	4	45	2	9
OMAS, violation of revenue laws	99	17	1	1
Do	18	17	2	1
AS, representative of	350	22	1	1
EBENEZER, title to lands in New Hampshire	855	27	2	2
JE and MARY, claim for relief	258	34	3	3
E, WISCONSIN, United States courts at	762	49	1	11
EPH, administrators of	162	28	2	2
Do	693	29	1	3
AMOS, sureties of	13	21	2	1
Do	64	22	1	1
, J. R., to remove political disabilities	2340	49	1	11
, expenses of, in House of Representatives	324	46	3	9
nterference, veto of act to prevent	†19	46	1	9
pervisors and special deputy marshals at	609	46	2	9
irginia, changing time of holding	912	47	1	10
VOTE OF MARYLAND, to give effect in late Presidential elec-				
	998	45	2	9
LAW, distribution of forfeited bonds under	455	27	2	2
OF GOVERNMENT, right of franchise	121	43	2	8
, salary of	59	42	3	8
Do	629	46	2	9
Do	43	47	1	10
Do	178	48	1	11
BERT, rejection of claim by reason of bankrupt proceedings	6	44	1	9
Do	910	45	2	9
Do	30	46	1	9
ARDEE, rejection of claim by reason of bankrupt proceedings	910	45	2	9
LIAM (paymaster of volunteers), relief of sureties	71	21	1	1
Do	247	22	1	1
Do	434	24	1	2

* Parts 1, 2. † Views of minority, Part 2.

* Parts 1 and 2. † And views of minority.

* And views of minority.

Subject.	Report.	Congress.	Session.	Volume.
HERRING & RICHARDSON, to indemnify for seizure of ship	140	23	2	1
Do	494	24	1	2
HERMANGE, ANTHONY, to issue letters patent to	164	29	1	1
HILLYER, Judge E. H., for relief of	1143	47	1	10
HOLT, CHARLES, claim for relief	113	26	2	1
Do	273	27	2	2
Do	206	28	1	2
Do	102	36	2	7
HOOD COUNTY, TEXAS, to attach to northern judicial district	102	49	1	11
HOOPER, JAMES, to indemnify for loss of vessel	481	48	1	11
Do	714	49	1	11
HORSE STEALING, to suppress, in Indian Territory	196	49	1	11
HOUSE OF REPRESENTATIVES,				
Organization of, to facilitate	102	36		7
Original papers, on files of, before court, production of	1	46		9
HOWE, SILAS Q., internal-revenue tax claim	27	44		9
HUMPHREYS, Judge WEST H., impeachment of	44	37		7
HUNTER, ALEXANDER, settlement of accounts	331	30		3
Do	122	30		3
HUNTER, THOMAS, recognizance bond, relief	205	28		2
HUNTINGTON, WILLIAM, settlement of accounts	1121	48		11
HUNTON, LOGAN, claim for fees	68	38		8
HURD, Hon. FRANK, payment for services in case of Hallet Kilbourn	153	46		9
HURST, FIELDING, claim for compensation	820	45	2	9
Do	1581	47	1	10
Do	666	48	1	11
ILLINOIS, judicial districts, to amend law relative to	438	48	1	11
Do	729	48	1	11
Do	344	49	1	11
IMPEACHMENT,				
Belknap, W. W. (Secretary of War)	222	44	1	9
Do	345	44	1	9
Busteed, Richard (judge)	778	43	1	8
Durell, E. H. (judge)	732	43	1	8
Humphreys, West H. (judge)	44	37	2	7
Johnson, Andrew (President of United States)	*31	39	2	8
Do	7	40	1	8
Peck, James H. (judge)	325	21	1	1
Watrous, John C. (judge)	7	32	2	3
Do	2	36	2	7
IMPRISONMENT, to secure the attendance of witnesses in court by	87	19	1	1
IMPORT DUTIES, right of the treaty-making powers of United States to admit any article free of, without the action of both Houses of Congress	4177	49	2	11
INDEBTEDNESS, Southern railroads, investigation of	78	41	2	8
Do	101	43	1	8
INDIANA, United States district court at Fort Wayne	628	46	2	9
INDIANS,				
Chickasaw, to carry out treaty stipulations with	41	41		8
Choctaw, to carry out treaty stipulations with	41	41		8
Miami Indians, payment of annuities	10	37		3
Prosecutions against	3922	49		11
Sac and Fox, determining northern boundary line of reservation of (treaty of 1824)	198	27		2
INDIAN DEPREDATION CLAIMS OF STATES AND TERRITORIES, providing for settlement	572	49	1	11
INDIAN TERRITORY,				
Boundary of, to define	1282	47	1	10
Horse stealing in, to suppress	196	49	1	11
Internal-revenue laws in, effect of	52	41	2	8
Do	30	41	3	8
Do	6	42	2	8
Do	920	45	2	9
Do	120	46	2	9
Robbery in, punishment for	314	49	1	11
United States courts in, conferring civil jurisdiction on	388	49	1	11
INSURRECTION, to repeal act of July 17, 1862, to suppress	1	39	2	8
INTEREST on claim to State of New Hampshire	63	31	2	3
Do	26	32	1	3
INTERNAL REVENUE,				
Judgments against bureau officers, payment of	1636	47	1	11
Laws, violation of, punishment for	1729	49	1	11
Tax on capital employed by banking associations, to refund	3964	49	2	11
Tax, erroneously collected, to refund	3923	49	2	11
Tax on liquor dealers, to amend law regulating	4046	49	2	11
Tax in States, Federal authority for collecting	85	22	2	1
INVALID PENSIONS, laws granting, validity of	259	34	3	3
IOWA,				
Judicial districts, dividing State into two	251	47	1	10
Do	2386	49	1	11

*And views of minority.

Subject.	Report.	Congress.	Session.	Volume.
tinued.				
f United States courts in northern district	2080	47	2	10
tasse circuit court in, where to be held	669	46	2	9
states district court, removal of, from Keokuk to Burlington	128	43	2	8
D OATH, modification of	51	38	1	8
m. THOMAS, charges against, preferred by James Dunlap, official act of	40	21	2	1
ILLIAM B., & CO., claim for money taken by United States troops	426	45	2	9
Do	616	46	2	9
General ANDREW, remission of fine imposed on	878	27	2	2
Do	123	27	3	2
S COUNTY, GEORGIA, to construct, in	612	36	1	7
BUREN, ARKANSAS, to construct, at	64	34	1	3
THOMAS, relief from judgments	36	24	2	2
EPHEN, surety on bond of United States purser	115	26	2	2
Do	250	27	2	2
President ANDREW, impeachment of	31	39	2	6
Do	7	40	1	6
Judge BENJAMIN, charges against the official conduct of	86	22	2	1
JAMES, relief from loss by embezzlement	302	48	2	9
SAMUEL, claim for relief	174	30	1	3
, GEORGE PEN, settlement of accounts	66	36	2	7
, JOHN, claim for relief	114	26	2	2
Do	262	27	2	2
OMAS AP CATESBY, surety on postmaster's bond	226	33	1	3
ALTER F., for relief of surety	226	33	1	3
LLIAM, sale of, as a slave	129	36	1	3
tirement of	3019	49	2	11
T LIENS, nature and extent of	395	44	1	9
TS. (*See also* COURT OF CLAIMS.)				
internal revenue officers	1629	47	1	10
of, against the United States	891	45	2	9
DISTRICTS,				
—				
thern and southern	12	47	1	10
hange	4100	49	2	11
Territory, to establish, in	122	42	3	8
divide, into two	251	47	1	10
ty, to establish eastern	141	43	1	8
ia, to divide into three	4155	49	2	11
n, to establish additional	482	29	1	3
Do	272	35	1	3
l,				
daries of	98	48	1	11
ding eastern	1285	47	1	10
arolina, to change	3542	49	2	11
divide State of, into two	838	29	1	3
vania, to provide additional	20	42	3	8
PROCEEDINGS of each State in the Union under act May 26, 1790	17	15	1	1
REMEDIES, to provide for overcharge of duties on tonnage and im- rts	95	43	2	8
SALES, land in Texas, to set aside conveyance of	3649	49	2	11
SYSTEM,				
ng the law relating to	207	19	1	1
Do	134	20	1	1
Do	429	23	1	1
al twenty-fifth section of act of September 4, 1789, establishing the	43	21	2	1
TERMS, to increase the, of holding the judicial courts of the United ates in New York	355	21	1	1
Y,				
lges to concur on constitutional questions	34	20	2	1
ization of	45	44	1	9
Y COMMITTEE, resolution to make special order, business from	2636	49	1	11
Y SYSTEM, to alter and amend	207	19	1	1
Do	134	20	1	1
Do	429	23	1	1
TION of United States circuit courts, to amend act of March 3, 1875, gulating	680	47	1	10
nterchangeably used by district and circuit courts when sitting at me time and place	3806	49	2	11
of, to punish	1269	47	1	10
in United States courts	49	21	1	1
of, limiting term of	1571	47	1	10
UNITED STATES, an additional, for Dakota Territory	4096	49	2	11
t court at Wichita	122	46	3	9
Do	545	47	1	10
da, into two judicial districts	1676	48	1	11
US, PETER A., claims under the French spoliation act	437	25	2	2

* Part 2. † And views of minority.

* And views of minority.

Subject.	Report.	Congress.	Session.	Volume.
ROCK AND FORT SMITH RAILROAD COMPANY, land grant to.	1205	47	1	10
FISHERY, to amend law regulating	79	21	1	1
Ion. JAMES W., relative to impeachment of	1442	48	1	11
, SAMUEL H., to remove political disabilities	759	47	1	10
C. M., surety on bond of J. C. Hobbs, relief	4111	49	2	11
OUNTY, OHIO, to transfer county to southern judicial district	1261	48	1	11
NA,				
g State into two judicial districts	1323	46	2	9
Do	261	46	3	9
g State into three judicial districts	4155	49	2	11
UFUS, surety on bond of J. C. Hobbs, relief	4111	49	2	11
BENJAMIN P., to remove political disabilities	3484	49	2	11
,				
of oath required of applicants for pension	144	43	1	8
nd law requiring proof of	1641	49	1	11
ATTHEW, to refund to heirs fine illegally imposed on	218	22	1	1
Do	491	23	1	1
Do	304	24	1	2
Do	377	25	2	2
Do	86	26	1	2
TER, JOHN, claim for relief	439	29	1	3
, JAMES, surety on bond	82	23	1	1
Do	345	25	1	3
AND, THOMAS, for relief as surety	430	23	1	1
Do	91	24	1	2
Do	357	25	2	2
ALD, JAMES, extension of patent	102	17	1	1
AND & DOWNEY, claim for rent of real estate	85	36	1	7
EUGENE E., to remove political disabilities	2635	49	1	11
Hon. JOHN, charges against	583	26	1	2
'ILLE AND MANCHESTER RAILROAD, to settle accounts with	2612	48	2	11
General ALEXANDER, and others, surety on paymaster's bond	594	27	2	2
TER, JOHN, claim for relief	392	26	1	2
ELIZA JANE, cotton claim	1132	46	2	9
THOMAS J., claim to seat as additional member from Nebraska	1863	47	2	10
FAYETTE, claim for relief	66	31	2	3
Do	37	31	1	3
E LIENS, Congressional action on	1698	46	2	9
M, WILLIAM, surety on bond	77	27	2	2
AHAN, WILLIAM, private land claim of	5	40	1	8
Do	30	40	2	8
Do	24	41	3	8
Do	*992	48	1	11
GE AND DIVORCE, to collect statistics of	1857	48	1	11
, PATRICK P., surety on bond	434	45	2	9
LS, bonds in certain cases to be taken by United States	6	46	3	9
WASHINGTON (steamer), prosecution of persons charged with burning of	135	33	1	3
EDWARD B., to relieve from judgments	421	23	1	1
Do	455	24	1	2
ND,				
re, purchase of sites for court-house and post-office in	257	34	3	3
al vote, to give effect to	*998	45	2	9
advanced in 1792 and 1793, reimbursement for	278	33	1	3
1812, to settle accounts for money expended during	1670	48	1	11
gton, D. C., to pay advances made for public buildings in	*1563	48	1	11
ERMAIN H., settlement of accounts	622	46	2	9
USETTS, to settle account for money expended during war of 1812	1670	48	1	11
LY, GEORGE, title to land in Washington, D.C	210	33	1	3
L, WILLIAM, relief from judgment	413	31	1	3
. HENRY (a Representative from Maryland), investigation of loyalty	2	37	1	7
IODIJAH (administrator), to renew copyright	1052	25	2	2
, BENJAMIN, and others, relief from judgments	759	29	1	3
E, DAVID (administrator), settlement of accounts	778	27	2	2
S OF CONGRESS,				
to, defining law granting	4	40	1	8
office, where and by whom administered	3745	49	2	11
deduction from, for absence	37	41	2	8
PIERRE, and others (heirs), claim for relief	233	33	1	3
HUGH W., reimbursement of proceeds of mining stock sold under legal decree of United States district court	348	44	1	9
ST. ANDERSON, to remove political disabilities of	758	47	1	10
T, NICHOLAS JOSÉ, claim for seizure of schooner, 1863	620	43	1	8
LITAN POLICE FORCE. (See DISTRICT OF COLUMBIA.)				
CITIZENS, right to citizenship of certain, in New Mexico	145	37	2	7
DIANS. (See INDIANS.)				
N,				
ion of, into the Union	380	24	1	2

* And views of minority.

Subject.	Report.	Congress.	Session.	Volume.
MICHIGAN—Continued.				
Bay City, to hold terms of United States courts at	1562	48	1	11
Do	1318	49	1	11
Do	2909	49	1	11
Judicial districts, to divide into two	482	29	1	3
Do	272	25	1	3
Ontonagon and State Line Railroad Company, to protect title to lands granted to	1266	47	1	10
MIFFLIN, KENNEDY, Mexican claim	116	47	1	10
MILEAGE to members of Congress	4	40	1	3
MILITARY BOUNTY LANDS, land patent in Virginia military district of Ohio	1414	47	1	10
MILITARY RESERVATION at Point San José, in State of California	527	43	1	6
MILLER, HENRY, to commute sentence of	32	39	2	6
MILLER, RAPHAEL M., claim for relief	114	43	2	6
MINNEAPOLIS, MINNESOTA, to hold term of United States circuit court at	2029	48	1	11
MINNESOTA, to hold term of circuit court at Minneapolis	2029	48	1	11
MINT, ratifying issuance of duplicate checks by superintendent of San Francisco	248	47	1	10
MISPRISON OF FELONY, to amend law relative to (sec. 5390 Revised Statutes)	1270	47	1	10
MISSISSIPPI.				
Claims between United States and, to adjudicate	35	34	1	3
Courts in, to create additional	1877	49	1	11
Judicial districts in	2714	49	1	11
Newton County, swamp and overflowed lands in	107	34	3	3
Vicksburg, to hold terms of United States court at	1317	49	1	11
MISSISSIPPI CITY, MISSISSIPPI, providing for holding terms of United States court at	3492	49	2	11
MISSISSIPPI LAND COMPANY OF NEW ENGLAND	956	25	2	3
Do	164	28	2	3
MISSOURI.				
Judicial district, eastern, to divide	1285	47	1	10
Judicial districts and courts in, to regulate	98	48	1	11
Do	370	49	1	11
Two per cent. land fund	440	35	1	3
MITCHELL, JOHN K., to remove political disabilities	1559	48	1	11
Do	3156	49	1	11
MITCHELL, SOPHIA G., cotton claim	1132	46	2	9
MITCHELL & RAMMELSBERG, claim for relief	190	36	1	7
MOBILE AND OHIO RAILROAD, to settle accounts with	2245	48	2	11
Do	312	49	1	11
MODIFICATION OF OATH OF OFFICE, to all employés in public service	51	39	1	6
MONEYS UNCLAIMED FROM ESTATES OF BANKRUPTS, redistribution of	3920	49	2	11
MONROE RAILROAD COMPANY, to relieve from bonds	337	31	1	3
Do	51	32	1	3
MONTANA, supreme court of	1454	49	1	11
Do	2910	49	1	11
MONTGOMERY, A. B., to remove political disabilities	2181	48	2	11
MORENO, FRANCIS, claim for relief	51	30	2	3
MORRIS, GOUVERNEUR, to remove political disabilities	738	47	1	10
Do	815	47	1	10
MORRIS, L. A., claim for relief	1131	46	2	9
Do	1261	47	1	10
Do	610	48	1	11
MORROW, JAMES, claim for relief	272	27	2	3
MOUNT VERNON RELICS, proper disposition of	36	41	2	6
MULVIHILL, THOMAS, reconveyance of certain lands erroneously conveyed by him to the United States	249	48	1	11
MUNICIPAL BONDS, appeals from judgments on	2723	49	1	11
MUNOZ, ALONZO B., claim for seizure of vessel	107	17	1	1
MURPHY, NEWTON S., compensation for services rendered United States officers	428	44	1	9
Do	825	45	3	9
NALLE, THOMAS B., removal of political disabilities	4097	49	2	12
NATCHEZ, MISSISSIPPI, to release American Baptist Home Mission Society from conditions of sale of marine hospital building at	53	48	1	11
NATURALIZATION, to amend laws relative to	88	17		1
Do	47	17	2	1
Do	87	26	2	2
Do	231	29		3
Do	1030	48		11
Do	731	49		11
NAVAL VESSELS FOR THE REPUBLIC OF TEXAS, claims of citizens for furnishing	13	30	2	3
NEBRASKA.				
Northern boundary, to establish	253	46	3	9
Representative, claim to additional	923	45	2	9
Do	91	47	1	10
Do	1863	47	2	10
United States courts in, to regulate terms of	1320	49		11
NEVADA, an additional judge for the district of	1143	47		10
NEWARK, NEW JERSEY, providing for holding terms of United States courts at	3526	49		11

Subject.	Report.	Congress.	Session.	Volume.
LAND MISSISSIPPI LAND COMPANY, claim for land in Mississippi	256	25	2	2
Do	164	26	2	2
Do	785	26	1	3
Do	200	26	1	3
PSHIRE, interest on claims to State of	62	31	2	3
Do	28	34	1	3
A MINING COMPANY, quieting titles to certain lands held by	5	46	1	9
Do	80	40	2	8
Do	24	41	2	8
EY, to ratify agreement relative to boundary between State of New rk and	2086	48	1	11
HENRY, to remove political disabilities	191	48	1	11
ICO,				
ssed at twenty-sixth session of legislature, to repeal operation of	1565	48	1	11
g all acts of legislature authorizing slavery or imprisonment except crimes	*508	36	1	7
court of, additional justice in	2816	48	1	11
EANS, LOUISIANA, claims of city to certain lands	466	23	1	1
Do	504	26	1	2
EANS, BATON ROUGE AND VICKSBURG RAILROAD, forfeit of land grant	†1850	49	1	11
ERS, defining jurisdiction of Postmaster-General over transmission papers through mail	51	37	3	7
NATIONAL BANK, loss of money by acts of United States Subtreasury Agent Hartwell	352	47	1	10
K (State),				
y between New Jersey and	2096	49	1	11
f district court, application of	136	16	1	1
judicial districts of, provisions for holding terms in	859	47	1	10
Do	990	48	1	11
im of 1812, to adjudicate	1670	48	1	11
K CITY TEMPERANCE ALLIANCE, memorial relative to intemperance in Washington, D. C	325	33	1	8
MUEL, cotton claim	*1728	49	1	11
Do	2365	49	1	11
DENT LANDHOLDERS, to withdraw the protection of Congress m	103	36	2	7
ROLINA,				
court in eastern district of, to confer jurisdiction on	799	48	1	11
districts of, to change	3542	49	2	11
gton, to hold United States circuit court at	799	48	1	11
Do	4	49	1	11
N BOUNDARY of the State of Ohio	380	24	1	2
N PACIFIC RAILROAD COMPANY, land grants to	*1283	47	1	10
PUBLIC, appointed by the President	1394	46	2	9
OSEPH, legal representatives, claim of, for interest on judgment	80	33	2	3
Do	110	34	1	3
Do	50	35	2	7
MARIA L., additional compensation	548	28	1	2
Do	375	29	1	3
SENORA DE REGLA (ferry-boat), to carry into effect decree of urt in case of	152	48	1	11
ENRY, surety on bond	142	23	1	1
LOYALTY, repeal of, required of applicants for pension	144	43	1	8
OFFICE,				
bers of Congress, where and by whom administered	3745	49	2	11
fy oath to employés in Government service	51	39	1	8
n of subcommittees to administer	194	48	1	11
house, to be administered by notaries public	1673	48	1	11
Do	1143	40	1	11
CHARLES, and others, titles to lands in California	614	43	1	8
of Cincinnati, ask for extension of jurisdiction of district courts	72	31	1	3
districts, to divide into two	838	29	1	3
County, to transfer to southern judicial district of	1261	48	1	11
n boundary of State of	380	24	1	2
ver, bridge across	387	21	1	1
's purchase, unsold land in	243	33	1	3
States courts in northern district of, to fix times of holding	182	47	1	10
ER, bridge across	387	21	1	1
IA, to establish judicial district of	122	43	2	8
ON AND STATE LINE RAILROAD COMPANY, to protect titles lands located on land grant to	1266	47	1	10
ATION, to facilitate the, of House of Representatives	102	30	2	7
PAPERS, production before courts-martial prohibited	1	46	1	9
NAVIGATION COMPANY, to secure free navigation of Bayou or River Saint John	89	19	2	1
Do	138	20	1	1
Do	62	20	2	1

* And views of minority. † Parts 1, 2.

*And views of minority. †Part 2.

*And views of minority. †Part 2.

Subject.	Report.	Congress.	Session.	Volume.
T OF THE UNITED STATES—Continued.				
ables of	31	[illegible]	2	[illegible]
to approve a bill after adjournment of Congress	108	36	1	6
ty in cases of suspension of writ of habeas corpus	45	37	2	6
against certain proceedings of the House of Representatives by	394	36	1	7
IAL PERMITS to purchase products of insurrectionary States	626	45	2	9
ablishment of a telegraphic censorship of, in Washington	64	37	2	7
ITED STATES, establish and erect buildings for	4007	49	2	11
, UNITED STATES, condition of, and number of commitments,				
-'88	4007	49	2	11
LAND CLAIMS in Napa County, California	70	33	1	3
PROPERTY, condemnation for public use	90	20	1	1
of members of Congress	2	39	2	5
,				
State courts	222	19	1	1
in patent and other cases	621	36	1	7
IONS against Indians	[illegible]	49	2	11
ON, withdrawal of, of Congress from non-resident land-holders	108	36	2	7
f President against certain proceedings of the House of Representa-				
tives	394	36	1	7
UCK, RHODE ISLAND, land adjacent to custom-house at	1464	46	2	9
GEE A., removal of political disabilities of	611	46	2	9
COUNTS and CLAIMS, to amend law relative to	1831	49	1	11
ND STRIP, to extend laws of United States over unorganized terri-				
y between New Mexico and Indian Territory, known as	3960	49	1	11
Do	869	49	1	11
NDS,				
wood, grass, or forests on, defining penalty for	4107	49	2	11
s of	2077	49	1	11
t, Chicago, Ill., rights of United States to	4006	49	2	11
r, suits for setting aside fraudulent	1830	49	1	11
Do	1827	49	1	11
ount of proceeds of sales, in certain States	40	41	2	8
Do	21	42	2	8
Do	47	42	3	8
INTING, to be done in District of Columbia	198	28	2	1
CURITIES, amendment to laws in relation to offenses against	671	29	1	2
SAMUEL M., relief from judgment	158	34	3	3
Do	274	35	1	3
SAN FRANCISCO, resolution in House relative to	2163	48	1	11
THOMAS F., to refund money awarded for capture of	2263	48	2	11
S (*see also* under titles of respective railroad companies).				
t of accounts with	969	45	2	9
cific, opinion of the Attorney-General relating to the	3746	49	2	11
OSEPH, *et al.*, fraudulent claim	669	26	1	2
Do	857	27	2	2
Do	122	28	1	2
JOHN, surety on bond	271	27	2	2
SUSAN C., claim for extra compensation	209	30	1	3
Do	175	31	1	3
Do	29	32	1	3
I, EDMUND M., compensation for legal services	27	43	1	8
I, PEYTON (administrator of), to renew copyright	1052	25	2	2
JOHN O. (sureties of), claim for relief	1828	47	2	10
S, to adjust consular accounts of	1004	45	3	9
Do	624	46	2	9
ATE, evidence to quiet titles to	2349	48	2	11
JOSEPH W., additional compensation	1023	27	2	2
cost of printing, for Supreme Court	318	25	3	2
WILLIAM C., claim for relief	49	35	2	7
ON lands sold under direct tax, 1823	6	19	1	1
F GREEN, to remove political disabilities	2077	49	1	11
N, and others, settlement of accounts	5	31	2	3
MARY, claim for relief	163	28	1	2
OF SURETY ON BOND	3025	49	2	11
CREED OR DOCTRINE, giving expression of, in the Constitution	143	43	1	8
sections 12 and 25 of act establishing the judicial courts of the United				
ates, approved September 24, 1789	86	36	1	7
, fixing compensation and defining duties of, of the Supreme Court				
the United States	861	47	1	10
distribution of, of United States Supreme Court	60	31	2	3
Do	861	47	1	10
TATIVES TO CONGRESS,				
nment prior to ninth census	2	41	3	8
g to ninth census	28	42	2	8
ation of	269	34	3	3
ION, boundary of Sac and Fox Indian (treaty of 1824)	198	27	3	2
LAWS.				
ent for violation of	252	23	1	3
for defects in customs	66	41	2	8

*Parts 1, 2, 3.

Subject.	Report.	Congress.	Session.	Volume.
SUFFRAGE IN DISTRICT OF COLUMBIA, to extend, to colored people	2	39	1	8
SUGAR, right of treaty-making-power to admit, free of duty into the United States	4177	49	2	11
SUPERVISORS OF ELECTIONS, fixing pay of	600	46	2	9
SUPREME COURT OF THE UNITED STATES,				
Appeals to,				
In certain criminal cases	84	36	1	7
Regulating	1572	47	1	10
Do	2728	49	1	11
To regulate, from supreme courts of District of Columbia and Territories	1260	48	1	11
Fees charged by clerk of	318	25	2	2
Judges, number of, to concur on constitutional questions	94	29	2	2
Jurisdiction of	103	45	2	9
Reporter of, duties and compensation of	861	47	1	10
Reports of, distribution of	69	31	2	3
Reorganization of	45	44	1	9
Writs of mandamus in, amending laws regulating issue of	632	47	1	10
SURETY ON BOND OF DISTILLER, release of	4111	49	2	11
SURRATT, JOHN H., arrest of	33	39	2	8
SWEENY, RITTENHOUSE, FANT & CO., deposit on Government loan	189	36	1	7
SYMMES'S PURCHASE, unsold land in	243	33	1	3
SYPHAX, MARIA, title to land	3407	49	1	11
TARIFF LAWS OF 1883, validity of	943	27	2	2
TARIFF ON SUGAR, inquiry into the right of the treaty-making power of the United States to remove	4177	49	2	11
TATE, JUDGE, charges against official conduct of	69	17	2	2
TAXES,				
Direct, collecting, in insurrectionary States	46	44	1	9
Government, in selling lands for taxes does not warrant title	855	27	2	2
Internal-revenue, to refund on capital employed in banking	3964	49	2	11
Refunding, to parties in thirty-second collection district of New York	919	45	2	9
Do	30	46	2	9
TAYLOR, ENOCH, claim for relief	1038	47	1	10
TEED, THEODORE, title to lands near Alexandria, Va	627	46	2	9
TELEGRAPH CENSORSHIP, regarding the existence of a, in Washington	64	37	2	
TELEGRAPH LINES, power of Government to regulate and equalize tariff of rates	125	43	2	
TENNESSEE,				
Chattanooga, United States court at	1206	46	2	
Grundy County, to attach to middle judicial district of	594	48	1	11
Relief of State of	100	43	1	
TEN EYCK, CONRAD, settlement of accounts	174	31	1	
TENNILL, FRANCIS, claim for relief	40	21	1	
TENNILLE, WILLIAM A., claim for relief	72	21	2	
TERRITORIAL COURTS,				
Dakota, an additional justice for	4096	49	2	
Processes of, to authorize service on reservations of	1390	49	1	
TERRITORIAL SUPREME COURTS, writs of error to	667	46	2	
TERRITORIAL VACANCIES, power of governors to fill	4005	49	2	
TERRITORIES,				
Courts of, to authorize service within reservations of processes issued by	1034	48	1	
Incorporation laws of, to amend laws relating to	501	46	1	
Polygamy in	27	39	2	
Do	83	36	1	
Supreme courts of, to authorize appeals from	1260	48	1	
TESTIMONY of accomplices in criminal cases	359	44	1	
TEXARKANA, ARKANSAS, to hold United States courts at	2637	49	1	
TEXAS,				
To define boundaries	1282	47	1	
Courts, United States, location of, in State of	3774	49	2	
Creditors of the late Republic of	236	45	2	
District and circuit courts for western district of	114	46	3	
Eastern and northern judicial districts and to attach part of Indian Territory to them	797	48	1	
Hood County, to attach, to Graham branch of northern judicial district in	102	48	1	
Judicial districts in	691	46	2	
Do	623	49	1	
Lands acquired by judicial proceedings in, to set aside sale of	3640	49	2	
Northern judicial district of	131	46	2	
Republic of, liability of United States for vessels of war transferred to United States Navy at time of annexation of	13	31	2	
TEXAS AND PACIFIC RAILROAD COMPANY, to forfeit land grant to	1803	47	1	
THIERMAN & FROST, compensation for property sold	1815	47	2	
THODY, THOMAS, claim for relief	328	29	1	
Do	38	32	1	
THOMAS, JAMES, settlement of accounts	571	36	1	
THOMPSON, JOHN G., Sergeant-at-Arms of House, payment of judgment and counsel fees	2435	48	2	
Do	2512	46	2	
THOMPSON, MANLIUS V., claim for compensation	440	25	1	
THORBURN, ROBERT D., to remove political disabilities	589	41	2	
THORNTON, J. H. F., and others, for relief of sureties	169	34	1	

Subject.	Report.	Congress.	Session.	Volume.
', Judge BUCKNER, investigating official conduct of	85	18	2	1
Do	327	24	1	2
AC P., compensation for meters furnished distilleries	1972	48	1	11
JOHN, relief from judgment	513	22	1	1
)NATHAN, relief from judgment	272	27	2	2
a, lands in	634	46	2	9
a, title to lands located on grant to Ontonagon and State Line Rail- ad Company	1266	47	1	10
RAISED IN INDIAN TERRITORY, right of United States to col- t internal-revenue tax upon	52	41	2	8
Do	30	41	3	8
Do	6	42	2	8
Do	920	45	2	9
Do	120	46	2	9
)MAS (heirs of), settlement of claims	249	47	1	10
, RAY, and others (governor of New York), settlement of accounts	200	29	1	3
and IMPORTS, judicial remedies for overcharge of duties on	93	43	2	8
OSEPH W., compensation for professional services	44	21	2	1
Do	49	22	1	1
DAH (legal representatives), private land claim	86	33	2	3
.RKS, registration of	561	46	2	9
:R OF UNITED STATES, to provide for absence or disability of	387	49	1	11
s Nation, enforcement of treaty with	30	41	3	8
pe Hidalgo, claimants to land under treaty of	14	41	2	8
laimants under first article of treaty of	208	20	1	1
Do	18	20	2	1
s Islands, inquiry into the power of the President and Senate to make extend treaties involving the admission of any article free of duty o the United States	4177	49	2	11
eaty of February 22, 1819, to carry into effect	16	20	1	1
ower of Executive in making treaties affecting	2680	48	2	11
.THANIEL (heirs of), land claim	337	23	1	1
Do	73	24	1	2
:D MONEYS FROM ESTATES OF BANKRUPTS, redistribution	3920	49	2	11
CIFIC RAILROAD COMPANY,				
Branch, meaning of acts of July 1, 1862, July 1, 1864, and July 3, 1866, cerning	615	43	1	8
l of Edward Learned concerning the organization and conduct of	5	40	3	8
of Attorney-General relating to	3746	49	2	11
TATES,				
of Columbia and, legal relations existing between	627	43	1	8
Ferry, to adjust claim of United States upon purchasers of prop- y at	616	43	1	8
force, employing, by	85	22	2	1
pi, settlement of accounts between	35	44	1	3
:ATES CIRCUIT COURTS. (*See* COURTS OF UNITED STATES.)				
:ATES CONVICTS, claim of Kentucky for maintenance of	443	28	1	2
:ATES PRISON,				
in city of New York	244	33	1	3
lish and erect buildings for	4007	49	2	11
:ATES REGULATION FIRE-ARMS COMPANY, claim for roy- y	1326	46	2	9
Do	1072	47	1	10
TATES SENATORS, election of, by popular vote	3796	49	2	11
'SE, JAMES, land warrant issued to	414	31	1	3
:RITORY, to amend act of 1882 relative to suppression of polygamy	2735	49	1	11
arms and supplies furnished in suppressing the rebellion, settle- nt of claim for	3602	49	2	11
o (schooner), for relief of owners	439	45	2	9
Vashington (steamboat), relief of owners	135	33	1	3
Senora De Regla (ferry-boat), relative to	52	48	1	11
(brig), claim of Noah Brown against	122	15	1	1
ation bills, to amend Constitution giving President power to veto arate items in	1879	49	1	11
, veto of act to prevent military interference with	*19	46	1	9
3, MISSISSIPPI, to hold terms of United States court at	1317	49	1	11
made by, to pay	†1563	48	1	11
transfer of certain, to West Virginia, from	6	39	1	8
listricts, to divide State into two	617	43	1	8
bounty lands of Ohio	1414	47	1	10
tates courts to regulate terms of, in western district	618	43	1	8
Do	1320	48	1	11
812, to settle accounts for money expended during	1670	48	1	11

* And views of minority. (Part 2). †And views of minority.

*And views of minority.

Subject.	Report.	Congress.	Session.	Volume.
IGTON, THOMAS (executors of), claim for relief	21	21	2	1
Do	181	22	1	1
JOEL, claim for relief	95	22	1	1
Do	51	23	1	1
WILLIAM, memorial of, relating to Commonwealth Bank of Boston, Lses	257	28	1	2
se of, by United States courts	228	44	1	9
tion and mandamus in the Supreme Court	683	47	1	10
F ERROR (see also COURTS OF UNITED STATES),				
reme courts of Territories	607	46	2	9
alate, for middle district of Alabama	114	29	1	3
F MANDAMUS, Supreme Court to issue, when sitting as court of admiralty	683	47	1	10
STONE PARK, to authorize service of process within	1084	48	1	11
WILLIAM, pardon of	118	38	1	8
ARLES, surety on bond	271	27	2	2

O

REPORTS

OF THE

OMMITTEE ON LABOR,

HOUSE OF REPRESENTATIVES,

FROM THE ORGANIZATION OF THE COMMITTEE, DECEMBER 23, 1883, TO THE CLOSE OF THE FORTY-NINTH CONGRESS, 1887, INCLUSIVE,

IN ONE VOLUME.

OMPILED, UNDER THE DIRECTION OF THE JOINT COMMITTEE ON PRINTING,

BY

T. H. McKEE,

CLERK, DOCUMENT ROOM, UNITED STATES SENATE.

WASHINGTON:
GOVERNMENT PRINTING OFFICE.
1887.

)213

FORTY-NINTH CONGRESS, FIRST SESSION.

[PUBLIC RESOLUTION—No. 24.]

Joint resolution authorizing the preparation of a compilation of the reports of committees of the Senate and House of Representatives.

Resolved by the Senate and House of Representatives of the United States of America in Congress assembled, That there be prepared under the direction of the Joint Committee of Printing, a compilation of the reports of the Senate and House of Representatives from the Fourteenth to the Forty-eighth Congress, inclusive, classified by committees, arranged, indexed, and bound in suitable volumes for the use of the standing committees of the two Houses of Congress. And the sum of seven thousand seven hundred and fifty dollars, or so much thereof as may be found necessary, is hereby appropriated out of any money in the Treasury not otherwise appropriated, for the preparation of said work, which sum may be paid by the Secretary of the Treasury upon the order of the chairman of said Joint Committee, as additional pay or compensation to any officer or employee of the United States.

Resolved further, That the Clerk of the House and Secretary of the Senate be, and they are hereby directed, to procure and file, for the use of their respective Houses, copies of all reports made by each committee of all succeeding Congresses; and that the Clerk of the House and the Secretary of the Senate be, and they are hereby, authorized and directed at the close of each session of Congress, to cause said reports to be indexed and bound, one copy to be deposited in the library of each House and one copy in the room of the committee from which the reports emanated.

Approved, July 29, 1886.

COMPILER'S NOTICE.

This compilation embraces all the printed reports made by both ouses of Congress from the commencement of the Fourteenth to the ose of the Forty-ninth Congress. They are classified by committees id arranged in numerical order. The collection for each committee is vided into volumes of suitable size. Each committee has a separate dex, a copy being bound in each volume.

The SPECIAL and SELECT reports are all compiled in one collection ving one index, a copy of which is bound in each volume.

The plan throughout the compilation is to place each report to the mmittee from which it was reported, without reference to the subject-atter.

The House and Senate reports are compiled separately. Care will required in noticing the chronological order, as in some instances an tire session or Congress may not appear in certain volumes from the t that during this period no reports were made by this committee.

T. H. McKEE.

INDEX

TO

RTS OF THE COMMITTEE ON LABOR,

HOUSE OF REPRESENTATIVES.

FROM DECEMBER 23, 1883, TO MARCH 4, 1887.

Subject.	Report.	Congress.	Session.	Volume.
OR, prohibiting employment of	369	49	1	1
ibiting employment of, on public works	2045	48	1	1
Do	444	48	1	1
Do	2901	49	1	1
WORKMEN, giving preference to, on public works	2045	48	1	1
ION, creating board for settlement of controversies between common iers and employers	1447	49	1	1
OCCUPIED BY GOVERNMENT. (See GOVERNMENT BUILDINGS.)				
F ENGRAVING AND PRINTING, employés of, relief	515	49	1	1
F LABOR STATISTICS, establishing	342	48	1	1
F UNITED STATES, giving preference to, on public works	2045	48	1	1
CHOOL,				
d in establishment of, fixing date for consideration of, in House of resentatives by Committee on Labor	3554	49	2	
ment and temporary support of	*1993	49	1	
E ON LABOR, fixing date for consideration of bill to aid in support ommon schools	3554	49	2	1
powers of, to limit hours of labor of employés	2044	48	1	1
ION,				
bor, to prohibit States employing	2043	48	1	1
labor, giving Congress power to limit	2044	48	1	1
LABOR, prohibiting importation into United States of	444	48	1	1
Do	2901	49	1	1
ABOR,				
g employment of	1064	48	1	1
Do	217	49	1	1
Do	369	49	1	1
nt to Constitution prohibiting	2043	48	1	1
NT BUILDINGS IN THE DISTRICT OF COLUMBIA, sanitary lition of, investigation of	932	48	1	1
NT OF INTERIOR, establishment of Bureau of Labor Statistics in	342	48	1	1
R LAW,				
ent of	1065	48	1	1
Do	368	49	1	1
employed under, adjusting accounts of	1285	48	1	1
Engraving and Printing, relief to	515	49	1	1
nt Printing Office,				
ing leave of absence to	2015	48	1	1
s of, regulating	3815	49	2	1
s of, restoring	1413	49	1	1
labor required by United States Government of	932	48	1	1
eekly payment of, by Government contractors	4011	49	2	1
print copies of report on condition of labor in	2256	48	2	1
, hours of labor in, to regulate	2044	48	1	1
ABORERS, prohibiting importation of	2901	49	1	1
NT BUILDINGS, sanitary condition of	932	48	1	1
NT CONTRACTORS, payment of wages by, weekly to employés er	4011	49	2	1
NT EMPLOYÉS, enforcing eight hour law for	1065	48	1	1

*And views of minority. Part 1.

Subject.	Report.	Congress.	Session.	Volume.
GOVERNMENT PRINTING OFFICE EMPLOYÉS,				
Granting leave of absence to	2015	48	1	1
Restoring wages to	1418	49	1	1
Wages of	3815	48	2	1
HOURS OF LABOR,				
Of Government employés, to investigate	982	48	1	1
Giving Congress power to limit	2044	42	1	1
LABOR,				
Convict, prohibiting employment of	1064	46	1	1
Do	217	48	1	1
Do	369	48	1	1
Do	1359	49	1	1
Foreign contract, prohibiting importation of	444	48	1	1
Do	369	49	1	1
Do	2901	48	1	1
LABORERS,				
Accounts of, under eight-hour law, to adjust	1285	48	1	1
Wages of, protection to	514	48	1	1
LABOR IN EUROPE, report on condition of, printing of	2256	48	2	1
LABOR STATISTICS, Bureau of, establishment of	342	48	1	1
LABOR TROUBLES, arbitration of, appointment of a commission for	1447	49	1	1
Do	1472	49	1	1
LETTER-CARRIERS, hours of employment of	2732	48	1	1
MECHANICS,				
Accounts of, under eight-hour law, to adjust	1285	48	1	1
Wages, protection of	514	49	1	1
NAVY-YARDS, employés of, leave of absence to	2900	49	1	1
PUBLIC BUILDINGS, sanitary condition of, to investigate	982	48	1	1
PUBLIC WORKS, employment on, to give preference to American workmen	2045	48	1	1
REVISED STATUTES, to amend or repeal section 3738, eight hour law	366	49	1	1
SILK CULTURE, bureau of, to establish	1722	48	1	1
TRADES UNIONS, incorporating national	2699	48	1	1
TREASURY BUILDING, sanitary condition of, improving	982	48	1	1
WAGES,				
Employés, Government Printing Office	3815	48	2	1
Weekly payment of, by Government contractors	4011	49	2	1
WORKMEN, accounts of, under eight-hour law, to adjust	1285	48	1	1

○

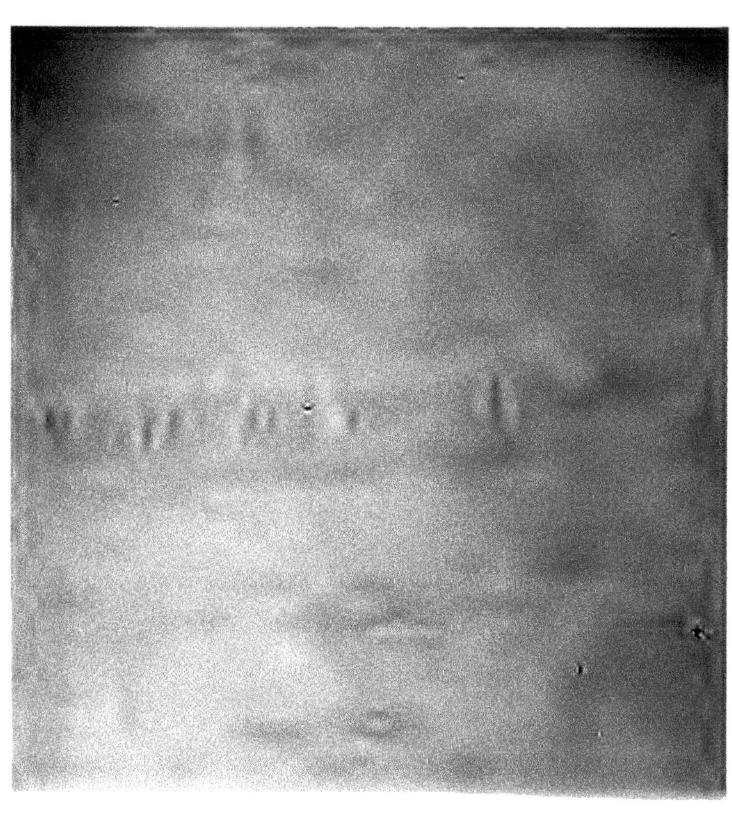

REPORTS

OF THE

MMITTEE ON THE LIB A

HOUSE OF REPRESENTATIVES,

FROM THE FOURTEENTH CONGRESS, 1815, TO THE FORTY-NINTH CONGRESS, 1887, INCLUSIVE.

IN ONE VOLUME.

IPILED, UNDER THE DIRECTION OF THE JOINT COMMITTEE ON PRINTING,

BY

T. H. McKEE,

CLERK, DOCUMENT ROOM, UNITED STATES SENATE.

WASHINGTON:
GOVERNMENT PRINTING OFFICE.
1887.

!245

FORTY-NINTH CONGRESS, FIRST SESSION.

[PUBLIC RESOLUTION—No. 24.]

Joint resolution authorizing the preparation of a compilation of the reports of committees of the Senate and House of Representatives.

Resolved by the Senate and House of Representatives of the United States of America in Congress assembled, That there be prepared under the direction of the Joint Committee of Printing, a compilation of the reports of the Senate and House of Representatives from the Fourteenth to the Forty-eighth Congress, inclusive, classified by committees, arranged, indexed, and bound in suitable volumes for the use of the standing committees of the two Houses of Congress. And the sum of seven thousand seven hundred and fifty dollars, or so much thereof as may be found necessary, is hereby appropriated out of any money in the Treasury not otherwise appropriated, for the preparation of said work, which sum may be paid by the Secretary of the Treasury upon the order of the chairman of said Joint Committee, as additional pay or compensation to any officer or employee of the United States.

Resolved further, That the Clerk of the House and Secretary of the Senate be, and they are hereby directed, to procure and file, for the use of their respective Houses, copies of all reports made by each committee of all succeeding Congresses; and that the Clerk of the House and the Secretary of the Senate be, and they are hereby, authorized and directed at the close of each session of Congress, to cause said reports to be indexed and bound, one copy to be deposited in the library of each House and one copy in the room of the committee from which the reports emanated.

Approved, July 29, 1886.

COMPILER'S NOTICE.

ompilation embraces all the printed reports made by both of Congress from the commencement of the Fourteenth to the the Forty-ninth Congress. They are classified by committees nged in numerical order. The collection for each committee is into volumes of suitable size. Each committee has a separate copy being bound in each volume.

'ECIAL and SELECT reports are all compiled in one collection ne index, a copy of which is bound in each volume.

an throughout the compilation is to place each report to the ee from which it was reported, without reference to the subject-

ouse and Senate reports are compiled separately. Care will red in noticing the chronological order, as in some instances an ssion or Congress may not appear in certain volumes from the during this period no reports were made by this committee.

T. H. McKEE.

INDEX

TO

RTS OF COMMITTEE ON THE LIBRARY,

HOUSE OF REPRESENTATIVES.

FROM 1815 TO 1887, INCLUSIVE.

Subject.	Report.	Congress.	Session.	Volume.
OF SCIENCES. (*See* NATIONAL ACADEMY OF SCIENCES.)				
ONGRESS, distribution of	261	20	1	1
international exhibition commemorative of discovery of	3822	49	2	1
COLONIES, history of, to procure from England and other places pers relating to	91	19	2	1
ajor, captors of, monument to	988	47	1	1
copyright laws to protect, in foreign countries	16	40	2	1
I FOUNTAIN, removal of	1316	48	1	1
I STATUE, pedestal of, making appropriation for	2259	48	2	1
IELDS OF THE REVOLUTION, monuments on, erection of	2123	48	1	1
F BENNINGTON, monument commemorative of	4092	49	2	1
L GARDEN, consolidate, with other public grounds	1315	48	1	1
B., historical portraits, purchase of collection of	46	41	3	1
IUSEUM, publications presented to the Library of Congress by, correspondence relative to	6	37	3	1
LAWRENCE S., relief of	930	48	1	1
E. EDWARD, monument in memory of	2426	48	2	1
OLLECTION OF JAPANESE WORKS OF ART, purchase of	4000	49	2	1
INDIAN GALLERY, purchase of	806	28	1	1
Do	820	30	1	1
S, statue to, selecting site for	3054	49	1	1
E REPORTS, digest of, purchase of	543	28	1	1
tion of acts of	261	20	1	1
as to present condition of work ordered by	186	33	1	1
hanks to John F. Slater by	869	49	1	1
IONAL LIBRARY. (*See* LIBRARY OF CONGRESS.)				
T, American authors in foreign countries, laws to protect	16	40	2	1
steamer), thanks of Congress to officers and crew of	2507	48	2	1
ND (Lake Champlain), monument, commemorative of battle of Plattsrg at	3355	49	1	1
D, CHARLES, gold medal to	*4171	49	2	1
orts of committees, purchase of	543	28	1	1
IC CORRESPONDENCE, publication of, from 1783 to 1789	356	22	1	1
OF COLUMBIA, statues of William Penn and Anthony Wayne, in	2793	49	1	1
TS RELATING TO AMERICA, catalogue of, in Europe	3962	49	2	1
LIBRARY, purchase of	553	28	1	1
EDALS, purchase of medals relating to events of war of Revolution	62	17	1	1
JAMES A., site for statue to	3054	49	1	1
LYSSES S., monument to	1727	49	1	1
H, HORATIO, statue of Washington executed by, removing from rotunda	219	27	3	1
L PORTRAITS, Brady's collection of, purchase of	46	41	3	1
D LAW, monument commemorative of passage of	1317	48	1	1
LLECTION, purchase of, prepared by Catlin	806	28	1	1
Do	820	30	1	1
IONAL COPYRIGHT, American authors in foreign countries, laws to protect	16	40	2	1
IONAL EXHIBITION, commemorative of discovery of	3822	49	2	1
N, THOMAS, manuscript papers of, purchase of	39	29	2	1

* Views of minority, Part 2.

Subject.	Report.	Congress.	Session.	Volume.
LAFAYETTE, General,				
Waln's Biography of, printing of	86	18	2	1
Site for statue to	3054	49	1	1
LAWS OF THE UNITED STATES,				
Printing of stereotype edition of	46	21	2	1
Printing of eighth volume of	608	24	1	1
L'ENFANT, PIERRE CHARLES, monument to memory of	2427	48	2	1
LIBERTY ENLIGHTENING THE WORLD. (*See* BARTHOLDI STATUE.)				
LIBRARY OF CONGRESS,				
Fire in	22	19		1
Making the, fire proof	68	19		1
Publications presented to, by British Museum, correspondence relative to	6	37		1
Additional accommodations for	85	46		1
Do	164	47		1
Building for accommodation of	471	43		1
Do	173	49		1
LINCOLN, ABRAHAM, monument to	3053	49		1
MANUSCRIPTS, list of, and printed books relating to America, in possession of Obadiah Rich	37	20	1	1
MAPS, by Samuel A. Ruddock, of North and South America, printing of	178	19	1	1
MEDALS, purchase of collection of medals in France relating to events of American war of Revolution	62	17	1	1
MERRIL, J. H., relief of	987	47	1	1
MEUCCI, ANTONIO, siege of Yorktown, painting of, by	88	18	2	1
MONMOUTH, commemorative of battle of	907	47	1	1
MONUMENTS,				
Commemorative of Revolutionary battles	795	47	1	1
Commemorative to battle of Monmouth	907	47	1	1
Wyandot Mission, Sandusky, Ohio, at	1376	47	1	1
Do	2428	48	2	1
Statues and tablets for, at Saratoga, N. Y	929	48	1	1
Commemorative of passage of homestead law	1317	48	1	1
Mary, mother of Washington, to complete the	1512	48	1	1
Do	3703	49	2	1
Battle-fields of Revolution, erection of, on	2123	48	1	1
Erecting, to—				
Col. Edward Buncombe	2426	48	2	1
Captors of André	988	47		1
Pierre Charles L'Enfant	2427	48	2	1
Ulysses S. Grant	1727	49	1	1
Daniel Morgan	1869	49		1
Abraham Lincoln	3053	49		1
Crab Island, Lake Champlain, commemorative of battle of Plattsburg, at	3355	49		1
Commemorative of battle of Bennington	4092	49		1
Stony Point, New York, at	2506	49		1
Do	3752	49		1
MORGAN, DANIEL, monument to	1869	49		1
MORRISTOWN, NEW JERSEY, monument at	2123	48		1
NATIONAL ACADEMY OF SCIENCES, trust funds, to receive and hold	1656	48		1
NATIONAL INSTITUTE,				
Russel's planetarium for use of	287	28	1	1
Charter of	539	28	1	1
NEW YORK, statues for subtreasury building in	587	46	2	1
PEALE, TITIAN R., relief of	167	33	1	1
PENN, WILLIAM, statue in District of Columbia of	2793	49	1	1
PLANETARIUM, purchasing Russell's, propriety of	287	28	1	1
PORTRAIT, General George H. Thomas, purchase of	3687	49	2	1
POWELL, WILLIAM H., relief of	47	41	3	1
PRICE, General S. W., purchase of portrait of General George H. Thomas, painted by	3687	49	2	1
PUBLIC DOCUMENTS,				
Distribution of acts of Congress	261	20	1	1
International exchange of	586	26	1	1
Do	590	30	1	1
Classifying, collecting, and publishing of	502	35	1	1
Commission on printing manuscripts belonging to Government	1633	49	1	1
Congress, present condition of work ordered by	186	33	1	1
Diplomatic correspondence, to publish, from 1783 to 1789	356	22	1	1
Laws of United States, to print stereotype edition of	46	21	2	1
Reports of committees, to purchase digest of	543	28	1	1
Vans Murray papers, purchase of	3356	49	1	1
PUBLIC LAWS, distribution of	261	20	1	1
PUBLIC PARKS AND GROUNDS, DISTRICT OF COLUMBIA, consolidation of	1315	48	1	1
REPORTS OF COMMITTEES, digest of	543	28	1	1
REVOLUTIONARY WAR. (*See* WAR OF REVOLUTION.)				
RICH, OBADIAH, Esq., list of manuscripts and printed books relating to America, in possession of	37	20	1	1
RUDDOCK, SAMUEL A., maps of North and South America, printing of	178	19	1	1
RUSSELL'S PLANETARIUM, National Institute, purchase of, for use of	287	28	1	1

Subject.	Report.	Congress.	Session.	Volume.
KY, OHIO, Wyandot Mission, monument at	1376	47	1	1
Do.	2428	48	2	1
GA, NEW YORK, statues and tablets for monument at	920	48	1	1
JOHN F., thanks and medal to	869	49	1	1
AWS, copies of laws of the several States, purchase of	77	20	2	1
S,				
Washington, of	459	22	1	1
Washington, of, removal of	219	27	3	1
easury building in New York, for	587	46	2	1
m Penn and Anthony Wayne, in District of Columbia	2793	49	1	1
bus, Lafayette, and James A. Garfield, sites for	3054	49	1	1
y Taylor	3427	49	1	1
OINT, NEW YORK, monument at	2566	49	1	1
, ZACHARY, statue to	3427	49	1	1
, General GEORGE H., portrait of, by General S. W. Price, to purchase.	3687	49	2	1
RY BUILDING, statues for subtreasury building in New York	587	46	2	1
ES, stereotype edition of United States, printing of	46	21	2	1
UNDS, National Academy of Sciences, to hold	1656	48	1	1
STATES, history of, to procure from England and other places papers relating to the	91	19	2	1
FORGE, monument at	2123	48	1	1
URRAY, WILLIAM, purchase of manuscript belonging to	3256	49	1	1
ARE, ALEXANDRE, international exchange of public documents, plan for	566	28	1	1
Do.	590	30	1	1
THANKS, Congress, to John F. Slater	869	49	1	1
OBERT, Lafayette's biography by, purchase of	86	18	2	1
REVOLUTION,				
ase of medals struck in France commemorating events of	62	17	1	1
ase of paintings of	8	19	2	1
nents commemorative of battles during	795	47	1	1
nents on battle-fields of	2123	48	1	1
GTON, GEORGE,				
of	459	22	1	1
al of statue of	219	27	3	1
GTON'S HEADQUARTERS. (See MORRISTOWN, N. J.)				
GTON, Mary, mother of, monument to, completion of	1513	48	1	1
ANTHONY, statue in District of Columbia of	2793	49	1	1
OF ART, Capron collection of Japanese, purchase of	4000	49	2	1
OT MISSION, OHIO, monument at	1376	47	1	1
Do	2428	48	2	1
WN, VIRGINIA, picture of siege, Antonio Meucci to paint	88	18	2	1

REPORTS

OF THE

EE ON LEVEES AND IMPROVEMENTS O

HOUSE OF REPRESENTATIVES,

THE ORGANIZATION OF COMMITTEE, DECEMBER 10, 18 TO THE CLOSE OF THE FORTY-NINTH CONGRESS, 1887, INCLUSIVE.

IN ONE VOLUME.

LED, UNDER THE DIRECTION OF THE JOINT COMMITTEE ON PRINTING,

BY

T. H. McKEE,

CLERK, DOCUMENT ROOM, UNITED STATES SENATE.

WASHINGTON:
GOVERNMENT PRINTING OFFICE.
1887.

256

FORTY-NINTH CONGRESS, FIRST SESSION.

[PUBLIC RESOLUTION—No. 24.]

Joint resolution authorizing the preparation of a compilation of the reports c mittees of the Senate and House of Representatives.

Resolved by the Senate and House of Representatives of the States of America in Congress assembled, That there be prepared the direction of the Joint Committee of Printing, a compilation reports of the Senate and House of Representatives from the teenth to the Forty-eighth Congress, inclusive, classified by comm arranged, indexed, and bound in suitable volumes for the use standing committees of the two Houses of Congress. And the s seven thousand seven hundred and fifty dollars, or so much then may be found necessary, is hereby appropriated out of any mo the Treasury not otherwise appropriated, for the preparation o work, which sum may be paid by the Secretary of the Treasury the order of the chairman of said Joint Committee, as additional compensation to any officer or employee of the United States.

Resolved further, That the Clerk of the House and Secretary Senate be, and they are hereby directed, to procure and file, for t of their respective Houses, copies of all reports made by each co tee of all succeeding Congresses; and that the Clerk of the Hous the Secretary of the Senate be, and they are hereby, authorize directed at the close of each session of Congress, to cause said r to be indexed and bound, one copy to be deposited in the libr each House and one copy in the room of the committee from whic reports emanated.

Approved, July 29, 1886.

2

COMPILER'S NOTICE.

This compilation embraces all the printed reports made by both Houses of Congress from the commencement of the Fourteenth to the close of the Forty-ninth Congress. They are classified by committees and arranged in numerical order. The collection for each committee is divided into volumes of suitable size. Each committee has a separate index, a copy being bound in each volume.

The SPECIAL and SELECT reports are all compiled in one collection, having one index, a copy of which is bound in each volume.

The plan throughout the compilation is to place each report to the committee from which it was reported, without reference to the subject-matter.

The House and Senate reports are compiled separately. Care will be required in noticing the chronological order, as in some instances an entire session or Congress may not appear in certain volumes from the fact that during this period no reports were made by this committee.

T. H. McKEE.

INDEX

TO

[R]EPORTS OF COMMITTEE ON LEVEES AND IMPROVEMENTS OF MISSISSIPPI RIVER,

HOUSE OF REPRESENTATIVES.

FROM 1875 TO 1887, INCLUSIVE.

Subject.	Report.	Congress.	Session.	Volume.
ANNEL, geology of the Mississippi River	44	42	2	1
TON MANUFACTURERS' ASSOCIATION, statement giving number of cotton mills in Southern States in 1868	44	42	1	1
TON MILLS, returns of National Association of Cotton Manufacturers and Planters in 1868	44	42	2	1
LTA,				
Area of the delta of the Mississippi River	44	42	2	1
Reclaiming and protecting levees along Mississippi River	418	43	1	1
Do	494	44	1	1
VEES,				
Mississippi River,				
Improvement of, from Saint Louis to Gulf of Mexico	714	45	2	1
History of	418	43	1	1
Advantages of the outlet system for protection of	44	42	2	1
Protection by artificial means of	494	44	1	1
Outlet system, advantages of, for protection of	44	42	2	1
WER MISSISSIPPI RIVER, historic account of great floods occurring in	44	42	2	1
SSISSIPPI RIVER,				
Channel of, geology of	44	42	2	1
Delta, defining the limits of the Mississippi River delta	44	42	2	1
Diverting tributaries from	494	44	1	1
Estimate, appropriations for improvement of	848	47	1	1
Floods, detailed notice of some of the great floods occurring in the Lower Mississippi River	44	42	2	1
Improvement of,				
From Saint Louis to Gulf of Mexico	714	45	2	1
Historical notes on	714	45	2	1
Best method of	1575	46	2	1
From Cairo to Gulf of Mexico	*1985	47	2	1
Jetties, prolongation of channel by	*1985	47	2	1
Levees,				
Organization of, in different States	44	42	2	1
Advantages of the outlet system for protection of	44	42	2	1
Protection from inundation of	44	42	2	1
Delta, improvement of	418	43	1	1
Efforts of the States towards protection and reclamation	418	43	1	1
Climate and physical geography	418	43	1	1
History of, description of alluvial basin of	418	43	1	1
Basin, improvement of	418	43	1	1
National character of the work	418	43	1	1
Results of partial reclamation	418	43	1	1
Improving low water by	*1985	47	2	1
Appropriation for preservation and repair of	4170	49	2	1
National highway, improvement of	714	45	2	1
Outlet system, advantages for protecting levees by the	44	42	2	1

* And views of minority.

	Report.	Congress.	Session.	Volume.
MISSISSIPPI RIVER COMMISSION, estimates, plans, and specifications for improvement of Mississippi River, submitted by	848	47	1	1
MISSISSIPPI RIVER LEVEES,				
Arkansas, diverting tributaries from	494	44	1	1
Delta, reclaiming and protecting from overflow the land contained in the	494	44	1	1
Outlets, relief from overflows by system of	494	44	1	1
Preservation and repair of, appropriation for	4176	49	2	1
Reservoirs, protection in flood season to	494	44	1	1
MISSISSIPPI VALLEY, reclamation of lands in	44	42	2	1
OHIO RIVER,				
Reservoirs at the headwaters of	494	44	1	1
Tributaries to	494	44	1	1
OUTLET SYSTEM, advantages of for protection of Mississippi River levees	44	42	1	1
RECLAMATION, value of reclaiming lands along the Mississippi River	44	42	2	1
RESERVOIRS, Mississippi River levees, improvement to navigation	494	44	1	1

REPORTS

OF THE

MMITTEE ON MA UF CT

HOUSE OF REPRESENTATIVES,

FROM THE FOURTEENTH CONGRESS, 1815, TO THE
FORTY-NINTH CONGRESS, 1887, INCLUSIVE,

IN ONE VOLUME.

OMPILED, UNDER THE DIRECTION OF THE JOINT COMMITTEE ON PRINTING,

BY

T. H. McKEE,

CLERK, DOCUMENT ROOM, UNITED STATES SENATE.

WASHINGTON:
GOVERNMENT PRINTING OFFICE.
1887.

10 MAN H

FORTY-NINTH CONGRESS, FIRST SESSION.

[PUBLIC RESOLUTION—No. 24.]

Joint resolution authorizing the preparation of a compilation of the reports of committees of the Senate and House of Representatives.

Resolved by the Senate and House of Representatives of the United States of America in Congress assembled, That there be prepared under the direction of the Joint Committee of Printing, a compilation of the reports of the Senate and House of Representatives from the Fourteenth to the Forty-eighth Congress, inclusive, classified by committees, arranged, indexed, and bound in suitable volumes for the use of the standing committees of the two Houses of Congress. And the sum of seven thousand seven hundred and fifty dollars, or so much thereof as may be found necessary, is hereby appropriated out of any money in the Treasury not otherwise appropriated, for the preparation of said work, which sum may be paid by the Secretary of the Treasury upon the order of the chairman of said Joint Committee, as additional pay or compensation to any officer or employee of the United States.

Resolved further, That the Clerk of the House and Secretary of the Senate be, and they are hereby directed, to procure and file, for the use of their respective Houses, copies of all reports made by each committee of all succeeding Congresses; and that the Clerk of the House and the Secretary of the Senate be, and they are hereby, authorized and directed at the close of each session of Congress, to cause said reports to be indexed and bound, one copy to be deposited in the library of each House and one copy in the room of the committee from which the reports emanated.

Approved, July 29, 1886.

COMPILER'S NOTICE.

This compilation embraces all the printed reports made by both
uses of Congress from the commencement of the Fourteenth to the
se of the Forty-ninth Congress. They are classified by committees
l arranged in numerical order. The collection for each committee is
ided into volumes of suitable size. Each committee has a separate
lex, a copy being bound in each volume.

The SPECIAL and SELECT reports are all compiled in one collection
ving one index, a copy of which is bound in each volume.

The plan throughout the compilation is to place each report to the
mmittee from which it was reported, without reference to the subject-
atter.

The House and Senate reports are compiled separately. Care will
required in noticing the chronological order, as in some instances an
tire session or Congress may not appear in certain volumes from the
ct that during this period no reports were made by this committee.

T. H. McKEE.

INDEX

TO

RTS OF THE COMMITTEE ON MANUFACTURES,

HOUSE OF REPRESENTATIVES.

FROM 1815 TO 1887, INCLUSIVE.

Subject.	Report.	Congress.	Session.	Volume.
TION in articles of food and drink	346	46	2	1
RAL PRODUCTS, necessity of protection to secure a market for..	67	40	2	1
RE, liability of protective duties to destroy	34	16	2	1
LABOR, providing for the protection of	95	39	1	1
INDUSTRY, protection of	67	40	2	1
ALES, modifying law regulating	34	16	2	1
STEEL, effects of tariff on	*72	41	2	1
MATERIAL, appointment of commission to investigate production use of metallic and other structural material	1307	47	1	1
Do	629	48	1	1
Do	508	49	1	1
TTON, protective tariff on	*461	27	2	1
ND LABOR, relations between	67	40	2	1
tive tariff on	*461	27	2	1
Do	*72	41	2	1
s on	*72	41	2	1
protective duties upon	34	16	2	1
.L TRAVELERS, for relief	1321	48	1	1
S, amending act to revise and consolidate statute referring to	3	46	2	1
rotective tariff on.	*461	27	2	1
reign, repeal of	324	25	3	1
ving exportations from East India of	*461	27	2	1
TH, manufacture of	115	20	1	1
Do	*461	27	2	1
NUFACTURE, tariff system, effect of, on	*72	41	2	1
TIES. (*See* IMPORT DUTIES.)				
ILLIAM, and others, memorial for repeal of duty on importation reign cotton	324	25	3	1
.TING DUTIES. (*See* IMPORT DUTIES.)				
MANUFACTURES,				
law protecting	115	20	1	1
of, message on	122	22	2	1
S, on import duties, remonstrance against abolition of	7	16	2	1
IMPORTS. (*See* IMPORT DUTIES.)				
. COTTON. (*See* COTTON.)				
EBBING, duty on, rate of	*72	41	2	1
omparative benefits of tariff system to	*72	41	2	1
RAILROAD, extension of	113	28	1	1
o HEMP), duty on, fixing rate	115	20	1	1
NN, CHARLES LEWIS, manufacture sugar-beet, by	319	25	3	1
DRINK, protection of, against adulteration	346	46	2	1
OTTON. (*See* COTTON.)				
ARBLE. (*See* MARBLE; IMPORT DUTIES.)				
facture of	115		1	1
Do	*461		2	1
TH AND GUNNY BAGS, comparative benefits of tariff system on.	*72		2	1
FLAX, amending law fixing rate of duty on imported	115	20	1	1
JFACTURES, progress of	*72	[illegible]	2	1

*And views of minority.

Subject.	Report.	Congress.	Session.
IMPORT DUTIES,			
Auction sales, modifying law regulating	34	16	2
Cash payments, to amend law regulating	34	16	2
Discriminating duties, amending law for	34	16	2
Do	*461	27	2
Domestic manufactures	122	22	2
Drawbacks	7	16	2
Increase of	34	16	2
On marble	551	23	1
Modifying acts, regulating	420	23	1
Do	67	40	2
Rates on, regulating	34	16	2
Do	115	20	1
Do	64	21	1
Do	36	21	2
IMPORTS,			
Revenue from	*72	41	2
Salt, restoration of duty on imported	70	21	2
Wool, increase of duty on	48	38	1
INCOME TAX, amending law regulating	344	46	1
INDUSTRIES,			
Growth of	*72	41	2
American, protection of	67	40	2
INTERNAL REVENUE, report of special commissioner on	72	41	2
IRON, duty on, rate of	115	20	1
Do	208	21	1
Do	72	41	2
LABOR, AMERICAN, protection of	95	39	1
LABOR AND CAPITAL, relations between	67	40	2
LEGACIES, amending law taxing	344	46	2
LUMBER, tariff on, effect of	72	41	2
MANUFACTURES,			
Authorizing printing of reports on	64	22	2
Domestic, protecting	115	20	1
Do	122	22	2
Do	95	39	1
Do	67	40	2
Do	72	41	2
Number of persons employed in	*72	41	2
METALS, providing for tests of	234	46	2
Do	1307	47	1
Do	629	48	1
Do	508	49	1
MARBLE, duty on, increasing	551	23	1
MERCANTILE SOCIETY OF NEW YORK, statement made before Committee on Manufactures by representatives of	34	16	2
MIDDLE STATES, silk culture in	287	24	2
MINERS, WELSH. (*See* WELSH MINERS)			
MORALS, effect of manufactures upon	34	16	2
NEW ENGLAND STATES, silk culture in	287	24	2
PAPER, duty on, fix rate	115	20	1
Do	461	27	2
PATENTS, to revise and consolidate statute referring to	3	46	2
PAUPERISM, liability of manufactures to produce	34	16	2
PRINTING. (*See* PUBLIC DOCUMENTS.)			
PROTECTION, views of early statesmen on	67	40	2
PROTECTIVE DUTIES, constitutionality of	34	16	2
RATES. (*See* IMPORT DUTIES.)			
REPORTS ON MANUFACTURES, printing of	64	22	2
REVISED STATUTES, section 17, chapter 10, income and legacy tax, to repeal	344	46	2
SALT, duty on	70	21	2
Do	72	41	2
SHOE AND LEATHER BUSINESS, protective tariff for	*461	27	2
SILK, manufacture and culture of	287	24	2
SMUGGLING, liability of protective duties to increase	34	16	2
SOUTHERN STATES, silk culture in	287	24	2
SPIRITS MADE FROM GRAIN, manufacture of	115	20	1
SPIRITS MADE FROM MOLASSES, manufacture of	115	20	1
STEEL,			
Duty on	115	20	1
Undervaluations of	72	41	2
SUGAR, duty on	461	27	2
Do	72	41	2
TARIFF. (*See also* IMPORT DUTIES.)			
Canvas	*461	27	2
Coal	*461	27	2
Cordage	*461	27	2
Discrimination in, assessment of duties	*461	27	2
Domestic manufactures	115	20	1

* And views of minority.

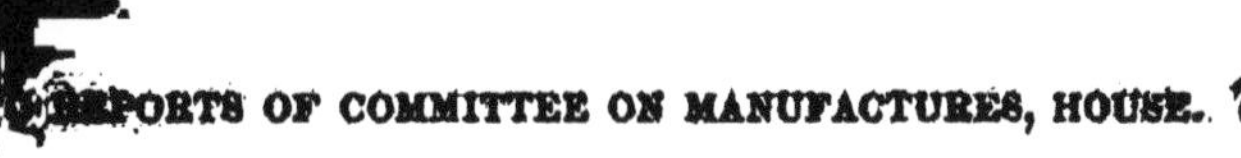

Subject.	Report.	Congress.	Session.	Volume.
se also IMPORT DUTIES)—Continued.				
flax	115	20	1	1
	115	20	1	1
Do	266	21	1	1
Do	72	41	2	1
egulate	481	22	1	1
Do	420	28	1	1
	551	23	1	1
	115	20	1	1
	84	21	1	1
Do	461	23	1	1
	70	21	2	1
	287	24	2	1
eather business	*461	27	2	1
	*461	27	2	1
	*72	41	2	1
lace	115	20	1	1
	48	28	1	1
woolens	115	20	1	1
ETALS, investigation of	224	*46	2	1
ariff on	*461	27	2	1
DUTIES, regulating	67	40	2	1
RKS, protection of	8	46	2	1
ING SYSTEM, modifying law governing	67	40	2	1
ates of duty upon elastic	*72	41	2	1
ERS IN AMERICA, condition of	*96	30	1	1
STATES, silk culture in	287	24	2	1
LASS, duty on	115	2	1	1
on	48	28	1	1
WOOLENS,				
	115	20	1	1
are of	*461	27	2	1
Do	72	41	2	1

*And views of minority.

REPORTS

OF THE

OMMITTEE ON MILEAGE,

HOUSE OF REPRESENTATIVES,

FROM THE ORGANIZATION OF COMMITTEE, SEPTEMBER 15, 1837, TO THE CLOSE OF THE FORTY-NINTH CONGRESS, 1887, INCLUSIVE.

IN ONE VOLUME.

COMPILED, UNDER THE DIRECTION OF THE JOINT COMMITTEE ON PRINTING,

BY

T. H. McKEE,

CLERK, DOCUMENT ROOM, UNITED STATES SENATE.

WASHINGTON:
GOVERNMENT PRINTING OFFICE.
1887.

9269

FORTY-NINTH CONGRESS, FIRST SESSION.

[PUBLIC RESOLUTION—No. 24.]

Joint resolution authorizing the preparation of a compilation of the reports of c mittees of the Senate and House of Representatives.

Resolved by the Senate and House of Representatives of the Un States of America in Congress assembled, That there be prepared ui the direction of the Joint Committee of Printing, a compilation of reports of the Senate and House of Representatives from the F teenth to the Forty-eighth Congress, inclusive, classified by committ arranged, indexed, and bound in suitable volumes for the use of standing committees of the two Houses of Congress. And the su seven thousand seven hundred and fifty dollars, or so much there may be found necessary, is hereby appropriated out of any mone the Treasury not otherwise appropriated, for the preparation of work, which sum may be paid by the Secretary of the Treasury i the order of the chairman of said Joint Committee, as additional pa compensation to any officer or employee of the United States.

Resolved further, That the Clerk of the House and Secretary of Senate be, and they are hereby directed, to procure and file, for the of their respective Houses, copies of all reports made by each com tee of all succeeding Congresses; and that the Clerk of the House the Secretary of the Senate be, and they are hereby, authorized directed at the close of each session of Congress, to cause said rep to be indexed and bound, one copy to be deposited in the librar each House and one copy in the room of the committee from which reports emanated.

Approved, July 29, 1886.

COMPILER'S NOTICE.

This compilation embraces all the printed reports made by both Houses of Congress from the commencement of the Fourteenth to the close of the Forty-ninth Congress. They are classified by committees and arranged in numerical order. The collection for each committee is divided into volumes of suitable size. Each committee has a separate index, a copy being bound in each volume.

The SPECIAL and SELECT reports are all compiled in one collection having one index, a copy of which is bound in each volume.

The plan throughout the compilation is to place each report to the committee from which it was reported, without reference to the subject-matter.

The House and Senate reports are compiled separately. Care will be required in noticing the chronological order, as in some instances an entire session or Congress may not appear in certain volumes from the fact that during this period no reports were made by this committee.

T. H. McKEE.

INDEX

TO

RTS OF COMMITTEE ON MILEAGE,

HOUSE OF REPRESENTATIVES.

FROM 1837 TO 1887, INCLUSIVE.

Subject.	Report.	Congress.	Session.	Volume.
IILEAGE, Sherrod Williams asking for	376	27	2	1
NS OF CONGRESS, for payment of mileage to members of s for attendance upon	2	45	1	1
CONGRESS,				
uniform rule for computing mileage of	587	26	1	1
o	72	34	3	1
amount of mileage drawn by	23	30	2	1
uniform rule for computing mileage of members of Congress	587	26	1	1
to members of Congress for attendance upon extra sessions of s	2	45	1	1
IZABETH F., to pay additional mileage due late Hon. Samuel ston to	41	31	1	1

REPORTS

OF THE

MMITTEE ON MILITARY AFFAIRS,

HOUSE OF REPRESENTATIVES,

FROM THE FOURTEENTH CONGRESS, 1815, TO THE FORTY-NINTH CONGRESS, 1887, INCLUSIVE,

IN FIFTEEN VOLUMES.

OMPILED, UNDER THE DIRECTION OF THE JOINT COMMITTEE ON PRINTING,

BY

T. H. McKEE,
CLERK, DOCUMENT ROOM, UNITED STATES SENATE.

WASHINGTON:
GOVERNMENT PRINTING OFFICE.
1887.

9215 MIL H

FORTY-NINTH CONGRESS, FIRST SESSION.

[PUBLIC RESOLUTION—No. 24.]

Joint resolution authorizing the preparation of a compilation of the reports of mittees of the Senate and House of Representatives.

Resolved by the Senate and House of Representatives of the Ui States of America in Congress assembled, That there be prepared u the direction of the Joint Committee of Printing, a compilation of reports of the Senate and House of Representatives from the F teenth to the Forty-eighth Congress, inclusive, classified by commit arranged, indexed, and bound in suitable volumes for the use of standing committees of the two Houses of Congress. And the su seven thousand seven hundred and fifty dollars, or so much there may be found necessary, is hereby appropriated out of any mone the Treasury not otherwise appropriated, for the preparation of work, which sum may be paid by the Secretary of the Treasury the order of the chairman of said Joint Committee, as additional p compensation to any officer or employee of the United States.

Resolved further, That the Clerk of the House and Secretary of Senate be, and they are hereby directed, to procure and file, for th of their respective Houses, copies of all reports made by each com tee of all succeeding Congresses; and that the Clerk of the House the Secretary of the Senate be, and they are hereby, authorized directed at the close of each session of Congress, to cause said rep to be indexed and bound, one copy to be deposited in the librar each House and one copy in the room of the committee from which reports emanated.

Approved, July 29, 1886.

2

COMPILER'S NOTICE.

This compilation embraces all the printed reports made by both ouses of Congress from the commencement of the Fourteenth to the se of the Forty-ninth Congress. They are classified by committees d arranged in numerical order. The collection for each committee is vided into volumes of suitable size. Each committee has a separate dex, a copy being bound in each volume.

The SPECIAL and SELECT reports are all compiled in one collection ving one index, a copy of which is bound in each volume.

The plan throughout the compilation is to place each report to the mmittee from which it was reported, without reference to the subject-atter.

The House and Senate reports are compiled separately. Care will e required in noticing the chronological order, as in some instances an ntire session or Congress may not appear in certain volumes from the ct that during this period no reports were made by this committee.

T. H. McKEE.

INDEX

TO

RTS OF COMMITTEE ON MILITARY AFFAIRS,

HOUSE OF REPRESENTATIVES.

FROM 1815 TO 1887, INCLUSIVE.

Subject.	Report.	Congress.	Session.	Volume.
ANNUITY FUND, Army officers, to create for	56	43	2	9
ANTISELL, THOMAS, medical services rendered to United States troops, claim for	204	35	1	5
APPLING, DANIEL, prize money, claim of legal representatives for	68	16	1	1
APPOINTMENTS, sale of, to Military and Naval Academies by members of Congress	29	41		
Do	39	41		
Do	42	41		
APPROPRIATION,				
Army, making annual appropriation for support of, 1887-'88	3489	49		15
Fort Douglas military reservation, to purchase lands at	3973	49		15
Military Academy, annual appropriation for support of, 1887-'88	3491	49		15
Military post, to establish, near Denver, Colo	3544	49		15
Pensacola, Fla., for fortifications at	119	20		1
ARBUTHNOTT, ALEXANDER, court-martial, trial of	82	15		1
ARIZONA, cavalry in, to raise regiment of volunteer	*531	49		15
Lawlessness in, use United States troops as *posse comitatus* to suppress	1151	47		12
Military roads in, to construct	300	44		11
ARKANSAS,				
Arkansas volunteers,				
Relief for services in war of rebellion	2170	48	2	13
To remove charges of desertion from Third Regiment of	914	49	1	15
Frontiers of, protection of	255	23	1	2
Do	442	24	1	2
Natchitoches, La., to construct military road to Gibson Cantonment in	67	19	1	1
ARLINGTON, VIRGINIA.				
Cemetery at, to improve road to	1185	47	1	12
Title of United States to grounds at	13	41	3	7
ARMBRISTER, ROBERT C., court-martial trial of	82	15	2	1
ARMES, GEORGE A., Army, to restore to	19	42	3	8
Do	620	44	1	10
ARMORIES (*see also* NATIONAL ARMORIES),				
Harper's Ferry, to establish at	194	44	1	10
Massac, Ill., to establish at	441	28	1	3
Do	451	29	1	4
Do	214	31	1	4
Shelby County, Alabama, to establish in	152	35	2	5
Western waters, to establish on	349	23	1	2
Do	378	24	1	2
ARMS (*see also* MILITIA),				
Indiana, issue to State	388	31	1	4
Iowa, issue to State of	489	28	1	3
Militia in Territories, to issue to	83	18	1	1
Sale, distribution, and disposal since January, 1860	85	36	2	6
Washington Territory,				
Erection of depository for, in	85	33	2	5
To credit, on books of Ordnance Department, loaned Oregon	4053	49	2	15
ARMSTRONG, FRANCIS, injuries received in line of duty, claim for	680	44	1	10
Do	237	45	2	11
ARMSTRONG, JAMES, money expended for rent of quarters, to reimburse	399	31	1	4
Do	237	35	1	5
ARMSTRONG, WILLIAM C., relief of	1964	49	1	15
ARMY,				
Accounts,				
Settlement of officers'	1	41	1	7
Do	296	44	1	10
To continue act of 1870 for settlement of officers'	670	48	1	13
Adjutant-General, grades in office of, to rearrange	3758	49	1	15
Appointments in,				
Captains of the line, prohibiting in, the staff from	286	22		2
Dental surgeons	743	44		10
Hospital stewards in, to regulate and pay	1405	47		12
Lieutenants in, additional	2538	48	2	13
Non-commissioned officers, to commission from meritorious	60	21	2	2
Surgeons and assistant surgeons in	782	29	1	4
Appropriations for, making annual (1886-'87, 1887-'88)	862	49		15
Do	3489	49		15
Ardent spirits, use by soldiers in	166	21		2
Articles of war, to amend article 103	674	46		11
Bounty and pay due to enlisted men serving during war of 1812	68	14	2	1
Boys, enlistment of, for instruction	125	26	2	3
Brevets,				
Duties and rights of officers holding commissions by	58	20		2
Do	47	21		2
Supernumerary second lieutenants by, to discharge	60	21		2
To confer, for Indian wars	1290	47	1	12
Do	623	48	1	13
Civil process in, discharging recruits who are infants under	58	29	2	4
Clothing, gratuitous issue in cases of loss of	812	47		12
Desertion in, remedy for	63	22		2

*Parts 1, 2.

Subject.	Report.	Congress.	Session.	Volume.
MY—Continued.				
Courts-martial, compensation for officers serving on	1300	47	1	12
Deposits, savings deposit of soldiers, to amend law of	15	43	2	9
Discharges from,				
Claim of soldiers who enlisted to fill old regiments	14	38	2	7
Mounted Riflemen	542	30	1	4
Supernumerary second lieutenants by brevet	60	21	2	2
Under civil process in cases of enlistment	58	29	2	4
Dragoons,				
To convert battalion of mounted rangers into regiment of	17	22	2	2
To remount Second Regiment of	77	28	1	3
Efficiency of, to promote	1408	49	1	15
Engineers,				
Increase and reorganization of corps	35	18	2	1
Do	36	19	1	1
Do	42	21	1	2
Do	4	23	2	2
Do	5	23	2	2
Do	95	24	1	2
Do	29	31	2	4
Additional force in office of	96	24	1	2
Extra allowance to officers stationed at Fort Kearney	128	34	3	5
General, to continue grade of	615	48	1	13
General-service men in, enlistment and pay of	1947	49	1	15
Headstones, furnishing soldiers'	802	44	1	10
Horses lost in,				
Changing mode and place of adjudicating claims for	295	28	1	4
To extend time for filing claims for	1278	46	2	11
Hospital stewards in, appointment and pay of	1405	47	1	12
Do	3658	49	2	15
Indian wars, brevets for service in	1290	47	1	12
Do	623	48	1	13
Increase of, adding four new regiments	107	35	1	5
Inspector-General's Department,				
Promotions in	196	43	1	9
Reorganization of	330	48	1	13
To increase and fix	321	28	1	3
Do	1839	47	2	12
Judge-advocates, promotion in corps of	812	48	1	13
Laundresses, relative to	204	49	1	15
Lieutenant-General, to continue grade of	615	48	1	13
Major-general, to abolish grade of	46	23	2	2
Medical Corps,				
Dental surgeons in, appointment of	743	44	1	10
Promotion in, to regulate	2883	49	1	15
Surgeons and assistant surgeons in, to amend law for admission	782	29	1	4
Missouri Cavalry, to adjudicate claim of Fifteenth and Sixteenth	902	45	2	11
Mounted Rangers, to convert battalion into regiment of dragoons	17	22	2	2
National armories,				
Increasing salaries of officers at	403	24	1	2
Appointing Army officers superintendents of	596	27	2	3
Non-commissioned officers,				
Appointments in line from meritorious	60	21	2	2
Do	286	22	1	2
Re-enlistment of	904	27	2	4
Sergeants, to increase pay of	51	18	2	1
Non-commissioned staff, increasing pay of	1162	47	1	12
Do	1209	47	1	12
Officers in,				
Accounts, settlement of	1	41	2	7
Do	206	44	1	10
Employment in departments	61	16	2	1
Lieutenants in, appointment of additional	2538	48	2	13
Muster and pay of, to regulate	51	40	2	7
Number of commissioned, to reduce	220	27	3	3
Pay of, to regulate	9	22	1	2
Rank and pay, to regulate	684	47	1	12
Record of volunteers, to correct	1341	48	1	13
Second Regiment of Artillery, vacant colonelcy in	85	21	1	2
Supernumerary power of President to muster out	27	42	2	8
Trial of incompetent, to organize board for	20	46	3	11
Volunteers, pay of	2251	48	2	13
Officers' families, apportionment of pay to	2045	49	1	15
Organization of,				
Peace establishment	40	19	2	1
Do	40	33	2	5
Do	384	43	1	9
Do	354	44	1	10
Re-enlistment of non-commissioned officers	904	27	2	4
Paymasters in,				
Rank of	16	22	2	2

Subject.	Report.	Congress.	Session.	Volume.
ARMY—Continued.				
Paymasters in—Continued.				
Additional	4	25	2	[illegible]
Do	166	26	1	[illegible]
Paymasters clerks, salaries of	730	45	1	13
Posse comitatus, employment of United States troops in Territories as	1251	45	1	[illegible]
Post schools, schoolmasters for, enlistment of	1436	47	1	12
Private property lost in,				
By officers at Fort Delaware, to reimburse for	213	32	1	[illegible]
By soldiers at Fort Sumter, to reimburse for	79	38	2	[illegible]
By officers at Hancock barracks, to reimburse for	112	32	1	[illegible]
By officers and soldiers on board steamships Winfield Scott and San Francisco, to reimburse for	50	34	2	5
By soldiers while on march or in battle, to reimburse for	22	35	1	7
Third Cavalry, Company F, to reimburse for	816	43	1	9
Ninth Infantry, to reimburse for	292	43	2	[illegible]
Fourteenth Infantry, Company B, to reimburse for	824	43	1	9
Do	1524	47	1	12
Settlement of claims for	984	48	1	13
Do	1045	48	1	13
Sixth Cavalry, Company C, to reimburse for	53	44	1	10
Third Artillery, officers of, to reimburse for	105	44	1	10
Promotion in,				
Of officers in regiments below minimum strength	136	49	1	[illegible]
Of officers from the ranks	189	44	2	11
Quartermaster-General,				
Rental of buildings for offices of	787	44	1	10
Quartermaster's Department, organization of	4	18	2	[illegible]
Do	22	19	1	[illegible]
Recruiting stations, one thousand additional men for instruction at	1403	47	1	12
Recruits, post trader and laundrymen to give credit to	1147	47	1	12
Re-enlistments in, to extend period for	1570	48	1	13
Regulations for, President authorized to promulgate	592	43	1	[illegible]
Reorganization of, explanatory of act of March 2, 1821	52	17	1	[illegible]
Do	5	17	2	[illegible]
Do	46	18	2	[illegible]
Do	85	21	1	5
Restoration to, of officers	189	49	1	15
Retired officers,				
Detail in colleges as instructors	676	48	2	11
To hold civil office in Territories	18	47	1	12
Retiring in,				
Of enlisted men, to amend act for	1225	47	1	12
Do	616	48	1	13
Of Army officers, to amend sections 1224 and 1253 Revised Statutes for	125	46	2	11
Do	1157	47	1	12
Sappers and miners, to organize company of	559	37	2	3
Do	131	28	2	3
School of instruction, to establish, for cavalry and light artillery	1948	49	1	15
Schoolmasters, enlistment of, for post schools	1425	47	1	12
Signal Service in,				
Assistant to Chief Signal Officer in	2539	48	2	13
Signal Service, efficiency of the	1156	47	1	12
Staff of,				
Pay of officers of	308	24	1	[illegible]
Reorganization of	33	40	3	[illegible]
Do	74	42	3	[illegible]
Strength of, distribution and	24	16	[illegible]	[illegible]
Subsistence Department, reorganization of	315	23	[illegible]	[illegible]
Supplies for, transportation of	17	43	[illegible]	[illegible]
Tactics, printing of copies of cavalry, infantry, and artillery	419	23	[illegible]	[illegible]
Telegraph, to establish, at Point Jupiter, Florida	639	49	[illegible]	[illegible]
Tobacco for, mode of purchasing	679	46	[illegible]	11
Do	207	49	[illegible]	15
Transportation, army supplies	17	43	[illegible]	[illegible]
Troops,				
Cause for ordering troops from Fort Union to Colfax	16	44	[illegible]	11
Efficiency of volunteer forces	[illegible]	37	[illegible]	[illegible]
Wagonmasters in, retirement of	200	49	[illegible]	15
Widows and children, provisions for, officers'	56	43	[illegible]	[illegible]
ARMY ASYLUM (*see also* SOLDIERS' HOMES),				
Carlisle barracks, to convert, into	266	20	1	[illegible]
Invalid soldiers, to establish, for	94	20	2	[illegible]
Do	74	26	2	[illegible]
Do	109	28	2	[illegible]
Do	201	28	1	[illegible]
ARMY MEDICAL MUSEUM,				
Anatomical catalogue of, to print descriptive	56	42	3	[illegible]
Property adjoining, to purchase	607	43	1	[illegible]
ARMY REGULATIONS. (*See* RULES AND ARTICLES OF WAR.)				
ARNOLD, SEYMOUR F., for relief	1569	49	1	[illegible]

Subject.	Report.	Congress.	Session.	Volume.
ES (see also WAR OF REBELLION).				
ension of	[illegible]	44	1	10
Do	[illegible]	45	2	11
governing granting, to amend	34	43	2	7
al State militia, granting to	67	42	2	7
a volunteers who were commissioned, to pay bounty withheld from	[illegible]	48	1	12
Do	1758	49	1	15
LANDS.				
ectors not entitled to, while serving as such	125	35	1	5
, Mass., lands to citizens of	297	34	1	5
f 1812, to amend act of March 3, 1855, granting, for service in	197	34	2	5
, JOHN, accounts of, to adjust	122	44	2	11
, THOMAS, charge of desertion, to remove	1076	49	1	15
, WILLIAM, military services prior to muster	736	44	1	10
Do	213	44	2	11
, FRANCIS L., pension to widow of	225	35	1	5
ARLISLE, restoration to Army	369	45	2	11
Do	65	47	1	12
ETHRO M., arrears of pay, claim for	192	47	1	12
, STEPHEN A., arrears of pay, claim for	192	47	1	12
LOUIS J., additional pay, claim for	279	43	1	9
RD, GEORGE S. P., retired list of Army, to place on	1949	47	2	13
RD, WILLIAM S., pension to	472	35	1	5
N, ELIJAH, relief of widow of	795	29	1	4
, JOSEPH B., relief of	861	44	1	10
N, VERMONT, cannon for monument at	844	47	1	12
JAMES W., relief of	1406	47	1	12
Do	621	48	1	13
Do	1262	49	1	15
N, ALTAMIRAH, arrears of pay and bounty, claim for	[illegible]	45	2	9
N, NATHAN, relief of	861	48	2	15
CHENRY, arrears of pay, claim for	192	47	1	12
HBRIDGE, JOSEPH C., services in Army, claim for	297	43	1	9
ER, SHERIDAN O., additional pay, claim for	404	43	1	9
N, CATHERINE, relief of	[illegible]	49	1	15
ROBERT, accounts of, to settle	604	35	1	5
Do	5	37	2	6
COMMISSIONS. (See also ARMY.)				
war, for service in	1290	47	1	12
officers having	47	21	1	2
of officers in Army holding	58	20	2	1
. RICHARD D., relief of	624	48	1	13
URG ARSENAL. (See FRANKFORT ARSENAL.)				
'S PASS, military road to Great Salt Lake City, Utah Territory, from	185	34	1	5
(see also under titles of respective rivers over which proposed to be ..ilt, and under titles of respective railroads asking authority to build), , construction of, in	36	33	2	5
ande River, memorial of assembly of New Mexico for bridges over	190	34	1	5
THOMAS S., arrears of pay, claim for	262	46	2	11
LD, MASSACHUSETTS, cannon for monument at	1402	45	2	11
. NATHAN S., public funds, relief for loss of	123	38	1	7
H, ANNE E., judgment against estate, to release	225	34	1	5
Do	59	35	2	5
, ALTAMIRAH, relief of	211	44	2	11
Do	38	45	2	11
ENRY K., cannon for statue of Washington, request for, by	271	33	1	4
GEORGE W., enrollment of militia in 1862, pay for	183	46	2	11
HARLES E., arrears of pay, claim for	192	47	1	12
IENRY, relief of widow	504	48	1	13
. W., patent for manufacture of arms, to sell to Government	88	35	2	5
OHN T., carrier of dispatches, claim for services as	669	44	1	10
ICE M., pay and bounty land, claim for extra	350	35	1	5
Do	147	35	2	5
Do	141	37	3	6
Do	81	43	1	9
UHAMY, pay and bounty as widow of Henry Brown	29	43	2	9
N, HENRY F., retired list of Army, to place on	478	47	1	12
RT, WASHINGTON TERRITORY, military road to Cowlitz Landing om	187	34	1	5
AVID, arrears of pay, claim for	192	47	1	12
ROBERT E., military services, claim for	345	43	2	9
S. E., arrears of pay, claim for	192	47	1	12
WILLIAM F., additional pay, claim for	256	44	1	10
N, ROBERT C.,				
n for portable boat, use of, by United States	73	44	2	11
Do	187	45	2	11
list of Army, to advance in rank on	71	45	2	11
N, W. JESSE, military record, to correct	75	45	2	11
. AUGUSTUS, relief of	26	31	2	4
CHARLES A., relief of	3670	49	2	17
neral DON CARLOS, loss of records in case of	97	42	2	
Do	93	42	3	

Subject.	Report.	Congress.	Session.	Volume.
BUFFALO, NEW YORK, paving streets near Fort Porter, expenses of, Government to pay portion	222	34	1	5
BUFORD, THOMAS (deputy quartermaster-general),				
Additional pay to	43	21	1	1
Advances made as contractor for Government, to reimburse	422	22	1	2
Do	2	22	2	2
BULLINGTON, LUCINDA, relief of	330	46	2	11
Do	505	48	1	13
BULOW, JOHN J., Jr., relief of heirs	70	35	1	5
BUNDY, MARTIN L., accounts of, to settle	288	46	2	11
BURBANK, JACOB E., public funds stolen, to reimburse for	142	46	2	11
Do	143	47	1	12
BURCHELL, JOHN T., medical services, claim for	576	43	1	9
Do	27	44	1	10
BURGESS, CHARLES J., bounty land, claim for	270	33	1	4
BURKE, JOHN, additional pay, claim for	281	43	1	9
BURKE, MARTIN S., relief of	218	35	2	5
BURKE, ORVILLE, retired list of Army, to place on	943	47	1	12
Do	205	48	1	13
Do	3165	49	1	15
BURNET, DAVID G., relief of	219	35	2	5
BURRELL, SAMUEL, relief of	1845	49	1	15
BURTCH, ALEXANDER, charge of desertion, to remove	88	43	1	9
BUSH, ISAAC, services in Florida war	740	30	1	4
Do	70	32	1	4
BUTCHER, WILLIAM, relief of	701	44	1	10
BUTLER, ANNE W., relief of	121	35	2	5
BUTLER, JOHN, charge of desertion, to remove	3686	49	2	15
BUTLER, Hon. R. R., appointments to Military and Naval Academies, sale of, by	39	41	2	7
BYRD, ROBERT K., relief of	133	44	2	11
BYRNE, EDWARD, restoration to Army	208	47	1	12
Do	206	48	1	13
Do	3161	49	1	15
CABET, PETER, relief of heirs	99	21	1	1
CADETS, expulsion from Military Academy at West Point	28	41	3	7
CAIN, JAMES, relief of	*434	49	1	15
CALIFORNIA,				
Indian hostilities, payment of expenses and money advanced by State for suppressing	817	30	1	4
Do	137	33	1	4
Do	660	36	1	6
Indian hostility claims in, to adjudicate	807	48	1	13
Inyo and Mono Counties, land for high school in	746	47	1	12
Modoc war of 1872-'73, to adjudicate claims of citizens and State on account of	218	43	2	9
Do	297	44	1	10
Do	843	47	1	12
Soldiers' home in, to establish	496	49	1	15
CALKINS, ALMERON E., pay from date of commission to date of muster	27	43	2	9
Do	505	44	1	10
CALLAN, PATRICK, relief of	51	15	2	1
CAMERON, JOHN W., services as officer previous to muster in	49	44	2	11
CAMP CADY, CALIFORNIA, military reservation at, transfer to Interior Department	19	44	1	10
CAMP CROOK, CALIFORNIA, military reservation of, transfer to Interior Department	19	44	1	10
CAMP DOUGLAS, UTAH, military reservation of, transfer to Interior Department	706	46	2	11
Do	203	48	1	13
CAMP INDEPENDENCE, CALIFORNIA, Inyo and Mono Counties, to grant portions to	746	47	1	12
CAMP McDOWELL, military road to San Carlos from	200	44	2	11
CAMP STEWART, military road from Scottsbury to	842	47	1	12
CAMPBELL, CHARLES H., restoration to Army	3183	49	1	15
CAMPBELL, CHARLES L., relief of	1849	49	1	15
CAMPBELL, J. B., judgment against, to release	91	45	3	11
Do	31	46	2	11
CAMPBELL, L. S., relief of	20	43	1	9
CANADY, WILLIAM N., relief of	2231	49	1	15
CANALS, Erie and Oswego, to enlarge	114	37	2	6
CANDEE, Maj. G. W., public funds, relief from loss of	58	47	1	12
CANFIELD, BAKER, additional pay, claim for	237	45	2	11
CANNON, CONDEMNED. (*See* CONDEMNED CANNON.)				
CARL, WILLIAM, discharge from Army	403	43	1	9
CARLIN, CHARLES J., additional pay, claim for	839	43	1	9
CARLISLE BARRACKS, PENNSYLVANIA, Army asylum, to convert into	266	29	1	3
CARMEN, W. H., arrears of pay, claim for	666	44	1	10
Do	287	45	2	11
CARPENTER, THOMAS H., relief of	3190	49	1	15
CARRICK, ROBERT, relief of	661	48	1	13
Do	3168	49	1	15
CARROLL, ANN ELLA, reward for services	386	46	3	11

* Parts 1, 2.

Subject.	Report.	Congress.	Session.	Volume.
L, CHARLES W., arrest of, damages for	258	33	1	4
VALLEY, NEVADA, military road from Missouri to	355	34	1	5
THOMAS F., relief of	670	44	1	10
WILLIAM, charge of desertion against, to remove	3074	49	2	15
IERS, WILLIAM, pay as acting second lieutenant	40	44	2	11
HOMAS, charge of desertion against, to remove	2245	49	1	15
E MOUNTAINS, military wagon road across	186	34	1	5
ACKSON, additional pay, claim for	573	43	1	9
AVID C., conduct in Quartermaster's Department, liability for	4	32	1	4
Do	41	33	1	4
JAMES T., relief of	952	49	1	15
Y, GEORGE A., relief of	2228	49	1	15
ISLAND, MASSACHUSETTS,				
ancy of, by municipal authorities of Boston, Mass	288	48	1	13
r of	81	23	2	2
JOHN T., military record, to correct	203	44	2	11
GUE of Army Medical Museum, to print anatomical	56	42	3	8
Y, tactics for	419	23	1	2
HN, relief of	114	23	1	2
GEORGE, property destroyed, claim for	204	29	1	4
URNE, R. H., sentence of court-martial, to set aside	33	43	2	9
ETTE. (*See* SAINT BERNARD PARISH.)				
ERLAIN, LOWELL A.,				
ency in quartermaster's stores, responsibility for	706	45	2	11
nation of, under apprehension of dismissal	100	43	2	9
ERLAIN, WILBUR F., arrears of pay, claim for	823	43	1	9
Do	52	44	1	10
Do	192	47	1	12
ERLIN, JOHN F., hotel on reservation at Fortress Monroe, to erect	3436	49	1	15
ERS, COLONEL, composition of court for trial of	229	19	1	1
ERSBURG, PENNSYLVANIA, cannon for monument at	1208	47	1	12
LISS, WILLIAM P., retired list of Army, to place on	53	47	1	12
Do	44	49	1	15
NEY, J. A., *et al.*, cannon for monumental purposes	36	44	2	11
LER, JOHN, relief of	134	44	2	11
LER, LOUISA G., court-martial proceedings, to set aside	122	44	2	11
Fort Columbus, New York Harbor, to erect at	95	28	2	3
S CITY, IOWA, cannon for soldiers' monument at	434	46	2	11
STON, SOUTH CAROLINA, property in, transfer of Porter Academy	4020	49	2	15
UGAY RAILROAD COMPANY, right of way across Plattsburgh reservation, New York	402	47	1	12
EE, IOWA, cannon for monument at	1564	47	1	12
EAKE AND OHIO RAILROAD, right of way across reservation at Fortress Monroe	1967	47	2	12
Do	331	48	1	13
NE, BLACK HILLS, AND MONTANA RAILWAY, right of way across Fort Russell and Fort Laramie reservations	756	48	1	13
NE AND NORTHERN RAILWAY, right of way across Fort Russell and Fort Laramie military reservations	2486	49	1	15
Do	2647	49	1	15
), ILLINOIS, donation of land by, for military post near	3543	49	2	15
RING JOHN W., restoration to Army	985	45	2	11
Do	3184	49	1	15
E, MASSACHUSETTS, cannon for monument at	1439	47	1	12
ZRA, relief of	59	15	2	1
WILLIAM E., additional pay, claim for	90	43	1	9
N, ROBERT P., services as assistant surgeon	15	41	3	7
AN, WILLIAM E., relief of	1251	49	1	15
, MARY E., relief of	964	49	1	15
ILL, SYLVESTER, services as Inspector-General	159	34	3	5
Do	103	35	1	5
ILL, THOMAS J., relief of	30	31	2	4
ILL, WILLIAM H., relief of widow	84	34	3	5
J. F., for relief	926	49	1	15
L ACADEMY,				
, to State militia	70	43	1	9
of South Carolina for rent of	2315	48	2	13
Do	456	49	1	15
FICES, retired Army officers to hold, in Territories	18	47	1	12
OCESS IN ARMY, discharging recruits who are infants, under	58	29	2	4
ERVICE, amending section 1754 Revised Statutes, employment of honorably discharged soldiers or sailors	1777	48	1	13
AR. (*See* WAR OF THE REBELLION.)				
rnia, for suppressing Indian hostilities	817	30	1	4
Do	137	33	1	4
Do	660	36	1	6
ng, or other property, to reimburse soldiers for, lost or destroyed while on march or in battle	32	38	1	7
are, interest on militia claims of	185	21	1	2
a, militia in Seminole war	893	27	2	3

Subject.	Report.	Congress.	Session.	Volume.
CLAIMS—Continued.				
Florida, Militia in Seminole war	108	28	2	3
Georgia, to adjudicate militia claims of	77	19	2	1
Do	584	27	2	3
Do	684	27	2	3
Horses lost in service,				
Extending time for filing claim for	1278	46	2	11
To refer to other tribunal than Third Auditor	295	29	1	3
Illinois, Bayley's Battalion of Illinois Volunteers for services in the Black Hawk war	71	35	1	5
Iowa, to reimburse for services by militia	543	26	1	2
Louisiana, to reimburse for militia services	364	27	2	3
Maine, to adjudicate, for militia services	566	26	1	2
Do	78	26	2	2
Do	363	27	2	3
Massachusetts, to adjudicate, for militia services	122	24	2	2
Do	144	35	2	5
Mexican war, pay of volunteers for services in	120	38	1	7
Michigan, to adjudicate for militia services	125	27	3	3
Missouri,				
Third Regiment of Volunteers for three months' extra pay	194	33	1	4
To adjudicate for militia services during civil war	37	38	1	7
To pay certain companies of volunteers	602	27	2	3
Do	167	28	1	3
New Hampshire, to adjudicate, for militia services	833	29	1	4
Do	47	29	2	4
Do	149	30	1	4
Do	170	32	1	4
New Mexico, payment of militia taken into service of Territorial government in 1854	196	34	1	5
Ohio, two companies of Ohio volunteers for military services rendered in 1846	149	35	2	5
Do	501	36	1	6
South Carolina, to refund to State moneys paid troops who served in Florida war	66	21	1	2
Do	1	22	1	2
Do	201	31	1	4
Texas, to reimburse State for moneys expended in support of volunteer troops	352	31	1	4
Do	143	35	2	5
Utah, to indemnify Territory for expenses incurred in suppressing Indian hostilities in 1853	201	36	1	6
Vermont, to reimburse for militia services	126	28	2	3
Do	23	31	1	4
Do	138	34	1	5
Washington Territory, to pay volunteers from Territory for services against Indians at Puget Sound	189	34	3	5
Winfield Scott and San Francisco, to reimburse officers and sailors for losses sustained by disasters to steamers	59	34	3	5
CLANCY, JOSEPH, relief of	1408	49	1	15
CLANCY, MICHAEL, charge of desertion, to remove	2872	49	1	15
CLARK, JOHN, arrears of pay	46	33	2	5
CLAYTON, JOHN G., loss of horse, claim for	136	35	1	5
CLERKS TO COMMITTEES. (*See* COMMITTEES; CONGRESS.)				
CLIFT, JAMES, arrears of pay	39	45	2	11
CLINTON GUARDS, services on Canadian frontier in 1838, pay for	86	34	3	5
CLITHERALL, CAROLINE E., relief of	363	23	1	2
Do	353	27	2	3
CLYMER, JOSEPH, transporting army supplies, to pay for	110	33	2	5
COBB, Lieut. JAMES D.,				
Legality of court-martial proceedings in case of	59	18	2	1
Do	67	20	2	1
Do	18	21	1	2
Restoration to Army	204	35		
COCHRAN, GEORGE T., sentence of court-martial, to commute	81	43		
COCHRAN'S BOMB-CANNON, purchase of	1	26		
COCKE, WILLIAM, military services, claim for	105	18		1
COCKERILL, GILES J., arrears of pay	192	47		12
CODY, SAMUEL, military record, to correct	129	44		11
COFFEY, CORNELIUS, bounty land to	240	33	1	4
COLD SPRING, NEW YORK, military road from Fishkill to	72	19	2	1
COLE, CLEMENT H., charge of desertion against, to remove	2868	49		15
COLFAX, NEW MEXICO, cause for ordering troops from Fort Union to	116	44	2	11
COLLEGES, retired Army officers to, detail of	676	46	2	11
COLLEY, HERMAN, charge of desertion against, to remove	130	44	2	11
COLLINGS, W. H., arrears of pay, claim for	105	44	3	11
COLORADO,				
Indian hostility claims in, to adjudicate	807	48		13
Military post near Ute Indian Reservation in, to construct	199	44	3	11
Ordnance account, to credit	3230	49		15
COLQUHOUN, WILLIAM S., extra pay for services in Subsistence Department	320	24		2
Do	352	25		

Subject.	Report.	Congress.	Session.	Volume.
IX, JEAN LOUIS, services in recruiting	46	44	2	11
GER, FRANK Y., additional pay to	74	43	1	6
SARIAT, mode of supplying Army, to make permanent	315	32	1	3
TEE ON MILITARY AFFAIRS, resolution making bills from, special order	1818	49	1	15
TEES IN HOUSE OF REPRESENTATIVES, clerical services rendered to	10	30	1	7
SATION. (See SALARY.)				
I, NEW HAMPSHIRE, cannon for monument at	770	47	1	12
NED CANNON (see also under head of respective place to which granted),				
ting of,				
ases, Edward, for statue to	195	44	1	10
earney, General Philip H., for monument to	652	44	1	10
ytle, General W. H., for statue to	1521	47	2	12
arion Artillery, to issue to	488	46	2	11
onumental purposes, for	260	47	1	12
orton, Hon. O. P., for statue of	265	47	1	12
eynolds, J. J., for statue to	266	47	1	12
oldiers' monuments, principle of granting for	192	44	2	11
'ashington, for equestrian statue of	271	32	1	4
ing, for soldiers' monuments and cemeteries at,				
Ilion, N. Y	1730	47	1	12
lbion, N. Y	1661	49	1	15
llegheny County, Pa	1741	47	1	12
nna M. Ross Post, G. A. R	256	47	1	12
uburn, N. Y	827	44	1	10
urora, Ill	1402	46	2	11
voca, Iowa	2379	49	1	15
von, N. Y	1402	46	2	11
angor, Me	1505	47	2	12
ellaire, Ohio	262	47	1	12
ellefonte, Pa	1449	47	1	12
erlin, Wis	1450	47	1	12
irmingham, Conn	190	47	1	12
Do	194	47	1	12
oston, Mass	1402	46	2	11
randon, Vt	844	47	1	12
rimfield, Mass	1402	46	2	11
hambersburg, Pa	1298	47	1	12
hampney, J. A., et al	36	44	2	11
harles City, Iowa	434	46	2	11
herokee, Iowa	1564	47	1	12
hicopee, Mass	1439	47	1	12
oncord, N. H	770	47	1	12
ornwall, N. Y	1435	47	1	12
anville, Pa	1440	47	1	12
anville Light Battery	1402	46	2	11
elaware, Ohio	1297	47	1	12
epartment of Potomac, G. A. R	1048	48	1	13
etroit, Mich	1402	46	2	11
over, N. H	1296	47	1	12
ast Bloomfield, N. Y	1402	46	2	11
aton, Ohio	2766	49	1	15
airfield, Iowa	1617	47	1	12
all River, Mass	1442	47	1	12
ranklin, Pa	1402	46	2	11
remont, Ohio	1402	46	2	11
D. Bailey Post, G. A. R., of New York	1868	47	2	12
allipolis, Ohio	1402	46	2	11
Do	261	47	1	12
rand Army of the Republic	448	46	2	11
reenville, Ohio	2029	49	1	15
roveland, Mass	1443	47	1	12
amilton, Ohio	769	47	1	12
atfield, Mass	1616	47	1	12
averstraw, N. Y	1619	47	1	12
onesdale, Pa	1868	47	2	12
udson, N. Y	1560	47	1	12
ndianapolis, Ind	1618	47	1	12
ronton, Ohio	1446	47	1	12
anesville, Wis	1451	47	1	12
ohn Ennis Post	1402	46	2	11
illingly, Conn	1402	46	2	11
noxville, Tenn	1294	47	1	12
okomo, Ind	1562	47	1	12
awrence, Mass	1617	47	1	12
ogansport, Ind	1447	47	1	12
ouisville, Ky. (McLean Post, G. A. R.)	845	47	1	12
ycoming County, Pennsylvania	773	47	1	12
ynn, Mass	1296	47	1	12

Subject.	Report.	Congress.	Session.	Volume.
CONDEMNED CANNON—Continued.				
Donating, for soldiers' monuments and cemeteries at—Continued.				
McGregor, Iowa	1402	46	2	11
Do	1868	47	2	13
McLean Post, G. A. R	845	47	1	12
Malden, Mass	1436	47	1	12
Mansfield, Ohio	768	47	1	12
Maquoketa, Iowa	1617	47	1	13
Marblehead, Mass	1445	47	1	13
Mason, Mich	1868	47	2	13
Medina, Ohio	1292	47	1	12
Milan, Ohio	779	47	1	12
Milford Centre, Ohio	1402	46	2	11
Mount Vernon, Ohio	1448	47	1	12
Muskingum County, Ohio	1444	47	1	12
Mystic, Conn	1742	47	1	12
Nevada, Iowa	1565	47	1	13
New Bedford, Mass	168	44	2	11
Do	1441	47	1	13
New Brighton, Pa	1783	47	1	12
Newburg, N. Y	826	44	1	10
New Hampshire Veteran Association	1868	47	2	13
Newport, Ky	1293	47	1	12
Newport, Vt	1437	47	1	12
Nunda, N. Y	1662	49	1	15
Otsego, Mich	264	47	1	12
Paxton	1402	46	2	11
Peabody, Mass	1618	47	1	12
Peru, Ind	1366	47	1	13
Philadelphia, Pa., Anna M. Ross Post, G. A. R	256	47	1	12
Pickaway County, Ohio	1744	47	1	12
Piqua, Ohio	1561	47	1	13
Portland, Me	259	47	1	12
Portsmouth, Ohio	1158	47	1	12
Posts 73 and 78, Massachusetts	1402	46	2	11
Poughkeepsie, N. Y	1402	46	2	11
Rochester, N. H	263	47	1	12
Roser Post, G. A. R	2030	49	1	15
Saint Johnsbury, Vt	1436	47	1	12
Salem, Ohio	1868	47	2	13
Saltsburg, Pa	444	46	2	11
Saratoga, N. Y	1076	47	1	12
Scranton, Pa	810	48	1	13
Do	811	48	1	13
Shingle House, Pa., Post 175, G. A. R	1783	47	1	12
Slaterville, N. H	1748	47	1	12
Somerville, Mass	492	49	1	15
Stoneham, Mass	1160	47	1	12
Susquehanna County, Pennsylvania	651	44	1	10
Taunton, Mass	1402	46	2	11
Tecumseh, Mich	1868	47	2	13
Topeka, Kans	258	47	1	12
Utica, N. Y	1740	47	1	12
Wakefield, Mass	1402	46	2	11
Washington Court House, Ohio	1868	47	2	13
Waterloo, Iowa	228	46	2	11
Do	257	47	1	12
Waterville, Me	1161	47	1	12
Wayne, Ind	1402	46	2	11
White Haven, Pa	1879	47	1	12
William L. Curry Post	1402	46	2	11
Winchester, Mass	1402	46	2	11
Woburn, Mass	1402	46	2	11
Do	260	47	1	12
CONFEDERATE SOLDIERS, burying dead, in national cemeteries	61	40	2	7
CONGRESS.				
Sale of appointments to Military and Naval Academies by members of	38	41	2	7
Do	39	41	2	7
Do	42	41	2	7
Powers of, to control and establish post-routes	51	38	1	4
CONLAN, FRANCIS J., relief of	1654	49	1	15
CONLY, MARY, relief of	570	43	1	9
CONRAD, JOSEPH, retired list of Army, to place on, with rank of colonel	616	47	1	12
CONSTABLE, ROBERT A., loss of horse and equipments, pay for	12	30	2	1
CONTRACTORS, bounty lands, not entitled to	135	35	1	2
COOK, C. J., relief of	546	28	1	1
COOK, CASPER B., *et al.*, services as members of Nineteenth Regiment band, New York Militia, claim for	241	39	1	4
COOK, HENRY, change name to Henry Jones	1979	47	2	13
COONEY, JAMES, relief of	917	49	1	15
COOPER, WICKLIFFE, military record, to correct	1269	47	1	12

Subject.	Report.	Congress.	Session.	Volume.
ND, JESSE, relief of heirs	612	36	1	2
ND, THOMAS, additional compensation to	595	27	2	3
, military road from Fort Ellis to	616	44	1	10
, BENJAMIN L., additional pay to	444	44	1	10
LLE, NEW YORK, cannon for monument at	1435	47	1	12
ILLIAM O., restoration to Army	400	44	1	10
AM, relief of	596	42	1	9
RISTOPHER, relief of	2230	49	1	15
, POLLY W., additional pension to	14	41	3	7
N, JAMES, charge of desertion against, to remove	3073	49	1	15
N, MARTIN, relief of	1030	49	1	15
R, JAMES, relief of	309	31	1	4
L BLUFFS, IOWA,				
ry road to Fort Kearney from	186	34	3	5
d, cost of, from New York to	12	46	3	11
OF CLAIMS, restricting jurisdiction of, and to provide for payment of certain demands for quartermaster stores and subsistence supplies	42	42	3	7
Do	187	44	1	10
MARTIAL,				
les of war, to amend	3307	49	2	15
ensation for officers serving on	1360	47	1	12
ous militia, validity of proceedings in trial of	140	20	1	1
Do	225	20	1	1
, Lieutenant-colonel, proceedings in case of	269	22	1	2
, GEORGE W., relief of	2344	49	2	13
Do	1828	49	1	15
, JAMES H., relief of	1286	49	1	15
, JAMES P., relief of	1163	49	1	15
L, VALENTINE, to be discharged from Army	268	23	1	2
E LANDING, military road to Bruceport, in Washington Territory, from	187	34	1	5
RD, ISAAC, relief of	3115	49	1	15
RD, SAMUEL W., retired list of Army, to place on	164	42	1	9
RD, THOMAS, relief of	962	49	1	15
C. H., charge of desertion, to remove	191	44	1	10
THURMAN, extra compensation to	442	24	1	2
Do	324	25	1	3
, ISABELLA, relief of	67	33	2	5
ER, ROBERT P., relief of	455	49	1	15
DAVID, charge of desertion against, to remove	2224	49	1	15
, J. B., *et al.*, relief of	72	28	2	3
NGTON, ELIJAH, pay as second lieutenant	53	43	2	9
, HENRY V., slave hire, claim for	146	27	3	3
GTON, ELIJAH, compensation as scout	470	44	1	10
OHN, administrator, relief of	213	31	1	4
IGS, Rev. JAMES, relief of	686	25	2	2
GHAM, ALBERT P., relief of	1108	49	1	15
GHAM JAMES, relief of	2217	49	1	15
, WILLIAM H., relief of	263	45	2	11
C. A., additional pay to	190	44	2	11
, JOHN, relief of	15	15	2	1
S HILLS NATIONAL CEMETERY, NEW YORK, purchase of additional grounds for	1607	47	1	12
, NICHOLAS, charge of desertion against, to remove	1163	49	1	15
,				
hostilities in 1862, to adjudicate expenses incurred in	35	42	3	8
nce account of, to credit	2291	49	1	15
ILLIAM A. W., first lieutenant, pay as	563	44	1	10
, SAMUEL W., relief of	2863	49	1	15
LE, PENNSYLVANIA, cannon for monument at	1440	47	1	12
LE, VIRGINIA, road to national cemetery at	1649	47	1	12
Do	3380	49	1	15
LE LIGHT BATTERY A, cannon for monument to	1402	46	2	11
G, JOHN A., relief of	458	49	1	15
LL, JEREMIAH Y., relief of	138	35	1	5
N ISLAND, ALABAMA, fortifications in Mobile Bay, on	94	17	1	1
Do	103	17	2	1
Do	450	29	1	4
Do	33	31	2	4
ON, CHARLES, relief of	1177	49	1	15
ENOCH, charge of desertion, to remove	442	46	2	11
ROBERT R., services previous to muster in, pay for	41	44	2	11
LVESTER, relief of	111	23	2	2
Do	401	25	2	2
A. H. C., military services, pay for	124	38	1	7
ER, FRANCISCO V., relief of	22	43	3	9
F UNITED STATES, payment of all debts contracted by Government in certain States	*68	45	2	11
ARE,				
ses incurred in defense of the United States, to indemnify loyal citizens for	57	37	2	6
claims of State, payment of interest on	183	21	1	2

* And Part 2.

Subject.	Report.	Congress.	Session.	Volume.
N, LANGDON C., relief of	209	31	1	4
N, THOMAS, relief of	1164	49	1	15
NESS, WASHINGTON TERRITORY, military road from, to intersect one from Vancouver	189	34	1	5
P, MYRON E., relief of	873	47	1	12
Do	50	48	1	13
Do	671	49	1	15
IATILDA B., relief of	216	21	1	2
MICHAEL J., relief of	993	48	1	13
S, HENRY, relief of	2881	49	1	15
B., relief of	78	43	1	9
OEL HENRY, services as judge-advocate, Florida campaign, 1836	230	25	3	2
Do	381	31	1	4
JAMES F., relief of	31	42	3	8
LOOMFIELD, NEW YORK, cannon for monument at	1402	46	2	11
LORIDA SEMINARY, relief of	599	48	1	13
ENRY, charge of desertion against, to remove	3366	49	1	15
ENNESSEE, VIRGINIA AND GEORGIA RAILROAD COMPANY, settlement of accounts with	832	44	1	10
N, HENRY B., relief of	183	46	2	11
ND, OSCAR, relief of	819	48	1	13
Do	532	49	1	15
AMOS B., accounts of, to audit	165	34	1	5
JOHN, charge of desertion against, to remove	283	45	2	11
JOSEPH, relief of	370	21	1	2
Do	92	22	1	2
JOSEPH B., relief of	56	36	1	6
Do	117	36	1	6
Do	7	37	2	6
Do	12	43	2	9
W., relief of heirs	211	28	1	3
EDWIN, loss of horse, pay for	500	44	1	10
N, FRED. H. E., subsistence funds, to relieve, for loss of	681	46	2	11
IARY J., relief of	123	44	2	11
JESSE, charge of desertion against, to remove	2864	49	1	15
Y, ANDREW J., relief of	3756	49	2	15
SON, MANLEY B., relief of	2226	49	1	15
TION, Fort Scott Reserve to Kansas for	37	33	2	5
DS, CHARLES, relief of	121	44	2	11
Do	1695	46	2	11
Do	192	47	1	12
DS, JAMES (administrator), relief of	556	29	1	4
DS, JOHN H., arrears of pay, claim for	192	47	1	12
I CEVALRY, MISSOURI STATE MILITIA, charge of desertion, to emove, from enlisted men of	666	44	1	10
WILLIAM R., negro killed by Indians, claim for	129	34	1	5
T, EDWARD G., relief of widow	503	36	1	6
T, MARTHA, pension to	282	34	1	5
GILES W., relief of	57	30	2	4
Do	4	32	1	4
Do	41	33	1	4
IENRY, charge of desertion against, to remove	2216	49	1	15
IMON B., charge of desertion against, to remove	87	46	3	11
OUIS F., medal of honor to	533	49	1	15
WILLIAM H., retired list of Army, to place on, with rank of brigadier-general	363	44	1	10
ER CORPS,				
s in office of Chief, to increase number of	96	24	1	2
anization of	35	18	2	1
Do	36	19	1	1
Do	42	21	1	2
Do	29	31	2	4
graphical Engineers, to reorganize Corps of	4	23	2	2
Do	5	23	2	2
Do	95	24	1	2
IENTS IN ARMY.				
arges under civil process in cases of	58	29	2	4
s in Army, for instruction	125	26	2	3
its enlisted to fill old regiments to be discharged with organization	14	38	2	7
listment period, special extension of	1570	48	1	13
ZATION OF BOUNTIES. (*See* BOUNTIES.)				
NAL, locks of, to enlarge	114	37	2	6
ENNSYLVANIA, Home for Indigent Soldiers and Sailors at	1631	46	2	11
Do	26	47	1	12
Do	379	48	1	13
JOHN H., relief of heirs	833	43	1	9
Do	40	45	2	11
JOHN S., sentence of court-martial, to annul	331	43	1	9
N. G., relief of	245	33	1	4
Do	244	34	3	5
T, EDWARD, services in Quartermaster Department, pay for	86	31	1	4
Do	3	32	1	4

Subject.	Report.	Congress.	Session.
EVEY, SAMUEL T., relief of	1859	49	1
EXCHANGE NATIONAL BANK OF NORFOLK, soldiers' homes, to reimburse for losses caused by failure of	500	49	1
EXECUTIVE DEPARTMENTS, Army officers in, employment of	61	16	2
EXTRA PAY, Fort Kearney, extending benefit of two acts for, to troops stationed at	128	34	1
EZEKIEL, DAVID I., promotion of	479	44	1
FACION, RICHARD, charge of desertion against, to remove	3369	49	1
FAIRFIELD, IOWA, cannon for monument at	1617	47	1
FALES, JOHN, bounty lands to	13	30	
FALL RIVER, MASSACHUSETTS, cannon for monument at	1442	47	1
FANNING, JAMES, relief of	924	49	1
FAUST, CHARLES W., relief of	1666	49	1
FAYETTEVILLE, NORTH CAROLINA, arsenal site at, sale of	53	33	
FECHET, EDWARD G., military record, to correct	189	47	
Do	290	48	
Do	3103	49	
FELARD, JOHN, relief of	757	48	
FERGUSON, AMOS B., additional pay to	672	44	
FERGUSON, HUGH, additional bounty land to	412	36	
Do	38	36	
FERGUSON, WILLIAM, arrears of pension to	100	20	
FERRY, JOHN H., accounts as quartermaster, to settle	194	44	
FIELD, H. B., relief of	52	33	
FIFTEENTH and SIXTEENTH MISSOURI CAVALRY, bounty to	992	45	
Do	437	46	
FIGLEY, WILLIAM, charge of desertion against, to remove	1968	49	
FILBECK, NICHOLAS, relief of	958	49	
FINDLEY & DEAS, relief of	270	24	
FINLEY, CLEMENT A., retired list of Army, to place on	361	44	
FISH, JOSHUA, relief of	91	25	
FISHBURN, JOSHUA J., arrears of pay to	192	47	
FISHER, GEORGE, relief of heirs	330	43	
Do	212	44	
FISHER, HARRIET F. (*See* FISHER, MARVIN W.)			
FISHER, JOSEPH W., arrears of pay to	192	47	
Do	1128	48	
FISHER, MARVIN, machine for charging percussion caps, pay for use of	58	30	
Do	197	31	1
Do	283	34	1
Do	479	36	1
FISHKILL, NEW YORK, military road from Cold Spring to	72	19	1
FITZPATRICK, RICHARD,			
Military services, pay for	7	23	2
Property destroyed, pay for	479	29	1
Do	72	23	2
FLAGS, One hundred and eighth Ohio Volunteers, to return, to	1527	47	1
FLETCHER, LYDIA, relief of	488	35	1
Do	653	36	1
FLORIDA,			
Black's volunteer company, claim for services in Seminole war	133	34	1
Fortifications at Pensacola, appropriations for	119	20	1
Key West and Dry Tortugas, in, occupation of	407	23	
Militia, claims for services in	892	27	
Do	108	28	
To adjudicate claims	600	45	
Sea-wall at Saint Augustine, to construct	59	25	
Volunteers in 1863, to accept 20,000 additional, for services in	5	37	
FLYNN, PATRICK, arrears of pay to	92	47	
Do	1957	49	
FONES, HARRY, arrears of pay to	1504	46	
Do	191	47	
FORBES HISTORICAL COLLECTION, Secretary of War to purchase	2440	45	
FORBES, LEVI, bounty land to	31	34	
FORD, WILLIAM P., relief of	93	36	
FORRENCE, GEORGE W., injuries received in action near Jalapa, Mexico	136	34	
FORT ATKINSON, military post at, to re-establish	223	33	
FORT BENTON, MONTANA, reservation at, to abolish	761	47	
FORT BLISS, TEXAS, right of way to Rio Grande and El Paso Railway through military reservation at	3067	49	
FORT BRADY, MICHIGAN, sale of old site at	2623	47	
Do	497	49	
FORT BRIDGER, WYOMING, military reservation at, relief of citizens on	521	43	
FORT BROWN, TEXAS, site for purchase	3146	46	
FORT BUFORD, DAKOTA,			
Ferry at, to permit F. W. Hunt to erect	527	48	
Do	213	48	
Coal at, to permit F. W. Hunt to mine	524	48	
Do	213	49	
FORT CROOK, CALIFORNIA, sale of, transfer to Interior Department	89	44	
FORT CUMMINGS, NEW MEXICO, transfer to Interior Department	19	44	

Subject.	Report.	Congress.	Session.	Volume.
AWARE,				
sement to officers for losses sustained by destruction of	313	22	1	2
ion at, to adjudicate title to	50	23	2	2
Do	92	24	1	2
GLAS, UTAH,				
iation for securing title to land adjoining	3973	49	2	15
r at, granting portion for	4052	49	2	15
S. mililitary road from Corinne to	616	44	1	10
ON, INDIAN TERRITORY, wagon road from Natchitoches, La., to	67	19	1	1
TIOT, MICHIGAN, church on reservation at, to erect	501	44	1	10
EN, RHODE ISLAND, site of, use for park to Newport, R. I	2576	49	1	15
S, KANSAS,				
Texas and Southwestern Railroad to build road across reservation at	4127	49	2	15
ortion of reservation at	735	48	1	13
Do	1958	49	1	15
RNEY,				
road from Council Bluffs to, to construct	180	34	3	5
erving at, extra pay to	128	34	3	5
AMIE,				
a, Black Hills and Montana Railway across lands at, right of way to	756	48	1	13
e and Northern Railway across military reservation at, right of y to	2486	49	1	15
Do	2647	49	1	15
VENWORTH, KANSAS,				
orth Street Railroad Company across reservation at, right of way to	475	44	1	10
road to Fort Pierre from	192	34	1	5
road to Fort Riley from	172	34	3	5
ION, FLORIDA, sea-wall at	39	23	2	2
SAC, ILLINOIS, armory at, to establish	214	31	1	4
DE, Fremont, Elkhorn and Missouri Valley Railroad, to build road oss reservation at	3059	49	2	15
LTRIE, SOUTH CAROLINA, preservation of	767	25	2	2
RARA, DAKOTA, Fremont, Elkhorn and Missouri Valley Railroad, ht of way across reservation at	546	47	1	12
RE, DAKOTA, military road from Fort Leavenworth to	192	34	1	5
ER, NEW YORK, United States Government to pay portion of ring streets in vicinity of	222	34	1	5
DALL, DAKOTA, reservation at, to vacate portion of	846	47	1	12
Do	201	48	1	13
DING, reservation at, to appraise and sell	35	44	2	11
, DAKOTA, reservation at, to vacate	847	47	1	12
Do	202	48	1	13
ELY, MINNESOTA,				
road from Winona to	191	34	1	5
committed by United States soldiers at	205	36	1	6
EY, KANSAS,				
Valley Railroad, right of way to, through reservation at	4112	49	2	15
road from Fort Leavenworth to	172	34	3	5
nts on, to open portion for	530	48	1	13
EY, MINNESOTA,				
f reservation, to reduce and open to settlement	118	34	3	5
Railroad Company, right of way through reservation	252	45	2	11
SELL,				
e, Black Hills and Montana Railway across reservation at, right of y to	756	48	1	13
e and Northern Railway across military reservation at, right of way	2486	49	1	15
Do	2647	49	1	15
TT, KANSAS, Fort Scott reserve to Kansas, for school purposes	37	33	2	5
DEN, NEW MEXICO, Rio Grande, Mexico and Pacific Railroad, ht of way through reservation at	501	49	1	15
TH, Saint Louis and San Francisco Railroad, right of way through ervation at	1889	47	2	12
LLING, MINNESOTA, reservation at, to cede to State of Minnesota rtion of	4051	49	2	15
IPPLE, ARIZONA, Prescott and Arizona Central Railway Compa , right of way through reservation at	3503	49	2	15
ILACOOM, military road to Bellingham Bay, in Washington Terri- ry, from	184	34	1	5
Do	360	35	1	5
ITER, soldiers at, claim for loss of property at	70	36	2	6
ON, NEW MEXICO,				
road from Santa Fé to	372	35	1	5
Do	509	36	1	6
from, ordering, to Colfax	116	44	2	11
NCOUVER, OREGON, military road from Cowlitz to	369	35	1	5
SHAKIE, WYOMING TERRITORY, wagon road to Yellowstone ark from	1006	47	1	12
SHINGTON, MARYLAND, additional land for site of	74	18	2	1
Do	125	19	1	1
Do	195	20	1	2
Do	151	21	1	2

Subject.	Report.	Congress.	Session.	Volume.
FORT WAYNE RESERVATION, sale of, at Savannah, Ga	364	28	1	2
FORT WILKINS, MICHIGAN, sale of reservation at	126	43	2	9
FORTIFICATIONS,				
Additional, to build, throughout United States	35	28	2	2
Alabama, memorial of legislature on	51	17	1	1
Condition of, in 1866	85	36	2	6
Condition of, in 1874	384	43	1	9
Defenses (permanent), examination of system	86	37	2	6
Examination of system of permanent defenses	86	37	2	6
Expenditures on,				
Amount of	93	16	1	1
To reduce or suspend	93	16	1	1
Harbors, protection of	94	24	1	2
Rivers and harbors, appropriations for general defense of	94	24	1	2
Florida,				
At Pensacola, in	46	19	1	1
Do	119	20	1	1
Occupation of, at Key West and Dry Tortugas	407	28	1	3
Sea-wall at Saint Augustine, repair	39	23	2	2
Alabama,				
On Dauphin Island, in Mobile Bay	94	17	1	1
Do	108	17	2	1
Do	450	29	1	4
Do	33	31	2	4
Louisiana, at Proctor's Point, in	450	29	1	4
Maine, at entrance to Penobscot River, in	333	28	1	3
Maryland, for Baltimore and Patapsco River, in	310	23	1	2
Massachusetts,				
At New Bedford	329	29	1	4
Do	21	31	2	4
At Castle Island	81	23	2	2
Mobile Point and Dauphin Island, Alabama, at	108	17	2	1
New York, at Sackett's Harbor	36	28	2	3
Do	392	29	1	4
Do	449	29	1	4
South Carolina, preservation at Fort Moultrie	767	25	2	2
FORTRESS MONROE, VIRGINIA,				
Chesapeake and Ohio Railroad, right of way across reservation at	1967	47	2	12
Do	331	48	1	13
Hotel at,				
Lease of grounds for	268	46	3	11
Do	1005	47	1	12
Do	1966	47	2	12
To erect	3436	49	1	15
Iron pier at	1149	49	1	15
Do	3191	49	1	15
Land in vicinity of, to purchase additional	92	35	2	5
FOSTER, ASHER W., charge of desertion against, to remove	3373	49	1	15
FOULK, W. L., restoration to Army	826	44	1	10
FOUNDRIES, NATIONAL. (*See* NATIONAL FOUNDRIES.)				
FOURTH BRIGADE, SOUTH CAROLINA VOLUNTEERS, board of field officers of, for relief	456	49	1	15
FOUTS, RICHARD H., relief of	744	44	1	10
FOWLER, FRANCES, pension to	353	27	2	3
FRANCESCO, ALEXANDER, military record, to correct	1967	47	2	12
FRANKFORD ARSENAL,				
Explosion at, relief of sufferers by	703	47	1	15
Right of way through grounds of	1709	47	1	12
FRANKLIN, JOHN H., for relief	25	43	2	9
FRANKLIN, PENNSYLVANIA, cannon for monument at	1402	49	2	11
FRANKLIN, WILLIAM E., relief of	32	42	3	8
FREDERICKSBURG, VIRGINIA, road to national cemetery near	1573	48	1	13
FREEMAN, HENRY, bounty to	216	44	2	11
FREEMAN, RUTH, relief of	212	31	1	4
FREEMAN, SAMUEL M., bounty to	61	46	3	11
FREMONT, ELKHORN AND MISSOURI RAILROAD COMPANY, right of way across Fort Niobrara reservation	546	47	1	12
Do	3650	49	2	15
FREMONT, J. L., continuance of rank given him	31	31	2	4
FREMONT, OHIO, cannon for monument at	1402	46	2	11
FREMONT, S. L., relief of	135	34	1	5
Do	14	35	2	5
FRENCH, WILLIAM H., retired list of Army, to place on, with rank of general officer	821	46	2	11
FRICK, A. P., appointment as assistant surgeon in Army	1046	48	1	23
FRISBEE, RACHEL, relief of	19	43	2	9
FRONTIERS, defense of Arkansas	255	23	1	2
Do	401	24	1	2
Do	442	24	1	2
FRY, ALFRED, additional pay to	442	43	1	9
Do	650	44	1	10

Subject.	Report.	Congress.	Session.	Volume.
NATHAN, claim for bounty land to	181	34	3	5
SAMUEL P., arrears of pay to	192	47	1	12
LEY POST, GRAND ARMY OF THE REPUBLIC, cannon for monument	1868	47	2	12
HN W., relief of representatives	136	44	2	11
LIS, OHIO, cannon for monument at	1402	46	2	11
Do	261	47	1	12
WILLIAM, services as brigadier-general	560	44	1	10
JAMES, arrears of pay to	192	47	1	12
R, EMMA E., relief of	12	43	3	8
R, FRANCES P., pension to	194	26	2	3
R, L. A., pension to	353	27	2	3
REDERICK, charge of desertion against, to remove	3372	49	1	15
VILLIAM, relief of	323	25	3	2
Do	502	30	1	6
OHN, Jr., relief of	477	45	2	11
ANDREW, restoration to Army	404	47	1	12
WILLIAM, increased pay to	54	44	2	11
, WILLIAM, relief of	460	44	1	10
, to continue grade in Army	615	48	1	13
SERVICE, pay of men enlisted in	1947	49	1	15
, to ascertain, of each State	106	22	2	2
WILSON B., relief of	208	49	1	15
l at Augusta, sanitary condition of	110	19	1	1
claims of, to adjudicate	91	17	1	1
Do	45	18	1	1
Do	77	19	2	1
Do	584	27	2	3
Do	684	27	2	3
BATTALION, employment in office of Third Auditor	28	31	2	4
EORGE W., retired list of Army, to place on	75-	48	1	13
Do	3176	49	1	15
URG, PENNSYLVANIA,				
' reunion at, camp equipage for	685	47	1	12
Do	1998	47	2	12
of battle-field at	1632	46	2	11
TTI, PETER, relief of	949	49	1	15
S, N. B., loss of powder seized by Government	245	34	3	5
Do	18	41	2	7
PIERRE, relief of	25	29	1	4
ORGE W., relief of	818	48	1	13
Do	3186	49	1	15
LLIAM H., restoration to Army	254	46	3	11
Do	57	47	1	12
Do	687	48	1	13
RESTON, services rendered	746	25	2	2
G., memorial placing veterinary surgeons on equal footing with army urgeons	508	44	1	10
ITTLETON O., charge of desertion against, to remove	955	40	1	15
, JOHN M., retired list of Army, to place on	207	44	2	11
Do	258	45	2	11
, MORRIS, charge of desertion against, to remove	109	44	1	10
R'S ISLAND, chapel at Fort Columbus, New York Harbor, to erect	95	28	2	3
JOHN,				
relief of	260	44	1	10
y record, to correct	832	43	1	9
, GEORGE W., additional pay to	21	43	2	9
RMY OF THE REPUBLIC (for reports relative to donating condemned cannon to posts of Grand Army of Republic see under titles of espective towns and cities in which located),				
, Colo., to loan tents for reunion at	1866	47	2	12
burg, Pa., to loan tents for encampment at	685	47	1	12
Do	1998	47	2	12
Island, Nebr., to loan tents for encampment at	686	47	1	12
SLAND, NEBRASKA, tents and camp equipage for soldiers' reunion t	686	47	1	12
JAMES H., relief of	746	25	2	2
PEMBERTON MONUMENT, purchase of land adjoining grounds surounding	558	44	1	10
Do	288	45	2	11
ULYSSES S.,				
ent to, at New York City	181	49	1	15
l list of Army, to place on, with rank and pay of General	92	46	3	11
W. S., relief of	65	37	2	6
EDEDIAH, back pension to	58	34	3	5
RESTON, relief of	90	22	2	2
JAMES, relief of heirs	104	28	1	3
Do	250	33	1	4
JAMES, charge of desertion against, to remove	260	44	1	10
Do	259	45	2	11

Subject.	Report.	Congress.	Session.	Volume.
GREGG, JAMES A., *et al.*, memorial to amend law admitting surgeons into Army	782	29	1	4
GREEK, SAMUEL, removal of charge of desertion against C. H. Creek	191	44	1	16
GREEN, DAVID A., charge of desertion against, to remove	1831	49	1	15
GREEN, L. T., relief of	88	45	2	11
GREEN, MARIE B., services as hospital nurse	58	43	1	9
GREENWOOD, CYRIL, relief of	1064	49	1	15
GRIERSON, B. H., military record, to correct	3180	49	1	15
GRIFFIN, JOHN C., relief of	440	43	1	9
Do	466	44	1	10
GRIFFITH, WILLIAM K., relief of heirs	19	44	2	11
GRIGGS, ALONZO H., relief of	3153	49	1	15
GROOMES, HORATIO, pension to	105	24	3	3
GROOMS, GEORGE, charge of desertion against, to remove	107	44	1	11
GROOSE, AUGUST, charge of desertion against, to remove	3671	49		15
GROTON, CONNECTICUT, right of way through Fort Griswold military reservation	1623	45	2	11
GROTON HEIGHTS, appropriation to celebrate battle of	1135	45	2	11
GROVELAND, MASSACHUSETTS, cannon for monument at	1443	47	1	12
GRUMBLING, JONATHAN C., charge of desertion against, to remove	2229	49	1	15
GUEDELLA, ROWENA, Twiggs swords, to return to	3650	49	2	15
GUMMO, JOHN W., charge of desertion against, to remove	403	47	1	12
GUNPOWDER. (*See also* ORDNANCE AND ORDNANCE STORES.)				
Depot for preservation of, erection of	737	29	1	4
Loans to private citizens of	58	17	2	1
Do	67	17	2	1
GUNS, manufacture of, for Navy and sea-coast defenses	4147	49	2	15
GUNTER, ALLEN, relief of	3632	49	2	15
GUSTIN, GEORGE S., bounty to	14	43	3	8
Do	84	44	2	11
GUY, LEVI, charge of desertion against, to remove	3374	49	1	15
GWIN, FRANCIS M., services rendered during Mexican war	234	33	1	4
HADDOCK, JOHN A., charge of desertion against, to remove	477	47	1	12
HAIGHT, SAMUEL S., relief of	281	34	1	5
HAIL, W. P. A., services rendered as assistant surgeon	37	34	1	5
HAINE, ELIAS, relief of	1160	49	1	15
HAINES, ELI, charge of desertion against, to remove	1171	49	1	15
HAINES, JOHN, charge of desertion against, to remove	78	45	2	11
HAKES, DWIGHT W., relief of	255	45	2	11
HALLER, GRANVILLE O., court of inquiry in case of	375	45	2	11
HALE, JONATHAN D., relief of	83	42	3	8
HALEY, WILLIAM D., relief of	962	49	1	15
HALL, JOHN H., indemnity for patent rifle	375	24	1	2
Do	257	25	2	2
Do	453	26	1	3
HALL, WILLIAM S., relief of	891	49	1	15
HALLOCK, THEODORE F., charge of desertion against, to remove	828	44	1	10
HALPIN, WILLIAM G., relief of	474	45	2	11
HALWICK, PETER M., pay from date of commission to date of muster	79	45	2	11
HAMILTON, J. M., priority of rank as captain	671	44	1	10
HAMILTON, JOHN, relief of	1	35	1	5
Do	2	35	1	5
HAMILTON, JOHN R., relief of	201	44	1	10
HAMILTON, OHIO, cannon for monument at	769	47	1	12
HAMILTON, SCHUYLER, restore to rank in Army	3759	49	2	15
HAMMOND, CHARLES H., charge of desertion against, to remove	1673	49	1	15
HAMPTON, VIRGINIA, soldiers' home at, management of	1867	47	2	12
HAMPTON AND OLD POINT RAILROAD COMPANY, right of way across military reservation of Old Point Comfort to	4093	49	2	15
HANCOCK BARRACKS, reimbursement of officers for losses by fire at	112	23	1	1
HANSELL, WILLIAM S, & SONS, royalty on knapsacks furnished Government	491	45	2	11
Do	705	47	1	12
HANWAY, SAMUEL B., additional pay to	127	44	2	11
HARBORS. (*See* RIVERS AND HARBORS.)				
HARDAWAY, JOHN F. S., charge of desertion against, to remove	1667	49	1	15
HARDIN, JOHN, relief of heirs	20	33	2	4
Do	52	34	1	5
HARLAN, THEODORE B., relief of	269	46	2	11
HARPER, SAMUEL D., charge of desertion against, to remove	3406	49	1	15
HARPER'S FERRY, VIRGINIA,				
Armory at, to re-establish	194	44	1	10
Assignment of officers for duty at	403	24	1	2
Property at, purchasers of	21	42	3	8
Winchester and Potomac Railroad Company through reservation at, right of way to	432	23	1	1
Do	3	23	2	1
HARRIS, ELLEN R., relief of	2171	48	2	14
HARRIS, WILLIAM A., arrears of pay	182	47	1	12
HARRISON, SAMUEL F., services as teamster	496	36	1	6
HARRODSBURG, KENTUCKY, soldiers' home at, sale of property belonging to	1820	47	2	12
HARTMAN, JACOB C., services previous to muster in	204	44	2	11
HARTMAN, JOHN M., relief of	3545	49	2	15

Subject.	Report.	Congress.	Session.	Volume.
MULTICHARGE GUN, tests of	2641	49	[illegible]	15
JOHN P., accounts of, to settle	48	24	1	4
, MASSACHUSETTS, cannon for monument at	1605	47	1	12
, JOHN H., charge of desertion against, to remove	880	49	1	15
NATHANIEL, relief of	212	22	1	2
HAW, NEW YORK, cannon for monument at	1619	47	1	12
ERT A., relief of	247	24	2	3
M., relief of	37	27	2	[illegible]
AT. C., additional pay to	67	43	1	9
, WILLIAM, relief of	296	27	2	3
Do	190	21	1	4
Do	63	[illegible]	2	[illegible]
JOHN C., relief of	734	47	1	12
ATWELL, relief of	203	35	1	[illegible]
NITRO-GLYCERINE SHELL, resolution in House relative to	[illegible]	49	1	15
EXANDER, relief of	[illegible]	35	1	5
WILLIAM P., military services, claim for	[illegible]	45	2	11
NES, contracts for furnishing	893	44	1	10
ENRY G., additional pay to	178	44	2	11
C., relief of	1690	49	1	15
, JOHN, relief of	340	43	1	9
Do	477	44	1	10
, ALFRED, relief of	1050	48	1	13
Do	1041	49	1	15
PATRICK, arrears of pay to	182	47	1	12
ROBERT, relief of	1545	49	1	15
AN, FREDERICK, relief of	843	43	1	9
N, ANN S., pension to	[illegible]	24	2	3
Do	591	25	2	3
Do	358	27	2	3
H., relief of	697	46	2	11
ON, TENNESSEE, raid by Confederate troops on, assessment for damages by	184	44	2	11
UY V., relief of	1861	47	2	12
WESLEY, arrears of pay to	906	45	2	11
ARLES, relief of	1172	49	1	15
, HELENA, relief of	182	47	1	12
GEORGE H., charge of desertion, to remove	60	43	1	9
RAIM, relief of	1176	49	1	15
RGER, GUSTAV A., accounts of, to settle	348	45	2	11
G. W., relief of	2236	49	1	15
, ELIZA P., relief of	92	23	2	2
Do	260	23	1	2
, GEORGE H., additional pay to	72	43	1	9
OHN D., additional pay to	27	47	1	12
IES A., military record, to correct	820	43	1	9
Do	26	44	1	10
ERT, relief of	2241	49	1	15
RLES W., traveling expenses, to compensate for	193	44	1	10
RGE D., military record, to correct	114	44	2	11
N, charge of desertion against, to remove	3364	49	1	15
EBT G., military record, to correct	1052	47	2	12
Do	1124	48	1	13
GUNNEGLE, relief of	204	36	1	6
LLIAM, relief of	487	45	2	11
NRY C., extra pay to	26	43	2	9
STER A., relief of	85	43	1	9
Do	476	44	1	10
ORGE, military history, to correct	74	45	2	11
, CHARLES, additional pay to	819	43	1	9
, JOHN, relief of	209	44	2	11
, WILLIAM P., retired list of Army, to advance in rank on	436	46	2	11
F. W., North Carolina Home Guards, memorial for relief	997	48	1	13
Do	920	49	1	15
ES, relief of	214	21	1	2
Do	75	22	1	2
ONARD, military bounty land to	423	22	1	2
HARLES E. H., military record, to correct	834	43	1	9
R DISABLED VOLUNTEERS (*See* SOLDIERS' HOMES.)				
LE, PENNSYLVANIA, cannon for monument at	1868	47	2	12
TT, STEPHEN M., relief of	875	43	1	9
Do	1407	47	1	12
Do	688	48	1	13
VID F., relief of	925	49	1	15
N., additional pay to	681	44	1	10
MES H., relief of	618	21	1	2
ELEANOR, relief of	252	33	1	4
GUSTAVUS B., relief of heirs	120	44	2	11
STEWARDS, appointment in Army of, to regulate	1405	47	1	12
Do	3654	49	2	15
N, JACOB, relief of	207	27	2	3

Subject.	Report.	Congress.	Session.	Volume.
HOUSÊR, ELI, relief of	908	49	1	15
HOWARD, C. A., to change name to Allen Henry Budlary	31	47	1	12
HOWARD, JAMES G., military record, to correct	192	47	1	12
HOWARD, STEPHEN, relief of	71	17	1	1
HOWE, HARRIET B., services as spy in war of 1812	500	36	1	6
HUDDLESTON, ELKANAH, relief of	468	44	1	10
HUDRY, JEAN, relief of	664	36	1	6
HUDSON, NEW YORK, cannon for monument at	1560	47		12
HUFF, JOHN, relief of	350	34		5
HUGHES, EDWARD B., charge of desertion against, to remove	905	49		15
HUGHES, IVAN, relief of	1956	49		15
HUGHES, JAMES, relief of	31	23		3
HUGHES, SAMUEL M., relief of	342	29		4
HUMPHREYS, HENRY H., relief of	3188	49		15
HUMPHREYS, GAD, relief of	203	29		4
HUNLEY, ARCHIBALD, back pay to	1705	46	2	11
Do	611	47		12
HUNT, FRANK W.,				
Ferry at Fort Buford, Dakota, to erect	527	48	1	13
Do	213	49	1	15
Coal on Fort Buford reservation, Dakota, to mine	528	48	1	13
Do	213	49	1	15
HUNT, HENRY J., to retire as major-general	122	48	1	13
Do	212	49	1	15
HUNT, REUBEN, improvement in ordnance, to test	400	25	2	2
HUNT, ROBERT, relief of	617	48	1	13
HUNT, THOMAS, relief of	328	25	2	2
HUNT, THOMAS B., relief of	1256	49	1	15
HUNTER, BENWOOD, relief of	3664	49	2	15
HUTCHINGS, J. M., relief of	2	41	2	7
HUTCHINSON, WILLIAM, services as spy, claim for	72	35	1	5
Do	119	36	1	6
HYAM, BENJAMIN D., relief of	298	35	1	5
HYDE, MICHAEL, charge of desertion against, to remove	918	49	1	15
IDAHO, Indian hostilities in, to adjudicate claims for losses by	1505	46	2	11
Do	333	46	3	11
Do	141	47	1	12
Do	807	48	1	13
IDDINGS, WILLIAM C., relief of	2313	48	2	13
ILLINOIS,				
Armory at Massac, to establish	441	28	1	3
Do	451	29	1	4
Do	214	31	1	4
Bayley's battalion, to pay for services in Black Hawk war	71	35	1	5
Soldiers' reunions in, to loan tents for	1291	47	1	12
IMES, JAMES O., arrears of pay to	192	47	1	12
INCOMPETENT OFFICERS. (*See* ARMY.)				
INDIAN BUREAU, transfer to War Department of	354	44	1	10
INDIAN HOSTILITIES (*see also* INDIAN WARS),				
Expenditures in, to amend act of 1882 for adjudicating claims of States and Territories for	807	48	1	13
Idaho, to adjudicate claims of, for losses	1505	46	2	11
Do	333	46	3	11
Do	141	47	1	12
Do	807	48	1	13
INDIAN TERRITORY, inquiry into firing of United States troops upon certain persons in	4050	49	2	15
INDIAN WAR CLAIMS,				
California,				
To adjudicate claim of, for supplies and service in Modoc war	843	47	1	12
Payment of expenses incurred in suppressing hostilities from 1854 to 1859	680	36	1	6
California and Oregon, for expenses incurred in Indian hostilities in 1872 and 1873	248	43	2	9
Dakota, expenses incurred in Indian rebellion of 1862	35	42	3	8
Idaho, to adjudicate claims for losses and services in Nez Percé war	1505	46	2	11
Do	833	46	3	11
Illinois, to pay Bayley's battalion of, for services in Black Hawk war	71	35	1	5
Kansas, to settle Indian war expenses of	440	46	2	11
Do	141	47	1	12
Missouri, to reimburse expenses for repelling invasion of Osage Indians	40	36	1	6
Montana, to audit for services in Nez Percé war	285	45	2	11
Do	134	46	2	11
Nebraska, to reimburse expenses incurred in defense of frontier settlements	193	34	1	5
Nevada, to adjudicate claims of, for expenses incurred in	141	47	1	12
New Mexico, to pay volunteer troops for suppressing hostilities in	52	37	3	6
Oregon,				
For expenses in 1855–'56	195	34	1	5
Do	837	43	1	9
Citizens of, on account of Modoc war	248	43	2	9
For expenses in Modoc war	843	47	1	12
To audit claim for expenditures in suppressing Indian hostilities	141	47	1	13

Subject.	Report.	Congress.	Session.	Volume.
WAR CLAIMS—Continued.				
n, to adjudicate	141	47	1	12
, for expenses in suppressing Indian hostilities	39	33	2	6
Do	201	33	1	6
ington Territory,				
for expenses in suppressing hostilities in 1855–'56	195	34	1	5
Do.	637	42	1	9
for services of volunteers at Puget Sound	198	34	2	5
to compensate citizens of, for service in Nez Percé war	1505	46	2	11
Do	538	46	2	11
Do	141	47	1	12
WARS,				
et rank, to confer, for services in	688	48	1	13
Do	1967	49	1	15
ole Indians, conduct of war against	82	18	2	1
A,				
to, distribution of	288	31	1	4
ted rangers from, compensation for	62	19	1	1
militia encampment, to loan tents to	771	47	1	12
nieth Regiment of Volunteers, for clothing lost	82	38	1	7
APOLIS, INDIANA, cannon for monument at	1618	47	1	12
S, RUFUS, retired list of Army, to place on	3170	49	1	15
, H. P., additional pay to	348	43	1	9
, HENRY, relief of	627	43	1	9
, WILLIAM P., relief of	44	44	2	11
TOR-GENERAL'S DEPARTMENT (*see also* ARMY),				
ector-generals in, to increase number of	331	30	1	3
ganization of	1580	47	2	13
Do	336	48	1	13
IGATION, United States troops, firing upon persons in Indian Territory by	4060	49	2	15
to, issue of	469	30	1	3
, cannon, &c., to loan for soldiers' reunions in	773	47	1	12
claims of, to adjudicate	545	30	1	3
Do	2	40	3	7
DOROTHEA, relief of	302	44	1	10
N, OHIO, cannon for monument at	1446	47	1	12
B. J. D., relief of	284	45	2	11
RG. HENRY, military record, to correct	88	46	3	11
CAMERON (steamer), relief of sufferers by loss of	476	47	1	12
Do	622	48	1	13
N, HENRY, relief of	13	43	2	9
Do	25	44	1	10
N, MATTHEW E., relief of	1946	49	1	15
NVILLE, FLORIDA, military site at, purchase of land for	3143	49	1	15
NVILLE, TAMPA AND KEY WEST RAILROAD COMPANY, right of way through reservation at Tampa	1574	47	1	12
S, WILLIAM, bounty land to	74	20	2	1
Do	17	21	1	2
JOHN, relief of assignee	13	38	1	7
N, JANE, services as nurse	474	44	1	10
ILLE, WISCONSIN, cannon for monument at	1451	47	1	12
, JOHN H., charge of desertion against, to remove	3835	49	2	15
T, ELI H., military services, pay for	13	42	3	8
, CHARLES C., relief of sureties	51	24	1	5
NRY B., relief of	3494	49	2	15
S, JOHN, relief of heirs	565	44	1	19
, CHARLES K., charge of desertion, to remove	3656	49	2	15
W., military record, to correct	256	44	2	11
NNIS POST, cannon for monument at	1403	46	2	11
N, CHARLES H., additional pay to	580	44	1	10
N, DANIEL, relief of	330	21	1	2
Do	83	22	1	2
N, EDWARD P., arrears of pay to	8	43	1	9
Do	192	47	1	12
N, ISAAC, charge of desertion against, to remove	1671	49	1	15
N, JAMES, relief of	2347	48	2	13
N, ROBERT, arrears of pay to	132	34	3	5
N, WILLIAM, relief of	812	47	1	12
CHARLES LEE, relief of	285	31	1	4
Do	292	31	1	4
Do	7	33	1	4
. S., relief of	667	44	1	10
OHN,				
on to	131	34	3	5
Do	525	35	1	5
ed list of Army, to place on	1406	49	1	15
EVI, relief of	690	48	1	13
ROGER, pay and emoluments of brevet rank, claim for	485	25	2	2
SARAH, pension to	255	20	1	1

Subject.	Report.	Congress.	Session.	Volume.
JONES, WILLIAM C., charge of desertion against, to remove	1675	49	1	15
JORDAN, THOMAS, relief of	290	33	1	4
JOSEPH, ADOLPH, additional back pay to	108	44	1	10
JOYCE, HERBERT, charge of desertion, to remove	838	47	1	12
JUDGE, PETER, military history, to correct	940	47	1	12
JUDGE-ADVOCATES IN ARMY, promotion in corps of	812	48	1	13
JURISDICTION, Court of Claims, restricting	42	42	2	7
Do	197	44	1	10
KANE, JAMES, relief of	678	46	2	11
Do	503	48	1	13
Do	3360	49	1	15
KANSAS,				
Fort Scott Reserve, for educational purposes, to State	37	33	2	5
Fourteenth Kansas Cavalry, relief of recruits	3365	49	1	15
Geological survey of, providing for	36	33	2	5
Indian war claims, to adjudicate	440	46	2	11
Do	141	47	1	12
Do	807	48	1	13
Military roads in, to improve	36	33	2	5
Ordnance account, to credit	2235	49	1	15
Do	3113	49	1	15
Rivers in, to improve	36	33	2	5
War claims, to adjudicate	64	41	2	7
KANSAS AND TEXAS RAILROAD, right of way across Fort Hays military reservation	4127	49	2	15
KANSAS VALLEY RAILROAD COMPANY, right of way across Fort Riley military reservation	4112	49	2	15
KEARNEY, General PHILIP H., cannon for monument to	652	44	1	10
KEIFER, CORNELIUS W., pay, arrears	192	47	1	12
KELLOGG, HARRY S (administrator), relief of	809	48	1	13
KELLOGG, JOHN F., relief of	1405	49	1	15
KELLY, ANDREW B., charge of desertion against, to remove	1855	49	1	15
KELLY, H. A., pay, additional	73	43	1	9
KELLY, MOSES J., property destroyed by fire, claim for	986	45	2	11
Do	80	47	1	12
KEMP, ISAAC R., charge of desertion against, to remove	1843	49	1	15
KENDALL, WILLIAM, sutler stores sold to recruits, claim for	227	34	1	5
KENNEDY, JAMES K., relief of	1854	49	1	15
KENNEDY, JOHN, relief of	1245	49	1	15
KENSINGTON AND TACONY RAILWAY, right of way through arsenal grounds at Bridesburg, Philadelphia, Pa., to	1650	49	1	15
Do	1990	49	1	15
KENT, LEWIS A., pension, increase	181	46	2	11
KER, WILLIAM H., sutler's supplies, claim for	283	31	1	4
KERR, BEVERLY & CO., private property destroyed by Indians, claim for	280	34	1	5
Do	100	34	3	5
KETCHUM, WILLIAM F., hand grenades, to test	328	29	1	4
KEY, GEORGE L., military history, to correct	1351	46	2	11
Do	192	47	1	12
KEY WEST, FLORIDA, cemetery at, to purchase land for	329	43	1	9
KIERNAN, JOHN, pay, additional	468	45	2	11
KILBOURN, DAVID, relief of	189	21	1	2
Do	174	23	1	2
Do	107	24		2
KILLINGLY, CONNECTICUT, cannon for monument at	1403	46	2	11
KIMBALL, RICHARD I., relief of	1241	49		15
KINCADE, EDWARD, charge of desertion against, to remove	1959	49		15
KING, JAMES S., private property lost by fire and shipwreck, claim for	72	45	2	11
KING, JOHN H., relief of	251	33		4
Do	272	33	1	4
KING, MARION M., relief of	913	49	1	15
KINGON, JAMES W., relief of	3226	49		15
KING'S MOUNTAIN, centennial celebration of battle of	1270	46	2	11
KIRBY, D. T., restoration to Army	680	46	2	11
Do	28	47		12
KIRBY, FRANCIS M., relief of	1047	48		13
Do	2223	49		15
KITZMILLER, A. M., relief of	17	28		3
KLAUSER, EMANUEL, relief of	1406	46	2	11
Do	617	47	1	12
Do	986	48		13
Do	1669	49		15
KNAPP, PETER J., military record, to correct	446	43		9
KNIGHT, EBENEZER, arrears of pay	192	47		12
KNIGHT, SIMEON, relief of	1025	25		2
KNOCKELMANN, JOHN, charge of desertion against, to remove	1657	49		15
KNOX, T. T., relief of	609	44		10
Do	261	45		11
KNOXVILLE, TENNESSEE,				
National cemetery near, road to	590	49		15
Soldiers' cemetery at, condemned cannon for	1294	47		12

Subject.	Report.	Congress.	Session.	Volume.
NDIANA, condemned mortars for monument at	[illegible]	47	1	12
EHMAN J., relief of	[illegible]	46	2	11
DOLPH, relief of	[illegible]	49	1	15
MILLER, judgment against, to be relieved from	17	42	3	8
AMES, bounty and re-enlistment pay, claim for	36	44	1	10
DAVID, charge of desertion against, to remove	[illegible]	49	2	15
STER, relief of	1247	49	1	15
ACOB, alias JOHN WALTERS, charge of desertion, to remove	[illegible]	49	1	15
IN G., funeral expenses of, to pay	1781	47	1	12
Do	257	48	1	13
T, A. F. S. S., relief of	4049	49	2	15
H, HENRY, relief of	[illegible]	49	2	15
WIN E. (lieutenant), muster of, to correct	[illegible]	49	2	15
ORGE, relief of heirs	127	34	1	5
RENZO, charge of desertion against, to remove	[illegible]	49	1	15
U., relief of	3	41	2	7
ANTS. (See PUBLIC LANDS.)				
W., compensation for exploration of Pacific railroad	801	35	1	5
Do	125	36	1	7
R, LEONARD L., arrears of pay	281	46	2	11
S., pension to	37	44	2	11
SAMUEL M., land near Fortress Monroe, Va., claim for	[illegible]	33	1	6
SSES. (See ARMY.)				
BENJAMIN and THOMAS, damages for breach of covenants of warranty, claim for	64	35	2	5
SIMON F., arrears of pay	102	47	1	12
J. W., pay as colonel, claim for	675	44	1	10
R, MASSACHUSETTS, cannon for monument at	1617	47	1	12
WILLIS, charge of desertion against, to remove	[illegible]	49	2	15
AMES T., army record, to correct	187	46	2	11
ORTH STREET RAILROAD COMPANY, right of way across Fort Leavenworth military reservation	475	44	1	10
ORTH, NORTHERN AND SOUTHERN RAILWAY, right of way across Fort Leavenworth military reservation	1801	49	1	15
Y, relief of	237	36	2	7
S M., service previous to muster in, claim for	184	44	2	11
Y A., relief of	106	47	1	12
Do	123	48	1	13
ELL, relief of heirs	327	23	1	2
PERCY S., relief of heirs	1301	47	1	12
HARRIET B., interment of remains in national cemetery at New rne, N. C	2013	49	1	15
CYRUS, relief of	44	39	1	7
GEORGE A., loss of horse, claim for	677	44	1	10
ENRY R., United States of Colombia, to accept position under Government of	483	47	1	12
MARIA B., relief of	403	44	1	10
EORGE, relief of	2230	49	1	15
ILLIAM L., additional pay to	128	44	2	11
J. H., accounts as assistant quartermaster, to audit	153	33	1	4
HILIP, salary, overpayment	677	46	2	11
RTH, HARRIETT, pension to	353	27	2	3
AS P., bounty land as Government contractor	135	35	1	5
HN F., restoration to army	3179	49	1	15
NT-GENERAL, grade in Army, to continue	615	48	1	13
CK ARSENAL, grounds at, disposition of	745	44	1	10
HOMAS, restoration to Army	450	46	2	11
Do	29	47	1	12
Do	3173	49	1	15
ON, JAMES C., charge of desertion, to remove	87	43	1	9
D, A. A., relief of	540	36	1	6
BERNHARD, military record, to correct	1978	47	2	12
NGELINE, pay as laundress	756	44	1	10
AVID M., relief of	1254	49	1	15
RT, INDIANA, cannon for monument at	1447	47	1	12
IES, additional pay	77	43	1	9
UGH, JOHN, relief of	902	49	1	15
JCY, pension to	95	22	2	2
ES, pay and bounty to	51	44	2	11
ATHANIEL HALL, *et al.*, conduct at Military Academy	87	16	1	1
Do	90	16	1	1
A,				
tions on Lake Borgne at Proctor's Point	459	29	1	4
road from Cantonment Gibson to Natchitoches in	67	19	1	1
road from mouth of Red River to Sabine River	643	29	1	4
asylum at New Orleans	65	30	2	4
laims, to audit	364	27	2	3
of, to return	3151	49	1	15
E AND BARDSTOWN TURNPIKE COMPANY, bridges destroyed by United States forces, claim for	121	38	1	7
E, KENTUCKY, cannon for monument at	845	47	1	12

Subject.	Report.	Congress.	Session.	Volume.
MAN, relief of	47	44	2	11
ATHAN L., back pay, claim for	34	43	3	8
Do.	80	43	1	9
LIAM, extra services during war of 1812, claim for	87	26	1	4
OHIO, cannon for monument at	769	47	1	12
OHN J., relief of	484	45	2	11
A, IOWA, cannon for monument at	1617	47	1	12
AD, MASSACHUSETTS, cannon for monument at	1445	47	1	12
HENRY, retired list of Army, to advance in rank on	1321	46	2	11
Do.	204	48	1	13
JOSEPH, relief of	43	18	1	1
GEORGIA, road to national cemetery near	2273	48	2	13
RPS, reorganization of	136	21	1	2
TILLERY, cannon for use of	428	46	2	11
ONZO J., military record, to correct	84	43	2	8
NDREW, relief of	1830	49	1	15
ARLES T., arrears of pay to	183	47	1	12
ARRY W., relief of	2364	48	2	13
LIUS, stores furnished United States troops, claim for	86	36	2	5
Do.	279	36	1	6
ARCELLUS, military record, to correct	766	47	1	12
,				
ions for defense of Baltimore	310	22	1	2
of, to adjudicate	152	43	2	9
CHIGAN, cannon for monument at	1868	47	2	12
SETTS,				
Springfield, purchase of land for	396	25	2	2
Posts 73 and 78, Grand Army of the Republic	1092	46	2	11
ions, to erect, at New Bedford	827	29	2	4
Do.	71	31	2	4
ims of, to adjudicate	16	19	1	1
Do.	123	26	2	3
Do.	195	27	1	4
Do.	144	25	3	5
12, expenses for	190	18	1	1
SETTS HEAVY ARTILLERY, bounties to First Battalion of	22	42	3	8
BRAHAM A., relief of	176	22	1	2
ARMORER AT SPRINGFIELD, MASSACHUSETTS, salary of, to	187	47	1	12
, WILLIAM B., services as chaplain, claim for	109	37	2	6
FRANCIS W., pay as second lieutenant, claim for	1136	46	2	11
R, WILLIAM M., relief of	54	47	1	12
ANDREW C., charge of desertion against, to remove	60	46	3	11
NRY B., relief of	11	43	3	8
' HONOR, to Louis F. Ellis	533	49	1	15
IUSEUM, property adjoining, in Washington, D. C., to purchase	607	43	1	9
HIO, cannon for monument at	1292	47	1	12
ral MONTGOMERY C., retirement of	337	47	1	12
ORGE H., relief of	1656	49	1	15
TENNESSEE,				
emetery near, road to	759	48	1	13
Do	1954	49	1	15
Do	1955	49	1	15
emetery near, to erect rostrum in	1856	49	1	15
, CHARLES G., pension to widow	202	36	1	6
LEWIS, date of commission, claim for pay from	76	44	2	11
B., services as chaplain, pay for	110	37	2	6
EPISCOPAL CHURCH, missionary society of, claim for land m at the Dalles, Oregon	145	35	2	5
Do	120	36	1	6
WAR,				
ents by Pay Department during	502	31	1	4
s in, pay of	120	38	1	7
uards, of, claim for services on Canadian frontier in 1838	86	34	3	5
oads in, to construct	42	19	1	1
militia for services, to settle	125	22	2	3
Home, to establish branch in	1514	48	1	13
N, WILLIAM M., relief of	3152	49	1	15
IO, cannon for monument at	772	47	1	12
, relief of	668	44	1	10
ENTRE, OHIO, cannon for monument at	1402	46	2	11
ACADEMY, WEST POINT, NEW YORK,				
g of	406	23	1	2
Do	476	28	1	3
, investigation of	87	16	1	1
Do	90	16	1	1
ppropriation,				
86–'87	719	49	1	15
87–'88	3491	49	2	15
ondition of	606	43	1	9

Subject.	Report.	Congress.	Session.	Volume.
SERVATIONS—Continued.				
—Continued.				
way to Chesapeake and Ohio Railroad across	221	48	1	12
way to Hampton and Old Point Comfort across	4068	49	2	15
ra, right of way to Fremont, Elkhorn and Missouri Railroad Company across	546	47	1	12
l, to vacate portion of	346	47	1	12
g, to sell	35	44	2	11
vacate	846	47	1	12
Kans., right of way to Kansas Valley Railroad Company across	4112	49	2	15
limits and open reservation to settlement	118	34	3	5
way to Western Railroad Company of Minnesota through	252	45	2	11
right of way to Saint Louis and San Francisco Railroad through	1869	47	2	12
g, to cede portion, to Minnesota	4051	49	2	15
sale of site of old	364	28	1	3
le, Ariz., right of way to Prescott and Arizona Central Railway Company across	2902	49	2	15
a, Mich., sale of	126	43	2	9
rry, right of way to Winchester and Potomac Railroad Company through	432	22	1	2
Do.	3	23	2	2
Comfort, Va., right of way to Hampton and Old Point Railroad Company across	4068	49	2	15
N. Y., right of way to Chateaugay Railroad across	492	47	1	12
sed, Cal., land titles at	4	41	3	7
right of way to Utah Western Railroad across	680	44	1	10
River, boundaries of reservation on	89	31	3	4
Arsenal, Mass., right of way to Springfield Street Railroad Company through	446	46	2	11
Do.	66	47	1	12
, right of way to Jacksonville, Tampa and Key West Railroad through	1574	47	1	12
Miss., right of way for railroad through cemetery near	1260	46	2	11
ROADS. (*See* WAGON ROADS.)				
ORE-KEEPERS. (*See* STOREKEEPERS.)				
ORES, sale of unfit	81	18	1	1
LEGRAPHS. (*See* TELEGRAPH.)				
appropriation for	94	17	2	1
, to replace unserviceable	1086	49	1	15
olumbia, reorganization of	666	36	1	6
ary States with appropriation for, to credit	2574	49	1	15
of	934	48	1	12
crease	567	26	1	3
urnishing	419	23	1	2
oops, court-martial proceedings in trial of	140	20	1	1
Do.	225	20	1	1
of States, to adjudicate	600	48	1	13
ate militia from,				
	893	27	2	3
Do.	108	28	2	3
	91	17	1	1
Do.	62	17	2	1
Do.	77	19	2	1
Do.	45	18	1	1
Do.	584	27	2	3
Do.	684	27	2	3
	543	26	1	3
a	364	27	2	3
	506	26	1	3
Do.	78	26	2	3
Do.	363	27	2	3
usetts	18	19	1	1
Do.	123	28	2	3
Do.	168	32	1	4
n	125	27	3	3
l	87	38	1	7
Do.	67	42	3	7
mpshire	833	29	1	4
Do.	47	29	2	4
Do.	149	30	1	4
Do.	170	32	1	4
xico	38	33	2	5
Do	196	34	1	6
t	126	26	2	3
Do.	23	31	2	4
Do.	188	34	1	5
M, money paid for substitute, to reimburse	524	43	1	9
REW C., relief of	1179	49	1	15
D, bounty land and back pay, claim for	20	36	2	6

Subject.	Report.	Congress.	Session.	Volume.
NATIONAL PARK. (*See* YELLOWSTONE NATIONAL PARK.)				
NAVY AND SEA-COAST DEFENSES, manufacture of guns for	4147	49	2	15
NAWRY, JOHN J., relief of	1238	49	1	15
NEALE, HOSEA, relief of widow	391	25	2	2
NEBRASKA.				
Indian hostility claims, to adjudicate	192	34	1	5
Do	807	48	1	13
Military posts in, to complete	3112	49	1	15
Roads in	34	33	2	5
NEEDHAM, WILLIAM H., additional pay to	678	44	1	10
NELSON, H., loss of horse and equipments, claim for	656	44	1	10
NEVADA, Indian hostility claims, to adjudicate	*141	47	1	12
Do	807	48	1	13
NEVADA, IOWA, cannon for monument at	1565	47	1	12
NEW ALBANY, INDIANA, road to national cemetery at	1517	47	1	12
NEW BEDFORD, MASSACHUSETTS,				
Cannon for monument at	168	44	2	11
Do	1441	47	1	12
Fortification at harbor of	327	29	1	4
Do	21	31	2	4
NEW BERNE, NORTH CAROLINA, interment of remains of Mrs. Harriet B. Lehman in national cemetery at	2013	49	1	15
NEW BRIGHTON, PENNSYLVANIA, cannonfor monument at	1783	47	1	12
NEWBURG, NEW YORK, cannon to Post Ellis, G. A. R., at	836	44	1	10
NEW HAMPSHIRE, militia claims, to adjudicate	833	29	1	4
Do	47	29	2	4
Do	149	30	1	4
Do	170	32	1	4
NEW HAMPSHIRE VETERAN ASSOCIATION, cannon for monument	1868	47	2	12
NEWKIRK, CHARLES, loss of baggage, claim	420	26	1	3
NEWMAN, Col. DANIEL, pension to	50	23	2	2
Do	674	25	2	2
NEWMAN, JOHN N., additional pay to	79	43	1	9
NEWMAN, WADE H., charge of desertion against, to remove	2225	49	1	15
NEW MEXICO,				
Cavalry in, to raise regiment of volunteer	*531	49	1	15
Indian hostilities in,				
To raise regiment of volunteers to suppress	155	35	2	5
Payment of volunteers for service in	537	36	1	6
Do	52	37	2	6
NEW MEXICO, militia called out in 1854, payment of	38	33	2	5
Do	196	34	1	5
NEW, NICHOLAS W., arrears of pay to	192	47	1	12
NEWPORT, KENTUCKY,				
Barracks at, to improve	3963	49	1	15
Cannon for monument at	1293	47	1	12
NEWPORT, RHODE ISLAND, site of Fort Greene for park purposes to city of, use of	2576	49	1	15
NEWPORT, VERMONT, cannon for monument at	1437	47	1	12
NEWS, JOHN, Soldiers' Home, Washington, D. C., permission to enter	75	44	1	10
NEWTON, WALKER A., restoration to Army	690	46	2	11
Do	1690	46	2	11
NEW YORK (CITY), arsenal in harbor, to establish	16	37	3	6
NEW YORK (STATE),				
Arsenal at Watervliet, additional land for	148	19	1	1
Fortifications at Sackett's Harbor, to construct	36	28	2	3
Do	202	29	1	4
Do	449	29	1	4
Niagara barracks, to repair	442	26	1	3
Seventh New York Cavalry Volunteers, relief of	1343	49	1	15
Twenty-first Regiment New York Volunteers, claims of	299	15	2	1
NIAGARA BARRACKS, repair of	442	26	1	3
NICHOLS, J. W., relief of	128	43	2	9
NINTH UNITED STATES INFANTRY, loss of personal property, claim for	993	45	3	11
NITRO-GLYCERINE SHELL. (*See* ORDNANCE AND ORDNANCE STORES.)				
NODINE, RICHARD H., *et al.*, discharge from army, petition for	96	31	2	*4
NON-COMMISSIONED OFFICERS, (*see also* ARMY),				
Recruiting stations, appointment of, at	2370	48	2	13
Sergeants, to increase pay of	51	18	2	1
NORTH, ALBERT A., arrears of pay to	193	47	1	12
NORTH CAROLINA,				
Arsenal in, to establish	373	24	1	2
Arsenal at Fayetteville, sale of site of	53	32	2	5
Executive letter-book of, to furnish copies of official	2375	48	1	13
Militia claims of State, to adjudicate	690	48	1	13
NORTH CAROLINA HOME GUARDS, relief of Capt. W. W. Hegeed's company of	997	48	1	13
Do	320	49	1	15
NORTH PLATTE RIVER, military bridge across, at Fort Laramie	829	44	1	10
NORTHWESTERN MISSOURI AND SOUTHWESTERN IOWA SOLDIERS' ASSOCIATION, tents to, loan of	687	47	1	12
Do	1562	47	1	12

* Parts 1, 2.

Subject.	Report.	Congress.	Session.	Volume.
ERN OVERLAND MAIL ROUTE, military posts from Saint Cloud, Minn., to Fort Walla Walla, Oregon, to establish on	45	39	1	7
CH UNIVERSITY, VERMONT, field pieces, to loan two, to	61	30	2	4
OOD, SAMUEL C., loss of horse and equipage, claim for	357	34	1	5
E, JOSEPHINE, relief of	510	25	2	2
Do	353	27	2	3
Do	407	28	1	3
AN, LORENZO D., for funds to rescue sister captured by Mohave Indians	55	34	3	5
N, AGATHA, relief of	317	36	1	6
N, JAMES, relief of	44	36	2	6
ELL, PATRICK, pay as brigadier-general, claim for	657	44	1	10
OR, STEPHEN, relief of	3162	49	1	15
ERS. (*See* ARMY; BREVET RANK; RANK AND PAY.)				
non to Pickaway County for soldiers' monuments at	1744	47	1	12
g to One hundred and eighth Regiment Infantry Volunteers, to restore	1527	47	1	12
inteers in 1846, pay of two companies of	149	35	2	5
Do	501	36	1	6
Do	122	38	1	7
OINT COMFORT. (*See* FORTRESS MONROE.)				
R, ROBERT, arrears of pay to	192	47	1	12
EAD, JAMES, arrears of pay to	192	47	1	12
, STEPHEN, relief of	53	21	1	2
. O. C., to retire as major-general	58	46	3	11
ANCE AND ORDNANCE STORES,				
rado, to credit, on account of	3230	49	1	15
s, manufacture of, for Navy and sea-coast defenses	4147	49	2	15
kell's multicharge gun, to test	2641	48	2	13
Do	3065	49	1	15
es's nitro-glycerine shell, purchase of	3065	49	1	15
sas, to credit, on account of	3113	49	1	15
n of, to States	58	17	2	1
Do	67	17	2	1
of, unfit for public service	81	18	1	1
ANCE DEPOT, New York Harbor, to establish, in	16	37	3	6
N,				
an hostility claims, to adjudicate	195	34	1	5
Do	248	43	2	9
Do	837	43	1	9
Do	297	44	1	10
Do	141	47	1	12
Do	843	47	1	12
Do	1114	47	1	12
Do	807	48	1	13
tary road to Astoria	29	33	2	5
ds in, to establish	34	33	2	5
Do	188	34	1	5
shington Territory on books of Ordnance Department for arms loaned, to credit	4053	49	2	15
N VOLUNTEERS, claims of, to adjudicate	529	48	1	13
JESSE N., relief of	2227	49	1	15
OHN G., muster rolls of Army, to place on	2237	49	1	15
RKE, PATRICK J., relief of	617	44	1	10
HELD, HENRY, pay from date of commission to date of muster, claim for	199	44	1	10
Do	1402	46	2	11
Do	192	47	1	12
GO CANAL, locks of, enlargement	114	37	2	6
O, MICHIGAN, cannon for monument at	264	47	1	12
HAN, RICHARD, arrears of pay to	192	47	1	12
WILLIAM H., loss of horse, claim for	435	31	1	4
CO, ANTONIO, relief of legal representatives	*187	30	1	4
, ALBERT F., charge of desertion against, to remove	1159	47	1	12
, PETER E., arrears of pay to	192	47	1	12
H, JOSEPH W., relief of	125	44	2	11
R, DANIEL, relief of	731	24	1	2
Do	206	25	2	2
Do	104	26	1	3
Do	124	26	2	3
R, GEORGE HENRY, charge of desertion against, to remove	1658	49	1	15
, HENRY C., retired list of Army, to place on	130	43	2	9
IDGE, ALDEN, ammunition to, for instruction of pupils in gunnery, issue of	82	18	1	1
SCO RIVER, MARYLAND, fortifications on, to erect	310	23	1	2
K, ALEXANDER H., relief of	93	26	2	3
K, MARY A., relief of	512	25	2	2
RSON, JAMES, relief of	906	49	1	15
RSON, JOHN, pension to	146	35	2	5
N, S. K., arrears of pay to	192	47	1	12
AUGUSTUS C., to place on retired list as first lieutenant	524	48	1	13

*And views of minority.

Subject.	Report.	Congress.	Session.	Volume.
...R ALBERT C., relief of	3672	49	2	15
...CHANCY J., relief of	382	42	1	10
...BENJAMIN F., relief of	434	48	1	13
Do	3189	49	1	15
...M, WILLIAM, relief of	1961	49	1	15
...R ACADEMY, CHARLESTON, SOUTH CAROLINA, transfer of land to	4090	49	2	15
...R, General FITZ JOHN, to restore to Army	139	46	2	11
Do	*1	48	1	13
Do	*42	49	1	15
...AND, MAINE, cannon for monument at	259	47	1	12
...AND, OREGON, military road, to Vancouver, Wash., from	841	47	1	12
...OUTH, OHIO, cannon to Ladies' Soldiers' Monument Society at	1155	47	1	12
...COMITATUS, employment of Army in Territories as	1151	47	1	12
...OUTES, power of Congress to establish	31	38	1	7
...CHOOL, enlistment of school masters in Army	1425	47	1	13
...RADERS, recruits, authorized to give credit to	1147	47	1	12
... ANDREW R., back pay, claim for	63	34	3	6
...KEEPSIE, NEW YORK, cannon for monumental purposes to	1408	46	2	11
...SON, WALLACE E. H., military record, to amend	478	47	1	12
...T GUN CARRIAGE, test of	2369	48	2	13
... JOHNSON S., relief of	1652	49	1	15
...ER, HIRAM, additional pay to	525	43	1	9
... JOSEPH R., loss of horse, claim for	489	45	2	11
...PTION. (See PUBLIC LANDS.)				
...YTERIAN CHURCH OF GRATIOT, permission to erect church on Fort Gratiot reservation	501	44	1	10
...OTT AND ARIZONA CENTRAL RAILWAY COMPANY, right of way to cross Fort Whipple military reservation in Arizona	3608	49	2	15
...ENT OF UNITED STATES,				
...nance stores, to direct sale of unserviceable	61	18	1	1
...er to muster out officers under certain conditions	27	42	2	7
...ON, WILLIAM G., relief of	52	33	2	5
... JACOB, pension to	49	34	1	5
... JOHN, service of self and command during Florida war, claim for	740	30	1	4
Do.	79	32	1	4
... SHIPS, monument to victims who died in (Revolutionary war)	176	28	2	3
Do	3975	49	2	15
...OR'S LANDING, LOUISIANA, fortifications at, on Lake Borgne	450	29	1	4
... HEALTH, to extend observations of Signal Service so as to benefit	526	43	1	9
Do	55	43	2	9
Do	661	44	1	10
... LANDS,				
Ripley reservation, to reduce limits of, and open to pre-emption	118	34	3	5
Francisco and vicinity, to relinquish title to lands in	177	44	2	11
...amette Valley and Cascade Mountain Wagon Road Company, land grant to	332	46	3	11
...RD, JOHN, relief of	504	44	1	10
...M, LEWIS I., arrears of pay to	192	47	1	12
...NTINE, islands in harbor of San Francisco to be used for	1704	46	2	11
...ERMASTER'S DEPARTMENT,				
...ganization of	4	18	2	1
Do	23	19	1	1
...al of buildings for	767	44	1	10
...IN, JULIUS, court-martial proceedings, to review, in case of	472	45	2	11
... ISAAC, relief of	3150	49	1	15
... THOMAS, relief of	471	44	1	10
..., A. P., additional pay to	755	44	1	10
...LPH, JOHN, bounty land to	347	36	1	6
...N, JOHN, relief of heirs	360	33	1	4
..., PETER D., back pay, claim for	117	44	2	11
...S, SAMUEL E., additional pay to	83	43	1	9
...N, JAMES M., relief of	478	44	1	10
...NS, BENJAMIN S., relief of	931	49	1	15
...NS, JOHN A., removal of statue of	107	49	1	15
...JOHN B., claim for improvement in ordnance	1938	47	2	12
Do	816	48	1	13
...R, JOHN, pension to	296	34	1	5
...ITING STATIONS, appointment of sergeant-majors and first sergeants for	2370	48	2	13
...ITS,				
traders, to give credit to	1147	47	1	12
...ld regiments to be mustered out with their commands	14	38	2	7
...N, SUSANNAH, increase of pension	140	35	1	5
...OHN, relief of	3675	49	2	15
...PARIS L., arrears of pay to	192	47	1	12
...WILLIAM, relief of	2239	49	1	15
...ISTMENT,				
commissioned officers, providing for, of	904	27	2	4
...d for, extension of	1570	48	1	13
...E, JOHN E., relief of	11	40	3	7

*And views of minority.

Subject.	Report.	Congress.	Session.	Volume.
RENTZ, JOHN, charge of desertion against, to remove	506	44	1	[illegible]
RESERVATIONS,				
Camp Douglas, Utah, to relinquish certain parts of	208	48	1	13
Fort Bliss, Texas, right of way to Rio Grande and El Paso Railway through	3067	49	1	15
Fort Brady, Michigan, sale of old site	2622	48	2	13
Do	497	49	1	15
Fort Buford, Dakota, Frank W. Hunt to mine coal on	528	48	1	13
Do	213	49	1	15
Frank W. Hunt to construct ferry at	527	48	1	13
Do	213	49	1	15
Fort Hays, Kansas, sale of portion of	755	48	1	13
Do	1958	49	1	15
Fort Randall, Dakota, to vacate portion east of Missouri River	201	48	1	13
Fort Rice, Dakota, to abolish	202	48	1	13
Fort Riley, Kans., to open portion for settlement	590	48	1	13
Fort Russell, right of way to Cheyenne, Black Hills and Montana Railroad across	756	48	1	13
Fort Russell, right of way to Cheyenne and Northern Railroad across	2486	49	1	15
Do	2847	49	1	15
Fort Selden, New Mexico, right of way to Rio Grande, Mexico and Pacific Railroad through	501	49	1	15
Fortress Monroe, to extend Chesapeake and Ohio Railway to lands of	331	48	1	13
Plattsburg, N. Y., dedicating same for park purposes to	2393	48	2	13
West Point, N. Y.,				
Permission to dig for treasure at	732	48	1	13
Providing for erection of buildings at	1684	48	1	13
RESTORATION OF OFFICERS. (*See* ARMY.)				
RETIRED OFFICERS. (*See* ARMY.)				
REVERE, GEORGE W., relief of	915	49	1	15
REVISED STATUTES,				
To amend act of March 3, 1855, granting bounty lands to soldiers in the war of 1812	107	34	3	5
To amend,				
1244, 1253, retirement of Army officers	135	46	2	11
1298, 1302, Army clothing issues	812	47	1	12
1190, salary of paymasters' clerks	840	47	1	12
1754, employment of soldiers and sailors	1777	48	1	13
REXFORD, WILLIAM H., relief of	4	46	3	11
Do	525	48	1	13
REYNOLDS, General J. J., cannon for statue to	266	47	1	12
REYNOLDS, SAMUEL M., relief of	219	44	2	11
REYNOLDS, WILLIAM B., relief of	620	48	1	13
RHEA, DAVID, relief of	881	44	1	10
RICE, ORRIN H., timber furnished to United States, claim for	148	35	2	3
RICE, RUSSELL, bounty land to	269	33	1	4
RICHAND, JOHN, relief of	114	23	1	2
RICHARDS, A. V., relief of	16	41	3	7
Do	396	43	1	9
RICHARDSON, HARLAND, relief of	619	48	1	13
RICHARDSON, JAMES, military record, to correct	53	44	2	11
RICHMOND, VIRGINIA, road to national cemetery near	1136	47	1	12
Do	832	48	1	13
Do	1249	49	1	15
RIGDEN, JAMES, relief of	232	25	2	3
RIGGS, WILLIAM J., relief of	919	49	1	15
RIGHT OF WAY. (*See* under name of railroad to which granted; under name of State, Territory, or reservation)				
RILEY, THOMAS F., relief of	3187	49	1	15
RIO GRANDE, MEXICO AND PACIFIC RAILROAD,				
Lands, authority to purchase certain	1653	49	1	15
Right of way through Fort Selden military reservation	501	49	1	15
RIO GRANDE AND EL PASO RAILWAY, right of way through Fort Bliss military reservation to	3067	49	1	15
RIO GRANDE RIVER, bridges over, memorial to construct	190	34	1	5
RISEDEN, ISAAC, additional pay to	443	43	1	9
RIVERS AND HARBORS, defense for all harbors and ports	94	24	1	2
ROACH, JAMES,				
Charge of desertion against, to remove	2878	49	1	15
Relief of	3367	49	1	15
ROBALDO, FRANCISCO, relief of	473	35	1	3
Do	600	36	1	4
ROBERTS, CASSIUS C., relief of	835	43	1	9
Do	192	47	1	12
ROBERTS, CHARLES S., relief of	968	45	2	11
ROBERTS, JACKSON, arrears of pay, claims for	25	42	2	8
Do	106	44	2	11
ROBERTSON, CHRISTOPHER W., charge of desertion against, to remove	742	44	1	10
Do	201	44	2	11
ROBERTSON, JAMES M., military record, to correct	335	43	1	9
ROBIDOUX, ANTONE, relief of	226	36	1	5
Do	80	35	2	5
Do	484	36	1	6

Subject.	Report.	Congress.	Session.	Volume.
NAL, Mississippi River and Lake Michigan, to connect, by	37	37	2	6
. AMOS, charge of desertion against, to remove	2685	49	2	15
Do	4173	49	2	15
, STANTON, relief of	37	15	2	1
TTEN, EPHRIAM, relief of	65	42	1	9
ST, JOHN H., charge of desertion against, to remove	982	45	2	11
Do	130	45	2	11
Do	3	47	1	12
RT, ROBERT F., charge of desertion against, to remove	982	45	2	11
Do	139	46	3	11
Do	3	47	1	12
SERVICE (*see also* ARMY),				
ency of, to increase	1130	47	1	12
Jupiter, Florida, to establish station at	659	49	1	15
Do	3658	49	1	15
stations in, to authorise	[illegible]	48	1	13
c health, to extend observations, to benefit	586	43	1	9
Do	55	43	2	9
Do	651	44	1	10
India Island, to establish stations in	[illegible]	49	1	15
NAGLE, JOHN J., relief of	[illegible]	49	1	15
. MARY A., bounty, claim for	136	44	2	11
R SENECA G., relief of	201	36	2	6
THOMAS, relief of	409	43	1	9
, MAURICE K., relief of	422	36	1	6
N, MOSES W., relief of	746	26	2	3
OHN A., relief of	325	34	1	5
IR, JAMES B., retired list of Army, to place on	190	44	1	10
IUS, FRANK, relief of	107	44	1	10
JACOB A., charge of desertion against, to remove	3904	49	1	15
UNITED STATES CAVALRY, claim of members of Company C, for loss of clothing destroyed	59	44	1	10
R, LEONARD, relief of	61	32	1	4
VILLE, NEW YORK, cannon for monument at	1748	47	1	12
, indemnity for loss of, by Government	287	30	1	4
TER, BENJ. F., arrears of pay, claim for	193	47	1	12
, HENRY, relief of	[illegible]	25	2	2
I. JACOB, relief of	97	18	1	1
MICHAEL P., relief of	1150	49	1	15
General A. J., relief of	695	44	1	10
ANDERSON J., medical services rendered to United States prisoners of war, claim for	51	44	1	10
CHARLES B., accounts of heirs, to settle	262	45	2	11
D. C., relief of	735	44	1	10
ELIZABETH, bounty land, claim for	497	36	1	6
GEORGE ?., relief of sureties	25	31	2	4
GEORGE W., pay as brigade forage-master, claim for	101	24	3	5
JACOB, charge of desertion against, to remove	1174	49	1	15
JAMES, relief of	11	45	3	11
LEONIDAS, relief of	68	40	2	7
MARTHA, relief of	2222	49	1	15
RICHARD, bounty land to	131	34	1	5
R, ROBERT G., lineal list of captains, to be advanced on	942	47	1	12
RS, THOMAS, pension for war of 1812	54	34	1	5
ON, BENJAMIN W., back pay, claim for	27	34	3	5
AMANDA M., relief of	406	43	1	9
, JAMES M., relief of	655	44	1	10
RASS, WILLIAM A., military record, to correct	159	43	1	9
R, ABRAM G., relief of	15	37	3	6
RS, ardent spirits, to discontinue issue of, to	166	21	1	2
RS' HOME, WASHINGTON, D. C.,				
lishment of	109	28	2	4
Do	391	29	1	4
Do	65	30	2	4
lations for	1984	47	2	12
deburg, Ky., sale of property at, belonging to	1820	47	2	12
RS' HOMES (*see also* NATIONAL HOMES FOR DISABLED VOLUNTEERS),				
rnia, to establish branch in	2392	48	2	13
Pa., to establish, at	1631	46	2	11
Do	26	47	1	12
Do	379	48	1	13
ange National Bank of Norfolk, to reimburse, for failure	500	49	1	15
pton, Va., management of home at	1867	47	2	12
gement of, investigation of	45	41	3	7
Do	783	44	1	10
gers for, appointment of	1122	46	2	11
igan, to establish branch in	1514	48	1	13
ssippi River, to establish branch west of	1552	48	1	13
Do	493	49	1	15
Do	494	49	1	15
Do	495	49	1	15

Subject.	Report.	Congress.	Session.	Volume.
SOLDIERS' MONUMENTS. (*See* CONDEMNED CANNON.)				
SOLDIERS' REUNION (*see also* TENTS), arms for, to loan	814	48	1	13
SOMERVILLE, MASSACHUSETTS, cannon to Grand Army of the Republic Post for monumental purposes at	492	49	1	15
SONNTAG, LOUIS, military record to correct	42	44	2	11
SOPAR, ENOS, relief of	801	25	2	2
SOUTH CAROLINA,				
Arms furnished to, to settle account for	878	47	1	12
Do	2252	48	2	13
Arsenal at Charleston, repairs of	444	24	1	2
Citadel Academy, to settle claim for rent of	2315	48	2	13
Florida war by, to refund moneys advanced in	201	31	1	4
Fort Moultrie, preservation of fortifications at	767	25	2	2
Fourth Brigade, State Volunteers, relief of board of field officers of	456	49	1	15
Military claims, to adjudicate	66	21	1	2
Do	1	22	1	2
Do	600	48	1	12
Mount Dearborn arsenal, retrocession of land occupied by, to State	128	19	1	1
SOUTHWICK, JOHN, relief of	956	49	1	15
SOWELL, WILLIAM J., relief of	954	49	1	15
SOWARD, THOMAS H., arrears of pay, claim for	192	47	1	12
SPANG, ROBERT W., relief of	3661	49	2	15
SPAULDING, COLUMBIA, military record, to correct	1840	49	1	15
SPAULDING, HENRY H., arrears of pay, claim for	192	47	1	12
SPENCER, T. J., restoration to Army	21	44	2	11
Do	3166	49	1	15
SPENCER, WILLIAM C., accounts to settle	3757	49	2	15
SPENCER, W. C., restoration to Army	78	44	1	10
Do	689	48	1	12
Do	3169	49	1	15
SPRAGUE, AUGUSTUS, relief of	563	44	1	10
SPRAGUE, WILLIAM D., relief of	948	49	1	15
SPRINGFIELD, ARMORY,				
Army officers, assignment of, to	403	24	1	2
Master armorer at, to regulate salary of	187	47	1	12
SPRINGFIELD STREET RAILROAD COMPANY, right of way through arsenal grounds at Springfield, Mass., to	446	46	2	11
Do	66	47	1	12
SPRINGFIELD, MISSOURI, road to national cemetery near	889	48	1	13
SQUIRES, EUGENE M., relief of	951	49	1	15
STAFF OFFICERS. (*See* ARMY.)				
STANHOPE, PHILLIP W., restoration to Army	253	45	2	11
STASER, JOHN F., bounty land, claim for	622	30	1	4
STATES,				
Instruction of militia of, providing for	934	48	1	12
Records of troops to, Secretary of War to furnish copies of	1776	48	1	13
STEADMAN, SIMEON,				
Charge of desertion against, to remove	82	34	3	5
Relief of	129	35	1	5
STEELE, FREDERICK, relief of	37	34	3	5
STEELE, MASON A., charge of desertion against, to remove	77	45		11
STEINBACH, RUDOLPH, *et al.*, title to lands at Point San José Reservation by	4	41		7
STEPHENS, FREDERICK, relief of	158	34		5
Do	87	35		5
Do	47	36		6
STEPHENSON, ANN C., relief of	712	25	2	2
Do	266	25	3	2
STERNBERG, GEORGE M., promotion in Medical Corps of Army, claim for	131	42	2	8
STEUBER, BERNHARD, charge of desertion against, to remove	3228	49		15
STEVENS, CHARLES A., arrears of pay, claim for	192	47	1	12
STEWART, GEORGE W., charge of desertion against, to remove	1709	47		12
STEWART, JAMES E., relief of	4	33		5
Do	106	34	1	5
STILLMAN, CHARLES., relief of	55	35	2	5
Do	57	35	2	5
Do	46	36		6
STOCKSTILL, DAVID W., substitute in Army, to refund money paid for	380	43		9
Do	454	44	1	10
Do	261	46	2	11
STOCKTON, JOHN, superintendent of mineral lands, claim for services as	548	29	1	4
STODDARD, LEWIS, arrears of pay, claim for	192	47	1	12
STONE, CUDBERTH, relief of	1403	49	1	15
STONE, D. C., back pay, claim for	990	45	2	11
STONE, JAMES, charge of desertion against, to remove	958	49	1	15
STONEHAM, MASSACHUSETTS, cannons for monument at	1160	47	1	12
STOREKEEPERS, arsenals, pay of, at	450	24	1	2
STOUFFER, ALBERT D., charge of desertion against, to remove	1223	49	1	15
STOUT, CHARLES M., relief of	69	30	1	7
STRASER, JOHN F., bounty land, claim for	622	30	1	4
STREET, HARLOW L., restoration to Army	445	46	2	11
STRICKLAND, FRANCIS M., charge of desertion against, to remove	196	44	2	11

Subject.	Report.	Congress.	Session.	Volume.
THOMAS B., pay from date of commission to date of muster, claim for.	1628	46	2	11
Do	19	47	1	12
Do	339	47	1	12
J. P. L., *et al.*, protest against burying Confederate dead in cemetery at Antietam	61	40	2	7
THOMAS, relief of	740	30	1	4
Do	70	32	1	4
ENCE AND TRANSPORTATION, furnishing volunteers, prior to muster in	229	30	1	4
N, KERRY, military record, to correct	347	43	1	9
S, CHARLES G., relief of	996	45	2	11
Do	997	45	2	11
FREDERICK, charge of desertion against, to remove	752	44	1	10
TENDENTS, appointment of officers of Army at national armories as.	306	27	2	3
Do	169	32	1	4
S, transportation of Army	17	43	2	9
NS, alteration of laws in reference to admission into Army of	782	29	1	4
LEA & CO., relief of	601	36	1	6
LAND, ROBERT, relief of	441	43	1	9
ISAAC R., relief of	208	44	2	11
LEVI, charge of desertion against, to remove	107	44	2	11
VOUT, ROBERT, relief of	58	15	2	1
JAMES, relief of	114	24	3	5
JOSEPH P., charge of desertion against, to remove	1169	49	1	15
, publication for use of Army and militia	419	23	1	1
N, MASSACHUSETTS, cannon for monument to	1402	46	2	11
JACOB, to place name on muster rolls of Company K, First Regiment Missouri Cavalry	43	44	2	11
, MORSE K., correction of date of commission	1504	46	2	11
, PETER, restoration to Army	131	44	2	11
, PHILIP, charge of desertion against, to remove	1668	49	1	15
EH, MICHIGAN, cannon for monument at	1868	47	2	12
APHS (*see also* POSTAL TELEGRAPHS),				
ry line from Sandford to Point Jupiter, Fla., to establish	639	49	1	15
Do	3058	49	1	15
ry telegraph operators during war of rebellion, relief of	682	48	1	13
MPF, Dr. THEODORE, professional services, claim for	28	42	3	8
K, TENODOR, restoration to Army	*1125	48	1	13
Do	2915	49	1	15
SEE,				
to State of, return of	54	34	3	5
martial proceedings in trial of certain militiamen, to investigate	140	20	1	1
Do	225	20	1	1
r's company of volunteers, to pay	72	28	2	3
teers for military services in Florida war from, to pay	32	31	2	4
a, Kans., to loan for soldiers' reunion at	767	47	1	12
r, Colo., to loan for reunion at	1806	47	2	12
burg, Pa., to loan camp equipage for reunion at	685	47	1	12
Do	1998	47	2	12
Islands, Nebr., to loan camp equipage for reunion at	686	47	1	12
a, to loan for soldiers' reunion in	1291	47	1	12
a, to loan for military encampment in	771	47	1	12
to loan tents for soldiers' reunion in	775	47	1	12
western Missouri and Southwestern Iowa Soldiers' Association, to loan to.	687	47	1	12
Do	1563	47	1	12
western Iowa Veteran Association, to loan to	3160	49	1	15
RIES,				
to citizens for defense against Indians, issue of	83	18	1	1
d Army officers to hold civil office in	18	47	1	12
ditures made for support of volunteer troops from	143	35	2	5
er defense, expense of	184	46	2	11
hostilities in, to audit claims for expenditures in suppressing	141	47	1	12
Do	807	48	1	13
ed volunteers from, expediency of raising regiment of	107	35	1	5
ry posts in, purchase of grounds for sites of	26	42	3	8
teers from, payment of	352	31	1	4
ER, MARSHAL P., relief of	581	44	1	10
NITED STATES ARTILLERY, private property destroyed by fire, to reimburse officers for	196	44	1	10
, ALFRED H., military record, to correct	190	47	1	12
, JAMES M.,				
ry record, to correct	439	46	2	11
of	55	48	1	13
, JOHN, relief of	28	18	1	1
ON, DAVID H., relief of	1858	49	1	15
ON, FRANCIS P., pay prior to muster in, claim for	16	45	2	11
ON, FRANKLIN, charge of desertion, to remove	820	48	1	13
Do	929	49	1	15

*Parts 1, 2

Subject.	Report.	Congress.	Session.	Volume.
THOMPSON, JOHN H., relief of	238	35	1	5
THOMPSON, MARY W., pension to	511	28	1	3
THOMPSON, SIMEON J., relief of	128	43	1	9
THOMBURG, J. H., relief of	3375	49	1	15
THORNHILL, MARY, relief of	205	44	2	11
THURSTON, RUSSELL S., charge of desertion against, to remove	2244	49	1	15
TICHNOR, ISAAC S., payment for twenty-four days as a captain	12	38	1	7
TOBACCO (*see also* ARMY; INTERNAL REVENUE), mode of purchasing, for Army	679	46	2	11
TODD, J. W., relief of	183	34	1	5
TOMPKINS, CHARLES H., relief of	817	47	1	12
TOPEKA, KANSAS,				
Cannon for monument at	485	46	2	11
Do	258	47	1	12
Soldiers' reunion at, to loan artillery and tents for	767	47	1	12
TOPOGRAPHICAL ENGINEERS, reorganization of corps	86	19	1	1
TOPP, JOHN, relief of	114	18	1	1
TORRENCE, GEORGE W., relief of	136	34	1	5
TOWN, LEVERETTE H., charge of desertion against, to remove	196	44	2	11
TRANSPORTATION. (*See* SUPPLIES; ARMY.)				
TRASPER, LEWIS J., relief of	2877	49		15
TREADWELL, DANIEL, improvements in construction of ordnance, to test	301	34	3	6
TREASURY DEPARTMENT, captured articles deposited in, to return to owners boxes of	1250	49		15
TREEN, LEWIS A., charge of desertion against, to remove	2240	49		15
TRICHLER, CHARLES, relief of	33	42		8
TRIMBLE, ISAAC R., relief of trustees of	333	48		13
TROOPS, UNITED STATES, firing upon supposed trespassers upon Indian reservation	4050	49		15
TRYON, CLARKSON, relief of	2869	49		15
TULLY, REDMOND, restoration to Army	135	46		11
TUNNARD, R. P., charge of desertion against, to remove	3669	49		15
TURNER, JUNIUS, travel pay, claim for	482	45	2	11
TURNLEY, PARMENAS T., retired list of Army, to restore to	257	46	2	11
TWENTY-FIRST NEW YORK CAVALRY, claim for the payment of traveling expenses of	289	45		11
TWIGGS SWORDS, President to return, to Rowena Guedella	3650	49		15
ULRICH, JULIUS W., military record, to correct	71	43		9
UNDERWOOD, C. S., relief of	383	43		9
UNION PACIFIC RAILROAD COMPANY, to extend eastern division as a military necessity	43	40	2	7
UNITED STATES, military districts in, to divide into two	341	28	1	3
UNSERVICEABLE ORDNANCE. (*See* ORDNANCE AND ORDNANCE STORES.)				
UPCRAFT, JOHN, relief of	1237	49	1	15
UPSEN, CHARLES, Army bill, on draft of amendment to	135	44	2	11
UTAH,				
Indian hostilities in, to refund expenses incurred in 1853 in suppressing	39	33	2	5
Do	201	36	1	6
Right of way through certain public lands in	3973	49	1	15
UTAH WESTERN RAILROAD, right of way through Rush Lake military reservation to	680	44	1	10
UTICA, NEW YORK, cannon for monument at	1740	47		12
VALDEZ, JOSÉ MARIA, relief of	89	35		5
VALIER, CHARLES, relief of	507	44	1	10
VAN BRUNT, relief of	6	31	1	4
VAN COLT, JOHN, relief of	538	36	1	6
VANCOUVER BARRACKS, WASHINGTON TERRITORY, military road from Portland, Oreg., to	841	47	1	12
VAUGHN, JAMES, relief of	90	35	2	5
VERMILLION LAKE, MISSOURI, military post at	43	39	1	7
VERMONT MILITIA CLAIMS, to settle	126	26	2	2
Do	198	31	1	4
Do	23	31	2	4
Do	138	34	1	5
VETERINARY SURGEONS, to place on equal footing with Army surgeons	508	44	1	10
VIBBART, HEZEKIAH E., charge of desertion against, to remove	3673	49	1	15
VICKSBURG, MISSISSIPPI,				
Right of way for railroad through military cemetery tract near	1350	46	2	11
Road to national cemetery near, to construct	2246	49	1	15
VIGIL, DON JUAN JESUS, relief of	200	31	1	4
VINNEDGE, ALEXANDER M., charge of desertion, to remove	206	46	2	11
Do	76	45	2	11
VIRGINIA, to reimburse, for moneys expended in organizing troops for Mexican war	165	32	1	4
VIRGINIA WOOLEN COMPANY, relief of	283	31	1	4
Do		32	1	4
VOLUNTEERS (*see also* WAR OF REBELLION),				
Black's company of Florida, for military services rendered in Seminole war, to pay	132	34	3	5
Crozier's company, of Tennessee, to pay	72	28	2	3
Efficiency of force of United States, report on	1	37	1	6
Mexican war, claim for pay of, in	120	38	1	7

Subject.	Report.	Congress.	Session.	Volume.
VOLUNTEERS—Continued.				
Officers of, for relief of certain	2	48	1	13
Pay of officers and men of	2251	48	2	13
Subsistence and transportation prior to being mustered in	329	30	1	4
Tennessee, for services in Florida war, to pay troops from	32	31	2	4
Texas militia, payment of	352	31	1	4
Third Regiment of Missouri, for three months' extra pay, claim of	194	33	1	4
Virginia, for moneys expended in organizing, for Mexican war, to reimburse	165	32	1	4
VOLUNTEER ARMY OFFICERS, records of, to correct	1841	46	1	13
VON HAACKE, ADOLPH, military history, to correct	326	42	1	9
Do	471	45	2	11
VON LUETTWITZ, ADOLPH H.,				
Claim to be advanced in rank	569	42	1	9
Do	72	44	1	10
Claim for pay from date of dismissal to date of restoration	1802	46	2	11
Relief of	3178	49	1	15
VON PUECHELSTEIN, LOUISE, relief of	874	44	1	10
VON STEINHOUSEN, ALBERT, military record, to correct	15	42	2	9
VOORHEES, GEORGE W., court-martial of, to set aside finding and sentence of	840	42	1	9
WAGONMASTERS. (*See* ARMY.)				
WAGON ROADS,				
To construct and survey,				
Willamette Valley and Cascade Mountain	332	46	2	11
Astoria, in Oregon	25	33	2	5
Bruceford to Cowlitz Landing	187	34	1	5
Do	369	35	1	5
Camp McDowell to San Carlos	300	44	2	11
Cascade Mountains, in Washington Territory	186	34	1	5
Corinne to Fort Ellis	616	44	1	10
Council Bluffs to Fort Kearney	180	34	2	5
Dungeness, Wash., to intersect with one from Fort Vancouver	188	34	1	5
Fishkill Landing to Cold Spring	72	19	2	1
Fort Leavenworth to Fort Pierre	192	34	1	5
Fort Leavenworth to Fort Riley	172	34	2	5
Fort Steilacoom to Bellingham Bay	184	34	1	5
Do	369	35	1	5
Fort Union to Santa Fé	272	35	1	5
Do	509	36	1	6
Gibson, Ark., to Natchitoches, La	67	19	1	1
Great Salt Lake City from Bridger's Pass	185	34	1	5
Kansas Territory	36	33	2	5
Michigan, general, in	42	19	1	1
Missouri to frontier of California, via Salt Lake City	355	34	1	5
Nebraska, Washington, and Oregon Territories	34	33	2	5
Do	369	35	1	5
Oregon, completion in	188	34	1	5
Red River to Sabine River	648	29	1	4
Scottsburg to Camp Stewart	842	47	1	12
Vancouver Barracks, Washington Territory, to Portland, Oreg	841	47	1	12
Wallula to Seattle, in Washington Territory	32	43	2	9
Washakie to Yellowstone Park	1006	47	1	12
Winona to Fort Ridgely, in Minnesota	191	34	1	5
WAGONER, J. R., relief of	338	43	1	9
WAINWRIGHT, R. A., relief of	106	34	3	5
WAKEFIELD, HARVEY, relief of	40	15	2	1
WAKEFIELD, MASSACHUSETTS, cannon for monument	1402	46	2	11
WALDO, DANIEL, & CO., relief of	56	35	2	5
WALDO, DAVID, relief of	284	34	1	5
WALKER, JOHN O., arrears of pay, claim for	192	47	1	12
WALTERS, JOHN H., charge of desertion against, to remove	1670	49	1	15
WALKER, MARK, restoration to Army	269	46	2	11
Do	1528	47	1	12
WALKER, MOSES B., relief of	757	48	1	13
Do	628	49	1	15
WALL, WILLIAM, relief of	1252	49	1	15
WALLACE, WILLIAM P., relief of	121	31	1	4
WALLULA, WASHINGTON TERRITORY, wagon road from Seattle to	32	43	2	9
WALSH, JOHN J., adoption of gun-carriage and shell of his invention	46	39	1	7
WAR CLAIMS,				
Iowa, for services and expenses incurred during war of rebellion, to adjudicate	2	40	3	7
Kansas, for expenses incurred during the civil war, to adjudicate	64	41	2	7
Missouri, for militia service in war of rebellion, to adjudicate claims	37	38	1	7
Montana, for expenses incurred in suppressing Indian hostilities, to adjudicate	82	42	2	7
WAR OF REBELLION,				
Arkansas Volunteers, charge of desertion, to remove, from Third Regiment of	2170	48	2	13
Do	914	49	1	15
Desertion during, to remove charges from all in service at close of war	28	43	2	9
Do	774	47	1	12
Florida, to accept 20,000 volunteers from	*5	37	2	6
Horses lost during, to extend time for filing claims for	1378	46	2	11

* Parts 1, 2.

Subject.	Report.	Congress.	Session.	Volume.
WAR OF REBELLION—Continued.				
Maryland, to reimburse, for arms and munitions of war taken by Government during	153	43	2	9
Muster and pay of volunteer officers, to amend act of 1884	640	49	1	15
Officers commissioned and not mustered, to pay	192	47	1	12
Do	618	48	1	13
Officers in, to amend act of July 26, 1866, for relief	51	40	2	7
Payments for military services in, approving certain	1138	47	1	12
Record of officers in, to correct	1841	48	1	13
Do	1844	49	1	15
Do	1847	49	1	15
Record of certain soldiers in, to correct	2628	48	2	13
Do	1656	49	1	15
States for moneys advanced during, to settle claims of	600	48	1	13
Telegraph operators during, giving military status to	682	48	1	13
Do	1677½	49	1	15
Veteran bounties withheld on account of promotion, to pay	1029	48	1	13
Do	1756	49	1	15
WAR OF REVOLUTION,				
Georgia, claims for moneys advanced in, to adjudicate	91	17	1	1
Monuments to memory of general officers of the, to carry into effect resolutions of Congress granting	414	25	2	2
Monument to persons who died in prison ships, to erect	176	28	2	3
WAR WITH GREAT BRITAIN (1812),				
Bigger's Rangers for service in, to adjudicate claims of	90	15	1	1
Bounty lands to soldiers of, to amend act of March 3, 1855	107	34	3	5
Massachusetts for expenses during war of 1812, to adjudicate claims of	120	18	1	1
Do	18	19	1	1
Pay and bounty land due enlisted men who served in	68	14	2	1
WARD, PETER M., military record, to correct	831	43	1	9
WARDWELL, EMERY S., relief of	2882	49	1	15
WARDWELL, ERNEST H., relief of	815	48	1	13
WARNER, JASON (administrator), relief of	100	20	2	1
WARREN, G. K., monument to	2316	48	2	13
WATERLOO, IOWA, cannon for monument	228	46	3	11
Do	257	47	1	12
WATERVILLE, MAINE, cannon for monument at	1161	47	1	12
WATERVLIET ARSENAL, NEW YORK, purchase of additional land for	31	19	2	1
WATKINS, J. A., Fort Monroe, use of land at, to	1966	47	2	12
WATSON, A., *et al.*, Signal Service, reflection upon	38	44	2	11
WASHINGTON COURT-HOUSE, OHIO, cannon for monument	1868	47	2	12
WASHINGTON TERRITORY,				
Depository for arms in, appropriation for erection of	35	33	2	5
Indian hostility claims, in 1855 and 1856 to adjudicate	195	34	1	5
Do	837	43	1	9
Do	141	47	1	12
Do	807	48	1	13
Roads in, to establish	34	33	2	5
Do	369	35	1	6
Do	82	43	2	9
Volunteers for military service,				
Against Indians, claim of	169	34	3	5
In Nez Percé war, 1877, claim of	1505	46	2	11
WATSON, CHARLES, relief of	533	48	1	13
WAYNE, INDIANA, cannon for monument	1402	46	2	11
WEATHERFORD, NANCY, increase of pension to	40	34	1	5
WEAVER, ELDRIDGE, military record, to correct	828	43	1	9
Do	195	44	2	11
WEBB, WEBSTER C.,				
Military record, to correct	59	46	3	11
Relief of	1126	48	1	13
WEBB, WILLIAM W., retired list of Army, to place on	706	47	1	12
Do	289	48	1	13
Do	3185	49	1	15
WEBER, JOHN B., relief of	3	43	1	9
WEBSTER, GEORGE P., relief of sureties	1423	47	1	12
Do	817	48	1	13
WEBSTER, LUCIEN B., relief of	22	29	1	4
WEIRICK, WILLIAM H., mileage, claim for	248	33	1	4
WELCH, JAMES, military record, to correct	69	45	2	11
WELLER, ELIZA R., relief of	192	47	1	12
WELLINGS, JAMES H., relief of	481	47	1	12
WELLS, DANIEL T., military record, to correct	482	47	1	12
WELLS, EUGENE, Army, to restore to	1567	47	1	12
Do	905	48	1	13
Do	3175	49	1	15
WELLS, JOHN, charge of desertion against, to remove	1677	49	1	15
WELSH, WILLIAM, Army, to restore to rolls of	480	44	1	10
WELSH, WILLIAM, retired list of Army, to place on	1166	49	1	15
WELTON, ALBERT, charge of desertion against, to remove	2074	49	2	15
WEMPE, FRANK, charge of desertion against, to remove	1170	49	1	15

Subject.	Report.	Congress.	Session.	Volume.
NG, HENRY, relief of	[illegible]	[illegible]	2	6
GER ALSTORPHEUS, relief of	536	44	1	10
DIA ISLANDS, signal station in, to establish	1536	49	1	15
INT ACADEMY. (See MILITARY ACADEMY.)				
INT, NEW YORK,				
ngs on military reservation at, to erect	1094	48	1	13
re at, permission to dig for	732	48	1	13
N FRONTIER, inland frontier, condition of	401	24	1	2
N RAILROAD COMPANY, right of way through military reservation f Fort Ripley	252	45	2	11
N STATES, armory in, to establish	373	24	1	2
TH, DEAN, relief of	111	18	1	1
N, HENRY D., relief of	832	43	1	9
R, JOHN F., arrears of pay, claim for	238	43	1	9
Do	192	47	1	12
, JOSEPH H., relief of	56	34	1	5
CHARLES B., promotion in Medical Corps of Army, claim for	131	43	2	9
AVEN, PENNSYLVANIA, cannon for monument at	1379	47	1	12
EAD, MATTHIAS, charge of desertion, to remove	84	43	1	9
, CHARLES J., relief for	3181	49	1	15
Y, W. SCOTT, relief of	188	47	1	12
MORE, B. F., appointments to the Military and Naval Academies by, nquiry into sale of	20	41	2	7
RE, CHARLES, relief of	1983	49	1	15
AN, WILLIAM A., charge of desertion against, to remove	2210	49	1	15
ORRA, bounty to	662	44	1	10
ENRY C., charge of desertion against, to remove	2626	49	2	15
CHARLES H., relief of	196	33	1	4
Do	208	35	2	5
, LITTLEJOHN, relief of	46	36	1	8
ON, HENRY E., relief of	196	44	1	10
Do	280	45	3	11
ON, M. C., relief of	1127	48	1	13
ETTE VALLEY AND CASCADE MOUNTAIN WAGON-ROAD OMPANY, lands granted to	282	46	2	11
L. CURRY POST, 18, cannon to, for monumental purposes	1402	46	2	11
S, CHARLES D. C., relief of	74	44	1	10
Do	469	44	1	10
S, ISAAC, relief of	1248	49	1	15
S, LAWRENCE A., Army, to restore to	482	44	1	10
S, MARY ANN, relief of	83	34	3	5
Do	303	35	1	5
S, ROBERT, retired list, to place on	1409	49	1	15
S, WILLIAM N., relief of	82	43	1	9
SON, JOHN C., relief of	282	45	2	11
ANTHONY G., relief of heirs	24	31	2	4
Do	62	32	1	4
Do	58	33	1	4
EWIS B., claim for judgment against the Government	1	33	1	4
ESTHER, relief of	102	34	3	5
TER, MASSACHUSETTS, cannon to, for monument at	1402	46	2	11
TER AND POTOMAC RAILROAD COMPANY, right of way hrough Harper's Ferry reservation to	432	23	1	2
Do	3	23	2	2
CHARLES, relief of	921	49	1	15
CHARLES L., relief of	218	35	2	5
D SCOTT (steamship), claim of officers and soldiers for losses sustained y disaster to	59	34	3	5
, S. C., relief of	192	47	1	12
JACOB, relief of	2243	49	1	15
MINNESOTA, military road from Fort Ridgely, Minn., to	191	34	1	5
, ROBERT F., relief of	66	37	2	6
, ALEXANDER, relief of	378	48	1	13
W, WILLIAM, relief of	473	44	1	10
, MASSACHUSETTS, cannon for monument at	1402	46	2	11
Do	260	47	1	12
ARLES W.,				
, claim for	734	44	1	10
of desertion against, to remove	10	45	2	11
AVID, charge of desertion against, to remove	1572	48	1	13
CLAY, relief of	140	37	2	6
D., relief of	479	45	2	11
AMES B., relief of	81	34	3	5
HN S., relief of	329	43	2	9
ESLEY, charge of desertion against, to remove	994	45	2	11
FF, MATTHEW, charge of desertion against, to remove	89	43	1	9
E, ANDREW J., relief of	2238	49	1	15
ARD, JOSEPH J., promotion in Medical Corps of Army	131	43	2	9
RTH, O. H., "Woodworth United States arm," to test	809	34	1	5
NERAL JOHN E., extra allowance of rations for commanding sepaate post, claim for	132	24	1	2

REPORTS

OF THE

MMITTEE ON THE MILITIA,

HOUSE OF REPRESENTATIVES,

FROM THE ORGANIZATION OF COMMITTEE, DECEMBER 10, 1835, TO THE CLOSE OF THE FORTY-NINTH CONGRESS, 1887, INCLUSIVE.

IN ONE VOLUME.

COMPILED, UNDER THE DIRECTION OF THE JOINT COMMITTEE ON PRINTING,

BY

T. H. McKEE,

CLERK, DOCUMENT ROOM, UNITED STATES SENATE.

WASHINGTON:
GOVERNMENT PRINTING OFFICE.
1887.

9266

FORTY-NINTH CONGRESS, FIRST SESSION.

[PUBLIC RESOLUTION—No. 24.]

Joint resolution authorizing the preparation of a compilation of the reports of committees of the Senate and House of Representatives.

Resolved by the Senate and House of Representatives of the United States of America in Congress assembled, That there be prepared under the direction of the Joint Committee of Printing, a compilation of the reports of the Senate and House of Representatives from the Fourteenth to the Forty-eighth Congress, inclusive, classified by committees, arranged, indexed, and bound in suitable volumes for the use of the standing committees of the two Houses of Congress. And the sum of seven thousand seven hundred and fifty dollars, or so much thereof as may be found necessary, is hereby appropriated out of any money in the Treasury not otherwise appropriated, for the preparation of said work, which sum may be paid by the Secretary of the Treasury upon the order of the chairman of said Joint Committee, as additional pay or compensation to any officer or employee of the United States.

Resolved further, That the Clerk of the House and Secretary of the Senate be, and they are hereby directed, to procure and file, for the use of their respective Houses, copies of all reports made by each committee of all succeeding Congresses; and that the Clerk of the House and the Secretary of the Senate be, and they are hereby, authorized and directed at the close of each session of Congress, to cause said reports to be indexed and bound, one copy to be deposited in the library of each House and one copy in the room of the committee from which the reports emanated.

Approved, July 29, 1886.

2

COMPILER'S NOTICE.

This compilation embraces all the printed reports made by both Houses of Congress from the commencement of the Fourteenth to the close of the Forty-ninth Congress. They are classified by committees and arranged in numerical order. The collection for each committee is divided into volumes of suitable size. Each committee has a separate index, a copy being bound in each volume.

The SPECIAL and SELECT reports are all compiled in one collection having one index, a copy of which is bound in each volume.

The plan throughout the compilation is to place each report to the committee from which it was reported, without reference to the subject-matter.

The House and Senate reports are compiled separately. Care will be required in noticing the chronological order, as in some instances an entire session or Congress may not appear in certain volumes from the fact that during this period no reports were made by this committee.

T. H. McKEE.

INDEX

TO

S OF COMMITTEE ON THE MILITIA,

HOUSE OF REPRESENTATIVES.

FROM 1835 TO 1887, INCLUSIVE.

Subject.	Report.	Congress.	Session.	Volume.
orising exchange of tents for Gatling guns with National Guard	1550	48	1	
ITIA, to amend Revised Statutes making annual appropriation	933	48	1	
	1267	49	1	
itroducing Colt's water-proof cartridges into militia service of tates	86	28	2	
TILLERY, authorizing Secretary of War to furnish battery and its to	451	46	2	1
introducing into service water-proof cartridges invented by	86	28	2	1
paring and adopting a plan of military discipline for the militia	44	14	2	1
providing for special and uniform instruction of State militia	1268	49	1	1
application by legislature of Iowa for payment for services ren-	371	28	1	1
	88	28	2	1
	678	29	1	1
RPS, to aid and encourage States respectively to raise and or-	453	29	1	1
IPLINE, preparing and adopting a plan of	44	14	2	1
reorganizing and classifying	44	14	2	1
	143	29	1	1
	452	29	1	1
	763	46	2	1
	590	47	1	1
organizing, arming, and disciplining	44	15	1	1
	108	15	2	1
	92	19	2	1
	68	20	2	1
	126	21	1	1
ining officers and sergeants of	108	15	2	1
clothing, when called into service of United States	38	16	1	1
uniform militia system	875	25	2	1
reorganizing	*584	26	1	1
r payment for services rendered by Iowa State forces	371	28	1	1
	88	28	2	1
	678	29	1	1
olt's water-proof cartridges into service of	86	28	2	1
calling forth militia in certain cases	*58	36	2	1
rs of Congress and rights of States over	763	46	2	1
ised Statutes relative to making annual appropriation for arms	933	48	1	1
	1267	49	1	1
pecial and uniform instruction of State	1268	49	1	1
	763	46	2	1
ional Guard Association for amendment of	590	47	1	1
ENSE, establishing a uniform militia to more effectually pro-	875	25	2	1
NDRIES, on expediency of establishing	205	29	1	1

* Views of minority.

Subject.	Report.	Congress.	Session.	Volume.
NATIONAL GUARD ASSOCIATION, on petition to reorganize and classify militia	[illegible]	47	1	1
NATIONAL GUARD OF ALABAMA, authorizing exchange of tents for Gatling guns with	1550	46	1	1
ORDNANCE AND ORDNANCE STORES, introducing Colt's water-proof cartridges into militia service of United States	86	28	2	1
REVISED STATUTES, to amend section 1661, making annual appropriation to provide arms for militia	923	48	1	1
Do	1267	49	1	1
ROME, GEORGIA, to furnish battery and equipments to Cherokee Artillery of	451	46	2	[illegible]
STATE MILITIA, providing for special and uniform instruction of	1268	49	1	[illegible]
UNIFORM MILITIA SYSTEM, to provide for national defense by establishing	875	25	2	[illegible]
WATER-PROOF CARTRIDGES, relative to introducing, into militia service	86	28	2	[illegible]

REPORTS

OF THE

)MMITTEE ON MINES AND MINING,

HOUSE OF REPRESENTATIVES,

FROM THE ORGANIZATION OF THE COMMITTEE, DECEMBER 19, 1865, TO THE CLOSE OF THE FORTY-NINTH CONGRESS, 1887, INCLUSIVE,

IN ONE VOLUME.

COMPILED, UNDER THE DIRECTION OF THE JOINT COMMITTEE ON PRINTING,

BY

T. H. McKEE
CLERK, DOCUMENT ROOM, UNITED STATES SENATE.

WASHINGTON:
GOVERNMENT PRINTING OFFICE.
1887.

9212

FORTY-NINTH CONGRESS, FIRST SESSION.

[PUBLIC RESOLUTION—No. 24.]

Joint resolution authorizing the preparation of a compilation of the reports of committees of the Senate and House of Representatives.

Resolved by the Senate and House of Representatives of the United States of America in Congress assembled, That there be prepared under the direction of the Joint Committee of Printing, a compilation of the reports of the Senate and House of Representatives from the Fourteenth to the Forty-eighth Congress, inclusive, classified by committees, arranged, indexed, and bound in suitable volumes for the use of the standing committees of the two Houses of Congress. And the sum of seven thousand seven hundred and fifty dollars, or so much thereof as may be found necessary, is hereby appropriated out of any money in the Treasury not otherwise appropriated, for the preparation of said work, which sum may be paid by the Secretary of the Treasury upon the order of the chairman of said Joint Committee, as additional pay or compensation to any officer or employee of the United States.

Resolved further, That the Clerk of the House and Secretary of the Senate be, and they are hereby directed, to procure and file, for the use of their respective Houses, copies of all reports made by each committee of all succeeding Congresses; and that the Clerk of the House and the Secretary of the Senate be, and they are hereby, authorized and directed at the close of each session of Congress, to cause said reports to be indexed and bound, one copy to be deposited in the library of each House and one copy in the room of the committee from which the reports emanated.

Approved, July 29, 1886.

COMPILER'S NOTICE.

This compilation embraces all the printed reports made by both louses of Congress from the commencement of the Fourteenth to the ose of the Forty-ninth Congress. They are classified by committees id arranged in numerical order. The collection for each committee is ivided into volumes of suitable size. Each committee has a separate idex, a copy being bound in each volume.

The SPECIAL and SELECT reports are all compiled in one collection aving one index, a copy of which is bound in each volume.

The plan throughout the compilation is to place each report to the mmittee from which it was reported, without reference to the subject-atter.

The House and Senate reports are compiled separately. Care will required in noticing the chronological order, as in some instances an itire session of Congress may not appear in certain volumes from the ct that during this period no reports were made by this committee.

T. H. McKEE.

INDEX

TO

RTS OF THE COMMITTEE ON MINES AND MINING,

HOUSE OF REPRESENTATIVES.

FROM DECEMBER 19, 1865, TO MARCH 4, 1887.

Subject.	Report.	Congress.	Session.	Volume.
RAL LANDS, detritus in beds of rivers of California, to restrain of	760	46	2	1
S, water for, obtaining of	260	43	1	1
mineral lands in, disposal of	614	47	1	1
MINES AND MINING, to establish	1065	47	1	1
Do	1881	49	1	1
A, agricultural lands, to restrain flow of detritus in beds of rivers	760	46	2	1
ing, to locate	1423	46	2	1
ON MINES AND MINING, making special order for considera- of business from	2345	49	1	1
LODE, geology of	1065	47	1	1
restrain flow of, on agricultural lands, in beds of rivers of California.	760	46	2	1
L SURVEY, management of	1065	47	1	1
AN, WILLIAM, relief of	1764	49	1	1
ULCH MINING AND TUNNEL COMPANY, granting privi- to	1860	48	1	1
ANDS,				
lisposal of	614	47	1	1
	270	47	1	1
l disposition of	1747	46	2	1
MINING, bureau of, to establish	1065	47	1	1
Do	1881	49	1	1
AIMS, location of, amend law for	1423	46	2	1
nel, construction of	50	40	2	1
Do	40	41	2	1
Do	94	42	2	1
Do	*44	42	3	1
arid land in	260	43	1	1
QUICKSILVER MINES, confirming title of William McGarra- to	1764	49	1	1
IDS, timber for mining and domestic purposes on	660	47	1	1
ATUTES, to amend,				
2, locators' rights of possession and enjoyment	1423	46	2	1
6, locating mineral lands	270	47	1	1
ashington Territory, scientific examination of	335	46	3	1
NEL, construction of	50	40	2	1
Do	40	41	2	1
Do	94	42	2	1
Do	*44	42	3	1
MINING PURPOSES, to provide	260	43	1	1
ON TERRITORY, survey and scientific examination of	335	46	3	1
D FLUME COMPANY, incorporating the	887	45	2	1
Do	36	46	1	1

*And views of minority.

REPORTS

OF THE

)MMITTEE ON NAVAL AFF I

HOUSE OF REPRESENTATIVES,

FROM THE ORGANIZATION OF THE COMMITTEE, MARCH 13, 1822, TO THE CLOSE OF THE FORTY-NINTH CONGRESS, 1887, INCLUSIVE,

IN TEN VOLUMES.

COMPILED, UNDER THE DIRECTION OF THE JOINT COMMITTEE ON PRINTING,

BY

T. H. McKEE,

CLERK, DOCUMENT ROOM, UNITED STATES SENATE.

WASHINGTON:
GOVERNMENT PRINTING OFFICE.
1887.

9216 NAV H

FORTY-NINTH CONGRESS, FIRST SESSION.

[PUBLIC RESOLUTION—No. 24.]

Joint resolution authorizing the preparation of a compilation of the reports of committees of the Senate and House of Representatives.

Resolved by the Senate and House of Representatives of the United States of America in Congress assembled, That there be prepared under the direction of the Joint Committee of Printing, a compilation of the reports of the Senate and House of Representatives from the Fourteenth to the Forty-eighth Congress, inclusive, classified by committees, arranged, indexed, and bound in suitable volumes for the use of the standing committees of the two Houses of Congress. And the sum seven thousand seven hundred and fifty dollars, or so much thereof may be found necessary, is hereby appropriated out of any money the Treasury not otherwise appropriated, for the preparation of said work, which sum may be paid by the Secretary of the Treasury upon the order of the chairman of said Joint Committee, as additional pay or compensation to any officer or employee of the United States.

Resolved further, That the Clerk of the House and Secretary of the Senate be, and they are hereby directed, to procure and file, for the use of their respective Houses, copies of all reports made by each committee of all succeeding Congresses; and that the Clerk of the House the Secretary of the Senate be, and they are hereby, authorized directed at the close of each session of Congress, to cause said to be indexed and bound, one copy to be deposited in the library each House and one copy in the room of the committee from which the reports emanated.

Approved, July 29, 1886.

COMPILER'S NOTICE.

---

compilation embraces all the printed reports made by both of Congress from the commencement of the Fourteenth to the the Forty-ninth Congress. They are classified by committees unged in numerical order. The collection for each committee is into volumes of suitable size. Each committee has a separate copy being bound in each volume.

PECIAL and SELECT reports are all compiled in one collection one index, a copy of which is bound in each volume.

lan throughout the compilation is to place each report to the ee from which it was reported, without reference to the subject-

Iouse and Senate reports are compiled separately. Care will red in noticing the chronological order, as in some instances an ession or Congress may not appear in certain volumes from the t during this period no reports were made by this committee.

T. H. McKEE.

INDEX

TO

ŁEPORTS OF COMMITTEE ON NAVAL AFFAIRS,

HOUSE OF REPRESENTATIVES.

FROM MARCH 13, 1822, TO MARCH 4, 1887, INCLUSIVE.

Subject.	Report.	Congress.	Session.	Volume.
ŁT. CHARLES W., relief of	146	45	2	8
Do	121	46	2	9
ŁS, Navy, to investigate in	77	23	2	2
Ł, ELIZABETH, pension to	705	29	1	4
Ł, JOHN, relief of	126	46	2	9
Ł, THEODORE, relief of	119	41	2	7
ŁKS, JOSEPH T., relief of	267	45	2	8
ŁON, S. R., additional pay, claim for	71	33	1	5
ŁAL, rank of, to establish	346	27	2	3
ŁA, mail steamers to, establishing line of	426	31	1	5
ŁAMA, tonnage duties in ports of Mobile and Blakely, resolution of State to levy, for benefit of disabled seamen	98	17	2	1
ŁAMA, FLORIDA AND GEORGIA RAILROAD COMPANY, land grant to	230	30	1	5
ŁARLE (ram), captors of, relief of	157	44	2	7
Do	97	45	2	8
Do	461	46	2	9
Do	90	47	1	9
ŁARLE AND CHESAPEAKE CANAL, claim of, to adjudicate	625	45	2	8
Do	1636	46	2	9
ŁRS, navy-yard at or near, to establish	20	47	1	9
ſ. JOHN, pension to	61	35	2	6
ſ. LYDIA, claim for pension to	6	18	1	1
ſ. THOMAS I. (administrator), prize money in war of 1812, claim for	20	14	3	1
ſ. W. A. H., relief of	160	46	2	9
ſ. W. H., pension to mother of	59	17	2	1
ſ. WILLIAM, pension to	560	27	2	3
ŁNCE (United States steamer), officers and crew of, relief to	1210	47	1	9
ŁONE. CHARLES O., navy record, to change	149	45	3	8
ŁCAN PRIME MERIDIAN. (*See* MERIDIAN.)				
ŁCAN SEAMEN. (*See* SEAMEN.)				
ŁSON, SAMUEL T., arrears of pension to	207	29	1	4
Do	444	30	1	5
Do	364	30	1	5
Do	266	31	1	5
ŁSON, SAMUEL T. (administrator of), relief of	630	45	2	8
ŁSON, THOMAS P., relief of widow	505	36	1	6
ŁWS, JOHN P., petition to dismantle Navy and disband Army	228	20	1	4
ŁWS, SARAH, pension to	597	27	2	3
Ł, ANNE W., pension to	37	27	3	3
Do	636	29	1	4
Do	74	30	1	5
Do	474	35	1	6
Do	48	36	1	6
Ł, SAMUEL, restoration of pay	43	19	1	1
ŁPOLIS, MARYLAND,				
Łnorial from merchants of	164	45	3	8
Łral Academy at,				
To equalize rank of graduates from, upon assignment to various corps	142	48	1	10
Do	2244	48	2	10
Do	4139	49	2	10
Do	4140	49	2	10

Subject.	Report.	Congress.	Session.	Volume.
ETT'S NAVAL BRIGADE. (*See* NAVAL BRIGADE.)				
TT, JAMES, prize money, claim for	172	15	1	1
Do	190	21	1	1
Do	416	25	2	2
TT, WILLIAM H., relief of	188	19	1	1
, FREDERICK F., retired list of Navy, to place on	107	43	1	7
, H. H., relief of	151	45	3	8
Do	1707	46	2	9
NG, SAMUEL, relief of	269	23	1	2
Do	105	26	1	3
. V., relief of	97	35	2	6
WS, EDWARD, relief of	1196	47	1	9
MAN, OTWAY H., accounts of, to settle	43	36	2	6
(*See* VESSELS.)				
GS, GEORGE W., memorial to furnish hemp for use of Navy	*120	31	1	5
Y, THOMAS, additional pay, claim for	544	26	1	3
Y, HENRY W., restoration to Navy	156	45	3	8
Do	1336	46	2	9
, WILLIAM, additional pay, claim for	56	34	1	6
KER, JOHN V. B., accounts of, to settle	1446	48	1	10
JOHN W., pension and loss of property, claim for	27	24	2	2
OF COMMISSIONERS OF NAVY,				
blishment of	662	45	2	8
Do	169	46	2	9
iding officer of, Secretary of Navy to act as	94	16	1	1
WAIN IN NAVY, increase pay to	74	32	1	5
M, Commander WILLIAM, pay as flag-captain, claim for	542	26	1	3
R, JULIUS S., restoration to Navy	59	44	2	7
JOHN R., additional pay, claim for	167	43	1	7
, DAVID S., prize money, claim for	1285	46	2	9
Do	44	47	1	9
LOUISA, pension to	104	20	2	1
(United States sloop of war), relief of officers of	278	24	2	2
, JACOB, pension to	509	28	1	3
Do	772	30	1	5
ICK, M. W., relief of sureties	269	23	1	2
Do	105	26	1	3
Y, Farragut fleet, bounty to officers and sailors of	313	46	3	9
Do	1132	47	1	9
Y LANDS,				
of 1855, to amend	95	35	2	6
ateers, to grant to officers and crews of	343	34	1	6
ELL, E. B., investigation in case of, to reopen	750	44	1	7
OSEPH K., prize money, claim for	43	22	2	2
Do	14	31	1	5
ROBERT, restoration to original position on Navy Register	158	45	3	8
ORD, PROFESSOR, relief of	437	31	1	5
EAR, SARAH, relief of	161	35	2	6
Do	349	36	1	6
EAR, W. C., relief of heirs	191	43	1	7
, JOHN P., pension to	148	24	2	2
EAD, EDGAR, relief of	1672	48	1	10
, CHARLES D., relief of	58	18	2	1
E, JOHN M., compensation for use of deep-sea sounding apparatus	260	34	3	6
Do	143	35	1	6
LYN, NEW YORK,				
lock at, to construct	100	20	1	1
Do	8	20	2	1
Do	40	27	3	3
l hospital at, for sale of	282	48	1	10
-yard at, purchase of land adjoining	126	27	3	3
op lands connected with navy-yard at, reclaiming of	115	43	2	7
about Bay, sale of land in, to city of	932	45	2	8
FREDERICK F., relief of legal representatives of	348	36	1	6
Do	10	37	2	6
, ELIPHALET, Jr., services in Japan expedition, claim for	26	35	1	6
Do	208	36	1	6
, URIAH,				
ship invented by	490	24	1	2
Do	36	29	2	4
Do	294	30	1	5
or and coast defense, plan for	252	20	1	1
ELL, THOMAS, pension to	168	28	2	3
SUSAN,				
ion to, extension of term of	759	27	2	3
ion to	601	29	1	4
WICK, GEORGIA, naval depot at, to establish	84	34	1	6
, JOSEPH, and others, line of mail steamers to Africa, memorial to establish	438	31	1	5

* And views of minority.

Subject.	Report.	Congress.	Session.	Volume.
CONTRACTS. (*See* SECRETARY OF NAVY; CONTRACTS.)				
, SAMUEL A., additional pay, claim for	130	35	2	6
Do	426	36	1	6
NG STATIONS,				
antic and Pacific coasts, to establish on	1411	46	2	9
Do	1760	47	1	9
public of New Granada, to establish in	568	36	1	6
DEFENSE,				
ention of Uriah Brown for, adoption of	262	20	1	1
ention of Taylor for	198	28	2	3
Do	409	29	1	4
IAN, JOHN, prize money to heirs, claim for	319	22	1	2
Do	188	23	1	2
SIONS AT SEA, commission to revise laws respecting	457	46	2	9
-BLINDNESS, laws for, to amend	1860	46	2	9
Do	445	47	1	9
SAMUEL, submarine battery invented by	46	28	2	3
ERCE,				
f of Mexico and West India seas, protection of, on	58	17	1	1
tection of, to increase naval force for	139	19	1	1
LIN, MARY, pension to	603	27	2	3
Y, JAMES H., back pay, claim for	764	29	1	4
Do	78	30	1	5
Do	1084	46	2	9
ECTICUT, navy-yard in River Thames, to establish	94	19	1	1
RUCTION FUND FOR NAVY, permanent, to create	189	46	2	9
Do	128	47	1	9
RACTS, coal to United States Navy, for supply of	566	36	1	6
Do	176	47	1	9
AY, FANNIE S., relief of	373	46	2	9
Do	1227	47	1	9
RIGHTS. (*See* PATENTS.)				
N, THOMAS G., relief of	116	46	3	9
Do	701	47	1	9
Do	1900	48	1	10
AGE, cotton cordage in Navy, introduction of	1286	46	2	9
ELL, J. B., *et al.*, relief of	984	45	2	8
ELL, WILLIAM H., prize money, claim for	827	45	2	8
N, MARTHA J., signal-lights, claim for use of patent for	334	43	2	7
N CORDAGE, introduction in Navy of	1286	46	2	9
S-MARTIAL, Mediterranean squadron, to investigate trial in case of Capt. O. H. Perry and officers of	183	15	1	1
DALE, NUNIS H., relief of	198	45	2	8
, HORATIO V., relief of	47	22	2	2
Do	29	23	1	2
Do	117	31	1	5
TON, WILLIAM, pension to heirs of	26	24	2	2
FORD, MARY, increase of pension to	564	27	2	3
Y, BENJAMIN, relief of	513	30	1	5
Do	231	31	1	5
CALEB, pension to children of	103	20	2	1
AN, ALEXANDER F., relief of widow	45	42	3	7
ELL, PRINCE S., relief of	72	36	2	6
ER, JOHN N., relief of	2037	48	1	10
Y, LANGLEY B., relief of	942	45	2	8
Do	275	46	2	9
Do	485	47	1	9
Do	58	48	1	10
NGHAM, J. S., relief of	145	45	3	8
Do	274	46	2	9
NG, MILTON B., accounts of, to adjudicate	768	44	1	7
NG, THOMAS B., additional pay, claim for	925	45	2	8
IAN, ROBERT W., additional pay, claim for	205	35	1	6
GREN, Mrs. M. V., relief of	133	43	2	7
Do	187	44	2	7
Do	885	45	3	8
NG, ELI, pension to	23	24	2	2
Do	289	31	1	5
SON, CHRISTOPHER P., pension to	1042	47	1	9
SON'S BOAT APPARATUS, purchase of	650	36	1	6
, LOT, pension to	30	24	2	2
Do	582	28	1	3
Do	512	30	1	5
Do	232	31	1	5
ON, LUCIEN L., restoration to Marine Corps	702	47	1	9
UR, SUSAN,				
litional pension to	306	34	1	6
e money (United States steamer Intrepid), claim for	48	19	1	1
Do	74	19	2	1
Do	201	20	1	1
Do	37	20	2	1

Subject.	Report.	Congress.	Session.	Volume.
DECATUR, SUSAN—Continued.				
Prize money (United States steamer Intrepid), claim for	60	21	1	1
Do	45	23	1	[illegible]
Do	237	24	1	[illegible]
DE KAY, GEORGE C., relief of	541	30	1	[illegible]
DE KAY, JANET H., relief	60	31	1	[illegible]
DE KRAFT, J. C. P., mileage, claim for	157	35	2	[illegible]
DE LA ROCHE, GEORGE F., additional pay, claim for	367	29	1	[illegible]
Do	130	30	1	[illegible]
DENNY, PENELOPE, pension to	62	17	2	[illegible]
Do	6	18	1	[illegible]
Do	1	19	1	[illegible]
Do	103	20	2	[illegible]
DEPOT OF CHARTS, superintendent of, to enlarge duties of	449	27	2	[illegible]
DE RUSSY, GEORGE A., additional compensation, claim for	744	29	1	4
Do	203	31	1	5
Do	33	32	1	5
DESERTION, Navy and Marine Corps, to remove charges from enlisted men of	664	48	1	10
Do	1866	49	1	10
DE SOTO (steamer), relief of owners	1707	46	2	9
DEVLIN, JOHN S., relief of	294	23	1	2
Do	154	24	1	3
Do	453	24	1	2
DEWLING, ISAIAH, retired list of Navy, to place on	79	44	1	7
Do	936	45	2	8
DICKERSON, JOHN, additional pay, claim for	546	26	1	3
DISTRICT OF COLUMBIA, Navy Department in, sale of certain land to	1415	48	2	9
DIX, ELLEN, pension to	103	20	2	1
DOBSON, EUPHEMIA, relief of	603	27	2	3
Do	518	28	1	3
DOCKAGE, amend section 3617, Revised Statutes, relating to private vessels at navy-yard dry docks	460	46	2	9
DOCKS and WHARVES, to construct at Washington, D. C	89	17	2	1
DOTY, H. H., torpedo invention, claim for use of	626	45	2	8
DOVILLIERS, L. V., relief of	1281	46	2	9
DOW, JESSE E., additional compensation, claim for	806	25	2	2
DRAPER, NEHEMIAH S., arrears of pension, claim for	300	35	1	6
DRAPER, PAUL, arrears of pension to heirs of	306	35	1	6
DRAPER, WILLIAM B., Japan expedition, claim for services on	304	35	1	6
Do	207	36	1	6
DRAWING. (*See* PROFESSORSHIPS.)				
DRY DOCKS.				
Establishment at certain yards of three additional, to be built of wood	2208	49	1	10
To establish, construct, and repair at,				
Brooklyn, N. Y	100	20	1	1
Do	80	20	2	1
Do	40	27	2	3
Kittery, Me	394	28	1	3
Do	156	30	1	5
Mare Island, California	829	45	2	8
New York Harbor	198	28	1	3
Pensacola, Fla	424	24	1	2
Do	106	30	1	5
Philadelphia, Pa	872	25	2	2
Do	394	28	1	3
Do	11	29	1	[illegible]
Do	649	29	1	[illegible]
Do	106	30	1	[illegible]
Portsmouth, N. H	100	20	1	[illegible]
Do	8	20	2	[illegible]
DU BARRY, EDMUND L., back pay, claim for	510	30	1	[illegible]
Do	205	31	1	[illegible]
DUNCAN, JONAS, relief of	65	18	1	[illegible]
DUNCAN, SARAH, pension to	100	30	1	[illegible]
Do	18	31	[illegible]	[illegible]
DUNCAN, SILAS, arrears of pension, claim for	41	19	[illegible]	[illegible]
Do	503	23	[illegible]	[illegible]
Do	600	29	[illegible]	[illegible]
DUNSEATH, DAVID, relief of	125	46	[illegible]	[illegible]
DURNELL, JESSE, additional pay, claim for	455	48	[illegible]	[illegible]
DURYEE, CHARLES H., relief of	177	24	[illegible]	[illegible]
EARLE, EDWARD, canvas and cordage, invention for protection of	598	29	1	[illegible]
EASBY, WILLIAM, additional compensation, claim for	162	28	1	[illegible]
ECKFORD, HENRY, relief of	84	30	[illegible]	[illegible]
Do	41	21	[illegible]	[illegible]
EDWARDS, JOHN, pension to	603	27	[illegible]	[illegible]
ELLIOTT, MARY, and others, pension to	44	23	[illegible]	[illegible]
Do	603	27	[illegible]	[illegible]
ELLIOTT, S. B., relief of	595	30	[illegible]	[illegible]
Do	158	35	[illegible]	[illegible]
Do	280	36	[illegible]	6

Subject.	Report.	Congress.	Session.	Volume.
SEAS, collisions on, for commission to revise laws and investigate	457	46	2	9
MOSES J., bombshell, to test patent for percussion	342	36	1	6
N, MICHAEL, relief of administrator	518	34	1	2
Do	273	34	2	2
EN, WILLIAM, arrears of pension	306	35	1	6
AND, JOHN, pension to	96	35	2	6
AND, JOHN E., relief of	66	29	1	4
ES & PEDRICK, hide rope, pay for machine for manufacture of	369	36	1	3
Do	117	29	1	4
YD, JOHN, payment for use of patent	159	45	3	8
Do	275	45	2	8
SQUADRON, permanent, providing for support of	8	27	1	3
ANTHONY S., relief of	161	45	3	8
TAL FUND, appropriation for	81	20	2	1
NS, ALFRED, relief of	763	48	1	10
NS, MARY E., relief of	2331	49	1	10
, HARRISON, relief of	106	33	2	6
Do	160	34	3	6
LL, GEORGE H., relief of	305	35	1	6
ELL, WILLIAM W., relief of	276	27	3	3
Do	75	28	1	3
Do	136	46	2	9
ISAAC, additional pay, claim for	81	22	2	2
Do	201	23	1	2
Do	147	25	2	3
Do	340	26	1	3
HREYS, JOSEPH, floating anchor, pay for use of patent	48	41	2	7
HRIES, JOSEPH, relief of	276	46	2	9
ER, CHARLES G., back pay, claim for	295	34	2	2
(United States steamer), monument commemorative of loss of	23	46	2	9
Do	352	47	1	9
Y, ANTHONY (administrator), relief of	477	23	1	2
T DUTIES, hemp, to amend tariff on	116	31	1	5
Do	120	31	1	5
HIP-BUILDING YARDS. (*See* NAVY-YARDS.)				
WOOD, B. F., promotion of, claim for	13	31	1	5
US OF PANAMA,				
munication across	56	19	2	1
road across, to construct	26	30	2	5
ANCE. (*See* LIFE INSURANCE.)				
NATIONAL LAWS, commission to frame rules in interest of	457	46	2	9
PID (United States ketch), claim by officers and crew of, for prize money	48	19	1	1
Do	74	19	2	1
Do	201	20	1	1
Do	37	20	2	1
Do	60	20	1	1
Do	45	23	1	2
Do	237	24	1	2
Do	14	31	1	5
TIONS. (*See* PATENTS.)				
TIGATIONS.				
ery navy-yard, investigation of affairs at	790	44	1	7
al cadetship, alleged sale of	124	43	2	7
y Department, errors, abuses or frauds existing in	784	44	1	7
Do	112	45	3	8
adelphia navy-yard, irregularities in purchase of tools at	4	40	3	7
Do	31	40	3	7
r & Co., contracts with	270	45	2	8
ON, JAMES, pension to heirs of	200	26	2	3
ON, MARY, pension to	742	29	1	4
MITCHELL (ship), claim of owners and consignees	197	23	1	2
Do	509	31	1	5
TOWN (United States steamer), officers and crew who manned the Ta-Kiang, claim of	343	43	1	7
ESE INDEMNITY FUND, officers and seamen of United States steamer Wyoming, prize money from, pay to	24	41	2	7
Do	343	43	1	7
E, HORACE, relief of	277	45	2	8
ETTE (steamer), loss of, to investigate	1759	47	1	9
ETTE EXPEDITION, survivors and heirs, relief of	2246	48	2	10
Do	2002	48	2	10
TS, THORNTON A., additional pay, claim for	637	45	2	8
Do	638	45	2	8
ON, H. D., services as judge advocate, claim for	208	29	1	4
Do	109	30	1	5
ON, OSCAR F., pay from date of warrant, claim for	149	34	3	6
ANDREW, bounty, claim for	270	46	2	9
EZEKIEL, relief of	487	25	2	2
JOHN PAUL, relief of heirs	206	29	1	4
THOMAS A. C., relief of	104	21	2	1
Do	108	22	2	2

Subject.	Report.	Congress.	Session.	Volume.
DSH, JAMES, relief of	768	29	1	4
Y, DONALD, relief of	274	45	2	8
Y, NATHANIEL, accounts of, to audit	271	45	2	8
Do	272	45	2	8
EVER, ISAAC, prize money to	159	19	1	1
E, JOHN, relief of	166	21	2	1
Do	126	22	2	2
LHON, JOHN, relief of	135	46	2	9
ERSON, MARY, arrears of pension to	129	28	2	3
MER, DAVID B., relief of	622	45	2	8
INISTS IN NAVY, permanence to, after certain re-enlistments	702	46	2	9
S,				
ines of ocean steamers for transportation of, to establish	685	29	1	4
ne of mail steamers to China and Sandwich Islands, to establish	596	29	1	5
Do	84	31	2	5
E, dry dock at Kittery, to establish	394	28	1	3
Do	166	30	1	5
TER, WILLIAM T., relief of	290	45	2	8
LEHEAD, MASSACHUSETTS, bounty and pensions to citizens of, for service in war of 1812	361	35	1	6
H, JOHN, pension to	768	24	1	2
Do	417	25	2	2
Do	191	25	3	2
ISLAND, CALIFORNIA,				
y dock at, to complete	839	46	2	8
d bars and deposits near, to remove	1636	46	2	9
NE CORPS,				
pointments in, to regulate	314	46	3	9
my, to abolish and transfer to	22	39	2	6
sertion in, to remove charges of	664	48	1	10
Do	1110	48	1	10
Do	1386	49	1	10
fe insurance in, system for officers of	920	45	2	7
icers of, to place on equal footing with officers of Army	117	22	2	2
Do	42	22	1	2
ganization of, explanatory of section 5 of act of June, 1834, for better	485	25	2	2
omotions in, to regulate	314	46	2	9
organization of	196	19	1	1
Do	243	27	2	3
Do	52	29	2	4
aff of, to regulate appointments and promotions in	1524	48	1	10
ansfer of, to Army	22	39	2	6
NE ENGINES, quality and kind used in war vessels, to investigate	8	38	2	6
NE HOSPITALS (*see also* NAVY HOSPITALS),				
arlestown, Mass., to establish, at	364	55	1	6
mphis, to establish, at	761	29	1	4
NE OFFICERS (*see also* FLEET OFFICERS), rank and pay of fleet	144	45	3	8
TON, WARD, retired list in Marine Corps as colonel, to place on	632	45	2	8
IN, FRANCIS, relief of	146	29	1	4
LAND, navy-yard at Baltimore, to establish	92	19	1	1
Do	139	34	1	6
ER-AT-ARMS (*see also* NAVY), commissioned as warrant officers	1409	46	2	9
S IN NAVY,				
omotion to rank of ensigns	311	46	3	9
tirement of	764	48	1	10
EMATICS, professors of, in Navy, to amend law regulating appointment of	464	46	2	9
IER, SARAH P., relief of	481	28	1	3
WELL, CHARLES D., additional pay to	23	35	1	6
S, ELIZABETH, pension to	180	20	1	1
Do	9	21	1	1
Do	431	25	2	2
Do	597	27	2	3
Do	75	30	1	5
E, HENRY M., accounts of, to audit	94	45	2	8
HER, PETER, claim for relief	631	45	2	8
S, JOHN O., accounts of to audit	42	33	1	6
CAL DEPARTMENT IN NAVY, reorganization of	47	19	2	1
TERRANEAN SQUADRON, court-martial trial of officers in	183	15	1	1
HIS, TENNESSEE,				
rine hospital at, to construct	761	29	1	4
val depot and dock yard at, to establish	991	27	2	3
Do	114	27	3	3
Do	120	28	1	3
ES, ANTHONY, pension to	27	24	2	2
DIAN, establishment of an American	286	31	1	5
ILL, CHESTER R., relief of	1973	48	1	10
ILL, J. H., relief of	456	46	2	9
LETON, EDWARD, relief of	308	47	1	9
IIPMEN,				
portioning of, among the States	92	17	2	1

*Parts 1, 2.

Subject.	Report.	Congress.	Session.	Volume.
VAL LAWS, code of, to revise	35	31	2	5
VAL OBSERVATORY,				
Astronomers at, to fix positions of assistant	1273	48	1	10
Cost of removing	454	45	2	8
Site for new, purchase of	90	46	2	9
VAL ORDNANCE. (*See* ORDNANCE.)				
VAL SCHOOLS. (*See* NAVY; SCHOOLS.)				
VAL STATIONS, lakes, to establish on	230	34	3	6
Do	67	39	1	6
VAL STORES, condition of, appertaining to Navy Department	55	17	1	1
VAL WHARF, Key West, Fla., to construct at	704	46	2	9
VY,				
Abuses in, alleged	77	22	2	2
Agents of, bonds required of	72	15	2	1
Apprentices in,				
Enlistment of	65	44	2	7
Additional ration to	152	45	3	8
Appropriations for,				
Annual, 1886-'87	2497	49	1	10
Annual, 1887-'88	3833	49	2	10
Transfer from one bureau to another	259	28	1	3
Arrears of pension, explanatory of law granting	129	23	2	2
Assistant engineers in,				
Promotion of	176	35	2	6
Retrospective pay of	440	36	1	6
Temporary increase of number of	3064	49	1	10
Boatswain in, increase pay to	74	32	1	5
Cadet engineers in, defining rank of	62	46	3	9
Cadet midshipmen in, appointment of	1414	46	2	9
Chaplains in,				
To reduce number of	930	45	2	8
Promoting efficiency of	1706	46	2	9
Civil engineers in, pay of	938	45	2	8
Color blindness, laws concerning	1569	46	2	9
Do	445	47	1	9
Condition of	258	28	1	3
Do	827	45	2	8
Construction fund in, to create permanent	169	46	2	9
Do	139	47	1	9
Constructors in, appointment of	1194	47	1	9
Cruisers for, to readvertise for bid for construction of the Newark (cruiser No. 1)	3910	49	2	10
Desertion from enlisted men in, removal of charges of	664	48	1	10
Do	1866	49	1	10
Efficiency of, to promote	115	46	3	9
Do	1009	47	1	9
Engineers in,				
Grade and rank of	699	46	2	9
Pay of	77	44	1	7
Do	2244	48	2	10
Pay of civil	938	45	2	8
To define rank of cadet	62	46	3	9
Enlistments in, to amend laws relating to	432	45	2	8
Expenses of naval establishment, to reduce	74	16	1	1
Graduates of Naval Academy at Annapolis, Md., to equalize rank of	142	48	1	8
Do	2244	48	2	8
Grog in, to discontinue issue of	73	28	2	3
Gunners in, increase pay to	74	32	1	5
Half-pay pensions. (*See* PENSIONS.)				
Hospitals in, appropriation for	61	20	2	1
Increase of,				
Ten additional sloops of war	33	18	1	1
Turler iron war steamers (with maps)	681	29	1	4
To protect commerce of United States	120	19	1	1
Expediency to	80	17	1	1
Do	785	24	1	2
Armed steam vessel for use on Lake Erie	1018	25	2	2
Judge-Advocate-General, fixing rank and pay of	459	46	2	9
Life insurance in	926	45	2	7
Machinists in, permanency of	702	46	2	9
Marine engines, kind and quality used in	8	38	2	6
Master-at-arms in, to make warrant officer	1408	46	2	9
Mates in,				
To appoint to rank of ensigns	311	46	3	9
Retirement of	764	48	1	10
Medical department in, the reorganization of	47	19	2	1
Midshipmen in, appointment of cadet	1414	46	2	9
Naval constructors in, appointment of assistant	1194	47	1	9
Do	1517	48	1	10
Naval depot at New Orleans	72	31	2	5

Subject.	Report.	Congress.	Session.	Volume.
NAVY—Continued				
Officers in,				
Pay, promotion, and duties of	85	21		1
Increase rank to	246	27	2	3
Relief of certain	924	45	2	8
Ordnance, fabrication of wrought-iron guns	479	28	1	5
Organization of,				
Reducing force in	40	16		1
Expenses of	74	16		1
Pay,				
In, to regulate and fix	511	24		2
To increase boatswains', gunners', and others	74	33		5
Modification of pursers' sea service	257	26	1	6
Retrospective pay to assistant engineers	440	26		6
To naval officers waiting orders	74	44	2	7
To regulate, of certain officers	748	44	1	7
Do	696	45	2	7
To equalize, of officers of Army and Navy	747	44		7
Sea pay to volunteer officers	706	46		9
Pension fund,				
Status of	147	15		1
Widows and orphans to be paid from	104	20		1
Do	86	21		1
Do	190	23		2
Do	444	30		5
To amend law on	451	34		3
Pensions,				
To extend term of half-pay pensions to widows and children of officers, seamen, and marines	5	18		1
Chargeable to privateer pension fund	85	20	2	1
Do	44	23	1	2
To re-enact law of March 3, 1837	531	28		3
To amend laws to embrace engineers, firemen, and coal-heavers	515	30		3
To amend laws relative to	1008	47		8
Privateer pension fund, to amend laws	175	21		1
Do	222	24		2
Prize money,				
To extend provisions of act	929	45	2	6
To abolish	1008	47		8
Professors of mathematics in, to amend law in appointment of	464	46		9
Prow-ship for, to construct	86	23		2
Do	674	24		2
Pursers, pay and allowance of	142	24	2	2
Do	586	25	2	3
Do	257	26	1	6
Ranks in, to establish additional	246	27	2	3
Rear-admirals in, to equalize pay of, on retired list	937	45	2	8
Reorganization of	35	31	2	5
Do	632	47	1	9
Repair and construction, to reimburse United States schooner Nonsuch	56	19	2	1
Retired officers in, relief of	806	47	1	8
Retiring in, voluntary	824	43	1	10
Do	96	43	1	10
Sail-makers in, to repeal section 1543 Revised Statutes, on employment of	66	44	2	7
Do	1413	46	2	9
Schools in, to improve condition of	121	23	1	2
Solicitor of, rank and pay of	459	46	2	9
Spirit ration, on discontinuance of	73	25	2	2
Warrant officers in, relief of	80	45	1	7
Do	277	46	2	8
Do	47	46	3	9
Vessels for, to construct additional	4056	46	2	10
War vessels in, construction and list of	653	47	1	9
NAVY AGENTS, bonds required of	72	15	2	1
NAVY AND MARINE CORPS LIFE INSURANCE, system of	926	45	2	8
NAVY DEPARTMENT,				
Bureaus of, to consolidate	1160	49	1	10
Investigations of	784	44	1	7
Do	312	45	2	8
Lands in District of Columbia, sale of, to	1115	46	2	8
Reorganization of	157	27	2	3
NAVAL HOSPITALS,				
Annapolis, Md., to transfer care of, to Secretary of Treasury	432	46	2	9
Do	936	47	1	9
Chelsea, Mass., sale of land attached to, at	490	28		5
Funds for establishing	78	17	2	1
NAVY HOSPITAL FUND. (*See* HOSPITAL FUND.)				
NAVY PENSION FUND (*see also* NAVY),				
Act of March 3, 1837, to re-enact	531	28		3
Arrears of pensions, to pay from	129	23		2
Condition of	1	27		3

Subject.	Report.	Congress.	Session.	Volume.
ENSION FUND—Continued.				
tment of	40	24	2	2
governing, to amend	451	24	1	2
of	147	15	2	1
ws and orphans of seamen to be granted pensions, payable from	190	23	1	2
SECRETARY OF. (*See* SECRETARY OF NAVY.)				
ARDS.				
rs, to establish at	20	47	1	9
nore, Md., to establish at	92	19	1	1
Do	139	34	1	6
lyn, N. Y.,				
o purchase land adjoining	126	27	3	3
o reclaim swamp land at	115	43	2	7
eston, S. C., to construct at	541	23	1	2
Do	199	24	1	2
estown, Mass., authorizing sale of	1077	47	1	9
s, regulating pay of, at first-class yards	247	27	2	3
ocks at,				
rooklyn, N. Y	100	20	1	1
Do	8	20	2	1
Do	40	27	3	3
are Island, Cal	829	45	2	8
ensacola, Fla	424	24	1	2
hiladelphia, Pa	872	25	2	2
Do	649	29	1	4
rtsmouth, N. H	100	20	1	1
Do	8	20	2	1
rt, to purchase land opposite	42	47	1	9
Do	140	47	1	9
hip-building yard on the Atlantic and Mississippi, to establish	345	43	1	7
y, Me., investigation of affairs at	790	44	1	7
his, to erect at	120	28	1	3
gansett Bay, Rhode Island, to establish in	93	19	1	1
London, Conn., to construct at	100	38	1	6
ern lakes, to construct on the	230	34	3	6
Do	1407	46	2	9
lelphia, Pa., relief of mechanics at	702	25	2	2
es River, Conn., to establish in	94	19	1	1
ington, D. C., relief of employés in	111	28	2	3
Do	169	28	2	3
MARY, relief of	68	27	3	3
K (United States cruiser No. 1), bids for construction of, to readvertise	3910	49	2	10
L, THOMAS N., relief of	706	29	1	4
NDON, CONNECTICUT, navy-yard at, to construct	100	38	1	6
LEANS, LOUISIANA, naval depot at, site for	72	31	2	5
RK.				
ock, to erect in New York Harbor	198	28	1	3
Do	40	27	3	3
tt's Harbor, sale of land at	177	28	2	3
A SHIP-CANAL, construction of	54	37	3	6
GUA, invasion of, by William Walker	74	35	1	6
SON, JOHN B., prize money to	240	28	1	3
SON, SOMERVILLE, restoration to active list of Navy	928	45	2	8
Do	1280	46	2	9
MARY and PHILOMEN, pension to	597	27	2	3
H (United States schooner), to rebuild	56	19	2	1
POLE. (*See* ARCTIC SEAS; EXPEDITIONS.)				
ERN FRONTIER, naval defense of	4	37	3	6
ELIHU, pension to	22	24	2	2
STEAMERS. (*See* VESSELS.)				
J, J., retired list of Navy, to place on	639	45	2	8
ELL, ELEANOR, pension to	597	27	2	3
RS OF NAVY (*see also* NAVY),				
otion of	85	21	1	1
itary retirement of certain	824	48	1	10
Do	96	49	1	10
, CHARLES, relief of	228	34	3	6
NCE AND ORDNANCE STORES, condition of naval	55	17	1	1
ovements in naval, to test value of	2	27	1	3
arine battery, invention by S. Colt	46	28	2	3
ght-iron guns, fabrication and testing of	479	28	1	3
DER, A. D., additional pay to	458	24	1	2
ER, DOUGLASS, retired list as captain in Navy, to place on	269	47	[illegible]	9
Do	1272	48	1	10
SEAS. (*See* SOUTH SEAS.)				
LIZABETH, relief of	273	46	2	9
R, B. W., and others, relief of	141	35	1	6
R, WILLIAM, and others, payments made by, to confirm	328	36	1	6
A, ISTHMUS OF. (*See* ISTHMUS OF PANAMA.)				
A RAILROAD COMPANY, transportation and supplies furnished General Walker's command, claim for	476	35	1	6

*And views of minority.

Subject.	Report.	Congress.	Session.	Volume.
condition of United States naval	121	23	1	
ZE, WILLIAM H., relief of	2188	48	2	10
NN, relief of	220	36	1	6
F. (administrator), relief of	125	46	2	9
VILLIAM B., relief of widow of	164	35	2	6
ER, JAMES, additional pay to	290	22	1	2
ST DEFENSES, Chesapeake Bay, steam batteries for defense of	448	27	2	3
disabled, providing for	309	46	3	9
CO., relief of	270	45	2	8
Do	272	45	2	8
ARY OF THE NAVY,				
of Commissioners of Navy, to act as presiding officer of	94	16	1	1
ntract with the Chiriqui Improvement Company made by	568	36	1	6
lists by, correction of errors in	188	43	1	7
IENRY B., relief of	1011	47	2	9
GE, THOMAS D., additional pay to	631	26	1	3
GE, THOMAS O., relief of	87	31	1	5
R, ELIZA, extra pay and prize money to	995	25	2	2
ER, ABRAM T., relief of	1005	48	1	10
THOMAS, pension to heirs	66	15	2	1
Do	454	29	1	4
NALS (*see also* CANALS).				
f Niagara, to construct around	54	37	3	6
nsin and Fox Rivers, to connect	55	37	3	6
K, E. R., relief of	124	22	2	2
Do	237	23	1	2
K, WILLIAM B., relief of	577	36	1	6
& COOK, patent "cut off," adoption of	834	29	1	4
storm and flood, to test plan of	90	42	2	7
CHARLES DWIGHT,				
n decorations, permission to accept	1652	47	1	9
n Navy, to establish	*1003	48	1	10
K, JOSEPH (guardian), pension to	103	20	2	1
LEWIS E., relief of	138	32	1	5
Do	228	33	1	6
N, J. W., and others, Key West, Fla., relief of	792	29	1	4
Do	189	30	1	5
Do	354	31	1	5
JOHN B., bounty to	454	46	2	9
ROBERT, retired list of Navy, to place on	1887	47	2	9
Do	1962	47	2	9
BRYAN, longitude, invention for determining	459	24	1	2
CHARLES, relief of	740	29	1	4
JOHN T., telegraph station at Charlestown navy-yard, to establish	562	36	1	6
MOSES, mariners' compass, pay for use of improvements made in	84	22	2	2
Col. R. (executor of), relief of	60	23	2	2
N, W. T. (administrator), relief of	207	36	1	6
JOSEPH, relief of widow	543	36	1	6
OR. (*See* JUDGE-ADVOCATE-GENERAL.)				
CAROLINA, navy-yard at Charleston, to establish	541	23	1	2
Do	199	24	1	2
EAS, EXPLORING EXPEDITION TO,				
ding for	209	20	1	1
of officers and men engaged in	270	27	3	3
ING, HARLOW, additional pay to	139	32	1	5
ING, LYMAN D., relief of	334	48	1	10
WILLIAM, additional pay to	284	31	1	5
ATION, discontinuance in Navy	73	28	2	3
ON, support of permanent home	3	27	1	3
N LIFE-BOAT, use in Navy of	148	33	2	5
N, OSCAR F., relief of	54	44	1	7
midshipmen, to apportion among the	92	17	2	1
ATTERIES, Chesapeake Bay by, providing for defense of	448	27	2	3
OILERS, explosion of, patent safety valve to prevent	115	28	2	3
ROW-SHIP, appropriation to construct	86	23	2	2
Do	674	24	1	2
WILLIAM A., accounts of, to audit	927	45	2	8
THOMAS B., pay from date of promotion	204	34	1	6
L, R. N., pay from date of promotion	157	45	3	8
Do	839	47	1	9
S, GEORGE A., restoration to Navy	195	47	1	9
S, JAMES A., steam navigation, pay for improvement in	510	28	1	3
S, THOMAS H., captain on active list, to advance as	22	40	2	7
T, CHARLES, prize money to	39	14	1	1
Do	40	14	2	1
WILLIAM B., relief of	76	44	1	7
ND FLOOD SIGNALS. (*See* SIGNALS.)				
JACOB J., additional pay to	72	32	1	5
L, WILLIAM H. H., naval cadetship by, alleged sale of	124	43	2	7
S, JOSIAH, and others, pension to	507	27	2	3
INE BATTERY. (*See* ORDNANCE.)				

* Parts 1, 2.

Subject.	Report.	Congress.	Session.	Volume.
-Continued.				
r construction of, to readvertise	2010	46	[illegible]	10
p, to readvertise bids for construction of Newark No. 1	2016	[illegible]	[illegible]	10
g of, to amend section 3617 Revised Statutes, relating to	[illegible]	[illegible]	[illegible]	[illegible]
-built, registry for	[illegible]	[illegible]	[illegible]	[illegible]
r steamers, to construct twelve	[illegible]	[illegible]	[illegible]	[illegible]
invention for paddle wheels on ocean and war steamers, to adopt	[illegible]	[illegible]	[illegible]	[illegible]
war, to 1883	[illegible]	[illegible]	[illegible]	[illegible]
teamers to China and Sandwich Islands, to establish line of	[illegible]	[illegible]	1	[illegible]
Do	[illegible]	31	[illegible]	[illegible]
eamers, to establish line to Africa	[illegible]	[illegible]	1	[illegible]
teamers for mail transportation, to establish lines	[illegible]	[illegible]	1	4
y for foreign-built, providing	[illegible]	46	[illegible]	[illegible]
IRAL, rank of, to establish	[illegible]	[illegible]	[illegible]	[illegible]
S, PHILIP F.,				
r	[illegible]	34	1	2
oney to	[illegible]	[illegible]	1	[illegible]
ARY D., pension to	743	[illegible]	1	[illegible]
BULON, relief of	109	34	[illegible]	[illegible]
Do	[illegible]	[illegible]	1	[illegible]
LD, BENJAMIN, increased pay to	[illegible]	35	1	6
, DUDLEY, relief of	411	34	1	2
Do	259	25	2	2
, WILLIAM, arrest of	74	35	1	6
OUT BAY, NEW YORK, navy-yard and naval-hospital land at, sale of	932	45	2	8
Do	762	46	1	10
YER, J., relief of	281	45	2	8
LL, WILLIAM T., professor of mathematics, pay as	765	29	1	4
REBELLION, relief of certain sailors and marines from charge of desertion	1110	46	1	10
AMERS. (*See* VESSELS.)				
SELS. (*See* VESSELS.)				
AMES, relief of	27	24	2	2
Do	597	27	2	3
T-OFFICERS. (*See* NAVY.)				
GTON, LEWIS, prize money to	240	28	1	3
Do	202	31	1	5
GTON CITY. (*See also* DISTRICT OF COLUMBIA.)				
GTON, DISTRICT OF COLUMBIA,				
nd wharf at, construction of	89	17	2	1
ard at, relief of employés in	111	28	2	3
Do	169	28	2	3
GTON TERRITORY, war vessel on coast of, to station	11	34	3	6
OTTED HEMP. (*See* HEMP; TARIFF.)				
JOHN, relief of	112	21	2	1
& POWERS, storm and flood signals, to test plan of	90	42	2	7
SA, relief of	63	45	3	8
Do	137	46	2	9
Do	484	47	1	9
WILLIAM, relief of	30	44	1	7
T, B. N., restoration to active list of Navy	937	47	1	9
DIA SEAS. (*See* GULF OF MEXICO.)				
EAD, ELIZABETH, pension to	103	20	2	1
, WILLIAM D., relief of	315	46	3	9
Do	19	47	1	9
Y, CHARLES W., relief of	22	40	3	7
Do	69	41	2	7
Y, HENRY, additional compensation to	181	23	1	2
HOLMES, assistant surgeon in Navy, appointment as	451	43	1	7
T (United States schooner), relief of heirs of officers and crew of	167	24	1	2
ON, ANSEL, pension to	283	31	1	5
Do	32	34	1	6
CHARLES, Jr., relief of	305	21	1	1
EXPLORING EXPEDITION. (*See* EXPLORING EXPEDITION.)				
, JAMES W., additional pay to	234	31	1	5
ON, JESSE, prize money to	192	20	1	1
ON, JOHN G., additional pay to	43	31	1	5
Do	117	46	3	9
), EDWARD, *et al.*, relief of	210	36	1	6
THEODORE D., relief of	933	45	2	8
K, JAMES, services as chaplain, claim for	99	28	2	2
Do	78	24	1	2
EBECCA, relief of	290	31	1	5
Do	49	33	2	6
, EDWARD K., accounts of, to audit	11	46	2	9
Do	1710	47	1	9
IN AND FOX RIVERS, improvement of	55	37	3	6
THARINE, relief of	66	18	2	1
Do	4	19	1	1
DEN, J., and others, Naval Asylum at Philadelphia, complaint of inmates of	253	28	1	3

WOOD, WILLIAM M.,
Back pay to
Relief of
WOOLSEY, ELLEN, pension to
WOOLSEY, MELANCTHON TAYLOR, relief of
WORDEN, JOHN L.,
Relief of
Retired list with highest pay of grade, to place on
WROUGHT-IRON GUNS. (*See* ORDNANCE.)
WYMAN, JAMES, pension to
WYOMING (United States steamer), officers and crew for prize money, claim of.
Do
YOUNG, EDWARD L., pension to
YOUNG, JOHN J.,
Pension to
Retired officer, pay as
ZANTZINGER, WILLIAM P., relief of
Do
ZELLER, THEODORE, investigation of purchase of tools by
Do

REPORTS

OF THE

IMITTEE ON PACIFIC RAILROADS,

HOUSE OF REPRESENTATIVES,

OM THE ORGANIZATION OF THE COMMITTEE, MARCH 2, 1865, TO THE CLOSE OF THE FORTY-NINTH CONGRESS, 1887, INCLUSIVE

IN ONE VOLUME.

COMPILED, UNDER THE DIRECTION OF THE JOINT COMMITTEE ON PRINTING,

BY

T. H. McKEE,

CLERK, DOCUMENT ROOM, UNITED STATES SENATE.

WASHINGTON:
GOVERNMENT PRINTING OFFICE.
1887.

)231

FORTY-NINTH CONGRESS, FIRST SESSION.

[PUBLIC RESOLUTION—NO. 24.]

Joint resolution authorizing the preparation of a compilation of the reports of committees of the Senate and House of Representatives.

Resolved by the Senate and House of Representatives of the United States of America in Congress assembled, That there be prepared under the direction of the Joint Committee of Printing, a compilation of the reports of the Senate and House of Representatives from the Fourteenth to the Forty-eighth Congress, inclusive, classified by committees, arranged, indexed, and bound in suitable volumes for the use of the standing committees of the two Houses of Congress. And the sum of seven thousand seven hundred and fifty dollars, or so much thereof as may be found necessary, is hereby appropriated out of any money in the Treasury not otherwise appropriated, for the preparation of said work, which sum may be paid by the Secretary of the Treasury upon the order of the chairman of said Joint Committee, as additional pay or compensation to any officer or employee of the United States.

Resolved further, That the Clerk of the House and Secretary of the Senate be, and they are hereby directed, to procure and file, for the use of their respective Houses, copies of all reports made by each committee of all succeeding Congresses; and that the Clerk of the House and the Secretary of the Senate be, and they are hereby, authorized and directed at the close of each session of Congress, to cause said reports to be indexed and bound, one copy to be deposited in the library of each House and one copy in the room of the committee from which the reports emanated.

Approved, July 29, 1886.

COMPILER'S NOTICE.

This compilation embraces all the printed reports made by both Houses of Congress from the commencement of the Fourteenth to the close of the Forty-ninth Congress. They are classified by committees and arranged in numerical order. The collection for each committee is divided into volumes of suitable size. Each committee has a separate index, a copy being bound in each volume.

The SPECIAL and SELECT reports are all compiled in one collection having one index, a copy of which is bound in each volume.

The plan throughout the compilation is to place each report to the committee from which it was reported, without reference to the subject-matter.

The House and Senate reports are compiled separately. Care will be required in noticing the chronological order, as in some instances an entire session or Congress may not appear in certain volumes from the fact that during this period no reports were made by this committee.

T. H. McKEE

INDEX

TO

REPORTS OF COMMITTEE ON PACIFIC RAILROADS,

HOUSE OF REPRESENTATIVES.

FROM 1865 TO 1887, INCLUSIVE.

Subject.	Report.	Congress.	Session.	Volume.
ACCOUNTS, Pacific railroad, investigation of	1691	49	1	1
ARKANSAS, NEW MEXICO AND PACIFIC RAILROAD, right of way through Indian Territory to	2582	49	1	1
ATLANTIC AND PACIFIC RAILROAD, requiring Government to guarantee payment of interest on bonds of	267	43	2	1
ATLANTIC AND PACIFIC TELEGRAPH, proposals for bids to construct	21	37	3	1
Do	31	37	3	1
AUSTIN-TOPOLOVAMPO PACIFIC ROUTE, survey for	359	44	1	1
Do	621	45	2	1
BOARD OF COMMISSIONERS, Pacific railroad, to establish	620	45	2	1
CENTRAL PACIFIC RAILROAD, indebtedness of, 1883	*1431	48	1	1
CINNABAR AND CLARK'S FORK RAILROAD, right of way to	832	48	1	1
COMMISSIONERS, Pacific railroad, board of, to establish	620	45	2	1
EXAMINATIONS, Pacific railroads, investigation of financial management of	2387	49	1	1
FINANCIAL MANAGEMENT, Pacific railroads, investigation of management of	2387	49	1	1
HOUSE OF REPRESENTATIVES, COMMITTEE ON PACIFIC RAILROADS,				
Fixing day for consideration of business of	2033	49	1	1
Fixing day for consideration of business reported from Committee on Pacific railroads	2033	49	1	1
Fixing day for consideration of business reported from	2033	49	1	1
IDAHO TERRITORY, Salmon City and North Fork County in, to incorporate	1575	48	1	1
INDEBTEDNESS OF PACIFIC RAILROADS, amending law relative to	622	45	2	1
INDIAN TERRITORY, Arkansas, New Mexico and Pacific Railroad through, right of way to	2582	49	1	1
INVESTIGATION,				
Northern Pacific Railroad, 1872	99	42	2	1
Pacific railroads, management of	1691	49	1	1
KANSAS PACIFIC RAILROAD, cost of operating	430	45	2	1
KANSAS PACIFIC *vs.* UNION PACIFIC,				
Letter of E. C. Smeed, 1878	430	45	2	1
To pay for surveying lands granted to	1312	47	1	1
Do	1857	47	2	1
Do	478	48	1	1
Indebtedness of, 1883	1431	48	1	1
LAND GRANTS,				
Relating to political platform, 1860	139	44	2	1
New Orleans, Baton Rouge and Vicksburg Railroad, forfeiture of grant to	1018	45	2	1
Pacific railroad system, Government aid for extension of	691	46	2	1
Kansas Pacific Railroad, to pay for surveying lands granted to	1312	47	1	1
Do	1857	47	2	1
Railroads, lands granted to, compelling companies to reimburse Government for surveying	607	49	1	1
Northern Pacific Railroad, cost of surveying lands granted to	1002	49	1	1
NEW ORLEANS, BATON ROUGE AND VICKSBURG RAILROAD, forfeiture of land grant to	1018	45	2	1
NORTHERN PACIFIC RAILROAD,				
Route, cost, and distance	428	36	1	1
Do	*428	36	1	1
Do	*428	36	1	1
Investigation of condition of	90	42	2	1

* Views of minority.

Subject.	Report.	Congress.	Session.	Volume.
NORTHERN PACIFIC RAILROAD—Continued.				
Extending time for completion of	120	45	2	1
Do	*615	45	2	1
Asking Government aid for completion of	691	46	3	1
Cost of surveying lands granted to	1002	49	1	1
Inquiring into violation of law by	2567	49	1	1
OCEAN Atlantic to Pacific, to construct railroad from	*428	36	1	1
OREGON SHORT-LINE RAILWAY COMPANY, to incorporate	1384	47	1	1
PACIFIC RAILROADS,				
Amending various acts incorporating	622	45	2	1
Do	478	48	1	1
Government aid for completion of	691	46	2	1
To consolidate continuous lines	755	47	1	1
Do	1168	47	1	1
Investigation of books and accounts of	1601	49	1	1
Examination of workings and financial management of	2287	49	1	1
Arkanfas and New Mexico, right of way through Indian Territory	2582	49	1	1
Atlantic and Pacific Railroad, asking Government guarantee to pay interest on bonds issued by	207	43	2	1
Claims of, for mail and other transportation	*1431	48	1	1
Commissioners, creating board of	*620	45		
Construction of, Government aid to assist in	428	36		
Humphrey, Captain, letter concerning different routes to the Pacific coast	*428	36		
Indebtedness of, statement of	*1431	48		
Interest on bonded debt, paid by United States, and amount due June 30, 1885	1929	49		
Kansas Pacific, to pay for surveying lands granted to	1312	47		
Do	478	48		
Lands granted to, cost of surveying to be paid by	607	49		
Murray, Lieut. M. F., letter relating to Pacific road from	*428	36		1
Niobrara Valley Branch, granting papers of incorporation to	1576	48	1	1
Northern Pacific Railroad,				
Defining line of duty of special committee investigating condition of	90	42	2	1
Extending time for completion of	120	45	2	1
Cost of surveying lands granted to	1002	49	1	1
Ocean, construction of road from Atlantic to Pacific	*428	36	1	1
Routes, relating to different routes for railroad to Pacific coast	428	36	1	1
Sinking fund, to amend act of May 7, 1878	762	46	2	1
Southern Pacific,				
Asking Government aid to complete line	1580	46	2	1
Consolidating other roads with	1856	47	2	1
Texas Pacific, amending original act chartering	*139	44	2	1
Texas and Pacific, asking guarantee by Government of interest on bonds issued by	207	43	2	1
Union Pacific, to pay for surveying lands granted to	478	48	1	1
Utah and Northern Railroad,				
Right of way through Montana to	1710	46	2	1
Through Montana, right of way to	1710	46	2	1
PACIFIC RAILROAD ACTS,				
Defining meaning and intent of act incorporating	430	45	2	1
Amending various	622	45	2	1
PACIFIC RAILROAD COMMISSIONERS, establishing board of	‡620	45	2	1
PACIFIC RAILWAY SYSTEM, extension of Government aid for	691	46	2	1
PACIFIC TELEGRAPH LINE, for purchase of	1505	47	1	1
PUBLIC LANDS, Salmon City and North Fork Toll-Road Company over, right of way to	1575	48	1	1
RAILROAD COMMISSIONERS, Pacific, creating board of	*620	45	2	1
RAILROADS, to consolidate continuous lines in the Territories	755	47	1	1
Do	1168	47	1	1
Do	1856	47	1	1
RIGHT OF WAY,				
Utah and Northern Railroad, through Montana	1710	46		1
To Cinnabar and Clark's Fork Railroad	832	48		1
To Salmon City and North Fork Toll-Road Company over public lands	1575	48		1
To Arkansas, New Mexico and Pacific Railroad through Indian Territory	2582	49		1
SALMON CITY AND NORTH FORK TOLL-ROAD COMPANY, to incorporate	1575	48		1
SINKING FUND, Pacific railroads, amending act of May 7, 1878	762	46		1
SIOUX CITY AND PACIFIC RAILROAD, indebtedness for 1883 of	*1431	48		1
SMEED, E. C., letter from, entitled "Kansas Pacific *vs.* Union Pacific," March 14, 1878	430	45	2	1
SOUTHERN PACIFIC RAILROAD,				
Condition of, in 1878	§238	45		1
Asking Government aid for completion of	691	46		1
Do	1580	46		1
Consolidating other roads with	1856	47		1
SPOKANE AND CŒUR D'ALENE RAILROAD COMPANY, to incorporate	[illegible]	48		1
Do	[illegible]	49		1
SURVEYS, Pacific railroad lines, payment of cost for surveying lands granted to	[illegible]	47		1
Do	1857	47	2	1
Do	1002	49	1	1

* Views of minority. † Parts, 1, 2, 3. ‡ Parts 1 and 2. § Part 2.

Subject.	Report.	Congress.	Session.	Volume.
APHS,				
Atlantic to Pacific Oceans, proposals for construction of	31	37	3	1
Do	31	37	3	1
continental, fixing schedule of prices	21	37	3	1
Do	31	37	3	1
tic and Pacific Ocean by electric, to facilitate communication between	21	37	3	1
Do	31	37	3	1
ern Pacific line, completion of	1560	46	3	1
e lines, to purchase	1505	47	1	1
ORIES, railroads in, to consolidate continuous lines of	755	47	1	1
Do	1166	47	1	1
PACIFIC RAILROAD,				
iring Government to guarantee interest on bonds of	267	42	2	1
g additional Government aid to complete	*238	45	2	1
Do	†619	45	2	1
itutionality of granting land by Government to assist in construction of	†139	44	2	1
y of line of route	139	44	2	1
ding original act chartering	†139	44	2	1
anteeing payment by Government of interest on bonded debt of	238	45	2	1
g Government aid for completion of	691	46	2	1
AN ACT,				
ading act of May 7, 1878	762	46	2	1
ic railroads, result of act of 1880 relating to	1929	49	1	1
OADS, Salmon City and North Fork road, to incorporate	1575	48	1	1
PACIFIC RAILROAD,				
of operating	430	45	2	1
y for surveying lands granted to	478	48	1	1
tedness for 1883	†1431	48	1	1
g fund, report of 1883	1929	49	1	1
tedness of	1929	49	1	1
ND NORTHERN RAILWAY COMPANY, right of way through Montana	1710	46	3	1

* Parts 1, 2, 3, 4. † Views of minority.

REPORTS

OF THE

)MMITTEE ON PATEN

HOUSE OF REPRESENTATIVES,

ROM THE ORGANIZATION OF THE COMMITTEE, SEPTEMBER 15, 1837, TO THE FORTY-NINTH CONGRESS, 1887, INCLUSIVE.

IN TWO VOLUMES.

COMPILED UNDER THE DIRECTION OF THE JOINT COMMITTEE ON PRINTING

BY

T. H. McKEE,

CLERK, DOCUMENT ROOM, UNITED STATES SENATE.

WASHINGTON:
GOVERNMENT PRINTING OFFICE.
1887.

9240 PAT H

FORTY-NINTH CONGRESS, FIRST SESSION.

[PUBLIC RESOLUTION—No. 24.]

Joint resolution authorizing the preparation of a compilation of the reports of mittees of the Senate and House of Representatives.

Resolved by the Senate and House of Representatives of the U
States of America in Congress assembled, That there be prepared u
the direction of the Joint Committee of Printing, a compilation of
reports of the Senate and House of Representatives from the F
teenth to the Forty-eighth Congress, inclusive, classified by commit
arranged, indexed, and bound in suitable volumes for the use of
standing committees of the two Houses of Congress. And the su
seven thousand seven hundred and fifty dollars, or so much there
may be found necessary, is hereby appropriated out of any mon
the Treasury not otherwise appropriated, for the preparation of
work, which sum may be paid by the Secretary of the Treasury
the order of the chairman of said Joint Committee, as additional p
compensation to any officer or employee of the United States.

Resolved further, That the Clerk of the House and Secretary of
Senate be, and they are hereby directed, to procure and file, for th
of their respective Houses, copies of all reports made by each com
tee of all succeeding Congresses; and that the Clerk of the House
the Secretary of the Senate be, and they are hereby, authorized
directed at the close of each session of Congress, to cause said re
to be indexed and bound, one copy to be deposited in the libra
each House and one copy in the room of the committee from whic
reports emanated.

Approved, July 29, 1886.

COMPILER'S NOTICE.

compilation embraces all the printed reports made by both s of Congress from the commencement of the Fourteenth to the f the Forty-ninth Congress. They are classified by committees ranged in numerical order. The collection for each committee is d into volumes of suitable size. . Each committee has a separate a copy being bound in each volume.

SPECIAL and SELECT reports are all compiled in one collection ; one index, a copy of which is bound in each volume.

plan throughout the compilation is to place each report to the ttee from which it was reported, without reference to the subject-
'.

House and Senate reports are compiled separately. Care will uired in noticing the chronological order, as in some instances an session or Congress may not appear in certain volumes from the at during this period no reports were made by this committee.

T. H. McKEE.

INDEX

TO

)RTS OF THE COMMITTEE ON PATENTS,

HOUSE OF REPRESENTATIVES.

FROM 1837 TO 1887, INCLUSIVE.

Subject.	Report.	Congress.	Session.	Volume.
:ALVIN, locks, improvement in	195	45	3	2
JOHN J., flattening window-glass cylinder, extension	32	30	1	1
SAAC, power printing press, improvements in	277	33	1	1
Do	168	34	1	1
, to facilitate, from Commissioner of Patents	237	46	3	2
& BISHOP, carding machine, extension	88	30	2	1
Do	151	31	1	1
Do	17	33	1	1
JERAUM, reaper and harvester, remuneration	184	45	3	2
Do	1062	47	1	2
Do	590	48	1	2
NATHAN, lining pipe with hydraulic cement invented, extension of	61	39	1	1
'ILLIAM, plow, improvement on, extension of	487	28	1	1
, WILLIAM H., hat-blocking machine, extension of letters patent for	3942	49	2	2
ISAIAH, act of 1836 relative to issuing of letters patent	506	28	1	1
, V., metallic cartridges, extension of	347	44	1	1
Do	191	45	3	2
BENJAMIN H., surveying instrument, extension	193	35	2	1
, JOHN C., claim for relief	181	45	3	2
OHN, claim for relief	666	25	2	1
ARD, THOMAS, wood-working machinery, renewal	397	23	1	1
Do	713	29	1	1
. JAMES ALBERT, claim for relief	2669	48	2	2
Do	900	49	1	2
N. STEPHEN, telegraph, system adopting	224	30	1	1
WILLIAM E., extension of patent	2751	49	1	2
AVID, type casting machinery, extension of	89	35	1	1
'HOMAS A., muck-dredging machine, extension	1714	48	1	2
WILLIAM M., pith of cornstalks, improvement in preparation of	3816	49	2	2
, WILLIAM G., shoe-pegging machinery, extension	1018	47	1	2
Do	1254	48	1	2
RDT, ornamenting the surface of india-rubber, extension	201	46	3	2
DMUND (Commissioner of Patents), investigation of charges preferred gainst	839	30	1	1
W. LEIGH, electro-heating system, extension	1570	49	1	2
Γ, JEREMIAH, musical instruments, letters patent	33	41	2	1
ILLIAM S., claim for relief of heirs	2174	48	2	2
, reducing fees for filing	64	46	3	2
MARGARET, vellum cloth, cutting	779	47	1	2
Do	102	48	1	2
Do	186	48	1	2
, EDWIN M., manufacture of india-rubber goods, extension	331	34	1	1
Do	156	35	1	1
ER, CHARLES F., refining sugar and sirup, extension	572	44	1	1
UCIUS C., extension of letters patent	87	43	2	1
NRIETTA H., fluting machines, extension	1466	47	1	2
Do	2243	48	2	2
Do	517	49	1	2
Do	3237	49	1	2
MICHAEL H., lamp burners, extension	492	47	1	2
MUEL, fire-arms, extension	6	33	1	1
Do	194	35	2	1

Subject.	Report.	Congress.	Session.	Volume.
...AR, gearing for wagons, extension	176	40	2	3
Do	182	41	2	3
Do	346	42	2	3
...S, prizes to inventors for meritorious	265	42	1	1
...and PATENTEES, on the encouragement and relief of	269	45	2	1
...FREDERICK S., relative to the extension of patent	2782	49	1	3
...JAMES J., process of generating heat, extension	1081	46	2	3
Do	885	47	1	2
Do	516	48	1	2
...ELES W., relative to extension of patent to assignees of	3665	49	1	3
...THAN L., armor for water and land batteries, compensation for ... by United States	294	43	2	1
...Y ANN, on petition for extension of patent No. 22135	182	49	1	3
...ARD N., purchase by Government of patent for separating gold ... silver	215	35	1	1
...IN E., coal chutes, extension	2820	48	1	3
...AH, reamer, boring holes in barrels	228	42	1	1
...HAZARD, reaping and mowing machine, completion of patent	676	37	3	1
...UEL A., plows, improvement, extension	344	43	2	1
Do	615	44	1	1
...H., preventing decay of vegetable matter, patent	568	25	2	1
...MINARD, steam-engine valve gear, extension	884	48	1	2
Do	736	49	1	2
...AMILTON, lard or tallow, method of separating, into two separate ...tances, patent	369	36	1	1
...UDOLPH, tool for boring rock, extension	1815	47	2	2
Do	449	48	2	2
...ATENT.				
...act of July 4, 1836, granting, to employés in Interior Department	679	37	3	1
...act of 1836, issuing of	506	25	1	1
...LIAM and WILLIAM H., claim for relief	2790	49	1	3
...F PATENTS. (*See* PATENT LAWS.)				
...EY, shutter hinge, extension	691	42	1	2
...RY A., cotton-bale tie, extension	122	49	2	1
Do	341	43	2	1
...CYRUS H., reaping machine, extension	118	35	2	1
...HUGH, claim for relief	3	42	3	1
...STEPHEN, claim for relief	421	28	1	1
...Y. (*See* under name of patentee and invention.)				
...A. S., self-feeding machine, patent for, extension	71	42	3	1
...REBECCA A., claim for relief	10	42	3	1
...ON A., *et al.*, steam-engine valve gear, extension	884	48	1	2
...ON A., claim for relief	736	49	1	2
...MOSES, knitting machines, extension	177	45	3	2
...N L., glass jar, screw top, extension	1189	46	2	2
...McKAY, machine for attaching the soles of shoes to their uppers, ...nsion	169	45	3	2
...RK, mode of taking casts from the face of living persons, extension	693	47	1	2
...ORGE, *et al.*, mode of unloading vessels, extension of	1377	47	1	2
...ALEXANDER, screw pile and screw mooring, extension	164	34	1	1
...C. H., heirs of, medical compound, extension	98	40	1	2
...THOMAS, hair-brush handles, improvement in, extension	293	43	2	1
...ASCALL, harvesting machine, extension	9	31	1	1
Do	103	32	1	1
Do	84	33	1	1
...WILLIAM, and others, floating excavator, extension	506	28	1	1
...REW, Jr., improved capstan, extension of patent	380	31	1	1
...RGE W., breech-loading fire-arms	1	45	3	2
Do	508	48	1	2
...MAN F., improvement in permutation locks, extension	194	45	3	2
...ANCIS, claim for relief	1862	48	1	2
...WATERS, removal of snags, &c., from	369	29	1	1
Do	30	30	1	1
...R, GABRIEL, improvement in process of preparing tobacco, exten...	535	48	1	2
...H, padlock, desk and chest locks, extension	114	30	1	1
Do	255	34	1	1
Do	501	35	1	1
...NCIS B., marine engine, patent	311	28	1	1
...r cutting spiral grooves in barrels of rifles, patent	667	25	2	1
...ting of percussion caps	212	29	1	1
...rnace, patent	468	30	1	1
...BULON and AUSTIN, water wheels, extension	208	31	1	1
Do	297	33	1	1
...tension or renewal for.				
...ing-power machine, patent	668	25	2	1
...for making ice, extension	112	41	2	1
...water and land batteries, compensation for use of, by United States	294	43	2	1
...t for steam boilers, extension	595	43	1	1
...ailroad cars, extension	640	30	1	1

Subject.	Report.	Congress.	Session.	Volume.
PATENTS, extension or renewal for—Continued.				
Baling press (perpetual), extension	833	48	1	2
Do	1095	49	1	2
Balls and shot, extension	160	26	2	1
Do	806	30	1	1
Belts for driving machinery, patent, extension	839	49	1	2
Broom machine, extension	32	41	2	1
Capstan (improvement), extension	380	31	1	1
Carding machine	88	30	2	1
Do	151	31	1	1
Do	17	33	1	1
Carpet lining, extension	2502	48	2	2
Do	645	49	1	2
Carriage wheels, extension	176	45	3	2
Chilled rollers and metallic cylinders, extension	6	30	2	1
Coal chutes, extension	2550	43	2	2
Compound to prevent the explosion of steam boilers, extension	247	36	1	1
Connecting links, extension	185	45	3	2
Cotton-bale tie, extension	182	43	2	2
Do	341	43	2	2
Cotton gin, extension	1321	46	2	2
Do	410	47	1	2
Cylinder window glass, extending	32	30	1	1
Design for an Army and Navy emblem, extension	1689	46	2	2
Door locks, extension	57	37	3	1
Double cultivator, extension	343	43	2	1
Do	609	44	1	1
Dredging machine, extension	160	29	1	1
Do	62	29	2	1
Do	293	30	1	1
Electro-heating machine	1570	49	1	2
Evaporating sugar, extension	103	45	3	2
Fire-arms, extension	63	33	1	1
Do	194	35	2	1
Do	84	42	3	1
Do	168	45	3	2
Do	1313	47	1	2
Do	731	48	1	2
Do	1518	48	1	2
Do	1778	48	1	2
Floating excavator, extension	505	28	1	1
Fluting machines, extension	1466	47	1	2
Do	2243	48	2	2
Do	517	49	1	2
Do	3237	49	1	2
Forks and spoons, extension	183	45	3	2
Forming button backs and affixing eyes, extension	91	39	1	1
Gearing for wagons, extension	170	45	3	2
Do	166	46	2	2
Do	146	47	1	2
Glass jar, extension	1139	46	2	2
Hair-brush handles, extension	295	43	2	1
Harvesting machine, extension	9	31	1	1
Do	103	32	1	1
Do	84	33	1	1
Hat-blocking machine	3942	49	2	2
Hat-forming machine, extension	172	45	3	2
Horse-power machinery, extension	112	37	2	1
Do	2	42		1
Ice, process and apparatus for manufacturing, Twining's patent, extension of	112	41	[illegible]	1
Improved pipe layer, extension	619	36		1
India-rubber, manufacture of, extending	183	34		1
Do	221	34		1
Indicating temperature and pressure of steam boilers	123	28		1
Indigo and paints, machine for grinding, extension	567	30		1
Iron buckle or clasp, extension	190	45		2
Iron-smelting furnace, extending	468	30		1
Knitting machine, extension	177	45		2
Lacing hooks for boots and shoes, patent for	445	48		2
Do	646	49		2
Do	3236	49		2
Lamp burners, extension	492	47	1	2
Lamp chimneys, extension	944	47	1	2
Lard, separating into two separate substances, patent for	340	38	1	1
Letters of patent, extension of	87	43	2	2
Linchpin, adopted for use in artillery in U. S. Army	498	47	1	2
Do	185	48	1	2
Lining pipe	61	39	1	1
Loading vessels, extension	1377	47	1	2
Locks, improvement in	195	45	3	2
Locomotive engine, extension	179	45	3	2

Subject.	Report.	Congress.	Session.	Volume.
, extension or renewal for—Continued.				
bag (folding), extension	1284	40	1	2
e for stripping cards, extension	373	44	1	1
acture of india-rubber goods, extension	321	34	1	1
Do	356	35	1	1
engine (Ericsson), patent for	311	33	1	1
compound, extension	39	40	1	2
cartridges, extension	367	44	1	2
Do	181	45	2	2
Do	86	46	2	2
Do	311	47	1	2
Do	1080	47	1	2
Do	659	48	1	2
of working ores, extension	179	45	2	2
taking casts from the faces of living persons, extension	666	47	1	2
candles, extension	362	44	1	1
boards for plows, extension	389	32	1	1
and conveying grain, extension	1068	48	1	2
dredging machine	1714	48	1	2
instruments	38	61	3	1
signals, extending	1603	47	1	2
ca canister, improved, purchase of, by United States	668	47	1	2
ating surface of india-rubber	361	46	2	2
green corn, extension	1875	47	1	2
desk and chest locks, extension	114	30	1	1
Do	303	34	1	1
Do	591	35	1	1
grinding machine, extending	307	30	1	1
ent, Schillinger's, extension	1834	40	1	2
sion cap. (*See* ORDNANCE AND ORDNANCE STORES.)				
sion caps, extension	232	32	1	2
sion projectiles, extension	175	45	2	2
ation locks, extension	196	46	2	2
yer, extension	518	35	1	1
machinery, extension	200	31	1	1
Do	158	33	1	1
Do	178	34	2	1
Do	89	34	2	1
Do	96	35	2	1
m scales, extension	174	45	3	2
extension	344	43	2	1
Do	610	44	1	1
loom, extension	88	35	1	1
Do	206	35	2	1
Do	486	43	1	1
printing press	277	33	1	1
Do	163	34	1	1
ing tobacco, extension	835	48	1	2
ting decay of vegetable matter, patent for	662	25	2	1
g press, improvement in, extension	277	33	1	1
Do	163	34	1	1
of generating heat, extension	1061	47	1	2
Do	985	48	1	2
Do	516	49	1	2
extension	549	44	1	1
Do	1253	48	1	2
Do	2173	48	2	2
d-car axle box, extension	1009	48	1	2
l-car brakes, extension	274	43	3	1
extension	290	43	1	1
(McCormick's), extension	119	33	2	1
g machine, extension	3	43	3	1
g and mowing machine, patent for	670	27	2	1
ing machine, extension	1017	45	2	2
g sugar and sirup, extension	572	44	1	1
rator furnace, extension	1380	47	1	2
l of snags from navigable streams, extension	369	29	1	1
Do	30	30	1	1
ers and harbors,				
raising mud, sand, and gravel from	160	29	1	1
Do	62	29	2	1
Do	293	30	1	1
deepening, patent	505	28	1	1
in cans, extension	190	35	2	1
e, extension	2318	48	2	2
Do	1414	49	1	2
wheel, extension	176	45	3	2
dle and screw moorings, extension	164	34	1	1
ling straw cutter, extension	71	42	3	1
machine, extension	129	48	2	1
Do	237	44	1	1

Subject.	Report.	Congress.	Session.	Volume.
PATENTS, extension or renewal for—Continued.				
Sewing machine (shoes), extension	169	45	3	2
Sheet-iron process (patent), extension	89	30	2	1
Shell-molding machine, extension	1522	46	2	2
Do	3037	49	1	2
Shoe-pegging machine	1018	47	1	2
Do	1254	48	1	2
Shot and shell, improvement in manufacturing of	918	47	1	2
Shovel or scraper, extension	91	30	2	1
Shutter hinge, extension	601	43	1	1
Silver spoon, extension	671	27	2	1
Snags, removal of	369	25	1	1
Do	30	30	1	1
Springs for steam engine pistons, extension	160	40	3	2
Steam engine, extension	126	30	2	1
Do	191	35	2	1
Do	620	36	1	1
Do	18	37	2	1
Do	46	42	3	1
Steam-engine valve gear, extension	834	48	1	2
Do	736	49	1	2
Steel and iron, manufacture of, extension,	178	45	3	2
Straw cutters, extension	207	35	2	1
Submarine telegraph cable, patent for	54	37	2	1
Surgical instruments, extension	587	48	2	2
Do	780	47	1	2
Surveying instruments	193	35	2	1
Tallow, separating into two separate substances, patent for	340	30	1	1
Telephones, patent for	1355	48	1	2
Thrashing machine, extension	813	30	1	1
Tool for boring rocks, extension	1915	47	2	2
Do	446	48	1	2
Type-casting machine	89	35	1	1
Type writer, extension	767	49	1	2
Washing and wringing machine, extension	473	43	1	1
Water wheels, extension	308	31	1	1
Do	297	33	1	1
Window glass, flattening cylinder	82	30	1	1
Wiring window-blind rods and slats, extension	550	44	1	1
Wood pulp for paper, machine for reducing	1638	46	2	2
Wood-splitting machine, extension	303	44	1	1
Do	193	45	3	2
Wood-working machine	397	23	1	1
Do	713	29	1	1
Wool-spinning machinery, extension	566	30	1	1
Do	47	37	2	1
PATENTS, amend land relating to	3682	49	2	2
PATENT ATTORNEYS' FEES, regulating	64	46	3	2
Do	2852	49	1	2
PATENT FUND, appropriation for purchase of arranging and displaying drawings of patents	551	28	1	1
PATENT LAWS,				
Act of July 4, 1836, as allows issue of letters patent to employés in Patent Office	670	27	2	1
Act of 1836 as relates to issuing of letters patent by Commissioner of Patents	506	28	1	1
Do	85	31	2	1
Amending	168	45	3	2
Do	1335	46	2	2
Do	1529	48	1	2
Do	2725	49	1	2
Amending law relative to voidance	1711	46	2	2
Do	1400	47	1	2
Do	4	48	1	2
Amending, relative to fees	64	46	3	2
Changing	84	31	2	1
Codifying	178	35	1	1
Do	358	14	1	1
Copyright law, amendment	1547	47	1	2
Do	1966	49	1	2
Foreign patented articles	66	48	1	2
Do	181	46	1	2
Limiting the life time of	972	48	1	2
Memorial of citizens of Philadelphia requesting alteration of	554	28	1	1
Protecting patents	1139	47	1	2
Do	66	48	1	2
Punishment of fraudulent vendors	130	48	1	2
Do	1862	49	1	2
Trade marks, registration of	1546	47	1	2
Do	2376	48	2	2
Do	1966	49	1	2

Subject.	Report.	Congress.	Session.	Volume.
...of delay in examining applications for	98	30	2	1
...Claims, jurisdiction, to regulate	501	47	1	2
...prizes for meritorious inventions	[illegible]	43	1	1
...and distribution of copyrights and patents issued	159	38	2	1
...OFFICE, organization of	797	25	2	1
...OFFICE LIBRARY, to prepare index to	590	46	2	2
...S, protecting	858	44	1	1
...EORGE W., cotton gin, extension	1821	46	2	1
Do	410	47	1	2
...ON, WILLIAM, inventing spiral grooves in barrels of rifles	887	25	2	1
...SE, DANIEL, balls and shot, extension	169	28	2	1
Do	506	30	1	1
...THOMAS, shovel or scraper, extension	91	30	2	1
..., CHARLES A., broom machine, extension	32	43	2	1
...ARY F., sad-irons, extension	2378	48	2	2
Do	2416	49	1	2
Do	3485	49	2	2
...ranting prizes for the encouragement of meritorious inventions	398	45	1	1
...SA C., platform scales, extension	174	44	2	2
...NG AIR STOVE, for use in United States Capitol	808	30	1	1
...FRANCIS A., surgical instrument, extension of	587	46	2	2
Do	780	47	1	2
...AND HARVESTERS,				
...unerate Jeraum Atkins for invention of	184	45	2	2
Do	1962	47	1	2
Do	584	48	1	2
...unerate Jeraum Atkins for invention of	184	45	2	2
Do	1962	47	1	2
Do	580	48	1	2
...IVIA C., claim for relief	172	46	2	2
...JOSEPH W., rectifying machine, extension	1617	45	2	2
...S, JOHN P., design for an Army and Navy emblem, extension	1830	46	2	2
...S, RENSSELAER, power looms, extension	466	45	1	1
...ON, JAMES H., telephones, patent	1256	49	1	2
..., JAMES, straw cutters, extension	207	35	2	1
...JAMES D., carriage wheels, extension	178	45	3	2
...S IMPROVED CANISTER, purchase by United States	892	47	1	2
...OSHUA, percussion caps, extension	212	29	1	1
...OD, JOHN P., door locks, extension	57	37	3	1
...HENRY M., removal of snags from navigable streams, extension	369	29	1	1
Do	30	30	1	1
...HRYSTIAN, manufacture of steel and iron, extension	178	45	3	2
...FREDERICK E., steam engines, extension	191	35	2	1
Do	620	36	1	1
Do	18	37	2	1
...CHARLES W. and FREDERICK, regenerator furnace, extension of	1380	47	1	2
...GEORGE B., submarine telegraph cable, patent	54	37	2	1
...LBA F., locomotive engines, extension	179	45	3	2
...G., claim for services rendered in Patent Office by	74	29	2	1
Do	31	30	1	1
...RANCIS PETTIT, claim for relief	166	33	1	1
...TEPHEN N., lacing hooks for boots and shoes, patent	415	48	1	2
Do	646	49	1	2
Do	3236	49	1	2
...G, HENRY C., metallic cartridges, extension	1660	47	1	2
...ORPE, JOHN, molding candles, extension	302	44	1	1
...NE CABLES, insulators	2018	48	1	2
Do	2650	49	1	2
...JACOB, hat-blocking machine, extension of letters patent for	3942	49	2	2
...BENJAMIN, *et al.*, claim for relief	534	29	1	1
...JOHN, *et al.*, laying "roving in cans," extension	190	35	2	1
...EMILY W., packing green corn, extension	1375	47	1	2
...N, CHARLES J., connecting link, extension	185	45	3	2
...N, LAFAYETTE, railroad-car brakes, extension	274	43	2	1
...ARKS, &c.,				
...laws relating to	3682	49	2	2
...ation of	1547	47	1	2
Do	2376	48	2	2
Do	1966	49	1	2
..., ALEXANDER C., apparatus for making ice, extension	112	41	2	1
...ETALLIC CARTRIDGE COMPANY, remuneration from Government for use of invention owned by	1964	47	2	2
Do	635	48	1	2
...CLOTH CUTTER, remuneration to inventor of, for use by United States	779	47	1	2
Do	102	48	1	2
Do	166	48	1	2
...LES, J. H. Kyan's new process for preservation of	662	25	2	1
..., HENRY, wood pulp, machine for reducing	1636	46	2	2

REPORTS

OF THE

)MMITTEE ON PENSIONS,

HOUSE OF REPRESENTATIVES,

FROM THE FOURTEENTH CONGRESS, 1815, TO THE FORTY-NINTH CONGRESS, 1887, INCLUSIVE.

IN SEVEN VOLUMES.

)MPILED, UNDER THE DIRECTION OF THE JOINT COMMITTEE ON PRINTING.

BY

T. H. McKEE,

CLERK DOCUMENT ROOM, UNITED STATES SENATE.

WASHINGTON:
GOVERNMENT PRINTING OFFICE.
1887.

9199 P H

FORTY-NINTH CONGRESS, FIRST SESSION.

[PUBLIC RESOLUTION—No. 24.]

Joint resolution authorizing the preparation of a compilation of the reports of committees of the Senate and House of Representatives.

Resolved by the Senate and House of Representatives of the United States of America in Congress assembled, That there be prepared under the direction of the Joint Committee of Printing, a compilation of the reports of the Senate and House of Representatives from the Fourteenth to the Forty-eighth Congress, inclusive, classified by committees, arranged, indexed, and bound in suitable volumes for the use of the standing committees of the two Houses of Congress. And the sum of seven thousand seven hundred and fifty dollars, or so much thereof as may be found necessary, is hereby appropriated out of any money in the Treasury not otherwise appropriated, for the preparation of said work, which sum may be paid by the Secretary of the Treasury upon the order of the chairman of said Joint Committee, as additional pay or compensation to any officer or employee of the United States.

Resolved further, That the Clerk of the House and Secretary of the Senate be, and they are hereby directed, to procure and file, for the use of their respective Houses, copies of all reports made by each committee of all succeeding Congresses; and that the Clerk of the House and the Secretary of the Senate be, and they are hereby, authorized and directed at the close of each session of Congress, to cause said reports to be indexed and bound, one copy to be deposited in the library of each House and one copy in the room of the committee from which the reports emanated.

Approved, July 29, 1886.

COMPILER'S NOTICE.

compilation embraces all the printed reports made by both of Congress from the commencement of the Fourteenth to the the Forty-ninth Congress. They are classified by committees anged in numerical order. The collection for each committee is into volumes of suitable size. Each committee has a separate copy being bound in each volume.

PECIAL and SELECT reports are all compiled in one collection one index a copy of which is bound in each volume.

lan throughout the compilation is to place each report to the tee from which it was reported, without reference to the subject-

House and Senate reports are compiled separately. Care will ired in noticing the chronological order, as in some instances an ession or Congress may not appear in certain volumes from the t during this period no reports were made by this committee.

T. H. McKEE.

INDEX

TO

PORTS OF COMMITTEE ON PENSIONS,

HOUSE OF REPRESENTATIVES.

FROM 1815 TO 1887, INCLUSIVE.

iis index is divided into two parts; the first division relates to the general subject-matter of pensions; the second division relates to purely personal matter.]

GENERAL MATTER.

Subject.	Report.	Congress.	Session.	Volume.
S,				
River, Kentucky, to establish, south of	74	23	2	1
polis, Ind., to establish at	85	23	2	1
OF PENSIONS,				
tionary war, amending act of February 3, 1853, granting	127	36	1	6
Do	486	36	1	6
ionary war, widows and children of soldiers in	241	35	1	5
Do	485	36	1	6
rebellion, extending time for	990	48	1	7
S, extension of law of 1832 to those excluded by limitations	196	23	1	1
LANDS,				
1850, to amend, increasing allowance of	76	31	2	5
of to soldiers of war 1812 and Indian wars	320	31	1	5
Do	321	31	1	5
Do	138	31	1	5
Do	454	31	1	5
wars, to soldiers for service in	138	31	1	5
Do	320	31	1	5
Do	321	31	1	5
Do	434	31	1	5
1812, to soldiers of	138	31	1	5
Do	320	31	1	5
Do	321	31	1	5
Do	484	31	1	5
ICUT, petition of citizens to pension officers and soldiers of war of 1812	164	19	1	1
NTAL ESTABLISHMENT, respecting construction of law granting pensions for services in	203	19	1	1
STEPHEN, JR., for relief of officers and crew serving at Tripoli under	520	30	1	4
N PENSION OFFICE, to investigate	37	23	2	1
COUNTY, TENNESSEE, memorial of citizens for relief of Jordan Milam	257	31	1	5
memorial of citizens asking bounties for soldiers serving in Indian wars, 1783 to 1795	263	31	1	5
VARS,				
lands, granting, to soldiers who served in	320	31	1	5
Do	321	31	1	5
Do	138	31	1	5
Do	454	31	1	5
s to soldiers who served from 1783 to 1795	263	31	1	5
ns for services in	96	24	2	2
Do	470	26	1	3
Do	566	29	1	4
Do	1838	47	2	6
Do	115	48	1	7
Do	151	48	1	7
Do	2007	48	1	7

General matter—Continued.

Subject.	Report.	Congress.	Session.	Volume.
INDIANA, memorials of citizens asking bounty lands for soldiers serving in war of 1812, and Indian wars	320	31	1	5
Do	321	31	1	5
INDIANAPOLIS, IND., to establish pension agency at	85	23	2	1
INDIANS, to pension, for service in war of 1812	264	45	3	6
INTREPID (ketch), for relief of officers and crew of	520	30	1	4
KENTUCKY,				
Green River, to establish pension agency south of	74	23	2	1
Pensions, resolution of legislature to grant, for services in Indian and other wars	74	23	2	1
LIFE-SAVING SERVICE, to pension dependent relatives of crew lost at Virginia Beach	3929	49		7
LOUISIANA, granting bounty lands to surviving defenders of New Orleans	369	31		5
McQUAIDE, THOMAS, *et al.*, for pension to soldiers of war of 1812	188	31		5
Do	216	31		5
Do	321	31		5
MAINE, pensions, petition of citizens for	164	19		1
Petition from widows for	606	29		4
MARINE CORPS, to amend section 4756 Revised Statutes, granting half pay for twenty years' service in	1729	49		7
Do	3294	49		7
MASSACHUSETTS, Bounty lands, claim of citizens for service in war of 1812	80	46		6
Marriage limitation, citizens of Essex County, for extension of pension laws without	33	30	2	4
"Old men," to pension	164	19	1	1
Pension laws, petition to extend, without marriage limitation	33	30	2	4
War of 1812, claim of citizens for bounty lands and pensions for service in	80	46	3	4
War of Revolution, petition to pension widows of soldiers serving in	295	27	3	2
MEXICAN WAR. (*See* WAR WITH MEXICO.)				
NAVY, twenty years' service in, to grant half pay for	1720	49	1	7
Do	3294	49	1	7
NEW HAMPSHIRE, memorial from citizens regarding granting of pensions	164	19	1	1
NEW ORLEANS, LA., granting bounty lands to defenders of	369	31	1	3
NEW YORK, petitions from citizens,				
For bounties to soldiers in Indian wars of 1783 to 1795	263	31	1	
To extend benefits of act of July 7, 1838, to widows from June, 1832, to August, 1843	322	31	1	3
To pension widows of all Revolutionary soldiers	446	31	1	3
For bounty lands to all heirs of Revolutionary soldiers	78	32	1	3
OHIO, memorial of citizens for relief of soldiers in war of 1812	216	31	1	3
Do	138	31	1	3
PENNSYLVANIA, petitions from citizens of,				
For relief to soldiers of war of 1812, Mexican war, and Indian wars	138	31	1	3
Do	216	31	1	3
Do	454	31	1	3
To extend benefits of act of March 18, 1818, relating to pensions	164	19	1	1
PENSION AGENCIES,				
Green River, Kentucky, to establish, south of	74	23	2	1
Indianapolis, Ind., to establish at	85	23	2	1
PENSION OFFICE,				
Business in, delay of	641	30	1	4
Frauds, committed in granting pensions and gratuities for services in Revolutionary war	37	23	2	1
PENSIONERS,				
Names of, on roll, publication of	37	23	2	1
Number in 1848	295	30	1	4
PENSIONS,				
Act of March, 1818, to amend, relative to granting	24	18	1	1
Do	79	19	1	1
Do	238	22	1	1
Arrears of,				
Extending time for claiming	990	46	1	7
To surviving children of soldiers of war of Revolution	2719	49	1	7
Bounty, extension of law of 1832 to those excluded by limitations	198	23	2	1
Increase of,				
For service in Revolutionary war	54	18	1	1
To extend amount to survivors of war of 1812	295	46	3	6
Indian wars,				
To pension for service in	96	24	2	1
Do	470	26	1	1
Do	263	31	1	1
Do	321	31	1	3
Do	434	31	1	3
Providing similar compensation for service in, as given for Revolutionary war service	566	29	1	4
Amending law granting pensions for services in	151	48	1	7
Life-Saving Service, to pension dependent relatives of crew lost at Virginia Beach	3929	49	2	7

General matter—Continued.

Subject.	Report.	Congress.	Session.	Volume.
-Continued.				
war.				
nsion all who served in	454	31	1	5
nsion survivors of	1836	47	2	6
Do	115	48	1	7
Do	151	48	1	7
Do	151	49	1	7
Do	972	49	1	7
Do	[illegible]	49	1	7
, granting pensions to	196	23	1	1
establishing	64	14	1	1
n of, to extend provisions of act of 1880 for	2757	49	2	7
Do	4037	49	2	7
, to pension for services in war of 1812	268	45	3	6
e campaign, granting pensions for services in	2007	48	1	7
command, to pension soldiers of	518	49	1	7
bellion, extending time for claiming arrears for service in	990	49	1	7
volution.				
y as to execution of act of March 18, 1818, granting pensions for serv- in	27	16	1	1
l of act of March 18, 1818, granting pensions for service in	36	16	1	1
sing, for service in	64	18	1	1
w pensions from date of declaration made under act of March 18, 18	79	19	1	1
nsion survivors of	197	19	1	1
natory of act of March 18, 1818, granting pension for service in	268	19	1	1
ding provisions of act of June 7, 1832, to survivors for three months	314	25	1	2
nsion for less than three months' service in	46	31	2	5
ng half pay for service in, to officers' widows and heirs	31	34	1	5
ding laws granting pensions for service in	316	34	3	5
Do	237	34	3	5
Do	241	35	1	5
Do	486	35	1	6
ding act of February 3, 1853, granting pension to widows subsequently married	127	36	1	6
Do	486	36	1	6
ng arrears, to children of soldiers serving in	2719	49	1	7
Great Britain (1812).				
sion all serving in	454	31	1	5
ding provisions of existing laws to survivors of	165	44	2	6
Do	280	45	3	6
ding provision of act of March 9, 1878, to soldiers of	265	45	3	6
Do	277	45	3	6
ding laws as to length of service to entitle to pension	274	45	3	6
sing pension for service in	285	45	3	6
ding law to pension for services in	151	48	1	7
ding acts of July, 1836 and 1838, relative to pensions to	123	26	1	3
Do	86	27	2	3
Do	784	27	2	3
Do	32	27	3	3
sion, who married previous to January 1, 1812	295	30	1	4
ding benefit of act of March 4, 1843, to certain	265	31	1	5
ng of.				
ding act of March 9, 1878, relative to	480	46	2	6
HIA (frigate), for relief of officers and crew who captured	520	30	1	4
RMED VESSELS.				
ding pension act of June 7, 1832, to those serving three months in	196	23	1	2
Do	210	24	1	2
S. (*See* PRIVATE ARMED VESSELS.)				
ATUTES.				
sections 4742 and 5354 pensioning heirs of soldiers serving in Revolutionary war	262	45	3	6
sections 4364, 4736, and 4738, granting pensions for services in war 1812	274	45	3	6
Do	277	45	3	6
NARY WAR. (*See* WAR OF REVOLUTION.)				
ND, petition relating to pensions from citizens of	164	19	1	1
REGULATIONS relating to substantiating claims to pensions	64	14	1	1
Do	17	16	1	1
OF WAR, letters relating to executing pension act of March 18, 8, to and from	17	16	1	1
, to pension for services in war of 1812	264	45	3	6
Do	267	45	3	6
Do	268	45	3	6
E CAMPAIGN, granting pensions for services in	2007	48	1	7
ompensate officers and seamen for capture of frigate Philadelphia port of	520	30	1	4

General matter—Continued.

General matter—Continued.

Subject.	Report.	Congress.	Session.	Volume.
DOWS—Continued.				
Marriage certificate, to extend law granting pensions without	33	30	2	4
Pensions to, to revive the act of July 7, 1838, in behalf of	32	27	3	3
Remarrying, between 1794 and 1812, granting pensions to	295	30	1	4
Revolutionary war,				
Extending provisions of act of June, 1832, granting pensions to soldiers who served three months in	210	24	1	2
To amend acts granting pensions to widows of soldiers serving in	123	26	1	3
Do	86	27	2	3
Do	216	34	3	5
Do	262	45	3	6
War of 1812, granting pensions to	264	45	3	6
Do	477	46	2	6
Do	3313	49	1	7
DOWS AND ORPHANS,				
Half pay, construction of act of February 3, 1853, relating to	127	36	1	6
Do	486	36	1	6
Revolutionary war, granting pensions	265	31	1	5
RGINIA BEACH, to pension dependent relatives of members of Life-Saving Service of	3929	49	2	7

PERSONAL.

Subject.	Report.	Congress.	Session.	Volume.
ABBOT, MATTHEW	784	27	2	3
ABEL, CATHARINE	784	27	2	3
Do	27	30	1	4
ABEL, PEGGY	684	24	1	2
ADAIR, CATHARINE	526	29	1	4
Do	254	31	1	5
ADAMS, FRANCIS	164	19	1	1
ADAMS, HENRY (widow of)	119	27	2	3
ADAMS, JACOB	139	26	1	3
ADAMS, JEREMIAH	391	22	1	1
Do	664	28	1	3
ADAMS, JOHN	374	31	1	5
ADAMS, LEMUEL	724	47	1	6
Do	1373	49	1	7
ADAMS, MOSES	402	21	1	1
ADAMS, NATH	164	19	1	1
ADAMS, SUSAN	279	45	3	6
ADAMS, THOMPSON, *et al.*	138	31	1	5
ADDOMS, MARY (children of)	714	26	1	3
Do	784	27	2	3
ADKINS, ELIZABETH	664	28	1	3
ADOMS, MARY	249	26	2	3
Do	714	26	1	3
ALBRECHT, SOPHIA	13	29	2	4
ALDRICH, SUSAN	528	29	1	4
ALDRICH, POLLY	519	30	1	4
ALEXANDER, JAMES (widow of)	217	31	1	5
ALFORD, BENEDICT	177	23	1	1
Do	136	24	1	2
ALFORD, GEORGE	19	29	2	4
ALLCOCK, THOMAS	975	47	1	6
ALLEN, ALATHEA	784	27	2	3
Do	295	27	3	3
ALLEN, AMOS	412	22	1	1
ALLEN, ARNOLD	365	22	1	1
ALLEN, CATHARINE	569	25	2	3
Do	73	25	3	2
Do	118	26	1	3
Do	44	28	2	3
Do	292	27	2	3
ALLEN, ETHAN	714	26	1	3
ALLEN, EZRA	411	22	1	1
ALLEN, JANE	784	27	2	3
ALLEN, JOHN	164	19	1	1
ALLEN, PHINEAS	490	26	1	3
Do	714	26	1	3
ALLEN, RICHARD	78	24	2	2
ALLEN, SARAH	40	29	2	4
ALLEN, STEPHEN	810	31	1	5
ALLEY, JOHN	784	27	2	3
ALLISON, JAMES M	1229	48	1	7
ALLISON, ROBERT (heirs of)	11	29	2	4
ALVORD, EMILY L	2299	48	2	7
AMBERSON, WILLIAM	164	19	1	1
AMBLER, SQUIRE (heirs of)	247	25	3	2
Do	218	28	1	3
ANDERSON, CHARITY	784	27	2	3
ANDERSON, JOHN	164	19	1	1
ANDREWS, HENRY	209	26	2	3
ANDREWS, LYDIA	784	27	2	3
ANDREWS, MARY	18	29	2	4
ANDREWS, WILLIAM	539	25	2	2
Do	163	26	1	3
ANGEL, EMILY	2099	48	1	7
Do	2418	48	2	7
ANGLEA, WILLIAM	249	26	2	3
Do	784	27	2	3
Do	295	27	3	3
ANNIS, PHINEAS (heir of)	628	30	1	4
ANSART, CATHARINE	490	26	1	3
Do	581	36	1	6
ARMBRECHT, LOUISE	3120	49	1	7
ARMENTROUT, J. J	3312	49	1	7
ARMSTRONG, NANCY	26	29	2	4

Personal—Continued.

Subject.	Report.	Congress.	Session.	Volume.
DANIEL	654	45	2	6
PETER (heirs of)	126	31	1	5
, MARGARET	826	29	1	4
ROBERT	164	19	1	1
ON, ANN	271	45	3	6
	478	46	2	6
	737	47	1	6
, MARGARY	3313	49	1	7
ESTHER	917	27	2	3
RICHARD (widow of)	450	29	1	4
EUSEBUIS	164	19	1	1
ISAAC	145	24	2	2
	155	25	2	2
	159	26	1	3
DAVID (heirs of)	607	29	1	4
	788	30	1	4
MARY	784	27	2	3
ACHSA	372	33	1	5
K, ROBERT	264	33	1	5
SAMUEL	371	22	1	1
LY, DAVID (widow of)	224	33	1	5
ANSELM	123	27	2	3
JOSEPH	587	25	2	2
	127	26	1	3
LOUDON	164	19	1	1
RICHARD	784	27	2	3
OHN	369	22	1	1
	424	26	1	3
	363	31	1	5
SAMUEL, *et al*	263	31	1	5
	690	46	2	6
	944	49	1	7
QUINCY A	3298	49	1	7
DGE, ISABELLA	151	29	1	4
N, NATHAN	136	26	1	3
	134	26	2	3
	298	27	2	3
IN	490	26	1	3
, JACOB	164	19	1	1
ONE, ELIZABETH	146	33	2	5
PATTY	424	26	1	3
ZACHARIAH	99	31	1	5
, ELIJAH	146	24	2	2
, ISAAC	244	23	1	1
, JAMES	50	18	2	1
, RUFUS	3692	49	2	7
WEALTHY	243	24	1	2
	218	25	2	2
	132	26	1	3
D, CAROLINE M	256	45	3	6
D, CYPRAIN	164	19	1	1
D, JOHN	164	19	1	1
BENNET	424	26	1	3
JOEL	784	27	2	3
RACHEL	2572	49	1	7
SIBEL (heirs of)	701	25	2	2
	68	25	3	2
T, JAMES (heirs of)	458	44	1	6
T, SAMUEL	381	22	1	1
SARAH	420	25	2	2
AMUEL	367	22	1	1
T, JAMES	490	26	1	3
TT, DEVEREUX D	52	31	2	5
TT, ESTHER	537	30	1	4
TT, JOANNA	253	25	3	2
TT, NATHANIEL	365	22	1	1
TT, ZADOCK	163	22	1	1
, LYDIA	784	27	2	3
LDER, ARCHELAUS (children of)	490	29	1	4
LDOR, JOHN A	164	19	1	1
HICKEY	784	27	2	3
MOWRY	587	36	1	6
A. H	3309	49	1	7
JACOB	362	26	1	3
MARY	49	31	2	5
	147	32	1	5
N, ELIZABETH	211	34	3	5
WILLIAM	487	30	1	6

Personal—Continued.

Subject.	Report.	Congress.	Session.	Volume.
BAYARD, SUSAN	1350	47	1	[illegible]
BAYLES, DAVID	125	33	2	[illegible]
BEACH, ISRAEL	38	22	1	[illegible]
BEACH, ROBERT	23	31	1	[illegible]
BEALE, ROBERT	422	24	1	[illegible]
BEAN, GEORGE W	2527	48	2	[illegible]
BEARD, MATILDA W	72	30	2	[illegible]
BEARD, WILLIAM	784	27	2	[illegible]
Do	271	29	1	[illegible]
BEARDSLEY, ICHABOD	156	24	2	[illegible]
Do	170	25	2	[illegible]
Do	67	25	2	[illegible]
Do	138	26	1	[illegible]
BECK, JOHN	162	27	3	[illegible]
BECKER, JACOB	607	25	2	[illegible]
Do	110	26	1	[illegible]
BECKER, JOHN P	376	24	1	[illegible]
Do	714	26	1	[illegible]
BECKET, HUMPHREY	50	21	2	[illegible]
BEDINGER, GEORGE M	464	26	1	[illegible]
Do	154	27	2	[illegible]
BEDINGER, HENRY	53	16	1	[illegible]
BEECHER, THANKFUL J	784	27	2	[illegible]
BEEKES, SALLY	618	29	1	[illegible]
BEELER, GEORGE	410	22	1	[illegible]
BELCHER, ANDREW	164	19	1	[illegible]
BELFIELD, MARY B	447	43	1	[illegible]
BELKNAP, SUSAN	492	29	1	[illegible]
BELL, MARY	214	34	2	[illegible]
BELL, PHINEAS	714	26	1	[illegible]
Do	784	27	2	[illegible]
BELLION, HENRY	2461	49	1	[illegible]
BENHAM, MRS. E A	983	49	1	[illegible]
BENJAMIN, EBENEZER	133	33	2	[illegible]
BENJAMIN, JOSEPH R	1412	48	1	[illegible]
BENNETT, AARON	714	26	1	[illegible]
BENNETT, LEMUEL J	2100	48	1	7
BENNETT, THOMAS	150	26	1	3
BENSELL, MARY	137	33	2	5
BENTLY, ELISHA	707	25	2	2
Do	302	25	3	2
BENTON, MARY E	164	19	1	1
Do	20	18	2	1
BENTON, STEPHEN P	863	46	2	6
BERRY, NICE	784	27	2	3
BESLEY, SARAH	119	27	2	3
BETTS, ELIZABETH	458	29	1	4
BETTS, TIMOTHY	193	19	1	1
BIBLE, MAGDALENE	784	27	2	3
BIGGS, MARY	664	28	1	3
BIGGS, PRICILLA	784	27	2	3
BILLINGS, KENNEDY G	[illegible]	49	1	7
BILLS, ALANSON	6	29	[illegible]	[illegible]
BINDON, JOSEPH	829	34	[illegible]	[illegible]
BIRD, MARY	487	36	1	[illegible]
BIRD, NATHANIEL	236	29	[illegible]	[illegible]
BIRDSALL, SARAH M	281	46	[illegible]	[illegible]
BISHOP, ELIZABETH	133	26	2	[illegible]
BISSELL, ANNA	527	29	[illegible]	[illegible]
BISSELL, SARAH M	2096	48	[illegible]	[illegible]
BLACK, BETHIAH	266	33	[illegible]	[illegible]
BLACK, CATHARINE	164	19	[illegible]	[illegible]
BLACK, DAVID	381	30	[illegible]	[illegible]
BLACK, JOHN	820	25	[illegible]	[illegible]
Do	160	26	[illegible]	[illegible]
Do	142	26	[illegible]	[illegible]
Do	107	27	[illegible]	[illegible]
BLACK, WILLIAM	22	22	[illegible]	[illegible]
BLACKEMORE, SARAH	262	28	[illegible]	[illegible]
BLACKSHIRE, EBENEZER (widow of)	211	26	[illegible]	[illegible]
BLACKWELL, ANN (heirs of)	784	27	[illegible]	[illegible]
Do	606	29	[illegible]	[illegible]
BLAIR, WILLIAM	164	19	1	[illegible]
BLAIR, WILLIAM K	448	31	1	[illegible]
Do	45	31	2	[illegible]
BLAKE, JONATHAN, *et al*	784	27	2	[illegible]
BLAKELY, NATHANIEL H	960	49	1	7

Personal—Continued.

Subject.	Report.	Congress.	Session.	Volume.
EY, MARY	606	29	1	4
	371	30	1	4
	181	33	1	5
TT, WILLIAM	640	45	2	6
ARD, WILLIAM L	164	19	1	1
NG, ORMSBY	147	48	1	7
NSHIP, HENRY	46	22	1	1
R, LEONARD	179	24	1	2
, G	164	19	1	1
LIJAH	484	36	1	6
MUEL	181	22	1	1
IELD, ANN	234	24	2	2
	272	25	2	2
	153	26	1	3
SAMUEL	164	19	1	1
, DICEY	750	47	1	6
ORGE	682	30	1	4
, ABAGAIL	786	29	1	4
LLEN M	3144	49	1	7
VE	826	29	1	4
	773	30	1	4
JOSEPH	578	27	2	3
	92	28	1	3
OHN	378	22	1	1
EDMOND	20	18	1	1
EDWARD	499	45	2	6
OHN	350	21	1	1
	390	21	1	1
	368	22	1	1
	446	24	1	2
OHN	194	19	1	1
OSEPH	164	19	1	1
N, THOMAS	551	26	1	3
BETSEY	295	27	3	3
N, JOHN (wife of)	784	29	1	4
OM, JOHN	32	30	2	4
TH, TOBITHA	132	24	2	2
BRAHAM, AND OTMANS	488	29	1	4
ON, MATTHEW	249	26	2	3
BALAAM	660	24	1	2
CATHARINE	292	45	2	6
WILLIAM	664	26	1	3
, DOROTHY	120	27	2	3
ORA	72	29	2	4
MES	419	25	2	2
ARY	234	33	1	5
BECCA	437	30	1	4
	525	49	1	4
JAMES	802	24	1	2
	326	25	2	2
	287	25	3	2
	133	26	1	3
RD, CHARLES	59	18	1	1
, NATHANIEL	714	26	1	3
OHN (widow of)	125	31	1	5
D, ELIJAH	164	19	1	1
HANNAH	784	27	2	3
LL, LUCRETIA	784	27	2	3
MARTHA C	2502	48	2	7
AMES D	2513	48	1	7
FRANCES ANN	164	19	1	1
E, CHARLES H	2005	48	1	7
SARAH	784	27	2	3
ELIZA	618	29	1	4
, JONATHAN	106	27	2	3
	7	27	3	3
, JAMES (heirs of)	128	31	1	5
ATER, CHARLES L	784	27	2	3
, BARTHOLOMEW (heirs of)	687	29	1	4
USER, MARY	784	27	2	3
EDMUND	42	15	1	1
	19	18	2	1
DAVID	353	21	1	1
	31	21	2	1
	273	22	1	1
EDWARD	249	26	2	3
JAMES	164	19	1	1
MARIAM	799	27	2	3

Personal—Continued.

Subject.	Report.	Congress.	Session.	Volume.
BROOKS, MICAJAH	207	26	1	5
BROUGHER, CHRISTIAN	304	25	3	2
Do	164	26	1	3
BROWER, JOHN	784	27	2	3
BROWN, ABIEL	164	19	1	1
BROWN, CHARLES	94	21	1	1
BROWN, EDWIN C	11	15	2	1
BROWN, JOHN (heirs of)	545	36	1	6
BROWN, JONATHAN	784	27	2	3
Do	455	28	1	4
Do	71	29	2	4
BROWN, JUDITH	919	46	2	6
BROWN, LABAN	164	19	1	1
BROWN, LUCRETIA	490	26	1	3
BROWN, PHEBE	218	36	1	6
BROWNFIELD, ROBERT	714	26	1	3
BRUNOT, ELIZABETH KREIDER	536	28	1	3
Do	462	29	1	4
Do	636	30	1	4
BRUSH, ROBERT	178	23	1	1
BUCK, MARY	234	29	1	4
Do	689	30	1	4
BUCKMAN, EUNICE	527	29	1	4
BUCKNER, DOROTHO B	784	27	2	3
BUDLONG, MARY C. J	1096	47	1	6
BUFORD, JANE	784	27	2	3
BUKEY, DRUSILLA	526	30	1	4
BULLARD, ISAAC	410	22	1	1
BULLMAN, HENRY	32	30	2	4
BULLOCK, ISRAEL	365	22	1	1
BULLOCK, MARY	312	36	1	6
BULLOCK, SIMEON	124	22	1	1
BUNNER, JACOB H	785	29	1	4
BURBANK, ABBY L	2459	49	1	7
BURCHAM, JOHN	914	27	2	3
BURGHER, MARY	229	34	1	5
BURKE, THOMAS	194	19	1	1
BURKETT, MARY	822	49	1	7
BURNHAM, CATY	638	30	1	4
BURNHAM, WALCOTT	696	30	1	4
BURNETT, WARD B	228	48	1	7
BURR, SAMUEL	165	15	1	1
BURRELL, WILLIAM	164	19	1	1
BURRETT, SAMUEL	434	26	1	3
BURROWS, HANNAH	164	19	1	1
BURT, JOSEPH	273	45	3	6
BURT, MARTIN	784	27	2	3
BUSH, HENRY	761	25	2	2
Do	154	26	1	3
BUSH, SARAH A	133	31	1	4
BUTLER, HULDAH (heirs of)	545	36	1	6
Do	25	38	1	6
BUTMAN, THOMAS	219	25	2	2
BUXTON, PETER	6	21	1	1
BYARLY, JAMES H., *et al*	210	31	1	5
BYERS, EBENEZER	784	27	2	3
BYRD, BRIGHT	644	45	2	6
BYRD, NANCY	572	27	2	3
BYXBE, SAMUEL	562	25	2	2
CABAN, WILLIAM W	164	19	1	1
CADY, JEREMIAH	714	26	1	3
CÆSAR, JULIUS	784	27	2	3
CAHILL, JAMES	44	31	2	5
CAKER, NEWTON	3301	49	1	7
CALDWELL, JOHN	826	29	1	4
Do	319	31	1	5
CALHOUN, VIOLET	219	28	1	3
CALKINS, ELIZABETH	770	29	1	4
CALLAHAN, JOEL	335	30	1	6
CALLENDER, CATHARINE W	305	27	2	3
CALLOWAY, VIOLET	422	48	1	7
CAMP, JESSE	164	19	1	1
CAMPBELL, ADAM P	689	30	1	4
Do	362	31	1	5
CAMPBELL, ASENATH	168	26	1	3
CAMPBELL, JACOB	167	21	1	1
CAMPBELL, JOHN W	446	31	1	5
CAMPBELL, JULIANA W	194	31	1	5

Personal—Continued.

Subject.	Report.	Congress.	Session.	Volume.
LL, MARY	468	28	1	3
o	94	27	2	3
o	626	29	1	4
LL, MARY E	85	44	2	6
LL, POLLY	253	20	1	1
LL, SAMUEL	210	26	2	3
LL, TRIPPHAY	118	29	1	4
JAMES	268	35	1	5
ARNOLD	1719	46	1	7
, SIMON	285	27	2	3
o	784	27	2	3
N, JOHN	164	19	1	1
SIMON	714	26	1	3
K, JOHN	290	23	1	1
N, BENJAMIN	369	22	1	1
, MARY E	499	26	1	3
TER, DAVID	784	27	2	3
AMES	164	19	1	1
HN (heir of)	536	26	2	2
o	22	27	2	3
o	51	28	1	3
o	6	28	2	3
o	14	29	1	4
GTON, HENRY (executor)	66	29	2	4
o	278	30	1	4
R, HANNAH	297	27	2	3
L, DAVID	424	26	1	3
, CHARLES C., *et al*	88	31	2	5
L, DAVID	164	19	1	1
, JOSEPH	172	28	2	3
o	88	29	1	4
o	451	31	1	5
o	287	44	1	6
, SARAH	3009	49	2	7
, STANLEY	784	27	2	3
GHT, H. P	3108	48	1	7
OHN	133	27	3	3
IZABETH	222	24	2	2
o	177	25	2	2
o	140	26	1	3
SEPH	164	19	1	1
JOHN	664	26	1	3
T. SUSAN	664	26	1	3
ELIZA	308	27	2	3
RACHEL FLEMING	2458	49	1	7
GRINDALL	411	22	1	1
RLAIN, EDWARD	490	24	1	3
RLIN, CHARLES	381	22	1	1
RLIN, ELIAS	381	22	1	1
RLIN, MILLEY	784	27	2	3
, JOHN (heirs of)	486	27	2	3
, PHEBE	508	25	2	2
ON, REUBEN J	68	34	3	5
ON, REUBEN AND RHODA H	125	36	1	6
ER, CARTER B	569	27	2	3
ER, FRANCES	552	25	2	2
o	664	26	1	3
ER, LEWIS	424	26	1	3
EK, MERIBAH	64	31	1	5
ER, RACHAEL	424	26	1	3
, JOHN	605	29	1	4
PRUDENCE	347	30	1	4
SETH (heirs of)	471	26	1	3
o	126	27	2	3
o	535	28	1	3
N, AZENATH	714	26	1	3
o	784	27	2	3
o	295	27	3	3
N, BENJAMIN	423	26	1	3
o	639	26	1	3
N, ELIZABETH	3307	49	1	7
N, ERASMUS	784	27	2	3
N, JAMES (widow of)	245	25	3	2
N, LYDIA	784	27	2	3
o	295	27	3	3
L, BENJAMIN (heirs of)	784	27	2	3
NT, PETER (heirs of)	330	34	1	5
ARAH	462	26	1	3

Personal—Continued.

Personal—Continued.

Subject.	Report.	Congress.	Session.	Volume.
N, CATHARINE	356	36	1	6
T, EBENEZER	44	24	2	2
Do	424	25	1	2
Do	272	29	1	4
AY, SAMUEL	164	19	1	1
AROLINE W	200	30	1	4
ASED	5	22	1	1
Y, WILLIAM	25	41	2	6
TON, MARY	125	27	2	3
N, JOHN	410	22	1	1
NG, WILLIAM, *et al*	228	29	1	4
, MARTHA	668	36	1	6
L, SARAH	784	27	2	3
, ELIZABETH	1028	47	2	6
Do	1090	48	1	7
BRAHAM	784	27	2	3
LGERNON M	2796	49	2	7
BAULAH	784	27	2	3
OHN W	411	22	1	1
USAN	56	21	2	5
, ADAM	194	19	1	1
, JOHN	822	25	2	2
, SAMUEL, *et al*	128	31	1	5
ADDISON M	2431	48	2	7
JACOB	3522	48	2	7
NATHAN	19	21	1	5
, EMERSON	164	19	1	1
EORGE W	258	45	2	6
L, THRUSTON	794	25	2	2
Do	142	26	1	3
ALL, AMOS	895	25	2	2
, MARGARET	524	29	1	4
, MARY	22	30	1	4
LL, JOHN	526	29	1	4
PRUDENCE	797	27	2	3
WILLIAM	118	28	2	3
NJAMIN	063	26	1	3
Do	714	26	1	3
IOMAS, *et al*	54	18	1	1
ANNA	153	48	1	7
MARY B	123	47	1	
R, SARAH	295	27	3	3
, SARAH N	1411	48	1	7
ELL, CAROLINE	784	27	2	3
, CHRISTOPHER	295	27	3	3
, COLONEL	164	19	1	1
ORD, JAMES	263	28	1	3
INS, MARY E	2449	49	1	7
, JOHN	690	30	1	4
ER, JONATHAN	20	21	2	1
OT, BENJAMIN	36	22	1	1
, LOUIS (alias Cronkhite)	784	27	2	3
Do	158	28	1	3
, JOSHUA	119	22	1	1
THOMAS	40	22	1	1
IAN, EUNICE	681	30	1	4
IAN, SAMUEL (heirs of)	483	36	1	6
LL, DELILAH	3313	49	1	7
LL, SALLY	3313	49	1	7
L, MARY	551	26	1	3
Do	720	29	1	4
RBACK, WILLIAM A	778	25	2	2
Do	125	25	3	2
Do	124	26	1	3
NGS, JAMES	498	24	1	2
NGS, JONAS	497	24	1	2
IGHAM, MOSES	500	45	2	6
GHAM, PATRICK	193	19	1	1
JOHN	164	19	1	1
S, JAMES	164	19	1	1
, JOHN	164	19	1	1
AN, ANDREW	164	19	1	1
AN, DANIEL	164	19	1	1
NG, EARL	164	19	1	1
T, ANTIS	490	26	1	3
A. M. (widow)	532	30	1	4
ETT, SAMUEL	784	27	2	3
Y, DENNIS	164	19	1	1

Personal—Continued.

Personal—Continued.

Subject.	Report.	Congress.	Session.	Volume.
H, *et al*	43	14	2	1
	19	16	2	1
ZER	497	24	1	2
	498	24	1	2
	663	26	1	3
	52	26	2	3
	181	27	3	3
N	436	30	1	4
L	45	31	1	5
S	194	19	1	1
OST	452	25	2	2
US	784	27	2	3
THANIEL (heirs of)	784	27	2	3
H	42	22	1	1
BE	112	26	1	3
LUCINDA C	607	43	2	6
	215	24	1	2
NY	800	46	2	6
ow of)	297	27	2	3
RIAH	164	19	1	1
S	164	19	1	1
ANDLEY	316	31	1	5
THARIO	380	22	1	1
(children of)	331	28	1	3
CHBELL	3155	49	1	7
CK	193	19	1	1
MES R., *et al*	263	31	1	5
	784	27	2	3
	205	27	3	3
W	784	27	2	3
	784	27	2	3
ILLIAM	367	22	1	1
AH	785	20	1	4
ISTOPHER	410	22	1	1
	784	27	2	3
SHA	164	19	1	1
MAS JAMES	164	19	1	1
N	436	24	1	2
RENCE	164	19	1	1
Y	44	31	1	5
I	295	27	3	3
E	784	27	2	3
Y	249	26	2	3
TER	364	23	1	1
	59	24	1	2
ACOB	89	31	1	5
RAH O.	936	49	1	7
AM	548	36	1	6
RY	284	45	3	6
A	784	27	2	3
R (heirs of)	520	29	1	4
ARET	919	46	2	6
HEN	164	19	1	1
	41	22	1	1
	16	22	1	1
BETH	881	25	2	2
	32	25	3	2
H	370	22	1	1
	879	25	2	2
AN	168	22	1	1
S	927	46	2	6
(heirs of)	55	31	2	5
ANNA	1289	48	1	7
THAN	551	26	1	3
MUEL	876	22	1	1
	138	24	2	2
	382	25	2	2
I	66	14	1	1
	75	17	1	1
	17	17	2	1
	164	19	1	1
	194	19	1	1
	164	19	1	1
MUEL	177	24	2	2
	152	25	2	2
	54	25	3	2
	249	26	2	3
	127	27	2	3
	65	27	3	3

Personal—Continued.

Personal—Continued.

Subject.	Report.	Congress.	Session.	Volume.
HERMAN	164	19	1	1
JAMES	561	26	1	3
JOHN	714	26	1	3
RELIA	217	34	2	5
LIZABETH	124	27	2	3
	212	28	1	3
	9	28	2	3
	766	30	1	4
AMES	231	24	1	2
ALD, CHARLES	521	25	2	2
	90	25	2	2
	455	28	1	3
ALD, WILLIAM	133	24	2	2
	164	25	2	2
	56	25	2	2
	468	26	1	3
	91	27	2	3
R, JACOB	472	22	1	1
, JAMES	1229	46	2	6
R, ELIZABETH	1228	46	2	6
AMES	498	24	1	2
ENJAMIN	372	22	1	1
ONATHAN	741	24	1	2
, GEORGE	164	19	1	1
EBENEZER (heir of)	206	33	1	5
A	304	31	1	5
NATHAN	49	21	2	1
	109	22	1	1
SBY, JAMES (widow of)	462	31	1	6
JEREMIAH	164	19	1	1
ELLIS H	35	21	1	1
Y, JOHN	164	19	1	1
E, ELIJAH	340	25	2	2
	198	25	3	2
	125	26	1	3
	784	27	2	3
IARY M	301	30	1	4
HUGH	164	19	1	1
ILLIAM	708	25	2	2
	70	25	3	2
, EBENEZER	164	19	1	1
ER, JOHN (heirs of)	129	36	1	6
BERT DE	152	49	1	7
MATHIAS	862	46	2	6
	722	47	1	6
	150	48	1	7
IAS	54	18	2	1
BENJAMIN	784	27	2	3
FORDYCE	3528	49	2	7
IDA	448	43	1	6
LATHROP	261	27	3	3
LEVI	317	31	1	5
MARY I	2464	49	1	7
POLLY	2313	49	1	7
SARAH	462	31	1	5
ACOB	898	48	1	7
, MARIA	97	27	2	3
	94	27	3	3
HER P	487	44	1	6
N	164	19	1	1
	472	22	1	1
EPH	410	22	1	1
CHAEL	161	34	3	5
LIAM	369	25	2	2
THY, WILLIAM	332	24	1	2
	2465	49	1	7
ER, JACOB	149	26	1	3
ER, JAMES	111	24	2	2
	271	25	2	2
, MARY	102	27	2	3
, MARY J	928	46	2	6
CO, MARY B	612	29	1	4
	253	31	1	5
BERGER, WILLIAM	508	45	2	6
IN, THOMAS P	238	29	1	4
, JAMES	57	31	2	5
E, DAVID	538	26	1	3
	93	27	2	3

Personal—Continued.

Personal—Continued.

Subject.	Report.	Congress.	Session.	Volume.
ALEXANDER	240	23	[illegible]	[illegible]
, PETER	410	21	1	1
, SAMUEL, *et al*	302	31	1	5
, WILLIAM	3505	49	2	7
ER, MARGARET	240	23	1	3
, EZEKIEL	164	19	1	1
o.	1017	23	[illegible]	[illegible]
, JOHN	3781	49	[illegible]	7
ITH, JEREMIAH	460	24	1	2
ATHARINE	305	27	3	3
L, EUNICE	25	30	1	4
IN, AMAZIAH	335	29	1	3
IN, WILLIAM B	425	31	1	5
, HANNAH	156	24	2	2
, JONATHAN	784	27	2	3
SAAC (heir of)	581	30	1	4
, JOHN	380	30	1	4
OMFORT	372	22	1	2
ASA	164	19	1	1
DANIEL	164	19	1	1
M, THOMAS	[illegible]	46	2	6
M, WILLIAM	164	19	1	1
IN, ADAM	472	22	1	1
ER, CHARLOTTE	41	31	2	5
ER, DANIEL	742	26	1	2
ER, JUSTIN	168	18	2	1
EER, BETSEY	836	30	1	4
DANIEL	164	19	1	1
, JAMES	164	19	1	1
, JAMES	410	22	1	1
, SARAH	34	26	2	3
o.	784	27	2	3
NDREW	566	30	1	3
DANIEL	565	22	1	1
EBENEZER (heirs of)	65	31	2	5
ELIZABETH	1253	47	1	6
LEAH	423	29	1	4
RESLY	54	24	2	2
o.	209	25	2	2
o.	461	26	1	3
o.	290	27	3	3
OBERT (widow of)	456	29	1	4
ANN TEMPLE, *et al*	460	31	1	5
ELIJAH	684	24	1	2
FRANCES	467	26	1	3
GIDEON	784	27	2	3
JAMES	715	29	1	4
o.	15	29	2	4
JOSEPH	611	29	1	4
, MARY A	2294	48	2	7
Y, ASAHEL	309	22	1	1
Y, SAMUEL	222	30	1	4
Y, SPITSBY	307	22	1	1
LL, WILLIAM	18	22	1	1
M, ELIZABETH	459	28	1	3
o.	99	27	2	3
o.	38	27	3	3
o.	261	28	1	3
MARY	164	19	1	1
, SIANA	259	31	1	5
LETTY	230	34	1	5
JOHN	423	26	1	3
LL, ELIZABETH	490	29	1	4
JACOB	608	25	2	2
MAN, LOUIS	1202	47	1	6
JOHN	490	28	1	3
SARAH	784	27	2	3
JESSE	158	22	1	1
, JOHN	63	31	1	5
CALVIN	1095	47	1	6
E, BENJAMIN	611	29	1	4
E, HENRY	474	24	1	2
E, JOHN	611	45	2	6
, JOHN (legal representative)	31	17	1	1
P, MARGARET	393	29	1	4
R, CAROLINE	700	30	1	4
o.	237	33	1	5

Personal—Continued.

Subject.	Report.	Congress.	Session.	Volume.
HADLOCK, LYDIA	2234	49	1	7
HAFFERMAN, ANN	490	26	1	3
HAGGETT, BENJAMIN	193	19	1	1
HAGIE, JOHN	436	25	2	2
Do	640	26	1	2
HALE, RICHARD	459	44	1	6
Do	25	46	2	6
HALEY, BARNABY	324	24	1	2
HALEY, BARBAS	330	29	1	4
HALL, BENJAMIN	785	29	1	4
HALL, CATHARINE	700	30	1	4
Do	237	33	1	5
HALL, JAMES	164	19	1	1
HALL, JOHN Y	194	19	1	1
HALL, NANCY	260	45	3	6
HALL, PRIMUS (alias Trask)	74	24	2	2
Do	275	25	[illegible]	2
HALL, SALLY	791	47	[illegible]	6
HALL, WILLIAM W	46	16	[illegible]	1
Do	164	19	[illegible]	1
HALLENBACK, RUTH	282	30	[illegible]	4
HALLS, THOMAS	371	25	2	2
HALSEY, JOB	699	25	[illegible]	2
Do	288	23	[illegible]	2
HALSEY, REBECCA	283	35	1	5
HALSEY, ZYPHANIAH	390	22	1	1
HALSEY, ZYPHANIAH (widow)	212	34	3	3
HAMBRIGHT, NANCY	579	27	2	3
HAMILTON, ANNA	207	30	1	4
HAMILTON, ELIZABETH	55	14	1	1
Do	969	47	1	6
HAMILTON, MARGARET	664	26	1	3
HAMILTON, POLLY	424	26	1	3
HAMM, JOHN	164	19	1	1
HAMMOND, ELISHA	373	22	1	1
HAMMOND, SARAH	528	29	1	4
HAMMONS, JOSEPH	974	48	1	7
HAMPTON, ELIZA	915	27	2	3
HAMPTON, HANNAH	382	30	1	4
HANDSBY, JOHN M	59	31	2	5
HANNA, CATHARINE (heirs of)	547	36	1	6
HARDESTY, OBEDIAH (heirs of)	435	36	1	6
HARDIE, MARGARET HUNTER	2450	49	1	7
HARDIE, ROBERT	449	43	1	5
HARDING, SAMUEL	164	22	1	1
HARDING, TRYPHENA F	3318	49	1	7
HARGAS, THOMAS	785	29	1	4
HARPER, WILLIAM	94	24	2	2
Do	263	23	2	2
Do	177	25	3	2
Do	536	26	1	2
Do	90	27	2	3
HARRELL, HELEN H	3300	49	1	7
HARRINGTON, JOHN T	196	44	2	[illegible]
HARRINGTON, WILLIAM	913	46	2	[illegible]
HARRIS, DANIEL	490	28	1	3
HARRIS, ELIZABETH	793	27	2	3
HARRIS, JAMES	920	46	2	6
HARRIS, JOHN	143	25	1	3
HARRIS, MARY	215	25	3	3
HARRIS, SIMPSON	301	43	1	[illegible]
HARRISON, MARY	661	28	1	3
HARRISON, ROBERT HANSON (heirs of)	164	19	1	1
HARRISON, SIDNEY	613	43	1	6
HARRISON, STEPHEN A	164	19	1	1
HARRISON, WILLIAM (heirs of)	458	31	1	5
HART, JOHN (widow of)	287	30	1	4
HART, SALLY	729	29	1	4
HARTLEY, JULIA	2487	43	1	7
HARTMAN, PHILLIP	509	24	2	2
Do	457	25	3	2
Do	232	25	2	2
Do	150	23	1	2
HARTSHORNE, KEZIAH	87	33	1	5
HARTWELL, ELIZABETH H	834	47	1	6
HARSON, DAVID	439	23	1	1
HARVEY, THOMAS	784	29	1	[illegible]
Do	293	25	3	2
Do	287	22	1	[illegible]

Personal—Continued.

Subject.	Report.	Congress.	Session.	Volume.
OD, MARGARET B.	2510	45	2	7
Do.	817	49	1	7
, MARY (heirs of)	504	30	1	5
, JOB	124	26	1	3
GS, JOHN	166	19	1	1
LEWIS	104	24	2	2
Do.	456	25	2	2
WAY, LEVI	194	19	1	1
, SAMUEL	775	23	2	2
Do.	71	25	2	2
, DANIEL	497	24	1	2
Do.	496	24	1	2
, JABEZ	106	22	1	1
S, BENJAMIN	1025	46	2	6
NS, CHRISTIANA	714	26	1	3
NS, JOB	453	26	1	3
Do.	88	27	2	3
Do.	300	29	1	4
NS, STEPHEN	171	22	1	1
NS, URIAH	164	19	1	1
ANIEL	409	27	2	3
N. ZEBA	365	22	1	1
BEDA	292	36	1	6
, ANN (heirs of)	578	36	1	6
RD, CATHARINE	734	26	1	3
D, SARAH	434	26	1	3
CHARLOTTE	784	27	2	3
EY, WILLIAM	26	22	1	1
WILLIAM J.	1807	49	1	7
Y, ELIPHAS	15	22	1	1
BETHIA	214	29	1	3
RACHEL W	812	49	1	7
K, PETER	766	25	2	2
Do.	250	25	2	2
Do	165	26	1	3
MAN, ANN	784	27	2	3
R, WILLIAM H	3472	49	1	7
INA T	164	19	1	1
Do.	194	19	1	1
AMUEL	784	27	2	3
Y. PERNETTA	1288	49	1	7
CKSON, ELIZABETH A	290	47	1	6
, LAURA	819	49	1	7
T, PETER (heirs of)	808	34	1	5
R, FERDINAND.	2616	48	2	7
TAILING, JAMES	411	22	1	1
ON, EDWARD	164	19	1	1
Do	396	22	1	1
ON, JOSEPH	449	31	1	5
K, ABEL	663	26	1	3
GTON, JAMES	164	19	1	1
WILLIAM	144	24	1	2
, JOSEPH	643	26	1	3
OSEPH	395	22	1	1
, JESSE	69	46	2	6
N, ELIZABETH (heirs of)	597	36	1	6
MARY	14	29	2	4
ABAGAIL	688	30	1	4
, MOSES	113	22	1	1
JACOB	488	22	1	1
LIZABETH	784	27	2	3
EDERICK	223	24	2	2
Do	168	25	2	3
ULDAH	784	27	2	3
OHN *et al.*	138	31	1	5
HN (heirs of)	314	31	1	5
, JAMES	75	29	1	4
Do	90	30	1	4
MARIA	50	31	2	5
AN, ELIZABETH	913	27	2	3
ISAAC	143	24	2	2
Do	153	25	2	2
, PETER	867	31	1	5
WILLIAM	785	29	1	4
D, SUSAN	784	27	2	3
EY, CHLOE	784	27	2	3
DANIEL	164	19	1	1
, WILLIAM	784	27	2	3

Personal—Continued.

Subject.	Report.	Congress.	Session.	Volume.
HITCHCOCK, ABIJAH	424	26		
HITCHCOCK, ABRAHAM	111	22		
HITCHCOCK, MARY	205	26	2	
HIX, H. H	968	47		
HOAGLAND, SUSANNAH	769	25		
Do	124	25		
HOARD, LYDIA	139	26		
Do	784	27		
HOBART, DANIEL (widow of)	518	29		
HOBBS, JOSIAH (widow of)	583	36		
HOHSTADT, JOHN	1227	46		
HOLDEN, ASA	365	22	1	
HOLDEN, MOSES	164	19	1	
HOLDEN, NEHEMIAH	350	31	1	
HOLLAND, JOHN	505	45	2	
HOLLISTER, JOSIAH	164	19	1	
HOLMES, ABIJAH	114	22	1	
HOLMES, EBENEZER	361	22	1	
HOLMES, NATHANIEL	107	24	2	
HOLMES, ORSAMUS	411	22	1	
HOLSTEIN, PETER	164	19	1	
HONEYWELL, ESTHER	663	26	1	
HOOK, MARY B	2569	49	1	
HOOKER, MARY	311	34	1	
HOOKS, ELIZABETH	164	19	1	
HOOPER, ANDREW J	751	47	1	
HOOVER, JOHN	423	26	1	
Do	490	26	1	
HOPKINS, FREDERICK	87	27	2	
Do	182	27	3	
Do	93	28	1	
Do	217	29		
HOPPER, MARY	427	36		
HOPPING, THOMAS	11	22		
HORN, PATRICK	714	26		
HORN, PHILIP	784	27		
HORNBECK, MARIA	982	25		
HORNER, GUSTAVUS B	1364	46		
HORROW, JOHN, *et al*	216	31		
HORTON, JULIA L	490	26		
HORTON, JULIA SHERBURNE	238	33		
HOSKINS, MARY	47	31		
HOUCK, PETER	714	26		
HOUGHTON, WILLIAM H	2128	48		
HOUSTON, LEONARD	101	22		
HOWARD, JAMES (widow of)	425	36		
HOWARD, JOHN D	100	22		
HOWARD, STEPHEN	395	31		
HOWARD, SUSAN	603	29		
HOWE, ELIZABETH	118	27		
HOWELL, SAMUEL	164	19		
HOWELL, WILLIAM	107	22		
Do	295	27		
HOYT, SAMUEL	325	43		
HUBBARD, ELISHA (estate of)	123	29	1	
HUBBARD, EMILY	694	30	1	
HUBBARD, WILLIAM	295	27	3	
HUDNUT, GRACE	16	29		
HUDSON, CHAMBERLAIN	164	19		
HUDSON, HALL	164	19		
HUDSON, JOHN	614	29		
HUDSON, JOSHUA	784	27		
HUEY, JAMES (heirs of)	312	34		
HUGGINS, LYDIA S	2101	48		
HUGHART, THOMAS	531	26		
HUGHES, SARAH	293	27		
HULL, EDWIN	784	27		
HUMPHREY, WILLIAM (heirs of)	89	34		
Do	356	36		
HUMPHREYS, REBECCA HOLLINGSWORTH	2643	49		
Do	*2643	49		
HUMPHRIES, ESTHER	527	29		
HUNNEWELL, JONATHAN	784	27		
HUNT, EPHRAIM	438	22		
HUNT, HENRIETTA M. DRUM	3019	49		
HUNT, SAMUEL	490	26	1	
HUNT, TIRZAH	714	26	1	

* Views of minority.

Personal—Continued.

Subject.	Report.	Congress.	Session.	Volume.
[...]RZAH	580	27	2	3
[...] ANN	784	27	2	3
	445	28	1	3
[...], AMOS	122	27	3	3
[...]TON, HIRAM	439	22	1	1
[...]TON, WILLIAM	377	22	1	1
[...], ABAGAIL, *et al.*	437	36	1	5
[...]AN, ELIZABETH	361	31	1	5
[...]ARITY	581	43	2	6
[...] ANNA	821	46	2	6
[...]B, BURKLEY	346	31	1	5
[...]S, JONATHAN	258	31	1	5
[...]SON, ISRAEL	287	22	1	1
[...]ON, SAMUEL	349	25	1	2
	301	30	2	4
	296	30	1	4
[...]SON, THOMPSON	107	26	1	3
	19	27	3	3
	56	28	1	3
	18	29	1	4
[...]SON, VALINCIA C	2104	48	1	7
	2462	48	1	7
[...]ON, WILLIAM	2746	48	1	7
[...]K, FRANCIS	464	30	1	4
	527	30	1	4
[...], WILLIAM	306	22	1	1
[...], BETSEY	465	28	1	3
[...], DANIEL	216	28	1	3
	78	29	1	4
[...], LUCY	486	26	1	3
[...], ZADOCH	363	22	1	1
[...] DAVID	164	19	1	1
[...]LL, BRIGGS	164	19	1	1
[...]M, FRANCIS	693	30	1	4
[...] SARAH (administratrix)	38	15	2	1
[...], JOHN	164	19	1	1
[...]. M	394	31	1	5
[...], ABAGAIL K	784	27	2	3
[...], CATHARINE	526	29	1	4
[...], JARVIS	493	45	2	6
[...], JOHN (heirs of)	358	31	1	5
	32	32	1	5
[...]ALLEN P	1607	40	1	7
[...]FRANCIS	62	35	2	5
[...]JOHN	784	27	2	3
[...]LISHA	414	21	1	1
[...]LIZABETH	784	27	2	3
[...]OHN	369	22	1	1
[...]ARY	164	19	1	1
	80	20	1	1
[...], WILLIS	612	45	2	6
[...]SOLOMON	664	26	1	3
[...], LUCY LEG	1437	48	1	7
	1507	48	1	7
[...]ON, HON. THOMAS (grandchild of)	1941	47	2	6
	38	48	1	7
	*38	48	1	7
[...], HANNAH	784	27	2	3
	132	27	3	3
[...]ON, WILLIAM	559	24	1	2
	171	24	2	2
	165	25	2	2
[...]YLVIA	916	46	2	6
	292	47	1	6
[...]COB	92	34	3	5
	40	35	1	5
[...] DAVID	164	19	1	1
[...] SOLOMON, *et al*	383	30	1	4
[...], ARCHIE	551	26	1	3
[...], BENJAMIN	615	29	1	4
	87	30	1	4
[...], EBENEZER	249	26	2	3
[...], HENRY	530	30	1	4
	20	31	1	5
	81	32	1	5
[...], IRA (children of)	93	34	3	5
[...], JACOB	784	27	2	3

*Views of minority.

Personal—Continued.

Personal—Continued.

Subject.	Report.	Congress.	Session.	Volume.
IOMAS (wife of)	259	31	1	5
N	391	22	1	1
, MARY	714	26	1	3
POLLY	503	24	1	2
SUSANNAH	767	30	1	4
RY	121	15	1	1
N	77	32	1	5
NCY	785	29	1	4
	538	30	1	4
VE	685	30	1	4
, ASAHEL	587	25	2	2
	454	26	1	3
	109	27	2	3
	295	27	3	3
ELIZABETH	684	30	1	4
HANNAH	774	30	1	4
IZA	447	31	1	5
ARY B	262	45	2	6
	926	46	2	6
ICK, KESIAH	784	27	2	3
, MICHAEL	164	19	1	1
, ELIZUR	884	25	2	2
URY, FREDERICK F	2484	48	2	7
ARY	423	26	1	3
BERGER, HENRY, *et al*	216	31	1	5
OSEPH	463	31	1	5
ARAH	27	29	2	4
	441	30	1	4
	129	31	1	5
NRY	164	19	1	1
EZEKIEL	164	19	1	1
CONRAD	268	24	1	2
IZABETH	594	45	2	6
	984	46	2	6
THANIEL	164	19	1	1
BERT	615	25	2	2
SSE, PRUDENT (heirs of)	228	30	1	4
EPH	43	31	2	5
CHRISTOPHER (heirs of)	56	31	2	5
CORNELIUS	110	22	1	1
, JERUSHA	784	27	2	3
MARY	743	24	1	2
MILES	784	27	2	3
L, THOMAS	3782	49	2	7
ALEM	216	36	1	6
JOHN	249	26	2	3
, JOHN	606	25	2	2
	72	25	3	2
	129	26	1	3
AY, TOUSANT (heirs of)	91	34	3	5
	126	36	1	6
E, ABRAHAM	411	22	1	1
E, JANE MARY	164	19	1	1
	122	20	1	1
JACOB	784	27	2	3
WILLIAM	164	19	1	1
ROBERT	784	27	2	3
R, ROWLAND	249	26	2	3
WILLIAM	232½	22	1	1
, ELIZABETH	938	49	1	7
, JOEL	480	26	1	3
	784	27	2	3
PAULINA	66	29	2	4
	276	30	1	4
CATHARINE	309	27	2	3
HANNAH (alias Davis)	714	26	1	3
MARTHA	664	26	1	3
HN	164	19	1	1
ATILDA	3301	49	1	7
IES	377	24	1	2
LOT	439	24	1	2
ANNAH	784	27	2	3
RAH	490	26	1	3
HN	315	31	1	5
AAC	490	26	1	3
	784	27	2	3
, MARY G	685	30	1	4
IZABETH M	1913	47	2	6

Personal—Continued.

Subject.	Report.	Congress.	Session.	Volume.
LEWIS, FRANCES	295	27	3	3
LIBBY, HARVEY	54	18	2	1
LIEUTAND, ANNIE	1773	48	1	[illegible]
LINDLEY, ABAGAIL	528	29	1	[illegible]
LINDSEY, JOHN	141	26	1	[illegible]
LINKER, J. W	625	47	1	[illegible]
LINKIN, L. W	149	48	1	[illegible]
LINTON, MARY ANN	277	27	2	[illegible]
Do	328	28	1	[illegible]
LISCOMB, SARAH	91	33	1	[illegible]
LITTLE, JAMES	367	22	1	[illegible]
LITTLEFIELD, DANIEL	124	24	2	[illegible]
LITTLEFIELD, PELATIAH	116	18	1	[illegible]
LIVINGSTON, HENRY B	51	16	1	[illegible]
LOCKHART, WILLIAM	2907	48	2	[illegible]
LOGAN, JOHN	372	23	1	[illegible]
Do	302	24	1	[illegible]
LOMAX, WILLIAM (heirs of)	114	26	1	[illegible]
Do	1097	27	2	[illegible]
LOOMIS, RUTH	384	30	1	4
LOOMIS, URIAH	324	28	1	3
LORD, MARY	784	27	2	3
LORING, JACOB	367	22	1	1
LOSKEY, ANDREW	423	26	1	3
LOUDERMAN, CATHARINE	58	18	1	1
LOUGH, GEORGE ANDREW	784	27	2	3
LOVEGROVE, HAMPTON	168	24	2	2
LOVEJOY, ESTHER	371	33	1	5
LOW, CHRISTIANA	300	27	2	3
LOWELL, JOHN	438	22	1	1
LOYD, THOMAS N	3784	49	2	7
LUCAS, ELISHA	261	23	1	1
Do	150	24	1	2
LUMPKINS, DICKINSON	782	30	1	4
LYBROOK, JOHN	151	26	1	3
Do	75	26	2	3
LYFORD, NATHANIEL	610	29	1	4
LYNAM, ANDREW	73	24	2	2
LYNCH, WILLIAM	2466	49	1	7
LYNN, JANE	310	30	1	4
LYON, ANN (heirs of)	968	47	1	6
LYON, BENJAMIN	551	26	1	3
LYON, JOSEPH	17	22	1	1
LYTLE, JAMES W	490	26	1	3
McADAMS, JOSEPH	784	27	2	3
McALPIN, DANIEL	2106	48	1	7
McAULEY, ANGUS	1252	47	1	6
MacBLAIR, MARY P	717	48	1	7
McCAIN, CHARLOTTE	206	30	1	4
McCARTY, DANIEL	204	26	2	3
McCARTY, JEREMIAH	2152	48	[illegible]	7
McCAW, MARGARET	664	26	[illegible]	3
McCLAIN, ELIZABETH	528	29	[illegible]	4
McCLELLAN, JOHN	144	24	2	2
Do	172	25	2	2
McCLELLAN, RODY	973	48	[illegible]	7
McCLURE, ALEXANDER	498	45	2	6
McCLURE, JANETTE	664	26	[illegible]	3
McCONNELL, NANCY	784	27	2	3
McCORMICK, JOHN	127	24	2	2
Do	270	25	2	2
McCOY, BARNABAS (widow of)	135	26	2	3
McCRAW, SALLY	306	27	2	3
Do	227	28	1	3
McCURDY, MARY	457	26	[illegible]	3
Do	784	27	2	3
McDANIEL, BERSHEBA	220	30	1	4
McDANIEL, JOHN (heirs of)	424	36	1	5
McDOUGAL, CAROLINE M	1943	47	2	6
Do	608	48	1	7
McDOUGAL, KATE C	1290	48	[illegible]	7
McDUFF, DANIEL	22	19	2	1
Do	9	16	2	1
McELHOISE, SAMUEL	784	27	2	3
McELROY, MARGARET	784	27	2	3
McEWEN, PATRICK	391	24	[illegible]	2
McFADDEN, AMANDA J	199	47	1	6
McFADDEN, E. A	2757	49	1	7

Personal—Continued.

Subject.	Report.	Congress.	Session.	Volume.
S, GEORGE	164	19	1	1
E, BARTHOLOMEW	164	19	1	1
E, JANE	83	27	3	3
D	10	28	1	3
AN, CELESTE	486	44	1	6
ON, JOHN	36	16	2	1
D	12	17	1	1
Y, ISAAC	489	26	1	3
D	784	27	3	3
E, MARGARET	602	28	1	3
H, MARY	1609	48	1	7
OHN	624	47	1	6
, SARAH P	2576	48	1	7
REBECCA REESE	1873	49	1	7
BARNABAS	164	19	1	1
ANDREW	781	30	1	4
EY, DANIEL	782	24	1	2
D	325	25	2	2
EY, DAVID	2505	48	2	7
D	1120	49	1	7
JOHN	784	27	2	3
SS, JOSEPH	582	43	1	6
AN, WILLIAM	147	22	1	1
EN, MARY	234	44	2	6
PHY, RACHEL	74	31	2	5
RY, MARGARET	294	27	2	3
NEIL	133	24	2	2
D	104	25	2	2
ROBERT (heirs of)	760	30	1	4
D	287	33	1	5
D	94	32	1	5
ALEXANDER	164	19	1	1
SON, MARK	164	19	1	1
DE, THOMAS, *et al*	138	31	1	5
D	216	31	1	5
D	321	31	1	5
DE, WILLIAM, *et al*	138	31	1	5
LEN, ALEXANDER	193	19	1	1
OLDS, ANDREW T	3524	49	2	7
N, NANCY, *et al*	227	34	3	5
, JOHN	635	26	1	3
D	764	27	2	3
, MRS. MARY H	3527	49	2	7
O	3695	49	2	7
POLLY	527	29	1	4
RD, POLLY	132	31	1	5
Y, SALLY	1413	48	1	7
E, LESLIE	105	24	2	2
BARTHOLOMEW	164	19	1	1
GO, DANIEL (heirs of)	41	35	1	5
GO, JUDAH	41	35	1	5
GO, JUDAH AND SARAH B (heirs of)	18	34	3	5
BARNABAS	164	19	1	1
, JAMES	820	29	1	4
Y, JOHN	110	30	1	4
NG, JOHN	164	19	1	1
NG ROSANNAH	824	29	1	4
, MEHITABLE	219	30	1	4
ARD, D. R., *et al*	138	31	1	5
AND, ALICE	223	31	1	5
EN, WILMOT	920	27	2	3
O	326	28	1	3
RICHARD	577	27	2	3
ALL, AMON	369	22	1	1
ALL, GEORGE A	897	48	1	7
N, DAVID	365	22	1	1
OTT, RUTH	567	27	2	3
, BETSEY	821	49	1	7
, ELIJAH	3302	49	1	7
, ELIZABETH	783	29	1	4
O	302	30	1	4
O	182	33	1	5
O	15	34	3	5
, FRANCIS (widow of)	17	34	3	5
, MARY	357	31	1	5
, MARY E	3611	49	2	7
, NANCY	5	29	2	4
, RICHARD	207	24	1	2

Personal—Continued.

* Minority report, Part 2.

Personal—Continued.

Subject.	Report.	Congress.	Session.	Volume.
GUE, NATHANIEL	381	22	1	1
, JOHN	125	24	2	5
, FANNY	196	31	1	5
, JOSEPH S.	2709	46	1	7
, NATHANIEL	3621	49	2	7
, LEMUEL	187	26	2	3
, THOMAS	87	34	2	6
Do.	224	36	1	6
Do.	213	36	1	6
CHRISTOPHER	547	30	1	4
, ASHBEL	609	30	1	4
, DANIEL	128	19	1	1
, ELIZABETH	784	27	2	3
, ELLEN	1548	47	1	6
, HENRIETTA, *et al.*	699	30	1	4
, ISAAC	476	22	1	1
, JANE	643	45	2	6
, JOHN (heirs of)	219	36	1	6
, JONATHAN	183	30	1	4
, MAGDALENA	9	29	2	4
, ROXANNA	529	29	1	4
, SARAH	346	26	1	3
Do.	113	27	2	3
IELD, NANCY	490	26	1	3
, JOSIAH	3785	49	2	7
T, HENRIETTA	76	24	2	2
N, ABNER	396	22	1	1
N, ELIZABETH (widow)	31	14	1	1
N, PERSIS	784	27	2	3
S, DELILA	424	26	1	3
S, GEORGE	129	26	1	3
Do.	287	27	2	3
S, JONATHAN	164	19	1	1
S, LESTER	22	22	1	1
S, REAMUS G.	3636	49	2	7
S, RICHARD G.	27	17	1	1
Do.	30	17	2	1
Do.	16	18	1	1
SON, JOHN	224	31	1	5
ELIHU	372	22	1	1
ISAAC	372	22	1	1
JEDEDIAH	140	30	1	4
SIMEON	806	24	1	2
Do.	178	25	2	2
ON, SIMEON	365	22	1	1
SON, JOHN	208	30	1	4
JEREMIAH (heirs of)	457	26	1	3
GAN, PATRICK	164	19	1	1
Do.	194	19	1	1
NGS, JAMES	274	24	1	2
IESTER, GERSHOM	46	31	2	5
AY, LEAH	638	26	1	3
Do.	295	27	3	3
R, PHILIP	164	19	1	1
DAVID	64	27	3	3
N, FRANCES	107	38	1	6
Y, JOHN	429	29	1	4
Y, MARY	1608	49	1	7
Y, REUBEN	919	25	2	2
Do.	212	25	3	2
Do.	131	26	1	3
Do.	784	27	2	3
Y, MILTON R.	366	49	1	7
, ELIZABETH	617	29	1	4
, H. L.	2107	48	1	7
JOHN (heirs of)	162	34	3	5
Do.	64	35	2	5
WILLIAM, *et al.*	216	31	1	5
AM, JEREMIAH	714	26	1	3
N, HUGH	164	19	1	1
N, MARY	784	27	2	3
Do.	1002	27	2	3
N, RUHANNA	1912	47	2	6
OHN	784	27	2	3
M, RANDOLPH	396	22	1	1
S, LEVI	529	29	1	4
Do.	458	31	1	5
SON, SAMUEL (heirs of)	460	31	1	5

Personal—Continued.

Subject.	Report.	Congress.	Session.	Volume.
NICKERSON, ESTHER	3313	49	1	7
NIELSSON, NIEL	1129	47	1	6
NIXON, SARAH	26	30	1	4
NOBLE, GOODMAN	379	22	1	1
NOEKS, JONATHAN	365	22	1	1
NOEL, ALEXANDER	784	27	2	3
NORRIS, HULDAH	525	29	1	4
NORRIS, THEOPHILUS	412	22	1	1
NORTON, HANNAH	786	29	1	4
Do	526	30	1	4
NORTON, MARTHA (heirs of)	83	29	2	4
NORVELL, HENRY H	164	19	1	1
NOURSE, JAMES	64	19	1	1
NOURSE, WILLIAM	254	24	1	2
NOYES, MOSES	52	16	2	1
NOYES, WALTER (heirs of)	52	16	2	1
NUGENT, JACOB	490	26	1	3
NUTTER, ELIZABETH	664	26	1	3
OAKLEY, SARAH	137	26	1	3
OLCOTT, ISAAC	410	22	1	1
ODELL, JEREMIAH	784	27	2	3
OLDHAM, ANNA	687	30	1	4
OLDS, MARCAY	784	27	2	3
Do	464	28	1	3
OLINGER, JACOB	424	26	1	3
Do	785	29	1	4
Do	221	30	1	4
OLIVER, WILLIAM	551	26	1	3
Do	784	27	2	3
OLMSTEAD, ESTHER	784	27	2	3
OLNEY, MARTHA	784	27	2	3
OLNEY, STEPHEN	705	25	2	2
Do	162	26	1	3
O'NEAL, CATHARINE	73	30	2	4
Do	701	30	1	4
O'NEIL, HUGH	2615	48	2	7
ONEY, AMOS (heirs of)	16	34	3	5
ONION, JULIET	134	33	2	5
ORVIS, ARSENATH	429	28	1	3
Do	19	28	2	3
OSBORN, JAMES	412	22	1	1
OSTERTROUT, ISAAC (widow of)	50	31	2	5
OSTRANDER, MARIA	330	28	1	3
OTMAN, NICHOLAS, PETER, AND WILLIAM	488	29	1	4
OVERTON, SETH	784	27	2	3
Do	239	29	1	4
OWEN, ALFRED M	934	49	1	7
OWEN, ELEAZER	439	22	1	[illegible]
OWEN, LIZZIE WRIGHT	4164	49	2	[illegible]
OWEN, POLLY	527	29	1	4
OWEN, THOMAS J	2644	49	1	[illegible]
OWINGS, WILLIAM J	820	49	1	[illegible]
PAGE, DANIEL	66	23	1	[illegible]
PAGE, EUNICE	359	31	1	[illegible]
PAINE, ABAGAIL	784	27	2	[illegible]
PAINE, FRANKLIN	503	45	2	[illegible]
PALMER, STEPHEN	424	26	1	[illegible]
PARDUE, WILLIAM	367	22	1	[illegible]
PARK, JONATHAN (wife of)	784	29	1	[illegible]
Do	137	30	1	[illegible]
PARKER, ABRAHAM	21	[illegible]	1	[illegible]
PARKER, EDMUND	164	19	1	[illegible]
PARKER, JOSEPH	281	24	1	[illegible]
Do	637	26	1	[illegible]
Do	568	27	2	[illegible]
PARKER, JOSHUA	164	19	1	[illegible]
PARKER, SARAH	898	27	2	[illegible]
Do	152	28	1	[illegible]
PARKER, WILLIAM	445	30	1	[illegible]
PARKHURST, BENJAMIN	497	24	1	[illegible]
Do	498	24	1	[illegible]
PARKMAN, WILLIAM E., *et al*	459	31	1	[illegible]
Do	322	31	1	[illegible]
PARKS, AARON	365	22	1	[illegible]
PARISH, OLIVER (heirs of)	395	22	1	1
Do	55	24	2	[illegible]
Do	301	27	2	[illegible]
PARISH, SARAH	925	46	2	[illegible]

Personal—Continued.

Subject.	Report.	Congress.	Session.	Volume.
IT, ESTHER	246	25	2	2
Do	626	26	1	3
Do	96	27	2	3
TT, MOSES	3043	49	2	7
ALL, DAVID	479	23	1	1
IS, ISRAEL	738	25	2	2
Do	155	26	1	3
, SAMUEL	136	25	2	3
Do	117	27	2	3
IN, SAMUEL	794	27	2	3
CK, JACOB	491	29	1	4
RSON, JAMES (widow of)	67	31	1	5
RSON, ROBERT	164	19	1	1
S, WILLIAM	591	24	1	2
Do	784	27	2	3
ON, RICHARD (administrator)	184	38	2	6
N, MARY	34	30	1	4
N, MILTON	714	26	1	3
N, SAMUEL	27	22	1	1
US, DAVID C	1650	49	1	7
Do	366	49	1	7
OCTAVE	3121	49	1	7
, JOHN, *et al*	318	31	1	5
R, ELIZABETH	262	24	1	2
E, JONATHAN	122	22	1	1
K, ELIZABETH	714	26	1	3
RE, ANNA	796	29	1	4
EY, ANN	526	29	1	4
Do	148	30	1	4
ON, JOSHUA, *et al*	76	31	2	5
ON, THOMAS	164	19	1	1
OLIVER	231	24	2	2
Do	39	25	3	2
Do	156	25	2	2
AM, WILLIAM	581	25	2	2
ES, ABNER	102	22	1	1
Y, WILLIAM	533	30	1	4
RTON, SARAH	139	24	2	2
Do	456	25	2	2
, THANKFUL	385	30	1	4
JOSHUA	454	24	1	2
MARGARET	664	26	1	3
. JOSEPH	528	43	1	6
MAN, HULDAH	235	24	2	2
VAL, JOHN	395	22	1	1
NS, ENOCH	727	29	1	4
NS, HECTOR	164	19	1	1
NS, ZOPHAR (heir of)	88	33	1	5
, JOHN (heirs of)	368	36	1	6
, MARY B., *et al*	331	28	1	3
, P. B., Sr	749	47	1	6
, ROBERT	786	30	1	4
S, WILLIAM (heirs of)	321	33	1	5
S, BISSEL	295	27	3	3
S, HANNAH	360	31	1	5
S, JAMES	113	26	1	3
Do	108	27	2	3
Do	310	34	1	5
S, MARY	609	25	2	2
Do	459	29	1	4
S, PHILENA	895	30	1	4
Do	77	31	2	5
S, RUFUS	590	36	1	6
STER, JOHN (heirs of)	626	47	1	6
S, GEORGE	164	19	1	1
S, STEPHEN (widow of)	390	28	1	3
Do	573	27	2	3
PS, GEORGE D	610	45	2	6
PS, ISAAC	12	34	3	5
PS, JOB	438	22	1	1
PS, JOHN	714	36	1	[illegible]
PS, SAMUEL	714	26	1	3
PS, WALTER	51	23	2	1
, JOSEPH	164	19	1	1
, WILLIAM	318	31	1	5
N, ERASTUS (heirs)	41	24	2	2
Do	538	25	2	2
Do	166	26		3

Personal—Continued.

Subject.	Report.	Congress.	Session.	Volume.
PIERSON, EUNICE	89	25	2	2
PIERSON, MOSES	816	22	2	2
Do	89	25	2	2
PIKE, MARY	249	26	2	3
Do	307	27	2	3
Do	45	27	3	3
Do	624	30	1	4
Do	139	31	1	5
PITMAN, JAMES	370	31	1	5
PLUMB, JOSEPH (children of)	714	26	1	3
Do	138	26	2	3
Do	100	27	2	3
Do	786	30	1	4
Do	450	31	1	5
PLUNKET, PENELOPE	428	26	1	3
PLUNKET, WILLIAM	714	26	1	3
PLYMPTON, EBENEZER	160	22	1	1
POLERECZKY, JOHN S.	59	16	1	1
POLERESKY, JOHN L.	103	19	1	1
POLK, RHODA	664	26	1	3
POND, ELIHU	371	22	1	1
POND, LETTIS	714	26	1	3
POND, NATHANIEL, JR.	2103	48	1	7
POOL, ELIZABETH	312	30	1	4
POOL, SAMUEL	210	30	1	4
POPE, RUTH	606	29	1	4
PORTER, BENJAMIN	164	19	1	1
PORTER, CANDACE	836	29	1	4
PORTER, JOHN	134	15	1	[illegible]
Do	20	26	2	[illegible]
Do	784	27	2	[illegible]
PORTER, ROSEMAN	125	31	1	[illegible]
POTTER, EBENEZER	164	19	1	[illegible]
POTTER, FRANCES McNEIL	899	48	1	[illegible]
Do	150	49	1	[illegible]
POTTER, THADDEUS	323	24	1	[illegible]
POWERS, ELIZABETH	784	27	2	[illegible]
Do	39	27	3	[illegible]
PRATT, CARY	164	19	1	[illegible]
PRATT, ELIZABETH	714	26	1	[illegible]
PRATT, SALLY	310	27	2	[illegible]
Do	295	27	2	[illegible]
PRATT, WILLIAM	618	29	1	[illegible]
PREWETT, SOLOMON	451	25	2	[illegible]
Do	26	25	[illegible]	[illegible]
PRICE, BENJAMIN	305	24	1	[illegible]
Do	207	25	2	[illegible]
Do	179	25	[illegible]	[illegible]
Do	144	26	[illegible]	[illegible]
Do	784	27	2	[illegible]
PRICE, WILLIAM	352	21	1	[illegible]
PUGH, DAVID	10	29	2	[illegible]
PURCHASE, ROBERT	172	35	1	[illegible]
Do	366	36	1	[illegible]
PURDY, DANIEL	51	22	1	[illegible]
PUTMAN, EDWARD	784	27	2	[illegible]
PUTNAM, EDWARD	537	26	1	[illegible]
QUAIT, WILLIAM	366	31	1	[illegible]
QUICK, GEORGE C.	1348	47	1	[illegible]
QUIN, FRANKY	664	26	1	[illegible]
QUINN, ROBERT	494	45	2	[illegible]
QUINTON, SAMUEL	73	21	2	[illegible]
RAGAN, CECILIA	819	25	2	[illegible]
Do	251	28	2	[illegible]
RAMEY, EDITH	710	29	1	[illegible]
RAMSAY, ELIZA H.	1570	47	1	[illegible]
RAMSDELL, ISABELLA J.	349	48	1	[illegible]
Do	814	49	1	[illegible]
RAND, MARY	301	27	2	[illegible]
RANDALL, JONAS	164	19	1	[illegible]
RANDALL, VIRGINIA TAYLOR	2561	49	1	[illegible]
RANDALL, WILLIAM	20	29	1	[illegible]
RANDOLPH, ELIZABETH	527	29	1	[illegible]
RANDOLPH, THOMAS F.	398	25	2	[illegible]
RANKIN, JANE	826	29	1	[illegible]
RANKIN, PEGGY	295	27	2	[illegible]
RANSOM, KEZIAH	208	26	2	[illegible]
RAPPLEYE, JOHN R.	59	21	2	[illegible]

Personal—Continued.

Subject.	Report.	Congress.	Session.	Volume.
ONE, PIBITUS	784	27	2	3
ILLIAM	164	19	1	1
ND, ELIZABETH, *et al.*	784	27	2	3
OND, NATHANIEL	164	19	1	1
ND, PHINEAS	217	30	1	4
WILLIAM (widow of)	1311	46	1	7
ABRAHAM J	489	29	1	4
RD, ELIJAH	462	28	1	3
TON, LAURA	367	23	1	1
JOHN	821	29	1	4
Do	1684	46	2	6
JOSEPH	164	19	1	1
MARY	135	28	2	3
LK, BARBARA	295	27	3	3
DMOND (heir of)	88	30	2	4
Do	376	30	1	4
AMES H	2482	48	2	7
K, REBECCA B	129	45	2	6
K, SAMUEL	436	26	1	3
T, ANN	687	25	2	2
LDS, AARON	153	21	1	1
LDS, ROBERT	400	22	1	1
Do	90	22	1	1
LDS, THANKFUL	789	29	1	4
VAULT, MARY (heirs of)	95	27	2	3
HAUNCEY	68	24	2	2
Do	180	26	2	2
Do	221	25	3	2
Do	122	26	1	3
Mrs. ELIZABETH	2026	49	2	7
AMES B	185	24	2	2
Do	454	25	2	2
Do	282	25	3	2
Do	484	26	1	3
Do	784	27	2	3
ACHEUS	164	19	1	1
Do	198	19	1	1
DS, EDMUND	372	22	1	1
DS, MARCY	550	25	2	2
DSON, DAVID (heirs of)	218	36	1	6
DSON, HANNAH	52	16	2	1
DSON, ISAAC	381	22	1	1
ND, JAMES	132	22	1	1
, RUBEN	193	19	1	1
D, ABNER	381	22	1	1
GTON, JACOB	342	24	1	2
, CATHARINE	536	30	1	4
ETER	218	29	1	4
Do	21	30	2	4
STEPHEN (heirs of)	312	31	1	5
HANNAH	57	15	2	1
LD, MARY C	835	47	1	6
, CATHARINE	784	27	2	3
Do	295	27	3	3
, EPAPHRAS	239	33	1	5
, JERUSHA	77	24	2	2
, MARY	129	26	2	3
Do	110	27	2	3
, PIRUM	396	22	1	1
, SARAH DENNY	2485	48	2	7
, DANIEL	368	31	1	5
MARGARET	784	27	2	3
S, JOHN	291	47	1	6
Do	435	48	1	7
S, SAMUEL	164	19	1	1
ON, LIFURS	3314	49	1	7
S, JESSE	7	29	2	4
S, JOHN	784	27	2	3
S, REUBEN	424	26	1	3
S, STEPHEN	164	19	1	1
ON, WILLIAM	313	24	1	2
ELL, SARAH	551	26	1	3
CK, LEWIS	269	45	3	6
S, AMANDA	350	49	1	7
S, JONATHAN	714	26	1	3
S, SAMUEL	295	27	3	3
S, SUSAN	490	26	1	3
LYDIA	664	26	1	3

Personal—Continued.

Subject.	Report.	Congress.	Session.	Volume.
ROGERS, SALLY	615	45	[illegible]	6
ROGERS, SARAH	784	27	[illegible]	3
ROGERS, SUSAN	784	27	[illegible]	3
ROOF, JANE ANN	261	45	[illegible]	6
ROOKE, AMOS	424	28	1	3
ROOT, CHESTER	253	45	[illegible]	6
ROLLINS, CATHARINE (alias Catharine Mosley)	273	25	[illegible]	2
ROLLS, SALLY	684	24	[illegible]	[illegible]
ROSE, JOHN	154	28	[illegible]	[illegible]
Do	530	29	1	4
ROSE, LIZA	784	27	2	3
ROSE, MALITTY (heirs of)	816	49	1	7
Do	3501	49	2	7
ROSE, ORPHA	826	29	1	4
ROSEBURY, JOHN	295	27	3	3
ROSEBERRY, JOHN M	789	30	1	4
ROSS, JOHN	276	45	3	6
ROSS, JULIA A	423	48	1	7
ROSS, SAMUEL	236	33	1	5
ROUSE, GEORGE	912	27	2	3
ROUSH, GEORGE	116	28	2	3
Do	215	29	1	4
ROWE, ELIZABETH	247	25	3	2
Do	218	28	1	3
ROWE, SUSANNAH	718	25	2	2
Do	30	25	3	2
ROWELL, RACHAEL (heirs of)	371	31	1	5
ROXBURGH, MATTHEW AND ELIZABETH	29	14	1	1
ROYAL, JAMES	89	20	2	1
ROYALL, ANNE	267	25	3	2
Do	491	26	1	3
Do	524	29	1	4
ROYALL, WILLIAM	796	27	3	3
RUCKER, COLLEY	354	36	1	6
RUGGLES, SOLOMON K	1965	47	2	6
RUSSELL, E. O	826	29	1	4
RUSSELL, ESTHER	112	30	1	4
RUST, GEORGE C	1431	47	1	6
RUTLEDGE, JOSHUA	60	16	1	1
RYAN, FRANCIS (widow of)	135	26	2	3
RYBURN, JAMES	164	19	1	1
SAMS, WARREN	671	47	1	6
Do	1414	48	1	7
SANBORN, PETER	367	22	1	1
SANDERS, EUNICE	816	25	2	2
Do	89	25	3	2
SANDERS, SALLY	664	26	1	3
SANDERS, ZACHARIAH	381	22	1	1
SANDS, COMFORT (heirs and assignees)	159	15	1	1
SANFORD, ELIHU	164	19	1	1
SARSFIELD, DAVID	853	49	1	7
SAUNDERS, JAMES	278	45	[illegible]	6
SAVAGE, JOHN	551	26	[illegible]	3
SAWYER, ESTHER	111	27	3	3
Do	163	27	3	3
SAWYER, JOHN	480	35	[illegible]	5
SAXTON, HULDAH	784	27	2	3
Do	526	29	1	4
SAXTON, JAMES	130	36	1	6
SAYER, JAMES	882	25	3	2
SCANLAND, LEWIS W	1808	49	1	7
SCHENK, JOHN H	784	27	2	3
SCHNEIDER, GEORGE	3506	49	2	7
SCHNETBERG, HENRY	152	48	1	7
SCHOFIELD, JOSEPH	3296	49	1	7
SCHOOMAKER, HENRY	164	19	1	1
SCOLLAY, ESTHER	89	30	1	4
SCOTT, ANNA L	258	31	1	5
SCOTT, ELEAZER	194	19	[illegible]	1
SCOTT, JAMES	437	24	[illegible]	[illegible]
SCOTT, JULIA T	2526	48	[illegible]	7
SCOTT, MARTHA	235	33	[illegible]	5
SCOTT, SUSANNAH	225	28	[illegible]	3
Do	7	28	2	3
Do	213	34	[illegible]	5
Do	128	38	[illegible]	[illegible]
SCOVEL, SARAH	295	27	3	3
SCOVILL, ROSWELL	254	45	3	6

Personal—Continued.

Subject.	Report.	Congress.	Session.	Volume.
LL, SARAH	[illegible]	[illegible]	1	4
T, WILLIAM (wife of)	[illegible]	[illegible]	1	4
AN, LAURA	642	45	2	6
S, ELNATHAN	[illegible]	[illegible]	[illegible]	[illegible]
Do	349	[illegible]	1	[illegible]
Do	784	27	[illegible]	[illegible]
Do	198	[illegible]	2	5
Do	218	34	2	[illegible]
Do	179	35	2	5
Do	214	[illegible]	1	[illegible]
S, GRACE	114	37	2	[illegible]
S, MARY J	467	45	2	[illegible]
Y, ISAAC	457	31	1	6
YR, EBENEZER	[illegible]	[illegible]	1	1
R, MARY	490	[illegible]	1	4
INGER, MICHAEL	167	[illegible]	1	[illegible]
ERS, DANIEL	167	34	2	[illegible]
ES, MARY MORTIMER	2443	49	1	7
RSON, RICHARD	438	34	1	9
ER, VALENTINE	[illegible]	30	1	5
LL, MARTHA	424	48	1	7
ON, JANE	872	51	1	8
, ARCHIBALD	873	22	1	1
, ELIZABETH	164	19	1	1
Do	34	19	2	1
Do	81	20	1	1
FER, HENRY	440	30	1	4
RER, SUSAN	1367	47	1	6
FIELD, MARY	346	30	1	4
LEY, MEDAD	542	30	1	4
TON, JONATHAN (administrator)	223	31	1	6
ARD, EDWARD	790	30	1	4
HERD, ZEMIA	906	47	1	6
Do	[illegible]	49	2	7
BURNE, JOHN SAMUEL (heirs of)	223	33	1	5
ER, DAVID	642	26	1	3
Do	784	27	2	3
MAN, BENJAMIN	367	22	1	1
WOOD, ABAGAIL	784	27	2	3
WOOD, MOSES	314	22	1	1
EY, REBECCA	971	47	1	6
EY, JOHN	40	20	1	1
LEY, DAVID	424	26	1	3
, HENSON	281	45	3	6
, SILOAM	411	22	1	1
ER, JOHN	410	22	1	1
M, JOHNSTON, *et al*	216	31	1	5
RICK, EDWARD R	3295	49	1	7
ATE, WILLIAM J	164	19	1	1
TLEFF, LYDIA	537	30	1	4
ES, DANIEL (alias Akerley)	784	27	2	3
, GEORGE	193	19	1	1
ONS, HANNAH	784	27	2	3
ONS, SYLVANUS	410	22	1	1
ON, JOHN	164	19	1	1
EY, GEORGE	322	25	1	3
E, HENRY	293	45	2	6
E, NICHOLAS	20	29	2	4
, JONATHAN	26	22	1	1
IER, MICAH	381	22	1	1
ER, THOMAS	784	27	2	3
EN, JOHN	20	22	1	1
SON, CHARLES	128	45	2	6
Do	1945	47	2	6
H, DAVID W	762	25	2	2
Do	145	26	1	3
, WILLIAM	714	26	1	3
ERLAND, JACOB	315	31	1	5
M, JOHN	164	19	1	1
, ELIZA	2097	48	1	7
L, DANIEL	54	18	2	1
Do	125	45	2	6
I, ABNER	133	22	1	1
I, ABRAM (widow of)	299	27	2	3
I, ADAH	44	29	2	4
Do	607	30	1	4
I, AGNES	551	28	1	3
I, ANNA	786	29	1	4

Personal—Continued.

Personal—Continued.

Subject.	Report.	Congress.	Session.	Volume.
..E, WILLIAM	714	26	1	3
Do	784	27	2	3
Do	285	27	3	3
..ENSON, DAVID T	790	47	1	6
..ENSON, OLIVE	273	46	3	6
Do	917	46	2	6
..ING, LORD	340	33	1	5
..ON, MARY	2213	49	1	7
.., CALEB	367	22	1	1
..INS, BENJAMIN (widow of)	496	45	2	6
..INS, JOHN	795	29	1	4
..INS, WILLIAM, *et al.*	216	31	1	5
..NSON, CATHARINE	706	29	1	4
..NSON, HANNAH	595	29	1	4
Do	45	29	2	4
..NSON, HUGH	164	19	1	1
..ART, ALEXANDER	487	26	1	3
..ART, DUNCAN	164	19	1	1
..ART, HENRIETTA M	444	31	1	5
..ART, NATHANIEL	369	22	1	1
..S, BERIAH	365	22	1	1
..ELL, JEREMIAH, *et al*	268	31	1	5
..HCOMB, AQUILLA (heirs of)	444	31	1	5
.., CATHARINE	164	19	1	1
..SDALE, ELIZABETH	267	49	1	7
..S, HAMPTON	551	26	1	3
..S, SARAH (children of)	111	30	1	4
Do	222	31	1	5
.., DAVID	164	19	1	1
.., ELIZABETH D	2305	49	1	7
.., JOHN H. (heirs)	520	26	1	3
Do	306	27	2	3
.., LEVI AND MARY (heirs of)	21	34	3	5
.., SAMUEL	784	27	2	3
.., SARAH J	973	47	1	6
..R, DOROTHY	66	14	1	1
Do	75	17	1	1
Do	17	17	2	1
Do	164	19	1	1
..R, EBENEZER	490	26	1	3
Do	784	27	2	3
..S, ELIZABETH (heirs of)	14	34	3	5
.., DANIEL	714	26	1	3
Do	5	26	2	3
Do	105	27	2	3
Do	62	31	1	5
.., JOHN	12	29	2	4
.., EBENEZER	423	26	1	3
..ELL, NATHANIEL (widow of)	217	34	3	5
..GHAN, REBECCA	122	45	3	6
..KLAND, WILLIAM	2098	48	1	7
..KLER, JOHN, *et al.*	138	31	1	5
..E, JACOB	257	45	3	6
Do	858	46	2	6
..G, HANNAH	714	26	1	3
..G, MARTHA	545	25	2	2
Do	91	25	3	2
Do	143	26	1	3
..G, ROGER	58	22	1	1
..P, JOHN (widow of)	63	35	2	5
..T, BUCKINGHAM	293	47	1	6
..EFIELD, WILLIAM	808	29	1	4
..S, JOEL H	826	29	1	4
..EVANT, JAMES K	995	47	1	6
..EVANT, JONATHAN	372	22	1	1
..IVANT, HANNAH	424	26	1	3
..ATH, DANIEL	529	43	1	6
..ERS, MARY	113	27	2	3
..RLAND, GEORGE	288	27	2	3
..RLAND, JOHN	826	29	1	4
Do	386	30	1	4
..N, LEROY D	614	45	2	6
..N, PHILIP	714	26	1	3
Do	784	27	2	3
.., ELIZABETH	221	23	1	1
Do	681	24	1	2
..T, ADAM	591	26	1	3
..TWOUT, SARAH (heirs of)	210	34	3	5

Personal—Continued.

Subject.	Report.	Congress.	Session.	Volume.
SWILLING, GEORGE (heirs of)	178	33	2	5
SWILLING, MARTHA (heirs of)	49	36	[illegible]	8
SYKES, JESSE	114	23	[illegible]	1
Do	143	24	[illegible]	2
SYUS, LEWIS	1154	42	[illegible]	7
TABOR, PHILIP	353	31	[illegible]	5
TALMAGE, STEPHEN	275	24	[illegible]	3
TAM, SUSANA	441	31	[illegible]	5
TARBOX, ROSWELL	42	31	[illegible]	5
TASKER, MATTHEW	728	32	[illegible]	6
TATE, ROBERT L	307	[illegible]	[illegible]	1
TATTON, PHILLIS	132	26	[illegible]	1
Do	289	27	[illegible]	1
TATUM, DOROTHEA	424	28	[illegible]	3
TAYLOR, ANNA	533	43	[illegible]	6
TAYLOR, ELIZABETH	669	32	[illegible]	6
TAYLOR, GEORGE	142	30	[illegible]	4
TAYLOR, HULDAH	10	24	[illegible]	2
Do	161	25	[illegible]	2
TAYLOR, JACOB (wife of)	116	30	[illegible]	4
TAYLOR, JAMES	57	23	2	1
Do	785	32	1	6
TAYLOR, MARY	669	25	2	2
TAYLOR, THOMAS	410	22	1	1
TEAS, SARAH	51	31	2	5
TEMPLE, TABITHA	307	30	1	4
TENURE, MICHAEL (widow of)	568	27	2	3
TERRY, NANCY	500	28	1	3
Do	963	27	2	3
TEVIS, WILLIAM	714	28	1	3
THAYER, JERIJAH	164	19	1	1
THEBANT, BARTOLA	3528	49	2	7
THOMAS, JOHN (heirs of)	482	36	1	8
THOMAS, JOSEPHINE DE COSTA	1121	49	1	7
THOMAS, JUDITH	80	21	2	1
THOMAS, NICHOLAS	784	27	2	3
THOMAS, POLLY	41	29	2	4
THOMAS, WILLIAM	60	31	2	5
THOMPSON, AMOS	79	24	2	2
Do	156	25	2	2
THOMPSON, HANNAH	784	27	2	3
Do.	295	27	3	3
THOMPSON, JAMES P	126	45	2	6
THOMPSON, MARY E	235	29	1	4
THOMPSON, NANCY	75	31	2	5
THOMPSON, SAMUEL (widow of)	296	27	[illegible]	3
THOMPSON, SAMUEL M	2606	43	2	7
THOMPSON, WILLIAM	457	44	[illegible]	6
Do	42	45	2	6
THORNBURGH, ELIZA W	2508	48	[illegible]	7
THORP, ELIZABETH	374	40	[illegible]	[illegible]
TIFFANY, HOSEA	369	22	[illegible]	[illegible]
TIFFANY, JOEL	101	27	[illegible]	[illegible]
TIFFANY, THOMAS	209	22	[illegible]	[illegible]
TILTON, ABAGAIL S	495	45	2	[illegible]
Do	593	46	2	[illegible]
TIPTON, JONATHAN	448	30	1	[illegible]
TIPTON, WILLIAM	235	20	1	[illegible]
Do.	37	21	1	[illegible]
TODD, ELONER	784	27	2	[illegible]
TO-HON-DO-CHE (or Big Skin)	104	19	1	1
TOLER, HOPEFUL	271	45	3	[illegible]
Do	478	46	2	[illegible]
Do.	737	47	1	[illegible]
TOMPKINS, ABRAHAM (heirs of)	672	47	1	[illegible]
TOMPKINS, CHRISTOPHER (widow of)	575	27	[illegible]	[illegible]
Do.	770	30	1	[illegible]
Do.	207	31	1	[illegible]
TOPHAM, COLONEL	164	19	1	[illegible]
TOWNSEND, SYLVANUS	162	23	1	[illegible]
TRABUE, DANIEL	510	24	1	[illegible]
TRACY, DOLLY	315	30	1	[illegible]
TRACY, DWYER	2718	47	1	[illegible]
TRACY, LEVI	438	23	1	[illegible]
TRAVERS, MATHIAS	412	24	1	[illegible]
TRIPLETT, PETER	168	19	1	[illegible]
TRIPLETT, SARAH	617	23	1	[illegible]
TRIPP, SALLY	2313	49	1	7

Personal—Continued.

Subject.	Report.	Congress.	Session.	Volume.
, ABRAHAM	164	19	1	3
, DAVID	605	20	1	4
	28	21	2	5
ILLIAM	960	47	1	6
, BENJAMIN	962	27	2	3
ALMON	12	34	2	5
DY	66	30	2	4
DA	311	31	1	5
DAVID	714	26	1	3
HULDAH	696	25	2	2
JESSE (widow of)	538	30	1	4
, ISAAC	194	19	1	1
JAMES	326	23	1	1
ILLE, GEORGE L. (heirs)	423	24	1	2
LYDIA	784	27	2	3
MOSES	295	27	3	3
ABEL	48	18	2	1
	164	19	1	1
CLARISSA	96	27	2	3
ELLEN	245	25	3	2
	42	26	2	3
	88	27	2	3
JOSEPH	410	24	1	2
THADDEUS	157	24	1	2
PRISCILLA DECATUR	426	30	1	4
	1180	47	1	6
ALLY	527	29	1	4
AFF, MARY	807	25	2	2
	178	25	3	2
LICE	978	27	2	3
	290	28	1	3
AMUEL	164	19	1	1
RAH	[illegible]	49	1	7
KIRK, PETER	188	34	3	5
BURGH, EVE	574	27	2	3
BURGH, JAMES	375	22	1	1
HOFF, JOHN A	2006	48	1	7
	3311	49	1	7
VEER, ALBERT	118	24	2	2
EN, JANE	424	26	1	3
ESEN, MARY MARGARET	784	27	2	3
ER, JOHN C., *et al.*	446	31	1	5
K, LAWRENCE, *et al.*	237	29	1	4
	84	29	2	4
	527	30	1	4
	66	31	1	5
N, ABRAHAM	921	27	2	3
S, EFFIE	472	26	1	3
	121	27	2	3
T, JAMES A	2463	49	1	7
EN, PETER	395	22	1	1
T, SARAH	328	34	1	5
SSELAER, HENRY K	588	36	1	6
SSELAER, NANCY G	714	26	1	3
	523	29	1	4
, JOHN C	610	29	1	4
KENBURG, JEHOACHIM	237	29	1	4
	84	29	2	4
	66	31	1	5
ST, JACOBUS	411	22	1	1
ST, GERSHOM	13	34	3	5
	589	36	1	6
RT, AMY	303	27	2	3
NKEN, JOHN J	784	27	2	3
, CATHARINE	784	27	2	3
, CHARLES	714	26	1	3
N, BENJAMIN	397	25	2	2
OSEPH	150	24	2	2
	166	25	2	2
E, ELIZA	457	31	1	5
LIAM	21	29	2	4
	446	30	1	4
N	522	29	1	4
ENEVIEVE (heirs of)	17	34	3	5
RUS	1372	49	1	7
D, JOHN	103	22	1	1
THEODORE	1352	47	1	6
GODFREY	370	24	1	2

Personal—Continued.

Personal—Continued.

Subject.	Report.	Congress.	Session.	Volume.
AMUEL L	1282	47	1	6
ANNA	19	14	2	1
L, JOHN H	119	21	1	1
NG, GEORGE	383	25	1	2
	48	25	2	2
ORTH, LYDIA	714	26	1	3
CATHARINE AND ELIZABETH	784	27	2	3
NNA	125	24	2	2
	168	25	2	2
AAC	371	22	1	1
OSEPH	460	26	1	3
HOMAS	179	24	2	2
	179	25	2	2
LL, DINAH	784	27	2	3
, HANNAH	535	30	1	4
	255	31	1	5
R, CHAUNCEY (administrator)	128	29	1	4
, OLIVE	460	26	1	3
Y, CATHARINE	1004	27	2	3
N, JOSEPH (heirs of)	90	35	1	5
R, ELIASHIB	502	45	2	6
R, OLIVER L	861	46	2	6
ER, EPHRAIM	117	21	1	1
ER, IRA	89	33	1	5
ER, NELL	391	22	1	1
DAVID	90	34	3	5
	512	35	1	5
ELIZABETH	551	26	1	3
GORDON	536	29	1	4
JACOB	807	25	2	2
	22	27	3	3
MOSES (executor)	65	16	1	1
JOHN (heirs of)	460	38	1	6
REBECCA	858	29	1	4
SARAH	571	27	2	3
	518	30	1	4
VASSEL	164	19	1	1
ZILPHA	136	30	1	4
AN, ELIZABETH	1105	27	2	3
RE, ENOCH	164	19	1	1
RE, LUCY	663	20	1	1
Y, SETH	783	24	1	2
	266	25	2	2
CAR, JOSEPH	164	19	1	1
ANNA JANE	24	29	2	4
CONRAD	211	24	2	2
	169	25	2	2
	180	25	3	2
	147	26	1	3
	249	26	2	3
	784	27	2	3
ILLIAM HAZZARD	176	32	1	5
TON, POLLY	714	26	1	3
RNE, LEWIS	784	27	2	3
HANNAH (heirs of)	90	34	3	5
	512	35	1	5
STEPHEN	164	19	1	1
JACOB	551	26	1	3
MATTHEW	642	25	2	2
	122	25	3	2
	157	26	1	3
D, FREDERICK	440	24	1	2
	176	26	2	3
. CARTER	265	44	1	6
SON, MOTT	519	29	1	4
	351	31	1	5
N, JOSEPH	714	26	1	3
MS, MARGARET	127	21	1	5
MS, MARY	347	26	1	3
	1003	27	2	3
MS, NANCY	551	26	1	3
	136	27	3	3
MS, RACHAEL	164	19	1	1
MS, RUAMAH	45	17	2	1
MS, TABITHA	784	27	2	3
MS, WILLIAM	784	27	2	3
MSON, ELIZABETH	517	30	1	4
MSON, JAMES	826	29	1	4

Personal—Continued.

Subject.	Report.	Congress.	Session.	Volume.
WILLIS, WILLIAM	916	27	2	3
WILLS, ELEANOR	22	29	2	4
WILSON, AMELIA A	1351	47	1	6
WILSON, AMY	58	24	1	2
WILSON, BENJAMIN (heirs of)	163	34	2	5
WILSON, CATHARINE	295	27	2	3
Do	18	27	3	3
WILSON, JOHN (heirs of)	596	36	1	6
WILSON, MARY	340	28	1	3
WILSON, NANCY	456	28	1	3
Do	66	27	3	3
Do	449	28	1	3
WILSON, PETER	329	28	1	3
Do	141	28	2	3
WILSON, ROBERT	443	31	1	5
WILSON, URIAH	120	30	2	4
Do	263	31	1	5
WILT, JACOB	263	27	3	3
WINANS, ISAAC	496	45	2	6
Do	2717	49	1	7
WINANS, SILAS (wife of)	770	29	1	4
WINCH, JOSEPH	134	24	1	2
WINCHELL, JOHN	283	45	3	6
WINCHESTER, JABEZ	105	22	1	1
WINCHESTER, SILAS	164	19	1	1
WINN, SAMUEL	223	34	2	5
Do	171	35	1	5
WINSLOW, JOHN (heirs of)	124	33	2	5
WINSTON, WILLIAM B	115	26	1	2
WINTER, JUVENAL	395	22	1	1
WISEMAN, NOAH (heirs of)	74	30	2	4
WITHEROW, DAVID	58	31	2	5
WOOD, EDMUND W	194	19	1	1
WOOD, ICHABOD	367	22	1	1
WOOD, JAMES	17	16	2	1
Do	46	17	2	1
WOODBURY, WILLIAM	87	33	1	5
WOODRUFF, GEDER	412	23	1	1
WOODS, AUKE	784	27	2	3
WOODS, HUGH (widow of)	21	31	1	5
WOODS, MARY	826	29	1	4
WOODS, SARAH	164	19	1	1
WOODWARD, ELIZABETH	784	27	2	3
WOODWARD, JONAS	784	27	2	3
WOODWARD, JOSHUA	309	31	1	5
WOODWARD, SARAH	103	27	2	3
WOODWORTH, ROSWELL	57	17	1	1
WOODY, JAMES	4095	49	2	7
WOLF, ELIZABETH BLISS	484	36	1	6
WOLF, FREDERICK (wife of)	484	36	1	6
WOLF, MARY	469	26	1	3
Do	116	27	2	3
WONDRAK, MATHIAS	2710	49	1	7
WORK, WILLIAM	164	19	1	1
WORRALL, JONATHAN	164	19	1	1
WORTH, MARGARET L	484	31	1	5
WORTH, MARGARET STAFFORD	2759	49	1	7
WORTHEN, JUDITH (heirs of)	356	29	1	4
Do	79	33	2	5
WRIGHT, ANN O	618	29	1	4
WRIGHT, ELIZABETH	388	30	1	4
Do	313	31	1	5
WRIGHT, GEORGE W	608	45	2	6
WRIGHT, ISAAC	164	19	1	1
WRIGHT, LUCY	826	29	1	4
Do	203	30	1	4
WRIGHTMAN, HANNAH	297	30	1	4
WYATT, SPEIRY	178	24	1	2
WYNNE, DANIEL	40	29	1	4
YANCY, ELIZABETH	579	36	1	6
YARRINGTON, ANNA	784	29	1	4
Do	197	30	1	4
YATES, JOHN	164	19	1	1
YATES, NANCY	490	26	1	3
Do	784	27	2	3
Do	295	27	3	3
YATES, WILLIAM (heirs of)	453	31	1	5
YORK, WILLIAM	169	23	2	2

Personal—Continued.

Subject.	Report.	Congress.	Session.	Volume.
RK, WILLIAM	158	26	1	3
RK, WILLIAM (heirs of)	70	34	3	5
Do	85	35	1	5
Do	211	36	1	6
RKE, ABAGAIL	423	26	1	3
RKE, SAWNEY (heirs)	62	24	2	2
Do	173	25	2	2
RKE, WILLIAM	11	24	2	2
ST, ESTHER	856	46	2	6
UMAN, JONAS	397	22	1	1
UNG, JOHN	211	30	1	4
UNG, RALPH	360	29	1	4
UNG, SAMUEL	164	19	1	1
UNG, URI, *et al.*	322	31	1	5
UNGS, SAMUEL	314	22	1	1
MERMAN, JACOB	194	19	1	1

O

REPORTS

OF THE

MITTEE ON PENSIONS, BOUNTY, AND BACK PAY,

HOUSE OF REPRESENTATIVES,

ROM THE ORGANIZATION OF THE COMMITTEE, MAY 16, 1879, TO THE CLOSE OF THE FORTY-EIGHTH CONGRESS,

IN TWO VOLUMES.

COMPILED, UNDER THE DIRECTION OF THE JOINT COMMITTEE ON PRINTING,

BY

T. H. McKEE,

CLERK, DOCUMENT ROOM, UNITED STATES SENATE.

WASHINGTON:
GOVERNMENT PRINTING OFFICE.
1887.

9255

FORTY-NINTH CONGRESS, FIRST SESSION.

[PUBLIC RESOLUTION—No. 24.]

Joint resolution authorizing the preparation of a compilation of the reports of committees of the Senate and House of Representatives.

Resolved by the Senate and House of Representatives of the United States of America in Congress assembled, That there be prepared under the direction of the Joint Committee of Printing, a compilation of the reports of the Senate and House of Representatives from the Fourteenth to the Forty-eighth Congress, inclusive, classified by committees, arranged, indexed, and bound in suitable volumes for the use of the standing committees of the two Houses of Congress. And the sum of seven thousand seven hundred and fifty dollars, or so much thereof as may be found necessary, is hereby appropriated out of any money in the Treasury not otherwise appropriated, for the preparation of said work, which sum may be paid by the Secretary of the Treasury upon the order of the chairman of said Joint Committee, as additional pay or compensation to any officer or employee of the United States.

Resolved further, That the Clerk of the House and Secretary of the Senate be, and they are hereby directed, to procure and file, for the use of their respective Houses, copies of all reports made by each committee of all succeeding Congresses; and that the Clerk of the House and the Secretary of the Senate be, and they are hereby, authorized and directed at the close of each session of Congress, to cause said reports to be indexed and bound, one copy to be deposited in the library of each House and one copy in the room of the committee from which the reports emanated.

Approved, July 29, 1886.

COMPILER'S NOTICE.

compilation embraces all the printed reports made by both
s of Congress from the commencement of the Fourteenth to the
f the Forty-ninth Congress. They are classified by committees
ranged in numerical order. The collection for each committee is
l into volumes of suitable size. Each committee has a separate
a copy being bound in each volume.

SPECIAL and SELECT reports are all compiled in one collection
; one index, a copy of which is bound in each volume.

plan throughout the compilation is to place each report to the
ttee from which it was reported, without reference to the subject-
.

House and Senate reports are compiled separately. Care will
uired in noticing the chronological order, as in some instances an
session or Congress may not appear in certain volumes from the
at during this period no reports were made by this committee.

T. H. McKEE.

INDEX

TO

TS OF COMMITTEE ON PENSIONS, BOUNTY, AND BACK PAY,

HOUSE OF REPRESENTATIVES.

FROM 1879 TO 1885, INCLUSIVE.

Subject.	Report.	Congress.	Session.	Volume.
DER, JOHN, claim for bounty land	2430	48	2	1
for loss of	908	47	1	1
for loss of, at shoulder-joint	434	47	1	1
S OF PENSIONS, providing for	*1502	47	1	1
EYS IN PENSION CASES, limiting fees of	2620	48	2	1
OHN W., back pay	2583	48	2	1
S, equalization of	*1315	46	2	1
S AND BACK PAY, delay in payment of	387	46	3	2
soldiers, providing for heirs of	1883	47	2	1
olunteers, granting bounty to Fourth Regiment	983	48	1	1
lvania volunteers, Sixty-second Regiment, claim for	2361	48	2	1
LAND CLAIMS, special examination of	435	47	1	1
LAND WARRANTS, to establish a board of review in Pension Bureau r	1108	47	1	1
N OF DECEASED PENSIONERS, providing pensions for	678	47	1	1
GENTS,				
ting fees of	2620	48	2	1
gation of practice of	2683	48	2	1
SOLDIERS, providing bounty and pension for service in war of rebellion	1883	47	2	1
PENSIONS, to establish	*606	46	2	1
Do	387	46	3	2
D CLAIMANTS, to amend law relating to	678	47	1	1
D PENSIONERS, providing pensions for children of	678	47	1	1
VILLIAM, claim for bounty	1784	48	1	1
NG SURGEONS, fixing fees of	433	47	1	1
NURSES, fixing compensation at $25 per month	1292	48	1	1
H, REBECCA, additional bounty	1513	48	1	1
AND, SYLVESTER F., claim for pension	1063	47	1	1
N, SAMUEL S., claim for bounty	1783	48	1	1
L-REVENUE SERVICE, providing pension for	1112	47	1	1
GATION, laws and practice in Pension Office	2683	48	2	1
GATION OF PENSION BUREAU, testimony and report	387	46	3	2
urth Regiment of Infantry, bounty for	983	48	1	1
RY ANN, claim for relief	2684	48	2	1
JOHN A., claim for relief	2584	48	2	1
g rate of pension for loss of	908	47	1	1
ING SERVICE, providing pensions for	1112	47	1	1
MEN, pensions for	677	47	1	1
ISTED MEN, pensions for	677	47	1	1
female), fixing compensation at $25 per month	1292	48	1	1
ON, EDWARD G., claim for pay	2685	48	2	1
VANIA VOLUNTEERS, to grant bounty to Sixty-second Regiment f	2361	48	2	1
AGENTS,				
igation of practice of	2683	48	2	1
iting fees of	2620	48	2	1
AND BOUNTY-LAND CLAIMS, to make special examinations into merit of	435	47	1	1

* And views of minority.

Subject.	Report.	Congress.	Session.	Volume.
PENSION AND BOUNTY-LAND WARRANT CASES, to establish a board of review of	1106	47	1	1
PENSION BUREAU.				
Management of	387	46	3	2
To create board of review to investigate bounty-land warrant cases	1106	47	1	1
PENSION CASES, testimony in	431	47	1	1
PENSIONERS, list of persons dropped from rolls	387	46	3	2
PENSION FRAUDS, statement of 500 cases	387	46	3	2
PENSION LAWS,				
To amend	1110	47	1	1
Do	1910	47	2	1
Investigation of passage of certain	2683	48	2	1
PENSION OFFICE, classification of the clerical force, 1880	387	46	3	2
PENSIONS,				
To establish court of	*606	46	2	1
Do	387	46	3	2
Agents, investigation of practice of	2683	48	2	1
Applications for, to extend time for filing	1140	47	1	1
Arm or leg, loss of	908	47	1	1
Arm at shoulder-joint, fixing rate for loss of	434	47	1	1
Arrears of	*1502	47	1	1
Arrears of, in certain cases	2382	48	2	1
Children of deceased claimants	1111	47	1	1
Do	1780	47	1	1
Claims for, providing for	676	47	1	1
Colored soldiers, pensions to heirs of	1883	47	2	1
Deceased claimants	678	47	1	1
Fees of attorneys in cases of	2620	48	2	1
Filing claims for, to extend time	1140	47	1	1
Granting, in certain cases	1257	48	1	1
Increase of, in certain cases	1516	48	1	1
Internal-revenue service, providing pensions for	1112	47	1	1
Life-saving service, providing pensions for	1112	47	1	1
Militia, to pension	677	47	1	1
Payment of	1109	47	1	1
Providing for	1141	47	1	1
Railway mail service, providing for	1112	47	1	1
Rates, to increase	908	47	1	1
Do	1110	47	1	1
Do	1910	47	2	1
Do	1516	48	1	1
PLOCHER, FERDINAND, claim for relief	2668	48	2	1
RAILWAY MAIL SERVICE, providing pension for	1112	47	1	1
REVISED STATUTES, to amend or repeal,				
Section 57, pensions, to amend	1141	47	1	1
Section 184, subpœnas for witnesses	431	47	1	1
Section 4693, referring to claims of militiamen and non-enlisted men	677	47	1	1
Section 4693, to extend time for filing claims for pensions	1140	47	1	1
Sections 4702, 4718, children of deceased claimants, amend	678	47	1	1
Do	1111	47	1	1
Do	1780	47	1	1
Section 4744, special examination of pension and bounty-land claims, to amend	435	47	1	1
Sections 5392, 5393, to amend	432	47	1	1
SHOULDER-JOINT, pension for loss of arm at	434	47	1	1
SIZER, ANDREW J., claim for pension	1281	47	1	1
STUCHELL, ANN, claim for pension	1062	47	1	1
SUBPŒNAS, issuing of, for witnesses in claims against United States	431	47	1	1
TESTIMONY,				
Relating to administration of Pension Office	387	46	3	2
Do	2683	48	2	1
Relating to certain pension laws and practice of pension agents	2683	48	2	2
WAR OF REBELLION,				
Providing bounty and pension for colored soldiers who served in	1883	47	2	1
Providing for payment of female nurses during	1292	48	1	1
WEST VIRGINIA TROOPS, for relief of	1906	48	1	1
WITNESSES IN CLAIMS AGAINST UNITED STATES, to amend Revised Statutes in regard to issuing subpœnas for	431	47	1	1

*And views of minority.

REPORTS

OF

IITTEE ON THE POST-OFFICE AND

HOUSE OF REPRESENTATIVES,

FROM THE FOURTEENTH CONGRESS, 1815, TO THE FORTY-NINTH CONGRESS, 1887, INCLUSIVE.

IN SIX VOLUMES.

IPILED, UNDER THE DIRECTION OF THE JOINT COMMITTEE ON PRINTING,

BY

T. H. McKEE,

CLERK, DOCUMENT ROOM, UNITED STATES SENATE.

WASHINGTON:
GOVERNMENT PRINTING OFFICE.
1887.

57 P O H

FORTY-NINTH CONGRESS, FIRST SESSION.

[PUBLIC RESOLUTION—No. 24.]

Joint resolution authorizing the preparation of a compilation of the reports of committees of the Senate and House of Representatives.

Resolved by the Senate and House of Representatives of the United States of America in Congress assembled, That there be prepared under the direction of the Joint Committee of Printing, a compilation of the reports of the Senate and House of Representatives from the Fourteenth to the Forty-eighth Congress, inclusive, classified by committees, arranged, indexed, and bound in suitable volumes for the use of the standing committees of the two Houses of Congress. And the sum of seven thousand seven hundred and fifty dollars, or so much thereof as may be found necessary, is hereby appropriated out of any money in the Treasury not otherwise appropriated, for the preparation of said work, which sum may be paid by the Secretary of the Treasury upon the order of the chairman of said Joint Committee, as additional pay or compensation to any officer or employee of the United States.

Resolved further, That the Clerk of the House and Secretary of the Senate be, and they are hereby directed, to procure and file, for the use of their respective Houses, copies of all reports made by each committee of all succeeding Congresses; and that the Clerk of the House and the Secretary of the Senate be, and they are hereby, authorized and directed at the close of each session of Congress, to cause said reports to be indexed and bound, one copy to be deposited in the library of each House and one copy in the room of the committee from which the reports emanated.

Approved, July 29, 1886.

2

COMPILER'S NOTICE.

compilation embraces all the printed reports made by both of Congress from the commencement of the Fourteenth to the the Forty-ninth Congress. They are classified by committees inged in numerical order. The collection for each committee is into volumes of suitable size. Each committee has a separate copy being bound in each volume.

PECIAL and SELECT reports are all compiled in one collection one index, a copy of which is bound in each volume.

lan throughout the compilation is to place each report to the ee from which it was reported, without reference to the subject-

Iouse and Senate reports are compiled separately. Care will red in noticing the chronological order, as in some instances an ssion or Congress may not appear in certain volumes from the t during this period no reports were made by this committee.

T. H. McKEE.

INDEX

TO

TS OF COMMITTEE ON THE POST-OFFICE AND POST-ROADS,

HOUSE OF REPRESENTATIVES.

FROM 1815 TO 1887, INCLUSIVE.

Subject.	Report.	Congress.	Session.	Volume.
IBIE, JOHN G., for relief	630	47	1	5
(*See* LEAVES OF ABSENCE.)				
EN, for relief	628	36	1	3
MES, for relief of executor	437	35	1	3
JCIEN B. (executor), for relief	437	35	1	3
AL CLERKS. (*See* CLERKS.)				
, special pay of postmaster at Maplesville in	168	26	2	1
IR AND WATER-TIGHT MAIL-BAGS, providing for introduction				
l use of	45	34	1	3
RVY, for relief	274	36	1	3
ADE, for relief	136	33	1	2
BIBLE SOCIETY, franking privilege to	52	14	1	1
, WILLIAM and SAMUEL B., for relief	628	25	2	1
Do	190	27	2	1
JOHN F., claim for relief	93	45	2	5
ATIONS,				
ric telegraph, to experiment with Richardson's patent	198	34	1	3
e Department, for payment of extra clerks in	122	21	1	1
anceling and post-marking machine, twenty-five thousand dollars for				
chase of Leavitt	928	47	1	5
e between United States and Europe, to establish	476	29	1	2
star routes, providing for deficiency for transportation of	1701	47	1	5
rder system, to provide for payment of expenses of	626	48	1	6
Do	380	49	1	6
ter at Maplesville, Ala., special, to pay	168	26	2	1
e Department.				
al for year ending June 30, 1887	720	49	1	6
Do	3653	49	2	6
l,				
Chicot County to Little Rock, Ark., making, for	218	21	1	1
Do	374	22	1	1
een Tuscumbia, Ala., and Memphis, Tenn., to improve	293	21	1	1
mail contractors, to reappropriate amount approved March 3, 1877, to				
	1051	48	1	6
ROBERT G., claim for relief	1138	46	2	5
S, appropriation to make post-road from Chicot County to Little Rock				
	218	21	1	1
Do	374	22	1	1
& TUCKER, claim for relief	19	46	2	5
MAIL STEAMERS. (*See* POSTAL SERVICE.)				
SAMUEL R., claim for relief	123	45	2	5
LTMARSH & CO., claim for relief	280	24	2	1
Do	561	25	2	1
EVI S., claim for relief	658	25	2	1
OMAS W., claim for relief	4	18	1	1
HN, claim for relief	548	26	1	1
ILLIAM, claim for relief	168	31	1	2
THOMAS E., *et al.*, claim for relief	126	48	1	6
E, MARYLAND, mail route between Philadelphia, Pa., and, to improve	51	19	1	1
WILLIAM F., claim for relief	40	42	2	3
THOMAS, claim for relief	174	32	1	2

Subject.	Report.	Congress.	Session.	Volume.
BARNEY, H. M., claim for relief	326	36	1	[illegible]
BARRON, JOHN E., claim for relief	602	35	1	[illegible]
BAUGHMAN & WYATT, claim for relief	252	46	2	[illegible]
BAYARD, WILLIAM, post-road from Fort Smith, Ark., to San Diego, Cal., proposition to construct	95	31	2	2
BEAMAN, JOEL, claim for relief	399	28	1	[illegible]
BEAN, G. S., *et al.*, claim for relief	332	34	1	[illegible]
BEDINGER, HENRY, claim for relief	219	19	1	[illegible]
Do	151	25	1	[illegible]
BELL, ANN P., claim for relief	18	45	2	[illegible]
BELL, DAVID W., claim for relief	1509	46	2	[illegible]
BELL, FRANCIS M., claim for relief	1533	47	1	[illegible]
BENTON, SAMUEL H., & CO., claim for relief	1051	25	2	[illegible]
BIBB COUNTY, ALABAMA, postmaster at Maplesville, in, special pay of	168	26	2	[illegible]
BLOUNTSVILLE, TENNESSEE, mail coaches to Knoxville, Tenn., from, to re-establish four-horse line of	56	29	2	[illegible]
BOGGESS, GILES S., claim for relief	805	25	2	1
BOSTON, MASSACHUSETTS,				
Mail between Washington, D. C., and, failure of	365	23	1	1
Post-office at, to prevent removal of	658	36	1	3
Post-office building at, to investigate construction of	*58	41	2	3
BOWEN, GEORGE,				
Claim for relief	354	22	1	1
Do	162	23	1	[illegible]
BOWLER, THOMAS F., claim for relief	339	36	1	[illegible]
BRASHEAR, LOUISIANA, to change name to Morgan City	572	47	1	[illegible]
BRAZIL, ocean mail steam service between United States and, to establish	261	34	3	[illegible]
Do	*346	45	2	[illegible]
BROOKS, JOHN S., claim for relief	550	28	1	[illegible]
BROWN, JOHN, & CO., claim for relief	594	25	2	[illegible]
BROWN, JOHN R., claim for relief	709	46	2	[illegible]
BROWN & TARBOX, claim for relief	37	31	1	[illegible]
BUCKLES, J. C., claim for relief	162	32	1	[illegible]
Do	129	33	1	[illegible]
BURGIN, JOHN, discharge from imprisonment of	74	17	2	[illegible]
BURLINGTON, CEDAR RAPIDS AND NORTHERN RAILROAD, payment of amount due for transportation of United States mails by	56	46	3	[illegible]
Do	341	47	1	[illegible]
BURNETT, JOHN S., claim for relief	228	25	3	[illegible]
BURNETT, SAMUEL M., claim for relief	477	36	1	[illegible]
BURTON, BENJAMIN, claim for relief	42	43	3	[illegible]
BUTTERFIELD, CARLOS, *et al.*, mail steamers between United States and Mexico, to authorize establishment of, by	607	36	1	[illegible]
CALDWELL, J. F., claim for relief	961	25	2	[illegible]
Do	988	25	2	[illegible]
Do	75	27	2	[illegible]
Do	186	28	1	[illegible]
Do	607	30	1	[illegible]
Do	109	31	1	[illegible]
CANNON, JOHN F., claim for relief	97	35	1	[illegible]
CARMEN, C. E., claim for relief	1807	47	1	[illegible]
CHENEY, THOMAS P., charges of alleged misconduct against, investigation of	128	45	3	[illegible]
CHICAGO, BURLINGTON AND QUINCY RAILROAD, payment for carrying mails by	1257	46	2	[illegible]
Do	342	47	1	[illegible]
CHICKASAW NATION, post-road through lands of, appropriation to improve	283	21	[illegible]	[illegible]
CHICOT COUNTY, ARKANSAS, appropriation to make post-road from, to Little Rock, Ark	218	21	[illegible]	[illegible]
Do	374	22	[illegible]	[illegible]
CHINA, Pacific Mail Steamship Company for carrying United States mails between United States and, forfeiture of contract with	1598	43	[illegible]	[illegible]
CHORPENNING, GEORGE, claim for relief	323	34	[illegible]	[illegible]
CITY POSTMASTER, examination of, relative to fire in Post-Office Department	134	28	2	[illegible]
CLERKS, Post-Office Department, appropriation for payment of additional, in	123	21	1	[illegible]
CLOWER, WILLIAM, claim for relief	371	21	1	[illegible]
COAN, J. C., claim for relief	195	35	2	[illegible]
COLLIER, THOMAS W., claim for relief	122	45	2	[illegible]
COLMESNIL, JOHN D., claim for relief	252	31	1	[illegible]
Do	142	33	1	[illegible]
Do	191	36	1	[illegible]
COMMITTEE ON POST-OFFICE AND POST-ROADS, business from, setting apart days for consideration of	1839	49	1	[illegible]
CONNECTICUT, post-route from Litchfield to Norfolk in, to discontinue	163	19	1	[illegible]
CONVERSE, JOHN P., claim for relief	154	32	[illegible]	[illegible]
COOK, NATHAN, claim for relief	180	34	[illegible]	[illegible]
CORRESPONDENCE DIVISION, POST-OFFICE DEPARTMENT, to reorganize	3621	49	2	[illegible]
CORSE, ALBERT C. (assignee), Norton's marking and cancelling stamp, pay for use of	98	30	1	[illegible]
CORSER, SOLOMON T., claim for relief	121	30	2	[illegible]

* And views of minority. † Parts 1, 2.

Subject.	Report.	Congress.	Session.	Volume.
[COUNT]ERFEITING POSTAL NOTES, to punish for	641	48	1	6
[COURT] OF CLAIMS, postmasters to institute certain proceedings in, to enable	167	46	2	5
[...], CORNELIUS, claim for relief	169	32	1	2
[...] ANDREW, claim for relief	401	26	1	1
[...]LAW, AARON A. L. H., claim for relief	698	36	1	3
[...]T, SAMUEL B., claim for relief	62	19	1	1
[...]G, ALEXANDER M., claim for relief	25	22	2	1
Do	169	29	1	2
[...]GHAM, JAMES, claim for relief	1416	46	2	5
[...]JOHN B., claim for relief	18	46	2	5
[...]TT, JOHN, claim for relief	169	31	1	2
Do	161	32	1	2
Do	267	35	1	3
[...]S, WILLIAM, claim for relief	*316	36	1	3
[...]ER, TERRENCE, claim for relief	1078	47	1	5
[...] & HUMPHREYS, claim for relief	871	29	1	2
[...], JOHN B., claim for relief	96	23	2	1
[...] POSTMASTERS,				
[comp]ensation of, to reduce	68	35	1	3
[...]ion of, by people, to provide for	92	36	1	3
[...]D, WILLIAM M., claim for relief	235	35	1	3
[...]Y, JOHN G., claim for relief	196	27	2	1
[...] OR RETURN ENVELOPES, law relative to, amending	1460	46	2	5
[...]SS & BEMAN, claim for relief	272	36	1	3
[...]SS, ROBERT, claim for relief	272	36	1	3
[...]RRIT L., for relief of sureties	166	21	1	1
[...]TER, claim for relief	169	21	1	1
[...]AVID, claim for relief	96	31	2	3
[...], J. H., claim for relief	23	45	2	5
[...]WILLIAM, Sr., for relief	73	29	1	2
[...]DS, ARTHUR, et al., claim for relief	96	36	1	3
[...]Hon. E. JOHN, charges against, in connection with star-route frauds, investigation of	967	48	1	6
[...]PES,				
[...]e or return envelopes, to amend law relating to	1460	46	2	5
[...]l request, to issue	177	46	2	5
[...]ed, abolishing of	36	42	2	3
[...], mail route between United States and, to establish	476	29	1	2
[...]B. N., claim for relief	713	46	2	5
[...]WILLIAM C., claim for relief	400	26	1	1
[...]. C., claim for relief	129	35	2	3
Do	101	36	1	3
[...] JOHN, claim for relief	547	26	1	1
[C]OMPTROLLER, duties of, to define	654	47	1	5
[...]G, JAMES P., claim for relief	199	34	1	3
[...]E FLAP POSTAL CARDS. (*See* POSTAL CARDS.)				
[...]N MAILS, management of, investigation of	1087	49	1	6
[...]Y, postal money-orders, to amend law for, of	522	48	1	6
[...]ITH, ARKANSAS, post-road to San Diego, Cal., from, proposal of William Bayard, to establish	95	31	2	2
[...], JOHN, claim for relief	06	33	1	1
[...]NG PRIVILEGE,				
[Ameri]can Bible Society, granting, to	52	14	1	1
[...] relating to, to define	608	30	1	2
[...]ers of Thirty-ninth Congress, to extend to	11	39	2	3
[Moun]t Vernon Association, to extend, to	136	35	2	3
[...]ings of, inquiry as to	909	25	2	1
Do	483	28	1	1
[...]LENT POST-OFFICES, penalty for keeping, prescribing	81	36	1	3
Do	1982	47	2	5
Do	1109	48	1	6
[...]ELIVERY SYSTEM (*see also* POSTAL SERVICE), to extend	2603	48	2	6
[...]N HENRY, claim for relief	47	19	1	1
[...]JOHN, claim for relief	348	33	1	2
Do	610	36	1	3
[...], WILLIAM, claim for relief	512	29	1	2
Do	102	30	1	2
[...]S, C. F., claim for relief	1511	46	2	5
[...]HER, JAMES A., claim for relief	124	35	2	3
[...]TON, TEXAS, transportation of United States mails between Vera Cruz, Mexico, and, providing for	†886	45	2	5
[...]Y, IRELAND, mail route between Jersey City and, to establish	152	32	1	2
[...]L, PETER, claim for relief	396	26	1	1
[S]TEPHEN O., claim for relief	105	36	1	3
[...]GS, GEORGE H., claim for relief	170	34	1	3
Do	26	44	2	4
Do	1	45	1	5
[...] JAMES M., claim for relief	23	34	1	3
[...]LL, JOHNSON, claim for relief	59	20	2	1
[...]d & FINNALL, claim for relief	38	31	1	2
Do	131	33	1	2

* And views of minority. † Parts 1, 2.

Subject.	Report.	Congress.	Session.	Volume.
GRANT, EDWAY A., claim for relief	387	46	1	6
GRANT, JULIA D., franking privilege to	573	49	1	6
Do	735	48	1	6
GRAY, WILLIAM F., claim for relief	93	18	1	1
GREAT BRITAIN, mail routes between United States and, to establish	137	35	2	3
GREAT SOUTHERN MAIL, transportation of, inquiring into best method for	171	30	1	3
GREEN, PATRICK, claim for relief	372	21	1	1
Do	179	22	1	1
Do	346	22	1	1
Do	155	24	1	1
Do	60	24	2	1
Do	102	25	2	1
Do	96	25	3	1
GREEN, SAMUEL S., claim for relief	270	36	1	3
GREEN, THOMAS F., for relief of sureties	451	22	1	1
GROVE, SAMUEL, claim for relief	365	46	2	5
GUION, E. P., claim for relief	49	30	2	2
HAGERTY, JOHN E., claim for relief	34	41	3	3
HALE, SILAS, claim for relief	1057	26	2	1
HALL, JACOB, claim for relief	299	34	1	3
HAMPSHIRE COUNTY, VIRGINIA, enforced specie payment of postage by citizens of	1019	25	2	1
HARD, BENJAMIN T., claim for relief	670	24	1	1
HARDESLY, R. C., claim for relief	743	25	2	1
HARRILL, DRURY D., claim for relief	3	36	2	3
HARRIS, JAMES, claim for relief	194	34	3	3
HARRIS, JAMES M., claim for relief	260	35	1	3
HARRIS & MORGAN, claim for relief	90	35	1	3
HARRIS & HODGE, claim for relief	526	36	1	3
HAVEN, FRANKLIN, *et al.*, claim for relief	13	36	2	3
HAYES, SHELDEN B., claim for relief	219	29	1	3
HECK, JOHN, claim for relief	26	18	1	1
HERNDON, EDWARD, claim for relief	374	29	1	3
HERRING, ASA, claim for relief	115	19	1	1
Do	50	20	1	1
HICK, JOHN, claim for relief	60	18	2	1
HIGHWAYS, post-roads, to make all public roads and	27	46	1	6
HILBURN, LEMUEL J., claim for relief	59	35	1	3
HILTON, JOSEPH W., claim for relief	*271	35	1	3
HOCKADAY & LEGGET, claim for relief	268	36	1	3
HOLMES, ANSEL D., claim for relief	20	46	2	5
HOOTEN, JAMES, claim for relief	99	36	1	3
HOPKINS, GEORGE W., claim for relief	113	35	1	3
HORTON, G. R., claim for relief	101	44	1	4
HOUSE, HILL W. and SAMUEL O., claim for relief	158	36	1	3
HOUSEWRIGHT, JOHN, claim for relief	396	26	1	1
HOWE, WILLARD, claim for relief	19	43		3
HOWELL, JOHN, claim for relief	110	31		
HUCKLEBERRY, J. H., claim for relief	1422	47		
HUMPHREYS, CURTIS, claim for relief	96	28		
HUNT, JAMES H., claim for relief	174	34		
ILLINOIS AND SAINT LOUIS BRIDGE COMPANY, Postmaster-General to make contract with, for carrying certain mails, authorizing	710	46		
IMLAY, RICHARD, metal mail chests patented by, to adopt	73	17		
INDIANA,				
Carrying of United States mails free of toll over roads in, to authorize	163	46		4
New Albany and Salem Railroad extra compensation for carrying mails between La Fayette and Michigan City in, to pay	252	35	2	
Post-road between Louisville, Ky., and Saint Louis, Mo., resolution of legislature in regard to	173	21		
IOWA, Mississippi and Missouri Railroad for carrying United States mails previous to August 15, 1857, in, to pay	208	35	2	3
JACKSON, ELISHA, claim for relief	560	25	2	1
JACKSON, JAMES A., *et al.*, claim for relief	101	44	1	4
JACKSON, JARVIS, claim for relief	36	18	2	1
JACKSONTOWN, OHIO, relief of postmaster at	438	26	1	1
JEMISON & WILLIAMSON, claim for relief	991	25	2	1
JENKINS, JAMES H., claim for relief	179	27	3	1
Do	552	28	1	1
Do	97	31	2	2
JENKINS, WILLIAM R., claim for relief	395	28	1	1
JERSEY CITY, NEW JERSEY, mail route between Galway, Ireland, and, to establish	152	32	1	3
JOSSLYN, CHARLES, relief of sureties	167	21	1	1
KELLEY, BERNARD, claim for relief	2	21	2	1
Do	67	22	1	1
KELLY, JOHN, claim for relief	438	35	1	3
KERR, JOSEPH, claim for relief	73	33	2	2
KIMBALL & MOORE, claim for relief	270	25	1	3
KINNEY, PETER, claim for relief	5	31	1	2

* And views of minority.

Subject.	Report.	Congress.	Session.	Volume.
LLE, TENNESSEE, Blountville, Tenn., to re-establish four-horse line of mail coaches from, to	56	29	2	2
. E., claim for relief	206	46	3	5
DALL, NATHANIEL, claim for relief	547	28	1	1
Do	809	30	1	2
NGE, GERRIT, claim for relief	109	21	1	1
RANT TELEGRAPH LINES. (See TELEGRAPHS.)				
WORTH, SETH M., claim for relief	130	29	1	2
OF ABSENCE, letter carriers and postal clerks, granting to	*1276	48	1	6
LETTER-CANCELING AND POST-MARKING MACHINE, authorizing Postmaster-General to purchase and adopt	928	47	1	5
D, FRANCIS DE P., claim for relief	196	34	3	2
D, SAMUEL, claim for relief	1083	27	2	1
CARRIERS (see also POSTAL SERVICE),				
, establishing	*117	45	2	5
ralate postage on second-class matter at offices of	125	48	1	6
S (see also POSTAL SERVICE),				
ge on,				
om three to two cents, to reduce	1816	47	2	5
ngle letters to one cent, to reduce	124	47	1	5
reduce	909	25	2	1
Do	1101	27	2	1
Do	477	28	1	1
Do	462	28	1	1
Do	781	30	1	2
e conveyance, to prohibit transmission of, by	228	28	1	1
boats, to regulate charges for carrying on	315	30	1	2
y delivery of, to prohibit	65	20	2	1
Do	*271	21	1	1
mission of, providing for safe	72	17	1	1
COUNTY, OHIO, postmaster at Jacksontown, in, relief of	486	28	1	1
VING SERVICE, free through mail, all newspapers and periodicals addressed to members of, to pass	133	47	1	5
ER, HENRY, claim for relief	78	16	1	1
BE, JESSE, claim for relief	725	25	2	1
ELD, CONNECTICUT, post-route between Norfolk, Conn., and, to discontinue	163	19	1	1
ROCK, ARKANSAS, post-road from Chicot County, Ark., to, appropriation to make	218	21	1	1
Do	374	22	1	1
TON, THOMAS R., claim for relief	100	36	1	3
REET, GILBERT, claim for relief	670	24	1	1
IES, to prohibit mailing all matter concerning	826	48	1	6
Do	*2678	48	1	6
LLE, KENTUCKY,				
oute from Saint Louis, Mo., to, establishing	173	21	1	)
nd Mississippi Mail Line, for carrying mail between New Orleans, La., and, to pay	252	31	1	2
Do	142	33	1	2
HN, claim for relief	725	25	2	1
& EASTHAM, claim for relief	163	32	1	2
Do	130	33	1	2
Y, A. B., claim for relief	195	34	3	3
AN, JOHN, relief of sureties	1058	25	2	1
AN, JAMES A., claim for relief	374	29	1	2
N, THOMAS, claim for relief	874	27	2	1
HLIN, B., claim for relief	49	30	2	2
DUNNING R., claim for relief	472	28	1	1
Do	626	29	1	2
Do	250	31	1	2
JOHN, claim for relief	375	30	1	2
V. WILLIAM M. F., claim for relief	6	34	1	3
JOHN, claim for relief	626	24	1	1
Do	714	25	2	1
GS, Allen's patent air and water tight, introduction and use of	45	34	1	3
ACHES, passengers to be carried in, to restrict number of	898	25	2	1
NTRACTS, (see also, POSTAL SERVICE),				
ving of, to amend law relative to	711	46	2	5
g of, to regulate	712	46	2	5
ATTER,				
ng of,				
prohibit, by private conveyance	228	28	1	1
test J. W. Post's invention for	179	34	1	3
straining individuals and corporations from	135	35	2	3
ry of, to facilitate	503	49	1	6
Do	506	49	1	6
rding of,				
ird class, to amend law relating to	1553	48	1	6
urth class, to amend law relating to	1553	48	1	6

* And views of minority.

Subject.	Report.	Congress.	Session.	Volume.
MAIL MATTER—Continued.				
Handling of, to prevent unlawful	164	46	2	5
Newspapers, to permit publishers to send marked copies as second class	1546	48	1	6
Postage on,				
First class, fixing rate of	1976	48	1	6
Second class,				
To secure uniform rates of	48	46	3	5
Do	126	47	1	5
Do	125	48	1	6
Fixing rate of	101	48	1	6
To reduce rate of	2498	48	1	6
Fourth class, to increase rate of	1355	48	1	6
MAIL ROUTES, Philadelphia, Pa., and Baltimore, Md., to improve, between	51	19	1	1
MAIL SERVICE, establishment of, in States and Territories, to regulate	502	49	1	6
MAIL STEAM SERVICE, additional, on Pacific coast, to provide for	62	34	1	3
MAIL TRANSPORTATION. (*See* POSTAL SERVICE.)				
MAILS OF UNITED STATES, (*see also* POSTAL SERVICE,)				
MAILS,				
Arrival and departure of, to punish postmasters for making false certificates.	1531	47	1	5
Contracts for carrying, to regulate subletting	507	49	1	6
Failures of, between Boston, Mass., and Washington, D. C., fines imposed for.	265	22	1	1
Obscene matter through, to amend law relative to transmission of	2676	49	1	6
Robbery of, to prevent	72	17	1	1
Transportation in United States and Territories of, inquiry into manner of	*38	42	2	3
Do	775	43	1	3
Do	783	43	1	3
Transportation and delivery on Sunday of, to prohibit	65	20	2	1
Do	*271	21	1	1
MANN, R. F. M., claim for relief	264	35	1	3
MAPLESVILLE, ALABAMA, postmaster at, for special pay of	168	26	2	1
MEANS, GEORGE F., claim for relief	278	36	1	3
MEDICINES,				
To restrict use of mails for advertising	533	48	1	6
MEMPHIS, TENNESSEE, appropriation to improve post-road between Tuscumbia, Ala., and	293	21	1	1
MERCHANT VESSELS, to carry foreign mails	*534	49	1	6
METAL MAIL CHESTS, authorizing Postmaster-General to adopt	72	17	1	1
MEXICO, line of mail steamers between United States and, to authorize Carlos Butterfield *et al.* to establish	607	36	1	3
MICHIGAN SOUTHERN RAILROAD, claim for relief	159	32	1	2
MILEY, AARON, claim for relief	714	46	2	5
MILLS, ADAM L., claim for relief	146	28	1	1
MISSISSIPPI AND MISSOURI RAILROAD, to compensate, for carrying United States mails in State of Iowa previous to August 15, 1857	208	35	2	3
MITCHILL, SAMUEL L., claim for relief	261	34	3	3
MOBILE, ALABAMA, post-road to Pascagoula, Miss., from, to open	63	20	2	1
MONEY-ORDER OFFICES, making postal notes payable at	641	49	1	6
MONEY-ORDER SYSTEM, deposit of receipts in Treasury, providing for	626	48	1	6
MONEY ORDERS (*see also* POSTAL MONEY ORDERS),				
Forging of, to amend law prescribing penalty for	1542	47	1	5
Payment of, to amend law for	†472	48	1	6
MONOPOLY OF TELEGRAPHIC FACILITIES, additional legislation to prevent	3501	49	2	6
MONROE, URIAH P., claim for relief	100	33	2	2
MOORE & WALKER, claim for relief	270	35	1	3
MORDECAI, M. C., claim for relief	34	36	2	3
MORGAN CITY, LOUISIANA, to change name of Brashear, La., to	572	47	1	5
MORRIS, Mrs. A. E., claim for relief	265	35	1	3
Do	22	36	1	3
MORRIS, ROBERT H., relief of legal representative	265	35	1	3
Do	22	36	1	3
MOSS, WILLIAM, claim for relief	114	35	1	3
MOUNT VERNON ASSOCIATION, franking privilege to	136	35	2	3
MUNGER, ASA, claim for relief	626	24	1	1
Do	14	25	2	1
MURPHY, JOHN H., claim for relief	874	27	2	1
NANTUCKET STEAMBOAT COMPANY, claim for relief	641	25	2	
NATIONAL STEAMSHIP COMPANY, to authorize carrying of United States mails by	137	35	2	
NEVADA, mail route from Austin to Bernice, to establish	536	49	1	6
NEW ALBANY AND SALEM RAILROAD, mails in State of Indiana, to pay extra amount for carrying	252	35	2	
NEW ORLEANS, LOUISIANA,				
Mails from Mobile, Ala., to, to compensate contractors for carrying	63	20	2	
Ohio and Mississippi Mail Line for carrying mail between Louisville, Ky., and, to pay	252	31	1	
Do	143	33	1	
NEWSPAPERS,				
Life-Saving Service to pass free through mail, all addressed to members of	125	47	1	
Postage on, to reduce	909	25	2	

* And views of minority. † Parts 1, 2.

*And views of minority. †Parts 1, 2.

Subject.	Report.	Congress.	Session.	Volume.
POSTAGE—Continued.				
Newspapers as second-class mail matter, to permit publishers to send marked copies of	1546	48	1	6
Rates of, upon,				
First-class matter, to amend	1976	48	1	6
Fourth-class, to increase	1355	49	1	6
Legal matter, establishing	223	44	1	4
Letters, to reduce, from three to two cents	1816	47	2	5
Second-class matter,				
To secure uniform	48	46	2	5
Do	126	47	1	5
To fix rates upon	101	48	1	6
At letter-carriers' offices	125	48	1	6
Reduction of,				
To one cent on single letters	124	47	1	5
On second-class mail matter	2498	48	2	6
On letters and newspapers	731	30	1	2
On letters to one cent	124	47	1	5
Second-class mail matter,				
To secure uniform rates upon	48	46	2	5
Do	126	47	1	5
To fix rate upon	101	48	1	6
Do	2498	48	2	6
At letter-carriers' offices, to regulate rate on	125	48	1	6
Special delivery provided by payment of extra postage	29	48	1	6
Do	336	48	1	6
Specie payment of, enforced	1019	25	2	1
Steamboats, defining law for postage upon letters carried by	315	30	1	2
Uniform rates of, to establish	411	31	1	2
Do	49	32	1	2
POSTAL CARDS, providing for issue of, with flexible flaps	715	46	2	5
POSTAL MONEY-ORDER SYSTEM, reorganizing	927	47	1	5
POSTAL MONEY ORDERS,				
Fees on domestic, reduction of	378	49	1	6
Forging of, to amend law prescribing penalty for	1542	47	1	5
Do.	522	48	1	6
Receipts from, to deposit in Treasury	380	49	1	6
POSTAL NOTES, payable at any money-order office, and punish counterfeiting of.	641	49	1	6
POSTAL PENALTY ENVELOPES, time of, to amend law as to	506	48	1	6
POSTAL SAVINGS BANKS, to establish	473	47	1	5
POSTAL SERVICE,				
Clerks, leave of absence in each year to	*1276	48	1	6
Contracts,				
To release Post-Office Department from present contract for carrying Great Southern mail	171	30	1	2
To fulfill contract with Ohio and Mississippi Mail Line	252	31	1	2
Do	142	31	1	2
To investigate, made by Post-Office Department for carrying mails in United States and Territories	*38	42	2	3
Do	775	43	1	3
Do	783	43	1	3
To authorize Postmaster-General to make contract with certain companies in Saint Louis, Mo., for carrying United States mails	710	46	2	5
To amend law relative to	711	46	2	5
To regulate letting of mail	712	46	2	5
To amend law regulating	1702	47	1	5
To pay Southern contractors	1051	48	1	6
To regulate letting of	1052	48	1	6
To regulate subletting	507	49	1	6
Employés in, relief of disabled	535	49	1	6
Foreign,				
Mail route between United States and Europe	476	29	1	2
Route between United States and South America and West Indies	261	34	3	3
Mail routes between United States and Great Britain	137	35	2	3
Carlos Butterfield, *et al.*, to establish line of mail steamers between United States and Mexico	607	36	1	3
To forfeit contract with Pacific Mail Steamship Company for carrying United States mails between United States and China	†598	42	1	3
Mail routes between United States and Brazil	*346	45	2	5
Transportation of United States mails between Galveston, Tex., and Vera Cruz, Mexico	†886	45	2	5
Requiring mails to be carried in American-built ships	1570	46	2	5
Mail routes between United States and foreign countries	542	47	1	5
Inquiring into management of	1087	49	1	6
Foreign mails, merchant vessels to carry	*534	49	1	6
Free delivery,				
Pay of letter-carriers in	*117	45	2	5
To extend benefits of	87	46	2	5
To extend system of	2215	49	1	6
Letter carriers,				
To regulate pay of	411	47	1	5

* And views of minority. † Parts 1, 2.

Subject.	Report.	Congress.	Session.	Volume.
POSTAL SERVICE—Continued.				
Letter carriers,				
Leave of absence in each year to	*1276	48	1	6
To extend system of	2808	48	2	6
Letters, safe transmission of	72	17	1	1
Mail messengers, employment of	2267	49	1	6
Railway,				
To pay Mississippi and Missouri Railroad for carrying United States mails in Iowa previous to August 15, 1857	286	35	2	2
To pay New Albany and Salem Railroad extra compensation for carrying United States mails in Indiana	263	35	2	3
Thomas P. Chaney, charges against	123	45	3	5
To pay Burlington, Cedar Rapids and Northern Railroad for carrying United States mails	56	46	3	5
Do	341	47	1	5
To pay Chicago, Burlington and Quincy Railroad for carrying United States mails	1257	46	2	5
Do	342	47	1	5
To fix salaries of employés in	1287	46	2	5
Do	412	47	1	5
Do	826	48	1	6
To compensate railroad companies for apartment service	2264	49	1	6
Do	3303	49	1	6
Regulations,				
Defining law for carrying United States mails on steamboats	318	30	1	2
To test invention of John W. Post for carrying mail matter	179	34	1	3
Expediency of reforming	66	36	1	3
To authorize United States mails to be carried free of toll over roads in Indiana	168	46	2	5
Unlawful handling of mail matter	164	46	2	5
Issue of special-request envelopes	177	46	2	5
Uniform rates on second-class mail matter	48	46	3	5
Postmaster-General in certain cases to extend post-routes	1532	47	1	5
Violation of certain laws a misdemeanor	1587	47	1	5
To restrict use of mails for advertising medicines, &c	523	48	1	6
To prohibit use of mails for lottery advertisements	836	48	1	6
Do	*2678	49	1	6
To facilitate delivery of mail matter	568	49	1	6
Do	506	49	1	6
Routes,				
Austin to Bernice, Nev	536	49	1	6
Blountsville to Knoxville, Tenn	56	29	2	2
From Louisville, Ky., to Saint Louis, Mo	173	21	1	1
Management of	731	30	1	2
Postmaster-General in certain cases to extend	1532	47	1	5
To establish, on Puget's Sound	172	34	1	3
From Sacramento, Cal., to Olympia, Wash. Ter	512	36	1	3
States and Territories, to regulate establishment of	502	49	1	6
Special delivery, to amend act for	1259	49	1	6
Star routes,				
Deficiency in appropriation for	1701	47	1	5
Compensation for increased speed in carrying mails on	1871	47	2	5
Contracts for carrying mails on certain	1931	47	2	5
Steamship, to provide for additional, on Pacific coast	62	34	1	3
POSTAL TELEGRAPHS,				
Appropriations to test Richardson's Atmospheric Telegraph	196	34	1	3
Establishing system of	32	40	3	3
Do	137	46	3	5
Do	2004	47	2	5
Do	1436	48	1	6
POSTMASTER-GENERAL.				
American-built vessels, contract for carrying United States mails in	1570	46	2	5
Annual reports of, to amend law relative to	2342	49	1	6
Claims of certain postmasters, to adjust	2994	49	1	6
Fire in Post-Office Department, examination of, relative to	134	24	2	1
Leavitt letter canceling and post-marking machine, to adopt and purchase	928	47	1	5
Mail routes, violations of postal laws, in establishment of private	228	28	1	1
Post-Office Department, to dispose of useless papers in	17	46	2	5
Post-offices of first, second, and third class, lease premises for	1275	48	1	6
Post-routes, to extend, in certain cases	1532	47	1	5
Post-routes, communication from, relative to establishment of new	964	25	2	1
Do	524	26	1	1
Richard Imlay's patent metal mail-case, authorized to use	72	17	1	1
Richmond, Fredericksburg and Potomac Railroad, for carrying great Southern mail, contract with	171	30	1	2
Saint Louis, Mo., contract with certain companies for carrying United States mails in	710	46	2	5
Salaries of certain postmasters, to authorize him to readjust	747	47	1	5
Specie payment of postage, communication from, relating to enforced	1019	25	2	1
Warrants, to delegate authority to sign	206	47	1	5

* And views of minority.

Subject.	Report.	Congress.	Session.	Volume.
POSTMASTERS,				
Claims of, for loss by burglary, fire, and other unavoidable casualties, to adjust	128	47	1	5
Classification and compensation of, to regulate (Revised Statutes 3860)	3970	49	2	6
Clerk hire, to regulate allowance for	379	49	1	6
Compensation for fourth-class, to fix	127	47	1	5
Election of, by the people	584	49	1	6
False certificate of arrival and departure of mails, to punish, for making	1531	47	1	5
Jacksontown, Ohio, for relief of postmaster	438	32	1	1
Mapleville, Ala., special appropriation for pay of postmaster at	168	32	2	[illegible]
Newspapers and periodicals at county seats of justice, to authorize them to receive subscriptions for	325	30	1	[illegible]
Claims of certain, Postmaster-General to adjust	2494	49	1	[illegible]
Salaries of, to adjust	167	46	2	[illegible]
Do	1786	46	2	[illegible]
Do	1969	47	2	[illegible]
Do	2376	49	1	6
Salaries of certain, to authorize Postmaster-General to readjust	747	47	1	5
Washington, D. C., to fix salary of postmaster at	1417	46	2	5
POST-OFFICE AND POST-ROADS COMMITTEE. (*See* COMMITTEE ON POST-OFFICE AND POST-ROADS.)				
POST-OFFICE DEPARTMENT,				
Abolishing of	135	25	2	2
Accountability of, for more effectual	450	22	1	1
Amount paid into Treasury by	285	22	1	1
Annual appropriations for year ending June 30, 1888	3653	49		6
Clerks in,				
Appropriation for employment of extra	122	21		1
Additional allowance to	630	25		1
Conduct and management of	*814	44	1	4
Conflagration in, cause of	134	24	2	1
Contracts for carrying mails in United States and Territories, made by	*38	43	2	3
Do	775	43	1	3
Do	783	43	1	3
Correspondence division in, to reorganize	3021	49	2	6
Disposal of useless papers in	17	46	2	5
Execution not to issue against officers of	1538	47	1	5
Management of	361	21	1	1
Do	524	28	1	1
Do	477	28	1	2
Do	731	30	1	2
Organization of, to authorize changes in	2743	49	1	6
Revised Statutes, section 5480, to correct irror of word in	1541	47	1	5
POST-OFFICE INSPECTOR, prescribing penalty for personating	1540	47	1	5
POST-OFFICES,				
Appropriation for year ending June 30, 1887	720	49	1	6
Appropriation for year ending June 30, 1888	3653	49	2	6
Boston, Mass., to prevent removal of, at	658	36	1	3
Boston, Mass., and New York city for, to investigate construction of buildings at	*58	41	3	[illegible]
Clerk-hire in, to reduce expense of	68	36	1	[illegible]
Delivery of letters from, to prohibit, Sunday	65	20	2	[illegible]
Do	*271	21	1	[illegible]
Delivery of mail matter at, to facilitate	503	49	1	[illegible]
Establishment of, in States and Territories, to regulate	502	49	1	[illegible]
Expenses of third-class, to regulate	381	49	1	[illegible]
Fraudulent, to prescribe penalty for keeping	[illegible]	[illegible]	1	[illegible]
Do	1982	47	[illegible]	[illegible]
Do	1109	48	1	[illegible]
Naming of, to regulate	505	49	1	[illegible]
New York city, to erect new post-office at	58	46	[illegible]	[illegible]
Philadelphia post-office, to make additional appropriation for site of	609	36	[illegible]	[illegible]
Postmaster-General to lease premises for, first, second, and third-class	1275	48	1	[illegible]
POST-ROADS,				
Chickasaw Nation, appropriation to improve post-road through lands of	[illegible]	[illegible]	1	1
Chicot County to Little Rock, Ark., appropriation to make post-road from	218	21	2	1
Do	374	22	1	[illegible]
Establishment of additional	361	21	1	[illegible]
Do	964	25	2	[illegible]
Do	524	26	1	[illegible]
Fort Smith, Ark., and San Diego, Cal., to establish	95	21	2	[illegible]
Litchfield and Norfolk, Conn., to discontinue post-route between	163	19	1	[illegible]
Louisville, Ky., to Saint Louis, Mo., to grant land in aid of post-road from	173	21	[illegible]	[illegible]
Mobile, Ala., to Pascagoula, Miss., to open, from	63	20	[illegible]	[illegible]
Philadelphia, Pa., and Baltimore, Md., to improve mail route between	51	19	1	[illegible]
Private, suppression of	228	28	1	[illegible]
Public roads and highways, post-roads, to make all	27	45	2	[illegible]
Wheeling bridges, post-routes and military roads, declaring	*158	32	1	[illegible]
PRIVATE LETTER BOXES. (*See* FRAUDULENT POST-OFFICES.)				
PRIVATE POST ROUTES, means for suppression of	228	28	1	1

* And views of minority.

Subject.	Report.	Congress.	Session.	Volume.
JOHN, claim for relief	549	26	1	1
SOUND (Washington Territory), mail route on	173	34	1	3
& STOKES, claim for relief	858	27	2	1
ES, SAMUEL (mail contract), claim for relief	167	26	2	1
ADS, to regulate compensation of, for transportation of mails	825	48	1	6
AY MAIL SERVICE. (*See* POSTAL SERVICE.)				
AY POSTAL CLERKS, to allow traveling expenses to	61	48	1	6
, THOMAS, claim for relief	261	34	2	3
, WILLIAM H., claim for relief	2195	48	2	6
, MARY, claim for relief	151	32	1	2
ERED LETTERS, to amend law for delivery of	*472	48	1	6
D STATUTES, to amend or repeal,				
on 969, execution not to issue against officers of Post Office Department	1536	47	1	5
on 3829, post-offices	1862	47	2	5
Do	1199	48	1	6
on 3860, post-office expenses	581	48	1	6
on 3893, obscene matter	1539	47	1	5
on 3940, forwarding mail matter	1553	48	1	6
on 3949, mail contracts	711	46	2	5
on 3958, mail contracts	1702	47	1	5
on 3961, mail contracts	1701	47	1	5
on 5463, postal money-orders	522	48	1	6
on 5463, postal crimes	1543	47	1	5
on 5480, Post-Office Department, to amend law relative to	1541	47	1	5
, THOMAS, claim for relief	131	30	1	2
& AUSTILL, claim for relief	745	25	2	1
Do	144	25	3	1
Do	325	26	1	1
DSON'S ATMOSPHERIC TELEGRAPH, appropriation to experiment with	198	34	1	3
S. and M., claim for relief	101	27	2	1
ND, FREDERICKSBURG AND POTOMAC RAILROAD AND STEAMBOAT COMPANY, authorizing the Postmaster-General to make contract with, for carrying Great Southern Mail	171	30	1	2
CS, JOHN S., for relief of executors	457	35	1	3
ON, JAMES H., claim for relief	164	32	1	2
ON, JOHN, claim for relief	161	28	2	1
, E. G. and L. F., claim for relief	193	34	2	3
JOHN B., claim for relief	118	35	1	3
D., claim for relief	846	27	2	1
TREE, FRANCIS, claim for relief	627	25	2	1
AGENTS, to curtail expenses of	68	36	1	3
, ELLIOTT, claim for relief	57	18	1	1
MENTO, CALIFORNIA, mail route from, to Olympia, Wash	512	36	1	3
LOUIS, MISSOURI,				
in aid of post-road between Louisville, Ky., and	173	21	1	1
aster-General to make contract with certain companies for carrying United States mails at	710	46	2	5
ES OF POSTMASTERS. (*See* POSTMASTERS.)				
RSH, ORLANDO, claim for relief	102	30	1	2
RSH & OVERTON, claim for relief	180	27	3	1
NS, ALLEN, claim for relief	166	26	2	1
GO, CALIFORNIA, proposal of William Bayard to establish post-road from Fort Smith, Ark., to	95	31	2	2
ANCISCO, CALIFORNIA, additional mail steam service from, to Oregon	62	34	1	3
, LORENZO P., claim for relief	610	36	1	3
ER, CHRISTIAN, claim for relief	394	26	1	1
JOHN, claim for relief	158	36	1	3
WILLIAM H., claim for relief	94	31	2	2
ON, JOHN H., claim for relief	174	34	1	3
, DANIEL, & Co., claim for relief	99	33	2	2
S & PENNOCK, claim for relief	491	28	1	1
Do	67	28	2	1
Do	220	29	1	2
, JOHN G., claim for relief	456	35	1	3
, JOHN Y., claim for relief	188	36	1	3
, JACOB (assignee), pay for use of Norton's marking and canceling stamp	98	39	1	3
DAVID, claim for relief	121	30	2	2
RD & CALDWELL, claim for relief	120	34	3	3
OOD, SAMUEL, claim for relief	8	33	2	2
UDITOR, to define duties of	654	47	1	5
KER, SAMUEL R., claim for relief	845	27	2	1
ELISHA, claim for relief	231	24	2	1
GEORGE R., claim for relief	717	29	1	2
Do	103	30	1	2
JOHN, claim for relief	813	25	2	1
LEWIS, claim for relief	110	31	1	2
P., claim for relief	3	46	1	5

*Parts 1, 2.

* And views of minority. † Parts 1, 2.

Subject.	Report.	Congress.	Session.	Volume.
CE, ROSA, claim for relief	1471	49	1	6
JOHN M., claim for relief	34	45	2	5
NTS, Postmaster-General to delegate authority to sign	206	47	1	5
NGTON, D. C.,				
re of mail between Boston, Mass., and	269	23	1	1
y of postmaster at	1417	46	2	5
NGTON TERRITORY, mail route on Puget Sound, in	172	34	1	3
JOSIAH H., claim for relief	183	21	1	1
Do	77	22	1	1
WILLIAM H., claim for relief	261	34	3	3
NDIES, ocean mail steam service between United States and	261	34	3	3
ING AND BELMONT BRIDGE COMPANY, memorial to Congress of, to make Wheeling Bridge a post-route	*156	32	1	2
ING BRIDGE, to make post-route of	*156	32	1	2
, FIELDING L., claim for relief	140	21	1	1
, RICHARD, claim for relief	8	23	2	2
EN LEGAL MATTER, fixing rate of postage on	223	44	1	4
JOHN V. N., claim for relief	112	21	1	1
Do	389	21	1	1
, JOSEPH, claim for relief	113	20	1	1
Do	164	21	1	1
RMAN, J. P., claim for relief	8	46	1	5

* And views of minority.

REPORTS

OF THE

MMITTEE ON PRINTING,

HOUSE OF REPRESENTATIVES,

FROM THE FOURTEENTH CONGRESS, 1815, TO
FORTY-NINTH CONGRESS, 1887, INCLUSIVE.

IN ONE VOLUME.

MPILED, UNDER THE DIRECTION OF THE JOINT COMMITTEE ON PRINTING,

BY

T. H. McKEE,

Clerk, Document Room, United States Senate.

WASHINGTON:
GOVERNMENT PRINTING OFFICE.
1887.

9228 PR H

[PUBLIC RESOLUTION—No. 24.]

Joint resolution authorizing the preparation of a compilation of the reports of mittees of the Senate and House of Representatives.

Resolved by the Senate and House of Representatives of the Ui States of America in Congress assembled, That there be prepared u the direction of the Joint Committee of Printing, a compilation of reports of the Senate and House of Representatives from the I teenth to the Forty-eighth Congress, inclusive, classified by commit arranged, indexed, and bound in suitable volumes for the use of standing committees of the two Houses of Congress. And the su seven thousand seven hundred and fifty dollars, or so much there may be found necessary, is hereby appropriated out of any mone the Treasury not otherwise appropriated, for the preparation of work, which sum may be paid by the Secretary of the Treasury the order of the chairman of said Joint Committee, as additional p compensation to any officer or employee of the United States.

Resolved further, That the Clerk of the House and Secretary of Senate be, and they are hereby directed, to procure and file, for the of their respective Houses, copies of all reports made by each com tee of all succeeding Congresses; and that the Clerk of the House the Secretary of the Senate be, and they are hereby, authorized directed at the close of each session of Congress, to cause said rep to be indexed and bound, one copy to be deposited in the librar each House and one copy in the room of the committee from which reports emanated.

Approved, July 29, 1886.

COMPILER'S NOTICE.

This compilation embraces all the printed reports made by both Houses of Congress from the commencement of the Fourteenth to the close of the Forty-ninth Congress. They are classified by committees and arranged in numerical order. The collection for each committee is divided into volumes of suitable size. Each committee has a separate index, a copy being bound in each volume.

The SPECIAL and SELECT reports are all compiled in one collection having one index, a copy of which is bound in each volume.

The plan throughout the compilation is to place each report to the committee from which it was reported, without reference to the subject-matter.

The House and Senate reports are compiled separately. Care will be required in noticing the chronological order, as in some instances an entire session or Congress may not appear in certain volumes from the fact that during this period no reports were made by this committee.

T. H. McKEE.

INDEX

TO

'RTS OF THE COMMITTEE ON PRINTING,

HOUSE OF REPRESENTATIVES.

FROM 1815 TO 1887.

Subject.	Report.	Congress.	Session.	Volume.
TURAL REPORTS, printing of, for 1883	2008	47	2	1
Turner's, L. M., report on, authorizing printing of	3060	49	1	1
OF CONGRESS, purchase of additional number of	113	37	2	1
MICAL OBSERVATIONS, observations for years 1883, 1884, and 1885, inting of	837	49	1	1
(*See* PRINTING AND BINDING.)				
IK. (*See* OFFICIAL REGISTER.)				
F MEDICAL EXPERTS, report of, printing of	1749	47	1	1
VS. (*See* PUBLIC DOCUMENTS.)				
OF ANIMAL INDUSTRY,				
nual report of, publication of	2213½	49	1	1
annual report of, printing of	3906	49	2	1
OF EDUCATION, annual report of Commissioner of Education for 84-'85, printing of	1635	49	1	1
OF ENGRAVING AND PRINTING, payment of wages to female nployés in	1733	46	2	1
OF ETHNOLOGY, annual bulletins of, printing of	964	48	1	1
Do	1330	49	1	1
OF NAVIGATION, navigation and customs laws issued by, printing of	612	49	1	1
UE OF GOVERNMENT PUBLICATIONS, to print, from 1870 to ite	319	46	3	1
REEDING AND DAIRY FARMING, consular reports upon, printing of	943	49	1	1
)	80	37	2	1
third, fourth, and tenth censuses of United States, schedules of, nding of	2206	49	1	1
, printing and binding of	3	32	2	1
statistics of population for use of Interior Department, printing of	909	47	1	1
reports of tenth	1784	47	1	1
dium of, printing of additional copies of tenth	2008	47	2	1
IAL COMMISSION, publication of additional copies of reports of	265	46	2	1
ommissioners of, extra copies of cases rejected by	2	44	1	1
. M. (Congressional Printer), bid for publishing the debates of Congress	75	42	3	1
D, flora of, printing of 5,000 copies of the	1747	47	1	1
ONER OF AGRICULTURE,				
tional Sheep and Wool Exposition, printing report of, on	1382	49	1	1
report of, to print	3996	49	2	1
ONERS OF CLAIMS, extra copies of cases rejected by	2	44	1	1
EE REPORTS,				
ition of the reports of committees of the Senate and House of Representatives	2157	48	1	1
Do	2158	48	1	1
Do	3362	49	1	1
ing rule for printing of	989	49	1	1
;.				
d plates withheld from, custody of	179	28	2	1
tion in newspapers the proceedings of	576	46	2	1
ition of surplus journals of	2618	48	2	1
SIONAL GLOBE, contract with, for public printing	26	41	2	1

Subject.	Report.	Congress.	Session.	Volume.
CONGRESSIONAL RECORD,				
Reporting and publishing debates of Congress in, payments made for	23	42	2	1
Investigations of cost of publishing debates of Congress in	641	43	1	1
Daily copies to be furnished foreign legations in Washington, D. C., of	397	46	3	1
Free distribution of	1751	47	1	1
Furnished each United States legation abroad	284	48	1	1
Do	942	49	1	1
Distribution to States and Territories of copy of	174	49	1	1
CONSULAR AND DIPLOMATIC SERVICE, Daily Congressional Record to each United States legation abroad	284	48	1	1
Do	942	49	1	1
CONSULAR REPORTS, printing of reports relative to cattle-breeding and dairy farming	943	49	1	1
DAIRY FARMING, reports of consuls on, printing of	943	49	1	1
DEBATES OF CONGRESS,				
Investigating cost of publishing	641	43	1	1
Publication of, by contract	75	42	3	1
Reporting and publishing, payment for	23	42	2	1
To prohibit the publication of, at public expense	573	46	2	1
DEPARTMENT OF INTERIOR,				
Stationery contracts made by, investigation of	15	49	3	1
Copies of statistics of population to	909	47	1	1
DISTRICT OF COLUMBIA,				
Advertising for proposals in the	1785	47	1	1
Report of the health officer of, extra copies of the	3553	49	2	1
Do	4041	49	2	1
EDUCATION. (*See* BUREAU OF EDUCATION.)				
EMORY'S REPORTS, printing and distribution of, investigating the	390	30	1	1
EMPLOYÉS,				
Government Printing Office, pay of	199	45	2	1
Do	1752	47	1	1
Granting pay for legal holidays to	585	46	2	1
Pay for loss time during Garfield obsequies to, of Government Printing Office	166	47	1	1
Granting leave of absence annually to same	2429	48	2	1
Do	188	49	1	1
ENGRAVED PLATES, investigation of withholding from Congress the custody of	179	28	2	1
ENGRAVING AND PRINTING. (*See* BUREAU OF ENGRAVING AND PRINTING.)				
ENTOMOLOGICAL COMMISSION, Riley's report upon grasshoppers, printing of additional copies of	575	46	2	1
EUROPEAN DOCK-YARDS, report of Naval Constructor Philip Hichborn on, printing of	570	49	1	1
FISH AND FISHERIES, reports on, printing of	1605	47	1	1
FISHERIES, report of Senate Committee on Foreign Relations on, additional copies of, printing of	3993	49	2	1
FLAGS OF MARITIME NATIONS, printing 3,000 copies of	1758	47	1	1
FLORA OF COLORADO, printing of 5,000 copies of	1747	47	1	1
FOREIGN LEGATIONS, copies of Daily Congressional Record to, in Washington, D. C	397	46	3	1
FOREIGN RELATIONS, Senate Committee on, of report of, on fisheries, additional copies	3995	49	2	
FRANCE, statement of payment of awards under treaty with, printing of	1302	49	1	
FRENCH SPOLIATION CLAIMS, list of claimants for, printing of	2493	48	2	
GARFIELD, JAMES A., memorial address on, printing of	1712	47	1	
GEOLOGICAL SURVEY,				
Clarence King's geological report, cost of printing	64	42	2	
Clarence King's geological explorations, printing of additional copies	574	46	2	
Annual report of, printing of	963	48	1	
Authorizing reports for distribution, printing of	1331	49	1	
GLOBE BUILDING, rental of, for storage of material from Government Printing Office	884	49	1	
GOVERNMENT PRINTING OFFICE,				
Establishment of	139	15	2	
Do	*425	26	1	
Management of, investigation of	495	44	1	
Enlargement of building	30	44	2	1
Removal and proper storage of material from	884	49	1	1
Binding, investigating the binding by agreement or contract of public documents	665	20	1	1
Employés in,				
Regulating and establishing salaries of	199	45	2	
Do	1752	47	1	
Granting pay for legal holidays to	585	46	2	
Payment for loss time during Garfield obsequies	166	47		
Granting annual leave of absence to	2429	48	2	
Do	188	49	1	1
Leaves of absence, granting to employés	2429	48	2	1
Do	188	49	1	1
Legal holidays, granting pay to employés for	585	46	2	1
Salaries in, establishing and regulating of employés'	199	45	2	1
Do	1752	47		1

* Views of minority.

Subject.	Report.	Congress.	Session.	Volume.
[M]ENT PUBLICATIONS (*see also* PUBLIC DOCUMENTS), authorizing				
[th]e printing from 1870 to date of	319	46	2	1
[HO]PPERS (*see also* ROCKY MOUNTAIN LOCUST), Professor Riley's report				
[u]pon, additional copies of	575	46	2	1
[E]XPEDITION, printing reports of	634	49	1	1
Do	1884	49	1	1
OFFICER OF DISTRICT OF COLUMBIA, extra copies of the re-				
[p]ort of	2558	49	2	1
Do	4041	49	2	1
[C]apt. M. A., cruise of revenue steamer Corwin, printing of reports of,				
[i]n the	4066	49	2	1
[...]S. (*See* LEGAL HOLIDAYS.)				
[...]NGS COMMISSION, report of	399	46	2	1
[O]F REPRESENTATIVES,				
[...]ation, indexing, and binding of reports from committees of	2157	48	1	1
Do	2156	48	1	1
Do	3362	48	1	1
[...]ting rule for printing of committee reports of	989	49	1	1
[...]R DEPARTMENT,				
[...]gation of stationery contracts	15	40	3	1
[...]e to furnishing copies of statistics of population to	969	47	1	1
[INTERNA]TIONAL LAW, Wharton's digest of, publication of	3140	48	1	1
[INTERNA]TIONAL POLAR EXPEDITION. (*See* GREELY EXPEDITION.)				
[INTERNA]TIONAL SHEEP AND WOOL SHOW, report of Commissioner of				
[A]griculture on printing of	1382	49	1	1
[...]ATION,				
[...]ts, relating to contracts for stationery in the Interior Department	15	40	3	1
[...] of Congress, on cost of publishing	641	48	1	1
[...]s reports, relating to printing and distribution of	380	39	1	1
[...]ment Printing Office, of management of affairs in	496	44	1	1
[...] Department, stationery contracts made by	15	40	3	1
[...]ery, concerning contracts made by Interior Department, for	15	40	3	1
[...]D STEEL, tests of, distribution of reports on	309	47	1	1
[...]S OF CONGRESS, surplus copies of, distribution of	2018	48	2	1
[...], JOSEPH C. G., claim for relief	50	39	1	1
[...]LARENCE) REPORTS,				
printing	84	42	2	1
[...]nal copies of, printing of	574	46	2	1
[...]TOWERS, bid of, for publication of debates of Congress	75	42	3	1
[L]ANKLIN BAY EXPEDITION. (*See* GREELY EXPEDITION.)				
[...]ION, Alexander's survey of, printing of	1578	46	2	1
[...]E'S UNITED STATES GOVERNMENT, purchase of additional				
[co]pies of	1734	46	2	1
Do	1746	47	1	1
[CO]MMISSION. (*See* PUBLIC LAND COMMISSION.)				
[...]WS, codification of	400	46	3	1
[...]VERNING PUBLIC PRINTING, compilation of	398	46	3	1
[...]OF ABSENCE, employés in Government Printing Office annual, grant-				
[in]g to	2429	48	2	1
Do	188	49	1	1
[...]OLIDAYS, employés in Government Printing Office for, granting pay				
[...]	585	46	2	1
[...] and water transportation, preparation of	468	47	1	1
[...]ITED STATES, additional copies of	4040	49	2	1
[...] AND SURGICAL HISTORY OF THE WAR, extra copies of, re-				
[pr]inting of	1579	46	2	1
[...] EXPERTS, report of, printing of	1749	47	1	1
[...] OF CONGRESS, distribution of documents to members of Forty-				
[ei]ghth Congress	2619	48	2	1
[...]Y AND NAVY BULLETINS, printing of certain	2492	48	2	1
[...]Y CONFERENCES, reports of, for years 1878 and 1881, printing and				
[di]stribution	835	49	1	1
[...]H, W. J., bid of, for publication of debates of Congress	75	42	3	1
[...]L ACADEMY OF SCIENCES, annual report of, printing of	3934	49	2	1
[O]BSERVATORY, astronomical and meteorological observations for				
[y]ears 1883, 1884, and 1885, annual volumes, printing of	837	49	1	1
[...]ION AND CUSTOMS LAWS, printing of the	612	49	1	1
[...]D MILITARY BULLETINS, printing of certain	2492	48	2	1
[...]ERS, proceedings of Congress in, publication of	576	46	2	1
REGISTER,				
[...]ation of	965	48	1	1
Do	2380	48	2	1
Do	569	49	1	1
Do	3552	49	2	1
[...]ng designated depositories with copies of	569	49	1	1
[...]ULTURE, report of the Agricultural Department on insects affect-				
[in]g, revised edition of	4148	49	2	1
[...]E AND WAR SHIPS, additional reports of Select Committee on,				
[pr]inting of	567	49	1	1
[...] THOMAS A., bid of, for publication of debates of Congress	75	42	3	1
[...]OFFICE, copies of, report for 1860 destroyed by fire	53	37	2	1

Subject.	Report.	Congress.	Session.	Volume.
PATENT OFFICE REPORTS, delay in printing mechanical portion of, inquiring into cause of	62	36	2	1
POSTAL LAWS, publication of	568	43	1	1
PRINTING and BINDING, schedules for, second, third, fourth, and tenth censuses of the United States, binding of	2208	49	1	1
PROPOSALS, advertising of, for the District of Columbia	1765	47	1	1
PUBLIC DOCUMENTS,				
Agricultural reports, providing for printing reports for 1863	2008	47	2	1
Facilities for the more rapid printing of	95	30	1	1
Suspend printing of	378	35	1	1
Delay in printing certain reports, cause of	150	45	3	1
Distribution of documents to members of Forty-eighth Congress	2619	48	2	1
Agricultural Department, revised edition of report of, on insects affecting the orange culture, printing of	4148	49	2	1
Agriculture, Commissioner of, to print annual report of	3909	49	2	1
Alaska, printing of Turner's report on	3920	49	1	1
Annals of Congress, to purchase additional number of	113	37	2	1
Astronomical observations, printing observations for years 1883, 1884, and 1885	697	49	1	1
Binding of, investigation relative to contract or agreement for	665	39	1	1
Bulletins,				
Annual bulletins of Bureau of Ethnology, printing of	964	48	1	1
Do	1230	49	1	1
Military and Navy bulletins, printing of certain	2402	48	2	1
Bureau of Animal Industry,				
First annual report of, publication of	2213	49	1	1
Fourth annual report of, printing of	3906	49	2	1
Bureau of Education, annual report of Commissioner of Education for 1884–'85, printing of	1625	49	1	1
Bureau of Ethnology, annual bulletins of, printing of	964	48	1	1
Do	1230	49	1	1
Catalogue of, from 1870 to date, printing of	319	46	3	1
Census,				
Statistics of population for use of Interior Department, printing of	909	47	1	1
Reports of tenth, printing of	1784	47	1	1
Compendium of the tenth census, additional copies of	2008	47	2	1
Census schedules, second, third, fourth, and tenth censuses of the United States, binding of	2208	49	1	1
Clarence King's reports,				
Cost of printing	64	42	2	1
Additional copies of	574	46	2	1
Committee reports,				
Compilation of	2137	48	1	1
Do	2158	46	1	1
Do	3362	49	1	1
Regulating rule for printing of	989	48	1	1
Congressional Record,				
Payments made for publishing debates in	23	42	2	1
Investigation of cost of publishing debates	641	43	1	1
Foreign legations in Washington, D. C., to be furnished daily copies of	307	46	3	1
Providing for free distribution of	1751	47	1	1
Each United States legation abroad to be furnished with copy	284	48	1	1
Do	942	49	1	1
Providing for distribution to designated corporations, institutions, &c., in each State and Territory with copy of	174	48	1	1
Dairy farming, additional copies of consular reports on, printing of	948	49	1	1
Debates in Congress,				
Payments for reporting and publishing	23	42	2	1
Publication of, by contract	75	42	3	1
Investigating cost of publishing	641	43	1	1
Publication of	573	46	2	1
District of Columbia, extra copies of report of health officer of	2563	49	2	1
Do	4041	49	2	1
European dock-yards, report of Naval Constructor Philip Hichbornon, printing of	670	49	1	1
Fish and fisheries, reports on, printing of	1085	47	1	1
Fisheries, report of Senate Committee on Foreign Relations on, additional copies of	3995	49	2	1
Flags of maritime nations, printing 3,000 copies	1759	47	1	1
Flora of Colorado, printing of 5,000 copies of	1747	47	1	1
French spoliation, list of claimants, printing of	2493	48	2	1
Garfield, James A., memorial address of James G. Blaine on, printing of	1742	47	1	1
Geological surveys,				
Cost of printing Clarence King's report on his	64	42	2	1
Additional copies of King's geological explorations, printing of	574	46	2	1
Authorizing printing of annual reports of	989	48	1	1
Do	1231	49	1	1
Grasshoppers, additional copies of Professor Riley's report on, printing of	575	46	2	1
Healy, Capt. M. A., reports of, upon cruise of revenue steamer Corwin	4036	49	2	1
Lady Franklin Bay. (*See* GREELY EXPEDITION.)				
Greely expedition, reports of, printing of	894	48	1	1
Do	1634	48	1	1

Subject.	Report.	Congress.	Session.	Volume.
DOCUMENTS—Continued.				
...ringe Commission, report of	[illegible]	42	2	1
...ational law, Wharton's digest of, publication of	2149	45	1	1
...ational Sheep and Wool Show, report of Commissioner of Agriculture ...n, printing of	1282	48	1	1
...geological explorations,				
...st of printing	68	42	2	1
...dditional copies of, printing of	578	46	2	1
...ds of Congress, distribution of surplus of	2018	45	2	1
...tore's United States Government, purchase of copies of	1734	46	2	1
Do	1746	47	1	1
...ommission, report of, distribution of	99	49	1	1
...aws, codification of	690	46	2	1
...overning public printing, compilation of printing of	365	48	2	1
...United States, additional copies of	4050	49	2	1
...l and Surgical History of the War, extra copies of, reprinting of	1572	46	2	1
...l experts, report of	1749	47	1	1
...y and naval bulletins, printing of certain	2627	48	2	1
...ary conferences, reports for years 1878 and 1881 of, printing and distri...ution of	525	49	1	1
...al Academy of Sciences, annual report of	[illegible]	47	2	1
...ation and customs laws, printing of	912	48	1	1
...nd military bulletins, printing of certain	3482	48	2	1
...Register,				
...stribution of surplus copies of	286	45	1	1
Do	2607	45	2	1
Do	568	46	1	1
Do	3352	49	2	1
...pplying designated depositories with copies of	588	48	1	1
...ce and War Ships, Select Committee on, printing of additional reports ...f	567	49	1	1
...Office report,				
...se of delay in printing mechanical portion of	63	36	2	1
...pies of report for 1860, destroyed by fire, to furnish	52	37	2	1
...laws, publication of	568	49	1	1
...printing, laws governing printing of	398	46	3	1
...Mountain locust, additional copies of Professor Riley's report upon, ...rinting of	575	46	2	1
...Commander, additional copies of report on Greely search expedition, ...rinting of	4106	49	2	1
...h census, printing and binding of	3	32	2	1
...nal Alexander's survey of Lakes Union and Washington for, printing of	1578	46	2	1
...Office, reports of, printing of	96	48	1	1
...onian Institution, annual reports of, additional printing of	941	49	1	1
...cal abstract, 1886, additional copies of	3823	49	2	1
...s, States and Territories, the distribution of, to	174	49	1	1
...ontinental railway, Helper's report on, printing of	1750	47	1	1
...s, statement of awards under treaties between France and Spain, print...ig of	1302	49	1	1
...Pacific Railroad Company, the reports of the Government directors of, ...rinting of	836	49	1	1
...States Coast and Geodetic Survey, additional copies of, report of	3770	49	2	1
...the rebellion, records of, printing of	704	47	1	1
...r, reports on, printing of	1745	47	1	1
...AND COMMISSION, report of, distribution of	99	49	1	1
...RINTING,				
...for, to regulate	*298	26	1	1
...documents, to suspend printing of	378	35	1	1
...t for, with Congressional Globe	26	41	2	1
...n delay in printing certain reports	150	46	3	1
...pid execution of	35	30	1	1
...RINTING AND BINDING,				
...census, printing and binding the	3	32	2	1
...al of W. B. B. Willis and others to have, done in Washington, D. C., all ...paid for	48	35	1	1
...paid for	350	35	1	1
...ation of laws governing	398	46	3	1
...expenses of	586	46	2	1
...D WATER TRANSPORTATION, map showing routes of, prepara...on of	468	47	1	1
...D CASES, extra copies of Commissioners of Claims' report of list of	2	44	1	1
...OF COMMITTEES,				
...ation of reports of committees of Senate and House of Representatives	2157	48	1	1
Do	2158	48	1	1
Do	3362	49	1	1
...ling rule for printing of	989	49	1	1
...STATUTES,				
...ising proposals in District of Columbia, amending section 3709, relative ...	1785	47	1	1
...ution to States and Territories of	174	49	1	1

* And views of minority.

Subject.	Report.	Congress.	Session.	Volume.
RITCHIE, THOMAS, claim for relief	157	32	1	1
ROCKY MOUNTAIN LOCUST, Riley's report on, additional copies of	575	46	2	1
ROUTES, map of rail and water transportation, preparation of	465	47	1	1
SALARIES, employés in Government Printing Office, establishing and regulating salaries of	190	45	2	1
Do	1752	47	1	1
SCHLEY, Commander W. S., Greely search expedition, report of, on, additional copies of	4106	49	2	1
SENATE OF UNITED STATES, compilation, indexing, and binding of reports from committees of	2157	48	1	1
Do	2158	48	1	1
Do	3362	49	1	1
SHEEP AND WOOL SHOW. (*See* INTERNATIONAL SHEEP AND WOOL SHOW.)				
SHIP-CANAL, Lieutenant-Colonel Alexander's survey of Lakes Union and Washington for, printing of	1578	46	2	
SMITHSONIAN INSTITUTION, additional annual reports of, printing of	941	49	1	
SIGNAL OFFICE, printing of reports of	96	48	1	
SPAIN, statement of payment of awards under treaty with, printing of	1302	49	1	
STATISTICAL ABSTRACT, 1886, additional copies of	3823	49	2	
STATUTES OF UNITED STATES, furnishing States and Territories with copies of	174	49	1	1
TRANSCONTINENTAL RAILWAYS, Helper's report on, printing of	1750	47	1	1
TREATIES, statement of awards under treaties between France and Spain, printing of	1302	49	1	1
TURNER, L. M., Alaska, report on, by	3060	49	1	1
UNION PACIFIC RAILWAY COMPANY, reports of the Government directors of, printing of	836	49	1	1
UNITED STATES COAST AND GEODETIC SURVEY, report of Superintendent of, additional copies of	3770	49	2	1
UNITED STATES MAPS, additional copies of	4040	49	2	1
UNITED STATES STATISTICAL ABSTRACT, 1886, additional copies of	3823	49	2	1
WAGES. (*See* SALARIES; GOVERNMENT PRINTING OFFICE.)				
WAR OF THE REBELLION, records of the, printing of	704	47	1	1
WAR SHIPS. (*See* ORDNANCE AND WAR SHIPS.)				
WHARTON, FRANCIS, digest of international law by, publication of	3140	49	1	1
WILLIS, W. B. B., *et al.*, petition of, relative to the public printing	48	35	1	1
ZOOLOGY, reports on, printing of	1745	47	1	1

o

REPORTS

OF THE

MITTEE ON PRIVATE LAND CLAIMS,

HOUSE OF REPRESENTATIVES,

FROM THE FIFTEENTH CONGRESS, 1816, TO THE FORTY-NINTH CONGRESS, 1887, INCLUSIVE,

IN EIGHT VOLUMES.

COMPILED, UNDER THE DIRECTION OF THE JOINT COMMITTEE ON PRINTING,

BY

T. H. McKEE,

CLERK, DOCUMENT ROOM, UNITED STATES SENATE.

WASHINGTON:
GOVERNMENT PRINTING OFFICE.
1887.

9225 PR L H

[PUBLIC RESOLUTION—No. 24.]

Joint resolution authorizing the preparation of a compilation of the reports of committees of the Senate and House of Representatives.

Resolved by the Senate and House of Representatives of the United States of America in Congress assembled, That there be prepared under the direction of the Joint Committee of Printing, a compilation of the reports of the Senate and House of Representatives from the Fourteenth to the Forty-eighth Congress, inclusive, classified by committees, arranged, indexed, and bound in suitable volumes for the use of the standing committees of the two Houses of Congress. And the sum of seven thousand seven hundred and fifty dollars, or so much thereof as may be found necessary, is hereby appropriated out of any money in the Treasury not otherwise appropriated, for the preparation of said work, which sum may be paid by the Secretary of the Treasury upon the order of the chairman of said Joint Committee, as additional pay or compensation to any officer or employee of the United States.

Resolved further, That the Clerk of the House and Secretary of the Senate be, and they are hereby directed, to procure and file, for the use of their respective Houses, copies of all reports made by each committee of all succeeding Congresses; and that the Clerk of the House and the Secretary of the Senate be, and they are hereby, authorized and directed at the close of each session of Congress, to cause said reports to be indexed and bound, one copy to be deposited in the library of each House and one copy in the room of the committee from which the reports emanated.

Approved, July 29, 1886.

COMPILER'S NOTICE.

This compilation embraces all the printed reports made by both Houses of Congress from the commencement of the Fourteenth to the close of the Forty-ninth Congress. They are classified by committees and arranged in numerical order. The collection for each committee is divided into volumes of suitable size. Each committee has a separate index, a copy being bound in each volume.

The SPECIAL and SELECT reports are all compiled in one collection having one index, a copy of which is bound in each volume.

The plan throughout the compilation is to place each report to the committee from which it was reported, without reference to the subject-matter.

The House and Senate reports are compiled separately. Care will be required in noticing the chronological order, as in some instances an entire session or Congress may not appear in certain volumes from the fact that during this period no reports were made by this committee.

T. H. McKEE.

INDEX

TO

˛EPORTS OF COMMITTEE ON PRIVATE LAND CLAIMS,

HOUSE OF REPRESENTATIVES.

FROM 1816 TO 1887, INCLUSIVE.

Subject.	Report.	Congress.	Session.	Volume.
Г, JAMES, confirming title to lands on the Detroit River to heirs of	236	22	1	2
ROBERT, relief of	661	25	2	3
, **CHRISTOPHER**, confirming titles to lands in Louisiana	31	20	2	1
JAMES, relief of	350	25	2	3
MA, patenting of unconfirmed land south of thirty-first degree in	1314	49	1	8
JERQUE, NEW MEXICO, confirming private land claim of	1262	48	1	8
JUDAH, relief of	72	18	1	1
Г, **VALERIAN**, confirming title to land in Louisiana	129	26	2	3
Do	840	27	2	3
CHILTON, confirming title to land in Louisiana	93	26	1	3
GEORGE and **REUBEN**, confirming title to land in Louisiana	406	27	2	3
Do	121	28	1	3
LEWIS, relief of	948	45	2	7
N, **ROBERT**, relief of	106	23	2	2
Do	110	24	1	2
, JACOB, relief of	415	36	1	6
SANDOVAL Y MANZANARES, confirming title to land in Territory of New Mexico to legal representatives of	1500	47	1	7
ɔON, CHARLES, confirming title to lands in Alabama	80	19	1	1
?, RICHARD T., purchase of certain public land in Mississippi	32	23	2	2
ATHANIEL L., relief of	3601	49	2	8
A TERRITORY, conferring titles to,				
.te grants in	530	47	1	7
Do	172	48	1	8
Do	192	49	1	8
Do	1380	49	1	8
el Gaudara	518	48	1	8
Alamos grant	187	49	1	8
ɔAS.				
nuing act of August 30, 1850, donating lands to citizens of	25	34	1	4
Springs reservation in, extending time to establish title to	263	43	1	7
Do	3	43	2	7
Do	351	44	1	7
ıting of unconfirmed lands in	1314	49	1	8
?ONG, JOHN, relief of	945	25	2	3
) DE SAN LORENZO GRANT, confirming title to legal representatives of Antonio Chaves	1501	47	1	7
Do	173	48	1	8
Do	451	49	1	8
ION PARISH, LOUISIANA, confirming certain land to	25	34	3	4
, JOSIAH, relief of	111	36	1	6
, LITTLETON, relief of	726	25	2	3
JOHN, patent to heirs of	357	28	1	3
WILLIAM, confirming title to land in the province of Florida	357	24	1	2
IN, BARTHOLOMEW, *et al.*, relief of	52	34	3	4
IN, IRA, relief of	266	28	1	3
Do	484	29	1	4
Do	58	32	1	4
:LL, GEORGE F., confirming title to land in Florida	277	34	1	4
'R, PHILIP, relief of heirs of	495	25	2	3
'R, PHILIP C. S., relief of	16	15	2	1
Do	8	16	1	1
?, JOSIAH, relief of	187	22	1	2
;Y, JOHN, relief of	115	24	1	2
ı, DAVID, relief of	450	43	1	7

Subject.	Report.	Congress.	Session.	Volume.
BARNES, DEXTER, relief of	[illegible]	[illegible]	2	[illegible]
BARNES, JOHN A., relief of	[illegible]	[illegible]	1	[illegible]
BARON, MARGUERITE, confirming title to land in Louisiana	163	[illegible]	1	[illegible]
BARRET, JAMES, relief of	[illegible]	[illegible]	[illegible]	[illegible]
BARRETT, RICHARD H., confirming title to land in East Florida	[illegible]	[illegible]	[illegible]	[illegible]
Do	[illegible]	[illegible]	1	[illegible]
BASS, JOB, relief of	[illegible]	[illegible]	1	[illegible]
BASTROP, BARON, confirming title to land in Louisiana	[illegible]	[illegible]	1	[illegible]
BAUTA, JACOB, relief of	11	[illegible]	2	[illegible]
BAXTER, CHESTER, *et al.*, issue of patents to	[illegible]	27	[illegible]	[illegible]
BAXTER, ZEBULON, relief of	42	[illegible]	[illegible]	[illegible]
Do	[illegible]	[illegible]	[illegible]	[illegible]
BAY, ELIHU HALL (heirs of Gaillard), British patents in West Florida prior to 1783	[illegible]	[illegible]	2	[illegible]
Do	[illegible]	[illegible]	1	[illegible]
Do	[illegible]	[illegible]	[illegible]	[illegible]
BEARD, HUGH, relief of	[illegible]	[illegible]	1	[illegible]
BEAUBIEN, CHARLES, confirming title to claim of	[illegible]	[illegible]	[illegible]	[illegible]
Do	[illegible]	[illegible]	1	[illegible]
BECK, PRESTON, Jr. (assignee), claim of land in San Miguel County	457	[illegible]	1	5
Do	[illegible]	[illegible]	1	[illegible]
BEDFORD, DRAYTON P., confirming title to land in Louisiana	600	25	[illegible]	[illegible]
BELEU, VALENCIA COUNTY, COLORADO, claim of lands by town of	457	35	1	5
Do	321	[illegible]	1	[illegible]
BELGAR, JUAN, relief of	[illegible]	37	[illegible]	[illegible]
BELL, FREDERICK M., relief of heirs of	[illegible]	25	[illegible]	[illegible]
BELLINGER, PETER, relief of	[illegible]	[illegible]	1	[illegible]
BENEDICT, LEWIS,				
To enter public lands in Illinois	[illegible]	[illegible]	1	[illegible]
Relief of	[illegible]	[illegible]	[illegible]	[illegible]
BERARD, BAPTISTE, confirming title to land in Louisiana	[illegible]	[illegible]	[illegible]	[illegible]
BERZAT, GABRIEL, confirming titles of lands to heirs of	[illegible]	[illegible]	[illegible]	[illegible]
Do	[illegible]	27	1	1
BESSEE, ANTHONY, relief of	[illegible]	[illegible]	1	[illegible]
BESSY, ANTHONY, public land in Louisiana, to enter	[illegible]	[illegible]	1	[illegible]
BILLS, JOHN, public land in Louisiana, to purchase	[illegible]	[illegible]	1	[illegible]
Do	[illegible]	[illegible]	[illegible]	[illegible]
BLACK, JACOB, confirming title to land in Louisiana	[illegible]	[illegible]	[illegible]	2
BOAS, JOHN R., relinquishing Government title to Bruce's Island, in Mississippi River, to	[illegible]	45	3	[illegible]
Do	[illegible]	[illegible]	2	[illegible]
BOGERT, GILBERT, relief of	[illegible]	[illegible]	[illegible]	[illegible]
BOND, MARY ANN, relief of	[illegible]	[illegible]	1	1
BORELL, EUGENE, confirming title to land in Louisiana	[illegible]	21	1	1
Do	[illegible]	[illegible]	1	[illegible]
Do	370	[illegible]	[illegible]	[illegible]
BOREY, JOHN, relief of	[illegible]	[illegible]	[illegible]	[illegible]
BOSTON AND LAKE SUPERIOR MINERAL LAND COMPANY, lands at Sault Sainte Marie, to confirm	215	[illegible]	1	[illegible]
Do	3048	[illegible]	1	[illegible]
BOUDREAN, JEAN CHARLES, confirming title to land in Louisiana	[illegible]	22	1	[illegible]
Do	42	[illegible]	2	[illegible]
BOULIGNEY, J. E., relief of	30	27	[illegible]	[illegible]
BOULIGNY, JOHN, relief of heirs of	63	[illegible]	1	[illegible]
BOUNTY LANDS, widows and children of soldiers of 1813	121	34	1	[illegible]
BOWMAN, WILLIAM, relief of	53	[illegible]	1	[illegible]
BOYD, ALEXANDER,				
Confirming title to lands in Louisiana	[illegible]	[illegible]	1	1
Do	144	[illegible]	1	[illegible]
Confirming title to land in Louisiana	144	[illegible]	1	[illegible]
Do	[illegible]	[illegible]	1	[illegible]
BRADFORD, JAMES, relief of	[illegible]	[illegible]	1	[illegible]
Do	[illegible]	[illegible]	1	[illegible]
Do	[illegible]	[illegible]	[illegible]	[illegible]
Do	[illegible]	[illegible]	[illegible]	[illegible]
BRADY, JAMES, relief of	[illegible]	[illegible]	[illegible]	1
BRAGG, BRAXTON, confirming title to land in Louisiana	[illegible]	[illegible]	1	[illegible]
BRANNIN, JAMES W., relief of	[illegible]	[illegible]	1	[illegible]
BRASHEARS, ANN, confirming title to lands in Mississippi Territory	[illegible]	[illegible]	[illegible]	1
Do	[illegible]	[illegible]	[illegible]	[illegible]
BRAYTON, CALEB L., confirming title to land to heirs of	[illegible]	[illegible]	[illegible]	[illegible]
BREARLEY, JOSEPH HENRY, relief of	[illegible]	[illegible]	[illegible]	[illegible]
BREST, JOHN, confirming title to lands in Louisiana	[illegible]	[illegible]	[illegible]	[illegible]
Do	[illegible]	[illegible]	[illegible]	[illegible]
Do	[illegible]	[illegible]	[illegible]	[illegible]
BRIGHAM, JAMES H., confirming title to land in Louisiana to wife of	[illegible]	[illegible]	[illegible]	[illegible]
BRIGHT, HENRY, confirming title to lot in the city of Mobile	[illegible]	[illegible]	2	[illegible]
BRISBAN, JAMES, relief of	[illegible]	[illegible]	[illegible]	[illegible]
BROU, Mrs. AMBROISE, confirming title to land	[illegible]	[illegible]	[illegible]	[illegible]
BROUSSARD, PIERRE, confirming title to lands in Louisiana to heirs of	[illegible]	[illegible]	3	[illegible]
Do	[illegible]	[illegible]	[illegible]	[illegible]

Subject.	Report.	Congress.	Session.	Volume.
TIN, MAGDALENE, confirming title to land in Louisiana to heirs of	115	34	1	4
N, AMOS W., relief of	258	22	1	2
Do	91	23	1	2
N, JOHN, confirming title to land in Florida to heirs of	598	26	1	3
Do	83	27	2	3
'S ISLAND, MISSISSIPPI RIVER, relinquishing title of United States to	63	45	3	7
Do	256	46	2	7
, JEREMIAH, public lands in Louisiana, to locate	7	34	3	4
EY, JEREMIAH, relief of heirs of	85	19	2	1
Do	316	21	1	1
Do	71	22	1	2
ER, JOHN, confirming title to land in Louisiana	198	21	1	1
Do	81	22	1	2
, NANCY, relief of	416	36	1	6
WILLIAM G., confirming title to land on Blakely's Island	249	27	2	3
TT, BENJAMIN, confirming title to land in Louisiana	72	22	1	2
ANTHONY, relief of heirs of	10	16	1	1
AND, THOMAS M., relief of	158	25	3	3
NGTON, IOWA, granting certain land to	1007	45	2	7
, MALACHI, confirming title to lands in Louisiana	48	18	1	1
SS, ELIZABETH,				
firming title to land in Louisiana	565	27	2	3
Do	699	29	1	4
Do	181	30	1	4
ef of legal representatives of	1612	46	2	7
N, SIMON, Jr., relief of	190	24	2	2
GEORGE, confirming title to land in Washington Territory	54	33	2	4
R, ABEL M., relief of	166	35	1	5
INDIANS LANDS between Rio Hondo and Sabine Rivers, to confirm title to	50	24	2	2
ORNIA,				
una de la Marced, relief of settlers on	29	41	3	7
Do	811	45	2	7
cho de Napa in, confirming title to	380	48	1	8
cho Panoche Grande in, determine title to the	29	46	3	7
Do	273	46	3	7
Do	922	47	1	7
R, JAMES, confirming title to land near Mobile, to heirs of	415	25	2	3
Do	475	25	2	3
Do	476	25	2	3
BELL, JOHN, confirming title to land in Michigan Territory	382	23	1	2
Do	153	24	2	2
IAN VOLUNTEERS, granting bounty lands to	711	25	2	3
DE CHAMA GRANT, confirming title to owners of	1690	46	2	7
Do	131	47	1	7
L, CHARLES, confirming title to land in Louisiana	146	28	2	3
Do	595	29	1	4
CHAEL, J. F., confirming title to lands in Louisiana and Mississippi	57	20	1	1
UCH, NARCISSA, relief of	191	26	2	3
DELET, MISSOURI, conferring jurisdiction on Court of Claims to decide claim of city to Jefferson Barracks	523	25	2	3
Do	825	30	1	4
Do	35	41	3	7
THOMAS, and others, confirming titles to lands in Yazoo district	62	16	1	1
ER, ARTHUR, J., patent to land in Dakota Territory	3498	49	2	8
N, JAMES G., relief of	50	29	2	4
R, FARISH, relief of	270	23	1	2
Do	72	24	1	2
COLORADO, VALENCIA COUNTY, NEW MEXICO, confirming title to claim of lands by town of	457	35	1	5
Do	321	36	1	6
, MARY E., relief of	1075	49	1	8
, ROBERT, relief of	166	25	3	3
Do	450	26	1	3
IELD, JAMES, public lands in Alabama, to enter	336	22	1	2
Do	408	23	1	2
Do	77	24	1	2
LO, JOSÉ, confirming title to lands in Mississippi	445	29	1	4
LO, ROSALIE, relief of	216	33	1	4
AR, PIERRE, confirming title to land in Louisiana to legal representatives of	156	34	3	4
Do	240	35	2	5
KINSEY B., land patents to	1929	47	2	7
Do	860	49	1	8
, PASCAL L., relief of heirs of	29	34	1	4
IELD, LEWIS W., relief of	414	36	1	6
S, ANTONIO, confirming grant of Arroyo de San Lorenzo, in New Mexico, to legal representatives of	1501	47	1	7
Do	173	48	1	8
Do	458	49	1	8

Subject.	Report.	Congress.	Session.	Volume.
CHAVES, IGNACIO, *et al.*, confirming title to land in New Mexico to legal representatives of	285	47	1	[illegible]
Do	1833	47	2	[illegible]
Do	175	48	1	[illegible]
Do	186	49	1	[illegible]
CHEMINS (or public passways) in Missouri, disposal of	203	24	3	[illegible]
CHERINO, ANTONIO, confirming title to land between the Rio Hondo and Sabine Rivers	284	27	2	[illegible]
Do	320	28	1	[illegible]
CHIAPELLA, CELESTIN, relief of	33	23	1	[illegible]
CHILILI, BERNALILLO COUNTY, NEW MEXICO, confirming title to claim of lands by town of	457	25	1	[illegible]
Do	321	26	1	[illegible]
CHINN, THOMAS W., relief of	495	26	1	[illegible]
Do	283	27	2	[illegible]
CHOUTEAU, PIERRE, Jr., confirming title to Dubuque claim in Iowa Territory	632	28	1	[illegible]
Do	675	29	1	[illegible]
CHRETIEN, FRANCOIS, confirming title to land in Louisiana	460	28	1	[illegible]
CHRISTIE, GABRIEL, relief of heirs of	22	28	2	[illegible]
CHRISTOPHER, WILLIAM G., relief of heirs of	173	22	1	[illegible]
CLAMORGAN, HENRY, *et al.*, relief of	506	30	1	[illegible]
CLAMORGAN, JAQUES, *et al.*, confirming title to land	635	43	1	[illegible]
CLARK, ANNA M., confirming title to land on island of Amelia, Florida	464	45	2	[illegible]
CLARK, ETHAN RAY and SAMUEL WARD, confirming title to land in Florida	218	34	1	[illegible]
Do	27	41	3	[illegible]
CLARK, WILLIAM, relief of	726	24	1	[illegible]
Do	283	25	2	[illegible]
CLARKE, ELIJAH L., *et al.*, confirming titles to lands in Louisiana	28	19	2	[illegible]
CLARKE, THOMAS B., patent for certain land in Michigan Territory	458	23		
Do	55	30		
Do	344	31		
CLENDENIN, JOHN G., relief of estate of	232	33		
COCKERILLE, WILLIAM S., confirming title to land in Louisiana	152	23	1	[illegible]
COFFMAN, JOSEPH, relief of	49	42	3	[illegible]
COLORADO, private land claims in, settling	1380	49		[illegible]
COMB, CHARLES, confirming title to land in Louisiana to heirs of	186	21	1	[illegible]
Do	131	22	1	[illegible]
CONGER, JOHN S., relief of	97	23	2	[illegible]
CONGRESSIONAL TOWNSHIPS, WARREN COUNTY, OHIO, claim of citizens for school lands in	246	33	1	[illegible]
CONWAY, WILLIAM, relief of heirs	78	34	3	[illegible]
Do	16	35	1	[illegible]
COOK, BENJAMIN C., relief of	217	33	1	[illegible]
COOK, WILLIAM H., relief of	100	28	1	[illegible]
COOPER, JAMES, relief of	254	25	2	
CORDER, BOLUS, relief of heirs	446	25	2	
COURT OF CLAIMS, conferring jurisdiction to adjudicate claims of Carondelet to Jefferson Barracks	523	25	2	
Do	825	30	1	
Do	25	41	3	
COVILLION, AMELIA, public lands, to enter	24	30	2	
CRAMER, JACOB, relief of heirs of	640	44	1	
Do	247	45	2	
Do	46	46	3	
Do	603	49	1	
CRAWFORD, JOHN, public land in Mississippi, to enter	24	34	1	
CRIBBEN, LAWRENCE, *et al.*, relief of	220	33	1	
CROSBY, ELIAKIM, relief of	250	20	1	
Do	262	21	1	
Do	55	22	1	
CROSBY, MARY C., relief of	2565	49	1	[illegible]
CRUZAT, ANTOINE, confirming title to land in Louisiana	234	22	1	[illegible]
Do	105	23	1	[illegible]
CULVER, SYLVANUS, relief of	205	32	1	[illegible]
CURRAN, WILLIAM, confirming title to land	213	33	1	[illegible]
CURRY, JOHN, confirming title to land in Arizona Territory	558	47	1	[illegible]
CUYAMUNGUE PUEBLO TRACT, confirming title to claimants of	61	45	3	[illegible]
DAUTERIVE, JEAN A. B., confirming title to land in Louisiana	343	36	1	[illegible]
DAVENPORT, JAMES B., confirming title to land in Louisiana	696	29	1	[illegible]
Do	177	30	1	
DAVID, KENNEY, relief of heirs of	337	26		
DAVIDSON, ROBERT, relief of	84	31		
DAVIDSON, THOMAS GREEN, confirming title to land in Louisiana	1611	46	2	
DAVIS, DANIEL, relief of	60	19	1	
Do	86	25	2	
Do	252	26	1	[illegible]
DAVLIN, JOHN, relief of	850	27	2	[illegible]
DAWSON, JOHN, relief of	38	24	2	[illegible]
Do	295	25		[illegible]

Subject	Report.	Congress.	Session.	Volume.
UX, A. L., relief of	150	25	3	3
HOUSSAYE, LOUIS, confirming titles of lands in Louisiana to heirs of.	28	19	1	1
LANE, SAMUEL, relief of	827	35	1	5
IGNACIO, confirming title to land west of Pearl River	118	24	1	4
A, MANUEL and JOACHIN, confirming title to land in Louisiana	80	24	2	4
T, JOHN, relief of	351	23	1	3
Do	71	24	1	3
EY, WILLIAM, relief of	104	33	2	4
IAD, FRANCIS, relief of	2232	49	1	8
NNE, PIERRE S., relief of	148	28	1	3
RINE, JEAN BAPTISTE, confirming title to land in Louisiana	208	35	1	5
LEMONT, DON CARLOS, confirming title to land in Louisiana to heirs of	348	25	3	3
Do	97	26	1	3
Do	312	36	1	6
OHN, patent for certain land in Florida	230	35	1	5
ROON, THOMAS L., relief of	126	34	1	4
Do	124	34	3	4
ON, WILLIAM, public lands in Louisiana, to enter	143	28	2	3
Do	594	29	1	4
ELENA, relief of	116	28	1	3
JOHN, relief of	232	25	2	3
ER, R. K., relief of	41	36	1	6
AN, ARNOLD HENRY, granting certain sections of public lands in Ohio to heirs of	68	22	2	2
Do	56	23	1	2
Y, LLOYD, *et al.*, public lands in Louisiana, to enter	303	28	1	4
AS, GEORGE, *et al.*, sections of public land in Louisiana, to purchase	135	22	1	2
Do	61	22	2	2
Do	677	24	1	3
ASS, JAMES S., *et al.*, public lands in Louisiana, to purchase	198	25	2	3
AN, HERCULES L., confirming title to lots in Prairie du Chien	71	23	1	4
Do	122	24	1	4
AN, TALBOT C., confirming title to land in Michigan Territory	128	24	1	4
NG, THOMAS H., claim to island of Yerba Buena	50	41	3	7
, EDMUND, relief of	14	18	2	1
Do	37	18	1	1
UE CLAIM, confirming title to	482	29	1	4
Do	675	29	1	4
QUET, FRANCIS, confirming title to land in Ohio to legal representative of	330	23	1	2
Do	114	24	1	2
EL, CHARLES OLIVER, confirming title to land in Louisiana	43	36	1	6
Do	947	45	2	6
Do	5	46	1	7
EL, OLIVER, confirming title to land in Louisiana	947	45	2	7
Do	5	46	1	7
AT, JOSEPH SONIAT, relief of	32	22	1	2
N, THOMAS, relief of	6	34	3	4
, JOHN B., relief of	55	20	1	1
T, LEWIS, relief of heirs of	261	24	1	2
Do	601	26	1	3
E, FREDERICK, relief of	178	30	1	4
Do	196	31	1	4
L, ELLEN, relief of	1034	27	2	3
Do	281	27	3	3
ATON ROUGE, LOUISIANA, to confirm lands to inhabitants of	594	24	1	2
DS, BENJAMIN E., confirming title to land in New Mexico Territory	460	35	1	5
Do	221	45	2	7
DS, EVAN, renewal of land warrant to heirs of	209	22	1	2
OHN, relief of heirs of	20	20	2	1
Do	62	21	1	1
OHN L., confirming title to land in Louisiana	785	25	2	3
JOHN, confirming title to land in Louisiana	70	33	2	4
JOSEPH, relief of heirs of	599	26	1	3
, DON MIGUEL, confirming title to land in Alabama to heirs of	39	18	1	1
Do	575	25	2	3
R, ROBERT, confirming title to land near Mobile to heirs of	352	24	1	2
Do	139	25	2	3
, JOHN T., relief of	62	30	2	4
RE, JOHN S., relief of heirs of	2296	49	1	8
, COLEMAN, confirming title to land in Louisiana	296	21	1	1
Do	250	22	1	2
Do	47	23	1	2
, WILLIAM, relief of heirs of	132	28	2	3
RALD, PHILIP, public lands in Louisiana, to purchase	75	22	2	2
Do	77	23	1	2
C, GARRIQUES, relief of	270	22	1	2
Do	48	23	1	2
Y, HENRY M., claim on vacant land in Louisiana, to locate	149	25	3	3
, PEDRO, *et al.*, confirming title to Rio Hondo land claims	222	45	2	7

Subject.	Report.	Congress.	Session.	Volume.
FLORIDA.				
Confirming title of land in, to Anna M. Clark	[illegible]	45	2	[illegible]
Examination, approval, and patenting of unconfirmed lands in	1314	49	1	[illegible]
FLOURNOY, MATTHEWS, relief of	225	21	[illegible]	[illegible]
FLOWERS, SIDNEY, public land, in lieu of land erroneously entered, to enter	25	30	[illegible]	[illegible]
FORBES, ABRAHAM, relief of	229	22	[illegible]	[illegible]
Do	22	23		
Do	118	25	1	2
Do	170	24	2	2
Do	780	29	1	4
FORBES, JOHN, & CO., relief of	845	24	1	2
FORD, NATHANIEL, relief of	469	21	1	1
FOREMAN, ROBERT S., relief of	36	15	1	1
FORMAN, WILLIAM GORDON, confirming titles of lands to heirs of	75	16	1	1
FORT CHARTRES ISLAND. (*See* BRUCE'S ISLAND.)				
FORT LEAVENWORTH, alleged issue of patents for land included within military reservation at	56	37	3	7
FOSTER, HUGH, confirming homestead entry to	3612	49	2	8
FRAZER, JOHN, relief of	232	38	1	4
FRIDGE, ALEXANDER, confirming title to land in Louisiana	76	21	1	1
FROST, GEORGE P., relief of	32	20	2	1
FRUGE, JOHN, confirming title to land in Louisiana	256	21	1	1
Do	450	22	1	2
GAGNON, PIERRE, confirming title to land in Louisiana	66	35	1	5
GAINES, MYRA CLARK, confirming title to land	641	44	1	7
Do	58	45	3	7
Do	561	47	1	7
Do	95	48	1	8
Do	1261	49	1	8
GAMBLE, ARCHIBALD, relief of	152	22	1	2
GARDERE, FRANCIS, relief of	483	31	1	4
GASS, PATRICK, relief of	56	32	1	4
Do	215	33	1	4
GAUDARA, MANUEL MARIA, confirming title to land in Arizona Territory to heirs or assigns of	518	48	1	8
GAUTT, BENJAMIN R., confirming title to land in Louisiana	301	34	1	4
GEE, HENRY, relief of	309	49	1	8
GIBSON, R. L., confirming title to land in Louisiana	114	36	1	6
GILL, NAPOLEON B., public lands in Missouri, to enter	125	34	1	4
GILLET, SHADRACK, *et al.*, relief of	64	30	2	4
GIRAULT, JOHN, relief of heirs of	62	16	2	1
Do	21	17	1	1
GIROD, JOHN F., relief of	252	21	1	1
GLADNEY, SAMUEL, relief of	779	27	2	3
GLASS, CYRENIUS, relief of	128	35	1	5
GODFROY, JACQUES, patent for land on Detroit River	294	34		4
GOODENOUGH, ADINO, relief of heirs of	528	28		3
Do	435	29		
GOODENOUGH, JOHN B., relief of	485	29		
GORDON, GEORGE, confirming title to land	428	22	1	
GRAHAM, ROBERT, confirming title to land in district northwest of Ohio River	180	28	2	
Do	134	33		
GRAHAM, WILLIAM, relief of heirs of	210	23		
Do	704	25		
GRAINGER, JEAN BAPTISTE, relief of	305	25		
Do	166	24	1	2
Do	1	24	2	2
GRAMILLON, FRANCOIS, confirming title to land in Louisiana	38	22	2	4
Do	183	30		4
GRANTLAND, SEATON, relief of	270	23		2
GRANTSVILLE, UTAH TERRITORY, confirming title to land to Thomas McBride in	1313	46	2	7
GREEN BAY, WISCONSIN, patents for certain lands at, to issue	782	25	2	3
GREEN, CHRISTOPHER A., confirming title to land in Alabama to	61	22	2	2
GRIGNON, CHARLES A., confirming title to land in Michigan Territory	523	24	1	2
GRIGNON, PIERRE, patent for land near Green Bay	322	36	1	6
GUADALUPE, MIRANDA, confirming title to claim of land, Taos County, to	457	35	1	5
Do	321	36	1	6
GUEDRY, JOSEPH, *et al.*, confirming titles to lands in Louisiana	18	22	2	2
Do	72	22		3
GUEDRY, PEDRO, relief of	52	21		1
GUEDRY, PIERRE, relief of heirs of	82	20		2
GUERIN, EMILE, relief of	1011	49		8
GUESS, ISAAC, confirming title to land	655	29		4
GUILLORY, FRANCOIS, conferring title to land in Louisiana to heirs of	202	35		5
Do	44	36		6
GULLEDGE, THOMAS, relief of	76	19		1
GUTHRIE, ABELARD, confirming title to land in Ohio	418	28		3
HAAS, JACOB, confirming title to land	335	26		3
Do	407	27	2	3

Subject.	Report.	Congress.	Session.	Volume.
, JACOB, confirming title to land	[illegible]	27	3	[illegible]
, ELIZUR B., relief of	[illegible]	49	1	8
, JAMES, relief of	154	[illegible]	2	4
LY, WILLIAM, relief of	14	[illegible]	2	1
Do	37	19	1	1
Y, BELAH, et al., relief of	340	[illegible]	1	2
IE, ALLEN W., relief of	31	[illegible]	1	3
RIDGE, WILLIAM and JOSEPH (Indiana), land patents in fee simple to	[illegible]	[illegible]	1	[illegible]
IN, GEORGE, relief of	70	[illegible]	1	[illegible]
ES, WILLIAM R., relief of	[illegible]	[illegible]	[illegible]	[illegible]
, JOHN, relief of heirs of	410	[illegible]	[illegible]	[illegible]
, NICHOLAS, relief of	108	[illegible]	1	[illegible]
ES JESSE, relief of	55	24	[illegible]	[illegible]
RD, WILLIAM C., relief of	[illegible]	[illegible]	[illegible]	[illegible]
Do	[illegible]	[illegible]	[illegible]	[illegible]
, MOSES, relief of	12	31	2	4
ET, URSIN, refund of purchase money to	870	25	2	3
IN, BERNARD, confirming title to land in Louisiana	78	28	1	6
lief of heirs of	118	24	1	4
ERSON, ROBERT, confirming title to land in Louisiana to heirs of	[illegible]	[illegible]	1	[illegible]
ERSON, STEPHEN, relief of	[illegible]	17	1	1
Do	85	17	2	1
RSON, WILLIAM H., confirming title to land in Louisiana	[illegible]	[illegible]	1	[illegible]
ANDEZ, JOSEPH, relief of	19	24	[illegible]	[illegible]
ICK, NANCY A., relief of	9	[illegible]	[illegible]	7
ZOG, JEAN FRANCOIS, confirming title to land in Louisiana	[illegible]	[illegible]	[illegible]	[illegible]
IN, MARCUS, confirming title to land in Ohio to heirs of	178	[illegible]	[illegible]	[illegible]
MAN, JAMES L., granting public land in Indiana, Illinois, or Missouri to	[illegible]	[illegible]	[illegible]	[illegible]
EN, NATHANIEL, confirming title to land in Louisiana to heirs of	[illegible]	[illegible]	[illegible]	[illegible]
MAN, WILLIAM, relief of	[illegible]	[illegible]	[illegible]	[illegible]
EN, JOSHUA, relief of	14	[illegible]	[illegible]	[illegible]
Y, LEONARD, relief of	[illegible]	[illegible]	2	[illegible]
ES, CHARLES, relief of	[illegible]	26	1	[illegible]
YMAN, SUSANNA, confirming title to land in Louisiana to heirs of	[illegible]	[illegible]	1	[illegible]
AS, GEORGE, relief of	281	22	1	1
PRINGS RESERVATION, ARKANSAS, extending time to establish title to	268	43	1	7
Do	3	43	2	7
Do	351	44	1	7
RD, JOHN H., relief of	113	27	3	3
RD, PURNELL, relief of heirs of	50	42	3	7
ELL, AARON, relief of	423	28	1	3
TAS, JOHN, authorizing the entry of certain lands in Florida by claimants in right of	67	35	1	5
ES, CHARLES, relief of	409	21	1	1
ES, DAVID M., et al., confirming title to land in Mississippi	262	27	2	3
ES, JAMES, confirming titles to lands in Illinois Territory	123	15	2	1
, JOSEPH, relief of	232	21	1	1
NGER, JACOB, relief of	5	16	2	1
, ABIJAH, confirming titles of lands to heirs of	75	16	1	1
INITY SCRIP, to amend law relative to	1942	49	1	8
NA, MONROE COUNTY, petition from residents of, for school lands	272	23	1	2
Do	56	24	1	2
N TERRITORY, relief of persons in	184	43	1	7
, CORNELIUS, relief of	86	23	2	2
JOSEPH, et al., relief of	52	34	4	4
SON, ARCHIBALD, relief of	78	21	2	1
Do	184	22	1	2
ON, GEORGE K., relief of	136	23	1	2
S, THOMAS, relief of	734	25	2	3
S, W. A. and H., relief of	129	33	2	4
S, FRANCIS, relief of heirs of	35	24	2	2
Do	145	25	2	3
SONNE, BAPTISTE, relief of heirs of	60	22	2	2
Do	83	23	1	2
RSON BARRACKS, MISSOURI, conferring jurisdiction in Court of Claims to decide Carondelet claim to	523	25	2	3
Do	825	30	1	4
Do	25	41	3	7
INS, JOHN, relief of	11	17	2	1
Do	11	18	1	1
E, THOMAS, relief of	92	20	1	1
SON, ANDREW, relief of	502	26	1	3
STON, GABRIEL J., relief of	12	36	2	6
STON, STEPHEN, relief of heirs of	103	26	1	3
, ARTHUR, confirming title to lands in Alabama	80	19	1	1
J. and E., to confirm British patents in West Florida prior to 1783 to heirs of	54	22	2	2

Subject.	Report.	Congress.	Session.	Volume.
JONES, JOHN RICE, relief of	30	15	2	[illegible]
Do	150	22	1	[illegible]
Do	223	45	2	[illegible]
JOURNEY, JAMES, confirming title to land in Louisiana	554	27	2	[illegible]
Do	210	28	1	[illegible]
Do	444	29	1	[illegible]
KAMBER, JOSEPH, relief of	70	22	1	[illegible]
KANSAS TERRITORY, confirming titles of purchasers of school lands in	665	36	1	[illegible]
KEAZY, ELIZABETH, confirming title to lands between the States of Mississippi and Louisiana	50	19	1	[illegible]
KEENE, WILLIAM B., relief of	186	22	1	[illegible]
KELLY, THOMAS, relief of heirs of	268	29	1	[illegible]
KENDALL, WILLIAM, confirming title to lands in the Chillicothe district	84	17	2	[illegible]
Do	10	18	1	[illegible]
KENNEDY, JOSHUA, confirming title to land in Louisiana	227	21	1	[illegible]
KERR, JACOB, relief of	302	28	1	[illegible]
Do	486	29	1	[illegible]
Do	13	21	2	[illegible]
Do	346	33	1	[illegible]
KEYTES, JAMES, granting public land in Missouri to	347	23	1	[illegible]
Do	314	24	1	[illegible]
KINCAID, DAVID, confirming title to land in the district of Saint Charles	224	22	1	[illegible]
KINCAID, GEORGE W., relief of	792	30	1	4
KNAGGS, JOHN, relief of	301	23	1	2
KNOX, ANDREW A. H., *et al.*, confirming title to land in Louisiana	119	24	1	4
LABEAUME, LOUIS, relief of heirs of	131	33	2	4
LACEY, OBED P., relief of	120	36	2	3
LACOSTE, AUGUSTIN, fee simple for land in Alabama to grant	95	26	1	3
LAFITTE, PIERRE, confirming title to land in Louisiana	304	23	1	2
LA FONTE, BENJAMIN, relief of	124	34	1	4
LAFORGE, PIERRE A., relief of	340	25	2	3
LA LANDE, ETIENE, confirming title to land in Alabama	512	24	1	2
Do	141	25	2	3
LAMY, JOHN, confirming title to claim for land in Santa Fé County	457	35	1	5
Do	321	36	1	6
LANAUX, ARNAUD, confirming title to land	30	22	1	2
LAND CERTIFICATES, confirming title to purchasers for lands in Louisiana	210	21	1	1
LAND CLAIMS,				
Alabama, to revise law governing	905	27	2	3
Do	59	27	3	3
Arizona, to adjudicate, in	1380	49	1	8
Arkansas, to revise law governing	905	27	2	3
Do	59	27	3	3
Colorado, to adjudicate, in	1380	49	1	8
Louisiana, to revise law governing	905	27	2	3
Do	59	27	3	[illegible]
Mississippi,				
To revise law governing	905	27	2	[illegible]
Do	59	27	3	[illegible]
Survey and location of	222	30	1	[illegible]
Missouri,				
Confirming titles to certain lands in	30	34	1	4
Do	463	35	1	[illegible]
Do	130	23	1	[illegible]
Do	112	36	1	[illegible]
Do	72	40	2	[illegible]
Do	250	42	1	[illegible]
Do	407	43	1	[illegible]
Do	24	44	1	[illegible]
Do	28	46	2	[illegible]
To revise law governing	905	27	2	[illegible]
Do	59	27	3	[illegible]
New Mexico, confirming title to certain	71	40	2	[illegible]
Do	50	44	1	[illegible]
Do	110	44	2	[illegible]
Do	1380	49	1	[illegible]
Mississippi. Perdido, providing claim for the final decision upon	*616	25	2	3
States and Territories, providing for the adjudication of	1733	47	1	7
Do	985	48	1	8
LAND ENTRIES,				
Louisiana, to confirm	51	35	2	8
Missouri, to confirm	350	43	1	[illegible]
LAND SCRIP,				
Defining manner of locating	58	44	2	7
Do	248	45	2	7
Florida	249	45	2	7
Louisiana	249	45	2	7
Missouri	249	45	2	7
LAND TITLES IN MISSOURI, quieting titles to lands	36	40	2	7

*Parts 1, 2.

Subject.	Report.	Congress.	Session.	Volume.
WARRANTS. (See MILITARY LAND WARRANTS.)				
kansas, to donate lands to certain persons in	28	24	1	4
of the Mississippi and island of New Orleans, confirming titles to inhabitants of	694	24	1	2
, payments for, to amend act of 1831 making	2461	22	1	2
REAU, JOHN PIERRE, confirming titles of lands in Louisiana to heirs of	34	20	1	1
Do	33	20	2	1
Do	31	21	1	1
Do	346	26	1	3
RY, OLIVER, confirming title to land in Louisiana to heirs and legal representatives of	462	35	1	5
HERY, A. S., relief of	215	33	1	4
RMIGAS AND LA NANA GRANTS, LOUISIANA, confirming title to grants made by Spain prior to treaty of 1803	82	36	2	6
Do	1	37	2	7
ULGAS RANCHO, correcting boundary line of	819	45	2	7
EL, HYACINTH, relief of	161	25	1	3
AM, JAMES, relief of heirs of	25	23	2	2
Do	42	24	1	2
NTURE, FRANCIS, patent for land near Green Bay	322	36	1	6
RENCE, JAMES, relocate certain land in Arkansas	15	35	1	5
ON, ROBERT, confirming title to land in Alabama	61	22	2	2
H, AMELIA, relief of	116	24	1	2
Do	143	25	2	3
H, GEORGE, relief of	639	25	1	3
ANC, TERENCE, relief of	115	25	1	3
NDRE, BAPTISTE, confirming title to lands in Louisiana	73	21	1	1
AN, HAYEM & TAYLOR, relief of	1655	48	1	8
Do	2028	49	2	8
N, POLLY, relief of	29	24	2	2
ARD, BERNARD, confirming title to land in Louisiana	73	22	1	2
ERS PATENT FOR LAND, issue of	125	43	1	7
UM, GARLAND R., relief of	267	30	1	4
AY, JAMES M., confirming title to land in Alabama	168	32	2	4
L, HANNAH, relief of	167	33	1	5
GSTON, RICHARD and STEPHEN, issue of land warrant to	447	26	2	3
LLY, JOHN L., relief of	824	22	1	2
Do	34	23	1	2
L, REGIS, confirming title to land in Louisiana	79	34	2	4
Do	22	35	1	5
ALTON, relief of	167	28	1	3
OGALES DE ELIAS, confirming land grant to	530	47	1	7
HREY, ARCHIBALD, relief of heirs of	289	35	1	5
IANA, confirming titles to lands in	21	15	2	1
Do	210	21	1	1
Do	84	27	2	3
IANA.				
morial from inhabitants of Assumption and Terre Bonne, in State of	95	27	3	3
mination, approval, and patenting of unconfirmed lands in	1314	49	1	8
ALEXANDER, confirming title to land in Florida Territory	125	21	1	1
ESS, MARY, relief of	54	20	1	1
FRANCIS S., relief of	2	39	2	7
IANY, relief of	222	20	1	1
DE, THOMAS, confirming title to land in Grantsville, Utah	1313	46	2	7
E, EDMUND H., relocate on public lands in Missouri	4	34	3	4
EB, DAVID, confirming title to lands in the State of Tennessee	71	17	2	1
ROLL, JOHN, Jr., relief of	137	24	1	2
LOCK, ELLIOTT, relief of	68	32	1	4
AS, JOSIAH, confirming title to lands in Mississippi Territory	94	15	2	1
MACK, PETER P., relief of	13	20	2	1
Do	175	22	1	2
ARY, JOHN E., relief of	341	23	1	2
LY, W. P., relief of heirs of	413	36	1	6
NELL, FERDINAND D., confirming title to land in the island of Amelia, East Florida	110	23	2	2
OUGH, confirming title to land in Louisiana to legal representatives of	67	21	1	1
Do	13	22	1	2
Do	65	32	1	4
Do	358	35	1	5
INEY, WILLIAM J., *et al.*, relief of	230	33	1	4
RLAND, WILLIAM, confirming title to land in Louisiana to heirs of	55	32	1	4
RRAHAN, WILLIAM, determining his title to the Rancho Panoche Grande	29	46	3	7
Do	278	46	3	7
Do	922	47	1	7
E, MARY, *et al.*, relief of	849	27	2	3
RE, WILLIAM, relief of heirs of	543	30	1	4
NIS, JOHN, relief of	121	27	3	3
K, GEORGE, relief of heirs of	341	33	1	4
TH, ZACHARIAH, relief of	540	23	1	2
W, *et al.*, confirming titles to lands situated on the Tombigbee River	64	16	1	1

Subject.	Report.	Congress.	Session.	Volume.
McGUIRE, ROBERT F., confirming title to land in Louisiana	151	[illegible]	1	[illegible]
McHUGH, JOHN, relief of	59	[illegible]	1	[illegible]
McHUGH, SUSANNA, relief of	25	[illegible]	[illegible]	[illegible]
Do	197	21	[illegible]	[illegible]
MACKAY, JAMES, confirming title to lands in Missouri Territory	95	15	[illegible]	[illegible]
Do	41	16	[illegible]	[illegible]
McKIMM, HANNAH, confirming title to land in Louisiana	69	[illegible]	[illegible]	[illegible]
McKNEELY, JOHN F., relief of	212	33	[illegible]	[illegible]
McLAUGHLIN, GEORGE, relief of	526	35	1	[illegible]
McLAUGHLIN, JOHN, relief of	550	26	[illegible]	[illegible]
Do	7	22	[illegible]	[illegible]
Do	233	[illegible]	[illegible]	[illegible]
McMILLAN, A. B., relief of	134	22	[illegible]	[illegible]
McVEA, JOHN, relief of	212	22	[illegible]	[illegible]
MAGRUDER, THOMAS B., confirming title to land in Louisiana	469	22	[illegible]	[illegible]
MAIS, PIERRE JOSEPH, relief of heirs and legal representatives of	252	46	2	[illegible]
MAJOR, CHERI P., relief of	1011	49	1	[illegible]
MALLETTE, THERESE, relief of heirs of	555	29	1	[illegible]
MARBURY, WILLIAM, relief of	174	22	1	[illegible]
Do	299	26	2	[illegible]
Do	100	26	1	[illegible]
MARIGUY, BERNARD, confirming title to land in Louisiana	106	21	[illegible]	[illegible]
Do	3	22	1	[illegible]
Do	4	26	1	[illegible]
MARIGUY, PROSPER, relief of	12	22	1	[illegible]
MARIN, E., *et al.*, confirming titles to lands on the Terre aux Bœufs, La	6	22	1	[illegible]
MARTIN, HENRY, relief of	1027	48	1	8
Do	450	49	1	8
MARTIN, JOHN L., relief of	166	22	1	2
MARSHALL, ROBERT, relief of	364	25	2	3
MARSHALL, WILLIAM, relief of	363	30	1	4
MARTINEZ, MANUEL, confirming title to claim of lands in Rio Arriba County.	457	35	1	5
Do	321	36	1	6
MARVIN, WILLIAM, confirming title to land in Florida	465	35	1	5
MASON, ASHBEL, relief of	409	25	2	3
MATHEWS, E. P., *et al.*, relief of	220	33	1	6
MAXWELL, JAMES, relief of	109	23	2	2
Do	857	25	2	3
MAYFIELD, GEORGE, confirming title to land in Tennessee	18	21	2	1
Do	597	26	1	3
MEDANO SPRINGS GRANT, confirming title to claimants of	60	45	3	7
MELLEN, PEGGY, relief of	22	16	2	1
Do	2	17	1	1
MERRILL, ELI, relief of heirs of	71	28	2	3
Do	270	29	1	4
MESITA JUAN LOPEZ GRANT, confirming title to claimants of	59	45	3	7
METOYER, BENJAMIN, relief of	247	33	1	4
MEXICAN CLAIMS, prescribing method of settling	965	48	1	8
MILITARY LAND WARRANTS, Virginia, defining the act locating	88	20	2	1
Do	103	21	1	1
MILLANDON, LAURENT, *et al.*, confirming title to land in Louisiana	81	26	1	3
Do	219	35	1	5
MILLER, CHAD, relief of	52	19	2	1
MILLER, JOHN, relief of	299	28	[illegible]	[illegible]
MILLS, JOHN N., relief of	38	19	[illegible]	[illegible]
MILNE, WILLIAM C., relief of	959	27	[illegible]	[illegible]
MINARD ROSWELL, relief of	11	33	[illegible]	[illegible]
Do	219	34	[illegible]	[illegible]
Do	165	35	[illegible]	[illegible]
MISSION OF SAINT JAMES, WASHINGTON TERRITORY, confirming title to	650	43	1	[illegible]
Do	189	44	[illegible]	[illegible]
Do	254	46	[illegible]	[illegible]
MISSISSIPPI, patenting of unconfirmed land south of thirty-first degree in	1314	49	[illegible]	[illegible]
MISSOURI.				
To quiet titles to lands in	21	15	[illegible]	[illegible]
Do	36	40	[illegible]	[illegible]
Do	24	44	[illegible]	[illegible]
Do	28	46	[illegible]	[illegible]
To confirm land-entries in	350	43	[illegible]	[illegible]
Patenting of unconfirmed land in	1314	49	[illegible]	[illegible]
MOBILE HARBOR, confirming title to heirs of Robert Farmer of certain lands in	252	24	[illegible]	[illegible]
Do	139	25	[illegible]	[illegible]
MOFFIT, GEORGE, relief of heirs	493	25	[illegible]	[illegible]
Do	560	29	[illegible]	[illegible]
MOLAISON PIERRE, *et al.*, confirming title to land in Territory of Orleans	96	26	[illegible]	[illegible]
MOOR, JAMES, relief of	128	25	[illegible]	[illegible]
MOOR, WILLIAM, relief of	140	25	[illegible]	[illegible]
MOORE, EBENEZER, relief of heirs	514	26	[illegible]	[illegible]
Do	358	24	[illegible]	[illegible]
MOORE, ISIDORE, relief of	78	[illegible]	[illegible]	[illegible]

Subject.	Report.	Congress.	Session.	Volume.
[illegible]RE, ISIDORE, relief of	[illegible]	[illegible]	1	[illegible]
[illegible]ORE, SAMUEL, relief of	574	[illegible]	1	[illegible]
[illegible]ORE, SARAH, relief of heirs of	[illegible]	31	1	[illegible]
[illegible]TGOMERY, ALEXANDER, confirming titles of lands in Mississippi Territory to heirs of	[illegible]	15	2	1
Do	54	17	1	1
[illegible]RE, ENOCH S., relief of	214	[illegible]	[illegible]	[illegible]
[illegible]GAN ASHER, purchase certain public lands in Louisiana	75	[illegible]	[illegible]	[illegible]
[illegible]GAN, CHARLES, confirming title to land in Louisiana	1021	[illegible]	[illegible]	[illegible]
Do	[illegible]	[illegible]	1	3
[illegible], MANUEL GONZALES, certificate of location for confirmed land in Missouri	37	24	1	4
[illegible], JAMES, confirming title to land in Louisiana	[illegible]	[illegible]	[illegible]	[illegible]
[illegible], HENRY J. S., relief of	112	[illegible]	[illegible]	[illegible]
[illegible], WILLIAM, public lands in Missouri, to locate	[illegible]	29	1	4
[illegible], JACOB, relief of	[illegible]	[illegible]	[illegible]	4
[illegible], HENRY T., relief of	6	34	[illegible]	[illegible]
[illegible], JAMES FORT (heirs), confirming title to land in Louisiana	[illegible]	[illegible]	[illegible]	[illegible]
Do	[illegible]	37	[illegible]	[illegible]
[illegible], RICHARD, relief of	79	[illegible]	1	[illegible]
[illegible], MARY, relief of	[illegible]	[illegible]	1	4
[illegible], JOSEPH, confirming title to land in Louisiana	[illegible]	[illegible]	1	[illegible]
[illegible], GEORGE, relief of heirs of	[illegible]	[illegible]	[illegible]	[illegible]
[illegible], ROBERT, enter public lands in lieu of land erroneously entered	54	[illegible]	1	4
[illegible], JOSEPH, relief of	64	[illegible]	1	4
[illegible]W IDRIA MINING COMPANY, "Rancho Panoche Grande," title to	[illegible]	46	[illegible]	7
Do	[illegible]	46	[illegible]	7
Do	[illegible]	47	1	7
[illegible]W MADRID, MISSOURI, granting legal titles to locations in	[illegible]	44	1	7
Do	[illegible]	44	1	7
[illegible]W MEXICO,				
confirming titles to,				
Lands in	[illegible]	44	1	7
Do	110	44	2	7
Do	[illegible]	[illegible]	1	8
Aña de Sandoral y Manzanares	[illegible]	47	1	7
Arroyo de San Lorenzo	[illegible]	47	1	7
Do	173	48	1	8
Do	481	49	1	8
Cañon de Chama grant	1690	46	2	7
Do	131	46	3	7
Cuyamungue Pueblo tract	61	45	3	7
Ignacio Chaves	985	47	1	7
Do	1833	47	2	7
Do	175	48	1	8
Do	186	49	1	8
Medano Springs and Zapato grant	60	45	3	7
Mesita Juana Lopez grant	59	45	3	7
Myra Clark Gaines	96	48	1	8
Petaca land grant	45	46	3	7
San Clémente claim	123	48	1	8
Do	184	49	1	8
Socorro grant	1369	47	1	7
Do	380	41	1	8
W ORLEANS, LOUISIANA,				
Confirming title to land claim in southeastern district of	253	23	1	2
Confirmation of land to city of	384	36	1	6
BERT, JOSEPH, confirming title to land in Louisiana to heirs of	665	25	2	3
KON, ADELINE C., confirming title to certain land in Louisiana	127	35	1	5
RRIS, SAMUEL, confirming title to land between the Rio Hondo and Sabine Rivers to	338	26	1	3
RTHWEST TERRITORY, relief of persons in	184	48	1	7
EN, BENJAMIN, relief of	111	23	1	2
Do	392	23	1	2
Do	425	24	1	2
IO, confirming title to Marcus Heylin to land in	178	46	2	7
D MINES, MISSOURI, confirming titles of lands to inhabitants of	308	22	1	2
LLON, D. L. R., public lands in Louisiana, to locate	79	24	1	3
Do	654	25	2	3
R, ROBERT, relief of heirs of	238	35	2	5
VEGO, KANSAS, land warrant belonging to Catholic church at	2632	48	2	8
Do	3129	49	1	8
STINE, FREDERICK, relief of	33	19	2	1
Do	108	20	1	1
ERALL, JOHN, relief of	42	19	2	1
CKWOOD, WILLIAM, confirming title to land in Washington Territory	295	34	1	4
Do	112	36	1	6
LAO, PEDRO, confirming title to land in province of Florida	727	24	1	2
LMER, ARCHIBALD D., relief of heirs of	461	29	1	3
NOCHE GRANDE. (*See* RANCHO PANOCHE GRANDE.)				
VIE, CHARLES, confirming title to land in Louisiana	236	33	1	4

Subject.	Report.	Congress.	Session.	Volume.
PECK, ALEXANDER D., confirming title to land in Louisiana	334	30	1	[illegible]
PEET, HARRIET, confirming title to land warrant No. 66067	279	34	1	[illegible]
PELLERIN, LOUIS, confirming title of lands in Louisiana to heirs of	284	22	1	[illegible]
Do	40	23	2	[illegible]
PEPPER, JAMES, *et al.*, confirming title to land in Louisiana	161	27	2	[illegible]
Do	298	28	1	[illegible]
PEREA, JOSÉ LEANDRO, confirming title to claim of, in San Miguel County	457	35	1	[illegible]
Do	321	36	1	[illegible]
PERKINS, EDWARD T., relief of	3421	49	1	[illegible]
PERRY, JEAN FRANCOIS, relief of heirs of	826	45	2	[illegible]
PETACA LAND GRANT, confirming title to land in New Mexico known as	45	46	2	[illegible]
PETERS, JOHN, relief of heirs of	123	27	2	[illegible]
PETERS, SAMUEL, confirming title to lands in Mississippi Territory	44	18	2	1
PETERSON, T. F., purchase of island at the mouth of the Mississippi	727	25	2	3
Do	143	25	2	3
PETRE, JOSEPH PIERRE, relief of	60	22	2	3
Do	83	23	1	2
PETTIT, WILLIAM McD., relief of	748	25	2	3
PHELAN, NICHOLAS, relief of	142	35	2	3
PHILIBERT, PETER, *et al.*, patents for confirmed land claims in Louisiana, to issue	8	26	1	3
PIERCE, SUSAN, *et al.*, relief of	849	27	2	3
PLUMB, NATHANIEL, relief of	408	25	2	3
POISSOT, PAUL, confirming title to land in Louisiana	109	22	1	2
Do	241	24	1	3
Do	654	25	2	3
POLLARD, WILLIAM, confirming title to land in city of Mobile to heirs of	229	22	1	2
Do	226	23	1	2
Do	498	24	1	3
PONCE, CAMILLA C. A., relief of	417	30	1	5
PORCHE, ALEXIS, confirming title to land in Louisiana to legal representatives of	329	23	2	5
POWEL, JESSE, relief of	51	16	2	1
PRATT, JOHN, relief of	452	26	1	3
Do	85	27	2	3
PRIVATE LAND GRANTS,				
Arroyo de San Lorenzo	1501	47	1	7
Do	173	48	1	8
Do	451	49	1	5
Cañon de Chama	1800	46	2	[illegible]
Do	181	47	1	[illegible]
Cuyamungue Pueblo tract	61	45	2	[illegible]
Guadalupe, Miranda	457	35	1	[illegible]
Do	321	36	1	[illegible]
Lagunda de la Maroca	29	41	2	[illegible]
Do	811	45	2	[illegible]
Las Ormigas and La Nana	87	36	2	[illegible]
Do	1	37	2	[illegible]
Las Pulgas Rancho	810	45	2	[illegible]
Medano Springs and Zapato	60	45	3	[illegible]
Mesita Juana Lopez	59	45	3	[illegible]
Rancho Panoche Grande	29	46	2	[illegible]
Do	273	46	[illegible]	[illegible]
Do	922	47	[illegible]	[illegible]
Rancho de Napa	360	48	[illegible]	[illegible]
Petaca	45	46	[illegible]	[illegible]
Rio Hondo	222	45	[illegible]	[illegible]
San Clemente	133	48	[illegible]	[illegible]
Do	184	49	[illegible]	[illegible]
Santillan	344	44	[illegible]	[illegible]
Do	243	45	[illegible]	[illegible]
Do	186	45	[illegible]	[illegible]
Socorro	1369	47	[illegible]	[illegible]
Do	380	48	[illegible]	[illegible]
Tres Alamos	187	49	[illegible]	[illegible]
Yazoo	62	16	[illegible]	[illegible]
Zapato	60	45	[illegible]	[illegible]
PRE-EMPTION LAW, benefit to certain persons in Louisiana	155	23	[illegible]	[illegible]
PRESTON, FRANCIS, relief of	287	20	[illegible]	[illegible]
PROVINCHERE, PETER, *et al.*, confirming title to land	635	43	[illegible]	[illegible]
PRUDHOMME, ANTOINE, *et al.*, relief of	81	21	[illegible]	[illegible]
PRUDHOMME, ROSALINE, confirming title to land in Louisiana	143	25	[illegible]	[illegible]
PUBLIC LANDS, refunding overplus of purchase money paid by purchasers of	96	23	[illegible]	[illegible]
RACHAL, J. ELOY, relief of	240	24	1	[illegible]
Do	653	25	2	[illegible]
RACHAL, JULIAN, and others, confirming titles to lands in Louisiana	53	22	2	[illegible]
RAILROAD, to Mobile and Ohio, right of way in Alabama	615	30	1	[illegible]
RAMIREZ, SERAFIN, confirming title to claim of lands in Bernalillo County to	457	35	1	[illegible]
Do	321	36	1	[illegible]
RANCHO DE NAPA, confirming title to claimants of	360	48	1	[illegible]
RANCHO PANOCHE GRANDE, to determine title to tract of land known as the	29	46	2	[illegible]
Do	273	46	2	[illegible]

Subject.	Report.	Congress.	Session.	Volume.
O PANOCHE GRANDE, to determine title to tract of land known as the.	922	47	1	7
UAN, relief of heirs of	1498	46	2	7
HENRY, relief of	185	30	1	4
CK, THOMAS F., relief of heirs of	117	24	1	2
AMUEL, relief of	674	29	1	4
LEWIS, confirming title to land in Louisiana to heirs of	120	34	1	4
ER, JOHN, relief of	85	16	1	1
T, PHILIP, confirming title to land in Illinois to heirs of	8[illegible]	14	2	1
Do	120	20	1	1
Do	377	23	1	2
Do	951	27	2	3
S, JOSEPH, public lands in Louisiana to enter	15	30	2	4
Do	273	31	1	4
LDS, THOMAS, confirming title to land in Florida Territory	271	22	1	2
OPKINS, relief of	22	21	2	1
RDS, JOSEPH, relief of	83	31	1	4
Do	28	34	1	4
S, HUGH, relief of	600	26	1	3
Do	1080	27	2	3
ANNA M. E., and sisters, land warrant in lieu of one issued to father	240	35	1	5
NDO LAND CLAIMS, confirming title to	222	45	2	7
JAMES P., confirming title to land in Florida	345	31	1	4
Do	55	33	2	4
NS, JOSEPH, confirming title to land in Kentucky	65	32	1	4
IS, ROBERT M., public land in Louisiana, to purchase	936	25	2	3
TSON, MARY, *et al.*, relief of	22	38	2	7
RS, ELIZABETH, relief of	127	34	1	4
UES, EDWARD, *et al.*, confirming title to land in Louisiana	241	35	2	5
Do	418	36	1	6
UEZ, SIMON, confirming title to land in Louisiana	184	30	1	4
MATTHIAS, relief of	85	20	1	1
, A. B., relief of	170	33	1	4
OHN B., relief of	111	34	3	4
WILLIAM B., *et al.*, relief of	66	32	1	4
MAISON, confirming title to land in Louisiana	178	22	1	2
Do	554	24	1	2
, LUDWICK, relief of heirs of	521	24	1	2
Do	316	25	2	3
GEORGE, relief of	729	24	1	2
Do	483	25	2	3
ANSON, reconvey certain land in Colorado to	3800	49	2	8
E, JOHN, relief of	554	29	1	4
LIAS and ABIJAH, public lands, to locate	242	35	2	5
, JAMES, relief of	206	20	1	1
L, SOLOMON, relief of	317	29	1	4
RS, ARUND, relief of	22	21	1	1
D, JOSEPH, *et al.*, relief of	473	25	2	3
HELENA COURT HOUSE, LOUISIANA, right of pre-emption to settlers in the district of	108	18	1	1
JAMES MISSION. (*See* MISSION OF SAINT JAMES.)				
LOUIS, MISSOURI.				
d board of trustees in, lands granted to	12	20	2	1
rming titles to certain lands in city of	15	39	1	7
LOUIS COUNTY, MISSOURI, claims of inhabitants to public passways	268	34	3	4
VRAIN, CERAU, *et al.*, confirming title to claim of land in Taos County	457	35	1	5
Do	321	36	1	1
ICK RESERVATION, TENNESSEE, relief of inhabitants of	369	24	1	2
Do	407	25	2	3
Do	99	26	1	3
ÉMENTE CLAIM, confirming title to land in New Mexico known as	133	48	1	8
Do	184	49	1	8
VAL, ANTONIO, confirming title to claim of lands in San Miguel County	457	35	1	5
Do	321	36	1	6
ANCISCO, to confirm survey of pueblo of	1699	46	2	7
ANCISCO LAND ASSOCIATION OF PHILADELPHIA, relief of	344	44	1	7
Do	243	45	2	7
Do	186	45	3	7
Do	*694	46	2	7
NACIO DEL BABOCOMORI, confirming land grant to	530	47	1	7
SE DE SONOITA, confirming land grant to	530	47	1	7
AN DE LOS BOQUILLOS Y NOGALES, confirming land grant to	530	47	1	7
ATEO COUNTY, CALIFORNIA, correcting boundary lines in	†680	44	1	7
Do	*653	44	1	7
Do	*1095	46	2	7
Do	*849	47	1	7
GUEL COUNTY, CALIFORNIA, confirming title to land claim of Preston Beck, jr., in	457	35	1	5
Do	321	36	1	6

* Views of minority. † Part 1.

Subject.	Report.	Congress.	Session.	Volume.
SAN RAFAEL DEL VALLE, confirming land grant to	530	47	1	7
SANTA ANNA, confirming title to lands in New Mexico to Indians of pueblo of	70	40	2	7
SANTILLAN LAND GRANT, confirming title to purchasers of	344	44	1	
Do	243	43	2	
Do	186	45	1	
SAUCIER, JEAN BAPTISTE, confirming title to land in Louisiana	90	22	1	
SAULT SAINTE MARIE, confirming title to land at	215	34	1	
Do	3048	49	1	
SAUNDERS, ISAAC D., relief of	814	25	2	
SAWYER, WILLIAM, *et al.*, relief of	98	37	2	
Do	105	28	1	
SCHNABEL, GEORGE, relief of	682	27	2	
SCOLLEY, JOHN, *et al.*, confirming title to claim of lands in Taos County	457	35	1	
Do	321	36	1	
SCHOOL LANDS.				
Claim of citizens of Marion township, Mercer County, Ohio, for	246	33	1	4
Grant made to Saint Louis, Mo	12	20	2	1
Kansas Territory, confirming titles of purchasers of	985	36	1	6
Warren County, Missouri (Congressional township)	246	33	1	4
SCOTT COUNTY, MISSOURI, issuing patent for lands in	188	43	1	7
SCOTT, THOMAS B., confirming title to land in Louisiana	697	29	1	4
SCRIP. (*See* INDEMNITY SCRIP.)				
SEGURA, ELOY, *et al.*, granting public land in Louisiana to	383	23	1	2
SEMOICE (Indian), granting fee simple title to heirs of	28	30	2	4
Do	194	31		4
Do	195	31		4
Do	57	32		4
SENET, EUGENE, confirming title to land in Louisiana	271	23		2
SEWELL, JOTHAM, relief of	106	43	1	7
SEXTON, JAMES P., relief of	160	30	1	4
SHAFER, JACOB, relief of	46	18	1	1
SHEETS, ZEBULON, relief of	309	24	1	2
Do	348	25	2	3
SHIELDS, JAMES, relief of	451	26	1	3
SHINALT, JAMES, relief of	332	26	1	3
SIMPSON, BENJAMIN M., relief of	97	49	1	8
SINGLETON & ANDREWS, confirming title to land in Louisiana	221	22	1	2
Do	76	23	1	2
SMALL, ARCHIBALD, relief of	50	23	1	3
SMITH, DANIEL, confirming title to land in Louisiana	548	23	1	2
Do	69	24	1	2
SMITH, JACOB, confirming title to land in Michigan to heirs of	101	24	1	2
SMITH, JOSEPH, relief of	44	19	2	1
Do	55	20	1	1
SMITH, LUTHER L., confirming title to land in Louisiana	228½	22	1	2
Do	39	23	1	2
SMITH, McGEE, and SEMOICE (Indians), relief of	195	31	1	4
SMITH, MATTHEW, relief of	2353	48	1	8
SMITH, PHILANDER, confirming title to land in Louisiana to heirs of	58	27	3	3
SMITH, ROBERT K., *et al.*, confirming title to land in Louisiana	526	35	1	5
SMITH, THOMAS GREGORY, relief of	625	26	1	3
SMITH, WILLIAM, confirming title to land in Louisiana to heirs of	17	25	1	3
SLAUGHBOUGH JOHN, relief of	822	22	1	2
SOCORRO GRANT, confirming title to claimants of	1369	47	1	7
Do	380	48	1	8
SOILEAU, NOEL, confirming title to lands in Louisiana to heirs of	82	18	2	1
SPALDING, MARCUS, relief of	200	25	3	3
Do	232	29		4
Do	115	31		4
SPANISH CLAIMS, prescribing method of settling	985	48		8
SPRAGGINS, SAMUEL, confirming titles to lands in Louisiana	31	20	2	1
SPRIGG, SAMUEL, relief of	59	16	2	1
Do	84	20	1	1
Do	124	21		1
SROUFE, MARY, public lands in Ohio, to purchase	147	24		2
Do	285	25		3
Do	102	26		3
STAFFORD, JOB, relief of	268	35		5
STAPLES, ABRAM, relief of	469	35		5
STEELE, GEORGE BOONE, confirming title to land in Arkansas	334	26	1	3
STEELE, RICHARD W., relief of	229	26	1	1
Do	326	21	1	1
Do	68	22	1	2
STERRETT, ADAM, relief of	1094	27	2	3
Do	33	28	1	3
STEVENS, WILLIAM, relief of heirs of	71	46	1	7
STEVENSON, HUGH, *et al.*, confirming title to claim of lands in Doña Aña County	457	35	1	5
Do	321	36	1	6
STODDARD, HENRY, confirming title to land in Ohio	330	23	1	2
Do	114	24	1	2

Subject.	Report.	Congress.	Session.	Volume.
S, JAMES L., relief of	225	22	1	2
Do	89	23	1	2
Do	214	24	1	2
Do	1026	25	2	3
AARON, relief of	505	24	1	2
G, WALCOTT A., relief of	148	28	1	3
ING, CATHARINE, confirming title to land in Florida	130	33	2	4
ES, SOLOMON, relief of	417	28	1	3
IS, WILLIAM, *et al.*, relief of	52	34	3	4
R, JOHN A., relief of	718	44	1	7
N, JOSÉ, confirming title to land in New Mexico	66	40	2	7
Do	463	45	2	7
CHARLES P., confirming title to land in Arizona Territory	558	47	1	7
E AND OHIO RAILROAD COMPANY, right of way through public lands	615	30	1	4
IADGE, THEODORE W., relief of	185	49	1	8
OTE, SAN MIGUEL COUNTY, COLORADO, confirming title to claim of lands by town of	457	35	1	5
Do	321	36	1	6
E, JOHN R., confirming title to lands in Louisiana	155	34	3	4
Do	65	35	1	5
SE, MARIA, confirming title of lands to heirs of	83	17	1	1
ULT, JOHN B., confirming title to land in Missouri	51	42	3	7
AS, ISAAC, confirming title to land in Louisiana	382	22	1	2
AS, JACOB, relief of	192	26	2	3
AS, JOEL, confirming title to land	148	22	1	2
AS, JOHN, relief of heirs	336	26	1	3
AS, JOHN H., confirming title to land in Louisiana	336	21	1	1
Do	37	22	1	2
AS, MINOR, relief of	60	20	1	1
ASON, ELISHA, relief of	179	30	1	4
PSON, JOHN, confirming titles to lands in Louisiana	31	20	2	1
PSON, MARGARET, confirming title of lands in the district of Natchez, to heirs of	77	17	2	1
PSON, THOMAS, confirming title of lands in the district of Natchez, to heirs of	77	17	2	1
TON, MICHAEL, relief of	141	24	1	2
ON, NICHOLAS E., issue of land patent to	75	29	2	4
TS, W. H., relief of	1426	48	1	8
Do	1379	49	1	8
NY, SYLVESTER, relief of	468	35	1	5
ALBERT, confirming title to land in Missouri	780	27	2	3
THOMAS, relief of	678	24	1	2
Do	282	25	2	3
VALENCIA COUNTY, COLORADO, confirming title to claim of land by town of	457	35	1	5
Do	321	36	1	6
RT, JAMES A., relief of legal representatives of	3399	49	1	8
UD, JEAN MARIE, relief of	89	21	1	1
WILLIAM, relief of heirs of	449	26	1	3
LAMOS GRANT, confirming title to claim in Arizona Territory known as	187	49	1	8
CHARLES, *et al.*, confirming title to land in Louisiana	241	35	2	5
Do	418	36	1	6
L, LOUISA E., confirming title to land in Louisiana	280	27	2	3
TT, WILLIAM, confirming title to land in Missouri	57	29	2	4
Do	183	30	1	4
LE, JAMES, relief of	140	24	1	2
ER, FRANCOIS ISIDORE, confirming title to land in Louisiana	77	21	1	1
ER, JOHN, confirming title to land in Louisiana	86	21	1	1
ULL, ANDREW, relief of	23	20	1	1
THOMAS, relief of	26	41	3	7
WOOD, JEHU, confirming title to land in Florida to heirs of	461	35	1	5
WOOD, PHINEAS, relief of	73	19	1	1
ANTONIO, relief of legal representatives of	1526	47	1	7
AMUEL, confirming title to land in Louisiana	216	23	1	2
ALEXANDER, confirming title to claim of, of land in San Miguel County	457	35	1	5
Do	321	36	1	6
J. B. and FRANCIS, confirming title to land	635	43	1	7
JOHN BAPTISTE, relief of heirs of	347	31	1	4
RY, J. B., confirming title of lands in Louisiana to heirs of	323	22	1	2
ZEN, THOMAS, confirming title to land in Washington Territory	69	44	1	7
ESEN, FRANCIS B., relief of	174	48	1	8
S, ANTOINE, location of certain land claims in Missouri	185	27	3	3
Do	213	28	1	3
R, JOHN L., relief of	278	34	1	
ARTWELL, relief of	98	23	2	2
JACINTHA, confirming title of lands in the district of Natchez to heirs of	77	17	2	
DONACIAN, confirming title to claim of lands in San Miguel County	457	35	1	5
Do	321	36	1	

Subject.	Report.	Congress.	Session.	Volume.
VIRGINIA. (*See* MILITARY LAND WARRANTS.)				
VOLCKER, HENRY, confirming title to land in New Mexico	93	34	1	4
VOLCKER, HENRY (heirs of), confirming title to land in New Mexico	3509	49	2	5
WALKER, JEREMIAH, confirming title to lands in Louisiana	211	20	1	1
Do	161	21	1	1
WALL, JOHN, relief of	[illegible]	[illegible]	1	4
WALLER, WILLIAM, relief of	40	[illegible]	2	3
Do.	[illegible]	27	2	3
WAR OF 1812, bounty land to widows and children of soldiers of	121	[illegible]	1	4
WARD, R. J., relief of	[illegible]	21	1	1
WARD, REES BOWEN, relief of	[illegible]	[illegible]	2	3
WARE, SAMUEL, relief of legal representatives of	166	44	1	7
WARNER, DANIEL, issuing patent to heirs of	[illegible]	[illegible]	1	2
Do.	142	25	2	3
WARREN COUNTY, OHIO, claim of citizens for school lands	246	[illegible]	1	6
WASHINGTON TERRITORY, confirming title to land belonging to Saint James Mission in	180	44	1	7
Do.	254	46	2	7
WATERMAN, CHARLES, confirming title to lots in Milwaukee, Wis	325	34	1	4
WATSON, SAMUEL, relief of	231	21	1	1
WEATHERHEAE, ROBERT, purchase of land in Lafayette County, Missouri	276	22	1	2
WEEMS, N. C., confirming title to land in Louisiana	20	35	1	5
WELCH, OLIVER, relief of	144	25	2	3
Do	94	26	1	3
WELLS, DOROTHY, relief of	195	21	1	1
Do	60	22	1	2
WELLS, SILAS, relief of	627	26	1	3
WELLS, WILLIAM H., *et al.*, relief of	59	32	1	4
WELSH, NATHANIEL, relief of	560	23	1	2
WESTBROOK, ANDREW, relief of	58	19	2	1
Do.	20	20	1	1
WHEAT, CONRAD, Jr., land patent in Louisiana	219	33	1	4
WHITAKER, RUHAMA and REBECCA, confirming title to land in Louisiana.	69	33	2	4
Do.	117	34	1	4
WHITE, ELIJAH, confirming title to land in Washington Territory	56	33	2	4
WHITNEY, DANIEL, *et al.*, relief of	396	22	1	2
Do.	182	24	1	2
Do.	202	34	3	4
Do.	368	35	1	5
Do.	464	35	1	5
WILLIAMS, ISAAC, relief of heirs of	395	23	1	2
Do.	291	24	1	2
WILLIAMS, JOHN C., confirming title to land in Louisiana	197	22	1	2
Do.	36	23	1	2
WILLIAMSON, CHARLES, relief of heirs	72	24	1	2
WILLIS, HENRY, confirming title to lands in Mississippi Territory to heirs of	66	16	1	1
WILLIS, JENNETT, relief of	95	24	2	2
WILLIS, JESSE H., relief of	346	25	2	3
Do.	283	25	3	3
Do.	678	26	1	3
Do.	[illegible]	27	2	3
Do.	1166	27	2	3
WILSON, DANIEL, relief of	[illegible]	[illegible]	1	6
WILSON, HENRY, relief of	[illegible]	[illegible]	1	3
WILSON, JOSEPH F., relief of	[illegible]	45	2	7
Do.	[illegible]	47	1	7
Do.	[illegible]	[illegible]	1	8
Do	[illegible]	[illegible]	3	8
WINGATE, JEREMIAH, confirming title to land in Florida to heirs of	[illegible]	[illegible]	1	4
WINN, PETER, relief of heirs of	[illegible]	[illegible]	1	3
WINTER, ELISHA, confirming title to land in Arkansas to heirs of	[illegible]	[illegible]	[illegible]	2
WINTER, GABRIEL, confirming title to lands in Missouri Territory	[illegible]	[illegible]	2	1
Do.	[illegible]	15	1	1
WINTERS, E., confirming title to land in Louisiana	[illegible]	[illegible]	1	2
WINTON, JOHN, relief of	17	[illegible]	2	1
WISCONSIN TERRITORY, patents for certain land at Green Bay, issue of	[illegible]	25	2	3
WLODECKI, FRANCIS, relief of	[illegible]	34	1	6
Do.	21	35	1	5
WOOD, JAMES, relief of	[illegible]	31	1	4
WREN, WOODSON, confirming title to lands in Mississippi Territory	51	17	2	1
Do.	272	[illegible]	1	2
Do.	367	[illegible]	1	3
WRIGHT, MAURICE, public land in Arkansas, to purchase	[illegible]	26	1	3
WRINKLE, ABRAHAM, confirming title to land in Louisiana	166	[illegible]	1	2
YAZOO CLAIM, title of land in the Yazoo district	[illegible]	16	1	1
YERBA BUENA (island), claim of Thomas H. Dowling to	[illegible]	41	3	7
YOUNG, JAMES, confirming title to land in Louisiana to heirs of	[illegible]	27	3	2
ZAPATO GRANT, confirming title to claimants of	[illegible]	[illegible]	3	7

REPORTS

OF THE

E ON PUBLIC BUILDI

HOUSE OF REPRESENTATIVES,

FROM THE FOURTEENTH CONGRI
FORTY-NINTH CONGRESS, 1887,

IN THREE VOLUMES.

COMPILED, UNDER THE DIRECTION OF THE JOINT COMMITTEE ON PRINTING,

BY

T. H. McKEE,

CLERK DOCUMENT ROOM, UNITED STATES SENATE.

WASHINGTON:
GOVERNMENT PRINTING OFFICE.
1887.

9139

FORTY-NINTH CONGRESS, FIRST SESSION.

[PUBLIC RESOLUTION—No. 24.]

Joint resolution authorizing the preparation of a compilation of the reports of committees of the Senate and House of Representatives.

Resolved by the Senate and House of Representatives of the United States of America in Congress assembled, That there be prepared under the direction of the Joint Committee of Printing, a compilation of the reports of the Senate and House of Representatives from the Fourteenth to the Forty-eighth Congress, inclusive, classified by committees, arranged, indexed, and bound in suitable volumes for the use of the standing committees of the two Houses of Congress. And the sum of seven thousand seven hundred and fifty dollars, or so much thereof as may be found necessary, is hereby appropriated out of any money in the Treasury not otherwise appropriated, for the preparation of said work, which sum may be paid by the Secretary of the Treasury upon the order of the chairman of said Joint Committee, as additional pay or compensation to any officer or employee of the United States.

Resolved further, That the Clerk of the House and Secretary of the Senate be, and they are hereby directed, to procure and file, for the use of their respective Houses, copies of all reports made by each committee of all succeeding Congresses; and that the Clerk of the House and the Secretary of the Senate be, and they are hereby, authorized and directed at the close of each session of Congress, to cause said reports to be indexed and bound, one copy to be deposited in the library of each House and one copy in the room of the committee from which the reports emanated.

Approved, July 29, 1886.

COMPILER'S NOTICE.

ı compilation embraces all the printed reports made by both s of Congress from the commencement of the Fourteenth to the of the Forty-ninth Congress. They are classified by committees ranged in numerical order. The collection for each committee is d into volumes of suitable size. Each committee has a separate a copy being bound in each volume.

SPECIAL and SELECT reports are all compiled in one collection g one index, a copy of which is bound in each volume.

plan throughout the compilation is to place each report to the ittee from which it was reported, without reference to the subject-r.

House and Senate reports are compiled separately. Care will uired in noticing the chronological order, as in some instances an session or Congress may not appear in certain volumes from the ıat during this period no reports were made by this committee.

T. H. McKEE.

INDEX

TO

RTS OF COMMITTEE ON PUBLIC BUILDINGS AND

HOUSE OF REPRESENTATIVES.

FROM 1815 TO 1887, INCLUSIVE.

Subject.				
EEN, MASSACHUSETTS, public building at				
)ON, VIRGINIA, authorizing exchange of site for public building at				
'ICS. (*See* HOUSE OF REPRESENTATIVES.)				
AL FARRAGUT, relative to erection of statue of				
, OHIO, public building at				
Do				
IENY, PENNSYLVANIA, public building at				
TOWN, PENNSYLVANIA, public building at				
IA, PENNSYLVANIA, public building at				
OLIS, MARYLAND, public building at				
OLIS AND BALTIMORE SHORT-LINE RAILROAD COMPANY, granting right of way across reservations at Naval Academy to	2742		1	3
'ECT. (*See* SUPERVISING ARCHITECT.)				
MEDICAL MUSEUM, to construct fire-proof building for	1	47	2	2
Do		48	1	3
LLE, NORTH CAROLINA, public building at		47	1	2
Do		49	1	3
Do	1		1	3
ON, KANSAS, public building at	2851		1	3
N, NEW YORK, public building at	1283		1	3
TA, GEORGIA, public building at	1296		2	2
Do	280			2
Do	1262	40		3
TA, MAINE, public building at	1657	47		2
Do	114	48		3
Do	184	48		3
IORE, MARYLAND, relative to purchase of site for post-office building at	18	46		2
)LDI STATUE OF LIBERTY, authorizing exhibition of model of pedestal at Capitol	831	48	1	3
T, MAINE, providing for extension of public building at	392	49	1	3
DA HUNDRED, VIRGINIA, authorizing sale of certain land at	914	47	1	2
& HIGGINS, claim for relief	58	30	1	2
.MTON, NEW YORK, public building at	3808	49	2	3
GHAM, ALABAMA, public building at	3350	49	1	3
OF HOME MISSIONS, memorial for building for Indian school purposes in Alaska	236	47	1	2
ITY, IDAHO, public building at	1457	46	2	2
Do	453	47	1	2
CAL GARDEN, purchase of ground for	290	34	2	1
.EBOROUGH, VERMONT, public building at	1794	47	1	2
, JAMES A., claim for relief	117	32	1	1
'ELL (Chicago, Ill.), authorizing sale of lots to Chicago and Great Western Railroad	970	49	1	3
'ELL DOCK PROPERTY (Chicago, Ill.), with reference to disposition of	1898	47	2	2
.YN, NEW YORK, public building at	547	46	2	2
Do	273	47	1	2
Do	1844	48	1	3
Do	3418	49	1	3
Do	3535	49	2	3

Subject.	Report.	Congress.	Session.	Volume.
BROWNSVILLE, TEXAS, public building at	1356	46	2	2
BUCKLEY, JAMES S., claim for relief	90	21	2	1
BULFINCH, CHARLES, memorial relative to improving acoustics of Hall of House of Representatives	123	21	1	1
CAMDEN, NEW JERSEY, public building at	2656	48	2	3
Do	3361	49	1	3
CAPE VINCENT, NEW YORK, public building at	915	47	1	2
CAPITOL BUILDING, WASHINGTON, D. C.,				
Committee-rooms, renting building for temporary	190	15	1	1
Completion of, relative to	89	14	2	1
Do	33	16	1	1
Do	69	16	1	1
Do	79	16	1	1
Do	50	16	2	1
Do	76	17	1	1
Do	91	17	2	1
Fire-extinguishers for, authorizing purchase of	157	46	3	2
House of Representatives,				
Estimates and diagrams for altering the Library-room to be used for sittings of	516	28	1	1
Making changes in Hall of	23	47	1	2
Library-room in, estimates and diagrams for altering, to be used for sittings of House of Representatives	516	28	1	1
Lighting of, by electricity	235	46	2	2
Do	270	46	2	2
Water supply for, providing for	145	21	1	1
Do	344	21	1	1
CAPITOL GROUNDS, relative to improvement of	357	44	1	2
CARROLLTON TURNPIKE COMPANY, KENTUCKY, granting right of way to	1481	49	1	3
CARSON CITY, NEVADA, public building at	1065	47	1	2
Do	366	48	1	3
CASEY, STEPHEN, claim for relief	892	45	2	2
CHARLESTON, SOUTH CAROLINA, public building at	545	46	2	2
CHARLESTON, WEST VIRGINIA, public building at,				
To erect	545	46	2	2
To repair	644	49	1	3
CHARLOTTE, NORTH CAROLINA, public building at	1456	46	2	2
Do	884	47	1	2
Do	1060	48	1	3
Do	3609	49	2	3
CHATTANOOGA, TENNESSEE,				
Public building at, to erect	1311	47	1	2
Do	112	48	1	3
Do	1324	49	1	3
Streets in, to grant public land for	1356	49	1	3
CHESTER, PENNSYLVANIA, public building at	3814	49	2	3
CHEYENNE, WYOMING, public building at	1833	49	1	3
CHICAGO, ILLINOIS,				
Bridewell property at,				
Disposition of	1898	47	2	2
Authorizing sale to Chicago and Great Western Railroad of	970	49	1	3
Public building in,				
To erect	391	48	1	3
Do	4145	49	2	3
To erect, on Dearborn Park	4162	49	2	3
Public land at,				
Confirming title to certain	615	44	1	2
Do	427	45	2	2
Do	236	46	3	2
CHICAGO AND GREAT WESTERN RAILROAD, authorizing sale of certain property in Chicago to	970	49	1	3
CLARKSBURG, WEST VIRGINIA, public building at,				
To erect	555	46	2	2
Do	886	47	1	2
Do	1063	48	1	3
Do	3473	49	1	3
Extending limit of appropriation for	1094	49	1	3
CLEVELAND, OHIO, relative to extension of public building at	536	46	2	2
CLUSKEY, C. B., statement of condition of public buildings in Washington	90	30	2	1
COLUMBIAN INSTITUTE, to compensate for improvements made on public grounds	226	24	2	1
COLUMBUS, OHIO,				
Barracks at, granting right of way through	735	48	1	3
Public building at, to erect	1572	48	2	3
Do	452	47	1	2
COMMISSIONER OF PUBLIC BUILDINGS,				
Duties of, to transfer to principal architect	87	17	1	1
Expenditures by, for 1843	485	28	1	1
Office of, to abolish	152	27	3	1

Subject.	Report.	Congress.	Session.	Volume.
COMMITTEE ON PUBLIC BUILDINGS AND GROUNDS,				
Eight-hour law, investigation of violation of law in work on post-office building in New York City	390	43	1	2
New York City, investigation of violation of the eight-hour law in work on post-office building in	390	43	1	2
Order of business, making special order for consideration of business reported from	2496	49	1	3
Public buildings,				
Report on sundry bills for erection of certain	1006	45	2	2
Subcommittee to investigate erection in certain cities of	53	45	2	2
COMMITTEE-ROOMS,				
Building for, temporary rental of	190	15	1	1
Congressional Hotel for, authorizing rental of	313	47	1	2
CONCORD, NEW HAMPSHIRE, public building at	916	47	1	2
CONGRESSIONAL HOTEL, authorizing rental of, for additional committee-rooms	313	47	1	2
CONGRESSIONAL LIBRARY, converting room of Library for use of Hall of House	516	28	1	1
CONTRACTS, relative to expenditures for public buildings made under contracts by Architect of Treasury	51	41	3	2
COUNCIL BLUFFS, IOWA, public building at	1455	46	2	2
Do	277	47	1	2
Do	129	48	1	3
DALLAS, TEXAS, public building at	1295	46	2	2
Do	1309	47	1	2
Do	511	49	1	3
DANVILLE, VIRGINIA, public building at	785	45	2	2
DAVIS, HENRY S., claim for relief	106	39	1	2
DAVIS, SOLOMON, for relief of heirs	82	17	2	1
DAYTON, OHIO, public building at	1310	47	1	2
Do	966	49	1	3
DEARBORN PARK, CHICAGO, ILLINOIS, to erect public building on	4162	49	2	3
DENVER, COLORADO, public building at	558	46	2	2
Do	271	47	1	2
Do	3537	49	2	3
DEPARTMENT OF TREASURY, defining duties of Supervising Architect of	2445	48	2	3
DES MOINES, IOWA, extending limit of appropriation for public building at	1832	49	1	3
DETROIT, MICHIGAN, public building at,				
To erect	320	46	3	2
Do	583	47	1	2
Do	1061	48	1	3
Do	3448	49	1	3
Purchase of site for	2134	48	1	3
Extending limit of appropriation for	1264	49	1	3
DISTRICT OF COLUMBIA,				
Jail in, to erect new	595	36	1	1
Do	17	40	2	2
Public buildings and grounds in, letter from Secretary of Treasury showing expenditures made up to 1840 on	515	28	1	1
Water supply for use of public buildings in District of Columbia	77	15	2	1
DOVER, NEW HAMPSHIRE, public building at	1994	49	1	3
DRUMMOND LIGHT, relative to lighting Hall of House with	380	28	1	1
DULUTH, MINNESOTA, public building at	734	48	1	3
Do	399	49	1	3
DUVALL, WILLIAM T., claim for relief	889	45	2	2
EASTPORT, MAINE, public building at	3482	49	2	3
EAST SAGINAW, MICHIGAN, public building at	3406	49	1	3
ECHOLS, JOHN, quieting title to certain lands in Louisville, Ky	770	49	1	3
EDUCATION, memorial of Board of Missions for public building at Sitka for use of Indian school	236	47	1	2
EIGHT-HOUR LAW, relative to violation of law in work on New York City post-office building	390	43	1	2
ELECTRICAL ANNUNCIATORS, relative to placing annunciators in Hall of House	52	45	2	2
ELLISON, GEORGE C., investigation of character of	841	44	1	2
EL PASO, TEXAS, public building at	2663	48	2	3
Do	996	49	1	3
ERIE, PENNSYLVANIA, public building at	455	47	1	2
Do	128	48	1	3
EXECUTIVE DEPARTMENTS,				
Additional buildings for, to erect	62	15	1	1
Condition of	879	27	2	1
Do	267	28	1	1
Expenditures for year 1824 upon	60	18	1	1
Expenditures for year 1827 upon	75	19	2	1
Expenditures for year 1829 upon	69	20	2	1
Expenditures for year 1824 upon	60	18	1	1
Expenditures for year 1827 upon	75	19	2	1
Expenditures for year 1829 upon	69	20	2	1
Navy Department, additional appropriation for	20	28	2	1
Do	89	28	2	1

Subject.	Report.	Congress.	Session.	Volume.
HUNTSVILLE, ALABAMA, public building at	2672	48	2	3
Do	1265	49	1	3
INDIANAPOLIS, INDIANA, appropriation for improvement of public building at	1311	49	1	3
INDIANS, relative to purchase of building at Sitka for Indian school purposes	236	47	1	2
JACKSON, MICHIGAN, public building at	631	48	1	3
Do	3809	49	2	3
JACKSON, MISSISSIPPI,				
Public building at, to erect	544	46	2	2
To transfer certain United States rooms in, to city of	3603	49	2	3
Do	3979	49	2	3
JACKSON, TENNESSEE,				
Public building at, to erect	913	47	1	2
Extending limit of appropriation for	1152	49	1	3
JACKSONVILLE, FLORIDA, public building at	1281	48	1	3
Do	969	49	1	3
JEFFERSON, TEXAS, public building at	1294	46	2	2
Do	1464	47	1	2
Do	2918	49	1	3
JEFFERSON CITY, MISSOURI, public building at	1291	46	2	2
Do	1084	47	1	2
JEFFERSONVILLE, INDIANA, public building at	4104	49	2	3
JERSEY CITY, NEW JERSEY, public building at	4057	49	2	3
JONES, PATRICK H., claim for relief	890	45	2	2
KALAMAZOO, MICHIGAN, public building at	3980	49	2	3
KANSAS CITY, MISSOURI,				
Public building at	540	46	2	2
To enlarge	3754	49	2	3
KEOKUK, IOWA, public building at	388	48	1	3
Do	395	49	1	3
KEY WEST, FLORIDA, public building at	1299	46	2	2
Do	1058	48	1	3
LA CROSSE, WISCONSIN, public building at	390	48	1	3
Do	3453	49	1	3
LA FAYETTE, INDIANA, public building at	2145	48	1	3
Do	1939	49	1	3
Do	3811	49	2	3
LANCASTER, PENNSYLVANIA, public building at	1300	46	2	2
Do	584	47	1	2
Do	441	48	1	3
Do	3235	49	1	3
LEACH, WILLIAM, claim for relief	79	28	2	1
LEAVENWORTH, KANSAS, public building at	1302	46	2	2
Do	458	47	1	2
Do	2673	48	2	3
LEXINGTON, KENTUCKY, public building at	2549	48	2	3
LIBRARY. (*See* CONGRESSIONAL LIBRARY.)				
LOGANSPORT, INDIANA, public building at	613	49	1	3
LOONEY, DENNIS, claim for relief	893	45	2	2
LOS ANGELES, CALIFORNIA, public building at	932	49	1	3
LOUISVILLE, KENTUCKY,				
Public building at,				
To erect	560	46	2	2
Do	168	47	1	2
To increase limit of appropriation for	1685	48	1	3
Echols, John, quieting title to certain lands in, to	2375	48	2	3
Do	770	49	1	3
LOUISVILLE AND PORTLAND CANAL, authorizing use of basin in Louisville by	1725	49	1	3
LYNCHBURG, VIRGINIA, public building at	546	46	2	2
Do	314	47	1	2
LYNN, MASSACHUSETTS, public building at	2141	48	1	3
Do	997	49	1	3
Do	3480	49	2	3
MACON, GEORGIA, public building at	457	47	1	2
Do	213	48	1	3
MADISON, INDIANA, public building at	3416	49	1	3
MALL, relative to purchase by United States from Washington City of the	63	22	2	1
MANCHESTER, NEW HAMPSHIRE, public building at	2659	48	2	3
MARBLE. (*See* PUBLIC BUILDINGS.)				
MARINE CITY, MICHIGAN, public building at	3417	49	1	3
MARQUETTE, MICHIGAN,				
Public building at,				
To erect	1298	46	2	2
Do	274	47	1	2
To increase appropriation for	2255	48	2	3
MAYSVILLE, KENTUCKY, public building at	551	46	2	2
Do	1656	47	1	2
MEDICAL DEPARTMENT OF ARMY. (*See* ARMY AND MEDICAL MUSEUM.)				
MEMPHIS, TENNESSEE,				
Public building at, to erect	816	45	2	2
Public lands to, cession of certain	556	46	2	2

Subject.	Report.	Congress.	Session.	Volume.
MILWAUKEE, WISCONSIN, public building at	4144	49	2	3
MILLS, ROBERT, claim for relief	275	28	1	1
MILLS, ROBERT, memorial relative to improving acoustics of Hall of House of Representatives	53	21	1	1
MINNEAPOLIS, MINNESOTA, public building at	552	48	2	2
Do	170	47	1	2
MONROE, LOUISIANA, public building at	2691	48	2	3
Do	1261	49	1	3
MONTGOMERY, ALABAMA, public building at	543	46	2	2
MONTPELIER, VERMONT,				
Public building at,				
To erect	1793	47	1	2
Do	2060	48	2	3
To extend limit of appropriation for	1871	49	1	3
MONUMENT LOT. (*See* SMITHSONIAN GROUNDS.)				
MORRISTOWN, NEW JERSEY, relative to preservation of Washington's Headquarters at	2143	48	1	3
MUSEUM. (*See* ARMY MEDICAL MUSEUM.)				
NATIONAL MONUMENT, to erect, to memory of George Washington	434	28	1	1
NATIONAL MUSEUM, to construct building suitable for	244	45	2	2
NATIONAL TROPHIES, making disposition of foreign flags taken in battle and flags of the United States as have been used in memorable battles	80	28	2	1
NAVAL ACADEMY, ANNAPOLIS, MARYLAND, granting right of way to Annapolis and Baltimore Railroad Company across grounds at	2742	49	1	3
NAVY DEPARTMENT,				
Providing additional room for	20	28	2	1
Do	89	28	2	1
NEBRASKA CITY, NEBRASKA, public building at	3681	49	2	3
NEW ALBANY, INDIANA,				
Public building at	1458	46	2	2
Do	887	47	1	2
Do	65	48	1	3
NEWARK, NEW JERSEY, public building at	3813	49	2	3
NEW BEDFORD, MASSACHUSETTS, authorizing purchase of additional land for public buildings at	1955	47	2	2
Do	2253	48	2	3
NEW BERNE, NORTH CAROLINA, public building at	883	47	1	2
Do	3837	49	2	3
NEWBURG, NEW YORK, public building at, to erect	885	47	1	2
Do	1686	49	1	3
Washington's Headquarters at, to erect memorial column at	1167	47	1	2
NEW HAVEN, CONNECTICUT, additional appropriation for enlargement of public buildings at	1715	48	1	3
NEWPORT, KENTUCKY, public building at	2558	49	1	3
NEW STATE, WAR, AND NAVY BUILDING, relative to changing plan of construction of	629	43	1	2
NEW YORK ARSENAL, to erect officers' quarters at	2379	49	1	3
NEW YORK CITY,				
Eight-hour law, violation of, in work on post-office building of	390	43	1	2
Marine hospital at, to establish	3234	49	1	3
Post-office site at, sale of old	1062	47	1	2
Public building at, to erect	4035	49	2	3
Subtreasury building at, to erect statuary on buttresses in front of	1290	46	2	2
Warehouse property in, appraisal of	2665	48	2	3
NORFOLK, VIRGINIA,				
Marine hospital at, to erect	881	47	1	2
Public building at, to erect	3457	49	1	3
NORTHERN ELECTRIC LIGHT COMPANY, relative to lighting Capitol and grounds	235	46	3	2
Do	270	46	3	2
OMAHA, NEBRASKA, enlargement of public building at	4146	49	2	3
OPELOUSAS, LOUISIANA, public building at	1357	49	1	3
OSHKOSH, WISCONSIN, public building at	1013	49	1	3
OWENSBOROUGH, KENTUCKY, public building at	550	46	2	2
Do	281	47	1	2
Do	2671	48	2	3
Do	3119	49	1	3
Do	3761	49	2	3
OXFORD, MISSISSIPPI, public building at	1293	46	2	2
Do	379	47	1	2
Do	3283	49	1	3
PADUCAH, KENTUCKY, public building at	548	46	2	2
PATERSON, NEW JERSEY, public building at	1083	47	1	2
Do	389	48	1	3
Do	1867	49	1	3
PENSACOLA, FLORIDA, public building at	544	47	1	2
PENSION BUILDING,				
Plants and shrubs for, appropriation to supply	46	49	1	3
Purchase of, now occupied by Pension Office	1003	45	2	2
PENSION OFFICE, additional room for	585	47	1	2

Subject.	Report.	Congress.	Session.	Volume.
PEORIA, ILLINOIS,				
Public building at, to erect	557	46	2	2
Do	275	47	1	2
Do	2172	48	2	3
Extending limit of appropriation for	396	49	1	3
PETERSBURG, VIRGINIA, appropriation for improvement of public building at	1690	49	1	3
PETTIBONE, DANIEL, method of heating public buildings	90	14	2	1
PITTSBURGH, PENNSYLVANIA, public building at	539	46	2	2
Do	111	48	1	3
PLYMOUTH, MASSACHUSETTS, public building at	2144	48	1	3
PORTLAND, OREGON, public building at	3405	49	1	3
PORTSMOUTH, OHIO, public building at	558	46	2	2
Do	1093	49	1	3
PORT TOWNSEND, WASHINGTON TERRITORY, public building at	889	47	1	2
Do	442	48	1	3
POSTAL SERVICE. (*See* STAR ROUTE CASES.)				
POST-OFFICE BUILDING, purchase of additional lots adjoining	25	28	2	1
POST-OFFICE DEPARTMENT, providing for erection of fire-proof building for	737	25	2	1
POTOMAC RIVER, relative to collecting tolls of bridge over	159	28	1	1
POUGHKEEPSIE, NEW YORK, public building at	1388	46	2	2
Do	451	47	1	2
PRESIDENT'S HOUSE, cause of delay in completing	89	14	2	1
PROVEST, WINTER & CO., claim for relief	253	34	3	1
PROVIDENCE, RHODE ISLAND, custom-house at,				
To purchase land adjacent to	1795	47	1	2
Do	1263	49	1	3
To sell part of old lot occupied by	2042	48	1	3
PUBLIC BUILDINGS. (*See also name of locality.*)				
Capitol and President's House, cause of delay in completing	89	14	2	1
Commissioner of,				
To abolish office of	152	27	3	1
Expenditures for 1843 made by	485	28	1	1
Condition of,				
Report by C. B. Cluskey on, in Washington, D. C	90	30	2	1
At Washington, D. C	267	28	1	1
Construction of,				
To secure economy in	2146	48	1	3
Do	1757	49	1	3
Designating kind and character of material to be used in	305	25	3	1
Material found in State to be used in	691	47	1	2
District of Columbia,				
Statement of all moneys expended since location of seat of government within, up to 1840	515	28	1	1
To erect new jail in	595	36	1	1
Expenditures upon, statement of amounts expended in District of Columbia up to 1840	515	28	1	1
Fire-extinguishers and gas governors, to purchase for protection of	157	46	3	2
Fire-proof building, specification of William Strickland for	267	28	1	1
General Post-Office at Washington, D. C., enlargement of	2674	48	2	3
Ground for, appropriations for purchase of	77	15	2	1
Jail in District of Columbia, to erect new	595	36	1	1
List of buildings recommended by committee to be built	1006	45	2	2
Material used in, designating kind and character of	305	25	3	1
National Museum, to construct suitable building for	244	45	2	2
Strickland, William, specification for fire-proof buildings	267	28	1	1
Supervising Architect of, defining duties of	2445	48	2	3
Telegraphic and telephonic communications between, to construct underground	2395	48	2	3
Washington, D. C., condition of, at	267	28	1	1
Water for, providing for	77	15	2	1
Workmen on, petition for appropriation for continuance of work at Washing-	9	27	1	1
ton, D. C., from	9	27	1	1
PUBLIC LANDS.				
Chattanooga, Tenn., giving title to certain lands for streets to	1358	49	1	3
Louisville, Ky., giving title to John Echols of certain lands in	770	49	1	3
QUINCY, ILLINOIS, public building at,				
To erect	549	46	2	2
Do	276	47	1	2
To extend limit of appropriation for	2066	48	2	3
RAILROADS, granting right of way to certain railroads through Columbus barracks, Ohio	735	48	1	3
READING, PENNSYLVANIA, public building at,				
To erect	549	47	1	2
Do	340	48	1	3
To extend limit of appropriation for	995	49	1	3
RECORDS, providing building for preservation of Army medical	2041	48	1	3
RICHMOND, VIRGINIA, appropriation for extension of public building at	341	48	1	3
RILEY, WILLIAM L., claim for relief	1697	46	2	2
ROCHESTER, NEW YORK, public building at,				
To erect	541	46	2	2
Do	169	47	1	2

Subject.	Report.	Congress.	Session.	Volume.
ROCHESTER, NEW YORK, public building at—Continued.				
To extend limit of appropriation for	2864	48	2	3
Do	396	49	1	3
SACO, MAINE, public building at	1658	47		
SACRAMENTO, CALIFORNIA, public building at	1292	46		
Do	315	47		
Do	632	48		
SAINT JOSEPH, MISSOURI, public building at	560	46		
Do	171	47		
Do	1278	48		
SAINT LOUIS, MISSOURI, donating strip of land for street purposes at	1007	48		
SAN ANTONIO, TEXAS, public building at	459	47		
Do	1280	48		
Do	394	49		
Do	614	49	1	3
SANDY HOOK, NEW JERSEY, granting right of way through Government grounds at	1994	47	2	2
SAN FRANCISCO, CALIFORNIA, public building at	1305	46	2	2
Do	542	49	1	3
SANTA FÉ, NEW MEXICO, appropriation for completion of unfinished building at	2739	49	1	3
SARATOGA SPRINGS, NEW YORK, public building at	364	48	1	3
SAVANNAH, GEORGIA,				
Oglethorpe barracks at, authorizing sale of	167	47	1	2
Public building at,				
To erect	393	49	1	3
To purchase site for	3824	49	2	3
SCHNELL, JAMES L., plan for illuminating and ventilating Hall of House by	393	28	1	1
Do	78	28	2	1
SCHOOLS. (*See* EDUCATION.)				
SCRANTON, PENNSYLVANIA, public building,				
To erect	278	47	1	2
Do	1333	49	1	3
Do	4058	49	2	3
To increase appropriation for	1279	48	1	3
SEATON, WILLIAM W., asking Congress to appropriate money to erect public clock	286	28	1	1
SECRETARY OF TREASURY, statement from Secretary showing expenditures of all moneys appropriated in District of Columbia since location of the seat of government within District; also amounts so appropriated in lots, lands, or other public property up to 1840	515	28	1	1
SEDALIA, MISSOURI, public building at	1686	49	1	3
SENECA STONE. (*See* STATE, WAR, AND NAVY DEPARTMENT.)				
SHREVEPORT, LOUISIANA, public building at	456	47	1	2
SIOUX CITY, IOWA, public building at	968	49	1	3
SITKA, ALASKA, to erect school-house for Indians at	236	47	1	2
SKINNING, JOHN, claim for relief	1081	27	2	1
SKIRVING, JOHN, relative to ventilation of Hall of House by	140	28	2	1
SMITHSONIAN GROUNDS, purchase of property by Congress known as the Mall to be added to	514	28	1	1
SPRINGFIELD, ILLINOIS, authorizing purchase of additional grounds for public buildings at	1954	47	2	2
Do	214	48	1	3
SPRINGFIELD, MASSACHUSETTS,				
To erect public building at	2661	48	2	3
Do	512	49	1	3
National Armory, to erect milling shop at at	2223	49	1	3
SPRINGFIELD, MISSOURI, public building at	541	49	1	3
STANDARD UNDERGROUND CABLE COMPANY, appropriation for extension of	2335	48	2	
STATE, WAR, AND NAVY DEPARTMENT,				
Corridors of, to remove obstructions from	586	47		2
Seneca stone, use of, in laying foundation for new	93	42		2
STATESVILLE, NORTH CAROLINA, public building at	2886	49	1	
STATUE OF AMERICA, relative to executing an emblematic	92	31	2	
STATUES.				
Admiral Farragut, to erect to	97	42		
Subtreasury building, New York City, to erect, on buttresses in front of	1290	46		
George Washington, to erect to	21	22	2	1
Do	434	28	1	1
(*See also under respective names or titles for erection of memorial statues.*)				
STAUNTON, VIRGINIA, public building at	2642	49	1	3
STEUBENVILLE, OHIO, public building at	1606	47	1	2
STEWART, HUGH, claim for relief	161	26	2	1
Do	283	27	2	1
STILLWATER, MINNESOTA, to erect public building at	2610	48	2	3
STRICKLAND, WILLIAM, on plans and specification of construction of buildings by	267	28	1	1
SUPERVISING ARCHITECT OF TREASURY,				
Duties of, defining	2445	48	2	3
Expenditures made by, on public buildings	51	41	3	2

Subject.				
USE, NEW YORK, public building at				
Do				
HONE AND TELEGRAPHS, relative to communications betweer ecutive Mansion and Capitol				3
HAUTE, INDIANA, public building at,				
ırect				
Do				
extend limit of appropriation for				
RKANA, ARKANSAS, public building at				3
S, giving title to certain lands in Louisville to John Echols				3
IO, OHIO, public building at				2
URY BUILDING,				
struction of, condemning plans for			2	1
for, providing			2	1
argement and improvement of, to provide for			2	1
Do			1	1
URY DEPARTMENT. (*See* DEPARTMENT OF TREASURY.)				
NEW YORK, public building at,				
erect	436	48	1	3
extend limit of appropriation for	2721	49	1	3
, TEXAS, public building at	1303	46	2	2
Do	634	48	1	3
BURG, MISSISSIPPI, public building at	1412	49	1	3
, establishing new mode of taking yeas and nays in House of Representatives	184	28	2	1
Do	642	30	1	1
TEXAS, public building at	633	48	1	3
DEPARTMENT, additional room for use of	20	28	2	1
Do	89	28	2	1
HOUSE, on appraisal of warehouse property in New York City	2665	48	2	3
ER, CALEB, claim for relief	559	36	1	1
NGTON, DISTRICT OF COLUMBIA,				
of records at, to erect building for	778	47	1	2
d in, to purchase certain	1899	47	2	2
ical library and museum at, to erect building for	2041	48	1	3
-Office Department at, enlargement of	2674	48	2	3
al Office at, to erect building for Chief of	3626	49	2	3
NGTON GAS-LIGHT COMPANY, asking increase of their capital stock.	91	31	2	1
NGTON, GEORGE, relative to erecting statue to	21	22	2	1
Do	434	28	1	1
NGTON'S HEADQUARTERS,				
ristown, N. J., to preserve at	2143	48	1	3
burg, N. Y., to erect memorial column at	1167	47	1	2
NGTON, MARY, to complete monument to	1659	47	1	2
NGTON MONUMENT. (*See also* NATIONAL MONUMENT.)				
egulate use of grounds around	1758	49	1	3
, THOMAS C., claim for relief	79	28	2	1
TA, KANSAS, public building at,				
rect	1284	48	1	3
xtend limit of appropriations for	2022	49	1	3
S BARRE, PENNSYLVANIA, public building at	2142	48	1	3
Do	3454	49	1	3
AMSPORT, PENNSYLVANIA, public building at	454	47	1	2
Do	1277	48	1	3
Do	397	49	1	3
NGTON, DELAWARE, public building at	630	48	1	3
NGTON, NORTH CAROLINA, public building at	1389	46	2	2
Do	1282	48	1	3
Do	1153	49	1	3
R BUILDING,				
nsion of, for use of War Department	317	46	3	2
hase of, by Government	102	32	1	1
Do	193	33	1	1
A, MINNESOTA, public building at	1861	48	1	3
Do	3812	49	2	3
STER, MASSACHUSETTS, public building at	1325	49	1	3
ND NAY VOTES. (*See* VOTES.)				
RS, NEW YORK, public building at	1162	49	1	3
Do	3680	49	2	3
VILLE, OHIO, public building at	540	49	1	3

REPORTS

OF THE

MMITTEE ON PUBLIC EXPENDITURES,

HOUSE OF REPRESENTATIVES,

FROM THE FOURTEENTH CONGRESS, 1815, TO
FORTY-NINTH CONGRESS, 1887, INCLU .

IN THREE VOLUMES.

COMPILED, UNDER THE DIRECTION OF THE JOINT COMMITTEE ON PRINTING,

BY

T. H. McKEE,
CLERK, DOCUMENT ROOM, UNITED STATES SENATE.

WASHINGTON:
GOVERNMENT PRINTING OFFICE.
1887.

9258

FORTY-NINTH CONGRESS, FIRST SESSION.

[PUBLIC RESOLUTION—No. 24.]

Joint resolution authorizing the preparation of a compilation of the reports of committees of the Senate and House of Representatives.

Resolved by the Senate and House of Representatives of the United States of America in Congress assembled, That there be prepared under the direction of the Joint Committee of Printing, a compilation of the reports of the Senate and House of Representatives from the Fourteenth to the Forty-eighth Congress, inclusive, classified by committees, arranged, indexed, and bound in suitable volumes for the use of the standing committees of the two Houses of Congress. And the sum of seven thousand seven hundred and fifty dollars, or so much thereof as may be found necessary, is hereby appropriated out of any money in the Treasury not otherwise appropriated, for the preparation of said work, which sum may be paid by the Secretary of the Treasury upon the order of the chairman of said Joint Committee, as additional pay or compensation to any officer or employee of the United States.

Resolved further, That the Clerk of the House and Secretary of the Senate be, and they are hereby directed, to procure and file, for the use of their respective Houses, copies of all reports made by each committee of all succeeding Congresses; and that the Clerk of the House and the Secretary of the Senate be, and they are hereby, authorized and directed at the close of each session of Congress, to cause said reports to be indexed and bound, one copy to be deposited in the library of each House and one copy in the room of the committee from which the reports emanated.

Approved, July 29, 1886.

COMPILER'S NOTICE.

compilation embraces all the printed reports made by both ı of Congress from the commencement of the Fourteenth to the f the Forty-ninth Congress. They are classified by committees 'anged in numerical order. The collection for each committee is l into volumes of suitable size. Each committee has a separate a copy being bound in each volume.

SPECIAL and SELECT reports are all compiled in one collection one index, a copy of which is bound in each volume.

plan throughout the compilation is to place each report to the tee from which it was reported, without reference to the subject-

House and Senate reports are compiled separately. Care will ıired in noticing the chronological order, as in some instances an ession or Congress may not appear in certain volumes from the ıt during this period no reports were made by this committee.

T. H. McKEE.

INDEX

TO

'S OF COMMITTEE ON PUBLIC EXPENDITURES,

HOUSE OF REPRESENTATIVES.

FROM 1815 TO 1887, INCLUSIVE.

Subject.	Report.	Congress.	Session.	Volume.
MIGRATING COMPANY, investigation of contract for removal eek Indians	458	27	2	1
estigation into charges made by the "Worcester Spy" relative to paid for territory of (testimony)	35	40	3	3
OF PUBLIC BUILDINGS, investigation of the management	460	27	2	1
to construct depots for emigrating Indians in	604	27	2	1
'S, investigation of cost in Florida of contruction of	903	27	2	1
ERS, pay for time intervening between resignation and reinstate-	459	27	2	1
:KEEPER, investigating character of duty required at Frankford, f	932	27	2	1
.. Postmaster-General, investigation of payment to Blair & Rives ill for printing	995	27	2	1
ES, payment of, by Postmaster-General for printing	995	27	2	1
TOM-HOUSE, investigation of charges of official misconduct in mony)	*15	39	2	3
. Col. J. B., court-martial, as quartermaster-general at Saint Louis, aud, &c. (testimony)	996	27	2	1
IEON, to investigate the expenditure of money, and the removal of asaw Indians (1837)	454	27	2	1
IARLES J., examination of the settlement of his claim for tobacco oyed in 1814	1103	27	2	1
Do	211	27	3	1
INDIANS,				
om Memphis, Tenn. to Little Rock, Ark	454	27	2	1
es of funds belonging to	604	27	2	1
INST THE UNITED STATES, examination and decision of	100	17	1	1
). C.,				
s disbursing agent of Indian Department at Little Rock, Ark., igation of	453	27	2	1
cond Comptroller	453	27	2	1
cond Auditor	453	27	2	1
ON PUBLIC EXPENDITURES, relative sphere of its duties un- e rules	116	20	1	1
: FUND OF HOUSE, investigation of contracts of purchases made	880	27	2	1
erection by soldiers of forts and military defenses under Army and officers and not by	100	17	1	1
'IAL, trial of Lieut. Col. J. B. Brant for fraud as quartermaster- al at Saint Louis, Mo. (testimony)	996	27	2	1
ANS, to investigate expenditures of appropriations for removal 36)	458	27	2	1
(*See* INDIAN WARS.)				
SE (Boston, Mass.), investigation of charges of official misconduct 36) (testimony)	*15	39	2	3
SE (New York City),				
on of fraud and abuses in (testimony)	669	27	2	1
on of official misconduct in (1864) (testimony)	111	38	1	2
Do	25	38	2	2
Do	30	39	2	3

* And views of minority.

Subject.	Report.	Congress.	Session.	Volume.
DEMOCRATIC REVIEW, investigation of aid derived from purchases made from contingent fund of the House for benefit of	880	27	2	1
DEPOTS,				
To establish, in Arkansas for emigrating Indians	604	27	2	1
Investigation of cost of construction of depots in Florida for use of Army	903	27	2	1
DISTRICT OF COLUMBIA, remarks of architect upon new jail in	[illegible]	27	2	1
EMIGRATING INDIANS. (*See* INDIANS.)				
EXECUTIVE DEPARTMENTS, to investigate expenditures in	116	26	1	1
Do	456	27	2	1
EXPENDITURES,				
Army depots in Florida, construction of, investigating cost	903	27	2	1
Florida squadron, expenses of, investigating	582	28	1	2
Do	168	28	2	2
Mail bags and blanks, purchase of, by Post-Office Department	889	27	2	1
Public, investigation of	162	14	2	1
Do	116	26	1	1
Do	456	27	2	1
Public buildings at the national capital, investigating	92	41	3	3
Salaries and other expenses of Government, reduction of	756	27	2	1
FEDERAL FINANCES, review of statements of Secretary of Treasury concerning (1848)	*728	30	1	3
FEDERAL GOVERNMENT, reduction of all salaries of employés in	756	27	2	1
FINANCES OF GOVERNMENT, statements of Secretary of Treasury concerning (1848)	*728	30	1	3
FLORIDA SQUADRON, investigation of expenditures made by Navy Department for	582	28	1	2
Do	168	28	2	2
FLORIDA WAR. (*See* INDIAN WARS.)				
FORTS, erection by soldiers and mechanics under officers of the Army and Navy, and not by contracts	160	27	1	1
FRANKFORD, PENNSYLVANIA, investigation of military storekeeper at	[illegible]	27	2	1
FRAUDS ON THE REVENUE, investigation of	15	30	2	1
FUEL, commutation to officers in Seminole and Creek campaigns for	307	27	3	1
GENERAL POST-OFFICE DEPARTMENT, investigation of contracts for mail bags and blanks made by	889	27	2	1
GOVERNMENT PRINTING OFFICE, management of (testimony)	119	45	3	1
HARRIS, C. A., Commissioner of Indian Affairs, investigation as Commissioner of Indian Affairs	[illegible]	27	3	1
HOUSE OF REPRESENTATIVES,				
Investigation of fraudulent purchases and payments made from contingent fund of	880	27	2	1
Examination of laws in relation to public printing of	249	36	1	2
HOYT, JESSE, investigation of New York custom-house under management of	669	27	2	1
INDIAN WARS,				
Creeks, commutation for fuel to officers serving in campaign against	307	27	3	1
Florida, investigation of cost of construction of depots and other buildings for Army use in	903	27	2	1
Seminole, commutation for fuel to officers serving in	307	27	3	1
INDIANS,				
Chickasaw,				
Expenditure of appropriations for removal of (1837)	[illegible]	[illegible]	[illegible]	1
Expenditure of funds belonging to	[illegible]	[illegible]	[illegible]	1
Creek, expenditure of appropriations for removal of (1836)	[illegible]	[illegible]	[illegible]	1
Emigrating, establishing depots in Arkansas for	604	[illegible]	[illegible]	1
INVESTIGATION,				
Boston, Mass., custom-house at, official misconduct in management of	[illegible]	[illegible]	[illegible]	3
New York custom-house, frauds and abuses in	[illegible]	[illegible]	[illegible]	1
Do	111	[illegible]	1	2
Do	[illegible]	[illegible]	[illegible]	2
Do	[illegible]	[illegible]	[illegible]	3
Post-Office Department, offices created in, without authority of law	[illegible]	[illegible]	[illegible]	1
JAIL, remarks of architect upon new jail in District of Columbia	[illegible]	[illegible]	[illegible]	1
LARNER, THOMAS D., petition for employment as page	74	[illegible]	[illegible]	1
LINDSLEY, MALCOLM, petition for employment as page	74	[illegible]	[illegible]	1
McLAUGHLIN, JOHN T., investigating expenditures made as purser of Florida squadron by	[illegible]	[illegible]	1	2
Do	*[illegible]	[illegible]	[illegible]	2
MAIL BAGS AND BLANKS, investigation of contracts for	[illegible]	[illegible]	[illegible]	1
MEMBERS OF CONGRESS,				
Mileage, establishing a uniform rule of	[illegible]	[illegible]	[illegible]	1
Do	[illegible]	[illegible]	[illegible]	1
Salaries of	[illegible]	[illegible]	[illegible]	1
MILEAGE, establishing uniform rule for members of Congress	[illegible]	[illegible]	[illegible]	1
Do	[illegible]	[illegible]	[illegible]	1
MILITARY DEFENSES, providing for erection by soldiers and mechanics under Army and Navy officers, and not by contracts	160	27	1	1
MILITARY STOREKEEPER, investigation of, at Frankford, Pa	[illegible]	[illegible]	2	1
MILLS, ROBERT, memorial (*see* Part 2)	[illegible]	[illegible]	[illegible]	1
MINT, cost of erecting, at New Orleans	[illegible]	[illegible]	[illegible]	1.
MISSISSIPPI RIVER, investigation of expenditure of appropriation to improve navigation of the mouth of	[illegible]	[illegible]	2	1

* And views of minority.

Subject.	Report.	Congress.	Session.	Volume.
AL CAPITAL, removal of, to Mississippi Valley	*52	41	3	3
ay of officers between time of resignation and date of reinstatemen to	459	27	2	1
EPARTMENT, investigation of expenditures upon Florida squadron made by	582	36	1	2
Do	163	36	2	2
LEANS, LOUISIANA, cost of construction of and expenditures in mint at	462	27	2	1
RK (city), frauds and abuses in management of custom-house at	669	27	2	1
Do	111	33	1	2
Do	25	33	2	2
Do	30	39	2	2
, investigation of creating, in Post-Office Department without authority	457	27	2	1
morial of citizens of, asking for reduction of 20 per cent. in pay and salaries of Government employés	756	27	2	1
ND PACIFIC MAILS, investigation of contract to carry, by Wells, Fargo & Co., testimony	24	40	3	3
Do	37	40	3	3
MAILS, investigation of contract with Wells, Fargo & Co., for carrying United States mails overland	24	40	3	3
Do	37	40	3	3
OHN, investigation of contract to remove Creek Indians	458	27	2	1
OFFICE BUILDING, remarks of architect upon	460	27	2	1
XTER, GEORGE, report as commissioner appointed to investigate management of New York custom-house	669	27	2	1
THOMAS J., letter relating to expenditure of Chickasaw funds	664	27	2	1
SERVICE,				
estigate contract made with Wells, Fargo & Co. for transporting Pacific mails overland	24	40	3	3
Do	37	40	3	3
igation of contracts made by General Post-Office Department for mail bags and blanks for use of	969	27	2	1
FICE DEPARTMENT,				
estigate the creation of offices without authority of law in the	457	27	2	1
ination of expenditures in	969	27	2	1
nt of bill of Blair & Rives by	865	27	2	1
G. (*See* Public Printing.)				
BUILDINGS,				
ect, remarks of, upon building for General Post-Office and new jail in District of Columbia	460	27	2	1
f construction of and expenditures made for	549	27	2	1
ditures in management of, by superintendent and architect	460	27	2	1
ment buildings, cost of, at national capital	52	41	3	3
t New Orleans, La., cost of construction	462	27	2	1
EXPENDITURES,				
igation of	102	14	2	1
Do	116	20	1	1
Do	458	27	2	1
ittee on, defining duties of	100	17	1	2
PRINTER, duties of	249	36	1	1
PRINTING,				
igation of printing as done for House of Representatives	†249	36	1	2
igation into management of Government Printing Office, testimony	119	45	3	[illegible] 4
S,				
uct for time absent from session of Congress by members	34	21	2	1
tion of 20 per cent. of all pay of Federal officers	756	27	2	1
E WAR. (*See* Indian Wars.)				
WILLIAM B., petition for employment as page	74	27	2	1
EPER. (*See* Military Storekeeper.)				
TENDENT OF PUBLIC BUILDINGS, investigation of management under	460	27	2	1
T, Captain A., letter explanatory of purchase made by	‡458	27	2	1
JAMES, investigating expenditures on Niagara frontier	85	14	2	1
ORTATION OF MAILS, investigation of contract with Wells, Fargo & Co., to carry overland Pacific mails, testimony	37	40	3	3
RY BUILDING,				
ks of architect upon	460	27	2	1
estigate construction of	549	27	2	1
STATES MINTS. (*See* Mints.)				
STATES REVENUE, investigation of frauds committed on	15	39	2	3
Do	30	39	2	3
GTON (District of Columbia), cost of Government buildings in	52	41	3	3
TEPHEN H., investigation of charges against, as military storekeeper at Detroit	679	27	2	1
FARGO & COMPANY, investigation of contract to carry Pacific mails, testimony	24	40	3	3
Do	37	40	3	3

* Views of minority. † And views of minority. ‡ Parts 1, 2.

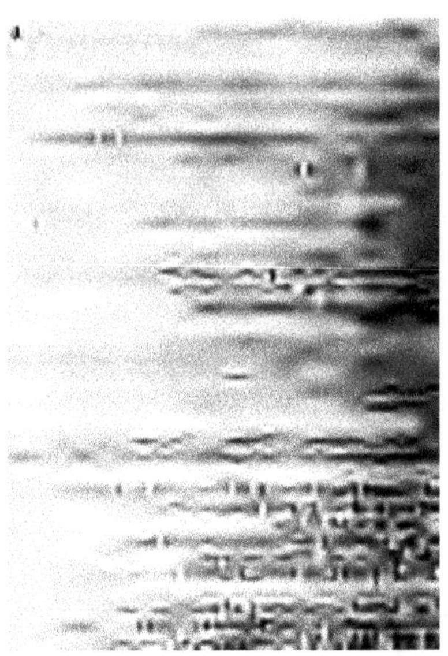

REPORTS

OF THE

OMMITTEE ON PUBLIC

HOUSE OF REPRESENTATIVES,

FROM THE FOURTEENTH CONGRESS, 1815, TO THE FORTY-NINTH CONGRESS, 1887, INCLUSIVE,

IN TEN VOLUMES.

COMPILED, UNDER THE DIRECTION OF THE JOINT COMMITTEE ON PRINTING,

BY

T. H. McKEE,

CLERK DOCUMENT ROOM, UNITED STATES SENATE.

WASHINGTON:
GOVERNMENT PRINTING OFFICE.
1887.

9206 P L

FORTY-NINTH CONGRESS, FIRST SESSION.

[PUBLIC RESOLUTION—No. 24.]

Joint resolution authorizing the preparation of a compilation of the reports of committees of the Senate and House of Representatives.

Resolved by the Senate and House of Representatives of the United States of America in Congress assembled, That there be prepared under the direction of the Joint Committee of Printing, a compilation of the reports of the Senate and House of Representatives from the Fourteenth to the Forty-eighth Congress, inclusive, classified by committees, arranged, indexed, and bound in suitable volumes for the use of the standing committees of the two Houses of Congress. And the sum of seven thousand seven hundred and fifty dollars, or so much thereof as may be found necessary, is hereby appropriated out of any money in the Treasury not otherwise appropriated, for the preparation of said work, which sum may be paid by the Secretary of the Treasury upon the order of the chairman of said Joint Committee, as additional pay or compensation to any officer or employee of the United States.

Resolved further, That the Clerk of the House and Secretary of the Senate be, and they are hereby directed, to procure and file, for the use of their respective Houses, copies of all reports made by each committee of all succeeding Congresses; and that the Clerk of the House and the Secretary of the Senate be, and they are hereby, authorized and directed at the close of each session of Congress, to cause said reports to be indexed and bound, one copy to be deposited in the library of each House and one copy in the room of the committee from which the reports emanated.

Approved, July 29, 1886.

COMPILER'S NOTICE.

This compilation embraces all the printed reports made by both Houses of Congress from the commencement of the Fourteenth to the close of the Forty-ninth Congress. They are classified by committees and arranged in numerical order. The collection for each committee is divided into volumes of suitable size. Each committee has a separate index, a copy being bound in each volume.

The SPECIAL and SELECT reports are all compiled in one collection having one index, a copy of which is bound in each volume.

The plan throughout the compilation is to place each report to the committee from which it was reported, without reference to the subject-matter.

The House and Senate reports are compiled separately. Care will be required in noticing the chronological order, as in some instances an entire session or Congress may not appear in certain volumes from the fact that during this period no reports were made by this committee.

T. H. McKEE.

INDEX

TO

;PORTS OF THE COMMITTEE ON PUBLIC LANDS,

HOUSE OF REPRESENTATIVES.

FROM 1815 TO 1887, INCLUSIVE.

Subject.	Report.	Congress.	Session.	Volume.
" SHAWNEE INDIANS, relative to sale of certain Shawnee Indian				
;, and providing homes for the "Black Bob" and	188	44	2	8
AAC, for relief	59	25	3	4
RAL COLLEGES (*see* SCHOOL LANDS), grant of land to the several				
;s for establishment of	261	35	1	7
ervations in, relinquishing United States title to	42	20	2	2
Do	69	21	1	3
Academy, to grant lands in aid of	381	26	1	5
ounty, relating to sale of public lands in	97	21	1	3
Do	204	21	1	3
ficates in, relief of holders of	9	21	2	3
ict in, to create additional	248	27	2	5
ts.				
road company in	607	24	1	4
to State for school purposes	746	30	1	6
ıds in, to dispose of the same as agricultural lands	203	46	3	9
Academy in, granting public land to	413	28	1	3
m rights, to allow, in purchase of lands in	115	18	1	1
ıd claims in, to settle	1859	48	1	10
ls in, exclusion of, from laws relating to mineral lands	117	48	1	10
Do	865	49	1	10
; of lands in 1818–'19 in	402	24	1	4
Do	239	25	2	4
ınd grants, to declare forfeited	2016	48	1	10
n, right of way over public lands to	607	24	1	4
Do	322	26	1	5
ed lands to, granting, for improving of rivers in State	11	20	2	2
Do	505	24	1	4
ls in, relative to worthless	815	30	1	6
rvations in, to amend act relative to 5 per cent. fund and	753	27	2	5
Do	145	28	1	5
Do	85	27	2	6
governor of State selection of any unsold land contiguous to Chick-				
cession for	753	27	2	5
Do	145	28	1	5
Do	85	29	2	6
ng land to aid	746	30	1	6
;eneral in, to discontinue office of	651	30	1	6
in, granting lands for	931	48	1	10
AND CHATTANOOGA RAILROAD, to forfeit land grant of	2443	49	1	10
FLORIDA AND GEORGIA RAILROAD COMPANY, granting				
lege of entering certain amount of public lands to	795	25	2	4
Do	269	25	3	4
horizing sale of certain lands in	174	44	2	8
R, for relief	408	23	1	3
Do	65	23	2	3
Do	389	24	1	4
Do	309	25	2	4
, ALEXANDER, for relief	102	36	1	7

Subject.	Report.	Congress.	Session.	Volume.
ALEXANDER, JAMES S., for relief	585	25	2	4
Do	76	26	1	5
ALEXANDRIA, LOUDON AND HAMPSHIRE RAILROAD, granting land in aid of construction to	267	34	3	7
ALIENS. (See FOREIGNERS.)				
ALLEN, BENJAMIN F., for relief	548	29		
ALSPECK, MICHAEL, for relief	31	34		
ALTMAN, MARZEL, for relief	562	46		
Do	32	47		
ALTON, ILLINOIS, fixing title to certain unsurveyed lands at	144	30		
AMBROZINE, JOHN, for relief	218	29		
Do	812	30		
AMERICAN COFFEE LAND ASSOCIATION, memorial for grant of land in Florida for cultivation of coffee, &c	47	17		
AMERICAN COLLEGE OF SCIENCE AND INDUSTRY, granting land in aid of	193	27		
ANDERSON, JAMES, for relief	318	26		
Do	348	24		
Do	165	29		
ARBUCKLE, MATTHEW, for relief	134	23		
Do	949	25		
ARCHIVES, to reduce number of keepers of public, in Florida	140	23	1	
ARCOTT, NICHOLAS, confirming title of lands to	2	16	2	
ARIZONA, granting lands for university purposes to	739	46		
ARKANSAS,				
Cherokee Indian reservation in, to sell	2021	48		13
Do	1004	49		11
Choctaw lands in, relief of settlers upon	93	19	2	
Do	208	24		
Do	99	25		4
Do	629	25		4
Do	600	27		5
Do	601	27	2	5
Claimants to lands in, of a larger amount than one league square authorized to institute proceedings to test validity of claim	48	18	2	1
Claims,				
To indemnify for loss of improvements ceded to Choctaw Indians	208	24	2	4
To adjust claim of State against United States	719	46	2	9
Authorizing location of the "Lovely Donation" claims	604	30	1	6
Fort Smith reservation, to grant part of, for school purposes	207	48	1	10
Indian depredations, to indemnify settlers for losses sustained by	321	22	1	3
Inundated lands of, to reclaim	549	24	1	4
Do	387	25	2	4
Land grants to,				
Additional, for erection of public building in	102	24	1	4
For construction of road for military purposes	651	24	1	4
Do	386	25	3	4
To certain persons in	509	27	2	5
Alternate sections near New Madrid and Saint Francis River for purpose of reclaiming same	310	28	1	5
Do	86	29	1	6
Do	108	31	1	7
Land titles in,				
To quiet certain	689	27	2	5
To quiet, under act of August 11, 1842	409	28	1	5
To quiet title to land known as "Bowie claims"	603	30	1	6
Military bounty-land warrants in, coercing holders to draw their patents for	257	23	1	3
Mineral lands in, to open to entry	9	43	3	8
Pre-emption rights in, relative to	56	18	1	1
Do	39	18	2	1
Private land claims in, to settle	1859	48	1	10
Public lands in, governor authorized to select six sections under act of June 23, 1836	166	28	1	5
Quapaw Indians in, lands granted to	60	19	2	1
Surveyor-general, to discontinue office of	651	30	1	6
Swamp lands, to indemnify State for sale of	547	47	1	9
ARMY.				
Bounty lands,				
Granted to persons promoted to commissioned officers	349	30	1	6
For military service	246	31	1	7
For service in "Wayne war," war of 1812, and Seminole war	246	31	1	7
Additional land bounties to veteran soldiers of the war of the Rebellion	37	39	1	8
Homestead law, granting privileges of, for ninety days' service in war of rebellion	6	44	3	8
ARREDONDO LAND GRANT, providing for settlement of conflicts between Spanish land claims and purchases under the United States	652	30	1	6
ASYLUM, to establish and support one in Minnesota for the benefit of the deaf, dumb, blind, and insane	315	34	1	7
ATKINSON, BENJAMIN, for relief	504	27	2	5
ATKINSON, THOMAS, for relief	17	36	1	7

* Views of minority.

*Views of minority.

Subject.	Report.	Congress.	Session.	Volume.
CARY, JESSE and PETER, for relief	595	25	2	4
CATNER, PHILIP, for relief	155	25	3	4
CAULFIELD, JAMES, for relief	77	24	1	4
CENTRAL PLANK-ROAD COMPANY, ALABAMA, granting right of way through the public lands to the	245	31	1	7
CERTIFICATES, relative to relinquishment of land	105	19	1	1
CHALLENGE (Cherokee Indian), for relief	42	20	2	2
Do	69	21	1	3
CHAMBERS, DAVID, for relief	68	48	2	1
CHANDLER, JOEL, for relief	504	24	1	4
Do	96	25	2	4
CHAPMAN, JAMES, for relief	145	30	1	6
CHAUDANIA, JOHN B., for relief	653	29	1	6
CHAZOTTE, PETER S., *et al.*, for grant of land in Florida for cultivation of coffee	47	17	1	1
Do	14	17	2	1
CHEROKEE RESERVATION. (*See* INDIANS.)				
CHEW & REFF, for relief	60	14	2	1
Do	73	14	2	1
CHICAGO, ILLINOIS, to confirm title to certain lands in, known as the Fort Dearborn Reservation	316	46	3	9
CHICAGO MILWAUKEE AND SAINT PATL RAILROAD COMPANY, granting authority to extend line of road to	735	46	2	9
CHICKASAW INDIANS (*see also* INDIANS), leasing of, certain reservation in Tennessee in treaty with	488	22	1	3
CHIPPEWA INDIANS (*see also* INDIANS), extending time of making homestead entries to	186	43	1	8
CHOCCHUMA, MISSISSIPPI, to quiet titles to lands sold at	36	27	3	5
Do	34	28	1	5
CHOCTAW INDIANS. (*See also* INDIANS.)				
Removal of, west of Mississippi River	10	15	2	1
Settlers upon lands of, for relief of	93	19	2	1
Do	102	20	1	2
Do	629	25	2	4
CHOCTAW TREATY (*see also* TREATIES; INDIANS), to indemnify citizens of Arkansas for losses incurred by	208	24	1	4
Do	99	25	2	4
CHURCH, RICHARD, *et al.*, for relief	180	29	1	6
CINNABAR AND CLARK'S FORK RAILROAD, granting right of way to	672	49	1	10
CLAIMS. (*See also* PUBLIC LANDS.)				
Arkansas, to adjust claim against United States	719	46	2	9
Board of commissioners,				
To establish, to decide finally on claims to land in Louisiana and Territory of Mississippi	82	14	1	1
Report on Florida land claims	24	19	1	1
Florida land claims,				
Letter from Alexander Hamilton respecting	130	18	1	1
Report of board of commissioners on	24	19	1	1
Providing for final settlement of	9	20	2	2
Do	162	21	1	3
Illinois, confirming title to lands in	52	46	1	1
Do	58	17	1	1
Ludlow's and Roberts's lines in Ohio, conflicting claims to lands lying between	192	10	1	1
Opelousas district in Louisiana, confirming titles to lands in	49	19	2	1
Do	93	24	1	4
Rio Hendo and Sabine Rivers, confirming claims to lands in district between	83	19	1	1
Saint Helena and Jackson districts, confirmation of certain claims to lands in	119	19	1	1
Spanish land claims, final adjustment of all claims to lands derived from Spain from 1803 to 1810	508	22	1	3
Do	652	30	1	6
Spanish and British grants, quieting and adjusting claims to lands in Mississippi held by citizens under	47	14	1	1
CLARK, JAMES A., for relief	94	25	3	4
CLERKS OF COMMITTEES. (*See* COMMITTEES; CONGRESS.)				
COINS AND COINAGE, assaying and coinage of products of mineral lands in the United States	66	39	1	8
COLE, GORDON E., for relief	49	37	2	7
COLE, HANNAH, for relief	123	30	2	6
COLE, JOHN, for relief	85	26	1	5
COLLEGES. (*See* SCHOOL LANDS.)				
COLLINS, GEORGE H., for relief	252	28	1	5
COLORADO,				
Boundary line, survey of, between Utah and	708	45	2	9
Desert lands in, to lease	197	47	1	9
Land district in, to create additional	593	43	1	8
Land office in, to establish at Akron	3479	49	2	10
Mineral school-lands, to allow State to exchange	627	48	1	10
Uncompahgre and White River Ute Indians, lands occupied by	561	47	1	9
COLORADO DESERT (*see also* DESERT LANDS COLORADO), relative to fresh water on	965	49	1	10
Do	1321	49	1	10

Subject.	Report.	Congress.	Session.	Volume.
COLUMBUS, MISSISSIPPI, quieting titles to certain lands sold at	36	27	3	
Do	34	28	1	[illegible]
COLUMBUS, FAYETTE AND DECATUR RAILROAD COMPANY, right of entry of public lands to	140	43	1	8
COLUMBUS AND EASTERN RAILROAD COMPANY, right of way through Columbus barracks grounds	2025	47	2	9
COMMERCE AND NAVIGATION, to perfect navigation of the Mississippi River at Falls of Saint Anthony	21	41	3	8
Do	17	42	2	8
COMMISSIONED OFFICERS. (*See* OFFICERS; ARMY.)				
COMMISSIONER OF GENERAL LAND OFFICE.				
Graham, George, investigation of charges against, as	94	19	2	1
Salary of, to increase	574	47	1	9
Timber-culture entry, authorized to allow persons to make a second or	875	47	1	9
Do	1013	47	1	9
COMMITTEES, relative to necessity for, and duties required of clerks to	32	39	1	8
COMPASS. (*See* SOLAR COMPASS.)				
COMPENSATION, increase, to deputy United States land surveyors	1042	25	2	4
COMPTON, JOHN and LEONARD, for relief	60	14	2	1
CONGER, JOHN S., for relief	324	30	1	6
CONGRESS, relative to the necessity of a clerk for the Committee on Public Lands	32	39	1	8
CONGRESS LANDS. (*See* PUBLIC LANDS.)				
CONKEY, SAMUEL T., for relief	595	25	2	4
CONNECTICUT WESTERN RESERVE, granting to State of Ohio increased quantity of land for support of schools in the	109	20	1	2
Do	84	23	1	3
COOLEY, EBENEZER, for relief	28	20	2	2
Do	146	23	1	3
COOSA AND TENNESSEE RIVER RAILROAD.				
Granting land to aid in construction of	62	33	1	7
Granting right of way through public lands to	62	33	1	7
COPENRATH, CAROLINE JUSTINA, *et al.*, for relief	261	30	1	6
COPES, THOMAS C., for relief	114	25	3	4
COUNCIL BLUFFS, IOWA, donating Carr Lake to city for public purposes	176	46	2	9
Do	24	46	3	9
COUSIN, BARTHOLOMEW, for relief of purchasers of lands from legal representatives of	117	41	2	8
CRAWFORD COUNTY, WISCONSIN, providing for survey of townships in	564	46	2	9
CREDITS, relative to relinquishment of certificates of further credits for land	105	19	1	1
CRESCENT CITY, CALIFORNIA, for relief of citizens of	18	36	2	7
CUMBERLAND HOSPITAL, KENTUCKY, to grant lands in Illinois for support of	43	20	2	2
CUNNINGHAM, ALEXANDER, for relief	78	20	2	2
CUSHING, MARY H., for relief	242	33	1	7
DADE INSTITUTE, FLORIDA, granting land to trustees of	321	25	3	4
Do	93	26	1	5
DAHLING, JOHN O., for relief	505	27	2	5
DAILY, JOHN, for relief	2159	48	1	10
DAKOTA.				
Fort Randall military reservation, to abolish all, lying north and east of Missouri River	744	46	2	9
Insane asylum in, to amend act granting land to establish	49	46	3	9
Land districts in,				
To create three additional	576	47	1	9
Do	1894	47	1	9
To create two additional	707	49	1	10
Pre-emption settlers in, for relief of	743	46	2	9
Reform school, granting land in aid of	2362	48	2	10
School lands in, granting an exchange of	255	46	3	9
University in, granting public land for	739	46	2	9
DAKOTA REFORM SCHOOL, granting land in aid of	2362	48	2	10
Do	2030	49	1	10
DAVIS, LEWIS C., for relief	115	18	1	1
DAWES, MARY, for relief	9	20	2	2
Do	162	21	1	3
Do	94	22	1	3
DAYTON AND MIAMI CANAL, relative to reducing price of public lands on the line of the	435	30	1	7
Do	83	31	1	7
DEAF AND DUMB (*see also* EDUCATION), to aid in education of	312	22	1	3
DEARDRUFF, DAVID, for relief of	508	28	1	5
DEARING, WILLIAM L. S., for relief	321	24	1	4
DECATUR COUNTY, INDIANA, on petition of citizens of, to pre-empt a township of land as a company	102	28	1	5
DEFIANCE, OHIO, relative to removing land office from Sandusky to	490	30	1	6
DE MAISON ROUGE, MARQUIS, confirming title of certain lands in Louisiana to	73	14	2	1
Do	123	20	1	2
DE NEVEM, GUSTAVE, for relief	641	29	1	6
DENEY, C. R., for relief	488	30	1	6
DENT, HATCH, for relief	60	14	2	1

Subject.	Report.	Congress.	Session.	Volume.
ENTRY OF LANDS—Continued.				
Fort Ridgely reservation, to be subject to pre-emption and timber-culture entry	733	46	2	9
Homestead entries,				
To regulate	34	33	1	7
According soldiers of war of rebellion privilege to make	37	39	1	8
Do	25	40	2	8
According soldiers of war of rebellion who served ninety days privilege to	6	41	3	8
Providing timber-culture or second	875	47	1	9
Do	1013	47	1	9
To allow original, to be increased to 160 acres	1163	47	1	9
To secure to actual settlers	41	43	1	8
Iowa, permission to enter lands for school purposes in lieu of those granted to the half-breeds of the Sac and Fox Indians	344	26	1	5
Do	882	27	2	5
Missouri, to confirm certain entries made in	603	33	1	7
Ottawa and Chippewa Indians, extending time for homestead entry	186	42	1	8
Pre-emption,				
For relief of persons deprived of right of entry under act of June, 1834, by the location of Indian reservations	606	24	1	4
Do	53	24	2	4
Do	434	25	2	5
Granting right to enter upon Dubuque claim in Iowa	894	27	2	5
Pre-emption laws, to repeal	1834	47	1	9
Reduced prices, to confirm entries made at, under act of June 15, 1880	874	47	1	9
Restrictions, to repeal law in regard to entry of forty-acre tracts of land	135	29	1	6
Terre Bonne, La., permission to citizens of, to enter back lands	873	27	2	5
Timber-culture, providing for second homestead or	875	47	1	9
Do	1013	47	1	9
Unsurveyed keys and lands, granting right to make entry upon all	1739	46	2	9
Void entries, to refund payment made on	344	47	1	9
EQUALIZATION, to equalize grants of land to the several States	263	34	3	7
ERROR, to correct error in law of June 16, 1880, relating to public lands	578	47	1	9
ESKRIDGE, THOMAS P., for relief	67	24	1	4
EVANS, A. H., for relief	41	27	3	5
EVERGLADES, FLORIDA, relative to draining of the	487	30	1	6
EWING, WILLIAM L. D., for relief	66	18	1	1
FARMER, LEONARD, for relief	727	46	2	9
FEES.				
Final certificates, to amend section 2238, Revised Statutes, for, in donation cases	718	46	2	9
Land patents, to reduce, in	4103	49	2	16
Registers' and receivers', to regulate	726	46	2	9
Do	1808	47	1	9
Repayment of, in certain land entry cases	717	46	2	9
FENCING, to prevent unlawful fencing and occupation of public lands	1325	48	1	10
FIELDS, JEREMIAH, for relief	7	26	2	5
FILLMORE, JOHN S., for relief of heirs	385	48	1	10
FISHER, SAMUEL, for relief	291	22	1	3
FISHER, SILAS D., for relief	37	22	2	3
FISK, ALVAREZ, for relief	67	24	1	4
FIVE PER CENT. FUND, to amend act relative to existing compacts with Alabama and Mississippi in regard to	758	27	2	5
Do	145	28	1	5
Do	85	29	2	6
FLEMING, SAMUEL, for relief	263	35	1	7
FLORIDA.				
Bounty lands, to persons engaged in suppressing Indian hostilities during 1854–'60 in	422	47	1	9
Dade Institute in, grant of land to aid in erection of	321	25	3	4
Do	93	26	1	5
Everglades in, to drain	487	30	1	6
Land claims in,				
Communication from Alexander Hamilton respecting	130	18	1	1
Report of boards of commissioners respecting	24	19	1	1
Final settlement of	9	20	2	2
Do	163	21	1	3
Coffee cultivation in, to grant land for	47	17	1	1
Land claims,				
To adjudicate and settle, between Mississippi and Perdido Rivers	508	22	1	3
To quiet title to	183	28	1	5
Palatka military reservation in, confirming entries to land on	746	46	2	9
Private land claims in, to settle	1859	48	1	10
Public archives in, to reduce force of keepers of	140	28	1	5
Public buildings in, grant of land to construct	503	28	1	5
Do	194	27	2	5
Railroad land grant in, to forfeit	2437	49	1	10
Reefers on south coast of, authorized to form separate and independent settlement	503	26	1	5
School lands in, to authorize selection of	143	28	1	5

Subject.	Report.	Congress.	Session.	Volume.
FLORIDA—Continued.				
Schools in, lands for	64	20	1	2
Seat of government in, granting land to	64	20	1	2
FLORIDA, ATLANTIC AND GULF CENTRAL RAILROAD,				
Granting certain lands to aid in construction of the	135	32	1	7
Granting right of way through public lands to	135	32	1	7
FLOURNEY, MATTHEWS, for relief	151	22	1	3
FOLEY, PATRICK, for relief of heirs	689	25	2	4
FOREIGNERS,				
Indigent, to donate lands to	242	28	1	5
Real estate by, to prevent acquisition of	2308	48	2	10
Do	3455	49	1	10
FORFEITURE (*see also* LAND GRANTS RAILROADS), relative to remission of forfeitures of partial payments on account of purchasers of public lands	17	20	1	2
FORESTRY,				
Forests, preservation of	259	43	1	8
Laws for, to repeal	1544	48	1	10
Timber, cultivation of	259	43	1	8
Timber-culture act, to amend	1418	46	2	9
Western prairies, to amend act of March 3, 1873, relative to encouraging growth of timber on the	66	43	1	8
FORT ABERCROMBIE RESERVATION, restoring to public domain the lands included within	731	46	2	9
Do	656	47	1	9
FORT DEARBORN, ILLINOIS, to confirm title to lands located within reservation of	316	46	3	9
FORT DODGE MILITARY RESERVATION, to allow actual settlers to enter lands under the homestead law on	723	46	2	9
FORT MADISON, IOWA, providing for sale of certain town lots in	350	34	1	7
FORT RANDALL, DAKOTA, to abolish all portion of reservation lying east and north of Missouri River, at	744	46	2	9
FORT RIDGELY, MINNESOTA, to subject lands to pre-emption and timber-culture entry embraced in the military reservation of	733	46	2	9
FORT SANDERS, WYOMING TERRITORY, granting portion for fish-hatching purposes	2293	49	1	10
FORT SMITH, ARKANSAS, military reservation at,				
Granting portion to city of	635	47	1	9
Granting portion for school purposes	207	48	1	10
To reappraise and sell abandoned	738	46	2	9
FORT SNELLING, MINNESOTA, for relief of settlers on military reservation near	853	27	2	5
FORT YUMA, CALIFORNIA, to encourage introduction of fresh water on the desert west of	380	45	2	9
FOX RIVER,				
Improvement of, granting lands for	112	28	2	5
Do	551	29	1	6
Island in, conveyance to Aurora, Ill., of	4010	49	2	10
FREDERICK, GEORGE, for relief	54	19	1	1
FREDERICKTOWN, MISSOURI, to remove land office from Jackson, Mo., to	316	28	1	5
FREELAND, BENJAMIN, for relief	73	20	1	2
FRIZZELL, WILLIAM, for relief	9	17	1	1
FULTON, ALEXANDER, confirming title to land on Bayou Bœuff, Louisiana	60	14	2	1
FULTON COUNTY, INDIANA, relative to change of land granted for school purposes to	433	30	1	6
FURSTENBERG, JOHN C., for relief	727	46	2	9
GAINES, W. D., for relief	85	22	1	3
GAINESVILLE AND NASKETAH RAILROAD COMPANY, granting right of way through the public lands to	322	26	1	5
GANN, WILLIAM, for relief	242	24	1	4
GARDIPIER, ALEXANDER, for relief	40	20	2	2
Do	81	21	1	3
Do	362	22	1	3
GARDNER, JAMES, for relief	33	34	3	7
GARDNER, JOHN M., for relief	47	34	3	7
GATES, JAMES, for relief	31	34	3	7
GEE, HENRY, for relief	478	27	2	
Do	427	44	1	8
Do	428	45	2	9
Do	565	46	2	9
Do	346	47	1	9
Do	966	48	1	10
GENERAL LAND OFFICE,				
Clerical force in, to reorganize	251	43	1	8
Commissioner of,				
Investigation of official conduct of	94	19	2	1
To increase salary of	574	47	1	9
Offices in, to create new	574	47	1	9
Reorganization of	482	27	2	5
GEOGRAPHICAL SURVEYS. (*See* SURVEYS.)				
GEOLOGICAL SURVEYS. (*See* SURVEYS.)				
GERVAIS, SINCLAIR D., for relief	387	22	1	3

Subject.	Report.	Congress.	Session.	Volume.
HOMESTEADS—Continued.				
Soldiers and sailors,				
To modify section 2305 Revised Statutes in relation to homestead entries..	365	46	2	9
Do	718	46	2	9
Granting lands for service in war of rebellion	87	43	1	8
Do	25	46	2	9
HOMESTEAD SETTLERS,				
Homesteads, to secure to actual	41	43	1	8
Protection within railroad limits of	218	49	1	10
Do	2231	49	1	10
Do	2213	49	1	10
Relief of	1117	46	2	9
Do	3	46	3	9
HOOE, NATHANIEL H., for relief	626	25	2	4
HOT SPRINGS, ARKANSAS,				
Improvements at, appropriation for	1061	47	1	9
Private property at, damages to	1635	47	1	9
Titles to land at, quieting	178	46	2	9
Woman's Library Association at, to use of lot	145	47	1	9
HOT SPRINGS, NEW MEXICO, to withdraw from sale	1665	48	1	10
HOT SPRINGS RAILROAD COMPANY, granting right of way over Hot Springs reservation in Arkansas	260	44	1	8
HOVER, JACOB, for relief	936	27	2	5
HOWE, AMOS, for relief	48	20	2	2
HOWELL, JOHN, for relief	294	24	1	4
HUBBERT, JAMES, for relief	84	26	2	7
HUGHES, JAMES, for relief	7	16	1	1
HURON (LAKE), relative to sale of lands located on islands in	390	30	1	6
HUTCHINS, J. M., confirming pre-emption claim to certain lands in Yosemite Valley	2	41	2	8
IDAHO,				
Flume in, granting John A. Post and others right of way for	472	47	1	9
Do	875	47	1	9
Land district in, to create additional	366	43	1	8
Land patents in, issue of, in mission-land cases	249	44	1	8
Mission lands in, issue of land patent to	249	44	1	8
University in, granting land for	729	46	2	9
IDAHO LAND AND IRRIGATION COMPANY, relative to	653	47	1	9
ILLINOIS,				
Cahokia, for relief of citizens of	380	26	1	5
Educational purposes in, to authorize sale of section of land for	465	24	1	4
Edwards County, for relief of citizens of	398	28	1	5
Emigrants from Ireland, to set aside lands in State for sale to	119	15	1	1
Land district in, to create additional	365	24	1	4
Do	236	25	2	4
Land titles in,				
Confirming certain	109	15	1	1
Do	52	16	1	1
Do	58	17	1	1
Respecting title to land for seat of government	43	16	2	1
Madison County, for relief of citizens of	718	24	1	4
Do	831	24	1	4
Mineral lands in, sale of	484	27	2	5
Do	269	28	1	6
Ohio and Mississippi Railroad Company, granting right of way through public lands to	653	30	1	6
Peoria County to enter land for a seat of justice at	196	22	1	3
Prairie du Chien, for relief of holders of property in	118	15	1	1
Randolph County in, granting lands to	1940	47	2	9
Road from Vincennes to Chicago, land to aid in construction of	510	23	1	3
Salt springs in, to sell lands reserved for	54	21	2	3
Do	322	30	1	6
School lands in, to authorize legislature of Indiana to sell	104	19	1	1
Seat of government at, title to land for	43	16	2	1
Surveyor-general's office, to establish	20	22	2	3
Vincennes district, for relief of settlers residing in	40	16	1	1
Wabash River, granting land to State in improvement of	397	24	1	4
ILLINOIS CENTRAL RAILROAD COMPANY,				
Lands to, granting additional	107	34	1	7
Railroad, authorized to locate and construct, through public lands	525	24	1	4
Do	121	24	2	4
ILLINOIS AND MICHIGAN CANAL,				
Canal scrip, to authorize issue by company	377	21	1	3
Land to,				
To grant additional	48	28	2	5
To authorize change in disposal of	377	21	1	3
INDEMNITY LANDS. (*See* PUBLIC LANDS.)				
INDIAN DEPREDATIONS,				
For relief of settlers in Arkansas for losses sustained prior to 1817 by	321	22	1	3
INDIAN TREATIES. (*See* TREATIES.)				
INDIAN TRUST FUND. (*See* TRUST FUNDS.)				

Subject.	Report.	Congress.	Session.	Volume.
INDIAN WARS,				
Wayne war, 1792-'95, bounty land for service in	246	27	1	7
Florida, between 1854 and 1860, bounty land for services in suppressing Indian hostilities in	422	47	1	9
Seminole war of 1835-'36, giving bounty land for services in	246	27	1	7
INDIANA,				
Beaver Lake, to release to State the lands known as the bed of	37	42		8
Land titles in, to confirm certain	109	15		1
Miami lands in, to reduce price of lands on	434	30		6
Do	434	31		7
Ohio and Mississippi Railroad Company, right of way through public lands to	653	30		6
Pre-emption,				
Granting right to settlers in northern limits of State	167	20		2
Granting right to citizens of Tipton and Richardville Counties	456	28		5
School lands in Illinois grant, legislature authorized to sell	104	19		1
Tipton and Richardville Counties in, granting pre-emption rights to	456	28		5
Union County, appropriating money for school purposes equal to value of certain lands in	68	20	1	2
Wabash River, granting lands to State for improvement of	327	24	1	4
INDIANA STATE SEMINARY OF LEARNING, to supply the deficiency in a township of land heretofore granted to	335	31	1	7
INDIANS,				
Black Bob, providing homes for	188	44	2	8
Cherokees, to provide for sale of reservation	1146	47	1	9
Do	2021	48	1	10
Do	1004	49	1	10
Chickasaws, relative to leasing of reservation in treaty with	488	22	1	3
Chippewas, extending time of making homestead entries of land to	186	43	1	8
Choctaws,				
Relative to removal of	10	15	2	1
For relief of settlers on lands ceded to	93	19	2	1
Do	102	20		2
Do	629	25	2	4
To indemnify citizens of Arkansas for losses incurred by	208	24		4
Do	99	25	2	4
Kansas, providing for sale of lands belonging to the	267	43	1	2
Ottawas, extending time of making homestead entries of lands to	186	43	1	8
Quapaw, to carry into effect the land grants made to the	60	19	2	1
Shawnee, providing homes for the Absentee	188	44		8
Sioux, for relief of half-breed	83	37		7
Ute, to open reservation to settlement	561	47		9
INDIGENT FOREIGNERS. (*See* FOREIGNERS.)				
INSANE,				
Donating public lands to the States and Territories for the benefit of indigent persons	125	33	1	7
INTERNAL IMPROVEMENTS, relative to granting land to State of Louisiana for	159	23	1	3
INTERNATIONAL LAND AND IMMIGRATION COMPANY, to incorporate	394	43	1	3
INUNDATED LANDS, relative to reclaiming those of Arkansas and Mississippi	549	24	1	4
Do	387	25	2	4
IONIA, MICHIGAN, relative to removal of land office to Grand Rapids from	512	27	2	5
IOWA,				
Boundary lines of, to extend western and northern	347	34	1	7
Council Bluffs, donating a lake for public use to town of	176	46	2	9
Dubuque claim in, right of pre-emption to land in	894	27	2	5
Dubuque County, granting certain lots in town of Dubuque to	351	28	1	5
Kanesville, for benefit of citizens of	150	32	1	7
Land office in, to create additional	68	27	2	5
Do	677	29	1	6
Linn County, granting land for county seat to	72	27	2	5
Mineral lands in, sale of	484	27	2	5
Do	269	28	1	6
Public buildings in, lands to aid in erection of	197	25	3	4
Railroads in,				
Granting land to aid in construction of	348	34		7
Do	349	34		7
Do	351	34	1	7
To forfeit land grants to	1793	48	1	10
School lands in lieu of those granted to Sac and Fox Indians	344	26	1	5
Do	882	27	2	5
Do	143	28	1	5
Sioux City and Saint Paul Railroad, to forfeit land grant of	2487	49	1	12
Town lots in, to provide for sale of certain	350	34	1	7
IOWA MECHANICS' MUTUAL AID SOCIETY, relative to donating public lands to	67	33	1	5
IRISH EMIGRANT ASSOCIATION, relative to sale of lands to emigrants from Ireland in Illinois	119	15	1	1
IRON MOUNTAIN RAILROAD, land grant to,				
In alternate sections	208	48	1	10
Forfeiture of	730	48	2	9
IRWIN, WILLIAM, for relief	563	27	3	5

Subject.	Report.	Congress.	Session.	Volume.
GTON ACADEMY, ALABAMA, relative to granting land in aid of.....	381	26	1	5
DS. (*See also* PUBLIC LANDS.)				
roit Straits, reserving from sale or entry islands in	496	30	1	6
at Miami River, granting pre-emption rights to islands in........	735	30	1	6
es Huron and Michigan, sale of lands upon islands in........	320	30	1	6
RD, PETER S., for relief........	157	25	3	4
ON, A. P., for relief........	2485	49	1	10
ON COUNTY, ALABAMA, relative to postponement of sale of public lands in........	97	21	1	3
ON, MISSOURI, to remove land office to Fredericktown from........	316	26	1	5
ONVILLE, ALABAMA, to remove land office from Lebanon, Ala., to....	216	26	1	5
LEY, THOMAS T., for relief	505	29	1	6
RS, JOHN, for relief........	226	24	1	4
MSON, ALABAMA, ceding certain lands to, to perfect titles of purchasers, and for school purposes	550	29	1	6
ON, ALLEN G., for relief	536	30	1	6
ON, JESSE, for relief	21	30	1	6
TON, JOSIAH S., for relief........	60	14	2	1
TON, ROBERT, for relief........	18	36	1	7
TON, STEPHEN, for relief of heirs	716	29	1	6
JOHN PAUL, for relief	115	28	1	5
M. P., for relief........	22	46	3	9
Do	261	48	1	10
N, JOHN, for relief........	291	23	1	3
DOMINGUEZ LAND GRANT. (*See* CALIFORNIA; LAND GRANTS.)				
IN, JOSEPH, for relief........	40	20	2	2
Do........	61	21	1	2
Do	263	22	1	3
AMZY, for relief	67	30	1	6
S, JOHN, for relief........	727	46	2	9
VILLE, IOWA, for the benefit of citizens of	150	33	1	7
AS.				
icultural college in, granting lands for	1942	47	2	9
thern Kansas Railroad grant, for relief of settlers on........	1939	47	2	9
d districts in, to create two additional........	386	43	1	8
d districts in, to create an additional........	724	46	2	9
emptors of lands in, for relief of........	727	46	2	9
road land grants in, to adjust	*1118	48	1	10
Do........	1619	49	1	10
Do........	†1619	49	1	10
ol lands in, authorizing Secretary of Interior to certify to State	721	46	2	9
lers, for relief of, on Northern Kansas Railroad grant	1939	47	2	9
lers, for relief of, on public lands in........	2133	48	1	10
S INDIAN LANDS, providing for sale to actual settlers and for distribution of proceeds of sale........	267	43	1	8
N, HENRY, for relief........	328	30	1	6
DY, ALVY, for relief........	144	28	1	5
DY, ROBERT L., for relief	137	24	2	4
Do.	92	25	2	4
Do........	175	25	3	4
Do	379	26	1	5
Do	591	26	1	5
Do	844	27	2	5
DY, WILLIAM M., for relief	137	24	2	4
Do	92	25	2	4
Do	175	25	3	4
Do	379	26	1	5
Do........	591	26	1	5
Do........	844	27	2	5
N, ROBERT L., for relief	160	20	1	2
CKY, relative to donating public lands for support of Transylvania College in	413	23	1	3
MARY, for relief	328	30	1	6
WILLIAM M., for relief	85	22	1	3
N, KANSAS, to donate cemetery site to city of	423	47	1	9
Do........	683	48	1	10
EL, ASA, for relief	35	14	1	1
TH INDIAN RESERVATION, to adjust claims of owners of lands within limits of........	183	44	1	8
Do	75	45	3	9
, JAMES for relief	595	25	2	4
, ABRAHAM, for relief	48	17	1	1
AW, SETH, for relief	330	28	1	5
ETTE, GENERAL, to amend act authorizing relocation of land warrants granted to	436	35	1	7
BEANS. (*See* SHORT CREEK LAKE.)				
HURON, relative to sale of lands on islands in	320	30	1	6
MICHIGAN, relative to sale of lands on islands in........	320	30	1	6
SAINT CLAIR, MICHIGAN, to set aside certain marsh lands in	2752	49	1	10

* Parts 1, 2. † Views of minority.

Subject.	Report.	Congress.	Session.	Volume.
LAMON, J. C., confirming pre-emption claim of, to certain lands in Yosemite Valley	2	41	2	8
LANCASTER, BARBARA, for relief	265	30	1	6
LAND CERTIFICATES, relative to relinquishment of	105	19	1	1
LAND DISTRICTS. (*See also* REGISTERS AND RECEIVERS.)				
Alabama,				
To create additional, in	248	27	2	5
To remove land office from Lebanon to Jacksonville	316	28	1	5
Colorado,				
To create additional, in	593	43	1	8
Do	3479	49	2	19
Consolidated, making additional provisions for	606	36	1	7
Dakota,				
To create land district at Bismarck in	284	43	1	8
To create three additional, in	576	47	1	9
Do	1894	47	1	9
Entry of lands at, providing for correction of	336	31	1	7
Errors of entry at, to provide for correction of	336	31	1	7
Fire-proof buildings in, to erect	1042	25	2	4
Florida, relative to removing land office from Newnansville to Ocala	495	30	1	6
Idaho, to create additional, in	266	43	1	8
Illinois, to create additional, in	365	24	1	4
Do	236	25	2	4
Iowa, to create an additional one in Territory of	69	26	2	5
Do	677	29	1	6
Kansas,				
To create two additional, in	265	43	1	8
To create an additional, in	724	46	2	9
Louisiana,				
To create an additional	229	24	1	4
To attach portion of northwestern land district to the district north of Red River	417	30	1	6
Michigan,				
To create an additional	434	26	1	5
Relative to consolidating Kalamazoo and Ionia districts	512	27	2	5
Relative to removal of land office from Ionia to Grand Rapids	512	27	2	5
Mississippi,				
To create additional, in	50	14	2	1
Do	14	22	2	1
To create one at Columbus, in	392	22	1	3
Missouri,				
To create an additional, in	289	24	1	4
To remove land office from Jackson to Fredericktown	316	28	1	5
To establish an additional land office in	8	30	2	6
New Mexico, to create additional, in	742	46	2	9
Ohio, to remove land office from Sandusky City to Defiance	490	30	1	6
Oregon, to establish additional, in	3478	49	2	19
Washington Territory,				
To create three additional, in	376	35	1	7
Creating the Yakima district, in	725	46	2	8
Wisconsin, to create two additional, west of Mississippi River	237	25	2	4
LAND GRANT RAILROADS. (*See* RAILROADS.)				
LAND GRANTS. (*See also* CANALS; EDUCATION; PUBLIC LANDS; RAILROADS; SCHOOL LANDS.)				
Agricultural colleges, donating lands to establish	261	35	1	7
Do	739	46	2	9
Alabama, to amend act of May 22, 1828, granting lands for improvement of rivers in	11	20	2	
Do	506	24		
Alexandria, Loudon and Hampshire Railroad, to aid in construction of	367	34		
Arkansas,				
Additional land for erection of legislative building in	182	24		
Lands to State to aid in construction of military roads	651	24		
Do	386	25		
Arredondo grant, relating to	652	30		
Canals,				
Additional land to aid in construction of Illinois and Michigan Canal	48	28		
To aid in construction of, in Louisiana	94	29		
To aid in construction of, in Ohio	139	20		
To aid in constructing Rock River and Lake Michigan Canal	851	25	2	
Do	483	26		4
Do	884	27		
To aid in construction of Sturgeon Bay Ship-Canal	57	41		
Lands for extension of Wabash and Erie Canal	403	28		
Cape Girardeau and Springfield Railroad, to aid in construction of	237	35		
Coosa and Tennessee River Railroad, to aid in construction of	62	33		
Deaf and dumb asylum in Ohio, to aid in support of	312	22		
Equalization of, among the States	263	24		
Florida, Atlantic and Gulf Central Railroad, land to aid in construction of	135	33		7
Forfeiture of,				
Lands granted to aid in construction of certain railroads	911	45	2	
Lands to Iron Mountain Railroad	730	46	2	

Subject.	Report.	Congress.	Session.	Volume.
LAND GRANTS—Continued.				
Illinois,				
Certain lands to aid in constructing road from Vincennes to Chicago	516	22	1	2
Lands to State for improvement of Wabash River	327	24	1	4
Illinois Central Railroad, additional to	107	34	1	7
Illinois and Michigan Canal, to aid in completion of	48	29	2	5
Indiana, lands to State for improvement of Wabash River	327	24	1	4
Indigent insane persons, for benefit of	125	33	1	7
Iowa, to aid in construction of railroad in	348	34	1	7
Do	349	34	1	7
Do	351	34	1	7
Iron Mountain Railroad, forfeiture of land granted to aid	730	46	2	9
José Domingues, to repeal act confirming grant to	111	41	2	8
Kansas Agricultural College, to aid	1942	47	2	9
Land patents, to prohibit issue to railroads of patent for unearned grants	1664	48	1	10
Do	*1664	48	1	10
Do	2030	48	1	10
Lawrence County Narrow-Gauge Railroad, to aid in construction of	16	43	2	8
Louisiana,				
To aid in construction of canals in	94	20	2	2
Land to State for construction of railroad from Texas State line to Vicksburg, Miss	42	43	1	8
Memphis and Charleston Railroad, to aid in construction of	131	33	1	7
Military land warrants, to pay States 5 per cent. of proceeds of sales of public lands, the amount due them for lands located under	706	44	1	8
Do	707	45	2	9
Do	161	46	2	9
Do	345	47	1	9
Military roads,				
To aid in constructing road from Vincennes to Chicago	516	22	1	2
To Arkansas and Missouri for construction of	651	24	1	4
Do	366	25	2	4
Missouri,				
Lands to State to aid in construction of military roads	651	24	1	4
Do	366	25	2	4
To aid in construction of railroads in	405	35	1	7
Missouri and Mississippi Railroad, to aid in construction of	262	24	1	4
Do	385	25	2	4
Mount Carmel and New Albany Railroad Company, to aid in construction of	590	26	1	5
Northern Cross Railroad, to aid in construction of	465	28	1	5
Ohio,				
To aid in constructing canals in	139	20	1	2
Granting to State conditionally all United States lands in	128	21	1	3
To aid in support of deaf and dumb asylum	312	22	1	3
Pacific railroads, to aid in construction of	324	34	1	7
Do	264	34	3	7
Public buildings, additional land for erection of legislative building in Arkansas	102	24	1	4
Quapaw Indians in Arkansas, lands granted to	60	19	2	1
Railroads, to prohibit issue of patents for unearned grants to	1664	48	1	10
Do	*1664	48	1	10
Do	2030	48	1	10
Rivers,				
To amend act of 1828 granting lands for improvement of rivers in Alabama	11	20	2	2
Do	505	24	1	4
Land to Illinois and Indiana for improvement of Wabash River	327	24	1	4
Rock River and Lake Michigan Canal, to aid in construction of	851	25	2	4
Do	432	26	1	5
Do	884	27	2	5
States,				
To equalize among the	263	34	3	7
To establish agricultural colleges in	261	35	1	7
Do	739	46	2	9
Stover College of West Virginia, lands to aid	1581	46	2	9
Sturgeon Bay Ship-Canal, to aid in construction of	57	41	2	8
Wabash and Erie Canal, for extension of	403	28	1	5
Winchester and Deposite Railroad, to aid in construction of	132	32	1	7
Woodward High School of Cincinnati, Ohio, land to	526	24	1	4
LAND OFFICES. (*See* LAND DISTRICTS; REGISTERS AND RECEIVERS.)				
LAND PATENTS.				
Fees for, to amend	4103	49	2	10
Homesteads, to grant patents for, after three years settlement	1708	46	2	9
Issue of,				
Delay in	16	36	2	7
To Chippewa and Ottawa Indians	186	43	1	8
Mission-land cases, to adjudicate and issue in	249	44	1	8
Ottawa and Chippewa Indians, to issue to	186	43	1	8
Records of, exemplification of	482	27	2	5
Secretary to sign, to abolish office of	161	28	1	5

*Views of minority.

Subject.	Report.	Congress.	Session.	Volume.
LOUISIANA—Continued.				
Lands in, sale of, north and south of Red River	22	18	1	1
Live Oak Reservation in, to cancel	2754	49	1	10
Opelousas district in, confirming titles to lands in	49	19	2	1
Do	93	24	1	4
Prairie lands in, reducing price of	23	18	1	1
Private land claims in, to settle	1859	48	1	10
Railroad from State line of Texas to Vicksburg, granting land to State to aid in constructing	43	42	1	8
Red River, sale of lands north and south of	23	18	1	1
Saint Helena district in, granting pre-emption rights to actual settlers on lands	12	19	2	1
Do	31	20	1	2
Surveyor's district in, to establish separate	23	18	1	1
Swamp lands in,				
To aid in reclaiming	316	30	1	6
To extend provisions of act of March, 1855, relative to	1953	47	2	9
Do	2083	48	1	10
Terre Bonne, entry of back lands in	673	27	2	5
LOVELY DONATION CLAIMS. (*See* ARKANSAS.)				
LUCAS, JOHN B. C., for relief	13	16	1	1
LUDLOW AND ROBERTS'S LINES. (*See* OHIO.)				
LYON, ISAAC S., for relief	747	46	2	9
McANULTY, GILES, for relief	69	21	1	2
McARTHUR, JOHN A., for relief	727	46	2	9
McCAFFREY, PHILLIP, for relief	1512	46	2	9
McCARROLL, JOHN, Jr., for relief	206	25	2	4
McCLASKEY, WILLIAM, for relief	362	30	1	6
McCLOUD, JOHN G., for relief	164	29	1	6
McDONALD, SARAH, for relief	496	47	1	9
McELROY, RANSOM, for relief	318	22	1	3
McELVAINE, PURDY, for relief	322	30	1	6
McFARLAND, JAMES, for relief	24	16	2	1
Do	9	17	1	1
McGARRAHAN, WILLIAM (*see also* PANOCHE GRANDE), for relief	951	45	2	9
Do	109	45	3	9
McGILL, JAMES, for relief	6	27	3	5
McILRATH, CHARLES, for relief	49	37	2	7
McINTOSH, WILLIAM, for relief	31	16	1	1
Do	1	16	2	1
McKAY, GEORGE, for relief	431	30	1	6
McKENZIE, CHARLES M., for relief	199	29	1	6
McNAMER, O'BRYANT, for relief	251	28	1	5
McPHERSON, WILLIAM, for relief	93	25	3	4
Do	35	18	1	1
MACOMB, ALEXANDER, for relief	70	17	2	1
MADISON COUNTY, ILLINOIS, for relief of certain citizens of	718	24	1	4
Do	831	24	1	4
MAGNESS, MORGAN, for relief	18	19	2	1
MAGRUDER, ELIZABETH, for relief	51	22	2	3
MAISON ROUGE, MARQUIS DE, to confirm title of certain land in Louisiana to	73	14	2	1
MALONE, DANIEL, for relief	489	24	1	4
Do	875	25	2	4
MALTBY, JASPER A., for relief	248	31	1	7
Do	145	32	1	7
MANNING, ENOS, to adjudicate claim to certain land	956	27	2	5
MANYPENNY, GEORGE, for relief	187	28	1	5
MARCUS, WILLIAM, for relief	664	25	2	4
MARICOPA AND PHŒNIX RAILROAD, to grant right of way through Gila River Indian Reservation	3192	49	1	10
MARQUETTE, MICHIGAN, granting city certain lands for park purposes	2706	49	1	10
MARQUETTE, HOUGHTON AND ONTONAGON RAILROAD,				
To forfeit land grant of	1053	48	1	10
Do	*1053	48	1	10
Do	†1928	49	1	10
MARTIN, JOSEPH, for relief	83	35	2	7
MASSEY, ESTHER, for relief	31	34	3	4
MASSEY & JAMES, claim for relief	890	25	2	4
MATHIAS, GEORGE, for relief	60	14	2	1
MATSON, ENOCH, for relief	635	25	2	4
MAY, JAMES L., for relief	481	27	2	5
MAYFIELD, GEORGE, to issue land patent to	182	22	1	3
MEANDERED LANDS. (*See* SWAMP LANDS.)				
MECHANICS' MUTUAL AID ASSOCIATION, IOWA, relative to granting tract of land to	507	27	2	5
Do	67	28	1	5
MEMPHIS AND CHARLESTON RAILROAD,				
Granting land to aid in construction of	131	32	1	7
Granting right of way through public lands to the	131	32	1	7

*Views of minority. †Parts 1, 2.

Subject.

MEMPHIS AND KANSAS CITY RAILROAD, declaring same to
MERCER COUNTY, OHIO, relative to quantity of land covere
Shane and Godfrey in Dublin township....................
Do..
Do..
Do ....
MERRICK, J. J., for relief ....
MESSINGER, B. F., for relief ....
MIAMI INDIAN LANDS,
Pre-emption rights to settlers on.............................
Do ....
Prices of, to reduce...
Do..
MICHIGAN,
Board of Fish Commissioners in State, to lease lands to ....
Detroit Straits, to reserve from sale, entry, or survey islands in
Grand Rapids, removal of land office from Ionia to.............
Ionia, removal of land office to Grand Rapids from.............
Islands in Detroit Straits, to reserve from entry, survey, or sale
Island in Saginaw Run, sale of ....
Land claims in, relative to...... ....
Land grants to, forfeiture of.................................
Land office in,
To create additional.....................................
Removal from Ionia to Grand Rapids ....
Lands in,
Authorizing State to make selections of.....................
To lease to Board of Fish Commissioners.....................
Marquette, Houghton and Ontonagon Railroad, to forfeit land g
Do..
Do.... ....
Marsh lands in, to set aside certain...........................
Mineral lands in, sale of.................................. ......
Monroe County, granting land to supervisors of ....
Ontonagon and State Line Railroad, to forfeit land grant of.....
Pre-emption rights to certain settlers in southern limits of Ter
Private land claims in, supplementary report of decisions on...
Saginaw Bay, to confirm title to certain lands in...............
Saginaw River, to sell island in................. ....
School lands in, authorizing legislative council to take charge c
Do ....
Surveyor in, to establish office of, west of Lake Michigan ......
Do..
Titles and claims to lands in, Secretary of Treasury authorized
Do. ....
MICHIGAN, LAKE, islands in, to sell lands located on ....
MICHIGAN LAND GRANTS, to declare forfeited ....
Do ....
MICHIGAN STATE NORMAL SCHOOL, relative to donating lan
MILITARY BOUNTY LANDS,
Coercing holders of, in Arkansas to draw their patents.........
Militia, granting lands for service in war of 1812 ....
Do ....
War of 1812,
To authorize soldiers of, to surrender bounty lands drawn
others in lieu thereof.......................................
To allow, to disbanded officers and others for service in ....
Do..
Do ....
Granting, to organized militia and volunteers for service in.
Do..
Virginia military, to extend time for obtaining land patents to
Ohio.. ....
Do........................ ....
MILITARY BOUNTY-LAND WARRANTS,
Heirs of deceased soldiers, to issue warrants to, without regard
Indian hostilities in Florida between 1854 and 1860, granting to pe
in suppressing ....
Issue of,
Extending time for, of scrip certificates......................
Do..
To continue and revive certain acts for.......... ....
To amend laws relative to ....
For services for less period than fourteen days ....
To heirs of deceased soldiers without regard to age.........
Laws, to amend, relative to issue of ....
Locating of,
To regulate..
Do..
To amend act of February, 1848, for ....

*Views of minority. †Parts 1,

Subject.	Report.	Congress.	Session.	Volume.
MILITARY BOUNTY-LAND WARRANTS—Continued.				
Scrip certificates, extending time for issue of	90	34	3	4
Do	817	29	1	5
Seminole war, 1835–'36, to issue, for service in	346	31	1	7
States, to ascertain amount of warrants located in States entitled to percentage of proceeds of sales of public lands	766	44	1	8
Do	707	45	3	9
Do	161	46	2	9
Do	345	47	1	9
War of rebellion, to soldiers of 1861 and 1862, and additional to veterans for service in	37	39	1	8
Do	35	40	2	8
War of 1812, to issue for service in	346	31	1	7
Wayne war, 1793–'95, to issue, for service in	346	31	1	7
MILITARY RESERVATIONS. (*See under titles of the various reservations.*)				
MILITARY ROADS. (*See* ROADS.)				
MILITIA,				
Granting bounty land to those organised and serving during the war of 1812	580	24	1	4
Do	756	25	2	4
MILL SEATS, relative to allowing pre-emption rights in the purchase of	315	18	1	1
MILLER, ISAAC, for relief	156	25	3	4
MILLER AND FUTTON, confirming title to land on Bayou Bœuf, Louisiana	69	14	2	1
MILLIKIN, DANIEL, for relief	195	27	2	5
Do	127	30	2	6
MILSTED, JOHN, for relief	406	28	1	5
Do	549	29	1	6
MILWAUKEE, WISCONSIN,				
To aid in construction of harbor at	661	27	2	5
MILWAUKEE AND ROCK RIVER CANAL,				
Land to aid in building	451	25	2	4
Do	452	26	1	5
Do	584	27	2	5
Grant heretofore made to aid in construction of	852	27	2	5
Do	884	27	2	5
Do	82	27	3	5
Do.	679	28	1	6
MINERAL LANDS. (*See also* PUBLIC LANDS.)				
Alabama, to place disposition of, in, upon same footing as agricultural lands	203	46	3	9
Arkansas, to open to entry in	9	43	2	8
Colorado, to allow exchange of mineral school lands in	627	48	1	10
Illinois, providing for sale of, in	1	26	2	5
Do	484	27	2	5
Do	269	29	1	6
Iowa, providing for sale of, in	1	26	2	5
Do	484	27	2	5
Do	269	29	1	6
Lead mines,				
To repeal law prohibiting sale of public lands in Missouri containing	114	20	1	2
Rental of lands in Missouri containing	171	25	3	4
Minnesota, to reduce price of, in Lake Superior district of	48	30	2	6
Missouri,				
To repeal law prohibiting sale of public lands containing lead mines in	114	20	1	2
To rent lands containing lead mines in	171	25	3	4
To open to entry in	9	43	2	8
Price of,				
To reduce, in Lake Superior district of Minnesota	48	30	2	6
To reduce, in Chippewa district of Wisconsin	48	30	2	6
Sale of,				
Providing for, in Illinois, Iowa, Michigan, Missouri, and Wisconsin	114	20	1	2
Do	1	26	2	5
Do	484	27	2	5
Do	269	29	1	6
Do	591	29	1	6
Providing for	66	39	1	8
Survey of,				
Providing for	66	39	1	8
Town lots and town sites on, designating rights of patents	745	46	2	9
Wisconsin,				
Providing for sale of, in	1	26	2	5
Do	484	27	2	5
Do	269	29	1	6
Do	591	29	1	6
To reduce price of, in Chippewa district of	48	30	2	6
MINERAL POINT, WISCONSIN, authorizing sale of certain lots in	625	25	2	4
Do	350	34	1	7
MINNESOTA,				
Allowing selections of lands in lieu of sixteenth and thirty-sixth sections for school purposes	344	34	1	7
Asylum for the deaf, dumb, blind, and insane in, to establish and support	345	34	1	7
Fort Snelling in, for relief of settlers on reservation near	853	27	2	5
Mississippi River improvement, to restore to market lands withdrawn for	573	47	1	9

Subject.

MINNESOTA—Continued.
Pre-emption rights to settlers on unsurveyed public lands in ..
School lands in, to authorize sale of section 36 of, for school pu
Sale of the thirty-sixth section......
Swamp lands in, for relief of settlers on
Do...
MINNESOTA STATE UNIVERSITY, donating land to aid.....
MISSION LANDS, to adjudicate and issue patents in mission-land c and certain Territories
MISSISSIPPI,
Board of commissioners to decide finally on claims to land in T
Chickasaw cession, giving to governor of State the selection c maining unsold, for school purposes contiguous to the...
Do
Do
Chickasaw trust fund, legalizing sale of lands in northwester passing money received to credit of
Choctaw district of, for relief of settlers on lands in
Claims to lands in,
To quiet titles and adjust
To establish board of commissioners to decide finally on ...
To confirm, Saint Helena and Jackson districts
Inundated lands in, to reclaim
Do
Private land claims in, to settle
Do
Public lands in, to confirm sales of
Purchasers of public lands in,
To extend indulgences to
To confirm title to, under act of June, 1834
Right of way to certain railroad companies over public lands t
River improvements, grant of lands for
Saint Helena and Jackson districts, to confirm claims to lands i
Sale of public lands in, to confirm
School reservations, to amend act relating to existing compac 5 per cent. fund and
Do
Do
Surveyor-general in, to discontinue office of
Two per cent. fund, to amend act of September 4, 1841, relating
MISSISSIPPI RIVER,
To amend act granting certain land to Minnesota for improvem
Do
Do
Survey of east bank of the
Do
MISSOURI,
Entries of land in, to confirm
Iron Mountain Railroad, declaring forfeited lands granted for c
Land grants in,
To construct military road in
Do
To Saint Genevieve, for school purposes
To Van Buren County, for court-house
To reclaim swamps of Saint Francis River
Do
Do
Land office in, to create additional
Do
Military road in, grant of land to construct
Do
Mineral lands in,
To repeal act prohibiting sale of
To rent
To open to entry
Private land claims in, to settle
Saint Francis River, alternate sections of land to reclaim swan
Do
Do
Saint Genevieve, lands for school purposes in town of
Saline lands in, for sale of
School lands in, memorial relating to
Valle, Francis, *et al.*, to confirm certain lands to, in
Do
Do
Van Buren County, land for court-house to
MISSOURI AND MISSISSIPPI RAILROAD, donating land to a tion of
Do
MITCHELL, DAVID, for relief
MOBILE AND GIRARD RAILROAD, to forfeit land grant of...

Subject.	Report.	Congress.	Session.	Volume.
MONROE COUNTY, MICHIGAN, to grant land to supervisors of	117	30	2	6
MONTANA,				
Mission-land cases, issue of patents in	249	44	1	8
University in, granting public lands for	799	46	2	9
MONTGOMERY, ALEXANDER, for relief	11	21	1	3
MONTGOMERY RAILROAD COMPANY, right of way through public lands in Alabama to	592	26	1	5
MONTGOMERY, WESLEY, for relief	576	47	1	9
MOORE, ELY, for relief of heirs of	59	42	2	8
MOORE, ISIDORE, for relief	89	19	1	1
Do	5	19	2	1
MOORE, JOHN M., for relief	493	30	1	6
MOORES, TIMOTHY, for relief	8	35	2	7
MORELAND, ELISHA, for relief	127	24	2	4
Do	92	25	2	4
Do	175	25	3	4
Do	379	26	1	5
Do	561	26	1	5
Do	544	27	2	5
MORRIS COUNTY RAILROAD, to grant right of way through United States powder-depot lands at Dover, N. J	605	49	1	10
MORROW, ISAAC, for relief	237	25	3	4
Do	323	26	1	5
MOULTON, FERDINAND, for relief	502	27	2	5
MOUNT CARMEL AND NEW ALBANY RAILROAD COMPANY, granting public lands in aid of	390	26	1	5
MURPHY, ALFRED C., for relief	654	36	1	7
MURRAY, ROBERT, for relief	304	25	2	4
MUTUAL AID ASSOCIATION, granting lands to	307	27	2	5
Do	67	28	1	5
NATIONAL GUARD. (*See* MILITIA.)				
NATIONAL PARK. (*See* YELLOWSTONE NATIONAL PARK.)				
NATIONAL ROADS, granting to State of Illinois certain lands to aid in construction of road from Vincennes to Chicago	510	22	1	3
NEALE, SEELEY, for relief	341	22	1	3
NEBRASKA,				
Land districts in, to create two additional	606	49	1	10
Northern Kansas Railroad grant	1939	47	2	9
Public lands in, relief of settlers on	2133	48	1	10
School lands in, for relief of settlers on	346	34	1	7
Settlers on,				
Northern Kansas Railroad grant, for relief of	1939	47	2	9
Public lands in, for relief of	2133	48	1	10
School land in, for relief of	346	34	1	7
University in, grant of land to aid	346	34	1	7
NEVADA, granting lands in lieu of sixteenth and thirty-sixth sections to	741	46	2	9
NEW IDRIA MINING COMPANY. (*See* RANCHO PANOCHE GRANDE GRANT.)				
NEWINGHAM, HENRY, for relief	592	26	1	5
Do	509	27	2	5
Do	401	28	1	5
NEWINGTON, CAROLINE, for relief	92	34	1	7
NEW MEXICO, to create additional land district in	742	46	2	9
NEWNANSVILLE, FLORIDA, relative to removing land office to Ocala from	495	30	1	6
NEW ORLEANS, BATON ROUGE AND VICKSBURG RAILROAD, to forfeit land grant of	678	48	1	10
Do	2698	49	1	10
NEWTON, JOHN, for relief	812	30	1	6
NIX, GEORGE, for relief	102	31	2	7
NIX, JOHN B., for relief	720	46	2	9
NOBLE, CHARLES, for relief	49	19	1	1
NORTHERN CROSS RAILROAD, granting right of way and lands to	465	28	1	5
NORTHERN KANSAS RAILROAD, for relief of settlers on land grant of	2133	48	1	10
NORTHERN PACIFIC RAILROAD, to forfeit land grant of	*1256	48	1	10
Do	†1226	49	1	10
NORTON, GARRET, for relief	144	28	1	5
OCALA, FLORIDA, relative to removing land office from Newnansville to	495	30	1	6
OFFICERS. (*See also* ARMY.)				
Granting privileges of bounty lands to persons promoted to commissioned	349	30	1	6
OHIO,				
Auglaize Seminary in, to grant land in aid of	192	27	2	5
Canals in, lands to aid in construction of	139	20	1	2
Claims to lands sold by United States in, to provide for relinquishment of certain	34	18	2	1
Do	145	19	1	1
Colleges in, additional lands for support of	124	20	1	2
Connecticut Western Reserve in, granting lands for support of schools in	109	20	1	2
Do	84	22	1	3
Dayton and Miami Canal, to reduce price of public land along line of	435	30	1	6
Do	82	31	1	7
Deaf and dumb asylum in, lands to aid in support of	312	22	1	3

* Views of minority. † Views of minority, parts 1 and 2.

Subject.

OHIO—Continued.
Deficient surveys in, relief of citizens for
Ludlow's and Roberts's lines in, conflicting claims to lands in
Ohio and Mississippi Railroad Company, right of way to, throu in
Oxford Township, Butler County, to enter land in lieu of secti purposes
Paulding County, commissioners authorized to enter land for
Perrysburg, right of pre-emption to lots in
Do
Do
Do
Do
Price of public lands in, to reduce, on line of Wabash and Erie Miami Canals
Public lands in,
Granting all, to State conditionally
o reduce price of, on line of Wabash and Erie and Day T Canals
Do
Refuse and unsold lands, for improving and draining, granting
School lands,
To enable certain townships to obtain
Do
Do
To confirm title to, located in Seneca County
Sciota Salt Springs in, authorizing State to sell
Seneca County, to confirm title to certain school lands in
Shaner and Godfrey, land covered by grant in Dublin Townsh
Do
Do
Do
Steubenville district, title to certain lands in, and donation of tional purposes
Surveys in,
Relief of citizens for deficient
To provide for certain
Swamp lands in, granting to State
Tymocktee Township, Wyandot County, to select certain lands poses in
Virginia military district of,
To extend time for obtaining land patents in
Do
Defining, ceding to State unsold lands in
Wabash and Erie Canal, to reduce price of public land along li
Do
Wyandot reservation, providing for sale of unsold lands in
Do
Wyandot treaty, relief of occupants of lands acquired under
Do
OHIO SALINE, authorizing legislature of Illinois to sell and co lands reserved to said State for use of the
OHIO AND MISSISSIPPI RAILROAD COMPANY, granting through public lands in Indiana, Ohio, and Illinois to
OLYMPIA, WASHINGTON TERRITORY, granting to town o of Budd's Inlet with power and authority to reclaim the
ONTONAGON AND STATE LINE RAILROAD, to forfeit land
ORE, JAMES, for relief
OREGON,
Geological survey of, appropriation for completing
Do
Klamath Indian Reservation in, to adjust claims of owners of
Do
Land district in, to establish additional
Land offices in, payment of clerks in registers
Mission-land cases in, issue of patents in
Surveyor-general in, to create office of
Timber lands in, providing for sale of
OREGON AND CALIFORNIA RAILROAD, to forfeit land gran
Do
*Views of minority.
Do
Do
*Views of minority.
OREGON CENTRAL RAILROAD, to forfeit lands granted to
OREGON CITY, OREGON, to pay clerks employed in land office
ORPHAN, declaring the meaning of the word
OSAGE INDIAN TRUST LANDS, to graduate the price and dis due of
OTIS, GEORGE K., for relief
Do
Do

Subject.	Report.	Congress.	Session.	Volume.
OTTAWA INDIANS, extending time of making homestead entries to certain	186	43	1	8
OVERFLOWED LANDS. (*See* SWAMP LANDS.)				
OZIAS, JOHN, for relief	264	30	1	6
Do	247	31	1	7
PACIFIC COAST, relative to granting public lands to aid in construction of railroads to the	324	34	1	7
Do	264	34	3	7
PACIFIC RAILROADS. (*See also* KANSAS PACIFIC RAILROAD; NORTHERN PACIFIC RAILROAD; RAILROADS; SOUTHERN PACIFIC RAILROAD; UNION PACIFIC RAILROAD.)				
Granting land to aid in construction of	2[illegible]4	34	1	7
PALATKA RESERVATION, FLORIDA, confirming certain entries and warrant locations in	746	46	2	9
PALMER, JAMES (guardian), for relief	15	36	2	7
PANKEY, HAMPTON, for relief	9	17	1	1
PARKS. (*See* YELLOWSTONE NATIONAL PARK.)				
PARNELL, WILY B., for relief	136	29	1	6
PATENTS TO LAND. (*See* LAND PATENTS.)				
PATRIDGE, JAMES, for relief	94	22	1	3
PAULDING COUNTY, OHIO, to authorize commissioners to enter certain lands for a seat of justice	636	25	2	4
PAULDING, W. K., for relief	163	23	1	3
PEARSON, GEORGE, claim for relief	52	15	1	1
PEGG, BENJAMIN, for relief	98	27	3	5
PENDLETON ACADEMY, ALABAMA, granting public lands for support of	413	23	1	3
PENROSE, CLEMENT B., for relief	14	16	1	1
Do	46	17	1	1
Do	23	21	2	3
PERRYSBURG, OHIO, granting pre-emption rights to certain lots in	511	23	1	3
Do	113	24	1	4
Do	895	25	2	4
Do	78	26	1	5
Do	70	27	2	5
PERUE, IOWA, providing for sale of lots in	2374	48	2	10
PLACER CLAIMS. (*See* MINERAL LANDS.)				
PLANKINGTON, DAKOTA, to grant land for reform school at	2362	48	2	10
Do	2039	49	1	10
PLAQUEMINES PARISH, LOUISIANA, donating land for public buildings at	104	28	2	5
POLK COUNTY, IOWA, authorizing trustees to pre-empt certain lands in, for seat of justice	590	29	1	6
PORCHÉ, SIMON, for relief of legal representative of	731	25	2	4
PORLIER, JAMES, for relief	40	20	2	2
Do	81	21	1	3
Do	362	22	1	3
PORTAGE LAKE AND LAKE SUPERIOR SHIP-CANAL, relative to land selected by	2631	48	2	10
Do	*2631	48	2	10
POST, JOHN A., *et al.*, granting right of way for flume to	472	47	1	9
Do	575	47	1	9
POTOSI, MISSOURI, granting additional aid to complete harbor at	143	30	1	6
POTTER, JOHN, *et al.*, for relief	262	30	1	6
POTTERFIELD, JOSEPH, for relief	328	30	1	6
PRAIRIE DU CHIEN, ILLINOIS, for relief of holders of lands at	118	15	1	1
PRAIRIES.				
Pre-emption rights extending to settlers upon the large	141	28	1	5
Timber on Western prairies, to amend act to encourage growth of	66	43	1	8
Do	1418	46	2	9
PRE-EMPTION. (*See also* ENTRY OF LANDS; PUBLIC LANDS.)				
Actual settlers, giving right of, to	290	24	1	4
Do	299	25	3	4
Act of March 2, 1833, to amend	79	23	2	3
Act of June, 1834, for relief of settlers deprived of benefits of	600	27	2	5
Do	601	27	2	5
Indian reservations, for relief of persons deprived of the right of, by the locations of	606	24	1	4
Indiana, granting right to settlers on lands contiguous to Big Saint Joseph River	167	20	1	2
Laws for, to repeal	1544	48	1	10
Do	1260	49	1	10
Do	1679	49	1	10
Michigan, granting right to settlers in, contiguous to Big Saint Joseph River	167	20	1	2
Mill seats on public lands, to allow rights in purchase of	115	18	1	1
Minnesota, granting right of entry to unsurveyed public lands in	107	31	1	7
Saint Helena district, Louisiana, right of preference in purchase of public lands to certain settlers in	12	19	2	1
Do	31	20	1	2
Settlers, granting right of, to actual	290	24	1	4
Do	299	25	3	4
Settlers on the large prairies, extending rights of, to	141	28	1	5
Wabash and Erie Canal, extending privileges to citizens of Ohio residing on line of	506	27	2	5

*Views of minority.

Subject.

PRESTON, FRANCIS, for relief ....
Do ....
PRICE OF LANDS. (*See also* PUBLIC LANDS.)
Graduating and fixing price to actual settlers ....
Do ....
Do ....
Do ....
Do ....
Do ....
Do ....
Do ....
Do ....
Do ....
Do ....
Do ....
Dayton and Miami Canal, to reduce price along line of ....
Do ....
Miami Reserve, to reduce price on ....
Do ....
Mineral lands in certain districts, to reduce the minimum pri
Railroad limits, to reduce price within ....
Do ....
Reduction in,
Dayton and Miami Canal ....
Do ....
Miami Reserve ....
Do ....
On certain mineral lands ....
Within railroad limits ....
Do ....
Do ....
Wabash and Erie Canal ....
Do ....
PRICE, WILLIAM J., for relief ....
Do ....
Do ....
Do ....
PRIVATE LAND CLAIMS, to settle claims in Arkansas, Fl
Missouri, Alabama, and Mississippi ....
PROTESTANT UNIVERSITY OF THE UNITED STATES, r
ing land in aid of ....
PRYOR, GREEN, for relief ....
PUBLIC ARCHIVES. (*See* ARCHIVES.)
PUBLIC DOMAIN. (*See* PUBLIC LANDS; HOMESTEADS.)
PUBLIC LAND SCRIP. (*See* SCRIP.)
PUBLIC LANDS. (*See also* DESERT LANDS; LAND DISTRICTS; M
LANDS; MINERAL LANDS; TIMBER LANDS; SWAMP LANI
Alabama,
To allow pre-emption rights to purchasers of lands in ....
Granting certain lands to improve rivers in ....
Do ....
Sale of public lands in Jackson County ....
Do ....
For relief of certain purchasers of public lands in 1818 an
Do ....
Ceding certain lands to town of Jefferson ....
To cede to State public land for educational purposes ...
Relative to act of March 3, 1883 ....
Granting lands to State to aid university ....
To exclude public lands of State from laws relating to mi
Alaska, authorizing sale of lands in ....
Arizona Territory, to amend law granting lands for universit
Arkansas,
Granting pre-emption rights to settlers in ....
Authorizing claimants of more than one league square
validity of claims ....
Concerning rights of pre-emption in Territory of ....
For relief of settlers upon Choctaw lands in ....
Do ....
Do ....
Do ....
Do ....
Do ....
Reclaiming inundated lands of ....
Do ....
To quiet title to tracts of land under act of August 11, 18
To sell Cherokee reservation in State ....
Do ....
California,
For relief of certain pre-emption and homestead settlers
To grant State 5 per cent. of net proceeds of public lands

Subject.	Report.	Congress.	Session.	Volume.
[PUB]LIC LANDS—Continued.				
California—Continued.				
To grant State 5 per cent. of net proceeds of public lands of	994	49	1	10
Do	4162	49	2	10
Granting seal rocks near San Francisco, Cal., to city	2649	49	1	10
Do	3415	49	1	10
Central Pacific Railroad, granting lands to aid in construction of road from Portland, Oreg., to	*2026	48	1	10
Colorado.				
Providing for leasing of desert lands in	197	47	1	9
Relative to introduction of fresh water on Colorado desert	965	49	1	10
Do	1321	49	1	10
Dakota, to amend law granting lands for university purposes to	1088	49	1	10
Desert lands, to amend act for sale of	1868	49	1	10
Dover, N. J., to grant right of way to Morris County Railroad through United States powder depot lands at	605	49	1	10
Entry of.				
Authorizing certain soldiers to surrender bounty lands drawn, and to locate others in lieu thereof	54	19	1	1
Providing for sale of relinquished lands, at certain fixed price, by	86	20	1	2
To amend act of March 2, 1833, in relation to pre-emption of settlers	79	23	2	3
Granting right of pre-emption to actual settlers	290	24	1	4
Do	290	25	2	4
To relieve certain persons deprived of the right of pre-emption by the locations of Indian reservations	606	24	1	4
Do	53	24	2	4
Do	484	25	2	5
Permission to enter back lands in Terre Bonne, La	873	27	2	5
Extending pre-emption rights to persons making improvements on public lands in the large prairies	141	28	1	5
Repeal of restrictions imposed by law in regard to entry of forty-acre tracts of land	185	29	1	5
Extending time for, claims to bounty lands	68	30	1	6
Granting right to islands in the Great Miami River	735	30	1	6
Regulating homestead entries	84	33	1	7
Providing for correction of errors in taking entries of land at land offices	336	31	1	7
Granting soldiers of war of rebellion homestead privileges to	37	39	1	8
Do	26	40	2	8
Privileges to soldiers who served ninety days in the war of rebellion	6	41	3	8
To secure homesteads to actual settlers on the public domain	41	43	1	8
Opening to entry mineral lands in Arkansas and Missouri	9	43	2	8
Repayment of fees for	717	46	2	9
Authorizing actual settlers to enter certain land on the Fort Dodge military reservation under homestead law	723	46	2	9
To subject lands embraced in Fort Abercrombie reservation to homestead and pre-emption entry	731	46	2	9
Do	656	47	1	9
To subject to pre-emption and timber-culture entry lands embraced in the Fort Ridgely reservation	733	46	2	9
For relief of settlers in, under the homestead law	1117	46	2	9
To subject to operation of law regulating disposal of public lands all unsurveyed lands, keys, and islands of the United States	1739	46	2	9
To refund payment on void entries	344	47	1	9
To confirm entries made at reduced prices under act of June 15, 1880	874	47	1	9
Providing for second entries	875	47	1	9
Do	1013	47	1	9
To allow original homestead entries to be increased to 160 acres	1163	47	1	9
To shorten time for final proofs in	1215	47	1	9
Repealing laws relative to pre-emption	1834	47	1	9
Equalization of, to the several States	263	34	3	7
Fencing of, to prevent unlawful occupation of	1325	48	1	10
Florida.				
Inspecting land claims in	130	18	1	1
Do	24	19	1	1
Relative to lands for schools and seat of government in Territory of	64	20	1	2
Foreign ownership of, to prohibit	2308	48	2	10
Do	3455	49	1	10
Fort Sanders reservation, granting portion of, to Wyoming Territory for fish-hatching purposes	2293	49	1	10
Grants of. (*See* LAND GRANTS.)				
Hot Springs, New Mexico, to withdraw from sale	1662	48	1	10
Idaho Territory, to amend law granting lands for university purposes to	1088	49	1	10
Illinois.				
Confirming titles to lands of settlers in	119	15	1	1
For relief of settlers residing within Vincennes district	40	16	1	1
Confirming certain claims to land in State	52	16	1	1
Do	58	17	1	1
To grant lands to Randolph County in State of	1681	49	1	10
Indemnity lands, to restore to public domain	1847	48	1	10

*Views of minority.

Subject.

PUBLIC LANDS—Continued.
Indiana.
Appropriating money in lieu of land for school purposes i State of ....
Right of pre-emption to certain settlers contiguous to I River in State of ....
To authorize a change of lands granted for school purpo sixteenth section............
Iowa.
Granting pre-emption rights to enter land in Dubuque cl
Granting pre-emption rights to authorities of Polk Coun for seat of justice ....
For sale of lots in town of Peru............
To quiet title of settlers on Des Moines River lands......
To confirm titles to land grant to ....
Iron Mountain Railroad, granting lands to ....
Kansas.
For relief of settlers on Northern Kansas Railroad grant
Granting lands for agricultural college in ....
For relief of settlers on public lands in ....
Adjustment of railroad land grants in State............
Do............
Kirwin, Kans., to donate cemetery site to city of ....
Land grants.
To forfeit grant to California and Oregon Railroad ....
Do............
Do............
Do............
To forfeit grant to Marquette, Houghton, and Ontonagon
Do............
Do............
To adjust grants to railroads in Kansas ....
To forfeit grant of Northern Pacific Railroad ....
Do............
Do............
Do............
To forfeit grant of Atlantic and Pacific Railroad ......
Do............
Do............
To prohibit issue of patents for unearned, to railroads ...
Do............
Do............
To forfeit to Sioux City and Saint Paul Railroad ....
Do............
To forfeit lands in Alabama granted to railroads............
To forfeit grant of Oregon and Pacific Railroad............
To forfeit grant to Girard and Mobile Railroad............
Do............
To forfeit grant of Selma, Rome and Dalton Railroad ....
Land selected by Portage Lake and Lake Superior Ship-C
Do............
To forfeit grant of Southern Pacific Railroad............
Do............
Do............
To declare forfeit in certain States, lands granted to railr
To forfeit grant of Ontonagon and State Line Railroad...
To forfeit grant of Oregon and California Railroad ......
Do............
To forfeit certain grants to railroads in State of Florida .
To forfeit grant of Alabama and Chattanooga Railroad ..
To forfeit grant of New Orleans, Baton Rouge and Vicksb
Land warrants, to regulate locating of............
Do............
Laws, to amend homestead ....
Louisiana.
To revive act relating to back concessions ....
To issue patents where claims have been confirmed.....
Relative to sale of lands south and north of Red River in
Establishing separate surveyor-general's district in .....
Reducing price of prairie lands in............
Pre-emption rights to actual settlers on lands in Saint Hel
Do............
Confirming certain claims to lands in district of Opelousa
Do............
Relative to granting lands for internal improvements to ..
To cancel certain live-oak reservations in State ....
Marquette, Mich., to grant certain lands for park purposes ...

*Views of minority.

Subject.	Report.	Congress.	Session.	Volume.
PUBLIC LANDS—Continued.				
Michigan,				
Authorizing Secretary of Treasury to examine and confirm certain titles and claims to land in	72	19	1	1
Do	42	20	1	2
Relative to school lands in Territory of	111	19	1	2
Do	71	20	1	2
Right of pre-emption to certain settlers contiguous to Big Saint Joseph River in Territory of	167	20	1	2
To lease certain lands in State to board of fish commissioners	384	48	1	10
To declare forfeit certain railroad-grant lands in State of	684	48	1	10
Do	*684	48	1	10
To quiet and confirm title to certain lands in Saginaw Bay in State of	1090	49	1	10
Do	3116	49	1	10
To authorize State to make selections	2982	49	1	10
Mineral lands,				
Relative to disposition of, in Alabama	117	48	1	10
To exclude public lands of Alabama from laws relating to	865	49	1	10
To enable State of California to take lands in lieu of sections 16 and 36	870	49	1	10
Minnesota,				
To restore to market lands withdrawn for Mississippi River improvement	573	47	1	9
Mississippi,				
Adjusting and quieting claims to lands held under Spanish and British grants in Territory of	47	14	1	1
Confirming certain claims to lands in Saint Helena and Jackson districts in	119	19	1	1
Extending indulgence to purchasers of public lands in Territory of	16	14	1	1
For relief of settlers upon lands in Choctaw district of	102	20	1	2
Surveying and reclaiming the inundated lands of	349	24	1	4
Do	367	25	2	4
To confirm purchases of land under act of June 19, 1834	479	27	2	5
To confirm certain private entries of land in northwestern part of	447	28	1	5
Missouri,				
Repeal of law prohibiting sale of mineral lands in	114	20	1	2
Relative to rental of lead mines in	171	25	3	4
Montana Territory, to amend law granting lands for university purposes to	1085	49	1	10
Nebraska,				
For relief of settlers on Northern Kansas Railroad grant	1989	47	2	9
For relief of settlers on public lands in	2183	48	1	10
New Orleans, Baton Rouge and Vicksburg Railroad, to forfeit land grant of	678	48	1	10
Ohio,				
Authorizing State to sell certain tract of land called the "Scioto Salt Springs"	119	18	1	1
Providing for relinquishment of certain claim to lands sold by the United States in	34	18	2	1
Do	145	19	1	1
Land patents in Virginia military district of	21	19	1	1
Do	317	26	1	5
Adjusting conflicting claims to lands lying between Ludlow's and Roberts's lines	192	19	1	1
Appointing surveyor for the Virginia military district in State of	53	20	1	2
Granting certain lands for school purposes in Connecticut Western Reserve, State of	109	20	1	2
Do	84	23	1	3
Additional lands for support of colleges in	124	20	1	2
To examine title to certain lands in Steubenville district and donate same for school purposes	411	21	1	3
Granting pre-emption to lots in Perrysburg, State of	511	23	1	3
Do	113	24	1	4
Do	805	25	2	4
Do	78	26	1	5
Do	70	27	2	5
To enable certain townships in, to obtain their school lands	812	25	2	4
Do	321	26	1	5
Do	73	27	2	5
Oregon Central Railroad, to forfeit lands granted to	883	48	1	10
Pre-emption of,				
Relating to rights of, in Territory of Arkansas	56	18	1	1
Allowing rights to purchasers of mill seats on public lands	115	18	1	1
To amend act of March 2, 1833, in relation to	79	23	2	3
To repeal laws for	1544	48	1	10
Do	1260	49	1	10
Do	1679	49	1	10
Price of,				
Graduating, reducing, and fixing	28	15	1	1
Do	125	20	1	2
Do	87	23	1	3
Do	1	23	2	3
Do	70	24	1	4
Do	202	25	2	4

*Views of minority.

Subject.	Report.	Congress.	Session.	Volume.
PUBLIC LANDS—Continued.				
Price of,				
Graduating, reducing, and fixing	80	28	1	5
Do	197	28	1	5
Do	732	30	1	6
Do	133	32	1	7
Do	33	33	1	7
Do	16	46	2	9
To reduce, lands on Miami Reserve	434	30	1	6
Do	434	31	1	7
Reducing, public lands along line of Wabash and Erie and Dayton and Miami Canals	435	30	1	6
Do	82	31	1	7
To reduce the minimum, mineral lands in certain districts	48	30	2	6
To reduce, within railroad limits	1165	47	1	9
Purchasers of,				
Extending indulgence to certain, public lands in Mississippi	16	14	1	1
Relative to continuing act of March 2, 1821, to	25	18	1	1
For relief of, which have reverted for non-payment of purchase money	17	20	1	2
Quieting of titles. (*See* TITLES.)				
Relinquishment of, relative to granting further privileges in the	103	19	1	1
Reserved lands, to authorize sale of	139	30	2	6
Right of way over,				
To Mississippi and Missouri Railroad Company	382	24	1	4
Do	385	25	2	4
To Illinois Central Railroad Company	523	24	1	4
To certain railroad companies in Alabama	607	24	1	4
To certain railroad companies in Alabama and Mississippi	322	26	1	5
To Montgomery Railroad Company in Alabama	593	26	1	5
To Northern Cross Railroad	465	28	1	5
To Great Western Railroad Company	467	28	1	5
Do	301	29	1	6
To the Ohio and Mississippi Railroad	653	30	1	6
To the Central Plank Road Company of Alabama	243	31	1	7
To Memphis and Charleston Railroad	131	32	1	7
To Winchester and Deposite Railroad	132	32	1	7
To Florida, Atlantic and Gulf Central Railroad	135	32	1	7
To Coosa and Tennessee Railroad	62	32	1	7
To the Boisé Basin Bed-Rock Fluming Company	255	43	1	8
To Hot Springs Railroad Company, through the Hot Springs reservation	250	44	1	8
To certain lands in Richmond County, New York, for railroad purposes	118	46	3	9
To Saginaw and Mount Pleasant Railroad Company	579	47	1	9
To Columbus and Eastern Railroad, through Columbus barracks grounds	2025	47	2	9
To grant, for irrigating purposes	2038	49	1	10
To Maricopa and Phœnix Railroad, through Gila River Indian Reservation	3192	49	1	10
Sale of,				
Providing for, relinquished lands, by entry, certain fixed prices	86	20	1	2
Relative to disposing of public lands to various States at a fair price	448	22	1	3
Relative to Vermillion Salt Springs in Illinois	54	21	2	3
Saline lands, relative to disposition of, in State of Missouri	96	21	1	3
San Francisco, Cal., to relinquish certain lands to city	2707	49	1	10
School lands,				
Relative to giving each State lands for school purposes	97	15	2	1
To amend act of 1843 donating to certain States	888	48	1	10
To enable State of California to take, in lieu of sections 16 and 36 found to be mineral	870	49	1	10
Schools, creating a fund from the sale of public lands for the support of common, throughout the States	83	19	1	1
Settlers,				
To secure, in public lands the benefit of the crop growing at time of sale	40	19	1	1
Do	19	19	2	1
Relative to the pre-emption right of becoming purchasers of lands at prices originally sold for	40	19	1	1
Do	19	19	2	1
For relief of, and to provide for repayment of certain fees paid on void entries of public lands	704	45	2	9
Surveys, of,				
For relief of certain citizens of Ohio for deficient	43	17	1	1
Relative to appointing a surveyor for the Virginia military district in Ohio	58	20	1	2
Swamp lands,				
To reimburse purchasers of, in certain States	566	46	2	9
To extend provisions of act of March 2, 1855, to State of Louisiana	2038	48	1	10
For relief of settlers on, in State of Minnesota	2373	48	2	10
To quiet title of settlers on Des Moines River lands	491	49	1	10
To set aside certain, in State of Michigan	2752	49	1	10
Tax, authorizing the several States in which the public land lie to levy and collect a tax thereon immediately after sale thereof by the United States	84	18	2	1
Tennessee, ceding certain lands to State of	134	29	1	6
Texas Pacific Railroad, to forfeit land grant of	678	48	1	10
Timber-culture lands, to repeal laws for entry of	1679	49	1	10
Titles to, to confirm in certain cases	2454	48	2	10

Subject.	Report.	Congress.	Session.	Volume.
PUBLIC LANDS—Continued.				
Trespassers on,				
Laws to punish	16	46	2	9
Do	1809	47	1	9
Do	1858	47	1	9
Do	1325	48	1	10
Regulating payment of costs in suits for	343	47	1	9
To prevent	1809	47	1	9
Do	1858	47	1	9
Wisconsin,				
For relief of certain settlers on public lands in	57	35	1	7
To restore to market public lands withdrawn for Mississippi River improvement	573	47	1	9
Wyoming Territory, to amend law granting lands for university purposes to	1088	49	1	10
PURCHASERS. (*See also* ENTRY OF LANDS; PUBLIC LANDS.)				
Act of March 2, 1821, to continue to purchasers of public lands	25	18	1	1
Mississippi, extending indulgence to certain purchasers of public lands in	16	14	1	1
Relief to certain purchasers of lands in 1818 and 1819	402	24	1	4
Do	239	25	2	4
Relief of purchasers of public lands which have reverted for non-payment of purchase money	17	20	1	2
QUAPAW INDIANS, to carry into effect the grants of lands made under treaty of November 15, 1824, with the	60	10	2	1
QUARANTINE ISLAND, relinquishing to city of Saint Louis said island and all vacant unappropriated lands within her corporate limits	502	31	1	7
QUIETING OF TITLES. (*See also* TITLES PUBLIC LANDS.)				
RAGAN, JOHN A., for relief	21	34	1	7
Do	404	35	1	7
RAILROAD LAND GRANTS (*see also* RAILROADS), to forfeit lands granted to aid in construction of certain railroads	8	48	1	10
Do	*8	48	1	10
RAILROAD LANDS,				
Taxation on, relative to	474	43	1	8
Do	709	45	2	9
Settlers on restored, for relief of	1512	46	2	9
Do	1013	47	1	9
RAILROADS (this title is limited to general matter). (*See also under titles of respective railroad companies.*)				
Alabama, to declare forfeited lands granted to, in	2016	48	1	10
Alabama and Chattanooga, forfeiture of grant to	2443	49	1	10
Atlantic and Pacific, forfeiture of grant to	1663	48	1	10
Do	193	49	1	10
Do	*193	49	1	10
California and Oregon Railroad, forfeiture of grant to	793	48	1	10
Do	*793	48	1	10
Do	931	49	1	10
Do	*931	49	1	10
Cinnabar and Clark's Fork Railroad, granting right of way to	672	49	1	10
Girard and Mobile Railroad, forfeiture of grant to	2501	48	2	10
Do	2640	49	1	10
Homestead settlers, for protection of settlers within railroad limits	215	49	1	10
Iron Mountain Railroad, to grant lands in alternate sections to	208	48	1	10
Land grants,				
To aid in constructing roads to the Pacific coast	324	34	1	7
Do	264	34	3	7
Forfeiture of grant to certain roads	911	45	2	9
Do	*8	48	1	10
To prohibit issue of patents for unearned	1664	48	1	10
Do	*1664	48	1	10
Do	2039	48	1	10
To declare forfeit in certain States	45	49	1	10
To forfeit grant of Alabama and Chattanooga Railroad	2443	49	1	10
To forfeit grant of Atlantic and Pacific Railroad	1663	48	1	10
Do	193	49	1	10
Do	*193	49	1	10
To declare forfeited grant to California and Oregon Railroad	793	48	1	10
Do	*793	48	1	10
Do	931	49	1	10
Do	*931	49	1	10
To forfeit grant of Girard and Mobile Railroad	2501	48	2	10
Do	2640	49	1	10
To Iron Mountain Railroad, alternate sections of land	208	48	1	10
To forfeit certain grants in State of Florida	2437	49	1	10
To provide for adjustment of grants to railroads in Kansas	†1113	48	1	10
Do	*1619	49	1	10
Do	1619	49	1	10
To forfeit grant of Northern Pacific Railroads	1256	48	1	10
Do	*1256	48	1	10
Do	1226	49	1	10
Do	*1226	49	1	10

* Views of Minority. † Parts 1 and 2.

Subject.

RAILROADS—Continued.
Land grants.
To forfeit land grant to Marquette, Houghton and Ontona
Do ....
Do ....
To forfeit grant of New Orleans, Baton Rouge and Vicksl
To forfeit grant of Ontonagon and State Line Railroad...
To forfeit grant of Oregon and California Railroad.......
Do..
Do ....
To forfeit grant of Selma, Rome and Dalton Railroad....
To forfeit grant to Sioux City and Saint Paul Railroad ...
Do ....
To forfeit grant of Southern Pacific Railroad ....
Do ....
Do..
To forfeit grant to Texas Pacific Railroad ....
To construct road from Texas State line to Vicksburg ..
Letter of Secretary of Interior relative to railroads in Ne
To declare forfeited, in Michigan.......................
Do ....
Marquette, Houghton and Ontonagon Railroad, forfeiture
Do..
Do ....
Morris County Railroad, granting right of way through Ui
der depot grounds at Dover, N. J ....
New Orleans, Baton Rouge and Vicksburg Railroad, forfe
Northern Pacific Railroad, forfeiture of grant to..........
Do..
Do..
Do ....
Ontonagon and State Line Railroad, forfeiture of grant to
Oregon and California Railroads, forfeiture of grant to....
Do..
Do..
Do..
Oregon Central Railroad, to forfeit lands granted to ......
Right of way.
Granting, for railroad purposes through certain lands in Ri
New York ....
To grant, to Cinnabar and Clark's Fork Railroad.........
To grant, to Morris County Railroad through United Stat
lands at Dover, N. J ....
Selma, Rome and Dalton Railroad, forfeiture of grant to......
Settlers on lands restored to, for relief...........
Sioux City and Saint Paul Railroad, forfeitures of grant to ...
Do ....
Southern Pacific Railroad, forfeiture of grant to.... ....
Do..
Do..
Texas Pacific Railroad, forfeiture of grant to.................
RAMEY, GEORGE, *et al.*, for relief...............................
Do ....
RANCHO PANOCHE GRANDE GRANT, to correct recor
tract of land in California called ....
Do..
RANDOLPH, A. F., for relief ....
RANDOLPH COUNTY, ILLINOIS, granting lands to ....
Do..
RECEIVERS. (*See* REGISTERS AND RECEIVERS.)
REDDICK, THOMAS F., confirming to heirs a tract of 640 acres
REEFERS OF FLORIDA, to form independent settlement on east
of Florida..
REEVES, THOMAS H., for relief ....
REFORM SCHOOL IN DAKOTA. (*See* DAKOTA REFORM SCH
REGISTERS AND RECEIVERS. (*See also* LAND DISTRICTS.)
Fees of, to regulate..
Oregon City and Winchester, State of Oregon, to pay cle
offices at..
Salaries of, to increase..
RELINQUISHED LANDS, relative to guarding the public l
fraudulent combinations in the resale of................
RESERVED LANDS, to authorize sale of ....
REVISED STATUTES,
To amend and repeal,
2305, relative to soldiers' and sailors' homesteads.........
Do ....
2238, in relation to fees for final certificates in donation ca
REVOLUTIONARY WAR. (*See* WAR OF REVOLUTION.)
REYNOLDS, BENJAMIN W., for relief........................
Do..

* Views of minority.

Subject.	Report.	Congress.	Session.	Volume.
for relief	[illegible]	46	2	9
WYATT, for relief	812	[illegible]	1	[illegible]
ILLE COUNTY, INDIANA, granting right of pre-emption to cer- lands for county purposes to	436	25	1	5
WAY. (*See also railroad companies by respective titles.*)				
to				
in railroad companies in Alabama, through the public lands	667	34	1	4
ed companies in Alabama and Mississippi, over public lands	832	[illegible]	1	5
ilroad purposes, through certain lands in Richmond County, New York	115	44	3	9
Basin, Bed-Rock, Fluming Company	[illegible]	42	1	8
al Plank Road Company of Alabama, through the public lands	345	31	1	7
bus and Eastern Railroad Company, through Columbus barracks grounds	[illegible]	47	3	9
and Tennessee River Railroad, through public lands	[illegible]	[illegible]	1	7
a, Atlantic and Gulf Central Railroad	183	[illegible]	1	7
Western Railroad Company, through public lands	467	[illegible]	1	5
Do	[illegible]	[illegible]	1	5
prings Railroad Company, through Hot Springs reservation	[illegible]	44	1	[illegible]
a Central Railroad Company, through United States lands	[illegible]	[illegible]	1	4
emphis and Charleston Railroad, through public lands	181	[illegible]	1	7
sippi and Ohio Railroad, through public lands in Ohio, Indiana, and Illinois	[illegible]	30	1	6
gomery Railroad Company, through public lands in Alabama	[illegible]	[illegible]	1	9
ern Cross Railroad, certain lands and	463	[illegible]	1	5
aw and Mount Pleasant Railroad Company	579	47	1	9
ester and Deposite Railroad, through public lands	[illegible]	[illegible]	1	7
MOTHY, for relief	[illegible]	[illegible]	1	2
D HARBORS.				
lands for improvement of certain, in	21	[illegible]	2	3
Do	[illegible]	24	1	4
e River, to amend act granting lands in aid of improvement of	[illegible]	[illegible]	1	6
Wisconsin Rivers, land for improvement of	[illegible]	[illegible]	2	5
Do	[illegible]	[illegible]	1	5
bash River, lands for improvement of	[illegible]	24	1	4
ver, granting pre-emption rights to certain islands in	[illegible]	[illegible]	1	6
e, Wis., to aid in the construction of harbor at	[illegible]	[illegible]	1	5
i, lands for improvement of certain rivers in	781	30	1	6
i River from Hickman, Ky., to mouth of Wolf River in Tennessee, truction of levees on east bank of	58	35	1	7
Do	318	36	1	7
i River, to amend act granting land to Minnesota for improvement of	21	41	3	8
Do	17	42	2	8
s, granting aid for completion of harbor at	143	30	1	6
ver, land on east side, for improvement of	795	30	1	6
, Wis., to construct harbor at	852	25	2	4
JAMIN, for relief	72	23	2	3
ting land to Missouri and Arkansas for construction of military s	651	24	1	4
Do	386	25	2	4
HARLES E., for relief	232	35	2	7
Do	542	36	1	7
AAC H., for relief	60	14	2	1
OHN H., for relief	378	26	1	5
V. H., for relief	109	35	1	7
VALLACE, for relief	70	21	1	3
D, ILLINOIS, relative to dividing the island into lots with reser- ons to distribute the water power through it	130	30	2	6
OSEPH, for relief	69	27	2	5
et al., for relief	652	30	1	6
SON, relative to the claim of Marquis de	128	20	1	2
ANNAH, for relief	15	36	2	7
LOMON, for relief	511	27	2	5
ER, granting lands for improvement of	795	30	1	6
OMAS, *et al.*, for relief	513	27	2	5
AND MOUNT PLEASANT RAILROAD COMPANY, granting of way to	579	47	1	9
AY, MICHIGAN, to confirm and quiet title to certain lands in	1090	49	1	10
Do	3116	49	1	10
R COUNTY, ILLINOIS, relative to granting lands for school pur- s in	79	26	1	6
EVIEVE, MISSOURI, granting certain lands for school purposes wn of	207	34	1	7
S, MISSOURI, ceding to city of, Quarantine Island and all vacant propriated lands within corporate limits of	502	31	1	7
ORGE, for relief	18	18	1	1
(*See also* COMPENSATION.)				
ner of General Land Office, to increase salary of	574	47	1	9
and receivers of public lands, to increase salaries of	122	35	2	7
general of public lands, to equalize compensation of	567	29	1	6
DS, authorizing sale of, by State of Missouri	96	21	1	3

Subject.	Report.	Congress.	Session.	Volume.
SALT SPRINGS,				
Arkansas, to select six sections of land in, under act of June 23, 1836	168	28	1	5
Illinois, sale of residue of lands in, reserved for use of	100	19	2	1
Do	322	30	1	6
Sciota, Ohio, to authorize sale of land in	119	18	1	1
SANDUSKY, OHIO, relative to removing land office to Defiance from	490	30	1	6
SAN FRANCISCO, CALIFORNIA,				
Granting Seal Rocks near, to city of	2619	49	1	10
Do	3415	49	1	10
To relinquish certain lands to city of	2707	49	1	10
Do	2755	49	1	10
Do	3056	49	1	10
SAN FRANCISCO LAND ASSOCIATION, for relief	1014	47	1	9
SAN MATEO COUNTY, CALIFORNIA, to authorize correction of boundaries of certain lands in	1448	48	1	10
SANTA CLARA RESERVATION, CALIFORNIA, for relief of certain settlers on the	217	44	2	8
SAVAGE, EDWARD, for relief	67	43	1	8
SCHNIBEL, TOTTENGEN, for relief	328	30	1	6
SCHOOL FUND, relative to appropriating a portion of the nett annual proceeds of the sale of public lands exclusively for the support of common schools throughout the States	88	19	1	1
SCHOOL LANDS,				
Act of 1843, to amend, donating to certain States	338	48	1	10
Agricultural colleges, granting, in aid of	261	35	1	7
Alabama authorized to select other lands in lieu of worthless lands	813	30	1	6
Alabama and Mississippi, to carry into effect the compacts with those States in regard to	753	27	2	5
Do	145	28	1	5
Do	85	29	2	6
California, authorized to exchange mineral lands in	3825	49	2	10
Colorado, authorized to exchange mineral lands	627	48	1	10
Connecticut Western Reserve, further grant of land for support of schools in	109	20	1	2
Do	84	23	1	3
Florida, certain quarter sections in	61	20	1	2
Florida, Iowa, and Wisconsin, authorizing the selection of certain lands in	143	28	1	5
Illinois grant, vesting the fee simple of lands set apart for schools in the, under direction of the legislature of Indiana	104	19	1	1
Kansas, authorizing Secretary of Interior to certify to	721	46	2	9
Lease of, granted to States	577	47	1	9
Michigan, authorizing legislative council of, to take charge of	111	19	1	1
Do	71	20	1	2
Minnesota, sale of thirty-sixth section of land in	270	31	1	7
Missouri, sale of, in	96	21	1	3
Ohio, to enable certain townships in, to obtain their	81	23	2	4
Do	321	26	1	5
Do	73	27	2	5
Relocation of sixteenth sections, in the various new States and Territories	164	28	1	5
Sac and Fox Indians, authorizing selection of, in lieu of those, granted to the half-breeds	344	26	1	5
Do	882	27	2	5
Seneca County, Ohio, to confirm title to certain lands in	650	30	1	6
Steubenville district in Ohio, to examine title to lands in certain sections of, and donation of same for school purposes	411	21	1	3
Substitution,				
Authorizing Alabama to substitute other lands in lieu of worthless lands	815	30	1	6
Authorizing, in lieu of worthless lands	794	30	1	6
Do	130	32	1	7
Tennessee, to sell certain	92	29	1	6
Tymochtee township, trustees of, to select lands for school purposes in Wyandot cession	10	29	1	6
Union County, Indiana, relating to, in	68	20	1	2
Utah, granting of certain town cites for school purposes in	8	40	2	8
SCIOTO SALT SPRINGS,				
Authorizing State of Ohio to sell and convey certain tract of land called the	119	18	1	1
SCOTT, JOSIAH, for relief	121	22	2	3
SCOTT, THOMAS, for relief	568	29	1	6
SCOTT, WILLIAM, for relief of heir	519	27	2	5
SCRIP,				
Military land warrants,				
Extending time for issuing certificates on	90	24	2	4
Do	317	28	1	5
Issuing scrip in exchange for	437	28	1	5
SCULL, JAMES, *et al.*, for relief	60	19	2	1
SEAL ROCKS, granting to city of San Francisco, Cal	2619	49	1	10
Do	3415	49	1	10
SEATTLE, WASHINGTON TERRITORY, granting to town of, the tide flats in Dwamish Bay, with authority to reclaim them	416	43	1	8
SECRETARY OF INTERIOR,				
Fort Abercrombie military reservation, authorized to have lands embraced in, subject to homestead and pre-emption entry	781	46	2	9
Do	656	47	1	9

Subject.	Report.	Congress.	Session.	Volume.
TARY OF INTERIOR—Continued.				
ana, authorized to certify school lands to	721	48	2	9
tary warrants in certain States, to ascertain and certify amount of land located with	706	34	1	8
Do	*707	45	2	9
Do	161	46	2	9
Do	345	47	1	9
TARY OF TREASURY, authorizing, to confirm certain titles and claims to lands in the Territory of Michigan	72	19	1	1
Do	42	20	1	2
. AND TENNESSEE RAILROAD COMPANY, granting right of way through the public lands to the	322	26	1	5
., ROME AND DALTON RAILROAD, to forfeit land grant of	2604	48	2	10
OLE WAR, 1835–36. (*See* INDIAN WARS.)				
A COUNTY, OHIO, to confirm title to certain school lands in	660	30	1	6
KES,				
omesteads, to secure, to actual	41	42	1	8
Do	1117	46	2	9
emption,				
Right of becoming the purchasers of lands at prices originally sold for	46	19	1	1
Do	19	19	2	1
Granting of, to actual	280	24	1	4
Do	120	25	2	4
For relief of those deprived of the benefits of act of June, 1834	606	24	1	4
Do	58	24	2	4
Do	434	25	2	5
Do	600	27	2	5
Do	601	27	2	5
lic lands, to secure to settlers on, benefit of crop growing at time of sale	46	18	1	1
Do	18	19	2	1
road lands restored, for relief of settlers on	1512	46	2	9
Do	1012	47	1	9
es of lands, to protect, to bona fide settlers	1860	47	1	9
Do	1856	47	1	9
l entries of public lands by, for relief of, and providing for repayment of certain fees paid on	704	45	2	9
E, JOHN, for relief	83	35	2	7
D, DANIEL, for relief	4	16	2	1
Do	78	19	1	1
ON, WILSON, *et al.*, for relief	68	30	1	1
EE INDIANS, finding homes for the Black Bob and Absentee	188	41	2	8
S, JAMES, granting right of pre-emption to	73	16	1	1
ANALS. (*See* CANALS.)				
CREEK LAKE, MISSOURI, to donate to State	2304	48	2	10
Do	2040	49	1	10
E, HENRY M., granting right of pre-emption to certain lands on Red River, in Louisiana	509	23	1	3
Do	383	24	1	4
Z, GERHART, *et al.*, granting permission to select school lands to	10	29	1	6
COB, for relief	100	31	2	7
CITY AND SAINT PAUL RAILROAD, to forfeit land grant to	1792	48	1	10
Do	2487	49	1	10
INDIANS, for relief of the half-breed or mixed-bloods of the	83	37	2	7
HTER, GEORGE H., for relief	72	26	2	5
RY, relative to applying proceeds of sales of public lands in aid of the extinction of	660	30	1	6
IARTIN, for relief	328	30	1	6
JANE, for relief	196	35	1	7
JOHN G., for relief	94	22	1	3
T. JOHN, for relief of heirs of	198	29	1	6
R, GEORGE G., for relief	1738	46	2	9
Do	754	47	1	9
COMPASS, to enable the United States to make use of the, for surveys	20	34	1	7
RS' HOMESTEADS. (*See* HOMESTEADS.)				
EVANDER M., for relief	612	30	1	6
RANCH, CALIFORNIA,				
mption settlers in, to indemnify	424	45	2	9
to, confirming to owners	20	37	3	7
ERN PACIFIC RAILROAD, to forfeit land grant of	2670	48	2	10
Do	†706	49	1	10
PORT, WISCONSIN, relative to sale of town lots in and construction of harbor at	852	25	2	4
ORD, AMOS, for relief	55	44	1	1
relative to final adjustment of all claims to land derived from, from date of 1803 to 1810	508	22	1	3
H GRANTS, relative to adjusting claims to lands in Territory of Mississippi held under	47	14	1	1
H LAND CLAIMS. (*See* CLAIMS.)				
OLNG, SARAH, for relief	103	44	1	8

* Parts 1, 2. †Views of minority.

Subject.	Report.	Congress.	Session.
SPENCER, JOHN, for relief	758	29	1
SPAFFORD, BENANA, for relief	54	19	1
STALLINGS, ABRAHAM, for relief	266	34	3
STEALEY, JOHN, for relief	131	18	1
STEELE, WILBUR F., for relief	1130	48	1
Do	214	49	1
STEPHENS, PEGGY, for relief	42	20	2
STEPTOE, JAMES, *et al.*, for relief	84	18	1
STEVENSON, WILLIAM W., for relief	528	23	1
Do	201	24	1
STEWART, WILLIAM, for relief	398	21	1
STIFF, ABRAHAM, for relief	757	25	2
STIGERMIRE, HINER, for relief	57	24	2
Do	311	25	2
STIGGINS, GEORGE, for relief	69	21	1
STOKER, HENRY, for relief	420	23	1
Do	597	24	1
STONE, SAMUEL, for relief	34	34	3
STOVER COLLEGE, West Virginia, granting land to	1581	46	2
STRANGE, WASHINGTON, for relief	255	28	1
STRATTON, J. F., for relief	341	22	1
STRONG, WILLIAM Y., for relief	338	36	1
STURGEON BAY SHIP-CANAL,			
Completion of, to extend time for the	42	43	1
Land granted to, in aid of construction of canal	57	41	2
STURGES, SOLOMON, for relief	441	24	1
Do	558	25	2
SULLIVAN, JAMES B., to adjudicate claim of	950	27	3
SULLIVANT, MICHAEL, for relief	74	27	2
Do	238	26	1
SURVEYING DISTRICTS (*see also* LAND DISTRICTS), relative to consolidating or discontinuing certain	142	28	1
SURVEYOR-GENERAL,			
Discontinuance of office of, to amend act relative to, in certain districts	142	28	1
Do	651	30	1
Illinois, to establish an office of, in	20	23	2
Michigan, to establish office of, for west of Lake Michigan	476	24	1
Do	238	25	2
Oregon, to establish an office of, in	55	29	2
Salaries of, to equalize	567	29	1
Wisconsin, to establish office of, in	238	25	2
SURVEYORS, relative to increasing compensation of deputy land	1042	25	2
SURVEYS,			
Mississippi River, relative to geographical and geological surveys west of	612	43	1
Oregon and Washington Territories, making appropriation for completing geological survey of	171	34	3
Do	409	35	1
Solar compass, to enable United States to make use of, in public surveys	20	34	
SWAMP LANDS,			
Arkansas, granting alternate sections of land near New Madrid and Saint Francis Rivers for purpose of reclaiming and draining	310	28	
Do	86	29	
Do	108	31	
Providing for confirmation to, all selections made and reported to Commissioner of General Land Office	719	46	
To indemnify State for those sold	547	47	1
California, to confer legal title to State of, to certain overflowed and	119	46	3
Indiana, to release lands known as the bed of Beaver Lake	37	42	2
Islands, beds of lakes (not navigable), bayous, &c., transferring to the several States the United States title to all	566	46	2
Louisiana, to reclaim, in	816	30	1
To extend provisions of act of 1855, relative to	1953	47	2
Minnesota, for relief of settlers upon lands in	732	46	3
Missouri, to grant alternate sections of land near New Madrid and Saint Francis River for purpose of reclaiming said lands	310	28	1
Do	86	29	1
Do	108	31	1
Ohio, to grant all the refuse and unsold Congress lands for purpose of draining and improving	349	28	1
Olympia, to grant tide-flats of Budd's Inlet with power and authority to reclaim them	256	43	1
Purchasers and locators of, relief of	16	33	1
Do	265	34	1
Seattle, to grant tide-flats of Dwamish Bay with power and authority to reclaim them	416	43	1
SWAYZE, C. L., for relief	134	32	1
SYMMES, JOHN C., relative to right and title of United States to certain lands in contract with	88	18	1
TAGGERT, JOHN R., for relief	563	46	[illegible]
Do	33	47	1
TALBOTT, DAVID I., for relief	15a	24	1

Subject.	Report.	Congress.	Session.	Volume.
TALBOTT, GEORGE W., *et al.*, for relief	808	27	2	5
TALBOTT, JAMES, for relief	572	36	1	7
TALBOT, THOMAS F., for relief	740	46	2	9
TALLASSE FIXICO RESERVE, to settle title to lands on the	862	26	1	6
TAXES,				
Railroad lands, taxation of	474	43	1	8
Do	709	45	2	9
States, the right of taxing lands sold by the United States	84	18	2	1
To subject all lands sold by United States to taxation by the States in which they respectively lie immediately after sale thereof	84	19	2	1
TAYLOR, HOUSTON L., for relief	728	46	2	9
TAYLOR, JOHN W., for relief	65	36	1	7
TAYLOR, TILFORD, for relief	601	25	2	4
TENNESSEE,				
Act of April 18, 1806, to amend, relating to settlement of claims to vacant and unappropriated lands in	230	22	1	3
Do	67	24	1	4
Do	101	25	2	4
Do	119	25	3	4
Do	92	26	1	5
Congressional reservation line, ceding certain lands to State of, south and west of	134	29	1	6
Leasing of reservation in treaty with the Chickasaws in State of	486	22	1	3
School lands in, to authorize sale of	100	25	2	4
Do	92	26	1	5
Titles, to perfect lands therein described	230	22	1	3
Do	67	24	1	4
Do	101	25	2	4
Do	119	25	3	4
Do	92	26	1	5
TERRE BONNE, LOUISIANA, entry of back lands in	878	27	2	5
TERRITORIES,				
Timber lands in, providing sale of	8	43	2	8
University purposes, public lands for	730	46	2	9
TEXAS PACIFIC RAILROAD,				
Land grants to,				
To aid in construction of	92	48	1	10
Forfeiture of	678	48*	1	10
THOMPSON, JACOB, for relief	40	22	2	3
THORP, WILSON, for relief	112	24	2	4
TIDE FLATS. (*See* SEATTLE; OLYMPIA; SWAMP LANDS.)				
TIMBER,				
Cultivation of, and preservation of forests	259	43	1	8
Growth of, on western prairies, to amend act relating to encouragement of	1418	46	2	9
TIMBER CULTURE. (*See* FORESTRY.)				
TIMBER LANDS, providing for sale of, in California, Oregon, and Territories of the United States	8	43	2	8
TIPTON COUNTY, INDIANA, granting right of pre-emption to certain lands for seat of justice to	456	28	1	5
TITLE TO LANDS,				
Alton, Ill., quieting title to certain lands at	144	30	1	6
Arkansas, to settle title to certain tracts of land in	689	27	2	5
TITLES,				
Certificates of, extending further	105	19	1	1
Columbus and Cochchuma, Miss., quieting of, to certain lands sold at	86	27	3	5
Do	84	28	1	5
Exemplification of records of land patents and evidences of	482	27	2	5
Guadalupe Hidalgo treaty, to perfect and quiet titles to land under the	45	40	2	8
Islands, beds of lakes, sloughs, &c., transferring United States title to the several States of all	566	46	2	9
Mississippi.				
Adjusting claims and quieting titles to lands in, held by residents under Spanish grants and non-residents under British grants	47	14	1	1
To confirm to certain persons, to public lands in	479	27	2	5
Soscol Rancho, confirming to holders of property on	20	37	3	7
Steubenville district of Ohio, titles to certain sections of land in	411	21	1	3
TODD, ISAAC, for relief of heirs	6	27	3	5
TOWN SITES, relative to the location on mineral lands of	745	46	2	9
TRANSYLVANIA COLLEGE, KENTUCKY, donating land for support of	413	23	1	3
TREATIES,				
Arkansas, to indemnify for loss of improvements caused by treaty of 1821 with the Choctaws	208	24	1	4
Guadalupe Hidalgo treaty, to quiet and perfect titles to certain lands under	45	40	2	8
Quapaw Indians, to carry into effect grants of land made by treaty of November 15, 1824, with the	60	19	2	1
Wyandott treaty, relief of certain persons under	160	27	3	5
Do	279	28	1	5
Do	10	29	1	6
TRESPASS ON LANDS,				
Costs in suits for regulating payment of	343	47	1	9
Occupation of public lands, to prevent unlawful	1809	47	1	9
Do	1858	47	1	9

Subject.

TRIPPE, GEORGE W., for relief ....
TRUST FUNDS, legalizing sale of certain lands in Mississippi and received to the Chickasaw ....
TUCKER, MARY, for relief ....
Do ....
Do ....
TURNER, CHARLOTTE, for relief ....
TUTTLE, JAMES M., for relief ....
TWO PER CENT. FUND, to change mode of application of the, g sissippi under act of September 4, 1841 ....
TYMOCHTEE TOWNSHIP, OHIO, authorizing trustees of, to sele for school purposes ....
UNIVERSITY. (See EDUCATION.)
UNIVERSITY OF ALABAMA, granting land to aid in rebuildin
UNIVERSITY OF CALIFORNIA, for relief ....
UTAH.
Boundary line between Colorado and, providing for survey of..
School purposes in, donating of certain town sites for ....
UTE INDIANS, to open reservation to settlement ....
VALENTINE, BERNARD, for relief ....
VALLE, FRANCIS, *et al.*, confirming certain lands to heirs, and le tives of ....
Do ....
Do ....
VAN BUREN COUNTY, MISSOURI, granting tract of land for co
VAN NESS, ABNER E., for relief ....
VERMILLION SALT SPRINGS, ILLINOIS, granting authorit reserved for ....
VETERAN UNION ASSOCIATION, LEADVILLE, COLOR certain lands to ....
VETERANS. (See WAR OF REBELLION; ARMY.)
VICK, HARTWELL W., for relief ....
VINCENNES, INDIANA, vesting title to certain land in ....
VINCENNES LAND DISTRICT, for the relief of certain settlers Illinois, residing within the ....
VINE, JEAN BATTISTE, for relief ....
Do ....
Do ....
VIRGINIA, to amend act making provision for military land claim and soldiers of the Virginia Line of the Revolutionary w
Do ....
VIRGINIA INSTITUTION FOR DEAF AND DUMB, granting aid ....
VIRGINIA MILITARY DISTRICT, defining act ceding to Ohio the, in State of Ohio ....
Do ....
VIRGINIA MILITARY LAND DISTRICT.
Patents in the, extending time for making locations, and obtai
Do ....
Surveyor for, appointing, within the State of Ohio ....
To allow the location of, on a portion of the public lands, also rel
Scrip upon, reviving law authorizing issue of ....
Do ....
Revolutionary war, making further appropriations of land to s ices during ....
WABASH RIVER, granting lands to States of Illinois and Indian provement of navigation of ....
WABASH AND ERIE CANAL.
Extension of, donating certain lands for ....
Price of lands on, reducing ....
Do ....
WADE, ELISHA A., for relief ....
WALKER, GEORGE H., for relief ....
WALKER, WILLIAM, for relief ....
Do ....
Do ....
Do ....
WALLACE, CADWALLADER, for relief ....
Do ....
Do ....
Do ....
WAR OF THE REBELLION.
Land bounties, giving additional, to veteran soldiers who serve
Entry of land under homestead laws, to soldiers who served ni
WAR OF REVOLUTION, bounty-land claims, extending certai enter ....
WAR WITH GREAT BRITAIN (1812-'14).
Bounty lands.
To grant, to officers and others for service in ....
Do ....
Do ....
Do ....

Subject.

WISCONSIN—Continued.
Settlers in, for relief of
Do
Southport in, sale of town lots in, and construction of harbo
Surveyor-general in, to establish office of
Town lots in, to provide for sale of certain
WISCONSIN CENTRAL RAILROAD, extending time for co
WISCONSIN RIVER, donating certain land for improvement
Do
WOMAN'S CHRISTIAN LIBRARY ASSOCIATION, to sell l
to
WOOD, ELLIS, for relief
Do
WOOD, JOHN, for relief
WOOD, WILLIAM, for relief of heirs
WOODALL, ABRAHAM, for relief
Do
Do
WOODWARD HIGH SCHOOL, donation of land to
WORTHINGTON, SAMUEL, for relief
WORTHINGTON AND SIOUX FALLS RAILROAD COMP.
them to extend line of road
WRIGHT, MAURICE, for relief
WYANDOT RESERVE, authorizing sale of residue of public l
Do
WYANDOT TREATY. (*See* TREATIES.)
WYOMING TERRITORY,
Fish hatching in, granting part of Fort Sanders military re
Fort Sanders military reservation, to grant part for fish-hat
Land district in, to establish new
Do
University to, granting land for
YELLOWSTONE NATIONAL PARK, to set apart a certain
designated the
YIELDING, RICHARD, for relief
YOSEMITE VALLEY, confirming pre-emption claims of certa
in

REPORTS

OF THE

OMMITTEE ON RAILWAYS C

HOUSE OF REPRESENTATIVES,

FROM THE ORGANIZATION OF T
THE CLOSE OF THE FORTY-

IN FIVE VOLUMES.

COMPILED, UNDER THE DIRECTION OF THE JOINT COMMITTEE ON PRINTING,

BY

T. H. McKEE,
CLERK, DOCUMENT ROOM, UNITED STATES SENATE.

WASHINGTON:
GOVERNMENT PRINTING OFFICE.
1887.

9308

FORTY-NINTH CONGRESS, FIRST SESSION.

[PUBLIC RESOLUTION—No. 24.]

Joint resolution authorizing the preparation of a compilation of the reports of mittees of the Senate and House of Representatives.

Resolved by the Senate and House of Representatives of the U States of America in Congress assembled, That there be prepared u the direction of the Joint Committee of Printing, a compilation o reports of the Senate and House of Representatives from the I teenth to the Forty-eighth Congress, inclusive, classified by commit arranged, indexed, and bound in suitable volumes for the use o standing committees of the two Houses of Congress. And the su seven thousand seven hundred and fifty dollars, or so much there may be found necessary, is hereby appropriated out of any mon the Treasury not otherwise appropriated, for the preparation of work, which sum may be paid by the Secretary of the Treasury the order of the chairman of said Joint Committee, as additional p compensation to any officer or employee of the United States.

Resolved further, That the Clerk of the House and Secretary o Senate be, and they are hereby directed, to procure and file, for th of their respective Houses, copies of all reports made by each com tee of all succeeding Congresses; and that the Clerk of the House the Secretary of the Senate be, and they are hereby, authorized directed at the close of each session of Congress, to cause said re to be indexed and bound, one copy to be deposited in the libra each House and one copy in the room of the committee from which reports emanated.

Approved, July 29, 1886.

COMPILER'S NOTICE.

This compilation embraces all the printed reports made by both Houses of Congress from the commencement of the Fourteenth to the close of the Forty-ninth Congress. They are classified by committees and arranged in numerical order. The collection for each committee is divided into volumes of suitable size. Each committee has a separate index, a copy being bound in each volume.

The SPECIAL and SELECT reports are all compiled in one collection having one index, a copy of which is bound in each volume.

The plan throughout the compilation is to place each report to the committee from which it was reported, without reference to the subject-matter.

The House and Senate reports are compiled separately. Care will be required in noticing the chronological order, as in some instances an entire session or Congress may not appear in certain volumes from the fact that during this period no reports were made by this committee.

T. H. McKEE.

INDEX

TO

REPORTS OF COMMITTEE ON RAILWAYS AND CANALS,

HOUSE OF REPRESENTATIVES.

FROM 1831 TO 1887, INCLUSIVE.

Subject.	Report.	Congress.	Session.	Volume.
ALABAMA,				
Lands granted to, for improving Tennessee, Coosa, Catawba, and Black Warrior Rivers	24	23	2	3
Roads in, to improve	258	20	1	3
ALABAMA, FLORIDA AND GEORGIA RAILROAD COMPANY, land grant to aid in construction of road	796	29	1	5
ALBEMARLE SOUND TO ATLANTIC OCEAN CANAL, survey of	648	26	1	4
ALEXANDRIA, CORPORATION OF, payment of subscriptions to stock of Chesapeake and Ohio Canal Company	112	20	1	2
ALLEN, THOMAS, and others, memorial relating to construction of Pacific Railroad	140	31	1	5
APALACHICOLA RIVER, improvement of	583	27	2	5
APPROPRIATION, Cumberland road, to complete	211	29	1	5
Do	51	29	2	5
Do	99	30	1	5
ATLANTIC AND MISSISSIPPI, land grant to aid in completion of	189	29	1	5
ATLANTIC AND PACIFIC CANAL, across the Isthmus of Panama, to construct	322	25	3	4
BALTIMORE AND OHIO RAILROAD COMPANY, aid in constructing road	92	20	2	2
BLACK WARRIOR RIVER, improvement of	24	23	2	3
BOSTON HARBOR AND NARRAGANSETT BAY CANAL, survey of	214	19	1	1
BRIDGE,				
Ohio River at Wheeling, Va., construction of	672	24	1	4
Do	135	24	2	4
Do	993	25	2	4
Do	278	27	3	5
Do	28	28	1	5
Do	79	28	1	5
Ouachita River, construction of	857	46	2	5
Potomac River at Washington, construction of	264	23	1	3
White River, to cede to State of Indiana, by Cumberland road	368	20	1	5
CAHABA RIVER, improvement of	24	23	2	3
CANAL,				
Albemarle Sound to the Atlantic Ocean, survey of	648	26	1	4
Appropriation for	270	20	1	2
Atlantic-Pacific, across Isthmus of Panama, to construct	322	25	3	4
Boston to Narragansett Bay, survey of	214	19	1	1
Cape Cod ship-canal, breakwater and harbor of refuge at northern end of, to construct	2040	48	1	5
Charenton, construction of, appropriation for	63	46	3	5
Do	2378	49	1	5
Charleston Neck, to construct, across	1289	46	2	5
Chesapeake and Ohio,				
Subscription by United States to capital stock of	90	19	2	1
Do	47	20	1	2
Do	112	20	1	2
Works on, examination of	141	20	1	2
Completion of, to Cumberland	56	28	1	5
Early history of project	228	19	1	1
Extension of	216	19	1	1

Subject.

CANAL—Continued.
Chipola, to construct
Cost of, from 1815 to 1835
Delaware and Maryland Ship, construction of
Do
Do
Dismal Swamp, to improve
Erie, improvement of
Do
Falls of Ohio, at Louisville, Ky., construction of
Do
Do
Farmington and Hampden, Conn., completion of
Hennepin, construction of
Illinois and Michigan, granting land to Illinois in aid of
Do
Enlargement of
Granting, by State of Illinois to United States
Do
Do
Illinois and Mississippi, construction of
Do
Lake Champlain to Ontario, to construct
Lake Michigan to Lake Erie, construction of
Do
Lake Michigan to Detroit River
Do
Louisville and Portland,
Free navigation of and purchase of bonds of
Do
Do
Stock of, to purchase
Tolls on, to abolish
Miami, to extend, to Lake Erie
Michigan and Illinois, aid to State of Illinois for construction
Michigan and Mississippi River, to construct
Muscle Shoals, Tennessee River, survey of
Do
Do
Do
Niagara Ship,
Survey of
Do
Land grant to aid in construction of
Olean Point, N. Y., to Erie Canal, survey of route
Oswego, improvement of
Rock Island and Hennepin Canal, construction of
Do
Saint Mary's to Saint John's River, to construct
Ship,
Across State of Michigan, to construct
Washington Territory, aid in constructing
To connect Delaware River with Atlantic Ocean
CANALS,
Surveys and plans for improvment of
Do
Do.
Systems of, between Mississippi Valley and Atlantic Ocean, portation
Do
Tennessee and Alabama Rivers, to construct
Tennessee and Coosa Rivers, to construct
Do
Tennessee River to Mobile Bay, aid in construction of
Toledo, Ohio, to La Fayette, Ind., to construct
Wabash and Lake Erie, granting land in aid of
Do
CAPE COD SHIP CANAL, breakwater and harbor of refuge at to construct
CARS, coupling of, on railroads, to regulate
CHARENTON CANAL (Louisiana), construction of, appropriat
Do
CHARLESTON NECK, canal across, to construct
CHEROKEE AND ARKANSAS RIVER RAILROAD COMP. tion of
CHESAPEAKE AND OHIO CANAL,
Completion of, to Cumberland
Early history of project
Extension of

* Views of minority.

Subject.	Report.	Congress.	Session.	Volume.
CHESAPEAKE AND OHIO CANAL—Continued.				
Government aid to construct	90	19	2	1
Subscription to capital stock of, by United States	47	20	1	2
Do	112	20	1	2
Do	414	20	1	2
Works on, examination of	141	20	1	2
CHIPOLA CANAL COMPANY, to incorporate	191	20	1	2
COLUMBUS AND SANDUSKY TURNPIKE COMPANY, land grant to aid in constructing toll road	189	29	1	5
COMMITTEE ON PUBLIC IMPROVEMENT, to organize, in House of Representatives	1066	25	2	4
COMMITTEE ON ROADS AND CANALS, to change to Committee on Public Improvement	1066	25	2	4
[illegible]A RIVER, improvement of	34	22	2	3
CUMBERLAND AND HOLLIDAYSBURG ROAD, survey of	113	22	2	3
CUMBERLAND ROAD,				
Change route between Springfield, Ohio, and Richmond, Ind	267	24	1	4
Completion of	148	15	1	1
Do	136	24	2	4
Do	221	29	1	5
Do	51	29	2	5
Do	99	30	1	5
Continuation of, in Ohio, Indiana, and Illinois	671	24	1	4
Cost of, from 1806 to 1835	850	24	1	4
Extending eastern terminus to Washington, D. C	109	19	1	1
Improvement of, in vicinity of Indianapolis, Ind	1062	25	2	4
Ohio River, bridge over	672	24	1	4
Do	278	37	3	5
Do	28	38	1	5
Do	79	38	1	5
Preservation of, by repairs	148	19	1	1
DES MOINES RIVER, improvement of	566	29	1	5
DISMAL SWAMP CANAL COMPANY, aid to improve canal	*892	45	2	5
DISTRICT OF COLUMBIA,				
Bridge across Potomac at, construction of	384	22	1	3
Railroad, Falmouth and Alexandria, to extend into	228	24	2	4
EDUCATIONAL INSTITUTIONS, to promote and encourage, by aid	11	18	1	1
ERIE CANAL, improvement of	628	48	1	5
Do	643	49	1	5
FALLS OF STE. MARIE, construction of ship canal around	95	32	1	5
FALLS OF THE OHIO, to remove obstructions to navigation of	661	29	1	5
Do	166	32	1	5
FALMOUTH AND ALEXANDRIA RAILROAD, to extend, into District of Columbia	238	24	2	4
FARMINGTON CANAL, CONNECTICUT, completion of	221	21	1	3
FLORIDA TERRITORY,				
Inland channel from Saint Mary's to Saint John's River, to construct	70	19	2	1
Internal improvements in, appropriation for	583	27	2	5
Road between Saint Mary's and Saint John's River, to improve	61	20	1	2
Roads in, construction of	271	25	3	4
FORTY-FIRST PARALLEL RAILROAD COMPANY, to charter	156	43	2	5
GEORGETOWN, CORPORATION OF, payment of subscriptions to stock of Chesapeake and Ohio Canal Company	112	20	1	2
GOOD, JOHN, claim for damage by right of way for Cumberland road	140	19	1	1
GREAT SOUTHERN RAILWAY COMPANY, aid in construction of railroad	999	45	2	5
HENNEPIN CANAL, construction of	118	43	2	5
HOUSE OF REPRESENTATIVES, rules of, to amend 73, rule relating to public improvements	164	23	1	3
Do	1066	25	2	4
Do	13	45	2	5
ILLINOIS, land grant to aid in construction of railroad	158	29	1	5
ILLINOIS AND MICHIGAN CANAL,				
Enlargement of	96	37	2	5
Canal, granting land to Illinois in aid of	53	18	1	1
Do	147	19	1	1
Granting, by State of Illinois to United States	1294	48	1	5
Do	574	49	1	5
Do	2031	49	1	5
ILLINOIS AND MISSISSIPPI CANAL, construction of	*1000	47	1	5
Do	574	49	1	5
INDIANA, land grant, to aid in constructing road	234	20	1	2
INDIANS, lands ceded by, for a road from Miami Rapids to the Western Reserve in Ohio	61	17	1	1
Do	50	17	2	1
INLAND CHANNEL, to construct, from Saint Mary's to Saint John's River, Fla.	70	19	2	1
INTERNAL COMMERCE AMONG THE STATES, to promote	11	15	1	1
INTERNAL IMPROVEMENTS,				
Appropriation for	270	20	1	2
By the General Government, power and methods of	63	18	2	1

*And views of minority.

Subject.	Report.	Congress.	Session.	Volume.
INTERNAL IMPROVEMENTS—Continued.				
Estimated cost of, from 1815 to 1835	850	24	1	
Florida Territory	583	27	2	
Organizing stock companies among the States for	53	18	2	
INTERNATIONAL PACIFIC RAILROAD, aid in construction of	14	40	2	
INTERSTATE COMMERCE,				
Control of railroads	*57	49	2	
To regulate, among the States	28	42	1	
ISTHMUS OF PANAMA (South America), canal across, to construct	322	25	2	
KANSAS CITY, FORT SCOTT AND GULF RAILROAD COMPANY, aid to construct railroad	949	45	1	
Do	730	46	2	
Do	2708	48	1	
KENNEBEC RIVER, MAINE, improvement of	118	19	1	
LA FAYETTE, INDIANA, to construct canal from Toledo, Ohio, to	1421	46	2	
LAKE CHAMPLAIN, canal to connect Lake Ontario with	230	19	1	
LAKE ERIE, canal to connect Lake Michigan with	155	46	2	
LAKE MICHIGAN, canal to connect Lake Erie with	155	46	2	
LAKE ONTARIO, canal to connect Lake Champlain with	230	19	1	
LAND GRANT,				
Alabama, Florida and Georgia Railroad Company, aid in construction of road	793	29	1	
Canals, aid to, memorial for	222	28	1	
Illinois, aid in construction of railroad	158	29	1	
Illinois and Lake Michigan Canal, aid in construction of	53	18	1	
Do	147	19	1	
Indiana, to aid in constructing road	234	20	1	
Mississippi,				
To aid in improvement of Pearl River	175	20	1	
Aid in construction of railroad	189	29	1	
Niagara Ship Canal, to aid in construction of	374	35	1	
Ohio, to aid in extending Miami Canal	88	20	1	
Pacific Railroad, aid in construction of	199	28	2	
West Virginia, to aid in construction of railroads	49	39	1	
LANDS CEDED BY INDIANS IN OHIO FOR PUBLIC ROADS	61	17	1	
Do	50	17	2	
LOCKS AND DAMS, Monongahela River, to construct	443	23	1	
LOOMIS, DANIEL, claim for work on Cumberland road	131	19	1	
LOUISIANA,				
Land grant to aid in improvement of certain rivers in	186	20	1	
Roads in, land grant to aid in constructing	194	20	1	
LOUISVILLE AND PORTLAND CANAL,				
Construction of	96	18	1	
Free navigation of, and purchase of bonds	307	22	1	3
Do	661	25	2	4
Do	3	26	1	4
Tolls on, to abolish	348	46	2	
LOUISVILLE AND SAINT LOUIS ROAD, improvement of, aid from United States	352	23	1	
MARYLAND AND DELAWARE FREE SHIP CANAL, construction of	*1016	47	1	5
Do	602	48	1	
Do	723	49	1	
MEMPHIS AND FORT GIBSON WAGON ROAD, aid in improvement of	251	24	2	
MIAMI CANAL, to extend, to Lake Erie	56	20	1	
MICHIGAN,				
Rivers, improvement of, survey of	316	23	1	
Roads in,				
Survey of	316	23	1	
Aid in construction of	1954	25	2	
Ship canal across State of, to construct	*879	47	1	
MICHIGAN AND ILLINOIS CANAL, aid to the State of Illinois for construction of	646	23	1	
MICHIGAN AND MISSISSIPPI RIVER CANAL, construction of	339	48	1	
MILESBURG AND SMITHPORT TURNPIKE COMPANY, memorial of	61	20	1	
MINNESOTA TERRITORY, roads in, construction of	172	31	1	
MISSISSIPPI,				
Land grant to aid in improvement of Pearl River	175	20		
Land grant to aid in construction of railroad	189	29		
MISSISSIPPI RIVER, improvement of	73	18		
Do	98	18		
Do	177	22		
Do	213	20		
Do	425	23		
Do	14	21		
Do	670	29		
MONONGAHELA RIVER, PENNSYLVANIA, improvement of	443	23		
MUSCLE SHOALS CANAL,				
Survey of	215	19	1	
Tennessee River, aid to construct	704	24	1	
Do	365	25		

* Views of minority.

Subject.	Report.	Congress.	Session.	Volume.
NATIONAL ROAD,				
Northwestern part of New York and Pennsylvania, construction of	91	20	1	2
Penobscot River to New Brunswick, construction of	214	20	1	2
Uniontown through Pittsburgh, to Lake Erie, to construct	267	20	1	2
NAVIGATION OF RIVERS IN WISCONSIN, improvement of	96	26	2	4
NEW MEXICO, wagon road, aid to open, from Santa Fé to the Valley of Taos	142	32	1	5
NEW ORLEANS, LOUISIANA, to construct national road from Washington to	48	20	1	2
NEW YORK CITY, to secure increased railroad facilities between Washington and	61	37	2	5
NIAGARA SHIP CANAL,				
Land grant to aid in construction of	374	35	1	5
Survey of	201	24	1	4
Do	466	25	2	4
NORTH CAROLINA, canal from Albemarle Sound to the Atlantic Ocean, survey of	648	26	1	4
NORTHERN CROSS RAILROAD, land grant to aid in construction of	158	29	1	5
OHIO RIVER,				
Appropriation for surveys of sites for reservoirs on affluents of	94	32	1	5
Falls of, to remove obstructions to the navigation of	661	29	1	5
Do	166	32	1	5
Improvement of	75	18	1	1
Do	98	18	1	1
Do	213	20	1	2
Do	269	20	1	2
Do	306	25	3	4
OHIO, land grant to extend Miami Canal	88	20	1	2
OLEAN POINT, NEW YORK, TO ERIE CANAL, survey of route for a canal	151	19	1	1
OREGON, roads in, construction of	348	31	1	5
OSWEGO CANAL, improvement of	643	49	1	5
OUACHITA RIVER, right to build bridge over	857	46	2	5
PACIFIC RAILROAD, location and construction of	773	29	1	5
Do	140	31	1	5
Do	101	32	1	5
PASCAGOULA RIVER, improvement of	145	20	1	2
PEARL RIVER, improvement of	175	20	1	2
PITTSBURGH AND CONNELLSVILLE RAILROAD, aid to complete	134	37	2	5
POST ROAD between Baltimore and Philadelphia, to improve	254	20	1	2
POTOMAC RIVER, bridge across, at Washington, construction of	264	23	1	3
PUBLIC WORKS, regulation and use of	880	47	1	5
RAFT IN RED RIVER, removal of	141	26	2	4
RAILROAD FACILITIES BETWEEN NEW YORK AND WASHINGTON, to increase	61	37	2	5
RAILROADS,				
Alabama, Florida and Georgia, land grant to	793	29	1	5
Atlantic Ocean to the Mississippi, construction of	189	29	1	5
Atlantic Ocean to Missouri River, to construct double-track freight railway	479	43	1	5
Baltimore and Ohio, aid in constructing road	92	20	2	2
Cars on, coupling of, to regulate	950	48	1	5
Cherokee and Arkansas River, to incorporate	1422	46	2	5
Control of	28	43	1	5
Falmouth and Alexandria, to extend, within District of Columbia	238	24	2	4
Forty-first parallel, to charter	156	43	2	5
Great Southern, aid in construction of road	999	45	2	5
International Pacific, aid in construction of	14	40	3	5
Kansas City, Fort Scott and Gulf, aid to construct	949	48	1	5
Do	730	49	1	5
Do	2708	49	1	5
Northern Cross, land grant to aid in construction of	158	29	1	5
Pacific, land grant to aid in construction of	199	28	2	5
Do	773	29	1	5
Do	140	31	1	5
Do	101	32	1	5
Pittsburgh and Connellsville, aid to complete	134	37	2	5
Regulation and control of	*57	40	2	5
San Antonio and Mexican Border, aid to construct	165	46	2	5
Do	*756	46	2	5
Signals on, uniform code of, to establish	951	48	1	5
Southern Maryland, aid in construction of	271	43	2	5
Washington and Ohio, aid in construction of railroad	321	43	2	5
Washington, Cincinnati and Saint Louis, aid to construct	346	44	1	5
Do	4	45	3	5
Worthington and Sioux Falls, to extend road to Sioux Falls, Dakota Territory	187	45	2	5
Wyoming, Montana and Pacific, to grant charter to	757	46	2	5
RED RIVER,				
Improvement of	96	19	2	1
Raft in, removal of	141	26	2	4
Right to build bridge over	857	46	2	5

*And views of minority.

Subject.

RIVER,
Black Warrior, lands granted to Alabama for improvement o
Cahaba, lands granted to Alabama for improvement of......
Coosa, lands granted to Alabama for improvement of... ....
Des Moines, improvement of .. ..
Kennebec, Maine, improvement of.........................
Mississippi, improvement of.................................
Do..
Do ....
Do ....
Monongahela, Pennsylvania, improvement of................
Ohio, improvement of...
Do...
Do...
Do...
Do...
Do ....
Pascagoula, improvement of..................................
Pearl, improvement of...
Providing for surveys and plans for improvement of ....
Red, improvement of...
Tennessee, lands granted to Alabama for improvement of...
Wisconsin, improvement of, in ....
ROADS,
Appropriation for ....
Baltimore to Philadelphia, to improve.......................
Black Swamp to Cumberland, to construct..................
Buffalo, N. Y., to Hanover, survey of......................
Covington to Opelousas, land grant to aid in constructing ..
Cumberland,
Completion of ....
Extending eastern terminus to Washington, D. C ....
Preservation by repairs ....
Cumberland to Hollidaysburg, survey of ....
Detroit to Lake Michigan, to construct ....
Florida, to construct in ....
Franklinton to Saint Francisville, land grant to aid in constr
La Plaisance Bay Harbor, westward, to construct ....
Lawrenceburg to Fort Wayne, Ind., to construct............
Lead mines on Fever River to Wiggins Ferry, Ill., to open..
Louisville to Saint Louis, aid in construction of..... ......
Memphis to Tuscumbia, to improve..........................
Michigan,
Survey of ....
Aid in construction of.....................................
Minnesota Territory, construction of ....
Natchez to New Orleans, to remove obstructions in ....
National,
To construct, from Washington to New Orleans..........
To construct, from Washington to northwestern parts o
Pennsylvania..
New Mexico, aid to construct, from Santa Fé to Valley of Ta
Oregon, construction of.......................................
Penobscot River to New Brunswick, to construct ....
Pittsburgh to Rapids of Maimi of Lake Erie, to construct ..
Rapids of Miami to Western Reserve, in Ohio, lands ceded by
Do..
Saint Mary's and Saint John's Rivers, to improve...........
Surveys and plans for improvement of.......................
Do ....
Do...
Tenth Turnpike Road Company, aid to construct ....
Uniontown, through Pittsburgh, to Lake Erie, to construct .
Wagon and military, Memphis to Fort Gibson, aid for impro
Wisconsin Territory, to construct............................
ROADS AND CANALS,
Construction and improvement of ....
Do.... ....
Estimated cost of, from 1815 to 1835........................
ROCK ISLAND AND HENNEPIN CANAL, construction of
Do ....
RULES OF HOUSE OF REPRESENTATIVES, to amend, con
ment of canals, rivers, and harbors ....
Do...
Do ....
SAINT LOUIS, MISSOURI, river improvement at............
Do ....
SAN ANTONIO AND MEXICAN BORDER RAILWAY CO
construct road...
Do...

*Views of minority.

Subject.	Report.	Congress.	Session.	Volume.
THERD, MOSES, claim for work on Cumberland road	183	19	1	1
CANAL,				
Cape Cod, breakwater and harbor of refuge at northern end of, to construct	2040	48	1	5
construction of, around falls of Ste. Marie River	96	22	1	5
Delaware River with Atlantic Ocean	390	49	1	5
Isthmus of Panama, to construct across	322	25	3	4
jurisdiction of United States over	380	47	1	6
Maryland and Delaware, to construct	*1016	47	1	5
Do	602	48	1	5
Do	738	49	1	5
Niagara,				
Survey of	201	24	2	4
Do	462	25	2	4
To construct	274	25	1	5
survey of, across State of Michigan	579	47	1	5
Washington Territory, aid to construct	603	48	1	5
SIGNALS ON RAILROADS, uniform code of, to establish	951	48	1	5
SOUTHERN MARYLAND RAILROAD COMPANY, aid in construction of railroad	271	43	2	5
SHERROD, DANIEL, claim for repairs on Cumberland road	56	19	1	1
Do	183	19	1	1
BANK COMPANIES, organization of, among the States, for internal improvements	83	18	2	1
SURVEY OF ROADS AND RIVERS IN MICHIGAN	316	22	1	2
SUWANNEE RIVER, improvement of	583	27	2	5
TENNESSEE, Muscle Shoals Canal, aid to construct	764	24	1	4
Do	985	25	2	4
TENNESSEE RIVER,				
improvement of	24	22	2	2
Muscle Shoals Canal, improvement of	104	22	2	2
TENNESSEE AND COOSA RIVER CANAL, survey of	230	19	1	1
TENNESSEE CANAL COMMISSIONERS, memorial for improvement at Muscle Shoals, in Tennessee River	104	22	2	2
TENNESSEE RIVER AND MOBILE BAY CANAL, aid in construction of	228	21	1	2
TURNPIKE ROAD COMPANY, aid to repair road	228	20	1	2
THURSTON, SAMUEL, memorial of	348	31	1	6
TOLEDO, OHIO, to construct canal from, to La Fayette, Ind	1431	46	2	5
ROAD, land grant to aid Columbus and Sandusky Turnpike Company in constructing	188	29	1	5
TRANSPORTATION BETWEEN TIDE-WATER AND MISSISSIPPI VALLEY, system of, by canal and railroads	360	44	1	5
Do	379	45	2	5
TURNPIKE, from Washington, D. C., to Frederick, Md., to construct	57	19	1	1
WABASH AND LAKE ERIE CANAL, granting land in aid of	317	23	1	3
WABASH RIVER, improvement of	222	28	1	5
WASHINGTON, D. C.,				
construct national road from, to New Orleans	48	20	1	2
secure increased railroad facilities between New York City and	61	37	2	5
WASHINGTON, CORPORATION OF, payment of subscriptions to stock of Chesapeake and Ohio Canal Company	112	20	1	2
WASHINGTON TERRITORY, ship canal in, aid in construction of	603	48	1	5
WASHINGTON AND OHIO RAILROAD, Government aid to complete	321	48	2	5
WASHINGTON, CINCINNATI AND SAINT LOUIS RAILWAY COMPANY, to construct railroad from Atlantic to Saint Louis and Chicago	346	44	1	5
Do	4	45	3	5
WASHINGTON TURNPIKE ROAD COMPANY, to construct a road from Washington, D. C., to Frederick, Md	57	19	1	1
VIRGINIA, land grant to aid in construction of railroads	49	39	1	5
WHEELING, VIRGINIA, bridge across Ohio River at	672	24	1	4
Do	135	24	2	4
Do	993	25	2	4
Do	278	27	3	5
Do	28	28	1	5
Do	79	28	1	5
WHITNEY, ASA, plan of, for construction of Pacific railroad	140	31	1	5
Do	101	32	1	5
WILKES, GEORGE, memorial of, relating to construction of railroad	773	29	1	5
WISCONSIN TERRITORY,				
public lands in, roads through, to construct	95	26	2	4
rivers in, improvement of	96	26	2	4
road in, to construct	95	26	2	4
WORTHINGTON AND SIOUX FALLS RAILROAD COMPANY, to extend road to Sioux Falls, Dakota Territory	187	45	2	5
WYOMING, MONTANA AND PACIFIC RAILROAD COMPANY, to grant charter to	757	46	2	5

*And views of minority.

REPORTS

OF THE

OMMITTEE ON REFORM IN CIVIL SERVICE,

HOUSE OF REPRESENTATIVES,

FROM THE ORGANIZATION OF THE COMMITTEE, DECEMBER 6, 1875, TO THE CLOSE OF THE FORTY-NINTH CONGRESS, 1887, INCLUSIVE.

IN ONE VOLUME.

COMPILED, UNDER THE DIRECTION OF THE JOINT COMMITTEE ON PRINTING,

BY

T. H. McKEE,

CLERK, DOCUMENT ROOM, UNITED STATES SENATE.

WASHINGTON:
GOVERNMENT PRINTING OFFICE.
1887.

9254

REPORTS

OF THE

OMMITTEE ON REFORM IN CIVIL SERVICE,

HOUSE OF REPRESENTATIVES,

FROM THE ORGANIZATION OF THE COMMITTEE, DECEMBER 6, 1875, TO THE CLOSE OF THE FORTY-NINTH CONGRESS, 1887, INCLUSIVE.

IN ONE VOLUME.

COMPILED, UNDER THE DIRECTION OF THE JOINT COMMITTEE ON PRINTING,

BY

T. H. McKEE,

CLERK, DOCUMENT ROOM, UNITED STATES SENATE.

WASHINGTON:
GOVERNMENT PRINTING OFFICE.
1887.

9254

FORTY-NINTH CONGRESS, FIRST SESSION.

[PUBLIC RESOLUTION—No. 24.]

Joint resolution authorizing the preparation of a compilation of the reports of committees of the Senate and House of Representatives.

Resolved by the Senate and House of Representatives of the United States of America in Congress assembled, That there be prepared under the direction of the Joint Committee of Printing, a compilation of the reports of the Senate and House of Representatives from the Fourteenth to the Forty-eighth Congress, inclusive, classified by committees, arranged, indexed, and bound in suitable volumes for the use of the standing committees of the two Houses of Congress. And the sum of seven thousand seven hundred and fifty dollars, or so much thereof as may be found necessary, is hereby appropriated out of any money in the Treasury not otherwise appropriated, for the preparation of said work, which sum may be paid by the Secretary of the Treasury upon the order of the chairman of said Joint Committee, as additional pay or compensation to any officer or employee of the United States.

Resolved further, That the Clerk of the House and Secretary of the Senate be, and they are hereby directed, to procure and file, for the use of their respective Houses, copies of all reports made by each committee of all succeeding Congresses; and that the Clerk of the House and the Secretary of the Senate be, and they are hereby, authorized and directed at the close of each session of Congress, to cause said reports to be indexed and bound, one copy to be deposited in the library of each House and one copy in the room of the committee from which the reports emanated.

Approved, July 29, 1886.

COMPILER'S NOTICE.

This compilation embraces all the printed reports made by both Houses of Congress from the commencement of the Fourteenth to the close of the Forty-ninth Congress. They are classified by committees and arranged in numerical order. The collection for each committee is divided into volumes of suitable size. Each committee has a separate index, a copy being bound in each volume.

The SPECIAL and SELECT reports are all compiled in one collection having one index, a copy of which is bound in each volume.

The plan throughout the compilation is to place each report to the committee from which it was reported, without reference to the subject-matter.

The House and Senate reports are compiled separately. Care will be required in noticing the chronological order, as in some instances an entire session or Congress may not appear in certain volumes from the fact that during this period no reports were made by this committee.

T. H. McKEE.

INDEX

TO

REPORTS OF COMMITTEE ON REFORM IN THE CIVIL SERVICE,

HOUSE OF REPRESENTATIVES.

FROM 1875 TO 1887, INCLUSIVE.

Subject.	Report.	Congress.	Session.	Volume.
APPOINTMENT BOARD, for executive board in each judicial district	1318	48	1	1
APPOINTMENTS,				
Discharged soldiers and sailors, amending law relating to	1319	48	1	1
Rules establishing, in civil service	1826	47	2	1
Do	749	48	1	1
Sailors and soldiers, giving preference to, in civil service	*1830	49	1	1
BRIBERY, 3.65 bond bill in District of Columbia	44	45	3	1
CHICAGO, ILLINOIS, pension agency at, investigation of	678	44	1	1
Do	*796	44	1	1
CIVIL SERVICE.				
Act of 1883 for improving, repealing	1788	48	1	1
Appointments in the Departments, rules for	1826	47	2	1
Do	749	48	1	1
Assistant civil service examiner, to provide for	1133	49	1	1
Classification of labor and equalization of pay of employés	1636	49	1	1
Discharged sailors and soldiers.				
Amending law relating to appointment of	1319	48	1	1
Preference to, in public appointments	*1830	49	1	1
Executive appointment board in each judicial district	1318	48	1	1
Ex-soldiers, prohibiting discharge of, as clerks	2499	48	2	1
Officers in the Departments, equitable classification and compensation of	1303	49	1	1
Repeal of present law	*1001	49	1	1
Tenure of office laws, repealing	748	48	1	1
Do	1955	48	1	1
CIVIL SERVICE COMMISSIONERS, salaries of, to increase	3997	49	2	1
CONTESTED ELECTION CASES, to refer, in House of Representatives to Court of Claims	1524	47	1	1
COURT OF CLAIMS.				
To refer contested election cases of House of Representatives to	1524	47	1	1
Judicial ascertainment of private claims against the United States, providing for	812	45	2	1
Do	198	46	2	1
Do	471	47	1	1
Do	636	47	1	1
DISTRICT OF COLUMBIA, charge and bribery in connection with 3.65 bond bill	44	45	3	1
DOORKEEPER OF HOUSE, investigating charges against	*422	45	2	1
ELECTION CASES. (*See* CONTESTED ELECTION.)				
EMPLOYÉS, pay of, and classification of labor	1636	49	1	1
EXECUTIVE DEPARTMENT, political assessments in, to prohibit	2006	47	2	1
HEADS OF DEPARTMENTS, reducing salaries of	466	47	1	1
HOUSE OF REPRESENTATIVES,				
Doorkeeper of, charges against	*422	45	2	1
Officers of, inquiry into charges against certain	2337	49	1	1
INVESTIGATION, Jeffersonville, Indiana, levees, appropriation for	2337	49	1	1
JEFFERSONVILLE, INDIANA, LEVEE, appropriation for inquiry on charges against L. F. Warder and O. O. Stealey in connection with	2337	49	1	1
JUDICIAL DISTRICTS, executive appointment board in each	1318	48	1	1
LABOR classification of	1636	49	1	1
MEMBERS OF CONGRESS, charges against, in connection with the 3.65 bond bill	44	45	3	1

* Views of minority.

Subject.	Report.	Congress.	Session.	Volume.
PENSION AGENCIES, investigation of, at Chicago	678	44	1	1
Do	*676	44	1	1
POLITICAL ASSESSMENTS, prohibiting levy of	2006	47	2	1
POLK, JOHN W., charges against	*422	45	2	1
PRIVATE CLAIMS,				
Adjudication by Court of Claims of	612	45	2	1
Do	198	46	2	1
Do	471	47	1	1
Do	636	47	1	1
PURMAN, Hon. W. J., charges against, for sale of naval cadetships	796	44	1	1
REVISED STATUTES,				
To amend section 1754, giving preference to discharged soldiers and sailors in public appointments	*1830	49	1	1
To repeal,				
Section 769, limiting term of the office of district attorney to four years	748	48	1	1
Sections 1767, 1768, 1769, 1770, 1771, 1772, tenure of office law	3539	49	2	1
Section 1864, limiting terms of the chief justice and associate justices of the Territories to four years	748	48	1	1
Section 2217, limiting term of surveyors-general to four years	748	48	1	1
Section 2244, limiting term of registers and receivers to four years	748	48	1	1
Section 2613, limiting term of collectors of customs and naval officers and surveyors of customs to four years	748	48	1	[illegible]
Section 2713, limiting term of postmasters to four years	748	48	1	[illegible]
SALARIES,				
Civil Service Commissioners, to increase	3997	49	2	[illegible]
Heads of Departments, reduction of	466	47	1	[illegible]
Officers in Government employ	1903	49	1	[illegible]
SOLDIERS AND SAILORS,				
Appointment of, to office, regulating	1319	48	2	[illegible]
Discharge of, except for cause, prohibiting	*2499	48	1	[illegible]
Preference to discharged, for appointment	*1830	49	1	[illegible]
STEALEY, O. O., charge in connection with appropriation for Jeffersonville levee against	2337	49	2	1
SWEET, ADA C.,				
Chicago pension agency, investigating appointment of	678	44	1	1
Do	*796	44	1	1
TENURE OF OFFICE, repealing laws relating to civil service	748	48	1	1
Do	1955	48	1	1
TENURE OF OFFICE LAW, to repeal	3539	49	2	1
WARDER, L. F., investigation of charges in connection with Jeffersonville levee, against	2337	49	1	1

* Views of minority.

O

REPORTS

OF THE

MMITTEE ON

HOUSE OF REPRESENTATIVES,

rom the organization of Comm
close of the Forty-second C

IN ONE VOLUME.

COMPILED, UNDER THE DIRECTION OF THE JOINT
COMMITTEE ON PRINTING,

BY

T. H. McKEE,

CLERK, DOCUMENT ROOM, UNITED STATES SENATE.

WASHINGTON:
GOVERNMENT PRINTING OFFICE.
1887.

9250

FORTY-NINTH CONGRESS, FIRST SESSION.

[PUBLIC RESOLUTION—No. 24.]

Joint resolution authorizing the preparation of a compilation of the reports of co mittees of the Senate and House of Representatives.

Resolved by the Senate and House of Representatives of the Unit States of America in Congress assembled, That there be prepared und the direction of the Joint Committee of Printing, a compilation of t reports of the Senate and House of Representatives from the Fo teenth to the Forty-eighth Congress, inclusive, classified by committe arranged, indexed, and bound in suitable volumes for the use of t standing committees of the two Houses of Congress. And the sum seven thousand seven hundred and fifty dollars, or so much thereof may be found necessary, is hereby appropriated out of any money the Treasury not otherwise appropriated, for the preparation of sa work, which sum may be paid by the Secretary of the Treasury up the order of the chairman of said Joint Committee, as additional pay compensation to any officer or employee of the United States.

Resolved, further, That the Clerk of the House and Secretary of t Senate be, and they are hereby directed, to procure and file, for the u of their respective Houses, copies of all reports made by each comm tee of all succeeding Congresses; and that the Clerk of the House a the Secretary of the Senate be, and they are hereby, authorized a directed at the close of each session of Congress, to cause said repor to be indexed and bound, one copy to be deposited in the library each House and one copy in the room of the committee from which t reports emanated.

Approved, July 29, 1886.

COMPILER'S NOTICE.

This compilation embraces all the printed reports made by both Houses of Congress from the commencement of the Fourteenth to the close of the Forty-ninth Congress. They are classified by committees and arranged in numerical order. The collection for each committee is divided into volumes of suitable size. Each committee has a separate index, a copy being bound in each volume.

The SPECIAL and SELECT reports are all compiled in one collection having one index, a copy of which is bound in each volume.

The plan throughout the compilation is to place each report to the committee from which it was reported, without reference to the subject-matter.

The House and Senate reports are compiled separately. Care will be required in noticing the chronological order, as in some instances an entire session or Congress may not appear in certain volumes from the fact that during this period no reports were made by this committee.

T. H. McKEE.

INDEX

TO

REPORTS OF COMMITTEE ON RETRENCHMENT,

HOUSE OF REPRESENTATIVES.

FROM 1828 TO 1874, INCLUSIVE.

Subject.	Report.	Congress.	Session.	Volume.
APPROPRIATIONS, extending practice of granting specific	152	21	1	1
ARMY, regulating pay and correcting abuses in	353	28	1	1
BONDS OF THE UNITED STATES, issuance of false certificates relative to the destruction of, investigating the	23	40	2	1
CATAWBA (iron-clad), alleged frauadulent sale of	64	40	2	1
CHAPLAINS, Indiana citizens for abolition of office of	302	28	1	1
CIVIL SERVICE (Jenckes's report), amending laws relative to appointment to offices in public service	47	40	1	1
CONGRESS.				
To reduce salaries of employés of	95	17	1	1
Fixing salaries of both Houses	300	28	1	1
CUSTOMS DUTIES,				
Collectors of, reducing and fixing salaries of	10½	21	1	1
Cost of collection of, 1828 to 1840	741	27	2	1
DISTILLED SPIRITS, collection of tax on, reducing expenses in	24	40	2	1
DISTRICT OF COLUMBIA, buildings rented in, by the Government	70	41	2	1
DRAUGHTSMAN,				
Office of, abolishing, in House of Representatives	113	21	1	1
Office of, creating, in House of Representatives	338	21	1	1
EMPLOYÉS,				
Congress, reduction of salaries of	95	17	1	1
Executive Departments, reduction of number in	263	27	2	1
EXECUTIVE DEPARTMENTS,				
Clerks and employés in, reduction in number of	263	27	2	1
Reorganization of	741	27	2	1
Retrenchment in expenses of the	259	20	1	1
Salaries paid to clerks and employés from 1828 to 1840 serving in	741	27	2	1
Chiefs of bureaus, equalizing and fixing salaries of	300	28	1	1
FRANKING PRIVILEGE,				
Abolition of	452	27	2	1
Abolishing privilege except during session	829	27	2	1
GETTYSBURG ASYLUM, exemption of, from taxes	12	40	2	1
GOLD, subtreasuries, investigating sale of, in	14	39	2	1
HOUSE OF REPRESENTATIVES,				
Reduction of salaries of employés in	95	17	1	1
Do	300	28	1	1
Draughtsman, discontinuing office of	113	21	1	1
Draughtsman in, creating office of	338	21	1	1
Censure and expulsion of members	829	27	2	1
INSPECTORS OF REVENUE, salaries of, reducing and fixing	10½	21	1	1
INTERNAL REVENUE DEPARTMENT,				
Frauds in, investigating	3	40	3	1
Whisky frauds upon, to investigate the	24	40	2	1
IRON-CLADS ONEOTO and CATAWBA, fraudulent sale of	64	40	2	1
INVESTIGATION,				
Whisky frauds, in 1868	24	40	2	1
Sale of iron-clads, in Navy Department	64	40	2	1
LOTTERY, exempting Gettysburg Asylum from payment of special tax	12	40	2	1

Subject.

MEMBERS OF CONGRESS.
Salaries of, reducing..
Mileage of, regulating..
Mileage to, abolishing..
Censure and expulsion of, enforcing rule for..................
Fixing the salary of..
Do..
MILEAGE.
Of members of Congress, regulating............................
Members of Congress, to discontinue to........................
NAVY, pay of, regulating......................................
NAVY DEPARTMENT, sale of iron-clads by, investigating..
NEWSPAPERS, prohibiting use of, at public expense.........
ONEOTO (iron-clad), alleged fraudulent sale of................
PRINTING FOR CONGRESS, cost, prior to 1848...... ....
PRINTING, PUBLIC, cost of, from 1828 to 1840..................
Do..
PUBLIC BUILDINGS rented by Government, investigation as
PUBLIC DEBT, payment of.......................................
PUBLIC PRINTING.
Cost of, providing for reduction in...........................
Public Printer, expenditures in office of, from 1829 to 1843..
RETRENCHMENT.
Executive Departments, providing for general reduction of
Executive Departments, reducing expenses in the.........
Officers and employés of the Government, reduction of amou
to..
Army, regulating abuses in....................................
REVENUE INSPECTORS. (*See* INSPECTORS OF REVENUE.)
SALARIES, Navy, regulating and fixing salaries in...........
SENATE, employés of, reduction of salaries of.................
SENATORS, salaries of, reducing the...........................
SPECIFIC APPROPRIATIONS, extending practice of.......
SURVEYORS OF PORTS, salaries of, fixing and reducing....
SWIFT, ALEXANDER, & CO., fraudulent purchase of vesse
tawba by..
TAXATION, retrenchment of.....................................
UNITED STATES BONDS. (*See* BONDS OF UNITED STATES.)
WHISKY FRAUDS.
Whisky, tax on, modifying law governing expenditures in c
Investigation of..

○

REPORTS

OF THE

COMMITTEE ON REVISION OF LAWS

HOUSE OF REPRESENTATIVES,

FROM THE ORGANIZATION OF COMMITTEE, JULY 25, 1868, TO THE CLOSE OF THE FORTY-NINTH

IN ONE VOLUME.

COMPILED, UNDER THE DIRECTION OF THE JOINT COMMITTEE ON PRINTING,

BY

T. H. McKEE,

CLERK, DOCUMENT ROOM, UNITED STATES SENATE.

WASHINGTON:
GOVERNMENT PRINTING OFFICE.
1887.

9268

Subject.	Report.	Congress.	Session.	Volume.
MEMBERS OF CONGRESS.				
Salaries of, reducing	95	17	1	1
Mileage of, regulating	451	27	2	1
Mileage to, abolishing	829	27	3	1
Censure and expulsion of, enforcing rule for	829	27	2	1
Fixing the salary of	829	27	2	1
Do	300	28	1	1
MILEAGE.				
Of members of Congress, regulating	451	27	2	1
Members of Congress, to discontinue to	829	27	2	1
NAVY, pay of, regulating	373	28	1	1
NAVY DEPARTMENT, sale of iron-clads by, investigating	64	40	2	1
NEWSPAPERS, prohibiting use of, at public expense	823	27	2	1
ONEOTO (iron-clad), alleged fraudulent sale of	64	40	2	1
PRINTING FOR CONGRESS, cost, prior to 1848	230	28	1	1
PRINTING, PUBLIC, cost of, from 1828 to 1840	741	27	2	1
Do	230	28	1	1
PUBLIC BUILDINGS rented by Government, investigation as to number	70	41	2	1
PUBLIC DEBT, payment of	101	20	2	1
PUBLIC PRINTING.				
Cost of, providing for reduction in	90	20	2	1
Public Printer, expenditures in office of, from 1829 to 1843	280	28	1	1
RETRENCHMENT,				
Executive Departments, providing for general reduction of expenses in	203	27	2	1
Executive Departments, reducing expenses in the	259	20	1	1
Officers and employés of the Government, reduction of amount paid for salaries to	300	28	1	1
Army, regulating abuses in	853	28	1	1
REVENUE INSPECTORS. (*See* INSPECTORS OF REVENUE.)				
SALARIES, Navy, regulating and fixing salaries in	373	28	1	1
SENATE, employés of, reduction of salaries of	95	17	1	1
SENATORS, salaries of, reducing the	95	17	1	1
SPECIFIC APPROPRIATIONS, extending practice of	152	21	1	1
SURVEYORS OF PORTS, salaries of, fixing and reducing	10½	21	1	1
SWIFT, ALEXANDER, & CO., fraudulent purchase of vessels Oneoto and Catawba by	64	40	2	1
TAXATION, retrenchment of	101	20	3	1
UNITED STATES BONDS. (*See* BONDS OF UNITED STATES.)				
WHISKY FRAUDS,				
Whisky, tax on, modifying law governing expenditures in collection of	24	40	2	1
Investigation of	3	40	3	1

○

COMPILER'S NOTICE.

This compilation embraces all the printed reports made by both Houses of Congress from the commencement of the Fourteenth to the close of the Forty-ninth Congress. They are classified by committees and arranged in numerical order. The collection for each committee is divided into volumes of suitable size. Each committee has a separate index, a copy being bound in each volume.

The SPECIAL and SELECT reports are all compiled in one collection having one index, a copy of which is bound in each volume.

The plan throughout the compilation is to place each report to the committee from which it was reported, without reference to the subject-matter.

The House and Senate reports are compiled separately. Care will be required in noticing the chronological order, as in some instances an entire session or Congress may not appear in certain volumes from the fact that during this period no reports were made by this committee.

T. H. McKEE.

INDEX

TO

)RTS OF COMMITTEE LAWS.

HOUSE OF REPRESENTATIVES.

FROM 1868 TO 1887, INCLUSIVE.

Subject.				
TANT, abolishing office of, in War Department				
ES IN BANKRUPTCY, settlement of bankrupt estates by				
JPT ESTATES, to prevent settlement of estates by other than the duly elected assignees			₺	
JPTCY,				
nees in, modifying law relative to		40	3	1
s of, issuing and publishing		40	3	1
rm system of, establishing	10	40	3	1
Do	20	40	3	1
Do	38	41	3	1
TO SENATORS AND REPRESENTATIVES, compensation of	3905	49	2	1
Γ LABOR, to prevent working of convicts for more than ten hours a day	746	48	1	1
)F CLAIMS, to restore jurisdiction of, over certain claims against United States	387	43		1
OF UNITED STATES,				
nend section 819 of Revised Statutes relating to the standing aside of jurors until a *venire* be gone through with	113	48	1	1
iend law relating to question of liens created by judgments rendered by.	1263	46	2	1
.LS at public expense	3551	49	2	1
DUTIES, decision of collector as to the rate and amount of duty shall be final	747		1	1
AL REVENUE LAWS, to limit time within which prosecutions may be instituted against persons charged with violating	1255	48 48	1	1
to amend section 819 of Revised Statutes relating to standing aside of jurors until a *venire* be gone through with	113	48	1	1
F UNITED STATES,				
intants in War and Navy Departments, to abolish offices of	26	40	3	1
y civil expenses, appropriation for	9	40	3	1
rm system of bankruptcy, establishing	10	40	3	1
Do	20	40	3	1
Do	38	41	3	1
) modify law relating to, on real estate created by judgments of United States courts	1263	46	2	1
STATES, payment for loss of steamboats and other vessels owned by men in	23	41	2	1
RS OF CONGRESS, compensation of clerks to	3905	49	2	1
EPARTMENT, abolishing office of accountant in	26	40	3	1
SERVICE, modifying the Revised Statutes relating to use of mails as a medium for distribution of obscene writings	888	45	2	1
BUILDINGS, draping of, in mourning	3551	49	2	1
STATE, to amend law relating to liens created by judgments rendered by United States courts upon	1263	46	2	1

Subject.	Report.	Congress.	Session.	Volume.
REVISED STATUTES,				
To amend,				
Section 819, standing aside of jurors until a *venire* be gone through with	113	48	1	1
Section 3013, decision of collector as to rate and amount of duty shall be final	747	48	1	1
Section 4596, to extend punishment provided for in	1203	47	1	1
To repeal,				
Sections 1785, 2491, 3878, 3893, 5389, use of mails as medium for distribution of obscene writings	886	45	2	1
STEAMBOATS, allowing payment for loss of, belonging to loyal men	23	41	2	1
SUNDRY CIVIL EXPENSES, to amend law relative to	9	40	3	1
TELEGRAMS, to secure to, the same sanctity as now protects letters by mail	1262	46	2	1
VESSELS, allowing payment for loss of vessels belonging to loyal men	23	41	2	1
WAR DEPARTMENT, abolishing office of accountant in	20	40	3	1
WILLIAMS, ZADOCK, *et al.*, praying for passage of an act to restore jurisdiction of Court of Claims over certain cases	387	43	1	1

O

REPORTS

OF THE

OMMITTEE ON RIVERS AND HARBORS,

HOUSE OF REPRESENT

FROM THE ORGANIZATION OF THE
CLOSE OF THE FORTY-NI

IN ONE VOLUME.

COMPILED, UNDER THE DIRECTION OF THE JOINT
COMMITTEE ON PRINTING,

BY

T. H. McKEE,
CLERK, DOCUMENT ROOM, UNITED STATES SENATE.

WASHINGTON:
GOVERNMENT PRINTING OFFICE.
1887.

9246 R H H

[PUBLIC RESOLUTION—No. 24.]

Joint resolution authorizing the preparation of a compilation of the reports of committees of the Senate and House of Representatives.

Resolved by the Senate and House of Representatives of the United States of America in Congress assembled, That there be prepared under the direction of the Joint Committee of Printing, a compilation of the reports of the Senate and House of Representatives from the Fourteenth to the Forty-eighth Congress, inclusive, classified by committees, arranged, indexed, and bound in suitable volumes for the use of the standing committees of the two Houses of Congress. And the sum of seven thousand seven hundred and fifty dollars, or so much thereof as may be found necessary, is hereby appropriated out of any money in the Treasury not otherwise appropriated, for the preparation of said work, which sum may be paid by the Secretary of the Treasury upon the order of the chairman of said Joint Committee, as additional pay or compensation to any officer or employee of the United States.

Resolved further, That the Clerk of the House and Secretary of the Senate be, and they are hereby directed, to procure and file, for the use of their respective Houses, copies of all reports made by each committee of all succeeding Congresses; and that the Clerk of the House and the Secretary of the Senate be, and they are hereby, authorized and directed at the close of each session of Congress, to cause said reports to be indexed and bound, one copy to be deposited in the library of each House and one copy in the room of the committee from which the reports emanated.

Approved, July 29, 1886.

COMPILER'S NOTICE.

This compilation embraces all the printed reports made by both Houses of Congress from the commencement of the Fourteenth to the close of the Forty-ninth Congress. They are classified by committees and arranged in numerical order. The collection for each committee is divided into volumes of suitable size. Each committee has a separate index, a copy being bound in each volume.

The SPECIAL and SELECT reports are all compiled in one collection having one index, a copy of which is bound in each volume.

The plan throughout the compilation is to place each report to the committee from which it was reported, without reference to the subject-matter.

The House and Senate reports are compiled separately. Care will be required in noticing the chronological order, as in some instances an entire session or Congress may not appear in certain volumes from the fact that during this period no reports were made by this committee.

T. H. McKEE.

INDEX

TO

REPORTS OF COMMITTEE ON RIVERS AND HARBORS.

HOUSE OF REPRESENTATIVES.

FROM DECEMBER 19, 1883, TO MARCH 4, 1887, INCLUSIVE.

Subject.	Report.	Congress.	Session.	Volume.
PRIATIONS,				
nination of South Pass, Mississippi River, and to ascertain depth of water and width of channel	1233	49	1	1
ississippi River, improvement of	28	48	1	1
PRIATION BILLS for rivers and harbors	1526	48	1	1
Do	1554	48	1	1
Do	2307	48	2	1
Do	2387	48	2	1
Do	1448	49	1	1
Do	1565	49	1	1
Do	3541	49	2	1
ES, recommending removal of, interfering with navigation	1526	48	1	1
Do	1448	49	1	1
Do	1565	49	1	1
WAYS, recommending removal of, interfering with navigation	1526	48	1	1
Do	1448	49	1	1
Do	1565	49	1	1
EL AT SOUTH PASS, making appropriation to ascertain depth of water and width of	597	48	1	1
Do	1233	49	1	1
ESTON AND OTHER HARBORS, appropriations recommended for	1526	48	1	1
Do	1554	48	1	1
Do	1448	49	1	1
Do	1565	49	1	1
ACT SYSTEM, to adopt, by Secretary of War	1526	48	1	1
Do	1448	49	1	1
JAMES B., deficiency appropriation for examination of South Pass and to ascertain depth of water and width of channel	507	48	1	1
Do	1233	49	1	1
ATES may be directed by Secretary of War	1526	48	1	1
Do	1448	49	1	1
SIPPI RIVER,				
ident's message and report of Mississippi River Commission on improvement of	28	48	1	1
ropriations recommended for improvement of	1526	48	1	1
Do	1554	48	1	1
Do	1448	49	1	1
Do	1565	49	1	1
SIPPI RIVER COMMISSION,				
rt of	28	48	1	1
nding jurisdiction of	1526	48	1	1
Do	1554	48	1	1
ake report before December 1st in each year	2387	48	2	1
Do	1448	49	1	1
Do	1565	49	1	1
RI RIVER, appropriations recommended for improvement of, and other large rivers	1526	48	1	1
Do	1554	48	1	1
RI RIVER COMMISSION, to create, recommended	1526	48	1	1
Do	1554	48	1	1
UKEE, WISCONSIN, appropriations recommended for improving harbor at, and other harbors	1526	48	1	1
Do	1554	48	1	1
Do	1448	49	1	1
Do	1565	49	1	1

Subject.

REPORTS

OF THE

COMMITTEE ON RULES,

HOUSE OF REPRESENTATIVES,

FROM THE FOURTEENTH CONGRESS, 1815, TO THE FORTY-NINTH CONGRESS, 1887, INCLUSIVE.

IN TWO VOLUMES.

COMPILED, UNDER THE DIRECTION OF THE JOINT COMMITTEE ON PRINTING,

BY

T. H. McKEE,

CLERK, DOCUMENT ROOM, UNITED STATES SENATE.

WASHINGTON:
GOVERNMENT PRINTING OFFICE.
1887.

9267

FORTY-NINTH CONGRESS, FIRST SESSION.

[PUBLIC RESOLUTION—No. 24.]

Joint resolution authorizing the preparation of a compilation of the reports of committees of the Senate and House of Representatives.

Resolved by the Senate and House of Representatives of the United States of America in Congress assembled, That there be prepared under the direction of the Joint Committee of Printing, a compilation of the reports of the Senate and House of Representatives from the Fourteenth to the Forty-eighth Congress, inclusive, classified by committees, arranged, indexed, and bound in suitable volumes for the use of the standing committees of the two Houses of Congress. And the sum of seven thousand seven hundred and fifty dollars, or so much thereof as may be found necessary, is hereby appropriated out of any money in the Treasury not otherwise appropriated, for the preparation of said work, which sum may be paid by the Secretary of the Treasury upon the order of the chairman of said Joint Committee, as additional pay or compensation to any officer or employee of the United States.

Resolved further, That the Clerk of the House and Secretary of the Senate be, and they are hereby directed, to procure and file, for the use of their respective Houses, copies of all reports made by each committee of all succeeding Congresses; and that the Clerk of the House and the Secretary of the Senate be, and they are hereby, authorized and directed at the close of each session of Congress, to cause said reports to be indexed and bound, one copy to be deposited in the library of each House and one copy in the room of the committee from which the reports emanated.

Approved, July 29, 1886.

2

COMPILER'S NOTICE.

This compilation embraces all the printed reports made by both Houses of Congress from the commencement of the Fourteenth to the close of the Forty-ninth Congress. They are classified by committees and arranged in numerical order. The collection for each committee is divided into volumes of suitable size. Each committee has a separate index, a copy being bound in each volume.

The SPECIAL and SELECT reports are all compiled in one collection having one index, a copy of which is bound in each volume.

The plan throughout the compilation is to place each report to the committee from which it was reported, without reference to the subject-matter.

The House and Senate reports are compiled separately. Care will be required in noticing the chronological order, as in some instances an entire session or Congress may not appear in certain volumes from the fact that during this period no reports were made by this committee.

T. H. McKEE.

INDEX

TO

REPORTS OF COMMITTEE ON RULES,

HOUSE OF REPRESENTATIVES.

FROM 1815 TO 1887, INCLUSIVE.

Subject.	Report.	Congress.	Session.	Volume.
)URNMENT,				
mend rule 30, relating to	56	17	1	1
:otions for, regulating rule for	1	26	1	1
ROPRIATION BILLS, designating period in which to report general	83	24	1	1
ROPRIATIONS,				
ommittee on, to create	12	38	2	1
ension bills to provide by taxation for payment of, rule to allow amendments to	2213	49	1	1
KING AND CURRENCY, committee on, to create standing	12	38	2	1
S,				
pproval of, prohibiting presentation on last day of session of any bill for Presidential	20	17	1	1
nacting clause of, to amend rule 29, with reference to	56	17	1	1
:otion on subject not germane to, to amend rule 36, relative to consideration of	56	17	1	1
rivate, regulating printing of	240	20	1	1
o abolish rule 19, regulating consideration of	240	20	1	1
Do	83	24	1	1
eference of, to amend rules 29 and 30, regarding	56	17	1	1
MITTEE REPORTS. (*See* REPORTS OF COMMITTEES.)				
MITTEE ON APPROPRIATIONS (House of Representatives), created as standing committee	12	38	2	1
MITTEE ON BANKING AND CURRENCY, to create standing	12	38	2	1
MITTEE ON PACIFIC RAILROADS, to create	12	38	2	1
MITTEE ON PUBLIC EXPENDITURES, resolution to abolish	240	20	1	1
MITTEE ON RETRENCHMENT, to establish standing	240	20	1	1
MITTEE ON RULES, defining duties of	1	31	1	1
MITTEE ON WAYS AND MEANS, fixing period in which general appropriation bills shall be reported by	83	24	1	1
Do	1	25	1	1
MITTEES,				
dditional standing, created in House	13	14	1	1
Do	56	17	1	1
ommittee on Public Expenditures, to abolish	240	20	1	1
ommittee on Retrenchment in House, to establish standing	240	20	1	1
GRESS,				
ournals of				
General index of, specimen copy	52	45	3	2
From the First to Tenth Congress, inclusive	1776	46	2	2
From the Eleventh to Sixteenth Congress, inclusive	1559	47	1	2
Relating to general preparation and progress made with	23	46	2	1
Do	145	46	3	1
General personal index of, from the First to Eighth Congress, inclusive	2692	48	2	2
rder of business in the two Houses of, joint rule regulating	20	17	1	1
ublications of, method of indexing current	128	46	2	1
GRESSIONAL RECORD, indexing of, remodeling system of	128	46	2	1
TINGENT FUND, payments from, additional rule governing	1	31	1	1
ATE, consideration of motions when a question is under, to amend rule 29, regulating the	56	17	1	1
ime of, to amend rule 33, limiting	1	30	1	1
anner of conducting, substitute for rule 33, relating to	1	30	1	1
'ords spoken in, prescribing action for, excepted	1	25	1	1
CTION OF OFFICERS, all voting in House shall be *viva voce* for	240	20	1	1
CTING CLAUSE, to amend rule 29, giving effect to striking out from a bill the	56	17	1	1
MANE MATTER. (*See* BILLS.)				
L OF HOUSE, admission to floor of. (*See* RULES.)				
R OF MEETING OF HOUSE OF REPRESENTATIVES, designating	2212	49	1	1
R RULE, No. 33, substitute for	1	30	1	1
SE OF REPRESENTATIVES,				
dmission to the floor of, amending rule 17, relative to	1	31	1	1
election of officers, all voting shall be *viva voce* for	240	20	1	1

Subject.	Report.	Congress.	Session.	Volume.
HOUSE OF REPRESENTATIVES—Continued.				
Hour of meeting, to fix	2212	49	1	1
Officers of, defining duties of. (*See* RULES.)				
Printing, providing rule for printing private documents, bills, &c	240	20	1	1
Rules of,				
To amend, repeal, or revise	13	14		
Do	20	17		
Do	56	17		
Do	240	20		
Do		23		
Do		26		
Do	11	27		
Do	3	28		
Do		29		
Do		31		
Do		35		
Do	58	36		
Do	12	38		
Do	24	46	2	1
Do	390	46	2	1
Do	571	46	2	1
Do	610	47	1	1
Do	637	47	1	1
Do		49	1	1
Do	1542	49	1	1
To change, providing for payment of pensions	2213	49	1	1
Standing committees in, creating additional	13	14	1	1
Do	56	17	1	1
Do	1	25	1	1
Unfinished business in, statement of	110	17	1	1
Do	182	18	1	1
Do	1	19	2	1
INDEX, Congressional Record, method of preparing index for	128	46	2	1
INDEXES,				
Journals of Congress,				
Specimen copy	52	45	3	2
From the First to Tenth Congress, inclusive	1776	46	2	2
From the Eleventh to Sixteenth Congress, inclusive	1559	47	1	2
General progress made with indexing of	23	46	2	1
Do	145	46	3	1
General personal index of, from First to Eighth Congress	2692	48	2	2
Publications of Congress, adopting system of indexing public	128	46	2	1
JOINT RESOLUTIONS. (*See* BILLS.)				
JOINT RULES, regulating order of business in the two Houses	20	17	1	1
JOURNALS OF HOUSE,				
Examination and correction of, to amend rule 6 relating to the	240	20	1	1
General index of,				
Sample copy	53	45	3	2
From the First to Tenth Congress, inclusive	1776	46	2	2
From the Eleventh to Sixteenth Congress, inclusive	1559	47	1	2
General preparation and progress made with	23	46	2	1
Do	128	46	2	1
Do	145	46	3	1
General personal index of, from First to Eighth Congress, inclusive	2692	48	2	2
MEMORIALS. (*See* PRINTING.)				
OFFICERS OF HOUSE,				
Defining duties of. (*See* RULES.)				
Elections for, shall be *viva voce*	240	20	1	1
ORDER OF BUSINESS,				
Amending rules regulating	13	14	1	1
Do	20	17	1	1
Do	56	17	1	1
Do	240	20	1	1
Do	83	24	1	1
Do	1	25	1	1
Do	1	26	1	1
Do	11	27	1	1
Do	3	28	1	1
Do	1	30	1	1
Do	1	31	1	1
Do	1	35	1	1
Do	58	36	1	1
Do	12	38	2	1
Do	390	46	2	1
Do	571	46	2	1
Do	610	47	1	1
Do	637	47	1	1
Do	1	49	1	1
Do	1432	49	1	1
Joint rule regulating, in both Houses	20	17	1	1
List of unfinished business in House	110	17	1	1
Do	182	18	1	1
Do	1	19	2	1

Subject.	Report.	Congress.	Session.	Volume.
FIC RAILROADS, standing committee on, to create	12	38	2	1
IONS, rules of House, to amend, providing for payment of	2213	49	1	1
TIONS.				
seenting of, modifying rule 45, regulating manner of	83	24	1	1
inting of private, regulating	240	20	1	1
eception of, to amend rule 16, regulating	56	17	1	1
IDENT OF UNITED STATES, joint rule prohibiting bills that have passed both Houses to be presented on last day of session to, for approval	20	17	1	1
TING, prescribing rule for printing of private bills, petitions, &c.	240	20	1	1
ATE BUSINESS, to abolish rule 19, setting aside two days each week for consideration of	240	20	1	1
Do	82	24	1	1
ATE PRINTING. (*See* PRINTING.)				
ILEGE OF FLOOR. (*See* RULES.)				
IC EXPENDITURES, resolution to abolish Committee on	240	20	1	1
ROAD COMPANIES, select committee to investigate disturbed condition between employés and	1621	49	1	1
RTS OF COMMITTEES, to amend rule, 17 limiting time for consideration of	56	17	1	1
Do	240	20	1	1
ENCHMENT. (*See* COMMITTEE ON RETRENCHMENT.)				
S, JOINT. (*See* JOINT RULES.)				
S OF HOUSE.				
amend and repeal.				
Committees, to increase number of standing	13	14	1	1
Do	56	17	1	1
Election of officers, all voting shall be *viva voce* in	240	20	1	1
Journals of House, to amend rule 6, on examination and correction of	240	20	1	1
Order of business, prescribing rule for Speaker in disposing of	1	25	1	1
Rule 6, examination and correcting of House Journal	240	20	1	1
Rule 16, regulating reception of petitions	56	17	1	1
Rule 17, fixing limit for considering subject of reports from committees	56	17	1	1
Do	240	20	1	1
Rule 17, prescribing manner of conducting order of business	1	25	1	1
Rule 19, consideration of private business	240	20	1	1
Do	82	24	1	1
Rule 29, regulating debate and enacting clause in bills	56	17	1	1
Rule 30, daily adjournment	56	17	1	1
Rule 33, substitute for, called hour rule	1	30	1	1
Rule 45, prescribing manner of presenting petitions and other papers	83	24	1	1
Rule 58, appropriation bills	83	24	1	1
Rule 83, suspension of rules	56	17	1	1
amend, repeal, or revise	13	14	1	1
Do	20	17	1	1
Do	56	17	1	1
Do	240	20	1	1
Do	1	25	1	1
Do	1	26	1	1
Do	11	27	1	1
Do	3	28	1	1
Do	1	30	1	1
Do	1	31	1	1
Do	1	35	2	1
Do	58	36	1	1
Do	12	38	2	1
Do	24	46	2	1
Do	390	46	2	1
Do	571	46	2	1
Do	610	47	1	1
Do	637	47	1	1
Do	1	49	1	1
Do	1452	49	1	1
KER OF HOUSE. (*See* RULES.)				
DING COMMITTEES, additional, created in House	13	14	1	1
Do	56	17	1	1
Do	1	25	1	1
KES, railroad employés, creating select committee to investigate cause of	1621	49	1	1
ENSION OF RULES, amending rule 83, regulating	56	17	1	1
NISHED BUSINESS OF HOUSE OF REPRESENTATIVES.				
escribing rule for disposing of	1	26	1	1
itement of	110	17	1	1
Do	132	18	1	1
Do	1	19	2	1
A VOCE" VOTING. (*See* ELECTION OF OFFICERS.)				
NG. (*See* ELECTION OF OFFICERS.)				
S AND MEANS, general appropriation bills, to amend rule 58, for Committee on, to report	83	24	1	1
Do	1	25	1	1

REPORTS

OF THE

COMMITTEE ON THE TERRITORIES,

HOUSE OF REPRESENTATIVES,

FROM THE ORGANIZATION OF THE COMMITTEE, DECEMBER 13, 1825, TO THE CLOSE OF THE FORTY-NINTH CONGRESS, 1887, INCLUSIVE.

IN THREE VOLUMES.

COMPILED, UNDER THE DIRECTION OF THE JOINT COMMITTEE ON PRINTING,

BY

T. H. McKEE,

CLERK, DOCUMENT ROOM, UNITED STATES SENATE.

WASHINGTON:
GOVERNMENT PRINTING OFFICE.
1887.

9239 TER H

FORTY-NINTH CONGRESS, FIRST SESSION.

[PUBLIC RESOLUTION—No. 24.]

Joint resolution authorizing the preparation of a compilation of the reports of mittees of the Senate and House of Representatives.

Resolved by the Senate and House of Representatives of the Un States of America in Congress assembled, That there be prepared u the direction of the Joint Committee of Printing, a compilation of reports of the Senate and House of Representatives from the F teenth to the Forty-eighth Congress, inclusive, classified by commit arranged, indexed, and bound in suitable volumes for the use of standing committees of the two Houses of Congress. And the su seven thousand seven hundred and fifty dollars, or so much thereo may be found necessary, is hereby appropriated out of any mone the Treasury not otherwise appropriated, for the preparation of work, which sum may be paid by the Secretary of the Treasury the order of the chairman of said Joint Committee, as additional pa compensation to any officer or employee of the United States.

Resolved further, That the Clerk of the House and Secretary of Senate be, and they are hereby directed, to procure and file, for the of their respective Houses, copies of all reports made by each com tee of all succeeding Congresses; and that the Clerk of the House the Secretary of the Senate be, and they are hereby, authorized directed at the close of each session of Congress, to cause said rep to be indexed and bound, one copy to be deposited in the libra each House and one copy in the room of the committee from whic reports emanated.

Approved, July 29, 1886.

2

COMPILER'S NOTICE.

This compilation embraces all the printed reports made by both Houses of Congress from the commencement of the Fourteenth to the close of the Forty-ninth Congress. They are classified by committees and arranged in numerical order. The collection for each committee is divided into volumes of suitable size. Each committee has a separate index, a copy being bound in each volume.

The SPECIAL and SELECT reports are all compiled in one collection having one index, a copy of which is bound in each volume.

The plan throughout the compilation is to place each report to the committee from which it was reported, without reference to the subject-matter.

The House and Senate reports are compiled separately. Care will be required in noticing the chronological order, as in some instances an entire session or Congress may not appear in certain volumes from the fact that during this period no reports were made by this committee.

T. H. McKEE.

INDEX

TO

REPORTS OF COMMITTEE ON THE TERRITORIES,

HOUSE OF REPRESENTATIVES.

FROM 1825 TO 1887, INCLUSIVE.

Subject.	Report.	Congress.	Session.	Volume.
ALABAMA TERRITORY, admission of, as a State	79	20	1	1
ALASKA TERRITORY,				
Certificate of election of M. D. Ball as Delegate from	1306	47	1	2
Civil government, providing for	*1106	47	1	2
Do	476	48	1	3
Courts of justice, establishing, in	754	46	2	2
Homestead laws in	3232	49	1	3
Organization of	4088	49	2	3
Penal colony in	1685	49	1	3
Resources of, to develop	3749	49	2	3
Settlement of, to facilitate	3749	49	2	3
ALDEN & EDDY, right of way to construct a subterranean telegraph to the Pacific Ocean	5	33	2	1
ARIZONA TERRITORY,				
Deer Creek coal fields in, to detach from White Mountain Indian Reservation	406	48	1	3
Cattle in, diseased	2335	49	1	3
Insane asylum in	2034	49	1	3
Internal revenue collections to erect capitol building in	27	41	2	2
Organization of	2	34	3	1
Do	117	34	3	1
Appropriation to complete the prison at Yuma, in	475	46	2	2
Probate and county courts, jurisdiction of	1478	49	1	3
Railroad in, construction and maintenance of a	124	46	3	2
United States courts in, to regulate fees of clerks, marshals, &c	3751	49	2	3
White Mountain Indian Reservation in, to correct western and southern boundaries of	406	48	1	3
ARKANSAS TERRITORY,				
Appeals and writs of error to be taken from the superior court of the Territory to the Supreme Court of the United States	89	19	1	1
Census, taking of	334	23	1	1
Formation of	79	20	1	1
Governor and judges in, salary of	235	21	1	1
Do	242	22	1	1
Judges to perform circuit duties, to compel	89	19	1	1
Public buildings in Territory of	118	21	1	1
State government in, formation of	334	23	1	1
Territorial judge, appointment of fourth	89	19	1	1
Western boundary of	52	20	2	1
ARTESIAN WELLS, boring of,				
Montana	3118	49	1	3
New Mexico	1092	49	1	3
West of the Mississippi River	1479	49	1	3
BAKER, GRAFTON, claim for relief as messenger from New Mexico	81	33	1	1
BALL, M. D. (*See* ALASKA.)				
BOUNDARY,				
Arkansas Territory	52	20	2	1
Missouri	512	22	1	1
Do	768	25	2	1
Missouri and the Territory of Iowa	2	26	1	1
Do	791	27	2	1
Do	86	27	3	1
Northwestern and Western Territories defined	79	20	1	1

* And views of minority, Part 2.

Subject.

BOUNDARY—Continued.
Ohio and Michigan ....
Oregon Territory ....
Do ....
Texas and Indian Territory ....
BROTHERTON INDIANS, division of lands and citizenship of,
CALIFORNIA, eastern boundary of, to change. ....
CARSON VALLEY, UTAH, annexation of, to California .....
CENSUS,
Arkansas and Michigan ....
Mississippi Territory ....
Oregon, in 1850 ....
CHAMBERS, E. G., et al., memorial for a wagon-road from the to the Pacific Ocean ....
COLORADO TERRITORY, formation of constitution and Sta and admission into the Union ....
Do ....
COMMITTEE ON THE TERRITORIES, clerk for ....
CONVICTS in the Territorial prison of Idaho Territory.. ......
CORNELL, THOMAS F., claim for compensation as district at Florida ....
Do ....
COURTS OF THE UNITED STATES,
Alaska Territory, to establish ....
Appalachicola, Florida Territory, to establish ....
Arkansas Territory, salaries of judges in ....
Do ....
Dakota Territory, compensation of judge of first judicial dis
East Florida, compensation of district attorney for ....
Eastern Montana, to provide additional judge for ....
Fees, to regulate, of marshals, clerks, &c., in Territories of A Mexico ....
Florida Territory,
To reorganize ....
To establish, in western district of ....
All crimes committed in East Florida to be tried at Saint
Indian Territory, to establish ....
Iowa, salaries of judges of the supreme conrt in the Territor
Judges of, in the Territories, power to elect ....
Jurors and witnesses in Territorial courts ....
Michigan Territory,
To establish ....
Compensation of United States marshal of ....
Appointment of judges in ....
Salaries of judges in ....
New Mexico, to provide additional judge for........
Wyoming Territory,
To provide additional judge for ....
To enlarge jurisdiction of ....
Do ....
COURT OF APPEALS, to provide library for, in the Territory
Do ....
Do ....
CRIMINALS IN TERRITORIES, may be confined in any othe tory ....
DAKOTA TERRITORY,
Admission of, as a State ....
Do ....
Do ....
Do ....
Do ....
* Councilmen and members of the legislature, to increase numb
Insurance companies in ....
Internal revenue collections to erect capitol buildings in ....
Judge of the first judicial district of, compensation of ....
Pembina, to organize Territory of, in northern half ....
Do ....
Penitentiary for, to provide ....
Do ....
DEER CREEK COAL FIELDS IN ARIZONA, to detach, from Indian Reservation ....
DETROIT, MICHIGAN, plan and titles of city of, in 1831........
DISEASED CATTLE,
In New Mexico ....
In Arizona ....
DOTY, JAMES D., accounts of, as treasurer of funds given Wis for the erection of public buildings ....
DOUGHTY, WILLIAM, claim for relief ....
ELLIOTT, R. G., and others, claim for relief for property destr Territory ....
Do ....

* And views of minority, Part 2.

Subject.	Report.	Congress.	Session.	Volume.
FEES, to regulate, of marshals, clerks, &c., of United States courts, in Territories of Arizona and New Mexico	3751	49	2	3
FLORIDA TERRITORY,				
Acting secretary, compensation of	205	21	1	1
Acts of, repealing certain of	258	23	1	1
Admission into the Union	577	28	1	1
Appalachicola, to establish district court at	19	23	2	1
Choctawhatchie River, to build bridge across	605	27	2	1
Court of appeals in, library for	776	25	2	1
Do	150	25	3	1
Do	61	27	3	1
Courts in, organization of	53	19	1	1
Do	19	23	2	1
Division of	577	28	1	1
Election of certain officers by the citizens of	57	27	3	1
Formation of the Territory of	79	20	1	1
Government of	53	19	1	1
Jacksonville, charter for	202	26	2	1
Legislature of, to alter the time of meeting of the	130	26	2	1
Public buildings in, appropriation to complete	229	25	3	1
Do	345	26	1	1
Do	677	27	2	1
Public lands in, railroad through	942	25	2	1
Quincy, academy at, petition of trustee for land grant	87	27	3	1
Representation in, equalize	431	23	1	1
Saint Augustine, filling up space behind sea wall at	790	27	2	1
Slaves of non-residents, per capita tax on	258	23	1	1
Statutes, in relation to compilation of	781	25	2	1
Tallahassee, completion of capitol at	62	27	3	1
United States troops in, payment for losses sustained by operations of, in 1814	131	26	2	1
Do	668	27	2	1
GARNETT, JAMES M., and others, claim for relief	258	23	1	1
GEORGIA, rights of State to lands in Mississippi Territory	76	14	1	1
GOVERNORS OF TERRITORIES, required to be residents thereof	477	48	1	3
HIGHWAYS,				
Donation of public lands for the location of a wagon road from the Missouri River to the Pacific Ocean	2	32	2	1
In the Territory of Florida	605	27	2	1
In the Territory of Minnesota	183	35	2	2
HOMESTEAD LAWS in Alaska Territory	3232	49	1	3
HOVEY, OLIVER P., claim for relief, for printing code of New Mexico	60	34	3	1
HURON TERRITORY, formation and boundaries of (now Wisconsin)	79	20	1	1
Do	56	21	1	1
IDAHO TERRITORY,				
Admission into Union as a State	3689	49	2	3
Convicts in prisons of	468	46	2	2
Internal revenue collections to erect capitol buildings in	27	41	2	2
Justices of the peace in, to increase jurisdiction of	472	46	2	2
Do	1166	47	1	2
Lewis Collegiate Institute, to enlarge and improve	3747	49	2	3
Reapportionment of, into council and representative districts	440	48	1	3
To annex a portion of, to Washington Territory	216	49	1	3
ILLINOIS TERRITORY, creation and boundaries of	79	20	1	1
INDIANA TERRITORY,				
Creation and boundaries of	79	20	1	1
United States courts in, to establish	*755	46	2	2
INDIAN RESERVATION, correcting boundaries of the White Mountain, in Arizona	496	48	1	3
INDIAN TERRITORY,				
Boundary line between Texas and	63	48	1	3
Indians to, removal of	474	46	2	2
United States courts in	*755	46	2	2
INDIAN TRIBES,				
In Wisconsin, in 1804	79	20	1	1
In the Indian Territory	188	45	3	2
INDIAN WARS, expenses of Cayuse war in the Territory of Oregon	122	33	1	1
INDIANS,				
Depredations of, in Mississippi Territory	3[illegible]	14	1	1
Removal of, to the Indian Territory	474	46	2	2
Tribes of,				
Cayuse, to ascertain and adjudicate expenditures of citizens of Oregon in the war with in 1847 and 1848	122	33	1	1
Brotherton, to partition and divide lands among	244	25	3	1
INSANE ASYLUM, in Arizona Territory	2034	49	1	3
IOWA TERRITORY				
Admission of, as a State at the same time with Florida	577	28	1	1
Boundary of	791	27	2	1
Do	86	27	3	1
Disputed boundary between the State of Missouri and	2	26	1	1
Election of certain officers by the citizens of the Territory of	57	27	3	1

* Views of minority.

Subject	Report.	Congress.	Session.	Volume.
IOWA TERRITORY—Continued.				
Establishment of	585	25	2	1
Extending the jurisdiction of, over all Pacific and intermediate possessions	308	28	1	1
Judges of supreme court in, salary of	270	25	3	1
Militia, pay of, while protecting disputed territory threatened by Missouri	896	27	2	1
Penitentiary building in	297	26	1	1
Do	782	27	2	1
JURORS, to amend the law relative to, in the Territories	1288	46	2	2
JUSTICES OF THE PEACE, enlargement of jurisdiction in Wyoming	1056	48	1	3
KANSAS TERRITORY,				
Admission of, as a State	181	34	1	1
Do	*181	34	1	1
Do	173	34	3	1
Do	*255	36	1	2
Citizens of, compensating, for property destroyed	326	34	1	1
Do	185	34	3	1
Constitution, to authorize people to form	173	34	3	1
Constitution adopted at Wyandott, July 29, 1859	255	36	1	2
Legislative assembly, to annual all acts of	179	34	3	1
Public buildings in, appropriations for	184	34	3	1
To organize	*80	33	1	1
LAKE MICHIGAN, boundary line between Ohio and Michigan to run due east from the southern bend of	196	20	1	1
Do	2	20	2	1
LANDS,				
Division of, among the Brotherton Indians in Wisconsin Territory	244	25	3	1
Donation of same to the city of Detroit, Mich., by the United States Government	83	21	2	1
Sale of, for taxes, belonging to non-residents	127	19	1	1
Do	7	19	2	1
Sold for taxes in the Territories, redemption of	127	19	1	1
Do	7	19	2	1
LAWRENCE, KANSAS, compensation for property destroyed in	326	34	1	1
Do	185	34	1	1
LAWS, execution of, in Utah	21	41	2	2
LEWIS COLLEGIATE INSTITUTE (Idaho), to enlarge and improve corporation of	3747	49	2	3
LIBRARY, for court of appeals in the Territory of Florida	776	25	2	1
Do	159	25	3	1
Do	61	27	3	1
LINCOLN TERRITORY, organization of	2578	49	1	3
Do	2579	49	1	3
Do	2580	49	1	3
LIQUORS, INTOXICATING, manufacture and sale of, in Territories	2444	49	1	3
MASON, CHARLES H., heirs of, claim for relief	124	36	1	2
MAY, JAMES (marshal of Michigan), claim for relief	177	19	1	1
MICHIGAN TERRITORY,				
Admission into the Union	334	23	1	1
Boundary,				
Establishing	334	23	1	1
Southern, establishing	196	20	1	1
Do	334	23	1	1
Relating to southern bend of Lake Michigan	2	20	2	1
Census of, to authorize taking of	334	23	1	1
Courts of	304	21	1	1
Creation and boundaries of	79	20	1	1
Division of, and formation of a new Territory from	79	20	1	1
Do	56	21	1	1
Do	145	22	1	1
Judge for, additional	197	20	1	1
Judges in, increase of salary	304	21	1	1
Legislative council, memorial of, for a division of Territory and formation of Huron (now Wisconsin)	79	20	1	1
Legislature, memorial of, asking an additional body called council	141	21	1	1
MILITIA, pay of in the Territory of Iowa	896	27	2	1
MINNESOTA TERRITORY,				
Roads and bridges in	183	35	2	2
Territorial government for the Territory of	141	32	1	1
MISSISSIPPI TERRITORY,				
Admission into the Union	9	14	1	1
Do	14	14	2	1
Do	42	14	2	1
Ceded from the State of Georgia	76	14	1	1
Creation of	79	20	1	1
Creek war, relief of sufferers in	33	14	1	1
Public lands in, to indemnify claimants of	76	14	1	1
Rights of the State of Georgia in	76	14	1	1
MISSOURI,				
Boundary between, and Iowa Territory	791	27	2	1
Do	86	27	3	1

* Views of minority.

Subject.	Report.	Congress.	Session.	Volume.
MISSOURI—Continued.				
Creation and boundaries of	79	20	1	1
Limits of	512	22	1	1
Northern boundary of, to extend	768	25	2	1
MONTANA TERRITORY,				
Admission into Union as a State	3689	49	2	3
Capitol buildings in, to use internal revenue collections to erect	27	41	3	2
Judicial system of	470	46	2	2
Justice of the peace in, to increase jurisdiction of	472	46	2	2
Do	1169	47	1	2
NEBRASKA TERRITORY, to organize	*80	33	1	1
NEVADA TERRITORY, organization of	375	35	1	2
NEW MEXICO TERRITORY,				
Artesian wells in	1092	49	1	3
Capitol and jail at Santa Fé, in	1322	46	2	2
Constitution and State government, formation of	561	43	1	2
Do	†503	44	1	2
Diseased cattle in	3334	49	1	3
Division of Territory into council and representative districts	283	46	3	2
Legislative districts in, reapportioning	3489	49	1	3
Organization of, to include lands claimed by Texas	16	30	2	1
Southwestern part of, to be organized into Arizona Territory	*2	34	3	1
Do	117	34	3	1
Supreme court of, additional justice of	3486	49	2	3
United States courts in, to regulate fees of clerks, marshals, &c	3751	49	2	3
Weights and measures, to furnish set of standard	3911	49	2	3
NORTHWESTERN TERRITORY, formation and boundaries of the	79	20	1	1
OHIO, STATE OF, boundary line between, and Michigan Territory	2	20	2	1
Do	334	23	1	1
OKLAHOMA (*see also* INDIAN TERRITORY), Territory of, to organize	61	42	2	2
Do	89	42	2	2
Do	*82	44	2	2
Do	186	45	3	2
Do	‡755	46	2	2
Do	1232	49	1	3
Do	1684	49	1	3
OREGON TERRITORY,				
Admission of, as a State	*123	35	2	2
Do	123	35	2	2
Boundaries of the State of	*764	44	1	2
Cayuse Indian hostilities in 1847-'48, to audit claims for expenditures in suppressing	122	33	1	1
Organization of	308	*28	1	1
Population of, in 1850	271	31	1	1
Population, settlement, &c., grant of lands to American settlers	271	31	1	1
Provisional government, formation of	271	31	1	1
Territorial government in, establishing	141	32	1	1
ORLEANS, formation of the Territory of (now Louisiana)	79	20	1	1
PACIFIC OCEAN,				
Grant of land in aid of construction of a wagon road from the Missouri River to	2	32	2	1
In aid of the construction of subterranean telegraph to	5	33	2	1
PEMBINA TERRITORY, organization of	350	45	2	2
PENAL COLONY in Alaska	1685	49	1	3
PENITENTIARY,				
Territory of Wyoming, to establish	291	45	2	2
Territory of Dakota, to establish	915	45	2	2
Do	138	46	2	2
PUBLIC BUILDINGS,				
Capitols in the Territories	27	41	2	2
To erect, in Arkansas	118	21	1	1
Florida,				
For use of legislature of Territory of	229	25	3	1
For capitol of	677	27	2	1
For the use of courts of justice in the Territory of	345	26	1	1
Santa Fé, to complete capitol and jail at	1322	46	2	2
Wisconsin, for use of United States courts and legislature of the Territory of	941	25	2	1
PUBLIC LANDS,				
Grant of, for endowment of a female college at Quincy, Fla	87	27	3	1
In aid of the construction of a subterranean telegraph to the Pacific Ocean	5	33	2	1
Donation of,				
To settlers in the Territory of Oregon	271	31	1	1
For locating a wagon road from the Missouri River to the Pacific Ocean	2	32	2	1
Railroad through, in Florida	942	25	2	1
REVISED STATUTES, to amend,				
Section 1846, legislative sessions in Territories	469	46	2	2
Legislative powers, 1851	232	46	3	2
Section 1852, legislative sessions in Territories	469	46	2	2
Sections 1856 and 1857, Territorial offices	232	46	3	2

*Views of minority. †And views of minority, Part 2. ‡Parts 1 and 2.

Subject.	Report.	Congress.	Session.	Volume.
REVISED STATUTES, to amend—Continued.				
Section 1858, filling vacancies in Territorial offices	2557	49	1	3
Section 1889, relating to legislative assemblies of Territories creating corporations	3750	49	2	3
Section 1926, jurisdiction of justices of the peace in Territories	472	46	2	2
Sections 2474 and 2475, boundaries of Yellowstone Park	2383	48	2	3
RIGHT OF WAY, granting same through the public domain for the construction of subterranean telegraph to the Pacific Ocean	5	33	2	1
SAINT AUGUSTINE, FLORIDA, filling up behind the sea-wall at, to prevent disease	790	27	2	1
SANTE FÉ, to complete capitol and jail at	1322	46	2	2
SLAVERY, to permit, in Kansas	80	33	1	1
SLAUGHTER, WILLIAM B., Secretary of Wisconsin Territory, claim for relief	132	30	1	1
SUFFRAGE,				
To regulate in Territories	371	35	1	2
In the Territory of Utah	949	45	2	2
TAX SALES IN THE TERRITORIES, to regulate	127	19	1	1
Do	7	19	2	1
TELEGRAPHS, SUBTERRANEAN, granting land to aid in construction of, to Pacific Ocean	5	33	3	1
TERRITORIAL OFFICES, mode of filling	233	46	3	2
TERRITORIES (*see also* under their respective names),				
Admission of, into the Union	127	48		3
Capitol buildings in	27	41		2
Congress, constitutional right of, to legislate for	141	22		1
Criminals in, may be confined in any other State or Territory	471	46		2
Federal officers to be residents in	2581	49		3
Intoxicating liquors, manufacture and sale of	2444	49		3
Judges in, to increase number of	234	48		3
Jurors and witnesses in, compensation of	1283	46		2
Justices of the peace in, election of	473	46		2
Laws in, to prohibit local or special	1477	49	1	3
Legislative assemblies of	469	46	2	2
Legislatures in, to increase number and pay of members of	1322	48	1	3
Non-residents in, lands of	127	19	1	1
Do		19	2	1
Officers in, election of	212	48	1	3
Revised Statutes, to amend, relating to legislative assemblies creating corporations	3750	49	2	3
Suffrage in, to regulate	371	31	1	2
TEXAS,				
Territory of, boundary line of	52	20	2	1
Do	16	30	2	1
Boundary line between Indian Territory and	63	48	1	3
Dismemberment of the Territory of	*16	30	2	1
Protest of, to lands belonging to, being organized into Territory of New Mexico	16	30	2	1
TEXAS CATTLE DISEASE, in New Mexico and Arizona	2334	49	1	3
Do.	2335	49	1	3
TINGLE, GEORGE E., claim for compensation as acting secretary of Florida Territory	205	21	1	1
Do	235	22	1	1
UNITED STATES COURTS. (*See* COURTS OF THE UNITED STATES.)				
UTAH TERRITORY,				
Carson Valley, annexation of, to California	116	34	3	1
Condition of	96	39	1	2
Elective franchise in	949	45	2	2
Government of, by a commission to prevent polygamy	1351	48	1	3
Do	†1351	48	1	3
Laws in, execution of	21	41	2	2
Do	221	41	2	2
Laws of United States relating to	§1351	48	1	3
Legislative assembly in, to convene	2641	49	1	3
Western part of, formation of, into the Territory of Nevada	375	35	1	1
WASHINGTON TERRITORY,				
Act of legislative assembly, to validate	1057	48	1	3
Do	3748	49	2	3
Do	4089	49	2	3
Do	4161	49	2	3
Admission of, as a State	690	47	1	2
Do	3689	49	2	3
Annexation of a portion of Idaho to	216	49	1	3
Capitol buildings in, to use internal revenue collections to erect	27	41	2	2
Columbia County, to issue bonds to construct a court-house	1323	49	1	3
Justices of the peace in, to increase jurisdiction of	472	46	2	2
Do	1106	47	1	2
Legislative assembly, to change time of meeting of	1310	49	1	3
WEIGHTMAN, RICHARD H., claim for relief	228	31	1	1
Do	3	35	1	2

* Views of minority. † Views of minority, Part 2. ‡ Parts 1, 2, 3. § Part 2.

Subject.	Report.	Congress.	Session.	Volume.
WEIGHTS AND MEASURES, to furnish New Mexico set of	3911	49	2	3
WHITE MOUNTAIN INDIAN RESERVATION, to detach Deer Creek coal fields from	496	48	1	3
WHITING, DAVID, claim for relief	123	36	1	2
WILLIAMS, JOHN R., *et al.*, memorial on lands at Detroit, Mich	83	21	2	1
WITNESSES, to amend the law relative to, in the Territories	1288	46	2	2
WISCONSIN TERRITORY.				
Annexation of a portion of, to Missouri	768	25	2	1
Appropriations for the erection of public buildings	897	27	2	1
Assembly of, in 1842 and 1843, expenses of	155	28	1	1
Do	119	28	2	1
Bonds issued and held by William Doughty	578	28	1	1
Division of	535	25	2	1
Election of certain officers by the citizens of	57	27	2	1
Formation of	79	20	1	1
Do	56	21	1	1
Do	145	22	1	1
Publ c buildings, appropriation to complete	941	25	2	1
WYOMING TERRITORY.				
Capitol buildings in, to use internal revenue collections to erect	27	41	2	2
Justices of the peace, jurisdiction of, in	1056	48	1	3
Legislature, to validate certain acts of	35	49	1	3
Penitentiary in	291	45	2	3
Probate courts in, to enlarge jurisdiction of	1875	49	1	3
Do	1876	49	1	3
Supreme court of, additional justice of	3739	49	2	3
Yellowstone National Park, jurisdiction of laws in	2368	48	2	3
YELLOWSTONE NATIONAL PARK, boundaries, to amend Revised Statutes relating to	2383	48	2	3

O

REPORTS

OF THE

)MMITTEE ON VENTILAT

HOUSE OF REPRESENTATIVES,

FROM THE FORTIETH CONGRESS, 1868, TO THE FORTY-NINTH CONGRESS, 1887, INCLUSIVE.

IN ONE VOLUME.

COMPILED, UNDER THE DIRECTION OF THE JOINT COMMITTEE ON PRINTING,

BY

T. H. McKEE,

CLERK, DOCUMENT ROOM, UNITED STATES SENATE.

WASHINGTON:
GOVERNMENT PRINTING OFFICE.
1887.

9248

FORTY-NINTH CONGRESS, FIRST SESSION.

[PUBLIC RESOLUTION—No. 24.]

Joint resolution authorizing the preparation of a compilation of the reports of committees of the Senate and House of Representatives.

Resolved by the Senate and House of Representatives of the United States of America in Congress assembled, That there be prepared under the direction of the Joint Committee of Printing, a compilation of the reports of the Senate and House of Representatives from the Fourteenth to the Forty-eighth Congress, inclusive, classified by committees, arranged, indexed, and bound in suitable volumes for the use of the standing committees of the two Houses of Congress. And the sum of seven thousand seven hundred and fifty dollars, or so much thereof as may be found necessary, is hereby appropriated out of any money in the Treasury not otherwise appropriated, for the preparation of said work, which sum may be paid by the Secretary of the Treasury upon the order of the chairman of said Joint Committee, as additional pay or compensation to any officer or employee of the United States.

Resolved further, That the Clerk of the House and Secretary of the Senate be, and they are hereby directed, to procure and file, for the use of their respective Houses, copies of all reports made by each committee of all succeeding Congresses; and that the Clerk of the House and the Secretary of the Senate be, and they are hereby, authorized and directed at the close of each session of Congress, to cause said reports to be indexed and bound, one copy to be deposited in the library of each House and one copy in the room of the committee from which the reports emanated.

Approved, July 29, 1886.

COMPILER'S NOTICE.

This compilation embraces all the printed reports made by both Houses of Congress from the commencement of the Fourteenth to the close of the Forty-ninth Congress. They are classified by committees and arranged in numerical order. The collection for each committee is divided into volumes of suitable size. Each committee has a separate index, a copy being bound in each volume.

The SPECIAL and SELECT reports are all compiled in one collection having one index, a copy of which is bound in each volume.

The plan throughout the compilation is to place each report to the committee from which it was reported, without reference to the subject-matter.

The House and Senate reports are compiled separately. Care will be required in noticing the chronological order, as in some instances an entire session or Congress may not appear in certain volumes from the fact that during this period no reports were made by this committee.

T. H. McKEE.

INDEX

TO

REPORTS OF COMMITTEE ON VENTILATION AND ACOUSTICS,

HOUSE OF REPRESENTATIVES.

FROM 1868 TO 1887, INCLUSIVE.

Subject.				
CAPITOL, ventilation of, improvement in				
DISTRICT OF COLUMBIA, public buildings in, examination of				
ELECTRIC LIGHT, House of Representatives, to introduce in				
FOLDING-ROOM, House of Representatives, condition of				
HEATING OF HALL OF HOUSE OF REPRESENTATIVES,				
Mode of, to examine				
Do				
Do				
Changes in				
HOUSE OF REPRESENTATIVES,				
Folding-room of, condition of, to examine				
Hall of House,				
Alban C. Stimer's plan for ventilation of		40	3	1
Wilson's electrical lighter for	...	41	3	1
Lighting, heating, and ventilation of	49	41	3	1
Do	116	45	3	1
Do	1970	48	1	1
Ventilation of	119	45	2	1
Lighting, heating, and ventilation of, to make changes in	22	46	2	1
Ventilation of, to improve	*2026	48	1	1
Do	2632	48	2	1
LIGHTING HALL OF HOUSE OF REPRESENTATIVES,				
Changes in, to make	22	46	2	1
Method of, to examine	49	41	3	1
Do	116	45	3	1
Do	1970	48	1	1
PUBLIC BUILDINGS, District of Columbia, examination of those in	990	49	1	1
SENATE CHAMBER,				
Wilson's electrical lighter, to introduce in	48	41	3	1
Lighting, heating, and ventilation of	49	41	3	1
STIMER'S, ALBAN C., plan for ventilating Hall of House	19	40	3	1
VENTILATION, examination of public buildings in District of Columbia as relates to	990	49	1	1
VENTILATION OF HALL OF HOUSE OF REPRESENTATIVES,				
Alban C. Stimer's plan for ventilation of	19	40	3	1
Method of, to examine	49	41	3	1
Do	119	45	2	1
Do	116	45	3	1
Do	1970	48	1	1
Changes in	22	46	2	1
To improve ventilation of	*2026	48	1	1
Do	2632	48	2	1
WILSON'S ELECTRICAL LIGHTER, substitution of, in place of one now in use over Hall of House	48	41	3	1

* Views of minority.

REPORTS

OF THE

COMMITTEE ON WAR CLAIMS,

(INCLUDING REVOLUTIONARY CLAIMS),

HOUSE OF REPRESENTATIVES,

FROM THE FOURTEENTH CONGRESS, 1815, TO THE
CONGRESS, 1887, INCLUSIVE,

IN FOURTEEN VOLUMES.

COMPILED, UNDER THE DIRECTION OF THE JOINT
COMMITTEE ON PRINTING,

BY

T. H. McKEE,
CLERK DOCUMENT ROOM, UNITED STATES SENATE.

WASHINGTON:
GOVERNMENT PRINTING OFFICE.
1887.

9205 W C H

[PUBLIC RESOLUTION—

Joint resolution authorizing the preparation of a co mittees of the Senate and House of F

Resolved by the Senate and House of Re States of America in Congress assembled, Th the direction of the Joint Committee of Pri reports of the Senate and House of Repr teenth to the Forty-eighth Congress, inclusi arranged, indexed, and bound in suitable standing committees of the two Houses of seven thousand seven hundred and fifty do may be found necessary, is hereby approp the Treasury not otherwise appropriated, work, which sum may be paid by the Secr the order of the chairman of said Joint Con compensation to any officer or employee of t

Resolved further, That the Clerk of the Senate be, and they are hereby directed, to of their respective Houses, copies of all rep tee of all succeeding Congresses; and that the Secretary of the Senate be, and they directed at the close of each session of Con to be indexed and bound, one copy to be d each House and one copy in the room of the reports emanated.

Approved, July 29, 1886.

COMPILER'S NOTICE.

This compilation embraces all the printed reports made by both Houses of Congress from the commencement of the Fourteenth to the close of the Forty-ninth Congress. They are classified by committees and arranged in numerical order. The collection for each committee is divided into volumes of suitable size. Each committee has a separate index, a copy being bound in each volume.

The SPECIAL and SELECT reports are all compiled in one collection having one index, a copy of which is bound in each volume.

The plan throughout the compilation is to place each report to the committee from which it was reported, without reference to the subject-matter.

The House and Senate reports are compiled separately. Care will be required in noticing the chronological order, as in some instances an entire session or Congress may not appear in certain volumes from the fact that during this period no reports were made by this committee.

T. H. McKEE.

INDEX

TO

PORTS OF COMMITTEE ON WAR CLAIMS,

HOUSE OF REPRESENTATIVES.

FROM 1815 TO 1887, INCLUSIVE.

Subject.	Report.	Congress.	Session.	Volume.
QUARRIER (schooner), for relief of owner	238	48	1	13
TT, EMER G., for relief	1256	47	1	12
TT, EMMA G., for relief	191	46	2	11
TT, Mrs. E. G. C., for relief as widow of D. M. Carter	744	48	1	13
N, SAMUEL, for relief of executor	1083	25	2	4
R, ELISHA, for relief	914	25	2	4
MS, CHARLES H., for relief	1245	48	1	13
MS, CHARLES W., for relief	784	42	1	8
MS, HENRY, referring claims to Court of Claims	2643	48	2	13
MS, JACOB, R., referring claims to Court of Claims	2643	48	2	13
MS, JOHN, for relief	450	45	2	10
MS, NATHAN, for relief of heirs	104	25	2	4
MS, O. F., for relief	2329	49	1	14
MS, PETER, for relief of heirs	104	25	2	4
IS, PETER, NATHANIEL, and JOHN, for relief of estate	808	24	1	3
IS, SILAS, for relief	1495	46	2	11
IS, WILLIAM, for relief of heirs	104	25	2	4
ISON, GREENBURY,				
r relief	419	46	2	11
ferring claim to Court of Claims	2643	48	2	13
ISON, F. W., for relief	2187	49	1	14
N, JOHN, for relief	756	43	1	8
Do	1494	46	2	11
N, JUDAH, for relief	106	20	1	2
Do	90	21	1	2
EDGE, JOHN, for relief	314	43	1	8
ANDER, JOHN W., referring claim to Court of Claims	2643	48	2	13
ANDER, MITCHELL, for relief	1480	46	2	11
ANDER, MORGAN, for relief of heirs	1086	25	2	4
Do	365	27	2	5
ANDER, ROBERT, for relief	1479	46	2	11
ANDER, W. J., for relief	626	44	1	10
Do	211	45	2	10
Do	487	49	1	14
ANDER, WILLIAM, for relief of estate	240	33	1	6
N CLAIMS, to establish a court to adjudicate	262	42	1	8
Do	134	43	2	9
N, CHARLES R., for relief	300	47	1	12
N, D. C., for relief	1853	47	2	12
N, DANIEL M., for relief	490	44	1	10
N, ETHAN, for relief of heirs	213	34	1	6
N, GEORGE, for relief	160	24	2	3
N, JOHN, for relief	1028	46	2	11
N, LATHROP, for relief of heir	498	22	1	2
Do	169	24	1	3
Do	91	24	2	3
Do	131	25	2	4
Do	16	25	3	4
Do	619	26	1	5
Do	868	27	2	5
Do	139	29	1	6

Subject.	Report.	Congress.	Session.	Volume.
ALLEN, LEWIS D., for relief	1189	47	1	12
ALLEN, LUCINDA, referring claim to Court of Claims	2643	48	2	13
ALLISON, MATTHEW, for relief of heirs	1602	46	2	11
Do	586	48	1	13
ALLOWANCE OF CERTAIN CLAIMS. (*See* FOURTH OF JULY CLAIMS.)				
ALSTON, VOLNEY S., for relief	193	46	2	11
ALSUP, JOHN F., for relief	4026	49	2	14
ALVARADO (bark), for relief of owner	332	43	2	9
ALVORD, JOB, for relief of estate	102	21	1	2
Do	89	22	1	2
AMERICAN BOARD OF FOREIGN MISSIONS, for relief	2612	49	1	14
AMESBURY, MARVIN H., for relief	46	43	2	9
Do	493	44	1	10
AMONETT, JAMES I. (executor), referring claim to Court of Claims	2643	48	2	13
ANDERSON, ABBIE P., for relief	188	46	2	11
ANDERSON, ALLEN E., for relief	972	46	2	11
Do	896	47	1	12
ANDERSON, JAMES W., *et al.*, for relief	110	47	1	12
Do	465	48	1	13
ANDERSON, JOHN J., for relief	283	43	2	9
ANDERSON, JOSEPH, for relief	800	43	1	8
Do	254	44	1	10
Do	464	47	1	12
Do	656	48	1	13
ANDERSON, JOSIAH, for relief of heir	619	25	2	4
ANDERSON, WILLIAM, for relief	2609	49	1	14
ANDERSON, WILLIAM W., for relief	1484	46	2	11
Do	1855	47	2	12
ANDREWS, RICHARD L., for relief	194	46	2	11
Do	42	48	1	13
ANDRÉ, Maj. JOHN, to remunerate heirs of captors of	550	35	1	7
Do	59	36	1	7
Do	78	37	2	7
ANGLEA, WILLIAM, for relief	292	29	1	6
ANSART, LEWIS, for relief of heirs	138	35	2	7
ANTHONY, WILLIAM A., referring claim to Court of Claims	2643	48	2	13
APP, MATTHIAS, referring claim to Court of Claims	2643	48	2	13
APPERSON, RICHARD, for relief of heirs	319	24	1	3
Do	235	26	1	5
Do	306	27	2	5
APPROPRIATIONS,				
Estimates to pay Fourth of July claims	1129	49	1	14
War claims to pay	2630	48	1	13
Do	720	48	1	13
Do	21	49	1	14
ARELL, DAVID, for relief of heirs	622	25	2	4
ARKANSAS, for relief of Cane Hill College	1468	46	2	11
ARMAND, for relief of heirs	14	27	2	5
ARMOR, THOMAS, for relief of heirs	359	27	2	5
ARMSTRONG, GEORGE, for relief of representative	766	43	1	8
ARMSTRONG, JAMES, for relief	165	23	1	3
ARMSTRONG, JOHN T., for relief	811	44	1	10
Do	203	45	2	10
ARMY,				
Horses lost in, extending time for filing claims for	1335	47	1	12
Officer,				
Compensation	556	47	1	12
Muster, compensation prior to	229	48	1	13
Pensions to soldiers of war of 1812	64	14	1	1
ARNOLD, WILLIS N., for relief	563	47	1	12
Do	74	48	1	13
ARRINGTON, GEORGE C., for relief	226	46	2	11
ARTHUR, HAMILTON F., for relief	1088	46	2	11
ASHE, JOHN B., for relief of heirs	384	24	1	3
Do	122	25	2	4
ASHLEY, CHESTER, for relief	1342	48	1	13
ASHLEY, NATHANIEL, for relief of heirs	526	27	2	5
ASHWORTH, JASON, for relief	1037	46	2	11
ASKEW, ALEXANDER, for relief of administrator	2643	48	2	13
ASKEW, J. D., administrator, referring claim to Court of Claims	2643	48	2	13
ATKINS, J. C. and J. H., administrators, referring claim to Court of Claims	2643	48	2	13
ATLANTIC WORKS, for relief	3424	49	1	14
ATLEE, WILLIAM A., administrator of, for relief	418	31	1	6
AUSTIN, STERLING T., for relief of estate	733	47	1	12
AUSTIN, VALOROUS G., for relief	50	43	2	9
Do	315	48	1	13
AWARDS,				
Citizens of Marion County, Tennessee, payment of	230	48	1	13
Citizens of McMinnville, Tenn., payment of	1466	46	2	11
Commissioners of Claims, payment of	456	44	1	10
AXSON SAMUEL J., for relief of heirs	436	22	1	2

Subject.	Report.	Congress.	Session.	Volume.
RS, SAMUEL, for relief	2259	49	1	14
ETT, WILLIAM, for relief of heirs	204	27	2	5
ETT, WILLIAM, referring claim to Court of Claims	2643	48	2	13
TT, PIERRE (administrator of), for relief	446	35	1	7
Do	36	36	1	7
ES, Mrs. C. M., referring claim to Court of Claims	2643	48	2	13
ES, TREADWELLL S.				
or relief	517	43	1	8
eferring claim of, to Court of Claims	2643	48	2	13
ON, JAMES M., for relief	581	48	1	13
Do	308	49	2	13
EY, B. C., for relief	377	43	1	8
D, ABSALOM, for relief of heir	130	23	2	3
Do	64	24	1	3
Do	640	25	2	4
ER, DE LA PALM HARRIET, for relief of heirs	448	35	1	7
Do	107	36	1	7
ER, HARRIET, for relief	614	26	1	5
DWIN, CHARLES L., *et al.*, for relief	2117	48	1	13
Do	565	49	1	14
DWIN, GEORGE W., *et al.*, for relief	2117	48	1	13
Do	565	49	1	14
L, BURGESS, for relief of heirs	443	26	1	5
LARD, AUGUST W., for relief	2786	49	1	13
LARD, JANE W., for relief	212	34	1	6
LARD, SIDNEY, for relief	46	48	1	13
LISTER, JOSEPH, for relief	7	43	2	9
GS, BROWNELL & CO., for relief	1184	47	1	12
Do	618	49	1	14
K OF COLUMBIA, PENNSYLVANIA, for relief	335	49	1	14
K OF LOUISIANA, for relief of stockholders of	2044	47	2	12
KHEAD, Mrs. A. G., for relief	187	46	2	11
TIST FEMALE COLLEGE, at Lexington, Mo., for relief	3135	49	1	14
DEN, EARL D., for relief	1045	46	2	11
RER, JAMES M., for relief	975	46	2	11
NES, ALMONT, for relief	98	43	2	9
Do	290	44	1	10
NES, ANN, for relief	80	48	1	13
NES, HENRIETTA, for relief	498	22	1	2
Do	169	24	1	3
Do	16	25	3	4
NES, JOHN, for relief of heirs	693	25	2	4
Do	3	25	3	4
Do	367	27	2	5
NETT, JAMES, for relief	120	21	1	2
Do	510	43	1	8
NITZ, CHARLES A., for relief	332	30	1	6
NS, G. W., for relief	1436	49	1	14
NUM, THOMAS, referring claim to Court of Claims	2643	48	2	13
RETT, SIMEON S., for relief	43	48	1	13
RON, ANN MORTIMER, for relief	26	21	2	2
Do	307	22	1	2
Do	53	23	1	3
RON, MAGGIE, *et al.*, referring claim to Court of Claims	2643	48	2	13
RON, WILLIAM, for relief	307	22	1	2
THOLOMEW COUNTY AGRICULTURAL SOCIETY, for relief	307	43	2	9
Do	188	44	1	10
Do	7	45	2	10
Do	1485	46	2	11
TLET, JONAS, for relief	530	25	2	4
TOW, ANTHONY (executor of), for relief	251	23	1	3
TOW, ROBERT S. (executor), for relief	251	23	1	3
, ELISHA, for relief	1033	46	2	11
, REUBEN B., for relief	1253	46	2	11
Do	47	48	1	13
ES, ELIZABETH, for relief	483	49	1	14
ON ROUGE GAS-LIGHT COMPANY, for relief of	1032	46	2	11
MAN, JOHN E., for relief	794	43	1	8
ARD, JOHN (executor of), for relief	157	23	1	3
ARD, SAMUEL (executor), for relief	157	23	1	3
LOR, ANN D., for relief	52	19	1	1
Do	5	21	2	2
Do	237	21	1	2
Do	78	22	1	2
LOR, GEORGE, for relief of heirs	527	27	2	5
TOP, THOMAS, for relief of heirs	355	24	1	3
Do	478	25	2	4
NSKY, ABRAM, referring claim of heirs to Court of Claims	2643	48	2	13
INSKY, HENRY (administrator), for relief	1819	49	1	14
H, SAMUEL, for relief of heirs	7	30	2	6
HY, ELIZABETH W., for relief	1079	27	2	5

Subject.	Report.	Congress.	Session.	Volume.
BEALL, THOMAS, for relief of heirs	128	30	2	6
BEALLE, ROBERT, for relief of heirs	405	25	2	4
Do	368	27	2	5
BEAN, NANCY M., for relief	752	43		8
BEARD, NATHAN, for relief	360	30		6
BEASLEY, GEORGE W., referring claim to Court of Claims	2643	48		13
BEASLEY, WILLIAM M., referring claim to Court of Claims	2643	48	2	13
BEATTY, CATHERINE, for relief	455	35		7
BEATTY, PATIENCE, for relief	2121	48		13
BEAUCHERY, JULES, for relief	1038	46	2	11
BEAUFORT MOUNTED GUARD, pay for service	311	48	1	13
BEAVER, BLACK, for relief of heirs	1103	48	1	13
BEAVER, JAMES B., for relief	1204	47	1	12
BECTON, ELIZABETH, referring claim to Court of Claims	2643	48	2	13
BEDFORD, JULIAN, for relief	77	48	1	13
BEDINGER, DANIEL, for relief of estate	105	33	1	6
Do	139	35	2	7
Do	242	48	1	13
BEDINGER, HENRY, for relief	53	16	1	1
Do	371	27	2	5
BEEBER, MAX, for relief	359	48	1	13
BEECHEY, ELIZABETH W., for relief	416	31	1	6
BEELER, HARRISON, referring claim to Court of Claims	2643	48	2	13
BEHYMER, BARRINGTON, for relief	240	48	1	13
BELCHER, JOHN, for relief	979	46	2	11
BELCHER, S. E., for relief	1093	46	2	11
BELDEN, O. S., for relief	3138	49	1	14
BELL, JAMES, for relief of estate	184	22	1	3
Do	54	30	2	6
Do	447	35	1	7
Do	341	36	1	7
BELL, JAMES H., for relief	992	46	2	11
BELL, MARCUS A., *et al.*, for relief of administrator of	3531	49	2	14
BELL, MARTHA W., for relief	658	48	1	13
BELL, PIROMISA H., for relief	3531	49	2	14
BENJAMIN, SAMUEL, for relief	866	25	2	4
BENNET, STEPHEN, for relief	600	24	1	3
BENSON, JOHNSON, referring claim to Court of Claims	2643	48	2	13
BENTLEY, GIDEON, for relief	59	31	1	6
BENTON, MARY E., for relief	20	18	2	1
BERAULT, MARY A., for relief	28	36	2	7
Do	77	37	2	7
Do	21	38	2	7
BERRIEN, JOHN, for relief	100	23	1	3
BEST, J. MILTON, for relief of estate	536	47	1	12
Do	722	48	1	13
BETHEL COLLEGE, TENNESSEE, for relief of trustees of	98	43	2	9
BIGHAM, MARGRET and AGNES, for relief	359	27	2	5
BIGLEY, NICHOLAS J., for relief	309	43	2	9
Do	2030	47	2	12
Do	232	48	1	13
BILLS, JOHN H., for relief of estate	24	48	1	13
BIRD, BENJAMIN, for relief of heirs	126	23	1	3
BIRD, NATHANIEL, for relief	286	21	1	2
Do	576	25	2	4
Do	98	30	1	6
BIRD, STEPHEN (executor), referring claim to Court of Claims	2643	48	2	13
BISCOE, JOSIAH, for relief	184	26	2	5
BIVINS, Mrs. L., for relief	3351	49	1	14
BIXBY, SAMUEL, for relief	532	27	2	5
BLACK, BEAVER, for relief of heirs	1103	48	1	13
BLACK, DANIEL, for relief	3439	49	1	14
BLACK, ROSANNA H., for relief	251	46	2	11
BLACK, THOMAS, for relief	2677	48	2	13
Do	1753	49	1	14
BLACKMAN, LUTHER M., for relief	295	47	1	12
Do	3396	49	1	14
BLACKWELL, MARY A.,				
Referring claim to Court of Claims	2643	48	2	13
For relief	1826	49	1	14
BLACKWELL, THOMAS, for relief	199	20	1	2
Do	129	21	1	2
Do	68	22	1	3
BLAIR, OLIVER M. (administrator), referring claim to Court of Claims	2643	48	2	13
BLAIR, SAMUEL M., for relief	446	45	2	10
BLISS, C. C., for relief	741	43	1	8
BLOOM, A. S., for relief	85	49	1	14
BLOOMSTEIN, JACOB,				
For relief	317	43	2	9
Referring claim to Court of Claims	2643	48	2	13
BLOUNT, JAMES F., for relief	289	43	2	9

Subject.	Report.	Congress.	Session.	Volume.
) OF CLAIMS, to establish a board of commissioners to examine and decide certain claims against the United States	441	29	1	6
CHARLES G., for relief of estate	1880	47	2	12
W. R., for relief	318	43	2	9
Do	445	45	2	10
Do	2009	47	2	12
Do	588	48	1	13
)NNEL, CHARLES, for relief	496	43	1	8
Do	828	45	2	10
WILLIAM, for relief of heirs	138	23	1	3
ER, AUGUSTUS F.,				
relief of estate	422	46	2	11
erring claim to Court of Claims	2643	48	2	13
ER, EDMOND, for relief	20	18	1	1
HAWKINS, for relief of widow	596	26	1	5
Do	15	27	2	5
ELL, THOMAS H., for relief	985	46	2	11
ITON, HANNAH, for relief	274	27	2	5
TY, to volunteers in District of Columbia	2336	49	1	14
TY-LANDS, relative to issuing in certain cases warrants for	361	25	2	4
Do	18	25	3	4
N, EPHRAIM, for relief	171	26	2	5
Do	360	27	2	5
RS, CHARLES F., for relief	2332	49	1	14
ER, SARAH, for relief	57	31	1	6
ES. MARTHA A., for relief	1539	48	1	13
ING, JAMES A., for relief	185	46	2	11
Do	81	48	1	13
AN, ABRAHAM,				
relief	154	23	1	3
Do	601	24	1	3
relief of estate	442	29	1	6
MAN ACT." (*See* CLAIMS.)				
AN, ISAAC,				
relief	106	33	1	6
Do	275	33	1	6
relief of estate	15	37	2	7
RDUS, JAMES, for relief of heirs	105	25	3	4
HOMAS N. (administrator), for relief	810	24	1	3
, WILLIAM, for relief of heirs	163	24	1	3
Do	384	24	1	3
Do	481	25	2	4
N, JAMES B., referring claim to Court of Claims	2643	48	2	13
S, THOMAS H., for relief of heirs	692	25	2	4
FORD, CHARLES, for relief	59	18	1	1
LEY, H. L., for relief	1475	46	2	11
SHAW, JOHN JOSEPH, for relief	2794	49	1	14
, J. M., *et al.*, for relief	432	44	1	10
Do	66	45	3	10
FOOT, JOHN, for relief of heirs	174	24	1	3
Do	479	25	2	4
HALL, MOSES B., for relief	757	43	1	8
CH, NEEDHAM, for relief	186	46	2	11
CH, OLIVE, for relief	942	27	2	5
DEIS & CRAWFORD, for relief of owners	951	46	2	11
DON, G. R., for relief	1482	46	2	11
Do	2011	47	2	12
NEISS, REINHART, *et al.*, for relief	1084	46	2	11
Do	160	49	1	14
, GEORGE, for relief of heir	46	29	2	6
Do	354	30	1	6
, JOHN, for relief of heirs	202	27	2	5
Do	233	27	3	5
, ROBERT C., for relief of administrator of	46	29	2	6
Do	354	30	1	6
T, ALFRED, for relief	1346	46	2	11
ES, MARTHA, for relief	204	46	2	11
S, J. A., for relief	22	49	1	14
Y, JOSEPH A., for relief	1695	47	1	12
Do	86	48	1	13
ER, JACOB, for relief of heir	621	30	1	6
LEY, WILLIAM, for relief of heirs	1022	25	2	4
DE, JACKSON, for relief	2017	47	2	12
DUS, JAMES, for relief of heirs	276	24	2	3
Do	670	25	2	4
Do	105	25	3	4
Do	773	27	2	5
DWAY, JORDAN,				
relief	1089	46	2	11
erring claim to Court of Claims	2643	48	2	13
DWELL, MARCUS L., referring claim to Court of Claims	2643	48	2	13

REPORTS

OF THE

COMMITTEE ON WAR CLAIMS,

(INCLUDING REVOLUTIONARY CLAIMS),

HOUSE OF REPRESENTATIVES,

FROM THE FOURTEENTH CONGRESS, 1815, TO THE FORTY-NINTH CONGRESS, 1887, INCLUSIVE,

IN FOURTEEN VOLUMES.

COMPILED, UNDER THE DIRECTION OF THE JOINT COMMITTEE ON PRINTING,

BY

T. H. McKEE,

CLERK DOCUMENT ROOM, UNITED STATES SENATE.

WASHINGTON:
GOVERNMENT PRINTING OFFICE.
1887.

9205 W C H

COMPILER'S NOTICE.

This compilation embraces all the printed reports made by both Houses of Congress from the commencement of the Fourteenth to the close of the Forty-ninth Congress. They are classified by committees and arranged in numerical order. The collection for each committee is divided into volumes of suitable size. Each committee has a separate index, a copy being bound in each volume.

The SPECIAL and SELECT reports are all compiled in one collection having one index, a copy of which is bound in each volume.

The plan throughout the compilation is to place each report to the committee from which it was reported, without reference to the subject-matter.

The House and Senate reports are compiled separately. Care will be required in noticing the chronological order, as in some instances an entire session or Congress may not appear in certain volumes from the fact that during this period no reports were made by this committee.

T. H. McKEE.

INDEX

TO

[cut off]EPORTS OF COMMITTEE ON WAR CLAIMS,

HOUSE OF R[cut off]

FROM 1815 TO 1887, INCLUSIVE.

Subject.

CULBERTSON, JOSEPH, for relief
CUMMINGS, J. J., for relief
CURTIS, JOTHAM, for relief
CUSHMAN, GEORGE W., for relief
CURTIS, WILLIAM B., for relief
CUTTS, THOMAS, for relief
CYNTHIANA, KY.,
  Citizens of, for relief of
  Saint Andrew's Lodge of Masons, for relief of
DABNEY, CHARLES, for relief of heirs
DADDS, WILLIAM, for relief
  Do
DADE COUNTY, MISSOURI, for relief
DADE, JANE, for relief
DAGGET, NATHAN, for relief
  Do
DAILY, AMANDA, for relief
DALE, JEREMIAH, for relief of heir
DALE, JOHN, for relief
DALTON, CARSON R., for relief
DALTON, GA., Catholic Church at, relief
DAMAGES TO LANDS IN ERECTION OF FORTS, Governm
D'AMBRUGEAC, for relief
DANDRIDGE, PETER, for relief of widow
DANIEL, LEONARD F., referring claim to Court of Claims
DANIEL, WILLIAMS, for relief of heirs
DARDIN, ALFRED H., for relief
DARDIN, DAVID, for relief of heirs
  Do
DARLING, FLORA A., for relief
  Do
  Do
DAVENPORT, WILLIAM, for relief of heirs
DAVIDSON, ELIJAH, for relief
DAVIS, CHARLES J. (administrator), for relief
  Do
  Do
DAVIS, HUGH, for relief
  Do
DAVIS, JAMES, referring claim to Court of Claims
DAVIS, JOHN,
  For relief of estate
  Do
  Do
  Do
  For relief of heir
DAVIS, JOHN P. Y., for relief
  Do
  Do
DAVIS, MARK,
  For relief
  Do
  For relief of heirs
  Do
DAVIS, NANCY, for relief
DAVIS, RICHARD, for relief
  Do
DAVIS, RICHARD C., for relief
DAVIS, SAMUEL, for pay and allowances
DAVIS, SARAH C., for relief
DAVIS, WILEY J., for relief
DAVIS, WILLIAM H., for relief
  Do
  Do
  Do
  Do
DAWSON, ELIZA M., for relief of heirs
DAWSON, JOSEPH N., *et al.*, referring claim to Court of Clair
DAY, JOSEPH, for relief of estate
DAY, THOMAS, for relief
  Do
DEANE, SILAS, for relief
DE BREE, JOHN, for relief
DEENSCOMB, SAMUEL H., for relief
DE GRASSE, ——, for relief of heir
DE KALB, JOHN, baron, for relief of heirs
  Do
  Do
  Do
  Do

* Part 2.

Subject.	Report.	Congress.	Session.	Volume.
DUER, W. A., *et al.* (trustees), for relief	240	33	1	
DUGAN, MARGARET T., for relief	742	46	1	1
DULANY, DANIEL F., for relief	427	43	1	
Do	350	44	1	1
DUNCAN, ANDREW I., for relief of heirs	167	48	1	1
Do	2331	49	1	1
DUNCAN, JULIA, for relief	1477	46	2	1
Do	986	47	1	1
DUNCAN, MARY T., for relief	953	46	2	1
DUNPHE, N. H., for relief	508	43	1	
Do	1883	48	1	1
DUNSCOMB, SAMUEL H., for relief	444	45	2	
DUNSEATH, DAVID, for relief	450	45	2	
DUPORTAIL, ——, for relief of heirs	14	27	2	
DURANT, THOMAS, for relief of widow	32	25	3	
DUVALL, WILLIAM F., for relief	161	48	1	
DWIGHT MISSION, CHEROKEE NATION, for relief	2612	49	1	
DWYER, JOHN, for relief	1049	46	2	
DYE, JONATHAN, for relief of heirs	758	25	2	
Do	52	25	3	
Do	91	26	1	
Do	2	26	2	
Do	82	27	2	
Do	91	29	1	
Do	114	34	1	
DYE, SARAH ANN, for relief of administrator of	674	30	1	
DYER, ELIZABETH P.,				
For relief	213	46	2	1
Do	1827	49	1	1
Referring claim to Court of Claims	2643	48	2	1
DYER, HORATIO, for relief	769	30	1	
DYER, JANE C., for relief	601	49	1	1
DYGERT, PETER, for relief of heir	405	29	1	
Do	274	31	1	
Do	9	31	2	
DYSON, SAMUEL (administrator), for relief	1687	47	1	1
EARLE, SAMUEL, for relief	942	27	2	
EASTEN, WILLIAM A., for relief	666	49	1	1
EASTMAN, HARRY E., for relief	489	44	1	1
EASTON, SARAH, for relief	66	14	1	
Do	17	17	2	
Do	130	21	1	
Do	116	21	2	
Do	79	22	1	
EATON, ANN J., for relief	48	43	2	
EATON, HENRY Z., for relief	40	43	2	
Do	1011	45	2	1
Do	1080	46	2	1
EBERLE, JOHN G., for relief	921	48	1	
EDDY, JOHN M., *et al.*, for relief	1440	49	1	1
EDDY, JOSHUA, for relief of heirs	369	30	1	
Do	112	31	1	
EDDY, MARY J., for relief	993	46	2	1
EDELEN, ROBERT J., for relief	795	43	1	
EDGECOMB, SAMUEL, for relief	54	25	3	
EDMONSTON, WILLIAM, for relief of heirs	164	25	1	
EDMUNDSON, SAMUEL, referring claim to Court of Claims	2643	48	2	
EDWARDS, DANIEL, for relief	1379	46	2	
EDWARDS, DAVID, for relief of administrator of	3647	49	2	
EDWARDS, HANNAH B., referring claim to Court of Claims	2643	48	2	
EDWARDS, LE ROY, for relief	102	19	1	
EDWARDS, T. J., for relief	3647	49	2	
ELDER, JOHN M., referring claim to Court of Claims	2643	48	2	
ELDIS, MARTIN, for relief of widow	401	43	1	
ELIZABETHTOWN, N. J., for relief of First Presbyterian Church at	259	27	2	
ELK BRANCH, W. VA., for relief of Presbyterian Church at	829	49	1	
ELLIOTT, ENOCH E., for relief	1365	47	1	
ELLIOTT, W. W. R., for relief	211	46	2	
Do	226	47	1	
Do	91	48	1	
ELMER, MOSES,				
Claim for relief	259	24	2	
For relief of heirs	123	24	1	
ELY, ELISHA, for relief	166	24	2	
ELY, JOHN, for relief of heirs	66	21	2	
EMBRY, W. J. (executor), referring claim of, to Court of Claims	2643	48	2	
EMERSON, JOHN,				
For relief	134	22	1	
Do	671	25	2	
For relief of heirs	373	27	2	
EMMERT, SAMUEL, referring claim to Court of Claims	2643	48	2	

Subject.	Report.	Congress.	Session.	Volume.
ETT, JAMES, for relief of heirs	913	25	1	4
LAND, JOHN, for relief	27	25	3	4
LE, JOHN M., for relief	726	49	1	14
LISH, THOMAS, for relief of widow	397	43	1	8
ES, FRANCIS, for relief of heirs	251	25	2	4
Do	25	25	3	4
Do	513	26	1	5
Do	38	27	2	5
ES, WILLIAM, for relief of heirs	55	22	2	2
EIN, PHILIP, *et al.*, referring claim to Court of Claims	2643	48	2	13
DE, LEWIS, for relief	1243	46	2	11
IN, WILLIAM, for relief	1774	48	1	13
Do	1821	49	1	14
Do	2333	49	1	14
ACE, JOHN, for relief	168	19	1	1
NS, ELIZA M., for relief	248	35	2	7
NS, MARIA P., for relief	142	43	2	9
ER, ELIZA, referring claim to Court of Claims	2643	48	2	13
OMER, JOSEPH, for relief of heirs	56	20	2	2
Do	92	21	1	2
Do	65	22	2	2
Do	157	23	1	3
LS, WILLIAM, for relief	452	45	2	10
NING, JOSHUA, for relief of heirs	463	24	1	3
Do	110	25	2	4
NY BRANDEIS (vessel), for relief of owners	951	46	2	11
S, NATHAN, for relief of heirs	825	24	1	3
LEY, JOHN, for relief	1889	49	1	14
LEY, JOHN A.,				
or relief	405	46	2	11
eferring claim to Court of Claims	2643	48	2	13
R, E. A., for relief	1489	47	1	12
RINGTON, MARCH, for relief	143	30	2	6
Do	188	31	1	6
ROW, JOSEPH J., for relief	2022	47	2	12
Do	170	48	1	13
LKNER, ASA, *et al.*, for relief	1002	46	2	11
Do	467	48	1	13
Do	629	49	1	14
NTLEROY, ROBERT, for relief	780	24	1	3
JAMES, for relief of heirs	577	25	2	4
JOSEPH (alias Facy), for relief of heirs	103	24	2	3
ETTEVILLE, ARK., for relief of Christian Church in	1246	46	2	11
Y, TIMOTHY, for relief of heirs	628	24	1	3
Do	116	25	2	4
TS, HENRY J., for relief	1510	48	1	13
JOSEPH S., for relief of heirs	540	27	2	5
ALE NURSES. (*See* WAR OF REBELLION.)				
ALE INSTITUTE OF MADISON, ——, referring claim to Court of Claims	2643	48	2	13
AN, THOMAS K., for relief	195	46	3	11
NIT, EUGENE, referring claim to Court of Claims	2643	48	2	13
RY, JAMES D., for relief	3441	49	1	14
INBURGH, JANE, for relief	15	27	2	5
D, BENJAMIN, for relief	856	24	1	3
D, C. J., for relief of heirs	726	48	1	13
D, HENRY, for relief of heir	358	22	1	2
Do	31	23	1	3
D, JAMES G., referring claims to Court of Claims	2643	48	2	13
D, REUBEN, for relief of heirs	533	27	2	5
Do	215	27	3	5
Do	235	27	3	5
ER, CHARLES,				
or relief of heir	76	33	2	6
or relief of administrator	4	36	2	7
Y, JOHN H., referring claim to Court of Claims	2643	48	2	13
LEY, POLLY, for relief	617	30	1	6
EY, ANDREW, for relief of heirs	284	33	1	6
EY, SQUIRE, for relief	540	47	1	12
T NATIONAL BANK OF SAINT ALBANS, for relief	148	43	2	9
Do	104	44	1	10
T PRESBYTERIAN CHURCH, ELIZABETHTOWN, N. J., for relief	259	27	3	5
T PRESBYTERIAN CHURCH, YORKTOWN, N. Y.,				
or relief	807	24	1	3
or relief of trustees	433	25	2	4
H, JOHN A., for relief	948	46	2	11
EMMA H., for relief	169	49	1	14
ER, THOMAS, referring claim to Court of Claims	2643	48	2	13
JAMES, for relief	1386	46	2	11
MMONS, THOMAS, for relief	828	24	1	3
GERALD, BISHOP E., for relief	236	48	1	13
GERALD, EDWARD, for relief	1828	49	1	14

Subject.	Report.	Congress.	Session.	Volume.
FITZHUGH, EDWIN C., for relief	515	43	1	8
FITZPATRICK, PATRICK, for relief	1221	49	1	14
FLEMMING, JOHN S. (administrator), for relief	190	22	1	2
Do	97	23	1	3
FLENNEKIN, JOHN C., for relief	1823	47	2	12
FLETCHER, WILLIAM, for relief	2028	47	2	12
Do	2120	48	1	13
FLINT, JAMES, for relief of widow	865	25	2	4
FLOWERS, CLARA H., *et al.*, referring claim to Court of Claims	2643	48	2	13
FLYNN, PATRICK, for relief	2122	48	1	13
Do	760	49	1	14
FOLKES & WINSTON, for relief	43	43	2	9
Do	73	45	3	10
FOLSOM, A., for relief	961	46	2	11
FOLTZ, JOSHUA, for relief	156	20	1	2
FONDA, JELLIS, for relief of heirs	206	27	2	5
FONTAINE, WILLIAM, for relief of heirs	14	25	2	4
FORBES, C. H., for relief	768	43	1	8
FORD, FREDERICK, Capt., for relief	4027	49	2	14
FORD, WILLIAM G., for relief	1727	47	1	12
Do	1728	47	1	12
FOREST, URIAH, for relief of heirs	444	26	1	5
Do	374	27	2	5
FORT, ROBERT D., for relief	1063	46	2	11
FORT, SUGG, for relief	763	43	1	8
Do	316	43	2	9
FORTUNE, RICHARD, for relief of heirs	975	25	2	4
FOSTER, PETER, for relief	130	22	1	2
FOSTER, THOMAS, for relief	2610	49	1	14
FOUNTAIN, Mrs. C. S., *et al*, for relief	3129	49	1	14
FOUNTAIN, WILLIAM, for relief of heirs	676	24	1	3
Do	429	25	2	4
Do	375	27	2	5
FOURTH OF JULY CLAIMS. (*See* CLAIMS; COMMISSIONERS OF CLAIMS.)				
FOX, VAUSE (administrator), for relief	429	24	1	3
Do	246	25	2	4
Do	221	25	3	4
FRANK, CHARLES H., for relief	91	43	2	9
FRANK, LEON, for relief	818	44	1	10
FRANKLIN, JOHN W., for relief	1023	48	1	13
FRANKLIN, MESHACK (administrator), for relief	241	48	1	13
FRASER, ANTHONY R., for relief	961	47	1	12
FRASER, WILLIAM F., for relief	539	47	1	12
FRAZIER, JOEL C., for relief	1240	46	2	11
Do	191	49	1	14
FRAZIER, WILLIAM F., for relief	966	46	2	11
FREDERICK CITY, MD., for relief of town and the banks thereof	746	43	1	8
Do	547	44	1	10
FREEL, ROSETTA, for relief	214	46	2	11
FREEMAN, CONSTANT, for relief of heirs	236	27	3	5
FRENCH, HENRY S., for relief	805	43	1	8
Do	648	44	1	10
Do	447	45	2	10
Do	954	46	2	11
FRIED, HENRY, for relief	62	21	2	3
FRISBIE, EDWARD, for relief of heir	521	27	2	5
FRISBIE, ISRAEL, for relief of heirs	109	36	1	7
Do	5	37	2	7
FRIZELL, JAMES S.,				
For relief	1485	46	2	11
Referring claim to Court of Claims	2643	48	2	13
FROTHINGHAM, JOSHUA P., for relief	88	22	1	2
FROTHINGHAM, THOMAS, for relief of heirs	68	21	2	2
Do	88	22	1	2
FULTS, JOSHUA, for relief	41	19	2	1
GALBREATH, NANCY, for relief	1436	46	2	11
GALL, JOHN W., for relief of heirs	110	43	2	9
Do	252	44	1	10
Do	712	45	2	10
GALLAGER, EDWARD, for relief	749	43	1	8
GALLOWAY, JOHN, for relief of heirs	933	25	2	4
GALLOWAY, W. A., referring claim to Court of Claims	2643	48	2	13
GALLUP, ASA O., for relief	1914	47	2	12
GAMBLE, EDMUND, for relief of heir	1085	27	2	5
GANNEWAY, EDWARD, for relief	167	48	1	13
GANT, Mrs. E., referring claim to Court of Claims	2643	48	2	13
GARDEN, ALEXANDER, for relief	65	20	1	2
Do	430	22	1	2
Do	118	23	1	3
GARDNER, ALBERT, for relief	1346	46	2	11

Subject.	Report.	Congress.	Session.	Volume.
DNER, A. H., for relief	974	46	2	11
Do	79	48	1	13
SON, NANCY, for relief	1065	46	2	11
LAND, BURLEY, for relief of heirs	220	24	1	3
LAND, PETER, for relief of heirs	124	24	1	3
NETT, TABITHA, referring claim to Court of Claims	2043	48	2	13
RETT, RICHARD H., for relief	743	43	1	8
ELIN, CLEMENT, for relief of heirs	31	36	1	7
RING, CHARLES, for relief	1490	46	2	11
RY, MARY,				
or relief	51	43	2	9
eferring claim to Court of Claims	2648	48	2	13
R, JAMES, for relief	342	31	1	6
GIA,				
aims of, to adjudicate	1090	27	2	5
otton and other claims, adjudication of	406	48	1	13
ilitia claims, to adjudicate	1094	47	1	12
ezvant, Peter, to refund certain moneys to State, paid to	6	36	2	7
TNER, GEORGE, for relief	174	24	2	3
, WILLIAM E., for relief	229	46	2	11
R, JOHN C., for relief	958	48	1	13
d, JOSHUA P. FROTHE, for relief	68	21	2	2
ES & CO., for relief	200	45	2	10
ON, JAMES, for relief	251	21	1	2
ONS, FRANCIS A., for relief	672	43	1	8
S, BENJAMIN, for relief	166	21	1	2
Do	108	22	1	2
S, CHURCHILL, for relief of heirs	531	27	2	5
Do	86	29	2	6
Do	138	30	2	6
S, SAMUEL,				
r relief	67	16	1	1
r relief of heirs	166	23	1	3
ON, GEORGE, for relief of heirs	194	23	1	3
Do	345	24	1	3
Do	113	25	2	4
ON, WILLIAM R., for relief	1686	47	1	12
INGS, NAPOLEON B., for relief	373	47	1	12
EAU, FRANCIS, for relief	1072	49	1	14
ERT, ABIJAH B., for relief	3442	49	1	14
ERT, ANGELICA, for relief	784	25	2	4
SAMUEL, for relief	1491	46	2	11
THOMAS, for relief of heirs	201	34	1	6
ETT, THEODORE J., for relief	3343	49	1	14
CK, ELIZABETH, for relief	292	43	2	9
ER C. G., for relief	1244	46	2	11
N, JOHN A., for relief	1084	46	2	11
COCK, THOMAS, for relief of heirs	778	24	1	3
Do	432	25	2	4
Do	330	26	1	5
Do	1057	27	2	5
SIE, D. W. AND MINNIE H., for relief	745	43	1	8
Do	942	46	2	11
Do	3045	49	1	14
E, JOSEPH L., referring claim to Court of Claims	2643	48	2	13
E, ALEXANDER, for relief	665	49	1	14
REY, W. E., for relief of heir	1084	27	2	5
IN, W. F., for relief	1074	46	2	11
SBOROUGH, WILLIAM, for relief of heirs	658	27	2	5
ALL, JANE M., for relief	165	48	1	13
ELL, JOHN, for relief of heirs	180	26	2	5
Do	376	27	2	5
RUM, TURNER C., for relief	3338	49	1	14
WIN, DANIEL, for relief	154	20	1	2
Do	314	21	1	2
Do	149	22	1	2
WIN, FRANCIS LE BARON, for relief of heir	283	35	1	7
WIN, HOLLISTER E., AND SURETIES, for relief	2372	49	1	14
WIN, NATHANIEL, for relief of heirs	138	23	1	3
WIN, SAMUEL AND OTHERS, for relief	221	27	2	5
ON, JAMES, for relief	179	21	1	2
ON, THOMAS, for relief of heirs	310	22	1	2
Do	799	24	1	3
Do	120	25	2	4
Do	330	26	1	5
Do	237	27	3	5
Do	42	34	1	6
ON, WILLIAM H., for relief	924	48	1	13
AN, JAMES (administrator), for relief	450	45	2	10
LIN, CLEMENT, for relief of heirs	31	36	1	7
M, THOMAS B., for relief	1219	49	1	14

Subject.	Report.	Congress.	Session.	Volume.
GOULD, CHARLES C., for relief	796	43	1	4
GOULD, DAVID, for relief of heir	952	25	2	4
Do	53	25	3	4
GOULD, WILLIAM B., for relief	952	25	2	4
Do	53	25	3	4
GOYAUX, LUCIEN, for relief	2329	49	1	14
Do	3136	49	1	14
GRAHAM, C. A. S., for relief	491	36	1	7
GRAHAM, GEORGE W., for relief	294	47	1	12
Do	2613	49	1	14
GRAHAM, R., for relief of widow	91	23	2	3
GRAHAM, STEPHEN,				
For relief of heirs	621	26	1	5
Do	377	27	2	5
For relief of estate	5	36	2	7
GRANNISS, ENOS, for relief of heirs	118	22	2	2
Do	117	23	1	3
GRATZ, BENJAMIN, for relief	90	43	2	9
Do	1610	46	2	11
GRATZ, MICHAEL, for relief	71	23	1	8
GRAVES, BETTIE, referring claim to Court of Claims	2643	48	2	13
GRAVES, JOHN O., for relief	212	46	2	11
Do	375	47	1	12
Do	87	48	1	13
GRAVES, R. F., Jr., for relief	676	43	1	8
GRAVES, THOMAS, for relief	564	24	1	3
Do	81	24	2	3
Do	765	25	2	4
Do	199	27	2	5
GRAY, GEORGE, for relief of heirs	326	24	1	3
GRAY, THOMAS P., for relief	978	49	1	14
GRAYSON, WILLIAM, for relief of heirs	527	28	1	6
Do	11	29	1	6
GREANER, WILLIAM, for relief	751	43	1	8
GREEN, J. & T., for relief	376	43	1	8
Do	5	43	2	9
GREEN, L. T., *et al.*, for relief	2240	48	2	13
GREENE, HENRY A., for relief	1016	45	2	10
Do	1767	47	1	12
Do	759	49	1	14
GREENE, NATHANIEL, for relief of heirs	283	33	1	6
GREENFIELD, OLIVER H., for relief	732	47	1	12
GREENSLADE, WILLIAM, for relief	950	46	2	11
GREER, JACOB, for relief	480	25	2	4
GREER, PRISCILLA, for relief	738	25	2	4
GREER, ROBERT, for relief of heir	545	27	2	5
GREGORIE, FERDINAND, for relief	759	43	1	8
GREGORY, JOHN M., for relief of heirs	421	22	1	2
Do	124	23	1	3
GREGORY, WILLIAM, for relief of heirs	294	25	2	4
Do	8	25	3	4
Do	275	27	2	5
GREGORY, WILLIAM H., for relief of heirs	90	26	1	5
GRIFFIN, THOMAS, for relief of executor of	440	26	1	5
GRIGG, ELIZABETH,				
For relief	52	37	2	7
Referring claim to Court of Claims	2643	48	2	13
Do	1820	49	1	14
Do	2185	49	1	14
GRIGGS, GEORGE W., for relief	760	43	1	8
GRIMES, MILINDA, for relief	2119	48	1	13
Do	2860	49	1	14
GRIMES, WILLIAM H., referring claim to Court of Claims	2643	48	2	13
GROOMS, YARVIN C., for relief	356	48	1	13
GROSH, LEWIS A., referring claim to Court of Claims	2643	48	2	13
GRUBB, CURTIS, for relief of administrator	7	36	2	7
GRIER, DAVID, for relief of heir	332	30	1	6
GRYMES, WILLIAM, for relief of heir	112	23	2	3
Do	109	24	1	3
Do	250	25	2	4
Do	534	27	2	5
Do	32	29	2	6
Do	428	31		6
GUILBEAU, FRANCIS, for relief of heirs	2027	47	2	12
GUSTIN, SAMUEL L., for relief	33	45	2	10
Do	1001	46	2	11
GUY, ELLA M., referring claim to Court of Claims	2643	48	2	13
GWIN, ELIZABETH P., for relief	32	23	2	3
Do	250	24	1	3
Do	212	25	2	4
GWIN, JOHN A., for relief	88	48		13

Subject.	Report.	Congress.	Session.	Volume.
[NN, JOHN, for relief of heirs	87	20	1	2
KETT, ANN, for relief	1076	27	2	5
KLEY, JAMES, for relief	905	25	2	4
Do	378	27	2	5
ER, JONATHAN, for relief of heir	519	27	2	5
GARD, DAVID E., for relief	518	43	1	8
GART, NANCY, for relief	112	23	2	3
Do	109	24	1	3
Do	250	25	2	4
Do	534	27	2	5
Do	32	29	2	6
Do	428	31	1	6
NES, HARRIET, for relief	788	43	1	8
RE, MILTON S., referring claim to Court of Claims	2643	48	2	13
Do	2199	49	1	14
DEMAN, FRANCIS W., for relief	337	49	1	14
E, JONATHAN D., for relief	511	43	1	7
F-PAY ALLOWANCES. (*See* PENSIONS.)				
L, DUDLEY, for relief of estate	340	31	1	6
L, JOHN, for relief of heirs	633	25	2	4
L, JOSEPH, for relief	106	48	1	13
L, LOT, for relief of estate	511	26	1	5
Do	517	27	2	5
Do	443	29	1	6
Do	148	33	1	6
Do	85	35	2	7
L, WARREN, for relief	1604	46	2	11
Do	489	48	1	13
Do	3505	49	2	14
LER SAMUEL M., referring claim to Court of Claims	2643	48	2	13
ILTON, ALEXANDER, for relief of widow	55	14	1	1
ILTON, ELIZABETH, for relief	55	14	1	1
ILTON, LIZZIE, for relief	49	48	1	13
ITER, JOHN H., referring claim to Court of Claims	2643	48	2	13
LIN, WILLIAM B., for relief	408	46	2	11
MOND, ALLAN C., for relief	937	46	2	11
Do	63	47	1	12
MOND, J. H., for relief	2029	47	2	12
Do	83	48	1	13
MOND, JOHN, referring claim to Court of Claims	2643	48	2	13
MOND, WILLIAM K., for relief	362	49	1	14
NER, WILLIAM T., for relief	1087	46	2	11
PTON, ELIZABETH J., for relief	228	46	2	11
GER, PETER, *et al.*, for relief	2240	48	2	13
BISON, J. M., for relief	1191	47	1	12
DAWAY, JOEL, for relief of heirs	290	25	2	4
Do	379	27	2	5
Do	239	27	3	5
DESTY, OBADIAH, for relief	282	35	1	7
GUS, JOHN (alias Hargis), for relief	560	24	1	3
MAN, PRISCILLA B., for relief	156	23	1	3
MON, M. G., for relief	50	45	2	10
MON, MICKLE, for relief	1012	45	2	10
Do	109	47	1	12
Do	2195	49	1	14
PER, GEORGE C., for relief	1241	46	2	11
Do	905	47	1	12
Do	927	48	1	13
RIS, J. GEORGE, for relief	497	43	1	8
RIS, JOHN, for relief of heirs	218	23	1	3
RIS, NEWITT.				
or relief	2792	49	1	14
eferring claim to Court of Claims	2643	48	2	1
RIS, RANSOM L., for relief	2026	49	1	14
RIS, THOMAS, for relief of heirs	638	24	1	3
Do	393	25	2	4
RIS, THOMAS B., for relief	1041	46	2	11
RIS, THOMAS D., for relief	1564	49	1	14
RISON, BENJAMIN, Jr., for relief of heir	238	27	3	5
Do	228	35	1	7
RISON, JOHN P., for relief of heirs	935	25	2	4
Do	380	27	2	5
Do	231	35	1	7
RISON, R. H., relief of heirs	66	14	1	1
Do	130	21	1	2
Do	116	21	2	2
T, DANIEL, for relief of heirs	420	31	1	6
WELL, DELOS A., referring claim to Court of Claims	2643	48	2	13
WOOD, WILLIAM G., for relief	418	46	2	11
FIELD, ALFRED G., for relief	1682	47	1	12
Do	1509	48	1	13

Subject.	Report.	Congress.	Session.	Volume.
HATFIELD, JOHN,				
For relief	84	49	1	14
For relief of heirs	159	49	1	14
HATHAWAY, JOHN R., for relief	111	43	2	9
HAWK, MILLER & Co., for relief	284	43	2	9
HAWKINS, JOHN, for relief of heirs	637	24	1	3
HAWKS, RUTH, for relief	971	25	2	4
HAYDEN, JOHN J., for relief	378	43	1	8
HAYDEN, JOSIAH, for relief of heirs	119	24	2	3
HAYES, CHARLES F., for relief	2026	47	2	12
HAYWOOD, F. P., for relief	998	46	2	11
HAZARD, THOMAS, for relief of heirs	200	34	3	6
HAZARD, JOHN V. S. (administrator), for relief	97	38	2	7
HAZEN, G. M., referring claim to Court of Claims	2643	48	2	13
HAZEN, MOSES, for relief of estate	85	16	1	1
Do	191	19	1	1
Do	216	20	1	2
HAZZARD, THOMAS, for relief of heirs and legal representatives	491	36	1	7
HEARD, JOHN, for relief of heir	177	33	1	6
HEARD, NATHANIEL, for relief of heirs	201	35	1	7
Do	412	36	1	7
HEARD, W. D. C., for relief	26	34	1	6
HEATER, JOHN, for relief	35	45	2	10
HEBERER, JOHN for relief	956	48	1	13
HEBERT, ELIZA E., for relief	309	44	1	10
Do	216	45	2	10
Do	226	46	2	11
Do	1683	47	1	12
Do	235	48	1	13
Do	305	49	1	14
HEETER, SEBASTIAN, for relief	2256	49	1	14
HEFLEBOWER, JOHN, for relief	2787	49	1	14
HELM, THOMAS, for relief of heirs	842	24	1	3
Do	881	27	2	5
HELMER, MARY, for reliief	409	35	1	7
HELPHENSTON, PETER, for relief of heirs	707	24	2	3
Do	193	25	2	4
HENDERSON, ELIZABETH, for relief	1628	49	1	14
HENDERSON, FRANCIS, for relief	257	21	1	2
HENDERSON, R. J., for relief	803	43	1	8
Do	312	44	1	10
HENDERSON, SIDNEY, for relief of heirs and estate	26	48	1	13
Do	923	48	1	13
HENDERSON, TENN.,				
Assessments levied upon disloyal citizens by military order, payment of	*3038	49	1	14
Destruction of property at, by rebel raid, indemnity for	75	48	1	13
HENDERSONVILLE, N. C., Judson Female College, relief of	2476	49	1	14
HENDRICKS, W. P., for relief	1220	49	1	14
HENDRICKS, WILLIAM, for relief of heir	334	24	1	3
Do	194	25	2	4
HENRY, J. A., *et al.*, for relief	2242	48	2	13
Do	1299	49	1	14
Do	1300	49	1	14
HENRY, JAMES O., for relief	414	46	2	11
HENRY, JOHN, for relief of heirs	1061	27	2	5
HERKIMER, GENERAL, relative to the erection of a monument to	695	29	1	6
HERN, SAMUEL, for relief	415	25	2	4
HERNANDEZ, VIDAL, for relief	1603	46	2	11
Do	2424	48	2	13
HERNDON, JOHN C., for relief	726	47	1	12
Do	233	48	1	13
HERR, A. H., for relief	418	45	2	10
Do	155	48	1	13
HESKETT, THOMAS N., referring claim to Court of Claims	2643	48	2	13
HESS, FRED, for relief	912	48	1	13
HETH, WILLIAM, for relief of heirs	717	24	1	3
HEVENOR, J., for relief	1223	49	1	14
HEY, LUCY A., referring claim to Court of Claims	2643	48	2	13
HICKMAN, WILLIAM, for relief of heirs	281	35	1	7
HICKS, DAVID, referring claim to Court of Claims	2643	48	2	13
HIGGINS, ELIZABETH B., *et al.*, for relief	196	46	2	11
Do	1848	47	2	12
Do	104	48	1	13
HIGGINS, JOHN M., for relief	1258	47	1	12
Do	†600	49	1	14
Do	1131	49	1	14
HIGGINS, MARGARET T., for relief of executor of	3701	49	2	14
HIGGINS, THOMAS L., for relief	3341	49	1	14

* Views of minority. † Part 2.

Subject.	Report.	Congress.	Session.	Volume.
HILDERBRAND, DAVID H.,				
For relief	383	46	2	11
Do	2236	49	1	14
Referring claim to Court of Claims	2642	48	2	13
HILL, GEORGE, Jr., for relief	2411	49	1	14
HILL, HARRIET AND JAMES N., for relief	449	45	2	10
HILL, J. N., for relief	925	47	1	12
HILL, JOHN, for relief	612	25	2	4
HILL, JOHN L., for relief	190	46	2	11
HILL, JOHN J., for relief	92	48	1	13
HILL, S. H., for relief	1499	47	1	12
Do	1624	49	1	14
HILL, W. H.,				
For relief	2202	49	1	14
Referring claim to Court of Claims	2643	48	2	12
HILLARY, RIGNALD (alias Nick), for relief of heir	101	21	2	2
Do	891	25	2	4
Do	104	25	3	4
Do	116	26	1	5
Do	252	27	2	5
Do	511	29	1	6
Do	146	31	1	6
Do	349	32	1	6
HILLIARD, NANCY, for relief	8	25	3	4
Do	275	27	2	5
HILLS, AGNES W. and SARAH J., for relief	1265	47	1	12
Do	721	48	1	13
HINDS, BARTLETT, for relief of heirs	616	30	1	6
Do	114	31	1	6
Do	53	32	1	6
Do	126	33	1	7
HINE, ADAM,				
For relief	513	43	1	8
Do	1004	46	2	11
Referring claim to Court of Claims	2643	48	2	13
HINMAN, WILBUR F., for relief	1422	48	1	13
Do	1434	49	1	14
HIXT, WILLIAM, for relief of heirs	153	31	1	6
HOBSON, HORACE P., for relief	1825	49	1	14
HOBSON, JOHN, for relief	807	43	1	8
HOBSON, JOSEPH, for relief of heirs	178	26	2	5
HOFFMAN, HENRY,				
For relief	242	25	3	4
For relief of heirs	1024	27	2	5
Do	149	33	1	6
HOFFMAN, R. H., for relief	741	48	1	13
HOGAN, JAMES, for relief of heirs	531	25	2	4
HOGAN, ROSANNA, for relief	288	43	2	9
HOGE, JOHN, for relief of heir	180	31	1	6
HOLCOMBE, JOHN, for relief of heirs	477	25	2	4
HOLDEN, ASA, for relief	396	24	1	3
HLOKER, NANCY D., for relief of widow	211	34	1	6
Do	62	35	1	7
Do	9	35	2	7
HOLLIDAY, ALLEN J., for relief	421	46	2	11
Do	40	48	1	13
HOLLIDAY, JOSEPH, for relief of heirs	383	27	2	5
HOLLIDAYOKE, DANIEL, for relief of heirs	659	27	2	5
HOLLORAN, JOHN, for relief	1441	49	1	14
HOLMES, DAVID, for relief of heirs	138	23	1	3
HOLMS, ORSAMUS, for relief	14	19	2	1
HOMER, GUSTAVUS B., claim for relief	259	24	2	3
HONER, GUSTAVUS B., for relief of heirs	2	33	2	6
Do	124	35	1	7
Do	150	36	1	7
HONEYWELL, ISRAEL, for relief of heirs	469	25	3	4
HOOPER, JOHN H., for relief	812	43	1	8
HOPKINS, ARVAH, for relief	599	49	1	14
Do	3597	49	2	14
HOPKINS, DAVID, for relief of estate	271	30	1	6
Do	102	31	1	6
Do	98	36	2	7
HOPKINS, PERRY G., for relief	787	25	2	4
HOPPER, JOHN, for relief of heirs	694	25	2	4
Do	792	25	2	4
Do	261	27	3	5
Do	44	35	1	7
Do	110	36	1	7
Do	320	36	1	7
HOPPING, THOMAS, for relief	68	21	2	2
Do	88	22	1	2

Subject.	Report.	Congress.	Session.	Volume.
HOOD, THOMAS, for relief of estate	506	43	1	8
HORINE, JACOB, for relief of estate	925	25	2	4
HORNER, EATON G., for relief	742	43	1	8
HORNER, GUSTAVUS B., for relief of heirs	798	24	1	3
Do	140	29	1	6
Do	2	33	2	6
Do	113	34	1	6
Do	124	35	1	7
Do	150	36	1	7
HORSES. (*See* ARMY.)				
HOSACK, W. S., for relief	668	49	1	14
HOUGHTON, GEORGE W., for relief of administrator	2643	48	2	13
HOUGHTON, JOSEPH, for relief of heirs	159	24	2	3
HOUSEHOLDER, WILLIAM, referring claim to Court of Claims	2643	48	2	13
HOUSTON, ALFRED, for relief	23	48	1	13
HOUSTON, JAMES, for relief of heirs	820	24	1	3
HOWARD, SAMUEL, for relief	166	48	1	13
HOWELL, DELOS A., for relief	1035	46	2	11
HOWES, ABNER, for relief of heir	660	27	2	5
HOWSE, JOHN C., for relief of heirs	2510	47	1	14
HOYT, STEPHEN, for relief	424	31	1	6
HUBBLE, WILLIAM, for relief of estate	99	20	1	2
HUDDY, JOSHUA, for relief	535	27	2	5
HUESTISS, DAVID, for relief	567	43	1	8
HUFF, WILLIAM H., for relief	977	46	2	11
HUGH, W. H. (administrator), referring claim to Court of Claims	2643	48	2	13
HUGHES, G. W., referring claim to Court of Claims	2643	48	2	13
HUGHES, INDIANA E.,				
For relief	280	46	2	11
Do	89	48	1	13
Do	2791	49	1	14
Referring claim to Court of Claims	2643	48	2	13
HUGHEY, WILLIAM H., for relief	1001	46	2	11
HULL, WARREN, for relief	629	47	1	12
HUMES, THOMAS W., for relief	1439	49	1	14
HUMNER, MARY, for relief	563	24	1	3
HUMPHREYS, JOHN, for relief	1057	46	2	11
HUMPHREY, JOHN W., for relief	528	47	1	12
HUNT, ELIZABETH, for relief	334	24	1	3
Do	194	25	2	4
HUNT, FANNIE T., for relief	235	46	2	11
Do	169	48	1	13
HUNT, HARPER P., for relief	254	43	2	9
HUNT, JAMES, for relief	396	24	1	3
HUNT, MARY S., referring claim to Court of Claims	2643	48	2	13
HUNTER, JAMES N., for relief	970	46	2	11
Do	89	48	1	13
HUNTING, WILLIAM B., for relief	598	24	1	3
HURDLE, GEORGE W., for relief of widow	797	43	1	8
HURLBUT, GEORGE, for relief of estate	19	14	2	1
Do	60	23	1	3
HURLEY, ANNA, for relief	1882	46	2	11
HUTCHESON, WILLIAM C., for relief	3422	49	1	14
HUTCHINS, SARAH, for relief	436	43	1	8
HUTCHINSON, RANE C., for relief	382	49	1	14
HUYETT, JOHN H., referring claim to Court of Claims	2643	48	2	13
HYDE, JANE ANN, for relief	181	29	1	6
ICKES, HENRY, *et al.*, for relief	1473	46	2	11
IHMS, ANTHONY, for relief	1192	47	1	12
ILLINOIS EXPEDITION, to audit claims of State of Virginia for expenses incurred during the years 1778, 1779, in the	519	28	1	5
IMPORT DUTIES, to refund to State of New York moneys paid on imported arms.	1297	49	1	14
INDIANA METHODIST CHURCH, NORFOLK COUNTY, VIRGINIA, claim for relief	2013	47	2	12
INGRAM, SARAH, for relief	38	15	2	1
INMAN, JOHN T. (administrator), referring claim to Court of Claims	2643	48	2	13
INTEREST ON WAR CLAIMS, to reimburse States for	1102	48	1	13
IOWA, for relief of Fourth Infantry Regiment of State of	1437	49	1	14
IRISH, NATHANIEL, for relief of heirs	718	25	2	4
Do	117	26	2	5
Do	884	27	2	5
IRVIN, JOHN, for relief	1890	49	1	14
Referring claim to Court of Claims	2643	48	2	13
IRVINE, DAVID, for relief of heirs	726	48	1	13
IRWIN, HENRY, for relief of heirs	828	24	1	3
Do	107	25	2	4
IRWIN, RICHARD, for relief of heirs	107	25	2	4
ISAACS, SOLOMON,				
Referring claim to Court of Claims	2643	48	2	13
For relief	2200	49	1	14

Subject.	Report.	Congress.	Session.	Volume.
ISAACS, WILLIAM B., & CO., for relief	1417	47	1	12
Do	484	49	1	14
ISGRIG, THOMAS C., for relief	1486	46	2	11
ISH, CHRISTIAN, for relief of estate	56	21	2	2
Do	288	22	1	2
Do	98	23	1	3
ISLAND QUEEN (steamer), for relief of owner	*146	43	2	9
IVIE, WILLIAM P., for relief	986	46	2	11
JACK, MATTHEW, for relief of heir	8	31	2	6
Do	145	33	1	6
JACKMAN, LOUISA, for relief of estate	2118	48	1	13
Do	3345	49	1	14
JACKSON, ANDREW (colored), for relief	97	43	2	9
JACKSON, JAMES, for relief	566	24	1	3
Do	1050	27	2	5
JACKSON, JOHN,				
For relief of heirs	566	24	1	3
Do	819	30	1	6
For relief	941	46	2	11
Do	108	47	1	12
JACKSON, SAMUEL, for relief	624	24	1	3
JACKSON, WILLIAM, for relief of heirs	620	25	2	4
JACKSON, WILLIAM W., for relief	939	46	2	11
Do	1773	47	1	12
JACOBS, BENJAMIN, for relief of estate	157	23	1	3
JACOBS, JOHN J., for relief	29	22	1	2
JAMES, ANNA P., for relief	1372	46	2	11
JAMES, DUNCAN, for relief	1065	46	2	11
JAMESON, LUCIE A.,				
For relief	442	45	2	10
Do	413	46	2	11
Referring claim to Court of Claims	2643	48	2	13
JAQUETT, PETER, for relief	80	22	2	2
Do	262	23	1	3
JARRATT, GREGORY, for relief of estate	986	49	1	14
JARRATT, SALLIE, for relief of estate	1831	48	1	13
JEFFREY, ROSA VERTNER, for relief of estate	754	43	1	8
Do	215	45	2	10
Do	441	45	2	10
Do	1608	46	2	11
Do	1425	48	1	13
JEFFRIES, EVAN S., for relief	813	43	1	8
JEMISON, LUCIE A., for relief	685	44	1	10
JENKINS, JAMES C.,				
Referring claim to Court of Claims	2643	48	2	13
For relief	2182	49	1	14
JENNINGS, JOHN, for relief of heirs	852	24	1	3
Do	242	27	3	5
JENNINGS, W. S., for relief	240	46	2	11
Do	904	47	1	12
Do	164	48	1	13
JETT, THOMAS, for relief of heirs	360	25	2	4
Do	330	26	1	5
Do	1062	27	2	5
Do	241	27	3	5
Do	508	30	1	6
Do	7	31	1	6
JEWETT, JOSEPH, for relief of heirs	39	36	1	7
JOHN F. CARR (steamboat), for relief of owners	1489	46	2	11
JOHNSON, H., *et al.*, for relief	761	42	1	8
JOHNSON, HIRAM, *et al.*, for relief	214	45	2	10
Do	1345	46	2	11
Do	564	47	1	12
Do	75	48	1	13
Do	†3038	49	1	14
JOHNSON, JERUSHA, for relief	109	36	1	7
Do	5	37	2	7
JOHNSON, JOSHUA, for relief	1034	47	1	12
JOHNSON, THOMAS, for relief of heirs	331	25	2	4
Do	656	24	1	3
JOHNSTON, CRAWFORD, for relief	114	25	2	4
JOHNSTON, ELIZABETH M., for relief	2657	48	2	13
JOHNSTON, LEWIS, referring claim to Court of Claims	2643	48	2	13
JOHNSTON, PHILIP, for relief of heirs	454	35	1	7
Do	20	38	2	7
JOHNSTON, ROBERT, for relief of estate	63	20	1	2
JOHNSTON, WILLIAM,				
For relief	2	17	2	1
For relief of heirs	410	25	2	4

* Parts 1 and 2. † Minority report, Part 2.

Subject.	Report.	Congress.	Session.	Volume.
JOHONNOT, WILLIAM, for relief of heirs	214	22	1	2
Do	239	24	1	3
Do	117	25	2	4
Do	410	25	2	4
JONES, ELIZABETH, for relief	28	25	3	4
JONES, FURNEY, for relief	810	43	1	8
JONES, JAMES W., for relief of widow	4	43	2	9
JONES, JESSE M., for relief	1067	49	1	14
JONES, JOHN H., for relief	1564	49	1	14
JONES, JOHN L. T., for relief	502	43	1	8
JONES, LUCY A. M., referring claim to Court of Claims	2643	48	2	13
JONES, MARTHA, for relief	409	24	1	3
Do	430	25	2	4
Do	17	25	3	4
JONES, PAUL, for relief of heirs	1058	27	2	5
JONES, PHILLIP S., for relief	230	46	2	11
Do	41	48	1	13
JONES, RICHARD, for relief of heirs	494	36	1	7
JONES, SAMUEL, for relief of heirs	796	24	1	3
Do	125	25	2	4
Do	15	25	3	4
Do	618	26	1	5
Do	1092	27	2	5
Do	240	27	3	5
Do	329	30	1	6
Do	112	34	1	6
Do	121	35	1	7
Do	108	36	1	7
JONES, STROTHER, for relief of heirs	385	27	2	5
JONES, T. J., for relief	1248	48	1	13
JONES, THOMAS, referring claim to Court of Claims	2643	48	2	13
JONES, WOOD, for relief of heirs	386	27	2	5
JORDAN, JOHN, for relief of estate	536	24	1	3
Do	123	25	2	4
JORDAN, MARTHA, for relief	583	24	1	3
JORDAN, MARTHA A., for relief	1374	46	2	11
JOSEPHS, ALEXANDER, for relief	1346	46	2	11
JUDGMENTS, relative to liquidating any that have been or may be obtained against the State of Virginia	904	25	2	4
JUDSON FEMALE COLLEGE, for relief	2476	49	1	14
JULIAN, JOHN, for relief of heirs	537	27	2	5
KANE, JOHN, for relief	1877	47	2	12
KARPE, A., for relief	1247	46	2	11
KAUFMAN, JACOB, for relief	256	43	2	9
KEARNEY, WILLIAM R.,				
For relief	412	46	2	11
Referring claim, to Court Claims	2643	48	2	13
KEEDY, JOHN D., referring claim to Court of Claims	2643	48	2	13
KEEL, EZEKIEL T., for relief	408	46	2	11
KEEL, GEORGE, referring claim to Court of Claims	2643	48	2	13
KEENE, ALDERSON T., for relief	212	45	2	10
Do	1048	46	2	11
KEENE, SAMUEL V., for relief of heirs	798	24	1	3
KEENE, SAMUEL J.,				
Claim for relief	259	24	2	3
For relief of heirs	887	25	2	4
KELLEY, THOMAS, for relief	1076	27	2	5
KELLY, JOHN, for relief	93	43	2	9
Do	4021	49	2	14
KELLY, JOHN H., for relief	39	27	2	5
KELLY, WILLIAM, for relief of heir	595	26	1	5
Do	39	27	2	5
KENDALL, WILLIAM, for relief of estate	170	49	1	14
KENDRICK, JOHN S., for relief	336	49	1	14
KENNEDY, MILTON, for relief	932	46	2	11
KENNEDY, SAMUEL, for relief of heirs	351	21	1	2
Do	48	22	1	2
Do	56	22	2	2
Do	507	24	1	3
Do	387	27	2	5
KENNERLY, FLORIDA, for relief	1834	49	1	14
KENOFSKY, MARTIN, for relief of heirs	3130	49	1	14
KENT, HORACE L., referring claim to Court of Claims	2643	48	2	13
KENTUCKY,				
Baptist Church at Somerset, for relief of	1008	46	2	11
To indemnify, for expenses incurred in defense of United States	422	46	2	11
KERR, WILLIAM F., for relief	38	43	1	8
KEY, GEORGE L., for relief	1362	47	1	12
KILBURN, FRANCIS, for relief	1768	47	1	12
Do	659	48	1	13

Subject.	Report.	Congress.	Session.	Volume.
KILLENBERGER, FRANCIS, for relief	891	25	2	4
Do	104	25	3	4
KILLENGER, WILLIAM, for relief	450	45	2	10
KIMBALL, BENJAMIN, for relief	397	24	1	3
KING, HENRY, for relief of heirs	1023	25	2	4
Do	198	27	2	5
Do	319	28	1	6
Do	276	35	1	7
KING, JACOB B., for relief	914	48	1	13
KING, JOHN H., referring claim to Court of Claims	2643	48	2	13
KING, JOSIAH, for relief of heir	862	27	2	5
KING, MARGARET, for relief	583	24	1	3
KING, MILES,				
For relief	826	24	1	3
For relief of heirs	98	24	2	3
KINGSBURY, BYRON (administrator), for relief	168	29	1	6
KINNEY, J. F., for relief	731	47	1	12
KIRK, RICHARD S., referring claim to Court of Claims	2643	48	2	13
KIRK, SARAH, for relief	160	24	1	3
KIRTLEY, BELFORD H., for relief	1378	46	2	11
KITCHEN, JAMES B. and RICHARD, for relief	938	46	2	11
KLEIM, DAVID, for relief	318	43	1	8
KLOR, FREDERICK, for relief	983	49	1	14
KNIGHT, JONATHAN, for relief of heirs	617	24	1	3
KNODE, LOUISA A., referring claim to Court of Claims	2643	48	2	13
KNODE, WILLIAM H., referring claim to Court of Claims	2643	48	2	13
KNOWLES, LUCY, for relief	975	25	2	4
KNOWLTON, THOMAS, for relief of heirs	238	24	1	3
Do	130	25	2	4
Do	50	25	3	4
Do	118	26	2	5
Do	1078	27	2	5
Do	365	29	1	6
KNOX, JAMES H., for relief	995	46	2	11
KNOX, SILAS, for relief	233	46	2	11
KOUNS, JOHN, for relief	3348	49	1	14
KREIS, MICHAEL, for relief	1025	48	1	13
KYLER, A. A., referring claim to Court of Claims	2643	48	2	13
LA BONTE, JOHN BABTIST, for relief of heirs	34	36	1	7
LACHANCE, NICHOLAS, for relief of heirs	179	31	1	6
LACHMAN, HENRY, for relief	57	45	3	10
LACHMAN, MARTHA ALLEN, for relief	930	46	2	11
Do	729	47	1	12
LACY, MOSES, for relief	466	48	1	13
LA GRANGE SYNODICAL COLLEGE IN TENNESSEE, for relief	376	47	1	12
Do	922	48	1	13
Do	3340	49	1	14
LAKIN, BENJAMIN D., for relief	21	48	1	13
LAMB, JOHN M., for relief	326	43	1	8
LAMB, SETH, for relief of heirs	57	43	1	8
LAMKIN, GEORGE W. F., referring claim to Court of Claims	2643	48	2	13
LAMME, NATHAN, for relief	582	24	1	3
Do	313	25	2	4
Do	4	25	3	4
Do	389	26	1	5
LANCASTER, SAMUEL W., for relief	1070	46	2	11
LANDERMAN, CATHERINE, for relief	58	18	1	1
LANDS, bounty lands, relative to issuing warrants for	361	25	2	4
Do	18	25	3	4
LANGBOURNE, WILLIAM, for relief of heirs	400	24	1	3
Do	430	25	2	4
Do	17	25	3	4
Do	241	26	1	5
Do	338	27	2	5
LANIER, ABNER W., referring claim to Court of Claims	*2643	48	2	13
LANIER, JOHN H., Jr. (administrator), referring claim to Court of Claims	2643	48	2	13
LARKIN, BENJAMIN D., for relief	675	47	1	12
LATHROP, ERASTUS, for relief	1246	48	1	13
LAUGHLIN, ROBERT, for relief of heirs	467	30	1	6
LAURENS, EDWARDS R. (administrator), for relief	946	25	2	4
LAURENS, JOHN, for relief of heirs	257	21	1	2
Do	366	22	1	2
Do	134	23	2	3
LAVERY, WILLIAM, for relief	898	47	1	12
Do	*2788	49	1	14
LAWRENCE, GEORGE W., for relief	3425	49	1	14
LAWRENCE, SAMUEL, for relief	393	24	1	3
Do	133	25	2	4
Do	430	31	1	6

*Part 2.

Subject.	Report.	Congress.	Session.	Volume.
LEA, PRYOR N., for relief	2423	48	2	13
Do	93	49	1	14
LEATHERMAN, LELAND, for relief of estate	415	46	2	11
LE CAZE, JAMES, for relief of estate	107	36	2	7
Do	14	37	2	7
LEDBETTER, JOHN W., referring claim to Court of Claims	*2643	48	2	13
LEDYARD, ISAAC, for relief of heirs	52	22	2	2
LEE, A. GATES, for relief	230	48	1	13
Do	86	49	1	14
LEE, EDMUND J. (administrator), for relief	139	35	1	7
LEE, LUCY ANN and ALLEN G., for relief	1130	49	1	14
Do	1247	48	1	13
LEE, R. H., for relief	1070	49	1	14
LEE, SOLOMON J., for relief	706	25	2	4
Do	40	27	2	5
LEE, WALTER J., for relief	108	43	2	9
LEEBRICK, ELIZABETH, for relief	622	49	1	14
LEES, RAMSAY ROBB, referring claim to Court of Claims	2643	48	2	13
LEFFERTS, ESTHER, for relief	543	27		5
LEIGHTON, YANCY, for relief of heirs	306	25		4
LEITCH, ANDREW, for relief of heir	532	27		5
LELAND, EMILY, for relief	245	46		11
LEPAGE, EMILLE, for relief	316	43		8
LEVACHER DE VAN BRUN, JOHN, for relief of widow	302	24		3
Do	1030	25		4
LEVANWORTH, NATHAN, for relief of heirs	389	27		5
LEVERETT, ANNIE D., for relief	3002	49		14
LEVERIDGE, JOHN A., for relief	538	47	1	13
LEVY, CHERRIE M., for relief	[illegible]	48	2	9
LEWIS, ABNER D.,				
For relief	1031	46	2	11
Do	171	48	1	13
Referring claim to Court of Claims	2643	48	2	13
LEWIS, CHARLES, for relief of heirs	603	26	1	5
Do	201	27	2	5
LEWIS, HUGH, for relief of estate	1073	46	2	11
LEWIS, JOHN E., for relief	92	48	1	13
LEWIS, WILLIAM,				
For relief of widow	243	27	3	5
For relief of heirs	940	25	2	4
Do	37	27	2	5
Do	775	27	2	5
LEXINGTON, MO., Baptist Female College at	3125	49	1	14
LIABILITY OF UNITED STATES, property taken, destroyed, damaged, occupied in time of war	262	43	1	8
LIEBURG, E. P., for relief	1000	46	2	11
LIGHTFOOT, PHILIP, for relief of heir	812	24	1	3
Do	274	24	2	3
Do	759	25	2	4
Do	390	27	2	5
Do	110	34	3	6
LINDERMAN, CHARLES, for relief	450	45	2	10
LINDSAY, JAMES, for relief	285	43	2	9
LINES, HENRY F., for relief	398	46	2	11
LINNANE, JAMES, for relief	450	45	2	10
LITLE, CATHARINE, referring claim to Court of Claims	2643	48	2	13
LITLEFIELD, NOAH M., for relief of estate	16	18	1	1
LIVERMORE, FIDUS, for relief	979	49	1	14
Do	4151	49	2	14
LIVINGSTON, ABRAHAM, for relief of heirs	236	26	1	5
Do	249	29	1	6
Do	443	35	1	7
Do	421	36	1	7
LIVINGSTON, HENRY B.				
For relief	51	16	1	1
Do	54	16	1	1
For relief of heirs	237	35	2	7
Do	196	36	1	7
LIVINGSTON, JAMES, for relief of estate	181	28	3	6
LIVINGSTON, RICHARD, for relief	83	19		1
Do	172	21		2
Do	329	22		2
Do	61	23	1	3
LIVINGSTON, RICHARD M. (administrator), for relief	181	28	2	6
LIVINGSTON, ROBERT L., for relief of estate	227	20		2
Do	254	22		2
Do	56	23		3
LIVINGSTON, STEPHEN, for relief	329	22		2

*Part 2.

Subject.	Report.	Congress.	Session.	Volume.
LIVINGSTON, WALTER, for relief of estate	227	20	1	2
Do	93	21	1	2
Do	254	22	1	2
Do	56	23	1	3
LLOYD, FRANCIS (administrator), for relief	532	29	1	6
LOAGUE, JOHN (administrator), for relief	3941	49	2	14
Do	4022	49	2	14
LOCKWOOD, MILLINGTON, for relief of heir	971	25	2	4
LOHMAN, W. L. E., for relief	792	43	1	8
Do	823	44	1	10
LONDON, JOHN A., for relief	2785	49	1	14
LORD, JOHN, for relief	178	21	1	2
LOUISIANA.				
Property to compensate parties for seizure of, by the Government	616	49	1	14
State National Bank of, for relief	4143	49	2	14
Union National Bank of, for relief of	4169	49	2	14
LOVE, HIRAM W., for relief	44	43	2	9
Do	205	46	2	11
LOW, FRANCIS, for relief	1474	46	2	11
LOY, DANIEL S., for relief	1485	47	1	12
Do	2239	48	2	13
Do	981	49	1	14
LOYD, ENOLS, for relief	363	49	1	14
LUCAS, MARY E., referring claims to Court of Claims	2643	48	2	13
LUCAS, WILLIAM, for relief of heirs	1050	46	2	11
LUMM, SOLOMON S., referring claim to Court of Claims	2643	48	2	13
LYNCH, WILLIAM B., for relief	1438	49	1	14
LYON, JEROME, for relief	1952	48	1	13
McADAMS, JOHN, for relief of heirs	421	31	1	6
McALLISTER, A. J., referring claim to Court of Claims	2643	48	2	13
McANULTY, JOSEPH,				
For relief	2186	49	1	14
Referring claim to Court of Claims	2643	48	2	13
McBRIDE, THOMAS, for relief	1030	46	2	11
Do	1919	47	2	12
Do	587	48	1	13
Do	165	49	1	14
McCAULEY, HENRY, referring claim to Court of Claims	2643	48	2	13
McCLANAHAN, THOMAS, for relief	25	19	2	1
McCLELLAND, HARRIETT E., referring claim to Court of Claims	2643	48	2	13
McCLELLAND, JOHN H., for relief	410	46	2	11
Do	2643	48	2	13
Do	2198	49	1	14
McCLELLAND, JOHN, for relief of heir	733	25	2	4
McCLINTOCK, JOSEPH B., referring claim to Court of Claims	2643	48	2	13
McCLURE, JOHN P., for relief	1366	47	1	12
McCLUNG, D. W., for relief	96	43	2	9
McCLURG, JOSEPH W., for relief	138	43	2	9
Do	18	44	1	10
Do	829	49	1	14
Do	859	49	1	14
McCOLLAM, JOHN, for relief of heirs	607	26	1	5
McCOLLISTER, LOUISA, referring claim to Court of Claims	2643	48	2	13
McCONNELL, ALEXANDER, for relief	1083	46	2	11
McCONNELL, J. C., for relief	824	44	1	10
McCOOL, WELLS C., for relief	486	49	1	14
McCORD, MOSES S., for relief	2359	48	2	13
McCORMICK, GEORGE, for relief of heirs	740	25	2	4
McCREADY, ROBERT, for relief	682	25	2	4
McCURDY, ARCHIBALD, for relief	748	24	1	3
McCURDY, JOHN, for relief	13	35	1	7
McDAVITT, EDGAR, for relief	444	45	2	10
Do.	416	46	2	11
McDONALD, ANDREW, for relief of heir	614	25	2	4
McDONALD, MICHAEL, for relief of heir	1079	27	2	5
Do	416	31	1	6
McDONALD, ROBERT S., referring claim to Court of Claims	2643	48	2	13
McDOWEL, JOHN, for relief	287	22	1	2
Do	188	24	1	3
Do	197	25	2	4
Do	110	25	3	4
Do	538	27	2	5
Do	284	35	1	7
Referring claim to Court of Claims	2643	48	2	13
McDOWELL, JOHN R. (administrator), for relief	3937	49	2	14
McDOWELL, W. W., for relief of estate	1024	48	1	13
Do.	1898	49	1	14
McDUFF, DANIEL, for relief	22	19	2	1
McFERRIN, SARAH, for relief	2183	49	1	14
McGHEE, JAMES, for relief	919	48	1	13
McGREGOR, MARY E. O., for relief	391	46	2	11

Subject.	Report.	Congress.	Session.	Volume.
McGUIRE, LUCINDA, for relief	291	43	2	9
Do	43	45	3	10
Do	1488	46	2	11
McHANEY, M. C., referring claim to Court of Claims	2643	48	2	13
McHANEY, W. C., for relief	403	46	2	11
McHATTON, JOHN, for relief	38	16	2	1
Do	12	17	1	1
Do	42	17	1	1
McHATTON (or McIlhatton) (administrator), for relief	826	25	2	4
McINTYRE, WILLIAM J., for relief	317	43	1	8
McKAY, NATHAN (executor),				
For relief	1951	48	1	13
Do	3039	49	1	14
Referring claim to Court of Claims	2643	48	2	13
McKENNA, SAMUEL, for relief	1042	46	2	11
McKINLEY, JOHN, for relief	1064	27	2	5
McKINNEY, CHARLES J., for relief	56	43	1	8
McKINNEY, MARY A., for relief	1076	46	2	11
McKINNEY, MARY E., referring claim to Court of Claims	2643	48	2	13
McKINNIE, JAMES R. (administrator), referring claim to Court of Claims	*2643	48	2	13
McKINNIE, JOHN R. (administrator), for relief	3985	49	2	14
McKNIGHT, CHARLES, for relief of estate	119	23	2	3
McKNIGHT, JOSEPH, for relief	942	27	2	5
McLACHLIN, COLIN, for relief	194	21	1	2
McLAUGHLIN, AMMON, for relief	3347	49	1	14
McLAUGHLIN, JOHN, for relief	806	43	1	8
McLEAN, CHARLES D., for relief	399	46	2	11
McLEMORE, SARAH, referring claim to Court of Claims	2643	48	2	13
McMAHONE, DANIEL, for relief of heir	972	27	2	5
McMAHON, JOHN, for relief	450	45	2	10
McMILLIN, ANDREW F., for relief of heirs	87	49	1	14
McMILLAN, WILLIAM, for relief	441	26	1	5
McMINNVILLE AND MANCHESTER RAILROAD, claim for relief	304	49	1	14
McMURTRIE, ALFRED, for relief	1840	48	1	13
Do	164	49	1	14
McNAUGHTON, JOHN, for relief	9:	49	1	14
McNEAL, E. P., for relief	443	45	2	10
Do	1067	46	2	11
Do	45	48	1	13
Do	183	49	1	14
McNEIL, DANIEL, for relief of heirs	309	22	1	2
Do	240	26	1	5
McPHAIL, JAMES L., *et al.*, for relief	325	43	1	8
Do	742	43	1	8
McREA, JAMES M., for relief	224	46	2	11
MACK, RICHARD, for relief	610	26	1	5
MACKLIN, SALLIE H., referring claim to Court of Claims	*2643	48	2	13
MACOMB, WILLIAM, for relief of estate	44	16	2	1
MACOMBER, CHARLES W., for relief	247	27	3	5
MADDOX, JOSEPH H., for relief	790	43	1	8
Do	39	45	3	10
Do	209	46	2	11
Do	3137	49	1	14
MADISON FEMALE ACADEMY,				
For relief	983	46	2	11
Do	296	47	1	12
Referring claim to Court of Claims	2643	48	2	13
MADISON, WILLIAM, for relief	728	28	2	4
MAGRUDER, ELIZABETH, for relief	101	21	2	2
Do	97	22	1	2
MAHON, ELIZA JANE, for relief	316	48	1	13
MAHONY, JOHN, for relief	420	46	2	11
MAIN, J. H. T., referring claim to Court of Claims	2643	48	2	13
MALONE, FRANCIS, for relief	615	26	1	5
MALONE, JOHN, for relief of estate	653	24	1	3
MALONE, RICHARD (administrator), for relief	652	24	1	3
MANCHESTER AND McMINNVILLE RAILROAD, for relief	304	49	1	14
MANDEVILLE, JOHN, for relief of estate	470	25	3	4
Do	1070	27	2	5
Do	675	30	1	6
Do	452	35	1	7
Do	558	36	1	7
MANN, JOEL, referring claim to Court of Claims	2643	48	2	13
MANSON, W. T., referring claim to Court of Claims	2643	48	2	13
MARAT, LOUIS, referring claim to Court of Claims	2643	48	2	13
MARCH, PETER, *et al.*, for relief	1730	47	1	12
MARCINKOWSKI, FELIX, for pay as surgeon	3106	49	1	14
MARCK, PETER, *et al.*, for relief	1613	49	1	14
MARIETTA, GA., PRESBYTERIAN CHURCH AT, for relief of trustees	488	48	1	13

* Part 2.

Subject.	Report.	Congress.	Session.	Volume.
MARION COUNTY, TENNESSEE, citizens of, for relief	1257	47	1	12
Do	[illegible]	48	1	13
MARKS, JOHN, for relief of heirs	475	34	1	3
Do	182	35	2	4
Do	774	27	2	5
MARNAY, LOUIS, for relief of heir	444	36	1	7
Do	80	36	1	7
MARSHALL, FRANCES, for relief	2046	49	1	14
MARTIN, FRANCIS, for relief of heirs	240	35	2	7
MARTIN, BETTY, for relief	261	49	1	14
MARTIN, HUDSON, for relief of heirs	391	27	3	5
MARTIN, JOHN W., for relief	810	46	1	12
MARTIN, STERLING A., for relief	308	43	2	9
MARYVILLE, TENN., for relief of college at	791	43	1	8
Do	1807	46	2	11
MASHER, JOHN	106	36	1	7
MASON, DAVID, for relief of heirs	626	34	1	3
MASSACRE WYOMING, to compensate the survivors and their descendants in	1082	25	2	4
MASSIE, THOMAS, for relief	636	34	1	3
MATHEWS, MOSES, for relief of heirs	679	30	1	6
Do	58	31	1	6
MATHEWS, WILLIAM, referring claim to Court of Claims	2643	48	2	13
MAY, JAMES, for relief	44	16	2	1
MAY, SAMUEL,				
For relief	186	48	1	13
Referring claim to Court of Claims	2643	48	2	13
MAY, WILLIAM J., referring claim to Court of Claims	2643	48	2	13
MAYES, RICHARD, for relief	1781	47	1	12
MAYSON, JAMES, for relief	975	27	2	5
MEAD, HORACE D., for relief	1072	46	2	11
MEAD, JOHN, for relief of heirs	81	32	2	6
MEAD, EVERARD, for relief of heirs	508	22	1	3
Do	64	23	1	3
Do	406	23	2	4
Do	930	25	2	4
Do	382	27	2	5
Do	806	33	1	6
MEADOWS, ANDREW C., for relief	1254	46	2	11
MEEHON, ANN M., for relief	239	46	2	11
MEMPHIS, TENN., compensation to, for occupancy of land as navy-yard	1250	46	2	11
Do	1850	47	2	12
Do	17	48	1	13
MENARD, PIERRE, for relief	519	26	1	5
Do	29	27	2	5
MENDENHALL, FRANCIS M.,				
For relief	400	46	2	11
Referring claim to Court of Claims	2643	46	2	13
MENDENHALL, SARAH E., for relief	2184	49	1	14
MEREDITH, WILLIAM, for relief of heir	245	27	3	5
MERIAM, GEORGE H., for relief of heirs	1496	47	1	12
MERRILL, AYRES P., for relief of heirs	657	48	1	13
MERRILL, K. C. B. (executrix), for relief	1627	49	1	14
MERRITT, STEPHEN, for relief of heirs	445	26	1	5
MERRITT, TURNER, for relief	286	43	2	9
MESSINGALE, JANE P., for relief	1360	47	1	12
MICHAUX, JOSEPH, for relief of heirs	176	26	2	5
Do	393	27	2	5
Do	244	27	3	5
MICKLE, HARMON, for relief	2195	49	1	14
MIDDLEKAUFF, JOSEPH M., referring claim to Court of Claims	2643	48	2	13
MIDDLEKAUFF, LEVI (administrator), referring claim to Court of Claims	2643	48	2	13
MIDDLETON, RICHARD, for relief	1188	47	1	12
Do	663	48	1	13
Do	566	49	1	14
MIDDLETON, THEODORE, for relief	579	25	2	4
Do	1011	25	2	4
Do	613	26	1	5
MIFFLETON, GEORGE W., for relief	1047	46	2	11
MIGNAULT, BASIL, for relief of heirs	32	36	1	7
MILITIA, to amend law relative to proof to establish claim to pensions	64	14	1	1
MILLARD, BENJAMIN F., for relief	73	46	1	13
MILLER, EMILY, for relief	770	43	1	8
MILLER, HENRY, for relief of heirs	300	34	1	6
MILLER, JAMES, for relief	68	45	3	10
Do	952	46	2	11
MILLER, RALPH P., for relief	1254	47	1	12
Do	87	48	1	13
MILLER, SAMUEL, for relief of heirs	163	35	1	7
Do	28	36	1	7
MILLIKEN, CYNTHIA, referring claim to Court of Claims	2643	48	2	13
MILLING, HUGH, for relief of heirs	735	26	2	4

Subject.	Report.	Congress.	Session.	Volume.
MILLINGER, JAMES, for relief	1691	47	1	
Do	583	48	1	
Do	90	49	1	
Do	2675	49	1	
MILLS, DANIEL, for relief	274	27	2	
MILLS, JOHN, for relief	741	43	1	
MINOR, REBECCA A., referring claim to Court of Claims	2643	48	2	
MINOR, THOMAS, for relief	503	22	1	
Do	33	23	1	
MISSIONS, FOREIGN, AMERICAN BOARD OF, claim for relief	2612	49	1	
MISSOURI, DADE COUNTY, for relief	15	48	1	
MISSOURI, vouchers filed in Treasury Department, examination of	2490	48	2	
Do	3133	49	1	
MITCHELL, JOHN H.,				
Referring claim to Court of Claims	2643	48	2	
For relief	4024	49	2	
MITCHELL, SOPHIA G.,				
For relief	316	48	1	1
Referring claim to Court of Claims	2643	48	2	1
MITCHELL, THOMAS, referring claim to Court of Claims	2643	48	2	1
MITCHELL, WARREN, for relief	424	46	2	1
Do	529	47	1	1
Do	408	49	2	1
MOBILE AND GIRARD RAILROAD, for relief	1563	49	1	1
MOBILE MARINE DRY-DOCK COMPANY, for relief	*1822	47	1	1
MOER, SAMUEL H., for relief	755	49	1	1
MOFFETT, JOHN, for relief	65	19	2	
Do	121	20	2	
Do	91	21	1	
MOFFITT, ALEXANDER, for relief	2843	49	1	1
MOFFITT, JAMES, for relief	247	46	2	1
MOLITOR, FRANCIS, for relief	402	46	2	1
MOLLY, ELLEN P., for relief	1059	46	2	1
Do	2037	49	1	1
MONROW, BARNEY, for relief of heir	452	24	1	
MONTANYE, BENJAMIN, for relief of heir	4	37	2	
MONTGOMERY, ALEXANDER, for relief	1073	49	1	1
MONTGOMERY, HUGH, for relief of heir	445	35	1	
MONTGOMERY, JOHN, for relief	2177	49	1	1
MONTGOMERY, PEARSON C., to compensate for use of steamboat	1100	48	1	1
MONTGOMERY, ROBERT H., for relief	514	43	1	
Do	246	45	2	1
Do	208	46	2	1
Do	3334	49	1	1
MONTY, AMABLE, for relief of heir	504	25	2	
MONTY, JOHN, for relief	340	36	1	
MONUMENTS,				
Herkimer, General, to erect, in memory of	695	29	1	
Prison ships (English), to erect, over remains of those who died in	1026	27	2	
Warren, General Joseph, to erect, in memory of	167	29	1	
MOON, JACOB, for relief of heir	85	24	2	
MOORE, ELIAS B., for relief	247	46	2	
Do	1249	48	1	
Do	667	49	1	
MOORE, EVA, *et al.*, for relief	926	48	1	
MOORE, FRANCES, for relief	15	21	2	
MOORE, JAMES, for relief	911	25	2	
MOORE, JAMES G.,				
Referring claims to Court of Claims	2643	48	2	
For relief	2196	49	1	
MOORE, JOHN, for relief of heirs	583	24	1	
MOORE, LAWSON, for relief	920	48	1	
MOORE, PETER, for relief of heirs	539	27	2	
MOORE, SOPHIA B., for relief	723	48	1	
MOORE, THOMAS A., for relief	242	46	2	
MOORE, WILLIAM F., for relief	52	46	2	
MORAN, EDMUND, for relief of heirs	394	27	2	
MOREAU, ANN, for relief	3940	49	2	
MORELL, JAMES, for relief of heir	661	27	2	
MORFIT, HENRY, for relief of heirs	521	25	2	
MORGAN, ELIZABETH, for relief	160	19	1	
MORGAN, WILLIS J., for relief	967	46	2	
MORGAN, ZAQUILLE, for relief of widow and heirs	81	14	1	
MORHISER, WILLIAM H., for relief	620	49	1	
MORRIS, CLARA, for relief	767	43	1	
MORRIS, ELIZABETH P., for relief	661	27	2	
MORRIS, GEORGE W.,				
Referring claim to Court of Claims	†2643	48	2	
For relief	3190	49	2	

* Parts 1, 2. † Part 2.

Subject.	Report.	Congress.	Session.	Volume.
IS, RICHARD G., for relief	27	17	1	1
Do	20	17	2	1
Do	16	18	1	1
IS, THOMAS, for relief of heirs	67	32	2	6
IS, WILLIAM S., for relief	73	45	2	10
ISON, JOHN A., for relief	1497	46	2	11
ISS, RICHARD G., for relief	128	20	1	2
Do	274	21	1	2
ELL, RICHARD T., for relief	796	43	1	8
ER, JOHN, for relief of heirs	209	35	2	7
IER, JOHN, for relief of heirs	106	36	1	7
Y CREEK, TENN., BAPTIST CHURCH, for relief of trustees	1384	46	2	11
Y CREEK, TENN., COLLEGE, for relief of trustees	1385	46	2	11
, THOMAS, for relief of heirs	346	27	2	5
T, ADAM D., for relief	665	27	2	5
T OLIVET CEMETERY, DISTRICT OF COLUMBIA, for relief of	1371	46	2	11
Do	298	47	1	12
T SAVAGE, MD., IRON COMPANY, for relief of trustees	1708	47	1	12
T VERNON MANUFACTURING COMPANY, OF ALEXANDRIA, VA., for relief	740	43	1	8
TJOY, JOHN, for relief of heirs	770	30	1	6
Do	53	37	2	7
TJOY, WILLIAM, for relief of heirs	646	24	1	3
R, JOSEPH D., for relief	509	43	1	8
AN, STEPHEN, for relief of heirs	457	24	1	3
Do	330	33	1	6
LER, ADOLPH, for relief	225	46	2	11
ORD, JAMES, for relief of heirs	77	34	2	6
OLLAND, MICHAEL, for relief	431	42	1	8
Do	1006	46	2	11
EN, HENRY, for relief	1856	47	1	12
Do	387	46	1	12
EHILL, ELIZABETH, for relief	2179	49	1	14
MA, HENRY C. and SAMUEL (executors), referring claim to Court of Claims	2642	48	2	13
DAY, JOHN, referring claim to Court of Claims	2642	48	2	13
HESON, JOHN, for relief	1075	27	2	5
OCK, WILLIAM D. C., for relief	921	47	1	12
REE, FANNY PRISCILLA, for relief	1873	46	2	11
HY, CHARLES, for relief of estate	1820	49	1	14
HY, DENNIS, for relief of heirs	3396	49	1	14
AY, ELIZABETH, for relief of estate	343	31	1	6
AY, FRANCIS M., for relief of heirs	3350	49	1	14
AY, JAMES, for relief of heirs	170	26	2	5
Do	520	27	2	5
AY, JOSIAH, for relief of estate	343	31	1	6
AY, LACKIE, for relief of estate	343	31	1	6
ELL, HARRIET F., for relief	1498	47	1	12
S, H. A., for relief	830	49	1	14
S, STEPHEN H.,				
for relief	1689	47	1	12
Referring claim to Court of Claims	2643	48	2	13
IS, VICTOR, for relief	39	43	1	8
CK, R. M., for relief	1039	46	2	11
EY, SAMUEL M., for relief	1301	49	1	14
E, WILLIAM L., for relief	89	43	2	9
, JOSEPH C., for relief	745	43	1	8
Do	942	46	2	11
Do	3045	49	1	14
VILLE, TENN., for relief of Mount Olivet Cemetery at	1371	46	2	11
Do	298	47	1	12
N, RICHARD, for relief	735	25	2	4
HEZ, MISS., for relief of trustees of orphan asylum at	711	44	1	10
Do	1903	47	2	12
Do	756	49	1	14
L CONTRACTOR. (*See* CONTRACTORS.)				
THOMAS G., for relief	1060	46	2	11
E, JOHN T., for relief	451	45	2	10
Y, HESTER, for relief	1375	46	2	11
N, ELISHA, referring claim to Court of Claims	2643	48	2	13
N, Mrs. M. A. C., for relief	229	45	2	10
N, WILLIAM, for relief of heirs	603	25	2	4
Do	442	26	1	5
Do	395	27	2	5
Do	423	31	1	6
Do	282	33	1	6
OMB, JOSEPH W.,				
relief	754	27	2	5
morial to erect monument to General Joseph Warren	167	29	1	6
OMER, JOSHUA, referring claim to Court of Claims	2643	48	2	13
OMER, SOLOMON, referring claim to Court of Claims	2643	48	2	13

Subject.	Report.	Congress.
NEW JERSEY, for relief of First Presbyterian Church of Elizabethtown	259	27
NEWLIN, HELEN A., for relief	2016	47
NEWMAN, JAMES C.,		
Referring claim to Court of Claims	2643	48
For relief	2188	49
NEWMAN, WILLIAM H., for relief	748	43
Do	551	44
Do	8	45
NEW MEXICO, to authorize Secretary of War to ascertain and report amount expended in organizing and maintaining militia force during war of rebellion by Territory of	333	43
NEWTON, LYTLE, for relief	409	46
NEW YORK (State),		
Arms, to refund duties paid by State on imported	1297	49
Canada frontier, expenditures by State in 1864 for defense of	925	48
Import duties, to refund to State for arms imported	1297	49
Yorktown Church, for relief	202	27
NICHOLS, FRANK H., for relief	1026	48
NILES, THOMAS, for relief	435	43
NIMITZ, ADOLPH (trustee), for relief	949	46
NOBLE, DAVID, for relief	49	26
Do	278	27
Do	101	33
Do	285	35
Do	251	36
NODINE, PETER, for relief	435	44
Do	314	48
NOEL, RICHARD, for relief of heirs	1027	27
NOLAN, PETER, for relief of heirs	628	49
NOLEN, JOHN, for relief	700	43
NOLEN, Z. C., for relief	398	46
Do	1726	47
Do	25	48
NOONAN, MARY H., for relief	42	43
NORRIS, O. P., for relief	825	44
NORTHEDGE, WILLIAM, for relief	156	43
NORTHUP, HENRY, for relief	412	25
NORTON, GEORGE A., for relief	1822	49
NORTON, SARAH E., for relief	401	46
Do	980	47
Do	34	48
NOYES, KIRK W., for relief	1186	47
NOYES, MOSES, claim for relief	52	16
NOYES, WADLEIGH, for relief of heirs	52	16
Do	634	24
Do	192	25
Do	22	30
Do	111	34
NURSES, to provide for payment of female	1940	49
NUTT, JULIA, for relief	167	44
Do	710	45
Do	251	46
Do	1259	47
Do	2010	47
OATES, JOHN T., for relief	957	46
O'BANNON, ANDREW, for relief of widow	173	24
Do	973	25
O'BRIEN, WILLIAM, for relief	633	44
ODD FELLOWS' LODGE, PULASKI, TENN., for relief	54	46
Do	2734	49
ODENDORFF, CHRISTIAN, for relief	422	31
ODEND'HAL, JEAN, for relief	660	48
OGLESBY, ROSCOE C., for relief	1081	46
OLDHAM, MOSES, for relief of heir	203	27
OLDNER, JOSHUA, for relief	230	35
OLIVER, WILLIAM, for relief of heirs	818	24
Do	277	25
OLNEY, JOSEPH, for relief of heir	784	24
O'NEILL, HENRY, Jr., for relief	1542	48
ORENDORF, CHRISTIAN, for relief of heir	866	27
Do	133	28
Do	422	31
ORSBORNE, JOHN, for relief	980	46
Do	982	47
OSGOOD, EBENEZER, for relief of heir	409	36
OURSLER, JOHN A.,		
For relief	3041	49
Referring claim of heirs to Court of Claims	2643	48
OVERSTREET, JOHN H., for relief of heirs	520	25
Do	396	27
OVERTON HOTEL COMPANY, referring claim to Court of Claims	2643	48

* Part 2.

Subject.	Report.	Congress.	Session.	Volume.
PENSIONS—Continued.				
Revolutionary war, making provision for final settlement of half-pay allowance for services in	125	35	1	7
Do	250	36	1	7
War of 1812, to increase, for service in	64	14	1	1
PERINE, SARAH E. E., for relief	3044	49	1	14
Do	3131	49	1	14
PERKINS, NEWTON C.,				
For relief	2189	49	1	14
Referring claim to Court of Claims	2643	48	2	13
PERKINS, THOMAS F. (administrator), for relief	1079	46	2	11
Do	2643	48	2	13
Do	3042	49	1	14
PERROW, CHARLES (administrator), for relief	42	22	2	
Do	116	23	1	
PERRY, ANNA, for relief	1251	46	2	11
PETERSON, JOHN, for relief	684	25	2	4
PETTUS, SAMUEL G., for relief of heir	20	25	3	4
PETTUS, SAMUEL O., for relief of heir	208	25	2	4
PHILIPS, W. C., for relief	1161	49	1	14
PHILLIPS, WILLIAM, for relief	312	43	2	9
PHILO PARSONS (steamer), for relief of owners of	146	43	2	9
PIATT, MARTHA, for relief	535	27	2	5
PIATT, WILLIAM, for relief of heirs	695	25	2	4
PICKARD, JOHN, for relief	206	24	1	3
PICKERELL & BROOKS, for relief	728	44	1	10
PIERCE, STEPHEN, for relief of widow	633	27	2	5
PIGGOTT, ISAAC N., for relief	970	25	2	4
PIKE, WILLIAM, for relief	2115	48	1	13
Do	564	49	1	14
PILLOW, GIDEON J., for relief	677	43	1	8
PINCKNEY, SUSANNAH HAYNE, for relief	468	25	2	4
PINKHAM, CALVIN, for relief	473	22	1	2
PIPER JOHN, for relief	27	27	2	5
PITZER, THOMAS J., for relief	1625	49	1	14
PLACY, JOSEPH, for relief	519	26	1	5
Do	20	27	2	5
PLANCHE, T. B., referring claim to Court of Claims	2643	48	2	13
PLANT, THOMAS, for relief	253	43	2	9
PLANTER (steamer), for relief of pilot and crew of	3595	49	2	14
PLEASANTS, MARY R. J., for relief	816	24	1	3
PLOWDEN, WALTER D., for relief	206	46	2	11
PLUMMER, FRANCES H., for relief	1015	45	2	10
Do	1495	47	1	12
Do	1312	48	1	13
Do	619	49	1	14
POINTER, SAMUEL, for relief	978	46	2	11
POITEVENT, WILLIAM J., claim for property seized by authority of United States Government at Gainesville, Miss., 1863	3530	49	2	14
POLAND, MARGARET, for relief	2761	49	1	14
POLERECZKY, JOHN S., for relief	59	16	1	1
POLEVESKY, JOHN L., for relief of heirs	96	36	2	7
POLHEMUS, JOHN, for relief	275	22	1	2
Do	80	23	1	3
POLLARD ROBERT (administrator), for relief	175	24	1	3
POLLOCK, OLIVER, for relief	50	15	2	1
POMEROY, GROVE, for relief of heirs	126	23	1	3
PORCH, EMMA A., for relief	432	43	1	8
Do	687	44	1	10
Do	207	45	2	10
PORTER, BENJAMIN J., for relief	259	24	2	3
Do	165	28	2	6
PORTER, ISAAC, for relief	942	27	2	5
Do	186	30	1	6
PORTER, MARY H., for relief	1859	47	1	12
PORTER, MARY S., for relief	537	47	1	12
PORTER, NIMROD, for relief	1638	47	1	12
PORTER, WILLIAM, for relief	1891	49	1	14
PORTERFIELD, CHARLES, for relief of legal representatives	23	36	1	7
PORTLOCK, MAHALA H., for relief	2191	49	1	14
POTTER, ELIZA, for relief	331	43	2	9
POTTER, NELSON, for relief	1068	46	2	11
POTTS, JESSE, for relief	173	24	1	3
Do	275	24	2	3
POTTS, SARAH B. for relief	156	23	1	3
POWEL, ROBERT, for relief of heirs	760	24	1	3
Do	825	24	1	3
POWELL, T. J., administrator, for relief	4023	49	2	14
PRESCOTT, JOSEPH, for relief	251	24	1	3
Do	314	25	2	4
PREWETT, SOLOMON, for relief	26	25	3	4

Subject.	Report.	Congress.	Session.	Volume.
PRICE, ABNER, for relief	827	24	1	3
PRICE, JAMES,				
For relief of heir	867	27	2	5
For relief	190	49	1	14
PRICE, JOHN, for relief of heir	1080	27	2	5
PRIDDY, JAMES M., for relief	90	48	1	13
PRIEST, FRANCIS, for relief	323	43	1	8
PRIMA DONNA (steamer), for relief of employés on	1613	49	1	14
PRINCETON, N. J., for the relief of trustees of Presbyterian church at	277	35	1	7
Do	530	36	1	7
PRIOR, ABNER, for relief of heirs	856	25	2	4
PRISON-SHIPS, relative to removal of remains and erection of monument to those who died in English	1026	27	2	5
PRORERTY,				
Captured and abandoned	262	43	1	8
Classification of, hostile organization	262	43	1	8
Confiscated	262	43	1	8
Destroyed to prevent it falling into enemy's hands, liability of Government for	262	43	1	8
Hostile organizations, belonging to	262	43	1	8
Prize, on seas, capture of	262	43	1	8
PROSISE, THOMAS J., for relief	1415	47	1	12
PROTESTANT EPISCOPAL SEMINARY, VIRGINIA, for relief	2643	48	2	13
Do	4125	49	2	14
PROTESTANT ORPHAN ASYLUM, NATCHEZ, MISS., for relief of trustees of	711	44	1	10
Do	756	49	1	14
PUGH, WILLIAM, for relief of heirs	621	25	2	4
PULASKI, TENN., for relief of Odd Fellows' lodge at	54	46	3	11
Do	2734	49	1	14
PULLIAM, J. J., for relief of estate	1561	49	1	14
PURCELL, DENNIS, for relief	624	26	1	5
Do	799	30	1	6
Do	193	31	1	6
PURCELL, GEORGE, for relief of heirs	248	27	3	5
PURCELL, HENRY D., for relief of heirs	867	25	2	4
PURNELL, MARY E., for relief	789	43	1	8
Do	797	44	1	10
PURRIENCE, CAROLINE M., for relief	251	44	1	10
PURVIANCE & WYETH, for relief	251	44	1	10
PURVIS, JAMES, for relief of estate	298	24	2	3
Do	135	25	2	4
Do	23	25	3	4
Do	88	26	2	5
PUTNAM, ELIZABETH, referring claim to Court of Claims	2643	48	2	13
PUTNAM, LUKE, for relief	410	36	1	7
QUACKENBUSH, C. L., for relief	1383	46	2	11
QUACKENBUSH, SILAS, for relief	2116	48	1	13
Do	563	49	1	14
QUARLES, JAMES, for relief of heirs	75	23	1	3
QUARLES, ROBERT, for relief of widow	639	24	1	3
QUARLES, WHARTON, for relief of estate	175	24	1	3
Do	730	24	1	3
Do	106	25	2	4
RADICH, MARCOS, for relief	1680	47	1	12
Do	162	48	1	13
RAILROADS,				
Manchester and McMinnville Railroad, for relief	304	49	1	14
Mobile and Girard Railroad, for relief	1563	49	1	14
RAINES, GILES, for relief of heirs	1086	27	2	5
RAINS, AMANDA, for relief	573	44	1	10
Do	5	45	2	10
RAMSBURG, JOHN W., for relief	900	47	1	12
RAMSEY, JOHN, for relief	1442	49	1	14
RAMSEY, WILLIAM, for relief of heirs	798	24	1	3
RANDALL, VOLTAIRE, for relief	742	43	1	8
RANSOM, ELI, for relief	822	24	1	3
RANSOM, SAMUEL, for relief of heirs	823	30	1	6
Do	187	31	1	6
RAVENCROFT, THOMAS, for relief	856	24	1	3
RAWLINS, MARY V., referring claim to Court of Claims	2643	48	2	13
RAY, JOHN C., for relief	208	45	2	10
RAY, UONEY, for relief of heir	181	29	1	6
RAYMER, FREDERICK, for relief	46	21	1	2
Do	17	21	2	2
Do	93	22	1	2
Do	104	23	1	3
RAYMOND, W. G., for relief	984	47	1	12
READ, WILLIAM B., for relief	395	46	2	11
READING, WILLIAM, referring claim to Court of Claims	2643	48	2	13
REAMY SON & ARCHBOLD, for relief	4149	49	2	14
REBEL ARMY, for losses sustained by invasion of Pennsylvania by	41	43	2	9

Subject.	Report.	Congress.	Session.	Volume.
REDDICK, WILLIS, for relief of heirs	412	23	1	3
Do	273	24	1	3
Do	119	25	2	4
Do	822	30	1	6
Do	41	31	1	6
Do	108	33	1	6
REDFORD, GEORGE R., for relief	404	46	2	11
REED, JOHN B., referring claim to Court of Claims	2643	48	2	13
REED, JULIA A., referring claim to Court of Claims	2643	48	2	13
REED, PARIS L., for relief	231	43	1	8
REESER, ULRICH, for relief of heirs	104	21	1	2
REEVES, W. C.,				
Referring claim to Court of Claims	2643	48	2	13
For relief	1900	49	1	14
REID, JOHN, for relief	485	48	1	13
REID, JOHN B., for relief	1824	49	1	14
REINHARDT, J. D., *et al.*, for relief	990	46	2	11
REPLOGLE, FREDERICK A., for relief	2020	48	1	13
REVELL, HENNIE E., referring claim to Court of Claims	2643	48	2	13
REVOLUTIONARY CLAIMS. (*See* CLAIMS.)				
REVOLUTIONARY WAR. (*See* WAR OF REVOLUTION.)				
REYNOLDS, BENJAMIN F., for relief	638	44	1	10
REYNOLDS, DAVID, for relief of heirs	225	27	2	5
REYNOLDS, JOHN, for relief	160	24	2	3
REYNOLDS, JOHN R., for relief	4025	49	2	14
REYNOLDS, MARY, for relief	89	20	1	2
RHODES, LEWALLEN, for relief	962	46	2	11
RIBINSON, ELIZABETH, for relief	357	27	2	5
RICE, GEORGE, for relief of heirs	654	24	1	3
Do	908	25	2	4
Do	398	27	2	5
RICE, PHILIP R., for relief	781	27	2	5
Do	107	28	2	6
Do	429	31	1	6
Do	42	33	2	6
RICHARDS, AMELIA A. H., for relief of estate	552	44	1	10
Do	204	45	2	10
RICHARDS, SAMUEL, for relief of estate	80	27	2	5
Do	16	27	3	5
Do	318	28	1	6
RICHARDSON, HANNAH, claim for relief	52	16	2	1
RICHARDSON, HUMPHREY, for relief	438	25	2	4
RICHARDSON, IDA A., *et al.*, for relief	429	43	1	8
Do	496	44	1	10
Do	6	45	2	10
Do	918	48	1	13
Do	163	49	1	14
RICHARDSON, JAMES R., for relief	1489	46	2	11
RICHARDSON, JOSEPH A., for relief	244	48	1	13
RICHARDSON, RALPH (executor), for relief	341	36	1	7
RICHARDSON, WILLIAM R., for relief of heir	617	25	2	4
RICHMOND, KY., for the benefit of the Madison Female Academy at	933	46	2	11
RICKMAN, WILLIAM, for relief of heirs	606	26	1	5
Do	776	27	2	5
Do	281	35	1	7
RIDDICK, NATHANIEL, for relief of estate	211	33	1	6
Do	64	35	1	7
RIDGEWAY, LINDSAY, referring claim to Court of Claims	2643	48	2	13
RIDGEWAY, THOMAS, for relief	396	24		3
RIKER, MARGARET, for relief of widow	139	22		3
RIPLEY, JOHN, for relief of heirs	278	35		7
Do	26	36		7
Do	19	37		7
RIPLEY, MARY A., for relief	1685	47		12
RISLEY, LEMUEL C., for relief	229	43		8
ROBB, WILLIAM N., for relief	831	49		14
ROBBINS, DAVID, for relief	244	46	2	11
ROBERTS, JAMES M., for relief	973	46	2	11
ROBERTS, JOHN, for relief	6	21	1	2
Do	45	22	1	3
Do	640	24	1	3
Do	390	26	1	5
Do	541	27	2	5
Do	871	27	2	5
Do	532	29	1	6
Do	35	36	2	7
ROBERTS, WILLIAM, for relief	856	24	1	3
Do	963	25	2	4
ROBERTSON, JOHN, for relief of heirs	663	27	2	5
ROBERTSON, MITCHELL, for relief	499	22	1	3
ROBINS, JOHN, for relief of heirs	119	23	1	

Subject.	Report.	Congress.	Session.	Volume.
BINSON, FRANCES A., for relief	1823	48	1	13
BINSON, GEORGE M., for relief	32	48	1	13
BINSON, Mrs. J. E., referring claim to Court of Claims	3642	48	2	13
BINSON, JACOB, for relief	961	47	1	12
BINSON, JAMES, for relief	485	42	1	8
BINSON, JOHN, for relief of heirs	121	21	1	2
BINSON, JOHN M., for relief of estate	727	49	1	14
BINSON, JULIA A., for relief	2204	49	1	14
BINSON, MELCHISEDEC, for relief	108	48	1	13
BINSON, ZOPHAR, for relief of heirs	325	25	2	4
CHAMBEAU, MARSHAL, for relief of heirs	307	24	1	3
Do	325	25	2	4
Do	1071	27	2	5
Do	201	29	1	6
DGERS, WILLIAM, for relief of heirs	543	27	2	5
GERS, LIZZIE, for relief	1346	46	2	11
GERS, WILLIAM, for relief of heirs	156	23	1	2
Do	130	24	1	3
Do	287	25	2	4
HR, PHILIP, for relief	865	44	1	10
Do	36	45	2	10
Do	962	47	1	12
MAN CATHOLIC CLERGYMEN OF MARYLAND, for relief of corporation of	338	43	2	9
Do	3048	49	1	14
SAMON, JOHN W., for relief	393	46	2	11
SE, ALEXANDER, for relief of heir	817	24	1	3
SE, ALEXANDER P., for relief	14	48	1	13
Do	3410	49	1	14
SSY, ALEXANDER, for relief of widow and heirs	107	47	1	12
THERMEL, LEWIS, referring claim to Court of Claims	3643	48	2	13
USE, CASPER, for relief of heirs	426	31	1	5
USE, CASPER M., for relief	943	27	2	5
UTZAHN, BENJAMIN, for relief	1768	47	1	12
WE, JOHN, for relief of widow	80	25	3	4
WLAND, J. W. and C., for relief	256	42	2	8
WLETT, JOHN W., for relief	550	47	1	12
XBURG, MATTHEW and ELIZABETH, for relief	29	14	1	1
YER, SAMUEL, for relief of heirs	249	27	3	5
BY, HENRY, for relief	1562	49	1	14
E, ARCHIBALD B., for relief	1609	46	2	11
GGLES, FREDERICK W., for relief	2477	49	1	14
Do	2478	49	1	14
MBAUGH, MARTHA J. A., for relief	1556	49	1	14
MNEY, WILLIAM, for relief of heir	250	27	3	5
SSEL, CORNELIUS, for relief of heirs	532	24	1	3
SSELL, ANDREW, for relief of heirs	278½	35	1	7
Do	493	36	1	7
Do	104	38	1	7
SSELL, CHARLES, for relief of heirs	232	24	1	3
SSELL, ELVEY, for relief	1046	46	2	11
SSELL, JAMES, for relief	897	47	1	12
SSELL, JOHN H., for relief	147	43	2	9
Do	1044	46	2	11
TH, SAMUEL, for relief	792	43	1	8
Do	823	44	1	10
THERFORD, BENJAMIN F., for relief	397	46	2	11
TLEDGE, JOSHUA, for relief	60	16	1	1
TLEDGE, THOMAS, for relief of estate	946	25	2	4
Do	177	26	2	5
AN, J. D., & CO., for relief	1490	47	1	12
AN, MARGARET F., for relief	1554	49	1	14
INT ALBAN'S RAID CLAIMS, to adjudicate	148	43	2	9
Do	104	44	1	10
INT CECILIA ACADEMY, Nashville, Tenn., referring claim to Court of Claims	2643	48	2	13
JOHN, A. F. and N. C., for relief	402	44	1	10
INT LOUIS, MO., for relief of trustees of Christian Brothers' College at	1841	48	1	13
Do	3332	49	1	14
AINT THOMAS' MANOR," for relief of corporation of Roman Catholic Clergymen of Maryland, known as	338	43	2	9
LOMON, HAYM, for relief of heir	504	30	1	6
MMONS, JACOB, for relief of heirs	228	24	2	3
MPSON, CROCKER, for relief of heirs	179	23	1	2
Do	553	24	1	3
Do	134	25	2	4
MPSON, SIMON, for relief of heir	625	36	1	7
Do	3	37	2	7
NDERS, DAVID T., for relief	989	46	2	11
NDERSON, DAVID, for relief	830	24	1	3
TTERLY, ISAAC, for relief	120	24	2	3
Do	231	25	2	4

Subject.	Report.	Congress.	Session.	Volume.
SAULPAW, GEORGE W., for relief	807	47	1	12
Do	724	48	1	13
Do	3134	49	1	14
SAUNDERS CELEY, for relief of heirs	139	24	1	3
SAVAGE JOSEPH, for relief of heirs	855	25	2	4
Do	330	30	1	6
Do	189	31	1	6
Do	147	33	1	6
SAWYER, LUKE, for relief	824	24	1	3
SAWYERS, ETHAN A., for relief	1511	48	1	13
SCAMMON, NICHOLAS (administrator), for relief	310	22	1	2
SCHADEL HENRY A., for relief	3342	49	1	14
SCHAEFNOCKER, CHRISTOPHER, for relief	1834	48	1	13
SCHENCK W. L., for relief	741	43	1	8
SCHIFFER SAMUEL, for relief	243	48	1	13
SCHOEFNOCKER CHRISTOPHER, for relief	307	49	1	14
SCHONMAKER, FREDERICK, for relief of heirs	84	33	2	6
SCHREINER, GEORGE A., for relief	434	43	1	5
SCHUYLKILL COUNTY, PENNSYLVANIA, to adjudicate war claim of	1729	47	1	12
Do	1615	49	1	14
SCOTT, DAVID L., referring claim to Court of Claims	2643	48	2	13
SCOTT, JAMES, *et al.*, for relief	967	46	2	11
Do	158	48	1	13
SCOTT, JOSEPH Jr., for relief of heirs	506	24	1	3
SCOTT, MARY, for relief	798	44	1	10
SCOTT, OBEDIAH, for relief	450	45	2	10
SCOTT, SAMUEL, for relief of widow	121	29	1	6
SCOTT, WILLIAM, for relief of heirs	282	24	1	3
SEALS, LUCIEN J., referring claim to Court of Claims	2643	48	2	13
SEARS JAMES W., for relief of heirs	1486	47	1	12
SEAWRIGHT, NANCY, for relief	958	46	2	11
SEAY JOHN H., for relief	1068	49	1	14
SECRETARY OF TREASURY, for jurisdiction of accounting officers exercised in office of	1099	47	1	12
SECRETARY OF WAR, to authorize, to ascertain amount expended by New Mexico for defense during war of rebellion	333	43	2	9
SEEDS, JAMES M.,				
Claim for secret service	662	48	1	13
Referring claim to Court of Claims	2643	48	2	13
SELLECK, GEORGE F., for relief	45	43	2	9
SEVEN YEARS' HALF-PAY, relative to granting same to widows and heirs of officers who served in the Revolutionary war	362	25	2	4
SEWALL, CLEMENT, for relief of heir	83	33	2	6
SEWARD, ELIZABETH, referring claim to Court of Claims	2643	48	2	13
SEWARD, WILLIAM T., for relief	372	47	1	12
SHACKLETT, HARRIET W., for relief	924	47	1	12
Do	3061	49	1	14
SHADDON ELISHA M., referring claim to Court of Claims	2643	48	2	13
SHAFER, JONATHAN, for relief	866	27	2	5
Do	252	27	3	5
SHAFF, ABRAHAM, referring claim to Court of Claims	2643	48	2	13
SHAFFRAY, WILLIAM, for relief	568	43	1	8
SHAMBLIN, THOMAS L., for relief	903	47	1	12
SHANNON, JOSEPH R., for relief	429	44	1	10
Do	440	45	2	10
Do	1472	46	2	11
Do	238	48	1	13
SHARPE, LINCHFIELD, for relief of heirs	561	24	1	3
SHAW, JOSIAH Q.,				
Referring claim to Court of Claims	2643	48	2	13
For relief	1892	49	1	14
SHEELY, ANN, for relief	1052	46	2	11
SHELL, JOHN for relief	411	25	2	4
SHELTON, CLOUGH, for relief of heir	237	26	1	5
SHEPPARD, REEDER B., for relief	968	46	2	11
SHERRILL, SAMUEL, for relief	1899	49	1	14
SHIELDS, MARY C., for relief	983	47	1	12
Do	33	48	1	13
SHIELDS, MARY L., for relief	956	46	2	11
SHIELDS, MATILDA, for relief	1488	47	1	12
SHINKLE, JOSIAH, for relief	429	47	1	12
Do	1493	47	1	12
Do	485	49	1	14
SHINN, JACOB L., for relief	1003	46	2	11
SHIPPEN, WILLIAM, for relief	546	30	1	6
SHOENFELT, ANDREW, for relief	1329	49	1	14
SHOTWELL, A. L., for relief	55	45	3	10
Do	250	46	3	11
SHROPSHIRE R. H., for relief	1069	49	1	14
SHUBRICK, RICHARD, for relief of heirs	468	25	3	4
Do	160	25	3	4
Do	78	27	2	5

Subject.	Report.	Congress.	Session.	Volume.
SHUBRICK, WILLIAM, for relief of heirs	119	28	2	5
SHUMATE, JAMES H., for relief	1061	46	2	11
SHUMATE, VIRGINIA A., for relief	1481	47	1	12
SHURLEY, BENNETT, for relief of widow	611	25	2	4
SIGHTS, JACOB, for relief	36	19	2	1
SIGNOR, CHARLES B., for relief	624	49	1	14
SIMES, JANE E., for relief	1678	47	2	12
Do	78	48	1	13
SIMMONS, BENJAMIN, for relief	108	20	1	2
SIMMONS, FRANCIS, for relief	889	46	2	11
SIMMONS, JEREMIAH B., for relief	1076	46	2	11
SIMPSON, ELIZABETH J., for relief	1281	46	2	11
SIMS, WILLIAM B., referring claim to Court of Claims	2643	48	2	13
SINGLETON, DAVID, for relief	1632	47	2	12
Do	13	48	1	13
SKILES, JOHN W., for relief	178	44	2	10
Do	210	45	2	10
SKINNER, JONATHAN, for relief of heir	398	35	2	7
Do	126	36	1	7
SLACK, JOHN B., for relief	622	44	1	10
SLAUGHTER, JAMES, for relief	556	24	1	3
SLAUGHTER, PHILIP, for relief	146	20	1	2
Do	229	21	1	2
Do	230	22	1	2
SLAUGHTER, WILLIAM, for relief of heirs	252	24	1	3
Do	633	26	1	5
Do	663	27	2	5
SLAVIN, JOHN, for relief	75	19	2	1
Do	38	20	1	2
SLEMAKER, ELLEN G., for relief	1014	45	2	10
Do	289	47	1	12
SLOCOMB, CORA A., *et al.*, for relief	429	43	1	8
Do	486	44	1	10
Do	6	45	2	10
Do	918	48	1	13
Do	169	49	1	14
SLOCUM, ISSAC, for relief	909	46	2	11
SMALLS, ROBERT, for relief	3505	49	2	14
SMITH, ALEXANDER LAWSON, for relief of heirs	664	37	2	5
SMITH, ALFRED, for relief	2021	47	2	12
SMITH, BALLARD, for relief of heir	715	25	2	4
SMITH, BENJAMIN, for relief	625	49	1	14
SMITH, CATHERINE and JAMES, for relief	1066	46	2	11
SMITH, CHARLES, for relief of heir	769	30	1	6
SMITH, CHARLES B., for relief of heirs	1435	49	1	14
Do	3040	49	1	14
SMITH, EDWARD, for relief of estate	35	16	1	1
SMITH, EDWARD B., for relief	2019	47	2	12
SMITH, H. C., referring claim to Court of Claims	2643	48	2	13
SMITH, HENRY, for relief	739	30	1	6
Do	481	31	1	6
SMITH, JOHN H., for relief	29	27	3	5
Do	1028	27	2	5
SMITH, LARKIN, for relief	285	24	2	3
Do	672	25	2	4
Do	976	27	2	5
Do	67	29	1	6
Do	673	30	1	6
Do	113	31	1	6
Do	207	33	1	6
SMITH, LEONIDAS, for relief	2610	49	1	14
SMITH, NATHAN, for relief of widow	968	25	2	4
SMITH, NOAH, for relief	680	30	1	6
SMITH, ROBERT,				
For relief of heirs	248	29	1	6
Do	2789	49	1	14
Referring claim to Court of Claims	2643	48	2	13
SMITH, SIDNEY R., for relief	383	49	1	14
SMITH THOMAS B. (administrator), for relief	1091	46	2	11
Do	31	48	1	13
SMITH, WILLIAM HOOKER, for relief of heirs	405	24	1	3
Do	112	25	2	4
SMITH, WILLIAM T., for relief of executor	315	24	2	3
Do	103	25	2	4
Do	330	26	1	5
Do	80	27	2	5
Do	16	27	3	5
Do	190	31	1	6
SNEAD, CHARLES, for relief of heirs	708	24	1	3
Do	111	25	2	4
SNOW, AARON, for relief	171	21	1	2
Do	87	22	1	2

Subject.

SNOWDEN, JONATHAN, for relief of heirs
Do
SNOWDEN & MASON, for relief
SNYDER, GEORGE, referring claim to Court of Claims
SOLOMON, HAYM M., for relief of heirs
SOMERSET BAPTIST CHURCH, for relief
SOPER, AMASA, for relief of heirs
Do
SOTHORON, JOHN H., for relief
SOUTH CAROLINA, for relief of Beaufort Mounted Guards
SOUTH, WILLIAM, for relief
SOYER, JAMES, for relief
Do
SPAFFORD, ELIPHALET, for relief of heir
SPAH, FIDAL,
Referring claim to Court of Claims
For relief
SPAIDS, C. C., for relief
SPATES, GEORGE W., for relief
SPAULDING, SIMON, for relief of estate
SPEILMAN, JONAS, referring claim to Court of Claims
SPENCER, HORATIO N.,
For relief of heirs
Referring claim to Court of Claims
SPENCER JOHN, for relief of heirs
SPINEY, CALVIN, referring claim to Court of Claims
SPINKS, W. B., for relief of heirs
SPOTSWOOD, JOHN, for relief of heirs
Do
SPRAGUE, AUGUSTUS, for relief
SPRINGSTEEN, PETER, for relief
STACK, EDWARD, for relief
STACY, J. B., referring claim to Court of Claims
STAFFORD, ABIGAIL, for relief
Do
STAFFORD, JAMES BAYARD, for relief of heir
STANFIELD, Mrs. R., referring claims to Court of Claims
STAPLETON, ROBERT H., for relief
STAR, DANIEL, for relief of heirs
STARK, CALEB, for relief
STARWOOD, ELLEN, referring claim to Court of Claims
STATE CLAIMS, for public defense, settlement of
STATE NATIONAL BANK OF LOUISIANA, for relief
STATES,
War claims of, to adjudicate
Do
Do
War loans, to reimburse for interest paid on
Do
STAYNER, ROGER, for relief
Do
Do
STERN, EDWARD, for relief
STEVENS, ALBERT, for relief of executor
STEVENS, JOHN (executor), for relief
STEVENS, MARTHA A., for relief
STEVENS, WILLIAM S., for relief
Do
STEVENSON, ALEXANDER, for relief of heirs
Do
STEWART, FRANCES E., for relief
Do
STEWART, JOHN,
For relief of heir
For relief
STEWART, JOHN F., for relief of heirs
STILGEBOWER, MARY, AND OTHERS, for relief of heirs
STIRMAN, THOMAS V.,
For relief of estate
Referring claim of estate to Court of Claims
STOCKLEY, LUCY J., referring claim to Court of Claims
STOCKSTILL, DAVID W., for relief
Do
STOCKTON, ROBERT, for relief of heirs
STODDARD, WILLIAM, for relief
STODDERT, BENJAMIN, for relief of heirs
STOKELY, NEHEMIAH, for relief of heirs
Do
Do
Do
Do

Subject.	Report.	Congress.	Session.	Volume.
STOKES, JOHN, for relief of heirs	198	24	2	3
Do	682	28	1	5
STONE, JOHN H, for relief of heirs	128	24	1	3
Do	821	30	1	6
Do	46	31	1	6
Do	107	32	1	6
STONE, LOUISA F., for relief	1797	47	1	12
STORY, BENJAMIN, for relief	1054	27	2	5
STOVER, DOROTHY, for relief	98	14	1	1
Do	130	21	1	2
Do	116	21	2	2
Do	79	23	1	2
STRABER, PETER, for relief of heirs	6	31	2	6
STRAHAN, GREGORY, for relief of heirs	17	18	2	1
Do	17	19	1	1
Do	9	19	2	1
STRANGE, LUCY, for relief	505	26	1	5
STRATTON, JOHN F., for relief	441	45	2	10
Do	416	46	2	11
Do	1728	47	1	12
STRATTON, THOMAS, for relief	447	28	1	5
Do	858	27	2	5
STRAUS, LEOPOLD R, for relief	504	48	1	6
STRICKLAND, JESSE H., for relief	*1754	49	1	14
STRYKER, WILLIAM D., for relief	[illegible]	43	2	9
SUDLER, THOMAS E., for relief of heirs	243	25	2	4
Do	1082	27	2	5
SUGG, J. B., for relief	924	46	2	11
SUGG, L. D., for relief	3464	49	1	14
SULLIVAN, JAMES B., for relief	760	43	1	9
SUMMERS, SIMON,				
For relief	205	24	1	3
Do	282	25	2	4
For relief of heirs	1049	27	2	5
SUMMERS, THERESA, for relief	1805	46	2	11
SUMPTER, FRANCIS, for relief of estate	165	28	2	6
Do	440	29	1	6
SUMPTER, THOMAS, for relief of estate	230	25	2	4
Do	371	26	1	5
Do	1082	27	2	5
Do	166	28	2	6
Do	39	31	1	6
SUTHARD, WILLIAM W., for relief	1764	47	1	12
SUTTON, JOHN, for relief	99	24	2	3
Do	655	43	1	3
SWANN, GEORGE T., referring claim of heirs to Court of Claims	2643	48	2	13
SWART, BERNARD T., for relief	117	43	2	9
SWART, B. Y., referring claim to Court of Claims	2643	48	2	13
SWEARINGEN, JAMES M., for relief	238	46	2	11
SWEAT, ISAIAH, for relief	1064	46	2	11
Do	22	48	1	13
SWIFT, ALEXANDER & CO., for relief	3059	49	1	14
SYME, JOHN, for relief of estate	190	22	1	2
Do	97	23	1	2
TABB, WILLIAM, for relief	232	37	3	5
Do	109	44	2	10
Do	3532	49	2	14
TAGG, JOSEPH, for relief	943	46	2	11
TALBURTT, CATHARINE A., for relief	1487	46	2	11
TALLY, ROBERT, for relief	959	46	2	11
Do	234	48	1	13
TATES, GEORGE, for relief of heirs	257	27	3	5
TATURN, HENRY, for relief	978	27	2	5
TAVERNER, ELI, for relief	2193	49	1	14
TAYLOR, B. B., for relief	965	46	2	11
TAYLOR, CHARLES, for relief of heirs	563	24	1	3
Do	137	25	2	4
Do	24	25	3	4
Do	181	26	2	5
Do	401	27	2	5
TAYLOR, EDMUND H. administrator, for relief	380	29	1	6
TAYLOR, FRANCIS, for relief of heirs	492	24	1	3
Do	127	25	2	4
Do	400	27	2	5
Do	380	29	1	6
TAYLOR, FRANCIS and JUDITH, for relief	31	23	1	3
TAYLOR, GEORGE T., referring claim to Court of Claims	2643	48	2	13
TAYLOR, ISAAC, for relief	332	43	2	9
TAYLOR, JAMES, for relief	183	24	1	3
Do	277	36	1	7

* Views of minorty, Part 2.

Subject.	Report.	Congress.	Session.	Volume.
TAYLOR, JAMES T., for relief	973	46	2	11
TAYLOR, JOHN, for relief of heirs	22	22	2	2
Do	90	23	1	3
TAYLOR, JOHN, & SON, for relief	1051	46	2	11
Do	527	47	1	12
Do	20	48	1	13
TAYLOR, JUDITH, for relief	358	22	1	2
TAYLOR, RICHARD, for relief of estate	211	33	1	6
Do	64	33	1	7
TAYLOR, THORNTON, for relief of heirs	493	22	1	2
Do	249	25	2	4
Do	402	27	2	5
TAYS, ELIZABETH, for relief	248	29	1	6
TEAS, WILLIAM, for relief of estate	42	22	2	2
Do	116	23	1	3
TEBAULT, A. G., for relief	812	44	1	10
Do	12	48	1	13
TEBBS, THOMAS, for relief of heirs	365	25	2	4
TEEL, JOHN, for relief	132	21	1	2
Do	86	22	1	2
TELFAIR, CATHERINE, for relief	974	25	2	4
Do	172	26	2	5
TELFAIR, MARY M., for relief	427	31	1	6
TENNESSEE,				
Bethel College in, for relief of trustees of	93	43	2	8
Marion County, citizens of, claims	230	48	1	13
Marysville College, trustees, relief of	791	43	1	8
McMinnville, citizens of, payment of award to	1466	46	2	11
Mossy Creek,				
For relief of Baptist Church at	1384	46	2	11
For relief of college at	1385	46	2	11
Memphis, city of, relief	17	48	1	13
TERRILL, A. T., for relief	1239	46	2	11
Do	1105	48	1	13
THATCHER, E., *et al.*, for relief	785	27	2	5
THAYER, MARY A., for relief	509	43	1	8
THOMAS, JOHN, for relief of heirs	129	22	1	2
Do	336	25	2	4
Do	969	25	2	4
Do	403	27	2	5
THOMAS, Maj. Gen. GEORGE H., order directing payment of awards to certain parties	1466	46	2	11
THOMAS, MARK, for relief of heirs	253	27	3	5
THOMAS, SARAH M., for relief	1190	47	1	12
Do	103	48	1	13
THOMPSON, DORA, *et al.*, for relief	2117	48	1	13
Do	565	49	1	14
THOMPSON, PLEASANT H., for relief	1066	46	2	11
Do	2012	47	2	12
THOMPSON, RANSOM, for relief	906	47	1	12
Do	44	48	1	13
THOMPSON, WILLIAM, for relief of heirs	451	35	1	7
Do	28	36	1	7
Do	2606	49	1	14
THORN, WILLIAM, for relief of widow	543	27	2	5
THORNTON, FRANCIS A., for relief	470	22	1	2
Do	32	23	1	3
Do	250	24	1	3
THORNTON, JANE, for relief	55	21	2	2
Do	143	22	1	2
THORNTON, JOHN, for relief of widow	148	22	1	2
THORNTON, PRESLEY, for relief of estate	32	23	1	3
Do	250	24	1	3
Do	242	25	2	4
Do	35	25	3	4
Do	979	27	2	5
Do	356	28	1	6
Do	12	29	1	6
Do	672	30	1	6
Do	870	32	1	6
THOROWGOOD, LEMUEL, for relief	38	15	2	1
THWEATT, THOMAS, for relief	565	24	1	3
TIDWELL, GEORGE W., for relief	956	46	2	11
TILLSON, ROBERT, & CO., for relief	341	43	1	8
TINKER, SIDNEY, for relief	324	43	1	8
TIPTON, ABRAHAM, for relief of heirs	618	25	2	4
TIRCUIT, EUGENE, for relief	1893	49	1	14
TOBACCO, claims for captured and destroyed	262	43	1	8
TODD, LEVI, for relief of heirs	202	24	2	3
TOMLINSON, HARTUPU & CO., for relief	4172	49	2	14
TOMLINSON, W. E., for relief	1007	46	2	11
Do	1724	47	1	12

Subject.	Report.	Congress.	Session.	Volume.
TONGUE, ANNA, for relief	667	24	1	3
TOOF, ELIZABETH, for relief	963	46	2	11
Do	62	46	1	12
TORREY, JOHN, *et al.*, for relief	1106	47	1	12
TORREY, JOSEPH, for relief of heirs	133	23	1	3
TOWNLEY, GEORGE, for relief of heirs	450	35	1	7
Do	51	37	2	7
TOWNS, JOHN, for relief of heirs	853	25	2	4
Do	494	27	2	5
TOWNSLEY, SARAH, for relief	1679	47	2	12
TRABUE, JAMES, *et al.*, for relief	3960	49	2	14
TRACY, NATHANIEL, for relief of heirs	799	24	1	3
Do	120	25	2	4
Do	320	28	1	6
Do	76	29	2	6
TRAVERSIE, JOSEPH, for relief of heirs	38	36	1	7
TREADWELL, WILLIAM, for relief of heirs	156	21	1	2
Do	27	21	2	2
TREASURY DEPARTMENT,				
Captured property, to return to owners, deposited in Department	1558	49	1	14
Jurisdiction of, to adjudicate certain claims	1089	47	1	12
Revolutionary claims, transferring settlement of, to, from Congress	230	23	1	3
TRIPLTETT, THOMAS, for relief	96	23	1	3
Do	563	25	2	4
Do	188	25	3	4
TROW, BARTHOLOMEW, for relief of heirs	334	25	2	4
Do	226	27	2	5
TRUEHEART, DANIEL, for relief	1073	27	2	5
TRUNDLE, THOMAS, referring claim to Court of Claims	2643	46	2	13
TRUSTEE,				
Catholic Church, Dalton, Ga., relief	467	48	1	13
Christian Brothers' College, Saint Louis, Mo., relief	1841	48	1	13
Presbyterian Church, Marietta, Ga., relief	468	48	1	13
TUBMAN, HARRIET, for relief	787	43	1	8
TUBBS, SAMUEL, *et al.*, for relief	868	25	2	4
TUCK, FERDINAND N., for relief	1476	46	2	11
TUCKER, EDWARD J., for relief	168	48	1	13
TUCKER, JAMES,				
Referring claim, to Court of Claims	2643	48	2	13
For relief	2327	49	1	14
TUCKER, NATHANIEL, for relief of heir	862	25	2	4
TULEY, EDWARD P., for relief	1439	46	2	11
TUPPER, C. E., for relief	40	45	3	10
Do	1470	46	2	11
Do	312	48	1	13
TURLEY, WILLIAM H., for relief	1825	47	2	12
Do	1424	48	1	13
TURNER, ANN, for relief	138	24	1	3
TURNER, JOANNA W., for relief	935	46	2	11
TURNER, MARTHA, for husband's services as scout	469	48	1	13
TURNER, PHILIP, for relief of heirs	176	23	1	3
Do	298	24	1	3
Do	105	25	2	4
Do	405	27	2	5
TURNEY, ABEL, for relief	40	18	2	1
TWIFORD, MARY E., for relief	112	43	2	9
TYLER, JOHN B., for relief	602	43	1	8
TYRONE, PA., for relief of Church of United Brethren in Christ at	2617	49	1	14
UNDERHILL, THOMAS, for relief of estate	119	29	1	6
Do	202	33	1	6
UNDERWOOD, WILLIAM, for relief of widow	1089	27	2	5
UNION NATIONAL BANK OF LOUISIANA, for relief	4169	49	2	14
UNITED BRETHREN IN CHRIST, TYRONE, PA., for relief	2617	49	1	14
URQUHART, CAROLINA AUGUSTA, *et al.*, for relief	429	43	1	8
Do	496	44	1	10
Do	6	45	2	10
Do	918	48	1	13
Do	163	49	1	14
VALIER, CHARLES, for relief	808	43	1	8
Do	711	45	2	10
VAN ANTWERP, W. W., for relief	39	43	2	9
Do	255	44	1	10
VAN BUSKIRK, ABRAM, for relief of heirs	199	34	3	6
VAN BUSKIRK, THOMAS, for relief of heir	101	35	1	7
Do	10	35	2	7
Do	25	36	1	7
VAN CAMP, ISAAC, for relief	980	27	2	5
VAN CAMPEN, MOSES, for relief	581	24	1	3
Do	204	24	2	3
Do	987	25	2	4
Do	821	30	1	6

Subject.	Report.	Congress.	Session.	Volume.
WALKER, MARY E., for relief	799	43	1	8
Do	820	44	1	10
Do	4150	49	2	14
WALKER, TIMOTHY, *et al.*, for relief	582	24	1	3
WALL, RICHARD, for relief	231	20	1	2
Do	111	21	1	2
Do	288	22	1	2
Do	822	24	1	3
WALLACE, BEN. F., for relief	248	46	2	11
WALLACE, ED., for relief	1608	47	1	12
WALLACE, THOMAS, for relief of heirs	225	22	1	2
Do	87	23	1	3
WALLACE, THOMAS B., for relief	248	46	2	11
Do	720	47	1	12
WALLACE, WILLIAM, for relief of heir	230	25	2	4
Do	665	27	2	5
WALLER, ROBERT P. (executor), for relief	446	26	1	5
WALSH, ANNA, for relief of estate	19	14	2	1
WALSH, NORA, for relief	2014	47	2	12
Do	2015	47	2	12
Do	35	48	1	13
Do	36	48	1	13
WALSH, WILLIAM F., for relief	1390	46	2	11
WALTON, GEORGE, for relief of heirs	492	36	1	7
WALTON, JOHN, for relief of heirs	661	48	1	13
WALTON, ROBERT H.,				
Referring claim to Court of Claims	2043	48	2	13
For relief	2181	49	1	14
WAPLES, SAMUEL, for relief of heirs	415	31	1	6
WAR CLAIMS. (*See* CLAIMS.)				
War of rebellion, settlement	262	43	1	8
WAR LOANS, to reimburse States for interest paid on	1202	48	1	13
Do	1560	49	1	14
WAR OF REBELLION,				
Claims of officers, to adjudicate, for services in	556	47	1	12
Claims of States, to adjudicate for expenses incurred in late war	497	44	1	10
Do	209	45	2	10
Do	2489	48	1	13
Do	977	49	1	14
Desertion in, to remove charges against certain persons for	72	48	1	13
Female nurses in, to provide payment of	1940	49	1	14
Louisiana, to compensate parties for property seized by Government in.	616	49	1	14
Loans, to reimburse certain States for interest paid on	1102	48	1	13
Do	1560	49	1	14
Missouri, to adjudicate claims for payments made by	2490	48	1	13
Do	2133	49	1	14
New Mexico, Secretary of War authorized to ascertain amount expended during war by Territory of	383	42	2	9
Officers, to adjudicate claims for services in	556	47	1	12
Pennsylvania, to compensate citizens for losses sustained by invasion of	41	43	2	9
Schuylkill County, Pennsylvania, to adjudicate war claims of	1729	47	1	12
Do	1613	49	1	14
States,				
To adjudicate claims for expenses incurred by, during	497	44	1	10
Do	209	45	2	10
Do	2489	48	1	13
Do	977	49	1	14
To reimburse for interest paid on loans by certain	1102	48	1	13
Do	1560	49	1	14
WAR OF REVOLUTION,				
Claims,				
Providing for final settlement of all claims accruing during	125	35	1	7
For service in, providing final settlement of officers' and soldiers' claims	135	35	1	7
Do	250	36	1	7
Do	212	46	2	11
Half-pay,				
To officers of Virginia State Line for services in	856	24	1	3
Granting to widows and orphans of officers in	862	25	2	4
Massachusetts, to compensate citizens of, for losses sustained in	582	24	1	3
Monument, to erect to those who died in English prison-ships during	1026	27	2	5
Virginia, to reimburse and audit claims of State for advances made and services rendered by, during	436	26	1	5
Do	485	27	2	5
Virginia State Line, respecting half-pay to officers of	856	24	1	3
WARD, ICHABOD, for relief	320	21	1	2
WARD, JONATHAN, for relief	73	23	1	3
WARD, NAHUM, for relief	101	19	1	1
WARD, P. L. (executrix), for relief	1184	47	1	12
Do	917	48	1	13
Do	3337	49	1	14

Subject.	Report.	Congress.	Session.	Volume.
WARD, SAMUEL, for relief	49	16	1	1
Do	74	20	1	2
Do	242	21	1	2
WARDWELL, ERNEST H., for relief	338	49	1	14
Do	3737	49	2	14
WARE, FRANCIS, for relief of heirs	390	29	1	6
Do	176	30	1	6
Do	342	36	1	7
Do	964	49	1	14
WARE, HENRY, for relief	1868	47	1	12
WARFIELD, MARIA E., for relief	1881	47	2	11
WARNER, MARY, for relief	545	27	2	
WARNER, WILLIAM, for relief of estate	93	21	1	
WARR, AMERICUS V. (administrator),				
For relief of heirs	2228	49	1	
Referring claim to Court of Claims	2643	48	2	
WARRANTS. (*See* LANDS; BOUNTY LANDS.)				
WARREN, JOSEPH, for relief of heir	754	27		
Do	166	29		
WARREN, General JOSEPH, for erection of monument to	107	29		
WARREN, PEYTON S. and JOHN T., for relief	48	48		
WARREN, SAMUEL, for relief	280	24		
WARRINGTON, WILLIAM, for relief	870	27		
WASHINGTON, LEWIS W., for relief of heirs	1839	48		
WASHINGTON AND OHIO RAILROAD, for relief	804	43		
Do	1250	48		
WASSON, RICHARD F., for relief of heirs	3400	49		
WATERHOUSE, CHARLES, for relief	487	47		
WATERMAN, JOHN, for relief of heirs	508	24		
WATERMAN, LUTHER, for relief of heirs	508	24	1	
WATERS, JOHN, for relief of heirs	208	24	2	
Do	367	25	2	
WATERS, SARAH,				
For relief	53	46	3	1
Referring claim to Court of Claims	2643	48	2	1
WATHEN, WILLIAM A., for relief	1055	46	2	1
WATKINS, JOHN R. (administrator),				
For relief of heirs of Matilda W. Anderson	2790	49	1	1
Referring claim to Court of Claims	2643	48	2	1
WATKINS, WILLIAM, for relief	120	35	1	
WATT, ARCHIBALD, for relief	165	22	1	
WATTS, ROBERT H., for relief	762	43	1	
WATTS, WILLIAM, for relief of heirs	255	27	3	
WATSON, JOHN T., for relief	65	43	1	
WAUGH, HENRIETTA M., for relief	882	49	1	1
WAUGH, JOHN, for relief	765	43	1	
WEAVER, ALFRED H., for relief	468	48	1	1
WEAVER, ELIZABETH, for relief	6	43		
WEAVER, JOHN C., for relief	3123	49		1
WEAVER, OCTAVIUS A., *et al.*, for relief	1060	46		1
WEAVER, TILGHMAN, for relief of heirs	700	47		1
Do	160	48		1
WEBB, ISAAC N.,				
For relief	1483	46	2	1
Referring claim to Court of Claims	2643	48	2	1
WEBB, MARTIN, for relief of heirs	743	49		1
WEBBER, WILLIAM R., *et al.*, for relief	961	46	2	1
WEDDERBURN, GEORGE C., for relief	257	43	2	
WEEKS, THOMAS, for relief	290	48	2	
WELLBORN, A. C., for relief	249	46	2	1
WILLFORD, B. R., for relief	282	28	1	
WELLS, BENJAMIN, for relief	241	21	1	
WELLS, GEORGE H., referring claim to Court of Claims	2643	48	2	
WELLS, IDA M., *et al.*, referring claim to Court of Claims	2643	48	2	
WELLS, JAMES MADISON, for relief	793	43	1	
WEISSENFELS, FREDERICK, for relief of heir	614	26		
Do	1072	27		
WELSH, ANNA, for relief	19	15		
WELSH, W. W., for relief	1242	46		1
WENDELL, JOHN H.,				
For relief	24	21		
Do	57	22		
For relief of heirs	304	24		
WENWOOD, GODFREY, for relief of heirs	169	26	2	
Do	336	27	2	
Do	26	28		
WESTON, J. F., for relief	946	46	2	1
WHEATON, JOSEPH, for relief of estate	28	36	2	
Do	77	37	2	
Do	21	38	2	
WHEELER, FRANCIS I., for relief of estate	2479	49	1	

Subject.	Report.	Congress.	Session.	Volume.
WHEELER, RICHARD, for relief	716	24	1	3
WHEELER, WILLIAM H., for relief	1546	48	1	12
Do.	68	49	1	14
WHITAKER, AMELIA ANN, for relief	1029	46	2	11
WHITAKER, EPHRAIM, for relief	25	21	2	2
Do.	29	22	1	2
Do.	38	22	2	2
Do.	63	23	1	2
WHITE, ALEXANDER, for relief of heir	456	24	1	3
WHITE, ANTHONY WALTON, for relief of widow and heirs	69	23	2	3
Do.	145	24	1	3
Do.	815	25	2	4
Do.	330	26	1	5
Do	248	35	2	7
WHITE, BAKER, for relief of heir	906	42	1	8
WHITE, ELIZABETH, for relief	862	25	2	4
WHITE, JAMES, *et al.*, for relief	1541	48	1	13
WHITE, JOHN B., for relief of heir	915	23	2	4
WHITE, JOHN M., for relief of heir	165	24	1	3
Do.	456	24	1	3
Do.	52	30	2	6
WHITE, JOSEPH R., for relief	2625	49	1	14
WHITE, MOSES, for relief of estate	26	16	1	1
Do.	171	19	1	1
WHITE, NICHOLAS, for relief	2433	49	1	14
WHITE PLAINS, N. Y., for relief of the trustees of the Presbyterian Church in	514	25	2	4
WHITE, R. G. P., for relief	1428	46	2	11
Do	2340	48	2	13
WHITE, TARPLEY, for relief of heirs	165	24	1	3
Do.	247	25	2	4
Do.	5	25	3	4
Do.	617	26	1	5
Do.	547	27	2	5
Do	176	28	1	6
WHITEFIELD, WILLIAM H., for relief	1671	46	2	11
WHITEHEAD, MARY E., for relief	1062	46	2	11
Do.	1851	47	2	12
Do	168	49	1	14
WHITING, HARVEY, for relief	611	26	1	5
WHITING LEWIS, for relief of heirs	254	27	3	5
Do	644	29	1	6
WHITMARSH, MICAH, for relief of heirs	831	30	1	6
WHITMORE JONATHAN, for relief of heirs	662	27	2	5
WHITNEY, FRANKLIN S., for relief of estate	111	47	1	12
WHITTED, WILLIAM D.,				
For relief	1043	46	2	11
Referring claim to Court of Claims	2643	48	2	13
WHITTED, WILLIAM H., for relief	2194	49	1	14
WIARD, NORMAN, for relief	430	43	1	8
WIDOWS. (*See* PENSIONS.)				
WIGGINS, SARAH H., for relief	913	48	1	13
WILDE, RICHARD, for relief of heir	357	27	2	5
WILDER, JOHN W. (administrator), for relief	5	36	2	7
WILDEY LODGE (I. O. O. F.), for relief	546	44	1	10
Do	1058	46	2	11
WILKINSON, ROBERT W., referring claim to Court of Claims	2643	48	2	13
WILLARD, HUMPHREY, for relief	185	26	2	5
WILLARD, SUSAN E., for relief	488	44	1	10
WILLARD, WILLIAM F., and GEORGE E., for relief	982	46	2	11
WILLCOX, ORLANDO B., for relief	940	49	1	14
WILLETT, AUGUSTIN, for relief of heir	182	26	2	5
Do.	1088	27	2	5
Do.	229	35	1	7
WILLETT, JOHN W., for relief	231	46	2	11
WILLEY, Rev. W., for relief	2612	49	1	14
WILLEY, WORCESTER, for relief of Dwight Mission, Cherokee Nation	2612	49	1	14
WILLIAMS, ALFRED A., for relief	516	43	1	8
WILLIAMS, DANIEL, for relief of estate	717	25	2	4
WILLIAMS, DAVID, for relief of heirs	550	35	1	7
Do.	59	36	1	7
Do	78	37	2	7
WILLIAMS Mrs. J. P. for relief	2241	48	2	13
WILLIAMS, JAMES G., for relief	330	43	2	9
Do	187	44	1	10
Do.	484	44	1	10
Do	41	45	3	10
Do	920	47	1	12
WILLIAMS, JOHN S., for relief	507	43	1	8
WILLIAMS, MARGARET, for relief	975	25	2	4
WILLIAMS, NATHAN, for relief	174	26	2	5
Do	41	27	2	5

Subject.

WILLIAMS, PLEASANT M., for relief.
WILLIAMS, REBECCA., for relief
WILLIAMS, THOMAS, for relief of heirs
Do.
WILLIAMSON, LUCY, for relief
WILLIAMSON, WILLIAM A., referring claim to Court of Cl
WILLMOTT, ROBERT, for relief.
Do
WILLOUGHBY, WILLIAM H., for relief.
WILSON, BENJAMIN, for relief of heirs
Do
WILSON, JOHN, for relief of heirs
Do
WILSON, JOSEPH, for relief.
WILSON, MARGARET, for relief
WILSON, WILLIAM D., for relief.
Do
WILSON, WILLIS, for relief of heirs
Do.
WILT, JACOB, for relief.
WILTBERGER, CHARLES H., for relief.
WINBOURN, R. W., for relief.
Do.
Do.
WINFORD, GODFREY, for relief of heirs.
WINSLOW, ROBERT F., for relief
WINSTON, CATHARINE B., for relief.
WINSTON, J. H. C., for relief.
Do.
WINSTON, JOHN, for relief of heirs
Do.
Do.
Do.
Do
Do.
Do.
WIRT, FINEAS E., referring claim to Court of Claims
WISHART, SIDNEY, for relief.
WISHART, THOMAS, for relief of heirs.
Do.
Do.
Do.
Do
Do.
WITHERELL, JAMES, for relief
Do
WITKOUSKI, SIMON, for relief.
WOLF, DAVID, referring claim to Court of Claims
WOLF, EDMUND, for relief.
WOLFE, ANN, *et al.*, for relief.
WOLFF, EDMUND, *et al.*, for relief.
WOOD, DANIEL T., referring claim to Court of Claims
WOOD, EDWARD, for relief of estate
Do
Do
WOOD, GERARD, for relief of heirs.
Do
WOOD, JAMES, for relief of estate
Do.
Do.
Do.
Do.
WOOD, JAMES D., for relief.
WOOD, JAMES E., for relief.
WOOD, JESSE, for relief of heirs.
WOOD, PAYNE and THOMAS C., referring claim to Court of
WOOD, R. H., for relief of estate.
WOOD, SARAH H., for relief
WOOD, WILLIAM H., for relief of estate.
WOODARD, JAMES H., for relief.
WOODFORD, SAMUEL A. B., for relief.
WOODSIDE, JAMES D. (administrator), for relief
WOODSIDE, JOHN, for relief of estate
WOODSON, CHARLES, for relief of estate.
WOODSON, TARLTON, for relief of heirs.
Do.
Do.
Do.
Do.

*Views of minority, Part

Subject.	Report.			
IDSON, TARLTON, for relief of heirs—Continued.				
Do	173	26	2	4
Do	546	27	2	5
Do	256	27	3	5
Do	316	29	1	6
IDWARD, JOHN, for relief	519	24	1	3
Do	355	27	2	5
IDWORTH, ROSWELL, for relief	57	17	1	1
IL, ISAIAH, for relief of heirs	974	25	2	4
Do	172	26	2	5
Do	861	27	2	5
ISTER, ANN, for relief	31	37	2	7
IKS, ATLANTIC, for relief	3424	49	1	14
IMER, DANIEL, for relief	433	43	1	8
Do	49	44	1	10
IRALL, ALEXANDER, refunding damages	520	48	1	13
Do	761	49	1	14
ITHINGTON, HUGH, for relief	1040	46	2	11
Do	297	47	1	12
ITHINGTON, THOMAS, for relief	1443	46	2	11
Do	1690	47	1	12
Do	490	48	1	13
AY, GIDEON B., for relief	411	46	2	11
AY, JAMES R., referring claim to Court of Claims	*2643	48	2	13
AY, MARY G., referring claim of heirs to Court of Claims	2643	48	2	13
GHT, DAVID, for relief	666	27	2	5
GHT, DAVID L., for relief	622	49	1	14
GHT, WILLIAM, for relief	330	26	1	5
Do	1062	27	2	5
Do	564	48	1	13
Do	1445	49	1	14
GHT, WILLIAM H., for relief	1225	49	1	14
IE, MARTHA J., referring claim to Court of Claims	2643	48	2	13
AND FREDERICK, referring claim to Court of Claims	2643	48	2	13
ETH, FRANCIS, for relief	251	44	1	10
OMING MASSACRE, to compensate the survivors and decendants of those slain in	1032	25	2	4
CEY, LEIGHTON, for relief of heirs	366	25	2	4
Do	234	26	1	5
Do	548	27	2	5
CY, WILLIAM T., for relief	48	43	2	9
Do	78	45	3	10
ES, GEORGE, for relief of heirs	854	25	2	4
Do	257	27	3	5
Do	210	35	2	7
Do	24	36	1	7
ES, GEORGE W., for relief of widow	1460	46	2	11
ES, JOHN, for relief of heir	31	37	2	7
MANS, MARTHA, for relief	154	21	1	2
BY, ADDISON O., for relief of estate	315	43	1	8
KTOWN, N. Y., for relief of First Presbyterian Church in	807	24	1	3
Do	433	25	2	4
KTOWN CHURCH, NEW YORK, for relief of	262	27	3	5
CE, JONATHAN, referring claim to Court of Claims	2643	48	2	13
NGE, ABBY, for relief	274	27	2	5
NG, GUY, for relief of heir	815	24	1	3
NG, JAMES, for relief of widow	29	36	2	7
NG, M. W., for relief	394	46	2	11
NG, W. C., for relief	985	47	1	12
NG, WILLIAM, for relief	20	19	2	1
NGLOVE, ISAIAH, for relief of heirs	258	27	3	5
NGS, JOSEPH, for relief of heirs	154	19	1	1
Do	68	23	2	3
Do	272	24	1	3
Do	128	25	2	4
Do	1074	27	2	5
Do	260	27	3	5
NGS, THOMAS F., for relief of estate	1492	47	1	12
HARIE, ISSACHOR, for relief	817	43	1	8
STEIN, JOHN, for relief	572	43	1	8
Do	218	45	2	10

* Part 2.

REPORTS

OF THE

OMMITTEE ON WA

HOUSE OF REPRESENTATIVES,

FROM THE FOURTEENTH C
FORTY-NINTH CONGRESS,

IN EIGHT VOLUMES.

COMPILED, UNDER THE DIRECTION OF THE JOINT COMMITTEE ON PRINTING,

BY

T. H. McKEE,

CLERK, DOCUMENT ROOM, UNITED STATES SENATE.

WASHINGTON:
GOVERNMENT PRINTING OFFICE.
1887.

9243 W M H

Joint

Re
State
the d
repo
teen

stan
seve
may
the
work
the
comp
Re
Sena
of th
tee o
the

COMPILER'S NOTICE.

This compilation embraces all the printed reports made by both Houses of Congress from the commencement of the Fourteenth to the close of the Forty-ninth Congress. They are classified by committees and arranged in numerical order. The collection for each committee is divided into volumes of suitable size. Each committee has a separate index, a copy being bound in each volume.

The SPECIAL and SELECT reports are all compiled in one collection having one index, a copy of which is bound in each volume.

The plan throughout the compilation is to place each report to the committee from which it was reported, without reference to the subject-matter.

The House and Senate reports are compiled separately. Care will be required in noticing the chronological order, as in some instances an entire session or Congress may not appear in certain volumes from the fact that during this period no reports were made by this committee.

T. H. McKEE.

INDEX

TO

REPORTS OF COMMITTEE ON WAYS AND MEANS,

HOUSE OF REPRESENTATIVES.

FROM 1815 TO 1887, INCLUSIVE.

Subject.	Report.	Congress.	Session.	Volume.
ABRAHAMS, A. H., for relief	55	35	1	4
ADAMS, BENJAMIN, & CO., for relief	392	24	1	3
Do	6	26	1	3
ADAMS, GEORGE, for relief	329	27	2	3
ADAMS, SAMUEL, for relief	29	18	1	1
ADULTERATION, to prevent importation of adulterated teas	1927	47	2	7
AD VALOREM DUTIES. (*See* IMPORT DUTIES.)				
AFRICA (*see also* SLAVE TRADE), agency on coast of, support of	65	19	1	1
ALASKA COMMERCIAL COMPANY,				
Lease made between United States and	623	44	1	5
To investigate affairs of	2027	48	1	8
ALEXANDRIA, VIRGINIA, to fix salary of collector of port	1279	47	1	7
ALL SOULS' CHURCH (Washington, D. C.), to remit duty on glass window for	209	46	3	7
AMORY, JONATHAN, Jr., for relief	73	15	1	1
ANDERSON, S. T., for relief	987	25	2	3
APPLEBY & HELM, for relief	603	46	2	7
APPLETON, C. H., for relief	29	18	1	1
APPLETON, NATHANIEL W., for relief	29	18	1	1
APPRAISERS. (*See* CUSTOMS OFFICERS.)				
APPROPRIATION BILLS,				
Army, on Senate amendments to bill for support of, for 1855-'56	90	33	2	4
Civil and diplomatic service, on making appropriation for 1842 in	44	27	2	3
Consular and diplomatic service, on Senate amendments to bill making appropriations for 1859-'60	185	35	2	4
Deficiency, on Senate amendments to bill supplying deficiencies for year ending June, 1852	149	32	1	4
For year ending June, 1853	6	32	2	4
For year ending June, 1854	132	33	1	4
Indians (*see also* title INDIANS), relative to appropriations for current and contingent expenses of Indian Department,				
For 1842-'43	75	27	2	3
For year 1848-'49	738	30	1	4
For year 1854-'55	201	33	1	4
For year 1855-'56	92	33	2	4
For year 1859-'60	774	35	2	4
Legislative, executive, and judicial, on Senate amendments to bill making appropriations for the year 1859-'60	187	35	2	4
Navy, annual appropriations for support of, for 1842	678	27	2	3
Pensions, appropriations for 1859-'60 for	175	35	2	4
Post-office, on amendments to bill making appropriations for the year 1855-'56.	139	33	2	4
Sundry civil expenses, appropriations for	20	37	2	4
APPROPRIATIONS, unexpended balance of	303	25	2	3
ARIADNE (ship), for relief of former owners of	83	15	1	1
ARMINGTON, ASA, for relief	233	23	1	2
Do	112	24	1	3
Do	45	24	2	3
ASPINWALL, AUGUSTUS, for relief	155	20	1	1
ASSISTANT SECRETARY OF STATE, authorizing the appointment of	491	31	1	4
ATHERTON & CO., for relief	130	46	3	7
Do	245	47	1	7
ATLANTA, GEORGIA, to make a port of delivery	149	46	3	

Subject.	Report.	Congress.	Session.	Volume.
AUBIN, JOSHUA, *et al.*, Castine cases, imported goods	29	18	1	1
AUCTIONS, imposing regulations on sales of foreign merchandise at	44	20	2	1
AUTOMATIC METER. (*See* METERS.)				
AVERY, THATCHER, for relief	29	18	1	1
AZALIA (steamer), for relief of builders	393	43	1	5
BABBITT, JACOB, for relief	3	18	1	1
BALTIMORE AND SUSQUEHANNAH R. R. CO., for relief	224	24	2	3
Do	2	25	2	3
BANGS, GEORGE and WILLIAM, for relief	168	19	1	1
Do	46	20	1	1
Do	44	21	1	1
BANK CHECKS, to repeal stamp tax on	307	46	3	7
BANK OF UNITED STATES,				
Legality of transfer of public debt to	151	15	1	1
Renewal of charter of	358	21	1	1
Do	*283	22	2	1
Tabular statements of the condition of	358	21	1	1
Do	283	22	1	2
Do	121	22	2	2
Continuing deposits of the Government in the	†121	22	2	2
Refusal of, to deliver over books, papers, and pension funds on order of Secretary of War	†263	23	1	2
Removal of public deposits from the	312	23	1	2
Do	†313	23	1	2
Creation of	634	25	2	3
BANK TAXES, repeal, on deposits	307	46	3	7
BARLEY MALT, fixing rate of duty on	595	46	3	7
BATES & LACON, for relief	289	23	1	2
Do	286	24	1	3
Do	527	25	2	3
Do	4	26	1	3
BATTELLE, JONATHAN, for relief	25	17	1	1
BAYARD, WILLIAM, and others, for relief	95	16	1	1
BEARD, DAVID, for relief	85	18	1	1
BENDER, MARGARETTA, for relief	597	46	2	7
BENTLANE, ROBERT (administrator), for relief	260	21	1	1
BERKS COUNTY, PENNSYLVANIA, for relief of certain distillers of	18	18	1	1
BIBLES, to admit free of duty in Chinese language for gratuitous distribution	590	46	2	7
BILLS FOR RAISING REVENUE, power of the Senate to originate	42	41	3	4
BLAISDELL, JONATHAN M., for relief	6	20	2	1
Do	138	21	1	1
BLOUNT, JAMES M., for relief	579	26	1	3
BOEHM BROTHERS, for relief	1613	46	2	7
BOHLEN & BORIE, for relief	378	28	1	4
BONDS OF BREWERS. (*See* BREWERS' BONDS.)				
BONDS OF UNITED STATES (*see also* DEBT OF THE UNITED STATES),				
Internal tax on interest of	73	40	2	4
Placing of 5 per cent. bonds on the market by Secretary of Treasury	7	42	4	4
To authorize United States commissioners to take acknowledgments of transfers of	642	47	1	7
BOOKS,				
To empower postmaster to administer oaths to importers of	1737	47	1	7
To admit duty free, for use of the blind	1836	47	1	7
BOSTON, MASSACHUSETTS,				
To regulate duties and salary of inspector of drugs at	1859	47	2	7
To increase salary of special examiner of drugs at	685	48	1	8
BOTTLERS' PROTECTIVE ASSOCIATION, to remit duty on goods for exhibition of	3357	48	1	8
BRADLEY, WALTER, for relief	1016	25	2	3
BRANNIN, SUMMERS & CO., for relief	143	43	2	5
Do	557	44	1	5
Do	1128	46	2	7
Do	335	47	1	7
Do	177	48	1	8
BREED, EBENEZER, for relief	60	24	1	3
BREEDLOVE, J. W., for relief	1036	27	2	3
BREWERS' BONDS, to amend law relative to	1140	49	1	8
BRONSON, CALVIN, for relief	128	45	3	7
Do	22	46	1	7
BRONSON, FREDERICK, for relief	907	27	2	3
BROWN, NOAH, and others, for relief	877	27	2	3
BUCKNER, JAMES F., for relief	511	44	1	5
BULKLEY, ASA, for relief	14	20	1	1
BUOYS, to erect, at entrance to Vermillion Bay, Louisiana	342	28	1	4
BURNSIDE, ROBERT, for relief	58	14	2	1
BURR & SMITH, for relief	906	27	2	3
BURR, DAVID H., for relief	550	27	2	3
BURTON, JOHN, and others, for relief	204	19	1	1
Do	30	19	2	1
Do	147	20	1	1

* Majority and minority. † Views of minority.

Subject.	Report.	Congress.	Session.	Volume.
BUSH, JOHN P., for relief	2496	48	2	8
CALIFORNIA, to refund to State duties collected prior to admission into the Union	169	33	1	4
CAMP, J. C., for relief	1789	47	1	7
CANADA,				
To impose duties on fresh fish imported from	358	46	3	7
Granting permission to farmers from Canada to bring grain over border to be ground	1462	47	1	7
CAPE CHARLES, changing terminus of railroad from Cherrystone to	1619½	49	1	8
CAPITOL BUILDING, providing supply of water for use of	244	21	1	1
CARDOZA, J. N., for relief	306	21	1	1
CARPENTIER, JOSEPH LE, for relief	23	19	2	1
CARRIAGES, repealing duty on	79	14	2	1
CARROLLTOWN, PENNSYLVANIA, Catholic church, to admit free of duty altar and regalia for	2436	48	2	8
CASHAW, JOHN, for relief	126	45	2	7
Do	1261	47	1	7
CASTINE, MAINE, for relief of certain parties who paid duties on importations into	29	18	1	1
CATLIN, GEORGE, for relief	636	27	3	3
CAVELIER, A. and Z., for relief	162	20	1	1
CENT. (See COINS AND COINAGE.)				
CERTIFICATES OF DEPOSIT, to authorize the issue of, on deposit of gold and silver coin and bullion	54	35	1	4
CHAPMAN, JOHN S., for relief	144	43	2	5
CHARLESTON, SOUTH CAROLINA, Saint Michael's Church in, relief of	281	45	2	7
Do	1619	46	2	7
CHASE, PAUL, for relief	27	18	2	1
CHASTELAIN & POUVEST, for relief	49	22	1	2
Do	23	23	2	2
Do	285	24	1	2
Do	1	25	2	2
Do	8	26	1	2
CHENOWITH, JOHN B., for relief of heirs of	246	47	1	7
CHERRYSTONE, changing terminus of railroad to Cape Charles from	1619½	49	1	8
CHICAGO, ILLINOIS, to fix salary of collector of port as	1898	47	1	7
CHINA MAIL SERVICE. (See POSTAL SERVICE.)				
CHOUTEAU, N. S. (surety), for relief	180	46	3	7
Do	245	47	1	7
CHRETIEN, LOUIS, for relief of heirs of	9	19	1	1
CHURCH,				
Catholic, of Carrollton, Pa., altar and regalia for, to admit free of duty	2436	48	2	8
Holy Trinity, of Philadelphia, Pa., to remit duty on chime of bells for	1632	47	1	7
CIGARS,				
Bonds of manufacturers of	266	46	3	7
Taxes on, to abolish	*1818	47	1	7
CITY POINT RAILROAD COMPANY, for relief	464	27	2	3
CIVIL EXPENSES OF GOVERNMENT,				
Appropriations of, for 1842	44	27	2	3
For 1862	20	37	2	4
CLARKE & FORCE, suspending the publication of "Documentary History of the Revolution" prepared by	849	24	1	3
CLAY, RICHARD, for relief	208	24	2	3
Do	522	25	2	3
CLERKS,				
Increase of compensation to, in public offices	641	24	1	3
Do	161	24	2	3
Regulating the number, classification, and compensation of those employed in public office at Washington	294	27	3	3
CLINTON, CHARLES, for relief	124	45	3	7
Do	16	46	1	7
COBB, GEORGE G., for relief	1208	47	1	7
COFFEE, to repeal discriminating duties on, imported from the Netherlands	202	46	3	7
COFFIN, WILLIAM, for relief	53	15	2	1
Do	21	16	1	1
COIN,				
Coin certificates to be given for gold and silver coin or bullion deposited in certain named treasuries	54	35	1	4
Converting all foreign coin held by General Government into legal coin of United States	487	29	1	4
COINAGE,				
Coinage of one-dollar gold pieces, providing for	346	28	1	4
Do	418	29	1	4
Nickle as a substitute for copper in the one-cent coinage	53	35	1	4
COLLECTOR (schooner), for relief of owner	92	15	1	1
COLLEGEVILLE, MINNESOTA, to refund duties on six statues to Saint John's University at	2487	48	2	8
COLLINS, CHARLES, for relief	136	21	1	1
COLLINS, JOHN F., for relief	137	23	1	2

* Parts 1, 2.

Subject.

COLORED RACE EXPOSITION, to remit duty on articles fo
COMMISSIONERS OF COURTS, to take acknowledgment
United States bonds
COMMISSIONERS OF LOANS, directing transmission of un
of the public stock to the, and providing the paymen
COMMITTEE CLERKS, duties of
COMSTOCK, ELIZABETH, for relief
Do
CONGRESS, power of Senate to originate revenue bill
CONRAD, JOHN, for relief
Do
CONTINENTAL INSURANCE COMPANY, to refund intern
CONTRACTS, SANBORN, investigation of
CONWAY, A. V., for relief
COOK, JAMES P., for relief
COOK, THOMAS, for relief
CORONNA, TAUSSIG & CO., for relief
COURTENAY, WILLIAM A., for relief
Do
CRAMER, CHARLES, and others, for relief
Do
CRAWFORD, JAMES, for relief
CREEK INDIANS,
To indemnify friendly Creek for property destroyed by host
Do
Treaty of 1802 between United States and
CROCKER, URIEL, for relief
Do
CROOKE, JOHN J., for relief
Do
CROSSIN, JESSIE, for relief
CUMBERLAND ROAD. (*See* NATIONAL ROADS.)
CURRENCY, condition of national bank notes
CUSIMANO, A., & CO., for relief
CUSTOMS DISTRICTS,
To amend section 2633, Revised Statutes, relative to establi
the frontier
Alexandria, Va., salary of collector at
Chicago, Ill., salary of collector at
Consolidation of
Edgarton, Mass., salary of collector at
Kennebunk, Maine, salary of collector at
Middletown, Conn., salary of collector at
Plymouth, N. C., salary of collector at
CUSTOMS DUTIES. (*See* IMPORT DUTIES; TONNAGE DUES.
CUSTOMS OFFICERS, to increase compensation of appraiser
CUSTOMS-REVENUE LAWS, to amend
DALLAS COUNTY, IOWA, to sell lands devised to Unite
Gardner in
DANA, N. and L., & CO., for relief
DANA & CO., for relief
DAVIS, AMOS, Jr., for relief
Do
Do
Do
DE AHNA, HENRY C., for relief
DEBENTURE. (*See* DRAWBACKS; IMPORT DUTIES.)
DEBT OF UNITED STATES,
Preventing an addition to funded, of 1816
Extinguishment of
Redemption of 3 per cent. bonds of 1819–20
Authorizing a loan for $12,000,000, or an exchange of bonds
pay portion due of
Providing for payment of unclaimed dividends of
Appropriating surplus in Treasury to payment of
DEFREES, JOHN D., for relief
DE GRAFF, JOHN J., for relief
Do
DE LA HAILANDIERE, C., for relief
DELAUNEY, ALEXANDER, for relief
DENVER CITY, COLORADO, establishing branch mint at
DEPARTMENT OF STATE increase of clerks in
DEPARTMENT OF TREASURY (*see also* TREASURY DEPART
of the United States, establishing a board to be called
DEPOSITORIES, establishing United States depositories for d
bursement of public moneys
DEPOSITS,
Relative to continuing Government, in Bank of United Stat
Removal from Bank of United States of Government depos
United States money in local banks, to regulate

*Views of minority.

Subject.	Report.	Congress.	Session.	Volume.
DETROIT, MICHIGAN, to refund taxes to house of correction at	533	47	1	7
DEWING, LUKE, for relief	14	20	1	1
DIRECT TAXES,				
To amend act of February 27, 1815, relating to	14	14	1	1
Georgia, a rebate of 15 per cent. on, paid by said State	58	14	2	1
DIRECT TAX OF 1861, to refund to States and Territories taxes levied	903	48	1	8
DISCRIMINATING DUTIES, to repeal, on tea and coffee imported from the Netherlands	202	46	3	7
DISTILLED SPIRITS,				
Amend the internal-revenue law relative to	1119	46	2	7
Amount of revenue received from	14	14	1	1
Commissions allowed collectors on taxes on, to repeal	2282	49	1	8
Imposing additional duties on importation of foreign spirits	57	16	2	1
Extend time for payment of tax	473	48	1	8
Entry and withdrawal in bond	811	47	1	7
Do	1277	47	1	7
Do	2288	49	1	8
Fruit brandy, to reduce tax on	3358	49	1	8
Grape brandy used to fortify wine for exportation	2632	49	1	8
Meters for registering manufacture of, to test	321	46	3	7
Do	588	47	1	7
Refunding tax laid on domestic spirits under act of July, 1813	43	20	1	1
Tax on fractional parts of a gallon	100	49	1	8
Taxation of small distilleries	2024	49	1	8
DISTILLERIES,				
Tax on stills and tubs in	24	17	1	1
Tax on small	2024	49	1	8
DISTILLERS,				
Action of, towards Government	24	17	1	1
Payment to them of cost of Tice meters	69	42	3	4
DISTILLERS OF BERKS COUNTY, PENNSYLVANIA, relief of	13	18	1	1
DISTRICT OF COLUMBIA,				
All Souls' Church, Washington City, to remit duty on window glass for	209	46	3	7
Providing a supply of water for the use of the	344	21	1	1
DIVIDENDS UNCLAIMED OF THE FUNDED DEBT OF THE UNITED STATES, providing for disposal of	139	19	1	1
DIXON, JAMES and WILLIAM, for relief	44	18	1	1
DODSWORTH, C., for relief	130	46	3	7
Do	245	47	1	7
DORR, JOHN, for relief	21	20	1	1
DOUGLASS, JOHN W., for relief	37	45	3	7
DRAWBACKS (*see also* IMPORT DUTIES),				
To authorize Secretary of Treasury to grant relief in certain cases	10	18	2	1
Reducing time of limitation for presenting claims for	195	24	2	3
Cigars, exported, manufactured in United States of imported leaf tobacco	688	24	1	3
Rum, exported	143	21	1	1
Spirits, distilled from foreign materials	164	15	1	1
Stills, manufactured for exportation	679	47	1	7
Sugar, refined, exported	164	15	1	1
Do	67	18	2	1
DRUGS,				
Abolish duty on certain	307	46	3	7
Fixing compensation of examiner of, at Boston	1859	47	2	7
Do	685	48	1	8
DUNNINGTON, F. M., for relief	6	46	2	7
DUTIABLE GOODS. (*See* TRANSPORTATION IN BOND.)				
DUTIES ON IMPORTS. (*See* IMPORT DUTIES.)				
EASTMAN, JONATHAN, for relief of widow of	16	20	1	1
EASTMAN'S DIGEST of decisions by Treasury Department and of Supreme Court relating to tariff, navigation, &c., to purchase	217	46	3	7
EASTPORT, MAINE, sufferers by fire at, relief	4173	49	2	8
EATON, ROBERT, for relief	309	21	1	1
Do	136	22	1	2
ECCLESTON, MARY, release from official bond	55	14	1	1
EDGARTOWN, MASSACHUSETTS, relating to salary of collectors at	69	14	2	1
EDMONSTON, WILLIAM C., for relief	1116	46	2	7
EDUCATION, distribution of surplus revenue among the States for purposes of	851	24	1	3
EDWARD EVERETT (steamer), for relief of builders	393	43	1	5
EDWARDS, AMOS, for relief	166	20	1	1
ELLERY, JOSEPH F., for relief	126	45	3	7
Do	1281	47	1	7
ELSBERG, ALBERT (administrator), for relief	438	47	1	7
ELSBERG, GUSTAVE, for relief	1614	46	2	7
ENOS, ROGER, for relief	345	21	1	1
ENTERPRISE INSURANCE COMPANY, for relief	944	45	2	7
Do	2587	48	2	8
EVANS, LEMUEL D., for relief	765	44	1	5
Do	72	44	2	5
EWING, WILLIAM L. D., for relief	117	19	1	1
EXCHEQUER, BOARD OF, establishing, in the Treasury Department	35	27	3	3

Subject.	Report.	Congress.	Session.	Volume.
EXECUTIVE DEPARTMENTS.				
Clerks in the, increase of salary of	641	24	1	3
Do	161	24	2	3
Clerks, number, classification, and compensation of	294	27	3	3
EXPORT TOBACCO MANUFACTORIES, to authorize establishment of	2310	48	2	8
Do	1141	49	1	8
EXPOSITION, CHICAGO, ILLINOIS, colored race, to remit duty on articles imported from	2432	48	2	8
EYSTER, GEORGE for relief	665	44	1	5
Do	130	45	3	7
Do	5	46	2	7
F. W. LINCOLN (steamer), for relief of builders	393	43	1	5
FAGAN, LEVI, for relief	69	14	2	1
FAIRBANKS, JASON, relief on official bond	26	15	1	1
FARRAR, W. B., for relief	880	45	2	7
Do	8	46	2	7
FARREL, MICHAEL, for relief	493	26	1	3
FEARON, MARY, for relief	28	45	2	7
FENCHWANGER, LEWIS, adopting of a composition one-cent piece	53	35	1	4
FERGUSON & CHAMBERS, for relief	6	46	2	7
FINANCES, condition of	66	16	2	1
Do	103	17	1	1
FINANCE.				
Readjustment of	14	14	1	1
Report of Secretary of Treasury on,				
For year 1821	6	17	1	1
For year 1825	64	19	1	1
For year 1827	185	20	1	1
For year 1837	303	25	2	3
For year 1838	716	25	2	3
For year 1839	218	25	3	3
For year 1843	227	27	3	3
For year 1844	306	28	1	4
FIRE IN NEW YORK CITY, relief of sufferers	41	24	1	3
FIRE AT EASTPORT, MAINE, sufferers by, relief	4173	49	2	8
FISH.				
To impose duties on fresh fish imported from Canada	388	46	3	7
To prevent importation and landing of mackerel during spawning season	343	49	1	8
FISHER, M. C., for relief	384	46	3	7
Do	618	47	1	7
FISHER, WILLIAM, for relief	1384	49	1	8
FLAGET, BENEDICT JOSEPH, for relief	206	19	1	1
FLOOD, WILLIAM, for relief of widow	44	16	1	1
FOOD, to prevent importation of adulterated and spurious teas	665	48	1	8
FORD, C., Jr., and others, for relief	946	45	2	7
Do	6	46	2	7
FORD, JOHN GERARD, for relief	708	26	1	3
Do	987	27	2	3
FORD, MOORMAN & CO., for relief	129	45	3	7
FOREIGN MERCHANDISE, imposing regulation on sales at auction of	44	20	2	1
FOREIGN TRADE, regulating importation of raw materials used in construction and repair of vessels engaged in	1261	46	2	7
FOREIGN VESSELS, to fix tonnage duties on	29	30	1	1
FOSTER, HENRY G., relief	74	17	1	1
Do	55	17	2	1
Do	85	19	1	1
FRAZER, SOLOMON, release from official bond	55	14	1	1
FREEDMAN'S SAVINGS AND TRUST COMPANY, to abolish commission appointed to take charge of	1571	46	2	7
FRUIT BRANDY, to remit tax on, used to fortify wine for export	2682	49	1	8
FRUIT SPIRITS, to amend law relative to tax	3258	49	1	8
FRYE, NATHANIEL, Jr., for relief	256	22	1	2
FUNDED DEBT, payment of the unclaimed dividends of	139	19	1	1
GAFF, J. W., and others, for relief	69	42	3	6
GAFF, T. and J. W., & CO., for relief	374	45	2	7
GARDNER, JOHN, authorizing sale of lands in Iowa devised to United States by	1738	47	1	7
GAUGERS (*see* INTERNAL-REVENUE OFFICERS).				
GELSTON & SCHENCK, for relief	169	15	1	1
GEORGE, SAMUEL K., for relief	154	28	2	4
GEORGIA,				
Creek and Cherokee Indian Reservation in, to purchase	57	17	2	1
Refund to State 15 per cent. on direct tax paid by	46	14	2	1
Do	58	14	2	1
Resolution of legislature for total repeal of tariff act of 1828	98	21	1	1
GODARD, CHARLES W., for relief	126	45	3	7
Do	1281	47	1	7
GODDARD, N., for relief	83	15	1	1
GOODING, JOHN, for relief	1	15	2	1
Do	74	15	2	1
Do	1	16	1	1
GORDON, MORGAN S., for relief	149	23	1	2

Subject	Report.	Congress.	Session.	Volume.
GOVE, GEORGE B. R., for relief	60	17	2	1
GOVE, JESSE, for relief	304	28	1	2
GRAEFF, MARY, for relief	61	15	1	1
GRAEF, WILBER H., & CO., for relief	3401	49	1	8
GRAHAM, JAMES, for relief	29	16	1	1
GRAIN, to permit Canadian farmers to bring grain over border to be ground	1462	47	1	7
GRAND GULF RAILROAD, claim for relief	1013	27	2	3
GRANT, JAMES D., for relief	150	46	2	7
GRAPE BRANDY, to remit tax on, used to fortify wine for export	2882	49	1	8
GRAPESHOT (bark), for relief of owners of	59	45	3	7
Do	10	46	2	7
GREELY, PHILIP and ELIPHALET, for relief	582	21	1	1
Do	587	22	1	2
Do.*	109	24	1	3
GREEN, THOMAS, for relief	475	25	1	4
Do	71	29	1	4
GREENBACKS. (*See* TREASURY NOTES.)				
GREERLY & CO., for relief	336	23	1	2
GREGORY, JOHN W., for relief	275	46	3	7
GRIFFIN, THOMAS, for relief	144	15	1	1
GRIGSBY, MARTIN, for relief	2496	42	2	8
GWATHMEY, HUMPHREY B., for relief	208	23	1	2
HALDEAMAN, W. N., for relief	53	44	2	5
HALEY, D. W., and others, for relief	710	26	1	3
HALL, BENJAMIN F., for relief	52	25	1	4
HALL, DUDLEY & CO., for relief	2448	48	2	8
Do	83	49	1	8
HALL, JOHN P., for relief	912	45	3	7
Do	1617	46	2	7
HAMBURG, GERMANY, remission of certain discriminating duties imposed on vessels belonging to city of	176	19	1	1
HANCOCK & MOORMAN, for relief	6	45	2	7
HARPER, SAMUEL, for relief	584	46	2	7
HARRISON & SMALL, for relief	180	46	3	7
Do	245	47	1	7
HAWAIIAN ISLANDS.				
Duties on sugars, to regulate	1880	46	2	7
Treaty with the, to carry into effect	116	44	1	5
Treaty with, to terminate	*1759	49	1	8
HAWLEY, RICHARD, & SONS, for relief	563	43	1	5
HAY, to regulate import duty on	1736	47	1	7
HAY, R. D., for relief	2017	48	1	8
HAZLETINE, BENJAMIN, for relief	29	18	1	1
HEARD, JOHN (assignee), for relief	36	20	1	1
Do	184	20	1	1
Do	270	21	1	1
Do	58	22	1	2
HENDERLITE, GEORGE W., for relief	1348	46	2	7
HENDERSON, JOHN, for relief	185	43	1	5
Do	703	45	2	7
HENNAMAN, JOHN T., for relief	384	47	1	7
HERMAN, HENRY, for relief	1634	47	1	7
HIBBEN & CO., for relief	103	43	2	5
HICKS, SAMUEL, & SONS, for relief	1018	26	3	3
HODSDON, EBENEZER, for relief	29	18	1	1
HOLGATE, H. & M., for relief	419	29	1	4
HORWITZ, ORVILLE, for relief	646	47	1	7
Do	2497	48	2	8
HOUSE OF REPRESENTATIVES, power of, to originate revenue bills	42	41	3	4
HOWE, DAVID, for relief	29	18	1	1
HOWE, SILAS Q., for relief	2005	47	2	7
Do	188	48	1	8
HUME, W. S., for relief	130	46	3	7
Do	245	47	1	7
HUMES, JAMES, for relief	16	14	1	1
HUNT, FIDELIO S., for relief	810	44	1	5
HUNT, GEORGE S., & CO., for relief	2434	48	2	8
Do	80	49	1	8
HUNT, NATHANIEL, for relief	13	20	1	1
ILLINOIS, customs duties paid on uniforms, to Company G, Sixth Regiment National Guards, State of, to refund	265	46	3	7
Do	334	47	1	7
IMPORT DUTIES.				
Carriages and harness, relating to duty on	79	14	2	1
Coffee from Netherlands discriminating	202	46	3	7
Collection of, to amend laws relative to	323	23	1	2
Do	3446	49	1	8
Discriminating.				
Imposed on certain Hamburg vessels and cargoes	176	19	1	1
Tea and coffee imported from possessions of the Netherlands	202	46	3	7

* And views of minority

Subject.

IMPORT DUTIES—Continued.
Cigars manufactured in United States of imported leaf tobac
Limitation of
Revised Statutes relating to, section 3019
Secretary of Treasury to grant relief in certain cases withlaws in relation to drawbacks
Sugar exported, additional drawback on refined
Tobacco exported
Do
Foreign spirits, increasing duty on imported
Overcharge on, providing remedies for
Refunding of,
California duties collected from imports prior to ad Union as a State
Hamburg vessels, imposed upon cargoes
Goods on shipboard at date of tariff of 1883
Statues to St. John's University, Collegeville, Minn
Remission of,
Altar and regalia for Catholic church at Carrolltown, Pa
Altars for Catholic church in parish of La Fayette, La.
Articles for colored race exposition at Chicago
Bibles and other religious books in Chinese language
Books imported for use of the blind
Exhibits for Minneapolis industrial exposition
Goods for Bottlers' Protective Association
Lecturn for St. Luke's Episcopal church, Kalamazoo, M
Materials used in ship-building
Do
Merchandise duties imposed by act of May 19, 1828
Prize silver cup won by A. B. Van Heusen
St. Francis Xavier Cathedral
On statue of Washington imported into United States
Rates of, fixing
Salt, to repeal
Act of July 14, 1832, duties on imports
Act of July 14, 1832, to amend
Act of August 30, 1842, to modify
Do
Agricultural implements
Barley malt, fixing rate on
Books for blind
Cotton goods
Fish, fresh, from Canada
Hay, to regulate
Iron, hoop, band, and scroll
Iron manufactured
Laws, amending
Do
Do
Laws, modifying existing
Do
Machinery
Printing of documents relating to
Printing statistics of, into the United States
Sugar, amend law relative to
Do
Sugar, from Hawaiian Islands
Teas, equalize on the various grades of
Relative to tin manufacture
Raw materials used in construction and repair of vessels e trade
Reduce and equalize
Do
Reduction of, message of President
Do
Tea from Netherlands, discriminating
Do
Tobacco, to amend law relative to duties on
Do
Tonnage on vessels, relating to
Vessels, from foreign ports, fixing rate of tonnage tax
Vessels engaged in foreign trade, raw material used in const
Warehousing
Wines, reducing duties on certain
Wool, restoration of tariff of 1867
Woolen goods
INDEPENDENT TREASURY,
Establishment of a United States
Do
Security of public funds in

* Views of minority.

Subject.	Report.	Congress.	Session.	Volume.
INDIANS,				
Appropriations for,				
1842	*75	27	2	3
Do	†738	30	1	4
Do	301	33	1	4
1854	‡92	33	2	4
Do	174	35	2	4
Creeks, appropriation to satisfy claims of friendly	62	14	2	1
Do	101	18	1	1
Creek, depredations by, providing for payment of	343	22	1	2
Creek and Cherokee reservation in Georgia, appropriation for purchase of	57	17	2	1
Treaty of 1802 between United States and Creek	343	22	1	2
INSOLVENT DEBTORS OF THE UNITED STATES, relief of certain	300	22	1	3
INSPECTORS, appointment in the revenue department of secret	90	29	2	4
INTERNAL IMPROVEMENT, distribution of surplus revenue among the States for	551	24	1	3
INTERNAL REVENUE,				
Licenses upon retailers	80	14	2	1
Tax on domestic spirits by act of July, 1813	48	20	1	1
INTERNAL-REVENUE LAWS,				
Entry and withdrawal from warehouses of spirits, amend law relative to	2368	49	1	8
Small distilleries, amend law relative to	2094	49	1	8
Tobacco, cigars, and snuff, inspection of, to amend	2633	49	1	8
Tobacco,				
Leaf, amend act of March 3, 1883	2617	48	2	8
Cut, packing and selling, to amend law for	2760	49	1	8
To repeal	5	15	1	1
Vinegar made from grain, regulate manufacture of	3164	49	1	8
INTERNAL-REVENUE OFFICERS,				
Compensation of the collectors of Plymouth, N. C., Edgartown, Mass., Kennebunk. Me., and Middlebury, Conn	69	14	2	1
Gaugers, compensation of, to regulate	1306	47	1	7
Collectors, to fix term of office of	496	47	1	7
Authorizing the Secretary of the Treasury to pay certain	456	45	2	7
INTERNAL-REVENUE STAMPS,				
To repeal section 17 of act of March 1, 1879, relative to redemption of unused	1735	46	2	7
To repeal limitation on redemption of	698	47	1	7
INTERNAL-REVENUE TAXES (*see also* BANK TAXES; DISTILLED SPIRITS; TOBACCO),				
Report of conference committee relative to repeal of part of act of July 27, 1871, relating to	42	41	3	4
Payment of moieties to informers	559	43	1	5
Bank checks, to abolish	307	46	3	7
Bonds of cigar manufacturers, to amend law	2438	49	1	8
Continental Insurance Company, to refund to	2185	48	2	8
Deposits, to abolish	307	46	3	7
Distilled spirits, to extend time for payment on	473	48	1	8
Drafts, to abolish	307	46	3	7
Fractional parts of a gallon, amend law	100	49	1	8
Friction matches, to abolish	307	46	3	7
Grape brandy used to fortify wine for exportation, to remit tax on	2632	49	1	8
Licenses to retailers, relating to duty on	80	14	2	1
Proprietary articles, to abolish	307	46	3	7
Tobacco, to repeal tax on	3210	49	1	8
To reduce	3209	49	1	8
Collection of, amend act of March, 1868, exempting certain manufacturers from paying	81	40	2	4
Refunding,				
Distillers of the sixth collection district of Pennsylvania	24	17	1	1
Distillers of Berks County, Pennsylvania	18	18	1	1
Distilled spirits of 1813	43	20	1	1
Income tax collected on salaries of State officers	248	47	1	7
IOWA, authorizing sale of lands devised to United States by John Gardner, situate in Dallas County, State of	1738	47	1	7
IRON MOUNTAIN BANK, Saint Louis, Mo., for relief	596	46	2	7
IRON ORE, to correct error in law fixing rate of duties on	1280	47	1	7
IRON AND STEEL,				
To regulate duties	§1398	46	2	7
To regulate duties on manufactured	257	46	3	7
JELLISON, ZACHARIAH, for relief	440	25	2	3
Do	7	26	1	3
JOHNSON, LEWIS, & CO., for relief	1070	47	1	7
JOHNSTON, DANIEL, for relief	29	18	1	1
JONES, GEORGE, for relief	319	23	1	2
JUDAH, MANUEL, for relief	27	14	1	1
KEARNEY, THOMAS, for relief	140	44	2	5
Do	884	45	2	7
Do	7	46	2	7
KENDRICK & AVIS, for relief	414	44	1	5

* Same for 1848–'49. † Same for 1855. ‡ Same for 1858. § Parts 1, 2.

Subject.	Report.	Congress.	Session.	Volume.
KENNEBUNK, MAINE, relating to salary of collector at	69	14	2	
KEYS, PURLEY, relief on official bond	26	15	1	
KIMBALL, W. S. & CO., *et al.*, for relief	591	46	2	
Do	1508	47	1	
KING, WILLIAM S. (*See* PACIFIC MAIL STEAMSHIP COMPANY.)				
KNIGHTON, CHARLES J., for relief	145	43	2	
KNIT GOODS, to correct error in law fixing rate of duties on	1280	47	1	
KNOWLES, SETH, for relief	131	20	1	
KUNER, ZISEMAN & ZOTT, for relief	414	44	1	
LA FAYETTE, LOUISIANA, altars for Catholic church, to admit free of duty	1453	49	1	
LA MAITRE, JOHN B., for relief	34	20	1	
LA PORTENA (steamer), for relief of builders	393	43	1	
LARGE, HENRY, Jr., for relief	382	47	1	
LASALA, JOHN B., for relief	299	26	1	
LATHAM, THOMAS, for relief	278	25	3	
Do	300	26	1	
LAWSON & BREUIS, for relief	47	44	1	
LEE, ALFRED E., for relief	440	47	1	
LEE, JOHN, for relief	29	18	1	
LEE, RICHARD H., for relief	378	29	1	
LEGISLATIVE, EXECUTIVE, AND JUDICIAL EXPENSES, Senate amendments to bill making appropriations for the	187	35	2	
LEHMANN, L., for relief	712	49	1	
LEIBERT, FERDINAND, claim for relief	949	27	2	
LEWIS, JOHN F., for relief	95	23	2	
LEXINGTON AND OHIO RAILROAD COMPANY., for relief	152	24	1	
LIBRARY OF CONGRESS, relative to an appropriation for use of the	69	16	1	
LICENSES, modifying act laying duties on licenses to retailers of wines, spirituous liquors, and foreign merchandise	80	14	2	
LIENS ON IMPORTED GOODS, to amend section 2981 Revised Statutes relative to	1448	46	2	
LIFE-SAVING STATIONS, keepers of the, appointment and payment of	870	35	1	
LIGHT-HOUSE, to erect at mouth of Vermillion Bay, Louisiana	342	28	1	
LITTLE, OTIS, for relief	29	18	1	
LONERGAN, P. F., for relief	587	47	1	
LOW, A. A., & BROTHERS, for relief	2083	47	2	
LOW, ANDREW (assignee), for relief	5	26	1	
LOW, TAYLOR & CO., for relief of assignee of	5	26	1	
LOWELL, JAMES, for relief	208	24	2	
Do	522	25	2	
LOWENTHAL, BERTHOLD, for relief	102	43	2	
Do	393	44	1	
LYNCH, DOMINICK, for relief	200	23	1	
Do	394	23	1	
LYNCH, THOMAS, for relief	796	48	1	
McCLINTOCK, JOHN M., for relief	143	46	3	
Do	639	47	1	
Do	498	48	1	
McCOBB, PARKER, for relief	395	21	1	
Do	103	22	1	
McCOMB, SAMUEL, for relief	464	25	2	
McCULLAH, JAMES A., for relief	77	42	2	
Do	78	42	2	
Do	487	43	1	
McCULLOUGH, HUGH, for relief	11	16	1	
McDANIEL, ALFRED W., for relief of sureties	710	26	1	
McDONNELL, JOHN, for relief	69	20	1	
McDOWALL, HAYNE & CO., for relief	264	27	2	
McJIMSEY, ROBERT, for relief	331	23	1	
McKAY & ALDUS, for relief	393	43	1	
MACEY, FRANCIS G., for relief	32	18	1	
MACKEREL, to prohibit importation and landing of, during spawning season	343	49	1	
MALSTER, WILLIAM T., for relief	158	44	2	
MANLEY, DANIEL, *et al.*, for relief	74	15	1	
MARIA and LAUCERO (Spanish vessels), concerning the remission of duties on cargoes of	1099	27	2	
MARSH, THOMAS, for relief	12	20	1	
MARSHALS, UNITED STATES, EASTERN DISTRICT OF PENNSYLVANIA, to discharge sundry judgments against	486	22	1	
Do	103	22	2	
MARTIN, WILLIAM D., for relief	593	46	2	
Do	135	47	1	
MARYLAND, to adjudicate and settle claim of State for moneys advanced during war of 1812	41	33	2	
MATCHES, to repeal tax on	307	46	3	
MATHEWS, THOMAS, *et al.*, for relief	2608	48	2	
MAYS, ROBERT, for relief	6	46	2	
METERS FOR DISTILLERIES, to test	321	46	3	
Do	568	47	1	
MEXICO, to carry into effect convention of 1883 with	1848	48	1	
Do	*2615	49	1	

* And views of minority.

Subject.	Report.	Congress.	Session.	Volume.
MICHIGAN, to remit certain taxes and penalties claimed to be due from mining and other corporations in the sixth collection district of	360	42	2	6
MIDDLETOWN, CONNECTICUT, relating to salary of collectors at	69	14	2	1
MILITARY ACADEMY, appropriations for support of, for 1855-'56	26	33	2	4
MILITIA, expediency of increasing appropriation for arming the	15	17	1	1
MILLER, BARBARA, for relief	71	44	2	5
MILLER, JOHN S., for relief	71	44	2	5
Do	30	45	2	7
MILLER, WILLIAM D., for relief	6	46	2	7
MILLER, WILLIAM H., for relief	71	44	2	5
MILLER & BRO., for relief	130	46	2	7
Do	345	47	1	7
MILLS, W. W., for relief	131	45	3	7
MINNEAPOLIS INDUSTRIAL EXPOSITION, to remit duties on exhibits for	3643	48	1	8
MINT, UNITED STATES,				
Completing the buildings	372	21	1	1
Establishing branch at Denver, Colo	86	37	2	4
Establishing a branch in Nevada Territory	17	37	3	4
MIRANDA, PEDRO, for relief	186	19	1	1
MITCHELL, WILLIAM, for relief	62	34	1	3
MOIETIES, to repeal so much of act May 8, 1872, as provides for employment of persons to assist the proper officers in discovering and collecting money withheld	559	43	1	5
To repeal all	645	43	1	5
MONTELL, JAMES E., for relief	262	46	2	7
Do	644	47	1	7
MOORE & LEWIS, for relief	419	43	1	5
MORDECAI & CO., for relief	1609	47	1	7
MORGAN, THOMAS, for relief	144	15	1	1
MORRISON, J. D., for relief	2	46	3	7
Do	184	47	1	7
Do	1852	48	1	8
Do	186	49	1	8
MURPHY, R. C., for relief	106	35	1	4
N. P. BANKS (vessel), for relief of builders	398	43	1	5
N. & G. TAYLOR COMPANY, for relief	123	45	3	7
Do	187	46	2	7
NACHTRIEL & CO., for relief	414	44	1	5
NATIONAL BANKS. (*See* BANK OF UNITED STATES.)				
NATIONAL ROADS, repairing and continuing certain territorial roads, 1834	198	23	1	2
NAVY, appropriation bill for 1842 for the	673	27	2	3
NEAPOLITAN INDEMNITY STOCK, purchase by the United States of certain	441	25	2	3
NETHERLANDS, to repeal discriminating duties on tea and coffee from possessions of	202	46	3	7
NEVADA, to establish branch mint in Territory of	17	37	3	4
NEWMAN & TATHAM, for relief	1800	47	1	7
NEW ORLEANS AND NASHVILLE RAILROAD, for relief	910	27	2	3
NEW YORK CITY,				
For the relief of the sufferers by fire in	41	24	1	2
Relative to sale of old site of post-office in	123	45	3	7
Do	21	46	1	7
Do	1118	46	2	7
NICHOLSON, THOMAS A., for relief	4	45	1	7
NOBLE, BUTLER G., for relief	126	45	3	7
Do	1281	47	1	7
NORRISTOWN AND VALLEY RAILROAD COMPANY, for relief	463	27	2	3
NORTH GERMAN LLOYD STEAMSHIP COMPANY, for relief	1573	47	1	7
Do	1429	48	1	8
NORTH MISSOURI RAILROAD, to indemnify company for losses sustained to road during the rebellion	29	39	2	4
NORTHAM & WHITEHORNE, for relief	256	24	2	3
NORVELL, HENRY J., for relief	1615	46	2	7
OATHS, to empower postmasters to administer same to importers of books	1737	47	1	7
OCEAN INSURANCE COMPANY, and others, New York, for relief	486	22	1	2
Do	103	22	2	2
OHL, J. F., for relief	170	20	1	1
Do	406	21	1	1
Do	344	23	1	2
OLEOMARGARINE,				
Taxing manufacture of	1529	47	1	7
To regulate the sale of	1529	47	1	7
ONLEY, HENRY T., & SON, for relief	2591	48	2	8
OSBORN, JAMES W., for relief	537	24	1	3
OSBORN, WILLIAM, for relief	227	22	1	2
PACIFIC MAIL STEAMSHIP COMPANY. (*See* SUBSIDY.)				
PAINE, THOMAS, for relief	224	21	1	1
Do	14	22	1	2
PATE, WILLIAM T., & CO., for relief	1	46	3	7
PEABODY, JOSEPH, and others, purchase by United States of certain Neapolitan indemnity stock owned by	441	25	2	3
PEA PATCH ISLAND, relative to title to	1010	27	2	3

Subject.	Report.	Congress.	Session.
PEARSON, PAUL, for relief	319	22	1
PENDLETON, E. BOYD, for relief	141	43	2
PENNSYLVANIA,			
Distillers of the sixth collection district of, relief	24	17	1
Distillers of Berks County, relief	13	18	1
To discharge certain judgments against marshal of eastern district of	486	22	1
Do	103	22	2
PENNY, J. P. and E. B., for relief	88	21	2
Do	4	22	1
PENSIONS,			
Prescribing the mode of paying pensions granted by the United States	263	23	1
Appropriation bill granting	175	25	2
PEOPLE'S NATIONAL BANK, LAWRENCEBURG, INDIANA, to issue duplicate certificate of deposit to	2449	48	2
PERKINS, THOMAS H., for relief	43	24	2
PETREE, J. J., for relief	457	45	2
PHILADELPHIA, PENNSYLVANIA,			
Saint Peter's Church of, for relief of	19	27	3
Church of Holy Trinity, to remit duties to	1632	47	1
Saving Fund Society, for relief	512	28	1
PHILADELPHIA AND READING RAILROAD, for relief	259	46	3
Do	25	47	1
PHINNEY & JACKSON, for relief	2447	48	2
Do	31	49	1
PINKINTON, E. T., for relief	645	47	1
PLEMMONS, S. D., for relief	1802	47	1
PLYMOUTH, NORTH CAROLINA, relating to salary of collector of	69	14	2
POLLOCK, WILLIAM J., for relief	882	45	2
Do	592	46	2
Do	165	47	1
POOLE, BENJAMIN, for relief	117	15	1
PORT OF ENTRY AND DELIVERY, to constitute Atlanta, Ga., a	149	46	3
POSTS, FRONTIER, to amend section 2633 Revised Status, relative to establishment of	328	46	3
POST-OFFICE DEPARTMENT, appropriations for the service of the	189	23	2
POSTAL SERVICE, subsidy paid to the Pacific Mail Steamship Company for transportation of mails	268	43	2
POSTMASTERS, to empower, to administer oaths to importers of books	1737	47	1
POWELL, W. H., & CO., for relief	733	44	1
Do	132	45	3
Do	602	46	2
PRESIDENT AND VICE-PRESIDENT, relative to increasing allowance to persons employed in transmitting to Congress the votes of	21	16	2
PRICE, LEVI, for relief	1773	46	2
PRIZE MONEY, to allow owners, officers, and crew of the brig Warrior certain amount of	738	24	1
Do	966	25	2
Do	877	27	2
PROPRIETARY ARTICLES, to repeal tax on	307	48	3
PUBLIC DEBT. (*See* DEBT OF UNITED STATES.)			
PUBLIC DEPOSITS. (*See* DEPOSITS; BANK OF THE UNITED STATES.)			
QUINCY, WM. and CHARLES E., for relief	161	20	1
RAILROADS, (NOTE.—See under titles of respective railroad companies.)			
RAW MATERIALS, regulating importation of, used in construction and repair of vessels engaged in foreign trade	1261	46	2
RAY, ELIZA J., for relief	2450	48	2
Do	2375	49	1
RECEIPTS AND EXPENDITURES.			
Tabulated statement of public,			
For year 1816-'17	14	14	
For year 1820	91	16	
For year 1821	6	17	
For year 1825	64	19	
For year 1827	185	20	1
For year 1838	716	25	2
For year 1839	218	25	3
For year 1843	227	27	3
RED RIVER, to complete the removal of raft of	426	26	1
REVENUE (*see also* IMPORT DUTIES),			
Act of 1842 to amend	*306	28	1
Do	*406	28	1
Auction sales, regulations for	44	20	2
Amount necessary to meet public expenditures	57	16	2
Collection of, amend laws relative to	323	23	1
Collection and safe-keeping	634	25	2
Do	309	28	1
Creation and distribution of a stock of $200,000,000	851	24	1
Surplus, distributing the	851	24	1

* Views of minority

Subject.	Report.	Congress.	Session.	Volume.
REVENUE—Continued.				
President's message on	14	14	1	1
(NOTE.—Upon this report several bills were founded, repealing duties on certain articles and modifying others.)				
Receipts and expenditures for the year 1838	716	25	2	3
Tabulated statement of the sources from which annual revenue is derived (1814)	14	14	1	1
Do	91	16	1	1
Do	185	20	1	1
Tabular statement of state of public revenue for year 1820	91	16	1	1
Do. 1821	6	17	1	1
Do. 1825	64	19	1	1
To reduce	88	24	2	3
REVENUE BILLS, power of Senate to originate bills for raising	42	41	3	4
REVISED STATUTES,				
To amend and repeal,				
Section 2504, duties on manufactures of iron, &c	257	46	3	7
Section 2504, duty on knit goods	1280	47	1	7
Section 2504, 2505, duty on iron ore	1280	47	1	7
Section 2552, changing terminus of railroad to Cape Charles	1619½	49	1	8
Section 2632, frontier posts	328	46	3	7
Section 2743, examiner of drugs	1887	47	2	7
Section 2981, liens on imported goods	1448	46	2	7
Section 2983, sugar duties	1510	47	1	7
Section 3058, ownership of imports	3066	49	1	8
Section 3066, search warrants	786	47	1	7
Section 3151, inspection of tobacco, cigars, and snuff	2683	49	1	8
Section 3244, tax on oleomargarine	1529	47	1	7
Section 3244, to amend law relative to tax on leaf tobacco	1891	46	2	7
Section 3282, manufacture of vinegar	212	46	1	7
Section 3328, relative to tax on native wines	589	47	1	7
Section 3336, brewers' bonds	1146	49	1	8
Section 3357, tobacco manufactories	1363	49	1	8
Section 3385, cancellation of bonds on exportation of tobacco, &c	1384	46	2	7
Do	703	47	1	7
Section 3385, relative export stamp on tobacco	210	46	2	7
Do	184	47	1	7
Do	703	47	1	7
RICE, HENRY G., for relief	32	19	2	1
Do	7	20	1	1
RIDGWAY, RICHARD C., *et al.*, for relief	2193	48	2	8
RIVERS AND HARBORS,				
Appropriation for improvement of, for 1836–'37 and 1837–'38	297	24	1	3
Do	175	24	2	3
Public works on, estimates to close accounts in relation to	767	24	1	3
Red River, removal of the rafts on	426	26	1	3
RIVES, J. H., for relief	604	46	2	7
ROBERTS, GEORGE F. (administrator), for relief	2609	48	2	8
ROBERTSON, J. E., & CO., for relief	293	43	2	5
Do	355	44	1	5
ROBINSON, R. R., for relief	1316	46	2	7
RODDY, ALEXANDER, for relief	66	16	1	1
ROGERS, DAVID, & SON, for relief	36	20	2	1
Do	114	21	1	1
ROGERS, RICHARDSON & CO., for relief	861	45	2	7
ROLLINS, PINKNEY, for relief	23	44	2	5
ROSENFELD, S., & CO., for relief	1129	46	2	7
Do	185	47	1	7
ROSS, JAMES, for relief	16	17	1	1
ROWE, D. P., for relief	455	44	1	5
ROWLEY, WILLIAM H., & SONS, for relief	2317	48	2	8
RUM, drawbacks on exported	143	21	1	1
RUSSELL, SAMUEL P., for relief	126	45	3	7
Do	1281	47	1	7
RYAN, THOMAS F., for relief	145	43	2	5
SAINT CLAIR, F. O., to refund duties to	1633	47	1	7
SAINT FRANCIS XAVIER CATHEDRAL, VINCENNES, to remit duties to	1837	47	2	7
SAINT JOHN'S UNIVERSITY, COLLEGEVILLE, MINNESOTA, to refund duties on statues for	2487	48	2	8
SAINT LUKE'S CHURCH, KALAMAZOO, MICHIGAN, to remit duty on lecturn for use of	2287	49	1	8
SAINT MICHAEL'S CHURCH, CHARLESTON, SOUTH CAROLINA, for relief	381	45	2	7
Do	1619	46	2	7
SAINT PETER'S CHURCH, PHILADELPHIA, for relief	19	27	3	3
SALARIES,				
Appraisers of customs, increased compensation of local	640	47	1	7
Do	641	47	1	7
Clerks in public offices, increase of pay of	641	24	1	3
Do	161	24	2	3
Collector of port at Chicago, to fix salary of	1523	47	1	7
Gaugers, to regulate compensation of internal-revenue	1206	47	1	7

Subject.	Report.	Congress.	Session.	Volume.
SALT, to repeal the law laying duty on	132	15	1	
SAN ANTONIO, TEXAS, to extend privileges of act of June 10, 1880, to	1852	48	1	
SANBORN CONTRACTS, investigation relative to	559	43	1	
SANFORD, THOMAS, for relief	360	23	1	
SAUNDERS, CHARLES H., for relief	27	14	2	
SCULL, JAMES, for relief	5	20	2	
SEABURN, JAMES, for relief	465	27	2	
SEAMAN, EDWARD B., for relief	126	45	3	
Do	1281	47	1	
SEARCH WARRANTS, for smuggled goods, to amend law	756	47	1	
SECRET INSPECTORS, appointment in the revenue department	90	29	2	
SECRETARY OF STATE, authorizing appointment of an assistant	491	31	1	
SECRETARY OF TREASURY (*see also* FINANCES),				
Annual report concerning the public revenue	14	14	1	
Do	91	16	1	
Do	6	17	1	
Do	64	19	1	
Do	185	20	1	
Report of the, on the state of the finances for 1843	227	27	3	
Report of the, on the state of the finances for 1844	306	28	1	
Placing of the 5 per cent. bonds upon the market by	7	42	2	
Report, estimates of appropriations	303	25	2	
To make loan for $12,000,000 stock	26	18	2	
To authorize drawback after twenty days	10	18	2	
SELFRIDGE, JAMES L., for relief	836	47	1	
SENATE OF UNITED STATES, power to originate bills for raising revenue	42	41	3	
SEWALL, WILLIAMS & CO., for relief	166	19	1	
Do	180	19	1	
SHENNON, THOMAS B., for relief	1462	47	1	
Do	187	48	1	
SHERWOOD, HORATIO N., for relief	126	45	3	
Do	1281	47	1	
SHIP-BUILDING (*see also* COMMERCE AND NAVIGATION),				
To remit duties on materials used in construction and repair of vessels to be employed in foreign carrying trade	1261	46	2	
Do	1461	47	1	
SHIPLEY, SMITH & CO., for relief	2588	48	2	
SHOUSE, WILLIAM, for relief of widow of	457	45	2	
SIMPSON, GEORGE,				
For relief of widow of	165	20	1	
For relief of administrator	662	30	1	
SINKING FUND,				
To apply, after year 1816, the sum of $13,500,000 annually to	14	14	1	
Increasing the sum to be applied annually to	34	14	2	
SIXTH COLLECTION DISTRICT OF PENNSYLVANIA, for relief of certain distillers of the	24	17	1	
SIXTH ILLINOIS REGIMENT, NATIONAL GUARD, for relief of Company G	265	46	3	
Do	334	47	1	
SLAVE TRADE,				
Disposal of captured Africans, delivered from on board vessels seized by commanders of United States war vessels	65	19	1	
Measures for suppression of	65	19	1	
SMEATON, JOHN, for relief	244	47	1	
SMILEY, ALEXANDER, for relief	599	46	2	
SMITH, JOHN H., & CO., for relief	6	46	2	
SMITH, JOHN T., & CO., for relief	6	46	2	
SMITH, JONATHAN S., for relief	78	17	1	
Do	36	17	2	
SMITH & MATTHEWS, for relief	644	43	1	
SMUGGLING. (*See* SEARCH WARRANTS.)				
SNEAD, E. K., for relief	763	44	1	
SNUFF. (*See* TOBACCO.)				
SOULÉ, FRANK, for relief	1616	46	2	
SPALDING, GEORGE, for relief	137	23	1	
STATE BANKS, regulating the Government deposits in certain	422	23	1	
STATE DEBTS, payment by the United States of the various	120	27	3	
STATES, to refund money assessed under direct tax of 1861 to	903	48	1	
STATUES OF WASHINGTON, to admit free of duty a statue of Washington	181	19		
STAUBER, SAMUEL B., for relief	457	45		
STICKNEY, HENRY R., for relief	1029	25	3	
STILLS and WORMS, allowing drawback on exportation of	679	47		
STITZEL, F., & BROTHER, for relief	1447	46		
STOHRER, JOSEPH, for relief	69	14		
STONE, JOHN, for relief	29	20		
SUBSIDIES, investigation relative to the Pacific Mail Steamship Company	268	43		
SUGAR (*see also* HAWAIIAN ISLANDS),				
To allow an additional drawback on exportation of refined	67	18	2	
Duties on	1899	46	2	
Do	1510	47	1	
SUMATRA TOBACCO, to amend law relative to	2617	48	2	
SUMMIT COAL AND RAILROAD COMPANY, for relief	514	27	2	

Subject.	Report.	Congress.	Session.	Volume.
SUTHERLIN, JOHN F., & BROTHER, for relief	439	44	1	5
SWEENEY, JOHN, for relief	430	22	1	4
TANNER & ASHER, for relief	6	46	2	7
TAPP, W. J., & CO., for relief	681	46	2	7
TAPPAN, JOHN, for relief	29	18	1	1
TARIFF ACT OF 1828, resolution of Georgia legislature asking for total repeal of	96	21	1	1
TARIFF COMMISSION,				
Appointing, to investigate the question of tariff	305	47	1	7
Report of	1881	47	2	7
TATHAM, P. B., for relief	1601	47	1	7
TAYLOR, JOHN G., for relief	606	47	1	7
TAYLOR, N. and G., & CO., refunding duty erroneously assessed against	125	46	2	7
Do	197	46	2	7
TAYLOR & WALKER, for relief	74	15	1	1
TEAS,				
To equalize duties on the various grades of	169	20	1	1
To repeal discriminating duties on, from Netherlands	202	46	2	7
To prevent importation of adulterated	1937	47	2	7
Do	665	42	1	5
TELEGRAPHS, continuing, from Baltimore to New York	187	28	2	4
THAYER, WILLIAM B., for relief of administrator	2806	48	2	8
THEUS, SIMEON, for relief of administrator of	209	21	1	1
THIERMAN & FROST, for relief	519	44	1	5
THOMAS, JOHN L., Jr., for relief	20	41	3	4
THOMAS, WILLIAM B., for relief	180	43	1	5
THOMPKINS, MINTHORNE, et al., for relief	2541	48	2	8
THOMPSON, EDWARD, for relief	496	22	1	2
Do	108	22	2	2
THOMPSON, G. W., & CO., for relief	130	46	2	7
Do	245	47	1	7
THOMPSON, WILLIAM H., for relief	566	46	2	7
THOMPSON & CO., for relief	130	46	2	7
Do	245	47	1	7
THOMSON, JAMES W., for relief	126	45	3	7
Do	1281	47	1	7
THOOFT, BARNARD, for relief	31	18	1	1
THORN, JOSEPH, for relief	49	15	1	1
TICE METERS, paying to distillers the cost of the	60	42	3	4
TIN, duties on manufactured	1804	47	1	7
TOBACCO,				
Act of March 3, 1883, relative to internal revenue on, to amend	2617	48	2	8
Bonds of cigar manufacturers, to amend law relative to	2438	49	1	8
Cancellation of export bonds on exportation of cigars, snuff, and	1264	46	2	7
Dealers in leaf, to amend law relative to tax paid by	1391	46	2	7
Drawback on the exportation of cigars manufactured in the United States of imported leaf	688	24	1	3
Export manufactories of, to establish	2310	48	2	8
Do	1141	49	1	8
Inspection of, cigars, and snuff, to amend law providing for	2633	49	1	8
Manufactures, to repeal taxes on, and all	*1818	47	2	7
Manufactories, to amend law relative to	1352	49	1	8
Packing and selling cut, to amend law relative to	2760	49	1	8
Perique, tax on	1635	47	1	7
Tax on export of, to repeal	703	47	1	7
Taxes on, to repeal	3310	49	1	8
Tobacco and snuff, section 3385 Revised Statutes, relative to export stamp on	210	46	3	7
Do	184	47	1	7
TOMPKINS, DANIEL D., to adjudicate and settle accounts of, late governor of New York	1	18	1	1
Do	107	18	1	1
TOMPKINS, MINTHORNE, for relief	426	45	3	7
Do	1281	47	1	7
TONNAGE DUTIES,				
Amending act regulating	7	14	1	1
Repeal of	29	20	2	1
Rates on certain foreign vessels	29	20	2	1
Providing remedies for overcharge of	68	44	2	5
TRANSPORTATION IN BOND, to amend act relative to	1118	48	1	8
Do	1851	48	1	8
Do	2262	48	2	8
Do	843	49	1	8
Do	844	49	1	8
Do	845	49	1	8
Do	2041	49	1	8
Do	2736	49	1	8
TRAVIS, FRANKLIN, for relief of sureties of	945	45	2	7
Do	1618	46	2	7
TREASURY DEPARTMENT, relating to probable receipts and expenditures for year 1838 by the	716	25	2	3

* Parts 1, 2.

Subject.	Report.	Congress.	Session.
TREASURY NOTES,			
Issue of	379	28	1
Issue and redemption of	83	37	2
Indemnifying innocent holders of purloined	512	28	1
TREATIES,			
Creek Indian, 1802, relative to carrying into effect	243	22	1
Hawaiian Islands, to carry into effect and ratify, with the	116	44	1
TREATY OF FORT WILKINSON, claim for property destroyed under	243	22	1
TUFTS & BLACK, for relief	199	23	1
UNON GOLD MINING COMPANY, for relief	216	24	1
UNITED STATES, assumption and payment of State debts by	120	27	3
UNIVERSITY, SAINT JOHN'S, MINNESOTA, to refund duty on works of art for	2437	48	2
UNITED STATES DEPOSITORIES, denominating certain State banks as, for public moneys	422	23	1
UNCLAIMED DIVIDENDS OF THE FUNDED DEBT, disposal of	139	19	1
VAN HEUSEN, A. B., to remit duty on prize silver cup won by	116	48	1
VERMILLION BAY, LOUISIANA, light-house and buoys at mouth of, relative to repairing	342	28	1
VESSELS (*see also* FOREIGN VESSELS; SHIP-BUILDING; SEAMEN; STEAM VESSELS),			
Ariadne (ship), loss of cargo	83	15	1
American Eagle (ship), seizure of	169	15	1
Construction and repair of, engaged in foreign trade, importation of raw materials used in	1261	46	2
Foreign, to regulate tonnage tax on	7	14	2
Tonnage duties on, to repeal	29	20	2
VINEGAR,			
Manufacture of, alcoholic vaporizing process	218	46	3
Manufacture of, to regulate	3154	49	1
VIRGINIA, liquidating and paying certain claims of State for Revolutionary services	475	28	1
Do.	71	29	
W. J. SPICER (barge), for relief of owners	256	46	
WADE, AMOS, for relief	501	26	
Do.	298	27	
WADSWORTH, ELIJAH, discharging a judgment against representatives of	17	18	
WALKER, SAMUEL D., for relief	171	23	
Do.	104	24	
Do.	433	24	1
Do.	488	28	1
WALLEY, SAMUEL, for relief	74	17	1
Do.	55	17	2
Do.	85	19	1
WALN, S. MORRIS, & CO., for relief	642	24	1
Do.	1014	25	2
Do.	1015	25	2
Do.	997	27	2
Do.	140	32	1
WALSH, THOMAS, & CO., for relief	383	47	1
WALTON, JONATHAN, for relief	383	21	1
Do.	394	22	1
WAR OF 1812,			
Claim of Maryland for expenses incurred during	41	33	2
Claims of Virginia for moneys expended in	475	28	1
Do.	71	29	1
WAR OF REVOLUTION, documentary history of, publication of the	849	24	1
WARD, JOHN, & CO., for relief	507	28	1
WAREHOUSING,			
Establishing a system of	823	23	1
Do.	195	24	2
To amend laws for	3446	49	1
WARING, JAMES J., for relief	154	43	2
Do.	244	44	1
Do.	29	45	2
WARRIOR (armed brig), for relief of owners, officers, and crew of	738	24	1
Do.	986	25	2
Do.	877	27	2
WASHINGTON, General GEORGE, to remit duty on a monument to	306	47	1
WASHINGTON MONUMENT ASSOCIATION OF BOSTON, authorising company to import a statue of Washington free of duty	181	19	1
WATKINSON, DAVID, & CO., for relief	222	23	1
Do.	872	27	2
WEHRLE, WERK & SON, for relief	385	47	1
Do.	2028	48	1
WEISS BEER, to regulate tax on	206	46	3
Do.	442	47	1
WELLS, BENJAMIN, for relief	184	19	1
WEST POINT. (*See* MILITARY ACADEMY.)			
WESTERN UNION RAILROAD COMPANY, for relief	439	47	1
WHITEHEAD, WILLIAM, for relief	29	18	1

Subject.	Report.	Congress.	Session.	Volume.
WHITTIER, SIMEON C., for relief	14	21	2	1
WICKS, GEORGE W., & CO., for relief	615	47	1	7
WILKINSON, DAVID, & CO., for relief	709	26	1	3
WILKINSON, REUBEN, respecting claim against Creek Nation of Indians for property destroyed	243	22	1	2
WILLIAMS, JAMES, for relief	1	15	2	1
Do	74	15	2	1
Do	1	16	1	1
WILLINK, JOHN A., for relief	185	19	1	1
WILMER, WILLIAM R., for relief	62	44	2	5
Do	583	45	2	7
Do	600	46	2	7
WILMONT, JOHN, for relief	92	15	1	1
Do	56	16	1	1
WILSON, BENJAMIN W., for relief	126	45	3	7
Do	1351	47	1	7
WINE,				
Grape brandy used to fortify	2682	49	1	8
Reducing the duties on	23	15	2	1
Tax on native	569	47	1	7
WINFREE & ALLEN, for relief	6	40	2	7
WINSLOW, EDWARD, for relief	329	27	2	3
WOLCOTT, ALEXANDER, for relief	60	14	2	1
WOOD, JAQUELIN M., for relief	1727	46	2	7
WOODWARD, WILLIAM, for relief	62	24	1	2
WOOL,				
Restoration of tariff of 1867 on	*2847	49	1	8
Retain present rates on	2848	49	1	8
WORKS OF ART, to abolish discriminating duties on	1224	48	1	8
WRIGHT, PETER, & SONS, for relief	272	42	2	5
Do	301	44	1	5
WYLD, ROBERT S., for relief	606	46	2	7
YAW, JOSEPH, for relief	12	20	1	1
YELLOW METAL SHEATHING, regulating importation	1361	46	2	7

* Views of minority.

REPORTS

OF THE

SELECT AND SPEC

HOUSE OF REPRESENTATIVES,

FROM THE FOURTEENTH CONGRESS, 1815, TO
FORTY-NINTH CONGRESS, 1887, INCLUSIVE,

IN SEVENTY-SEVEN VOLUMES.

COMPILED, UNDER THE DIRECTION OF THE JOINT COMMITTEE ON PRINTING,

BY

T. H. McKEE,
CLERK DOCUMENT ROOM, UNITED STATES SENATE.

WASHINGTON:
GOVERNMENT PRINTING OFFICE.
1887.

9197 SEL II

FORTY-NINTH CONGRESS, FIRST SESSION.

[PUBLIC RESOLUTION—No. 24.]

Joint resolution authorizing the preparation of a compilation of the reports of co mittees of the Senate and House of Representatives.

Resolved by the Senate and House of Representatives of the Uni States of America in Congress assembled, That there be prepared un the direction of the Joint Committee of Printing, a compilation of reports of the Senate and House of Representatives from the Fo teenth to the Forty-eighth Congress, inclusive, classified by committ arranged, indexed, and bound in suitable volumes for the use of standing committees of the two Houses of Congress. And the sum seven thousand seven hundred and fifty dollars, or so much thereof may be found necessary, is hereby appropriated out of any money the Treasury not otherwise appropriated, for the preparation of s work, which sum may be paid by the Secretary of the Treasury u the order of the chairman of said Joint Committee, as additional pa compensation to any officer or employee of the United States.

Resolved further, That the Clerk of the House and Secretary of Senate be, and they are hereby directed, to procure and file, for the of their respective Houses, copies of all reports made by each com tee of all succeeding Congresses; and that the Clerk of the House the Secretary of the Senate be, and they are hereby, authorized directed at the close of each session of Congress, to cause said rep to be indexed and bound, one copy to be deposited in the library each House and one copy in the room of the committee from which reports emanated.

Approved, July 29, 1886.

COMPILER'S NOTICE.

This compilation embraces all the printed reports made by both Houses of Congress from the commencement of the Fourteenth to the close of the Forty-ninth Congress. They are classified by committees and arranged in numerical order. The collection for each committee is divided into volumes of suitable size. Each committee has a separate index, a copy being bound in each volume.

The SPECIAL and SELECT reports are all compiled in one collection having one index, a copy of which is bound in each volume.

The plan throughout the compilation is to place each report to the committee from which it was reported, without reference to the subject-matter.

The House and Senate reports are compiled separately. Care will be required in noticing the chronological order, as in some instances an entire session or Congress may not appear in certain volumes from the fact that during this period no reports were made by this committee.

T. H. McKEE.

INDEX

TO

SELECT COMMITTEE REPORTS,

HOUSE OF REPRESENTATIVES.

FROM 1815 TO 1887, INCLUSIVE.

Subject.	Report.	Congress.	Session.	Volume.
ACCOUNTS OF COMMISSIONERS to fix boundary line of the northwest under treaty of Ghent, settlement of	193	15	1	2
Do	56	16	1	4
ADAMS, JOHN, investigation of assault made by Jarvis Russell upon	*200	20	1	12
ADAMS, JOHN QUINCY, report upon Massachusetts resolutions proposing amendment to Constitution relating to direct taxes and representation among the States	†404	28	1	27
ADJOURNMENT OF THE NINETEENTH CONGRESS (first session)	141	19	1	19
ADMINISTRATION OF EXECUTIVE DEPARTMENTS, investigation of condition and management of	*194	24	2	19
ADMISSION OF KANSAS UNDER THE LECOMPTON CONSTITUTION	377	35	1	35
ADULTERATION OF DRUGS, IMPORTED	664	30	1	29
ADULTERATION OF FOOD. (*See* FOOD.)				
AFRICA, colonization of colored people of United States in	78	14	2	1
Do	9	15	2	2
Do	101	19	2	9
AFRICAN SLAVE TRADE,				
European powers, arrangements with, for suppression of	92	17	1	5
Liberia colony, efforts of, to suppress	348	21	1	13
To suppress, efforts of Government	70	18	2	6
AGRICULTURAL BANK, MISSISSIPPI, claim for relief	553	27	2	24
AGRICULTURE, creating bureau of	95	14	2	1
ALABAMA,				
Affairs in, Coburn's report upon	262	43	2	65
Kuklux investigation, 1871-'72 (testimony)	‡22	42	2	65
Reconstruction of	30	39	1	48
Do	21	40	2	55
ALEXANDER, J. H., memorial, on routes to the Pacific to reach California, by	145	30	2	30
ALIENS,				
Naturalization of, extend time for	1040	25	2	21
Patents, issuing of, to	458	22	1	14
ALVORD, JOHN W., connection with Freedman's Savings and Trust Company	502	44	1	67
AMELIA ISLAND, investigation as to the introduction of slaves from	46	15	1	2
AMERICA, exploration of northwest coast of	35	19	1	9
Do	213	19	1	9
AMERICAN ARTISTS,				
Employment of, to decorate and embellish walls and niches of the Capitol, illustrative of American life	198	35	2	38
Preference to be given for work upon Government buildings to	198	35	2	38
AMERICAN COLONIZATION SOCIETY, organization of free people of color in United States with view of colonizing in Africa	78	14	2	1
AMERICAN PHILOSOPHICAL SOCIETY, granting Government aid to carry on series of magnetic and meteorological observations to	680	26	1	23
AMERICAN TONNAGE, causes of reduction of	28	41	2	58
AMES, OAKES, investigation of alleged bribery by	77	42	3	60
AMISTAD CASE, investigation of alteration of House Doc. No. 18, first session Twenty-sixth Congress, relating to passport for certain slaves	51	26	2	23
ANDERSON, Hon. LUCIEN, investigation of charges of bribery and malfeasance in office against	29	38	2	47
ANDERSONVILLE PRISON, records of	30	39	1	49

* Views of minority. † Part 3. ‡ Parts 1, 2, 3.

Subject.

ANGELL, GEORGE T., evidence of poisonously adulterated markets ....
ANONYMOUS LETTER, author of one, addressed to Hon M. C. ....
APPOINTMENTS in Post-Office Department for political re also. ....
APPORTIONMENT OF CLERKS AND EMPLOYÉS A ERAL STATES ....
APPORTIONMENT OF REPRESENTATIVES,
Amendment to Constitution relating to ....
Under—
Fifth census ....
Sixth census ....
Do ....
APPROPRIATIONS for support of Army in 1818 ....
ARKANSAS,
Affairs in ....
Constitution of, 1861 ....
Election frauds in ....
Labor troubles in 1886, investigation of ....
Lands (swamp) reclaimed, donating to State ....
Memorial of legislature for national road from western fron
Poland's report on election frauds in ....
Poland's report on condition of affairs in ....
ARMORIES, to establish, west of Allighany Mountains ....
ARMS, investigation of Government contracts for purchase o
ARMY,
Appointments in altering mode of ....
Appropriations for conferrees' report on Senate amendme
Bounties, investigation of frauds in payment to colored t Pay Department ....
Bounty lands, granting, to officers in War of 1812 ....
Investigation of execution of act of September 28, 1850, gra ice in Army ....
Civil service, employment of Army officers in ....
Colored troops, investigation of frauds in payment of bou partment to ....
Fourth United States Infantry, making further provision viving soldiers of the old ....
Do ....
Do ....
Military posts, establishing, at mouth of Columbia River.
Do ....
Do ....
Officers of, employment in civil service of ....
Pay of, inquiry as to expenditure for, 1815 ....
Reorganization of, provisions for ....
Salaries, equalizing of officers', and fixing amount of pay lowance now made ....
Do ....
Subsistence, expenditure in 1815 for ....
Supplies for, investigation of the mode of purchasing (Go
Tactics, publication of ....
Troops, necessity in the South for ....
War of Revolution, adjustment of claims of officers for se
Additional compensation to officers for services in ...
War of 1812, granting bounty lands to officers for service
ARSENALS, seizure by seceding States of United States....
ARTISTS (American), work upon Government buildings to
ASHLEY, Hon. J. M., investigating official conduct of, in pr ment of F. M. Case as surveyor-general ....
ASSAULT,
Brooks, Preston S., upon Charles Sumner, investigation
Fields, A. P. upon Hon. W. D. Kelley, investigation of .
Grinnell, Josiah B., upon Lovell H. Rousseau, investigat
Houston, Samuel, upon William Stanberry, investigation
Lane, John, upon John F. Ewing, investigation of ....
McMullen, Fayette, upon Anson P. Granger, investigati
Russell, Jarvis, upon John Adams, investigation of ....
ASSAY OFFICES, to establish, within the gold districts of
Do ....
Do ....
ASSESSMENTS (political) upon Government employés for p
ASYLUM, DEAF AND DUMB, OF CONNECTICUT, gr
ASYLUM, DEAF AND DUMB, AT DANVILLE, KY., c
ASYLUM (SOLDIERS') AT GETTYSBURG, PA., claim fo
ATLANTIC AND PACIFIC TELEGRAPH,
Rates March 10, 1862 ....
Proposals for erection of ....
Do ....

* Views of minority. † Parts 1, 2, 3, 4

Subject.	Report.	Congress.	Session.	Volume.
ATTORNEY'S. (*See* UNITED STATES DISTRICT ATTORNEYS.)				
BACOT, ELIZABETH S. W., claim for relief	117	23	2	16
BAILEY, JOHN (chief clerk House of Representatives), investigation of charges against	2003	47	2	72
BALTIMORE, MD., purchase of site for post-office and custom-house at	148	33	2	32
BANK OF PENNSYLVANIA, purchase of site for post-office from	541	35	1	35
BANK OF UNITED STATES,				
Books of, examination of	*460	22	1	15
Charter, investigations of violations of	481	23	1	16
Condition of	461	23	1	16
Loans and discounts by	59	17	1	5
Management of	29	14	2	1
Notes, reissue of	272	24	2	18
Do	306	24	2	18
Do	358	27	3	24
BANKS. (*See also* BANKING AND CURRENCY.)				
Commonwealth Bank of Massachusetts, claim of United States against	678	27	2	24
Deposit banks, investigation of	*193	24	2	19
District of Columbia, renewal of charters of	800	24	1	18
District of Columbia, investigation into condition of	182	23	2	27
Freedman's, investigation of management of	*502	44	1	67
Government contracts with, investigation of	64	37	3	44
Mississippi Agricultural Bank, claim for relief	568	27	2	24
State, reissue of notes of	372	24	2	18
Do	306	24	2	18
Treasury agents of deposit banks, investigation of	*193	24	2	19
BARGY & VAN ALSTINE claim for relief of assignee of	525	26	1	27
BARRON, JAMES,				
Extending limitation of patent to	666	24	1	18
Investigating the payment of pension claim to administrator of	489	31	1	31
BARRY, W. T., investigation of loan by James Reeside to	*103	23	2	17
BARTLETT, JONATHAN, for relief	57	14	1	1
BASTROP'S LAND CLAIMS, to quiet title to	21	18	2	6
Do	3	19	1	9
Do	347	21	1	13
Do	223	22	1	14
BAXTER, JOHN W. C., for relief	57	14	1	1
BAYLY, Hon. THOMAS H., investigation of charges made by B. E. Green against	354	33	1	32
Do	142	33	2	32
BEAUFORT, S. C., direct tax sales of sea island lots in	108	41	2	58
BEAUMARCHAIS, BARON DE, claim of heirs for money advanced by French Government June 10, 1776	64	18	1	6
BELKNAP, W. W., House managers on the impeachment of	791	44	1	67
BENNET, J. & B., extra compensation for carrying mail	*103	23	2	17
BIENNIAL REGISTER,				
Compilation of, preparing	549	23	1	16
Delay in issuing	506	22	1	14
BILLS OF EXCHANGE. (*See* FOREIGN BILLS OF EXCHANGE.)				
BINDING, investigation of the management of binding done for the Executive Department (Covode)	648	36	1	42
BLAIR, Hon. F. P., Jr., investigation of charges made by Hon. J. W. McClurg against	61	38	1	47
BLAIR & RIVES, memorial relating to printing of the Compendium of Statistics of the United States	45	27	2	24
Do	1009	27	2	24
BLOUNT, WILLIE (late governor of Tennessee), for relief for advances in war of 1812	76	18	1	6
Do	121	19	1	9
Do	362	21	1	13
BLUE BOOK. (*See* BIENNIAL REGISTER.)				
BOATS,				
Lost on Western rivers	178	27	3	25
Snag-boat patented by H. M. Shreve, to adopt and use	272	27	3	25
BOYNTON, H. V., investigation of charges against	1112	48	1	74
BONDS OF DISTRICT OF COLUMBIA, relating to the payment of interest on	774	43	1	62
BONDS OF UNITED STATES, investigation of destruction of certain	23	40	2	55
BOOKS, abstraction from House Library by seceding members of Congress	90	36	2	41
BOON, DANIEL, claim for relief of heirs	1039	25	2	21
BOSTON, MASS.,				
Commonwealth Bank of, investigation of settlement of claims of United States against	678	27	2	27
Public building at, erection of	143	33	2	32
BOUNDARIES, establishing the southern boundary of Tennessee	445	23	1	16
BOUNTIES,				
Colored troops, frauds in payment to	83	40	2	55
Frauds in payment to colored troops	83	40	2	55
Payment of, delays in	5	40	2	55
BOUNTY LANDS,				
Act of September 28, 1850, execution of	4	31	2	31
Canadian volunteers, granting to	30	14	2	1

* Views of minority.

* Views of minority. † Part 2.

Subject.	Report.	Congress.	Session.	Volume.
CAPITOL BUILDING—Continued.				
Paintings, historical, providing for four, to be placed in rotunda of	294	24	2	18
Washington, entombment of remains of, in	69	14	1	1
Do	318	21	1	13
CAPITOL OF UNITED STATES,				
Longitude of, to determine	683	27	2	24
Seizure of, by secret organization in District of Columbia	79	36	2	41
CARBINES (HALL'S), investigation of contract for purchase of	2	37	2	45
CARR, THOMAS, and others, claim for relief	86	15	1	2
Do	31	15	2	3
Do	2	16	1	4
CARROLL COUNTY, INDIANA, petition of citizens relating to Executive interference in affairs of Rhode Island	546	28	1	28
Do	581	28	1	28
CASE, CALVIN, statement as to loss of boats on Mississippi and Missouri Rivers	178	27	3	25
CASS, LEWIS (Secretary of War), investigation of conduct of	334	31	1	31
CATALINE (steamer), investigation of chartering of (Government contracts)	*2	37	2	45
CATAWBA (ironclad), inquiry into alleged fraudulent sale of	64	40	2	55
CATTLE, investigation of purchase of (Government contracts)	*2	37	2	45
CENSUS,				
Apportionment,				
Of Representatives under fifth	463	22	1	4
Of Representatives under sixth	43	27	2	24
Error in sixth, investigation of	579	28	1	27
Do	580	28	1	27
Fifth, to provide for taking	295	21	1	13
Kansas, vote on Lecompton constitution in State of Kansas	377	35	1	35
Population,				
Of Mississippi at time of admission into the Union in 1816, as shown by the census taken	14	14	2	1
Of Kansas, as shown by elections and taking of census, 1855	200	34	1	34
Sixth, taken in 1840, error in	579	28	1	27
Do	580	28	1	27
CENSUS BUREAU, providing for the establishment in the Department of Treasury of a	579	28	1	27
CENTENNIAL CELEBRATION OF BATTLE AT GUILFORD COURT-HOUSE	1772	46	2	72
CENTENNIAL EXPOSITION, 1876,				
Completion of grounds, Government aid for	1	44	1	67
Government collection at, preservation of	144	44	2	67
CENTENNIAL MEMORIAL, purchase of edition prepared by J. D. McBride	94	45	3	71
CHANDLER, WALTER S., claim for relief	37	18	2	6
CHARTER GOVERNMENT OF RHODE ISLAND, upheld by United States military forces under order of Executive	546	28	1	27
Do	581	28	1	27
CHARTERS OF BANKS OF UNITED STATES, resolution of inquiry into the violation of, in 1818	92	15	2	3
Do	†460	22	1	14
CHARTERS OF BANKS OF DISTRICT OF COLUMBIA, renewal of	800	24	1	18
CHARTS OF SAINT JOSEPH'S BAY AND SHIP ISLAND INLETS, lithographing	899	27	2	25
CHAZOTTE, PETER STEPHEN, memorial on culture of vine, olives, coffee, cocoa, &c., in the Southern States	47	17	1	5
CHEMICALS (IMPORTED), inspection by custom-house officers of	664	30	1	29
CHEROKEE INDIANS. (*See* INDIANS.)				
CHINESE IMMIGRATION, restricting	†572	46	2	72
CHOLERA, authorizing President of United States to call an international sanitary conference for the purpose of suppressing	620	46	2	72
CILLEY, Hon. JONATHAN, investigation of cause of death of	825	25	2	21
CIPHER TELEGRAMS IN 1876, Potter's report on	‡140	45	3	71
CITIZENS (LOYAL) OF UNITED STATES, protection of, in life and liberty	37	41	3	58
CIVIL SERVICE,				
Apportionment of messengers and clerks in Government Departments under	406	35	1	35
Army officers, employment of	191	33	1	32
Efficiency of	8	39	2	48
Laws, appointment to offices in public service, amending	47	40	2	55
CLAIMS.				
Georgia, to adjudicate	16	15	1	2
Do	311	25	3	21
Loyal citizens, to perpetuate evidence of losses sustained during the war of rebellion	37	41	3	58
Massachusetts war claims, to adjudicate	147	15	1	2
Officer of Revolutionary war, to adjudicate	9	16	1	4
Do	19	19	1	9
Virginia war claims, to adjudicate	191	22	1	14
CLERK OF HOUSE OF REPRESENTATIVES,				
Defining power to control printing of special orders of House and binding of Congressional documents	101	26	2	23
Do	215	26	2	23

* Part 1. † Views of minority. ‡ Part 2.

Subject.	Report.	Congress.	Session.	Volume.
CLERK OF HOUSE OF REPRESENTATIVES—Continued.				
Investigating accounts of William Cullom, late Clerk	542	35	1	
Do	188	35	2	
CLERKS. (*See* GOVERNMENT EMPLOYÉS.)				
COAST SURVEY.				
Inquiry into report of, and management by Superintendent of	43	27	2	
Do	170	27	2	
COBB, Hon. HOWELL, investigation of charges made by Hon. Preston King against	218	31	1	
COBURN, Hon. JOHN, report upon investigation of condition of affairs in Alabama, 1875	262	43	2	
COCHINEAL, Chazotte's memorial on production in the Southern States of	47	17	1	
COCOA, Chazotte's memorial on production in the Southern States of	47	17	1	
COFFEE,				
Chazotte's memorial on production in Southern States of	47	17	1	
Investigation of agitation in Philadelphia as to reduction of duty on	282	21	1	
COINS AND COINAGE,				
American dollar, a legal tender for all debts	94	21	2	
Five franc (French coin), to make a legal tender	94	21	2	
Foreign coin,				
Continuing in force acts regulating	83	17	2	
To recoin	94	21	2	
Foreign gold and silver, to regulate the value of, in foreign trade	420	22	1	
Do	496	22	1	
Do	278	23	1	
Gold,				
Increasing amount to be coined	109	15	2	
Do	111	15	2	
Do	54	16	2	
A legal tender	420	22	1	
Do	496	22	1	
Do	278	23	1	
Gold coin,				
Modifying the standard value of	95	21	2	
To issue, of the denomination of $1, $2, $3 and $4	513	24	1	
Gold and silver, issuing of subsidiary coin	420	22	1	
Do	496	22	1	
Do	278	23	1	
Legal tender, to make American dollar and five franc	94	21	2	
Silver a legal tender	420	22	1	
Do	496	22	1	
Do	278	23	1	
Silver coin, to issue subsidiary	420	22	1	
Do	496	22	1	
Do	278	23	1	
COLONIZATION.				
Freedmen, providing for, in Africa	9	15	2	
Do	101	19	2	
Location of colony for emancipated slaves	148	37	2	
Do	120	37	2	
COLONIZATION SOCIETY, memorials from Kentucky, Ohio, &c., concerning	348	21	1	
COLORED TROOPS, investigation of frauds in payment of bounties to	83	40	2	
COLT PATENT, investigation of corrupt measures used to extend	353	33	1	
Do	132	33	2	
COLUMBIA RIVER, OREGON, expediency of occupying	45	16	2	
Do	18	17	1	
Do	110	18	1	
Do	35	19	1	
Do	213	19	1	
COMMERCE WITH GREAT BRITAIN, conference committee on bill to regulate	52	14	1	
COMMERCE AND NAVIGATION, cause of reduction of American tonnage	28	41	2	
COMMISSARY-GENERAL OF PRISONERS, communication relative to condition of returned Union prisoners made by	67	38	1	
COMMISSIONERS OF DISTRICT OF COLUMBIA, improper use of police force by	189	44	2	
COMMISSIONER OF INDIAN AFFAIRS, investigation of charges against official conduct of William Medill as	104	30	1	
COMMISSIONER OF PATENTS, investigation of charges against	48	37	2	
Do	26	38	2	
COMMISSIONER OF PENSIONS, investigating existing regulations adopted by	4	31	2	
COMMITTEE ON ACCOUNTS, investigation of charges against John A. Searing, chairman of	185	35	2	
COMMITTEE OF THIRTY-THREE, on disturbed condition of the country	31	36	2	
COMMONWEALTH BANK OF MASSACHUSETTS, investigation relating to the settlement of claims of United States against	678	27	2	
COMPENSATION, allowance in certain cases of extra	108	23	2	
CONFEDERATE STATES, reconstruction of	*30	39	1	

* Views of minority.

Subject.	Report.	Congress.	Session.	Volume.
CONGRESS,				
Adjournment of first session of Nineteenth Congress, and for the commencement of second session	141	19	1	9
Corrupt combinations of members of, investigation of	242	34	3	33
Election contest, J. W. Whitfield and Andrew H. Reeder, as Delegates from Kansas to	200	34	1	34
History of, publication of, in 1818	180	15	1	2
Jurisdiction of, over Indian lands in Georgia	98	19	2	11
Laws of, publication of	180	15	1	2
Mileage of members, reducing	964	27	2	24
Power of, to fix rate and rule of damages upon protested bills of foreign exchange	185	19	1	9
Power of, to secure to each State a republican form of government	546	28	1	28
Do	581	28	1	28
Power of, to abrogate State governments	10	40	2	55
Printing for	754	29	1	28
Salaries of members of, fixing	12	14	3	1
CONGRESSIONAL LIBRARY. (*See* LIBRARY OF CONGRESS.)				
CONKLING, Hon. ROSCOE, investigation of charges against Provost-Marshal-General Fry and his bureau by	93	38	1	50
CONNECTICUT, granting land to deaf and dumb asylum in	142	15	2	3
CONSTITUTION,				
Kansas, Lecompton	*377	35	1	35
Kansas, Topeka, 1855	200	34	1	34
CONSTITUTION OF UNITED STATES,				
To amend:				
By Mr. Underwood	1104	27	2	25
Apportionment of Representatives in Congress	404	28	1	27
Do	11	39	1	48
President and Vice-President, election of	18	18	1	6
Do	19	19	1	9
Do	69	21	2	16
Tenure of office, relating to eligibility	1104	27	2	25
Direct taxes among the States	404	28	1	27
Secretary of Treasury, appointment of	296	24	2	18
Slavery in the States, reported by Committee of Thirty-three	31	36	2	41
State banks, reissue of notes of	372	24	2	18
Do	906	46	2	16
States, to regulate representation among	11	39	1	48
Treasury, relative to appointment of Secretary of	296	24	2	18
Woman suffrage, providing for	1997	47	2	73
CONSULAR BUREAU, to establish, in State Department	714	29	1	29
CONSULAR AND DIPLOMATIC SERVICE, reorganization and improvement of	714	29	1	29
CONTINGENT EXPENSES OF HOUSE, investigation of	30	27	2	24
CONTRACTS. (*See also* NAVAL CONTRACTS.)				
Indian removals, investigating conduct of Secretary of War in	502	22	1	14
Investigation of letting of, mail routes	*103	23	2	17
Mix, Elijah, inquiry into contract of	109	17	1	5
Naval expenditures (1859), investigation of	184	35	2	40
CONVICT LABOR, prohibiting introduction from foreign countries of	1040	25	2	21
CORRUPT COMBINATIONS OF MEMBERS OF CONGRESS, investigation of	243	34	3	33
CORRUPTION. (*See* BRIBERY AND CORRUPTION.)				
CORWIN, THOMAS (Secretary of Treasury), investigation of connection with the Gardiner claims	1	32	2	31
COURTS-MARTIAL, collection of fines imposed by	97	17	1	5
COVODE INVESTIGATION, conduct of the Executive and management of the Executive Departments	*648	36	1	43
COYLE, THOMAS, to compensate for invention for manufacture of cement by	1021	25	2	21
CRAIN, JOHN, claim for relief	55	18	2	6
CRAWFORD, Hon. GEORGE W., investigation of the conduct and relation to the claim of George Galphin of	334	31	1	31
CRAWFORD, WILLIAM H. (Secretary of Treasury), investigation of charges against	128	18	1	6
Do	133	18	1	6
CREDIT MOBILIER, investigation of the	77	42	3	60
Do	78	42	3	60
CREEKS, INDIANS. (*See* INDIANS.)				
CREEK INDIAN LANDS IN GEORGIA, cession of, to United States	98	19	2	11
CUBA, Slaves imported from	231	19	1	9
CUMBERLAND NATIONAL ROAD, proceedings and estimates in constructing	75	14	1	1
CUSTOM-HOUSES,				
New Orleans, inquiry into conduct of affairs at (testimony)	25	39	2	48
New York, contract for moving public stores at	*647	36	1	41
Philadelphia, Pa., into management of affairs at (Covode)	648	36	1	42
CUSTOM-HOUSE OFFICERS, increase of	527	24	1	18

* Views of minority.

* Views of minority.

* Views of minority. † Part 2.

Subject.	Report.	Congress.	Session.	Volume.
EXECUTIVE INTERFERENCE, prevention of the people of Rhode Island from forming government under constitution adopted December, 1841, by	546	28	1	28
Do	581	28	1	28
EXECUTIVE MANSION, purchase of furniture for	79	18	2	8
EXECUTIVE OFFICERS, providing seats on floor of Congress for	43	38	1	47
EXECUTIVE PATRONAGE, investigation of	*194	24	2	28
EX-MEMBERS OF CONGRESS, violation of privileges of admission to floor of House by	3798	49	2	76
EXPENDITURES,				
Coast Survey, investigation for	43	27	3	25
Do	178	27	3	25
House of Representatives, retrenchment in	230	27	3	25
Mail contracts, investigation of (1859)	184	35	2	40
Reduction of public	407	35	1	35
Retrenchment of, in Executive Departments	*250	20	1	12
EXPLORATION OF THE NORTHWEST COAST OF AMERICA	35	19	1	9
Do	213	19	1	9
EXPLORING EXPEDITION (WILKES), printing maps of	160	28	2	27
EXTRA COMPENSATION, allowance to be made in certain cases	103	23	2	17
FALLS OF NIAGARA, granting land to aid in construction of canal around	374	25	1	25
Do	53	37	3	44
FEDERAL LAWS, suspending execution by certain States of	91	36	2	41
FEDERAL OFFICES IN LOUISIANA, investigation into conduct and management of	816	44	1	63
FIELD, A. P., investigation of assault on Hon. William D. Kelley, made by	10	38	2	47
FIELD SERVICE, adopted for government of the Army	108	17	1	5
FINES, collection of, imposed by courts-martial on Pennsylvania militia	97	17	1	5
FIVE-FRANC PIECES, making legal tender in United States of	111	15	2	2
Do	94	21	2	13
FLAG OF UNITED STATES, expediency of altering	23	14	2	1
Do	37	15	1	2
FLORIDA,				
Coffee and cochineal, production of, in	47	17	1	5
Election of 1876, investigation of	*143	44	2	60
Kuklux investigation, in 1871-'72 (testimony)	22	42	2	61
Reconstruction of	*30	39	1	49
Representation of	*30	39	1	49
FOLDING-ROOM OF HOUSE, sanitary condition of	1398	47	1	72
FOOD (ADULTERATION), providing for commission to examine	199	46	3	72
FOREIGN BILLS OF EXCHANGE, right of Congress to regulate	135	19	1	9
FOREIGN COINS,				
Regulating use of, in United States	109	15	2	2
Do	111	15	2	2
Do	83	17	2	5
Gold coins of Great Britain and France, receivable for payment of public lands	86	17	2	5
Regulating value of	420	22	1	14
Do	496	22	1	14
Do	278	23	1	16
FOREIGN COUNTRIES, unjust discrimination against tobacco exported from the United States by	239	24	2	18
Do	310	25	3	21
Do	810	30	1	29
Do	667	36	1	41
FOREIGN EMIGRATION, encouragement of	56	35	1	37
FOREIGN PAUPERS AND CONVICTS. (*See* PAUPERS; CONVICTS; IMMIGRATION.)				
FOREIGNERS. (*See* ALIENS.)				
FORT PILLOW MASSACRE, investigation of	65	38	1	47
FORT SNELLING, MINNESOTA, military reservation at, sale of	351	35	1	35
FORTIFICATIONS, purchase of, at Willets Point, New York	549	35	1	35
FORTS, United States, seizure of, by seceding States	91	36	2	41
FOUNDRIES, NATIONAL, to establish	141	23	2	16
Do	168	25	3	21
Do	455	28	1	27
Private, capacity of, for material for war-ships	1450	49	1	74
FRANCE, to reimburse for moneys advanced as represented in claims of heirs of Beaumarchais	64	18	1	4
FRANKING PRIVILEGE,				
Abolishment of, providing for	1	36	2	41
Abuses of, to correct	576	28	1	27
Do	1	36	2	41
Regulating, prescribing laws for	576	28	1	27
Do	1	36	2	41
FRAUDS. (*See* ELECTION FRAUDS.)				
FREE TRADE, relating to the adoption of	407	35	1	35
FREEDMAN'S SAVINGS AND TRUST COMPANY, investigating management and books of (testimony)	*502	44	1	67
FREEDMEN,				
Colonization of, providing for	9	15	2	2
Cruelty and hostility towards	30	39	1	49
Labor, disposition and fitness to perform	30	39	1	49

* Views of minority.

Subject.	Report.	Congress.	Session.	Volume.
FREEDMEN AND REFUGEES, to establish bureau of	2	38	1	47
Do	8	38	2	47
Do	30	40	2	55
FREEDMEN'S BUREAU, necessity in the South for	30	39	1	49
FRISBEE, GIDEON, for relief	38	14	1	1
FRONTIER TROUBLES IN TEXAS, report of commission appointed to investigate	343	44	1	67
FRY, General JAMES B., investigation of charges made by Hon. Roscoe Conkling against	93	39	1	50
FULTON, ROBERT, for relief of heirs	64	20	2	12
Do	267	21	1	13
GALES & SEATON, investigation of charges against	76	17	2	5
GALPHIN, GEORGE, investigation of conduct of Secretary of War in relation to claim of	364	31	1	31
GARDINER CLAIM, investigation of the, connection of Hon. Thomas Corwin with	1	32	2	31
GARFIELD, JAMES A. (President of United States), illness and burial expenses of	1060	47	1	73
GARLAND, Hon. RICE, altercation between Hon. Jesse A. Bynum and	488	26	1	23
GEOLOGICAL SURVEY, restricting publications of	2214	49	1	76
Do	2740	49	1	76
GEORGIA,				
Indian titles in, extinguishment of	109	18	1	6
Jurisdiction of State over lands of Creek Indians in	98	19	2	11
Kuklux investigation 1871–'72 (testimony)	*22	42	2	61
Militia, claims of, to adjudicate	55	14	2	1
Do	16	15	1	2
Reconstruction of	30	39	1	49
Representation in Congress	30	39	1	49
Treaty with Creek and Cherokee Indians, 1802	10	17	1	5
Do	1	17	2	5
War claim of, to adjudicate	311	25	3	21
GETTYSBURG, PA., to exempt from taxation lottery for an asylum for disabled soldiers at	12	40	2	55
GHENT TREATY, establishing the salaries of commissioners and agents appointed under the	56	16	2	4
GILBERT, Hon. W. A., investigation of charges against	243	34	3	33
GNADENHUTTEN, OHIO, recession of lands to United Brethren Church at	99	18	1	6
GOELL, ALIVEN C., claim for relief	138	28	2	27
Do	273	29	1	29
GOLD,				
Sales and loans of, in subtreasury at New York	14	39	2	48
Value of, to increase	54	16	2	4
Do	95	21	2	13
GOLD AND SILVER, value of, to fix standard	185	44	2	1
GOLD COINAGE, providing by law for coining gold pieces of small denominations	513	24	1	18
GOLD COINS. (*See also* COINS and COINAGE.)				
GONON, E., claim for relief	325	27	2	24
GOTTKILFF, AUGUSTUS, claim for relief	462	22	1	14
GOVERNMENT CONTRACTS,				
Employés of Government connected with banking-houses or engaged in	64	37	3	44
Fines, penalties, and forfeitures accrued in district of New York, 1858–1862	†149	37	3	44
Do	50	37	3	44
McKinstry, Justus, quartermaster U. S. Army, charged with corrupt practices in connection with	49	37	3	44
Testimony, giving out of	†149	37	3	44
Do	50	37	3	44
War of the rebellion, operations in suppressing	2	37	2	45
Do	11	37	2	46
GOVERNMENT EMPLOYÉS,				
Equalizing and reducing salaries of	547	23	1	17
Loyalty of, investigation of	16	37	2	44
Names and salaries of, in Departments at Washington	200	28	2	27
Official conduct in the Departments of	182	15	1	2
Tabular statement of employés in Government employ in 1857	406	35	1	35
GOVERNMENT EXHIBITS, PHILADELPHIA, making provision for preservation of, at Centennial Exposition	144	44	2	67
GRAND AND SPRING RIVERS, improvement of	186	27	3	25
GRANGER, Hon. AMOS P., assault made by Hon. Fayette McMullin upon	1	34	2	33
GRAY, GEORGE, claim for relief	451	22	1	14
GRAY, WILLIAM, AND OTHERS, claim for relief	458	22	1	14
GREAT BRITAIN,				
Commerce with, report of conference to regulate	52	14	1	1
Jurisdiction of, in State of Oregon	157	27	3	25
GREAT LAKES, providing for defenses and fortifications of the	23	37	2	44
GREEN, B. E., investigating charges made against Hon. T. H. Bayly by	354	33	1	32
Do	142	33	2	32
GREEN, DUFF, proposals to print laws of United States	286	25	2	21

* Parts 1, 2. † Part 2.

Subject.	Report.	Congress.	Session.
GRINNELL, Hon. JOSIAH B., investigating assault by Lovell H. Rousseau upon	90	39	1
GUANO (PERUVIAN), levying import duty on	347	33	1
GUILFORD COURT-HOUSE, providing for centennial celebration of battle at	1772	46	2
GUTHRIE, ABELARD, claim for mileage and per diem as Delegate from Nebraska	19	40	2
HACKLEY, RICHARD S., claim for relief	88	16	1
HACKNEY, R. B. (Doorkeeper House of Representatives), investigation of accounts of	412	35	1
HALE, Capt. NATHAN, monument to	171	24	1
Do	959	25	2
Do	713	26	1
Do	783	27	2
HALEY, DAVID D., and others, claim for relief	50	26	2
HALF-PAY, to soldiers of the Revolutionary war, for life	136	20	1
HALL & TROTTER, extra allowance for carrying mail	*103	23	2
HALL OF HOUSE OF REPRESENTATIVES,			
Alterations in	11	19	1
Do	495	22	1
Desks in, removal of	178	35	2
President of United States, investigation of, on floor of	26	39	2
Seats in, authorizing heads of Departments to occupy	43	38	1
Seat upon floor, granting to Mrs. President Madison	5	25	1
Ventilation of	19	40	3
Do	119	45	2
Do	116	45	3
HALL'S CARBINES, investigation of purchase by General Frémont of (Government contracts)	2	37	2
HARBORS. (*See* RIVERS AND HARBORS.)			
HARBOR DEFENSES, providing fortifications for	23	37	2
HARRINGTON, RICHARD, robbery of safe in office of	785	43	1
HARRIS, Hon. THOMAS L., proposition to expel from Congress	*179	35	1
HARRISON, WILLIAM H., notification of election as President of the United States of	165	26	2
HAWES, SILAS, extension of patent for carpenters' squares	657	24	1
HAYDEN, AARON, for relief	57	14	1
HEARD, STEPHEN, and others, for relief of	37	18	1
HEMP, water-rotted, inspector of, to appoint at Louisville, Ky	551	27	2
Purchasing agency for, to establish	184	27	3
HENNEN, DUNCAN N., investigation of charge against P. K. Lawrence	272	25	3
HIDES AND TALLOW (investigation of purchase by Government contract) of	† 2	37	2
HISTORY OF CONGRESS, 1818, publication of	180	15	1
HISTORY OF RAILROAD STRIKE, 1886, causes of strike	*4174	49	2
HOFFMAN, General WILLIAM, communication relative to condition of returned Union prisoners of war, from	67	38	1
HOLLOWAY, D. P., investigation of charges made by Andrew Whitely against	26	38	2
HOME DEPARTMENT, to create as an executive department	232	19	1
Do	10	19	2
HORSES AND WAGONS, purchase of (Government contract)	† 2	37	2
HOUSE OF REPRESENTATIVES,			
Assaults in, investigation of	260	20	1
Do	447	22	1
Do	135	23	2
Do	182	34	1
Do	1	34	2
Do	10	33	2
Do	90	39	1
Books, abstraction of, from library of	90	36	2
Cabinet officers, to occupy seats in	43	38	1
Clerk of, defining power in printing public documents	101	26	2
Do	215	26	2
Cobb, Howell (Speaker), investigation of charges against	218	31	1
Contingent expenses of, investigation of	30	27	2
Cullom, William, late Clerk of, investigating accounts of	543	35	1
Do	188	35	2
Darling, Nathan, (Doorkeeper), investigating accounts of	412	35	1
Desks and seats in, rearrangement of	178	35	2
Electoral vote, rules to govern counting of	41	18	2
Expenditures in, retrenchment of	95	17	1
Do	230	27	2
Folding-room, investigating sanitary condition of	1398	47	1
Hackney, R. B. (Doorkeeper), investigating accounts of	412	35	1
Hall of, alterations in	11	19	1
Do	495	22	1
Matteson, Orsamus B., expulsion of, as member of	179	35	1
Members of, compensation of	95	17	1
Members, election of	8	18	1
Officers and employés of, reducing	95	17	1
Order of business for second session Eighteenth Congress	71	18	2

* Views of minority. † Part 1.

Subject.	Report.	Congress.	Session.	Volume.
HOUSE OF REPRESENTATIVES—Continued.				
Order of business to be acted upon during remainder of first session Nineteenth Congress	175	19	1	9
Powers of, in counting electoral vote	100	44	2	69
Privilege of floor of, violation of, by the arrest of Whitelaw Reid	373	43	2	66
Privilege of floor of, abuse of, by Hon. W. H. English	2126	48	1	74
Relation of, to the Senate in the matter of notifying the President and Vice-President elect of the result of counting the electoral vote	84	14	2	1
Reporters' gallery, to expel W. Scott Smith from	104	41	2	56
Representation in, under the fifth census	127	21	1	13
Rule 34, relating to admission of ex-members to floor of	3798	49	2	76
Rules and orders of	20	17	1	5
Do	88	24	1	16
Do	1	25	1	21
Do	1	26	1	22
Do	56	36	1	41
Sergeant-at-Arms, acounts of, with Bank of Metropolis, Washington, D. C	512	25	2	21
Summons (*duces tecum*), refusal of Kilbourn to obey	242	44	1	67
Do	789	44	1	67
Unfinished business in	99	14	1	1
Do	7	15	1	2
Do	186	15	1	2
Do	141	15	2	3
Do	22	16	1	4
Do	64	16	2	4
Do	4	17	1	5
Do	117	18	1	6
Do	132	18	1	6
Do	20	19	2	9
Do	82	19	2	9
Do	88	19	2	9
Do	243	20	1	12
HOUSTON, Hon. SAMUEL,				
Assault on Hon. William Stanberry by	447	22	1	14
Investigating charges of fraudulent attempt to obtain contract for supplying rations to emigrating Indians	502	22	1	14
HUDDY, JOSHUA, claim for relief of heirs	227	24	2	18
HURLBUT, Hon. STEPHEN A., report on recent troubles in State of Mississippi	265	43	2	66
ILLINOIS.				
Labor troubles in, in 1886, investigation of	*4174	49	2	77
Land offices in, management of	81	17	1	5
Land-warrants of Revolutionary war, 3 per cent. claims to	79	29	1	29
Lands, swamp, donating to State	586	27	2	24
Swamp lands in, donating to State	586	27	2	24
ILLINOIS AND MICHIGAN CANAL, granting Government aid to construct	53	18	2	6
Do	446	22	1	14
ILLINOIS RIVER, giving Government aid to connect the waters of Lake Michigan with	53	18	2	6
Do	446	22	1	14
IMMIGRATION.				
Chinese, prohibiting	*572	46	2	72
Convicts, prohibiting introduction of	1040	25	2	21
Encouragement of, providing system for	56	38	1	47
Paupers, prohibiting introduction of	1040	25	2	21
IMPEACHMENT,				
Delahay, Mark W	92	42	3	59
Peck, Judge James H	385	21	1	13
Do	359	21	1	13
IMPORT DUTIES.				
Adulterated drugs and chemicals, special inspection of	664	30	1	29
Amending laws relating to	407	35	1	35
Collection of,				
Power of President to enforce	*998	27	2	24
providing for	50	36	2	41
Distilled spirits, to increase duty on imported	225	19	1	9
Effect of, at Pittsburgh, Pa	86	14	2	1
Guano, to levy duty on, imported from Peru	347	33	1	32
Imported splints, to increase duty on	225	19	1	9
Increase of, on imported spirits	225	19	1	9
Laws relating to, to amend	407	35	1	35
Peruvian guano, to levy duty on	347	33	1	32
Power of President to enforce collection of	*998	27	2	24
Tea and coffee, agitation in Philadelphia on	282	21	1	13
IMPRISONMENT FOR DEBT, to abolish	63	16	2	4
Do	194	22	1	14
Do	5	22	2	14
IMPROVEMENT OF MISSISSIPPI RIVER, Burrows's report on	†1985	47	2	73
INDEMNIFICATIONS, to adjudicate claims for damages sustained during war of 1812	102	18	1	6

* Views of minority. † Views of minority, Part 2.

Subject.	Report.	Congress.	Session.	Volume.
INDIAN AFFAIRS. (*See* BUREAU OF INDIAN AFFAIRS.)				
INDIAN AGENCIES, condition of	1076	49	1	73
INDIAN CLAIMS, making appropriation for the purpose of extinguishing	160	15	1	
INDIAN COMMISSION, to appoint	1076	49	1	73
INDIAN CONTACTS. (*See* CONTRACTS.)				
INDIAN TREATIES. (*See* TREATIES.)				
INDIAN TRUST BONDS, investigation of fraudulent abstraction of	78	36	2	43
INDIAN WARS, granting pensions for services in	284	23	1	16
Do	328	24	1	
Do	96	24	2	
Do	327	25	2	21
Do	361	27	2	
Do	88	29	1	
INDIANA,				
Land office in, management of	81	17	1	
Land warrants of Revolutionary war, 3 per cent. claims to	79	29	1	
Wabash and Erie Canal, granting land in aid of	78	18	2	
Do	544	28	1	
Do	545	28	1	
INDIANS,				
Cession of lands for public highway in Ohio and Michigan	98	16	1	
Cherokee,				
Making appropriation to carry into effect treaty with	10	17	1	
Do	1	17	2	
Removal from Georgia	109	18	1	
Christian Indians, recession to the United States of the title of lands belonging to	99	18	1	
Condition of	1076	49	1	
Contracts, investigating the assignment of contract for supplying rations to emigrating Indians	502	22	1	
Creek,				
Making appropriation to carry into effect treaty made with	10	17	1	
Do	1	17	2	
To adjudicate claim of, in Georgia	109	18	1	
Lands, jurisdiction over	98	19	2	
Lands, right of ownership to, in United States	109	18	1	
Pottawatomie, investigating claim of W. G. and G. W. Ewing against	*489	31	1	
Right of ownership to lands in United States	109	18	1	
Stockbridge, execution of treaty with	70	16	1	
Supplies, investigating the assignment of contract of supplies to emigrating Indians	502	22	1	
Treaties, making appropriation to carry into effect the Creek and Cherokee	10	17	1	
Do	1	17	2	
INDIGENT INSANE, memorial of Miss Dicks for grant of land for relief of	487	31	1	
INGERSOLL, J. R., report upon Massachusetts resolutions	†404	28	1	
INSANE (INDIGENT), granting land for aid to	487	31	1	
INSPECTORS. (*See* STEAMBOAT INSPECTORS; STEAM-VESSELS.)				
INSURRECTION (DORR), Rhode Island	546	28	1	
Do	581	28	1	
INSURRECTIONARY STATES,				
Affairs in, relating to safety of lives and property of citizens of	‡22	42	2	
Debt of, in 1872	‡22	42	2	
Election laws of 1872	‡22	42	2	
Kuklux investigation in 1871-'72	‡22	42	2	
Reconstruction and representation in Congress of	*30	39	1	
INTERIOR DEPARTMENT. (*See* DEPARTMENT OF INTERIOR.)				
INTERNAL IMPROVEMENTS,				
Canals, bays, harbors, roads and rivers	416	22	1	
Do	446	22	1	
Do	491	22	1	
Conference report on	257	20	1	
Debts contracted by States in	296	27	3	
INTERNAL-REVENUE FRAUDS, investigation of	24	39	2	
INTERNAL-REVENUE TAX, providing for	225	19	1	
Do	407	35	1	
Do	24	39	2	
INTERNATIONAL SANITARY CONFERENCE	620	46	2	
INTEROCEANIC SHIP-CANAL, PANAMA ROUTE	390	46	3	
INTEROCEANIC SHIP-RAILWAY, to incorporate	322	46	3	
INVESTIGATION,				
Alabama, condition of affairs in	263	43	2	
Amelia Island, introduction of slaves from	46	15	1	
Ames, Oakes, alleged bribery by	77	42	3	
Amistad case, falsified printing in	51	26	2	
Anderson, Hon. Lucien, of charges made against	29	38	2	
Army, disbursement for pay and subsistence since March 4, 1815	72	16	1	
Ashley, Hon. J. M., official conduct in procuring certain Government appointments and contracts	47	37	3	

* Views of minority. † Part 5. ‡ Part 1 and views of minority.

Subject.	Report.	Congress.	Session.	Volume.
INVESTIGATION—Continued.				
Assault by—				
Brooks, Preston S., upon Hon. Charles Sumner	182	34	1	28
Bynum, Jesse A., upon Rice Garland	488	26	1	28
Codd, Robert, upon Henry G. Wheeler	702	24	1	18
Field, A. P., upon Hon. W. D. Kelley	10	38	2	47
Houston, Hon. Samuel, upon William Stanberry	447	22	1	14
Lane, J. F., upon Hon. John Ewing	125	23	2	16
McMullen, Fayette, upon Amos P. Granger	1	34	2	33
Rousseau, Hon. Lovell H., upon Hon. Josiah B. Grinnell	90	39	1	41
Russell, Jarvis, upon President's private secretary	*380	20	1	12
Bailey, John, charges against	2008	47	2	73
Bank of Pennsylvania, purchase of property by General Government belonging to	541	25	1	26
Bank of United States, books and management of	*460	22	1	15
Banks of deposit	*193	24	2	19
Barron, Commodore James, commutation pay for naval service of	488	31	1	21
Bayly, Hon. T. H., charges made by B. E. Green against	354	32	1	22
Do	162	32	2	22
Bills, House of Representatives, alteration in	351	33	1	33
Do	353	33	1	33
Do	122	33	2	33
Blair, Hon. F. P., jr., charges against	61	38	1	47
Boynton, H. V., charges against	1112	48	1	74
Bonds of United States, false certificate as to destruction of	23	40	3	55
Books, abstraction by seceding members of Congress from House library	90	36	2	41
Bounties, delay in payment of	5	40	3	55
Bounty lands, execution of act September 28, 1850, granting	4	31	2	31
Breach of privilege, floor House of Representatives, by President of United States	26	38	2	46
Brooklyn, N. Y., election frauds in	218	46	2	70
Calhoun, J. C., participation in War Department contracts while Secretary of War	79	19	2	19
Cilley, Hon. Jonathan, cause and circumstances attending death of	325	25	2	31
Cipher telegrams, 1876	140	45	3	71
Clerk of House, investigating accounts of	542	35	1	35
Do	186	35	2	38
Cobb, Hon. Howell, charges by Hon. Preston King	218	31	1	21
Colt patent, corrupt measures used to extend	353	33	1	32
Commissioner of Patents, charges of fraud in office of	26	38	2	47
Commissioner of Pensions, regulations concerning bounty lands	4	31	2	31
Committee on Accounts, charges against chairman of	185	35	2	38
Commonwealth Bank of Massachusetts, settlement of claim of United States against	678	27	2	24
Contingent expenses of House	30	27	2	24
Corrupt combinations, by certain members of Congress	243	34	3	33
Corwin, Hon. Thomas, connection with the Gardiner claim	1	32	2	31
Covode, management of Executive Departments	648	36	1	42
Crawford, Hon. George W., relation to the claim of George Galphin	334	31	1	21
Credit Mobilier, testimony had in	77	42	3	60
Cullom, William, Clerk of House of Representatives	542	35	1	35
Do	186	35	2	38
District of Columbia,				
Government of	647	43	1	62
Real estate pool in	242	44	1	67
Do	789	44	1	67
Improper use of police force in	189	44	2	67
Donnelly, Ignatius, charges made against	48	40	2	56
Election frauds in New York	31	40	3	56
Do	41	40	3	56
Do	140	45	3	71
English, Hon. William H., charges against	2136	48	1	74
Elliott, Commodore Jesse, charges against	295	25	3	21
Executive Department, management of	648	36	1	42
Ewing, G. W. and W. G., payment of claims against Pottawatomie Indians made by	489	31	1	31
Florida elections in 1876	143	44	2	68
Fort Pillow massacre, testimony taken of	65	38	1	47
Fort Snelling, sale of military reservation at	351	35	1	36
Freedman's Bank, management	*502	44	1	67
Fry, Provost-Marshal-General, charges by Roscoe Conkling against	93	39	1	50
Gales & Seaton, charges against	76	17	2	5
Galphin, George, claim of	334	31	1	31
Gardiner claim, connection of Secretary of War with	1	32	2	31
Government contracts, frauds in	*49	37	3	44
Do	50	37	3	44
Grinnell, Hon. Josiah B., assault upon	90	39	1	1
House of Representatives, ventilation of	19	40	3	56
Do	119	45	2	71

* Views of minority.

Subject.	Report.	Congress.	Session.	Volume.
INVESTIGATION—Continued.				
House of Representatives, ventilation of	116	45	3	71
Impeachment of President Johnson, raising money to carry on	75	40	2	58
Indian Affairs, charges against Commissioner of	104	30	1	29
Indian contracts, fraudulent assignment by Secretary of War	502	22	1	14
Internal revenue, examination of frauds in	24	30	2	52
Ironclads, fraudulent sale by Navy Department of	64	40	2	55
Jersey City, election frauds in	218	44	2	70
Kilbourn, Hallet, refusal to obey orders of House of Representatives	242	44	1	67
Do	789	44	1	67
Labor troubles in 1886, Curtin committee	*4174	49	2	77
Lawrence, P. K., charges against	272	25	3	21
Library of House of Representatives, abstraction of books from	90	36	2	41
Louisiana,				
Condition of affairs in	16	39	2	51
Elections held in 1876 in	100	44	2	68
Do	156	44	2	68
Federal offices in	816	44	1	68
Maps and charts, frauds in engraving and printing of	305	23		47
Members of Congress, corrupt combinations of	243	34		33
Memphis riots, origin of	101	39		42
Minnesota land bill, alteration in text of	352	33		33
Do	122	33	2	32
Naval contracts, inquiry into	184	35	2	40
Navy Department,				
Fraudulent sale of ironclads by	64	40	2	55
Administration of affairs in	80	42	2	59
New Orleans, La.,				
Management of affairs in custom-house at	25	39	2	48
Do	816	44	1	68
Riot of July 30, 1866, at	16	39	2	51
New York, election frauds in	218	44	2	70
New York City post-office, tampering with mails in	138	44	2	67
New York Hotel Fund, creation of	*831	36	1	41
Ocean mail steamers, disbursement of money appropriated for	281	33	1	32
Paine, E. A., charges against	29	38	2	47
Pan Electric Telephone Company, charges against	3142	49	1	76
Patent Office, charges against management of	48	37	3	44
Do	26	33	2	47
Pay Department, frauds in payment of bounties to colored troops	83	40	2	55
Philadelphia, election frauds of	218	44	2	70
Post Office Department, condition of affairs in	65	16	2	4
Do	69	16	2	4
Do	77	44	1	67
President of United States, presence on floor of House of	26	39	2	48
Public Printer, investigating accounts of	189	35	2	39
Randall, Hon. Samuel J., certain charges against	139	45	3	71
Real-estate pool in District of Columbia	242	44	1	67
Do	789	44	1	67
Reid, Whitelaw, arrest in District of Columbia of	273	43	2	62
Safe burglary in District of Columbia	785	43	1	62
Searing, John A., charges against	185	35	2	38
Secretary of Navy, certain charges against	80	42	2	59
Secretary of State, official misconduct of Hon. Daniel Webster as	684	29	1	29
Secretary of War,				
In assigning contracts for Indians	502	22	1	14
Relation of, to the claim of George Galphin	384	31	1	31
Seizure of forts and arsenals by seceding States	91	36	2	41
Slaves, introduction from Amelia Island	46	15	1	2
Smithsonian Institution, management of affairs in	141	33	2	32
South Carolina,				
Murder of Union soldiers in	23	39	2	48
Elections held in 1876 in	175	44	2	68
Stamps, loss in office of subtreasury, New York City	70	42	2	59
Stephens, William, official conduct of	136	15	2	2
Sylvester, Henry H., removal from Pension Office of	945	27	2	24
Treasury Department, investigation of charges against	140	38	1	47
Treatment of prisoners of war by rebel authority	45	40	3	57
Van Ness, William P., official conduct of	136	15	2	2
Ventilation, Hall of House	19	40	3	55
Do	119	45	2	71
Do	116	45	3	71
Vicksburg, Miss., recent troubles at	265	43	2	66
Webster, Hon. Daniel, official misconduct as Secretary of State	684	29	1	29
Wetherill, Charles M., inquiry as to absence from his Department	35	38	1	47
Willets Point, New York, purchase of	549	35	1	35
Woolley, Charles W., conduct of, during impeachment of President	44	40	2	56
IRONCLADS, sale of Oneoto and Catawba	64	40	2	55
ISTHMUS OF PANAMA, to incorporate interoceanic ship-railway across	322	46	2	72

* Views of minority.

Subject.	Report.	Congress.	Session.	Volume.
JACKSON, ANDREW, claim for relief	12	16	1	3
Do	3	16	1	4
JARVIS, RUSSELL, investigation of assault upon Hon. John Adams by	*266	20	1	12
JERSEY CITY ELECTION, investigation of	218	44	2	70
JETTIES. (*See* MISSISSIPPI RIVER.)				
JOHNSON, ANDREW (President), investigation of corrupt means used to secure acquittal of	75	40	2	56
JOHNSON, ANDREW, military governor of Tennessee, proclamation of	30	39	1	49
JOURNAL OF CONGRESS, providing for general distribution among the people of the laws of the United States and	107	22	2	1
KANSAS, labor troubles in, 1886	*4174	49	2	77
KANSAS AFFAIRS, investigation of, 1856	*200	34	1	24
KANSAS CONSTITUTION, Lecompton, November 7, 1857	*377	35	1	35
KELLEY, Hon. WILLIAM D., investigation of assault made by A. P. Field upon	10	38	2	47
KENTUCKY,				
Asylum for Deaf and Dumb, Government aid to	28	18	2	6
Do	7	19	1	9
Shore of Mississippi River in, surveying	179	35	2	38
Slavery in, extinction of	148	37	2	44
KILBOURN, HALLET, refusal to comply with *subpœna duces tecum* issued by House of Representatives	242	44	1	67
Do	789	44	1	67
KILLBUCK, recession of lands to United States granted to	99	18	1	6
KING, Hon. PRESTON, charges made against Hon. Howell Cobb, Speaker of House, by	215	31	1	31
KING, WILLIAM, for relief	52	18	1	6
KREMER, Hon. GEORGE, investigation of a letter published in the Columbian Observer, January 25, 1825	64	18	2	7
KUKLUX INVESTIGATION,				
Alabama, 1871–'2 (testimony)	†22	42	2	61
Florida, 1871–'2, (testimony)	22	42	2	61
Georgia, 1871–'2 (testimony)	‡22	42	2	61
Mississippi, 1871–'2 (testimony)	‡22	42	2	61
North Carolina, 1871–'2, (testimony)	22	42	2	61
South Carolina, 1871–'2 (testimony)	†22	42	2	61
KUKLUX OUTRAGES, protection of loyal citizens from	37	41	3	58
LABOR, causes of depression of	*572	46	2	72
LABOR TROUBLES, 1886, investigation of	*4174	49	2	77
LAKE DEFENSES, providing for	23	37	2	44
LAKE ERIE, construction of canal to connect Lake Ontario with	53	37	3	44
LAKE MICHIGAN, granting Government aid in opening a canal to connect Illinois River with	53	18	2	6
Do	446	22	1	14
LAKE ONTARIO, construction of canal to connect Lake Erie with	53	37	3	44
LAND, granting, to Connecticut Deaf and Dumb Asylum	142	15	2	2
LAND GRANTS,				
Acts relating to	296	27	3	26
Public roads, aid in construction of	98	16	1	4
Railroads, forfeited lands granted in aid of certain	3	40	2	55
Do	15	40	2	55
LAND OFFICES, examination into the management of	81	17	1	5
LAND WARRANTS (Virginia military), to quiet claims of purchasers	121	18	1	6
LANDS OF VIRGINIA RESERVE IN OHIO, to quiet claims of	121	18	1	6
LANE, Lieut. JOHN F., investigating assault upon Hon. John Ewing by	135	23	2	1
LATHAM, WILLIAM, for relief	75	14	2	1
LAWRENCE, P. K., investigation of charges made by D. C. Henning against	272	25	3	21
LAWRENCE, STONE & CO., connection with passage of tariff act of 1857	*414	35	1	35
LAWS OF UNITED STATES,				
Distribution of	107	22	2	14
Do	286	25	2	21
Printing of	286	25	2	21
Do	659	29	1	29
Stereotyping, cost of	47	20	2	18
LECOMPTON CONSTITUTION of Kansas	377	35	1	35
Do	648	36	1	41
LEE, General R. E., increase of hostility after surrender of	30	39	1	49
LEGAL-TENDER COINS, fixing	94	21	2	13
Do	420	22	1	14
Do	496	22	1	14
Do	278	23	1	23
LEVEES, Mississippi River	179	35	2	38
Do	1985	47	2	73
LIBERIA, colonization of freedmen in	348	21	1	13
LIBRARY OF CONGRESS, providing additional accommodations for	65	46	3	72
Do	164	47	1	72
LIBRARY OF HOUSE, abstraction of books from	90	36	2	41
LINCOLN, ABRAHAM				
Memorial exercises on life and character of	17	39	1	48
Efforts to avert war in 1861	30	39	1	49

*Views of minority. † Parts 1, 2, 3. ‡ Parts 1, 2.

Subject.	Report.	Congress.	Session.	Volume.
LIVE-OAK CONTRACTS, investigation as to letting of	184	35	2	36
LOANS (French), by Baron De Beaumarchais, in 1776	64	18	1	6
LOANS, power of Postmaster-General to make	*103	23	2	17
LOANS AND DISCOUNTS, resolution of inquiry as to the per centum exacted by the Bank of United States on	59	17	1	5
LOANS FROM DEPOSIT BANKS, to members of Congress	846	24	2	18
LONGITUDE OF CAPITOL OF UNITED STATES, to determine	683	27	2	24
LOTTERY, exempting the Gettysburg Asylum, scheme from internal-revenue tax	12	40	2	1
LOUISIANA.				
Affairs in	16	39	2	51
Bastrop grant, claim of settlers upon, to adjudicate	21	18	2	6
Do	3	19	1	8
Do	347	21	1	13
Do	233	22	1	14
Difficulties between Government and State officials of	92	42	2	59
Election in 1876, investigation of	100	44	2	69
Do	*156	44	2	69
New Orleans custom-house, management of	816	44	1	68
Presidential election in, 1876	101	43	2	68
Reconstruction of	30	39	1	49
LOUISVILLE, KY.,				
Agency, to establish, for inspection of manufacture of water-rotted hemp at	551	27	2	24
Canal around falls at, appropriation to aid in construction of	98	18	1	6
LOYAL CITIZENS OF UNITED STATES, to protect in their rights	39	41	3	58
LOYALTY OF GOVERNMENT EMPLOYÉS	16	37	2	44
LUCAS, J. B. C., claim for relief	13	16	1	4
LYON, MATHEW, claim for relief	8	16	2	4
McBRIDE, JAMES D., purchasing for State Department the Centennial Memorial, prepared by	94	45	3	71
McCLURG, Hon. J. W., investigation of charges against Hon. F. P. Blair, jr., made by	61	38	1	47
McDUFF, DANIEL, claim for relief	10	16	2	4
Do	58	21	1	13
McINTIRE, MAKER, BIXBY & CRAIG, investigation of contract for removal of public stores in New York made with	*647	36	1	41
McKINSTRY, JUSTUS, court-martial proceedings upon charges of corruption in Government contracts in case of	49	37	3	44
McMULLEN, Hon. FAYETTE, investigation of assault made upon Hon. A. P. Granger by	1	34	2	33
MACHINE SHOPS, PRIVATE, capacity for making engines for war-ships	1450	49	1	76
MADISON, Mrs. PRESIDENT, allowing section in Hall of House to	5	28	1	27
MADISON PAPERS, providing for the purchase and publication of	410	29	1	39
MAGEE, JOHN, & CO., relative to contracts for carrying mail by	*103	23	2	17
MAIL CONRRACTS,				
Investigation of	*103	23	2	17
Investigation of (Covode)	648	36	1	3
MAIL PROPOSALS, relative to printing of	*103	23	2	17
MAIL ROUTES, to investigate letting of contracts for	*103	23	2	17
MAIL STEAMSHIP SERVICE, to insure established lines in Gulf of Mexico	18	41	3	58
MAILS (New York City post-office), investigation of	138	44	2	67
MAINE, providing for defense of northern frontier of	119	38	1	47
MANUFACTURES,				
Bureau of, to establish	95	14	2	1
Pittsburgh, Pa., condition of, at and their relation to protective tariff	86	14	2	1
MANUSCRIPT, alteration of House Doc. No. 185, of first session Twenty-sixth Congress, relating to the Amistad case	51	26	2	28
MAPS AND CHARTS, frauds in printing of	305	28	1	27
MARITIME CANAL, to incorporate Nicaragua Canal Company	211	46	3	72
MARKLE, ABRAHAM, for relief	30	14	1	1
MARYLAND,				
Mail routes in, contracted for by Stockton & Neil	*103	23	2	17
Slavery in, gradual emancipation of	148	37	2	44
MASSACHUSETTS RESOLUTIONS,				
Adams, John Quincy, report on	†404	28		27
Burke, Edmund, report on	‡404	28		27
Burt, Armistead, report on	§404	28		27
Davis, Garrett, report on	‖404	28		27
Direct tax, amending Constitution for a	¶404	28		27
Giddings, Joshua R., report on	†404	28		27
Gilmer, Thomas W., report on	§404	28		27
Ingersoll, J. R., report on	‖404	28		27
Instructions by the State legislatures concerning	‖404	28		27
Morse, Freeman H., report on	**404	28		27
Representation in Congress, amending Constitution	404	28	1	27
Sample, S. C., report on	††404	28	1	27
MASSACHUSETTS WAR CLAIMS OF 1812, to adjudicate	147	15	1	9
Do	223	21	1	13

*Views of minority. †Part 3. ‡Part 2. §Part 1. ‖Part 5. ¶Parts 1, 2, 3, 4, 5, 6. **Part 6. ††Part 4.

Subject.	Report.	Congress.	Session.	Volume.
MATTESON, Hon. ORSAMUS B., (of New York,) on resolution proposing expulsion of	179	35	1	35
MATTESON, Hon. O. B. (of New York), investigation of charges against	243	34	3	33
MAURY, JABES *et al.*, for relief	57	14	1	1
MEADE, RICHARD W., confinement in prison by Spanish authorities of	185½	15	1	2
MEDICINE (compound), amending patent laws to prevent the patenting of	52	30	1	29
MEDILL, WILLIAM (Commissioner of Indian Affairs), investigating official conduct of	104	30	1	29
MEMBERS OF CONGRESS,				
Admission to floor of House, violation by ex-members of privileges of	3798	49	2	76
Apportionment of, among the States under the sixth census	43	27	2	24
Banks of United States, accommodations from, to	846	24	2	18
Bribery of, by Oakes Ames	77	42	3	60
Compensation and mileage of, reduced	547	23	1	16
Do	964	27	2	24
Corrupt combinations, investigation of	243	34	3	33
Laws of State for election of	221	19	1	9
MEMPHIS NAVY-YARD, recommending completion and re-establishment of	61	33	2	32
MEMPHIS RIOTS, investigation as to origin, progress, and parties engaged in	101	39	1	54
METALLIC STANDARD COIN, continuing legal-tender, quality of	185	44	2	67
METEOROLOGICAL OBSERVATIONS, granting aid to American Philosophical Society to continue	630	26	1	23
MEXICAN WAR. (*See* WAR WITH MEXICO)				
MEXICO,				
Commission to investigate robberies committed in Texas along border	343	44	1	67
Establishing a tariff of duties in the forts held by United States forces during war with	110	30	2	29
Levying, in 1847–'48, of military contributions in	119	30	2	29
Steamship service between United States and	18	41	3	58
MICHIGAN, examination into management of land offices in	81	17	1	5
MILEAGE, reducing to members of Congress	95	17	1	5
Do	547	23	1	16
Do	964	27	2	24
MILITARY ACADEMY, WEST POINT,				
Modifying system of military instruction at	303	24	2	18
Report of Board of Visitors to	112	46	3	72
MILITARY CONTRIBUTIONS IN MEXICO, levying of, 1847–'8	119	30	2	29
MILITARY LAND WARRANTS,				
To adjudicate claims of States for land sold to satisfy issue of	79	29	1	29
Virginia, location in State of Ohio	121	18	1	6
MILITARY POSTS,				
Establishing one at mouth of Columbia River	18	17	1	5
Do	213	19	1	9
Do	35	19	1	9
To establish a line from Council Bluffs to mouth of Columbia River	110	18	1	6
MILITARY RESERVATION, sale of Fort Snelling	351	35	1	35
MILITARY AND POST ROADS, to establish between New York City and Washington	63	37	3	44
MILITIA,				
Calling out of, by the President	58	36	2	41
Georgia, claim for services during years 1793–'94	16	15	1	2
Massachusetts, claim of, for services during war of 1812	147	15	1	2
Pennsylvania, fines imposed upon, by courts-martial	97	17	1	5
Powers of President to call out	58	36	2	41
MILLER, CHRISTOPHER, claim for relief	37	16	1	4
MILROY, SAMUEL, investigation of Executive interference in affairs of Rhode Island	546	28	1	28
Do	581	28	1	28
MINES, granting permission to mine on public lands west of Mississippi River	48	14	1	1
MINISTERS PLENIPOTENTIARY OF UNITED STATES, regulating salaries, allowances, &c., of	79	18	2	8
MINNESOTA LAND BILL, investigation of alteration in text of bill granting lands to State	352	33	1	32
Do	122	33	2	32
MINTS. (*See also* UNITED STATES MINTS.)				
Providing regulations for	420	22	1	14
Do	496	22	1	14
Do	278	23	1	16
MINT (Philadelphia, Pa.), prolonging continuance of	80	17	2	5
MISSISSIPPI,				
Investigation of recent troubles in	*265	43	2	66
Kuklux investigation, 1871–'72 (testimony)	22	42	2	61
Reconstruction of	30	39	1	49
Representation in Congress	30	39	1	49
MISSISSIPPI LEVEE, construction in Tennessee and Kentucky of	179	35	2	36
MISSISSIPPI RIVER,				
Improvement of	†1985	47	2	2
List of boats lost in	178	27	3	25
Navigation of	98	18	1	6
Obstructions in, construction of boats for removal of	379	21	1	13

* Parts 1 2. † Views of minority, Part 2.

Subject.	Report.	Congress.	Session.	Volume.
MISSISSIPPI RIVER—Continued.				
Snags in, removal by Shreeve's patent of	272	27	3	25
Survey of eastern bank in Tennessee and Kentucky	179	35	2	36
MISSISSIPPI TERRITORY, admission as a State	14	14	2	1
Do	42	14	2	1
MISSOURI,				
Admission of, as a State	3	16	2	4
Do	60	16	2	4
Citizens of, investigation of voting in Kansas by	200	34	1	36
Labor troubles in, in 1886	*4174	49	2	7
Land office in, management of	81	17	1	5
Lands, swamp, donating to the State	130	30	2	29
Slavery in, gradual emancipation of	148	37	2	44
State claims, 3 per cent. on Revolutionary land warrants	79	29	1	29
MISSOURI RIVER, list of boats lost in	178	27	3	25
MISSOURI TERRITORY, permission to work mines of precious metals on public lands beyond Mississippi River	48	14	1	1
MIX, ELIJAH, settlement of contract	100	17	1	5
MONETARY COMMISSION, report of	185	44	2	6
MONROE, JAMES (President United States),				
Settlement of accounts growing out of his mission to France	79	18	2	8
Do	76	20	2	12
Do	96	20	2	12
To adjudicate claim of heirs	136	19	1	1
Do	276	21	1	13
MONUMENT,				
Hale, Nathan (captain), to erect, in memory of	171	24	1	18
Do	969	25	2	21
Do	713	26	1	23
Do	783	27	2	24
Washington, to erect	69	14	1	1
Do	94	34	2	3
Do	79	42	3	5
Do	485	43	1	6
Washington, Mary, to erect, to memory of	625	43	1	6
Williams, David (one of the capturers of André), to erect, to	811	24	1	1
Do	327	25	2	21
Yorktown, Va., to erect, at	488	23	1	1
Do	82	24	1	1
MOORE, WILLIAM S., investigation of attack made upon a police officer of the Capitol by	470	28	1	2
MORTON, WILLIAM T. J., to compensate for discovery of anæsthetic property of sulphuric ether	114	30	1	2
NATIONAL ARMORIES,				
Army officers as superintendents of	191	33	1	2
Location of, advantages of certain places for	43	37	2	44
West of Alleghany Mountains, to establish	43	37	2	44
NATIONAL DEBT, reluctance to pay, by people of reconstructed States	30	39	1	4
NATIONAL DISTURBANCES, proposing constitutional amendments and other guarantees for the perpetuity of the Union in view of	181	36	2	41
NATIONAL FLAG, alteration of	23	14	2	1
NATIONAL FOUNDRIES,				
Providing for establishment of	141	23	2	1
Do	168	25	3	2
Do	229	27	3	2
Do	455	28	1	2
NATIONAL OBSERVATORY, providing for erection of	124	19	1	1
NATIONAL PARK. (See YELLOWSTONE PARK.)				
NATIONAL UNIVERSITY, erection and endowment at Washington City, of	4	14	2	1
NATURALIZATION LAWS, amending	1040	25	2	2
NAVAL CONTRACTS, 1859, investigation of	184	35	2	4
NAVAL EXPENDITURES, investigation of	184	35	2	4
NAVAL FORCE, distribution and location of, in January, 1861	87	36	2	4
NAVAL OFFICER (New York City), official conduct of	313	25	3	2
NAVIGATION LAWS, amending	1033	27	2	3
Do	407	35	1	3
NAVY,				
Compensation of officers of	295	23	1	1
Do	467	23	1	1
Iron steamers, to construct for western lakes	985	27	2	2
List of vessels in commission and where stationed in January, 1861	87	36	2	4
NAVY DEPARTMENT,				
Affairs in, investigation of	*80	42	2	3
Do	*81	42	2	3
Investigation of, letting of naval contracts by	184	35	2	4
Sale of certain ironclads by	64	40	2	5
NAVY-YARDS,				
Capacity for constructing war-vessels	1450	49	1	7
Memphis, Tenn., to re-establish at	61	33	2	3

* Views of minority. *Nine parts.

Subject.	Report.	Congress.	Session.	Volume.
NEW ORLEANS, LA.,				
Custom-house at, management of	25	39	2	48
Do	816	44	1	68
Riots at (July 30, 1866), investigation of	16	39	2	51
NEWSPAPERS, effect of disloyal	30	38	1	49
NEW YORK, election frauds in, investigation of	31	40	3	55
Do	41	40	3	55
Do	218	44	2	70
NEW YORK CITY,				
Custom-house in, investigation (Swartwout)	*312	25	3	22
Completion and furnishing of	1066	27	2	25
Removal of public stores from	647	36	1	41
Post-office at, tampering with mails in	128	43	2	67
Public building at, to erect	148	32	2	32
Subtreasury in, sales and loans of gold at	14	39	2	48
Loss of stamps in	70	42	3	59
NEW YORK HOTEL FUND, investigation relative to creation of	*381	36	1	41
NEW YORK INSTITUTION FOR DEAF AND DUMB, granting an endowment of land to	16	16	1	4
Do	7	19	1	9
Do	185	19	1	9
Do	322	21	1	13
Do	65	29	2	29
NIAGARA CLAIMS, payment of	102	18	1	6
NIAGARA FALLS, grant of land to aid in construction of ship-canal around	374	35	1	35
Do	55	37	3	44
NIAGARA FRONTIER, for relief of inhabitants of, for property destroyed in 1813	48	14	2	1
Do	1	15	2	7
NICARAGUA CANAL COMPANY, to incorporate	211	46	3	73
NICARAGUA ISTHMUS, route for canal and railroad across	145	30	2	29
NORTH AMERICAN COLONIES, commercial intercourse with	87½	16	1	3
NORTH CAROLINA,				
Claim of, to public lands in Tennessee	57	14	2	1
Kuklux investigation, 1871–'72 (testimony)	22	42	2	62
Reconstruction of, plans for	30	39	1	49
NORTHEASTERN FRONTIER, defenses for	23	37	3	46
Do	119	38	1	47
NORTHERN CITIES, investigation of charges of fraud at elections of Congressmen and Presidential electors	218	44	2	70
NORTHWEST COAST, exploring of	18	17	1	5
Do	35	19	1	9
Do	213	19	1	9
NORTHWESTERN LAKES, providing for construction of iron steamer for protection of	965	27	2	24
NYE, J. W. (assignee), claim for relief	525	28	1	27
OBSERVATIONS, granting aid to carry on magnetic and meteorological	630	26	1	23
OBSERVATORY. (*See* NATIONAL OBSERVATORY.)				
OCEAN MAIL STEAMERS, investigating frauds in payment of money for mail service to the Collins and other lines of	281	33	1	32
OHIO,				
Claim of 3 per cent. on land to satisfy Revolutionary land warrants	79	29	1	29
Land office, management of	81	17	1	5
OHIO RIVER, removal of obstructions in	98	18	1	6
Do	379	21	1	13
ONEOTO (ironclad), inquiry into alleged fraudulent sale of	64	40	2	56
ORDER OF BUSINESS. (*See* BUSINESS OF HOUSE.)				
ORDNANCE,				
Improvements in, claim by Norman Wiard for	6	40	3	55
National foundry for, to establish	229	27	3	25
Steel-producing works, for casting heavy	1450	49	1	75
War-ship, location for manufacture of, for	1450	49	1	75
OREGON, settlement at mouth of Columbia River, in	45	16	2	4
Do	110	18	1	6
Do	157	27	3	25
PACIFIC OCEAN.				
Railroad to, survey for	145	30	2	29
Settlements on	45	16	2	4
Survey for railroad to	145	30	2	29
PACIFIC RAILROADS,				
Construction of, from Lake Michigan to Oregon	733	30	1	29
Establishment and construction of	145	30	2	29
Do	*274	34	1	33
Do	*358	34	1	33
Government aid in construction of	*428	36	1	41
Surveys, various routes for	*428	36	1	41
PAINE, E. A., investigation of charges of bribery and corruption against	29	38	2	47
PAINTINGS, providing, for Rotunda of Capitol	294	24	2	18
PANAMA ISTHMUS, route for canal and railroad across	145	30	2	29

* Views of minority.

Subject.	Report.	Congress.	Session.	Volume.
PAN-ELECTRIC TELEPHONE COMPANY, investigation of	3142	49	1	76
PARDONS, EXECUTIVE, effect of	30	39	1	49
PASSENGERS ON STEAMBOATS, amending law providing for safety of	1033	27	2	1
PATENT LAWS, to amend, so as to prevent the patenting of compound medicines.	52	30	1	29
PATENT MEDICINES, to amend patent laws so as to prevent the patenting of.	52	30	1	29
PATENT OFFICE,				
Additional force in, providing for	99	19	2	9
Frauds in, investigation of charges of	48	37	3	44
Do	26	38	2	47
Organization of	90	19	2	9
PATENTS,				
Aliens, to grant, to	458	22	1	14
Secret specifications, to issue, to Horatio Spofford on	351	22	1	14
PATTERSON, ELIZA W., for relief of	1432	47	1	72
PAUPER IMMIGRATION, to prohibit	1040	25	2	21
PAY DEPARTMENT, alleged frauds in payment of colored troops	83	40	2	38
PAY OF ARMY AND NAVY, to equalize	295	23	1	16
PECK, Judge JAMES H., impeachment of	359	21	1	13
Do	385	21	1	13
PENITENTIARY SYSTEM (District of Columbia), reforming and revising	140	30	2	29
PENNSYLVANIA,				
Election in (1856), corrupt use of money in	648	36	1	42
Militia fines, collection of	97	17	1	5
PENROSE, CLEMENT B., claim for relief	37	15	2	2
Do	13	15	1	2
Do	13	16	1	4
PENSIONS,				
Indian wars, to pension persons who served previous to 1795 in	284	23	1	16
Do	328	24	1	18
Do	96	24	2	18
Do	327	25	2	21
Do	361	27	2	24
Do	88	29	1	29
Mexican war, to widows and orphans of soldiers in	796	30	1	29
Revolutionary war, to persons who served in	136	20	1	12
PERSONAL LIBERTY, to protect loyal and peaceable citizens of United States in enjoyment of	37	41	3	58
PERU, to levy duty on guano imported from	347	33	1	32
PHILADELPHIA, PA.,				
Collector of port at (Jonathan Roberts), removal of	284	27	3	38
Custom-house at, investigation of	648	36	1	42
Election frauds in, investigation of	218	44	2	70
Government aid to	1	44	1	67
Import duties on tea and coffee	282	21	1	13
Mint at, continuing	80	17	2	5
Navy-yard in, investigation of naval contracts and expenditures made at	184	35	2	40
Post-office site, purchase from Bank of Pennsylvania of	541	35	1	35
Public building at, providing for	143	33	2	32
PIATT, JOHN H., for relief of heirs	21	18	1	13
PITTSBURGH, PA., inquiry into manufacturing interests of	86	14	2	1
POLAND, LUKE P.,				
Report on election frauds in Arkansas	5	42	2	59
Report upon condition of affairs in Arkansas	771	43	1	64
POLICE DEPARTMENT (DISTRICT OF COLUMBIA), alleged improper use of, by District Commissioners	189	44	2	67
POLITICAL ASSESSMENTS, investigation of assessments upon Government employés (Covode)	648	36	1	42
POLITICAL DISABILITIES, list of persons from whom is recommended the removal of	74	40	2	55
POLK, Hon. JAMES K., notification of his election as President	142	28	3	27
POOL, ISAAC, claim for relief	37	19	1	9
POSTAL MAIL ROUTES, letting of contracts for	*103	23	2	17
POSTAL SERVICE,				
Mails, United States, tampering with, in New York City post-office	138	44	2	67
Vaccine matter, free distribution, through mail	48	17	1	5
Do	93	17	1	5
Do	95	19	2	9
POSTAL TELEGRAPH SYSTEM, to establish	114	41	3	56
Do	115	41	2	58
POSTMASTER-GENERAL, authority of, to negotiate loans	*103	23	2	17
POSTMASTERS, removal of, for political causes	*103	23	2	17
POST OFFICE BLANKS, relative to purchases of	*103	23	2	17
POST-OFFICE CLERKS, statement showing number of and salaries paid to	*103	23	2	17
POST-OFFICE DEPARTMENT,				
Affairs in, investigation of	65	16	2	4
Do	69	16	2	4
Do	*103	23	2	17
Do	648	36	1	42
Franking privilege, investigating abuse of	576	28	1	27

* Views of minority.

Subject.	Report.	Congress.	Session.	Volume.
POST-OFFICE DEPARTMENT—Continued.				
Investigation, affairs in	65	16	2	4
Do	69	16	2	4
Do	*103	23	2	17
Do	648	36	1	42
Management and financial condition, investigation of	77	14	1	1
POST ROADS, to construct, from Washington, D. C., to New York City	63	37	3	44
POSTS, MILITARY, to establish line from Council Bluffs to mouth of Columbia River	110	18	1	6
POTTAWATOMIE INDIANS. (*See* INDIANS.)				
PRESIDENT'S MESSAGE, report upon message as relates to condition and management of various Executive Departments	194	24	2	3
PRESIDENT OF UNITED STATES,				
Apportionment bill, under sixth census, approval of	909	27	2	24
Conduct of, investigation of (1860)	*648	36	1	42
Constitutional power of, to negotiate with representatives of South Carolina relating to surrender of public property in	88	36	2	41
Customs duties, defining power of, in collection of	59	36	2	41
Frauds in election of	140	45	3	71
Investigation of, presence on floor of hall of House by	26	39	2	48
Investigation of conduct of, in 1860 (Covode)	*648	36	1	42
Militia, defining powers of, to call out the	58	36	2	41
Notification to Martin Van Buren of his election as	199	24	2	18
Notification to William H. Harrison of his election as	165	26	2	23
Rhode Island controversy	546	28	1	28
Do	581	28	1	28
Tariff act of 1842	*998	27	2	24
PRESIDENT AND VICE-PRESIDENT,				
Election of, to prevent, by House of Representatives	8	18	1	6
Do	9	19	1	9
Election of, by direct vote	69	23	2	16
Electorial votes for, counting	84	14	2	1
Do	41	18	2	6
Do	198	24	2	18
Do	106	28	2	27
Do	100	44	2	69
Notification of election	142	28	2	27
PRESIDENTIAL ELECTION, 1876,				
Investigation of, in Louisiana, Florida, and South Carolina	143	44	2	69
Do	156	44	2	69
Do	100	44	2	69
Do	175	44	2	69
PRESIDENTIAL ELECTORS, changing mode of choosing	8	18	1	1
PRESIDENTIAL VETO. (*See* VETO.)				
PRICE, WILLIAM M., defalcation of	313	25	3	22
PRINCE EDWARD ISLAND, establishing reciprocal trade between United States and	39	40	3	55
PRINTING. (*See* PUBLIC PRINTING.)				
PRINTING. (*See* REPORTS OF COMMITTEE ON PRINTING.)				
PRISONERS OF WAR,				
Condition of, in 1864	67	38	1	47
Treatment by rebel authorities during war of rebellion of (Shank report)	45	40	3	57
PRIVATE LAND CLAIMS,				
Bastrop grant, quiet title to	3	19	1	9
Do	347	21	1	13
Do	233	22	1	14
Marquis de Maison Rouge, to certain lands in Louisiana	18	18	2	6
Do	2	19	1	9
Do	347	21	1	13
PROPERTY, amending act of March 3, 1817, relating to captured, destroyed, or lost, in war of 1812	1	18	2	6
PROTESTED BILLS. (*See* CONGRESS.)				
PROVOST-MARSHAL GENERAL FRY, investigation of charges made by Roscoe Conkling against	93	39	1	50
PUBLIC BUILDING,				
Congressional library, providing additional accommodations for	164	47	1	72
Finishing and furnishing	122	19	1	9
Number rented by Government in District of Columbia	70	41	2	58
To erect, at—				
Baltimore, Md	143	33	2	32
Boston, Mass	143	33	2	32
New York City	143	33	2	32
Philadelphia, Pa	143	33	2	32
PUBLIC DOCUMENTS,				
Binding for Executive Departments (Covode)	848	36	1	41
Field-service tactics, publication of	108	17	1	5
Geological Survey, restricting publications of	2214	49	1	76
Do	2740	49	1	76
Journals of Congress, providing for the general distribution of	107	22	2	14

* Views of minority.

Subject.	Report.	Congress.	Session.	Volume.
PUBLIC DOCUMENTS—Continued.				
Laws of United States, providing for general distribution of	107	22	2	14
Do	286	25	2	21
Do	639	29	1	29
Maps and charts, fraudulent engraving and printing of, for Twenty-sixth and Twenty-seventh Congresses	305	28	1	27
Printing and binding of, defining powers of Clerk of House of Representatives in	101	26	2	23
Do	215	26	2	23
Wilkes exploring expedition, printing of maps and plates connected therewith	160	28	2	27
PUBLIC DOMAIN, cessions of various States to	296	27	3	26
PUBLIC LANDS,				
Appropriating among the several States for educational purposes the net proceeds of sales of	95	20	2	12
Do	312	21	2	13
Disposal of, in Tennessee	68	19	1	9
Do	137	21	1	13
Do	120	23	1	16
Educational purposes, net proceeds of sale of land to be distributed among the States for	95	20	2	12
Do	312	21	1	13
Foreign coins, receivable in purchase of	85	17	2	5
Granted to railroads, to forfeit all	3	40	2	56
Do	15	40	2	56
Granting				
To asylum for deaf and dumb in Connecticut	142	15	2	2
To Indiana, for construction of canal	78	18	2	6
Do	544	28	1	27
Do	545	28	1	27
For educational purposes to Tennessee, certain	32	20	1	12
For canal from Illinois River to Lake Michigan, aid in construction	446	22	1	14
To Arkansas, swamp and overflowed lands in	130	30	2	29
To Missouri, swamp and overflowed, in	130	30	2	29
To Niagara Ship-Canal	374	35	1	35
Granting bounty lands to survivors of the "old Fourth Regiment United States Infantry" serving in the war of 1812	798	25	2	21
Do	232	26	1	23
Do	322	27	2	24
Ohio, between Ludlow and Roberts' lines, relief of purchasers of	121	18	1	6
Proceeds of sale of, to be applied to the payment of State debts	296	27	3	28
Swamp and overflowed, granting to State of Missouri	130	30	2	29
Tennessee, donating certain vacant, for educational purposes to	32	20	1	12
PUBLIC MONEYS, inquiry whether banks for deposit of, have agents at the Treasury Department	193	24	2	19
PUBLIC PRINTER, investigating accounts of	189	35	2	30
PUBLIC PRINTING,				
Cost of, from 1828 to 1840	741	27	2	34
Execution of, defining manner of	754	29	1	29
Executive Departments, investigation of printing done for (Covode)	648	36	1	41
Expenses for, retrenchment of	90	20	2	12
House of Representatives, printing ordered by, to be executed by Public Printer	101	26	2	23
Do	215	26	2	23
Investigation of, done for Executive Departments (Covode)	648	36	1	41
Prices of, fixing	754	29	1	29
Retrenchment in, expenses of	90	20	2	12
PUBLIC PROPERTY, seizure of, by seceding States	91	36	2	41
PUBLIC REVENUE, collecting and disbursing	282	25	3	21
RAILROADS,				
Construction of,				
From Lake Michigan to Pacific Ocean	733	30	1	29
Do	145	30	2	30
From New York City to Washington	68	37	3	44
From Bangor to Saint John River, in Vermont	119	38	1	47
Lands granted to, to forfeit	3	40	2	56
Do	15	40	2	56
Southern, investigation of	34	39	2	43
RANDALL, Hon. SAMUEL J., investigation of certain charges against	139	45	3	71
RATHBUN, Hon. GEORGE, investigation of an encounter between Hon. John White and	470	28	1	21
RATIO OF REPRESENTATION IN CONGRESS, fixing, under fifth census	137	21	1	13
RAUBS SAFETY-VALVE, adoption by Government of	827	35	2	27
Do	82	36	2	28
REAL ESTATE POOL OF DISTRICT COLUMBIA, investigation into the nature and history of	242	44	1	67
Do	789	44	1	67
RECEIVERS OF PUBLIC MONEY, list of defaulters (1837–'39)	313	25	3	28
RECIPROCITY TREATY, to establish, with Prince Edward Island	39	40	3	55
RECONSTRUCTION of States lately in rebellion	*30	39	1	45
REESIDE, JAMES, combined bid of, for carrying mails	*103	23	2	17

* Views of minority

Subject.	Report.	Congress.	Session.	Volume.
REFRIGERATING-SHIP, providing for purchase of	1792	46	2	72
REGISTRATION, investigation into, at elections of Congressmen and Presidential electors	218	44	2	70
REID, WHITELAW, investigation of arrest in District of Columbia of	273	43	2	62
REILLY, BOYD, claim for relief	543	25	2	21
REMOVALS in Post-Office Department for partisan reasons	103	23	2	17
REPRESENTATIVES,				
Apportionment of, under fifth and sixth censuses	127	21	1	13
Do	463	22	1	14
Do	43	27	2	24
To regulate, among the States	11	39	1	48
RETRENCHMENT,				
Contingent fund, to reduce in House and Senate, in	101	20	2	12
Do	230	27	3	25
Employés, to reduce number of	*259	20	1	12
Salaries of employés, to reduce	*259	20	1	12
RETURNING BOARD, testimony in relation to the action of board in recent election in Louisiana	101	43	2	63
REVENUE. (*See* PUBLIC REVENUE.)				
REVENUE CUTTERS, seizure by seceding States of	91	36	2	41
REVENUE LAWS, violation of, amount of fines collected for, in district of New York	*49	37	3	44
Do	50	37	3	44
REVENUE STAMPS, loss in office of assistant treasurer, New York City	70	42	3	59
REVOLUTIONARY SOLDIERS, claims for relief	136	20	1	12
RHODE ISLAND,				
Brigade in Revolutionary war, compensation of	128	23	2	16
Do	337	24	1	18
Constitution of 1841, conflict over	546	28	1	28
Do	581	28	1	28
RIVERS AND HARBORS, providing for improvement of	491	22	1	14
ROADS, PUBLIC, construction of, from Western Reserve in Ohio into Michigan Territory	98	16	1	4
ROADS AND CANALS, improvement of	72	14	2	1
Do	92	14	2	1
ROANOKE INLET, reopening of	317	21	1	13
ROBERTS, JONATHAN, removal from office of collector of port of Philadelphia	284	27	3	25
RODGERS, Commodore JOHN, for relief	43	14	1	1
ROTUNDA OF CAPITOL. (*See* CAPITOL BUILDING.)				
ROUSSEAU, Hon. LOVELL H., investigating assault upon Josiah B. Grinnell, by	90	39	1	48
RUGGLES, ADIN, for relief of heirs	658	24	1	18
RULES OF HOUSE OF REPRESENTATIVES,				
Amendments to	1	25	1	21
Do	1	26	1	23
Counting electoral vote	41	18	2	6
Revision of	13	14	1	1
Do	20	17	1	5
Do	83	24	1	18
Do	58	36	1	41
Violation of Rule 34, admission of ex-members to floor	3798	49	2	76
SAFETY-VALVES FOR STEAM-ENGINES (Raub's), claim for use by Government	328	25	1	21
Do	92	26	2	23
SAINT JOSEPH'S BAY, cost of engraving charts of	899	27	2	24
SALARIES,				
Commissioners to fix boundary line of the Northwest under treaty of Ghent	193	15	1	2
Do	56	16	2	4
Employés of Government, to reduce	*259	20	1	12
Do	547	23	1	16
Members of Congress,				
Per diem pay of	12	14	2	1
To reduce	547	23	1	16
Northwest boundary commissioners, to fix salary of	193	15	1	2
Do	56	16	2	4
Officers of Army and Navy, to fix	295	23	1	16
Do	467	23	1	16
SAN FRANCISCO (steamship), to reward rescuers of passengers from	113	33	1	32
SANITARY CONFERENCE. (*See* INTERNATIONAL SANITARY CONFERENCE.)				
SCHELL, AUGUSTUS, refusal to produce certain papers	*331	36	1	41
SCHOOL FARM LANDS direct-tax sale in South Carolina of	108	41	3	58
SCHWEINITZ, LEWIS D. DE, recession of lands of missions of United Brethren on Muskingum, Ohio	99	18	1	6
SCIENTIFIC BUREAUS, limiting publications of	2214	49	1	76
Do	2740	49	1	76
SCOTT, J., Kuklux investigation in the late insurrectionary States	†22	42	2	61
SEA ISLANDS (Beaufort, S. C.), providing for the sale of, and confirming title to sales made under direct-tax sales	108		2	
SEAMAN, A. G. (Public Printer), investigating accounts of	189	41	2	58
SEARING, JOHN A., investigation of charges against	183	35	2	39
SECESSION. (*See* SOUTHERN STATES.)				

* Views of minority. † Part 1.

Subject.	Report.	Congress.	Session.
SECRET ORGANIZATION, hostile to United States Government, in District of Columbia, inquiry into	79	36	2
SECRETARY OF INTERIOR, investigating claim of W. G. and G. W. Ewing against Pottawatomie Indians, by	489	31	1
SECRETARY OF NAVY, investigating charges against George M. Robeson as	*80	42	2
Do	*81	42	2
SECRETARY OF STATE, investigating charges against Daniel Webster as	684	29	1
SECRETARY OF TREASURY,			
Appointment of, to change law regulating	296	24	2
Authority of, to establish customs duties in Mexican ports during war with Mexico	119	30	2
Investigation charges against William H. Crawford as	128	18	1
Do	133	18	1
Investigation of charges against Levi Woodbury as	*313	25	3
Investigation of charges against Thomas Corwin as	1	32	2
SECRETARY OF WAR, investigation of conduct of Lewis Cass as	334	31	1
SENATE, relation of, to House of Representatives in counting electoral vote	84	14	2
SENATORS. (*See* CONGRESS.)			
SERGEANT-AT-ARMS, House of Representatives, account between Bank of Metropolis and	513	25	2
SHEPHERD, MOSES, claim for relief	63	18	2
SHIP-CANALS. (*See also* CANALS.)			
Niagara, granting lands to aid in construction of	374	35	1
Do	53	37	3
Nicaragua Ship-Canal Company, to incorporate	211	46	3
Panama, selection of route for	390	46	3
Tehuantepec, survey of route for	145	30	2
Do	648	36	1
SHIP ISLAND INLETS, cost of engraving charts of	899	27	2
SHREN, HENRY M., claim for relief	556	27	2
Do	272	27	3
Do	538	28	1
SIGNATURES, to purchase those of executive, judicial, and legislative officers of the Government in service July 4, 1876	94	[illegible]	3
SILVER AND GOLD, report of commission upon the legal relation between	185	44	2
SILVER COINS. (*See* COINS AND COINAGE).			
SILVER DOLLAR, making legal tender of, in payment of all debts and demands	94	21	2
SIXTH CENSUS, apportionment of Representatives under	43	27	2
SLAVERY,			
Abolishment of,			
In District of Columbia	691	24	1
In certain States	148	37	2
Do	120	37	2
Action of the Committee of Thirty-three in 1861 relative to (9 parts)	31	36	2
Committee of Thirty-three, action of, in 1861, relative to (9 parts)	31	36	2
District of Columbia, to abolish in	691	24	1
Kansas, to establish in	200	34	1
Do	377	35	1
Do	648	36	1
SLAVES,			
Colonization of	148	37	2
Do	120	37	2
Compensation for	30	39	1
Emancipation of, belonging to persons in rebellion	148	37	2
Do	120	37	2
Introduction of, from Amelia Island	46	15	1
Passport for, alteration in (Amistad case)	51	26	2
SLAVE TRADE, suppression of	97	16	1
Do	92	17	1
Do	70	18	2
Do	231	19	1
Do	348	21	1
SMALL-POX, vaccination as a guard against	78	18	1
SMITH, Dr. JAMES, memorial on vaccination	78	18	1
SMITH, W. SCOTT, to expel from Reporters' gallery of House	104	41	2
SMITH, WILLIAM, contracts for carrying mail by	†103	23	2
SMITHSONIAN INSTITUTION,			
Appropriations for	587	27	2
Do	540	28	1
Establishment of	181	24	1
Do	277	26	1
Do	587	27	2
Do	540	28	1
Do	870	29	1
Funds of, transfer to the Treasury Department	587	27	2
Do	540	28	1
Do	144	33	2
Management of, investigation of	141	33	2
Regulations for	870	29	1
SOLDIERS, investigation, in South Carolina, of murder of United States	23	24	2

* Views of minority. † Parts 1, 2; views of minority.

Subject.	Report.	Congress.	Session.	Volume.
SOLDIERS' BOUNTIES. (*See* BOUNTIES.)				
SOUTH, condition of, investigation	101	43	2	52
SOUTH CAROLINA.				
Election in, in 1876	*175	44	2	69
Kuklux investigation, 1871–'72 (testimony)	†22	42	2	61
Murder of United States soldiers in, investigation of	23	39	2	48
Reconstruction of	30	39	1	49
Secession of, correspondence with President of United States on	88	36	1	41
SOUTHERN OUTRAGES, Kuklux investigation of, 1872	†22	42	2	61
SOUTHERN RAILROADS.				
Affairs of, investigation of	34	39	2	50
Land grants to, forfeiture of	2	40	2	55
Do	15	40	2	55
SOUTHERN STATES.				
Compromise measures, reported for, by Committee of Thirty-three in 1861 (9 parts)	31	36	2	41
Federal laws, suspending execution of, in 1861, within	91	36	2	41
SPAFFORD, HORATIO G., claim for secret letters-patent	351	22	1	14
SPAIN, investigation of imprisonment of Richard W. Meade, by authorities of	185‡	15	1	2
SPEAKER OF HOUSE OF REPRESENTATIVES, investigation of charges against Howell Cobb, as	218	31	1	51
SPECIE PAYMENT, resumption of	188	44	2	67
SPRING AND GRAND RIVERS, improvement of	196	27	3	25
SPRINGER, Hon. WILLIAM M., investigation of anonymous letter to	395	46	2	72
STANBERRY, Hon. WILLIAM, investigation of assault by Hon. Samuel Houston upon	447	22	1	14
STANDARD VALUE. (*See also* GOLD, SILVER.)				
Establishing, of gold coins of the United States	95	21	2	19
STANLEY, RUFUS, investigation of extra allowance to	§103	23	2	17
STATE BANKS. (*See also* BANKS.)				
Reissue of notes of	272	24	1	18
Do	306	24	1	18
Do	558	27	2	24
STATE DEBTS. (*See* DEBTS.)				
STATE DEPARTMENT. (*See* DEPARTMENT OF STATE.)				
STATE GOVERNMENTS, power of Congress to abrogate	10	40	2	55
STATE OF THE LAW RESPECTING ELECTION OF PRESIDENT AND VICE-PRESIDENT	5	46	1	72
Do	347	46	2	73
Do	1207	47	1	72
STATES.				
Customs duties in, authority of Government to collect	59	36	2	41
Loyal, to reimburse for debts contracted in suppression of rebellion	16	39	1	48
Proceeds of sale of public lands, distribution among	95	20	2	12
Relief of, by applying the proceeds of sales of public lands	296	27	3	26
Stock of $200,000,000, to distribute among, to be redeemed from sale of public land	296	27	3	26
STATE'S RIGHTS AND SECESSION, utterances since the war	30	39	1	49
STATISTICS. (*See* BUREAU OF STATISTICS.)				
STATUE OF WASHINGTON, to erect	318	21	1	13
STEAMBOAT.				
Inspectors of, appointment of	478	22	1	14
Inventor of, claim of heirs of James Rumsey for	317	24	2	18
Do	265	25	3	21
Do	650	26	1	...
Passengers on, safety of	1038	27	2	24
STEAM-ENGINES, making appropriation to test improvements made in	426	23	1	16
STEAMSHIP SAN FRANCISCO, to reward rescuers of passengers from	113	33	1	32
STEAM VESSELS.				
Inspectors of, appointment of	478	22	1	14
Iron, for northern lakes, to construct	965	27	2	24
Passengers on, safety of	1033	37	2	44
STEPHENS, EBENEZER, claim for relief	104	15	2	2
STEWARD, HUGH, claim for relief of assignee of	525	28	1	27
STOCKBRIDGE INDIANS. (*See* INDIANS.)				
STOCKHOLDERS OF UNITED STATES BANK (1818)	92	15	2	3
STOCKTON, RICHARD C., mail contract for Virginia	§103	23	2	17
STOCKTON & NEIL, list of mail routes contracted for by	§103	23	2	17
STOCKTON & STOKES, contracts for carrying mail by	§103	23	2	17
STRIKES, cause of railroad strikes in 1886	§4174	49	2	77
SUBSIDY to mail steamship in Gulf of Mexico	18	41	3	58
SUBTREASURY, UNITED STATES (New York City).				
Loss of revenue stamps in	70	42	3	59
Sales and loans of gold at	14	39	2	48
SULPHURIC ETHER, discovery by William T. Morton of anæsthetic property of	114	30	1	29
SUMNER, Hon. CHARLES, investigation of assault made by Preston S. Brooks upon	182	34	1	33
SUPERINTENDENTS OF NATIONAL ARMORIES, detail of Army officers as	191	33	1	32
SUPERINTENDENT OF PUBLIC PRINTING, investigating accounts of	189	35	2	39

* Parts 1, 2; views of minority. † Parts 1, 2, 3. ‡ Part 1; views of minority. § Views of minority.

Subject.

SURVEYS.
Eastern bank of Mississippi River, in States of Tennessee
Grand and Spring Rivers.............................. .
Indian lands, prohibiting...................................
Pacific Railroad...
Panama Ship-Canal.................. ....
Rivers and harbors, for improvement of ....
Tehuantepec Ship-Canal ....
Do...
SWAMP LANDS, donating to,
Arkansas ....
Illinois, conditionally......................................
Missouri ....
SWARTWOUT, SAMUEL, *et al.*, investigation of defalcatio
SWIFT, General JOSEPH G., estimates required for fortifi
ings at West Point.....................................
TALLMADGE, MATHIAS B., investigation of official cond
TARIFF,
Act of 1857, passage of, inquiry into.......................
Distilled spirits, to increase duty on imported.... . .....
Guano, fixing rate of duty on Peruvian.....................
Mexican ports held by United States forces during war of
Peruvian guano, fixing rate of ....
Spirits, to increase duty on imported ....
Tea and coffee, agitation in Philadelphia, Pa., upon tariff o
Tobacco, unjust discriminations by foreign powers on.....
Do...................... ....
Do..
Do..
Veto of 1842 ....
TEHUANTEPEC SHIP-CANAL, survey, 1842-'43...... ....
Do .. ..
TELEGRAPH, ATLANTIC AND PACIFIC,
Proposals for erection of ....
Do... ....
Rates, March 10, 1862......................................
TELEGRAPH SYSTEM, control by Government and union
Do ....
TELEGRAPH, WESTERN UNION COMPANY, cipher tel
tigation of..... ....
TELEPHONE COMPANIES, investigation of Pan-Electric..
TENNESSEE.
Boundary of, establishing southern ....
Eastern bank of Mississippi River, survey of..............
Public lands in,
Right of North Carolina to ....
Providing for the disposal of ....
Do..... ....
Do.... ....
Granting, for educational purposes ....
Reconstruction of ....
Slavery in, providing for gradual emancipation of ....
TENURE OF OFFICE,
President of United States fixing period of................
Rules regulating ....
TEXAS.
Frontier troubles in, report of commission on ....
Labor troubles in, investigation of (1886) ....
Reconstruction of...... ....
THOMAS, JAMES, account as deputy quartermaster ....
THOMPSON, SAMUEL, for relief..............................
Do ....
TOBACCO TRADE with foreign countries ....
Do..
Do..
Do ....
TONNAGE, AMERICAN, causes of reduction of.............
TOPEKA CONSTITUTION, vote on ....
TRANSPORTATION OF UNITED STATES TROOPS, inv
TRANSYLVANIA UNIVERSITY, national aid to rebuild. .
Do.................... ....
TREASON, conviction by jury in Virginia for................
TREASURY DEPARTMENT,
Consular Bureau in, to establish..........................
Deposit banks, investigation of agents of..................
Investigation of.......... ....
Smithsonian funds, transferred to ....
Statistical Bureau in, to establish............. ....
Do ....
TREASURY SURPLUS, to distribute among the States.....

* Views of minority †I

Subject.	Report.	Congress.	Session.	Volume.
TREATIES,				
Brownstone, Mich., made with Indians at	98	16	1	4
Cherokee Indians, to carry into effect treaty with	10	17	1	5
Do	1	17	2	5
Creek Indians, to carry into effect treaty with	10	17	1	5
Do	1	17	2	5
Indians, made at Brownstone, Mich., with	98	16	1	4
Oregon boundary, settlement of	157	27	3	25
Prince Edward Island, to establish reciprocity treaty with	39	40	3	55
Reciprocity, to establish, with Prince Edward Island	39	40	3	55
TRIPLET, HEDGEMAN, claim for relief	99	22	2	14
TURNER, MOSES, for relief	28	14	1	1
TYLER, JOHN and BENJAMIN, patent claim	15	14	1	1
UNFINISHED BUSINESS OF HOUSE OF REPRESENTATIVES. (*See* BUSINESS OF HOUSE.)				
UNION MEN, hostility toward	30	39	1	49
UNITED BRETHREN, recession of lands granted to, for Indian missions on the Muskingum River, Ohio	99	18	1	6
UNITED STATES, hostility toward	30	39	1	40
UNITED STATES BANK, inquiry into management of	29	14	2	1
Do	92	15	2	3
UNITED STATES BONDS. (*See* BONDS OF UNITED STATES.)				
UNITED STATES DEPOSITORIES. (*See* DEPOSITORIES.)				
UNPRODUCTIVE MAIL ROUTES, description and list of	*103	23	2	17
UNSETTLED BALANCES due United States	88	14	1	1
VACCINE VIRUS, authorizing free use of the mails for the distribution of	48	17	1	5
Do	93	17	1	5
Do	95	19	2	9
VACCINATION, memorial of Dr. James Smith in regard to	78	18	1	6
VAN BUREN, Hon. MARTIN, notification of being elected President of the United States	190	24	2	18
VAN NESS, WILLIAM P., investigation of official conduct of	136	15	2	2
VENTILATION, Hall of House of Representatives	119	45	2	71
Do	116	45	3	71
Do	19	40	3	71
VESSELS,				
Captured and confiscated for importing slaves from Cuba	231*	19	1	9
Catiline (steamer), chartering of	2	37	2	45
Iron steamer, construction of, for northwestern lakes	985	27	2	25
List of captured, engaged in African slave trade	92	18	1	6
San Francisco (steamship), to reward rescuers of passengers from	113	33	1	32
United States, purchase of	2	37	2	45
VETO,				
Passage over President's, by majority vote of two Houses	296	24	2	18
Tariff act of 1842	998	27	2	24
VICKSBURG, MISS., investigation upon recent trouble at	265	43	2	66
VIRGINIA,				
Bounty land,				
To soldiers of Revolutionary war	160	15	1	2
Settlement of	1063	27	2	24
Military land warrants, location of, in Ohio	121	18	1	6
Reconstruction of	30	39	1	49
Reserve in Ohio, quiet claim to land in	121	18	1	6
Secession of, how accomplished in 1861	30	39	1	49
Slavery in, gradual emancipation of	148	37	2	44
War claims, to adjudicate	191	22	1	14
Do	1063	27	2	24
VOTES. (*See also* PRESIDENT OF UNITED STATES.)				
Providing for election of President of United States by direct	69	23	2	16
WABASH AND ERIE CANAL, granting lands to State of Indiana for construction of Central Canal to connect with	78	18	2	6
Do	544	28	1	27
Do	545	28	1	27
WAGER, JOHN, Jr., for relief of heirs	68	16	2	4
WAR CLAIMS,				
Massachusetts, to settle	147	15	1	2
Virginia, to settle	191	22	1	14
Do	1063	27	2	24
WAR DEBT OF LOYAL STATES, to pay	16	39	1	48
WAR OF REVOLUTION,				
Bounty lands, to soldiers in	160	15	1	2
Claims, settlement of	9	16	1	4
Georgia claims, to settle	311	25	3	21
Officers in, additional compensation to	19	15	2	2
Do	9	16	1	4
Do	19	19	1	9
Do	6	19	2	9
Rhode Island claims, to settle	337	24	1	18
Virginia claims, to settle	191	22	1	14

* Views of minority.

* Part 2.

Lightning Source UK Ltd.
Milton Keynes UK
UKHW010049280219
338009UK00005B/174/P

9 780332 234304